D0207691

01/24
STRAND PRICE
$ 5.00

Psychology of Work Behavior

Fourth Edition

Frank J. Landy
Professor of Psychology
The Pennsylvania State University

Brooks/Cole Publishing Company
Pacific Grove, California

Brooks/Cole Publishing Company
A Division of Wadsworth, Inc.

Printed in the United States of America

10 9 8 7 6 5 4 3 2 1

Library of Congress Cataloging-in-Publication Data

Landy, Frank J.
Psychology of work behavior.

Bibliography: p.
Includes index.
1. Psychology, Industrial. 2. Work—Psychological aspects. 3. Personnel management. I. Title.
HF5548.8.L25 1989 158.7 88-28536
ISBN 0-534-11091-6

Preface

The history of industrial and organizational psychology is best characterized as the *application* of psychological principles and methods to problems in the work context. It represents one of the most direct attempts to put the principles of behavior to use.

Problems in the work context can be approached from several points of view. I have chosen to identify the individual worker as the unit of analysis. This means that I will most often be trying to evaluate the interactions of organizational and individual variables. While there is merit to studying these actions on work groups and perhaps even on the organization itself, I will leave these considerations to the industrial sociologist and social psychologist.

In the last two decades, there has been a rapid expansion in theory and research in almost every phase of industrial and organizational psychology. The most obvious expansion has involved the increasing appreciation of the role of cognitive activity in work-related behavior. As a result, theories of human performance, motivation, leadership, training, job satisfaction, and stress have been radically altered. Similar maturation has occurred in the more traditional areas of personnel psychology. Industrial and organizational psychologists have begun to apply the tools of science (both logical and empirical) to issues such as performance measurement, ability testing, and prediction. As a result, compromises have been reached between the scientist and the advocate in the area of equal employment and affirmative action. This is exciting from a professional perspective, since it represents the best indication that progress is being made. It is also exciting from the point of view of an author of an industrial text, since it represents an opportunity to make both students and colleagues aware of the changes that have occurred in the field and the challenges that lie ahead. After reading the text, I hope you will conclude that I have brought you "up to date" and have possibly even given you a glimpse of the future.

Texts differ in many important respects. One such difference that students often recognize is a "hard-nose"–"soft-nose" distinction. I would like to identify with the "hard-nose" approach. Specifically, I feel that the only way to ensure progress in thinking and research is through a dependence on the scientific method for posing and answering questions. Studies without a progression of thought and research and that depend strictly on armchair theorizing are processes that ultimately deprive the solution to the problem of any meaning at all. I have tried to provide a good theoretical and empirical background for every topic discussed in the text. In addition, I have tried to point out in each topic the major question of interest and to separate that major question from each of the varied attempts to answer it. I think that the value of such an approach will become obvious in the course of reading the text.

I expect that the text will have most appeal for students taking their first course in industrial and organizational psychology. I expect that the students in such a course would have had at least one previous course in psychology, most likely introductory psychology. The student also would benefit from prior familiarity with basic statistical theory and practice. In addition, I have high hopes that my emphasis on the *individual* as the unit of analysis will provide a unique and valuable approach to many students in the more traditional business school settings.

Recently, the issue of "sexist" treatments of topic areas has assumed major importance. The feeling is that stereotypes are developed and maintained by the way in which information is presented. I have chosen to deal with the problem by alternating the use of personal pronouns throughout the text. For any industrial position, you should be just as likely to encounter females in that position as males. The worker is just as likely to be a "she" as a "he." There is one exception to that treatment. I have chosen to retain the term *man-machine system*. In this context, I prefer to think of the term *man* as generic. In addition, there is a large body of information that is likely to appear under that heading rather than under another heading such as "worker-machine system." I think that such continuity of topic headings is important and feel that the reader will accept the spirit in which the term is used.

This edition of the text, the fourth, differs in some respects from the earlier editions. These differences are represented in both form and content. In form, there is one substantial change: I have altered the order of chapters. In earlier editions, I presented material on tests first and then material on performance measures. I did this because it represented an appropriate temporal sequence from the perspective of the employee—first, the person is hired and, later, performance is evaluated. Nevertheless, from the perspective of the I/O psychologist, this is not the correct order. First, a job analysis is done and measures of performance are identified. Then, predictors are chosen based on that job analysis. Thus, the new order of chapters places job analysis and performance measurement in front of chapters on predictors or tests. There are no other substantial changes in form, although there has been a change in "style." We have changed some formats to increase visual appeal and provide a "friendlier look" to the reader. There are many more relevant illustrations and photos than in earlier editions. In addition, I have added additional applied examples to help the student better understand the concepts.

In preparing this edition, I have not felt compelled to make any additional dramatic changes of form or substance. Most of those "big" changes have been made in earlier editions. Naturally, I have replaced many older references with more current research. In addition, I have expanded substantially in certain areas, for example, validity generalization in the personnel area and self-efficacy in the motivation area. I have also added new sections such as the material on hands-on performance measurement and behavioral accomplishment records in the performance evaluation area and the "vitamin" model of job satisfaction. In addition, I have maintained and deepened the cognitive orientation of the third edition. Beginning with the first edition, there have been requests to make the book less comprehensive, easier, or both. In this edition, as in others, I have maintained a rigorous approach to the substance of I/O psychology. Nevertheless, I have tried to present certain difficult topics in a way that would make them easier to understand, primarily through the use of examples and heuristics. I/O psychology deals with complex problems and, as a result, is a complex subdiscipline. Pretending that the world is simpler does not make the problems less complex—just more intractable.

Instructors who have used earlier editions of the text will notice one pervasive change in the personnel area. Many of my police examples have been replaced with fire fighter examples. For the past several years, I have been doing research on fire fighter performance. There are many challenges in this area, particularly predicting performance in an occupation that requires not only cognitive but also physical abilities. In the next edition, I may have moved on to nuclear power plant operators or sales personnel. But for this edition, the instructor and student will be exposed to many of the intricacies of fire suppression. This is my personal form of job rotation. I have been aided in this new area by Larry Isabella, a friend and fire fighter in Cleveland, Ohio.

The preparation of this edition of the text was aided by the efforts of friends and colleagues at Penn State and in the "real" world. Joe Vasey and Jeff Quinn were a big help in tracking down research material. Friends in government and industry provided me with many of the examples and illustrations that appear in the text. In particular, I would like to thank Gene Larson and friends in the police and fire departments in Columbus, Cleveland, and Akron, Ohio. In addition, civil service professionals such as Dave Kriska and Cathy Cline have been wonderful sources of professional stimulation. Rick Jacobs, Jim Farr, John Mathieu, and Janet Echemendia represent a wonderful group of I/O psychologists at Penn State, and they have helped me to refine many of the concepts that appear in the text. Haleh Rastegary, Joe Vasey, Jeff Quinn, Joy Struble, and Erin Landy assisted in manuscript production. Early drafts of the chapters were reviewed by Professor Robert S. Billings, The Ohio State University; Dr. Kurt F. Geisinger, Fordham University; Professor David C. Gilmore, University of North Carolina at Charlotte; Professor Lee A. Jackson, University of North Carolina at Wilmington; Professor Charles E. Lance, University of Georgia; and Professor Mary E. McLaughlin, University of Illinois. I am grateful for their insight and suggestions. Now that he has retired and can do me no more substantial harm, I would like to identify Bob Guion as the source of all points in the book with which the reader might disagree. Although it has been 20 years since I received my degree under Bob's supervision, I can't seem to shake his goofy way of approaching certain topics. In contrast, all the points with which the reader might agree were developed after I received my degree, so Bob should be given no credit for that.

Frank J. Landy

Contents

CHAPTER 1

Introduction

In comparison with the physical and biological sciences, psychology has a short history as a scientific discipline. While the disciplines of chemistry, physics, and biology have been around for hundreds of years, psychology, as a modern science, has a history of barely 100 years. Industrial psychology, as a special subdiscipline, has an even shorter history.

In 1917, it was impossible to receive an advanced degree in industrial psychology—this simply did not exist as an area of specialization in graduate training programs. Although there were psychologists who did research in industrial settings, they had received their degrees in either clinical or experimental psychology. In 1921, Bruce V. Moore was awarded the first Ph.D. in Industrial Psychology at Carnegie Institute (now Carnegie-Mellon Institute) in Pittsburgh, Pennsylvania.

In the approximately 70 years that have passed, the area has developed to the extent that there are now specialty areas within industrial psychology—areas such as personnel psychology, social-industrial psychology, and engineering psychology. As can be seen in Figure 1–1, employment announcements no longer solicit responses from "industrial psychologists" but specify individuals with backgrounds and interests in work motivation and job satisfaction, criterion development and validation, or systems analysis of man-machine designs. This is evidence of the expanding challenge and scope of industrial and organizational (I/O) psychology. In this introductory chapter, I will try to lay the groundwork for the later discussion of problems addressed by industrial and organizational psychologists.

HISTORY

Despite its youth, industrial and organizational psychology has an interesting and complex history. As is true of most areas within psychology, its roots can be found in experimental psychology, that traditional part of the discipline that seeks general principles or "laws" describing the behavior of its subject matter. In psychology such laws are attempts to describe how *people* (or other animals) respond to certain conditions, or "treatments," systematically manipulated by the experimenter. I emphasize *people* because the goal of experimental psychology has been to describe principles that characterize

FIGURE 1–1 Jobs for I/O Psychologists

Ph.D. in Behavioral Sciences for major consulting firm. Will design/implement performance appraisal systems to foster communication, reinforce culture, build productivity and effectiveness for Fortune 500 companies.

Industrial/Organizational Psychologist. BellSouth, a leader in the telecommunications industry, is seeking candidates for a position in our Human Resources Research group based in Atlanta, GA. The position involves working with a group of psychologists responsible for research support for personnel selection systems (ranging from paper-and-pencil ability tests to management assessment centers) and employee development programs. The immediate opening will involve research projects ranging from test development and validation to evaluation of existing training programs.

Human Factors/Engineering Psychologist. Industrial/Organizational Psychologist. The Department of Psychology anticipates being able to fill two or more positions with a starting date of September, 1988. Candidates should have strong preparation and an active research program in one of the following areas: (a) human factors or engineering psychology, human-computer interactions, computer displays, artificial intelligence/expert systems, or other human factors applications of cognitive psychology; (b) industrial or organizational psychology.

Personnel Psychologist, Columbus, Ohio. The City of Columbus Civil Service Commission is actively recruiting a Personnel Psychologist to direct the activities of the testing staff and to advise the Commission on technical matters related to testing. The qualified applicant must possess a doctorate in psychology with graduate course work in testing and statistics and five years of experience in personnel test construction, validation, and administration.

SOURCE: The Industrial Organizational Psychologist, 1988, *25*(2), pp. 84, 86; *25*(3), p. 77.

the behavior of people *in general.* Such principles are, of course, extremely useful for the understanding of behavior in an industrial setting. They are also useful in predicting how certain conditions of work—or the modification of these conditions—will affect the behavior of the worker.

Many of the studies I will describe in the text differ from classic laboratory studies of learning, perception, motivation, and the like only by virtue of the fact that they deal with the effects of work-related variables on behavior and, in many cases, are conducted in work settings rather than in the laboratory. Because the field conditions of the work setting differ from those of the laboratory, it is often hazardous to generalize from laboratory findings. Principles, or findings, obtained in the laboratory need to be verified (and sometimes modified) in the work setting.

Modern industrial and organizational psychology also has important historical roots in *differential psychology,* the study of individual differences. In the latter part of the nineteenth century, psychologists became interested in the identification, description, and measurement of the ways in which people differ in abilities, traits, interests, and the like. By combining the methods of scientific observation with the advances that were taking place in psychological measurement and data analysis, these psychologists developed the area known as differential psychology.

It is interesting to note that differential psychologists took as their area of investigation those individual differences in behavior that were (and are) sources of frustration to the experimental psychologist. They were sources of frustration because individual differences often obscure the general principles of behavior the experimentalist seeks. It would be a relatively simple matter to identify behavioral principles if *all* people behaved in one way under one set of experimental conditions and in another way under a second set of conditions. The differential psychologist found these individual differences interesting and challenging and sought to account for them through the measurement and interrelation of abilities, interests, aptitudes, and personality traits.

Industrial and organizational psychology has also been influenced by developments in industrial engineering, including time-and-motion study and the design and arrangements of work and machines. In fact, one of the fathers of industrial psychology, Morris Viteles, decided to become an industrial psychologist in 1920 because industrial engineering, through the medium of time-and-motion study, had demonstrated that changes in the behavior of an individual could result in changes in productivity and profitability for the organization. He was persuaded that there was a bottom-line impact that resulted from the application of psychological principles to industrial behavior.

These three distinct forces—experimental psychology, differential psychology, and industrial engineering—combined to define a new area, which Hugo Munsterberg, another pioneer in the field, called "economic psychology." It now became possible to identify differences as well as similarities among individuals, to take these differences and similarities into account in the design of machines, work stations, and work routines, and to evaluate the relative efficiency of various worker-machine-process combinations. In fact, this was the primary activity of the "economic" psychologist for the first 20 to 30 years of this century.

Work procedures and machines were becoming more standardized and homogeneous by 1930. As a consequence, differences in work behavior could not always be explained in terms of physical differences among individuals or variations in work methods or machines. The psychologists in work settings began to take the "human" characteristics of the worker more seriously. The feelings, the motivations, the social relations among workers—all these topics began to receive attention. In all likelihood, these human or social issues became more prominent *because* of the standardization of equipment and work methods. As the factory system, mass-production methods of manufacturing, and time-and-motion studies exerted their strangleholds on behavior at the workplace, opportunities for individual expression and feelings of accomplishment diminished. There was a tension created in this standardization and simplification movement that remains to this day in the industrial environment. We explore this tension and its effects on several occasions in this book.

The period immediately preceding World War II was a dramatic one for all areas of psychology. Social psychology was on the verge of dramatic breakthroughs in measuring and understanding attitudes. Clinical psychology was able to expand on the rather rigid propositions of Freudian psychology. Developmental psychology was on the threshold of combining the observations and insights of Piaget with advances in the measurement of individual differences.

The revolution in industrial psychology came in the form of the Hawthorne studies, a series of field experiments that helped to highlight the complexity of work behavior. The Hawthorne studies signaled the beginning of the human-relations movement in industrial psychology. The feelings and internal reactions of workers became important variables. At the same time, the enthusiasm for the industrial use of psychological tests, kindled by the success of intelligence testing for recruit placement in World War I, began to slacken.

During this period, there seem to have been three independent movements in industrial psychology: (1) the testing movement (known as personnel psychology), drawing heavily on the differential-psychology approach; (2) the human-relations movement ("social-industrial" psychology), sparked by the Hawthorne studies; and (3) the experimental-industrial engineering movement, using the methods of experimental psychology and industrial engineering. Each of these three areas appeared to develop relatively independently, each with its own techniques and proponents. In personnel psychology, the development of modern statistical techniques aided in the construction of test batteries and new approaches to the measurement of performance. The human-relations movement discovered the work of Maslow and Rogers. These two individuals emphasized issues of personal growth and the realization of one's potential. As a result, the human-relations theorists developed principles of job satisfaction and work motivation that also emphasized these issues. Psychologists who were interested in application of experimental methods and principles found new challenges during World War II with the rapid development of new man-machine systems. They also found a new identity in what has come to be known as engineering psychology.

Until recently, the overlap of these three distinct but related areas did not receive recognition. The interdependence of the social-organizational structure, machine and system design, and worker characteristics now defines the science of work behavior. In 1973, Division 14 of the American Psychological Association (APA) changed its name from Division of Industrial Psychology to Division of Industrial and Organizational Psychology to underscore this interdependence. While engineering psychology is often treated separately, it should be recognized that it shares the common goal of understand-

Control room in a nuclear power plant. (Philadelphia Electric Co.)

ing in the relationship of people and work with industrial and organizational psychology.

The recognition of this interdependence has made life both more difficult and more exciting for the student of industrial and organizational psychology: more difficult because the number of variables that must be considered in trying to understand even the simplest reaction of the individual in the work setting has become staggering; more exciting because the understanding of this simplest of behaviors has finally become possible.

Currently, industrial and organizational psychology (I/O psychology) is undergoing another revolution. This revolution is equal in magnitude to the one induced by the Hawthorne studies. It is the *cognitive revolution*. In the late 1960s, cognitive variables became very important in most areas of psychology. Social learning theory influenced personality theory, social psychology, and clinical psychology. New models of memory were introduced that quickly led to dramatic advances in understanding how people process information. This revolution had a delayed effect in I/O psychology but is clearly being felt right now. The problems of appraising performance have been almost completely recast as cognitive rather than as administrative or procedural (Landy & Farr, 1980, 1983). Instead of studies on the best type of rating form, current appraisal research covers issues such as cognitive complexity of raters, and the role of short- and long-term memory in rating. Similarly, motivation theories now emphasize the inferential skills of the worker, particularly the way in which reward probabilities are estimated. The most obvious influence of the cognitive revolution is in the area of system design. Information-processing capacities and limitations are playing a major role in the design of work environments and tasks. In addition, a better understanding of cognitive variables and processes is responsible for major advances in the identification of stressors and the reduction of stress at work. Earlier I identified the three major influences in the development of I/O psychology—differential psychology, human relations, and industrial engineering. Future development will add cognitive theory as a fourth major influence. Throughout the book, this influence will be identified when it appears.

The capacity to study industrial behavior in all its complexity is a result of the normal maturation that characterizes the development of any credible science. This development is well described by Dunnette (1976) in contrasting the *Handbook of Applied Psychology* published in 1950 (Fryer & Henry) with the *Handbook of Industrial and Organizational Psychology* (Dunnette) published in 1976:

> The 1950 *Handbook* was almost exclusively a handbook of practice, emphasizing techniques and applications and giving little attention to research or research methodology and no attention at all to theories of individual or organizational behavior. In contrast, the current *Handbook* gives heavy emphasis to strategies of research and research methodology, theories of behavior, and very strong emphasis to organizational characteristics and the impact of social psychological forces and influences involving interaction processes between organizations and persons. (pp. 2–8)

The difference between the two *Handbooks* that Dunnette highlights can also be seen in the differing professional activity of the industrial psychologist then and now. As early industrial psychologists became aware of the needs of society, they were able and willing to respond to these needs. World War II and the needs it presented caused industrial and differential psychologists to advance the testing movement that began around World War I. Engineering psychologists also responded magnificently by producing some of the finest knobs and dials ever to adorn an airplane's instrument panel. Nevertheless, it was not until the late 1950s and early 1960s that psychologists began to work on the *theories* that might explain the various successes and failures of the 1930s and 1940s.

Several excellent histories of the early phases of the field are available. DuBois (1970) traces the development of psychological testing; Fryer and Henry (1950) present an excellent view of both the roots and the status of I/O psychology in 1950; Ferguson (1962) gives a very personal account of the development of the field to 1960; and Dunnette (1976) provides a contemporary overview of I/O psychology. By examining these histories, we can see that industrial and organizational psychology is much more aggressive today than it was 25 years ago. Recently, industrial psychologists have been responsible for introducing and refining concepts such as job enrichment and task design. They have introduced taxonomies to cover physical and mental activities at the workplace and have developed elaborate methods of investigation and analysis in validation research. In short, they have adopted an *active* rather than a *reactive* mode. I believe that this change is a permanent one and that I/O psychologists will become increasingly active. This is a luxury afforded by a better understanding of the behaviors being studied.

There are several themes that I will follow throughout this book. The first is the importance of individual differences. It is my belief that advances in the understanding of behavior patterns in industry can be made from an analysis of the differences among individuals. I will look at those factors that might account for the fact that one individual succeeds in a particular job while another fails, or the fact that one individual is happy in a particular job while another is miserable. Although I will attempt to draw some generalizations from the material presented, these generalizations will be based on observation of such individual differences. This approach is in contrast to theories contending that the behavior of all individuals can be understood on the basis of a single rule or principle. Such approaches seem to follow the human preference to reduce information to its simplest form. While such a strategy may be pleasing, it is usually useless and circular. It is becoming more and more apparent that certain behavior patterns are more influenced by characteristics on which *individuals* differ than by characteristics on which *situations* differ. In each of the chapters of this book, I will try to identify some of these individual differences and the ways in which they affect the understanding and prediction of behavior in industrial settings.

Another theme I stress is that the various topic areas are inextricably bound together. It is impossible to select the best workers for a particular job until we are able to describe success on the job. Further, regardless of which individuals the selection scheme identifies as the most likely prospects for success, the reward system of the organization will have very definite and predictable consequences on whether that individual is, in fact, successful on the job. These kinds of interrelationships will emerge as the areas are introduced. I will alert you to some of the more important interrelationships.

A final theme that will be carried through every chapter is the total interdependence of research, theory, and practice. Sterile theories, developed in laboratories and tested only in the mind of the researcher, are useless. Ultimately, theories should be tested in several different settings and "packaged" somehow for local application. Unless the generality of a theory of behavior can be *demonstrated*, the theory is best abandoned. Conversely, dozens of studies on a similar topic are equally useless until and unless someone collects the findings, identifies consistencies in the results, and forms more general principles that might account for these results. In the various chapters,

I will identify models and theories that have guided research; where models and theories are not available, we will review available research and identify consistencies. Above all, I will attempt to show how theory complements practice.

There are undoubtedly other themes in this book that will be more evident to you than they are to me. When I present material that is open to speculation, I will identify it as such. This does not mean that I will hide my own preference; it means that the critical evidence or logic is missing from the argument, and I will warn you of this.

The book is separated into four areas. The first appears in Chapters 1 and 2. This material consists primarily of background or contextual information necessary for the interpretation of what will follow. It consists of descriptions aimed at establishing the uniqueness of industrial psychology from other sciences as well as from other areas within psychology. In addition, I describe what industrial psychologists do and where they are likely to do it. Chapter 2 consists of the methodological preparation necessary for working with the raw information (in the form of research results) that appears in the content chapters. Learning this is much like learning a language necessary for the understanding of later chapters. I also present the research methods related to the philosophy of individual differences. Then I show how this philosophy is applied in research related to industrial problems. Finally, I explore some of the favorite tools of the I/O psychologist—specifically, ways of collecting and analyzing data.

The second major group of chapters deals with what has been traditionally labeled as "personnel psychology." It would probably be more appropriate to call it the "psychology of personnel decisions." In most modern organizations, the term *human resources* has replaced the term *personnel*. This second section is composed of Chapters 3 through 9—predictor-related issues, alternative-selection devices, criterion-related issues, personnel decisions, and a chapter on the theory and application of industrial training. Historically, personnel psychology has been the backbone of industrial and organizational psychology. Since it deals so heavily with problems of measurement, prediction, and inference, it will undoubtedly continue to be an area of prime importance. Issues such as reliability and validity, raised in the sections on personnel decisions, carry equal importance in the evaluation of motivational programs and of man-machine systems. Criterion development, introduced as a preparation for performance appraisal, is equally crucial in studies of leadership and of skilled operator performance. In short, personnel psychology includes a collection of the techniques that are essential to the psychologist pursuing the understanding of behavior in industrial settings.

The topics in the personnel psychology chapters are critically related to human resource administration in any modern organization. Unless the important elements and implications of job analysis, validation, and performance assessment are understood, it is unlikely that the modern human resource department can perform its duties either efficiently or legally. New human resource issues are appearing at a rapid rate. As examples, many of today's organizations are routinely administering drug screening tests. These tests have an impact on hiring decisions, just as other tests do. There is an implicit assumption that the presence of certain substances in the blood or urine of an applicant is a predictor of failure on the job. As the use of these tests increases, so will assaults on the assumption of the substance-performance link. As many companies have discovered, the legal costs of having tests constructed and administered by the uninformed can be enormous. The complexity and increasing cost of selecting and training employees make the sections on tests, testing procedures, and training models and devices "must" reading for anyone responsible for personnel decisions. These chapters are relevant for both manager and psychologist equally.

The third area of interest deals with the individual's attempts to adjust to the characteristics of the job, coworkers, superiors, and the organization. It also deals with the modifications the organization makes in an attempt to coexist with the characteristics of its workers. Chapters 10, 11, 12, and 13 deal with work motivation, job satisfaction, leadership, and organizational theory, respectively. These chapters might be thought of as falling on a continuum that begins with the molecular view of the individual's motives and his affective or emotional responses to the work environment (work motivation and job satisfaction) and ends with the molar examination of the effect of the systematic expectancies of the organization on the employee's behavior on those expectancies. Another way of looking at the chapters in this section is that they deal with decisions that the individual makes while at the workplace: decisions about whether to expend energy and whether to accept the goals of the leader or the organization. In addition, I will explore the feelings that accompany these decisions and the effect of these feelings on later decisions. This section might be contrasted with the personnel section by stating that it concentrates on the *individual worker* as the decision maker rather than on the system or organization (as implied in the notion of a "personnel decision").

As was the case in the personnel section, these chapters are important for the manager as well as for the psychologist. The way individuals *feel* about their jobs may ultimately determine how long they *stay*. Job variety, opportunity to affect decisions, leadership style, and organizational climate may all affect the worker's feelings; for that reason, it is important to be familiar with current thinking on organizational variables. On a more humanistic note, the topics in this section deal with the "quality of work" as perceived by the individual employee. All other things being equal, it is reasonable for both managers and psychologists to have as one of their goals the desire to make workers happy.

The last two chapters deal with an area generally referred to as "engineering psychology." Chapters 14 and 15 deal with the extent to which the worker's environment—both physical and psychological—affects her effectiveness and well-being. This section differs from the two that precede it primarily because it views the human element in the man-machine–environment complex as a component in a system, communicating with machine elements and interacting with physical environmental conditions. It also treats the tasks assigned to the human components and the environmental conditions as potential sources of stress on the individual.

With the increasing complexity of the modern workplace, it is important for the practitioner, whether manager or psychologist, to understand the effects of drugs, alcohol, fatigue, information overload, shift work, and other stressors on industrial performance. In addition, the demands placed on the worker by the tasks that compose his job, as well as the resources placed at his disposal to meet those demands, need to be understood and included in the process of work and environmental design. As machine operators are replaced by machine tenders through automation, it is important to recognize that the skills necessary for successful performance and the costs of adapting to the new job demands are different from previous skills and costs. The final section will highlight these issues.

INDUSTRIAL AND ORGANIZATIONAL PSYCHOLOGY

Before presenting a formal definition of *I/O psychology,* I will provide a framework to help put it into the proper perspective.

As a Science. To describe a particular activity as "scientific" implies that the activity has certain goals and is carried out in a prescribed manner. The major goals of a scientific endeavor are understanding, prediction, and control. In that respect, I/O psychology is similar to experimental psychology, nuclear physics, and biochemistry. Each of those disciplines has understanding, prediction, and control as a major set of goals. But a scientific endeavor is characterized as much by the *way* in which it is carried out as by the *goals* it seeks. One of these characteristics is a system of logic that enables a researcher to draw inferences or form hypotheses about the relationships among variables. This system of logic may be inductive (one that proceeds from a broad data base to a principle), deductive (one that proceeds from a set of a priori principles to test those principles in the real world), or both. At the simplest level, I am saying that theories are central to a science. In addition to the role of a unifying theory, scientific activity must be accompanied by the collection of data (i.e., it must be related to empirical or observable investigation). A third characteristic of scientific activity is that it must be communicable; one must be able to describe procedures and analyses employed, as well as experimental manipulations, to the public at large. If the researchers cannot adequately explain the nature of their activities, then the activity is something less than science. As a matter of fact, this is one of the major distinctions between art and science. Art is something that depends on individual experience and cannot always be communicated to someone else; science, on the other hand, must be communicable if we are ever to add to the body of knowledge, whether that knowledge be related to blood flow, nuclear fission, or work motivation. Communication occurs in the form of scholarly articles in journals, books, talks, and the like. I/O psychology possesses all the important characteristics of a science. It is supported by theories and theory development. In almost every chapter in this book, you will be exposed to theories of different aspects of work behavior. I/O psychology is also dependent on data. In the next chapter, I will present some of the common techniques for gathering and analyzing those data, and in the chapters that follow, most of the discussion will revolve around data that have been collected in order to understand better a phenomenon of interest. Finally, I/O psychology is public. There are several major journals in the field. These include the *Journal of Applied Psychology, Personnel Psychology, Organizational Behavior and Human Decision Processes, Human Performance,* the *Administrative Science Quarterly,* the *Journal of Occupational Psychology,* the *Academy of Management Journal,* the *Academy of Management Review, Human Factors,* and *Ergonomics.* These journals carry the results of studies on work behavior as well as theoretical statements. This provides other I/O psychologists the opportunity to replicate the findings of colleagues, to extend theories, and to test research findings in varied settings. In fact, on several occasions in the book, I will identify scientific debates that are being carried on among I/O psychologists. These debates are possible only by virtue of the fact that we carry out our activities *publicly.* Given these characteristics, I/O psychology clearly qualifies as a science.

As a Behavioral Science. Psychology, and in particular I/O psychology, is classified as a behavioral science. This separates it from the physical sciences. The behavioral sciences, as their title implies, focus their efforts on the study of behavior of systems and subsystems in which individuals find themselves. A system may be as broad as a culture, as in the case of anthropology, or as narrow as the subjective reality a single individual has created for herself, as in the case of psychology. Some other disciplines that are characterized as behavioral sciences are sociology, political science, and economics. Psychology stands out from the rest of the behavioral sciences primarily because its emphasis is on the understanding, prediction, and control of behavior peculiar to the *individual.* Although individuals may form groups and respond to common antecedents, the psychologist continues to be concerned with the behavior of the individual and why the individual may belong to one group rather than another. The study of group process and group behaviors is in the province of the sociologist and social psychologist.

As an Interest Area in Psychology. I/O psychology has the industrial situation as its setting. Although work may be done in a laboratory or in a simulated work setting, the industrial psychologist is primarily concerned with the application of psychological principles to the problems workers encounter in the performance of their duties.

A comparison of I/O psychology with the other areas of psychology will give you an idea of its potential uniqueness. Here are some definitions of various areas from a publication of the APA, the primary professional organization for psychologists:

> *Clinical psychology.* Clinicians specialize in the assessment and treatment of persons suffering emotional or adjustment disorders.
>
> *Educational psychology.* Educational psychologists are concerned with the development and evaluation of materials and procedures for education and training.
>
> *Industrial and organizational psychology.* Industrial and organizational psychologists are interested in aspects of people's work such as their job satisfaction and their efficiency. (American Psychological Association [APA], 1976, pp. 5, 8, 10)

Industrial and organizational psychology is a popular specialty. A survey published in 1981 reveals that approximately 1,500 of a total of 21,000 Ph.D. psychologists who responded identified their specialty as industrial, engineering, or psychometrics. In terms of numbers, this places industrial and organizational third behind clinical (9,500) and counseling (2,400) as an interest area (Stapp, Fulcher, Nelson, Pallack, & Wicherski, 1981).

When comparing I/O psychology with each of the other areas of psychology, we might make that comparison along three dimensions: (1) the context—Where does the research and application go on? (2) the process of the research and application of the particular area; and (3) the content of the area—What are the antecedent and consequent variables that appear most often in research and application in that area of interest?

Context. Traditionally, I/O psychology has been bound to the industrial context, the world of work. This is true neither of social psychology nor clinical psychology. This is not to say that I/O psychology does not draw from findings in context other than the work context in research and application, but rather that it relates those findings to behavior in work settings. In that sense, I/O psychology, like school psychology, is closely allied to a particular setting. While this distinction is becoming more and more blurred, it may be useful for the time being to maintain it.

Process. When we look at the *way* in which I/O psychology approaches research or the application of principles, we find that it is not unique. The I/O psychologist characteristically makes use of the full range of experimental designs and analyses that are employed by other areas in conducting research, but—and it is an important exception—the I/O psychologist applies these findings to industrial settings. In the next chapter, we will see some of the more frequently employed designs and statistical tools of the I/O psychologist.

Content. A final dimension that can be used to characterize I/O psychology is the content of the discipline, that is, the variables under consideration. In this respect, the field is characterized by the three major subareas described above. It considers intraindividual variables such as job satisfaction and work motivation. It also considers prediction and measurement systems as they apply in industry in the form of selection and performance appraisal of employees, and it deals with certain stimulus variables such as information displays, effects of environmental conditions that might add to or reduce stress, and strategies for information processing as they relate to man-machine interactions.

What Is the Importance of the Term *Organizational*?

As I indicated earlier, the name of the specialty area was changed in 1973 from industrial psychology to industrial and organizational psychology. This was not simply an attempt to emphasize the fact that this type of psychologist worked in formal organizations. Instead, it was meant to emphasize something unique about the behavior that I/O psychologists study. For the most part, we examine *organized* behavior. The organization of behavior for each person often involves many other people and the organization of several tasks into job responsibilities for the individual. In any organization, we are dealing with interdependent units (e.g., people, jobs, or departments) rather than discrete ones. The very act of organizing effort creates a new behavior. The perspective of Gestalt psychology seems appropriate here—organized behavior is more than the simple sum of its parts, regardless of whether those parts are different members of a work group or different actions in a sequence of actions performed by a single individual. This interest in the organization of behavior in particular settings distinguishes the I/O psychologist from those in many other specialty areas. In addition to the emphasis on the entire organization rather than single individuals, the practice of organizational psychology has become identified to a great extent with organizational change. As a result, organizational psychologists are contributing to our understanding of the mechanisms that promote and obstacles that prevent organizations from growing or adapting to environmental demands.

The Role of an I/O Psychologist

I once asked my introductory psychology class to gather descriptions of what an I/O psychologist does from friends, relatives, and neighbors. Here are some of the most interesting of those descriptions:

> Industrial psychology is the process of making people do what they don't want to do.
>
> An industrial psychologist is one who reviews technical inventions to ascertain whether or not the effect of the invention will be beneficial to the society—for example, a nuclear power plant.
>
> A shrink for machines.

> An industrial psychologist interviews people to see that they are placed in the right positions in factories.
>
> An industrial psychologist is one who investigates the behavior of people at work as opposed to outside of work.

These observations confirm a statement made by a member of a task force commissioned to describe the effective practice of psychology in industry ("Task Force," 1971):

> People have the image of psychologists—either you're a numbers man, you're a kind of a nuts-and-bolts guy, or you're a clinical type who comes in to help sick people. But they don't realize that we know a great deal about the normal individual. (p. 77)

You can see that many of these definitions come close to the activities I have already described. Unfortunately, at least two of them confuse the I/O psychologist with an industrial engineer and a person who communicates with inanimate objects.

One way of describing the role of I/O psychologists might be to indicate where they are likely to be found and what they are likely to be doing.

Settings. There are four major settings for I/O psychologists—government and industry, consulting firms, academia, and research organizations. While the predominant work setting in which I/O psychologists are found is the industrial setting, this is not exclusive. The activities of the I/O psychologist in this setting might include developing testing programs for the selection of employees, determining equitable pay plans for employees through job analysis and evaluation, developing motivation programs for managers, conducting seminars on leadership for executives, evaluating training programs, or determining the characteristics of a new bank of turret lathes that will fit best with the capabilities and limitations of the organization's employees. Even though not *every* I/O psychologist would be concerned with *each* of the problems mentioned, the problems constitute a reasonable sample of those that confront industrial psychologists. Their activities generally consist of both long-term and short-term projects. The unique challenge of I/O psychologists in industry is that they must not only develop programs for an organization but must also be accountable for the results of those programs. This may also be the reward of such an activity—being able to develop and *implement* a program.

Generally, consulting firms make use of the skills of the I/O psychologist in much the same way as does industry. In these settings, the I/O psychologist is responsible for the development of a particular action program, such as constructing a performance-appraisal system, developing a recruiting program, or attempting to analyze "human-relations" problems. Unlike the psychologist who works for a single industrial organization, however, the consulting industrial psychologist is not always directly responsible for the implementation of an action program but may function in an advisory capacity to the management group of the particular organization. Activities are as varied as those of the psychologist in industrial settings.

I/O psychologists are also found in academic settings. An example of such a person might be your instructor in this course. The primary responsibilities of I/O psychologists in this setting are teaching and research, but they may also engage in consulting work for government and industry. A typical I/O psychologist in an academic setting might teach three courses during a semester; conduct a research project on a skilled motor-performance task, such as driving an automobile; and help a local company validate a test battery it has been using for the past decade.

Finally, the I/O psychologist might work for a research organization. Examples of this type of organization are the Educational Testing Service of Princeton, New Jersey, and the American Institutes for Research in Washington, D.C. These organizations concentrate on developing rather broad programs of action in areas germane to I/O psychology, such as selection programs for municipal police departments or training programs for hospital administrations. They are usually able to support the kind of long-term basic research necessary to advance the field and to solve the difficult and complex problems of modern society. In these settings, the I/O psychologist's time might be split between research and application, and more often than not, it will involve working with a small group of other psychologists in a team effort.

Of course, there are other settings in which an I/O psychologist might be found, such as government agencies like the U.S. Civil Service Commission, the Equal Employment Opportunity Commission (EEOC), or the National Institute of Occupational Safety and Health (NIOSH), but even so the problems they face will be as varied and challenging as those outlined above.

Stapp et al. (1981) have provided a glimpse of the work settings of I/O psychologists who hold the Ph.D. Approximately 60 percent of the I/O psychologists are found in business or governmental settings; 35 percent can be found in higher education settings; the other 5 percent may be found in independent practice, hospitals, and other human service settings. As a group, I/O psychologists engage in a full range of professional activities including teaching, training, conducting basic research and development, performing applied research, and carrying out personnel programs and the design of man-machine systems. Naturally, the particular activities that any one I/O psychologist engages in will depend to a great extent on the work setting.

I/O Psychology in Other Countries

One of the great failings of U.S. I/O psychology is the failure to recognize the importance of the work being done by scientific colleagues in other countries. There are two important aspects to that work. First, our international

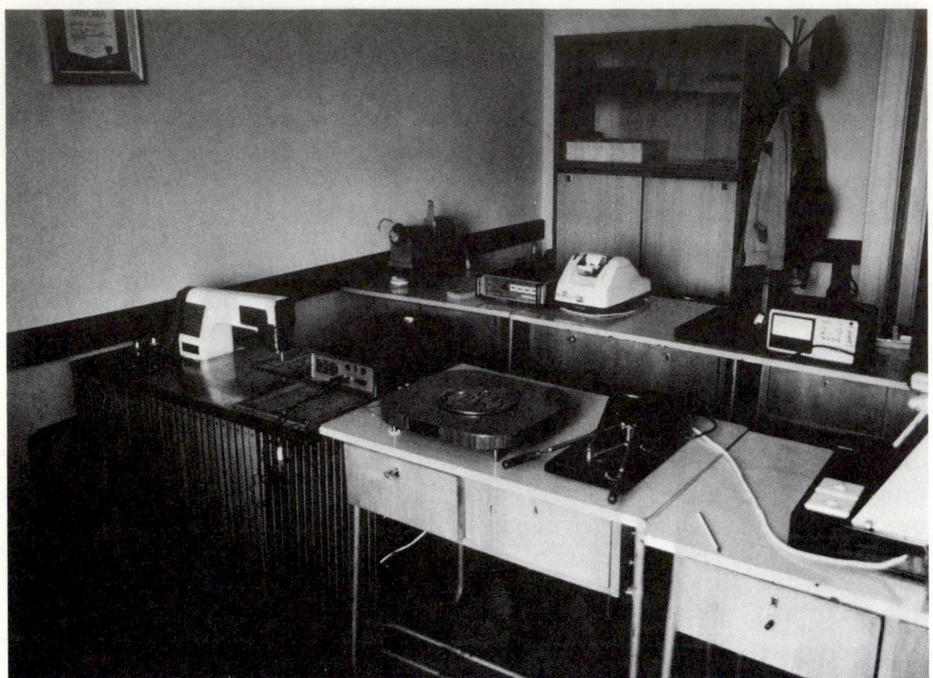

An industrial psychologist's testing laboratory in a Romanian factory. Candidates for jobs on knitting machines are tested here.

colleagues often deal with a much different work environment and sociopolitical environment than we do. For example, the challenges of worker motivation experienced by a manager in a socialist or communist country are very different than those facing the capitalist manager. It is not common (or in many instances, legal) to offer differential wages to workers. As another example, in many countries there is still a strong agricultural influence that pervades the value system of the industrial workers, making it difficult to hold them at their workplace during planting or harvest times.

The second aspect of international I/O psychology that deserves attention is the quality of research and theory being published by our colleagues in other countries. There is a tendency to examine only U.S. sources when conducting literature reviews. This is a mistake. There is a good deal of excellent research published in journals such as the *Journal of Occupational Psychology*, the *Journal of Organizational Behavior*, the *International Review of Applied Psychology*, the *Scandinavian Journal of Psychology*, and the *Bulletin of the International Test Commission*.

In many countries, industrial psychology plays a central role in strategic planning and decision making at policy levels. As an example, in Romania there is an industrial psychologist at almost every plant. The psychologist is

Candidates who do well on the tests are assigned to knitting and sewing machines.

responsible for helping the plant manager to maintain high levels of productivity. If a worker's performance falls below standards, the worker is sent to the psychologist for diagnosis and correction. The psychologist will explore health issues and nonwork factors in addition to assessing skills and abilities using standardized tests. If the psychologist decides that the problem is skill or ability based, the worker may be assigned to a training room for 30 days for monitoring and instruction. At the end of the 30-day period, the worker will be given a productivity test to determine whether he will be reassigned to his old position or fired. The opinions of the psychologist have substantial weight in making decisions about work methods and equipment. It is ironic that in many U.S. organizations the psychologist has considerably less status with respect to operating decisions than her Warsaw Pact colleague. It is well worthwhile for the student of industrial and organizational psychology to examine the work of non-U.S. colleagues in an attempt to develop generalized theories of work behavior. An excellent source of information regarding the practice of industrial psychology in other countries is *The Industrial and Organizational Psychologist* (also known as TIP), the newsletter of Division 14 of the APA. In the past several years, there have been articles describing industrial psychology in Great Britain, Sweden, Australia, and Romania.

How Will a Course in I/O Psychology Help You?

Most of the activities that I have described above involve advanced training in I/O psychology. It is unlikely that you could move directly into a position involving personnel administration or man-machine design after taking a first course in I/O. Nevertheless, there are some tangible benefits from even this one course. For example, virtually everything you do in the course of a day involves other people. This means that understanding the motivations and emotions of other people should make these interactions more pleasant and more efficient. And a large section of this course (and this book) will be devoted to human motivations and emotions. In addition, after taking this course, you should have a much greater appreciation for the role that measurement plays in making practical decisions. By *measurement* I do not mean simply statistics. Instead, this term includes the administration and interpretation of tests and test scores, the description of the performance of workers, and the evaluation of various strategies for staffing organizations. You need not be a manager to use or appreciate this information. It is safe to say that you will seldom be far from measurement issues regardless of your life-style or circumstances. You will take tests and interviews to get jobs, and you will receive pay increases based on performance levels. In short, your skills, abilities, and personality are "measured." Finally, in dealing with people and environments, you will be at an advantage if you know something about your capacities and limitations, particularly with respect to potential sources of stress. What are the basic cognitive and physical abilities that can be brought to bear on a particular task—any task? How can you rearrange your job or work setting to reduce stress?

As you can see, these issues are not trivial. If you know more about these areas as a result of taking this course and reading this book, you will have a useful knowledge base for both industrial and nonindustrial behavior. Much of this knowledge is unique to I/O psychology and is not represented in other advanced courses.

The Challenge to I/O Psychology

Most disciplines grow as a result of challenge. I/O psychology is no exception. Consider the growth experienced as a result of the classification pressures of World War I and World War II. Enormous advances in test development and administrative procedures resulted from this pressure. Similarly, engineering psychology has realized tremendous scientific growth as a result of changing technology. As new machinery, work procedures, and entire technologies were introduced, expanded descriptions of human capacities and limitations were required. Currently, the nuclear power and transportation industries are receiving a great deal of attention from I/O psychologists as a result of the pressure placed on these industries by the concern for safety of the public. Perhaps the most dramatic influence or pressure on personnel psychology has been the section of the Civil Rights Act that defines permissible employment procedures. Title VII of the Civil Rights Act of 1964 completely changed the way in which people were hired. In addition, it led to a tremendous advance in our conceptions of skills and aptitudes as well as methods for measuring productive effort.

In the next few years, some of these pressures will remain, some will be modified, and some new ones will be added. For example, it is unlikely that the pressure for fair employment will diminish. What will change will be the focus. As the work force ages, there will be an increased demand for models and theories of the behavior of older adults. Court cases involving mandatory retirement programs have also shown a rapid increase. The EEOC has clearly indicated its willingness to challenge the untested assumptions of many employers that older workers are less capable of effective work simply due to chronological age. In addition, the post–World War II baby boom has created organizations in which the opportunities for advancement are greatly reduced. Many employees find themselves supervised by someone their own age or only slightly older. This means that retirement-fueled promotions will be less frequent than in past years.

There are other pressures that may not be felt as much as they should but remain the responsibility of the I/O psychologist. During the last economic recession, certain dramatic changes occurred in the fabric of the work environment. First, many traditional jobs disappeared. It is unlikely that they will be back in their original form. These include jobs in the steel industry, auto industry, and lumber-construction industry. This means that a large number of people have skills that are no longer desired. How can these people be reintegrated into the work force? Retooling and retraining should be a critical concern of the I/O psychologist. A second change that has occurred relates to the demographics of unemployment. The groups hardest hit by the recession were teenagers, blacks, and blue-collar workers. In many major cities, the unemployment rate among young black males with primitive technological skills is a tragedy. This should represent a pressure on I/O psychology for solutions to the dilemma. Another effect of the recession was to point out the immense role that work plays in the lives of average adults. Most estimates of future levels of employment suggest that levels of unemployment in particular geographic areas (e.g., the heavily industrialized cities of the Midwest) will continue to create problems—economic and social—for society. We need to know more about the negative effects of unemployment and underemployment and how best to moderate or to reduce these effects.

Many feel that women's issues, like racial issues, have been largely resolved in the industrial setting. Nothing could be further from the truth. In fact, women's issues are just beginning to surface in the form of questions regarding the structural foundation of the organization. The tendency for women to be offered certain classes of jobs and men other classes, the issue of comparable worth and compensation plans generally, the issue of dual-career families and changing family roles—all these issues represent challenges for the I/O psychologist.

Finally, there is the issue of the handicapped. Traditionally, I/O psychologists have considered studies of the capacities and limitations of the handicapped to be in the province of the educational, vocational, clinical, or counseling psychologist. Unfortunately, these other professionals are often unprepared to deal with the issues of organization in the workplace. They may be unfamiliar with work procedures, reward policies, organizational structures, or supervisory styles. As a result, the handicapped applicant has an additional burden—unfamiliarity with the underlying structure of the work organization. I/O psychology can make substantial contributions to the utilization and development of impaired persons.

In the chapters that follow, I will cover research, practice, and theory that might be used to address many of these challenges as well as aid in the traditional activity of the I/O psychologist.

CHAPTER 2

Methods and Ethics of Industrial and Organizational Psychology

As you saw in the last chapter, the I/O psychologist is concerned with the behavior of individuals in work settings. Coworkers, gauges, salary, demanding tasks—these are all examples of stimuli that might be of interest to the I/O psychologist. Similarly, the work setting implies certain classes of unique responses on the part of the individual. These responses might include statements about satisfaction, levels of job performance, absence behavior, or willingness to accept directions from a supervisor.

The stimuli and the responses that interest the I/O psychologist are often different from those that might interest the developmental, clinical, or educational psychologist. For that reason, the I/O psychologist often makes use of certain "tools" or methods that are unique. Similarly, since data are often gathered outside of the laboratory in real-world settings, some statistical techniques are used more frequently than in other areas of psychology. Finally, since the circumstances under which data are gathered and the uses to which those data may be put are often unique, the ethical questions that arise in the course of carrying out the activities of the I/O psychologist are sometimes different from the ethical questions in other areas. In this chapter, we will consider those three aspects of I/O psychology: methodology, statistics, and ethics. The object will not be to repeat material that you may have already encountered or will encounter in another course. Instead, I will try to identify those aspects of methodology, data analysis, and ethics that are of particular importance for the I/O psychologist. This will also be the first instance in which I implement the technical appendix strategy that I outlined in the preface. This should allow you to consider the purpose and general procedures in certain analytic and statistical operations without being bogged down in detail. If you are interested in the particular operations, you can turn to the appendix at the end of the chapter.

METHODS OF INVESTIGATION

I/O psychology has accepted the scientific method as a general strategy for studying behavior in the context of work. The implication of this acceptance is that systematic observation will occur. In other words, data will be gathered and those data used to draw conclusions about the behavior under consideration. Naturally, there are many different ways to gather these data. As an example, if I were interested in understanding the behavior of the instructor for this course, I could gather data in several different ways. I could watch the instructor as she presented a lecture. I could ask you and your fellow students to describe her teaching behavior. I could ask her to come to a special room and present a lecture on a preselected topic. I could masquerade as a student having a problem understanding the material and ask her questions about the material. These would all be legitimate ways of gathering data and could qualify as applications of the scientific method. A study is nothing more than a set of observational procedures that allow at least *some* alternative explanations to be ruled out while other explanations (and ideally, *one* explanation) can be justified.

Experimental Controls

The rules of observation that I referred to above are often called *experimental controls.* These rules cannot be easily covered in a few sentences, but I can suggest some of the characteristics of experimental control. First, the scientist has rules or guiding principles dealing with the adequacy of the sample of observations made. One does not "jump to conclusions" on the basis of a single observation, especially in observing something as complex as human behavior (and as variable as human beings); a sample of observations or different "specimens" of the subject matter is required. Sampling adequacy means more than just the *number* of observations the researcher makes, however. The observations must be "fair," or unbiased; they must fairly sample representatives of the larger population from which the sample was taken and to which the researcher wants to generalize any conclusions. Thus, for example, the researcher who wants to draw conclusions about the effect of music on the productivity of "blue-collar workers" (the population) cannot limit herself to observing only young women assemblers in an electronics plant (the sample). Or, conversely, if she samples a small homogenous group, she must be cautious about generalizing the findings beyond the sample. Adequate sampling will be considered further in Chapter 3 under the heading "Reliability and Validity."

The tasks we set for people to do, the physical environment in which the tasks are carried out, the time of day, the instructions, the incentives, and in some cases the experimenter are factors that may affect the behavior being observed. Unless these conditions are standardized so that the only conditions varying are those that the researcher systematically manipulates (the independent variables), then the interpretation of the observations in terms of cause-effect relationships is extremely limited. The last sentence states the logic of the experiment: variations in A cause variations in B when we can rule out the possibilities that variations in other "extraneous" variables occurred. Recently, a national testing firm retained by the federal government to keep tabs on the reading effectiveness of public school students discovered that the reading level of a sample of these students plummeted almost one full year over a two-year period. This was a startling figure since it implied that most of the gains in national reading levels that had been realized in recent years had been wiped out—almost overnight. It wasn't long before it was discovered that some items had been changed between the 1984 and 1986 administrations of the critical reading examination. Thus, it was not clear whether the reading level of the students decreased or whether the difficulty of the test increased. This was an example of a missing experimental control that rendered a result uninterpretable. The changed items were the extraneous variables in this study.

The discussion leads us to another topic of concern: the nature of the research design. It should be obvious by now that control is related to the setting in which the research is done. There are several different settings in which an I/O psychologist may find himself. Four major approaches to gathering data are (1) the laboratory experiment, (2) the field experiment, (3) the field study, and (4) the simulation. Each of these has its own strengths and weaknesses and will be dealt with individually.

The principal differences among the four major designs for gathering data are in terms of (1) the extent to which the conditions of observation can be systematically controlled by the experimenter, (2) the extent to which the "treatments" (experimental or independent variables) can be systematically manipulated, and (3) the extent to which the behavior observations (dependent variables) can be prescribed so as to be representatives of some larger population.

Strategies of Investigation

A Laboratory Experiment. Many jobs require a person to search a screen for information. As an example, a radar operator is constantly attempting to keep track of one or more objects that may change position, that may increase or decrease in number, and that may change in their proximity to one another. If that radar operator happens to be an air traffic controller at Chicago's O'Hare airport, the "objects" to which we are referring take on a new meaning.

There are many aspects of this job that would be of interest to the industrial psychologist. For example, how are individuals selected and trained for this job? What types of variables affect their job satisfaction and work motivation? What kinds of training programs are most efficient for teaching trainees the multitude of tasks that make up this job? Another important

aspect of the job would be the nature of the equipment that the controller uses to accomplish task goals. Suppose we are interested in the question of whether the number of objects on the radar screen or "display" affects search time or the speed with which any *one* object can be found and identified.

Carter (1979) has studied exactly that question in the laboratory. He was concerned with the characteristics of the display that affect a subject's search time. He constructed an experimental apparatus that allowed him to vary two characteristics of the display: the number of objects present at any one time and the relative position of those objects on the screen. There were two levels of density—30 objects or 60 objects. There were three levels of object proximity to the outer edge of the screen. Objects had either 0, 1, or 2 adjoining "neighbors." In addition, the objects could appear in either the top half or the bottom half of the display. Thus, there were many different experimental conditions to which subjects could be assigned. Each of the various combinations of target positions was presented to a different experimental group. Figure 2–1 presents a few typical displays to which subjects might have been exposed.

The subjects were college students. They were asked to sit in a quiet,

FIGURE 2–1 Experimental Displays

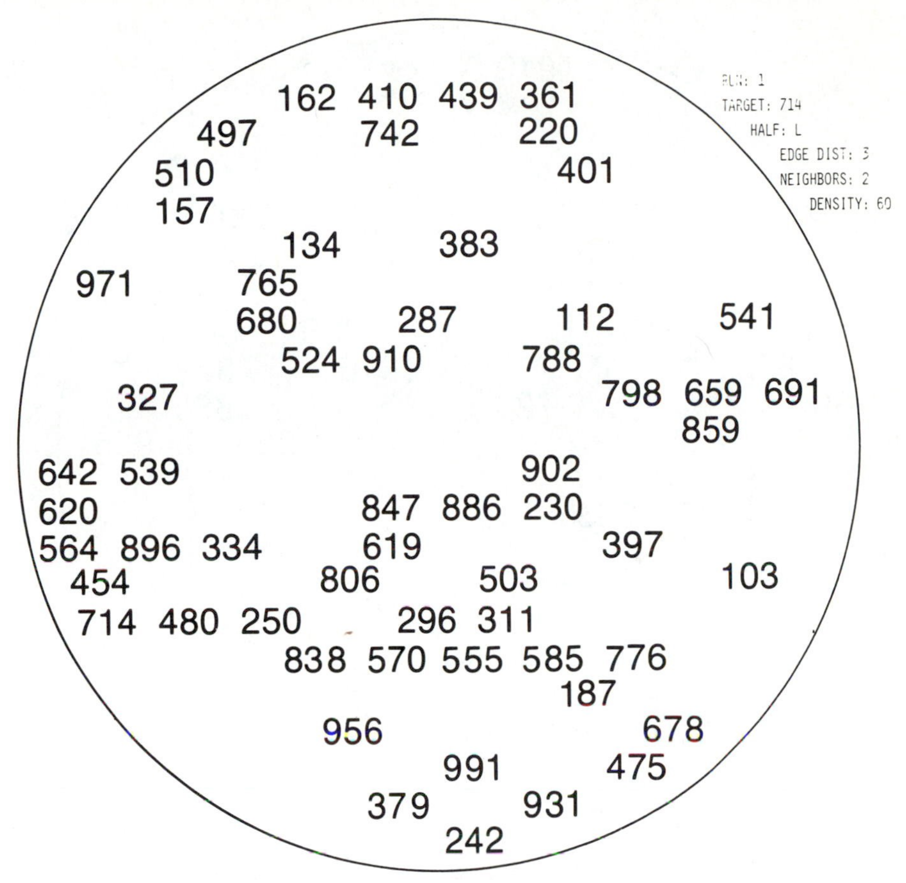

darkened room and view a screen like the one depicted in the photograph of the air traffic controller. They were given a number or "target" to search for, and the amount of time it took to find that number was the measure of search speed. Subjects were assigned to conditions randomly and were given training trials prior to test trials. They were also given vision tests prior to the experiment to eliminate any subjects with serious visual deficiencies.

An examination of the results revealed that density had a rather substantial effect on search time. When 30 objects were present, the average search time was 5.5 seconds. But when 60 objects were present, the average search time was 11 seconds. It was also found that targets in the center of the display could be found more quickly than targets toward the outside of the display. Search time was not affected by the number of neighboring

FIGURE 2–1 *(concluded)*

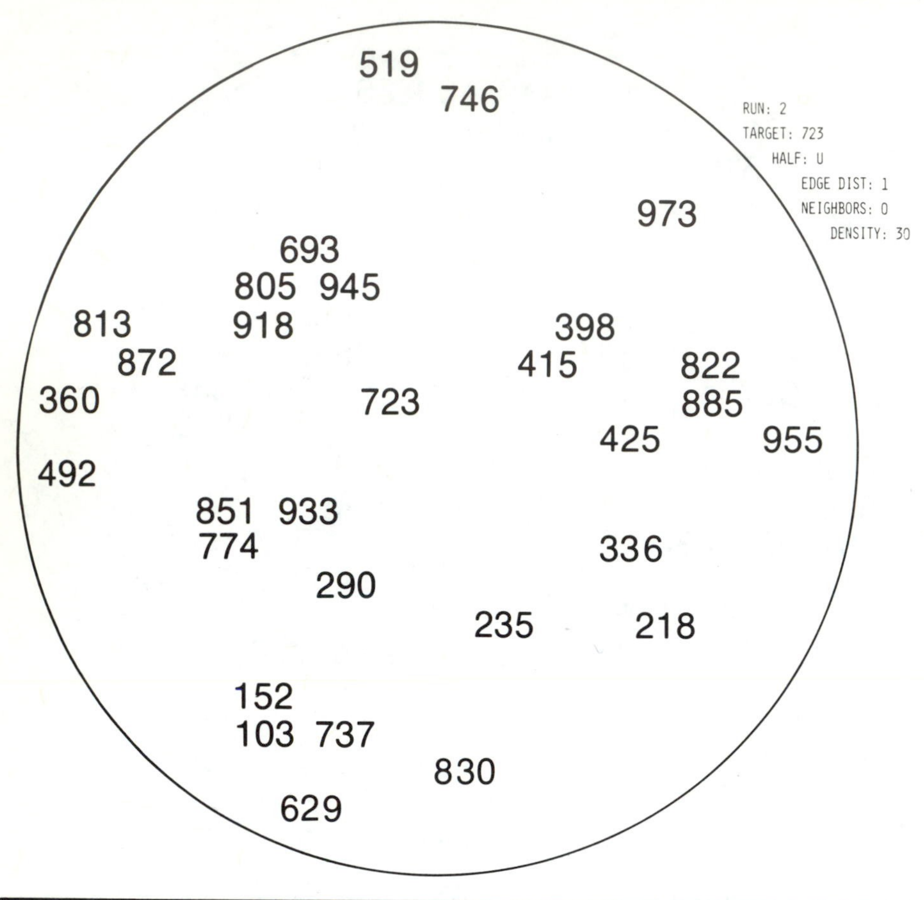

objects. Finally, search time was quicker for targets in the upper half of the display than it was for those in the lower half of the display.

There were a number of advantages to studying this problem in a laboratory experiment. First, operators could be selected and randomly assigned to various experimental conditions. Second, the effect of experience could be controlled through the training trials. (I will return to a discussion of the importance of these two characteristics of an experiment at the end of this section.) Third, it was possible to screen out individuals who might have physical disabilities that might hinder the investigation. Finally, it was possible to make very specific and refined manipulations of the independent variables (display characteristics) and to make very exact recordings of the dependent variable (search time).

There were some disadvantages to this approach also, especially if one were concerned with what people do in real job situations. The results of the experiment were based on observations of subjects who had only brief exposure to the task. Thus, the task was novel, and overall performance might have been quite different from what it would be with actual radar operators on several longer shifts or after several months on the job. Furthermore, the more difficult task conditions may have been seen as most challenging by the subjects in the brief period of the experiment, and they may have given more effort to those than to the easier conditions. Finally, the quiet, darkened room might have been very different from actual control tower conditions.

A Field Experiment. If you have ever ridden in a cab in a major city, you know something about terror. Cabs commonly weave through traffic at a high rate of speed. The cabs often change lanes without signaling, defy traffic signals, and start and stop abruptly to pick up or discharge passengers. As you might expect, cabs are frequently involved in accidents. A cab company in San Francisco decided to try and reduce a certain type of accident—the rear-end collision in which the cab was hit by another car (Voevodsky, 1974).

The company installed large yellow deceleration lights on the trunks of 343 cabs. These cabs were designated the experimental group. These lights were designed to begin blinking as soon as the cab began to slow down. The speed of the blinking was proportional to the rate of deceleration: the greater the rate of deceleration, the more quickly the lights blinked. The hypothesis of the experiment was that drivers following cabs were not receiving sufficient information about the changing speeds of the cabs to avoid hitting those cabs in the rear end when the cab stopped or slowed down dramatically. A second group of 160 cabs was designated as a control set, and no lights were added to the trunks of these cabs. The accident statistics were kept on the experimental and control cabs for 10 months. At the end of the 10-month period, it was clear that the lights made a difference. In the group of experimental cabs, the number of rear-end collisions, the cost of repairs, and the number of injuries to cab drivers were all reduced to a level 60 percent below what those numbers had been before the lights were installed. These numbers did not change for the control cabs. It was concluded that the blinking lights had a positive effect on safety.

Although you might agree that blinking lights had an effect on safety, you might argue that the effect was on the driving behavior of the cabbie rather than on the following behavior of the noncab vehicles. In other words, you might interpret the findings to mean that since the cab drivers with the lights on their trunks knew that they were in an experiment, they drove more carefully. Therefore, the lights were really accidental to the effect. That would be a clever explanation, but in this case it would be wrong. A comparison of the number of *front-end* collisions for these cabs showed that there were no differences between the experimental and control cabs. Both groups of cabs hit about the same number of other cars as they had before the lights were installed on the experimental cabs. This suggests that the drivers of the experimental cabs did not change their driving behavior appreciably.

This study is a good example of a field experiment. There was an actual manipulation of an independent variable (i.e., the presence or absence of deceleration lights). There were some variables, however, that could not be controlled. In the laboratory, the weather would not be a factor; in the cab experiment it could have been. In the laboratory, the testing conditions (e.g., traffic density) could have been held constant; on the streets of San Francisco, this would not be possible. In the laboratory, all aspects of the experimental equipment could have been identical for every subject; in this field experiment, the cabs differed with respect to age and condition. The advantages of the field study lie in its realism and the fact that one need not be concerned with generalizing from the laboratory to the job. This does not mean that the field study is free of problems, artifacts, or ambiguities. The basis for some of the problems in a field experiment is that the experimenter typically has much less control over the conditions of observation than in a laboratory experiment. In our cab example, suppose that some of the cabs were older models than others, that some drivers were much more experienced than others, or that there were snowstorms or strikes by the cab drivers or a host of other factors that might have influenced accident rates other than the blinkers. It is difficult to do well-controlled experiments in the field setting, and there is a certain amount of luck involved when one finds matched or replicate situations, groups, and equipment to provide the appropriate settings for the experimental conditions. Furthermore, there is always the possibility that the experimenter or the experiment as a social happening will be viewed as a more potent variable for behavioral change than the experimental manipulations. As we will see later, a famous series of field experiments—the Hawthorne studies—was plagued with problems, and the appropriate interpretations of those research findings continues to be a controversial topic.

When appropriately designed and conducted, there are two characteristics of experiments (regardless of whether they are conducted in the laboratory or in the field) that give them an advantage over field studies. You might think of these as characteristics of the "true" experiment. The first characteristic is the random assignment of subjects, and the second is the control of variables that are not being manipulated as part of the experiment.

Random Assignment. *Random assignment* means that each subject has an equal probability of ending up in either the control or the experimental group. The effect of random assignment is to equalize the groups *before* the experiment is carried out. This means that any differences noted *after* the experiment are more likely to have been caused by the experimental manipulation rather than by the initial group composition. To give a simple example, suppose that a psychologist wanted to examine the effect of watching violent TV programs on aggressive behavior in children. In deciding which children would be the experimental subjects (i.e., would be exposed to violent TV programs) and which would be the control subjects (i.e., which would watch nonviolent programs or perhaps watch no TV at all), suppose the experimenter decided that it would be easier to maintain control over nonaggressive children in the small TV room, so only nonaggressive children were assigned to the experimental group. After the experiment was conducted, the researcher might have found no differences between the experimental and control groups. Would it be appropriate to conclude that violent TV programs have no effect on aggressive behavior in children? Probably not. In fact, there was most likely a substantial increase in the aggressive behavior of the experimental subjects, but the nonrandom assignment made it difficult to observe. In the example above, the experimenter could have also noted these changes if measures of aggression taken before the experiment were compared with measures taken after the experiment. The point I am trying to illustrate, however, is that random assignment could have prevented this problem in interpretation.

Control of Third Variables. The second aspect of a true experiment is similar in function. If we can control levels of a third variable so that they do not vary when we are conducting the experiment, we can rule them out in explaining any observed effects of the experimental treatment. Suppose you decide to change the duties of a particular worker in the hope that the worker's productivity or satisfaction will increase. You decide to conduct a little "experiment" by changing the duties of one group of workers but leaving the duties of a second group unchanged. You find that the productivity and satisfaction of the second group has improved. Can you conclude that the change in duties was responsible for the improvement? Not necessarily. It may have been that when you changed the duties, you also changed the method or extent of supervision. You may have also had to change the pay rate. In addition, the workers in the experimental group might have been pleased that they were "chosen" for the experiment. In order to conclude that the change in job duties was responsible for the improvements in satisfaction and productivity, it would be necessary to hold every other variable *except* job duties constant. If we were able to hold third variables constant (i.e., not allow them to change during the experiment for either the experimental or control group subjects) and still noticed an improvement in satisfaction and productivity after the change in job duties, we would be in a much stronger position to claim that the change in duties was responsible for the change in worker behavior.

The Field Study. In the field study, the researcher observes, measures, and records what he finds *without* any experimental manipulation. If he finds work groups of different sizes and different levels of morale, he may determine the extent to which these two variables are associated. However, since he does not manipulate group size as an independent variable or institute other controls such as equal distribution of age, sex, and job tenure among his groups, he is not able to conclude that size of the work group bears a causal relationship to morale. It may be that small work groups tend to be involved in teamwork, and it is teamwork that affects morale. It is not likely that morale affects group size, but there are many other correlations in which a B→A causal interpretation is just as defensible as an A→B interpretation. We will return to this issue of correlation and causation later in the chapter.

Easily, the most recognizable field study method is the use of a survey or questionnaire to collect information. An investigator interested in the issue of life and work quality, for example, may ask subjects to complete questionnaires dealing with their relative satisfaction with various aspects of their life—for example, health, relations with spouse and children, and leisure activities. On a second occasion, the investigator might ask questions about individuals' relative satisfaction with aspects of their job—for example, supervision, pay, coworkers, and the nature of the work. These two sets of responses might then be compared in order to examine the extent to which satisfaction with work and satisfaction with life go together. Note that the investigator has engaged in no variable manipulation. He did not change pay or health or methods of supervision of leisure activities. Instead, he simply observed and noted the extent to which satisfaction with aspects of life in general were associated with aspects of the satisfaction that a person expressed with work.

Since most organizations are reluctant to allow psychologists to interfere with work procedures, equipment, or personnel, many I/O investigations are field studies rather than field experiments. Instead of exercising experimental control over all the aspects of the study, the investigator observes and records relevant data about the circumstances of the study and later examines the data to see if these circumstances might account for the findings. Thus, the field study usually employs statistical rather than experimental controls. In the case of studies based on records already existing in company files, the method is often referred to as a *file case* study since the data come not from subjects directly but from filing cabinets that hold records about those subjects.

The Simulation Study. The purpose of simulation is to gain some of the control that may be absent in a field experiment but at the same time to approximate a realistic operating situation so that one can generalize from the research findings to the operational task. The key word here is *realistic,* and the critical question for simulation is, . . . What aspects of the working situation have to be simulated to ensure that the research task is realistic in all those characteristics that may affect the performance of the operators on the task? This may include simulation of unusual environmental conditions, such as noise, heat, vibration, or even weightlessness. Thus, for example, simulators of the Gemini and Apollo space vehicles included such features as wide-screen projections of the stars and planets that the astronauts viewed from their cabin, just as they would later in actual space travel. Furthermore, computers were programmed to provide realistic information about the effects of control actions that the astronauts performed; in some cases, they lived in the simulator for several days with realistic life-support conditions, including space suits, special food supplies, and oxygen conditions. Some simulators were built to test an individual's endurance and ability to perform under conditions of gravitational forces such as would be experienced in takeoff and reentry.

A good example of a simulation is the driving test that a person takes to get a driver's license. The person is asked to guide the car around a measured course and demonstrate certain skills (e.g., parallel parking, backing, cornering) to an observer. It is assumed that the test course is a sufficiently faithful simulation of the "real world" such that basic flaws in driving ability can be identified if they are present.

In the past 10 years or so, one variation of the simulation study has become quite popular. Students are asked to pretend that they are managers. In that role, they are asked to make decisions (e.g., hiring, firing, salary increases) about hypothetical subordinates who are described on paper or portrayed on videotape. For the most part, these simulations are poor. The subjects represent a rather special group—college students unfamiliar with personnel decision making. The stimuli are quite unique as well. They are collections of words or scenes rather than real two-way interactions. This type of research has come to be known as *paper people research* and has not done much to increase our knowledge about behavior in work settings. Paper people research trades realism for control. Good simulations require a reasonable balance of these two factors.

Of course, there are problems in developing good simulations. For one thing, they can be quite expensive. Consider the cost of simulating the control room in a nuclear power plant, the cockpit of a 747, or the production line of an auto assembly plant. Recent estimates of the economic investment required for a state-of-the-art simulated nuclear control room run around $15 million. In addition to the cost of good simulation, even when all relevant factors are simulated, the subject still knows that the situation is not "for keeps." As a result, there is no way to ensure that the tensions, anxieties, and emotions of a real situation will not have a profound effect on a person's behavior. In a recent observation of a nuclear power plant control room simulation exercise being conducted for training purposes, I heard a supervisor comment about the performance of an operator in that simulation: "He always does great here; I wish to hell he would do the same thing back at the plant."

The greatest advantage in the use of simulations is often related to safety and cost factors involved in training individuals when the cost of a mistake is extremely high. Cost can be either an advantage or a disadvantage, depending on the benefit of the simulations. For example, training pilots in a 747 mock-up instead of in the cockpit of a real 747 where errors could be fatal represents an appropriate use of a simulation. The benefit clearly outweighs the cost.

A simulated nuclear power control room. Notice how closely this picture matches an actual control room as shown earlier on page 5. (Philadelphia Electric Co.)

I have discussed each of these approaches to investigation as if one were permitted to choose only one of them. This is seldom the case. In fact, many important behaviors can be examined from several different design perspectives. Surveys of employee satisfaction might be conducted. Based on the results of these surveys, the pay program might be changed and a survey taken again. This would represent a field study followed by a field experiment followed by a second field study. Astronauts might be observed for differential vulnerability to motion sickness in space flight and later brought into a space simulator to explore possible influences. This would be a field study followed by a simulation. This, in turn, might be followed up by a lab experiment that seeks to induce motion sickness in students who have the same characteristics that seemed to be implicated in the sickness of the astronauts. In fact, each of the methods of investigation gives us a different piece to the puzzle of understanding.

I will return to these issues throughout the book. Each of the four types of research discussed has its place in the search for knowledge in industrial and organizational psychology. Some questions may be best approached in the laboratory, whereas other questions can be assessed only in field experiments, field studies, or simulation research.

TECHNIQUES OF ANALYSIS

As you have seen in the last section, observation produces data. These data hold the key to understanding the behavior under consideration. The issue then becomes how to analyze these data in a way that will aid the understanding process. Statistical analysis of data from the industrial context is no different than analysis of any other type of data. The goals are both descriptive and inferential. There is a need to describe data sets in terms of distribution characteristics. Typically, these distribution characteristics include some measure of central tendency such as the average score, some measure of variation such as the range or standard deviation and some statement regarding the symmetry of the distribution such as an index of skewness. The concepts of central tendency, variability, and shape are standard statistical concepts and will not be considered in any great detail in this book. They are simply ways of describing a distribution of scores.

Inferential statistics are also common to all areas of psychology. In analyzing data, an investigator is often testing a hypothesis about the relationship among several variables. At the most basic level, the investigator would like to be sure that the results that he obtained were not due to chance but instead were the result of some systematic influence. The most common obstacle to such a conclusion is sampling error. In other words, there is always the possibility that a different result would have been obtained if a different subject sample had been used. The issue in inferential statistics is one of confidence. Can the investigator be confident that the conclusions based on a sample of people would hold for the entire population from which that sample was taken? Statistical tests are used to help determine the confidence that the investigator should have.

The common inferential tests with which you may be familiar are the t-test, the F-test, and the chi-square test. These tests help the investigator determine if two or more groups of subjects (e.g., an experimental and a control group) differ on some variable of interest. The results are interpreted by way of a significance level. Two groups may be said to be "significantly" different. This is another way of saying that the investigator is *confident* that the two groups in question are really different in some important respect (i.e., on a measure of the behavior under consideration). Significance is defined in terms of a probability statement. To say that a finding of difference is significant at a probability level of .05 (or in statistical terms, $p < .05$) is to say that such a difference could be expected as *a result of chance alone* only 5 times out of 100. A more confident statement would be that a difference this large would be expected only 1 time out of 100 as a result of chance ($p < .01$). A less confident statement would be that such a difference would be found 10 times out of 100 as a result of chance alone ($p = .10$).

The terms *confidence* and *significance* are often used interchangeably. As long as you keep the discussion in a statistical context, either term is acceptable. A problem arises, however, when the term *significance* is used as a synonym for importance or strength of a treatment or effect. This is an inappropriate use of the term *significance*. There are separate techniques available for determining the importance or strength of a result, and these techniques should not be confused with significance testing.

Correlational Analysis

As I suggested earlier, there are many occasions when the I/O psychologist cannot manipulate variables and examine the effect of that manipulation. Instead, natural variation is observed and inferences are drawn based on those variations. This means that distorting influences must be controlled statistically rather than experimentally. We cannot assign levels of intelligence or assertiveness or satisfaction or visual acuity to our subjects. Instead, we observe the extent to which those variables are related to other variables of interest such as satisfaction, productivity, or tendency to quit. We pay close attention to covariation.

In statistics, there are various ways of analyzing covariation. Generally, we compute measures of association as indexes of covariation. The two most common measures of association are the chi-square index and the correlation coefficient. The chi-square index is used for examining the degree of association between two categorical variables. By *categorical*, I mean that we cannot easily assign a number that indicates some level on a variable. Gender is an example of a categorical variable; so is hair color and job title.

In I/O research and practice, we can typically use numbers to characterize the variables that interest us. A person can be assigned a number that roughly represents how well she did on a test or how much she produced or how happy she is with her supervision. In this case, our data are more informative than simply categorical data such as group membership (e.g., male versus female or red hair versus brown hair). As a result, the most common measure of association is the correlation coefficient. The correlation coefficient is used as the point of departure for many other forms of analysis that you will encounter throughout the book. For that reason, it is best to spend a little time describing this statistical index and the other statistical techniques based on it. In the "Technical Appendix" at the end of the chapter, I present the most common formulas for computing the correlation coefficient.

THE CONCEPT OF CORRELATION

Francis Galton, a cousin of Charles Darwin, was interested in the hereditary aspects of height and weight. To get an idea of the relationship between the heights of parents and the heights of offspring, he plotted the respective heights on a graph much like the one displayed in Figure 2–2.

Next, Galton computed the average scores of the heights of those offspring whose parents had a certain height. For example, in Figure 2–2, he would have computed the average heights of all children whose fathers were

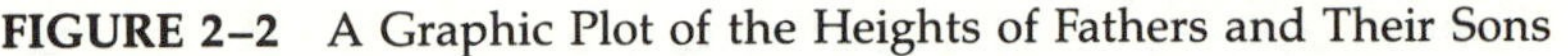

FIGURE 2–2 A Graphic Plot of the Heights of Fathers and Their Sons

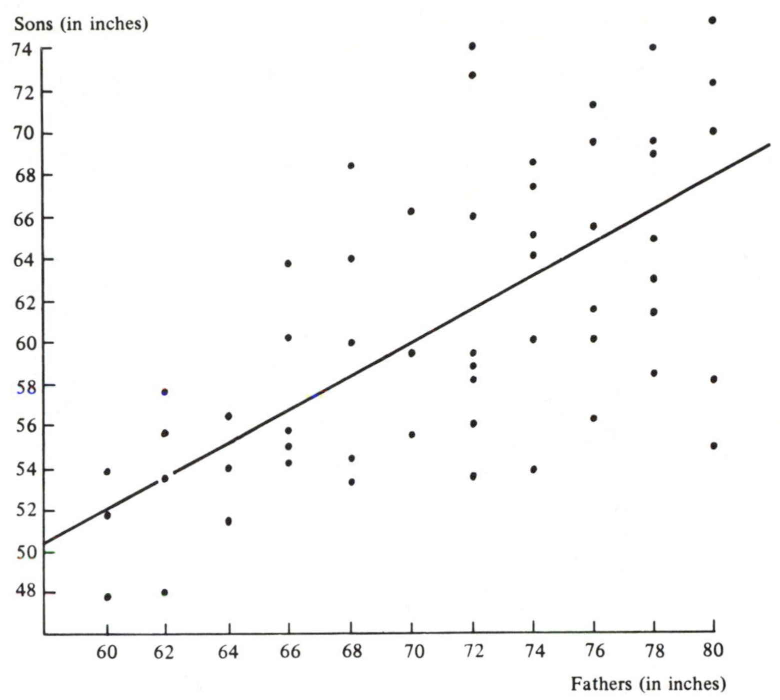

in the first category (60 inches), then the second category (62 inches), the third, and so on. He found that the means of these columns fell along a straight line represented by the solid line in Figure 2–2.

Examine Figure 2–2 for a moment. You will see that if the line were horizontal instead of tilted up and to the right, we might conclude that fathers' heights were not associated with sons' heights. But Figure 2–2 seems to show that the heights of sons whose fathers are of a *particular* height show less variability than the heights of all sons, regardless of fathers' heights. In our example, the heights of sons whose fathers are 60 inches tall vary between 48 and 54 inches, whereas the heights of all sons (regardless of fathers' height) vary from 48 inches to 74 inches. In this case, knowledge of fathers' heights reduces the observed variance or variability of sons' heights.

Although psychologists of today are not that interested in the relationships between the heights of parents and offspring, the nature of Galton's analysis lends itself to many other areas of concern. As an example, look at the data in Figure 2–3. These data represent the scores for a sample of people on two variables: years of formal education *(X)* and performance on the job *(Y)*. Look at the distribution of the data points for each of the two variables—

FIGURE 2–3 Scatterplot of Education and Performance

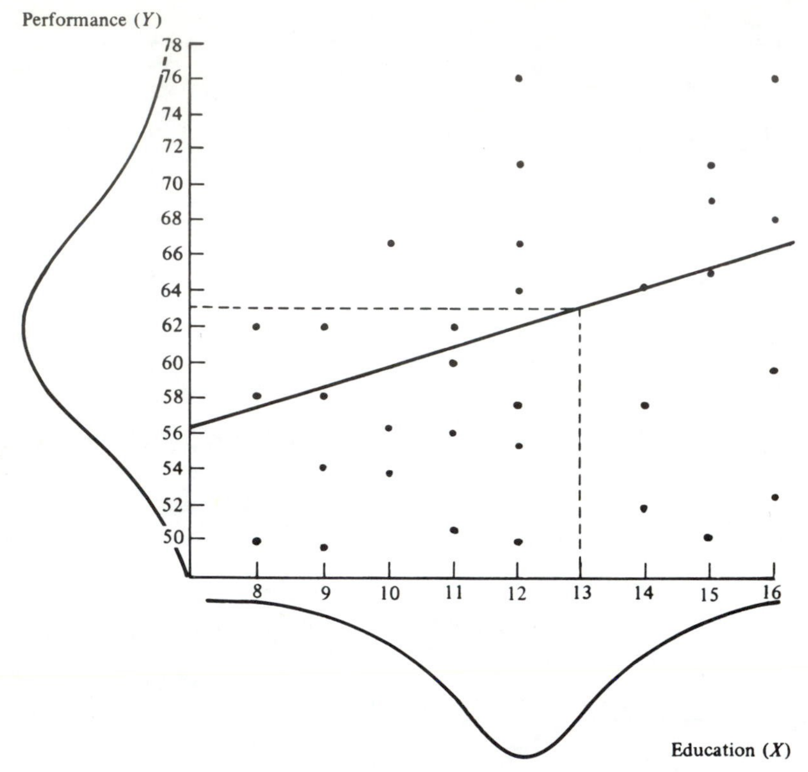

these distributions appear at the edge of each of the axes of the graph.

If you know the number of years of formal education an individual possesses, you also know something about the range of performance scores that individual is likely to exhibit. In other words, the variation of performance scores is reduced when we know something about the amount of formal education. This is the essence of using correlational analyses to predict behavior. It doesn't matter whether we are trying to predict performance from job satisfaction, group effectiveness from leadership style, or job success from a test score—the operations are basically the same as those identified and formalized by Galton.

You will notice in Figure 2–3 that no one in the sample had 13 years of formal education. How would we predict a performance score for someone with 13 years of formal education who applied for a job? We would simply interpolate from the available data. We could use the straight line that we plotted through the column means to predict that performance score. We would go up the column representing 13 years of formal education until we

FIGURE 2–4 Scatterplots Representing Varying Degrees of Correlation

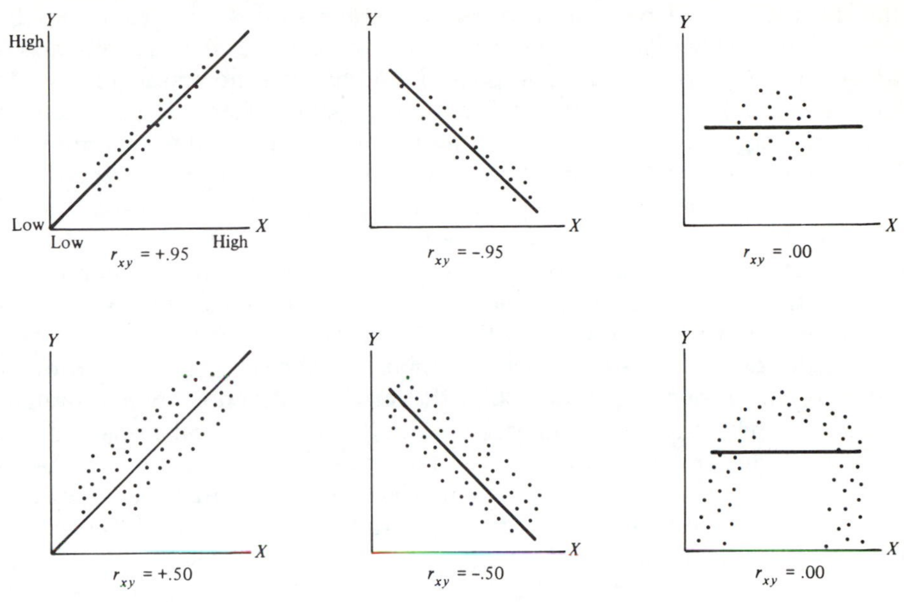

reached the line, then read across for the predicted performance score (63).

A coworker of Galton, Karl Pearson, suggested an index—a single number—that could be used to describe the extent of linear relationship between any two variables. This index has come to be known as the *correlation coefficient* or the *Pearson correlation coefficient* in honor of the man who suggested this index.

Correlation coefficients consist of two distinct parts. They have a sign (that can be either positive or negative), and they have a numerical value (that can range from .00 to 1.00). Consider the different correlation coefficients that would be used to describe the relationships illustrated in Figure 2–4. As you can see, the plus (+) sign indicates a positive relationship between two variables; as one variable increases in value, so does the other. A minus (−) sign indicates an inverse relationship; as the value of one of the variables increases, the value of the other variable decreases. An example of a positive relationship might be height and weight, whereas an example of a negative relationship might be age and visual acuity. This also indicates that as the value of the correlation coefficient increases, prediction becomes more accurate.

Occasionally, you may run into some forms of the correlation coefficient that are intended for special situations. If one of the variables under consideration is dichotomous (the scores fall in one or the other of two categories) and the other variable is continuous (scores may assume any value), the resulting correlation coefficient may be called a *point-biserial* correlation coefficient; if both variables are dichotomous, the resulting coefficient may be referred to as a *phi coefficient*. Finally, you may encounter a correlation between two sets of rank orders. For example, you might read the results of a study that examined the correlation between high school class standing and college class standing. In this case, each person would be represented by a number that signified their relative position in a score distribution rather than by a score indicating how much of some trait they possessed. Two sets of ordered data can be correlated using a coefficient called the *Spearman rank-order correlation coefficient*. This can be interpreted in exactly the same manner as any other correlation coefficient. It describes the extent of linear relationship between the two variables on which the subjects are ordered.

All the discussion so far has been about linear relationships. In other words, we are discussing relationships that could be described with a straight line. Not all relationships are linear. You can think of some relationships that might be better described by a curved line instead of a straight one. As an example, think of food and satisfaction. Too little results in a feeling of discomfort (that we might label "hunger"). The right amount results in a pleasant feeling (that we might label "satiation"). Too much produces a feeling of discomfort again (that we might call "indigestion"). Consider a more relevant example. Figure 2–5 presents a hypothetical relationship between intellectual ability and performance on an ordinary assembly-line task (such as bolting a transmission to a frame). People with too little intellectual ability may do poorly because they cannot remember the correct procedures or learn how to use certain pieces of equipment. People with too much intellectual ability may do poorly because they become bored very quickly. As a result, their attention wanders and their work suffers. People with an intermediate amount of intellectual ability may do just fine; they have sufficient ability to learn the tasks but not too much to yield boredom.

If you were to calculate a correlation coefficient for the data in Figure 2–5 it would be .00, implying that there was no relationship between intellectual ability and job performance in the hypothetical bolting operation. This would be an inaccurate statement. An accurate statement would be that there is no *linear* relationship between the two variables. It is possible to calculate correlation coefficients that can take into account nonlinear (or curvilinear) relationships. I won't describe them here. Simply be aware that a Pearson correlation coefficient does not necessarily tell you all you need to know about a possible relationship. A good safeguard against ignoring a potential curvilinear relationship is actually to plot your data on a scatterplot and visually examine it. Often, you will notice certain nonlinear trends in the data. This will be the cue to calculate a nonlinear correlation coefficient.

Another question related to the association among and between variables is the treatment of multiple variables. What do we do when we have scores from seven different tests and want to predict performance from them? Do

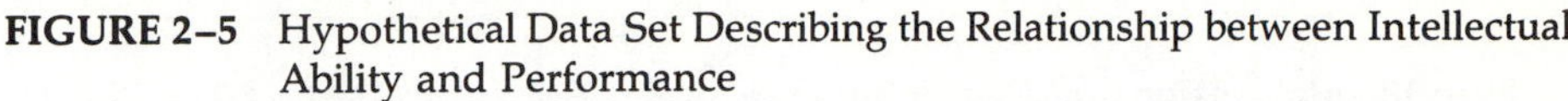

FIGURE 2–5 Hypothetical Data Set Describing the Relationship between Intellectual Ability and Performance

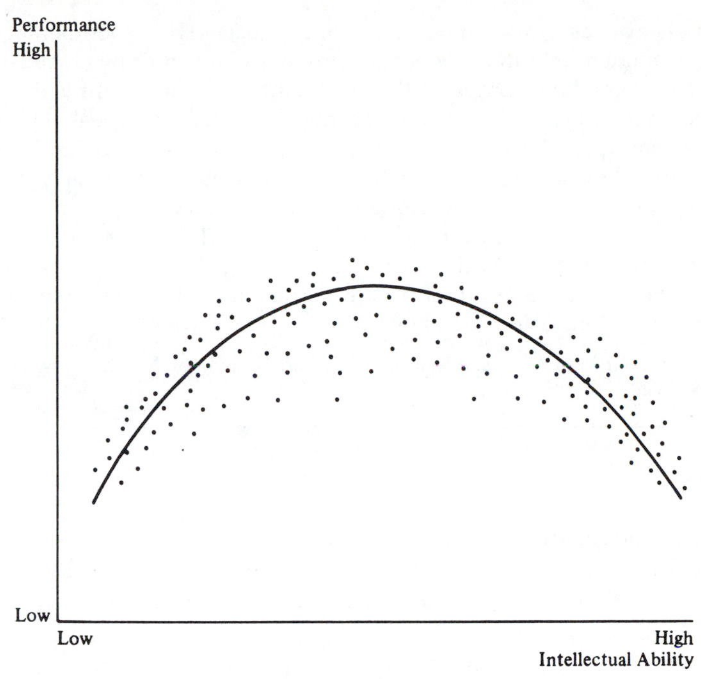

we compute the correlation coefficients one at a time, or do we first add the test scores together? As it turns out, we use a procedure known as *multiple regression*. In this procedure, the variables are combined in a way that is most efficient for predicting scores on the dependent variable, performance. What we actually do is to form a new variable that is a combination (in technical terms, a *linear composite*) of the test scores and correlate this new variable with the dependent variable, performance. In effect, then, we are still correlating only two variables, the one that we are attempting to predict and the other derived from the several scores. We will see some specific examples of the use of multiple regression analysis in Chapter 5.

One challenge faced by psychologists is to account for the differences among and within individuals. The correlation coefficient is an attempt to account for variations of behavior on one dimension in terms of variation on a second dimension. So, for example, we attempt to account for and predict variation in job performance in terms of a second variable, perhaps a measure of particular aptitude. To the degree to which these two variables covary, we have explained the differences among individuals on the performance dimension. In a sense, the larger the correlation coefficient, the more we have

Experimental Design and Causation

It is not always easy to separate causes and effects. The experimental design that you use often determines what conclusions you can draw. A story is told of the researcher who interviewed the inhabitants of a particular neighborhood. He noted that the young people spoke fluent English. In speaking with the middle aged people who would be the parent generation of the younger people, he found that they spoke English with a slight Italian accent. Finally, he spoke with older people (who would represent the grandparent generation of the youngest group) and heard a heavy Italian accent. The researcher concluded that as you grow older, you develop an Italian accent. It is a safe bet that had the researcher studied a group of people as they aged, he would have come to a very different conclusion, perhaps even an opposite one.

SOURCE: Adapted from *Aging and Human Performance* (p. xvii) by N. Charness (Ed.), 1985, New York: Wiley.

reduced the unexplained variability among individuals on some dimension of interest. In terms of *predicting behavior,* this means that we have increased the accuracy with which we can predict performance scores from test, or "predictor," scores.

Multiple regression is another way of approaching the same basic problem. In this case, however, we are hoping to reduce the unexplained variability in some dependent or consequent variable by *combining* independent or antecedent variables. In the case of the simple correlation problem, we attempt to account for the variation in one variable by noting the variation in a *second variable.* In the case of multiple correlation or regression, we have attempted to account for the variation in one variable by noting the joint variation in *several other variables.*

Correlation and Causation

Correlation coefficients are simply numbers that represent the extent to which two variables are associated. These coefficients provide no information about cause-effect relations between the two variables. To give a simple example, height and weight are positively correlated. If you are taller, you tend to be heavier. This does not mean that height *causes* weight or that weight *causes* height. If that were the case, short people could increase their height by simply gaining weight. It is inappropriate to assume that correlation means causation.

In many of the topics that will be considered in the book, the issue of correlation and causality will be important. To give an example, there have been many studies that have demonstrated that considerate leaders (i.e., those who are people oriented) have more satisfied subordinates. The temptation is to assume that considerate styles of leadership result in (i.e., cause) satisfied coworkers. There are some problems with that interpretation. Let's consider two of them.

The first problem is one of direction. Does the leadership style cause the satisfaction, or might the relationship be the other way around, that is, satisfaction causes considerate behavior? It may very well be that a relaxed and satisfied group of workers allows their leader to relax as well. This leader relaxation might result in a greater tendency to chat informally with subordinates, to ask how things are going at home, to engage in pleasant conversation. Conversely, when the subordinates are dissatisfied, grumbling, and bickering, the leader might "tighten up," concentrate more on work-related issues, and avoid interacting with the workers until things calm down. As you can see, in this case, even if we do admit to the possibility of a causal relationship, the correlation coefficient does not tell us anything about which variable is the cause and which is the effect.

There is another problem with interpreting correlation coefficients in a causal way. It may be that there is a third variable that is really responsible for the relationship between the two variables of interest. To continue with the leader style–subordinate satisfaction example, it might be that these two are positively correlated because of their individual relationships with a third variable—work group productivity. It may be that productive work groups are happy with what they have been able to accomplish and their supervisors can afford the luxury of concentrating on positive human relations because things are running smoothly. It may be that the leader uses a considerate style as the *reward* for high productivity. In this case, a considerate leadership style does not cause employee satisfaction, nor does employee satisfaction cause a considerate leadership style. Instead, both a considerate leadership style *and* employee satisfaction are the result of work group productivity.

Factor Analysis

Often the I/O psychologist must understand the relationships among many variables simultaneously. For example, we might have a set of statements such as those posed in Figure 2–6. The question we might ask of ourselves in analyzing the responses of individuals to these questions is, Although there are 20 questions, are there really 20 *different* categories of information represented? The answer is probably no. Just from inspection, we would expect the answers to items 1, 5, 7, 15, and 18 to be correlated; they all seem to deal with pay. We would expect that the same would be true for items 2, 3, 11, 14, and 17—each of these items asks the person to indicate satisfaction with supervision. If that is actually the case, it would be easier to compare the questionnaire responses to two persons (or two groups) by looking at their responses to some subsets of items *taken as a group*. In other words, we can reduce the 20 questions to several subsets or groups of similar

FIGURE 2–6 Job Satisfaction Statements

1. My pay is pretty good.
2. On the whole, my supervisor is pretty fair.
3. I wish my supervisor paid more attention to me.
4. I do not get along with my coworkers particularly well.
5. I make about the amount of money that I am worth.
6. I like to pal around with my coworkers off the job.
7. I would like to make more money.
8. My job is quite interesting.
9. The promotional policy at this organization leaves a lot to be desired.
10. There is little challenge in my work.
11. My supervisor is thought of as a fair individual.
12. I prefer to work alone rather than with others.
13. I have no freedom in my work.
14. I can't seem to get the help I need from my supervisor.
15. I would gladly change jobs for the opportunity to make more money.
16. I am happy with the vacation plan.
17. I could do more work if it were not for the interference from my supervisor.
18. An individual's pay should be determined on the basis of the worth of the individual to the company.
19. I occasionally have to do things that go against my conscience in this job.
20. I am in a "dead-end" job.

questions. The technique most often used to accomplish this goal is called *factor analysis*. The logic behind this statistical technique is the assumption that there is a *factor* underlying the observed association between two variables. For example, consider the variables of height, weight, shoe length, and shirtsleeve length. For any individual, we might expect positive correlations between any two of these variables. The correlations may not be perfect, but they will probably be reasonably high (say, +.50). You might reasonably suggest that all these correlations are the result of a factor called *body size*. Similarly, in the questionnaire that appears in Figure 2–6, you might propose that the answers to questions 1, 5, 7, 15, and 18 are all the result of a factor called *satisfaction with pay*. Factor analysis begins with the intercorrelations among a number of variables and extracts or identifies components or factors that might be used to account for those intercorrelations.

Since tests often have many different items and questionnaires often include many different questions, factor analysis is a very useful technique for reducing data sets to manageable proportions. It would be impossible to make sense out of the intercorrelations among 10 or 12 variables. As an example, look at Table 2–1 in the "Technical Appendix" at the end of this chapter. Could you have made sense out of this table by just looking at it? In this appendix, I explain in somewhat more detail how you would interpret the results of a factor analysis. For those who are not interested in the mechanics of factor analysis, the important thing to keep in mind is that factors are based on observed intercorrelations among variables and that once a factor has been identified, it is then used as a substitute (conceptually) for the variables from which it has been composed.

Some New Statistical Concepts

There are a few terms that you may see used more frequently in the research literature of I/O psychology in the future. Those terms are *path analysis* or *causal modeling* and *meta-analysis.* As I indicated above, *correlation* simply means an association between two variables. It does not necessarily say anything about cause-effect relationships. Even though one cannot draw causal inferences from correlations, techniques are available that permit these data to be broken down or decomposed in a way that permits some statement about which variables may be acting as antecedent variables and which as consequent variables. In other words, it is possible to say something about the path or sequence of behavior in a complex situation. Path analysis is based on the intercorrelations among many different variables, often on several different occasions. When dealing with such important relationships as satisfaction and performance or leadership and motivation, it is important to know which variable comes first and which comes second. In other words, it is important to know the *path* of the relationship. Does satisfaction lead to performance, or does performance lead to satisfaction? Does employee motivation result in leader behaviors, or do leader behaviors precede employee motivation? These are the kinds of questions that path analysis addresses. Path analysis might have been able to help us interpret the leadership style–employee satisfaction finding that we considered in the earlier section on correlation and causality. The more general theoretical process that path analysis serves is known as *causal modeling.* This simply means that the researcher is trying to develop a model or statistical simulation of which cause-effect relationships are more plausible given a set of data.

The second analytic technique to receive attention is called *meta-analysis.* If you read the research literature, you will find dozens, sometimes hundreds, of studies on the same general topic. Each study is done with a different subject sample, a different sample size, and often a different observational or experimental environment. For example, there have been well over 3,000 studies of job satisfaction published in the past several decades (Locke, 1976). How are all those studies to be considered? Should each study be considered by itself? Should the "best" study be identified and used for explanatory purposes, or can the studies somehow be averaged to yield a general conclusion? Meta-analysis is a specific analytic technique for averaging the results of many studies on the same topic. There are several good sources that describe the techniques of meta-analysis (G. V. Glass, 1976; Hunter, Schmidt, & Jackson, 1982). I/O psychologists have been conducting and publishing research results for over 60 years. The field has now reached the stage where these studies can be examined and conclusions drawn about basic relationships. In the next few years, meta-analysis will become a more common technique for inference and theory building. A very specific application of meta-analysis that is becoming quite important in personnel testing is called *validity generalization.* In this application, a statistical analysis is done to determine if the differences between patterns of associations noticed in several different studies mean that the actual relationship changes from one location to another or that there are other variables (e.g., sample size) that could account for these differences. As you can see, in some respects meta-analysis permits us to exercise statistical control over third variables that might be obscuring a relationship. We will go into this technique in greater detail when we deal with validity generalization in a later chapter.

ETHICAL CONSIDERATIONS IN RESEARCH AND PRACTICE

Virtually every occupation has an implicit or explicit code of ethical behavior. Psychology is no exception. Within the field of psychology, each specialty area confronts different ethical dilemmas. The clinical psychologist may find it necessary to choose between confidentiality of the client-therapist relationship and the safety of the public at large; the social psychologist may struggle over the ethical implications of a deception experiment; the developmental psychologist may be concerned with the possible long-term effects of a particular learning environment on preschool children.

In research settings, the I/O psychologist must be concerned with the rights and well-being of subjects. In this respect, she is no different from the clinical or social or developmental psychologist. In the field, however, as an applied psychologist, many unique situations develop that are peculiar to the I/O psychologist. I will briefly cover a few of them.

Testing and Evaluation

Perhaps the most common activity of the I/O psychologist is evaluation of one form or another. This might be the evaluation of training effects, the evaluation of performance, or the evaluation of abilities. Evaluation presents one of the most significant tests of ethical behavior. London and Bray (1980) have considered this aspect of industrial and organizational psychology. They have suggested that the I/O psychologist has three interrelated sets of responsibilities or obligations. One obligation is to the profession itself. Since the I/O psychologist is acting on behalf of all psychologists, it is unethical not to be aware of the most recent advances in the field. Practically, this would mean staying abreast of new tests and testing procedures, new ways of measuring work performance, and recent developments in substantive theory such as those dealing with intellectual abilities or work motivation or accident prevention. Naturally, the I/O psychologist cannot be aware of every development in the field. Nevertheless, if he deals extensively with testing issues or employee safety or worker motivation, then he has a responsibility to stay up to date in these areas at least. This is accomplished primarily through reading and discussions with colleagues.

A second obligation that the I/O psychologist has is to individual workers and those applying for employment. London and Bray (1980) identify several responsibilities in this area. Let's consider some of these responsibilities and examples of ethical problems related to them.

1. Guarding against invasion of privacy of the person. The I/O psychologist should not administer a questionnaire that touches on personal information that may be of a sensitive nature if there is no clear or defensible reason for gathering that information.
2. Guaranteeing confidentiality. The I/O psychologist should not engage in casual discussion about test scores or performance evaluations of particular individuals. Only those who have a right to know should be privy to such individual difference data.
3. Providing a person with feedback about evaluation. If an individual requests feedback concerning his performance on a battery of tests that the psychologist administered, provision should be made for giving that feedback in an appropriate manner. This would mean making sure that the information is interpreted correctly and presented in such a way that the person who was evaluated understands what the test score means.
4. Getting informed consent from individuals with respect to information about them. An individual who has been evaluated has the right to know how that information will be used. Similarly, an individual who evaluates another (e.g., a supervisor who rates the performance of a subordinate) has a right to know how those data will be used. It would be unethical to tell a supervisor that ratings were for research purposes only and then to use those ratings to make salary decisions.
5. Making sure that data are not kept for too long a period of time. Data, like bread, can become stale. If an individual completes a battery of preemployment tests and is hired, those test scores typically become a permanent part of the individual's personnel file. If the person applies for a new job in that organization 15 years later, it would be unethical (and stupid) to use those preemployment test scores to make the promotion decision. It is unlikely that they accurately represent the individual at the time he applies for the promotion. It is the responsibility of the I/O psychologist to ensure the currency of evaluative information.

The I/O psychologist has a third obligation. He has an obligation to his employer. It is tempting to "oversell" an idea or to misrepresent the research literature when pushing for a particular program. For example, an I/O psychologist might claim that a new test of intellectual ability will solve all the

FIGURE 2–7 Ethical Categories in the Practice of I/O Psychology

Test validation techniques
Test validation strategies
Assessment techniques
Inadequate resources to comply with ethical and technical standards
Misuse of assessment procedures
Conducting individual assessments
Use of management development results for employee assessment
Miskeyed test items on commercially marketed tests
Personnel screening for emotional stability
Misuse of psychological services
Misleading reporting of results
Accurately reporting research results
Misrepresentation of results in test validation
Disposition of psychological reports
Training requirements in I/O psychology
Practice of I/O psychology by a clinical psychologist
Career switching
Licensing and credentialing
"Realistic job previews" and the selection of female employees
Marketing psychological products
Advertising and public statements
Publicity and advertising
Use of copyrighted material in new instrumentation
Authorship and publication agreements
Publication credit
Plagiarizing
Fairness in book reviews
Ethical responsibilities of reviewers
Evaluating colleagues' competencies
Confronting unethical behavior
The right not to participate in psychological activities
Protecting confidentiality
Confidentiality of employee interview data
Confidentiality
Misuse of data obtained through one's employment
Dual relationships
Conflict of interest
Psychologists as employers of other psychologists
Pressures to prematurely implement psychological programs
Sensitivity training groups
Referral to an employee assistance program
Academia-industry relationships
Misuse of attitude surveys to prevent unionization

SOURCE: From *Casebook on Ethics and Standards for the Practice of Psychology in Organizations* (pp. 2–3) by R. L. Lowman (Ed.), 1985, College Park, MD: SIOP, University of Maryland, Department of Psychology.

quality control problems of a manufacturing organization. It is unlikely that a manager or vice president in that company would or could dispute such a claim. It is the psychologist's ethical responsibility to represent fairly the current state of the art when discussing possible programs of intervention. It does not matter if these interventions involve selection, motivation, or machine design. Similarly, the psychologist has the responsibility of fairly representing a data set to the employer. If test scores unfairly discriminate against one or another group of employees, it is the psychologist's ethical responsibility to inform the employer of this circumstance. In this case, unfair discrimination would mean that the differences in test scores are unrelated to probable success on the job but that these scores *are* related to race or sex

FIGURE 2–8 An Example of a Situation Giving Rise to Ethical Considerations

Use of Copyrighted Material in New Instrumentation

A. Statement of the Problem

An I/O psychologist in the role of consultant developed a job analysis data collection form for use with clients. This instrument embodied significant features and numerous items from a well-known and widely used copyrighted instrument. No permission was obtained from the copyright holder to use the copyrighted material, nor was credit given to the original source.

B. Applicable Policies

Principle 3 (Moral and Legal Standards). In their professional roles, psychologists avoid any action that will violate or diminish the legal and civil rights of clients or of others who may be affected by their actions. (3-c)

Principle 7 (Professional Relationships). Publication credit is assigned to those who have contributed to a publication in proportion to their professional contributions. . . . All contributors are to be acknowledged and named. (7-f)

C. Interpretation of Policy Principles in Light of the Major Questions Posed by the Case

If this case constituted plagiarism of copyrighted material, then the psychologist's behavior was both illegal and unethical. There are, however, many examples of materials in the I/O field (e.g., performance appraisal forms) which may be quite similar even if developed independently, as may have been the case here. When a source is directly used as a "model," even if it is in the public domain, due credit should be given. When the material is copyrighted, of course, appropriate permission must be obtained.

D. Educative Ramifications

Psychologists should be made aware, beginning with their graduate student training, of the appropriate uses of copyrighted material and of acceptable professional practices in the utilization of the results from research activities and programs of their professional colleagues. Appropriate actions to confront and/or to report ethical violations by psychologists who plagiarize the work of others should be taken promptly by psychologists encountering such behavior.

SOURCE: From *Casebook on Ethics and Standards for the Practice of Psychology in Organizations* (p. 34) by R. L. Lowman (Ed.), 1985, College Park, MD: SIOP, University of Maryland, Department of Psychology.

or age, effectively limiting employment to certain favored subgroups. If test scores contain so much error that it is impossible to distinguish accurately among job applicants in terms of their true ability (in spite of the fact that their test scores differ), the psychologist is ethically bound to consider those limiting factors when providing advice concerning how those test scores will be used. In each of these instances, the psychologist has an obligation to protect the employer from inadvertent error.

Ethical dilemmas are seldom as clear as those presented above. Instead of black and white, the issues are usually gray. Nevertheless, there is ultimately one course of action that is more ethical than another. There are some principles that can be studied. The APA publishes a general set of ethical standards that apply to the entire profession (American Psychological Association [APA], 1981). Within these general guidelines, there are descriptions of specific instances that are relevant to I/O psychology. A much more useful document for I/O psychologists has been published recently by the Society for Industrial and Organizational Psychology (SIOP) (the formal corporate name of Division 14 of the APA). This document (Lowman, 1985) is a casebook that identifies most of the important facets of ethical behavior that an I/O psychologist might need to consider. Figure 2–7 presents a listing of the major headings of that document. Each of those headings presents an example of a salient ethical problem, relates that example to the appropriate section of the APA ethical principles, presents an interpretation or diagnosis of the ethical issue, and then presents a concise directive for avoiding or dealing with that type of ethical problem. Figure 2–8 on page 47 presents an excerpt from the casebook. This is an excellent document with a wealth of real-world examples of ethical dilemmas facing I/O psychologists.

There is a need to consider continually the consequences of certain professional activities for the profession, the employee, and the employer. Since no two situations are identical, it is best to think of ethical behavior as something that is learned rather than as something that is endorsed or adopted. The I/O psychologist must stay alert to possible violations of one or more of the obligations described above.

Technical Appendix

CORRELATION

A correlation coefficient can be computed from either raw scores or standard scores. The raw score formula can be expressed as follows:

$$r = \frac{n\sum xy - \sum x \sum y}{\sqrt{n\sum x^2 - (\sum x)^2}\sqrt{n\sum y^2 - (\sum y)^2}}$$

where

n = the number of pairs of scores (i.e., subjects)
x = the scores on the x variable
y = the scores on the y variable
xy = the value of each person's x score multiplied by the value of their y score
r = the resulting correlation coefficient

The raw score formula for the correlation coefficient, in effect, transforms the raw scores into standard score form as part of the calculation process. A standard score is a raw score converted to standard deviation units. A standard score (or Z score) is obtained using the following formula:

$$Z_i = \frac{X_i - M}{S.D.}$$

where

X_i = the raw score
M = the sample mean
$S.D.$ = the sample standard deviation
Z_i = the standard score equivalent of the raw score

By definition, the Z score distribution has a $M = 0$ and a $S.D. = 1.00$. If the variables that you would like to correlate are already in Z score form, the formula for computing the correlation coefficient is much simpler:

$$r = \frac{\sum Z_x Z_y}{n}$$

where

Z_x = standard score on the X variable for an individual
Z_y = standard score on the Y variable for that individual
n = the number of pairs of scores (i.e., subjects)
r = the correlation coefficient

Expressed verbally, this formula says that the correlation is equal to the sum of the cross-products of the standard scores divided by the number of pairs of scores. In other words, the correlation is equal to the average of the cross-products of the standardized scores.

Factor Analysis

Factor analysis is a term used to describe a family of analytic strategies. In other words, there are many different kinds of factor analysis. I will not describe the different types, but keep in mind that the description that follows is of a "typical" factor analysis. There are many variations on this general technique.

There are two basic operations in the factor analysis. The first consists of identifying the *number* of factors in a data set. This is the factor solution. The second operation takes the basic solution and helps make psychological sense out of it. This second operation is called the *factor rotation*. These two operations together comprise factor analysis. The analysis begins with a matrix containing all the possible correlations between the variables to be analyzed. As an example, let's take the satisfaction questionnaire that

I described in Figure 2–6. There were 20 questions. In Table 2–1, you will see the correlations between all the possible question pairs. The bottom half of that matrix is missing since it would be identical to the top half. The correlation of question 1 with question 3 would be the same as the correlation of question 3 with question 1. The task is to reduce that correlation matrix to more manageable proportions. Instead of 20 different dimensions of job satisfaction (represented by the 20 different questions), we want to identify some smaller number of dimensions (that we will call *factors*) that will accurately represent the domain of job satisfaction covered by these 20 questions. These factors are identified through a series of mathematical operations that are performed on the intercorrelation matrix.

Once the number of factors has been identified through the mathematical operations, it is necessary to perform a second set of operations on those factors in order to turn them into concepts that can be useful psychologically. This second set of operations is called factor rotation because in the early days of factor analysis, before the advent of high-speed computers, factor analysts actually plotted the factors geometrically and moved or rotated these geometric representations around axes on graph paper until they made psychological sense.

The result of a factor solution and factor rotation is a table similar to the one illustrated in Table 2–2. This is called a *factor loading table.* The numbers that appear in the table are actually correlations. They are the correlations between variables and the hypothetical factors that have been identified mathematically. Since they are correlations, they vary from +1.00 to −1.00. These correlations are commonly referred to as loadings because they tell us something about how much of a particular variable is represented in a given factor. A high correlation or loading means that the variable is central to understanding or interpreting the factor—the variable loads heavily on the factor. In order to make Table 2–2 easier to read, I have underlined the highest factor loading in each row. This tells you at a glance which factor each variable is most highly correlated with.

Within a factor (column) the sign of the loading tells us something about *how* the variable relates to the factor. Consider factor I in Table 2–2. As you can see, question 1 has a loading of +.80. This is a high positive correlation. Question 7 has a loading of −.40. This is a moderate negative correlation. This means that the two variables have opposite relationships to the factor. If we look at the original questions, we can understand why this has occurred. Question 1 is a positive statement about pay. If a person agrees with the statement, it means that they are happy with pay. Question 7 is a negative statement about pay. If they agree with question 7, they are *unhappy* with pay. Together, the two questions (along with questions 4, 15, and 18) describe a pattern of responses dealing with an employee's satisfaction with pay.

TABLE 2–1 Intercorrelations among Responses to 20 Job Satisfaction Statements

	Variable																			
Variable	*1*	*2*	*3*	*4*	*5*	*6*	*7*	*8*	*9*	*10*	*11*	*12*	*13*	*14*	*15*	*16*	*17*	*18*	*19*	*20*
1	X	.14	.31	.04	.71	.34	−.63	.41	.21	.07	.19	.19	.21	.23	−.75	.32	.01	.64	.07	.07
2		X	−.64	.07	.04	.22	.22	.32	.10	.13	.64	.17	.14	−.71	.01	.04	−.62	.21	.13	.41
3			X	.43	.17	.09	.11	.01	.13	.40	−.48	.06	.31	.54	.07	.31	.39	.40	.23	.36
4				X	.21	−.75	.26	.07	.22	.23	−.41	.61	.09	.01	.21	.26	.21	.27	.22	.02
5					X	.36	−.60	.14	.27	.22	.19	.27	.17	.04	−.48	.43	.14	.71	.06	.26
6						X	.09	.01	.32	.27	.06	−.49	.14	.31	.10	.14	.17	.21	.14	.31
7							X	.27	.02	.01	.17	.41	.39	.28	.60	.29	.34	−.85	.27	.02
8								X	.41	−.64	.31	.64	−.75	.21	.06	.06	.07	.26	.17	−.81
9									X	.13	.17	.13	.01	.06	.13	.14	.07	.07	.19	.19
10										X	.02	.19	.61	.14	.05	.74	.29	.22	.14	.58
11											X	.17	.23	−.64	.22	.41	−.81	.48	−.17	.45
12												X	.19	.36	.06	.09	.13	.13	.04	.17
13													X	.19	.27	.41	.07	.21	.31	.68
14														X	.14	.00	.58	.19	.26	.06
15															X	.15	.26	−.64	.04	.07
16																X	.36	.14	.11	.40
17																	X	.28	.04	.32
18																		X	.33	.17
19																			X	.14
20																				X

TABLE 2–2 Factor Loadings for Factor Analysis of Responses to Job Satisfaction Statements

	Factor				
Variable	*I*	*II*	*III*	*IV*	*V*
1	.80	.03	.24	.17	.01
2	.35	.71	.06	.11	.06
3	.21	−.72	.19	.01	.19
4	.06	.05	.19	−.71	.43
5	.64	.43	.27	.06	.22
6	.17	.01	.41	.62	.07
7	−.40	.02	.13	.22	.03
8	.21	.14	.56	.17	.27
9	.02	.07	.07	.14	.17
10	.06	.44	−.54	.08	.24
11	.14	.60	.09	.16	.41
12	.21	.19	.01	−.74	.15
13	.26	.14	−.46	.21	.34
14	.09	−.61	.21	.30	.30
15	.64	.01	.17	.02	.01
16	.14	.07	.29	.16	.32
17	.22	−.53	.31	.17	.07
18	.81	.04	.02	.31	.14
19	.19	.02	.11	.01	−.41
20	.01	.14	−.71	.23	.26
Percent variance accounted for	14%	11%	10%	10%	06%

The factor loading table permits us to interpret or understand the factor that was identified mathematically. Let's consider our loading matrix. In Table 2–2, some possible labels for the factors might be "satisfaction with pay" (I), "satisfaction with supervision" (II), "satisfaction with the work itself" (III), and "satisfaction with coworkers" (IV). The fifth factor has no clear interpretation.

There is a second characteristic of factor analysis to which I will refer in some later discussions of research results. If we assume that our initial problem is to account for all the joint variability in responses to the 20 items, we can determine the *relative importance* of the various factors in reducing or explaining this variability. The term usually used to describe this characteristic of factors is the *percentage of variance accounted for* by the factor. In Table 2–2, this value is indicated in the last entry in each column. From an inspection of these values, you will see that satisfaction with pay accounts for the greatest amount of the variation in responses. In a sense, this means that the psychological aspect of pay seems to pervade (or possibly override) responses to other questions.

CENTRAL POINTS FOR STUDY

1. I/O psychology adheres to the scientific method.
2. In order to draw conclusions from research, controls are necessary. These controls can be experimental or statistical.
3. Four common strategies for collecting research data include the lab experiment, the field experiment, the field study, and the simulation.
4. Data analysis can be either descriptive or inferential.
5. Correlation coefficients indicate extent of association.
6. Testing and evaluation represent an ethical challenge to the I/O psychologist.

CHAPTER 3

Prediction in Industrial Settings

The introductory chapter targeted testing and applied prediction as one of the major challenges for I/O psychology in the next decade. The methodology chapter described many of the basic statistical and design tools that have proved useful for prediction. In this chapter, the process of prediction and the nature of tests as individual predictors will be dealt with more fully.

Consider the following definition of a *test: A psychological test is the measurement of some phase of a carefully chosen sample of an individual's behavior*. This definition, provided by Clark Hull in 1928, is broad enough to encompass devices other than the standard paper-and-pencil test. It also includes such diverse things as interviews and actual attempts at performing the duties of a particular job (called *work samples*). A relatively broad definition of the word *test* is accepted. With such a definition in mind, certain other pieces of information must be categorized: answers to questions usually found on application blanks (e.g., "How many brothers and sisters do you have?") and physical examination data. We have a lot of material to cover in order to appreciate the role that testing might play in industrial settings. In this chapter, we will examine principles of testing. In the next chapter, we will consider methods for determining what the performance requirements of jobs are and how to measure the performance of an actual worker. In Chapter 5, we will consider a particular form of performance measurement, the performance rating. Then, in Chapter 6 we will look at particular tests that may be used so to predict performance. In Chapter 7, we will examine the interview and several nontraditional methods for predicting work performance. Finally, in Chapter 8 we will examine the way in which the testing process contributes to personnel decision making. This sequence of chapters will provide a good basis for a consideration of performance in the work setting.

The logic for developing and using tests for personnel decisions is a simple one. The major assumption is that different individuals have different probabilities of success in different jobs. You have often run across teachers who you felt were remarkably ill-suited for their chosen profession. The same could be said of bus drivers, senators, steelworkers, and police officers. Based on that belief, a search is begun for those elements of the particular job on which the well-suited and the ill-suited can be discriminated. For an offensive guard on a football team, this might be the ability to move laterally; for a crane operator, it might be the ability to notice events in the periphery of the visual field; for a textbook writer, it might be knowing when to stop belaboring an obvious point. On the basis of an identification of crucial job elements (a process called *job analysis*), a sample of behavior, or test, can be identified that will help to distinguish well-suited applicants from ill-suited ones *before* they are placed on the job. The great promise of testing for industry and the individual workers has been the possibility of identifying those individuals who will best fit into a particular job opening. Another name for this process is *differential placement*. The implications of such placement are fulfillment for the individual and profitability for the organization. Most of the early history of industrial testing shows attempts by the new discipline of industrial psychology to find a perfect match between the abilities of the worker and the requirements of the job. Douglas Fryer set up a series of vocational counseling programs at YMCAs all over metropolitan New York City in the mid-1920s. The aim of these counseling centers was to provide people with insight about their interests and abilities and thus allow them the opportunity to seek employment that would be pleasing to them. The placement notion was a very strong influence in the early testing movement.

Test Development and Use: An Example

It might be easier to get an idea of test use from a real-life example. Let's take the case of an assembler in the electronics industry (Figure 3–1). There are many different electronics components that are assembled by hand. One such component is called a transducer—a device that takes power from one electrical system and transfers it to another system. For our example, we will consider an assembler who constructs a transducer used in X-ray machines. The transducer is about the size of a child's fingernail and may have as many as 30 different components in it. Physically, the transducer has a round ceramic shell with two electrical leads attached to it. Inside the shell are the components of the transducer. Each of these components is linked to each other component so that if any one component does not function properly, the transducer cannot perform its function. An acquaintance of mine in this field compares making transducers to packing parachutes: If every operation is not done perfectly, the result is disaster. A transducer that is "almost perfect" is worthless.

Consider a fictitious organization called Transducers, Inc. that is having problems with production. In particular, the transducers must be reassembled several times before they can meet quality control standards. Some faulty transducers are being shipped and orders are several weeks behind promised delivery dates. In the past, Transducers, Inc. hired most of their production workers in one of three ways: they offered jobs to workers currently employed by a competitor in the area, they offered jobs to relatives of current employees,

FIGURE 3–1 Transducer Assembler

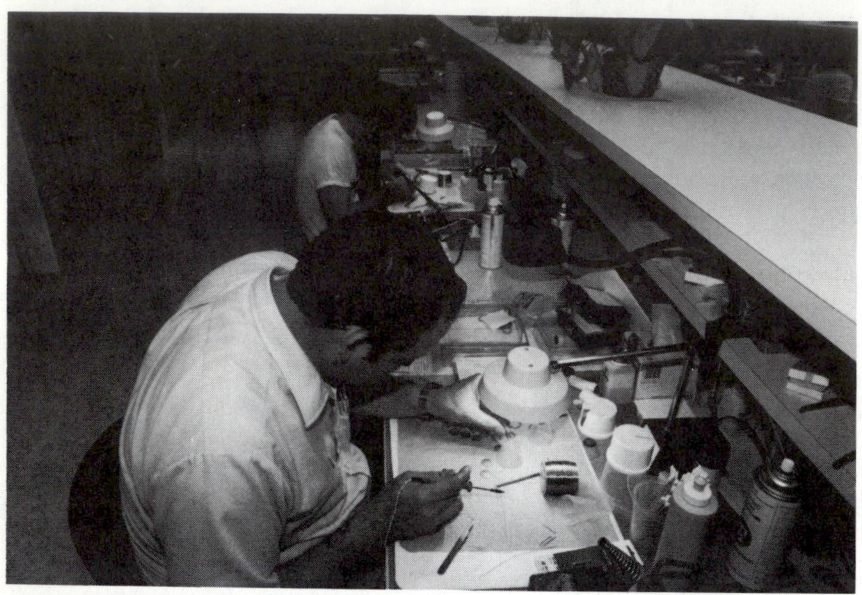

or they had production supervisors interview applicants who walked in off the street in response to an ad in the help-wanted column of the local newspaper. As the company has grown from a dozen production workers to over 100, production has steadily declined in both quality and timeliness. The president of Transducers, Inc. has come to a personnel psychologist for help. How would the personnel psychologist proceed?

First, a job analysis would be completed. The psychologist would go to the plant and watch transducers being assembled, talk to assemblers and supervisors, and possibly have assemblers and supervisors complete a questionnaire or checklist dealing with various aspects of the job of assembler. This would be a job analysis. The job analysis would identify the most critical aspects of the job—those that are most important in producing a high-quality transducer. At Transducers, Inc. these tasks turn out to be the following:

1. Soldering the electrical leads that are attached to the transducer body
2. Assembling the transducer shell with glue
3. Testing the assembled transducer to make sure that it has the correct electrical properties
4. Visually inspecting the assembled transducer before it is packed and shipped

There are many other specific operations that are involved as well, but these particular operations seem to be the ones most likely to be leading to the production problems.

The psychologist now tries to identify the human skills and abilities that would be necessary to perform the critical operations successfully. For soldering, the abilities might include visual acuity, eye-hand coordination, and finger dexterity. For transducer assembly, the required abilities might be hand steadiness, visual acuity, and finger dexterity. For transducer testing, abilities such as reading specifications, sequencing actions, and reading test equipment accurately might be required. Finally, the visual inspection of the assembled transducer might involve abilities such as color vision, visual acuity, and attention to detail.

The next step for the psychologist would be to identify commercially available tests that could be used to provide estimates of these abilities in candidates for assembler positions. If tests are not currently available, the psychologist would construct a test to measure the particular ability. In our case, the test battery might include the following tests:

Finger dexterity
Eye-hand coordination
Visual acuity
Reading comprehension
Hand steadiness
Information sequencing
Test equipment reading and recording
Color vision
Attention to detail

Assume that Transducers, Inc. can arrange their production workers from best to worst. This might be done through supervisory ratings or through examinations of scrap and reject records. The next step would be to explain the purpose of the testing and the anticipated use of the results to the employees. It is critical that they understand the importance of accurate prediction to organizational health. In organizations where the employees are represented by a union, it is essential to explain the process to appropriate union officers and enlist their aid in the validation project. The psychologist might now administer the battery of tests described above to all present employees of Transducers, Inc. The purpose of this step would be to compare test scores with performance scores. In the best of circumstances, several of the tests would show substantial relations to performance measures. In other words, the best performers on the job would receive the highest scores on the test. After various statistical analyses, the psychologist would present Transducers, Inc. with a strategy for hiring applicants. This strategy would include the administration of the tests shown to be related to performance of applicants, the transformation of test scores into anticipated performance scores (or probabilities of success on the assembler job), and the method for deciding which of the applicants actually to hire. If the psychologist has done a good job, production problems should begin to disappear as new employees are added using the suggested system.

Of course, the example above has been greatly simplified for the purposes of this chapter. In addition to testing, the psychologist would also examine machine and task design to make sure that the right equipment and task setup was being used. An examination of possible motivational issues might be completed also. There would also be an investigation of assembler training programs. Nevertheless, if we were to consider the testing component in isolation, it might be developed along the lines described above. The next several chapters will deal with all the operations you have seen in this example in greater detail.

On the basis of this brief description of the testing process and the role of tests, you can see that there are many components to the well-developed and administered system. These components are:

1. *Job analysis.* Identifying the elements of the job that are critical to success
2. *Predictor identification.* Locating tests or other devices that might be predictive of future job success
3. *Measurement of success.* Obtaining measures of work performance in order to determine if any of the potential predictors would have identified superior performers

These are the basic elements necessary for developing and evaluating a testing program.

Testing in Perspective

While the logic of testing is well-rooted historically, going back considerably farther than Plato, for all practical purposes the modern history of aptitude testing begins with Alfred Binet. In 1904, Binet was charged by the French government with the identification of those children likely to have "difficulties" in the school system. The assumption was that the difficulties were related to the mental capacity of the children. Within a few years, Binet and Theodore Simon (a coworker) had developed a series of tests aimed at identifying those children who could not benefit from the standard school curriculum. Lewis Terman, a psychologist at Stanford University, adapted the tests for use in the United States. Shortly thereafter, variations on the test were used in industrial settings. In the very first issue of the *Journal of Applied Psychology,* which appeared in 1917, Terman describes a study in which he used a variation of the Stanford-Binet intelligence test to predict the success of police officers and fire fighters in San Jose, California.

World War I provided an excellent opportunity for people interested in

YELLOW CAB COMPANY

OF PHILADELPHIA

Test for Drivers

Compiled by

Morris S. Viteles, Ph.D., Consulting Psychologist

A ....
R ....
SCORE

page 7

34. In the drawing below make a line to show the SHORTEST route from house 1 to house 2 to house 3 following the traffic rules.
THE NUMBERED SQUARES STAND FOR HOUSES.
There are TWO TRAFFIC rules
    1. ALWAYS TURN TO THE RIGHT. No left-hand turns are allowed.
    2. Keep off the part of the street marked "CLOSED."

1 ↓
Closed
2
3

35. If you charge 30 cents per mile and 15 cents for each extra passenger more than one, how much will you collect for a 6-mile ride on which you carry 4 passengers?
    Answer: ....

36. If a taxicab bill is $7.55 and you are given a ten dollar bill, what is the SMALLEST number of coins you can give back in change?
    .... Dollars .... Halves .... Quarters
    .... Dimes .... Nickels

37. Answer the following question about the picture of the automobile accident which you observed:
    From what State is the automobile?
    Answer: ....

38. Above the first letter below make a cross. Draw a circle around the letter which follows it in the alphabet and a line from this to the last letter below.

J A R N P K L O S T V A

An example of a test used in 1930 for hiring cab drivers. (From Industrial Psychology *[p. 227] by M. Viteles, 1932, New York: Norton.)*

applied aptitude testing to try out their new skills. There was a problem, however. How could recruits be efficiently tested by means of individually administered intelligence tests? The answer was that they could not. There were some group tests that were being developed at the time by Otis (see Hull, 1928, for a more detailed description). These tests became known as the Army Alpha and the Army Beta (primarily for illiterates) and served the purposes for which they were intended quite well. In less than 50 minutes, the test could be administered to groups as large as 500. This procedure certainly satisfied what Hull (1928) later described as one of the essential characteristics of an aptitude test: "A method of prognosis which is not at the same time reasonably quick and reasonably inexpensive has no excuse for existence" (p. 2). It is good that Hull is not around today to see the extent and cost of many testing programs in industry.

It is interesting to note that at the outset of World War I there was an internal dispute among applied psychologists with respect to how to use tests to place new recruits in various functional positions. On the one hand, Robert Yerkes, the president of the American Psychological Association at the time, was interested in individually administered tests patterned after the Stanford-Binet. Walter Dill Scott, an eminent applied psychologist of the era, was more interested in a group-administered test similar to those he had been administering for sales personnel for some time. The dispute became so bitter that Scott and Yerkes pursued completely different programs in attempting to help the services. In the end, it was the work of Walter Bingham, Terman, and Otis that resulted in the Army Alpha test. But by the time this technology had been worked out and approved, the war was almost over. As a result, few actual placement decisions were actually made using the new tests, although military personnel already in place were tested to ensure that they were suited for their positions (Sokal, 1987). Thus, the technology for mass testing had been developed and would be used frequently in the decades to follow.

As Ghiselli (1966) pointed out, an implied promise was made to the industrial community by the procedural success of World War I testing. If it could be done so quickly and efficiently for the army, it could be done equally well for industry. Unfortunately, procedure could not make up for content, and there was a good deal of disappointment among the leaders of industry in the value of testing. There was a brief rekindling of interest during the time of the Great Depression and an enormous reawakening of interest with the commencement of World War II. Once again, millions of recruits had to be classified, and once again, it was primarily the applied measurement, personnel, and industrial psychologists who developed the programs. After the war, testing became more widespread in industry, with more specific aptitude testing occurring (e.g., tests for mechanical aptitude or hand-eye coordination). Industry was ready to accept testing as "the answer." Unfortunately, no one had taken the time to ask "the question."

Testing as an activity proceeded rapidly and relatively unchecked at the industrial level until the 1960s. About then, social critics such as Gross (1962) and Whyte (1956) began to question the implications of testing for some traditionally cherished values such as "privacy." Testing also came under fire from psychologists for its overwhelmingly empirical flavor. The implication was that there was no *theory* that related aptitudes and abilities to job success. It is interesting to note that when Morris Viteles wrote the first textbook on modern industrial psychology in 1932, his concern was that there was too much theory and too little data.

In the 1960s, the critics demanded both a demonstration of job relatedness (those critics concerned with invasion of privacy) and a theory relating mental measurement to constructs such as job performance (those critics concerned with the single-mindedness of the empirical approach). The critics could never have had the impact they had if the public at large had not also experienced a disenchantment with testing in general. Consequently, it was not too great a leap to include some of these specific objections and general feelings of uneasiness into the Civil Rights Act of 1964 (Title VII). Shortly thereafter, two federal agencies were created to identify abuses of testing as they affected minority groups and to employ economic sanctions against organizations so identified. The first agency, the EEOC, produced a set of guidelines defining fair employment practices. The heart of these guidelines was the assertion that tests could not be used to discriminate unfairly against certain protected groups. Guion (1966) has since defined *unfair discrimination* as "individuals with equal probability of success on the job having unequal opportunities for employment." The second agency, the Office of Federal Contract Compliance (OFCC), was given the power to withhold or recall federal funds from employers who did not comply with the fair employment practices outlined by the EEOC.

As a result of the possible economic sanctions that might be directed against them, many organizations abandoned their testing programs in favor of interviews, background checks, and biographical information that might be obtained on an application blank. This simply postponed the problem; it did not solve it. The most recent version of the guidelines (now known as the "Uniform Guidelines") imposes a much broader definition of a test that includes, among other things, interviews, biographical data, and performance ratings (if they are used to make promotion decisions). All this has led to great activity in the theory and application of testing, activity that was absent for so much of the history of the applied testing movement.

Testing has made great strides since the turn of the century, and there is little doubt that tests and testing have added substantially to the common good. Nevertheless, there were some periods in the history of testing that cannot be viewed with pride. A good example is the role of intelligence testing in the immigration policy following World War I. In the process of screening enlisted men for armed service, it became apparent that there were substantial differences among national and cultural groups. American blacks did very poorly on the Army Alpha. The same was true of southern Europeans. White American and northern European immigrants did best.

Since it was clear that language facility was a problem, the Army Beta test was developed for immigrants with poor English facility and native-born illiterates. The test scores produced through this mass testing were later used to limit the immigration of certain "undesirable" nationalities. Immigration quotas were set at percentages that represented the U.S. population distribution *prior* to the mass immigration of the late nineteenth and early twentieth century. This effectively limited any further "dilution of the American stock" by immigrants of supposed inferior capacities. Chief among those responsible for producing the data used by Congress in establishing these restrictive quotas were people like Yerkes, Goddard, and Brigham. These individuals were all involved in the development and application of standardized ability tests. Brigham was a strong advocate of a position called *racial determinism*, that is, that the observed inferiority of certain immigrant groups on intelligence tests had a strong genetic component. He was later to accept and argue the opposite position, but during the mid- and late 1920s he and other testing experts exercised a strong influence over Congress as they made decisions about immigration policies. There are some excellent descriptions of this period of testing history provided by the National Research Council (Garner & Wigdor, 1982) and in two recent and fascinating books. The first is by Stephen Jay Gould entitled *The Mismeasure of Man* (1980). In this book, Gould suggests strongly that the history of mental testing is something of a national disgrace. He feels that many tests have been developed simply to illustrate prejudices of majority groups. A second book that has recently appeared (Sokal, 1987) deals more evenly with the history of applied testing and illuminates many of the influences in the early testing movement. Recently, some have contended that it was not the psychological or testing establishment that was at fault in the misguided use of test results for determining immigration quotas but rather ill-informed and unscrupulous political forces (Snyderman & Herrnstein, 1983). For all practical purposes, however, it is not really important whether these psychologists intended to misuse test information, were unaware that test information would be misused, or were ineffective in combating this misinformation. Testing information was used inappropriately and millions suffered as a result. This is the legacy that forms the core of the current dispute regarding the role of tests in a free society. We will return to this discussion in Chapter 8 when we examine the use of test scores for decision making.

Test constructors and test users must share in the blame equally for the public distrust of testing. For their part, the professionals developing tests did not or would not take the time to consider logical and theoretical relationships among tests and on-the-job behaviors. The test users were equally uninterested in theory—they wanted *results*. The person taking the test was often caught in the middle. The whole testing movement is in the process of correcting past deficiencies in both test development and test use. The rest of this chapter is concerned with the logical, methodological, and theoretical principles that are being currently practiced in the use of personnel tests.

Evaluation in Psychological Measurement

It was stated in the opening paragraph of this chapter that "a psychological test is the measurement of a . . . sample of . . . behavior." To equate testing and measurement indicates that tests are used to quantify (measure) observations of behavior. Some tests may quite adequately fulfill the purposes for which they were designed just by consistently classifying people into two or more categories. Such tests "measure" at a primitive level and may yield only binary information—that a person has or does not have a certain blood type or disease, for example. Nevertheless, most psychological testing is concerned with assigning a score to an individual that is indicative of his position along some continuum or dimension of individual difference. In this sense, a psychological test is an *operational definition* of a concept—an ability, an aptitude, or an area of achievement—a set of standard procedures or operations for measuring the abstract concept.

Each item of a test may be thought of as an observation of the individual's behavior. The total test of *n* items constituting a behavior sample of stimuli (the test questions) is representative of the population (or "universe") of stimuli that might be presented to elicit behaviors relevant to the concept being considered. Thus, for example, a test of "achievement in arithmetic" presents a sample of stimuli (problems) from the nearly infinite universe of arithmetic problems that might be presented. The responses to these problems constitute a sample of the individual's behavior and, at the same time, a sample of the concept, or attribute, "arithmetic skill."

Because psychological test scores are based on a *sample* of observations, they are subject to error. Just as we know that our confidence in a sample mean depends in part on the size of the sample, our confidence in a test score depends on an adequate sample of behavior.

RELIABILITY AND VALIDITY

If I were to ask someone about the characteristics of a good measuring device, she would probably respond with terms like *accuracy, precision,* or *adequacy for the job at hand.* The carpenter may find a yardstick graduated to eighths or sixteenths of an inch sufficiently accurate and precise for a job, but the machinist would insist upon calipers accurate to the thousandth or ten-thousandth of an inch. Neither would suggest that a good measuring device ought to measure that dimension or attribute that it was designed to measure; that is, neither would raise the issue of whether the yardstick—or the calipers—measured "length," or the distance between two points. Yet the surveyor might well be concerned that a measuring tape measures length and that it be relatively uncontaminated by temperature changes that expand and contract the materials from which the tape is made.

In psychological measurement, however, the question of *what* is being measured is at least as important as the questions of accuracy, precision, or consistency of measurement, since the attribute that one attempts to measure is an abstract theoretical concept, such as "intelligence," "clerical aptitude," and "authoritarianism." Of course, it is also true that "length" and "time" are abstractions, but the yardstick and the clock function very well, for most purposes, as operational definitions of these constructs. The psychologist, like the surveyor, but to a greater degree, is plagued by potential and real sources of contamination in attempts to define concepts or theoretical constructs operationally. Furthermore, one person's conceptual definition may differ from that of a colleague's.

The terms *accuracy* or *precision* of measurement may be thought of in both a relative and an absolute sense. When we speak of the *tolerance* of a measuring device (e.g., "accurate to ± one-thousandth of an inch"), we are describing the absolute accuracy for assessing the length of the object. On the other hand, if we speak of the confidence we can have of ordering a set of objects on a scale or dimension (i.e., of stating which of each pair of objects is longer or larger), then we are concerned with relative accuracy of measurement.

Two concepts central to the problems of evaluating psychological measurement are reliability and validity. *Reliability* refers to the issues in psychological measurement that are like those of precision or accuracy in physical measurement. However, as Guion (1965) points out, the word *accuracy* implies something more than or different from what is meant by either *reliability* or *validity*. *Accuracy* implies the confidence we have in: (1) the reproducibility of an individual measurement (absolute accuracy), (2) the ordering of a set of objects (relative accuracy), and (3) the extent to which the value or score agrees with some absolute standard. Guion offered the example of a thermometer that has slipped in its moorings on a board marked with degree readings. The thermometer may yield dependable measurement both in the sense that it accurately reflects differences among days in warmness and that it yields highly similar readings under identical conditions, but the fact that it reads 20 degrees higher than the local standard makes it inaccurate—though reliable. In other words, accuracy is concerned with both constant and variable error, whereas reliability is concerned with variable errors in measurement.

Validity, as implied by the word, has something to do with the *truth* of a measurement. Thus, validity of a measurement answers the question, Does this number truly represent what I want it to represent? This suggests that it is possible to collect the wrong information reliably and precisely. It is possible, and often the case, that we have reliable but not valid measurements. There are separate sets of operations for determining reliability and validity, and I will try to keep them distinct in the following discussion. Nevertheless, bear in mind that reliability and validity are both distinct and related. They are distinct in that they deal with different characteristics of measurements;

they are related in that measures must be reliable before they can be shown to be valid. In fact, this connection between reliability and validity can be stated quite forcefully: reliability sets the upper limit for validity.

Reliability

The operational definitions of reliability, which are presented below, reflect the consistency and reproducibility of an observation (score) or set of observations (distribution of scores). If a measuring instrument is to be of any value, it should produce highly reliable measurements. In terms of a correlation coefficient, acceptable reliabilities are of the order .70 and above. Perfect reliability would be represented by a correlation of 1.00 between two sets of measurements on the same sample of people with the same or equivalent measuring devices. Correlation coefficients representing reliability estimates are usually much higher than those representing validity estimates. Validity coefficients in applied settings seldom exceed .50. Although the size of the validity coefficients is disturbing (since low values of the correlation coefficient indicate a lack of predictability of one variable from another), it makes sense that the correlation of a variable with itself (reliability) should be higher than the correlation of a variable with another variable (validity). More will be said about validity later in this chapter. First, we will consider the procedures for estimating the reliability of a test.

Sources of Unreliability. Suppose that you wished to measure each of several new trees planted in your yard. You would get your measuring device, stand it up beside each tree, and determine as best you could the mark on the scale that corresponded to the highest tip on the tree. You would then record the reading and go on to the next tree. When you were finished, you could order the trees from tallest to shortest (by name or location). Now suppose, for the sake of the example, that you misplaced your recordings and, a week later, went through the whole measuring process again. Then, as always happens, having done the job over, you would find your first set of observations. Out of curiosity, you might compare the two sets of numbers. If they agreed very well, both with respect to *order* and *magnitude,* then you would conclude that: (1) the trees had not changed appreciably with respect to the attribute (height), (2) you had a good measuring device, and (3) you had done a good job—each time—in using the measuring device. If, on the other hand, the two sets of measures agreed very well in designating the *order* but not the *height,* you might conclude that the user and the instrument were accurate, but the trees had changed (i.e., grown by a fixed amount in the time interval between measures). Finally, if you found that the two sets of measures did not agree with respect to order or magnitude, then you would be in somewhat of a dilemma, not knowing whether you had: (1) a poor measuring device, subject to a good deal of error or contamination (e.g., it measures differently in the sun than in the shade; (2) a poor user of the device, careless in aligning the object and instrument, in reading the instrument, or in recording the values; or (3) an unstable attribute—height—subject to growth spurts and differential rates from one tree to the next, with some trees shrinking, some growing taller, and some remaining unchanged. Frequently, it is difficult to determine if the lack of reliability is the result of the device (yielding an inadequate sample of the attribute), lack of skill on the part of the user, or a lack of stability in the attribute measured.

Estimates of Reliability. The Technical Appendix at the end of the chapter will cover the statistical issues of reliability measurement. In this section, we will consider the reliability from a conceptual perspective.

Operational Definition 1: Test-Retest. One way to obtain an estimate of reliability is to test and then retest the same set of individuals on the same test items. Thus, each individual has two scores, X_1 and X_2, each an estimate of the "true" score. The correlation, $r_{x_1x_2}$, between these two sets of scores taken over the sample of individuals constitutes our estimate. Figure 3–2 illustrates how a high test-retest correlation documents a consistency in the *ordering* of individuals, whereas Figure 3–3 shows that low reliability means high *uncertainty* as to the relative position of an individual in the distribution. Figure 3–4 demonstrates that a perfect correlation, $r_{x_1x_2} = 1.00$, does *not* necessarily mean that the estimate of the individual's score remains unchanged: if there is a constant change, such as a fixed growth rate, the correlation can be perfect, while the two observations of each individual differ widely (but systematically).

The appropriate time interval between test and retest is difficult to determine exactly. It should be long enough so that the individual cannot remember responses on the first test. It should be short enough so that dramatic changes have not occurred in the individual as a function of some experience (such as training).

Operational Definition 2: Equivalent Forms. Test and retest scores might differ (either as in Figure 3–2 or Figure 3–3) as a result of the *effects of the initial testing* on retest performance. Thus, the two sets of observations may not be independent.

Although guessing is a common test behavior, there is a problem that is introduced by *consistent* guessing behavior. On a multiple-choice test, you may use a common decision rule for all items that you cannot answer. For example, using student folklore, you might always choose alternative c. If you use the same decision rule on the retest, the consistency of your score (and the reliability of the test) will be an artificially inflated estimate of the true score consistency and reliability owing to the consistency of your guessing pattern. This would be an example of a systematic error that affects the reliability estimate. For these and other reasons, test developers have often sought to assess reliability by developing and using different forms rather than the identical form at the original and retest sessions. These forms are usually carefully constructed to be equivalent in content, types of questions,

FIGURE 3–2 Score Distributions of Individuals Tested on Two Different Occasions—High Test-Retest Reliability

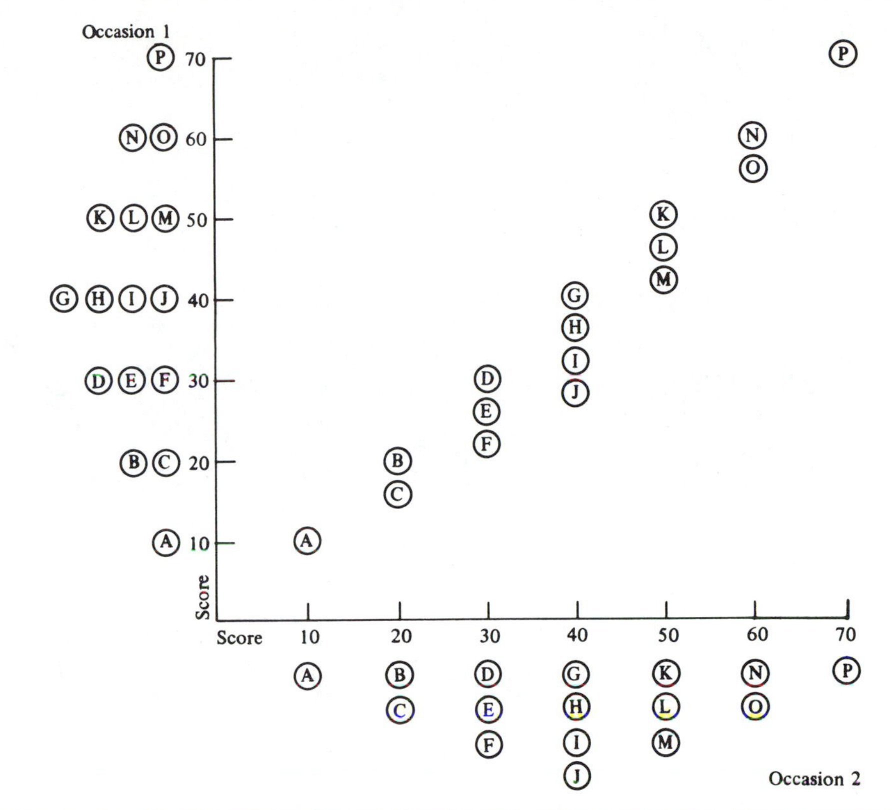

difficulty levels, and so on. The analysis of possible outcomes for the test-retest approach is equally true for equivalent forms. To appreciate this, simply substitute "Form A" and "Form B" for "Occasion 1" and "Occasion 2," respectively, in Figures 3–2, 3–3, and 3–4. However, as we shall see, sources of error variance and of systematic variance are not the same in any two estimates of reliability.

Both the test-retest and the equivalent-forms method yield a *coefficient of stability* if some time interval is allowed between first and second measures. Without an appreciable interval between administrations, the correlation between equivalent forms is called a *coefficient of equivalence.* Each form is presumed to yield a representative sample of the individual's behavior. Low estimates of equivalence, therefore, can be interpreted in terms of inadequate or unrepresentative sampling of the behavioral domain. In terms of a traditional paper-and-pencil test, the domain might consist of all possible test items

FIGURE 3–3 Score Distributions of Individuals Tested on Two Different Occasions—Low Test-Retest Reliability

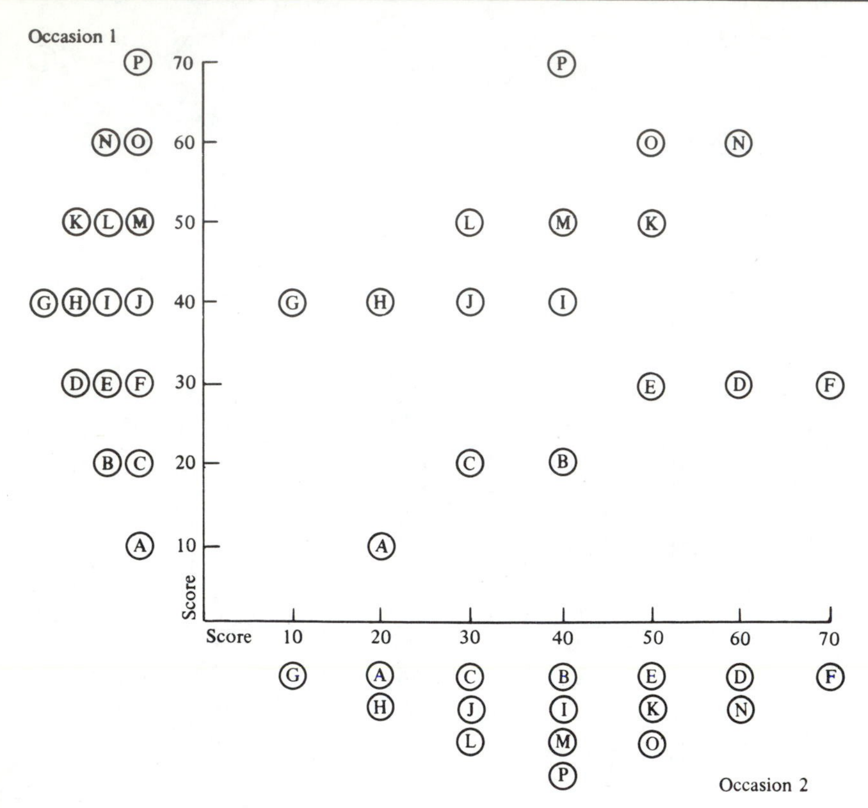

designed to measure the attribute under consideration. The domain of test items for a test on this chapter might consist of 500 to 600 questions dealing with predictor-related issues. If the coefficient of equivalence for two equivalent 20-question tests of this material were low, we might conclude that the domain had been poorly sampled by one test, the other, or both tests.

Operational Definition 3: Internal Consistency. A good yardstick should measure equally from both ends, and it should not really matter whether we start at the end or in the middle—the results should be the same. Somewhat analogous to this example is the rationale for internal consistency estimates of reliability. Basically, the approach is to divide a test into two equivalent halves (e.g., odd versus even items), score each half for each individual, then correlate the two sets of scores. A high correlation indicates that the two halves yield consistent information: if one half indicates a high score for individual A, the second half signals the same thing. Thus, where two sessions

FIGURE 3–4 Score Distributions of Individuals Tested on Two Different Occasions—High Test-Retest Reliability

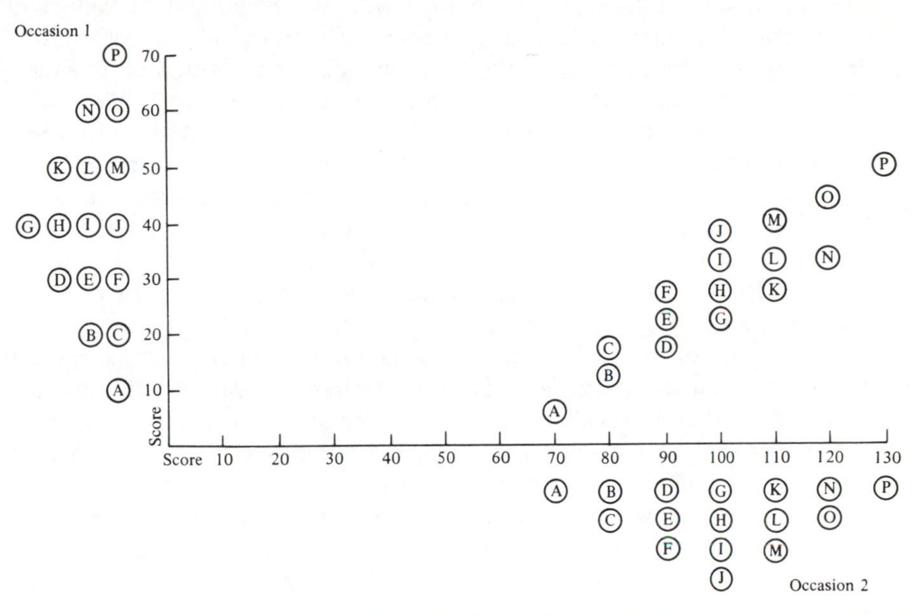

or two forms are not available, they are created (and, it is hoped, are equivalent) from a single administration of a test. The reliability must be adjusted upward since you would actually be estimating the reliability of a test with only one-half the items that the full test has. This adjustment is accomplished using the Spearman-Brown prophecy formula. This formula is described in the Technical Appendix at the end of the chapter.

Validity

At one level of analysis, the question of the validity of a test or other predictor is simply, How well does the predictor predict that which it was designed or chosen to predict? In other words, if we know an individual's score on the predictor, how accurately can we predict his score on a criterion? Validity typically is operationally defined as the correlation between the predictor and the criterion scores of a sample of individuals. The result is known as the *validity* coefficient, or simply the predictive validity of the test *for that specific criterion*. It should be clear that while scores on a test may predict, say, quantity of production, they might be unrelated to another criterion—say, turnover. *Validity in this sense is not an inherent property of the test but is only an empirically demonstrated relationship to a specific criterion.* A test may have as many different validity coefficients as there are different criteria to correlate with it.

For a long time, personnel psychology was concerned almost exclusively with this empirical, nontheoretical definition of validity. It did not matter if the test measured memory capacity, reading skill, or general ability, as long as it yielded scores predictive of some measure of success on the job. More recently, however, industrial psychologists have recognized the limitations of a nontheoretical "shotgun" approach to testing and have begun to ask questions about the logical as well as the empirical validity of their predictors. While empirical validity is concerned with the accuracy with which test scores can predict criterion scores, logical validity is concerned with how well the operational definition (i.e., the test) measures the construct (construct validity) or how adequately it samples the domain (content validity).

Instead of empirical and logical validities, Guion (1976) refers to criterion-related validities and descriptive validities. Criterion-related validities (concurrent and predictive) evaluate inferences about the relationship between test scores and criterion scores. Descriptive validities (content and construct) evaluate the intrinsic meaning of test scores.

As one might expect, the federal agency responsible for enforcing compliance with the Equal Employment Opportunity law, the EEOC, presents a more mechanical view of the various ways that might be used to validate a selection procedure:

> In criterion related validity, a selection procedure is justified by a statistical relationship between scores on the test or other selection procedure and measures of job performance. In content validity, a selection procedure is justified by showing that it representatively samples significant parts of the job, such as a typing test for a typist. Construct validity involves identifying the psychological trait (the construct) which underlies successful performance on the job and then devising a selection procedure to measure the presence and degree of that construct. An example would be a test of leadership ability. (Federal Register, 1978, p. 38292)

Predictive, concurrent, content, and *construct validity* were introduced as terms to describe different experimental designs for validating a selection procedure (American Psychological Association (APA), 1954). As with most experimental designs, they could be well applied or poorly applied. In practice, this meant that some content validity studies might have led to stronger support for a selection strategy than some criterion-related studies that were poorly done. Eventually, psychologists, lawyers, judges, plaintiffs, and defendants fell to arguing about which type of validity was "acceptable" or "permissible." Unfortunately, in the course of these arguments, the essence of the validation *process* was obscured.

At the heart of the validity discussion is the issue of how well the validity study was designed. If we consider a validity study as an experiment or, more appropriately, a field study, the issue is really one of deciding if we should

FIGURE 3–5 Validation Process from the Conceptual and Operational Levels

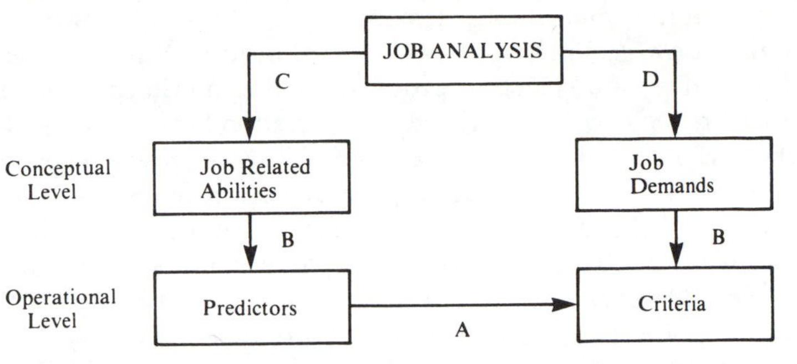

support or reject a hypothesis about job performance. The implied hypothesis states that job performance is a function of certain attributes as measured by certain procedures. These attributes are the psychological variables that are represented by the predictors. The procedures are the actual tests. When we consider the validation process as really just hypothesis testing, the importance of the three common models of validity can be seen in the appropriate perspective. These three types of validity—content, construct, and criterion-related—are simply three of many different approaches that might be taken to test our job performance–psychological attribute hypothesis. This broader view of the validation process is becoming more commonly accepted (Guion & Gibson, 1988; Landy, 1986).

One way of looking at the validation process is from the conceptual and operational levels. The conceptual level is abstract and depends more on logic than on particular tests or criteria or data. The operational level is more concrete. It is concerned with which tests will be used, which criteria will be considered, and how these tests and criteria may be statistically related. Figure 3–5 presents a diagram of various relationships within each level and between the conceptual and abstract levels. As I described in the earlier example of transducer assemblers, the process begins with a job analysis. This analysis is intended to accomplish two goals. First, it should identify the critical demands of the job in question. In addition, the job analysis should be useful in identifying the human abilities that can be used in meeting those job demands. The process of getting from the job analysis to an understanding of the job demands and the ability requirements is a logical process. As you will see below, the technical name for this logical process is *content validity.*

At the operational level, we still have the problem of deciding which ability tests to use and which criterion information to gather. Further, after gathering that information, we must still examine the relationship between test performance and job performance. Most of the common types of validity can be described using the model in Figure 3–5 as a point of departure. Keep in mind that by describing three commonly used validity designs, I am not suggesting that these designs exhaust the possibilities. These should be thought of as "traditional validity designs" rather than as "approved" designs.

Criterion-Related Validity: Concurrent Design. When we are investigating the validity of a selection procedure using a criterion-related design, typically we are looking for a significant correlation between a test (predictor) and job behavior (criterion). The two major forms of criterion-related validity differ in terms of the time separating the predictor or test information from the behavior to be predicted, or the criterion information. The *concurrent* approach means that we test *present* employees for whom individual job performance criteria are available. Test scores are then correlated with criterion scores to determine if performance can be predicted from test information. The resulting correlation coefficient (now known as the *validity coefficient)* describes the degree of concurrent validity of the test.

As part of a testing project, I developed a physical ability test for fire fighter applicants in a midwestern city. Female applicants did more poorly on this test than male applicants. As a result, a suit was filed by the female applicants in federal court. The judge in that case ruled that a concurrent criterion-related study should be conducted to demonstrate the validity of the physical ability test. The study was carried out by identifying a representative sample of currently employed fire fighters in that city, administering the physical ability test to them, and also gathering performance data on those fire fighters. The primary performance data gathered were the rating of their immediate supervisors on the effectiveness of the fire fighters in various work-related tasks (e.g., rescue, fire-fighting operations, first aid, etc.). The pattern of correlations was significant and positive. Fire fighters who did better on the physical ability tests also received higher supervisory ratings. Naturally, precautions were taken to ensure that the supervisors did not know what test scores the fire fighters had achieved on the physical ability tests.

There are substantial advantages to concurrent studies. One clear advantage is in the availability of the necessary data. Had we employed a predictive design in the fire fighter study, it might have taken five to six years before a sufficient number of new fire fighters were hired to enable the validity analysis. In this city, they typically hired 36 fire fighters each year. Some feel that there is a disadvantage in this design as well. It has been feared that the predictive value of the resulting validity coefficient might be artificially low since it was assumed that the size of the correlation coefficient is affected by having only part of the population of potential workers available. We do not have information about those who are not currently employed by the organization (either because they were not hired or because they quit or were fired). A recent meta-analysis by Schmitt, Noe, Gooding, and Kirsch (1984) has demonstrated that the concurrent design may actually produce stronger correlation coefficients than predictive designs. They conclude that there is little difference between the two designs for all practical purposes.

Criterion-Related Validity: Predictive Design. In the predictive approach to test validation, there is an interval of time that separates the test information from the criterion information. Predictive validation is concerned with the extent to which earlier observations (test scores) are predictive of later behavior (criterion scores). Thus, the predictive validity of IQ scores or reading-readiness measures obtained on preschoolers might be evaluated against performance measures taken after the first year of school.

In an industrial setting, a mechanical comprehension test might be administered to all applicants for the job of machinist and the scores on that test correlated with production figures after those hired had been on the job for several months. The resulting correlation coefficient would be known as the *predictive validity coefficient* of the test.

Recently, I conducted a predictive criterion-related validity study of a test that had been used to hire police officers in New York City in 1980. This test had been the subject of a court suit brought by black candidates who had failed this examination, and as a result of this suit, the city of New York was ordered to use the test results in a very special manner. They were told to identify a passing point and hire all those above the passing point without regard to their actual score on the test. In this way, black candidates would have a greater probability of being hired. In essence, the court had created the opportunity for a real predictive validity study. Tests had been administered, but individual test results for all those above the pass point were ignored in the hiring process. My job was to collect performance information on the individuals actually hired and to investigate the extent to which the test scores *would have predicted* job performance had they been used in the traditional manner (i.e., the better test scorers hired before the poorer test scorers). I gathered the performance data in the police academy (i.e., academy success) and two years after the individuals graduated from the police academy. The performance data included supervisory ratings and productivity information (e.g., numbers of arrests made, number of summonses written, etc.). The data indicated that the test was valid for predicting many aspects of performance in the academy and on the street. At the very least, this study showed that the test was a reasonable device for making hire–no-hire decisions, as the court had permitted. Further, however, the study indicated that the test could have been even more valuably used if individual scores had been taken into account and those candidates with higher scores given preference over those with lower scores.

An important consideration in the predictive approach is that the test scores not be used to make hiring decisions until *after* the validity coefficient has been computed. If the test in question is used to screen applicants, we have the same problem that we encountered in the concurrent approach—we are missing the data from those who are not hired; that is, our sample is inappropriate. In the police study described above, we had a hybrid design. We were missing *some* of the full sample that would make up a truly predictive

FIGURE 3–6 Variations of Predictive Validity Designs

Type of Validity	*Procedure*
1. Follow up—random	Test applicants; select randomly; collect criterion data later; correlate test scores and criterion data
2. Follow up—present system	Test applicants; select using procedures used in past; collect criterion data later; correlate test scores and criterion data
3. Select by test	Test applicants; select based on test scores; collect criterion data later; correlate test scores and criterion data
4. Hire, then test	Hire applicants; test during orientation or training; collect criterion data later; correlate test scores and criterion data
5. Shelf research	Hire applicants; collect criterion data later; examine personnel folders for potential predictors; correlate potential predictors and criterion data

SOURCE: Based on "A Note on Concurrent and Predictive Validity Designs: A Critical Re-analysis" by R. M. Guion and C. J. Cranny, 1982, *Journal of Applied Psychology, 67*(2), 239–244.

study (i.e., those who had not achieved a passing mark). On the other hand, there were still many individuals hired who might not have been, had the passing applicants been arranged from highest to lowest scorer and only the higher scorers chosen for employment.

Regardless of whether the test data and job performance data are gathered at the same time (concurrent design) or whether the test data are gathered before performance data and not used (predictive design), the validation is being carried out at the operational level. In Figure 3–5, criterion-related validity is represented by arrow *A* connecting predictors and criteria.

Neither predictive nor concurrent validity is a unitary concept. In fact, there are many different versions of each. As an example, Figure 3–6 describes five different versions of predictive validity. Similarly, there are several versions of concurrent validity. Recently, there has been some debate concerning the interchangeability of predictive and concurrent designs. The two sides of the argument are succinctly presented in a pair of papers. Barrett, Phillips, and Alexander (1981) argue that the two designs are rendered interchangeable through statistical and logical transformations. Guion and Cranny (1982) argue that the two different generic designs cannot be freely substituted for one another. Further, they argue that even within a design (e.g., predictive) different variations allow for different inferences about test scores and performance. Both arguments are interesting and plausible. I would agree with Barrett et al. that the distinction between concurrent and predictive designs is not clear-cut and in some instances is arbitrary. I would agree with Guion and Cranny that each validity design (even *within* the generic categories of concurrent and predictive) must be evaluated on its own merits rather than by association with the concurrent or predictive label. There will be continued discussion of the differences between these two designs, since the real issue is, What inferences do certain data collection techniques permit? This is a question that has not been satisfactorily resolved in *any* area of psychology. For the present discussion, the predictive validity designs presented by Guion and Cranny emphasize once again the proposition that there are many different ways to test the job performance hypothesis, not just three "approved" designs (Landy, 1986).

Content Validity. Content validity is concerned with the extent to which the sample of items in a test (and the sample behavior elicited by these items) is an unbiased representation of the domain (i.e., attribute or trait) being sampled. Keep in mind the earlier definition of a test: *a measurement of some phase of a carefully chosen sample of an individual's behavior.* Since this definition included measures other than just paper-and-pencil tests, this also means that test *items* should be broadly defined as well. These items can be in a form other than questions on a paper-and-pencil test. They might include questions in an oral interview, questions on an application blank, performance tasks such as tweezer dexterity tasks, or physical strength tests.

For example, if one were attempting to select from among a group of applicants for the job of typist, the test battery might include a typing test. The domain under consideration (typing ability) would have been well represented by the "test item" (i.e., material the individual applicant was asked to type). Similarly, suppose an instructor assigns 100 pages of a text treating one topic and devotes 5 lectures to the topic, but assigns 200 pages and devotes 10 lectures to another topic. Content validity of a test covering these two topics might be demonstrated if approximately one-third of the test items were devoted to the first topic and two-thirds to the second topic. Content validity is determined on the basis of how well the test material samples the job performance domain. This means that content validity is more judgmental than the criterion-related validities.

Consider the examples presented in Figure 3–7. A job analysis of the job of fire fighter showed that among the important tasks were those listed in the left column of Figure 3–7. In an attempt to simulate these tasks in a testing environment, the test events in the right column were developed. As you can see, the test events closely match important tasks of the job and thus would be considered content valid. In other words, if candidates did well on the test events listed in the right-hand column, it would be expected that they would do well on the tasks listed in the left-hand column.

To return to Figure 3–5, content validity is based at the conceptual level. Consider arrows *C* and *D*. If there is a logical error in specifying the necessary job-related abilities (arrow *C*) or in specifying the critical demands of the job (arrow *D*), then content validity will suffer.

Current practice in industrial psychology is leaning toward a greater quantification of certain aspects of content validity. It is now common to find

FIGURE 3–7 Test Events Designed to Match Tasks

Tasks	*Test Events*
1. Advance hose lines inside a residence	1. Pull 50 ft. of 2 in. hose line filled with water
2. Shuttle equipment to higher floors in a multistory fire	2. Carry seven different pieces of equipment up three flights of stairs one piece at a time
3. Set up ladders	3. Remove a 16 ft. ladder from a ladder truck, place it on the ground, and then replace it in the ladder truck rack
4. Search for victims in smoke-filled rooms	4. Travel through a plywood maze on hands and knees with a blindfold on
5. Hang fans for ventilation	5. Hang a 16 in. fan on a doorframe
6. Drag victims staying close to floor	6. Drag a 125 lb. sandbag over a 40 ft. course, keeping one knee on the ground at all times

groups of job experts making judgments about job demands and necessary abilities. This is an attempt to improve the strength of the relationship between the job analysis and the ability-demands specifications through expert consensus. It makes it less likely that the possibly incorrect logic and concepts of one person will distort the ability-performance relationship.

Construct Validity. The construct validity of a test of intelligence is essentially an answer to the question, Does this set of operations [the test] really measure that something [hypothetical construct] we refer to as intelligence? It is the most theoretical of the definitions of validity, since it is concerned with the abstractions used in referring to psychological structures, functions, or traits, rather than to the prediction of some external criterion. Nevertheless, the evaluation of construct validity may well use predictive validity as evidence that the test measures the construct. For example, the empirical evidence that IQ scores are somewhat predictive of school performance and of success in various occupations and training programs may be cited as evidence of construct validity. Our confidence in *what* it is that a test measures grows with the accumulation of evidence as to its relationship to other measures. As Guion (1965) explained:

> This [construct validity] is not a concept permitting easy operational definition. Only in one limited sense may a specific statement of correlation be considered an operational definition of construct validity. In general, construct validity must be expressed as a judgment, inferred from the weight of research evidence gathered in many independent studies. (p. 128)

Construct validity, while a difficult concept to grasp, may be one of the most important forms of validity for understanding the meaning of a test score. If a test has construct validity, something is known about how it relates to other tests that measure similar but not identical attributes. More specifically, in order to understand what is measured by a new test, we must know how it is related to other tests and behaviors. If it is thought to be a test of general intellectual ability, it should have positive correlations with other similar tests, such as the Stanford-Binet or the Wechsler Intelligence Scale. In addition, our new test should correlate with many of the behaviors that the Stanford-Binet and other intelligence tests correlate with—behaviors such as academic performance. In short, to understand the new test score, it is necessary to discover its theoretical context or the domain of behaviors it measures.

The fire fighter selection battery that I have described earlier in the chapter can provide a good example of construct validity. Most job analyses of the fire fighter's job show that stamina (or more technically, cardiovascular endurance) is important for success. It is the oxygen that is used as fuel for the muscles that actually do the physical work. In fighting fires while wearing heavy protective equipment and clothing and carrying heavy equipment, fire fighters consume large amounts of oxygen. The more oxygen the fire fighter can consume, the more effective will be that fire fighter's performance. As a result, it would be a good idea to get a measure of an applicant's capacity to consume oxygen. As you can see in the right column of Figure 3–7, there is a test event that requires candidates to carry equipment up a stairwell, making several trips. This might be considered a test of stamina or cardiovascular endurance. In order to make sure that this was a test of this ability, we administered a standard test of cardiovascular endurance to the concurrent validity sample of fire fighters described earlier. This standard test was a bicycle stress (ergometer) test. Subjects rode an exercise bicycle at a particular work load (i.e., predetermined revolutions per minute [RPMs] at a predetermined work load level) for seven minutes. By measuring heart rate at the end of that period, it is possible to estimate oxygen-consumption capacity (Arstrand & Rohdahl, 1977). Since we also had the scores of all these subjects on the stairway climb test, it was a simple matter to correlate their stairway climb scores with their bicycle test scores. The correlation was approximately +.80. This indicates that the stairway climb test is a good measure of the construct of cardiovascular endurance. We know this because the stairway climb score (the new test) correlates highly with an accepted measure (the bicycle test) of the construct (cardiovascular endurance). In this particular study, the bicycle test was also administered to applicants for the fire fighter job who had already taken the stairway climb test as well. The results were virtually identical to those of the real fire fighters—the correlation was high and positive. Other data were also gathered on basic strength and flexibility measures. These measures also correlated significantly with test events, demonstrating that those test events (e.g., the pike pole test, the dummy drag) were measures of the constructs of strength and flexibility.

Let's return again to Figure 3–5. In that model, construct validity is

A candidate for a fire fighter position carries equipment up a stairwell. (Rick Jacobs)

represented by the two arrows (*B*) connecting abilities to predictors and performance to criteria, respectively. If the predictors chosen do not fairly represent the ability construct in question, or if the criteria chosen do not fairly represent the performance construct in question, then construct validity will be deficient.

It is now possible to make a final summarizing observation. From Figure 3–5 it can be seen that conceptual and operational levels of validity are interdependent. If ability or job demand specifications do not follow logically from the job analysis, the observed correlation between the particular predictor and the particular criterion is irrelevant. In other words, if content validity has been compromised, there can be no reasonable interpretation or inference drawn from an examination of the predictor-criterion relationship. Similarly, if predictor or criterion choice do not follow logically from the specification of abilities or job demands, predictor-criterion relationships are uninterpretable. Once again, we are left with the conclusion that validity is not a unitary thing. One does not choose a single design as one might pick an item from a supermarket shelf. Instead, the issue is, What inferences can be drawn from the design employed to study the ability–job demand relationship?

The fire fighter example is a good one to make the point more concretely. In developing that test battery, three different types of design were used to support the inference that candidates with higher scores would be more likely to be successful than candidates with lower scores. First, the content validity design illustrated that important parts of the job were included as test events (as shown in Figure 3–7). Second, the criterion-related study demonstrated that actual fire fighters who did better on the test were also rated as better by their supervisors. Finally, evidence of construct validity was illustrated by the correlations between the test event scores and standard measures of physical capacities such as strength, cardiovascular endurance, and flexibility. All the evidence pointed to the same conclusion: valid inferences about probable job success could be drawn from this test battery. The strength of the design of the "experiments" that had been conducted using the fire fighter test permitted this inference.

Face Validity. The *face validity* of a measure is not really validity in the technical sense. It refers to a judgment made by those who are being measured, for example, the individual taking the test. An engineer who is applying for a position may have some doubts about the validity of a vocabulary test that includes words such as *leprechaun, unicorn,* or *veracity,* but might judge a test with *stress, conductance,* or *mass* as valid, that is, measuring concepts predictive of success in engineering. Face validity is important to ensure a positive attitude toward both the testing and the organization. Face validity is more closely related to the motivation of the person being measured than his ability and, as such, is a critical part of overall test performance. Because they were designed for different purposes to be used in different contexts, many tests used in personnel selection lack face validity. The effect of this deficiency on attitudes toward testing and toward industrial psychologists can only detract from the value of the obtained scores and also reduce the acceptance of psychologists in the world of work. The fire fighter tests described above had high face validity. Candidates for hire perceived these events as the type of activities that fire fighters carry out. In fact, the mean of the candidates' scores was better than the mean of the actual fire fighters' scores in the validation study described above. The candidates were clearly motivated to perform well. Generally speaking, the closer the simulation of test events to job duties, the higher the face validity.

As students of personnel psychology, it is important for you to understand that validity is not a *thing*—it is the result of a *process* called validation. The manner in which the validation might be carried out will vary, just as other experimental designs vary. We should pick the design that best suits our individual situation. The various "types" of validity describe some of the available designs.

Criterion-Related Validity: Myths and Reality

Test construction and validation is a big business. A typical criterion-related validity study in a medium-sized company might cost $30,000 if it involves a job analysis, test administration and scoring, criterion development (e.g., developing rating scales for estimating performance), and statistical analyses designed to demonstrate that the test does not discriminate unfairly. In theory, the same procedure could be used for each job in the company. In addition, if the company has multiple locations, it might be done for each job at each location. As you can see, the cost would build rapidly.

In the years that followed the passage of the Civil Rights Act of 1964, some assumptions were widely accepted. The first assumption was that tests that were valid for whites were not for blacks, Hispanics, or other ethnic minorities. This meant that tests had to be validated separately for majority and minority groups. Occasionally, this meant that separate tests were developed for majority and minority job applicants. The second assumption was that a test that was shown to be valid in one situation would not necessarily be valid in another situation. This meant that separate validity studies were needed for each new situation. The third assumption was that a test valid for selecting among applicants for one job would not necessarily be valid for selecting among applicants for another job. Each of these three assumptions added time and cost to the general process of validation. Schmidt and Hunter (1981) have argued that these assumptions can be shown to be myths rather than realities. Let's consider the assumptions one at a time in light of the Schmidt and Hunter argument.

Myth 1:

Ability tests have lower validity for minority than majority groups.

In the early 1970s, studies appeared demonstrating that validity coefficients between common predictors and criteria were significant for whites but not for blacks. This was taken as evidence that these predictors were not valid for selecting among black applicants. Several large-scale reviews of these early validity studies (Boehm, 1977; Hunter, Schmidt, & Hunter, 1979; Katzell & Dyer, 1977; O'Connor, Wexley, & Alexander, 1975) have shown that these apparent differences in validity were really the result of differences in sample sizes between the black and white subgroups. In a typical concurrent validity study, there might have been 158 white employees and 26 black employees. The validity coefficient for the white subgroup might have been +.22 (significant at the .01 level). The validity coefficient for the black subgroup might have been +.29 (not significant). The conclusion might have been drawn that the test was valid for whites but not for blacks. In fact, the lack of significance in the black subgroup was the result of a small sample size. In statistical terms, the power of the test of significance (i.e., the power to detect a difference between the observed value of +.29 and a hypothesized value of .00) was very low—much lower than the power of the test of significance for the white subgroup. Power is closely related to sample size. When sample size differences are taken into account, most of the black-white differences disappear. Thus, Schmidt and Hunter (1981) claim that the assumption of different validities for majority and minority applicants is largely a myth and should be dismissed.

Myth 2:

A test that is valid in one situation is not necessarily valid in another situation.

When a scientific study is conducted with a sample from a population, the object is to make an inference or reasoned guess about characteristics of that population from the behavior of members of the sample. In the case of validity, one conducts a validity study in order to determine whether a particular test might help predict the performance of individuals who come from the same population from which the sample was drawn. That is the logic of inferential statistics. The problem is that over the years a particular test might have shown a wide range of validities. For example, an arithmetic test might have correlated +.45 with a measure of production accuracy for a tool and die maker in one company, +.10 with a supervisory rating of performance for a tool and die maker in a second company, and −.18 with a production quantity measure for a tool and die maker in a third company. As a result of the many different validity coefficients that accompanied a given test, the assumption was made that the nature of the situation modified or moderated the validity of a given test. This means that it was impossible to use the results of a study done in one situation in another situation. It suggested that a separate validity study was required for every use of the particular test.

This was a problem for two reasons. First, it added enormously to the cost of administering a reasonable personnel decision system. Under these circumstances, many companies might choose to flip a coin rather than to go to the time and expense of revalidating a test for each use. From a scientific point of view, there is a second, more serious problem. If it is necessary to revalidate a test every time it is used, it means nothing was learned from its previous use. The object of scientific inquiry is to extrapolate from observable behavior to basic relationships. Schmidt and Hunter (1981) suggested that situational specificity—that is, the variation of validity coefficients from one situation to another—was a myth. After studying many purported instances of this variation in coefficients, they concluded that variations were the result of several statistical artifacts. There are certain statistical circumstances that have the effect of lowering a validity coefficient. One of these circumstances is called *restriction of range*. This means that the score range of those who are measured (by either the test or the criterion measure or both) is artificially low or restricted. As an example, if you gave an intelligence test to a group of high school Merit scholars, the scores would probably be high but with much less variability than if you gave the intelligence test to a random sample of people chosen at the local shopping mall. The second circumstance that lowers validity is using measures with low reliability. In fact, it is safe to say that validity is limited by reliability. An unreliable measure is not likely to have high correlations with any other measure. When Schmidt and Hunter controlled for such factors as the reliability of the tests and criteria, the sample sizes in the various studies, and the restriction of range in predictor and criterion scores, much of the variability among validity coefficients disappeared. As an example, one study might have found that the correlation between a given test and a measure of job performance was +.45 (significant at the $p < .01$ level); a second study conducted with a different sample might have resulted in a validity coefficient of +.15 (not significant). One might conclude that the test was valid in the first situation but not in the second. But what if the reliability of the criterion was .95 in the first situation and .45 in the second? Further, what if the range of test scores in the first situation was four times greater than the range of test scores in the second? Both of these circumstances would have the effect of suppressing any true relationship between test scores and performance scores in the second sample. In this case, the apparent difference would be a statistical artifact rather than a substantively different relationship between predictor and criterion. Schmidt, Hunter, and their colleagues (Pearlman, Schmidt, & Hunter, 1980; Schmidt, Gast-Rosenberg, & Hunter, 1980; Schmidt, Hunter, Pearlman, & Shane, 1979) have been able to demonstrate that most "situational specificity" is actually the result of statistical influences similar to those described above. As a result, the second troublesome assumption about validity—that it must be demonstrated situation by situation—also appears to be more myth than reality.

Myth 3:

A test that is valid for one job is not necessarily valid for another job.

Just as variability in validity coefficients can be shown from one situation to another, variability can also be shown from one job title to another with the same test. Again, it was assumed that this variability was the result of the fact that something in the jobs themselves was responsible for the variation. For example, a clerical accuracy test might have a correlation of +.54 with a performance measure for an accounts receivable clerk but only a correlation of +.21 with a performance measure for a billing clerk. It might be assumed that this difference stems from the fact that the two jobs are different. Using the same approach as outlined above, Schmidt and Hunter (Schmidt, Hunter, & Pearlman, 1981) were able to demonstrate that many of the differences in validity coefficients calculated for different job titles were the result of differences in sample sizes, reliabilities of predictor and criterion, and range restriction. When these influences were eliminated, the variability among validity coefficients was drastically reduced. Once again, an assumption was shown to be a myth. This should be interpreted with some caution, however. This does not mean that validity information from *any* job transfers to *any other* job. It means that within a *job family* (e.g., clerical jobs or maintenance jobs), generalization is possible.

Validity Generalization. As a result of the propositions and research findings of Schmidt, Hunter, and their colleagues, a new concept has emerged. It has been called *validity generalization* (or *VG*). It means that groups of validity coefficients that seem to vary from one study to another can be examined to determine the extent to which these variations are the results of the statistical artifacts described above (e.g., unreliability, sample size, range restriction). This has important implications for validity studies in industry. If it can be shown (a) that variations in validity coefficients are due to statistical artifacts and (b) that once these artifacts are removed, the average validity coefficient is positive and significant, then the stage is set for using the results of validity studies done in the past on a particular test or type of test as documentation of the validity for the use of that same test in a new situation. The only necessity is that of showing that the job for which the test is being used is highly similar to the job on which the original validity studies were done. In essence, VG permits one to transport results from a range of studies to a particular situation without the necessity of carrying out a full validity study.

There has been a good deal of discussion of the logic and the statistical foundation for VG. The strongest advocates of VG argue that most cognitive tests are valid predictors of success in a wide range of occupations. They cite the fact that after making corrections for unreliability, sample size, and restriction of range, the average validity coefficient is positive and significant. Others are more cautious in accepting the logic and the techniques of validity generalization. An excellent discussion of the differing points of view appears in two articles appearing in a special issue of *Personnel Psychology* (Sackett, Tenopyr, Schmitt, & Kehoe, 1985; Schmidt, Hunter, Pearlman, & Hirsh, 1985).

There is a great deal of uneasiness in the scientific community regarding validity generalization techniques. The uneasiness is not with the concept. It is easy enough to accept the notion that a good deal of the variation among observed correlation coefficients is artifactual. Similarly, it is easy enough to accept the notion that validity can be transported from one situation to another if the situations are sufficiently similar. The problem arises in broad claims that imply that any well-designed cognitive test is a valid predictor of most aspects of industrial behavior. To many, that appears to be an inductive leap not over a crevice but over a chasm. It carries with it the implication that there are not many different cognitive abilities but really only one general intellectual ability. In fact, in later chapters I will discuss research that does point in that direction. Nevertheless, this notion of the importance of "general intelligence" has not yet been so widely accepted as to warrant the more ambitious VG claims. In addition to the conceptual reservations, there has been some discomfort with statistical assumptions underlying the VG strategies. Papers by L. R. James, Demaree, and Mulaik (1986), Sackett et al. (1985), and Specter and Levine (1987) all raise questions about techniques and methodology.

It is clear that validity generalization is a concept that will be with us for some time to come. There is sufficient confirmation in studies conducted by Schmidt and his colleagues to warrant acceptance of basic propositions. Further, it has clear and important policy implications. As an example, the National Research Council (the operational unit of the Academy of Sciences) has just begun a substantial evaluation of the General Aptitude Test Battery (GATB), a test used widely for public sector employment decisions, to determine the extent to which validity information currently available for 400 job titles can be generalized to a full range of 12,000 job titles. Since such a decision would rest on the adequacy of the validity generalization model and propositions, the National Research Council committee will undertake a thorough review of both the VG theory and its application to employment settings. Thus, within a few years, there should be a definitive answer to the questions raised in the VG debate. Keep in mind, however, that the issue is not whether the basic propositions of VG are reasonable—they are. The issue is how far these propositions can be stretched and what the implications will be for the conduct of validity studies.

The conclusion to be drawn from this consideration of assumptions and myths is that validity coefficients are probably a good deal more stable than had been previously assumed. Within limits, they seem to resist the influences of ethnic differences, situational differences, and job differences. In other words, one can make inferences from well-designed studies. Of course, there are limits to these inferences. There may be some occasions in which tests are not equally valid predictors for minority and majority applicants, but these cases are exceptions rather than rules. The same is true of differing situations and jobs. This is an extremely important piece of information since it suggests that tests and testing programs can be administered in a cost-efficient manner. It is not necessary to conduct a new validation study every time a new situation arises.

THE EQUAL EMPLOYMENT OPPORTUNITY COMMISSION

The EEOC has played a rather dramatic role in the development and administration of tests in industry. As the federal government's main administrative agency for the enforcement of the Civil Rights Act in the employment context, it has taken its role seriously. The EEOC has evolved from a weak public advocate status to a strong and active enforcement agency, with broad powers to initiate and negotiate legal and administrative action on behalf of protected minority groups.

As a result of this evolution, accompanied by some sensational court settlements on behalf of minority plaintiffs, employers have become justifiably cautious in the use of tests for employment decisions. As indicated earlier, the first reaction of personnel officers was to abandon traditional tests in favor of "nontest" predictors rather than take a chance on accidentally discriminating unfairly against a minority applicant. This was not the best action for several reasons. In the first place, in the view of psychologists and administrative agencies alike ("Uniform Guidelines," 1978), the label "test" was not restricted to traditional paper-and-pencil question-and-answer formats exclusively. A test could include a physical examination, an application blank, an interview, a work sample, or even a performance rating (if this rating was used to predict future success in another position). Consequently, employers were often abandoning a standardized measure with some technical documentation for a loosely constructed and poorly documented measure.

This seems almost like rats swimming *toward* a sinking ship instead of away from it. As far as EEOC was concerned, the employer would have to validate the interview, just as it would have been necessary to validate the traditional test.

In addition, regardless of the pressures from EEOC to be fair, there remained the very real need to identify those individuals who would be most likely to help an organization meet its production or service goals. Consequently, employers could not afford to abandon any promising technique for finding such employees, including traditional testing.

It should have been obvious to employers that a more appropriate response would have been to look more carefully at the jobs in question (on the basis of a job analysis) and consider more carefully what kinds of behaviors were required on that job and how these behaviors might be successfully predicted. This is happening to a much greater extent now than it was five years ago and for several reasons. For one thing, the federal guidelines regarding equal employment opportunity stabilized in 1978. There had been a good deal of disagreement among federal agencies concerning how strictly and literally the EEOC rules should be interpreted. Finally, the EEOC, the Department of Labor, the Department of Justice, and the U.S. Civil Service Commission agreed on a single interpretation of the guidelines (hence their label—"Uniform Guidelines"; see "Uniform Guidelines," 1978). These uniform guidelines were the result of long and complicated discussions among legal experts, psychologists, employers, and federal administrators. As a result of the agreement among these parties, the employer's responsibility was made clearer than at any time in the previous 15 years. Unfortunately, these guidelines are becoming obsolete. They are now over 10 years old, and there have been substantial changes in both theory and practice of personnel research since their initial publication. Thus, the attempt to use these guidelines to evaluate the adequacy of a selection system is becoming increasingly clumsy. Instead, greater reliance is being placed on two more recently published documents. The first of these deals with the general issue of evaluating educational and psychological tests and was published by the American Psychological Association in 1985. It is known as the *Standards for Educational and Psychological Testing,* or usually as just *Standards.* The second document was published in 1987 by the Society for Industrial and Organizational Psychology (SIOP) and is known as the *Principles for the Validation and Use of Personnel Selection Procedures* and is most often referred to as simply *Principles.* It is inevitable that the guidelines will be rewritten in the next several years. When that revision is undertaken, there will no doubt be a good deal of heated debate about what administrative procedures the government will approve or require.

Another interesting aspect of the issue of tests and discrimination is the shift that seems to have occurred in social and political thought since the Civil Rights Act was passed in 1964 (Garner & Wigdor, 1982). The original intention of Title VII (Employment Opportunity) had been to ensure that every individual had an equal opportunity for employment regardless of race, sex, or religion. As a result, there was considerable emphasis on test use and validity in employment settings. With the introduction of the concept of affirmative action, the emphasis changed to adding minority members to the work force at a rate that might make up for past deficiencies. While tests remained a central mechanism in the hiring and promotion process, there was clear emphasis on changing the profile of the work force to match some negotiated or predetermined set of figures. Employers filed plans with the government indicating how many minority members would be added over a fixed time period. In this new environment, certain tests became attractive or unattractive based on their capacity to aid or hinder the completion of the affirmative action plan. The final shift was from affirmative action to group parity. In group parity, the notion seems to be that applicants should be hired or promoted in proportion to their numbers in the applicant pool or the current employee pool, respectively. The discussions in this new context have tended not to revolve around the validity of the test but rather around what is known as the "bottom line." Do the numbers of minority applicants hired proportionally match the minority representation in the applicant pool? The group parity philosophy is only vaguely related to the notion of ability and job demands. As a result, in environments characterized by the group parity philosophy, tests play a much less central role. In the long run, group parity models are philosophical or social or political. They are not based on issues of measurement or validity. To the extent that these models *ignore* issues of validity, they are ultimately self-defeating and should not deter psychologists and managers from seeking to understand the relationship between ability and performance.

Technical Appendix

ESTIMATES OF RELIABILITY

In measurement theory, reliability is based on the notion that an obtained measurement (score), X, represents a true score, t, plus some error, e, or $X = t + e$. Actually, as Guion (1965) pointed out, e should refer only to the random unpredictable error, not systematic error, such as the 20-degree constant error in the thermometer. Guion prefers the expression, $X = s + e$, where s is the composite of true score and constant error and e is only the random, unpredictable error of measurement. Reliability is then defined as the freedom of a set of measurements (or observations) from this random variance. As we saw, the instrument, the attribute, and the user can all contribute random variability to the obtained score and, therefore, to the unreliability of the observations.

To the extent that obtained scores (X) agree with true scores (t), error variance (e) is reduced. Thus, the correlation r_{xt} is a measure of reliability, since it is the correlation of the obtained score with the true score. Since t values are hypothetical and not accessible to measurement, r_{xt} cannot be obtained directly. Instead, a number of alternative methods have been devised to estimate reliability. Before describing these, however, it should be pointed out that if one assumes the true score of an individual to be unchanging, then the variable error of measurement could be described in terms of the standard deviation of a sample of repeated measurements of the individual.

Thus, for example, with our tree measurements we might measure a given tree 100 times and then obtain the standard deviation of this set of observations as an estimate of variable error. This standard deviation is technically known as the *standard error of measurement*.

Fortunately, there is a statistical method for computing the standard error of measurement that saves us the labor of gathering so many different samples. The formula for the standard error is:

$$SE_x \text{ or } \sigma_e = \sigma_x \sqrt{1 - r_{xx}}$$

By means of this formula, we can see that the standard error of measurement is related both to the reliability of the measure being considered (represented by the term r_{xx}) and to the variability in the sample (represented by the term σ_x). The formula states that as the reliability of the measure increases, the standard error decreases, but as the sample variability increases, so does the standard error.

Corrections for Test Length in Split-Half Reliability

In *split-half reliability*, each half test used in the estimation is only a half sample of behavior of the whole test for which the reliability is sought. Small samples are more vulnerable to sampling error, so a split-half reliability estimate is likely to be very conservative. For this reason, it should be corrected using the Spearman-Brown prophecy formula:

$$r_{nn} = \frac{nr_{11}}{1 + (n - 1)r_{11}}$$

where r_{nn} is the reliability of a test n times as long as the one used to obtain the estimate, and r_{11} is the obtained estimate of reliability. Thus, if n is two times the length of the half tests used to estimate reliability, then

$$r_{\text{corrected}} = \frac{2r_{\text{obtained}}}{1 + (2 - 1)r_{\text{obtained}}}$$

or for $r_{\text{obt}} = .60$, the corrected estimate would be;

$$r_{\text{corrected}} = \frac{2(.60)}{1 + (1).60} = \frac{1.2}{1.6} = .75$$

(Note that this formula can be used with whole-test estimates of reliability to predict the effects on reliability of doubling or otherwise increasing the length of a test.)

Other internal consistency estimates of reliability are basically variations of the test-splitting procedure. The best known of these methods are those resulting in the Kuder-Richardson formula (K-R 20), which provides an estimate of the reliability coefficient that would be obtained if the test were split into all possible halves and the individual split-half correlations computed and averaged. The K-R formula (Richardson & Kuder, 1939) save the researcher the labor of splitting, computing, and averaging. Another similar reliability estimate that is becoming popular is L. J. Cronbach's Alpha coefficient (Cronbach, 1970), which is also a summary reliability statistic.

Relationship between Reliability and Validity

As indicated in the chapter, reliability sets the upper limit for validity. The equation expressing this relationship is:

$$r_{xy} \leq \sqrt{r_{xx}}$$

In words, this means that the validity coefficient can be no higher than the square root of the reliability coefficient. This relationship can be used to advantage if the reliability of the criterion is known. In that case, the obtained validity coefficient can be adjusted to take into account the unreliability of the criterion. This is a legitimate correction to make. It would be inappropriate to correct for unreliability in the predictor, however, since we plan to use the predictor to make hiring decisions and must take that unreliability into account when making those decisions. The equation for making an adjustment for unreliability in the criterion variable is as follows:

$$r_{xyc} = \frac{r_{xy}}{\sqrt{r_{yy}}}$$

In words, this equation says that the corrected or adjusted validity coefficient can be obtained by dividing the observed validity coefficient by the square root of the reliability of the criterion variable. As you can see, the higher the reliability, the less the effect of the adjustment.

CENTRAL POINTS FOR STUDY

1. A psychological test is a measure of some phase of a carefully chosen sample of an individual's behavior.
2. A test is an operational definition of a concept (i.e., an aptitude, an ability, or an area of achievement).
3. Good measuring instruments possess both reliability and validity.
4. Reliability deals with consistency.
5. Validity addresses the issue of whether a measure accomplished its purpose.

6. **Four common validity designs are predictive, concurrent, content, and construct.**
7. **The Equal Employment Opportunity Commission has been charged with administering the section of the Civil Rights Act that addresses employment decisions.**

CHAPTER 4

Job Analysis and the Measurement of Performance

Historically, industrial psychology has been the application of principles of measurement and behavior to personnel decisions—personnel psychology. The field has become much broader than it was originally and now encompasses such constructs as job satisfaction, work motivation, computer-assisted training programs, and work simulation. Nevertheless, some of the basic issues comprising the traditional area of personnel psychology are indispensable for the extensions of the field as well.

One of the most basic problems in personnel psychology is defining *the criterion*. A criterion is a way of describing success. The criterion for measuring student success in this course might be the course grade. A criterion for a football team might be the number of wins versus the number of losses in a season. The criterion for the salesperson might be the dollar volume of her sales in a one-month period. In personnel psychology, the criterion usually occupies the role of the variable to be predicted.

The last chapter should have sensitized you to the importance of the criterion in personnel decision making. In personnel testing, we are not primarily interested in how people do on tests. Instead, we use their test performance as a substitute for job performance. We assume that if the test is positively correlated with job performance, then the higher the test score, the more likely it will be for performance to be good. This means that in the logical sequence of developing or evaluating a test, we must first know something about the performance required on the job in question—the criterion. In this chapter, we will consider the issue of the criterion, and in later chapters we will deal with specific predictors.

The criterion will be approached from a number of vantage points. First, its role in a personnel decision system will be described. Next, some basic issues relating to the development and the use of criteria will be introduced. I will then introduce the technical, statistical aspects of criteria. Since performance rating is so universal and so central to the activity of the personnel psychologist, I will consider it separately in a later chapter. Just keep in mind that the general principles introduced in this chapter apply with equal force to performance rating.

Performance in athletic events is often easier to judge than performance at work. One of these individuals will win. (Penn State University)

The Criterion Construct

The increasing importance of the criterion in both research and application of behavioral principles is becoming apparent from several different sources. Employees are becoming increasingly dissatisfied with the way in which their performance is measured. Employment bulletins directed toward behavioral scientists are filled with job offers for individuals who have the technical and practical abilities necessary "to evaluate the success of a drug therapy program," "to evaluate the success of a day-care program," or "to evaluate the success of a community mental health clinic." Researchers are required to include in their grant applications the way in which they will evaluate the outcomes of their research efforts. Schoolteachers are being trained in the development of "behavioral objectives" for their pupils. Pupils are being trained to interact with the teaching system in terms of "meeting behavioral objects" and "completing behavioral units." Training programs in industry are no longer being structured solely on the basis of available training equipment in the plant but instead are expected to meet some concrete behavioral goal.

All these developments are variations on the theme of criterion development. They may be responses to earlier excesses and oversights. Employees now realize that performance evaluation systems that were introduced to eliminate favoritism are so subjective that they actually make favoritism easier. Many social programs that were accepted on face value as being valuable have come off poorly under examination, and consequently, checks and balances are being built into the programs. The federal government is becoming much more "product-oriented" in its interaction with researchers. School systems are quickly discovering that it is actually impossible to determine the intended effect of the educational process under existing evaluation procedures; they are redefining the effect in terms of the expected effect of the treatment on the behavior of the pupils.

The previous examples are global descriptions of the role and impact of a criterion in a given situation. You might get a better feel for the importance of the criterion by examining some specific uses of criterion information.

1. *Validation.* Tests suitable for predicting job success cannot be identified until job success has been defined. In addition, after suitable tests have been identified, the validation procedure usually requires some specific measure of job success to compare with test success.
2. *Selection.* After a valid test or predictor has been identified, it is still necessary to provide the personnel office with a decision rule for hiring. This decision rule is usually in the form of a cutoff score on the predictor—for example, reject individuals with scores lower than 45 on test A and schedule the others for an interview. This cutoff score was determined on the basis of "minimal acceptable *job* performance." Once this level of job performance has been defined, it is possible to work backward to "minimal acceptable *test* performance."
3. *Compensation.* Since most organizations would prefer to pay workers in proportion to their value, it is necessary to have some measure of that value when making compensation decisions. Performance criteria usually represent that measure of value.
4. *Training.* In many organizations, training is a rather haphazard endeavor, influenced more by fad than by logic. Training needs can be easily identified on the basis of demonstrated performance levels.
5. *Motivation and satisfaction of employees.* Many organizations have elaborate programs of motivation and satisfaction for their employees. These programs are intended both to increase the satisfaction of the employee and to maximize individual performance. Performance measurement is critical for the evaluation of the success of these programs. If they are successful, it should be possible to demonstrate changes in performance levels.
6. *Feedback.* It seems more and more obvious that people seek feedback on the effectiveness of their actions. In the work setting, this means feedback on work performance. This type of feedback requires fair and accurate performance information. The adequacy of performance measurement determines the adequacy of feedback.

Criterion information might also be used for making promotional decisions, evaluating the effectiveness of training programs, providing long-term vocational counseling, and changing organizational structure. The object has not been to overwhelm you with the uses of criterion information but to point out how important the criterion is in almost every aspect of industrial and organizational psychology.

Criterion Characteristics

Most texts in industrial psychology contain lengthy lists of requirements for criteria. These texts invariably mention such requirements as freedom from contamination, relevance, and freedom from deficiency. The list also includes such things as freedom from bias, acceptability by management, cost, and predictability. All these criterion characteristics might be reduced to three requirements: reliability, validity, and practicality. Conceptually, there is much to be gained from reducing requirements to these three categories. First and foremost, it helps to point out that in spite of their unique position in the personnel system, criterion data must satisfy the same requirements as all other forms of data. If inferences are to be drawn based on criterion data, those data must be reliable and representative. In addition, there must be a practical scheme for gathering the data so that the cost does not greatly exceed the potential benefit. Great advances in the area of criterion measurement and development can be made if three requirements are kept in mind: reliability, validity, and practicality. This should come as no surprise to you. In Chapter 3, we considered the broad issues of accurate, meaningful, and trustworthy measurement. At that time, we were considering the issue of predictors. As you can see, the same issues are reappearing in our discussion of criteria. The requirements for adequate measurement do not change simply because we are looking at job performance instead of test performance.

JOB ANALYSIS

Unlike published tests, it is virtually unheard of to purchase a criterion instrument. Such instruments are generally developed on a situation-by-situation basis. In this section, I will describe how criterion instruments are constructed.

At the outset, the differences among job analysis, job evaluation, and performance evaluation must be understood. Job analysis and evaluation make statements and inferences about a job, regardless of the person in that job. Job analysis describes important aspects of a job that help to distinguish it from other jobs. Job evaluation attaches a dollar value to a job and derives a logical scheme for relating the dollar value of that job to the value of other jobs. Performance evaluation distinguishes between workers on the basis of their relative performance, independent of the particular job that they are performing. Figure 4–1 presents a graphic description of the functional relationship of job analysis to criterion development.

It might be best to start by describing what job analysis is like rather than by describing how it is accomplished. Its purpose is the same as that of a videotape system with stop-action and slow-motion capabilities. Just as the videotape system might be used to break down a golf swing into a number of discrete operations for purposes of correction, a job analysis might be completed to break job performance down into a number of discrete elements.

FIGURE 4–1 Relationships among Job Analysis, Job Evaluation, Job Description, Criterion Development, and Performance Appraisal

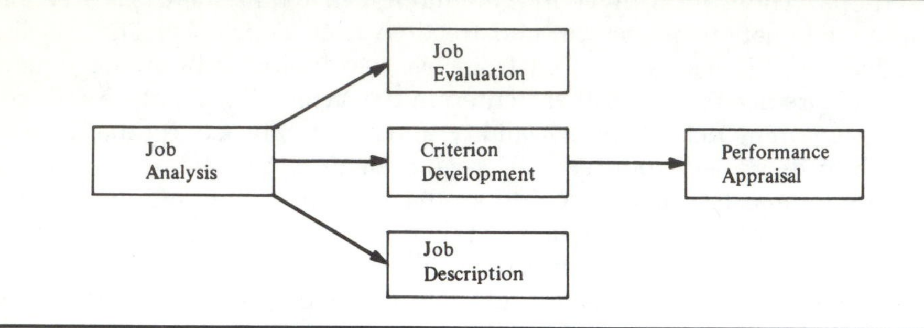

Just as we would want to know what the elements of a good golf swing are, we would also want to know what the elements of successful punchpress operation are.

It is the search for these elementary units of performance that best defines job analysis. It is one of the first steps in the process of criterion development. Before we can distinguish behaviorally among individuals with respect to job performance, we must determine the nature of the dimensions on which we will make this distinction.

Assuming that a job analysis was needed in a particular situation, how would you go about conducting one? There are really only three ways to get information about the critical elements in a job. You can ask someone about the job who knows it well, you can watch an individual try to carry out the tasks that compose the job, or you can try to do the job yourself.

Interviews and Questionnaires

By far, the most common method for conducting a job analysis is a combination of interview and questionnaire. Typically, the job analyst will first read any existing information about the job duties and responsibilities and then schedule discussions with one or more individuals who currently hold the job title in question. In addition, the analyst will usually interview the supervisor for that position as well since the supervisor can often see certain aspects of the job that are less obvious to the incumbent. The interview is usually unstructured, and the incumbent or supervisor is asked to describe in his own words the most important and frequently occurring job duties. These two dimensions of duties—importance and frequency—are at the heart of job analysis. Regardless of why the job analysis is being conducted, the object is to describe the essence of the job and the importance and frequency of duties to accomplish that end.

Occasionally, the interview will also include questions about which duties are critical to safety or essential for cost-effectiveness, but the importance-frequency focus is most common.

As a substitute for or in addition to interviews, questionnaires and checklists of various types are also used often. Incumbents and supervisors are asked to rate various potential job characteristics on frequency or importance. The questionnaire may be a standardized one consisting of a fixed group of behavioral statements that can be used for any job, or it can be a specific one constructed for the particular job analysis. In Figures 4–2 and 4–3 you can see examples of the two different types. In the first figure, you can see several questions that have been taken from an instrument known as the PAQ (Position Analysis Questionnaire) developed by McCormick and his colleagues over the past several decades (McCormick, Jeanneret, & Mecham, 1972). In Figure 4–3 you will find sample questions from a job analysis questionnaire that was completed by fire fighters and their supervisors in a job analysis of a municipal fire fighter position. As you can see, the two forms are quite different. The PAQ is general and could be applied to almost any job (including the fire fighter job). That is a strength. On the other hand, the person filling it out must make applications of these general questions to her own job. This is sometimes difficult. The specific job analysis questionnaire illustrated in Figure 4–3 needs no translation. It was constructed specifically for the job analysis being conducted. The weakness of this approach is that a new instrument must be developed when a new job analysis is to be conducted, for example, a job analysis of a heavy equipment repair technician in the fire department.

Besides the question of whether to use a specific or a general questionnaire, there is also the issue of job-oriented versus worker-oriented questionnaires. The job-oriented approach tends to emphasize the conditions of work, the results of work, or both. It concentrates on the accomplishments rather than the behavior of a worker. In contrast, the worker-oriented approach focuses more directly on the human behaviors that compose the job in question. As a simple example for the job of fire fighter, the job-oriented questionnaire might include a statement such as: "Applies water or chemical agents to extinguish flames." A worker-oriented questionnaire might restate that duty as: "Correctly identifies the nature of a fire and chooses the correct fire-suppressing or -retarding agent." Both of these statements involve putting out a fire, but the first emphasizes the results of behavior and the second highlights the behavior itself.

Because the worker-oriented elements tend to be more generalized descriptions of human behavior and behavior patterns and less tied to the technological aspects of the particular job, worker-oriented analyses produce data that are more useful in structuring training programs and giving feedback to employees in the form of performance appraisal in-

FIGURE 4–2 Information Input

1. INFORMATION INPUT

1.1 Sources of Job Information

Rate each of the following items in terms of the extent to which it is used by the worker as a source of information in performing his job.

Code	*Extent of Use (U)*
N	Does not apply
1	Nominal; very infrequent
2	Occasional
3	Moderate
4	Considerable
5	Very substantial

1.1.1 Visual Sources of Job Information

1 ______ Written materials (books, reports, office notes, articles, job instructions, signs, etc.).

2 ______ Quantitative materials (materials that deal with quantities or amounts, such as graphs, accounts, specifications, tables of numbers, etc.).

3 ______ Pictorial materials (pictures or picturelike materials used as *sources* of information, for example, drawings, blueprints, diagrams, maps, tracings, photographic films, X-ray films, TV pictures, etc.).

4 ______ Patterns/related devices (templates, stencils, patterns, etc., used as *sources* of information when *observed* during use; do *not* include here materials described in item 3 above).

5 ______ Visual displays (dials, gauges, signal lights, radarscopes, speedometers, clocks, etc.).

6 ______ Measuring devices (rulers, calipers, tire pressure gauges, scales, thickness gauges, pipettes, thermometers, protractors, etc., used to obtain visual information about physical measurements; do *not* include here devices described in item 5 above).

7 ______ Mechanical devices (tools, equipment, machinery, and other mechanical devices that are *sources* of information when *observed* during use or operation).

8 ______ Materials in process (parts, materials, objects, etc., that are *sources* of information when being modified, worked on, or otherwise processed, such as bread dough being mixed, workpiece being turned in a lathe, fabric being cut, shoe being resoled, etc.).

9 ______ Materials *not* in process (parts, materials, objects, etc., not in the process of being changed or modified, which are *sources* of information when being inspected, handled, packaged, distributed, or selected, etc., such as items or materials in inventory, storage, or distribution channels, items being inspected, etc.).

10 ______ Features of nature (landscapes, fields, geological samples, vegetation, cloud formations, and other features of nature that are observed or inspected to provide information).

FIGURE 4–2 *(concluded)*

11 ______ Man-made features of environment (structures, buildings, dams, highways, bridges, docks, railroads, and other "man-made" or altered aspects of the indoor or outdoor environment that are *observed* or *inspected* to provide job information; do not consider equipment, machines, etc., that an individual uses in his work, as covered by item 7).

FIGURE 4–3 Task Statements Used in Fire Fighter Job Analysis

D. *Ladder (truck) Operation:* Stabilizes ladder trucks and elevates and operates aerial ladders, snorkels, squirts, and platforms in order to rescue victims, provide access for ventilation, operate master stream devices, etc., using wheel chocks, stabilizing pads, stabilizing jacks, and outriggers.

Stabilizes elevating apparatus using wheel chocks, stabilizing pads, stabilizing jacks and outriggers

Elevates, rotates, and extends aerial ladder bed and fly sections for supported and unsupported operation, while watching for power lines, trees, and other overhead obstructions

Operates snorkel and elevating platforms from ground controls or from platform controls, while watching for power lines, trees, and other overhead obstructions

Sets up water tower operations with aerial ladders by clamping master stream appliances to end of ladder, strapping 3" or 4" fabric or plastic hose to fly section, and then extending the ladder

F. *Forcible Entry:* Pries open doors or windows, kicks in doors, breaks out windows, or otherwise forcibly enters buildings and vehicles in order to search for and rescue victims and provide access to the fire for offensive fire fighting, using axes, pry bars, pike poles, hux bars, battering rams, sledge hammers, bolt cutters, and other tools, while wearing full turnout gear.

Kicks in or breaks down doors using axes, sledge hammers, battering rams, halligan tools, and other forcible-entry tools

Breaks out windows and crawls into structures using pike poles, axes, ladders, and other equipment

Pries open doors and windows in structures and vehicles using pry bars, hux bars, bolt cutters, and other tools

Breaches holes in wooden, brick, and masonry walls using sledge hammers, battering rams, axes, and other tools

Cuts open doors, walls, floors, or roofs using power saws and axes formation. In addition, an organization can generalize from one occupation to another without having to deal with a different set of elements for each job.

The PAQ described above is an excellent example of a worker-oriented instrument (McCormick et al., 1972). The PAQ consists of worker-oriented job statements comprising six major divisions of worker activity. Four of these divisions deal directly with behavioral categories of worker activity. These four divisions are Information Input, Mediation Processes, Work Output, and Interpersonal Activities. Each division has a series of questions similar to those in Figure 4–2. Information Input questions deal with how the worker receives information concerning the job. Does it come from dials or gauges or written orders or verbal requests? Mediation Processes include such things as decision making, reasoning and judgment, ordering or sequencing information, and selecting stored (e.g., memorized) information for use. Work Output deals primarily with the execution of a response and would include things such as manipulating hands and feet to accomplish a task, using equipment in a skilled manner, or incorporating any one of a broad range of general body activities. Interpersonal Activities involve communications and interpersonal relationships.

In addition to these four behavioral categories, the PAQ also collects information about the Work Situation and Job Context (e.g., physical working conditions and social environment of the job) and Miscellaneous aspects such as the method of pay (e.g., hourly versus piece rate) and the work schedule (e.g., fixed-day work versus rotating shift).

Recently, some issues have arisen with respect to when it might be appropriate to use the PAQ and when it might be more appropriate to use a questionnaire specifically developed for the job in question. DeNisi, Cornelius, and Blencoe (1987) discovered that the PAQ had a large number of items that dealt with machine and equipment use. This meant that it might not be that appropriate for jobs that did not have a heavy dependence on machines and equipment (e.g., personnel manager, adult education instructor). The PAQ, like many such instruments, provides the job analyst with the option of responding DNA (does not apply) to any task statement that is unrelated to the job in question. It is reasonable to assume that the larger the number of DNA responses on the PAQ (or any other similar instrument), the less well described is the job in question. DeNisi et al. showed that there was a correlation of +.66 between the number of DNA responses and the extent to which a job was high on a machine-equipment rating. In the examples listed above, the personnel director job analysis yielded 63 DNA responses (from slightly less than 200 statements), and the adult education instructor yielded 62 DNA responses. In contrast, the job of appliance service repair technician produced 5 DNA responses, and a TV repair technician 12 DNA responses. This is an important finding because it demonstrates rather clearly that one should not use the PAQ (or any job analysis instrument) without some initial decision that its format or structure suits the job being considered.

Occasionally, observation of work activities can be challenging. Here is a picture of the author with two colleagues shortly after emerging from a burning house where we observed fire fighters extinguishing a bedroom fire. (S.D. Kriska)

Observation

Questionnaires, interviews, and checklists can be very useful ways of gathering information about a job, but they have some weaknesses. The major problem is that experienced workers are not always aware of how they carry out their duties. As a simple example, try to explain to someone how to tie a shoelace or ride a bicycle. Many of our actions are so habitual that we often forget we are making them. As a result, it can be very useful to watch someone performing a job. Recently, I was carrying out a job analysis for the position of quality control (QC) inspector in a metal fabricating company. I had interviewed several of the inspectors and was watching one perform inspections. I noticed that over the course of an hour or so, she had made brief notations in a little notebook that she kept in her pocket. On her break, I asked her what she was writing down. She replied that she had jotted down the times when the frequency of errors seemed to increase appreciably. At the end of her shift, she would compare notes with a production supervisor who recorded any changes in the operating characteristics of various pieces of fabricating equipment. This turned out to be an important part of the QC inspector's job, yet it had never been mentioned in the interviews. The questionnaires described in the previous section can be very useful as a checklist for observing a particular job.

There is another problem that occasionally occurs. Workers will often report how the job should be done *in theory* or according to organizational rules, but in fact they carry out the job in a different way. In discussions with police sergeants on a recent job analysis, they assured me that they used a book with various criminal codes in it to decide on which charges should be filed by the patrol officers who reported to them. When one of these sergeants reported this activity to me while I rode with him in his patrol car, I asked him to show me the copy of the book he used. My plan was to see what pages were most dog-eared and dirty and, in that way, to get an idea of the most important sections of the book. He said it was in the trunk of the cruiser and he would get it out when we stopped for coffee. When we did stop, I asked him to get the book. He opened the trunk and couldn't find the book but assured me that it was in a briefcase in his locker and he had simply forgotten to put the briefcase in the trunk that morning. When we returned to the precinct, I asked him to retrieve the book from the briefcase. He went to his locker and returned with the book and a sheepish grin on his face. The book was still in the clear wrapper that covered it when it was issued to him six months earlier. He modified his description of the job to an indication that it would be *possible* to check the book if one wanted to, but it was not absolutely necessary (or, as I discovered in his case, frequent).

Work Participation

The final method of conducting a job analysis—actually having the job analyst perform the work operations—is not particularly practical. In the first place, many jobs cannot be entrusted to a job analyst. A major airline will not be excited about handing the controls of a jumbo jet to the analyst. In addition, since high levels of various skills are often required to perform job duties correctly, the analyst is not likely to perform the job in the way in which it is accomplished by more experienced incumbents. There are occasions when work participation can be an effective tool for the job analyst, but these occasions usually involve a relatively simple task.

What Is Covered in a Job Analysis

The term *job analysis* can be used broadly or narrowly. In the narrow use, it means the tasks carried out by the person who holds the job under consideration. A slightly broader use would include various equipment that might be used by the incumbent. As an example, in a job analysis of the position of fire fighter, we might be concerned with the extent to which various firefighting apparatus is used. Figure 4–4 presents an example of such a list. In the broadest use of the term, a job analysis would also include a consideration of the knowledges, skills, and abilities necessary to carry out the important and frequent tasks that compose the job. Figure 4–5 illustrates just a fraction of the knowledge sources used by a lieutenant in the New York City Police Department in carrying out her duties. The full list includes over 300 specific knowledge sources.

FIGURE 4–4 Partial Equipment List Used in Fire Fighter Job Analysis

Rating Sheet for Frequency Ratings: Equipment

5 = Used every workday
4 = Used once every two or three working days
3 = Used once every four or five working days
2 = Used once each month
1 = Used once each year
0 = Never used by the average fire fighter

_____ Fire axe
_____ Halligan bar
_____ Heywood bar
_____ Pinch bar
_____ Kelly tool
_____ Battering ram
_____ Electrical cord reel
_____ Bolt cutters
_____ CO_2 extinguisher
_____ Dry chemical extinguisher
_____ 2 1/2 cal. water pressure extinguisher
_____ First responder kit w/liteflow 0_2 bottle
_____ Backboard and straps
_____ Burn kit
_____ 5 gal. foam pail
_____ Foam play pipe and P/U tube
_____ Task force tip
_____ Small tool kit
_____ Sprinkler kit
_____ Portable hydrant
_____ Chain tongs
_____ Shovel
_____ Broom
_____ Ajax tool (complete)
_____ Life line in bage
_____ Wheel chocks w/chains
_____ Smoke ejector (small)
_____ Smoke ejector (large)
_____ Adjustable door hanger for smoke ejector
_____ Standpipe bag
(2—50′ sections of 1 3/4″ line
1—1/2″ to 2 1/2″ adapter
Pipe wrenches
Combination nozzle
Bonner nipple
Small pry axe)
_____ Hard suction hose

Subject Matter Experts

Fifteen years ago, a job analysis was conducted by having a particular person (usually a staff person in the personnel department) learn as much as possible about the job in question. This person would interview and observe incumbents and then write a job description listing the important and frequent job duties. The list might include 20 broad task statements. As a result of the necessity for demonstrating the validity of tests, this process has changed substantially. It is now common to do a job analysis by asking a large number of incumbents (often called subject matter experts or SMEs) to complete an extensive task list by assigning importance and frequency ratings. These lists might be several hundred items long. It is common to get these ratings from as many as 100 respondents in job titles with many incumbents.

A question naturally arises about the nature of these subject matter ex-

FIGURE 4–5 Partial Knowledge Source List from Knowledge Analysis of Police Supervisory Position

Knowledge of Subject Matter Covered in Patrol Guide and Interim Orders Regarding:

1. Patrol Duties and Responsibilities of all Uniformed and Civilian Personnel
2. General Regulations
3. Order of Rank—General Regulations

Uniforms and Equipment

4. Uniforms and Equipment—General Regulations
5. Uniforms of All Uniformed Personnel
6. Required Equipment for All Uniformed Personnel
7. The Wearing of Emblems and Insignia and Breast Bars

Aided Cases (Including Aided at Accident Scenes)

8. General Procedures
9. Preparation of Aided Reports
10. Preparing the Aided Report
11. Preparing the Aided and Accident Index
12. Procedures Regarding Supplementary Aided Reports
13. Example of an Aided and Accident Index

perts. Does it matter if they are experienced or inexperienced, trained in job analysis or untrained, careful or casual in their ratings? Recently, there have been a number of studies that have provided good data about these issues. Here are a few of the results.

1. *Naive raters produce low-quality job analysis information.* Friedman and Harvey (1986) and DeNisi et al. (1987) compared the accuracy of students to the accuracy of professional job analysts looking at various jobs using the PAQ. There was a clear superiority for the trained job analysts. Interestingly, it did not seem to matter if the students were given a great deal of information about the job (i.e., detailed list of task statements) or a minimal amount (just the job title).

2. *Some raters are more careless than others in completing a job analysis questionnaire.* S. B. Green and Stutzman (1986) conducted a study using 290 mental health workers as SMEs to analyze the job of entry-level mental health worker. The position was basically one of an orderly in a mental health facility. Embedded in 115 salient task statements were 5 other statements that had nothing to do with the job in question. For example, one statement read, "Prepares budget for the facility"; another read, "Evaluates the performance of employees." The study examined the extent to which SMEs reported that they carried out one or more of

the five tasks that were unrelated to the job. A number was created called the *carelessness index* and indicated the extent to which an SME reported carrying out the five unrelated tasks. They discovered that 145 of the SMEs reported carrying out one or more of the unrelated tasks. Additional analyses were even more revealing. If they calculated the interrater reliabilities using all 290 SMEs, the correlation was +.56. If, on the other hand, they considered only those SMEs who had a carelessness index of zero (i.e., did not report carrying out any of the unrelated tasks), the reliability value climbed to +.79.

Green and Stutzman also suggested that in many job analyses it was necessary to have more than three SMEs to achieve reasonably accurate data. In addition, they suggested that the more complex the job in question, the more important the characteristics of the SMEs.

3. *Work experience makes a difference in the ratings made by SMEs.* In a study that I conducted with patrol officers (Landy & Vasey, 1988), I discovered that experienced officers performed some tasks more frequently than new officers. As an example, less experienced officers (those with one to five years on the job) reported spending more time in traffic-related activities. In contrast, more experienced officers (those who had been police officers for more than 11 years) spent more time in non–crime-related interaction with the public, for example, giving advice and information.

In this same study, there were no differences between the reported activities of white, black, and Hispanic officers, nor were any differences noted when the educational levels of the SMEs were contrasted. Similar results have been reported by Silverman, Wexley, and Johnson (1984) and Schmitt and Cohen (in press). The conclusion to be drawn from these results is that the experience of the SMEs should be taken into account when developing the sample who will respond to the job analysis questionnaire. In order to get a full picture of the relative importance and frequency of various tasks, a full range of experience should be sampled.

A Typical Job Analysis

In practice, a job analysis consists of a combination of activities. The job analyst first reads any information that is available concerning the job in question. Often, there is a job description available that is based on some earlier and less systematic job analysis. After reading up on the job, the analysts will then have a conversation with a middle-level supervisor. During this conversation, the analyst picks up some of the critical terminology of the job, identifies what may be important job dimensions, and develops questions to ask in an interview and things to look for while observing the job. Next, the analyst might watch three or four different people perform the job in question. Finally, the analyst might schedule a series of interviews with incumbents and supervisors or distribute questionnaires for them to fill out and

Cleveland fire fighters using a pike pole to extinguish a dumpster fire. (F. Landy)

return regarding job duties. As an example, in a recent job analysis of the position of fire fighter in the city of Cleveland, I began by reading fire fighter job analyses conducted earlier in Cleveland and other major cities. Next, I discussed the job with a sample of fire fighters and supervisors. Then I spent many hours living in firehouses in Cleveland. Since actual fires occur relatively infrequently, it may take several 24-hour shift observations before one can observe important job-related behavior. This meant actually living with the fire fighters and going out with them on all calls (even those at 3:00 A.M.!). While I was at the firehouse, I took an inventory of all the equipment that fire fighters used, noting the size and weight of each piece. Finally, I distributed questionnaires to several dozen fire fighters and supervisors, asking them to respond to a series of statements about their job duties, the equipment that they used, and the knowledges and abilities that helped them to carry out their tasks and use their equipment effectively. Their responses included both judged importance and estimated frequency ratings for each statement. I was then able to combine all this information to form a coherent view of what duties made up the job "fire fighter."

The last activity described above is the most important part of job analysis. It is up to the analyst to combine information from many different sources and describe the essence of the job. Job analysis is not simply a mechanical operation of collecting standard information. Instead, it is more like trying to solve a riddle. How can the job under consideration be decomposed into its critical elements? All the techniques provide clues. Some clues come from watching, others from talking, and still others from having people respond to standard questions. Effective job analysis does not depend exclusively on the accumulation of abstract knowledge. It also requires some creativity, some dedication to identifying important behaviors that are not obvious, and some skill at eliciting information from incumbents who may be hostile, suspicious, or very busy.

JOB EVALUATION

Job evaluation is the process by which wage rates are applied differentially to jobs. The job evaluator takes a series of factors into account, weights these factors, and places each job at a point on a continuum. This continuum is then broken into a series of classes, usually corresponding to the wage categories. Although there *should* be some relationship between job analysis and job evaluation, there seldom is unless the evaluation was designed and implemented by a compensation specialist. If the evaluation system is set up by someone unaware of compensation principles, at best there is some relationship between the job-oriented approach to job analysis and job evaluation.

Historically, job evaluations have tended to consist of factors such as those found in Figure 4–6. The organization determines the relative worth of each of these factors and then breaks down each of the factors into a series of steps. The job to be evaluated is then considered on each of these factors and points assigned depending on the step represented. Figure 4–6 describes a job as seen from the point of view of the job evaluator. This is only one example of a possible evaluation scheme. It relies on the detailed allocation of points in graded steps. There are other methods of assigning dollar values to jobs. Perhaps the simplest is to arrange all jobs to be evaluated on a continuum describing their relative worth to the organization. Money may then be allocated to each of the jobs depending upon its position on the continuum.

Job evaluation schemes may sometimes appear arbitrary. After a very careful analysis and evaluation is completed, it is not unusual to see the personnel department change the wage rate assigned to the job. There are many reasons for this. The most common reason is that accepting the evaluation would result in lowering the pay for certain jobs, and both organizations and unions often find this totally unacceptable. In addition, personnel departments consider prevailing wage rates when making final decisions on compensation. They are reluctant to pay significantly more or less than other employers in the area unless there is a good reason for such deviation. This does not mean that the job evaluation is arbitrary. Instead, it simply indicates that the relative position of jobs within an organization is one of *several* factors that are taken into account in setting wage rates. A fuller description of procedures and principles has recently been published jointly by the American Society for Personnel Administration and the American Compensation Association (1981). The publication is entitled *Elements of Sound Base Pay Administration* and should be read by those with a deeper interest in evaluation procedures.

FIGURE 4–6 Job Evaluation: Fork Truck Driver

	Points
Experience Must learn to operate fork truck and hand truck if he does not have this skill. Two to three weeks on-the-job training	48
Education Requires ability to speak, read, and write English and understand simple written instructions. Should have knowledge of simple mathematics in order to complete certain daily reports. Grammar school education desirable	32
Responsibility for Equipment, Tools, Product, or Material Could damage products if not stacked properly in freezer. Cost would vary from $100 to $500	94
Resourcefulness Some variety in the job. Exercises some discretion in keeping freezer in order	52
Responsibility for Work of Others None	35
Monotony Has a number of tasks to perform. Works in several places and moves around	10
Pressure of Work Occasionally has problems keeping up with work pace	46
Physical Effort On feet most of day when not driving lift truck. Pushes and/or pulls stack of empty pallets with truck or moves full pallet with hand truck. Lifting involved in carrying boxes of damaged packages	30
Surroundings In freezer (0°) for approximate total of 1½ to 2 hours daily. Occasionally on dock. Noisy in Cartoning Department	38
Hazards Operates fork truck. Often ice on freezer floor; could skid. When driving fork truck on dock must be cautious—ice and water. Pallets of cases incorrectly stacked in freezer could topple on him	30
Concentration Duties require close attention most of the time	75
Total	490

Job evaluation is sometimes known as *job classification,* particularly in public-sector personnel work, such as federal, state, or city government. The term implies that a job is placed in a class with several other jobs that demand similar levels of effort for the purpose of assigning wage or salary rates. Although job evaluations or classifications may be updated only every seven years or so in private organizations, there is an elaborate mechanism for public employees to request a review of job duties and responsibilities, with an eye toward increasing the monetary value of the particular position. London (1976) studied the perceptions of workers concerning the reclassification process. He noted that pay increases based on reclassification decisions are usually considerably more than increases resulting from either cost-of-living or merit increases. He also noted that requests for reclassification in public-sector organizations were increasing at a rapid rate, an indication that the individual employee sees some value in requesting the review—most likely a monetary one! The study was conducted in a university setting, and the subjects were predominantly female clerical workers. In spite of the fact that reclassification should depend almost exclusively on the nature and conditions of work, the subjects believed that factors such as perseverance and job success (on the part of the person requesting the reclassification) significantly affected the reclassification decision. The subjects were also concerned that the evaluator's accuracy would affect the resulting decision.

London's findings allow for some interesting speculation and extension to the private sector. It seems as if the employees in his study saw classification decisions as potential rewards for good work. The problem with this logic is that it puts the decision to give or withhold a reward in the hands of someone who is unfamiliar with the level of performance. In addition, the focus of the evaluator is on the job, not the person. Because of the disparities in monetary results from merit increases versus increases resulting from reclassification, it may not be long before private-sector employees decide to pursue the reclassification route for increasing monetary rewards, rather than the more traditional merit-increase procedure.

Job Evaluation and Comparable Worth

In determining how much money a particular job should be worth to the organization, there are two schools of thought. The first approach is, Take the market perspective and say that the worth of a job will be determined by how easy it is to fill it. If it is simple to find someone to take the job, it is worth less; if it is difficult to fill the position, it may be worth substantially more. An alternative approach is one based on a job analysis procedure. In this approach, dollar values are assigned to various factors, such as those described above, and the worth of a job is based on the accumulation of the values assigned to various tasks that are performed on the job. Naturally, there is an association between the marketplace approach and the job analysis approach. Tasks that are difficult to carry out well will probably define a job that demands high levels of skill, effort, or both. Generally speaking, there will be fewer people capable of fulfilling the requirements of these demanding jobs. Thus, both the marketplace and the job analysis tell us that the job should pay well.

Recently, job evaluation has emerged as a central component in discussion on the concept of *comparable worth*. The major theme of the Equal Pay

TABLE 4–1 Annualized Median Earnings[a] by Sex for Census Major Occupation Groups, 1970

Census Major Group	*Men*	*Women*	*Women's Earnings as a Percentage of Men's*
Professional, technical, and kindred workers	$9,701	$7,731	79.7%
Managers and administrators, except farm	9,496	5,514	58.1
Sales workers	7,684	3,185	41.4
Clerical and kindred workers	7,298	4,805	65.8
Craft and kindred workers	7,840	4,676	59.6
Operatives, except transport	6,544	3,936	60.1
Transport equipment operatives	6,351	4,064	64.0
Laborers, except farm	5,025	3,556	70.8
Farmers and farm managers	4,663	2,442	52.4
Farm laborers and foremen	2,364	1,495	63.2
Service workers, except private household	5,117	3,032	59.3
Private household workers	2,170	1,525	70.3
Total	$7,394	$4,603	62.3%
Average within-category earnings ratio[b]	—	—	63.4%

[a] Adjusted to correct for differences in the number of hours worked per year. Annualized median earnings = median earnings × [2080 (mean hours worked last week × median weeks worked last year)]. The constant (= 40 × 52) is an estimate of the hours of labor contributed by full-time year-round workers.

[b] Weighted average of within-category ratios, with weights equal to total labor force in each category.

SOURCE: From U.S. Bureau of the Census, 1973, table 24.

Act of 1963 was "equal pay for *equal* work." This was a concept that was used to support efforts by women and minority group members to achieve financial parity with their white male counterparts. In terms of our discussion above, those in favor of comparable worth are against the marketplace definition of job value.

Let's consider an example of an issue that would have been adequately addressed by the Equal Pay Act. If a female machine operator is paid less than a male operator of identical equipment, the female operator can file an equal-pay claim against the employer. In most cases, the jobs in question are either identical (e.g., machine operator) or very similar (e.g., janitor and maid; orderly and nurse's aide).

The principle of comparable worth takes such comparisons one step further and suggests that the compensation plans should be guided by the notion of "equal pay for *comparable* work" (Treiman & Hartmann, 1981). Consider Table 4–1. There is little dispute about what this table says—women are paid less than men overall as well as by occupational grouping. The Equal Pay Act has not been of much help in eliminating these differences since men and women often hold different job titles, even within occupational groupings. As a result, the emphasis has shifted from equal work to comparable work. Further, the administrative mechanism for claims has shifted, to some extent, from the Equal Pay Act to the laws governing equal employment opportunity ("Uniform Guidelines," 1978). Women and minority workers have attempted to prove that the employers are in violation of Title VII of the Civil Rights Act of 1964 by paying lower rates to employee classes specifically protected by the Civil Rights Act (e.g., women) when these employees are performing jobs that are of a value equal to the value of jobs performed by white males. As an example, female nursing supervisors employed by the city of Denver claimed that they were being discriminated against because their jobs were placed in a low pay class that was predominantly populated with other jobs held by women (e.g., beginning nurses and dental hygienists) rather than in a higher and more appropriate pay class populated with jobs held predominantly by men (e.g., hospital administration officers). The nursing supervisors claimed that their jobs were comparable in scope to jobs held by men in higher pay classes and, as a result, that they should be paid on an equal level (Treiman & Hartmann, 1981). In other words, they claimed that their jobs were *comparable in value or worth* to those of the higher paid men. The court rejected this case, deciding that the wage differences were not based on sex discrimination. In another example, it was determined that clerk typists (jobs held predominantly by women) employed by the city of San Francisco were paid 64 percent less than storekeepers (jobs held predominantly by men). It was suggested that the jobs of clerk-typist and storekeeper were equal with respect to contribution or worth to the employer and that the jobs should have paid equally (Treiman & Hartmann, 1981). A recent case involving state employees in Washington will have enormous repercussions. A federal judge ruled that the state of Washington was guilty of overt wage discrimination against 14,000 female employees. The plaintiffs argued that they had been placed in job categories and paid 20 percent less simply because they were women. They further argued that the jobs that they performed were comparable to jobs performed by male employees in other job categories and that they deserved equal pay. The judge agreed and the state of Washington may end up paying as much as $500 to each of the plaintiffs. Similar rulings have appeared in other states since the Washington decision.

If you accept the possibility that discrimination may be present in the differences in wage rates between men and women or whites and blacks and that continued discrimination is likely to be maintained by virtue of the fact that women and minorities have greater access to some job titles (i.e., those in lower pay classes) than other job titles (i.e., those in higher paying classes), then job evaluation represents a strategy for restoring equity. Since job evaluation typically places monetary values on four major factors (skill, effort, responsibility, and working conditions), it would be possible through job evaluation techniques to create pay classes that contained jobs of equal worth regardless of the similarity or dissimilarity of actual job duties. As an example, a pay class in a municipal school district might include librarians, computer programmers, bus dispatchers, and kitchen supervisors. Each of these jobs would pay the same basic wage. For purposes of compensation, it would not matter if librarians were predominantly female and bus dispatchers predominantly male (although this might be a problem from other perspectives, for example, advancement opportunities). They would be paid a similar wage because it could be demonstrated that the jobs were equal with respect to skill and effort demands, responsibility, and working conditions.

The issue of comparable worth is only now beginning to receive careful attention from psychologists. As you have seen above, the techniques of job evaluation are well developed and have been around for many decades. The question is whether these techniques can be applied to solve the problem of potential discrimination in compensation practices. Some claim that job evaluation techniques are simply ratings and that they are subject to all the biases that plague other types of ratings. These biases would include sexist and racist biases. In other words, job evaluators might very well rate jobs held by women and blacks lower than those held by white males. This would simply be using the mechanics of job evaluation to prop up long-standing patterns of discrimination (Treiman & Hartmann, 1981). There are others who claim that job evaluation can be shown to be free from bias and sensitive to real differences among jobs in terms of skill, effort, responsibility, and working conditions (Doverspike, Carlisi, Barrett, & Alexander, 1983; McCormick, 1981).

It is much too early to come to any firm conclusion on this issue with respect to the eventual contribution of job evaluation and job analysis techniques to illuminating the comparable worth debate. Nevertheless, a recent review of the comparable worth issue by Arvey (1986) clearly identifies some of the potential technical obstacles involved in the use of job evaluation and job analysis techniques. Arvey talks about "ports of entry" for wage discrimination. By this, he means that unfair discrimination influences can enter into the process of setting wage rates at several different stages. For example, in developing the job form, a decision might be made to include factors that cover heavy physical exertion but to ignore factors that deal with attention to detail or concentration. This might have the effect of artificially inflating the value of jobs held by men compared with those held by women. Similarly, in developing a task list for a job analysis of the positions in question, more tasks carried out by males in the jobs being examined may be included and tasks carried out by females excluded. Through these influences, the results of the job analysis and job evaluation might, on the surface, appear to document the appropriateness of the wage differentials between the jobs of men and the jobs of women, but this is more apparent than real since the structure of the questionnaire–task list all but guaranteed such an outcome.

Even when task lists are appropriately prepared, examples may be given that influence the way the task lists are used. Consider the example that Arvey presents on equipment use. This example appears in Figure 4–7. If

FIGURE 4–7 Narrow versus Broad Statements in Job Evaluation

Importance of setting up or adjusting equipment (setting up lathe or drill press, adjusting an engine carburetor, etc.)

vs.

Importance of setting up or adjusting equipment (attaching devices to patients, setting up a lathe or drill press, adjusting office equipment, etc.)

SOURCE: From "Sex Bias in Job Evaluation Procedures" by R. D. Arvey, 1986, Personnel Psychology, *39*(2), p. 322.

the example includes only lathe use, it would be tempting to report that a secretary did not use equipment. On the other hand, if the example includes setting up office equipment such as printers, mimeograph machines, and the like, people holding the job of a secretary are likely to be rated higher on the importance and frequency of such a task. The Arvey review is a comprehensive and provocative statement of the technical challenges to addressing the comparable worth issue.

Madigan (1986) identifies an additional problem in using job analysis–evaluation procedures in deciding questions of comparable worth. He demonstrates that even though the reliability of the job analysis and evaluation judgments may be high, so might the standard error of those judgments. He cites an example in which, even with a reliability coefficient of .95 for the job evaluation judgments, the standard error might be ±40 points in a factor-point job evaluation scheme. Thus, assuming a 95 percent confidence interval of 160 points (i.e., 2 standard errors on either side of the scope in question), a particular job could be classified as many as four pay classes away (above or below) the pay class in which it actually belongs. This means that when real decisions are being made about the differences between pay classes of various jobs, the standard error must be taken into account in addition to the reliability. Madigan is actually arguing that the typical job evaluation–job analysis rating scales are not well suited for resolving the comparable worth debate.

It is likely that the comparable worth issue will assume even greater importance in the next several years as various states pass laws requiring parity between the jobs typically held by men and the jobs typically held by women. This may, in turn, put pressure on the job analysis and evaluation procedure and result in substantially more precise measurement scales and procedures.

PERFORMANCE EVALUATION

Performance evaluation is the more specific term for criterion measurement for the purpose of describing performance strengths and weaknesses within and between workers. The most general use for performance evaluation is for administrative personnel decisions such as promotions, salary increases, or layoffs. Cummings (1973) has termed this use one of providing structure for a reward-punishment system. He suggests that there are at least three other uses for performance evaluation systems: (1) providing criterion information for the selection process, (2) providing objectives for training programs, and (3) providing elements for supervisory feedback and control.

One logical conclusion of a job analysis is the development of a performance evaluation system. Once the elements of the job are determined, successful performance on that job can be described. There are several kinds of data that can be used to provide such a description. Guion (1965) identified at least three different kinds of measures of job behavior: *objective data* in the form of production information, *personnel data,* and *judgmental data*. The multidimensionality of "job performance" becomes apparent when these categories are considered simultaneously. Is a successful worker one who turns out the greatest numbers of units (objective data), the one who has not been absent for 11 years (personnel data), or the one who is rated high on quality of work and judgment by a supervisor (judgmental data)? The first and second of these categories will be considered in the following sections. Judgmental forms of performance evaluation will be covered in the next chapter.

It is instructive to consider the results of a recent study that illustrates the diversity of various performance measures. In a recent meta-analysis of 23 performance studies, Heneman (1986) found a very low correlation between supervisory ratings (judgmental data) and results-oriented measures such as sales volume, complaint letters, and output (objective data). The average correlation was approximately +.20. This value was obtained after adjusting for the unreliability of the different measures. Given the fact that this result was based on 23 independent studies, it is more powerful than if it were only a single study result. What it says is that these criterion types—that is, supervisory ratings and objective performance data—address independent aspects of job performance and should not be considered substitutes for each other. This means that we must consider carefully the results of the validity generalization studies described in the last chapter. When it is proposed that a test or test type is valid for a particular job or job family, it is important to know what criteria were represented in the studies included in the VG analysis.

Objective Production Data

After introducing the link between job analysis and performance evaluation, it is somewhat embarrassing to note that seldom is there any explicit relationship between a job analysis and objective indexes of performance, such as rate of production. At best, there is a naive faith that embedded somewhere in the production data are the important job elements as identified by the job analysis. This is a very serious problem that must be dealt with if any advances are to be made in predicting the results of behavior. We must know how individual behaviors (job elements) combine to yield certain performance profiles and, further, how a particular profile combines with environmental factors to yield an organizational outcome. This lack of attention to the relationship between job analysis and performance evaluation is most apparent in objective production criteria but exists to a certain degree in the other two categories of criterion information as well. The most widely used variables are in the form of output measurements—or, as Guion (1965) describes the process, "simply a count of the results of work". This count can take many different forms. It might be the number of arrests for a police officer, the number of decisions rendered by a judge in a district court, the number of hamburgers prepared by a grill worker, or the number of swings taken by a professional golfer in completing 18 holes at Augusta. Measures of productivity come in every shape and form. Consider the examples in Table 4–2. This is just a sample. Even *within* jobs, the variety of objective measures is often staggering. Consider the potential measures of productivity for patrol officers that appear in Table 4–3.

Unfortunately, there is ample opportunity for variability to be introduced into these measures that has nothing at all to do with the individual being evaluated. The number of arrests made by a police officer may depend heavily on the district or shift to which that officer is assigned. The number of cases heard by a judge may depend heavily on the degree to which the district attorney engages in plea bargaining before the cases reach court. The number of shots required by a professional golfer may depend heavily on the knowledge and judgment of a caddy. Similar objections may be raised to all the objective criteria mentioned above. There is a seductive appeal to these variables. After all, they define the goals of the organization. Although this is true, variance in these measures is often unrelated to the behaviors of the individual. It is interesting to note that one of the reasons often advanced for using objective measures rather than judgmental measures is the presumed resistance to race effects. In other words, it is assumed that with objective measures there will be no differences between the mean performance of majority and minority group members. There is one big qualification to that belief, however. The qualification that must be added is ". . . other than the true score differences that might exist between the two subgroups." In a recent meta-analysis by Ford, Kraiger, and Schechtman (1986), it was demonstrated that race effects were as apparent in objective measures as in judgmental measures of performance.

There are three basic problems with the use of objective production data as criterion measures for individual job success. The first is the simple measurement problem of reliability. Each objective measure probably has an observation period that is not stable. For example, if we were to take the total number of arrests for a patrol officer for a one-week period, the relationship between one week and any other week might be very low. The relationship would increase greatly if we extended the period of observation from one week to one month. A reliable measurement implies a sufficient period of time to observe variations in the target behavior.

The reliability problem is not limited to the period of observation. Rothe

TABLE 4–2 Representative Performance Measures from Varied Job Titles

Job Title	*Measure*	*Reference*
Typist	Lines per week	Yukl & Latham (1978)
Forester	Cords cut	Latham & Kinne (1974)
Keypuncher	Number of characters; number of errors	Johnson (1975)
Service representative	Errors in processing customer orders	Hackman & Porter (1968)
Toll collector	Dollar accuracy/axle accuracy	Farr, O'Leary, & Bartlett (1971)
Clerk	Errors per 100 documents checked; number of documents processed	Bassett (1979)
Wood harvesters	Number of cords delivered	Latham & Locke (1975)
Tree planters	Bags of tree seedlings planted	Yukl & Latham (1975)
Typist	Number of strokes; number of errors	West (1969)
Skateboard makers	Number produced; number rejected	Newman, Hunt, & Rhodes (1966)
Sewing machine operators	Minutes per operation	Lefkowitz (1970)
Loggers	Weight of wood legally hauled	Latham & Baldes (1975)
Dentists	Errors in reading radiographs	Goldstein & Mobley (1971)
Foreman in open hearth	Time between "Taps"	Cleven & Fiedler (1956)
Inspectors	Errors detected in finished product	Chaney & Teel (1967)
Tool makers/die makers	Dies produced	Ivancevich (1978)
Helicopter pilots	Deviations from proper instrument readings	Isley & Caro (1970)
Bank tellers	Number of shortages; number of overages	Bass & Turner (1973)
Air traffic controllers	Speed of movement of aircraft through the system Correction of pilot error Errors in positioning aircraft for final approach Errors in aircraft separation	Kidd & Christy (1961)

SOURCE: From *The Measurement of Work Performance* (table 2.3) by F. J. Landy and J. L. Farr, 1983, New York: Academic Press.

TABLE 4–3 Common Measures of Police Officer Performance

Number of arrests for felony offenses	Number of chargeable accidents
Number of arrests for misdeameanor offenses	Danger-tension index: Number of arrests divided by sick days taken × 100
Number of traffic citations issued	Clearance rates: number of incidents reported divided by number of arrests for such incidents
Number of accident reports taken	Average time required to respond to calls in various categories (felony, traffic, etc.)
Number of nontraffic cases in court	Percent of crimes solved in less than "x" days
Number of convictions on court cases	Time required to solve a crime
Number of letters of commendation from the public	Number of arrests without use of force
Number of trial board hearings	Number of resisting arrest charges filed by officer[a]
Number of written reprimands	
Number of sick days used	
Number of department citations	
Number of precinct citations	
Number of shots fired in line of duty	
Number of citizen complaints sustained	

[a]This may seem like an unusual measure of police officer performance, but some suggest that this index, at least when abnormally high, represents brutality on the part of the officer. The charge is filed by the officer to shift the focus to the suspect.

SOURCE: From *The Measurement of Work Performance* (table 2.5) by F. J. Landy and J. L. Farr, 1983, New York: Academic Press.

and Nye (1959) completed a series of studies designed to assess the stability of output rates for machine operators. They discovered that the *type of pay* can affect the stability of the production data. Greater stability was found for output measures when workers were paid on an incentive system than when they were paid on a day-rate plan. They concluded that performance on the predictors of job performance is often more stable than the performance that is to be predicted. A distinction between accuracy and reliability should be evident from this example. Many objective criteria are accurate in that there is little error in the counting of output as indicated by a counter on the machine or a record of gross sales; yet taken over a short period, this count may not provide a representative estimate of the typical output of the employee.

A second problem that arises with the use of objective data is the changing nature of skilled and semiskilled work. Many former machine *operators* are now machine *tenders*. Manual machines are being replaced with automatic and semiautomatic machines. If only objective data are considered, no differential performance data on these individuals can be obtained unless a machine malfunctions.

Finally, there are many jobs for which no good objective measures are available. This becomes more troublesome as we go up the occupational ladder. It is very difficult to describe the performance of a middle-level supervisor in objective terms. The problem is one of reducing the supervisory responsibility for the allocation of human resources and delegation of responsibility to units that can be counted.

Typical versus Maximum Performance. An interesting sidelight of the issue of objective production measures relates to the distinction between typical and maximum measures of performance. If I appear at your workplace and tell you that I am going to record information about the effectiveness of your performance, you will probably try hard to perform effectively. A good example of this would be the elementary school teacher whose behavior is being observed by a principal while a class is taught. This would be considered a measure of maximum performance. On the other hand, consider what your performance profile might look like if I observed it without your awareness. You would still be engaging in work-related behavior, but it would probably look different than it did when you knew you were being observed. This second type of measure is referred to as a *measure of typical performance.*

Sackett, Zedeck, and Fogli (1988) carried out an ingenious study in which they compared the effectiveness of supermarket cashiers on typical and maximum performance measures. For the typical measures, the researchers simply examined the register tapes for their sample of cashiers and noted how many times the cashiers voided an item (an example of an error in ringing the item up) and how many items they were able to ring in a fixed period of time (a measure of speed). For the maximum measure, the researchers loaded up a market basket with a specific set of products and asked the cashier to ring up the purchases while the researcher recorded speed and accuracy. The results were surprising. The correlation between maximum and typical performance was quite low for new employees (only +.14) and only slightly higher for experienced employees (+.32). Since it could be demonstrated that both measures (i.e., typical and maximum) were reliable, we are left with the conclusion that the two types of measures are not substitutes for one another. Further, it means that we should be careful in our validity studies to distinguish between maximum and typical criterion measurements.

Personnel Data

The second general class of criterion information is personnel data, those data usually available in the personnel folder of an individual. Some of the more common variables are absences, tardiness, turnover, rate of advancement, type of salary adjustment, and accidents. Although there are other potential variables in this category (such as commendations and disciplinary actions), they are usually present in fewer than 5 percent of the cases examined, making them rather useless criteria. Almost all these measures tend to affect the well-being of the organization but are rather global in nature. In addition, they also tend to fall prey to the potential confounding effects of other variables and in much the same manner as described for objective production data. Absences might be separated into "excused" and "unex-

TABLE 4–4 Sources of Unreliability in Absence Data

Individual
- General health and resistance to illness
- Work-induced fatigue
- Nonwork-induced fatigue
- Current hobbies, leisure activities
- Shift

Environmental
- Ambient flu, virus, etc.
- Fluctuations in atmospheric conditions

Suborganizational
- Accuracy of supervisor in recording incident and reason

Administrative
- Accuracy of personnel office in transcribing supervisory attendance reports
- Administrative categories used for attribution of absence
- Level of aggregation of absence data (day, week, month, quarter, individual, work group, shift, plant, etc.)
- Index of absence used (i.e., number of total days per unit time, number of periods, ratio of total days to periods)

SOURCE: From *The Measurement of Work Performance* (table 2.2) by F. J. Landy and J. L. Farr, 1983, New York: Academic Press.

cused." Although it may be difficult to predict from psychological test data the number of times an individual will contract a bad head cold each year, it may be easier to predict the number of times a day or more of work will be missed for nonlegitimate reasons. In addition, absences might be recorded as either absolute number of days absent or number of absences regardless of the length of each absence.

The reliability of absence data is generally poor, at least over periods of time up to one year. In other words, it is very difficult to identify a measure of absence that represents a stable characteristic of the worker. Managers are fond of the concept of the "absence-prone" worker or the "sick-leave abuser." These kinds of employees may exist, but they cannot be easily identified using absence data commonly available in company records. Reliability estimates for absence are commonly in the range of .30 to .50. This is considerably below what might be expected of a suitable measure of performance. There are many reasons for this low reliability. Some of these sources are listed in Table 4–4. As you can see, there are many opportunities for absence data to become distorted.

It seems clear that more work must be done in refining both the concept and the measurement of absence. There do seem to be differences between measures of absence. For example, the frequency of absence (i.e., the number of periods or "spells" regardless of duration) seems to be more reliable than the duration or severity of absence (i.e., the average or total number of days absent) (Chadwick-Jones, Brown, Nicholson, & Sheppard, 1971; Landy & Farr, 1983; Muchinsky, 1977). Similarly, some recent research has suggested that half-day absences are considerably more reliable than full-day absences and that some administrative categories (e.g., funeral or bereavement absence) are more reliable than other categories (e.g., personal day excused with pay) (Hedrick, 1983). In order to make absence measures more appropriate for administrative and research use, two things will be necessary. First, companies must take the classification and recording of absence more seriously. This might involve developing a standard form. In addition, the phenomenon of absence must be decomposed more carefully. Not all absence will be of interest to the I/O psychologist. This means that some careful consideration must be given to the *validity* of possible absence measures. Of those forms of absence that are valid and are of interest, several may be too unreliable for all practical purposes. Absence measures are seductive but have not been very useful in helping to create more efficient or satisfying work environments.

Turnover is another difficult variable to deal with. The question is one of classifying turnover as voluntary (quitting) or involuntary (being fired). It is not always that easy to distinguish between them. For example, a professor who knows that his contract is not likely to be renewed the following year looks for a new job before he is fired. Should that be considered voluntary or involuntary turnover?

Rate of advancement might be controlled more by an informal quota system or the expected life span of first-level supervisors than by the behavior of the worker. Type of salary adjustment might reflect more the economic profile of the organization than the behavior of the individual on the job. In short, although there are perfectly acceptable reasons for using personnel data as indexes of performance, we often encounter problems in their use.

The arguments that have been raised in relation to the use of objective production data and personnel data do not mean that they are useless as criteria. But if they are to be useful, a careful analysis of the relationship between the elements of the job as identified by job analysis and the elements of behavior as related to the performance appraisal is necessary. Even if this is successfully accomplished, there are still many jobs for which performance will have to be described in terms other than those provided by objective and personnel data. This leads to the most pervasive set of performance evaluation data—judgmental data. We will consider this type of performance evaluation in the next chapter.

A New Measure: Hands-on Performance

A very recent development in the field of performance measurement is known as the hands-on measure of performance. As you will see in the next chapter, hands-on measures are frequently used as predictors and are called *work samples*. A typing test for clerical workers, a programming test for computer programmers, and a one-game "tryout" for an aspiring

Hands-on tests can assess proficiency of tank crewmen. (Booz, Allen, & Hamilton, Inc.)

athlete are all examples of work samples as predictors. Conceptually, the work sample as a criterion is no different and as a criterion measure has some attractive characteristics not possessed by alternative criterion measures. In the first place, the criterion work sample or hands-on performance measure is a carefully developed and clearly delimited *piece* of the entire job. It is selected and developed to represent a central or important part of the job. It is administered in carefully controlled conditions that permit accurate observation of behavior and the standardization of equipment and environment. This accomplishes two things. First, it reduces the common contaminating influences in most attempts to measure performance on the job—factors such as equipment differences, production demands, and day-to-day environmental variation. In addition, it permits one to observe certain behaviors that occur infrequently or that could not be observed easily on the actual job.

Currently, the U.S. Department of Defense is supporting a large-scale validation of the Armed Services Vocational Aptitude Battery (ASVAB) in each of the branches of the military. Each service has identified one or more job titles for study and is developing multiple criterion measures for a criterion-related validity study of the ASVAB. In each of these service projects, one or more hands-on measures is being developed as a criterion variable (Harris, 1987; Wigdor & Green, 1986).

As an example of hands-on measures, in the armed services study, the army is studying the position of tank crewman. As part of the study, they have developed a hands-on battery that is administered to incumbent crewmen. The battery requires the subject to complete several different exercises for which a tank crewman would be expected to possess proficiency. This battery requires the subject to climb into an actual tank and

1. Operate the radio system that would be used to communicate with friendly ground forces outside the tank

2. Operate the internal communication system that would be used to speak with other tank crew personnel in that tank when it is in operation
3. Position the tank cannon for firing
4. Disassemble and reassemble an automatic hand-held weapon

Each subject is asked to complete these tasks one at a time. The subject is carefully observed and scored on a checklist for the various operations necessary to complete the action in question successfully. The scoring is done by trained observers. These scores represent criterion measures, and they will ultimately be correlated with ASVAB scores as part of the criterion-related validity study of that predictor.

The hands-on measures seem to produce reliable scores, and since they are samples of tasks identified as important in a job analysis, their validity seems to be well grounded. Nevertheless, as is the case with work samples as predictors, these measures are complex, expensive to develop, and demanding to administer. It may be that their expense and complexity place them out of the reach of the garden-variety validity study. Nevertheless, just as predictor work samples are becoming more popular, inexpensive, and feasible, so might criterion work samples. There is little doubt about the potential that they offer for validation research. They seem to eliminate the most obvious disadvantages of the other forms of performance information.

Multiple versus Composite Criteria

You have been exposed to several different potential sources of performance information. For any given person, it might be possible to gather information on absences, scrap rate, and production rate as well as secure supervisory ratings on interpersonal skills, reasoning, decision-making skills, and communication skills. The question then arises regarding what to do with this information. Should it be combined, or should it be considered one piece at a time? If performance information is somehow combined, it is often referred to as a *composite criterion*. Consider the following simple example. A company finds itself in a slump and decides that it must lay off 20 percent of its workers. Since the company is relatively young, there is little variation in seniority. The company calls in its upper-level managers to determine the way of characterizing each employee in terms of "worth to the company." The managers decide to use a measure of *quality of production*, a measure of *quantity of production*, and a rating of *initiative*. Furthermore, they decide that quantity of production is twice as important as quality of production, which is, in turn, twice as important as initiative. Consequently, they construct an equation like this:

$$(4 \times \text{quantity}) + (2 \times \text{quality}) + (1 \times \text{initiative}) = Y$$

They then arrange all the Y scores from high to low, and they lay off those with scores in the bottom 20 percent. These Y scores would be an example of using a composite criterion for making an administrative decision. A new variable, or index of success, is formed by combining three other variables. The controversy is centered on the question of whether the data justify such a combination.

Perhaps another example will strike closer to home. Assume that a student receives a grade report at the end of the term that states that the student received two As and three Fs. If someone were to take those grades, assign a point value to each of the grades (e.g., A = 4, B = 3, C = 2, D = 1, F = 0), add up the point values, and divide by 5, the student might be described as slightly worse than average. The student would justifiably argue that the averaging process distorted the real state of affairs. This highlights the different purposes that might be served by the same criterion information in *two different forms.* The university is interested primarily in the average of the grades, to determine if the student should be allowed to continue in the academic program. The student and the student's adviser take the information on the grade report and use it to determine what deficiencies must be made up, what general goals might be set for the next term, and how career goals might be changed or modified by the term report. The student's academic dean might argue that any single grade is simply a sample of that student's academic ability and a grade point average derived from several grades is a more stable index of that ability. For that reason, the dean might be unimpressed by the fact that the student received two As. On the other hand, it is of little use to either the student or the adviser to know that the student's grade point average is 1.60. The adviser must have specific pieces of information, the components of that single index called the grade point average, to advise the student efficiently.

Most psychologists who have confronted the problem of multiple versus composite criteria recognize that there is ample justification for either approach. There will always be a need for a single index in making administrative decisions. In addition, there will always be a need for specific performance information of a multidimensional nature for counseling, regardless of how these dimensions might be combined to form a single dimension.

The argument about composite versus multiple criteria is usually presented as if one form of criterion information *excludes* the other, and this is by no means the case. The argument is not about how the information will be gathered but about how it will be used. There are good reasons to consider presenting the information in both forms, since the information often serves two distinct purposes, one administrative and the other diagnostic. Since it makes sense to use performance information in many different contexts, and since each of those contexts may require the information in a different form, I would suggest that performance information be gathered and recorded in a "multiple" or uncollapsed form. A composite index can always be computed when needed.

Another issue related to the composite-multiple controversy is the compensatory nature of various criteria. For any given job, it may be that there are some areas of performance so critical that an individual cannot make up for deficiencies in that area with an abundance in another area. For example, it may be that a crane operator cannot substitute exceptional interpersonal skills for deficiency in reading work orders. In that case, unless some minimal amount of reading accuracy can be assured, performance will consistently be disastrous. In this case, one would not want to use an equation such as the one given earlier to combine performance scores. Interpersonal skills and reading accuracy should remain separate in describing the performance of the crane operator. While most jobs allow for compensatory relationships among performance measures, it is important to recognize that there are instances in which performance scores should not be combined or, at the very least, should not be combined in a strictly linear additive fashion. This point will be discussed in Chapter 8, when we discuss the combination of test scores for prediction purposes.

Performance Evaluation and the Law

As I indicated in Chapter 3, the definition of a test is broad. In fact, it is broad enough to encompass many forms of performance measurement. To the extent that a measure of performance is used as a standardized sample of behavior, it is a test and subject to the same scrutiny as a test of intellectual abilities. This means that performance evaluation may be subject to litigation if the performance data will be used to make promotions or to determine salary increases or will influence similar personnel decisions. Currently, there is a major case being decided by the U.S. Supreme Court involving performance evaluation *(Clara Watson v. Fort Worth Bank and Trust, 1988)* that will have substantial implications for the extent to which performance ratings require validation when used for making promotional decisions. The plaintiff, Clara Watson, contends that she was denied promotions on several occasions and that this was due to performance ratings that had not been validated. The defendants, Fort Worth Bank and Trust, claim that Title VII does not require them to support the validity of these ratings, only to demonstrate that all candidates were evaluated in the same manner. It is interesting to note that there is substantial fire power on both sides. The APA has sided with the plaintiff in a supporting belief and argues that performance ratings can be subjected to the same validation procedures as any other selection device. The Department of Justice, the EEOC, the American Society of Personnel Administration, and the International Personnel Management Association, on the other hand, are supporting the defendant in this case. An excellent review of the issues has been provided by Sharf (1988). It is clear that the decision of the Supreme Court will have a tremendous impact on the manner by which performance evaluations are used for making personnel decisions. Regardless, however, of the Supreme Court's decision, from a psychometric standpoint the issue is crystal clear—we are assuming that performance information is reliable and valid in making personnel decisions. It is not unreasonable for an individual (e.g., Clara Watson) to demand that these assumptions be verified, particularly when the use of the device may be violating the Civil Rights Act.

Performance data often play a role in litigation for another reason as well. In criterion-related validity studies, one must be concerned with the integrity not only of the predictor(s) but also of any criterion used in calculating the validity coefficient. Consider what the "Uniform Guidelines" have to say about criteria:

> Whatever criteria are used should represent important or crucial work behavior(s) or work outcomes . . . The bases for the selection of the criterion measures should be provided, together with references to the evidence considered in making the selection of criterion measures. A full description of all criteria on which data were collected and means by which they were observed, recorded, evaluated, and quantified should be provided. If rating techniques are used as criterion measures, the appraisal form(s) and instructions to the raters should be provided as part of the validation evidence or should be explicitly described and available. All steps taken to insure that criterion measures are free from factors which would unfairly alter the scores of members of any group should be described. (Uniform Guidelines, 1978, pp. 38300-38301)

There is no mistaking the need for a well-developed measure of performance.

Several excellent reviews have been done that summarize the recent history of court cases in which the integrity of performance measures played a central role. The conclusions of those reviews are instructive. Feild and Holley (1980) looked at the question from the perspective of verdicts. They attempted to determine what factors in performance evaluation systems influenced a judgment for or against a defendant (i.e., management). Although their review dealt predominantly with performance ratings as evaluative devices, their conclusions might be generalized to all forms of performance measurement. They concluded that the critical factors were the type of organization, the presence of written instructions for the conduct of the performance evaluation, the extent to which the performance dimensions dealt with traits rather than behaviors, the extent to which the performance evaluation system was tied to a job analysis, and if the performance evaluation results were reviewed with the employee who was evaluated. In concrete terms, they concluded that if a performance evaluation system being considered was used by an industrial employer, if no job analysis was used to develop the evaluation system, if there were no written instructions for the procedure, if traits were considered rather than behaviors, and if the employee did not have an opportunity to review the evaluation, then a judgment would likely be given on behalf of the employee rather than the employer. Although they could not come to any conclusion about the *relative* importance of these factors, two things seem obvious. First, the absence of a good job analysis is probably a fatal flaw in any performance measurement system. No matter

TABLE 4–5

1. Purpose of the appraisal system (promotion versus layoffs, transfers, discharges, etc.)
2. Job analysis used as basis for development of the performance appraisal system
3. Type of appraisal system used (trait versus behavioral)
4. Presence of reliability information
5. Frequency of appraisals
6. Number of evaluators used for providing performance information
7. Presence of training programs for evaluators
8. Specific appraisal instructions given to performance evaluators
9. Provisions for discussion of evaluation results with employee
10. Evidence provided with respect to the validity of the appraisal system
11. Basis for employment discrimination charge (race versus sex)
12. Type of organization (industrial versus nonindustrial)
13. Geographical location of organization

SOURCE: From *The Measurement of Work Performance* (pp. 208–209) by F. J. Landy and J. L. Farr, 1983, New York: Academic Press.

what other factors are present or absent, if a job analysis has not been conducted, the performance measurement system will be viewed with great suspicion. In addition, even if a job analysis has been done, the integrity of the performance evaluation system will be eroded with the addition of each negative aspect. A system that has no written instructions *and* is trait based will be in greater jeopardy than one that is only missing adequate written instructions. The point is that a performance evaluation system that is deficient in some important respect is the equivalent of a cocked gun pointed at the employer.

Feild and Holley (1980) have identified factors in court decisions that may lead to a judgment for the employer or employee. Cascio and Bernardin (1981) completed an independent review of recent court cases involving performance appraisal and have shown how these court cases can be linked to principles or prescriptions for developing performance evaluation systems. They are able to show that a performance evaluation system that is developed according to sound psychological principles will also meet legal standards. The principles that they identify appear in Table 4–5.

They conclude that the integrity (and defensibility) of a performance evaluation system does not depend exclusively (or even predominantly) on physical characteristics such as format. Instead, they suggest that employers pay closer attention to the process by which these systems are developed, to the training and involvement of raters, and to the administration of the system as it is used on a day-to-day basis. This is good advice. A more recent review of similar data has been conducted by Kleiman and Faley (1985). The results confirm the earlier observations of both Feild and Holley (1980) and of Cascio and Bernardin (1981).

Challenges for Criterion Research

Performance measurement issues have generated a renewed enthusiasm for personnel psychology. This enthusiasm has provided some rather clear challenges for I/O psychologists. The challenges can be thought of as coming from two distinct directions: (1) the government and (2) the workers.

The Government. In the past two decades, the EEOC has become a pervading force in personnel psychology. The recently published guidelines for testing, constructed by a loose confederation of federal agencies ("Uniform Guidelines," 1978), have clearly placed a major emphasis on criterion development as a means of eliminating unfair hiring practices. In addition, it appears that if performance information is used to make promotional decisions, performance evaluation systems will have to be validated in much the same manner as selection systems. There are major disagreements among government agencies, private industry, and I/O psychologists concerning fair employment issues. Many of the disagreements center around issues such as job analysis and criterion development.

Comparable worth represents a clear challenge to the integrity of job analysis and job evaluation. The recent ruling in the state of Washington condemning past patterns of job segregation and wage inequities between male and female workers is a signal for renewed research and development in strategies for job analysis and evaluation. It would seem that techniques such as job evaluation are bound to be implicated in litigation dealing with patterns of discrimination in pay. As a result, it will be necessary to demonstrate the integrity of these methods and develop new techniques that will prevent future inequities based on irrelevant characteristics such as race, sex, or age.

The Workers. Perhaps a bigger challenge to the adequacy of criterion development and performance evaluation systems will be provided by the workers themselves. More and more, their discontent with many traditional personnel practices such as performance evaluation is surfacing. Too often, performance evaluation, as a device, has been used to justify an arbitrary personnel decision. In other instances, the performance information is religiously gathered and just as religiously ignored.

A great credibility gap is developing between what we say we are doing as professionals and the fruits of our work as seen by the worker. Most workers truly desire a fair and rational system of performance evaluation that will help them understand the relationship between their individual efforts and organizational goals. Unfortunately, their patience with such attempts may be wearing thin.

CENTRAL POINTS FOR STUDY

1. Criterion information can be used for selection, validation, compensation, training, motivation and satisfaction programs, and feedback.

2. Criteria should be valid and reliable.
3. Job analysis describes the important characteristics of a job.
4. Job evaluation places dollar values on jobs.
5. Performance evaluation identifies strengths and weaknesses of individual workers.
6. Performance data can come in the form of objective measures, personnel data, or judgments.
7. Multiple and composite criteria satisfy different purposes.
8. Performance measures, like predictors, may not unfairly discriminate against protected groups.

CHAPTER 5

Judgmental Measures of Performance

Performance judgments seem to be an almost natural act for most of us. We watch a football game and conclude that the quarterback had a bad day because he had lots of incomplete passes. We stop for a meal and leave the restaurant labeling the service "terrific." We listen to a lecture and later tell a friend that it was boring. Each of these is a judgment. We did not take the time to count the number of incomplete passes by the quarterback. In fact, since the incomplete passes might have been the fault of the receivers, it is interesting that we have no problem assigning the responsibility to the quarterback. In the restaurant, it might have been that the waiter smiled or that the beer was served within seconds after your order or that your coffee cup was filled without asking. All those things together resulted in your positive evaluation. The boring lecture could be the result of a monotone voice, dull material, or both. In each of these instances, we take in some information, combine it in particular ways, and end up with some judgment about the event or object that is a synthesis of any number of impressions.

Judgments also occur commonly at the workplace. Sometimes these judgments are informal and just represent your opinion of the performance level of a coworker or supervisor. No one asked you to make that evaluation, and no one is particularly interested in recording your judgment once you have made it. Most of the time you keep it to yourself. On the other hand, organizations often ask their members to judge and be judged. Owing to the fact that objective measures are often impossible to obtain, as well as the fact that they represent results of behavior rather than behavior itself, organizations must often depend on judgments to estimate the adequacy of performance. These judgments take several forms. They may be a simple comparison of one employee with another on one or more dimensions; they may be a list of statements that are applied to each employee; or they may be some form of rating by which the employee is placed on a continuum, the individual's position determined by the amount or degree of proficiency demonstrated. Occasionally, these judgments have rather dramatic consequences, such as those described in the article on page 129, which was taken from the *Chronicle of Higher Education* (1978).

Judges are often called on to evaluate intricate pieces of performance. (Penn State University)

Rating Scales

By far the most widely used judgmental measure is the rating scale. Guion (1965) reports that 81 percent of the validation studies reported in the *Journal of Applied Psychology* between January 1950 and July 1955 relied on some form of rating as the criterion. A review of the literature published since Guion's report show that performance ratings still play a major part in validation. (Landy and Rastegary, 1988)

Figure 5–1, taken from a book in personnel testing by Guion (1965), presents most of the common forms of rating scales. The scales can be distinguished from one another on three different dimensions: (1) the degree to which the meaning of the response categories is defined, (2) the degree to

Administrator Charged in Killing of Colleague

A University of Michigan administrator has been charged by police with shooting a colleague to death in a dispute over a job-performance evaluation.

Police said Donald Koos's uncomplimentary evaluation of William Aparicio's work apparently motivated Mr. Aparicio to kill the assistant director of the university's Neuro-Psychiatric Institute last week.

University officials said Mr. Koos, 30, and Mr. Aparicio, 46, had worked together for more than a year and seemed to get along well. Mr. Aparicio has been serving as the institute's administrative manager.

Police believe Mr. Aparicio learned recently that he had been turned down in his bid to become the institute's top administrator and that he blamed his rejection on an assessment of his performance by Mr. Koos, also a candidate for the job.

which the person interpreting the ratings (e.g., personnel manager) can tell what response was intended by the rater, and (3) the degree to which the performance dimension rated is defined for the rater.

The first dimension, the ambiguity of the response categories, is usually handled through the process of "anchoring." Anchors are placed along a rating scale to define each of the response categories. Just as a ruler is marked off in inches or millimeters, the rating scale must be marked off in units of some type that allow the rater to make meaningful statements about the performance of individuals. These anchors are extremely important. Rating scale *(a)* in Figure 5–1 is an example of the use of "end anchors" without accompanying numerical anchors, whereas scale *(b)* has qualitative "end anchors" as well as numerical anchors. These anchors are of little use, since the interpretation of what characterizes high and low quality is left completely up to the rater. Scale *(c)* specifies more clearly what is meant by each of the categories on the scale; the same is true of scale *(h)*. Consider for yourself the potential ease encountered in using scale *(h)* as opposed to scale *(a)*.

The second major descriptive characteristic of rating scales is the degree to which the person interpreting the ratings can tell what response was intended. Another name for this characteristic is *response clarity*. If your task were to determine what value the rater had in mind, you would probably find that scales *(e)*, *(f)*, and *(g)* were easier to work with than scales *(a)*, *(b)*, *(c)*, *(d)*, and *(i)*.

The third characteristic is the degree to which the performance dimension rated is defined for the rater. Consider all the possible interpretations that raters might apply to the term *quality of work*. This allows for the possibility that a set of ratings on workers might be worthless because they are based on different interpretations by various raters of the dimensions to be consid-

FIGURE 5–1 Examples of Graphic Rating Scales

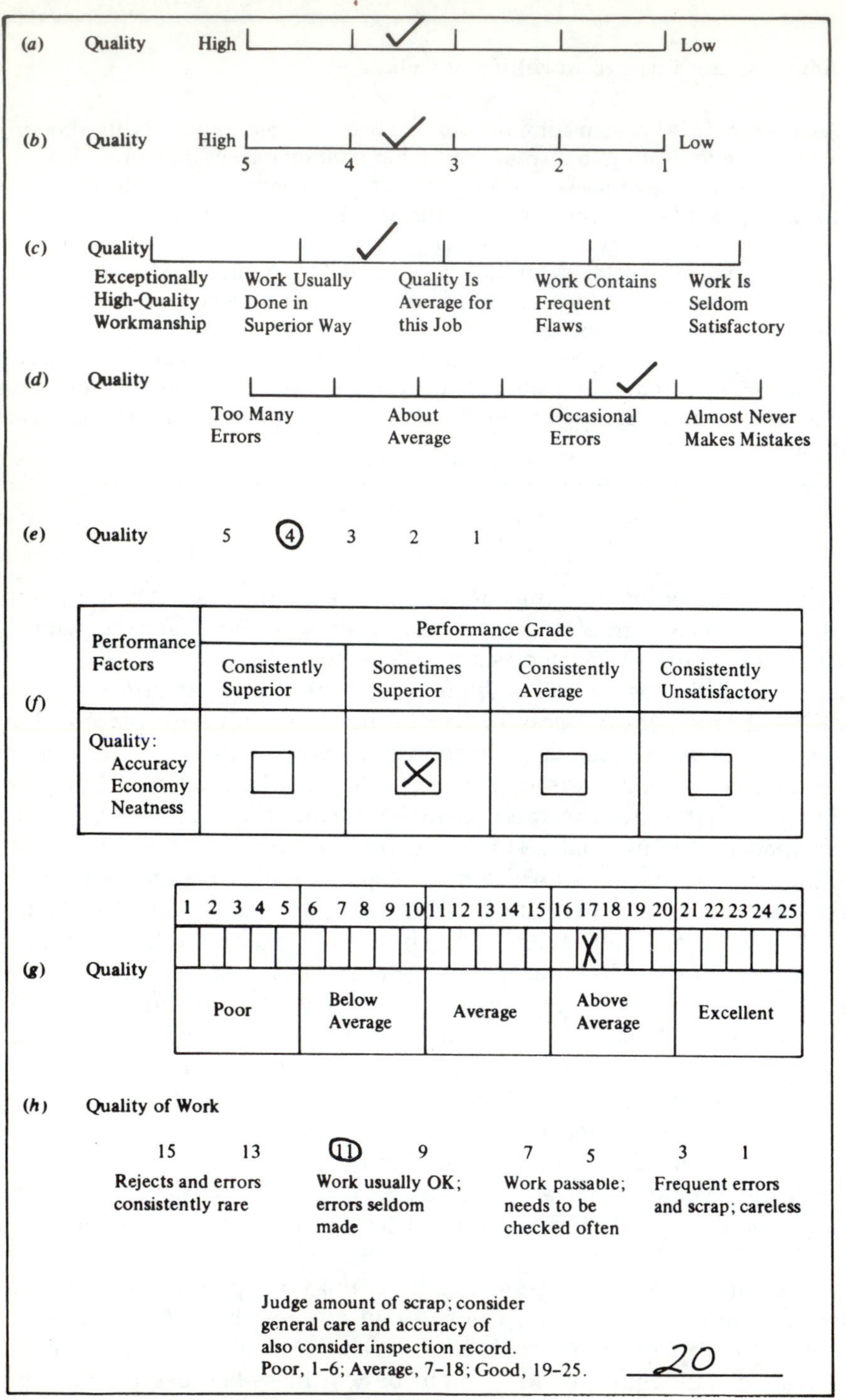

SOURCE: From *Personnel Testing* by R. M. Guion, 1965, New York: McGraw-Hill.

FIGURE 5–2 Graphic Description of Leniency Error on Hypothetical 5-Point Rating Scale: Positive (+) and Negative (−)

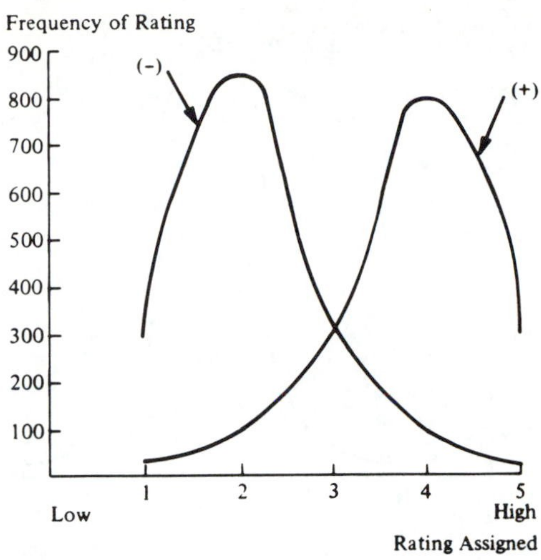

ered. Scales *(a)*, *(b)*, *(e)*, and *(g)* give little or no structure to the rater regarding the performance dimension to be rated. On the other hand, scales *(f)* and *(i)*, and to a certain degree *(c)* and *(h)*, give the rater a pretty good idea of what performance dimension is being considered.

Rating Errors. It should be possible to see from the description of the various types of rating scales how ambiguity can lead to errors in ratings that make them useless. These errors can be placed into three major categories: leniency-severity errors, halo errors, and central tendency errors. Figures 5–2 and 5–3 depict leniency-severity and central tendency errors.

Leniency-Severity Errors. It is common to encounter raters who would be described as unusually harsh (severe) or unusually easy (lenient) in their ratings. The harsh individual tends to give ratings that are lower than the average level of the subordinates on the rated dimension. The easy individual tends to give ratings that are higher than the average level of subordinates. In other words, if one could accurately measure the amount of a given attribute in a group of ratees, the ratings of the harsh rater could be consistently lower than the actual amount of the attribute possessed by the ratees, whereas the ratings of the easy rater would be consistently higher. These kinds of errors usually come about because the rater is applying personal standards to the rating scale. For example, the anchor "excellent" may have completely different meanings to different raters. Two suggestions have been offered to eliminate these errors: (1) a forced distribution in which the rater is required

FIGURE 5–3 Graphic Description of Central Tendency Error on Hypothetical 5-Point Rating Scale

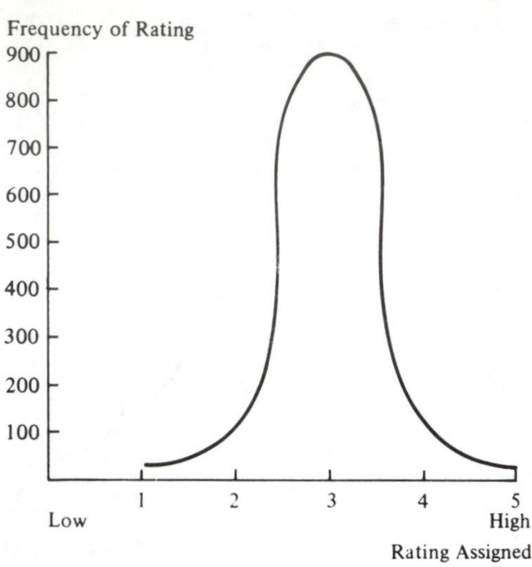

to allocate the ratings so that a given percentage of the ratees fall in the top category, a given percentage in the next category, and so on; and (2) a reduction in the degree of ambiguity of the scales by improving the definition of the dimension and the nature of the anchors. The second suggestion is somewhat easier to implement than the first. The forced distribution implies some knowledge of what the distribution should look like or how the attribute should be distributed in the ratees. This type of knowledge is not easily acquired, and raters frequently object to being told that "10 percent of your ratees must be rated poor [or excellent]."

Halo Errors. The term *halo* is meant to imply that there is a general aura surrounding all the individual judgments that are made about a given worker. The rater has a generally favorable or unfavorable impression of the ratee. Ratings are then assigned that are consistent with the impression. Halo errors may also come into play when a rater feels that a particular dimension of performance is extremely important. Ratings are then assigned on the other dimensions that are consistent with the rating on the most important one. Forced distributions of ratings may be of little value, since the rater is still free to distribute ratees on the basis of overall impressions of favorability. One method that has been suggested for the solution of this problem is to rate all the ratees on one trait, then all of them on another, until all ratees have been rated on all traits or dimensions. The hope is that the rater will be able to distinguish between dimensions if forced to consider all the ratees on one dimension at a time. It might also be that the problem lies in the definition of the dimensions for the raters. If the dimensions were clearly defined and anchored, the raters would be less likely to depend on overall impressions.

Central Tendency Errors. Central tendency error is characterized by an unwillingness on the part of the rater to assign extreme ratings—either extremely high or extremely low. This error has a potentially serious effect on attempts to establish empirical validity for selection devices. Since the range of variability is restricted on the criterion (see Figure 5–3), the value of the obtained validity coefficient may be drastically reduced. Once again, the forced distribution method has been suggested as a way of eliminating central tendency errors. Central tendency error often appears when raters are required to "justify" above average or below average ratings with a paragraph describing the behavior of the person in question. In such a case, the rater can reduce any hassle or potential problems by just giving an average rating, thus creating the central tendency problem. A recent article in the *Washington Post* highlights some of the administrative problems that surround appraisal in the real world.

Attempts have been made to minimize the effects of halo, leniency-severity, and central tendency errors by using alternative evaluation schemes. Two of the most popular of these alternatives have been the employee comparison methods and the forced-choice checklist.

Employee Comparison Methods

The two most widely used employee comparison methods are the *ranking* procedure and the *pair-comparison* procedure. In the ranking procedure, the rater simply arranges the set of ratees in rank order from high to low on a given dimension of performance. This process can be simplified by using an alternating procedure in which the rater picks out the best and the worst worker, sets them aside, then picks out the best and worst from the remaining set of names until all the ratees are ranked. One of the problems introduced by the use of this method is the nature of the data that result from the ranking. It is of little use to know that an individual is ranked third of 30 on some performance dimension unless you have some notion of whether that represents adequate, good, or bad performance. Rankings do not give you that information. Another criticism of the ranking methods currently in use is that the ranking is usually done on one overall suitability category. When more than one dimension is used, ranking may suffer from halo error to the same degree as rating scales.

Instead of simply ranking the workers on an absolute basis, or using an alternating ranking procedure, each individual may be compared with every other individual in the set to be evaluated. The number of resulting pairs can be calculated from the formula $n(n - 1)/2$, where n = the number of people to be evaluated. If there are 10 people to be evaluated, there will be 45 pairs. The task of the evaluator is to choose the better of each pair. Each

THE FEDERAL DIARY
2nd Look at Job Ratings

By Mike Causey,
Washington Post Staff Writer

Bosses who give subordinates job ratings that could deny them raises or promotions or result in pink slips can be ordered by an arbitrator to review and upgrade performance appraisals, according to a new decision by the Federal Labor Relations Authority.

The decision, which the government may challenge in court, says that performance appraisals deemed unfair or illegal by arbitrators can be sent back to agencies with instructions to change them.

Every year each of the government's million-plus white-collar workers is supposed to get a performance rating. Some bosses spend considerable time on the procedure. Others consider it to be such a hassle that they leave the job to subordinates or give everybody the same satisfactory rating.

While the procedure varies by agency, appraisals generally are based in part on guidelines established for particular job and grade levels, and also on how well the boss thinks employees have met mutually agreed goals for the year.

Typically, performance appraisal systems have six levels: "Outstanding, exceeds fully successful, fully successful, minimally successful, unacceptable" or a "not rated," or similar terms.

Workers who get any of the top three ratings qualify for within grade (seniority) pay raises and promotions and get job retention points that agencies consider when undergoing layoffs. The vast majority of all federal workers are rated "fully successful" or better.

Many workers contend that the rating system makes it easy for bosses to play favorites or unfairly punish employees whose work is good but who may have personality clashes with their superior. Many bosses say that the complexity of the procedures and the backlash when they rate a problem worker poorly make it conducive to giving everyone the same rating.

The Federal Labor Relations Authority's decision came in a job rating challenge brought by the American Federation of Government Employees union against a Social Security Administration supervisor in Baltimore. SSA had no comment on the overall effect of the ruling, or whether it would comply with the arbitrator's order to review and upgrade the performance rating.

SOURCE: "2nd Look at Job Ratings" by M. Causey, February 5, 1988, *Washington Post*, Metro Section, p. 2.

person's rank is defined as the total number of times that person was chosen as the better of the pair. As in the ranking procedures, in most instances a global dimension of suitability is used as the criterion for making the choice.

The employee comparison methods have the following weaknesses. First,

FIGURE 5–4 Summated Checklist

	*Scale Value**
Statements checked for Officer Smith	
Goes out of the way to help the public	4.3
Is occasionally sarcastic with juveniles	1.9
Keeps equipment in top shape	3.2
Total for Officer Smith	9.4
Statements checked for Officer Jones	
Can be counted on to "back up" fellow officer	4.2
Fails to keep gun clean and well oiled	1.4
Takes continuing education courses in law enforcement on own time	4.6
Total for Officer Jones	10.2

*Highest statement value possible = 5; lowest statement value possible = 1.

comparability of evaluations across groups of locations is often lacking; for example, there is no assurance that the top-ranking individual in one group is comparable with the top-ranking individual in another. Second, the use of one global dimension may yield information that is unsuitable for making specific personnel decisions such as job changes. Third, as the number of individuals in the group becomes larger, the task becomes more tedious. For example, if one were to use a pair-comparison format in a work group with 15 individuals, 105 separate comparisons would be necessary.

Checklist

Another major category of judgmental data is the checklist. In the checklist, a set of statements is presented to the rater. The rater's task is to check those items that best (or sometimes, least) describe the person to be rated. Each of these items has been judged; a numerical value representing the degree of performance represented by that particular statement has been determined. In one treatment of checklist responses, known as *summated ratings,* the numerical values of each of the statements checked are added to yield a total score for the individual. An example of such a procedure is presented in Figure 5–4.

One variation on this basic theme is the *forced-choice format.* In the general checklist approach as described, the rater is not required to check any of the statements. Consequently, the rater may choose those items to check that have high social desirability but say little about performance. In an effort to

FIGURE 5–5 Example of Forced-Choice Item for Describing Performance of College Teachers

a. Is impatient with slow learners
b. Lectures with confidence
c. Acquaints class with objectives for each class in advance
d. Does not tell enough jokes

avoid such nondiscriminating responses and possibly to identify those raters who were giving socially desirable responses, an effort was made to introduce socially desirable items systematically into the evalulation procedure. The forced-choice format usually presents the rater with a group of statements that have been judged previously for social desirability as well as for their ability to discriminate good from poor performance. The rater is asked to pick two of four statements that best describe the ratee; or the rater might be asked to pick the statements *most* and *least* descriptive of an individual. An example of a set of forced-choice statements appears in Figure 5–5. Items *a* and *c* have been found to distinguish between the good and poor college instructor; items *b* and *d* do not distinguish the good from the poor instructor but are high and low, respectively, on social desirability. Since the rater must choose two statements—and it would be logically difficult to choose both the desirable *and* the undesirable items—at least one discriminating item is usually chosen. The forced format was originally introduced in an attempt to reduce or control leniency error and has had some success in accomplishing that end.

One of the problems with the forced-choice method is that it is not constructed to give diagnostic information. The rater does not know the scale values of the items chosen—this is an important aspect of the method—therefore, the method cannot provide a basis for appraisal feedback from the rater to the ratee. Instead, the scales are usually directed at providing some index of overall performance. The major stumbling block to developing sets of items for each of several dimensions is the time involved in writing and scaling items that are both matched on desirability and have adequate power of discrimination.

New Methods of Obtaining Judgments

Mixed Standard Rating Scales. A variation on the rating format that has been introduced by Blanz and Ghiselli (1972) is known as the mixed standard scale. In this procedure, items that discriminate good from poor performance are obtained from experts (usually supervisors). Subsequently, three items are chosen to form a scale for a particular performance dimension. One of the items represents good performance, one represents average performance, and one represents poor performance. These items are randomly mixed with items from scales measuring other dimensions. We present an example of a mixed standard scale format used in the measurement of police performance. The letters to the left of the items correspond to the performance dimension. Dimension *A* is *judgment*, dimension *B* is *knowledge*, and dimension *C* is *relation with others*. The instructions and the items given to the rater are as follows.

> Listed below are a number of descriptions of behavior relevant to the job of patrol officer. Your task is to examine each example carefully and then to determine in your own mind the answer to the following question: Is the patrol officer to be rated "better than this statement," "worse than this statement," or "does this statement fit this patrol officer?"
>
> If you believe that the person you are rating is "better than the statement," put a + in the space to the right of the statement. If you believe that the person is "worse than the statement," put a − in that space. If you believe that the statement "fits" the patrol officer, put a 0 in that space.
>
> Be sure that you write either a +, a −, or a 0 after each of the statements listed below.

		Rating
(*B*)	1. The officer could be expected to misinform the public on legal matters through lack of knowledge. (*P*)	+
(*C*)	2. The officer could be expected to take the time to answer a rookie's question carefully. (*G*)	0
(*B*)	3. This patrol officer never has to ask others about points of law. (*G*)	−
(*A*)	4. The officer could be expected to refrain from writing tickets for traffic violations that occur at a particular intersection that is unusually confusing to motorists. (*G*)	+
(*A*)	5. The patrol officer could be expected to call for assistance and clear the area of bystanders before confronting a barricaded, heavily armed suspect. (*A*)	+
(*C*)	6. The officer could be expected to use racially toned language in front of minority group members. (*P*)	+
(*B*)	7. This officer follows correct procedures for evidence preservation at the scene of a crime. (*A*)	0
(*A*)	8. The patrol officer could be expected to continue to write a traffic violation in spite of hearing a report of a nearby robbery in progress. (*P*)	+
(*C*)	9. This officer is considered friendly by the other officers on the shift. (*A*)	+

The letters *G*, *A*, and *P* immediately following the statements indicate whether the item describes good, average, or poor performance. In practice, the rater is not told which item relates to which scale or the level of performance represented by each item. The scoring scheme for the format is presented in Table 5–1. From this scheme, we derive the following scores for the hypothetical patrol officer rated above. On dimension *A*, judgment, the

TABLE 5–1 Mixed Standard Scoring

Descriptive Statements			
G	*A*	*P*	*Points*
+	+	+	7
0	+	+	6
−	+	+	5
−	0	+	4
−	−	+	3
−	−	0	2
−	−	−	1

\+ = The ratee is better than the statement.
0 = The statement fits the ratee.
− = The ratee is worse than the statement.

officer receives a score of 7; on dimension *B*, job knowledge, the score is 4; on dimension *C*, relations with others, the hypothetical patrol officer received a rating of 6. It should be obvious that not all raters will respond as logically as our hypothetical rater. For example, the rater might have said that the ratee was better than the good statement but worse than the average statement. In that case, the scoring scheme presented in Table 5–1 would not apply. Blanz and Ghiselli have extended their scoring scheme to include such rating errors, and alternative error scoring schemes have been developed (Saal, 1979).

The logic for the mixed standard format is derived from some early findings indicating that halo errors are smaller when ratings are not made on an obvious scale. The random arrangement of performance statements is thought to make it difficult for the rater to determine what the exact nature of the performance scale is, that is, what order of merit each of the statements represents. Such a random arrangement is thought to lead to fewer halo and leniency errors.

Aside from the reduction of some traditional rating errors, one of the proposed strengths of the mixed standard format may be that it provides an opportunity to identify those raters who are making logical errors. A rating error implies that the rater is not using the scale as it was intended. If many raters have many errors, it is likely the fault of the scale and the way in which the three statements were derived and arranged. If few raters make few errors, or a few raters are responsible for many errors, the problem is likely to be centered in the rater rather than in the scale for measuring performance.

Recent data suggest that the number of errors or inconsistent responses made in the use of the mixed standard scale is substantial. Barnes-Farrell and Weiss (1984) found that 50 percent of the raters made one or more errors in using the scale. Prien and Hughes (1987) found an even larger percentage of rater errors—70 percent. The purpose of the Prien and Hughes study was to see if the errors could be reduced by improving the scales that the raters used. As a result, they evaluated consecutive administrations of the mixed standard scales. After the first administration (in which they obtained the 70 percent error rate), they examined the various scales to see which yielded the greatest number of errors. After identifying those scales, they improved the actual statements or anchors that were used and formed a revised set of scales. These revised scales were readministered and the error rates recalculated. The error rate dropped from 70 percent to 50 percent in the second administration. This seems like an instance of winning the battle but losing the war. Even though the error rate was reduced, it was still enormously high. In addition, few employers will be willing to go through the effort expended by Prien and Hughes to revise and readminister rating scales. The study seems to be saying that efforts in initially developing high-quality scale anchors will have payoffs in the quality of eventual ratings. In summary, it is difficult to generate much enthusiasm for the mixed standard scale until there is a better understanding of why so many inconsistent responses (logical errors) appear.

Behaviorally Anchored Scales. Another variation in rating scales was introduced in 1963 by Smith and Kendall. In an attempt to develop scales that had unambiguous anchors, they developed a procedure for constructing a performance scale based on Flanagan's (1954) work with "critical incidents." Critical incidents are examples of behavior that appeared *critical* in determining whether performance would be good, average, or poor. The logic of the procedure is that anchors on rating scales should be statements that can discriminate the good from the poor performer. Based on that assumption, groups of judges are asked to provide examples of behavior that characterize the high, the average, and the low performer on some aspect of job behavior.

It might be best in this instance to put the cart before the horse and present examples of the end products or the behaviorally anchored scales, then describe how they were constructed. Figure 5–6 describes a scale used to measure performance of fire fighters. If you go back to our earlier discussion of the adequacy of rating scales, you can see that these scales have the potential for satisfying the three criteria. The dimensions are well defined for the rater, the anchors adequately define the response categories of the scale, and depending on rating instructions, the response made by the rater is well defined.

The procedure is tedious and occasionally expensive. A brief summary of the steps involved in constructing a behaviorally anchored scale such as the one in Figure 5–6 will shed some light on this practical difficulty.

Constructing a Behaviorally Anchored Scale. To construct a behaviorally anchored scale, groups of workers, supervisors, or both are gathered together for group conferences in which they attempt to identify and define

FIGURE 5–6 Behaviorally Anchored Rating Scale for Fire Fighters

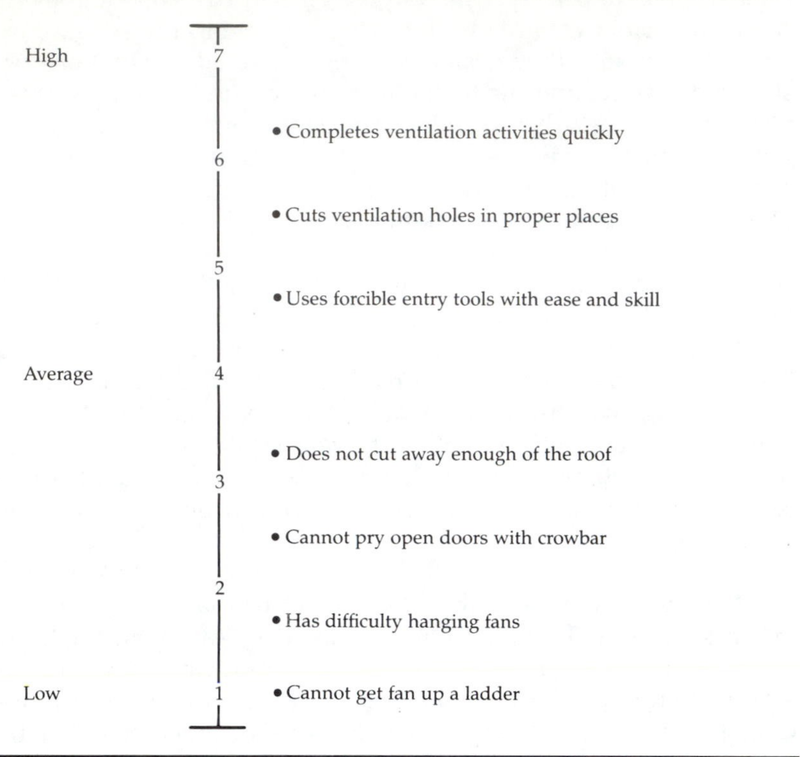

all the important aspects necessary for successful performance on a particular job. Next, a second group is asked to take the aspects as they have been defined by the first group and provide examples of high, average, and low performance on each of the aspects of performance. Then, a third group is given a list of each of the aspects and a randomized list of the examples provided by the second group. They are asked to place or allocate each example in the category or aspect for which it is written. This is known as *retranslation*. It resembles the quality control check often used to determine whether a translation from one language to another is an adequate one. If examples cannot be allocated to the category for which they are written, they do not represent unambiguous anchors and should not be used.

A fourth group is then asked to consider each of the examples that survived the retranslation and place a scale value on it, indicating the level of performance on a particular aspect that that example represents. The means and standard deviations are then computed, and items are chosen for the scale that have the following properties: (1) they have mean values that provide anchors for the entire scale, and (2) they have low standard deviations.

If an item has a high standard deviation, it means that judges cannot agree on the level of performance that the example represents, and if they cannot agree, the eventual raters will also probably disagree. The item is then discarded because the level of performance it represents is not clear.

Finally, the resulting scales are administered to a sample of supervisors who are asked to rate the performance of their subordinates on each of the scales. Each subordinate is rated independently by two supervisors, and the ratings of those supervisors are correlated to provide an estimate of interrater reliability. In addition, the scale scores are intercorrelated to provide an estimate of the degree to which each of the scales is measuring some unique aspect of performance.

This process can take many months and involve large numbers of people. Consequently, it may not be practical for many organizations to undertake such a project by themselves. On the other hand, as the procedure grows in popularity, it is likely that scales will be developed that will have wide generality and can be used in many different settings. For example, I have used behaviorally anchored scales developed in one police department for measuring the performance of officers in a second police department. The same has been true for scales developed for measuring fire fighter performance. The only modifications have involved minor changes in language. This has been possible because the job analyses in these cities have demonstrated that the job in question (e.g., police officer) is performed in a highly similar manner in the two cities.

One of the major advantages of this procedure may have nothing to do with the measurement of performance per se. The degree of involvement of the workers and supervisors in the procedure is very high. In the process of developing the scales, the participants are required to take a long, hard look at performance as it is behaviorally defined. In doing this, they are required to drop many inaccurate stereotypes of the unsuccessful worker. They are no longer permitted simply to label someone as a "loser." They must now describe this individual in terms of what actually qualifies him or her for the "loser" category. It would appear that the procedure provides excellent rater training as well as good rating scales. As we will see later in the chapter, several successful rater training programs depend on the same principles as those used to develop behaviorally anchored rating scales.

Another advantage of the procedure is that it seems to have face validity for both the rater and the person rated. This is due to the fact that the anchors consist of behaviors that subordinates and supervisors have already identified as critical. In addition, these examples are presented in the language of the worker rather than the language of the psychologist or personnel director. After administering behaviorally anchored rating scales as part of a research project, I have often been asked by supervisors if they could keep the scale booklets to help them fairly evaluate subordinates in the future in an actual operational setting. Some have even asked if they could take the form home to show a spouse because the scales do an excellent job of illuminating the complexity of their jobs.

A Comparison of Behaviorally Anchored Scales with Other Formats. Because of the time and expense involved in constructing this type of scale, it is reasonable to expect that behaviorally anchored scales would have some advantage over other methods. Even though the logic on which the system is based is compelling, the results have been disappointing. There have been several extensive reviews of the relative advantages of the behaviorally anchored system, and the conclusion seems to be that they are not much better than carefully constructed graphic scales or summated checklists (Bernardin, 1977; Bernardin, Alvares, & Cranny, 1976; Landy & Farr, 1980, 1983; Schwab, Heneman, & DeCotiis, 1975). There may be a hidden blessing in this finding that supports the use of behaviorally anchored scales. The procedures for scale construction, as described, almost guarantee that the scales will be carefully developed. This is not the case with other formats. It is relatively simple for a manager to develop his own graphic form using sloppy procedures and gather suitably sloppy performance measures. At least the behaviorally anchored scales ensure some quality control in the final product. Thus, it may be that in spite of the fact that well-developed graphic rating scales are as resistant to error as behaviorally anchored scales, it is harder to construct a *good graphic rating scale* than it is to develop a *good behaviorally anchored scale*.

Recently, K. R. Murphy and Constans (1987) have sounded a note of caution in the use of behaviorally anchored rating scales. They discovered that behavioral anchors such as those found on behaviorally anchored rating scales may actually *create* distortions. They carefully constructed some videotaped depictions of performance with various examples of good and bad behavior embedded in those videotapes. They discovered that if a rater saw an actual example of behavior that was listed as a scale anchor on the videotape, this behavioral incident had a substantial influence on the ratings given to the person on the videotape. At first glance, this might seem to be an appropriate use of the rating scales. The problem was that even if the behavior was uncharacteristic of the rest of the behavior seen on the videotape, the rater could clearly remember the particular incident when using the rating scale and tended to rate the person at the level occupied by that incident on the scale. Thus, if the specific incident was an example of good behavior (even if the general level of performance was poor), the rater assigned the ratee a rating close to that good example or anchor. Similarly, if the specific incident was an example of poor behavior (even if the general level of performance was good), a poor rating was assigned. Murphy and Constans do not conclude that behaviorally anchored scales should not be used. Rather, they suggest that the anchors be chosen carefully to be truly representative (i.e., commonly encountered examples) of various levels of performance. Nevertheless, they do point to a particular weakness that could affect the value of behaviorally anchored rating scales.

Behavioral Observation Scales. Even before the research of Murphy and Constans (1987), there had been some misgivings about the use of behaviorally anchored rating scales. Traditionally, the anchors include the phrase "expected to" as is the case with the scales illustrated in Figure 5–6. This represents a problem to the rater since the ratee may never have had an opportunity to perform in a way described by the anchor. Murphy and Constans demonstrate that the opposite situation could also be a problem—seeing the exact behavior that appears as a scale anchor—even though it may be unrepresentative.

From a legal standpoint, the fact that you may never actually see a worker perform the behaviors that appear as anchors may create an additional problem, particularly if the performance rating will be used to make a personnel decision such as termination, promotion, or merit pay award. The *Watson v. Fort Worth Bank and Trust* (1988) Supreme Court case mentioned in the last chapter will focus close attention on performance evaluation from the legal perspective based on the opinion issued by the justices. Since the scales are really directed toward hypothetical or future behavior, the ratee is being considered in the abstract rather than in the concrete. The "Uniform Guidelines" (1978) are less than enthusiastic about such an abstract treatment of the employee when concrete decisions are being made. For these and other more technical reasons, a new method of performance rating called the *Behavioral Observation Scales (BOS)* was introduced by Latham and his colleagues (Latham, Fay, & Saari, 1979; Latham & Wexley, 1977). The BOS method is similar to the Behaviorally Anchored Rating Scales (BARS) method in some respects. As is the case with BARS, the scales are formed from the initial recording of critical incidents, that is, those instances of worker behavior that seem to make the difference between success and failure. In addition, the actual scale anchors are suggested and written by incumbents and their supervisors. This makes the anchors more meaningful for the raters. There is one critical difference between the BARS and BOS methods, however. In BARS use the rater identifies a point on the performance continuum that represents his or her judgment concerning how effective the ratee is on the dimension in question. In addition, the BARS scales ask the rater to consider what the ratee might be *expected* to do.

In contrast to the BARS method, the BOS method asks the rater to consider how frequently the ratee has been observed behaving in a particular manner. An example of a BOS scale appears in Figure 5–7. As you can see, there are five categories to choose from. These categories range from "almost never" (1) to "almost always" (5). The logic of this type of scale is that the better performers will be seen engaged in behaviors critical to success more frequently than the poorer performers. The full set of BOS scales may cover several different aspects of performance. For example, there might be three scales similar to the one illustrated above that measure communication skills, two scales that tap interpersonal skills, four scales that ask for ratings of decision-making skills, and three scales that measure skill in meeting dead-

FIGURE 5–7 Example of One BOS Criterion or Performance Dimension for Evaluating Managers

1. Overcoming Resistance to Change*

(1)	Describes the details of the change to subordinates						
	Almost Never	1	2	3	4	5	Almost Always
(2)	Explains why the change is necessary						
	Almost Never	1	2	3	4	5	Almost Always
(3)	Discusses how the change will affect the employee						
	Almost Never	1	2	3	4	5	Almost Always
(4)	Listens to the employee's concerns						
	Almost Never	1	2	3	4	5	Almost Always
(5)	Asks the employee for help in making the change work						
	Almost Never	1	2	3	4	5	Almost Always
(6)	If necessary, specifies the date for a follow-up meeting to respond to the employee's concerns						
	Almost Never	1	2	3	4	5	Almost Always
	Total = ________						

Below Adequate	*Adequate*	*Full*	*Excellent*	*Superior**
6–10	11–15	16–20	21–25	26–30

*Scores are set by management.

SOURCE: From G.P. Latham and K.N. Wexley, *Increasing Productivity Through Performance Appraisal*, copyright 1981, Addison-Wesley Publishing Co., Inc., Reading, Massachusetts. Fig. 3.8 on page 56. Reprinted with permission.

lines. This could result in four scores—communication skills, interpersonal skills, decision-making skills, and ability to meet deadlines. In addition, one could calculate an overall performance score by adding or averaging the four dimension scores. Since every ratee is considered on every scale, this method is similar to the summated checklist procedure we considered earlier. This means that ratees can be compared with one another on each dimension and on overall scores.

On the surface, this method would seem to solve some of the problems that are present in other methods, particularly the expectation emphasis of the BARS method. It also seems clear that such a rating technique might solve the problem highlighted by Murphy and Constans since the rater would be required to assign a frequency rating to each behavioral anchor. On the other hand, this problem may remain if only one of the anchors is apparent in the recent work of the employee. The rater might simply overestimate the frequency of that behavior. Social cognition theory (Nisbett & Ross, 1980) suggests that there are several cognitive mechanisms working to exaggerate the representativeness of recent and concrete behavioral examples. In addition, Latham and Wexley (1977) suggest that the method should be preferred over others because it can be accomplished with less effort and in less time by the raters. They say that "this decrease in the number of items required for appraisal is extremely important for managers who often complain that they do not have enough time to conduct lengthy performance appraisal sessions" (p. 264). In spite of these presumed advantages, the BOS seems to have as many shortcomings as the methods it purports to replace. The first problem is related to the response categories. A rating of 3 (74 to 85 percent) might be an indication of outstanding performance if the behavior being observed is winning a 10-kilometer road race. On the other hand, if the behavior being observed is turning off the headlights of the car when parking, then the ratee would be spending a good deal of time waiting for road service. The same percentage or frequency can mean many different things (Bernardin & Kane, 1980).

A second problem with the BOS method is suggested by the research of K. R. Murphy, Martin, and Garcia (1982). They had students consider the teaching behavior of instructors on a videotape. The students provided two types of performance evaluation—traditional trait ratings and BOS ratings. Immediately after viewing the tapes, the correlation between the performance ratings using the two different methods was significantly lower than the correlation one day later. This means that over the space of one day, BOS judgments "degenerated" in the memory of the student rater. Murphy et al. conclude that any BOS advantage disappears quickly (e.g., in less than 24 hours). This is a serious problem since most performance evaluations are done after observing behavior for six months to one year. Loftus (1975), Bransford, and Franks (1971), and other cognitive psychologists have clearly demonstrated that memory is constructive; that is, after we store information in memory, things continue to happen to that information. The BOS method does not eliminate that type of cognitive influence.

The final problem with BOS scales is more basic and represents a personal bias of mine. I have carefully considered the research to date in performance evaluation generally and in performance rating specifically (Landy & Farr, 1980, 1983). One major conclusion to be drawn from this research is that there is no "easy way" to get accurate and informative performance information. Methods that aim toward easing the pain for managers who are busy will pay a price in terms of the accuracy and value of the information obtained. The research record suggests that if basic requirements of good measurement are present, formats and mechanical techniques play a minor role in shaping performance judgments. This is as true of BARS and mixed standard scales as it is of the BOS approach. As I will suggest shortly, improving performance evaluation is more likely to depend on a better understanding of cognitive processes of raters (such as memory and reasoning) than on the construction of "better" performance scales. Recently, Wiersma and Latham (1986) have suggested that the BOS method is more acceptable to users and lawyers who must defend it. There is no doubt that evaluation techniques should be acceptable to those who will use them, but the fact remains that it is the job of the scientist to develop scales of high integrity. It is the job of the consultant to keep clients happy.

Factors Affecting Rating

It is not unusual to hear people complain about performance ratings they have received. The most common complaint is that the ratings are "unfair" in some respect. They may feel that either their personality or the personality of the rater has played an inappropriate role in the evaluation of their performance. They may feel that their supervisor has not had sufficient opportunity really to observe their day-to-day performance. They may also feel the rating process works against them since the supervisor is asked to complete ratings on 15 people in one day, thus limiting the attention paid to any individual.

There has been a good deal of research that supports the feelings of these "complainers" as well as research that is at odds with their assumptions. As an example, Schoorman (1988) demonstrated that supervisors who played a role in the selection of an employee and had suggested that the individual be hired rated that same individual higher when evaluating the employee's performance at some later time. Conversely, if the supervisor had been against hiring the individual but had been overruled, the supervisor assigned lower ratings when evaluating the performance of this employee at some later time.

Even a brief examination of rating research demonstrates that the process of performance rating is incredibly complex, with many opportunities for the ratings to be influenced by factors other than the performance of the person rated. Jim Farr and I have reviewed this research extensively (Landy & Farr, 1980, 1983) and have proposed a model that purports to describe the task of performance rating from a process perspective. This model appears in Figure 5–8. When I presented this model several years ago, a colleague suggested that it looked more like a diagram of the plumbing in a Scottish castle than a model of behavior. It does bear some similarities to plumbing. It is a flowchart, and it does have the characteristics of a closed system. Fortunately, it also differs in certain important respects from the plumbing metaphor. Each component of our model has a research history to it. As an example, consider Table 5–2, which I have adapted from our review (Landy & Farr, 1983). There are dozens of studies that have dealt with characteristics of raters. These studies allow the conclusions that appear in the table. (The particular studies are identified in the table from which this table was adapted.) One thing to keep in mind when considering this model is that the goal of performance rating is to provide an accurate performance description of the person in

FIGURE 5–8 A Process Model of Performance Rating

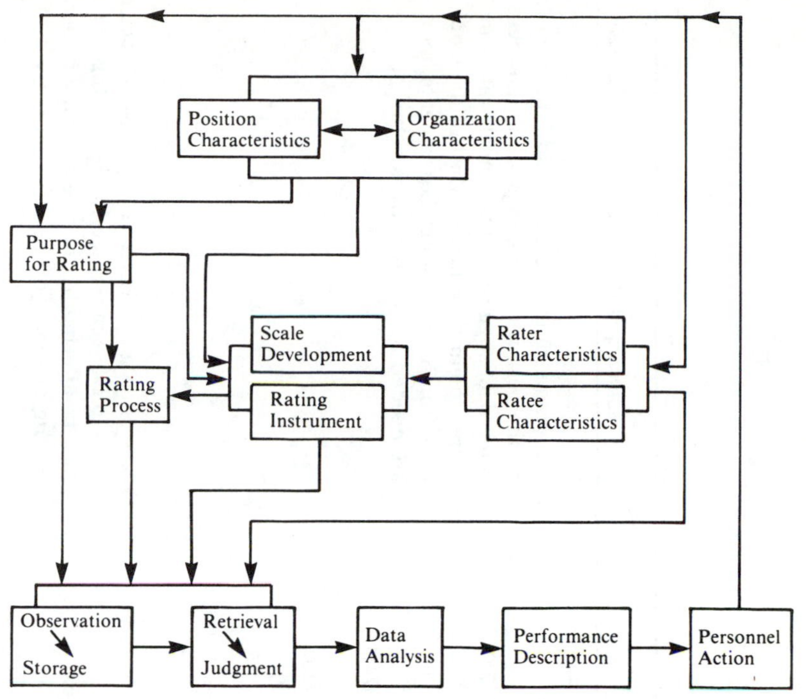

SOURCE: From "Performance Rating" by F. J. Landy and J. L. Farr, 1980, *87,* p. 94. Copyright 1980 by the American Psychological Association. Reprinted by permission of the publisher and author.

question. In the model (Figure 5–8), this is represented as the box on the right-hand side labeled "Performance Description." Most of the other boxes might be thought of as potential obstacles to accurate performance description. I will describe some of them below.

Rater Characteristics. The rater possesses certain characteristics that may be related to sets or biases brought to the rating task—for example, dislike for women or younger employees or Catholics. These biases may influence the ratings assigned to members of the classes the rater dislikes.

Ratee Characteristics. In addition to the general sets that a rater might have for or against particular groups, ratees "possess" certain characteristics that they carry with them from job to job and setting to setting. The characteristic we are most interested in is their level of performance. Nevertheless, ratees have other accidental characteristics such as sex, age, and race that are their individual properties, not properties of raters.

As the figure indicates, these two boxes meet or interact. It is this *inter-*

TABLE 5–2 Studies Investigating Rater Characteristics

Variable Investigated	*Study*	*Summary of Results Concerning Variable*
I. Demographic factors		
A. Rater gender	Centra & Linn (1973) Dipboye et al. (1977) Elmore & LaPointe (1974) Elmore & LaPointe (1975) Gupta et al (1980) Hamner et al. (1974) Jacobson & Effertz (1974) Lee & Alvares (1977) London & Poplawski (1976) Mai-Dalton et al. (1979) Mischel (1974) Rose (1978) Rosen & Jerdee (1973) Schmitt & Lappin (1980)	Rater gender in most studies had little or no effect on the performance ratings, although there are some data suggesting that female raters may be more lenient than males. Most of the studies are laboratory or simulation experiments; more data are needed from actual work settings.
B. Rater race	Cos & Krumboltz (1958) Crooks (1972) DeJung & Kaplan (1962) Hamner et al. (1974) Schmidt & Johnson (1973) Schmitt & Lappin (1980) Wendelken & Inn (1981)	Raters often give higher ratings to same-race ratees than to cross-race ratees, although this effect may be affected by the degree of interaction among members of the different races.

C. Rater age	Barnes (1980) Cleveland & Landy (1981) Klores (1966) Mandell (1956) Schwab & Heneman (1978)	Rater age does not appear to have a substantial main effect on performance ratings.
D. Rater education	Cascio & Valenzi (1977)	Although a statistically significant effect of education was found, Cascio and Valenzi concluded that it was so small as to have little or no practical significance.
II. Psychological factors		
A. Personality variables	Lewis & Taylor (1955) Mandell (1956) Rothaus et al. (1965)	A lack of systematic research effort makes general comments impossible.
B. Cognitive variables	Bernardin, Cardy, & Carlyle (1982) Lahey & Saal (1981) Saurer & Pond (1981) Schneier (1977) Vance & Kuhnert (1980) Zedeck & Kafry (1977)	Zedeck and Kafry found no effect of several cognitive measures on rating strategies. Schneier found that cognitive complexity affected the psychometric properties of ratings. Subsequent research has failed to replicate Schneier's findings regarding cognitive complexity.
III. Job-related factors		
A. Job experience	Cascio & Valenzi (1977) Jurgensen (1950) Klores (1966) Mandell (1956)	Job experience seems to affect positively the quality of ratings, but it is not clear exactly why experience functions in this way.

SOURCE: Adapted from *The Measurement of Work Performance* (pp. 120–122) by F. J. Landy and J. L. Farr, 1983, New York: Academic Press.

TABLE 5–2 *(concluded)*

Variable Investigated	*Study*	*Summary of Results Concerning Variable*
B. Job performance level	Bayroff et al. (1954) Kirchner & Reisberg (1962) Mandell (1956) Mullins & Force (1962) Schneider & Bayroff (1953)	Better performers seem to provide performance ratings of higher quality, but there is no recent work in this area.
C. Leadership style	Bernardin (1980) Klores (1966) Taylor et al. (1969)	Production-oriented leaders seem to be less lenient than interaction-oriented leaders. The causal relationship between ratings and leadership may be complex and reciprocal.
D. Type of rater	Bartlett (1959) Booker & Miller (1966) Borman (1974) Centra (1975) Fiske and Cox (1960) Freeberg (1969) Gordon & Medlund (1965) Heneman (1974) Kirchner (1965) Klieger & Mosel (1953) Klimoski & London (1974) Kraut (1975) Landy et al. (1976) Lawler (1967) Parker et al. (1959) Rothaus et al. (1965) Springer (1953) Zedeck et al. (1974)	Different types of raters (i.e., supervisors, peers, self, subordinates) are likely to have different perspectives on and information about the ratee's job performance. Thus, cross-rating correlations are usually low to moderate in magnitude. No one type of rater appears to be more valid than any other type. The differences among types may be useful for organizational problem diagnosis.

E. Organizational level relative to ratee	Berry et al. (1966) Borman & Dunnette (1975) Campbell et al. (1973) Whitla & Tirrell (1953) Zedeck & Baker (1972)	Usually only low to moderate agreement has been found among ratings from supervisors at differing levels in the organization vis-à-vis the ratee. Whitla and Tirrell and Zedeck and Baker found higher quality in ratings by first-level supervisors than by higher-level supervisors.
F. Knowledge of job requirements	Amir et al. (1970) Wagner & Hoover (1974)	More knowledgeable raters gave more valid ratings (Amir et al.) and were less affected by serial position of ratees (Wagner & Hoover).
G. Amount and type of rater-ratee contact	Amir et al. (1970) Bowen (1968) Ferguson (1949) Fiske & Cox (1960) Freeberg (1969) Gordon & Medland (1965) Hollander (1957) Hollander (1965) Klieger & Mosel (1953) Klores (1966) Landy & Guion (1970) Suci et al. (1956) Waters & Waters (1970)	Frequency of contact does not appear to be as important as the relevancy of the contact with regard to the performance being evaluated.

action of rater and ratee characteristics that produces the effect on the performance description rather than either the rater or ratee characteristics alone.

Position Characteristics. In addition to the rater and ratee components, there are characteristics peculiar to the position that the ratee occupies in the organization that may influence the accuracy of the performance description. Some of these characteristics might be line versus staff status, the level in the organization, or the formal reporting relationship of ratee to rater.

Rating Instrument. The particular format used to gather the ratings might influence the performance description. For example, one might choose to use a forced-choice scale rather than a simple graphic rating scale or a behaviorally anchored scale rather than one anchored with descriptive adjectives such as "outstanding," "average," or "poor." The nature of the format that is used may distort the performance description.

Scale Development. The manner in which the scale was developed will directly affect the nature of the scale and thus indirectly affect the accuracy of performance description. For example, there is some question as to whether the eventual raters should be directly involved in the development of the rating scales. The procedures for developing behaviorally anchored rating scales imply that this involvement is good both in terms of yielding better scales and in terms of increasing rater motivation.

Rating Process. There are a number of *procedures* that may influence the accuracy of ratings. For example, there may be differences in accuracy depending on whether the ratee gets to see the ratings or whether they are kept secret. Completing ratings at one time during the year for everyone may produce different results from ratings that are staggered throughout the year. Ratings that require elaborate justification might be significantly different from those that need not be documented.

Organizational Characteristics. The organization in which the ratings are gathered might have certain characteristics that influence the accuracy of ratings. These characteristics are independent of the characteristics of the rater, ratee, or position. Some examples of these characteristics are organization size, union-nonunion status, profitability, turnover levels, and full-time–part-time employee ratio.

Observation/Storage. The ultimate accuracy of performance description can be affected by the care and methods used by an individual to consider the behavior of another. If you pay close attention to the behavior you are observing, the eventual description will be more accurate than if you were casual in your observation. It naturally follows that if you have not carefully observed, you will not be storing completely accurate information. In addition, regardless of how carefully you observe behavior, the scheme you use to place those data in memory will have an effect on what is available to remember at a later time. If you encode (i.e., place in memory) only performance information that interests you, that is the only information that will be available several months later when it is time for evaluation.

Retrieval/Judgment. The way in which a rater prepares for a performance evaluation will have an impact on the outcome of that evaluation. A careful examination of the job description of the ratee should help to provide the cues necessary for retrieving salient performance information about the ratee (assuming it was stored at some earlier point). Similarly, the judgment task that confronts the evaluator will affect the accuracy of the eventual judgment. For example, it might be considerably easier to identify the best and worst performers in a group of 30 subordinates than it is to make an absolute judgment about how much interpersonal sensitivity or communication skill a particular subordinate possesses.

Data Analysis. Once the ratings are gathered, there are still some decisions to be made regarding data analysis that may affect the accuracy of the performance description. For example, should ratings be averaged or left independent? Should ratings from multiple raters be combined? Should the ratings be factor analyzed? The answers to these and other similar data questions will determine the characteristics of the eventual performance description.

The Performance Description. The combination of all these elements produces a performance description. On the basis of this performance description, certain personnel actions are taken. Performance information is fed back to employees, salary changes are proposed, layoff lists are established, promotions are made. In many instances, performance descriptions are produced and nothing happens as a result of them; they are "filed." In a sense, this is also a personnel action, although it is an action by default. This type of nonaction has very special meaning to both the ratee and the rater. It tells both of them very clearly that nothing they do makes a difference to the organization.

The arrows from the box labeled "Personnel Action" to the boxes labeled "Rater Characteristics" and "Ratee Characteristics" imply that both action and inaction have an effect on how the rater and ratee approach their jobs. In an ideal setting, performance descriptions allow accurate feedback to the ratee, who subsequently changes his behavior to make it more efficient. This increased efficiency is suitably rewarded, and the rater feels as if the ratings were a positive force in improving the skills of the subordinate and increasing the efficiency of the organization. Things are not always the way we would like them to be, however. It is also possible that punishments are distributed on the basis of ratings (e.g., layoffs, reprimands). In that case, the supervisor may think twice about being truthful the next time ratings are gathered. As another example, ratees may discover that individuals who always agree with the rater tend to receive the highest ratings, and they may subsequently change their behavior so that they always agree with the supervisor in conversations. These latter two instances are examples of counterproductive effects of the feedback.

Although this model does not offer much in the way of explanation concerning *why* these elements may have adverse effects on the accuracy of performance descriptions, it does present a reasonable view of the complexity of the process. A good deal of research has been conducted over the past few decades that addresses the effect of several of these components, and it may be useful to review the findings of these studies. A much more complete review of these effects can be found in other sources (Landy & Farr, 1980, 1983).

1. Rater experience (i.e., training in rating, familiarity with the rating scales) appears to affect the quality of the ratings positively.
2. The relevance of the rater-ratee interaction is more important than the simple frequency of interaction.
3. The sex stereotype of the occupation (i.e., whether a particular job is typically perceived as masculine or feminine) interacts with the sex of the ratee to distort ratings. Thus, males are evaluated more favorably than females in perceived masculine tasks, but females are evaluated more favorably than males in tasks typically characterized as feminine.
4. Experimental studies of the effect of the performance level of the ratee upon performance ratings generally support the validity of the ratings.
5. While people may have preferences for various rating formats (e.g., the "good" portion of the rating scale is on the top or bottom, left or right), these preferences have little or no effect on actual rating behavior.
6. The number of response alternatives available to a rater should not be less than five or more than nine.
7. Whether the rating format is behaviorally anchored or forced-choice, or even traditional graphic, is less important than whether the anchors were chosen carefully to distinguish between good and poor performance.
8. Ratings for administrative purposes will be more lenient than ratings for research purposes.
9. Rater training is effective in reducing rating errors.

This last point is generally taken as a "given"—raters should be trained. But how should they be trained? Should they be trained to make judgments in a particular manner, to observe behavior in some special way, to use one particular set of rating scales? Figure 5–8 does not specifically deal with the issue of training. In the next section, I will present some information on the extent to which rater training is a factor that influences performance judgments.

Rater Training. It makes sense to train raters. Performance evaluation requires certain skills. In addition, the rater must be knowledgeable about how to use the particular rating form or system of evaluation. Traditionally, an important part of rater training has involved a description of the traditional rating errors of leniency and halo and suggestions of how to avoid those errors. For example, Ivancevich (1979) demonstrated that extensive rater training involving a discussion of leniency and halo reduced these errors. That would seem to be desirable. A later study puts a new perspective on that result. Bernardin and Pence (1980) considered the issue of accuracy, in addition to the problem of rating errors. Lenient ratings or ratings on different dimensions that are almost perfectly correlated do create problems. On the other hand, the object is not simply to eliminate these statistical characteristics; the object is to produce more accurate ratings. Bernardin and Pence used a set of verbal descriptions that depicted teacher performance. Several groups of students evaluated the performance of the lecturers as described by these vignettes. These descriptions were created such that there were certain "true" characteristics of the performance being considered. A lecturer could be made to behave in particular ways, for example, organized, interesting, sensitive. Furthermore, all the subjects would be considering exactly the same performance. This allowed for the comparison of various training methods with respect to not only errors but also accuracy.

There were three groups of subjects in the study. One group received training that involved a discussion of traditional errors of leniency and halo and instruction on how to avoid them. The second group devoted the training session to a consideration of the dimensions of teacher performance and to constructing stereotypes of good and bad teacher behavior. In addition, they generated actual rating scales for evaluating the instructors. A third group acted as a control and received no formal training. The results were surprising. The group that received training in avoiding rating errors was able to avoid these errors to a greater extent than the other two groups. The problem was that they also were less accurate in describing "true" performance than either the other training group or the control group subjects *who received no training*. In this case, training did more harm than good. The battle was won (i.e., reducing leniency and halo), but the war was lost (performance was less accurately described). Bernardin and Pence suggest that the subjects receiving training in avoiding rating errors adopted a "set" or a cognitive control mechanism that was geared toward producing numbers (ratings) that had certain statistical properties rather than numbers that described behavior.

Research in the area of rater training suggests that it might be more effective to train raters in observation skills than to exhort them to avoid certain errors (Murphy, Garcia, Kerkar, Martin, & Balzar, 1982). K. R. Murphy and his colleagues have been able to demonstrate that raters who are more accurate observers are also more accurate evaluators. This should come as no great surprise. Common sense dictates that accurate evaluation depends on accurate perception. Nevertheless, the history of rater training has been characterized by an obsession with rating errors and their elimination.

Recent research results have expanded the understanding of what the important aspects of rater training include. Very similar studies by McIntyre,

Smith, and Hassett (1984) and Pulakos (1984) come to virtually identical conclusions. McIntyre et al. label their training technique "frame of reference" (FOR) training. Pulakos describes "rater accuracy training" (RAT). Both these approaches present the rater with information about (1) the multidimensional nature of the performance being considered, (2) the meaning of anchors on the scales, (3) a practice exercise in rating a standard performance stimulus, and (4) feedback on that practice exercise. The results of this type of training have been encouraging. The accuracy of raters exposed to this type of rating is considerably better than those exposed to no training or to training in simply avoiding errors. Recently, Athey and McIntyre (1987) have replicated these results and presented a theoretical rationale for the superiority of this type of training. They suggest that the positive effects come from the fact that the additional information and rating practice sessions permit a more efficient encoding of the performance information and thus a more accurate retrieval of that information.

Cognition and Rating

Throughout the discussion of factors affecting rating, you have seen examples of cognitive processes at work. By implication, most of the factors that we have considered so far could be thought of as "cognitive" factors. Let's consider the issue of cognition and rating more directly.

The material on rater training suggests that the obstacles to effective performance evaluation are not really rating formats or tendencies toward leniency and halo. Instead, the problem seems to be in the perceptual and cognitive strategies of the raters—how they observe and classify information, how they store and retrieve it, how they make comparisons among individuals being considered simultaneously. Consider the simple model that appears in Figure 5–9. This is an elaboration of the cognitive portion (i.e., observation/storage and retrieval/judgment) of Figure 5–8. As you can see, the cognitive operations are quite complex. This is not the time for a consideration of theories of information processing. Nevertheless, you should recognize that operations such as perceptual organization, stimulus categorization, memory, and reasoning will play critical roles in accurate performance assessment. The training studies of McIntyre and Pulakos support this cognitive interpretation. To take a simple example, a male supervisor watches a female subordinate complete a work-related task and says to himself, "Not bad for a woman." This implies that he has organized the information in a particular way. It also means that it will be remembered in a particular way. The details of the performance might be lost, but the evaluation (e.g., 70th percentile for a comparison group of *women*) will be retrieved at a later time. If the supervisor further believes that most men are better than most women, when the time comes for an evaluation of the entire work group, this particular woman might receive evaluations that place her below all male work group members and above all female work group members. Of course the process is not as

FIGURE 5–9 Cognitive Components in Rating

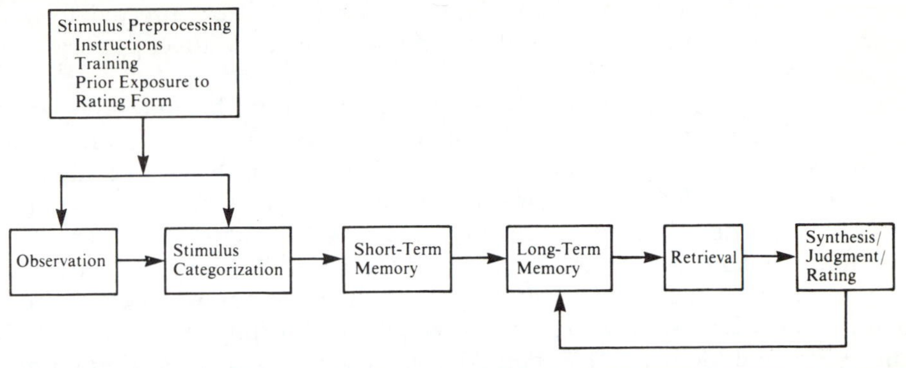

SOURCE: From *The Measurement of Work Performance* (Fig. 4.2) by F. J. Landy and J. L. Farr, 1983, New York: Academic Press.

simplistic as the example implies. Remember the study that I described by Schoorman (1988) in which he found that a supervisor who approved of a hire gave better ratings to that individual. This is another example of this cognitive process.

Both reviews (Landy & Farr, 1980, 1983) and theory (Feldman, 1981) have suggested many fruitful avenues for research and application of cognitive principles to performance evaluation. These avenues include exploration of long- and short-term memory dynamics, the role of encoding on information retrieval, the use of judgment heuristics (cognitive "habits" used in processing complex information), and the role of evaluator attributions on performance judgments. There are two assumptions that underscore the importance of research into cognitive factors in performance evaluation. The first assumption relates to the basic notion of perception. It is self-evident that perceptions depend on sensations. It is less evident but no less true that most perception is an extension (i.e., a creative interpretation) of incomplete sensation. We constantly *add* information to raw sensations in order to make sense out of those sensations (Landy, 1987). The second assumption is that in most industrial situations, information overload is the rule rather than the exception. Supervisors do not have time (or do not take time) to record and evaluate performance accurately of subordinates when it actually occurs. As a result, they are always trying to make up for an information-processing inefficiency. They are always playing catch-up. As an example, Srinivas and Motowidlo (1987) demonstrated that stress, in the form of information overload, resulted in ratings with higher halo (less differentiation) than ratings following low information loads. The brain is magnificently prepared to adapt to both of these circumstances, that is, incomplete sensation and information overload. But the brain is adapted to reduce stress, not necessarily to preserve completely accurate information. There are many techniques that humans use to correct for these two problems. For the most part, they are habitual and we are not normally aware of them. Future research will be directed toward uncovering these mechanisms and determining how they affect performance judgments.

Some of these studies have just begun to appear in the literature. As an example, Cardy and Kehoe (1984) demonstrated that a rater's accuracy was related to the selective attention of that rater. In this case, selective attention was measured as the rater's score on a test that measures the extent to which a person can identify many different aspects of the environment. The idea was that the more capable the rater was in this area, the more likely it would be that the rater could accurately assess the many complex aspects of work performance. Similarly, the recent work of K. R. Murphy and Balzer (1986) and Athey and McIntyre (1987) on the role of memory and encoding in performance evaluation has begun to shed some light on the cognitive processes that might be involved in performance rating.

A Cautionary Note

Most of the recent research on cognitive processes in performance evaluation has been done in the laboratory. The performance evaluated has been presented on paper in the form of vignettes or on videotape in the form of behavioral incidents. The typical subjects have been students (either undergraduate or graduate), and the rating has occurred either immediately following observation/reading or within a few hours or days. I will simply add my concern to that already expressed by Hakel (1986) and Guion and Gibson (1988). These experimental situations are so far removed from the actual challenges of performance evaluation in an industrial setting as to be almost caricatures. That is not to say that this research is useless, wasted, or wrong. Those conducting the research and those who support these designs (e.g., Greenberg, 1986) assert that the nature of the beast is such that this type of research cannot be conducted without careful experimental control. Further, they assert that lots of other types of research (e.g., goal setting) has demonstrated that lab results can be replicated in field settings. Although these arguments have some merit, they will continue to ring hollow until it can be demonstrated that the same phenomena uncovered in the laboratory are present in the field. It is only necessary to look at the typical laboratory task and compare it to the typical performance evaluation in work settings to become skeptical. It is time to demonstrate the transcendence of the laboratory findings.

True Halo and Leniency

To this point, I have suggested that performance rating is plagued with errors of various types. The two most commonly cited rater errors are halo and leniency. But are high ratings and significant correlations between dimensional ratings always signs of rating errors? There are good reasons to think not. Consider the circumstance in which the selection system being used by the organization is valid and correctly implemented. Further, assume that the employees have been appropriately trained and motivated. Under such circumstances, why would you not expect the ratings to be skewed toward high performance? You might very well obtain a distribution similar to one of those that was used to identify leniency in Figure 5–2. Would this be leniency? Would the ratings be in error? In this case, probably not.

Another case in point is halo. Should you expect the intercorrelations between performance dimensions to be .00? There is good reason to doubt such a state of affairs. Most definitions of a job assume that the tasks performed in that job are homogeneous or similar in some respect. As an example, police officers are charged with preserving the public good and enforcing a body of law. All their assigned duties are directed toward these ends. Similarly, a clerk in a supermarket is concerned with moving customers through a checkout line in a fast and accurate manner. Again, this goal has a major influence on the behaviors directed toward satisfying it. Since this homogeneity exists, it is likely that there is a natural correlation between dimensions of performance that can be used to describe the behavior of people who hold a particular job. This is a case of what has come to be known as "true" halo. The expected value of the correlation between any two performance rating dimensions for a single job is not .00 but instead some positive value.

Generations of personnel managers and researchers have attempted to produce distributions of performance scores that are uncorrelated and are normally or symmetrically distributed with means at or near the physical center of the rating scale. As you saw in the Bernardin and Pence (1980) research described above, this may be a case of drowning the baby in the bathwater. In the course of eliminating the "errors," accuracy may also be eliminated.

The point of this discussion is that rating errors need to be defined relatively rather than absolutely. *Halo* might be defined as a higher correlation between dimensions *than might be expected under a given set of circumstances.* A similar definition might be suggested for *leniency.* We should not lose sight of the fact that our task in performance evaluation is to describe performance, even if that performance happens to be considerably above average or if the various facets of performance are substantially correlated with one another.

The Social Context of Performance Appraisal

Up to this point, we have been considering performance evaluation as one component of a comprehensive human resources program. Certainly it is. But if you have ever had your performance appraised (or wanted feedback from a supervisor), you know that the process can have some very personal and emotional effects as well. As an example, a recent study by Pearce and Porter (1986) demonstrated that when someone is labeled "satisfactory," it displeases them. Most of us think that we are making a substantial and unique

FIGURE 5–10 Process Model of the Effects of Feedback on Recipients

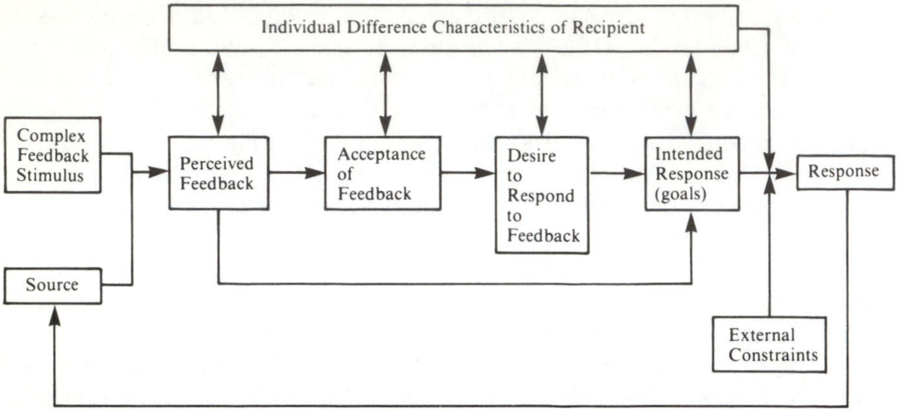

Individual Difference Characteristics of Recipient

Complex Feedback Stimulus

Source

Perceived Feedback

Acceptance of Feedback

Desire to Respond to Feedback

Intended Response (goals)

Response

External Constraints

SOURCE: From "Consequences of Individual Feedback on Behavior in Organizations" by D. R. Ilgen, C. D. Fisher, and M. S. Taylor, 1979, *Journal of Applied Psychology, 64,* p. 352. Copyright 1979 by the American Psychological Association. Reprinted by permission of the publisher and author.

contribution to the organization for which we work. To be told that you are "satisfactory" conveys a very different message. In this section, we will consider several aspects of performance evaluation that are more social than administrative in nature. The consideration will focus on the manner in which the ratee is made aware of performance strengths and weaknesses. The process is typically labeled *feedback.*

Feedback as a Communication Process. Once performance information is gathered and evaluations made, it is appropriate to present the person who was evaluated with some version of the information. Considered from this perspective, we are faced with the problem of sending a message (i.e., the feedback) to a recipient (the worker) from a source (a supervisor, coworker, or the task itself). Ilgen, Fisher, and Taylor (1979) have developed a process model of the manner by which this type of communication proceeds in work settings. The model appears in Figure 5–10. As you can see, the stimulus to the recipient is not simply the *message* but also the *source.* In other words, when interpreting performance feedback information, the worker typically not only makes inferences based on the raw information (i.e., performance-based statements) but also takes into account characteristics of the source. The source might be a supervisor, a fellow worker, or the task itself. In some instances, the source might include customers or clients. As is true with any communication source, some are more credible than others. For example, we might be inclined to take the comments of a supervisor more seriously than those of a coworker or casual observer. The model assumes that the nature of the source and the credibility of that source will influence the extent to which a person will pay attention to performance feedback. The message is the actual information about the appropriateness of past performance (Ilgen et al., 1979).

Those two elements—the message itself and the perceived characteristics of the source—represent the information to be processed by the person receiving the feedback, the recipient. Ilgen et al. suggest that when the information reaches the recipient, a four-stage operation of information processing begins. The first stage is labeled *perception* and implies that the person applied certain grouping or sorting principles as initial organizers of the information. As an example, the person might first look for information with implications about pay and benefits; next, a search might be made for information about individual job duties; finally the person might search for information about social interactions. These would be the organizing principles that would aid the recipient in interpreting the information. The next phase is *acceptance* of feedback. Acceptance represents the person's belief that the feedback correctly describes her performance. Note that the belief could be either correct or inaccurate—the point is that acceptance represents belief, not fact. We will return to the issue of acceptance shortly. The third phase is a behavior intention. It is labeled the *desire to respond*. This means the intention to maintain behavior that was evaluated as effective and change or eliminate behavior identified as ineffective. There are personal characteristics of the recipient that seem to affect the desire to respond. For example, individuals who desire to perform competently will have a greater desire to respond than those who are unconcerned about successful performance (Ilgen et al., 1979).

The final phase is called the *intended response*. In this phase, the individual may actually set performance improvement goals such as "I won't get mad at the shipping clerk this week" or "I will try to reduce scrap by three units per day." We will consider goal setting more extensively in the motivation chapter.

Ilgen's model is a very attractive one since it supports the increasingly cognitive view that is being imposed on the consideration of worker responses. It further reinforces the view that performance information should be reliable and valid. Can you imagine what the impact of either inaccurate or unreliable information would be by following it through the model? At the very least, it would suggest intended responses (goals) that would be irrelevant or even counterproductive. At the very worst, the entire credibility of the system and the information would be undermined, eventually rendering the feedback powerless to affect behavior.

The discussion of Ilgen's process model of feedback is informative from the broad system's perspective. We can also consider feedback from a more personal viewpoint. Frequently, performance feedback is dreaded by supervisor and worker alike. One reason for this is the arbitrary nature of the information. The supervisor is given a form by the personnel department and told to evaluate all the workers with that form. The form usually has three dimensions or performance categories on it—quality of work (high, average, or low), quantity of work (high, average, or low), and overall performance (high, average, or low). The supervisor is usually as uncomfortable describing a worker in these terms as the worker is in being described in them. Consequently, supervisors give generally high ratings, since they do not know how to counsel the worker on low ratings. Everyone concerned realizes that the process is little more than ritual, and it loses any value it might have had. Adequate criterion development and measurement are crucial to the continuing development of both subordinates and supervisors.

Regardless of how the information about individual performance is collected—whether a ranking system, a rating system, or a collection of incidents that are critical to job performance—there must be a *formal* feedback system connected to the data collection. We stress the term *formal* because unless one is built into the system, one will develop informally. The most common *informal* feedback system is a result of no *formal* feedback to the subordinate or the rater. In the absence of such feedback, subordinates assume that either they have not been considered or evaluated in a long time, or if they had been, it is irrelevant. Time after time, I have run into situations in industry where the employee complains that no one has even bothered to look at the quality or quantity of his work for the past two years. In checking into the complaint, we find that the employee's job performance has been rated by a supervisor each six months for the past three years. The supervisor, upon questioning, contends that 30 different people must be rated and that he can hardly "hold each of their hands" while he is doing it. "Besides, no one uses the information anyway."

In this case, the time and money that went into the preparation of the appraisal system is not only wasted, but it is counterproductive. For that reason, it is essential that a feedback system be incorporated into the appraisal system from the very beginning. This usually takes the form of a discussion between the supervisor and the subordinate that is related to the behavior of the subordinate. Such a discussion can be quite uncomfortable for all concerned in its initial stages or until each party gets used to the procedure. There is often a tendency for supervisors to avoid uncomfortable issues, and consequently they defeat the purpose of the session. There is also a tendency on the part of the subordinate to explain away deficiencies rather than face up to them. Although this situation may be more in the domain of a clinical psychologist rather than an industrial and organizational psychologist, I will mention one research study that makes a point about the dynamics of the feedback session. Kay, Meyer, and French (1965) examined the relationship between critical comments in a feedback session and the number of defensive comments made by the subordinate. Their general finding was that as threats or critical comments increased, defensiveness also increased. Further, they concluded that praise accomplished very little—and the reason is fascinating: most supervisors use praise to cushion criticism, forming a "praise-criticism-

FIGURE 5–11 Hypothetical Relationship between Negative Comments by Supervisor and Defensive Responses by Subordinate

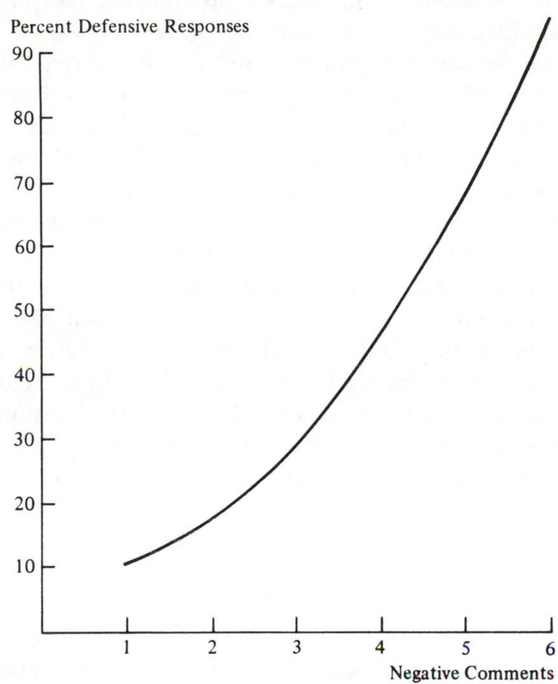

praise sandwich." A few positive statements begin the feedback session to "put the employee at ease." Then come the negative comments, followed by a few more positive comments so the employee will "leave the session with a positive attitude." In effect, praise becomes a conditioned stimulus announcing the arrival of criticism, exactly as a tone signaled the presentation of food to the dog in Pavlov's classic experiment. In the feedback situation, the individual is put on the alert by positive comments; the positive comments following the criticism merely signal the individual that no more negative comments will come for a while.

Another interesting finding of the Kay et al. study was the shape of the relationship between negative comments and defensiveness. The function does not seem to be a linear one but rather a curvilinear, positively accelerating one such as described in Figure 5–11. They suggest that an individual has some critical level of criticism that can be absorbed before defensive tendencies begin to appear. Based on this premise, they suggest that such a problem may be solved by having more frequent sessions with the individual so that the absolute number of negative comments in any one session is reduced. A recent study by Stone, Gueutal, and McIntosh (1984) has questioned the findings of Kay et al. Stone et al. discovered that the recipient of feedback will consider that feedback to be more accurate if positive information is presented first and negative information second. If the negative information is presented first, the recipient has a greater tendency to doubt the accuracy of that information. The Stone et al. study was a laboratory study with role playing, and I would expect that, at the very least, it should be demonstrated that the same findings appear in real work settings. Nevertheless, it is an issue that deserves more attention since virtually all performance feedback involves a mixture of positive and negative information.

The preceding discussion of the feedback mechanism in the appraisal process suggests several things: (1) it should be a formal part of the system; (2) supervisors should analyze their feedback style to identify such things as the praise-criticism-praise sandwich; (3) it should be done frequently enough so that an individual is not overwhelmed by negative comments; and (4) supervisors should be made aware of the relationship between the data they collect on individual performance and the overall personnel decision system.

Perceived Fairness and Accuracy

As you can see from our consideration of the performance evaluation interview, the very process of evaluating performance can have an emotional impact on a worker. Under certain circumstances, the evaluation may be seen as unfair and inaccurate. As you saw in the Ilgen et al. (1979) model, this will have certain consequences. If feedback is considered unfair or inaccurate, the information is unlikely to be accepted, it is unlikely that there will be a desire to respond, and no goals will be set for performance improvement.

For these reasons, as well as the job satisfaction of the worker in question, it is important that feedback be seen as fair and accurate. In a study that I conducted with two colleagues (Landy, Barnes, & Murphy, 1978), managers were asked to describe the elements that affect their perceptions of fairness and accuracy in performance appraisal. The four predominant elements they mentioned were: (1) frequency of appraisal, (2) plans developed with the supervisor for eliminating weaknesses, (3) supervisor's knowledge of the ratee's job duties, and (4) supervisor's knowledge of ratee's level of performance.

Two follow-up studies have been conducted that shed a little more light on the importance of this finding. One way of explaining perceived fairness and accuracy is to say that those individuals who received the highest performance scores were most likely to perceive the performance appraisal as fair and accurate. We repeated the study with a different group of managers six months after their performances had been evaluated and feedback discussions held. Once again, we asked them to assess the fairness and accuracy of their performance evaluation. There was no relationship between the actual performance ratings assigned by supervisors and the perceived fairness and accuracy of the process. The same factors remained important in the perception of fairness.

In a test of these findings, Brief, Fulk, and Barr (1981) suggested that supervisor's knowledge of subordinate's performance and the development of action plans related to performance weaknesses were the most important factors in fairness perceptions. In addition, they showed that trust in supervisor also played an important role.

A study by J. R. Burke, Weitzel, and Weir (1978) suggests another interesting aspect of perceived fairness. This aspect has more to do with how the subordinate prepares for the feedback interview than with how the supervisor behaves. They found that the more time a subordinate took to prepare for the performance discussion (e.g., analyzing job responsibilities, considering problems that occur), the more positive the outcomes of the performance discussion. Under these circumstances, the subordinate was able to exert more control over the discussion and to discuss performance problems in some detail—the subordinate was a much more active participant in the interview.

Greenberg (1986) suggests that all these variables that seem to influence perceived fairness can be lumped into two broad categories—procedural factors and distributive factors. Procedural factors include issues such as the extent to which input was solicited from the worker prior to evaluation, the presence of two-way communication during the evaluation interview, the possibility for the worker to challenge information or evaluations, and the extent to which the rater was familiar with the ratee's job and performance. The distributive factor is defined by the extent to which rewards based on performance were considered fair and the extent to which rewards (such as salary increases) were at all related to the performance evaluation process.

All these studies suggest that the Ilgen et al. model is a good one. It seems clear that subordinates have attitudes about performance evaluation that affect the way they process information provided in that interview. The information-processing strategy, in turn, affects future intentions and behavior. In order to maximize the benefit of performance evaluation and feedback, an organization should impress on supervisors the importance of a good knowledge of the person and the job being evaluated and attempt to suggest methods for improvement. Further, subordinates should be encouraged to prepare for the performance evaluation interview by considering the duties and responsibilities of the job (perhaps by simply going over a job description) as well as performance problems that have occurred since the last evaluation. This latter suggestion implies that subordinates must be trained to receive feedback. Zedeck (Landy, Zedeck, & Cleveland, 1983) has recently made a similar observation.

CENTRAL POINTS FOR STUDY

1. Performance judgments can be rankings, ratings, or comparisons.
2. Ratings often suffer from errors of various types.
3. Behaviorally based rating scales are preferable to trait rating scales.
4. There are many factors that affect the accuracy of a rating.
5. There is a social context to employee rating.
6. Several factors affect the perceived fairness and accuracy of ratings.

CHAPTER 6

Tests and Testing Techniques

From what has been said in the earlier chapter on personnel selection, you may have concluded that selection of a test is a straightforward process where you find a reliable and valid test and use it. The fallacy in this is that predictive validity for a situation can be evaluated only after a test has been chosen and a sample of test and criterion data has been obtained. That is not to deny that evidence of test reliability and validity are important information in choosing a test. On the contrary, evidence that a test has been a valid predictor of "success" with a sample of jobs similar to the one being examined is one of the best indicators that the test may be a wise choice. As we have already seen, the whole concept of validity generalization depends on the potential of transporting the validity of a test in one situation to another similar situation. Similarly, in the absence of empirical validity data, evidence of logical validity, of reliability, or of both may serve as bases for choosing among tests. It should be evident that these two criteria for evaluation in psychological measurement—reliability and validity—are of first-order importance in test selection decisions.

However, there are a number of other factors that must be considered. One does not select a test simply because it is reliable and valid for *some* purpose. A test is selected because it looks as though it may be valid for a *particular* purpose—that it will be a good measure of some attribute that is important for performance on a particular job. The test selection process starts with a hypothesis (or hunch) based on systematic job analysis and worker analysis data regarding those attributes most important for job success. Then tests are sought to measure one or more of those attributes. At that point, reliability and validity become an important consideration. Other important factors are: (1) the availability of appropriate normative data ("norms") to permit evaluation of obtained scores; (2) standardized administration and scoring procedures, without which test scores may be meaningless; (3) professional training requirements for administration and scoring; and (4) costs and other factors.

This chapter is concerned with how one goes about finding, evaluating, and selecting a test likely to yield information that will be relevant to personnel decisions.

Remember the last time you took a standardized test? It might have been the Scholastic Aptitude Test (SAT) or the Graduate Record Examination (GRE). Did you wonder who thought it up or where it came from? If you had to give a test to someone for some purpose, would you know how to go about finding and evaluating a test? Probably not, as most people give little thought to identifying an appropriate test and then evaluating its properties. But this may represent a real problem for the personnel manager. What if a new employee has to be hired to run a rather complicated lathe? If the personnel manager wants to explore the possibility of using a test of some kind, how is this done?

There are several sources she might use. We will discuss one such source later (*Ninth Mental Measurements Yearbook* [J. V. Mitchell, 1985]), but simply because an appropriate test is found does not mean that it can be purchased and incorporated into the employment process. Ideally, the test publisher exercises some control over the sale of the test so that society is not abused by the unethical or inappropriate use of tests by those not qualified to administer and interpret them. There must also be some safeguard against a person buying a copy of a test that he will be given as part of a selection or promotion process. So, there are really two questions to consider. First, Who may purchase a test? Second, How may a test be identified and evaluated?

Test Users

In 1953 the American Psychological Association provided a scheme for the classification of tests that helps publishers determine the degree of professional training necessary for the potential user of a particular test. This helps individuals considering various tests determine which tests they are capable of administering and interpreting. In addition, it helps the publisher determine whether an individual should be permitted to purchase a particular test. This classification scheme follows.

Level A Tests. Level A tests are relatively low-level tests requiring little in the way of formal training in administration or interpretation. They can be administered with the help of an instruction manual and can be easily scored and interpreted. These tests are generally of the achievement variety, which check on present proficiency rather than potential achievement (aptitude). An example of a level A test would be a standardized language-proficiency examination used to determine placement of a student in a foreign-language curriculum.

Level B Tests. Level B tests require some degree of training and familiarity with concepts of psychological testing on the part of the purchaser. Unlike the tests of level A, level B tests cannot be mechanically interpreted from a manual. They require some knowledge of concepts such as standardization, norm groups, and errors of measurement. This is primarily due to the inferential nature of the tests. Aptitude tests fall in this category. We are attempting to predict some potential on the part of the individual rather than describe some current level of achievement. This added element of prediction requires specialized training. Such training might be an advanced college course in tests and measurements, with a supporting statistics background.

Level C Tests. Level C tests are the most demanding of the user. In addition to the necessary training described for level B, level C tests require specialized supervision in administration, scoring, and interpretation. An example of such a test would be the Rorschach inkblot test. Graduate courses are dedicated solely to the use of that test (this includes supervised administration as well as classroom instruction).

This classification procedure provides some general form of protection against the abuse of psychological and educational tests. Let us assume that an individual is aware of such restrictions on the purchase of tests and wants to identify some possible tests for use in an industrial setting. How can these tests be found and evaluated? In 1938, Oscar K. Buros published the *First Mental Measurements Yearbook* (*MMY*—by designation) with the following purposes in mind:

1. To provide information about tests published throughout the English-speaking world
2. To present frankly critical test reviews written by testing and subject specialists representing various viewpoints
3. To provide extensive bibliographies of verified references on the construction, use, and validity of specific tests
4. To make readily available the critical portions of test reviews appearing in professional journals
5. To provide fairly exhaustive reviews of new and revised books on testing

This was a rather ambitious set of goals, and an index of the success of Buros is the fact that the *Yearbook* has appeared eight more times since then. It is a kind of bible for test users. Figure 6–1 presents a typical entry from a *Mental Measurements Yearbook* (Buros, 1972). As you can see from the figure, information such as target populations of subjects, cost, length, time to administer, author, and publisher is included. This information is normally followed by two or more reviews of the test and a bibliography of publications in which information about the test has appeared. The *MMY* serves the dual purpose (1) of identifying those tests that are poorly constructed and poorly supported with appropriate documentation and also (2) of highlighting tests with exceptional promise for a particular purpose. (Another book, entitled *Tests in Print III* [J. V. Mitchell, 1983] has also been published. It serves the purpose of an index for the *MMY*.)

In addition to Buros, there is another source that should prove useful in determination of the value of a particular test for a given situation. The source is called the *Test Validity Yearbook: Organizational* (Landy, 1989), and it will be

FIGURE 6–1 A Typical Entry from the *Mental Measurements Yearbook*

[675]

Flanagan Aptitude Classification Tests. Grades 9–12, 10–12 and adults; 1951–60; FACT; 2 editions; postage extra; John C. Flanagan; Science Research Associates, Inc. *

a) SEPARATE BOOKLET 16-TEST EDITION. Grades 10–12 and adults; 1951–60; 16 tests; examiner's manual ('53, 27 pages); technical supplement ('54, 16 pages); personnel director's booklet ('53, 27 pages); manual for interpreting scores ('56, 12 pages); $5.10 per 25 self-marking tests; 40¢ per technical supplement; 55¢ per manual for interpreting scores; 80¢ per personnel director's booklet; $6.10 per specimen set; 258(388) minutes in 2 sessions.

1) *FACT 1A, Inspection.* 1953–56; form A ('53, 6 pages); 6(12) minutes.
2) *FACT 2A and 2B, Coding.* 1953–56; forms A ('53, 6 pages), B ('54, 6 pages); 10(30) minutes.
3) *FACT 3A and 3B, Memory.* 1953–56; forms A ('53, 3 pages), B ('54, 3 pages); 4(5) minutes.
4) *FACT 4A, Precision.* 1953–56; form A ('53, 4 pages); 8(15) minutes.
5) *FACT 5A, Assembly.* 1953–56; form A ('53, 6 pages); 12(18) minutes.
6) *FACT 6A, Scales.* 1953–56; form A ('53, 6 pages); 16(28) minutes.
7) *FACT 7A, Coordination.* 1953–56; form A ('53, 8 pages); 2⅔(8) minutes.
8) *FACT 8A, Judgment and Comprehension.* 1953–56; form A ('53, 7 pages); (35–40) minutes.
9) *FACT 9A, Arithmetic.* 1953–56; form A ('53, 6 pages); 10(20) minutes.
10) *FACT 10A, Patterns.* 1953–56; form A ('53, 6 pages); 20(28) minutes.
11) *FACT 11A, Components.* 1953–56; form A ('53, 6 pages); 20(24) minutes.
12) *FACT 12A, Tables.* 1953–56; form A ('53, 6 pages); 10(15) minutes.
13) *FACT 13A and 13B, Mechanics.* 1953–56; forms A ('53, 6 pages), B ('54, 6 pages); 20(25) minutes.
14) *FACT 14A, Expression.* 1953–56; form A ('53, 6 pages); (35–45) minutes.
15) *FACT 15A, Reasoning.* 1957–60; form A ('57, 6 pages); supplementary manual ('60, 6 pages); 40¢ per supplementary manual; 24(30) minutes.
16) *FACT 16A, Ingenuity.* 1957–60; form A ('57, 7 pages); supplementary manual ('60, 6 pages); 40¢ per supplementary manual; 24(30) minutes.

b) 19-TEST EDITION. Grades 9–12; 1957–60; 19 tests (same as for *a* plus vocabulary, planning, alertness) in 2 booklets: gray book ('57, 64 pages), blue book ('57, 24 pages); examiner's manual ('58, 70 pages); mimeographed norms ['58, 23 pages]; administrator's manual ('58, 17 pages); technical report ('59, 65 pages); mimeographed manual for planning short batteries ('60, 10 pages); score interpretation booklet for students ('58, 25 pages); separate answer sheets (MRC) must be used with gray book (blue book is scored by students); $3.25 per specimen set; (630) minutes in 3 sessions.

1) *SRA Scored.* Scoring service available only for MRC answer sheets used with gray books.
(*a*) Complete Rental Plan. Rental and scoring service, $1.60 per student.
(*b*) Scoring Only Plan. $8.50 per 25 blue books; $25 per 25 gray books; scoring service, $1.36 per student.
2) *School Scored.* $8.50 per 25 blue books; $25 per 25 gray books; $11.25 per 100 MRC answer sheets and 3 examiner's manuals; $2 per set of MRC hand scoring stencils for gray books; $10.75 per 25 score interpretation booklets; $3.25 per set of interpretive materials (administrator's manual, technical report, norms, and manual for planning).

SOURCE: From *The Seventh Mental Measurements Yearbook* (Vol. 2, p. 1053) by O. K. Buros, 1972, Highland Park, NJ: Gryphon Press.

published annually. The first issue is to appear in 1989. This volume will take up where a well-established industrial psychology journal left off over two decades ago. Until 1963, *Personnel Psychology* published basic validity information about tests and testing techniques in a particular section called the "Validity Information Exchange." When this section was eliminated, there was no available source for basic validity information. The *Test Validity Yearbook* should fill that role nicely.

TYPES OF TESTS

There are many ways in which the thousands of available tests could be categorized. I will use three different schemes. The first consists of the traditional distinctions you are likely to find in a discussion of testing and deals primarily with the administrative aspects of the test. The second set of categories is nontraditional and includes some behavioral categories as suggested by Cleary and her associates (Cleary, Humphreys, Kendrick, & Wesman, 1975) as well as a new development known as *computer adaptive testing*. The third set of categories is the traditional content category approach, breaking tests down into areas such as intelligence tests, interest tests, and special aptitude tests.

Traditional Administrative Categories

When considering the administrative aspects of tests, the user must often make choices as to the type of test that will be administered. As a result, I have arranged these administrative categories as a series of choices.

1. Speed Tests versus Power Tests. You have probably taken tests that had rigid and demanding time limits (so demanding that almost everyone who took them was unable to complete them). These were probably speed tests. The score on this type of test is the amount of work done per unit of time. In a sense, these might be characterized as tests of maximum rather than average performance. In classroom settings, these tests are often disguised as "open-book" tests. In most cases, the individual must have the information necessary to answer the questions readily at hand; if time is taken to go to the book for the answer, the test cannot be completed. The logic of speed tests is that the individual may be called upon to solve a problem or find an answer in a short period of time, and the necessary information must be readily at hand and quickly retrieved. There is some question about how frequent or important this kind of activity is in day-to-day behavior on most jobs. Of course, in many skills such as typing, speed is an important aspect of performance.

As opposed to speed tests, power tests have no rigid time limits. The individual is given ample time to complete the test. This might be considered a maximum performance test of another kind (i.e., do your best when time limits are not a factor). Although there are some time limits on these tests, the limits are more for the convenience of the person administering the test than anything else. If you ever administer a test to an appreciable number of people, you will discover that some percentage of them will need 5 percent more time than allotted, *regardless of the time allotted*. Most power tests are constructed such that the items increase in difficulty over the course of the test, and some items are so difficult that no one is expected to get them correct.

The same test can be given under conditions of either speed or power. It is likely that under the two sets of conditions something quite different is being measured in each.

2. Group Tests versus Individual Tests. As the name implies, group tests are tests that can be easily administered to groups of people at one time. As mentioned in the first chapter, one of the significant accomplishments of the psychologists attempting to institute a testing program for placement of

World War I recruits was the translation of the individual intelligence test of Binet/Terman into a test that could be administered to 500 individuals at one time. I have administered entry tests for appointment to the police academy in New York City to over 40,000 candidates on one day! It is not uncommon to administer tests for civil service jobs (e.g., police, fire, streets, courts, etc.) to several thousand applicants in large cities. Most tests administered in organizations for the purpose of selection or placement are group tests. Of course, group tests could be administered to single individuals. The point is that this type of test could be administered to large groups of applicants.

Individual tests can be given to only one person at a time. It is clear that the benefit from an individual test must be large enough to outweigh the cost of such a process. For this reason, individual tests are generally administered in special situations. Individual tests are often administered to applicants for high-level managerial positions, for instance. An example of such a test might be one sampling the applicant's ability to solve problems that would normally confront a manager on a day-to-day basis. Since one of the outcomes of the test is intended to be an assessment of the *styles* of problem solving as much as the *products,* a group test is often inappropriate. Other examples of individual tests would be those requiring a certain interpersonal rapport between the person taking and the person administering the test. This characteristic is claimed to be of the utmost importance by those involved in using high-level diagnostic tests such as the Rorschach inkblot test.

3. Paper-and-Pencil Tests versus Performance Tests. The paper-and-pencil test is by far the most common in industrial settings (with the exception of the preemployment interview, if that is considered as a test). The important characteristic of this test is that no manipulation of physical objects or equipment is directly related to the score that the individual is given. The facility with a pencil should be unrelated to the score that a person receives on a test (assuming some minimal level of proficiency). These tests range from the more common, general intelligence test that presents items dealing with vocabulary, or numerical operations, to a test such as the Bennett Mechanical Comprehension Test that requires the individual to visualize some particular mechanical operation and answer a question about it. The common element is that the response is made on paper with a pencil.

Performance tests require the individual to make a response by manipulating a particular physical object or piece of equipment. The score that the individual receives on the test is directly related to the quality or quantity of that manipulation. An example might be a test that requires the individual to assemble nuts and bolts. There are many situations in which one might be interested in knowing how well an individual can perform a particular operation rather than simply whether the person knows the principles of the operation. An example of this type of test that most of us have encountered is the actual driving part of the driver's examination for certification.

Taking tests on computers is becoming more common. This is the modern version of the paper-and-pencil test, assuming that the test is not intended to determine how well you use a computer; rather, the computer is simply a convenient medium for presenting the test stimulus information. Many of you may have prepared for the SAT or similar paper-and-pencil tests by taking a tutorial course on your personal computer. Thus, you can see that the computer version was simply a surrogate or replacement for the paper-and-pencil version of that test. On the other hand, if a person is given a test to see how facile she is with the use of certain computer hardware (e.g., a floppy disk drive or a printer) or software (e.g., the use of WordStar, a word processing program), this would be an example of a performance test.

4. Aptitude Tests versus Achievement Tests. The claim is often made that aptitude tests measure the *future potential* of an individual for a particular activity. An example of such a test would be the SAT or the College Board Entrance Examination (CBEE), both of which are intended to identify the aptitude of the individual for academic curricula of a particular sort.

In contrast to aptitude tests, achievement tests are thought to measure some degree of proficiency that the individual possesses *at the time of testing.* Most examinations related to specific courses, such as your midterm or the final examination in industrial and organizational psychology, are like that. The distinction between these categories is often difficult to make since the same test can be used in two different ways. If the test is used to determine what you have learned (e.g., a typical class examination), it would be an achievement test. On the other hand, if that test were used to determine who would be permitted to enroll in an advanced class on the same subject matter, it might be considered an aptitude test (i.e., a measure of your potential for learning more difficult material).

Nontraditional Administrative Categories

Behavioral Repertories Sampled. Cleary et al. (1975) suggested another method or set of dimensions for categorizing tests. This method emphasizes the repertory of behavior that is sampled by the test, rather than administrative aspects. They suggest the following four dimensions:

1. Breadth. Breadth is the amount of coverage of the test. A test can vary from a very narrow test of a particular content area (such as knowledge of performance appraisal techniques) to a very broad test of general intellectual ability. The interview might also be used as an example. Frequently, candidates have two interviews. The first is with someone from the human resources department and is very broad in scope, covering issues of motivation, background and communication, or interpersonal behavior. The second interview is much narrower and is with the individual who will be the immediate supervisor of the candidate if she is hired. This interview often deals with technical information related to the job in question.

2. Relation of Test to a Particular Training or Educational Program. This is the degree to which a test is independent of a particular curriculum. Police recruits who complete the academy training program are usually given an examination that will be used as the index of whether they successfully completed the training program. The nature of that test is closely tied to the curriculum of the academy, requiring a knowledge of laws and procedures that was provided by the training program. If the academy training program were to change, the test would undoubtedly change with it. On the other hand, many tests, such as general intelligence tests or tests of eye-hand coordination, are unrelated to the nature of any particular training program and would remain unchanged if the training program were to be modified.

3. Recency of Learning Sampled. Another factor is the passage of time since the individual first displayed the behaviors sampled. As an example of this distinction, Cleary and associates cite the GRE, which has an arithmetic-operations section based on high school algebra. On the other hand, the advanced subject area of the GRE might sample information that the individual encountered for the first time only 10 minutes before beginning the examination.

4. Purpose of the Test. How is information to be used? At least two ways in which test information might be used would be (1) to assess the amount of learning that *has occurred* over some specifiable period of time and (2) to predict how much learning is *likely to occur* in the future. This is another way of making the aptitude-achievement distinction that was discussed above. As I indicated in the last section, this distinction clearly implies that the concepts of aptitude and achievement are not tied to the test; they are related to the reason for which the test is given.

Computer Adaptive Testing

Since the computer has become such an integral part of everyday life, it should come as no surprise that computer-based test administration schemes have appeared. The computer offers a dramatically enhanced flexibility over standard paper-and-pencil tests. This is a result of the power to monitor a person's test performance when the test is actually being taken and choose items that will best get at the skill or ability being tested. The same flexibility is not possible with a standard paper-and-pencil test.

Computer adaptive testing (or *individually tailored testing*, as it is often called) is based on the principle of getting a reliable estimate of an individual's skill level by choosing items with specific difficulty levels. Items are added to the test until one can be confident that a good estimate of the true skill level of the person has been obtained. Since items are retrieved from a memory component of the computer presented on a computer screen, there are no difficulties procedurally in carrying out the test. The item appears and the person answers using a computer keyboard or other peripheral device such as a light pen. The value of this type of testing is that a test can be tailored

Occasionally, a computer can be used to test candidates. (Booz, Allen, & Hamilton, Inc.)

to the individual taking the test. Some individuals may take long tests; and others, short tests. The final test score depends not only on the number of items that were correctly answered but also on the difficulty of those items. Someone who answered a few very difficult items would receive a higher score than someone who answered many easy questions.

Figure 6–2 presents an example of how adaptive testing might be used in two stages. An individual first takes a preliminary test to determine general skill level. This is called the *routing test* and might consist of 10 or 15 questions. Based on the individual's routing test score, she is then given a second test that is geared more specifically to her probable skill level. This is a fairly simple procedure that is possible even without a computer, although it can be done very efficiently using computer selection and presentation of test items. A second, more complex version of adaptive testing is not possible without a computer-based retrieval and presentation system. Anastasi (1982) presents an example of what she has labeled *pyramidal testing*. Figure 6–3 illustrates this scheme. An individual begins with the same test item of moderate difficulty. If he answers that item correctly, he moves to a slightly more difficult item. If he answers incorrectly, he moves to a slightly less difficult item.

The logic of tailored testing is that each test item is geared toward estimating a person's skill or ability level. Since the object is to come to a reliable estimate of that level, the actual number of items becomes less important than in traditional testing. You have had many occasions to take tests that were considerably longer than they had to be. This was probably because the instructor wanted to be sure that the test was of sufficient length to be reliable.

FIGURE 6–2 Two-Stage Adaptive Testing with Three Measurement Levels

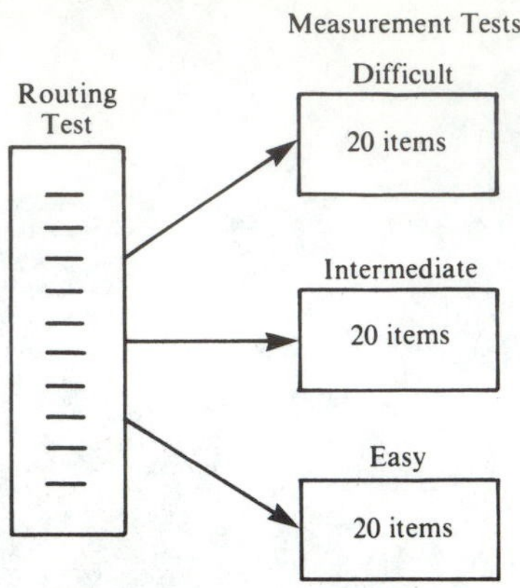

Each examinee takes routing test and one measurement test.

SOURCE: Reprinted with permission of Macmillan Publishing Company from *Psychological Testing,* 5th ed. by Anne Anastasi. Copyright © 1982 by Anne Anastasi.

The point is that for many people, the test was too long. Possibly for some, it was too short. After reviewing the literature on adaptive testing, Anastasi (1982) concludes that there are several advantages to adaptive testing. First, it results in reliability and validity equal to or better than conventional paper-and-pencil tests but with many fewer items and less testing time. In addition, it can provide a more accurate estimate of the ability levels of persons on the high or low end of the ability range.

In many settings, adaptive testing would be too expensive to be practical. In other settings, however, adaptive testing could save substantial amounts of time and money. For example, in professional licensing programs, adaptive testing could be a very efficient way of coping with the needs of single individuals who appear for licensing or certification at random periods. It would be possible for these individuals to come to a central testing center for computer-based examination. In training programs, adaptive testing could more accurately determine when the person had learned a sufficient amount. This would have the effect of preventing overtraining (often a costly activity) and permit the individual quicker access to the operational aspects of the job (clearly a substantial economic benefit to the organization). Similarly, when large numbers of individuals are being screened on certain basic abilities (e.g., verbal, numerical, spatial), the screening could be accomplished more efficiently by using a variation on adaptive testing than by using traditional paper-and-pencil methods. The armed forces are currently conducting research studies to test the feasibility of using adaptive testing for screening recruits. It is

FIGURE 6–3 Pyramidal Testing Model

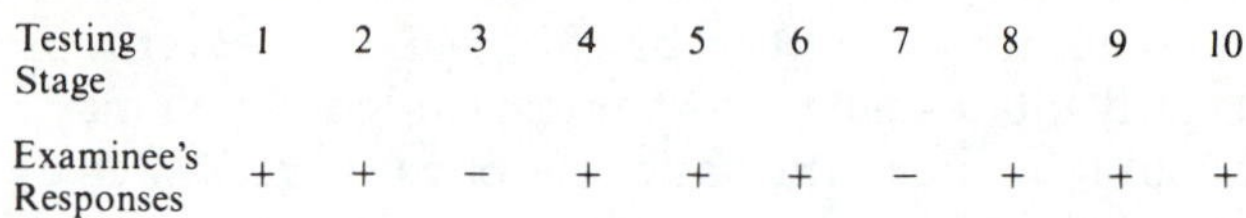

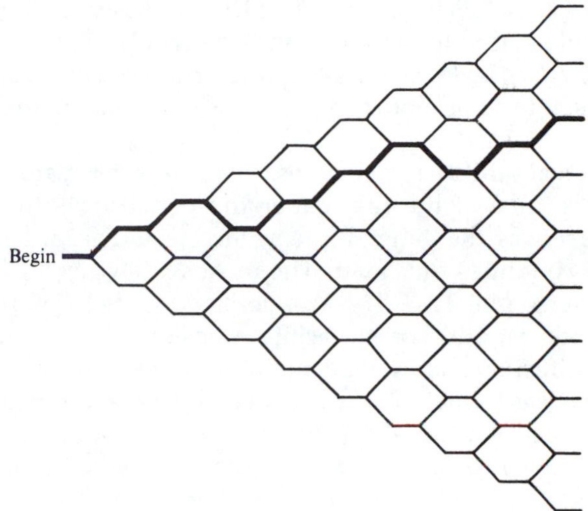

Heavy line shows route of examinee whose item scores are listed across top.

SOURCE: Reprinted with permission of Macmillan Publishing Company from *Psychological Testing,* 5th ed. by Anne Anastasi. Copyright © 1982 by Anne Anastasi.

likely that this innovative testing methodology will become considerably more popular as computers proliferate in work settings. In addition, as more of these types of tests become available and commercially feasible, the cost is bound to drop substantially. This, in turn, should lead to an increase in the popularity of the method.

Test Content Categories

In addition to categorizing tests according to traditional and nontraditional administrative characteristics, it is possible to describe tests in terms of their content area. Mitchell (1985) has 16 different major headings for tests in the ninth *MMY*. Many of these tests are irrelevant for our present purposes, for example, courtship and marriage tests. We are primarily interested in categories of tests that have some potential use in organizational settings. For this purpose, I will adopt the classification scheme that Ghiselli has used for reviewing the validity of occupational tests (Ghiselli, 1955, 1966, 1973; Ghiselli & Brown, 1955). I will give examples of the tests represented by the various headings, but I will not attempt to be exhaustive or even representative. If you are particularly interested in a test or test category, you may find adequate information about it in one of the basic reference sources such as Buros (1978) or in one of several good personnel and psychological testing books such as the ones by Guion (1965), Cronbach (1970), or Anastasi (1988). The following headings will be used to categorize tests generally used in industrial settings: tests of intellectual abilities, tests of spatial and mechanical abilities, perceptual accuracy tests, tests of motor abilities, and personality and interest tests.

Intellectual Abilities. As we saw in the brief history of industrial aptitude testing, one of the first paper-and-pencil tests to be introduced for industrial use was the general intelligence test. The popularity of this kind of measure continues unabated. The most widely used of these tests is the Wonderlic Personnel Test. The Wonderlic consists of 50 items dealing with verbal, numerical, and spatial facility. These items are mixed together and increase in difficulty from the beginning to the end of the test (this is known as a *spiral omnibus* format). There are several parallel forms for the tests. Guion (1966) has suggested that the Wonderlic is primarily a test of verbal facility, although the test also deals to some degree with deductive logic and numerical facility. Its wide popularity is probably due as much to the ease of administration and scoring as to its psychometric properties (although the norms are quite extensive, including minority group norms). One of the forms takes only 12 minutes to complete and can be given to groups. A single score is derived from the test responses.

There is a strong feeling on the part of many personnel departments that "general intelligence" *must be* related in some way to most of the positions for which hiring and placement are done. However, there are several reasons to question the indiscriminate administration of "general intelligence" tests.

The first and probably most important reservation is that we do not know what "general intelligence" is; a debate of a sort has continued unabated for more than 70 years about the nature of intelligence. Second, there seems to be a good deal of correlation between tests of verbal facility and short spiral omnibus tests of "general intelligence," which raises some concern about how "general" these tests actually are. Third, if intelligence is not a unitary concept, we should at least have some reasoned guesses about how particular aspects of intelligence relate to job-related criteria. Finally, there is no particular reason to think that general intelligence is the only, or even most important, dimension for success in many positions.

In support of this last point, Table 6–1, taken from Ghiselli's review (1973), shows the range of relationships between measures of intellectual ability and success for several different occupational categories.

Recent work by Hunter and Schmidt (e.g., Hunter, 1983; Hunter & Hunter, 1984; McDaniel, Schmidt, & Hunter, 1988; Schmidt, Hunter, &

TABLE 6–1 Validity Coefficients for Industrial Occupations

	Machine Tenders	*Bench Workers*	*Inspectors*	*Packers and Wrappers*	*Gross Manual Workers*	*All Industrial Workers*
Intellectual abilities	$.21^{F}$	$.18^{F}$	$.21^{D}$	$.18^{D}$	$.22^{F}$	$.20^{F}$
Intelligence	$.21^{E}$	$.18^{F}$	$.23^{D}$	$.17^{D}$	$.21^{D}$	$.20^{F}$
Immediate memory	$.17^{D}$	$.06^{D}$	$.14^{B}$	$.24^{D}$	—	$.15^{D}$
Substitution	$.19^{C}$	$.12^{D}$	$-.01^{D}$	$.16^{D}$	—	$.14^{D}$
Arithmetic	$.21^{E}$	$.20^{E}$	$.24^{D}$	$.16^{D}$	$.24^{D}$	$.21^{F}$

A = less than 100 cases.
B = 100 to 499 cases.
C = 500 to 999 cases.
D = 1000 to 4999 cases.
E = 5000 to 9999 cases.
F = 10,000 or more cases.

SOURCE: Adapted from "The Validity of Aptitude Tests in Personnel Selection" by E. E. Ghiselli, 1973, *Personnel Psychology, 26,* p. 476.

Outerbridge, 1986) suggests that many of the cognitive tests currently in use measure a general factor of intellectual ability. These researchers go on to show that this general cognitive ability is related to job success. As I indicated in an earlier chapter, this is the "content" part of the validity generalization thrust of Schmidt, Hunter, and their colleagues. They suggest that most industrial jobs depend on cognitive abilities for successful completion. Further, they suggest that, within some limits, cognitive ability is unidimensional. As an example, they suggest that the General Aptitude Test Battery (GATB) produces a measure of "general learning ability" or intelligence. This is defined as

> the ability to "catch on" or understand instructions and underlying principles; the ability to reason and make judgments. Closely related to doing well in school. (U.S. Department of Labor, 1970, p. 17)

General learning ability is calculated by combining scores from three of the nine GATB subtests—three-dimensional space, vocabulary, and arithmetic reasoning.

Schmidt, Hunter, and their colleagues are not alone in suggesting that we can measure and use general intellectual ability in applied settings. Gottfredson (1986) edited a special issue of the *Journal of Vocational Behavior* devoted to the topic of general intellectual ability in the workplace. In my opinion, this is an intriguing possibility and one worthy of careful examination, but the research to date is simply too sparse to warrant a sweeping conclusion about the existence of a general intellectual factor. To cite just two examples of some potential problems in this approach, consider the studies described in earlier chapters by Sackett et al. (1988) and by Heneman (1986). The Sackett study of supermarket cashiers showed very low levels of association between measures of typical performance and measures of maximum performance. If we accept the notion of general intellectual ability, we need to know the separate relationships of this ability to maximum and typical performance if we are to understand its contribution to work behavior. Similarly, Heneman (1986) demonstrated that there was a low correlation between judgmental measures of performance and objective measures. Again, if for the sake of argument, we accept the construct of general intellectual ability, we need to know the specific relationship of that construct to various performance measures (e.g., supervisory ratings, production measures, absences, accidents, etc.). I think that we can all be enthusiastic about the research effort currently under way involving the construct of general intellectual ability. I suspect that we will know a great deal more about it four years from now.

Although there is probably some value in pursuing and trying to understand the relationship between the construct of intelligence and the construct of industrial proficiency, we should not abandon the search for relationships between specific aspects of "intelligence" (if we can define the construct adequately) and specific aspects of job performance.

FIGURE 6–4 Sample Item from Bennett Mechanical Comprehension Test

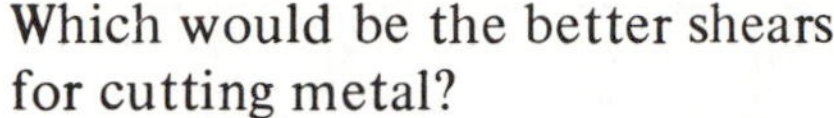

Which would be the better shears
for cutting metal?

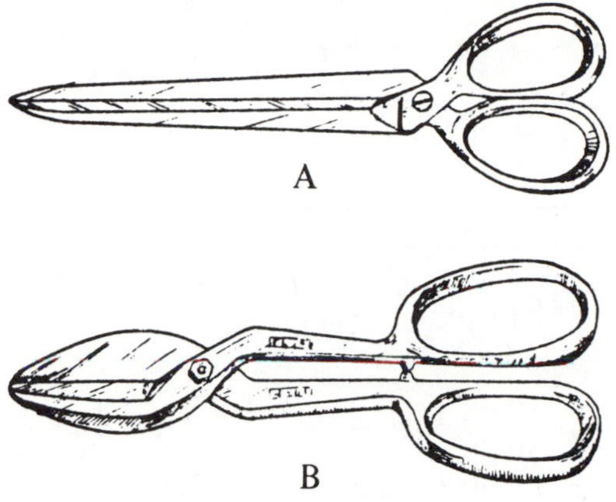

SOURCE: Bennett Mechanical Comprehension Test, Form BB, Item Y. Reproduced by permission. Copyright 1941, renewed 1969 by The Psychological Corporation, New York, NY All rights reserved.

Mechanical and Spatial Abilities. Paper-and-pencil tests of mechanical abilities generally require the individual to identify, recognize, or apply a mechanical principle suggested by the test item. Figure 6–4 presents an item from one of the most popular of these tests, the Bennett Mechanical Comprehension Test. This type of test has high face validity for many blue-collar skilled and unskilled positions.

Spatial relations and reasoning would seem to be important for many occupations. A multiple aptitude test battery known as the DAT (Differential Aptitude Test) describes spatial relations as follows:

> The *Spatial Relations* test is a measure of ability to deal with concrete materials through visualization. There are many vocations in which one is required to imagine how a specified object would appear if rotated in a given way. This ability to manipulate things mentally, to create a structure in one's mind from a plan, is what the test is designed to evaluate. It is an ability needed in such fields as drafting, dress designing, architecture, art, die-making, and decoration, or wherever there is a need to visualize objects in three dimensions. (DAT, 1973, p. 6)

Figure 6–5 is an example of a relatively simple spatial relations test item. The individual is required to visualize some property of the stimulus that is not immediately apparent. This requires some mental manipulation of the stimulus. This is an ability that seems to be modifiable by training. Figure 6–5 comes from the DAT. Consider how that ability, spatial relations, might

FIGURE 6–5 Spatial Relations Test Item

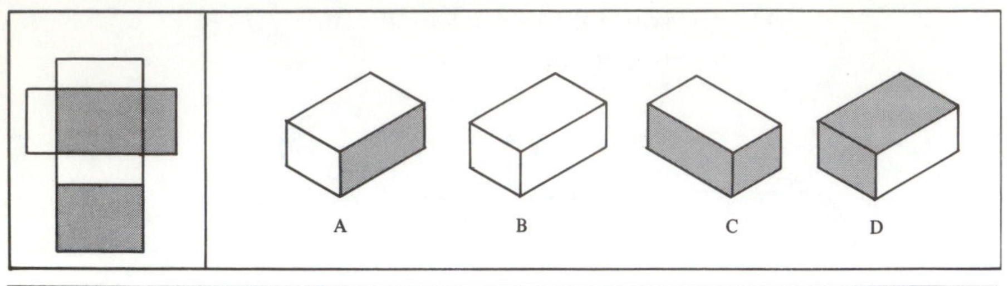

SOURCE: DAT Space Relations Test. Reproduced by permission.

enter into the job of a fire fighter. The test item in Figure 6–6 comes from a test administered to candidates for a fire fighter job in a midwestern city. It should be apparent that these items really address the same basic skill except one of the test items has a good deal more face validity than the other.

Perceptual Accuracy. Perceptual accuracy tests are usually straightforward and, like mechanical comprehension tests, have high face validity for many occupations. These tests usually involve some kind of comparison. The individual is presented with a standard stimulus of some kind and asked to determine if a test stimulus is the same or different. Figure 6–7 presents an example of such a test item. The task of the individual is to compare the two columns of numbers and letters and identify pairs that do not match, such as those checked. For many clerical jobs, this kind of test amounts to a work-sample test, since the job requires exactly the behavior tested. In other cases, it is assumed to measure an aptitude necessary for the development of clerical skills. As Ghiselli points out (1973), these tests do have reasonable validity for many clerical positions. He reports some validity coefficients in the .40s.

Motor Abilities. Tests of motor abilities involve the movement of the limbs in one fashion or another. It may be a complex task in which the individual is required to move arms and legs in coordination, as in the task of flying an airplane or playing an organ; it may be a simple task such as placing pins in slots with the use of tweezers. Motor abilities represent characteristics of the individual that have some potential relationship to job performance not accounted for by tests of intellectual abilities, of mechanical and spatial abilities, or of perceptual accuracy.

The terms *sensorimotor* and *psychomotor* are often applied to manipulation tests such as those described above. Guion (1965) provides a useful distinction between these two terms. Psychomotor abilities are those primarily requiring

FIGURE 6–6 Spatial Relations Item from a Test for Fire Fighters

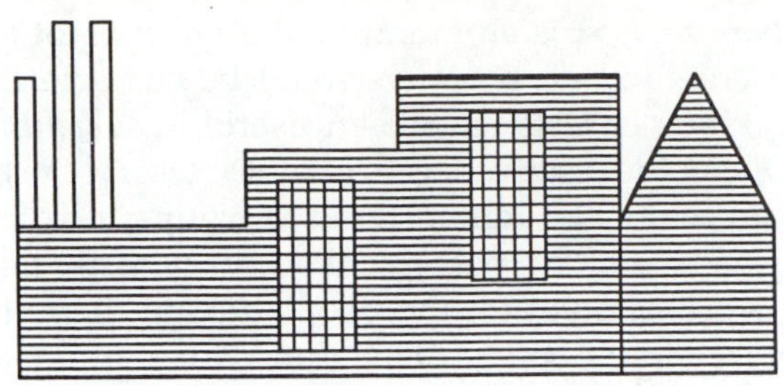

Above is a picture of a factory shown from the front. From the back, it would look like:

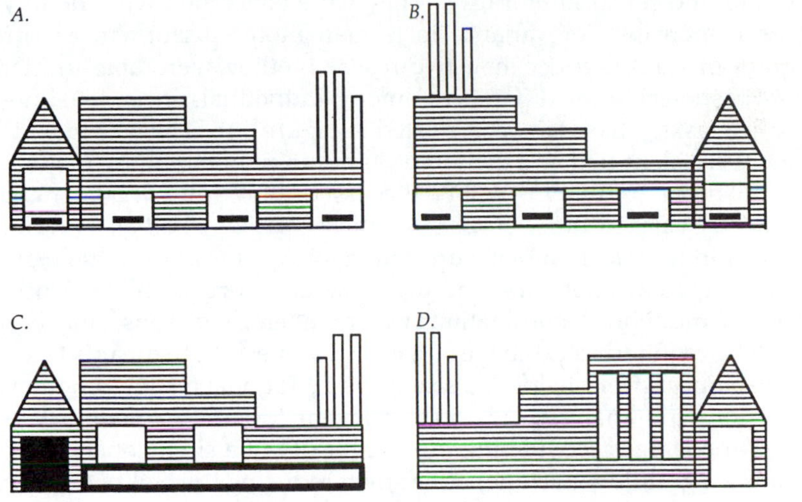

FIGURE 6–7 A Perceptual Accuracy Test

A	*B*
170-CU-7Z25B43-W47	170-CU-7Z25B43-W47
248-RT-67F896H-T62	248-RT76F-896H-T62 √
991-PP-943G56V-55J	991-PP-943G56U-55J √
693-LD-T754DF9-BB6	

muscular movement and control; sensorimotor tests basically require some initial involvement of sense receptors, followed by some muscular movement and control. A tweezer test is an example of a psychomotor test; driving an automobile on a crowded expressway would be characterized as a sensorimotor test. Both kinds of tests have been useful in selection and placement over the years. One of the disadvantages of motor tests is the time and expense involved. They can seldom be administered to groups and often involve costly equipment. As was true of the perceptual accuracy tests, many of the motor tests amount to work samples for the people taking them: in many jobs, an individual is required in the course of job duties to manipulate nuts and bolts, small pins, and the like.

Fleishman and his associates (Fleishman, 1966; Fleishman & Quaintance, 1984) have been extremely successful in refining our understanding of psychomotor and sensorimotor tests. They were concerned with identifying the factors responsible for variance in human motor performance. Through a program of careful and exhaustive research, they were able to identify 11 factors responsible for differences among individuals in various motor performance tasks. These factors are listed in Figure 6–8. The way in which these factors were identified and their importance in understanding the capabilities and limitations of humans will be discussed more fully in a later chapter. It is relatively easy to think of tests for these various abilities as well as their relationship to tasks that make up certain jobs. For example, crane operators, heavy-equipment operators, and organists are all required to exhibit a high degree of multilimb coordination; watchmakers, surgeons, and bartenders may all be required to exhibit arm-hand steadiness. Fleishman's taxonomy of motor abilities is very helpful in structuring a rational testing program around a well-done job analysis; it is quite relevant to current models of selection since it encourages considering the complexity of a single operation (such as operating a grinding machine) rather than reducing the ability test to one task that might be a simulation of the job (such as a tweezer dexterity test).

Often, it is necessary to measure broad physical abilities that are necessary in testing candidates for physically demanding jobs. One example of such a job is that of fire fighter. These individuals must often work for extended periods of time, exerting substantial physical effort in difficult circumstances. It is common for a fire fighter to pull a 2-inch fire hose weighing 100 pounds or more into a burning residence, unable to see through the smoke, wearing 60 pounds of protective gear (clothing, air tank, etc.), and then to stay in that environment (at temperatures between 300 and 1,000 degrees) for 15 to 30 minutes. Those situations place heavy physical demands on the incumbent and require above average amounts of stamina, muscular strength, muscular endurance, and flexibility. As a result, many testing programs for physically demanding jobs include tests of these broader physical abilities. Table 6–2 describes a series of physical ability tests that I developed for use in screening fire fighter applicants.

FIGURE 6–8 Taxonomy of Abilities

The taxonomy of the more important abilities resulting from this programmatic research as briefly described by Fleishman (1966):

Control precision: This factor is common to tasks which require fine, highly controlled, but not overcontrolled, muscular adjustments, primarily where larger muscle groups are involved . . .

Multilimb coordinations: This is the ability to coordinate the movements of a number of limbs simultaneously . . .

Response orientation: This ability factor . . . appears to involve the ability to *select* the correct movement in relation to the correct stimulus, especially under highly speeded conditions . . .

Reaction time: This represents simply the speed with which an individual is able to respond to a stimulus when it appears . . .

Speed of arm movement: This represents simply the speed with which an individual can make a gross, discrete arm movement where accuracy is not the requirement . . .

Rate control: This ability involves the making of continuous anticipatory motor adjustments relative to changes in speed and direction of a continuously moving target or object . . .

Manual dexterity: This ability involves skillful, well-directed arm-hand movements in manipulating fairly large objects under speed conditions . . .

Finger dexterity: This is the ability to make skill-controlled manipulations of tiny objects involving, primarily, the fingers.

Arm-hand steadiness: This is the ability to make precise arm-hand positioning movements where strength and speed are minimized; the critical feature, as the name implies, is the steadiness with which such movements can be made . . .

Wrist, finger speed: This ability has been called "tapping" in many previous studies . . .

Aiming: This ability appears to be measured by printed tests which provide the subject with very small circles. . . . The subject typically goes from circle to circle placing one dot in each circle as rapidly as possible.

SOURCE: From "Human Abilities and the Acquisition of Skill" (pp. 152–156) by E. A. Fleishman, in E. A. Bilodeau (Ed.), *Acquisition of Skill,* 1966, New York: Academic Press.

Physical Abilities: Fitness versus Performance. It is important to distinguish between *physical abilities* and *physical fitness.* Many organizations test for fitness. These tests might include a bicycle stress test of cardiovascular (heart) strength, a flexibility test, and a muscular-strength test. In spite of the fact that these tests might also be used to differentiate among candidates, when they are administered as fitness tests, it is only to assure the employer that the applicant has at least some minimum amount of an attribute. The notion is that if an individual falls below some minimal standard, the individual is more likely to suffer an illness or injury. It can be easily shown that poor

" 'Oops!' has no place in the vocabulary of a surgeon."

From *The Wall Street Journal,* with permission of Cartoon Features Syndicate

cardiovascular fitness can lead to coronary and cardiovascular disease for those with physically demanding jobs. Similarly, workers who have low flexibility or strength can be shown to have a much higher probability of lower back injuries in physically demanding jobs (Davis & Mount, 1984). The value

TABLE 6–2 Physical Ability Tests for Fire Fighters

Stairway climb: Candidate wears fire protective clothing and air tank and carries seven pieces of equipment up three flights of stairs, one piece at a time. Each piece of equipment weighs between 25 and 55 pounds.

Hose pull: Candidate wears air tank, stands in one spot, and pulls 50 feet of fire hose filled with water using a hand-over-hand technique.

Ladder pull: Candidate wears air tank and pulls a 16-foot ladder from the ladder bed of a fire truck, places it on the ground, picks it back up, and replaces it in the ladder bed.

Dummy drag: Candidate drags a 125-pound sandbag around a serpentine course of 40 feet. The candidate must keep one knee in contact with the ground and may not lift or carry the sandbag but must drag it.

Blind crawl: Candidate wears fire protective clothing and an air tank. After putting on a blackened face mask, the candidate must crawl through a plywood maze that has several turns in it. In addition, there are sandbags located strategically throughout the maze. The maze is approximately 40 feet in length.

Pike pole: Candidate wears an air tank and alternately pulls and pushes a 75-pound weight attached to a pole hanging from a frame. The candidate must complete as many repetitions as possible in a four-minute period. A repetition is defined as one push and two pulls.

Fan hang: Candidate wears fire protective clothing and an air tank and lifts a 50-pound fan from ground level, hanging it on a standard door frame.

of fitness tests can be demonstrated by looking at things such as lost time and injuries for fit and nonfit workers. The logic is that an individual who is not at work because of illness or injury can hardly make a contribution.

The role of physical abilities in *performance* is another issue. When performance is the central issue, the assumption is that the individual with more of the physical ability (e.g., stamina) will perform better (i.e., faster or longer) than the individual with less of the physical ability. A recent review by Campion (1983) and research projects by J. D. Arnold, Rauschenberger, Soubel, and Guion, (1982) and Reilly, Zedeck, and Tenopy (1979) demonstrate the validity of physical ability tests for physically demanding jobs. It can be demonstrated for many jobs that the greater the physical ability possessed by the worker, the higher the performance.

What Typical Ability Tests Do Not Measure

There is no doubt that from the time at which large-scale ability testing was introduced to educational and employment contexts, the role, value, and accuracy of tests has been exaggerated. There are some things that ability tests can do and do quite well. They can highlight subgroups of strengths and weaknesses in applicants and allow a reasonable comparison to be made between the demands of a job and the characteristics of an applicant. Further,

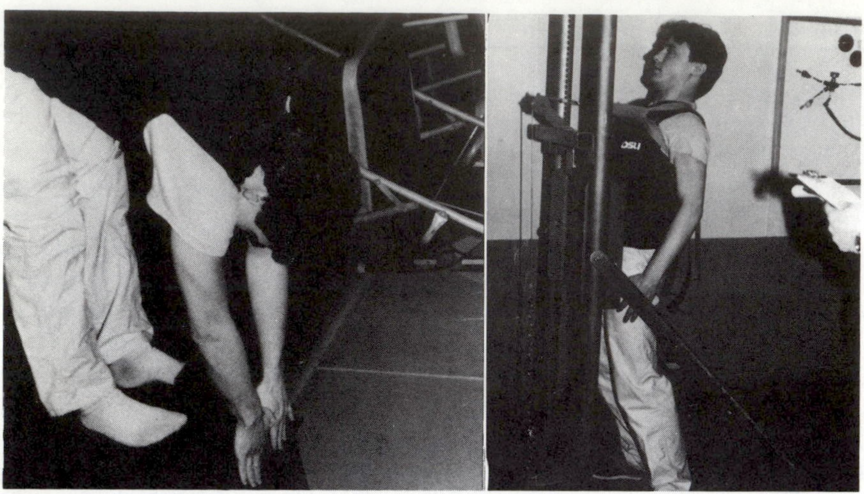

(a) Here an individual takes a sit-and-reach test to measure flexibility. (Mike Gill)
(b) This device was created to measure lower back strength. (Mike Gill)

they can place an applicant in perspective with respect to others who might have applied for the same position. This can be accomplished by comparing observed scores to norm tables of the percentages of people from a given population achieving certain scores.

In balance, however, there are many uses of ability test scores that are inappropriate. In Chapter 8, I will discuss various strategies for using test information to make employment decisions. Nevertheless, it is important in this chapter to point out the limitations of content in many commonly used ability tests. For example, consider a test battery that includes a general test of intellectual ability, a hand-eye coordination test, and a mechanical aptitude test. For a particular position such as transducer assembler, abilities measured by these tests might be quite important to successful performance. There are other skills, abilities, and tendencies that will also play a role in the success of the transducer assembler that are *not* measured by these tests. In a review of the state of the art in ability testing, the National Research Council (Garner & Wigdor, 1982) made several observations with respect to limitations of ability tests. First, large-scale group tests do not permit much opportunity for getting estimates of written or oral expression (as opposed to comprehension). In addition, the typical group test expects the applicant to *react* rather than take independent action. As a result, it is impossible to assess creativity, independent action, or imagination—characteristics that are important in many occupations. Finally, these typical tests provide little opportunity for estimates of intuition, perseverance, or insight.

That is not to say that typical ability tests do not play an important role in personnel decisions. Rather, it suggests that they have a specific role and should not be stretched to serve purposes beyond that role. In most situations, measured abilities will represent several pieces of the puzzle, but other pieces will be necessary.

Personality and Interest Inventories. It might be more appropriate to label these tests as motivational rather than personality and interest tests. The distinction between motivational and personality variables is becoming less clear. For example, you are likely to see "need for achievement" described as both a personality and a motivational variable. However, in keeping with Ghiselli's categorization, I will refer to these tests as personality and interest tests. Two major subcategories of personality tests are *objective* and *projective.* By objective tests, I refer to those paper-and-pencil tests that provide a clear stimulus, such as a statement about preferences for various life-styles, and a clear set of responses from which to choose. This type of test is often referred to as a personality *inventory.* A projective test, on the other hand, presents an ambiguous stimulus to the individual and does not restrict response format. The Rorschach inkblot test is an example of a projective test.

The logic of personality testing is that knowing the habitual manner in which an individual responds in many different situations should help in determining whether the individual will be successful in a particular class of jobs. Although this rationale makes sense, it has been hard to demonstrate. Guion and Gottier (1965) reviewed the validity information on personality tests used in industrial settings. Their review covered studies published between 1952 and 1963. Here is their conclusion:

> In brief, it is difficult in the face of this summary to advocate with a clear conscience the use of personality measures in most situations as a basis of making employment decisions about people. It seems clear that the only acceptable reason for using personality measures as instruments of decision is found only after doing considerable research with the measure in the specific situation and for the specific purpose for which it is to be used. Sometimes, unvalidated personality measures are used as instruments of decision because of "clinical insight" or of gullibility or superstition or of evidence accumulated in some other setting. All of these may be equally condemned unless specific situational data can be gathered that the insight, superstition, or borrowed validity is in fact predictive. (p. 160)

The invasion of privacy issue raised by critics in the early 1960s (Gross, 1962) has done much to temper the use of personality tests in industry. This tempering has received an additional boost from current concerns for fair employment. The responsibility for demonstrating that a particular personality test is job-related could be overwhelming in the case of a projective test, such as the Rorschach. A review of the three journals cited as sources by Guion and Gottier for the years following the publication of their article reveals few published reports of attempts to relate personality measures to job performance. This will change, no doubt, in the next several years. A technique known as the *assessment center* is becoming more and more popular, particularly in the identification of managerial talent. I will describe this technique in some detail shortly, but for the present discussion it is useful to know that a significant part of the "assessment" in such centers is the measurement of motivational or personality variables.

Individual Assessment. It is interesting to note that in spite of the paucity of research on personality testing for selection since the Guion and Gottier review, this type of testing still seems to be quite popular. It is most often embedded in a procedure known as *individual assessment,* a term meant to connote several things. First, it generally implies that the psychologist will be combining information in some clinical rather than statistical manner in order to make a decision about whether to hire or promote someone. In addition, it usually means that the psychologist will be considering only one person at a time and will not be administering group tests of any sort. Third, it commonly means that the psychologist will be using one or more personality tests or inventories in the assessment process.

Ryan and Sackett (1987) recently completed a survey of the extensiveness of individual assessment by industrial and organizational psychologists, and the results are surprising. There are many more I/O professionals involved in this activity than might be expected, based on the absence of research on the topic. Ryan and Sackett originally mailed surveys to 1,000 I/O psychologists who indicated some involvement in personnel selection. They received responses from 316 of these individuals. Of those responding, over 50 percent indicated that they were involved in individual assessment. Of those conducting individual assessments, the majority conducted assessment sessions that lasted anywhere from two hours to two days, typically charged $500 for the assessment, and used personality inventories liberally. There was one anomaly in the data that was interesting. Although only 40 percent of those conducting individual assessment reported conducting formal job analyses for the positions in question, 64 percent claimed that what they were doing met the requirements of the "Uniform Guidelines" (1978) for valid test procedures. Another 30 percent were unsure of the extent to which they were following the guidelines. I would be willing to bet that a distressing number of those individuals do not even have a copy of the guidelines! It is hard to reconcile the extensiveness of the use of personality tests and individual assessment with the absence of solid research and the casual attitude toward job analysis.

This problem may be in the process of being addressed. The topic of individual assessment has emerged as a legitimate area for research and theory building. As an example, Bernardin and Bownas (1985) published a book devoted to personality assessment in industrial settings. By publishing that book, the authors hoped to bring about a revival in research in this area, almost as a defensive strategy. If people continue to use personality inventories for selection, promotion, and placement, it is best that serious research be undertaken. In the introduction to that book, the authors describe, with

Novice Monk Driven to Crime

By Anthony Hopkins

The pressures of the monastic life boiled over for a young novice monk at St Hugh's Charter House, Partridge Green, Sussex, and he took a 30-ton lorry loaded with 7,000 bricks and drove it away, knocking down a traffic bollard, a magistrates court was told yesterday.

Michael Brims, 25, was conditionally discharged by Horsham magistrates when they were told that he had taken vows of poverty and had no money although the monastery had offered to pay costs.

Mr Terence Coghlan, defending, said that the offence had happened during Lent—an onerous time when life at the monastery was particularly hard. Rations had been meagre and gradually life there had begun to get Brims down.

Wearing a suit in court, Brims admitted taking a lorry without consent from outside a house in Cowfold, Sussex. He got into the cab, found the ignition keys there and drove it off.

He reached Epsom in Surrey where he decided to call his family in Glasgow and it was while he was reversing the lorry down a narrow street that he hit and damaged the bollard.

Brims, who also pleaded guilty to using the vehicle without a heavy goods vehicle licence and without insurance, was ordered to pay £18 costs.

He was described as the youngest member of the community and—as an assistant cook in the company of senior monks who practised almost total silence—life had got too much for him.

Mr Coghlan said that it was a mistake to expect Brims to spend so much time—up to seven hours—in the company of an 80-year-old monk because it meant that he was not getting out into the monastery garden for exercise.

Brims, who had not realised he suffered from dyslexia, had trouble reading from the scriptures—a major part of the life of a monk, said Mr Coghlan. Gradually the pressures built up until he could stand them no longer. He suddenly walked out without telling anyone.

Prior Bernard O'Donovan said: "Brother Michael always gave the impression of being very peaceful going about his work. If he had come along to me that morning, things could have been resolved. I have not the slightest doubt that this was a temporary aberration."

SOURCE: From "Novice Monk Driven to Crime" by A. Hopkins, May 20, 1987, *London Daily Telegraph*, p. 1.

Brother Michael might have been well served with some individual assessment before taking his position at the monastery.

painful precision, the way in which the personality test is introduced into the workplace. That description is reproduced in Figure 6–9.

Interest Inventories. The most widely used interest test is probably the Strong Vocational Interest Blank (SVIB). This type of test compares the responses of the individual taking the test with the responses of individuals

FIGURE 6–9 The "Selling" of a Personality Test

The typical adoption scenario is for the practitioner first to be influenced by a slick brochure from the publisher of "Snake Oil Extraordinaire (SOE)." The brochure probably has guarded and ambiguous statements of support for the use of SOE. Testimonials may make such claims as "my productivity went up 20% after I started to select my managers using the SOE" or "preliminary evidence shows the SOE increases productivity, decreases turnover and absenteeism, and reverses male pattern baldness." The probability that the practitioner will purchase the test may be more a function of the slickness of the brochure and the fast-talking sales representative than of the actual validity of the instrument being peddled. One common marketing strategy in this area is to publish related articles in magazines and soft trade journals that are read by organizational decision makers. These outlets often lack the expertise to critically assess the veracity of claims regarding the instrument. Airline magazines are a great target for this strategy. For example, three articles appeared in airline magazines in 1983 extolling the virtues of handwriting analysis for predicting sales and managerial success. All were by the same author, who happens to have a consulting firm specializing in graphology. In fact, there is virtually no evidence to support the use of handwriting analysis to predict work performance.

SOURCE: *Personality Assessment in Organizations,* H. John Bernardin and David A. Bownas, Eds. (Praeger Publishers, New York, 1985), p.vi. Copyright © 1985 by Praeger Publishers. Reprinted with permission.

already successful in particular fields. The implication is that the individual has the greatest likelihood for success (on motivational grounds) in the occupation most closely matching his or her response pattern. Interest tests are used more widely for vocational counseling and guidance than for selection and placement decisions.

Multiple-Aptitude Test Batteries

A final category of tests is defined by structure rather than content. This category includes test batteries that compose many of the content categories already mentioned. They are generally lengthy tests lasting several hours and have subsections dealing with items such as numerical abilities, verbal abilities, and spatial relations. There have been several prominent batteries over the years. One of the first was Thurstone's (1938) Primary Mental Abilities test (PMA), which closely paralleled his theory of intelligence. As opposed to many of the early researchers in the area of intelligence, Thurstone concluded on the basis of factor analyses that intelligence was composed of several basic or primary mental abilities. He set about constructing a scale to measure each of these abilities. The scales currently composing the PMA are as follows: verbal meaning, number facility, reasoning, spatial relations, perceptual speed, memory, and word fluency. These clearly represent a collection of several of the content categories that we have dealt with so far.

There are advantages to having information related to many different abilities. Such information would be particularly valuable for differential job placement purposes. The trade-off, of course, is the cost and time involved in administration. Although the PMA represents one of the few attempts to tie tests specifically to a theory of intellectual abilities, there are some complaints that it has not changed appreciably since its introduction (Buros, 1972). Two other more recent batteries in use are the General Aptitude Battery (GATB) and the DAT. The GATB will be receiving a great deal of attention in the next two years. As I indicated in an earlier chapter, a committee of the National Research Council is considering the extent to which the GATB provides predictive information for all the jobs in the federal government. In addition, it is the GATB that forms the foundation for the proposals of Schmidt, Hunter, and their colleagues about general intellectual ability. A similar test is one that has been used by the armed services for 40 years in the testing of applicants and recruits. It is known as the Armed Services Vocational Aptitude Battery (ASVAB) and consists of various subtests to measure different facets of intellectual functioning.

Assessment Centers

A logical extension of the multiple-aptitude battery is the *assessment center*. This label derives from the fact that groups of individuals (both those to be assessed and those doing the assessment) are brought together for the purpose of determining the potential of a group of individuals currently employed by an organization. This assessment may imply promotion, placement, or simply career guidance. Finkle (1976) has done a comprehensive review of the development of this technique over the past few decades. In that review, he says that "assessment center . . . refers to a group-oriented, standardized series of activities that provides a basis for judgments or predictions of human behaviors believed or known to be relevant to work performed in an organizational setting" (p. 861). The earliest systematic assessment center approach was by AT&T. An excellent description of the development and logic of the AT&T effort is contained in a book by the psychologists primarily responsible for that program (Bray, Campbell, & Grant, 1974). This program was begun in 1956.

Most assessment centers are similar in several respects (Finkle, 1976):

1. Assessment is done in groups. Groups of 12 individuals are usually assessed simultaneously. They may be broken into smaller groups of six or three for particular exercises. Group assessment provides the opportunity for peer evaluation.
2. Assessment is done by groups. Evaluators or assessors work in teams to produce and evaluate information. These groups usually consist of man-

agers from the organization who are not personally acquainted with the person being assessed. The team may also include a psychologist.

3. Multiple methods. Several different methods are used to gather information about the person being considered. These might include objective testing, projective testing, and group and individual interviews, as well as individual and group-based situational exercises. One favorite individual exercise is known as the *in basket*. In this exercise, the assessee deals with a series of memos by rerouting them, responding to them in writing, or filing them. A typical group exercise might be a leaderless group discussion. The objective and projective tests might be chosen from the list described earlier in the chapter.
4. Face validity. There is almost universal agreement among individuals being assessed and acting as assessors that the process has the appearance of relevance—to a much greater degree than the typical paper-and-pencil test for the selection of managers.

As a result of completing the various tests, exercises, and interviews, the person being assessed has provided the assessment team with a large amount of information. On the basis of this information, the team typically rates each assessee on a series of dimensions. Typical of these dimensions are the following: decision making, human relations skills, administrative ability, persuasiveness, resistance to stress, impact, personal acceptability, flexibility, realism of expectations, motivation, and intellectual ability.

On the basis of these ratings, as well as other notes kept during the assessment period, a rather lengthy narrative report is prepared for each person who was assessed. In Figure 6–10, portions of a typical report are produced.

This report is then condensed, and portions of it are fed back to the person who was assessed by one or more members of the assessment team. The actual activities usually occur over a several-day period, often in a conference center geographically separate from the normal workplace. The members of the assessment team are usually given training in assessment procedures and the particular instruments to be used. This training may last anywhere from three hours to several days.

As part of the promotional process for appointing sergeants in a midwestern police department, my colleagues (Rick Jacobs and Janet Echemendia) and I developed an assessment center. This assessment center followed a written examination on technical and managerial knowledge and was administered to 135 candidates. The candidates reported to a local conference center in groups of six. Group membership was randomly assigned. After arriving at the location, the candidates picked up a packet of materials that described what their activities would be for the next four hours. Candidates

FIGURE 6–10

"There were several indications from his behavior that his strong desire to make a favorable impression promoted above average tenseness in the assessment situation. On several occasions, his behavior was characterized by nervousness and controlled quietness, as though he were reluctant to enter into a situation until he felt absolutely sure of himself."

"The picture he created was that of a young man eager to cooperate, comply, and do his best in order to fulfill the expectations others had for him."

"In most respects, the trainee's general abilities compare favorably with the total sample of men in the Management Progress study."

"Most members of the staff anticipated a very successful career in the Bell System for the trainee. . . . There was a mild amount of disagreement concerning the speed with which he is likely to reach the district level of management. Everyone agreed that he presently displays the abilities and potential to perform effectively at the district level."

SOURCE: From *Formative Years in Business: A Long-term AT&T Study of Managerial Lives,* by D. W. Bray, R. J. Campbell, and D. L. Grant, 1974, New York: Wiley & Sons. Copyright © by John Wiley & Sons, Inc. Reprinted by permission of John Wiley & Sons, Inc.

were assessed by a four-person assessment panel consisting of three upper-level police supervisors (captains and deputy chiefs) and one professional human resource consultant. All candidates were assessed by the same panel.

The first task for each candidate was to meet individually with the board and describe the work experiences that qualified them to be a first-level supervisor. They had been told in advance about this component and were able to prepare their presentation prior to their meeting with the board. Next, the candidates were asked to complete several written reports that might be filed by a sergeant. Finally, the candidates were asked to meet as a group and discuss two problems that they might encounter as actual sergeants while the assessment panel observed the discussion. The first problem dealt with a new department policy regarding meal breaks that was unpopular with the police officers reporting to the sergeants. The second problem was related to a string of armed robberies that seemed to be occurring in all precincts and were disrupting normal work routines and creating pressure on the sergeants from their supervisors.

After the candidates had completed the group discussions, the assessors had one hour to review their notes on the performance of the various candidates and assign ratings to them on various performance areas including communication skills, interpersonal skills, and problem-solving skills. Based on these ratings, candidates were assigned an assessment center score that was combined with their written examination scores to determine their final promotional score. The candidates uniformly praised the assessment center as job-related and fair.

On the basis of the results of an assessment center, organizations may make many different types of decisions. Among them are the following (Finkle, 1976):

1. An assessee does or does not qualify for a particular job or job level.
2. Assessees may be ranked on a series of variables and placed into different categories of anticipated speed of promotion.
3. Predictions of long-range potential may be made.
4. Development programs for aiding the assessee in personal growth may be provided.
5. Team members may be aided in their role as assessors.

The results of assessment center approaches are encouraging. This approach supports the process of differential placement rather than the more traditional and less useful selection ethic. The strengths and weaknesses of the applicants can be matched with the requirements of various positions in the organization. Data on predictive validities are promising. For example, Schmitt et al. (1984) show strong patterns of validities for predicting success as school administrators (assistant principals and principals in elementary and secondary schools) using an assessment center approach. There are now several private organizations that conduct assessment centers for client companies. This provides an opportunity for small organizations with too few employees to do traditional validation projects to take advantage of the cumulative data of the assessment center in drawing inferences about the potential of its people.

In spite of its logical and cosmetic appeal, there have been some misgivings expressed concerning assessment centers. Dunnette and Borman (1979) warned that the "rapid growth of assessment methods may be accompanied by sloppy or improper application of assessment procedures" (p. 32). The lack of quality control on assessment procedures could easily lead to indiscriminate and damaging results, similar to those encountered by the random application of "sensitivity training" in the late 1960s. The general use of assessment centers (whether they are appropriate or not) is a particularly important issue, owing to the cost of this technique. It is extremely expensive, and the benefit should clearly be evaluated in terms of its cost.

Reservations have also been expressed concerning the reliability of the ratings that are made of the assessees (Hinrichs & Haanpera, 1976) as well as the validity of those ratings (Klimoski & Strickland, 1977). There is some concern that instead of predicting future performance, the team members are actually identifying those assessees who fit in the company "mold" most neatly. In effect, they are actually predicting the promotion decisions that will ultimately be made concerning the assessees. This criticism could not be easily dismissed, since most validation studies of assessment centers used promotions or salary success as the criterion. The only way to answer this type of criticism is to show that assessment centers are capable of predicting the actual behavior of the individual being assessed. Studies such as the one reported by Schmitt et al. (1984) directly address those criticisms and, to some extent, dispel the concerns.

Similarly, Borman (1982) was able to demonstrate that an assessment center approach to the selection of army recruiters was considerably more effective than traditional paper-and-pencil devices when a behavioral (rather than "progress") criterion was employed. In this study, the criterion was the performance of recruiters in a telephone conversation with a prospective recruit and the recruit's family.

The Schmitt et al. and Borman research represent a step in the right direction. Nevertheless, there is still a great need for studies documenting the relationship between assessed abilities and assessee job performance. More important, we need to know *why* assessment centers are valid. Klimoski and Brickner (1987) have written a provocative article that directly addresses the potential explanations for why assessment centers seem to work. Their concern is based primarily on the fact that there seems to be no discriminant validity for the various dimensions assessed in the exercises, nor is there discriminant validity for the various exercises themselves. Operationally, this is seen in the high intercorrelations among the dimension scores (e.g., communication skills, interpersonal skills, problem solving) and in the high intercorrelations among the scores assigned for different exercises. In other words, the assessment center does not seem to be able to distinguish clearly among various attributes. This is a problem since the exercises are usually developed for the purpose of illuminating specific skills and abilities. Klimoski and Brickner suggest six different alternative explanations to account for the correlations between assessment center scores and various criteria. These alternatives are:

1. *Legitimate validity.* The attributes measured by the assessment center are required for successful performance on the job in question. Although they suggest this as a possibility, they cannot be enthusiastic about this explanation since it cannot account for the high intercorrelations among the dimensions, intercorrelations that should be in the low to medium range.
2. *Criterion contamination (direct).* Assessment center scores are used to make later promotions. This explanation would be relevant only if salary or promotional history is used as a criterion.
3. *Criterion contamination (indirect).* This explanation is the original suggestion of Klimoski and Strickland; that is, the assessors can recognize the attributes that are favored by the organization and can predict who will be considered successful in the organization. Note that this could also account for ratings as criteria and is not necessarily limited to salary and promotion history as criteria.

4. *Self-fulfilling prophecy.* Candidates who do well in the assessment center will begin to think more highly of themselves and, as a result, aspire to higher levels of performance with enhanced self-confidence.
5. *Performance consistency.* Since many assessment centers include components that require the candidate to disclose information related to past work assignments, successes, failures, and the like, the assessors are simply working from the premise that the best predictor of future behavior is past behavior and use those historical data to make their predictions.
6. *Managerial intelligence.* This explanation assumes that both assessor and eventual supervisors value apparent intellectuality. As a result, apparently intelligent assessees receive higher scores in the assessment center and more promotions/raises or higher ratings from their eventual supervisors. This is independent of the extent to which general intelligence is required for the job in question. This is a form of institutional help.

Value of Requiring Consensus among Assessors. A common characteristic of assessment centers is a discussion called the *consensus review.* After individual assessors have assigned ratings to the candidates, they reveal those ratings to each other and agree to record a single score for the candidate that represents their "consensus" view of the candidate's performance. In Borman's study described above, the value of this consensus process was evaluated. Borman found that consensus was not a critical part of the success of the assessment approach. In fact, he found that predictive accuracy of assessments was better when the ratings of the various assessors were simply averaged than when they got together to talk about their impressions of the individual assessees. In an independent study, Sackett and Wilson (1982) found that the consensus ratings of assessors could be predicted with a great degree of accuracy from the simple average of their individual ratings. This meant that, at best, the process of arriving at consensus was redundant. Consensus could have been achieved by simply averaging ratings. Together, these findings suggest that if an assessment center is being used for purposes of identifying particular individuals who will be selected or promoted, the consensus phase is either redundant (Sackett et al.) or counterproductive (Borman, 1982). In other words, it is best left out of the process. On the other hand, if the purpose is identifying strengths and weaknesses, providing feedback, or assessing general organization resources, then the consensus phase would be critical since substance is more important than the simple identification of applicants of high potential.

The assessment center remains an intriguing annoyance. It is intriguing because it is widely accepted by candidates and produces some very encouraging validity coefficients. It is an annoyance because we still do not know *why* these validities are obtained. Certainly the high intercorrelations among dimension scores should be reason for discouragement and a warning sign that something is not right. Both Guion (1987) and Sackett and Dreher

TABLE 6–3 Possible Components of Test Preparation

1. Supplying correct answers (cheating)
2. Taking the test for practice
3. Maximizing motivation
4. Optimizing test anxiety
5. Instructing test wiseness
   a. General test wiseness (being careful, following directions, using good guessing strategies, using time well, etc.)
   b. Taking advantage of test construction flaws and cues
   c. Using special strategies appropriate to a novel or complex question format
6. Instructing test content
   a. Instructing in areas related to the interpretation to be made from the scores (the content domain for an achievement measure, the ability being measured, requisite skills or knowledge for eventual success for an admissions or selection measure)
   b. Reviewing previous instruction in areas related to the interpretation to be made
   c. Instructing test-specific content unrelated to the interpretation to be made

(1984) suggest that assessment centers move away from the assessment of personalitylike traits (e.g., leadership, judgment) and move toward the assessment of observable skills and abilities. Then we might find out whether the king might be naked, as Klimoski has been suggesting for some time. Additionally, it seems obvious to me that since the assessors are rating candidates, it might make sense to provide these assessors with the type of rating training advocated by McIntyre (frame of reference) and Pulakos (rating accuracy training) described in the last chapter.

Coaching

The value of personnel testing rests on the assumption that we can obtain an "honest" and accurate estimate of an individual's ability. We expect that the score will be free from artifacts that superficially raise or lower the score. In recent years, there has been increased concern that the score that an individual receives on a paper-and-pencil cognitive test might be artificially inflated through special preparation exercises. The general name for this special preparation is *coaching.* Let's consider the issue of coaching and try to come to some conclusion with respect to whether coaching can affect the interpretation or usefulness of a test score.

Tests are often assumed to tap some relatively stable underlying ability. It is assumed that if a test is well developed, the score obtained from any single administration should depart from the true score of the individual only as a function of change. The variation between true and observed score is a function of the reliability. The less reliable the test, the greater the variation. There are some individuals making millions of dollars challenging that assumption. Stanley Kaplan is one of those people. Kaplan is the head of an empire of test preparation schools devoted to helping individuals improve their scores on standardized tests used to screen applicants for college and professional schools. As an example, in 1982, Kaplan's learning centers enrolled over 80,000 students preparing for tests such as the SAT (for college entrance, LSAT (for law school admissions), and the GMAT (for business school admission). This effort produced $25 million in revenue for Kaplan.

Kaplan's efforts represent the best example of test coaching. Similar efforts can be found wherever large numbers of people are preparing for a standardized examination. As an example, in New York City, there is a very active coaching industry that revolves around various examinations for city employment. In 1983, 37,000 applicants took the examination that would be used to determine who would be admitted to the police academy. Many of these individuals bought study guides and attended coaching sessions geared toward improving their scores on that examination. In fact, after an examination is administered, personnel departments often sell that examination to coaching services for use in later test preparation classes. This raises a question: Can coaching significantly improve an individual's test scores? To a certain extent, the answer depends on how you define *coaching*.

Table 6–3 describes various potential components of a test preparation (coaching) program. There have been many studies of the effect of coaching on test performance, but few of them have been well controlled. Good reviews of this research are provided in a recent report by the National Research Council (Garner & Wigdor, 1982) and in an article by Anastasi (1981). The conclusions of these reviews are as follows:

1. Taking examinations for practice can have a small but positive effect on test scores. Scores will improve simply as a result of exposure to the test in question. Many coaching centers depend on this fact in "guaranteeing" that test scores will improve as a result of their instruction. If the individual has already taken a test and done poorly, his or her test score would probably improve regardless of enrollment in the program. In this way, the program can easily claim credit for the improvement. If the person has not yet taken the test, the coaching program will most likely expose the student to sample tests patterned after the test that will be taken, thus ensuring the practice effect.

2. "Cram" courses intended to teach substance over a short but intense time period will have little impact on test scores beyond the practice effect described above. Again, it won't matter whether the cram courses are conducted by a formal training program or whether the person buys a study guide and crams alone. The effect will be minimal.

3. There is some advantage in learning techniques of test taking. These techniques constitute the skill called *test wiseness*. Individuals can

be taught how to analyze a multiple-choice question, how to spot false assertions in true-false formats, how to use time wisely, and so on. Many students take advantage of these techniques in taking course examinations. In a sense, instructions in test wiseness are attempts to take advantage of weaknesses in the test itself—clues or cues that can narrow the alternatives or make one answer more likely than another. As such, they have little to do with the particular ability being tested for (unless that ability happens to be the analytic decomposition of a test item).

4. Coaching can have significant effects on such variables as motivation, self-esteem, and anxiety. As a result, many obstacles to successful test performance can be eliminated. Being "test wise" implies a confidence in dealing with the basic device being used to estimate the skills or abilities in question. Exposure to the sample test that is similar to the test to be taken relieves a good deal of apprehension and anxiety. The reduction of anxiety can have a positive impact on test performance.

5. Coaching that is directed toward the basic skills being measured by the test can have substantial long-lasting effect on both test performance and skill level. In this case, the improved test performance is a symptom of increased skill or ability. As an example, instruction in memory techniques in preparation for a test that taps memory ability should have a positive and long-lasting effect on the efficiency of a person's memory. This improvement will show up in both test performance and day-to-day behavior.

There are two interrelated problems to consider with respect to coaching. First, although it may not have a major impact on test scores, it may provide the edge necessary in a competitive setting (e.g., civil services testing, college and professional school admissions). In many instances, differences of 1 or 2 percentage points can result in acceptance or rejection. As an example, in the case where 40,000 people take a civil service examination, it is not unusual for over 70 percent of those taking the test to answer over 80 percent of the questions on the test. This means that even a few extra correct answers can move someone from the "reject" to the "accept" category. Related to this problem is the issue of who is exposed to coaching. Coaching costs money. It is likely that the culturally and educationally disadvantaged will have less access to coaching programs than others, in spite of the fact that these are exactly the people with the greatest need for such programs. The most obvious solution to both problems is to make coaching available on a broad basis. For the employer, this might mean providing opportunity for taking a practice examination. It might also suggest that instructions in test wiseness and test-taking strategies be given to all applicants. Finally, it might suggest that employers develop in-house coaching programs that precede employment testing. This coaching might include not only exposure to sample tests and instructions in test wiseness but also to basic skill training in verbal, numerical, and reasoning abilities. There is no doubt that many employers are rejecting applicants whose basic skills are suitable for the position but who suffer from one or more temporary obstacles to test performance. The employer must keep in mind that the search is for an individual who will perform the job well, not for an individual who will produce good test scores.

CENTRAL POINTS FOR STUDY

1. There are resources available for identifying good tests.
2. Tests can be categorized along several different dimensions.
3. Assessment centers are multimethod testing formats.
4. Coaching can affect test scores.

CHAPTER 7

Interviews and Other Predictors

In this chapter, we will consider some sources of data, other than standardized tests, that are used to gather information and impressions used in personnel decision making. As a matter of fact, data from psychological tests constitute only a small part of the total information used in personnel decisions. Interviews and biographical information blanks (or application blanks) are used almost universally in business and industry. Thus, for example, Scott, Clothier, and Spriegel (1949) found that over 99 percent of 325 business organizations reported using the interview as a part of the personnel selection process, and Uhrbrock (1948) reported yearly averages of from 5.4 to 20.8 interviews *per person hired* in one company over a seven-year period. Biographical inventories, or application blanks, appear to be used almost as universally. Similarly, reference checks and letters of recommendation are also used frequently in making personnel decisions.

Somewhat less well-known and less frequently used sources of information are work sample and situational tests and the ratings of peers who interact with other applicants. Yet these methods show some promise as sources of information that can be used to improve personnel decisions. Finally, there are some nontraditional predictors that deserve some mention, including self-appraisal, handwriting analysis, and lie detection.

THE INTERVIEW

The preemployment or selection interview is part of a decision-making process. Both the interview and the process of which it is a part can be evaluated, but the two should not be confused. The interview (the face-to-face interaction between the interviewer and the applicant) is one component of the total process leading to a decision about the applicant. Frequently, studies purporting to evaluate the interview have instead examined the validity of the interviewer's predictions or decisions. However, these decisions are based on the total information and impressions that the interviewer has gained about the applicant and not solely on the face-to-face interview. Typically, the interviewer has had access to biographical and work history data, letters of recommendation, telephone conversations with former employers, and psychological test scores, or some subset of these. Each of these sources of information may contribute to the predictions or decisions about the applicant, but to assume that the predictive validity of the final rating or recommendations indicates the value of the face-to-face interview or any other source of information is, of course, fallacious. Without some knowledge of an interviewer's strategy, we cannot determine how the information received is used. The face-to-face interview may play a determining role, or it may have a trivial influence on the interviewer's decisions.

The time order in which the interviewer receives the information may be important. If the interview occurs before any other information is received, it may "color" the impression of the individual, and nonconfirming or contrary evidence from other sources may be discounted or overlooked. On the other hand, an interview that comes late in the total information-gathering, impression-forming process may serve only to confirm the impressions of the interviewer, contributing little or nothing to the decision process. I will have more to say later about the order effects of information on overall evaluations. For the present, my only point is that the fact that an interview is included in the total decision process provides no indication of the contribution of that face-to-face interaction to the final impressions and evaluations of the interviewer.

The Role of the Interviewer

The first purpose of the interview is to gather information about the applicant. In the most limited conception, the only role of the interviewer would be to report "factual" information about the applicant obtained by asking questions in the interview. This is the type of interviewing used in survey research, where the interview competes with the questionnaire as a method of data collection. The applicant, like the survey respondent, is presented with standardized questions and a limited choice of responses. These answers to open-ended questions are recorded verbatim by the interviewer for later coding. In many surveys the interviewer's role ends with the gathering of information; the coding or interpretation of responses is left to experts in the survey research headquarters.

In contrast, preemployment interviewers seldom function strictly as gatherers of information. Usually, they are required to interpret the information gained from the interview and to draw inferences about certain traits, attributes, attitudes, and potentials that the applicants possess. These inferences frequently take the form of ratings along several dimensions, together with overall ratings (or rankings) of the applicants. The latter often constitute predictions or recommendations by the interviewers. Distinctions as to the role of interviewers can be made again at this point: they may provide ratings as one source of information to a decision maker, with or without overall ratings or recommendations, and these ratings may be based exclusively on the face-to-face interview, or they may be based on the interview and whatever ancillary data are available.

Clinical versus Actuarial Predictions

If the interviewer is expected to integrate interview and other data, weighing different sources and resolving conflicting evidence to arrive at an evaluation, the interviewer is being asked to use *clinical skills* and to function as a sort of human computer. If, on the other hand, the interviewer's ratings are integrated with the other items of information by means of a statistical equation (e.g., a multiple-regression equation), with each variable assigned its own optimum weight, then the predictions are *actuarial,* or statistical, rather than clinical in nature. Although the interviewer's ratings are a matter of clinical judgment, the strategy whereby they are combined and used to arrive at predictions or decisions may be either a matter of judgment or of statistical methods.

There have been several excellent comparisons of clinical versus actuarial methods of information combination. A series of studies by Paul Meehl (1954, 1957, 1965) suggest that acturial combination of information is superior to clinical combinations. In a review of 51 studies, Meehl (1965) found that 33 clearly favored statistical over clinical prediction, 17 failed to establish one method as superior to the other, and only 1 study (Lindzey, 1965) favored clinical over statistical methods. The evidence strongly suggests that the general practice of clinical combination of data must be challenged. This is not to deny the value of interviewing or observational-judgmental methods for gathering data and making inferences about traits or attributes. Rather, it is to bring into question the use of clinical methods for combining the observations and judgments into a composite prediction. In medical terms, the distinction is between observing and recording information about symptoms, on the one hand, and making a diagnosis, on the other. (Incidentally, in that context, Overall and Hollister [1964] have demonstrated the power of statistical models for accurate diagnosis of diseases from observations of symptoms.)

The implications of these findings for decision making in industry and other organizations are far-reaching. They go well beyond questions of the role of the interviewer in the decision process, suggesting, first, that a clear distinction be made between data-gathering and decision-making functions and, second, that statistical techniques be used to a greater extent in combining information into predictions and decisions. This approach has the added advantage of making the decision-making strategy explicit and, consequently, more susceptible to analysis and refinement. Human decision makers are likely to resist the idea of turning over their decision-making responsibilities to a computer. However, they might be less resistant to a compromise strategy in which they would give primary weight to a statistical prediction but reserve a "veto" power in the final decision. Subsequent analysis of the outcomes of those decisions where the decision maker overruled the computer would provide an objective test of his clinical skills. In this respect, the interviewer is in much the same position as a clinical psychologist trying to estimate certain characteristics on the basis of verbal interaction in combination with certain written records. In fact, Wiggins (1973) has done an outstanding job of evaluating the clinical-actuarial argument from the perspective of personality assessment. Although it is inappropriate to review Wiggins's conclusions here, if the general question of clinical versus actuarial prediction interests you, it would be useful to examine Wiggins's book.

Evaluation of the Interview

There are literally hundreds of studies that have investigated the selection interview. It is beyond the scope of this text and the endurance of the reader to review each of these studies. Fortunately, there are several systematic literature reviews that enable the interested student to trace the history of interview research as well as to accumulate substantiated research findings about the interview. These reviews, historically sequenced are: Wagner (1949), Mayfield (1964), Ulrich and Trumbo (1965), Wright (1969), Schmitt (1976), Arvey and Campion (1982), and Webster (1982). For all practical purposes, the last three reviews are sufficient for a current view of interview research since each of them incorporates information from these earlier reviews.

The change in emphasis and approach to the interview is well described in Schmitt's (1976) review. He examined the previous reviews, and in addition to contrasting earlier conclusions with his own, he considered more current evidence concerning the influences on decision making in the interview. His findings are quite detailed and will not be reproduced here. Instead, I will simply summarize the results and invite you to consult the original article for details. What I will do is to pose each of the major findings of the Schmitt review as a question and provide the answer in summary form.

1. *Negative-positive nature of the information.* Does favorable information have the same effect as unfavorable information in the interview? It seems clear that negative information plays a greater role than positive information.
2. *Temporal placement of information.* Does it make any difference if favorable information comes early or late in the interview? It does not seem to. Some studies show one directional effect and other studies show the opposite.
3. *Interviewer stereotypes.* Do interviewers have an "ideal" applicant in mind when they are interviewing real applicants? If so, does this stereotype come from the nature of the job or from the past history of the interviewer? Interviewers do commonly have an "ideal" in mind when they are interviewing candidates, but the ideal of one interviewer is not necessarily the same as the ideal of another interviewer.
4. *Job information.* Does it help to give the interviewer a detailed picture of the job for which the applicant is being considered? Absolutely! We saw

the same effect in frame-of-reference and rater-accuracy training in the performance rating chapter.

5. *Individual differences.* Do all interviewers use basically the same method of combining information? Can interviewers describe how they combine information? Interviewers use different methods for combining information, and they are not very good at describing in words how they do it.
6. *Visual cues.* Are there nonverbal or postural-facial applicant cues that influence interviewer decisions? Yes. In fact, some recent studies (Baron, 1983) show that even the presence of a pleasant scent may have an impact on evaluations. Surprisingly, the effect is not always positive. Male interviewers seem to be negatively affected by the smell of cologne or perfume. In addition, Gifford, Ng, and Wilkinson (1985) have shown that nonverbal cues (such as gestures, the amount of time talked, and dress style) have an influence on estimates of social skill of applicants.
7. *Attitudinal and racial similarity.* Are interviewers more lenient toward applicants of their own race or applicants with similar attitudes? It is complicated, but there do seem to be some effects on particular types of decisions such as starting salaries. The effects do not seem to extend to actual hiring decisions.
8. *Sex.* Are interviewers more lenient toward applicants of the same sex? There do not seem to be strong sex-based influences on hiring decisions.
9. *Contrast effects.* Is an applicant's favorability affected by the favorability of others in the applicant group? The evidence is not particularly strong here. In addition, many of the studies are done with students acting as interviewers rather than real employment interviewers.
10. *Interviewer experience.* Do experienced interviewers produce more valid and reliable decisions than inexperienced interviewers? The problem is not so much of differences in reliability and validity. Instead, it seems that inexperienced interviewers can often panic if they do not see any real talent and have a tendency to accept mediocre or poor applicants.
11. *Appearance.* Does the personal appearance of the applicant have an effect on interviewer decisions? As we saw above, there is an effect for appearance (e.g., dress and smell), but it affects evaluations on some but not all the dimensions being considered (e.g., social skills) rather than directly on the hiring decision itself.
12. *Accuracy of interviewer as measured by number of factual questions she is able to answer.* Do more accurate interviewers actually gather more information? Yes. The more information the interviewer can elicit and retain, the more accurate the ratings and eventual decision. Again, this is similar to the results of performance rating training studies.
13. *Structure of interview.* Does a standard interview format for every applicant

FIGURE 7–1 Information Seeking, Receipt, and Processing

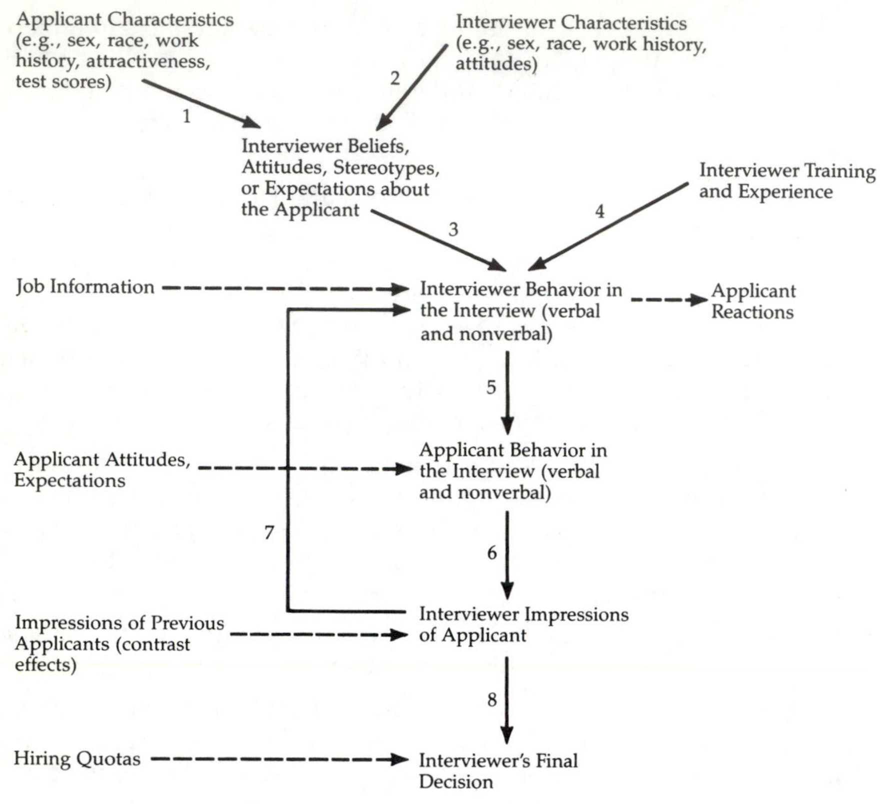

SOURCE: From Perspectives on Staffing and Selection by G. F. Dreher and P. R. Sackett, 1983, Homewood, IL: Irwin.

improve the reliability of the interview? Absolutely. Every year a study confirming this conclusion is published. A good recent example is a study by Orpen (1985) contrasting the unstructured with the structured interview for choosing sales personnel for an insurance company. Similarly, Arvey, Bouchard, Segal, and Abraham (1987) demonstrated the validity of the structured interview for selecting sales clerks.

Dreher and Sackett (1983) have presented a model that demonstrates the various types of influences that may be present in the typical interview. The model is presented in Figure 7–1. It is presented as a flowchart of the way in which the interviewer goes about getting information and using that information to make evaluations and a final decision. One interesting aspect of the model is that it emphasizes the interaction among the applicant, interviewer, and psychosocial environment in which the interview is conducted.

A recent study by Rynes and Miller (1983) helps illustrate this dynamic element. Undergraduate students watched videotaped interviews and made judgments about the probability of a job offer and the desirability of the job under consideration in the interviews they were watching. The videotapes were constructed so that various interviewers showed positive and negative behaviors. For example, positive behaviors included steady eye contact, smiling, nods of encouragement, and verbal approval of applicant comments; negative interview behaviors included no smiling, fidgeting, and appearing anxious to finish the interview. In addition to varying interviewer behavior, the experimenters varied the type of information provided by the interviewer. High information conditions were characterized by specific information about salary, fringe benefits, and geographic location of the work setting. The low information condition provided only vague data about salary, benefits, and location. The results were interesting. Interviewer behavior (positive or negative) had an impact on the perceived probability of receiving a job offer. In other words, interviewers who were positive were seen as more likely to make an offer of employment. On the other hand, level of information affected the desirability of the position under consideration. Specific information made the position seem more attractive, regardless of the interviewer's behavior. Rynes and Miller suggest that the interviewer's behavior might be a critical factor when the job is neither particularly desirable nor undesirable. As I will suggest later in the chapter, great caution should be exercised in generalizing from interview research that involves simulations and nonprofessional interviewers. Nevertheless, this is the type of effect that Dreher and Sackett suggest by the arrow that runs from *Interviewer Behavior* to *Applicant Reactions* and to *Applicant Behavior* in Figure 7–1. To take a concrete example, the interviewer might engage in negative behaviors as described above. As a result, the interviewee might assume that a job offer is unlikely, and subsequently, the interviewee might act less interested, strengthening the interviewer's initial negative impression. The point is that the interview itself is a dynamic event with characteristics that go beyond the static properties of the applicant or interviewer.

Current Interpretations of Interview Research

Schmitt's review was a good one for several reasons. First, it provided a model for thinking about the various components of the interview. As we saw above, the model helps to understand the dynamic properties of the interview process. In addition, the review outlined what was known to that point about influences on the interview. By default, it also illustrated what was *not* known. Since Schmitt's review, two additional reviews of research on the interview have appeared. One (Webster, 1982) covers much the same research as Schmitt but from a different perspective. The second (Arvey & Campion, 1982) updates the Schmitt review and makes suggestions for future avenues of exploration.

Webster has been engaged in interview research for over 30 years. His program of research at McGill University illustrates the value of careful programmatic research in the behavioral sciences. He reviews that research as well as the research of contemporaries in a small book that is as much an essay as a review. The title of the book gives away the theme of the essay. It is called *The Employment Interview: A Social Judgment Process*. He feels very firmly that the interview can only be understood in the context of a complex decision task being performed in stressful circumstances. He emphasizes such processes as impression formation and theories that interviewers hold of applicants. The stressful circumstances that interest him are not those that affect the applicant but rather those that affect the interviewer. The point is that most of the information is being processed by the interviewer, not by the applicant. As a result, interviewer stress is more likely to lead to inaccurate decisions than applicant stress.

This concern for interviewer stress has interesting implications. The most important of these implications is that Webster considers a good deal of the recent research using resumés of fictitious applicants and videotapes of simulated interviews as irrelevant. Further, he is not impressed by research using students as make-believe personnel managers or recruiters or interviewers. He has some support in this concern from a study by Gorman, Clover, and Doherty (1978) who show substantial differences between the process by which real people are evaluated in the face-to-face interview context and the analysis of "paper-people" who exist only as resumés or descriptions on paper. The same objections can be leveled against "videotape" people. As far as Webster is concerned, there is no stress on the interviewer in these artificial settings. Thus, nothing can be learned from these studies that has any value for understanding interview dynamics.

Arvey and Campion (1982) set out to update the Schmitt review and come to some interesting conclusions in the process. First, they agree with Webster that there may be an overreliance on paper-people research (although they are not as willing to disregard completely this type of research). In addition, they agree with Webster that more studies of a cognitive variety must be done. They feel that much more needs to be known about how interviewers process information, what shortcuts they use, how they form impressions, and the extent to which biases influence interviewer decisions. I am less tolerant of the paper-people research than Arvey and Campion. I agree with Hakel (1986) and Guion and Gibson (1988) who have come to the conclusion that research done with undergraduate students making artificial judgments about make-believe people produced make-believe conclusions. A recent study by Barr and Hitt (1986) demonstrated that there were substantial differences in both form and level between student "interviewers" and real interviewers with respect to decisions and decision processes.

Arvey and Campion also emphasize some suggestions implied by the earlier Schmitt review. They stress the potential value of using structured interviews and a panel of several interviewers rather than a single interviewer.

TABLE 7–1 Examples of Situational Interview Questions and Their Corresponding Critical Incidents Used for Selection of Emergency Telephone Operators

Interview Question	*Critical Incident*
1. Imagine that you tried to help a stranger, for example, with traffic directions or to get up after a fall and that person blamed you for their misfortune or yelled at you. How would you respond?	1. Telephone operator tries to verify address information for an ambulance call. The caller yells at them for being stupid and slow. The operator quietly assures the caller an ambulance is on the way and that she is merely reaffirming the address.
2. Suppose a friend calls you and is extremely upset? Apparently, her child has been injured. She begins to tell you, in a hysterical manner, all about her difficulty in getting babysitters, what the child is wearing, what words the child can speak, etc. What would you do?	2. A caller is hysterical because her infant is dead. She yells incoherently about the incident. The operator talks in a clear calm voice and manages to secure the woman's address, dispatches the call, and then tries to secure more information about the child's status.
3. How would you react if you were a salesclerk, waitress, or gas station attendant, and one of your customers talked back to you, indicated you should have known something you did not, or told you that you were not waiting on them fast enough?	3. A clearly angry caller calls for the third time in an hour complaining about the 911 service because no one has arrived to investigate a busted water pipe. The operator tells the caller to go to ______ and hangs up.

SOURCE: From STAFFING ORGANIZATIONS by Benjamin Schneider and Neal Schmitt. Copyright © 1986, 1976 by Scott, Foresman and Company. Reprinted by permission.

With respect to structure, they review the research of Latham and his colleagues (Latham, Saari, Pursell, & Campion, 1980) on the "situational interview." In this approach, applicants are asked questions that are based on critical incidents provided by those familiar with the job in question. A critical incident is a description of an event that was central (or critical) to success or failure on a particular task. In the Latham approach, applicants are given questions based on these critical incidents and asked how they might respond. Table 7–1 presents examples of questions and the critical incidents from which they were derived. One important characteristic of this technique is that there is some agreement with respect to what constitutes a "good," "average," and "poor" answer to the question. As an example, the applicant might be asked what a response would be if a spouse and two children were sick in bed with bad colds and had no one to take care of them. A "good" response might be that since the illness was not serious, the applicant would come to work. An "average" response might be that the applicant would call the supervisor to say that he or she would not be in that day. A "poor" response would be simply to stay home without informing the supervisor. Latham et al. demonstrated interrater reliabilities in the .80s with this format of scoring. In addition, using supervisory ratings as a criterion, the validity of the interview decision was .33. There has been little published research on the situational interview to the point, but it does have intuitive appeal since it is job related with the possibility of a structured scoring format. One recent study by Latham and Saari (1984) demonstrates a substantial relationship between what applicants say they will do in a situation and what their supervisors actually see them do on the job in that situation. This is encouraging from the validity perspective. It seems as if we can make accurate inferences from the situational interview.

The "modern" point of view is that the result of an interview is a decision or evaluation of some sort. As a result, the interview really consists of two different components—the interview and the interviewer. Below, I will briefly consider some of the issues implied by this distinction.

Interview versus Interviewer Validity. One of the problems with evaluating the interview is that we must separate the characteristics of the interview (e.g., the traits rated, the questions asked) from the characteristics of the interviewer (e.g., What follow-up questions does she ask? How does she combine information in making a final decision?). We can conceive of a good interview structure and an incompetent interviewer–decision maker; conversely, we can picture a poorly constructed interview format and a terrific interviewer–decision maker. Since both the interview and the interviewer are components of the predictor, the validity and reliability of each component should be considered separately. Carlson (1972) provides support for the distinction between interview and interviewer validity by showing that the validity coefficients for studies in which the interview was the sole source of information tend to be lower than coefficients in studies where the interviewer had access to additional information. This conclusion must remain tenuous at this point. What we can be sure of is that interviewers vary in their capacity to combine information, regardless of its source.

Reliability of Interviewer Ratings. Carlson (1967a, 1967b, 1968) has shown that interviewer self-consistency increases as the judgment task is made easier by (1) providing a relative standard for comparison, (2) increasing the variability among the interviewees, and (3) increasing the consistency of information about each interviewee. In other words, when the "objects" are made more discriminable and less ambiguous, judges are more consistent from initial to repeat evaluations. These findings also suggest that the interviewer's interpretation of the traits to be rated, his stereotype of the "ideal" applicant, or both remain quite stable over time. Schmitt (1976), Arvey and Campion (1982), and Webster (1982) all confirm one or more of these observations. Conversely, the absence of these conditions can reduce reliability.

Since many interview evaluations are based on trait ratings made during or after the interview, it should be apparent that these ratings may suffer from the same distortions as other types of ratings. We covered these distorting influences in Chapter 5 when we considered performance evaluation. In general, however, it appears that interviewers have a better chance of agreement in rating some traits than others, probably because (1) they are more likely to possess more common behavioral referents for, say, "intelligence" or "mental ability" than for "submissiveness"; (2) behaviors that are the basis for rating some traits are more consistently displayed by an interviewee from one interview to the next; or (3) ancillary data available to the interviewer provide more reliable information for judging some traits than others. It must be remembered that these reliability data do not reflect the reliability of ratings based solely on the face-to-face interview; rather they are estimates of the reliability (agreement) of interviewers who have used interviews and whatever other sources were available and combined the data according to largely unknown and probably idiosyncratic strategies to arrive at their ratings. It is also likely that interviewer trait-rating reliability increases with standardization of the interviews, though there is little evidence to support this.

Standardization does appear to increase interviewers' agreement on their overall evaluations or predictions, and as one would expect, more detailed job information also increases agreement. This latter finding is consistent with the notion that agreement depends on the possession of similar stereotypes of the ideal worker; it is also consistent with the notion that the interviewer's ability to predict job performance depends, in part, on knowing *what* job is being performed. This increase in agreement (reliability) is important for prediction. Remember that reliability sets the limits for validity. If we cannot make reliable measurements of predictor variables, we certainly can't make valid inferences about eventual performance.

Scope of the Interview

The typical selection interview is a jumble of several different types of information. This information ranges from that *given* to the applicant about "the way we do things here" to that *obtained* from the applicant about personal history, preferences, and skills.

Let's concentrate on the interviewer for a moment. What should she look for in the face-to-face interview? There is some evidence that factual information about work history and other biographical items can be obtained with reasonable accuracy in the interview. As you would expect, applicants tend to give socially desirable answers to certain questions (e.g., they might deny they had ever been on welfare when in fact they had received welfare payments; Weiss & Dawis, 1960). Other less threatening information tends to be reported quite reliably in the interview: things such as previous wages, duration of prior employment, age, and education (Keating, Patterson, & Stone,

1950; Vaughn & Reynolds, 1951). But the question remains as to whether the interview is the most efficient means of gathering such information. Most of the items could easily be reported on a preemployment information sheet (application blank). In this form, at least errors of reporting by the interviewer would be eliminated. Furthermore, the released interview time could be used to collect information or impressions that cannot be obtained more efficiently and accurately in other ways. It is difficult to see how the preemployment interview can be defended as a means of gathering strictly factual, biographical data.

Given that we will not gather biographical information in the interview, we must still decide whether the goal of the interview should be a broad-band or global assessment of the individual or a consideration of only a few traits that are presumed to be related to success on the job. As a systematic approach, we might expect the personnel manager to begin with a list of worker characteristics assumed to be important for the job (on the basis of systematic job analysis), then to decide on the most reliable and economical way to obtain information about each characteristic or attribute. Presumably, the interview would be utilized to assess only those traits that could *not* be evaluated more efficiently by other means. Which traits or areas might then be assessed by the interview?

In a review of interview research, Ulrich and Trumbo (1965) concluded:

> [Research] results rather consistently indicate two areas which both contribute heavily to interviewer decisions and show greatest evidence of validity. These two areas of assessment may be described roughly as *personal relations* and *motivation to work*. In other words, perhaps the interviewer should seek information on two questions: "What is the applicant's motivation to work?" and "Will he adjust to the social context of the job?" Such an approach would leave the assessment of abilities, aptitudes, experience, and biographical data to other, and, in all likelihood, more reliable and valid sources. (p. 113, emphasis added)

Is this good advice? It depends on the role of the interviewer in the selection program. Schmitt (1976) suggests that the information to be gathered should depend, to some extent, on whether the interviewer is part of the decision-making process or is simply an information gatherer. If the interviewer is part of the decision-making process, it is likely that she has a good deal of information about the job to be filled. This, in turn, suggests that she is likely to be more accurate in her assessment of candidates. On the other hand, if the interviewer is gathering information for any number of different jobs (most of which she knows little about), her assessment may be less accurate. As a result, a reasonable conclusion might be to have interviewers concentrate on communication skills, personal relations, and motivation to work if they are not well informed about the positions under consideration. If, on the other hand, they know a good deal about the positions in question and may be asked for a hiring recommendation, then it may be advantageous to have them gather more detailed information on technical and professional matters as well.

We have spent a good deal of time on the "scientific" aspects of the interview, but how about the interpersonal and administrative aspects? What is the best way actually to conduct an interview? Hakel (1982) has provided a valuable set of guidelines that are based on the accumulation of interview research results and what we know about interpersonal behavior and stress. These guidelines are presented in Figure 7–2. Hakel prepared these guidelines for selecting applicants for the job of "interviewer," but they could be easily adapted to fit interviews for almost any job title.

Equal Employment Opportunity and the Interview

Several times I have alluded to the potential for unfair discrimination when the selection interview is used for decision making. This issue is of particular concern in the interview because so many decisions are left up to the discretion of the interviewer: decisions about questions to ask and follow-up questions, decisions as to the length of the interview, the number of questions asked, and often the ultimate decision of whether to employ the applicant. Arvey (1979) has reviewed all the available literature concerning unfair discrimination in the interview. He cites the Washington State Human Relations Commission as an example of a body that has carefully regulated the nature of the preemployment interview. That commission has stated that it is unfair and illegal to make the following inquiries unless they can be shown to be job-related (valid):

1. Information regarding arrests
2. Information regarding citizenship
3. Information regarding spouse's salary, children, child-care arrangements, or dependents
4. Overgeneral information (e.g., "Do you have any handicaps?"), which might highlight health conditions unrelated to job performance
5. Marital status of the applicant
6. Military discharge information
7. Information related to pregnancy
8. Whether the applicant owns or rents a home

All these pieces of information might be used to the disadvantage of one minority group or another. Consequently, unless they are related to job success, the answers to these questions might result in differential hiring rates for minority and majority applicants. In certain situations, however, it may be illegal to hire someone with a criminal record (e.g., police departments, prisons) or someone who is not a citizen or resident of the city in which the

FIGURE 7–2 An Abbreviated Interview Guide for Use in Evaluating Selection Interviewer Applicants

Opening

- Give a warm, friendly greeting—smile.
- Names are important—yours and the applicant's. Pronounce it correctly and use first and last names consistently. Tell the applicant what to call you and then ask the applicant for his or her preferred form of address.
- Talk briefly about yourself (your position in the company and then your personal background, hobbies, interests, etc.) to put the applicant at ease so that she or he might reciprocate with personal information.
- Ask the applicant about hobbies, activities, or some other topic that you believe will be of interest to "break the ice."

Structure the Interview

- State the purpose of interview: "The purpose of this interview is to discuss your qualifications and to see whether they match the skills needed to work as a selection interviewer. First, let's talk about your work experience and next your education and training. Then I will give you a preview of what the interviewer's job is really like. Finally, there will be a chance to ask about anything you want. How's that?"
- Since you plan to take notes, mention this to the applicant: "By the way, I will be taking some notes during the interview so that I don't miss any pertinent information that may come from our discussion. Okay?"

Work Experience: Most Relevant Job

- Use this comprehensive opening question: "Let's talk about your work experience. How about starting with the job that you feel gave you the best preparation for working as a selection interviewer. Tell me all about the job: how you got it, why you chose it, your actual job duties, what you learned on the job, the hours and your attendance record, the pay, why you left (or are leaving), and things like that."
- Probe and follow up to cover each of these items thoroughly: how the applicant got the job, reasons for choosing it, job duties, etc.
- Summarize the major facts and findings from the applicant's most relevant job. For example: "Let me summarize what we have covered to make sure that I've got it right. You worked as a ________ where most of your time was spent doing ________ and ________ , and you used these skills, ________ and ________ . You chose the job because of ________ and your reasons for leaving it are ________ and ________ . Anything else to add?"

Other Work Experience

- If time is available, discuss other jobs the applicant has held that might be pertinent. Get a brief overview of each job the applicant has held. Emphasize jobs held in the last five years or less, since older expereience is less likely to be relevant for your decision.
- Ask the work experience questions you specifically prepared for this applicant when you planned the interview.
- Summarize your major finding about all jobs. When the summary is satisfactory to the applicant, go on to discuss education and training.

Education and Training

- Use this question to start the discussion: "Now let's talk about your education and training—schools, courses, likes and dislikes, things like that. Let's start with this:

FIGURE 7-2 ***(concluded)***

What did you learn in school that might be helpful for you in working as a selection interviewer?"

- Probe to get specific answers to these questions: "What training have you had in interviewing techniques? What courses have you had in psychology or personnel management?" and so on.
- Ask the education and training questions you specifically prepared for this applicant when you planned the interview.
- Summarize the applicant's education and training, just as you summarized work experience. When the applicant is satisfied with your summary, go on to discuss the Job Preview List.

Job Preview List

- Introduce the Job Preview List: "As a selection interviewer, you have many responsibilities and duties. Here is a list of some major factors."
- Give the applicant the Job Preview List. Discuss it point by point. Be sure that you describe the job realistically. Don't "paint a rosy picture."

SELECTION INTERVIEW JOB PREVIEW LIST

1. Conduct screening and final evaluation interviews with all applicants for nonexempt factory and clerical positions.
2. Administer and score screening tests and weighted application blanks.
3. Maintain records and compile reports on all applicants for Affirmative Action purposes.

    •

    •

    •

10. Recommend two candidates for each position for interviews by the hiring manager.

Applicant's Questions

- Turn the interview over to the applicant: "As I mentioned at the start, you would have a chance to ask anything you would like. We've just had a short preview of what the job would be like, but here is a chance to ask anything you want about the company, training, and so on."
- Respond fully and frankly to all of the applicant's questions, and note any further information that the applicant volunteers that will aid you in making your evaluation.

Closing the Interview

- Conclude with a warm, friendly close—smile.
- Outline the next steps in the decision process.
- Tell the applicant when to expect a decision.
- Thank the applicant.

After the Interview

- Take time to write summary notes immediately. Describe the applicant's behavior and the impressions he or she created. Cite facts and specific incidents from the interview or from the person's work or educational history.
- Wait a day and then complete the Evaluation Form.

SOURCE: From Milton D. Hakel, "Employment Interviewing" from Rowland and Ferris, PERSONNEL MANAGEMENT. Copyright © 1982 by Allyn and Bacon, Inc. Reprinted with permission.

work will occur. Similarly, the new Immigration Reform and Control Act does require employers to seek information about citizenship on certain occasions. In those cases, it will be important for the employer to consider the conflicting requirements and decide which requirement has priority.

One might expect that the applicant groups suffering the greatest adverse impact are nonwhites, women, and older applicants. Arvey reviewed research dealing with these three variables and came to the following conclusions:

1. The older applicant is often described in less favorable terms than the younger applicant; this suggests that decisions are often less favorable in the case of the older applicant.
2. Women are generally given lower evaluations than men when these candidates have similar or identical qualifications.
3. There seems to be an interaction between sex and type of job being considered that affects evaluations. Female applicants for historically male roles (police officer) receive lower evaluations than male applicants for the same jobs. Arvey calls this the "sex-congruency" hypothesis; we will see similar dynamics operating in the performance evaluation process.
4. Few studies have directly examined applicant race as an influence on interview evaluations. The evidence that was available did not indicate that nonwhite applicants were at a disadvantage in the interview.
5. The qualification of the applicant plays a major role in the eventual applicant evaluation (that's a relief!).
6. Little is known concerning handicapped applicants. Anecdotal evidence suggests that they may be viewed more positively owing to higher motivation than the normal applicant (consider the obvious obstacle that they had to overcome in applying for work at all).

THE APPLICATION BLANK

The application blank is generally recognized as having three purposes. First, it can be used to determine whether an applicant is hireable, that is, whether he meets minimum hiring requirements as set by the organization or by law. For example, the company may require a high school education as a minimum educational requirement, the state may require a chauffeur's license, and the federal government may require a social security registration or security clearance for a particular job. Usually the issue of hireability can be determined with a small number of questions. Information dealing with other questions need not be included in the initial form: one does not need to know the number of dependents or marital status of the applicant (unless these determine his hireability) for the purposes of withholding tax until it is determined that he is hireable or, indeed, until he is actually hired. Thus, it might be well to consider a preemployment blank where information essential to the hireability issue is obtained and a postemployment blank to obtain the information needed for personnel programs and the like.

A second purpose of the application blank has been as a supplement to and preparation for the interview. From this view, the application blank provides "leads" to be pursued in the face-to-face interview, or, put another way, the interview may be used to check on first impressions gained from the application blank and other credentials or psychometric data. Thus, McMurray (1945), in an early plea for the "patterned" interview, recommended that the interviewer become familiar with the applicant's credentials in preparation for the interview. At any rate, used in this way, information from the application blank is combined with data and impressions from the interview in a clinical evaluation by the interviewer. In this case, its contribution to the impressions, ratings, or predictions of the interviewer are confounded with other sources of information and therefore not readily determined.

A third purpose of the application blank is to obtain biographical data and work history information that may be used actuarially to predict some assessable aspect of job proficiency. That is, the application blank can be used to gather items of personal data that are predictive of performance, turnover, absenteeism, or whatever, and that can be combined and weighted into a multiple predictor, with or without other (e.g., psychometric) types of information. In this sense, the information that the applicant has four dependents or has held five different jobs in the past three years is treated in the same way as a score of 78 on a test of some ability—potentially, both items of information may be predictive of some aspect of success.

These three purposes represent criteria for deciding what items should be included in the application blank. Here is a list of specific questions that may be asked of items that are candidates for inclusion on an application blank (Ahern, 1949). If an item cannot be justified on the basis of a positive answer to at least one of the questions, it should be rejected.

1. Is the item necessary for identifying the applicant?
2. Is it necessary for screening out those who are ineligible under the company's basic hiring policies? Specifically, what policy does it pertain to?
3. Does it help to decide whether the candidate is qualified?
4. Is it based on analysis of the job or jobs for which the applicant will be selected?
5. Has it been pretested on the company's employees and found to correlate with success?
6. Will the information be used? How?
7. Is the application form the proper place for it?

8. Will answers provide information not obtained in another step in the selection procedure—for example, through interviews, tests, or medical examinations?
9. Is the information needed for selection at all, or should it be obtained at induction or even later?
10. Is it probable that applicants' replies will be reliable?
11. Does the question conform to any applicable federal or state legislation?

Evaluating Personal Data Items

It should be apparent that personal data items can be evaluated in the same way as test scores. The validity of the item could be determined as well as its contribution to a multiple prediction equation. Although these procedures would be appropriate, they have not been the practice with personal data items. Instead, a relatively simple method has been used in most cases.

The Horizontal Percent Method. Just as with the analysis of items in a test, the items on an application blank can be evaluated in terms of their ability to discriminate among criterion scores or criterion groups. Items that do not discriminate have zero validity for that criterion measure and should not be used; items that have high discriminability should receive greater weights than items that show modest discriminability, that is, low correlations with the criterion. The horizontal percent method (Stead & Shartle, 1940) provides a simple means of assessing the validity of personal data items and a straightforward rationale for weighting each item in a composite score.

The first step, as with any validation procedure, is to choose a criterion measure. Since most of the research on personal data items has used a criterion of job tenure, I will follow that example. Keep in mind, however, that any single or multiple criterion could be used. What items of personal data might be predictive of job tenure (or turnover)? In most personnel offices, this question could be answered by identifying two samples of employees, those who remained with the organization more than one year and those who left within the first year. The next step is simply to compare these two criterion groups ("good" and "poor" workers) with respect to personal data items. Table 7–2 provides a hypothetical example, using sex of the applicant as the personal datum. In the sample presented, 40 employees were male, 60 female. Each of these subgroups is tallied under good and poor worker categories, depending on whether they stayed one year or more with the organization. In the sixth column of the figure, the percentage of good workers to the total within each subgroup is calculated. Thus, we see that 20 of the 40 men, or 50 percent, were "successful," whereas 45 of the 60 women, or 75 percent, were successful. A woman, then, has a higher probability of being successful

TABLE 7–2 Evaluation of Personal Data Item by the Horizontal Percent Method

Personal Data Item	*Categories*	*"Successes" (+1 year)*	*"Failures" (−1 year)*	*Total*	*Successes*	*Weight*
Sex	Males	20	20	40	20/40 = 50%	50
	Females	45	15	60	45/60 = 75%	75

on this criterion than a man, and women should receive more points. This is reflected in the last column of Table 7–2, headed "Weight." The category "Female" is given a weight equal to the percentage obtained in the previous column (75), whereas males receive a lower weight (50). The rationale of this scoring procedure may be clearer if we consider an alternative outcome: suppose that of the 65 successful employees, 26 were men and 39 women. This would result in percentages of 65 for each category, and the weights would be equal for men and women, reflecting the fact that this item was not differentially predictive. (In this case, it would not make sense to score the item at all, once its lack of validity was determined.)

The validity of other items could be determined and weighted scores assigned in precisely the same way. Of course, the method is not limited to dichotomized variables; age, for example, might be categorized into three or four levels representing approximately equal proportions of the total sample. Likewise, the criterion measure could be represented in three or more levels, such as zero to two, three to five, or six or more absences per quarter. England and Patterson (1960) have described the development of scoring keys for application blanks. Essentially, a stencil or overlay can be prepared for each job, such that only those items that are valid for a given job appear through the windows of the stencil, and the appropriate weights to assign to the various response categories are listed beside each window.

Studies of the Validity of Personal Data. Personal data items may appear in many different forms. Some deal with obvious life history items such as age, education, number of brothers and sisters, and parents' occupations. Presumably, these items are easily verifiable. There are other items, however, that request self-reports from the applicant that are not easily verified. Examples of these items would be: "Were your parents happy with your schoolwork?" or "Were you considered a 'joiner' in your circle of friends?" Traditionally, application blanks have been made up of the former type of items—uncomplicated life history items that require little or no evaluation by the applicant; they simply require a reasonable long-term memory. In the past decade, however, more and more organizations have been looking into the possibility that some other type of self-report items are valid for predicting success in various positions. This latter class of items is generally known as *bio data* (short for *biographical data*) and often includes information far removed from job activities.

Cascio (1976) reported substantial relationships between life history items and turnover for clerical employees. The predictors were: age, marital status, children's ages, education, tenure on previous job, previous salary, presence of a friend or relative in the company, location of residence, home ownership, and length of time at the present address. He attempted to use this information to predict those employees who would stay with the organization for longer than one year. He was able to look at the predictor-criterion relationships separately for a sample of minority workers ($n = 80$) and a sample of majority workers ($n = 80$). All subjects were women. The results appear in Table 7–3. As you can see, Cascio was able to predict who would stay and who would leave. The trustworthiness of this prediction scheme is shown by the cross-validated correlation coefficients, which represent the validity of the prediction scheme on an independent sample of subjects.

These data are encouraging for two reasons. Not only do they demonstrate the potential value of application blank information, but they also indicate that application blanks can be used to make employment decisions in a manner that is fair to both majority and minority applicants.

Cascio's items were fairly traditional and would not be obvious targets for rejected applicants claiming unfair treatment due to minority status. A study by Nevo (1976) provides an example of items that might come under substantial attack from rejected applicants. The study looked at the validity of biographical information for identifying individuals who would be successful in the Israeli army. The criterion was rank attained by the time the individual left the army. Data for male and female soldiers were examined separately. Most of the items dealt with characteristics of the subjects' parents. These included father's and mother's age, father's and mother's education, and so on. One item in particular would send chills down the spine of most personnel administrators. It requested information regarding the father's country of origin, that is, *nationality*. This represents one of the categories of protected applicants under the EEOC guidelines. On the surface, this type of item might represent prima facie evidence of intent to discriminate unfairly. Many employers are currently concerned about just this issue. They carefully comb their application blanks for any hints of items that might be interpreted as potentially unfair discriminators. Cascio (1976) points out that employers are permitted to use even the most patently discriminatory items if they can be demonstrated to be job related. Unfortunately, theory and practice would probably clash on this issue. Although Cascio has a reasonable argument based on the guidelines, there is another argument that is equally compelling and could also be made on the basis of the guidelines: employers who are engaging in a personnel practice that has an adverse impact on a particular minority group are required to search for decision-making mechanisms that are equally valid but that have less of an adverse impact. Thus, in this case

TABLE 7–3 Correlation of Application Blank Responses with Turnover

	Validity Coefficient	*Cross-Validity Coefficient*
Majority sample	.77	.56
Minority sample	.79	.58

the employer might have to expend considerable effort and money to show that the application blank is the most valid device available. It is possible that the organization might spend more money in comparing the application blank to other techniques than it did in the development of the application blank in the first place. The wise employer will avoid the *appearance* as well as the practice of unfair discrimination.

Do Applicants Lie? One of the possibilities that has nagged researchers and personnel managers has been the degree to which the answers to application blank items are either intentionally or unintentionally distorted. Do people actually report the truth, or do they shade it in a manner that makes them look like better applicants? Cascio (1975) examined the application blanks for 112 applicants to the Dade County, Florida, police department. He examined 17 items and verified the answers to these items for the 112 applicants. He found a very high correlation between fact and self-report. The median correlation between the applicant's answer and the verified truthful answer to the question was .94. Cascio took this as evidence that items that can be easily verified are unlikely to yield distorted responses. This finding may have been a little optimistic, since the applicants were being considered for a position as police officers and were aware that background checks were common in the employment procedure. Nevertheless, it is a comforting finding.

As you might suspect, there is some contradictory evidence as well. Cohen and Lefkowitz (1974) examined the distortion on biodata items and distortions on a standard personality test, the Minnesota Multiphasic Personality Inventory (MMPI). They were able to show significant correlations between distortions on the two instruments. As a general principle, it might be wise for the employer to include at least some items that can be easily verified or to verify all responses of a sample of applicants to assess possible distortion.

A Rational Approach to Life History Items. One of the most prominent researchers in the area of biodata prediction has been William Owens. He and his colleagues have been refining a life history questionnaire for several decades. He has described this research in a monograph (Owens & Schoenfeldt, 1979). He suggests that there are two different components that one might address with a life history questionnaire — the things that were done *to* a person (by teachers, parents, friends, employers, etc.) and the experiences that a person had. Owens's life history questionnaire includes both kinds of items. On the basis of responses to 118 items, Owens is able to identify groups of individuals with varying psychological characteristics. For example, he has identified male biodata groups such as "indifferent low achieving artists," "bright achieving leaders", and "approval seeking humanitarians." Female biodata groups include "goal oriented social leaders," "conservative athletes," and "unconventional achievers." In other words, he has used the responses of people to a carefully developed questionnaire to form clusters or subgroups of people with similar interests. He then attempts to predict college success, life adjustment, and career success on the basis of what is known about these subgroups.

The approach that Owens takes is very different from the early approach to life history prediction. The traditional manner of validating life history items is simply to weight responses in a manner that maximizes the predictability of some criterion. You saw examples of this in Table 7–2 that illustrated the horizontal percent method. There is no "theory" of the relationship between the items and the criterion. For this reason, the traditional method is known as the *empirical* method. This approach implies that if the item predicts and doesn't unfairly discriminate, use it. This is a type of "dust-bowl empiricism" that has given applied psychology a bad name over the years. Although there is nothing wrong with identifying correlated variables (e.g., an answer to a life history item and a supervisory rating), eventually a theory should emerge to explain that relationship. Owens and the modern biodata researchers are more concerned with this theory than their predecessors had been. For this reason, their approach has been referred to as the *rational* approach. Owens developed his questionnaire using factor analysis to identify underlying life history factors rather than dealing with hundreds of unconnected items. Further, he assumes that certain profiles of past experiences can be predictive of some broad range of future interests and capabilities. As a result, his approach lends itself more readily to counseling, career development, and assessment than do the simpler criterion weighting methods. In addition, it makes a contribution to selection and placement.

Recently, there have been some tests of the differences between the empirical and the rational approach to biodata prediction. As an example, Mitchell and Klimoski (1982) attempted to predict the success of students preparing for a real estate license. They compared the predictive efficiency of a life history questionnaire that was traditionally (empirically) weighted to one that was developed more intuitively and subsequently factor analyzed (rational). In the latter case, factor scores were used as the predictors rather than individual items. There was a significant difference between the methods—the empirical method was a better prediction scheme. They conclude by suggesting that the rational method is best for research and understanding, but the empirical method might be better for prediction and application.

On the other hand, Neiner and Owens (1982) show that the dimensions underlying the rational approach that Owens used in the development of his life history questionnaire as quite stable over long periods of time. They gathered data on college freshmen and then gathered a second set of data seven years later. They were able to demonstrate stability in biodata scores in spite of the fact that the questionnaires were different at the two different points in time. The first questionnaire dealt with life history up to and including the college experience. The second questionnaire dealt with postcollege experiences. They conclude that life history scores, developed on the basis of a rationally scored life history form, can predict future behavior and interests. Two other studies (Eberhardt & Muchinsky, 1982a, 1982b) confirm the internal stability of the Owens's life history form and illustrate its usefulness for vocational counseling. Shaffer, Saunders, and Owens (1986) have recently demonstrated that the rational approach produces quite good test-retest reliabilities even after a separation of five years between administrations of the biodata form. In addition, they show that there is good agreement between the individual in question and those who know that individual with respect to how the individual answers certain questions (e.g., those dealing with academic achievement, socioeconomic status, etc.). This is comforting since it appears that social desirability or other response sets are not exerting a strong influence. It takes a special person to remember how he intentionally distorted the response to a biodata item five years earlier!

There is no "winner" in the empirical-rational discussion. There is too little comparative research to answer the question of predictive efficiency. On the other hand, it seems obvious that atheoretical prediction must eventually be supported with theory or logic. It is dangerous and inefficient to be the servant of a correlation coefficient. For that reason, I favor continued development of the rational approach. The straight empirical approach might be used to generate hypotheses or to fill a prediction void until another measure becomes available, but it is not an approach that can promise any long-range confidence. Empirical results may vary wildly from one study to another. This variation can only be reduced by having a logical understanding of why certain questions *should* be predictive of future success.

Some Additional Comments on Biographical Data. The utility of biographical data for predicting job tenure and, to a lesser extent, job proficiency has been adequately demonstrated. Identifying a number of discriminating items leads to a "sketch" of the most promising applicants, and items such as "amount of life insurance," "hobbies," or "leisure-time activities" may lead to inferences about more basic characteristics of the individual.

Lee and Booth (1974) provide a dramatic example of the potential economic advantages of the weighted application blank. They attempted to predict turnover among clerical employees, using an application blank. They were able to estimate the costs of turnover through various cost accounting procedures. These costs included things like recruiting costs, wages to trainees during training, wages to trainers during training, fringe benefits, and so on.

Individuals who leave shortly after completing the training program are not able to offset training costs through productive effort. Therefore, it is to the advantage of an organization to reduce turnover. Lee and Booth were able to demonstrate potential savings of $250,000 over a 25-month period through the use of a simple application form. While part of this savings was based on the large number of applicants (1,700 for 400 positions), it is still impressive evidence regarding the potential of the application blank as a selection device.

SELF-ASSESSMENT

Application blanks depend on self-report of demographic data and past experiences. The application blank is an attractive device because of its ease of administration and low cost. Some have suggested that the application blank be taken a step further. It has been suggested that applicants be asked to estimate their own abilities in different areas that are relevant to the job in question. Consider the checklist that appears in Figure 7–3. This could be administered to applicants for semiskilled positions in order to identify those who claim to have suitable skill levels and past experience. Those who are identified might pass on to the next level of screening prior to an employment decision.

Levine, Flory, and Ash (1977) asked 73 clerical employees to assess their abilities in several different areas. Subsequently, these individuals took a series of tests that provided independent estimates of these skills. There were significant correlations between self-assessments and demonstrated skills in the areas of grammar, spelling, word meaning, reading, and arithmetic. In addition, Levine et al. examined the relationships between self-assessments and supervisory ratings of proficiency in these clerical skill areas. There were significant correlations between self-assessed skill levels and supervisory ratings of skill in spelling, reading, grammar, proofreading speed and accuracy, comparing names and numbers, and accuracy for details. The most dramatic example of the capability of individuals to provide self-assessments was illustrated by self-assessed typing skills of 569 typists. The correlation was .62. These results are intriguing since they present the possibility of a more efficient method of applicant screening. Shrauger and Osberg (1981) review self-assessment in a broad context including instances of vocational choice, Peace Corps performance, posthospital adjustment of former psychiatric patients, academic achievement, and reactions to therapy and conclude that self-assessment can be useful in two ways. First, it can be demonstrated that under certain circumstances self-assessment can be more accurate than other forms of assessment. In addition, they suggest that self-assessment may actually exert a motivational force to behave in a manner consistent with the self-assessment after this assessment has been made — almost a self-fulfilling prophecy dynamic. This latter possibility is fascinating but as yet untested.

FIGURE 7–3 Skills Inventory

For each of the items listed below, rate your level of skills/experience. Use the following scale to indicate skill level in the blank at the left of each item.

3 Highly skilled	2 Basic skill	1 Minimum/No skills

Production Operations
___ Operate various machine tools
___ Machine maintenance
___ Blueprint reading
___ Welding: gas and electric
___ Machine troubleshooting
___ Mechanical maintenance
___ Electronic troubleshooting
___ Calibration of gauges and controls
___ Boiler operation
___ Boiler maintenance
___ Lift truck operation
___ Lift truck maintenance
___ Electrical troubleshooting
___ Building maintenance
___ Graphic arts
___ Pipe fitting
___ Hydraulic maintenance
___ Pneumatic maintenance
___ Chemical analysis
___ Heating and air conditioning
___ Other production and maintenance skills
____
____
____

Finance and Accounting
___ Accounts payable
___ Payroll and labor accounting
___ Cost accounting
___ Accounting for scrap
___ Fixed asset accounting
___ Planning and budgeting
___ Inventory and accounting
___ Other finance and accounting skills
____
____
____

Customer Service
___ Written communications
___ Verbal communications
___ Deal with customer problems
___ Order initiation and follow-up
___ Other customer service skills
____
____
____

Materials/Purchasing
___ Order inventory
___ Maintain inventory
___ Expediting
___ Scheduling production
___ Forecast inventory
___ Prepare materials report
___ Deal with supplier problems
___ Other material-purchasing skills
____
____
____

Systems (Data Processing)
___ Computer operations
___ Systems analysis–design skills
___ Programming
___ Data entry
___ Business process knowledge
___ Other systems (D.P.) skills
____
____
____

Quality Control
___ Statistical analysis
___ Process control
___ Machine capability study
___ Supplier quality assurance
___ Use of measuring equipment
___ Inspection planning
___ Color analysis
___ Proofreading
___ Other quality control skills
____
____
____

Training
___ Developing training program
___ Administer training programs
___ Operate media equipment
___ Use of photographic equipment
___ Evaluate instructional effectiveness
___ Facilitate term-building skills
___ Other training skills

Naturally, there are concerns about the tendency for an applicant to provide overestimates of skills. Similarly, there is some concern about exactly what applicants should be asked to assess — past, present, or future capabilities. With respect to the concern about accuracy (or more bluntly put, honesty), Mabe and West (1982) suggest that this can be handled by telling applicants that the assessments are subject to verification with actual tests. With respect to the actual task that should be presented to the applicant, there have been several suggestions. On the basis of a meta-analysis of 55 self-assessment studies, Mabe and West suggest that applicants be asked to assess *performance* (both past and future) rather than abilities. In addition, they suggest that applicants be instructed to use a relative rather than absolute standard of judgment. For example, instead of attempting to estimate themselves in abstract terms, applicants should be instructed to compare themselves with others they have known. With respect to manual dexterity, a mechanic might compare herself to other mechanics she has known rather than estimate how competent she will be in some abstract sense. Shrauger and Osberg (1981) suggest that self-assessment can be improved by asking the applicant to assess maximum performance rather than typical performance. They further suggest that the applicant be given assistance in recalling previous relevant experience or events.

Pannone (1984) has suggested a novel approach to self-assessment. He proposes to use self-assessment to screen applicants in order to determine who should be given a test. In his strategy, candidates for a job would be given a list of tasks that were taken directly from the job analysis for the job in question. They would then be asked how frequently they performed those tasks and the extent of supervision that was required if they performed the tasks. He suggests that those who have most frequently performed the tasks that compose the job with the least supervision imposed on them be permitted to move on to the next stage and actually take a qualifying test for that job. He found that the correlation between that variable (i.e., number of tasks performed frequently without supervision) and the eventual test score of the candidate was +.55. Although this is intriguing, there are several problems with the proposal. First, many jobs are entry-level jobs, and the individual would not be expected to have performed any of the tasks of the job previously. Second, it would seem to disadvantage those who were not already "in the network." This would most often include ethnic minority and female applicants, particularly for jobs that had been primarily filled in the past with white males. Finally, it seems obvious that an individual could "cheat" by simply claiming that she had done all the tasks listed frequently and without supervision. Pannone developed a strategy for dealing with the last objection. He suggested putting in task statements that seemed plausible but were not part of the job in question. Anyone who indicated that he or she had performed that task previously would be excluded from further consideration. This is reminiscent of the "carelessness index" proposed by Green and Stutzman (1986) in weeding out inaccurate subject matter experts in job analysis.

Although Pannone's research is interesting, it is not a realistic strategy for dealing with the screening process.

Self-assessment has not been widely studied as a potential predictor. Instead, it is usually considered as a way of identifying discrepancies in perceptions between two individuals (e.g., supervisor and subordinate in a performance review). It deserves more attention from both a practical and a theoretical standpoint. Although the use of self-assessment may be problematic for filling positions in normal industrial settings, it might prove useful in volunteer organizations or even as an aid in determining training needs or placement decisions in the traditional work setting.

WORK SAMPLE AND SITUATIONAL TESTS

Work Sample Tests

As the name implies, *work sample* tests measure job skills by taking a sample of behavior under realistic joblike conditions. Actually, the performance may not be measured at the job station but instead on a standard test machine and with a standardized task. For example, applicants for the job of sewing-machine operator might be given a standard set of tasks reflecting the various techniques required on the job.

Work sample tests have been used both as predictors of job performance and as criteria for job proficiency. As predictors, they are obviously designed to assess present skill achievement, not aptitude or potential. Therefore, they would be of greatest use in situations in which experienced workers were being recruited. The work sample test is a simple demonstration of proficiency under standardized, controlled conditions, and comparisons can be made with accumulated normative data. As an example of a predictor work sample, consider the form reproduced in Figure 7–4. This form was presented to candidates for promotion to police sergeant in a medium-sized midwestern city. The candidates were asked to review the form and identify and correct any errors in the information on the form. The form was identical to forms submitted by patrol officers at the end of every shift. In this city (as in most), it was the sergeant's responsibility to make sure that all the forms were filled out correctly before she turned them in for processing to the records office. Further, since there was no training program for sergeants in this particular city, it was necessary for the new sergeant to be able to carry out this task on the very first day on the job. Although the errors may not be apparent to you, they would be to a proficient patrol sergeant. For example, in box 16 the wrong charge is listed and in box 9 an incorrect abbreviation is used. The candidate's score was based on how many errors were detected and corrected on the several forms that he was given to review.

As criterion measures, work sample tests provide a means of overcoming machine contamination and factors due to the interdependence of jobs. That

A candidate for a fire fighter position moves a ladder. This is an example of the actual job of fire fighter. (Rick Jacobs)

is, they provide standardized tasks to be administered under standardized conditions, whereas performance on the job may be biased by a poor machine or inept coworkers. As an example of the criterion work samples, remember the category of performance measures that I referred to in Chapter 5 as "hands-on performance" measures. The examples that I gave were related to the job of tank crewman. Criterion work samples also provide a solution to the problem of equating performance on jobs involving somewhat different tasks but basically the same skills. Thus, sewing-machine operators sewing pajama tops may be compared with those sewing nightshirts, providing that the same sort of stitching is involved.

The limitation of the work sample test as a criterion measure may be apparent. Although the work sample test may provide an accurate assessment of what the employee *can do* (that is, her skill level), there is no assurance that her test score reflects what she *will do* on the job. Even though we may assume that being capable of skillful performance is intrinsically rewarding and should be an incentive to perform, it is also possible that when the skill requirements are low or moderate, even the most skillful worker may become bored and unmotivated. Yet, under the artificial conditions of the work sample test, they may be motivated to "show their stuff." Naturally, the same arguments can be raised against work samples as predictors: they measure the

FIGURE 7–4 Work Sample for Position of Police Sergeant

DEPARTMENT Wilmington

CRIME REPORT

18. PAGE 1 OF 2
19. DATE OF REPORT 2 FEB 86
1. VICTIM'S NAME (LAST-FIRST-MIDDLE) (FIRM NAME OR BUSINESS) ADAMS JOHN QUINCY
2. COMPLAINT NO. 86-27381
20. PERSON NOTIFIED IN CRIMINAL INVESTIGATION N-A
21. REFERRED TO
3. VICTIM'S RESIDENCE ADDRESS 1302 N. CLAYTON ST. COMMUNITY CITY Wilmington
22. POINT OF ENTRY Basement window
23. SCHEDULED INTAKE DATE N/A
4. VICTIM'S RACE-SEX-AGE WM 33
5. D.O.B. 6 MAR 52
6. RESIDENCE PHONE 652-7871 ☑ DAY ☐ NIGHT
BUSINESS PHONE ☐ DAY ☑ NIGHT 773-8267
24. TYPE OF PREMISE SEMI-DETACHED DWELLING
7. WHERE VICTIM IS EMPLOYED OR SCHOOL ATTENDS Wilmington Latex CITY Wilmington
8. VICTIM TO OFFENDER NO
25. NATURE OF INJURIES N/A
9. LOCATION OF INCIDENT (ADDRESS OR BLOCK NO.) 1302 N. CLAYTON ST (A-2)
10. GRID 18C
26. WEAPONS OR MEANS OF ATTACK N/A
11. REPORTED DAY DATE TIME SUN 2 FEB 86 1630
12. SECTOR 18
13. COUNTY NC
27. VICTIM HOSPITALIZED · WHERE? N/A
14. OCCURRED DAY DATE TIME SUN 2 FEB 86 0800 TO SUN 2 FEB 86
DAY DATE TIME
15. SUPPLEMENT CODE
28. 4-F-14 SENT YES ☐ NO ☐ DATE N/A
29. GENERAL BROADCAST YES ☐ NO ☑
16. CRIME OR INCIDENT BURGLARY III (11-824) (F)
17. U.C.R. CLASSIFICATION

WAS THERE A WITNESS TO THE CRIME? IF NO, PLACE AN X IN BOX A → A ☒

INDICATE RELATIONSHIP TO INVESTIGATION: W-1, W-2 WITNESS, NI NOT INTERVIEWED, RP REPORTING PERSON, PC PERSON CONTACTED, P PARENT

CODE	30. NAME	RACE-SEX-AGE	RESIDENCE ADDRESS	ADDRESS CONTACTED	PHONE
	N/A		N/A	N/A	

IS THERE A SIGNIFICANT M.O. PRESENT? IF NO, PLACE AN X IN BOX B → B

31. METHODS USED TO COMMIT CRIME
UNKNOWN PERSON(S) PRIED OPEN BASEMENT WINDOW, ENTERED DWELLING, REMOVED ITEMS FROM FIRST FLOOR OF DWELLING
34. M.O. CLASS

IS THERE SIGNIFICANT PHYSICAL EVIDENCE PRESENT? IF NO, PLACE AN X IN BOX C → C ☒

32. EVIDENCE WORK PERFORMED ☐ YES ☒ NO PERFORMED BY: N/A ☐ REFUSED TYPE PROCESSING N/A

IS STOLEN PROPERTY TRACEABLE? IF NO, PLACE AN X IN BOX D → D ☒

CODE	33-1 DESCRIBE PROPERTY TAKEN	REMOVED FROM	IDENTIFICATION NO.	PROPERTY VALUE
H	RCA 19" PORTABLE COLOR TV, BROWN PLASTIC CHASSIS	LIVING ROOM	UNK	$250
	33-2			
	33-3			
	33-4			
	33-5			
	33-6			

TYPE OF PROPERTY CODE (A) Currency, Notes, etc. (B) Jewelry and Precious Metals (C) Furs (D) Clothing (E) Locally Stolen M. Veh. (F) Miscellaneous (G) Office Equip. (H) Televisions, Radios, Cameras, etc. (I) Firearms (J) Household Goods (K) Consumable Goods (L) Livestock (M) Bicycles (N) No Property Stolen (P) Pending Stolen Property (R) Any Two-way Radios, or Equipment attached thereto Except Aerials (S) Marine Equipment.

39. VALUE DAMAGED 35.00 40. VALUE RECOVERED -0- 41. VALUE STOLEN 285.00

CAN SUSPECT BE NAMED? IF NO, PLACE AN X IN BOX E → E ☒

42. SUSPECT 1. NAME N-A 43. SUSPECT 2. NAME N-A

CAN SUSPECT BE (F) LOCATED, (G) DESCRIBED, OR (H) IDENTIFIED? IF NO, PLACE AN X IN BOX F, G, AND/OR H → F ☒ G ☒ H ☒

N/A N/A

CAN SUSPECT VEHICLE BE IDENTIFIED? IF NO, PLACE AN X IN BOX I → I ☒

44. REGISTRATION NO. STATE N-A YEAR MAKE BODY MODEL N-A COLOR(S) IDENTIFYING CHARACTERISTICS OF VEHICLE

CAN CRIME BE SOLVED WITH A REASONABLE AMOUNT OF INVESTIGATIVE EFFORT? IF NO, PLACE AN X IN BOX J → J ☒

CODE 45. CONTINUATION OF ABOVE ITEMS
22 ON SOUTH SIDE OF DWELLING
REPORTING PERSON STATES THAT BETWEEN THE ABOVE TIMES OF OCCURRENCE PERSON(S) UNKNOWN PRIED OPEN A SOUTH SIDE BASEMENT WINDOW AND ENTERED THE BASEMENT AREA. PERPETRATORS THEN PROCEEDED TO THE FIRST FLOOR AREA AND INTO THE DINING ROOM. THERE THEY OPENED SEVERAL DRAWERS TO A CUPBOARD, AND SPILLED

ONE OF THE SOLVABILITY FACTORS PRESENT IN REPORT | NO-OFFICE | NO-BUT, FOLLOW-UP NEEDED | YES-FOLLOW-UP | YES-CLOSED | FIELD SUPVR. DECISION.

46. REPORTING OFFICER Ptlm. Abel Baker NO. 23/417 DIV. CPLT
48. STATUS ☐ UNFOUNDED ☐ PENDING ACTIVE ☐ PENDING INACTIVE ☐ ARREST-ADULT ☐ ARREST-JUV ☐ EXCEPT. CLEAR ☐ SERVICE CLEAR
IF FOLLOW UP · SOLVABILITY FACTORS SHOULD BE INVESTIGATED
OFFICE FOLLOW-UP CLOSED
47. REPORTING PERSONS SIGNATURE Ptlm. Paul Smith 23/419 CPLT.
49. REVIEWER

DOC # 45-06-78/06/06 DSP 6014

RECORDS

ability but not the motivational determinant of on-the-job performance. It may well be, however, that those who have been motivated to learn a set of skills and who were motivated to perform them in the work sample test are at least more likely to find practicing the skill on the job a satisfying experience. Some indirect evidence of this with respect to job information tests (rather than job-skill work sample tests) was summarized by Ghiselli and Brown (1948). They found significant validities for supervisors' ratings of proficiency for six of eight jobs with a median of .33. Apparently, proficient workers are knowledgeable about their jobs (or vice versa), and this may be true for skill as well.

Situational Tests

I have intentionally grouped work sample and situational tests together in this section. In a sense, situational tests are the work samples of the managerial and professional occupations. Although the problems provided in situational tests are not always intended to be realistic samples of problems on the job, there is some evidence that they should share this characteristic with work sample tests. Both work sample and situational tests that do present realistic samples of the job are more easily defended with respect to EEOC guidelines than are standard psychological tests.

Situational tests may be individual problem-solving situations, such as the "in-basket" test (Meyer, 1961), in which the applicant responds to a standardized set of situations such as he might find in the in-basket on his desk, or group problem-solving (or discussion) situations. The best example of the latter is the "leaderless group discussion" method developed and investigated by Bass (1954). In this method, observers rate the behavior of each individual in the group, usually in areas of "individual prominence," "group goal facilitation," and "sociability." Both interrater and test-retest reliabilities tend to be high (Bass, 1954; Bray & Grant, 1966; Greenwood & McNamara, 1967). Greenwood and McNamara (1967) found that nonprofessional observer-assessors were as reliable as professionals. However, interrater agreement seems to depend in an important way on the size of the group. Thus, Bass and Norton (1951) found increases in reliability from two-person groups ($r = .72$) to a maximum with six-person groups ($r = .89$), and L. Carter et al. (1951) reported similar results for four- ($r = .70$) and eight- ($r = .85$) person groups. Test-retest estimates seem to follow the same pattern. Furthermore, the greater the similarity (problem, personnel, etc.) of the retest to the test situation, the higher the reliability estimate, as would be expected (Bass & Norton, 1951).

Bass (1954) reported evidence of validity of leaderless group discussions for a number of jobs and occupational levels, including shipyard foremen, oil-refinery administrators, administrative trainees, and civil and foreign service administrators. These validities tended to be somewhat lower than for peer nominations. More recently, Bray and Grant (1966) reported that both in-basket and group situational tests proved to be predictive of assessment ratings (internal validity) and of salary progress, taken as one criterion of job proficiency (external validity). In fact, the results with these two techniques yielded consistently higher validities than with a number of standardized ability tests and personality questionnaires, although it was concluded that both sources of information contributed to the assessment ratings that were quite predictive of progress in management. While reliability seems to be relatively independent of the *content* of the group situational test, suggesting—as Carlson (1972) pointed out—that observers can agree on ratings or rankings of "general person quality" (probably involving a "valid halo" effect), validity depends somewhat more on content. Thus, Freeberg (1969) found that a relevant task (mathematics problems) not only was better for predicting a math criterion (scores on a math test) than irrelevant content but was also better for predicting two other criteria (grade point average and general ability scores) for which no specific content was available. Freeberg suggested that the rater's halo "worked," that she generalized from the specific (math) content to the other two inferred traits on the basis of her "psychological theory" of the relationship among these traits. Factor analyses of the ratings (by both peers and observers) indicated a general factor of "cognitive ability," a secondary factor of "math ability," and four specific factors related to relevant-irrelevant tasks and observer-participant raters.

A Closer Look at Work Sample Tests

Asher and Sciarrino (1974) reviewed the available research evidence with respect to the validity of work sample tests. They classified work samples as belonging to one of two classes: motor work samples (requiring physical manipulation) and verbal work samples (requiring communication or interpersonal relations skills). Figure 7–5 presents some of the typical content of these two different types of work samples.

The results of these authors' review were very encouraging. They compared the validity of work sample tests to the estimates of the validity of other common predictors published periodically by Ghiselli (1966). I reported some of Ghiselli's estimates in Chapter 4 in the discussion of IQ tests. Figure 7–6 compares the validities of work sample tests with the validities of other predictors. As you can see, a large percentage of studies using the work sample approach report validities in excess of .50. When you drop the validity coefficient to .30, 78 percent of the motor work sample studies and 60 percent of the verbal work sample studies report significant validities.

Another interesting aspect of this review was a comparison of the results of motor and verbal work sample validation studies. Asher and Sciarrino were able to demonstrate that verbal work samples were better at predicting training success, and motor work samples were better at predicting job proficiency. They account for their results by proposing a "point-to-point" validation the-

FIGURE 7–5

Motor Work Samples	*Verbal Work Samples*
Carving dexterity test for dental students	A test of common facts of law for law students
Blueprint reading test	Group discussion test for supervisor
Shorthand and stenography test	Judgment and decision-making test for administrators
Rudder control test for pilots	Speech interview for foreign student
Programming test for computer programmers	Test of basic information in chemistry
Map reading test for traffic control officers	Test of ability to follow oral directions

ory. They contend that the greater the number of common elements in predictor and criteria, the higher the validity of the predictor. Thus, since most training programs are highly verbally loaded, it makes sense that verbal work samples do a better job of predicting training success.

In a later study, Gordon and Kleiman (1976) suggested that the value of work sample tests had not been adequately assessed, since few studies directly compared the validity of work samples and more traditional predictors by using the same subjects and the same criterion. They made a direct comparison of the value of work samples versus traditional predictors with several classes of police academy recruits. They found that a verbal work sample was a better predictor of academy success (essentially training success) than was an IQ test administered prior to the beginning of the training program. This result also lends support to the Asher and Sciarrino (1974) conclusion that verbal work samples are good predictors of training success. In spite of a general support of the Asher and Sciarrino results, Gordon and Kleiman were not yet ready to accept the "point-to-point" theory. They suggest that an equally plausible explanation for the good showing of work samples is that since these tests tend to be more realistic than traditional paper-and-pencil tests, the applicant's level of interest, motivation, or both may be substantially higher. There is not enough information available to choose between the two competing explanations, but one thing is clear: work samples deserve and will undoubtedly receive a good deal of attention from managers and personnel researchers alike in the coming years. They represent a technique that seems to be both legally and technically defensible. In fact, it is the system by which amateur and professional sports teams have been making selection decisions for decades.

In a summarizing section at the end of this chapter, I will have more to say about the relative validity of work sample tests. Nevertheless, at this point it is fair to say that they have much to recommend them both from a legal and a psychometric standpoint.

FIGURE 7–6 Proportion of Validity Coefficients .50 or Higher with Job Proficiency as the Criterion

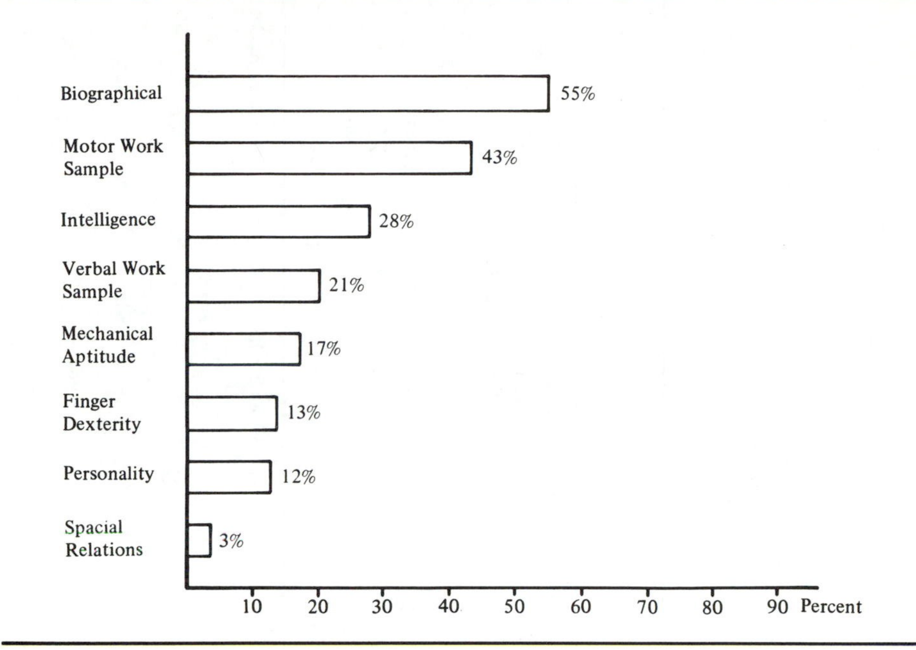

A COMPARISON OF STANDARDIZED TESTS VERSUS OTHER PREDICTORS

We have considered many different devices that might be used to predict occupational success. In the last chapter, we examined various standardized paper-and-pencil tests as well as assessment centers and physical ability tests. In this chapter, we have considered a heterogeneous set of alternative or additional predictor devices. A natural question that arises is, How do these alternatives stack up against tests with respect to validity? A recent meta-analysis by Schmitt and his colleagues (Schmitt et al., 1984) provides substantial data for answering this quetion. They reviewed the results of 99 studies published in IsolidusO journals between 1965 and 1982. These studies covered a broad range of occupations from professional through unskilled labor. In all, they examined 366 validity coefficients. I have reproduced some of their results in Tables 7–4 and 7–5. Table 7–4 summarizes the validity coefficients by predictor, and Table 7–5 breaks those results down further by criterion type. As can be seen in Table 7–4, personality tests do most poorly; aptitude, general mental ability, and biodata predictors are slightly more predictive; and work samples, assessment centers, physical ability tests, and supervisory-peer evaluations seem to do best. In Table 7–5, specific relation-

TABLE 7–4 Validity Coefficients as a Function of Type of Predictor

Predictor	*Number of Validities*	*Sample Range*	*Sample Total*	$\bar{r}$	σ_r^2	σ_e^2	σ_Q^2	*Percent Unexplained*
Special aptitude	31	19–1,091	4,315	.268	.02083	.00619	.01464	70
Personality	62	24–3,964	23,413	.149	.01109	.00253	.00856	77
General mental ability	53	24–8,885	40,230	.248	.01908	.00117	.01791	94
Biodata	99	22–14,738	58,107	.243	.01831	.00151	.01680	92
Work sample	18	19–1,091	3,512	.378	.01139	.00377	.00762	67
Assessment center	21	35–8,885	15,345	.407	.00250	.00095	.00155	62
Supervisor/peer evaluations	31	30–1,979	6,620	.427	.03046	.00313	.02733	89
Physical ability	22	55–588	3,103	.315	.04865	.00575	.04290	88
Total	337	19–68,616	154,645	.280	.01750	.00133	.01617	92

SOURCE: From "Metaanalyses of Validity Studies Published between 1964 and 1982 and the Investigation of Study Characteristics" by N. Schmitt, R. Z. Gooding, R. D. Noe, and M. Kirsch, 1984, *Personnel Psychology*, *37* (3), p. 415.

TABLE 7–5 Validity Coefficients as a Function of Type of Criterion

Criterion	*Number of Validities*	*Sample Range*	*Sample Total*	$\bar{r}$	σ_r^2	σ_e^2	σ_Q^2	*Percent Unexplained*
Performance ratings	140	22–520	17,559	.260	.03051	.00693	.02358	77
Turnover	48	37–68,616	127,021	.246	.01104	.00033	.01071	97
Achievement/grades	43	19–453	7,156	.270	.03971	.00516	.03455	87
Productivity	30	50–3,590	14,869	.208	.00584	.00185	.00399	68
Status change	46	30–8,885	52,686	.359	.01303	.00066	.01237	95
Wages	33	47–443	5,470	.378	.02278	.00443	.01835	81
Work samples	24	77–1,091	8,244	.401	.02638	.00205	.02433	92
Total	364	19–68,616	233,005	.280	.01750	.00133	.01617	90

SOURCE: From "Metaanalyses of Validity Studies Published between 1964 and 1982 and the Investigation of Study Characteristics" by N. Schmitt, R. Z. Gooding, R. D. Noe, and M. Kirsch, 1984, *Personnel Psychology, 37* (3), p. 416.

ships can be examined more closely. As an example, it is apparent that general mental ability tests do best in predicting general mental ability activities (such as progress in academic settings). Similarly, physical ability tests do quite well in predicting work sample criteria. The answer to the question, Which types of predictors do best? would seem to depend on the type of criterion that you are interested in predicting. If you are interested in predicting turnover, it would seem that biodata items provide the best (but still not very attractive) alternatives. On the other hand, if you are interested in predicting training grades or other instances of academiclike achievement, your best bet might be general mental ability tests. It should be clear from these tables that the relationships are complex and need a great deal more careful examination.

A SAMPLER OF OTHER POSSIBILITIES

The techniques that I have covered to this point are traditional alternatives to paper-and-pencil assessment devices. They are supported by theory or data or both. There are other techniques that have been suggested (and even utilized) in making personnel decisions that have a much leaner history or conceptual basis. I will not dwell on them at any great length, but you should know something about them. I will cover five topics in this sampler—graphology, lie detection, recommendations, seniority, and unassembled testing.

Graphology

Handwriting analysis has been popular as a parlor game for centuries. Commonly, it is asserted that traits can be assessed from various characteristics of an individual's handwriting. This technique has had some popularity in Europe (Jansen, 1973). Recently, Rafaeli and Klimoski (1983) looked at the validity of handwriting assessments gathered from expert graphologists. The handwriting samples came from 104 real estate sales personnel. The criteria included both supervisory ratings and sales data. They found that there was some reliability to the judgments of the graphologists but no validity. In other words, there was some agreement with respect to the characteristics of a given individual's handwriting, but these characteristics were unrelated to sales success.

Ben-Shakhar, Bar-Hillel, Bilu, Ben-Abba, and Flug (1986) have provided additional data on graphology. They compared professional graphologists with clinical psychologists and discovered that clinical psychologists could do as well as graphologists in assessing characteristics of writers if the handwriting samples included a range of biographical statements. Thus, it was the content, not the style, of writing that was being used for information.

Several years ago, I managed to get into a dispute with a handwriting expert with respect to the validity of handwriting analysis for employment selection. I had made an intemperate comment in the newspaper that he noticed. As luck would have it, he was also the president of the state association of graphologists. The dispute was carried on in the local newspaper with letters from me and letters from the handwriting expert (who suggested that the more "scientifically correct" term was *graphologist*—I continued to use the term *handwriting expert!*). I ended the dispute abruptly with one swift stroke of the letter: I asked if he had been chosen for the position of president based on an analysis of his handwriting. No more letters appeared from the handwriting expert.

Lie Detection

It is not illogical for an employer to prefer an honest to a dishonest employee. It is both the right and the responsibility of any employer to reject an individual who is likely to engage in dishonest or deceptive behavior in the work setting. In many instances, this dishonesty is costly to the employer (in the form of pilferage). In other instances, it is costly or dangerous to the consumer (in the form of inferior products or services that result from intentional poor performance). There are two occasions when employers attempt to identify dishonest employees. The first occasion is when something has happened at the workplace (e.g., an information leak, a theft), and the employer seeks to identify the guilty party. The second instance is when the employer seeks to identify those individuals who *might* engage in dishonest behavior if they were to be hired.

There are several different devices that are currently available that purport to measure honesty (either in the abstract, in the case of a prospective employee, or in the concrete, with respect to a particular incident). Two common devices are the polygraph (commonly known as the lie detector) and the voice stress analyzer. Both work on a common principle. It is assumed that the dishonest or guilty person will display a pattern of emotions that is substantially different from the pattern displayed by an honest or innocent individual. In the case of the polygraph, various electrodes are attached to the person to be examined. These electrodes provide measures of such things as dampness of the skin (Galvanic Skin response), respiration, blood pressure, and heart rate. A trained polygraph examiner then asks a series of questions that are intended to provide data related to guilt or innocence (or in the abstract case, honesty or dishonesty).

Sackett and Decker (1979) have published a review of studies relating to the industrial use of polygraphs. They conclude that the use of polygraphs is not warranted because of differences between the criminal context and the employment context. In other words, one cannot generalize from the accuracy of the polygraph for criminal investigation to its potential for employment use.

I would like to make some broader points about lie detection. First, there have been attempts since the turn of the century to identify unique physiological patterns that accompany reported emotions. These attempts have been uniformly and spectacularly unsuccessful (e.g., Ax, 1953). Over 3,000 emotions have been labeled (Plutchik, 1980). So far, the only distinctions that seem possible are between fear and rage. There has never been any serious claim for having identified "guilt." In addition, many studies have demonstrated the extent to which psychophysiological responses (e.g., heart rate, blood pressure, respiration, and skin conductance) can be intentionally moderated (e.g., Stern, Botto, & Herrick, 1972; Stern & Lewis, 1968). Finally, and most important, the predominant theory of emotion—the Schachter-Singer theory (Schachter & Singer, 1962)—proposes that an emotion is the result of generalized arousal that is interpreted by the person in terms of contextual cues. In other words, emotions have only one physiological dimension—arousal. The individuality of emotions comes from context, not unique physiological response mechanisms.

David Lykken has spent many years considering the reliability and validity of lie detection techniques. His book entitled *A Tremor in the Blood* (1981) is an excellent critique of the logic and theory of lie detection. Most damning (and problematic) from the perspective of applied prediction is the error rate. The most common error is to identify someone as guilty (or dishonest) when in fact they are innocent (or honest). The polygraph is biased against the person telling the truth. In three studies reviewed by Lykken (1983), 49 percent, 39 percent, and 55 percent of truthful respondents were identified as deceptive. Lykken further points out that the typical claims of a polygraph expert to be "99 percent" accurate are nonsense since the polygrapher almost never discovers if the test was correct or not. There is no independent confirming evidence. In our terminology, there is no criterion with which to assess the validity of the device. To quote Lykken (1983):

> False positive polygraph tests result in honest persons being refused jobs in and out of government, in blameless persons being fired from their jobs and losing their good reputations, in innocent suspects of being prosecuted and even convicted for crimes they did not commit. (p. 4)

The problems of the polygraph seem trivial when compared with those of the voice stress analyzer. These devices purport to measure microtremors in the speech of individuals and use these microtremors to detect deception. The machines vary in price from $150 to $3,000 and are often labeled "truth machines." The microtremors they purport to measure have never been associated with any stable pattern of autonomic nervous system (ANS) responsiveness (the ANS is central to all theories of emotion).

My advice is simple. The current state of the field provides no support for the use of polygraphs in industrial settings. The use of voice stress analyzers is equally questionable. Both state and federal legislation has now caught up with the questionable use of polygraphs, and their use in employment settings has been rapidly declining. The House of Representatives has passed a very strong anti–lie detection bill (HR1212), and the Senate has followed suit with a slightly milder version. The House and Senate are now working out a compromise bill. It will not be long before most use of lie detection equipment will be banned from the workplace. This is good.

Paper-and-Pencil Honesty Tests. Sackett and Harris (1984, 1985) have identified written honesty tests as another cause for concern in the employment arena. These tests have become more popular with the increase in antipolygraph legislation. In a review of currently available honesty tests, they identify five different types of items that appear on these tests. These items deal with beliefs about (1) the extensiveness of theft in the workplace, (2) the propriety of various penalties for theft, (3) the ease of theft, (4) personal knowledge of thefts, and (5) the assessment of one's own relative honesty compared to coworkers. Validity for these tests is typically assessed in several ways. First, validity is assessed by comparing the results of the honesty test to the recommendations of a polygrapher. Sometimes, the honesty test results are compared to admissions of past thefts. The real test would be to compare the results of the honesty test for employees caught stealing with those of employees not caught stealing. The fact is, however, few employees are caught stealing so this type of study is not feasible.

Sackett and Harris conclude that the risks to individual liberties are too great to encourage the use of honesty tests given the current knowledge about what they measure. I agree. If honesty tests were a new drug, the Food and Drug Administration would require considerably more testing before permitting them into the marketplace.

One final note might be appropriate on the topic of honesty testing regardless of the technique used. Murphy (1987) provides a sobering analysis of the level of accuracy necessary for detecting infrequent deception. He points out that most employers are interested in detecting the risk of serious dishonesty (e.g., a theft of more than $5) not trivial dishonesty (e.g., taking a pencil from work to home). The incidence of serious dishonesty at the workplace is low. In statistical terms this would be called a *low base rate*. Murphy demonstrates that none of the techniques currently available (e.g., polygraphs, honesty tests, voice stress analyzers) could possibly be of any value in detecting dishonesty if they are used as screening devices. Thus, theoretical arguments aside, the small numbers of people who engage in serious deception make it impossible to place any confidence in current methods for evaluating honesty.

Recommendations

It is common for applicants to be asked for references. These references are then contacted by phone or by mail and asked to provide judgments regarding various ability- and temperament-based characteristics of the applicant. For example, they may be asked to write a paragraph describing the strengths or weaknesses of the person, or they might be asked to rate the applicant on characteristics such as trustworthiness, initiative, emotional stability, or creativity. Even a brief consideration of recommendations suggests that they are seldom based on a job analysis. They either solicit or encourage unanchored trait-based judgments that may have little relevance for the job under consideration. Baxter, Brock, Hill, and Rozelle (1981) contend that letter writers apply their own theories of success to the job in question. In a sense, they do their own quick and intuitive job analysis and decide what information they should provide. In all likelihood, they know little about the job in question and, as a result, provide useless or even misleading information. In other words, letters of recommendation may tell us more about the recommender than about the applicant.

There may be other forces at work as well. Many employers are cautious in saying anything that might be construed as evaluative about a former employee for fear of precipitating a lawsuit. In spite of a desire to be honest and helpful, they feel that the risk is too great and the benefit to them nonexistent.

Shaffer and Tomarelli (1981) examined an issue related to letters of recommendation. The Buckley Amendment provides for the right of an applicant to discover what someone may have said about his qualifications in a letter. The applicant can waive this right or retain it. As an example, I might receive a form from a student asking me to provide a recommendation in support of a graduate application. On that form is a box that the student can check to tell me whether she keeps or retains this right. Shaffer and Tomarelli found that graduate admissions officers favored applicants who waived their right to examine the letter of recommendation. They found this effect at all levels of ability. They reasoned that the graduate admissions officer "trusted" the information more when they felt that the student was unable to see the letters. In this instance, a characteristic incidental to the purpose of the letter was having an influence. As Shaffer and Tomarelli point out, the purpose of the Buckley Amendment was to inform the person requesting the letter of his or her rights and the letter writer of possible requests for disclosure. It was not intended to be used as a device by decision makers. They suggest that individuals receiving such letters be kept "blind" with respect to the confidentiality of the letter. This information can be recorded and filed in the institution or organization but denied the decision maker.

Knouse (1983) examined a number of specific aspects of recommendation letters and made several interesting discoveries. First, he found that, as was the case in the interview, negative information played a much more powerful role than positive information, as if the reader were looking for an opportunity to eliminate as many candidates as possible from consideration using the letter. In addition, he found that specific behavioral examples produced more positive evaluations of the candidate in contrast to more general nonbehavioral statements. Nevertheless, Knouse's research did not address the validity of the letter of recommendation, only the perceived favorability of the letter from the reader's perspective.

There has been little serious research on the validity of recommendations. Given the importance that they often play in the decision process, this is a serious problem. As is the case with any predictor, more must be known about the circumstances favoring or diminishing the validity of these devices.

Seniority

In many organizations, decisions regarding job duties, promotions, and financial rewards are made on the basis of seniority. Seniority can be defined in several ways. It can be accumulated time in a particular job or accumulated time in the organization. Certainly, an important element of seniority influence is the notion of rewards for stability and loyalty. Union contracts provide that those individuals who have served the longest (i.e., had the greatest opportunity to make a contribution to the vitality of the organization) be given preference in personnel decisions. Another component of seniority, however, should be experience (in terms of either the organization or the particular job title). One might expect that more senior employees display greater skill, knowledge, or both than less senior individuals.

Gordon and Johnson (1982) have recently reviewed the literature on seniority and have found little empirical evidence to suggest that seniority is a valid index of ability or performance. In fact, what little evidence they did find suggested the opposite. In examining a training program, Gordon and Cohen (1973) discovered that those most likely to succeed in a later position spent less time in the training program under examination. Gordon and Johnson (1982) conclude that much more must be known about seniority and its validity for personnel decisions since it is generally accepted as a legal and defensible basis for staffing decisions.

Gordon and Fitzgibbons (1982) compared five different policies for making promotions. These policies were:

1. Promote on the basis of past performance.
2. Promote on the basis of seniority.
3. Select the most senior candidate from those equally qualified.
4. Select the most senior candidate only when the old and new jobs are similar.
5. Select the most senior candidate from those equally qualified only when the old and new jobs are similar.

The subjects of the study were 162 sewing-machine operators who had been promoted and remained in the new job for a minimum of nine months. The criterion was output. This was easy to measure since the operators were paid on a piece-rate basis and their productivity was simply a transformation of their pay. Seniority was defined both in the job and in the company. Job similarity was determined through existing job evaluation information. The results were fairly clear. Seniority—either by itself or in combinations with other variables—did not predict future performance. The two most significant predictors were past performance and interjob similarity, regardless of seniority. In other words, the best performers were likely to be those who had been good performers on other jobs, those who had held jobs similar to the one they were promoted to, or both. In a more recent study, Gordon, Cofer, and McCullough (1986) replicated the Gordon and associates earlier results—but this time with a training criterion. Those with higher seniority were no more trainable than those with less seniority.

Once again, one is struck with the irrelevance (or possibly counterproductive value) of a commonly held assumption. As was the case with recommendations, much more needs to be known about seniority if it is to continue to be used as an influence on personnel decisions. From the personnel psychologist's perspective, the sacred characteristics of a union management agreement do not provide sufficient logic for the continued use of seniority for decision making. Most of us would agree that *experience* should be related to performance. The problem is that seniority is not a good substitute for experience. Simply "being there" is not enough.

There is one final point that might be made with respect to the observed correlations between seniority and performance. There may be a serious problem of range restriction in most studies. If an organization recognizes potential and develops talent, the best people may have the least seniority. They are promoted or transferred or go to work for other organizations. This explanation follows directly from the results of the Gordon and Johnson study described earlier. If that is the case, one would reasonably expect the correlations to be low or negative.

Unassembled Testing

Recently, a new type of predictor has been suggested that is a good deal freer in form than many of the devices we have considered previously. In most situations, the candidate is given a standard set of questions, problems, scales, or tasks. These "items" are uniform from one candidate to the next. Unassembled testing has a very different approach. On the basis of a job analysis, the important and frequent characteristics of the job are identified, and the candidate is asked to provide evidence about past accomplishments that are similar in some important respects to the requirements of the job under consideration. For example, the job of high school track coach might involve intensive interaction with adolescents and young adults. The candidate might be asked to describe past successes in working with similar groups. One applicant might list supervisory responsibilities with a 4-H group, including a successful exhibit at a county fair. A second applicant might reply that she had no previous experience with such groups. The third applicant

FIGURE 7–7 Items Appearing on Final Budget Analyst Behavioral Consistency Supplemental Form

1. *Analytical and Quantitative Reasoning Abilities*
   Budget analysts must analyze complex technical data and other information, using their logic and quantitative reasoning abilities. In doing this, they must be able to distinguish essential from unessential information. On a separate sheet of paper give examples of your past achievements demonstrating these abilities.
2. *Interpersonal and Organizational Skills*
   Budget analysts must be able to work with all kinds of people—different ethnic groups, personalities, age group and occupational levels. In addition, they must be able to determine where to go within their organization for needed information and to judge what information should be passed on to different levels of management. They must also be sensitive to the needs and requirements of people at different organizational levels and realize the extent to which they can aggressively promote their own ideas. On a separate sheet of paper give examples of your past achievements which demonstrate that you possess these skills.
3. *Motivation, Initiative, and Ability to Organize Work*
   Budget analysts must possess initiative and motivation to learn new ideas and techniques. They must be able to budget their time for accomplishing tasks and assignments within given guidelines. How willing are you to seek out and assume additional responsibility and to explore better methods for accomplishing your work? How well can you work with more than one complex project or assignment at a time, organize them as to their importance? On a separate sheet of paper give examples of your past achievements which demonstrate that you possess these skills.
4. *Writing Ability*
   Budget analysts must be able to communicate well in writing. Can you write clearly and concisely? On a separate sheet of paper describe your past achievements demonstrating your writing ability.
5. *Oral Communication Ability*
   Budget analysts must be able to react quickly, confidently, and with composure in stressful, interpersonal situations and present ideas or information in an organized manner on short notice. How successful are you in this type of oral communication? On a separate sheet of paper give examples of your past achievements demonstrating your ability to communicate effectively in such situations.

SOURCE: From *The Behavior Consistency Method of Unassembled Examining* by F. L. Schmidt, J. R. Caplan, S. E. Bemis, R. Decuir, L. Dunn, and L. Antone, 1979, Washington, D.C.: U.S. Office of Personnel Management.

might report that she had been a junior high school track coordinator in another school district for three years and had produced a team that won the league championship. It is up to the candidate to identify past successes that are relevant to the present position.

In a recent report issued by the Office of Personnel Management (OPM) (Schmidt et al., 1979), the method of unassembled examining was used to develop a selection scheme for the position of budget analyst. Figure 7–7 presents examples of questions that could be used to elicit salient information about past accomplishments from candidates for this position. The scoring of answers to those questions is complex, and there is no need to go into it in any detail. The point is that the candidate has the responsibility for listing accomplishments that are relevant. The "examiner" is responsible for arranging those experiences in terms of salience and level. The reason it is called "unassembled" testing is because the test can be given to individuals one at a time and can be completed by mail. Since the answers are verifiable (in theory), the method avoids the shortcomings of other types of self-assessment. The OPM report concludes that this new method of testing is reliable and efficient. Furthermore, it seems to be a more direct measure of education and experience than more traditional-type application blanks. Finally, since it is developed from a job analysis, it would seem to increase the likelihood of content validity. This technique is quite new, and there has been little published research to this point, but the contribution of unassembled testing may turn out to be substantial.

Accomplishments Record. Hough and her colleagues (Hough, 1984; Hough, Keyes, & Dunnette, 1983) have developed a variation of unassembled testing that has a great deal of promise. It is called the "accomplishment record." The logic is the same as that of unassembled testing. The candidate is expected to provide evidence of his accomplishments in a number of areas determined by the job analysis to be salient or critical aspects of the job. In fact, the job analysis is usually done using the critical incidents methods described earlier in the performance chapter. Incumbents are asked to identify incidents that were critical to success or failure of the job in question. These incidents are then sorted into categories of items that are similar, and from those categories, dimensions of the job are identified and defined.

Based on these critical job dimensions, candidates for the job in question are asked to supply evidence of accomplishments in each of those areas. They are provided with a particular form that they use in providing this information. An example of such a form appears in Figure 7–8. This form is taken from the Hough (1984) study in which a promotional scheme for the job of attorney was being constructed. As you can see, candidates were given the definition of each area (e.g., using knowledge) and asked to provide information about the time period when the accomplishment occurred, a statement of what was accomplished, a description of the exact contribution of the candidate (in contrast to the contribution of others who may have been involved), any formal recognitions for that accomplishment, and the name of someone who could verify that accomplishment.

In her study of attorneys, Hough (1984) received over 2,600 accomplishment examples from 300 attorneys who took part in the study. Her next steps were similar to those used in developing BARS performance scales. She had some expert judges sort these examples into categories for which they thought the examples had been written. In the BARS technique, this was called *retranslation*. This had the effect of identifying incidents that were unambiguous examples of the eight dimensions of attorney job performance that had been

FIGURE 7–8 One Dimension of the "Accomplishment Record" Inventory and an Example of a Response.

Using Knowledge

Interpreting and synthesizing information to form legal strategies, approaches, lines of argument, etc.; developing new configurations of knowledge, innovative approaches, solutions, strategies, etc.; selecting the proper legal theory; using appropriate lines of argument, weighing alternatives and drawing sound conclusions.

Time Period: *1974–75*

General statement of what you accomplished:

I was given the task of transferring our anti-trust investigation of into a coherent set of pleadings presentable to and the Commission for review and approval within the context of the Commission's involvement in shopping centers nationwide.

Description of exactly what you did:

I drafted the complaint and proposed order and wrote the underlying legal memo justifying all charges and proposed remedies. I wrote the memo to the Commission recommending approval of the consent agreement. For the first time, we applied anti-trust principles to this novel factual situation.

Awards or formal recognition:

None

The information verified by: *John , Compliance*

SOURCE: From "Development and Evaluation of 'Accomplishment Record' Method of Selecting and Promoting Professionals" by L. Hough, 1984, *Journal of Applied Psychology, 69*(1), p. 137. Copyright 1984 by the American Psychological Association. Reprinted by permission of the publisher and author.

identified in the job analysis. Next, she had another group of expert judges rate the incidents within a given performance area in terms of the level of performance illustrated by the incident, similar to the scaling phase of BARS development. This produced a set of rating scales, one for each performance dimension, anchored with real incidents that illustrated various levels of performance from impressive to trivial in each performance area. The scale that was constructed to evaluate accomplishments in the area of "Using Knowledge" appears in Figure 7–9. As you can see from this figure, the scale is very much like a behaviorally anchored scale, but it has accomplishments as anchors instead of the broader behavioral examples common on BARS instruments. Once the scales have been established, it is then possible to evaluate the accomplishments of the candidates by "scoring" the accomplishments that they submit through the use of the rating scales. In other words, in this case, each candidate would receive eight scores or ratings, one for each dimension being considered.

The results of the accomplishment record strategy in the Hough study were encouraging. Reliabilities were quite high for the rating scales developed

FIGURE 7–9 Rating Scale for Dimension "Using Knowledge" of Accomplishment-Record Inventory

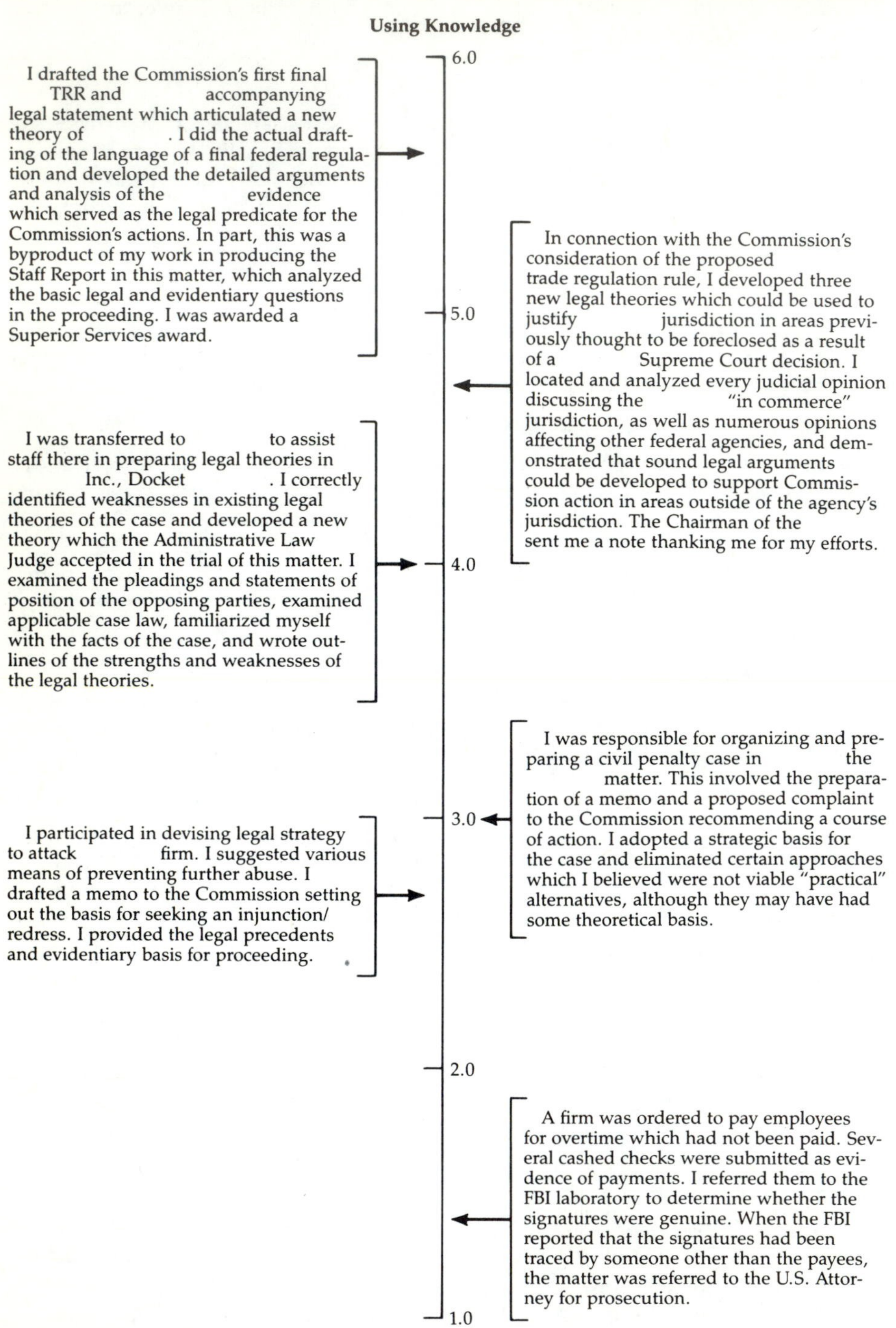

SOURCE: From "Development and Evaluation of the 'Accomplishment-Record' Method of Selecting and Promoting Professionals" by L. M. Hough, 1984, *Journal of Applied Psychology, 69*(1), p. 139.

using the technique. In addition, the scales seemed to be only modestly related to tenure and time since graduation from law school. Nevertheless, the scores were corrected statistically to eliminate the effect of experience. This was necessary since the accomplishments of an individual would logically be related to how long they had been in the position in question. By controlling for experience, in essence, candidates were being compared with others with the same level of experience. The validity coefficients representing the correlations between accomplishment record ratings and measures of job performance were positive and significant. Of equal importance and interest, the validity coefficients seemed to be unaffected by the race and gender of the applicants. Hough suggests that the accomplishment record be considered as one of several instruments composing a test battery for promotional decisions.

There has been little research appearing on accomplishment records since the initial illustration by Hough. This is surprising. The technique seems very promising because of its inherent logic, its psychometric integrity, and its apparent fairness from an equal employment perspective. Its most appealing characteristic is that it permits relevant and documented examples of previous performance to play a role in the personnel decision process. It is reasonable to think that a good predictor of future performance is past performance. I would expect to see more demonstrations of the effectiveness of the accomplishment record technique in the near future.

CENTRAL POINTS FOR STUDY

1. The interview is the most common nonpaper-and-pencil test.
2. The value of the interview can be considered separately from the value of the interviewer.
3. The interview is an exercise in social judgment.
4. Interviews should be based on a thorough job analysis.
5. The application blank can serve multiple purposes in the selection context.
6. There are methods available for scoring application blanks.
7. Life history items can be useful in prediction situations.
8. Self-assessment is a potentially valuable technique in the selection context.
9. Work sample tests measure job skills by sampling behavior in realistic situations.
10. Graphology and lie detection have problems as selection devices.
11. Recommendations and seniority are commonly used in making employment decisions but are supported with little formal research.
12. Unassembled testing is a new method that has been suggested for selection.

CHAPTER 8

Personnel Decisions

Personnel decisions are decisions about people: about hiring, classifying and placing, transferring and reclassifying, promoting and upgrading, training, and developing people. The objective of these decisions is to maximize the utilization of manpower as evaluated in terms of the growth and profit goals of the company. Personnel decisions are *institutional decisions* designed to maximize payoff in terms of institutional rather than individual goals. By contrast, *individual decisions* involving the selection of career, training, company, job, transfer, or retraining—decisions that are arrived at privately, with friends, or in vocational counseling—reflect the goals and values of the individual. Although an institution, such as a medical school, may look at an applicant who, based on her records and test scores, has less than a 50/50 chance of completing medical school training as a bad risk, the individual might feel that, in spite of any odds, life will be meaningless unless she becomes a doctor. Whereas *probability of success* can govern the institutional decision, it is not the sole consideration in the individual decision.

With the exception of a relatively few institutions with open admissions policies, institutions select people and thereby limit the number of choices available to the individual. For the most part, these two types of decisions are made at very different times and places. Only in the vocational counseling situation are the realities of the two decision processes brought face-to-face. The counselor knows that on an actuarial basis the institution will say yes to the individual, and he learns something about the values and preferences of the individual. Ideally, he can consider both the potential payoff to the institution and to the individual as a basis for counseling.

In recent years, there has been a general increase in the concern for the individual in our society. This is reflected in the civil rights movements, the concerns for invasion of privacy, equality of opportunity, and the like. Guion (1967) describes this trend in U.S. business and industry as an increased concern for the "wholeness and integrity of the applicant." Is such a personal approach inconsistent with the goals of the institution and with efficient personnel decisions? No. By and large, good institutional decisions will be good individual decisions, and bad institutional decisions, based on arbitrary biases, prejudices, and whims rather than on valid information, are bad, not only for the individuals rejected but also quite possibly for the "favored" individual. A good decision is one that results in a good match between individual and job, and decisions based on irrelevant information are often apt to result in mismatches between individuals and jobs. Korman (1971) has suggested that this new concern may lead to something like a placement-counseling approach in the personnel office, where employer and applicant might be seen as

> viewing the selection decision as one where the organization and the individual attempt to see whether the two can be or have the capacity to be mutually beneficial to one another . . . not too different from the general "career choice" process as it takes place in vocational counseling centers and the like. (p. 219)

THE EVALUATION OF TESTING PROGRAMS

Much of Chapters 6 and 7 were concerned with the evaluation of tests and other measuring devices, and a good deal of emphasis was placed on reliability and validity as criteria of a predictor's worth. It was emphasized that these and other criteria should be considered in choosing a predictor for use in a selection program. The present chapter takes up where Chapters 6 and 7 left off: having selected a test or other predictor on the basis of the criteria and procedures described, and having incorporated the predictor(s) into a testing program, how then can one determine the utility, or payoff, of that program? How and to what extent is the information in the predictor scores used? To what extent does it affect the personnel decisions made? Assuming that better decisions are made because of the predictor, what is the payoff in terms of increased efficiency of the organization, improved proficiency of the worker on the job, reduced turnover, increased satisfaction, or increased profitability? In the following sections, we will consider several of the issues that determine the utility of a particular test. Certainly, validity is one of those influences. Another influence is the number of people who will apply for a given job or the selection ratio. Finally, we can consider the percentage of people who would have been successful even if the test in question were not used. In this way, utility can be interpreted in terms of the *improvement* in success rate resulting from the use of the test.

The best measurement data from the best tests are of little value if they cannot be utilized to guide decisions, if the data cost more than the gains that result from improved decisions, or if they are highly redundant with information that is already available to the decision maker. To illustrate the last point with an example, suppose an organization administered a test to all applicants, even though scores from the same test were available from their schools or on their transcripts. No new information would be made available to the decision maker, and the testing program would be a liability equal to the direct and overhead costs of operating it, not to mention the imposition on the applicant.

Validity and Predictive Efficiency

Validity is not a concept that grew out of the legal arguments surrounding the Civil Rights Act of 1964. As we saw in Chapter 3, validity is a basic measurement concept. Conceptually, it relates to the meaning of a test or predictor. For example, a test that successfully predicted some aspect of job performance that it was developed to predict would warrant the label "valid." If such a test could be used to predict later job performance, it would add to the efficiency of the selection scheme. It would be more efficient than using a test that had no predictive power; it would be more efficient than hiring everyone who applied and firing all but those who score in the top 10 percent in performance. It would be more efficient than hiring randomly and finding that half of the new hires are unsuitable. In other words, validity also means efficiency.

Consider three examples of validity. In case 1, the predictor is correlated perfectly with the measure of performance ($r = +1.00$). In case 2, the predictor is correlated moderately with the performance in question ($r = +.50$). In case 3, the correlation between predictor and criterion is .00—there is no validity. Figure 8–1 illustrates these three conditions. Examine **(a)**, **(b)**, and **(c)** carefully. These figures represent the actual predictor and criterion scores for samples of individuals. Each point represents a particular subject in the sample who received the respective predictor and criterion scores. Pick any single predictor score and look at the range of criterion scores. For the sake of illustration, let's take the predictor score of 50. In **(a)**, there is one and only one criterion value associated with that predictor score—a criterion score of 85. Now consider **(b)**. Here, the correlation is less than perfect. This, in turn, means that the prediction is less than perfect. An individual who received a predictor score of 50 might obtain a criterion score anywhere between 70 and 100. You can see this by simply following the dotted line from the x (predictor) axis and reading what criterion scores are associated with that predictor score, The shaded area in the figure tells you that there are several criterion scores associated with a predictor score of 50. Finally, consider the case where the correlation between the predictor and criterion is .00 [**(c)**]. Again, consider a predictor score of 50. If you look at the criterion scores associated with that predictor score, you will find that a person who receives a score of 50 when the validity is .00 could receive *any* criterion score from the lowest to the highest. As before, the shaded area in **(c)** illustrates that range. So in the case where the validity is .00, knowledge of the predictor score tells us nothing about the probable criterion score.

In the case of perfect validity, every predictor score has one and only one criterion score associated with it. By knowing the predictor score, you

FIGURE 8–1 Three Instances of Validity

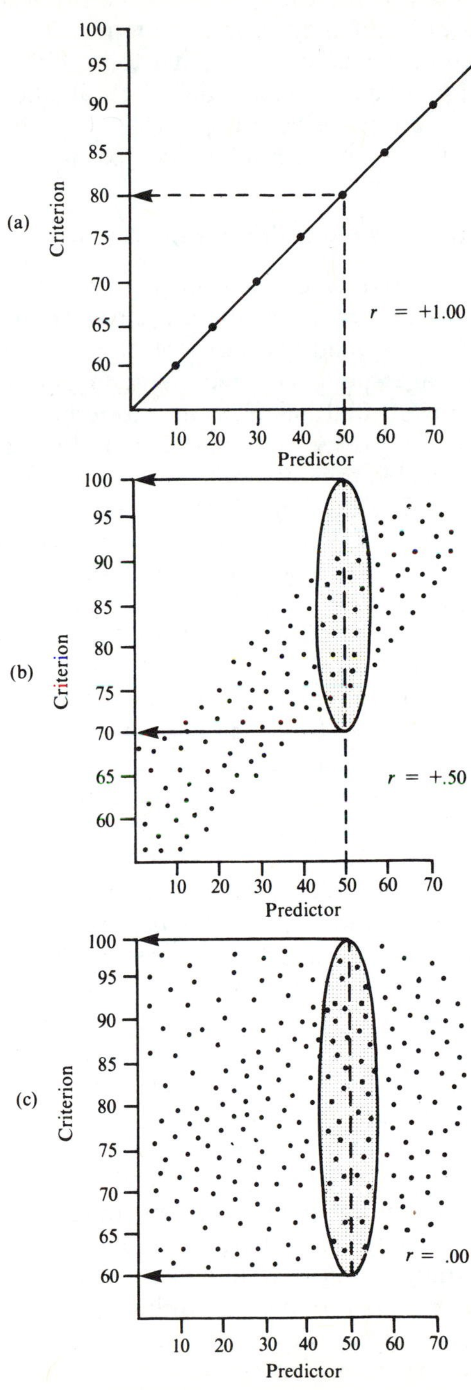

also know the criterion score. This is maximum efficiency. A validity coefficient of .00 represents no efficiency at all. Such a predictor would not make selection any more efficient than hiring randomly. The same performance score would be predicted regardless of what the predictor score was. From this simple illustration, you can see that the practical efficiency of a test varies as a function of the validity coefficient. The exact form of this relationship is described in section 1 of the "Technical Appendix" at the end of this chapter.

Decision Accuracy versus Prediction Accuracy

The discussion of predictive efficiency suggests that we can assess the value of a predictor or selection system on the basis of a validity coefficient. There is no doubt that the validity coefficient plays an important role in this evaluation, but the real issue for a personnel manager is not the calculation of a correlation coefficient that has pleasing properties but rather hiring applicants who will make good employees. This is the "bottom line" of the selection process. Basically, the decision maker is interested in improving his "batting average" in hiring the "right" people and in rejecting the "wrong" people. He wants to minimize both *false positive* errors (i.e., hiring a person who turns out to be a failure) and *false negative* errors (rejecting someone who would have been a success). The situation is illustrated in Figure 8–2. Assume again a validity of .50 and a cutoff score of X_i on the predictor. Assume further that the success rate on the job is 50 percent—half of the *selected* workers succeed (i.e., obtain criterion scores greater than Y_c). Decisions to hire, *prior* to use of the test, then, have been half correct and half incorrect—that is, half true positives and half false positives. It is not possible to know the accuracy of the rejection decisions, since no criterion data are available for those not hired. However, given a validity coefficient of .50, and assuming X_i to be a median score so that we would accept the 50 percent of the applicants who score above X_i, we would expect 67 percent of those accepted to be successful (true positives), and 33 percent to be unsuccessful (false positives). In other words, the correct "accept" decisions would be increased from 50 percent to 67 percent (see Taylor-Russell tables, discussed later). It should be noted that the choice of a cutoff score is critical in determining the ratio of "hits" to "misses"; with the cutoff at X_b, there would be few false positives, but a large proportion of the rejections would be false negatives. With the cutoff at X_a, however, there would be no rejections (hence, no false negatives), and since no selection would occur, the ratio of true to false positives would remain as it was before the predictor was available.

Thus, there are three numbers that combine in various ways to determine the utility of a particular test or selection strategy. These numbers are the validity coefficient, the percentage of individuals who were successful at the job *before* the predictor was introduced, and the cutoff score that is set on the predictor. Variations in any of these three values will result in variations in the success of the selection program. Fortunately, it is not necessary to draw scatterplots and superimpose lines on those plots at various possible cutting

FIGURE 8–2 Scatterplot of Predictor and Criterion Scores

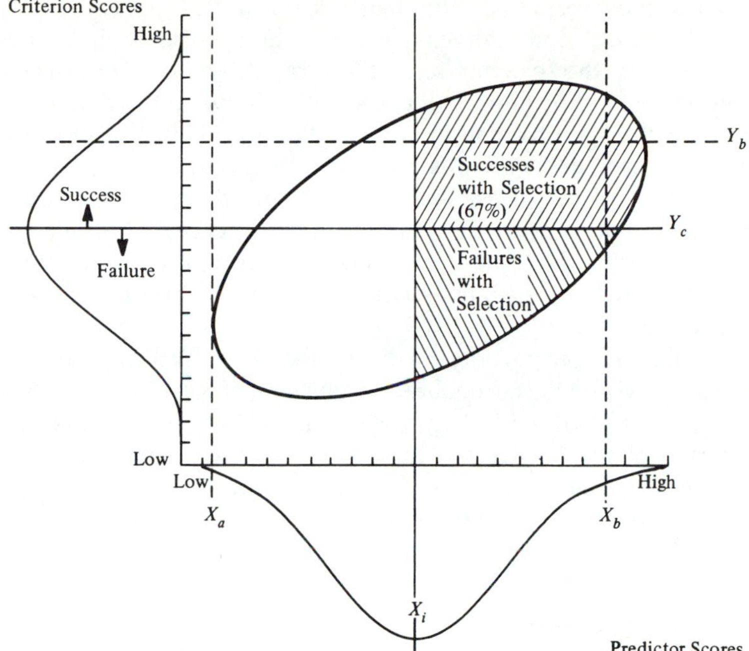

Without the use of the predictor, 50 percent of the employees are successful *($Y > Y_c$). With a cutoff score of X_i,* on the predictor scores 67 percent of those selected are successful. The success rate is nearly 100 percent with a very high cutoff score *(X_b).*

scores in order to determine the cutoff score that is associated with the highest utility. Instead, there are a series of tables and graphs that can be used. Not only do these tables and graphs give information about where to set a cutoff score, they also permit one to estimate the increase in productive efficiency (i.e., performance) associated with various cutoff scores. In other words, they permit one to estimate how much the average performance of the work group would increase if a particular test were used and a particular cutoff score set. A detailed description of these estimating procedures appears in section 2 of the "Technical Appendix."

Validity, Selection Ratio, and Success Rate

The above discussion pointed out that the *predictive validity of a test alone is not sufficient to determine its utility as a selection device.* Unless one can be selective and reject some portion of the applicants with low scores, the predictor score information cannot be used in decisions (there are *no* decisions in this case), and it is of no value. From Figure 8–2 it can be seen that, assuming a relatively fixed distribution of X scores in the applicant population, the setting of a cutoff score defines that proportion of the applicants that will be accepted, that is, the selection ratio. More typically, however, the selection ratio is determined by the supply of applicants relative to the demand created by job vacancies. This information is then used to set the cutoff score.

Figure 8–2 also serves to illustrate the interaction of selection ratio and success rate as it affects decision errors and the utility of selection. If, for example, only 20 percent of the employees were considered successful (Y scores $> Y_b$), then the decision errors would be quite different: false positives would increase and false negatives would decrease nearly to zero using the cutoff X_i in Figure 8–2.

To maximize the proportion of correct decisions (and minimize decision errors), a cutoff score should equate the number of false positives and false negatives. This is illustrated in Figure 8–3. Line $X—X'$ is a cutoff that results in equal errors of the two types. Line $W—W'$ would tend to reduce false positives (proportional to area A) but to produce a greater increase in false negatives (area B). Similarly, a cutoff at $Z—Z'$ increases false positive errors faster than it decreases false negatives.

Utility and Profitability

Once the payoff resulting from selection is translated into terms of increased proficiency, cost accounting procedures can be used to attach a dollar value to that gain. From that dollar value, one would subtract the cost of the testing to arrive at the final figure representing the net gain from testing.

Unfortunately, there are many jobs in which proficiency cannot be measured objectively, in terms of units produced or time expended. Nevertheless, it should be obvious that a valid selection decision is worth more to an organization than an invalid one. In 1979, Hunter and Schmidt tackled this problem. Instead of looking at the output of the individual in terms of productivity per se, they attempted to *estimate* the worth of the individual to the organization—to put a dollar value on performance, using expert judges.

In one study, they asked the supervisors of computer programmers in the federal government to estimate the value of those programmers in dollar terms. The instructions to the supervisors were as follows: "Consider the quantity and quality of output typical of the *average programmer* and the value of this output. In placing a dollar value on this output, it may help to consider what the cost would be of having an outside firm provide these products and services." The question that was used to obtain this information read as follows: "Based on my experience, I estimate the value to my agency of the average GS 9–11 programmer at ______ dollars per year. In addition, supervisors were also asked to estimate the dollar value of poor (15th percentile) and outstanding (85th percentile) programmers. This allowed the researchers

FIGURE 8–3 Cutoff and Decision Errors

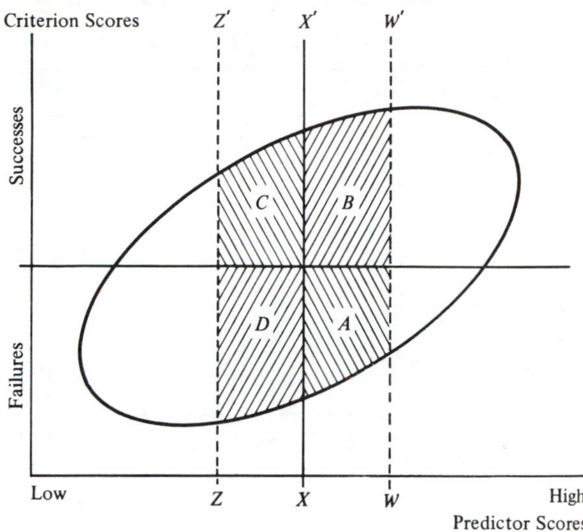

The cutoff, *X—X'*, equates false positive (lower right) and false negative (upper left) errors, resulting in a minimum of decision errors. Raising the cutoff to *W—W'* results in a decrease of false positives *(A)* but an even greater increase in false negatives *(B)*. Similarly, lowering the cutoff to *Z—Z'* yields a decrease in false negatives *(C)* but a larger increase in false positives *(D)*.

to calculate the distribution (and hence the standard deviation) of performance in dollars.

A total of 105 questionnaires was returned from supervisors. None had any difficulty in estimating the dollar value of computer programmers. In addition to this estimate, Hunter, Schmidt, and Pearlman had a number of additional pieces of information: (1) a test known as the Programmer Aptitude Test (PAT: McNamara & Hughes, 1961) had an estimated validity of .76 (this estimate was based on published studies); (2) the testing cost was approximately $10 per examinee; (3) there were approximately 4,400 programmers employed by the government at the levels in question; (4) there were approximately 618 new hires a year at these levels; and (5) the average tenure for computer programmers at these levels was 9.69 years.

On the basis of this information, the researchers were able to calculate the expected gain from using the PAT for hiring computer programmers in

TABLE 8–1 Estimated Productivity Increase from One Year's Use of the PAT to Select Computer Programmers in the Federal Government ($ millions)

	True Validity of Previous Procedure				
SR	*.00*	*.20*	*.30*	*.40*	*.50*
.05	97.2	71.7	58.9	46.1	33.3
.10	82.8	60.1	50.1	39.2	28.3
.20	66.0	48.6	40.0	31.3	22.6
.30	54.7	40.3	33.1	25.9	18.7
.40	45.6	3.4	27.6	21.6	15.6
.50	37.6	27.7	22.8	17.8	12.9
.60	30.4	22.4	18.4	14.4	10.4
.70	23.4	17.2	14.1	11.1	8.0
.80	16.5	12.2	10.0	7.8	5.6

SOURCE: From *Assessing the Impact of Intervention Programs on Workforce Productivity* by J.E. Hunter, F.L. Schmidt, and K. Pearlman, 1979, Washington, D.C.: Office of Personnel Management.

the federal government. While it might have been reasonable to assume that the previous method had *no* validity, Hunter and Schmidt estimated the gain on the basis of various previous validities ranging from .00 to .50. Remember, the PAT had an estimated true validity of .76. In addition to varying the validity level of the previous selection procedure, Schmidt also varied selection ratios from .05 (1 applicant out of every 20 is hired) to .80 (16 applicants out of every 20 are hired). The results are presented in Table 8–1. The numbers are staggering. The smallest dollar gain was $5.6 *million*. This gain was under the poorest conditions (i.e., a selection ratio [SR] of .80 and a previous procedure with high validity [.50]). Under the best conditions (SR = .05 validity of previous procedure = .00), the gain was $97.2 *million*. This would be a rather dramatic payoff for a testing procedure that cost approximately $6,000 per year. Since Hunter, Schmidt, and Pearlman had figures available for the number of programmers employed in the private sector, they were able to extrapolate these results to the U.S. economy as a whole. Their analyses showed that under the worst conditions (SR = .80, validity of previous procedure = .50), the estimated productivity increase as a result of using the PAT for hiring would be approximately $93 million. Under the best of conditions (SR = .05), validity of previous procedure = .00), the gain would be $1.5 *billion*. If a manager were ever tempted to doubt the potential monetary contribution of valid selection procedures to the effectiveness of an organization, these figures would promptly renew her faith.

Using these types of analyses, Hunter, Schmidt, and Hunter (1979) have estimated the "effectiveness gains" in other occupations. These results are summarized in Figure 8–4. Once again, these results help to make the notion of validity more concrete. The conclusion to be drawn from these results is

FIGURE 8–4 Estimates of Dollar Gain from Instituting New Selection Procedures

Study	*Job Title*	*Criterion*	*Dollar Gain*[a]
Lee & Booth (1974)	Clerical workers	Turnover	$250,000
Doppelt & Bennett (1953)	Checkout clerks	Training time	600/hire
	Adding machine operators	" "	540/hire
	Produce workers	" "	348/hire
Rusmore & Toorenaar (1956)	Telephone operators	Training costs	750,000
Schmidt & Hoffman (1973)	Nurses	Turnover	233,920
Roche (1961)	Radial drill operators	Productivity	350,000
van Naersson (1963)	Drivers	Reduction in accidents	No positive utility[b]
		Failure rate	88,000
		Training time	185,000
Hunter & Schmidt (1978)	Budget analyst	Productivity	28,000,000

[a]The time period for realizing these gains varies from one study to another.
[b]The selection procedure was estimated to cost more than would be gained in a reduction of accidents.

SOURCE: Adapted from "Fitting People to Jobs" (p. 257) by J.E. Hunter and F.L. Schmidt, in *Human Performance and Productivity* ed. E.A. Fleishman, 1982, Hillsdale, NJ: Erlbaum.

that *valid testing procedures contribute significantly to the cost effectiveness of organizations.* The level of this contribution will depend on: (1) the dollar value of the job being considered, (2) the validity of the previous selection procedure, (3) the selection ratio, (4) the cost of testing, and (5) the validity of the selection procedure being considered. With these types of analyses, it should be somewhat easier to determine the cost-benefit characteristics of a particular selection program.

Since Hunter, Schmidt, and Pearlman introduced the method for estimating the dollar value of performance, alternative estimators have been suggested. In 1984, Schmidt and Hunter proposed that instead of using the estimating procedure that they first introduced, it would be possible to simply take 40 percent of average salary. Similarly, Cascio and Ramos (1986) have suggested breaking the job down into unique elements through traditional job analysis, determining the value of these elements, estimating the performance level of incumbents on these elements, and deriving a final dollar value for the job. There is some disagreement about whether each of these techniques produces the same value. For example, Weekly et al. (1985) found that the original Hunter and Schmidt estimation procedure yielded values much higher than the 40 percent rule of the Cascio-Ramos technique. Clearly, the value of the standard deviation in dollar terms will have a substantial impact on the final utility of the test or intervention being considered.

In spite of the fact that utility analysis adds some "legitimacy" to the activities of industrial psychologists, there is very little that is psychological about the concept. There are dozens of articles appearing that describe refinements in calculating costs, or dollar values of performance. Unfortunately, there is little or no research to show how managers actually *use* utility information in making decisions about adopting a testing program. Although there is clearly a role for utility analysis in human resource system design, the psychological implications of utility data are not yet obvious.

USING MULTIPLE PREDICTOR INFORMATION

Thus far, we have dealt with a simple linear model of the relationship between a predictor and a criterion. In this case, given some predictive validity and some selectivity, the decision-making strategy is rather straightforward: accept applicants with the highest predictor scores and reject those with low scores. There are two common situations that destroy the simplicity of this model. The first is the availability of two or more relevant (valid) test scores or other predictors; the second is the choice between two or more jobs for the individual. The latter problem, differential placement, will be taken up later.

The availability of two or more pieces of information in personnel decision situations is surely the rule rather than the exception. Even though only a single standardized test is given, the decision maker is likely to have letters of reference, a high school transcript, biographical information, work history, and impressions or ratings from an interview.

The value of multiple sources of information depends on the predictive validities of the separate items and on the uniqueness or independence of the information obtained. If, for example, a standardized test score, high school transcript, and a letter of reference all tell us that an individual is superior in mathematical skills, we have one piece of information from three sources, not three pieces of information. Although the consistency of reports may increase our confidence that the information is reliable, it does not increase the amount of information. Similarly, having scores from two standardized tests of mathematical skills yields redundant information to the extent that performance on the two tests is highly correlated.

Strategies in the Use of Multiple Information

Faced with two or more items of information, the decision maker may explicitly adopt a strategy that relates decisions to the information. Probably the strategy he uses most frequently is not explicit and may vary unpredictably from time to time. Basically, such decision-making strategies are concerned with the way in which the data are combined or used sequentially. As you saw in Chapter 7, a fundamental distinction can be made between *statistical,* or mechanical, strategies and *clinical,* or intuitive, strategies. Statistical strategies are characterized by explicit formulas or rules that dictate decisions. Clinical strategies, on the other hand, require the decision maker to "weigh all the evidence" (usually qualitative impressions as well as quantitative biographical and psychometric data) and then choose among the alternative courses of action. It is possible, of course, to combine statistical and clinical methods. For example, data from several valid predictors might be combined statistically, yielding a predicted criterion score or a statement of expectancy of success, that the decision maker could then combine clinically with less readily quantifiable data, such as letters of reference or impressions gathered from an interview, but for the purposes of this chapter, let's consider the process of statistical combination.

Statistical Combination of Information

The decision is not simply whether to combine information clinically or statistically. If we decide on statistical combination, we still have another decision to make: What form of statistical combination will be used? There are several choices. The first, and most common, is the *compensatory* form. In this approach, the information is really averaged together so that a low test score in one area (e.g., mathematical skills) can be offset (or compensated for) by a high test score in another area (e.g., verbal skills). If a college looked only at total SAT scores, this would be an example of a compensatory combination of information.

The second form of combination involves setting specific cutoff scores for the different predictors. This is a noncompensatory system of prediction. To return to the SAT example, assume that the college was not interested in the overall score but instead set minimum acceptable scores as requirement for admission. The college might say that the minimum acceptable math score was 650, and the minimum verbal score was 665. By choosing certain minimums on both of those scores, the college could make sure that they accepted only a certain number of students who applied. In this instance, if your score on the math portion of the exam was 625, you would not be admitted regardless of your verbal score. Even a score of 775 on the verbal portion would not result in your admission.

The third form of statistical combination is really a compromise between the first two. In this joint cutoff-compensatory scheme, specific cutoffs are set on each of the predictors, but they are set considerably lower than in the straight cutoff scheme described above. All the applicants who score above the relevant cutoffs are then considered from a compensatory perspective in which exceptionally high scores on one or more predictors can improve the applicant's chances for selection.

FIGURE 8–5 Three Alternative Strategies for Sequential Decision Making

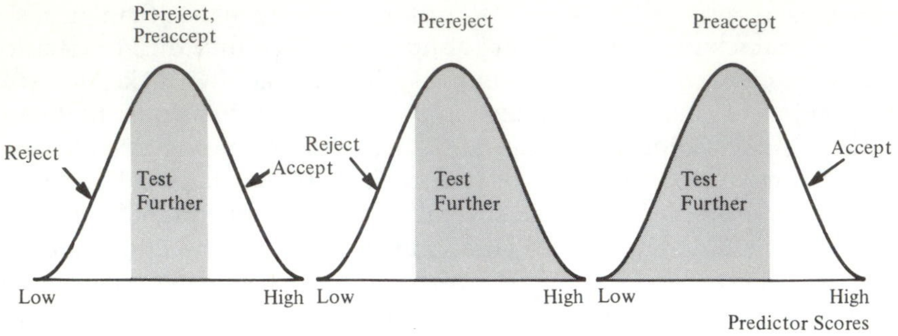

Multiple Hurdles and Sequential Decision Making

In the methods discussed thus far, it was implied that a more or less final decision was made on the basis of all the information available at one point in time. The applicant's folder is completed, including, in some cases, the results of an eight-hour battery of tests. Then a final decision is made. In simple selection, this decision is dichotomous; the applicant is hired for *the* job or she is rejected. In differential placement, job A is accepted for the new hire and jobs B and C are rejected for her. In practice, it is more likely that final decisions come only after a series of tentative decisions; in other words, information is received and evaluated sequentially over a period of time. Many management development programs employ successive hurdles in that evaluations are made first in accepting people into the program, then periodically after the completion of various phases of testing or training. Cronbach and Gleser (1965) identify three basic strategies of multiple hurdles or sequential selection. These are illustrated in Figure 8–5.

The most general case is illustrated on the left. Here, in contrast to the dichotomous decision of single-stage decision making, three outcomes are recognized. Candidates may be: (1) rejected, (2) accepted, or (3) held for further testing on the basis of the first item of information. This strategy assumes that terminal decisions can be made about some proportion of the applicants on the basis of one item of information. For example, finding that the applicant is a mathematical genius (or moron) may justify a final decision to hire (or reject) without seeking further information, especially when mathematical skills are essential to the job. On the other hand, the majority of "fair-to-good" mathematicians are held for further testing, which may include a period of training or observation on the job.

The two variations of sequential testing—prereject and preaccept—shown in Figure 8–5 indicate that only one type of final decision (accept or reject) is permitted on the basis of the first test score or item of information. For all others, the first-stage decision is to "test further," that is, to collect additional information.

The greatest disadvantage of multiple hurdles is the amount of time involved in arriving at final decisions. When "time is money," as when the individual is kept on in a management development program, one might wish for an earlier decision. On the other hand, testing costs, both to the institution and to the applicant (in time and convenience), are minimized when decisions are made on some proportion of the applicants after each test. The prospect of making final decisions about even a small percentage of the applicants after a single half hour of testing rather than requiring them to sit through an entire eight-hour battery is indeed an appealing one. As we saw in Chapter 6, to some extent, this is the goal of computerized adaptive testing.

Cross Validation

As you saw in earlier discussions, error is an inevitable part of prediction. Few things can be predicted with perfect accuracy. A corollary of this proposition is that as more predictors are added to the scheme, the errors of prediction increase proportionally. In practical terms, this means that there is a greater possibility of error when information is combined statistically. In order to understand this principle, it is necessary to introduce a few technical terms. *Simple correlation* is the relationship between one predictor and one criterion. If the compensatory model of combining information is used, the equivalent correlation coefficient is called the *multiple correlation coefficient*. Unlike the simple correlation, the multiple correlation (that has the symbol R as opposed to the symbol r associated with simple correlation) varies from $+1.00$ to $.00$, because it is calculated as a square root of R^2 rather than directly. Nevertheless, the value of R is interpreted the same as the simple correlation.

The problem is that when the individual validities from each of the predictors are combined, the errors associated with each of them become part of the prediction system. The effect of these errors is to make the resulting hiring equation less generally useful. Even though it might be effective in describing the relationship between the predictors and criterion in the particular sample on which it was developed, it may be less effective in predicting success for other individuals who are not part of that sample. As you saw in Chapter 2, this is sampling error. It means that the sample that we have drawn has certain idiosyncrasies that limit the generality of any relationships discovered. The greater the amount of error, the greater the limits on general application. It is the combination of individual predictor information in the compensatory model that increases the extent of this sampling error.

A multiple correlation coefficient describes the relationship between several predictors and the criterion for that specific sample of observations. Multiple correlation is a broad description of the extent of the relationship between a set of predictors and a criterion variable. It does not tell you how much to depend on one predictor rather than another. Nevertheless, to the extent to which individual predictors vary in validity, they must be given greater or less weight or emphasis in the final hiring decision. The actual equation or scheme that is used to weight or emphasize these various predictors is called a *regression equation.* (A technical description of multiple correlation and regression appears in section 3 of the "technical appendix" at the end of this chapter.) The validity coefficient for each of the predictors and the intercorrelations between predictors that are used in calculating R and in determining the statistical weight or emphasis assigned to each predictor in the regression equation are subject to sampling error. In other words, another sample taken from the same population of workers would, in all likelihood, yield somewhat different correlation coefficients and a different regression equation.

For this reason, the extent of this error must be considered in evaluating any decision system based on multiple information such as a compensatory or multiple regression system. This can be accomplished in two ways. One obvious way would be to select a second sample, apply the decision rule from the first sample, and see how accurate the predictions were with respect to job performance. This is known as *cross-validation.* If the multiple correlation drops substantially in the second sample, it means that there was a good deal of sampling error in the original decision scheme of equation. This drop in multiple correlation is often referred to as "shrinkage." Traditionally, the most common method for incorporating cross-validation into a validity study has been to hold out one-third to one-half of the available sample of subjects from the original validation. The multiple R and regression equation are obtained on the remainder of the sample and then cross-validated with the hold-out sample. Another procedure is to determine the regression equations on each of the two samples, then cross-validate each equation on the other sample. Naturally, the original and hold-out samples should be randomly assigned from the original study sample. K. R. Murphy (1983) has recently criticized this design and demonstrated that it is prone to distortion under certain circumstances. As a result, he suggests that the time and effort devoted to this type of cross-validation are not justified. Instead, he suggests another traditional method—the use of an estimating formula.

In addition to the method of collecting another sample of data in order to check for sampling error, there are formulas available for estimating the extent to which a multiple R might shrink owing to a capitalization on chance error in the original estimate. These equations deal predominantly with the issue of how *many* variables are being used as predictors and the effect of this number of sampling errors. Several equations for estimating shrinkage appear in the "Technical Appendix."

Although the foregoing discussion has used multiple R and multiple regression in illustrating cross-validation, it is equally important that any decision-making strategy established on one sample be checked for shrinkage. Nor should the empirical evaluation stop there. Validation should not be considered a one-time operation because jobs change and job applicants change. Therefore, predictor information and a selection strategy for using that information, both appropriate at one point in time, may lead to inappropriate decisions only a few years later.

There are three types of situations in which serious misuse of tests may occur: (1) where tests and a selection strategy have been adopted—perhaps with considerable care—but where no study has been conducted to establish empirically the validity of the procedures; (2) where a testing program and decision strategy were validated 10 or 20 years earlier and the procedures are continued as though the world never changed; and (3) where a serious misuse of tests occurs involving the assumption that cutoff scores or other decision strategies appropriate to a majority group or to a homogeneous sample are therefore equally appropriate to minority groups or identifiable subsamples.

SELECTION, PLACEMENT, AND CLASSIFICATION

To this point, I have been discussing the use of single and multiple predictors as if the information they provided would be used for making only one kind of decision—a selection decision. A typical selection situation involves many people applying for a single position. One applicant will be chosen and the rest rejected. There are other possible uses for the information, however. Instead of one job, there may be several different types of jobs to be filled. There might be an opening for an electrician, a welder, a motor pool mechanic, and a loading dock supervisor. Instead of advertising and testing separately for each of these positions, we might want to take advantage of the fact that we will be evaluating a large number of applicants and see if we can match applicants to jobs. In this case, we might administer a broad battery of tests that covers abilities needed in *all* the jobs in question. On the basis of the test scores, we might then consider each individual in terms of the job or jobs for which each person is best suited. This is a problem in classification rather than selection (Cascio, 1982). Figure 8–6 illustrates the classification situation and the various strategies that might be used to deal with it.

Still another situation might be deciding which applicants can be put on a particular job without any training, which ones will be suitable after successfully completing a training program, and which ones should simply be rejected. This is known as a *placement problem.*

Strategies for Classification

Implicit in the foregoing discussion is a strategy for placement—namely, use the predictor information to place each person so that the sum of the criterion scores (or the sum of the gains in utility) will be maximized. From the viewpoint of institutional goals, such a strategy would seem ideal. The picture presented by this model may be oversimplified, however. People vary along many dimensions, and while a composite score can always be obtained

FIGURE 8–6 Predicted Criterion Scores (in Zscore units) for Three Applicants to Each of Three Job and Assignments Made under Three Alternative Classification Strategies

	Job 1	*Job 2*	*Job 3*	*Number of Jobs Adequately Filled*	*Number of Workers Placed According to Their Highest Talent*
Worker A	1.0	0.8	1.5		
Worker B	0.7	0.5	−0.2		
Worker C	−0.4	−0.3	−1.6		
Minimum qualification score (in Zscore units)	0.9	0.0	−2.0		
Classification strategies:					
Place each according to his best talent (vocational guidance)	B	C	A	1	1
Fill each job with the most qualified person (pure selection)	A	A	A	1	1
Place workers so that all jobs are filled by those with adequate talent (cut and fit)	A	B	C	3	0

SOURCE: From *Applied Psychology in Personnel Management* (2nd ed.) by Wayne Cascio, 1982. Reprinted with permission of Reston Publishing Company, A Prentice-Hall Company, 11480 Sunset Hills Road, Reston, VA 22090.

from a multiple regression equation, it may be that the pattern or profile of attributes is both more analytic and more predictive for placement purposes than any composite score. Such a view was expressed by Guion (1965) when he stated that placement is more concerned with *intra*personal than with *inter*personal differences, reflecting the strengths and weaknesses of the individual *relative to his own average* or norm. The questions then become, (1) On what jobs will the individual's strengths be put to best use? and (2) On what job will this individual make his best contribution to the employing organization and to himself? (p. 11) The last sentence reflects a concern for the individual as well as the organization needs.

Placing Each Person in Accordance with His or Her Highest Potential. This strategy would look only at the intrapersonal differences. The individual's standard scores on several measures would be compared, and he would be placed on the job for which his highest aptitude score had the greatest predictive validity. This strategy is closely related to that described for component validity. Its greatest limitation is evident in that while an individual's highest aptitude might be at the 50th percentile, the job might require someone in the upper 25 percent of the population on this attribute. At the same time, the individual's second-highest aptitude might be at the 30th percentile, which might be an adequate level for the job with which that aptitude is associated. Assignment according to highest potential would leave the job inadequately filled, but *assignment to ensure that the greatest number of jobs were adequately filled* would place the person on the job for which his aptitude score was at a somewhat lower rank. Equally dubious would be a situation where an individual's highest aptitude is at the 90th percentile, but the only job requiring this aptitude is so easy that a person at the 20th percentile can handle the job. Assignment by highest potential would place the individual in a job for which she was tremendously overqualified, probably resulting in low satisfaction and short job tenure. Thus, either a strategy based on adequately filling the greatest number of jobs or one based on placing people according to their highest ability can lead to glaring mismatches of people and jobs.

None of these strategies considers the possibility that different priorities may exist in filling jobs. It may be much more important to fill a job where a crippling shortage of workers exists than one where present employees can handle the work if given a few hours overtime. Assuming that such priorities exist and the vacancies can be rank-ordered according to the urgency for filling them, then a strategy can be used that compares each new hire with the requirements of each job in order of urgency and *places him on the job with the highest priority for which he can qualify.*

Placing Each Person in Accordance with Needs and Abilities. Schoenfeldt (1974) has suggested a placement scheme that he has labeled the *assessment-classification model.* In his approach, he first identifies job families or clusters of jobs with similar activities or ability requirements. Next, he subgroups individuals in terms of motivational makeup as derived from past experience or biodata questions. Finally, he matches subgroups of individuals with job families for which their probability of success and satisfaction is greatest. This is a rather sophisticated vocational-guidance approach to placement, one that steps outside of the traditional ability approach to placement. In addition, the suggestion that individuals might be suited for a wide range of jobs with similar characteristics rather than a specific set of job titles provides the employer with considerably greater latitude for the best possible placement. Figure 8–7 presents a schematic representation of Schoenfeldt's approach.

Morrison (1977b) tested Schoenfeldt's assessment-classification model with a sample of blue-collar workers in a Canadian manufacturing organization. He was able to identify two homogeneous clusters of jobs or job families. One family consisted of process operators—those involved with the

FIGURE 8–7 A Modified Version of Schoenfeldt's Model

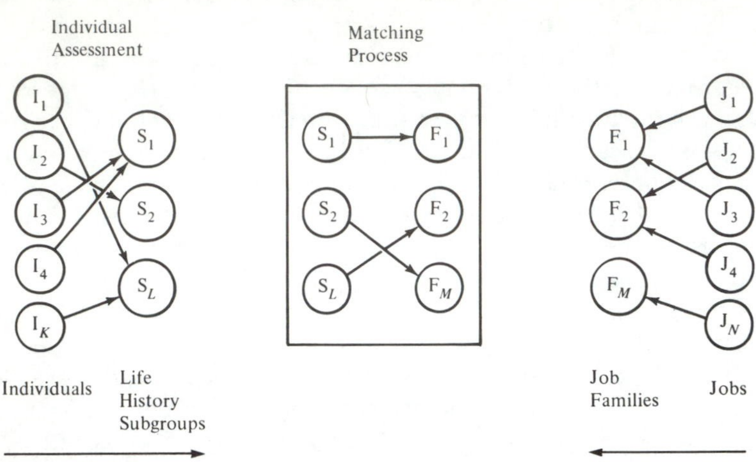

SOURCE: Adapted from "Assessment Classification Model to Match Individuals and Jobs" by L. F. Schoenfeldt, 1974, *Journal of Applied Psychology, 59,* p. 584. Copyright © 1974 by the American Psychological Association. Reprinted by permission of the author.

monitoring of ongoing operations such as the extraction of sulfur from substances. A second job family consisted of heavy-equipment operators, such as employees who operated power shovels or cranes. Morrison was able to demonstrate that three characteristics separated the process operators from the heavy-equipment operators. Successful process operators were more likely to have a more favorable self-image, to have been raised in an urban environment, and to prefer standardized work schedules. Since these data were gathered six months after the subjects joined the organization, and since it had been established that dissatisfied and unsuccessful employees left the organization prior to this six-month point, it was assumed that those remaining were reasonably capable and satisfied. While neither Schoenfeldt nor Morrison would claim that life experiences are sufficient for the accurate prediction of industrial success, they have demonstrated that life experiences and employee interests might also play a role in differential placement.

Placement in Sequential Jobs. *Sequential jobs* can refer to an assembly team or successive machine operations where each worker's operation depends on the completion of one or more prior operations. *Successive jobs* can also refer to a hierarchy of jobs based upon different levels of the same aptitude or skill. In the latter case, where the placement question may be "At what labor grade or wage level do we start this individual?" the absolute level of the predictor validity is important. The same aptitude is presumed to be relevant for each job; therefore, the higher the validity, the more accurately the employees can be classified. A prime example of this type of placement is in the allocation of ability-graded training classes to students or employees. In this situation, a highly valid measure more accurately measures the aptitude, achievement levels, or both for which the various training programs are designed.

When jobs are sequential in the sense that they represent successive and dependent operations, then the placement strategy may well be to attempt to select people for one line who constitute a homogeneous group with respect to output rate. In such situations, it may be reasonable to have "slow, medium, and fast" teams rather than three teams, or lines, forced to operate at the rate of their slowest worker. Thus, as with hierarchically related jobs or with ability-graded training, the goal is to establish homogeneous work groups with respect to speed of production. Absolute level of validity would be important for choosing the work groups, whereas differential validities would be important for choosing the jobs within the groups for the individual employee.

Coordinate Jobs. When the relationship between jobs involves coordinate rather than sequential activities, the efficiency of the system may depend on something more than the technical competence of the individuals to perform the individual functions in the group. It may depend on skills of communication, of interpersonal relations, or simply of coordination, not important in independent or even sequential jobs. The concept here is one of a multiman-machine system where systems performance measures, rather than individual performance measures, are particularly relevant. Selection and placement must both be concerned with the relationships among people and between performances of related jobs. Unfortunately, we know relatively little about the selection and placement of people on teams, although there is some evidence (Van Zelst, 1952) that teams based on sociometric choices are more efficient and rewarding to the members.

Further Considerations

Should initial selection and placement be concerned primarily with an ideal match of the employee to the present job, or should the strategy be to select and place those applicants with the highest overall potential for growth and advancement within the organization? In filling a position of machinist, should the personnel office be looking for the best available machinist and one who is apt to remain a machinist throughout her career, or should one look for a potential foreman, plant manager, or vice president? In a relatively "tight" labor market, the question may be more academic than real; persons with supervisory or administrative skills and experience are not likely to be candidates for semiskilled or skilled jobs. That is, self-selection of applicants will restrict the extent to which an organization can "overhire" for a job. However, in a period of high unemployment, it may be possible to pursue such a strategy. Engineers may be available for drafting positions, master mechanics as machinists, and supervisors as assemblers. Two problems may arise for the organization that seeks to "take advantage" of the labor market to hire highly skilled people who are overqualified for the available jobs. First, these employees may be bored, discontented, and restless in their routine jobs. Second, when there is a change in labor market conditions, the organization may have a higher turnover rate as these overqualified employees leave for more appropriate jobs. This is likely to occur unless the present organization is in a position to promote them to more responsible positions.

Another economic situation that tempts an organization to overhire is one in which the government issues defense contracts on a "cost-plus" basis. In such a situation, as during the post–World War II cold war period, hundreds of experimental and applied experimental (engineering) psychologists were hired into defense industries to "human-engineer" new military equipment. Actually, a large percentage of these research-oriented Ph.D. psychologists spent their time thumbing through handbooks or engaging in other relatively low-level tasks. The turnover was astounding as these people moved from company to company and out of industry into academia where they could use their research skills. Whether industry today is more aware of the possible drawbacks of overhiring is not clear. It is reported, however, that many students feel that the Ph.D. degree is a handicap in some hiring situations, and it is better to "forget to mention" that achievement.

Obviously, the questions discussed above are related to the organization's policy with respect to "promotion within" versus "hiring from without." If one adheres to a strong promotion-from-within policy, then it is imperative that one select for potential as well as immediate placement. If, on the other hand, the organization espouses a policy of hiring from without for all (or nearly all) management or technical-professional positions, then selection and placement should focus on finding the person to fit *the* job and—what is more—to seek those persons who will likely be content to remain at the job level at which they are hired and not be especially motivated by advancement or promotion opportunities. The issue is obviously not an either-or case; it is a complex one for which we do not have any clear answers or even adequate models.

DECISIONS VERSUS DECISION MAKERS

In describing the way in which information might be combined and utilized in making hiring or placement decisions, we have glossed over a rather substantial assumption—decision makers use information in a rational and accurate manner. Herbert Simon was awarded the Nobel prize in economics for his demonstrations that man's rationality is limited (Simon, 1960). The implications for personnel hiring and placement decisions are that employers (and maybe even psychologists) may use accurate information in an inaccurate manner. The most common example of this type of information misuse is the employment interview, which we examined in some detail in Chapter 7. More generally, several studies have demonstrated the misuse of information in other activities of the personnel decision process. In a study by Roose and Doherty (1976), judges were asked to assume the role of managers with the task of hiring life insurance sales personnel. They were given a test score but were instructed to use it only on a pass-fail or dichotomous basis; that is, if the individual applicant had achieved a passing score, the judges were instructed to ignore how much higher the particular score was than the cutting or passing score. The judges were unable to treat the data dichotomously when it was presented in continuous raw-score form. The researchers suggested that if the data were to be treated dichotomously by the judges, it should be presented to them dichotomously.

In a second study in which the employment process was simulated (Schaffer, Mays, & Ethridge, 1976), the effect of the Buckley amendment on employment decisions was examined. The Buckley amendment guaranteed to students the right to examine their permanent files if they requested such access. This amendment has led to two types of permanent files—open files and confidential files. Open files, as the name suggests, are open to the individual student's inspection. Presumably, for college students this would include the potential inspection of letters of recommendation. On the other hand, students may choose a closed or "confidential-file" option in which they give up the right to examine their file and accompanying letters of recommendation. The data indicated that judges acting as prospective employers were more favorable toward confidential-file applicants than they were toward open-file applicants when they made the simulated employment decisions.

As a final example, Peters and Terborg (1975) asked undergraduate students to assume the role of prospective employers and consider the qualifications of fictitious candidates for positions. The results showed that both the order in which information was presented as well as the similarities in attitudes between the prospective employer and the applicant affected the hiring decision. In addition, it was found that if an applicant with attitudes dissimilar to those of the employer was hired, the suggested starting salary was lower than that suggested for applicants with attitudes similar to those of the employer. In spite of some attempts to eliminate this attitudinal effect in subsequent studies, it remained an important influence on the hiring decision.

All these studies were simulations. They did not evaluate the behaviors of "real" employers making "actual" decisions about "real" applicants. As such, they are open to criticism. Nevertheless, they do raise disturbing possibilities. For example, a withdrawn-pass (WP) grade may mean one thing to a student and quite another to a prospective employer or medical school admissions board. A regular high school diploma and a General Education Development (GED) certificate may be functionally equivalent but may be treated very differently by employment offices. More studies of the decision processes of employers must be carried out in the field. No matter how elaborate and refined our knowledge of test theory and validity of tests, this information is relatively useless unless we know *how* predictor information is used by decision makers.

LEGAL AND PHILOSOPHICAL EVALUATIONS OF TESTING PROGRAMS

The Equal Employment Opportunity Commission

Title VII of the 1964 Civil Rights Act prohibited discrimination in employment on the basis of race, color, religion, sex, or national origin. The agency charged with administering that law was the EEOC. Over the years, this agency has probably had a greater impact on personnel decision making than any other source. The "rules" for fair employment practices have been published several times and have changed with each publication. These changes have been a result of both increases in knowledge concerning testing and validation and pressure from professional and business communities to implement more workable procedures. There have been significant disagreements even within the government concerning the interpretation and administration of the Civil Rights Act with regard to employment decisions. This disagreement resulted in the publication of two separate sets of rules in 1977. One set, published by EEOC, was very demanding of employers, requiring considerable attention to validation of tests in separate settings, or for each job title; these were considered the "hard-nosed rules." The second set, jointly published by the U.S. Civil Service Commission, the Department of Labor, and the Department of Justice was entitled the Federal Executive Agency (FEA) Guidelines and were more liberal in interpretation, leaving certain decisions to the discretion of the employer and asking for good-faith effort at fair employment rather than strict adherence to specific prescriptions; these were the "soft-nosed rules." The battle of the rules was awaited with apprehension by psychologist and employer alike. Fortunately for all concerned, the two different groups were able to reach a compromise and in August 1978 jointly published a set of principles known as the "Uniform Guidelines on Employee Selection Procedures" (1978). It has been over 10 years since those rules were published, and they have become obsolete. As a result, many judges are paying less attention to those guidelines than to other more recent documents such as the APA test standards (1985) and the Principles for test validation published by Division 14 of the APA in 1987. There is considerable pressure to rewrite the "Uniform Guidelines" to bring them into line with current professional practice. In all likelihood, a new set will be issued within the next two years.

Adverse Impact. The major mechanism for determining fairness in employment procedures is the consideration of *adverse impact*. In the simplest terms, adverse impact is a measure of the degree to which a particular procedure has a negative effect on the members of a protected minority group. Adverse impact is operationally defined by the "⅘ths" or "80-percent" rule. This rule states that the proportion of minority applicants hired should be no less than ⅘ths or 80 percent of the proportion of majority applicants hired. Thus, if 100 white males apply for employment and 10 are hired, and 100 black males apply for employment at the same company and 6 are hired, the hiring procedure would have had an adverse impact on a racial group, the blacks. Dividing 10 percent into 6 percent, we get a figure of 60 percent; thus, the proportion of black applicants hired was less than 80 percent of the proportion of white applicants hired, a violation of the ⅘ths or 80-percent rule. If eight black applicants had been hired instead of six, there would have been no problem, since we would then divide 10 percent (the white proportion) into 8 percent (the black proportion) and get a result of 80 percent, exactly what the law requires.

The determination of adverse impact is a critical step in examining the degree to which an employer is using legal selection procedures. As far as the federal government is concerned, if there is no adverse impact, the selection procedures are considered nondiscriminatory. This is not necessarily the definition of "fair" as accepted by other interested parties, such as psychologists and applicants. Guion's definition of test fairness is conceptually sounder: "Individuals with equal probabilities of success have equal probabilities of being hired" (Guion, 1966). Similarly, applicants might accept as a fair selection procedure one that selects individuals who worked hard to acquire the skills and experience necessary for successful performance on the job in question. Thus, while the federal government might accept a random lottery among all applicants as fair, neither Guion nor the applicants would. Nevertheless, as it now stands, adverse impact is the primary principle defining the fairness of selection procedures in the "Uniform Guidelines."

The demonstration of adverse impact is the responsibility of the plaintiffs, those claiming that they have been unfairly treated. While the employer must provide appropriate records, it is the responsibility of the complaining applicant to demonstrate unfairness. The 80-percent rule has the effect of ensuring that plaintiffs can only argue as a member of a *class* of individuals rather than as a single individual. Regardless of how a decision might have been made in a single case, it is necessary to show a pattern of such decisions before adverse impact is upheld.

If adverse impact is demonstrated, it is then the employer's responsibility to demonstrate a "business necessity" that requires the use of the particular selection strategy responsible for the adverse impact. In operational terms, the employer must demonstrate the *validity* of the selection procedure. Even if the employer is able to demonstrate the validity of the procedure, she may be required to demonstrate that there are no equally valid procedures that would result in less adverse impact. The requirement to demonstrate business necessity and to minimize the adverse impact of otherwise valid procedures has led some employers to address the legality of their selection procedures at the most basic level. They strive to hire in particular proportions regardless of the validity of the procedure. Their logic is that if the 80-percent rule is not violated, they will not have to go through the effort and expense of validation procedures, court fights, and potential damage payments. Rather than being fair to all groups, this logic seems more like being uniformly *unfair* to all concerned. At the very least, these employers are abandoning the opportunity to use selection procedures as a means of enhancing organizational effectiveness and profitability, as described earlier in the section on utility.

Affirmative Action. There is considerable confusion surrounding the issue of affirmative action. The terms *equal employment opportunity and affirmative action* often appear together in recruiting literature and are often uttered virtually simultaneously by personnel managers and recruiters. Nevertheless, the terms have quite different meanings and mechanisms. Equal employment opportunity is a law. If an employer violates that law, she is subject to penalties as imposed by the judicial branch of government. The law states that today, here and now, members of protected minority groups will have the same opportunity for employment as majority group members. Affirmative action is a social philosophy. The procedures related to it imply that an employer will go beyond the simple condition of equal employment on a day-to-day basis; instead, the employer will set goals for employment decisions over some period of time (e.g., five years) that will guarantee a certain profile of demographic characteristics of employees. The salient demographic characteristics are those pertaining to race, color, religion, sex, and national origin. In practice, the focus has been on blacks, Hispanics, and women. The effect of affirmative action programs is to accelerate what would normally come to pass through selection procedures that were equally fair to majority and minority applicants. In addition, affirmative action agreements require the employer actively to seek out or recruit minority applicants who might not otherwise apply for employment. But affirmative action is not a law. It is a voluntary agreement that employers enter into with local, state, and federal government agencies. These agencies can require affirmative action policies or plans through economic pressures. If an employer does not agree to construct an affirmative action policy setting specific targets for employment of minority group applicants, the governmental agency may withhold federal funds in the form of grants or contracts from that employer. In addition, the employer must also agree to purchase goods and services from organizations that have affirmative action plans. Thus, if your university refuses to file an affirmative action plan, they would most likely jeopardize any federal funds that they currently receive. In addition, faculty members at the university may become ineligible to receive federal research grants until their university complies with the affirmative action requirements of the federal department from which the funds are requested. A private employer might refuse to file an affirmative action plan and subsequently be denied access to Department of Defense contracts or Department of Labor training funds. This economic lever is a powerful one and for all practical purposes has an equal or greater impact than a legal lever. Nevertheless, affirmative action is not a law, and the fiercely independent employer can choose to ignore its implications—at the risk of financial disaster.

Other Pitfalls in the Employment Process

The employment decision process is actually a series of interrelated activities, and as we have seen, testing is only one part of the process. In addition to tests, other components in the system might be a recruiting mechanism, an employment receptionist, an application blank, and one or more interviewers. The American Psychological Association (1969) appointed a task force to consider the potential pitfalls in the entire employment process for members of minority groups. This task force identified the following potential sources of unfair discrimination in hiring:

1. *Recruiting.* An employer might restrict the number of applicants from minority groups by the pattern of contracts or visits to various schools or community organizations; recruiting might also be affected by the type of newspapers, magazines, or both in which vacancies are announced.
2. *Initial contact.* Receptionists might exercise some uncalled-for discretion in deciding to whom they shall give application forms. In effect, if an individual is refused an application form, a *reject* decision has been made not by the personnel director but by the receptionist.
3. *Application forms.* Many biographical items on application blanks have the potential for discriminating against minority applicants. Rejection decisions are often made on the basis of responses to biodata items, in spite of the fact that no relationship has been established between the answers and the probability of success on the job.
4. *Interviews.* Interviewers are prone to error in combining information and making decisions. These tendencies were well documented in Chapter 7. These errors are not always random; they are often systematic errors that have adverse effects on minority applicants.

The task force suggested the following remedies for the potential pitfalls of the employment process:

1. Develop a recruiting plan that includes all relevant segments of the local population, regardless of minority or majority status.
2. Inform receptionists daily of jobs available and of the responses that should be made to applicants. Do not allow screening by the receptionist—with the exception of clearly inappropriate applicants (e.g., drunks).
3. Train interviewers to be aware of systematic influences on their judgment

processes. Consider having one individual gather information and another combine it to make a decision.

4. Develop weighted application forms that ask only questions having demonstrated relevance for the job in question.

As you can see from the list of ills and cures, the employment process is a minefield for employer and applicant alike. The employer must be aware of potential obstacles to fair employment and take steps to guard against them. The employer's responsibility under the law for fair employment practices is a substantial one. If an organization has done little to develop accurate predictors of performance, it is unlikely that valid predictor-criterion relationships will be found.

Even when an employer has been validly selecting employees on the basis of a particular selection device, it would be difficult to demonstrate that relationship with present employees, since there would be a substantial restriction of range on the predictor variable. In other words, if only individuals with high test scores are hired, there will not be much variation in the predictor variable. The restriction in variability has a depressing effect on the validity coefficient. In one article (Landy, 1978a), I facetiously suggested that employers concentrate on hiring a small number of predicted failures (true negatives) to ensure that there is no restriction of range. It was further suggested that a side effect might be an increase in the self-esteem of the failures, since they have finally been able to succeed at something—failing. Unfortunately, the proposal is doomed to failure—*it is probably more difficult to predict failures than successes!*

It is unfortunate but true that most employers can no longer successfully plan, implement, and defend a valid selection procedure without the services of an industrial psychologist and a lawyer. This is not likely to change in the near future. As indicated earlier in the chapter, this may have the effect of making "quota hiring" more attractive to employers, a condition that would be unfair to applicant and employer alike.

Fair Employment Policies

Many organizations hint at affirmative action policies in their announcement of positions to be filled. For example, a company might state that they are an equal employment opportunity employer with a particular interest in women and minority applicants. Figure 8–8 illustrates a strong affirmative action statement in an announcement for an academic position. Such ads and recruiting practices are intended to increase women and minority workers, groups that may be underrepresented in the organization at that time. Many do not agree with this type of policy. They feel that it fosters reverse discrimination insofar as there are not an infinite number of jobs available. If a black or a woman has some special "edge," this must mean that white males are at a disadvantage. The debate here is really one of values and philosophies

FIGURE 8–8

DEPARTMENT OF PSYCHOLOGY: Is seeking an additional faculty member for a tenure track position to begin August 1984 at any professional level pending budgetary approval. All teaching and research areas will be considered. The department is also seeking an assistant director of the Psychological Clinic. Duties will include supervision of graduate students and some clinical service. Since both an off-campus and internal review of our program concluded that additional minority faculty and staff would significantly strengthen the department, special consideration will be given to minority applicants.

rather than personnel practices, so I won't deal with it directly. There is, however, a related issue that is of interest to the I/O psychologist. How do managers and employees feel and react when they must carry out staffing in a strong affirmative action environment? There are two separate but distinct issues. The first relates to the feelings of individuals hired through strong affirmative action programs. Occasionally, they feel like second-class citizens. Regardless of their talent, experience, or training, they may feel that they were hired because they are black or Hispanic or female. In Figure 8–9, Richard Cohen, a columnist for the *Washington Post,* describes the two sides of the coin in his description of a bias settlement that the *Post* entered into with female employees. In some respects and in some situations, equal opportunity and affirmative action are like apples and oranges; the two programs cannot be easily averaged to yield some level of social good. The fact is that when the two programs are reduced to particular individuals and particular personnel decisions, they may result in feelings of insecurity on the part of minority employees and inequity on the part of majority employees (and almost certainly on the part of rejected majority applicants).

A second related issue relates to how minority applicants are treated by those making personnel decisions under different types of fair employment policies. For example, are hiring decisions made differently when the organizational policy is a "strong" one such as the one illustrated in Figure 8–9? Is the manager more likely to hire a minority applicant? Rosen and Mericle (1979) conducted a study to see what the effects of stated fair employment policies might be on personnel decisions. The subjects were 67 male and 11 female municipal administrators. These subjects read a hypothetical job description, a statement of the hypothetical organization's fair employment policy, and a description of a hypothetical applicant. The two independent variables were the strength of the fair employment policy and the sex of the applicant. There are two different fair employment statements. One group of subjects received a strong statement that stated that the employer was "under considerable pressure to carry out its affirmative action goals and to hire more women and minorities." Another group of subjects received a

FIGURE 8–9 Some Side Effects of Affirmative Action

Muddy Thinking Behind Group Bias Settlements

A COLLEAGUE OF MINE has had a nagging doubt that she was hired here at The Washington Post not because she is a graduate of a really terrific college, not because she is she is a gifted writer and not even because she applied with examples of her work that knocked a few editors off their chairs. She thinks she was hired because she is a woman.

She has her reasons. She came to the paper at a time when it was trying to make amends for what is sometimes called past discrimination and she was told that being a woman helped her get her job. Now a whole generation of women can share her feelings. The Post, in settling a sex discrimination complaint, has agreed to hire whole bunches of women for no other reason than that they are women and maybe talented. Just which of the two is the more important will be left for the women themselves to figure out.

In addition, The Post has agreed to award $101,000 to women who worked at The Post during the years 1972 through 1974. It is these women, all 567 of them, who will share the money The Washington Post has bestowed on them in an agreement that skirts any admission of discrimination in either hiring or promotion.

I could point out, of course, that some of this is just plain silly. Among the women who can receive the maximum $250 are Katharine Graham, board chairman of The Post. Also sharing in this largesse is Meg Greenfield, who is editor of the Editorial Page and a columnist for both Newsweek and The Post, and Sally Quinn, a star reporter. As my aunt used to say when she gave me a gift, I hope they all spend it on something fun.

I could also point out, of course, that the money was awarded the women regardless of whether they actually suffered from discrimination or whether they complained of discrimination. In fact, some of the women who are eligible for the money say they had no complaints: They had neither been discriminated against nor thought discrimination even existed. To them, too, I offer my aunt's advice.

The truth is, of course, that whenever you make a group settlement you are going to have to give money to both the deserving and the undeserving. That's the way it goes. And the truth is also that there really was discrimination at The Washington Post. It was not an institutional thing, not policy, but it existed because the place was run mainly by male supervisors of a certain age. Some were better than others and some were really terrific, but a few were truly awful. No matter. None of their supervisors called them on the carpet for it.

And so some women suffered. There were some, probably, who left the paper because of discrimination and some who were never hired because of discrimination and some who were assigned differently because they were women and some who saw their careers stagnate because they were women. If anyone deserved the money, they do.

But that is not what is being done. Instead, the money is being awarded to a group—all women employed at The Post at a certain time. In addition, The Post is setting aside sabbaticals and scholarship programs just for women and has established certain employment targets. God and The Post willing, one third of the new employees on the foreign desk by 1985 will be women.

Some of this makes sense. A firm that has discriminated has a duty to show that it no longer does, and employment targets (not quotas) may be a way of doing that. A firm that has discriminated—that has, in effect, kept women out of journalism—has an obligation, maybe even to the nation, to make amends. In that sense, the scholarships may not be a bad idea.

But what is troublesome in the agreement is the notion that all women today are entitled to compensation because some women once suffered on account of their sex. It is the flip side of the same sort of thinking that holds an entire group—blacks, Jews, whatever—forever responsible for the actions of a few of their number.

The agreement condones this type of thinking. In agreeing to hiring standards and to agreeing in reserving certain sabbatical programs just for women, The Post and the women involved have agreed to consider certain people first as women and only secondarily as journalists. In other words, no need applying for a sabbatical reserved for women if you happen, by some bad luck, to be a man.

It is patronizing to treat women this way. It is insulting to reserve for them, solely on the basis of sex, programs or positions that they should be able to get on the basis of ability. I couldn't blame a woman if she wanted to wear a little tag saying that she got her job because she deserved it, not because The Post was making amends. After all, special consideration is a two-edged sword. The same man who gave up his seat on a bus for a woman, wouldn't hire her when he got off. He saw her only as a woman. In that sense, The Post, with the help of some women, is still a perfect gentleman.

Source: From "Muddy Thinking behind Group Bias Settlements" by R. Cohen, 1980, Washington Post.

weaker statement simply indicating that the organization was an equal opportunity employer. In addition, one group of subjects reviewed the credentials of a female applicant and the other group reviewed the application of a male. In fact, the only difference between the applicants was the first name (Charles or Charlotte).

Subjects were asked to make one of two decisions. First, they were to decide whether to offer a job to the applicant. If they did decide to make a job offer, they were then asked to determine a starting salary level. The results were interesting. Selection decisions were identical for male and female applicants. There was neither preference for nor resistance to female applicants in the strong policy condition. There were differences in the starting salary recommendations, however. Suggested salary levels for females chosen in the strong policy condition were significantly lower than the salary levels for females selected in the weak policy condition. Rosen and Mericle suggest that in the strong policy condition, decision makers were reacting against the pressure to hire women by starting them at a lower salary level. Somehow, these women were valued less because of their association with the affirmative action policy. In a way, this confirms the feelings of inadequacy that Cohen described in women at the *Washington Post*. This study was not a particularly strong one with respect to the real world. Decision makers were asked to consider hypothetical people for a hypothetical job and make decisions in a manner that was very different from the way in which they usually make decisions (i.e., they never saw or talked with the "person"). Nevertheless, there was some kind of effect on the decision that can be tied to the affirmative action statement. Furthermore, the effect seems to parallel the feelings expressed by many people in the real world. It would have been interesting to see if the effect was similar for the male and female decision makers, but results were not analyzed separately.

Evidence of Compliance

As I indicated earlier, many employers are required to adopt affirmative action programs in order to receive government contracts or subcontracts from other government contractors. The government examines the affirmative action efforts of an organization through several mechanisms. One mechanism is the quarterly report that employers must file. Another mechanism is the compliance review in which an individual called a *contract compliance officer* examines the efforts of the organization in some detail to determine if good-faith efforts are being made. Marino (1980) administered questionnaires to 50 federal compliance officers in an attempt to determine what they considered to be the critical characteristics of good-faith affirmative action effort. He found that there were several dimensions that compliance officers considered. Marino found that the characteristics of effective affirmative action programs (as seen through the eyes of compliance officers) included making attempts to seek community support (e.g., conducting plant tours), discussing equal employment matters in company newsletters and other employee publications, setting affirmative action goals for managers, instituting minority-oriented training programs, recruiting from predominantly minority colleges and high schools, and demonstrating top-level management support for affirmative action goals. All these strategies make sense and will very likely improve the climate for minority employees as well as increase their representation in the work force.

Truth in Testing

Recently, the testing industry has received a good deal of attention in both the educational and the industrial sector. This attention has come in the form of "truth-in-testing" discussions. The goal of this legislation is to guarantee the rights of test takers to question particular items or answers. The mechanism used to accomplish this goal is a requirement to provide test takers with answer keys following the test administration. The best known case of such legislation is the New York State legislation known as the La Valle bill (named after the New York State senator who introduced the legislation). This bill affects the "aptitude" portions of tests used by admissions officers in making decisions regarding applicants to college, professional schools, and graduate schools. The bill requires that reports related to the development and validity of the examination be filed in the office of the State Commissioner of Education. Prior to administering the test, the person taking the test must be told what the test measures and how the results will be used, how the test scores relate to later performance (i.e., validity), how the test scores are related to family income, and a description of the policy that the testing organization follows with respect to confidentiality of test scores. After the test has been administered, the testing organization must file (in the Commissioner of Education's office) a copy of all items used on the test and the correct answers to those questions as well as a description of how raw scores were transposed to standard scores. The person who took the test may also request a copy of the test items and the correct answers. The test taker must pay a fee for this information to cover the administrative costs of dissemination (Lefkowitz, 1980).

There have been a number of eloquent arguments both for and against bills such as this. Those who argue for such legislation contend that the testing industry has acted irresponsibly and, in effect, has been a party to inappropriate decisions (e.g., rejections from college admissions offices) based on flawed information. In its simplest form, the argument is that some test items do not tap what they are purported to, other test items may have several correct answers, and still other items may have *no* correct items. It is assumed that by allowing the test taker to examine the test and the correct answers, it is less likely that flawed items will be allowed to influence decisions.

Those arguing against such bills suggest that the attack on testing is based on more fundamental objections by the opponents (Lerner, 1980a, 1980b). The inferred objections are: (a) standardized tests don't measure everything that is important; (b) standardized tests are not 100 percent accurate and become less accurate as they are used to predict events occurring a long time after the tests are taken; and (c) standardized tests are biased against minorities and poor people (Lerner, 1980a). There seems to be no disagreement about the first two points. In an earlier chapter, I pointed out that there are many things that standardized ability tests do *not* measure. Similarly, the fact that validity coefficients are usually in the low (+.20) to modest (+.40) range suggests that there is a good deal of unexplained variance in criterion behaviors. Logically, few would argue that a test score produced today will be as useful in predicting behaviors 20 years from now as it would be in predicting behavior tomorrow. With respect to the third charge—that tests unfairly discriminate against the poor and members of minority groups—the opponents of truth-in-testing legislation answer that the tests only serve to highlight the abilities considered important in our society. As such, the standardized tests are no more (and no less) guilty than curricula developed in school systems, tests developed by teachers for assigning grades, and job duties as assigned by employers. They contend that our culture places a high emphasis on reading, writing, and arithmetic and that this emphasis is not likely to disappear in the next few decades. They suggest that the argument is really with current values in society rather than with standardized tests per se.

There are many issues involved in the debate. The test publishers contend that test questions and answers must be kept secret so that the test can be used again. The truth-in-testing response is that this is nonsense; most standardized tests are used only a few times, and as a matter of course, test publishers develop many more items than are used in any given examination. The test publishers argue that it will be extremely expensive to satisfy the requirements of legislation such as the La Valle bill. Those in favor of such legislation contend that this is an exaggerated claim, that on the average the cost would increase about 75 cents per student per test. Lefkowitz (1980) presents and rebuts most of the arguments against truth-in-testing legislation. Nevertheless, the most important issue remains in dispute: Does our society value (or overvalue) the wrong characteristics of its members? As we saw in our earlier reading, some careful studies (e.g., Garner & Wigdor, 1982) have concluded that ability testing can predict various aspects of educational and industrial success and that there is no substantial evidence that, on the whole, standardized ability tests unfairly discriminate against members of minority groups.

Neither the report of the National Academy of Sciences (Garner & Wigdor, 1982) nor the truth-in-testing debate is likely to solve the problem of cultural values. From a purely pragmatic perspective, the question is much simpler: What shall we use instead of standardized tests? As Lerner (1980a) states in her answer to the charge that tests are not perfect:

> So what? The choice before us is not between assessment methods available in utopia and those available in reality. The choice is among methods available in

> reality, and comparative studies show that valid tests measure a number of extremely important abilities more quickly and more accurately than anything else does. That is why predictions made with them are almost always better than predictions made without them, and that is as true for predictions about black students and workers as it is for predictions for white and Oriental ones. (pp. 132–133)

In short, no one claims that tests are perfect, only that they are better (i.e., more valid, more feasible, or both) than most alternatives that have been suggested.

AN EXAMPLE OF TEST CONSTRUCTION AND DECISION MAKING

In the last several chapters, we have examined most of the pieces of a modern selection system. We have considered job analysis, test construction, the testing process, criterion measurement, the reliability of behavioral measures, test validation, and personnel decision making. By necessity, we have dealt with each of these issues separately. This may have produced a familiarity with each of the trees in the personnel psychology forest, but you may still have little or no feel for the entire forest. A good way to provide an overview of the entire selection process is with an example that illustrates how these pieces go together to form a coherent program of test development, validation, and decision making. I will use as an example a recent project that my colleagues (Rick Jacobs, Dave Kriska) and I completed for the Columbus, Ohio, fire department.

As is the case with any large company, fire fighters quit, are fired, retire, and die. This means that in any given year there are jobs to be filled. There is a continual need for trained fire fighters to take the place of those who leave the department. This need is met by appointing individuals to the fire academy in preparation for assuming the responsibilities of a fire fighter. The appointment to the fire academy involves several different hurdles. First, the applicant must take a written and physical ability examination to demonstrate that he or she has the ability necessary both to complete academy training and to meet the demands of the job after the training is over. In addition, the applicant cannot have a criminal record (i.e., felony conviction), should receive good recommendations (from letters of reference), must pass a medical examination (including a drug test), and be free from problems of psychological adjustment.

The first step in this process is a paper-and-pencil examination that is intended to measure various mental abilities. Only a certain portion of those who take this test will move to the next stages of selection (e.g., physical abilities examination, background check, medical exam, psychiatric exam). Thus, for most applicants, the ability test is the first major hurdle to overcome. It is common for black and Hispanic applicants to do more poorly on this type of examination than white applicants. As an example, the average score for black males might be 71 percent and for white males, 82 percent. As a result, this type of test commonly has adverse impact since it can be demonstrated that a larger percentage of whites (as defined by the 80-percent or ⅘ths rule) pass the exam than blacks. The extent of this impact will depend on where the pass mark is set. If it is set very high, the impact will be greater; if it is set low, the impact will be much less. Herein lies the problem. A score must be set that at the same time selects those candidates most likely to succeed in the academy and on the street without creating a force of fire fighters composed exclusively of white incumbents. Similarly, women applicants invariably do more poorly on the physical abilities test than men, resulting in adverse impact. As you might expect, the fire fighter exam has been the focus of various court cases related to fair employment practices. Minority candidates usually initiate lawsuits related to the written examination, and female candidates initiate suits related to the physical ability tests. Since adverse impact is common, it is the employers' responsibility to demonstrate validity. I was asked to develop an examination to be administered to academy applicants.

The first step was to conduct a job analysis. The first step was camping out in firehouses for 24-hour shifts. I would sleep and eat with the fire fighters, go on calls with them, and generally observe them as they did their work. It was necessary to spend 24-hour shifts because in most fire departments "fires" such as we think of them occur infrequently. Fire fighters go to many false alarms, dumpster fires, and automobile fires. They may only have one "real" fire in a month. A fire fighter friend of mine gave me an interesting perspective on the issue number of fires fought. He told me that after a long dry period with no fires, when a real fire comes along, the fire fighters tend to attack that fire with unusual aggressiveness just because they have not had much opportunity to do so in the previous several weeks. For example, instead of just letting a roof burn through, they will get on the roof with axes and saws and chop a hole for ventilation. Inactivity can have strange effects on people.

In addition to observation and discussion of duties and responsibilities with fire fighters and their supervisors, a list of 200 different tasks was distributed to 150 fire fighters and several dozen fire fighter supervisors chosen to represent different firehouses, shifts, duty assignments, and levels of experience. The raters were asked to make judgments on the relative importance and frequency of each of the tasks in the job of fire fighter. A portion of that checklist is reproduced in Figure 8–10.

The next step was to take the 200 items of the job analysis and group them into homogeneous sets of job activities. This grouping was relatively easy to do. An earlier job analysis of the fire fighter's position had suggested that there were 16 basic tasks performed. These tasks and brief descriptions of them appear in Table 8–2. These, then, were the job demands that a fire fighter would be expected to meet. The next question was, What abilities could be used to meet these demands? One of the best ability taxonomies available is based on the work of Fleishman (1975). He has suggested a list

FIGURE 8–10 Task List for Fire Fighter Position

L. Transporting Supplies and Equipment. Carries hose, tools, extinguishers, air tanks, high-rise pack, medical equipment, and other supplies or equipment up and down stairs or across long distances in order to fight fires or provide medical treatment in tall buildings, isolated locations, or limited-access areas, (possibly) while wearing full turnout gear.

L1. Carries hose, tools, extinguishers, air tanks, medical equipment, and other supplies up and down stairs in high-rise buildings and across long distances in isolated locations or limited-access areas.

L2. Hoists hose line or other tools and equipment onto roofs or into windows using hose rollers and ropes.

M. Transport of Victims. Assists, lifts, or carries victims onto stretchers or backboards and into medics or squads in order to transport them to hospitals.

M1. Assists, lifts, or carries victims downstairs, upstairs, up or down ladders, and across distances.

M2. Lifts or assists victims onto stretchers, backboards, and gurneys.

M3. Restrains struggling and aggressive victims in order to transport them or provide medical treatment.

N. Extrication. Extricates victims from vehicles, cave-ins, collapsed buildings or other entrapments in order to save lives or remove bodies, using shovels, torches, drills, pry bars, saws, jacks, hurst tools, air bags, and other equipment.

N1. Pries, breaks, or cuts open doors, windows, or other parts of vehicles using pry bars, hurst tools, torches, hux bars, drills, pneumatic metal cutters, and other tools.

N2. Moves heavy objects, materials, and other obstructions in order to free or gain access to trapped victims or bodies, using air bags, chains and hoists, come-alongs, shoring materials, hurst tools, and other hydraulic tools.

N3. Digs to free victims trapped in tunnels, pipes excavations, cave-ins, or other entrapments using shovels, picks, spades, and other equipment.

N4. Dismantles machines in industrial accidents using shop tools and fire-fighting tools.

of 17 physical and 18 cognitive abilities that might be used in meeting the performance demands of any task. Not every ability is used in every task or job. Instead, certain ones are more important in completing certain tasks and others more important in completing other tasks. My job was to identify which abilities were important and then develop test items for those abilities, if possible. The full set of Fleishman abilities appears in Table 8–3. In order to determine which abilities were critical in the successful performance of fire fighter duties, a group of 70 fire fighters and supervisors were asked to make estimates of the relative importance of each ability in successful fire fighter performance. They were given a list of the 16 task groups as well so that they

TABLE 8–2 Basic Task Groups of Fire Fighters

A. *Driving.* Drives emergency vehicles (engines, ladders, crash trucks, squads, medics, and rescues) in order to transport fire fighters, victims, and equipment to and from emergency scenes, following emergency run procedures in response to alarms.

B. *Search.* Searches fire area in order to locate victims, while wearing full turnout gear following standard search procedures.

C. *Rescue.* Assists, carries, or drags victims from emergency area by means of interior access (stairs, hallways, etc.) or if necessary by ladders, fire escapes, platforms, or other means of escape, while wearing full turnout gear.

D. *Forcible entry.* Pries open doors or windows, kicks in doors, breaks out windows, or otherwise forcibly enters buildings and vehicles in order to search for and rescue victims and provide access to the fire for offensive fire fighting, using axes, pry bars, pike poles, hux bars, battering rams, sledgehammers, bolt cutters, and other tools, while wearing full turnout gear.

E. *Engine operation.* Operates engine (and ladder) pumps and fire hydrants in order to supply water for fire fighting, using hydrant wrenches, couplings, hoses, spanner wrenches, printed charts, and other tools.

F. *Ladder (truck) operation.* Stabilizes ladder trucks and elevates and operates aerial ladders, snorkels, squirts, and platforms in order to rescue victims, provide access for ventilation, operate master stream devices, etc., using wheel chocks, stabilizing pads, stabilizing jacks, and outriggers.

G. *Emergency medical treatment.* Provides emergency medical treatment to victims in order to save lives and minimize injuries, using splints, backboards, oxygen, cardiopulmonary resuscitation, and other techniques or equipment.

H. *Handling hose lines.* Lays and advances hose lines (plastic and fabric) and connects hose couplings, nozzles, and master stream appliances in order to supply water for fire fighting, using siamese kits, standpipe kits, portable hydrants, ropes, hose hooks, and hose rollers, while wearing full turnout gear.

I. *Fire fighting.* Operates and advances charged hose lines, master stream appliances, and fire extinguishers from defensive positions or while advancing toward the fire area in order to extinguish the fire, while wearing full turnout gear.

J. *Ventilation.* Opens or breaks open windows, chops or cuts holes in roofs, breaches walls or doors and hangs fans in windows, in holes in roof or wall, from doors or other structures in order to remove heat, smoke, and gas from burning buildings, using ground ladders, roof ladders, axes, pike poles, roof cutters, saws, battering rams, sledgehammers, fans, fog streams, and other equipment, while wearing full turnout gear.

K. *Illumination.* Sets up and starts generators and sets up floodlights in order to illuminate the emergency scene, using extension cords, cord reels, floodlights, and portable or nonportable generators.

L. *Transporting supplies and equipment.* Carries hose, tools, extinguishers, air tanks, high-rise pack, medical equipment, and other supplies or equipment up and down stairs or across long distances in order to fight fires or provide medical treatment in tall buildings, isolated locations, or limited-access areas, (possibly) while wearing full turnout gear.

TABLE 8–2 *(concluded)*

M. *Transport of victims.* Assists, lifts, or carries victims onto stretchers or backboards and into medics or squads in order to transport them to hospitals.
N. *Extrication.* Extricates victims from vehicles, cave-ins, collapsed buildings, or other entrapments in order to save lives or remove bodies, using shovels, torches, drills, pry bars, saws, jacks, hurst tools, air bags, and other equipment.
O. *Salvage.* Moves and covers furniture, appliances, merchandise, and other property, covers holes in buildings, and redirects or cleans up water, in order to minimize damage, using plastic and canvas covers, refrigerator straps, ropes, staple guns, mops, squeegees, and other tools, (possibly) while wearing full turnout gear.
P. *Overhaul.* Pulls down walls and ceilings, cuts or pulls up floors, and moves or turns over debris, in order to check for embers or flames and prevent rekindling or further spread of the fire, using pike poles, axes, saws, bale hooks, mattress hooks, and pitchforks, (possibly) while wearing full turnout gear.
Q. *Clean up/Pick up.* Picks up and returns equipment to vehicle and rolls up or folds up hose, so that the company can go back in service.
R. *Equipment maintenance.* Maintains equipment after fighting a fire as well as on a continual basis to ensure it is ready for immediate service.
S. *Station duties and chores.* Performs routine housekeeping chores and communications duties within the stationhouse.
T. *In-service preplanning and fire prevention inspection.* Inspects electrical and heating systems and makes recommendations to eliminate fire hazards. Inspects fire extinguishers and preconnected fire hoses, ladders, and stairways, fire alarm systems, and hazardous material storage. Preplans fires in areas to provide information regarding hydrant locations, exposures, and areas of high risk.

would keep the entire job in mind when making these decisions. The Fleishman abilities were translated into terms with which they would be familiar. An example of such a translation appears in Figure 8–11. On the basis of their responses, we were able to determine the relative importance of the various abilities. The most important abilities appear in boldface type in Table 8–3. As you might expect, the job of fire fighter depends on both cognitive and physical abilities in almost equal proportions.

Having identified the most important abilities in the job, we now had to decide which ones could be reasonably tested for in a group-administered paper-and-pencil examination and, subsequently, in a physical abilities examination. It was clear to us that certain abilities did not lend themselves to paper-and-pencil testing. Since 3,000 individuals had applied to take the examination, test items requiring equipment other than a pencil or test formats requiring extensive interaction with a test monitor were not feasible. There were a total of nine abilities that were amenable to the practical constraints of the test administration. The nine abilities represented on the examination appear in boldface in Table 8–3. These abilities covered over 80 percent of

TABLE 8–3 Fleishman's Taxonomy

Ability	*Description*
Verbal comprehension	Ability to understand language, either written or spoken; the ability to hear a description of an event and understand what happened.
Verbal expression	This ability involves using either oral or written language to communicate information or ideas to other people; includes vocabulary, knowledge of distinctions among words, and knowledge of grammar and the way words are ordered.
Fluency of ideas	The ability to produce a number of ideas about a given topic. Concerns only the *number* of ideas, not the quality of those ideas.
Originality	This is the ability to produce unusual or clever responses to a given topic or situation; the ability to improvise solutions in situations where standard operating procedures do not apply.
Memorization	This is the ability to memorize and retain new information that occurs as a routine part of the task or job.
Problem sensitivity	This is the ability to recognize or identify the existence of problems; involves both the recognition of the problem as a whole and the elements of the problem but does not include the ability to solve the problem.
Deductive reasoning	The ability to apply general rules or regulations to specific cases or to proceed from stated principles to logical conclusions.
Inductive reasoning	The ability to find a rule or concept that fits the situation; would include coming up with a logical explanation for a series of events that seem to be unrelated.
Information ordering	The ability to apply rules to a situation for the purpose of putting the information in the best or most appropriate sequence; involves the application of previously specified rules and procedures to a given situation.
Category flexibility	The ability to produce alternative groupings or categories for a set of things. These "things" might be people, cars, ideas, theories, etc.
Spatial orientation	The ability to keep a clear idea of where you are in relation to the space you happen to be in; helps you keep from getting lost in a particular space, whether it is a city, a building, a park, or a subway system.
Visualization	This ability involves forming mental images of what objects look like after they have been changed or transformed in some way.

TABLE 8–3 *(continued)*

Ability	*Description*
Speed of closure	This ability involves the speed with which a large number of elements can be combined and organized in a meaningful pattern when you do not know what the pattern is or what is to be identified. Means having to combine lots of information quickly.
Flexibility of closure	This ability involves the skill of finding an object that is somehow hidden in a bunch of other objects; would involve picking out a particular face in a crowd of faces. Speed not important.
Selective attention	This is the ability to complete a task in the presence of distraction or monotony.
Perceptual speed	This ability involves the speed with which the features of a person, place, or thing can be compared with other features of another person, place, or thing to determine how similar the two objects are.
Time sharing	This is the ability to pay attention to two sources of information at the same time. The information that is received from these two sources may be either combined or used separately. Important aspect is ability to deal with information that is coming *rapidly* from several different sources.
Static strength	Ability we generally think of when we hear the word *strength*. It is the amount of force exerted against a fairly heavy object—can involve pushing, pulling, or lifting.
Explosive strength	Ability to use energy in one or a series of explosive muscular acts—what is needed is a burst of muscular energy rather than a steady effort.
Dynamic strength	Involves using your arms and trunk in moving your own body weight for some period of time or across some distance—example is climbing a rope.
Stamina	Ability to maintain physical activity over a long period of time. Extent to which the cardiovascular system (heart and lungs) is exercised.
Extent flexibility	Ability involves stretching or extending arms and legs and their particular muscle groups.
Dynamic flexibility	Ability to make repeated or continuous arm and leg flexing movements with some speed—example is pulling in a rope hand over hand in a short time.
Gross body equilibrium	Ability to maintain the body in an upright position and keep one's balance.
Choice reaction-time	Ability to choose the correct response quickly when two or more responses are possible; important aspect is how quickly the response is begun.

TABLE 8–3 *(concluded)*

Ability	*Description*
Reaction time	Ability concerned with the speed with which a single response can be begun—no choice of reaction involved here, as above.
Speed of limb movement	Ability involves the speed with which arms and legs can be moved—the speed to carry out an arm or leg movement after it has been chosen and begun—example would be how quickly a boxer could throw a punch or a quarterback release a football.
Wrist-finger speed	Ability deals with how quickly wrists, fingers, and hands can be moved—example would be speed with which someone could tie complicated knots or sew an intricate pattern.
Gross body coordination	Ability to coordinate movement of trunk, arms, and legs—example might be running on an uneven or slanted surface and keeping your balance.
Multilimb coordination	Ability to use two limbs together—example is driving, where arms must be used in coordinated fashion with feet or legs.
Finger dexterity	Ability to make skillful and coordinated use of fingers—example, threading a needle.
Manual dexterity	Ability to make skillful use of hand, or arm and hand together.
Arm-hand steadiness	Ability to make precise, steady arm-hand movements (neither speed nor strength is important). Includes the elimination of shaking or tremors—example might be taking aim with a gun or stitching a wound.
Rate control	Ability to make timed movements in response to changes in the speed of continuously moving object—example is catching a ball thrown to you, ducking a punch or thrown object.
Control precision	Ability to make controlled muscular movements to adjust or position a piece of equipment—example is working the controls of a radio.

SOURCE: Adapted from "Toward a Taxonomy of Human Performance" by E. A. Fleishman, 1975, *American Psychologist, 30*, pp. 1127–1149.

the cognitive requirements of the job as estimated from the judgments of our 70 fire fighters and supervisors.

The next step was to develop test items that would tap these abilities. There were two issues to consider. The first was the content of the items, and the second was the number of items in each area. It was decided that the actual items would be tied to fire fighter tasks that were important and

FIGURE 8–11 Fleishman Taxonomy with Fire-Fighting Examples

Static Strength: This is the ability we generally think of when we hear the word *strength*. It is the amount of force that is exerted against a fairly immovable or heavy external object. Force is exerted continuously and might involve pushing, pulling, or lifting. Examples of this would include prying a door open, lifting a person, or holding hoses.

Explosive Strength. This is the ability to use energy in one or a series of explosive muscular acts. What is needed is a burst of muscular energy rather than a steady effort. Examples might be jumping over an obstacle, using an ax, or knocking open a door.

Dynamic Strength. This ability involves using your arms and trunk in moving your own body weight for some period of time or across some distance. An example would be climbing a rope or pulling yourself along using only your arms. Another important part of this ability is that you must use the same arm muscles repeatedly or continuously.

Stamina. This is the ability to maintain physical activity over a long period of time. This deals with the extent to which the cardiovascular system (heart and lungs) is exercised. A good example of the use of this ability would be climbing up 20 flights of stairs. Another example would be running a long distance.

Extent Flexibility. This ability involves stretching or extending arms and legs and their particular muscle groups. An example of this ability would be stretching a leg up above your waist to climb over a wall. A second example would be reaching with your arms at an extreme angle so that a ladder could be put in place.

Dynamic Flexibility. This is the ability to make repeated or continuous arm and leg flexing movements with some speed. An example would be pulling in a hose or rope, hand over hand, in a short time or quickly climbing up a ladder.

frequent. These tasks were easily identified from the job analysis ratings. The question regarding the number of test items in each area was also answered empirically by using the judgments of our 70 fire fighters and supervisors. Since we were able to determine the average importance of each of the nine abilities in completing fire fighter tasks, we used this importance estimate to determine the written test composition. The most important abilities were represented by the greatest number of items. The abilities of lesser importance had fewer items. The actual test items were written by civil service personnel technicians who were instructed on the results of the job analysis, the conceptual and operational characteristics of each of the nine abilities, and general procedures for writing test items. A total of seven technicians spent several weeks writing possible test items. Each item was tied to a job-related task and was written to represent an important ability. Each item writer was given separate ability areas to work on.

The resulting items were examined for clarity, possible discriminatory content, and internal structure. Alternatives were checked to make sure that there was only one acceptable answer per item. The result was a 100-item paper-and-pencil test administered to the applicants. In the next several weeks, the examinations were scored and item analyses reviewed. The reliability of the test was high for the entire group of applicants as well as minority subgroupings. There was no reliability coefficient lower then +.90. In all technical respects checked, the test had "worked" well.

The next challenge was to administer a physical abilities examination. Based on the Fleishman ability analysis, we were able to determine what physical abilities were most clearly impacted in fire fighting. These abilities were stamina, dynamic strength, explosive strength, static strength, and dynamic flexibility. We then set about constructing work samples that would include these abilities. These work samples were the actual test events of the physical abilities test. They included such tasks as dragging a 125-pound dummy along a marked course, climbing stairs with fire-fighting gear on and carrying equipment, and crawling through a wooden maze with a blackened facemask. Each of the tasks simulated in these work samples had been judged by the fire fighters to be an important task in their job.

After the physical abilities tests had been developed, they were performed by fire fighters, and that performance was videotaped. This videotape was then shown to a panel of 20 industrial psychologists, and they were asked to judge which of Fleishman's abilities were necessary for successful completion of each of the physical test events. In this way, it was possible to conduct a quality control check of our tests to make sure that they measured what we had intended them to measure. In short, we were establishing the validity of the test components.

Only those candidates who received a passing score on the written examination were permitted to take the physical ability examination. Approximately 900 applicants passed the written examination and were administered the physical abilities test. It took almost one month to administer these tests to all the applicants.

The issue now became how to *use* the test results. In other words, who had "passed" the total examination, and in what order would those people be considered? The written test counted 50 percent of the final score, and the physical abilities test accounted for the other 50 percent. Typically, those who pass a civil service examination are put on a list of "approved" candidates. This list remains current for several years and is used whenever new appointments need to be made. Thus, some applicants will be processed before others. The question is how this order is to be established. On the basis of anticipated personnel needs in the three years following the examination, it was assumed that there might be a need for as many as 300 replacement fire fighters.

After the physical abilities test had been constructed, it was administered to a sample of 150 Columbus fire fighters. Their scores were used to set cutoffs on the examination. The logic was that applicants should be able to perform as well as the average fire fighter on tasks that did require various physical

In a, a candidate completes a test of strength intended to simulate the use of a pike pole by a fire fighter. A fire fighter actually uses a pike pole in b.

abilities but did not require any particular skill. The actual test events did not involve elaborate equipment or familiarity with fire-fighting techniques. After these cutoffs were established, candidates were arranged from highest to lowest scorers and appointments were made. The cutoffs were necessary to determine how many men and how many women passed the physical ability examination. Since the city had been involved in litigation brought by unsuccessful female applicants on earlier tests, the federal court decided that the results of the present test would be used to correct earlier inequities. As a result, the court required the appointment of a specific number of women to the fire academy as long as these women passed the physical ability examination.

The next logical step would be to develop a method of measuring fire-fighting performance in Columbus and then to conduct a criterion-related validity study. In fact, that is just what we did. We identified a sample of 140 fire fighters who took part in a concurrent validity study. The criterion measures were behaviorally anchored scales constructed to represent the 16 task groups of the job listed above. In a sense, this guaranteed the validity of the criterion measures. An example of one of the scales appears in Figure 8–12. The supervisors of the members of our concurrent sample rated these fire

FIGURE 8–12 Behaviorally Anchored Rating Scale for Evaluating Fire-Fighter Performance

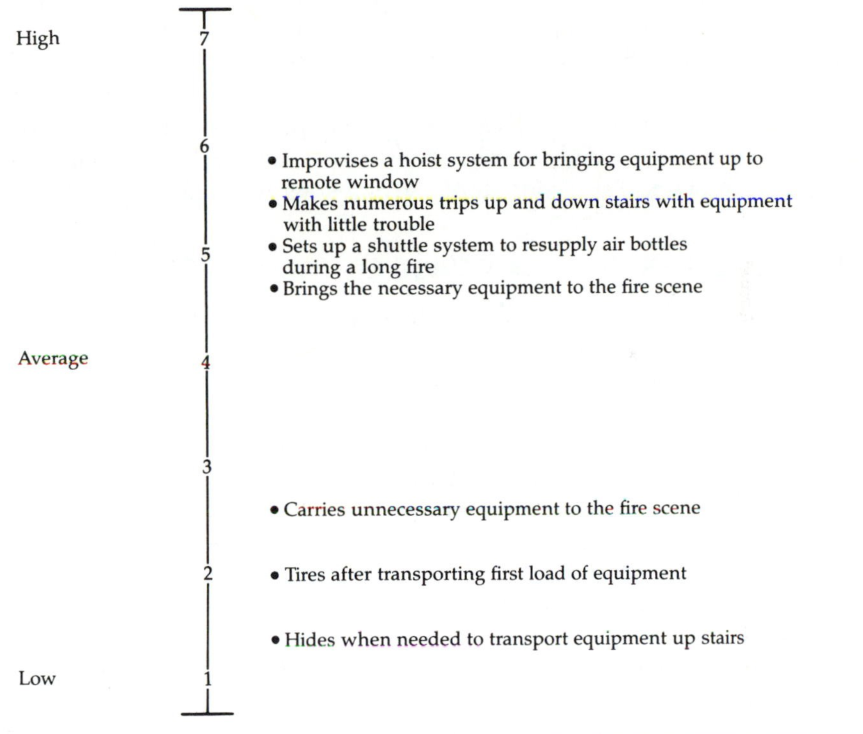
Transporting Supplies and Equipment
This area of performance involves carrying hoses, tools, extinguishers, air tanks, medical equipment, and other supplies or equipment up and down stairs or across long distances in order to fight fires or provide medical treatment in tall buildings, isolated locations, or limited access areas.
High
7
6
• Improvises a hoist system for bringing equipment up to remote window
• Makes numerous trips up and down stairs with equipment with little trouble
5
• Sets up a shuttle system to resupply air bottles during a long fire
• Brings the necessary equipment to the fire scene
Average
4
3
• Carries unnecessary equipment to the fire scene
2
• Tires after transporting first load of equipment
• Hides when needed to transport equipment up stairs
Low
1

fighters on the performance dimensions. The predictor variables were the written test scores and the physical ability test scores for the incumbent sample. The results of the concurrent validity study were encouraging. There was a strong pattern of significant correlations between the physical ability test scores and the ratings on the physical dimensions of the job. Similarly, there were significant correlations between the written test scores and the cognitive performance aspects of the job. We are currently completing a predictive validity study on these tests by tracking the progress of those hired with the test and getting supervisory evaluations of these fire fighters. Since an academy class consists of 38 fire fighters, it will take a few years before a sufficient number have been hired from the list to permit a predictive validity calculation. Nevertheless, based on the results of the concurrent study, we felt secure that those who did better on the tests would do better on the job.

This was a long and elaborate example of test development, validation, administration, and decision making. It should have the effect of pulling all the independent pieces of a testing program together for you. The Columbus Fire Department is not substantially different from the Nationwide Insurance Co. or Pennsylvania State University or your local hardware store with respect to the issue of making personnel decisions. The same procedures that I used to develop, validate, administer, and use the results of the fire fighter exam can be used in any setting. Test development is more than simply writing items. Furthermore, personnel decisions involve more than simply ordering test scores. The integrity of standardized testing depends on high-quality test development and logical and consistent use of test scores in making decisions.

REALISTIC JOB PREVIEWS: A CASE OF SELF-SELECTION

There is one final topic that should be covered in order to complete our view of the selection process. To this point, we have considered various predictors and prediction systems that might maximize the probability of identifying candidates with a high probability of success. There is another way in which we can maximize our "hit" rate in hiring. If we consider that the task of selection is not just the identification of talent but also keeping that talent in the organization for some reasonable period of time, then the definition of a "hit" changes slightly. It has been suggested that there are strategies that can be applied in the context of the selection process that can improve our capacity to identify *and retain* talented employees.

Why should we worry about the issue of retention? The simplest example is an applicant who looks terrific on paper, is offered and accepts a job, and then quits two months later. The problem is that the organization has devoted time and energy to the applicant, and this expenditure is lost when the employee leaves. In addition, a new expense is incurred in looking for a replacement employee. As an example, Dean and Wanous (1984) estimate that a bank teller who quits after 23 weeks will cost the bank approximately $1,400 more than one who leaves shortly after training (3 weeks) or who does not take the job in the first place.

The perspective of this chapter has been the adequacy of a selection decision and the ways in which that decision is made. It would seem that a good selection decision is made not only on the basis of who will be a productive employee but also in terms of who will stay long enough to return the investment in selection and training. Recruiting is one example of a process that can affect the utility or payoff of selection and training costs. For example, Decker and Cornelius (1979) compared the "survival" rates of employees who became aware of openings through newspaper ads, through employment agencies, and by way of referrals from acquaintances currently working for

FIGURE 8–13 Comparison of Realistic Job Preview Booklets

Topic	*Specific RJP*	*General RJP*
Training	Training described Failure rate	Not mentioned
Work	Banking transactions Accuracy important Working under pressure Manager schedules work	Banking transactions
Customers	Courtesy required Rude customers	Courtesy required
Career opportunities	Promotion criteria Promotion rates How to move into branch management	The various teller positions described
Compensation	Pay rates How increases are determined	Pay rates Employee benefits
Summary of major points	Included	Not included

SOURCE: From "The Effects of Realistic Job Previews on Hiring Bank Tellers" by J. P. Wanous and R. A. Dean, 1984, *Journal of Applied Psychology, 69*.

the company. The worst survival rates were associated with employees who had been referred by an employment agency. In a sample of bank employees (n = 514), a total of 47 percent of the applicants who came via this route were gone after one year. The best survival rates were associated with an employee referral. Only 31 percent of these applicants were gone after a year. As Dean and Wanous point out, this difference could be a substantial one in terms of selection and training costs. One way of addressing this problem has been suggested. It is known as the realistic job preview (RJP).

A realistic job preview is an attempt to provide applicants with information about the organization that paints a realistic picture. Sometimes company literature and recruiters paint an overly attractive picture of the organization. This has a negative effect on the new employee for several reasons. In the first place, it creates unrealistic expectations with respect to rewards and job duties. In addition, it diminishes the credibility of the organization since it quickly becomes clear that the applicant was misled. Both of these effects are thought to lead to increased turnover (Wanous, 1980). Instead of this inaccurate view of the organization, RJPs are based on accurate descriptions of various aspects of the job and the organization. For example, in Figure 8–13 (Dean & Wanous, 1984), a booklet was prepared for prospective bank tellers describing not only the positive aspects of pay and advancement but

FIGURE 8–14 Psychological Effects of the Realistic Job Preview (RJP)

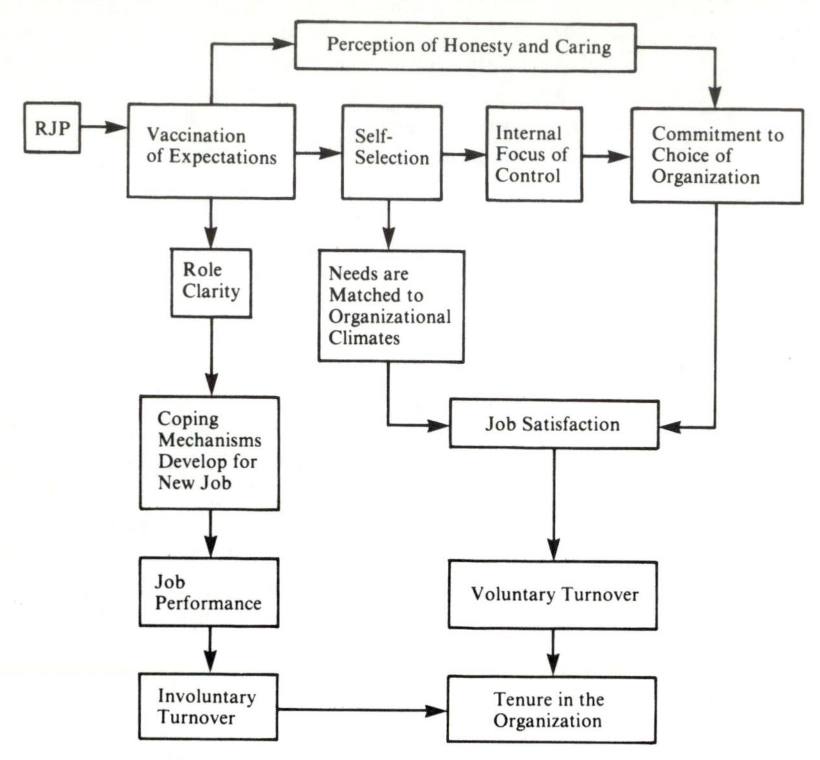

SOURCE: From "Realistic Job Previews: Can a Procedure to Reduce Turnover Also Influence the Relationship between Abilities and Performance?" by J. P. Wanous, 1978, *Personnel Psychology, 31* p. 251. Reprinted by permission.

also some negative aspects of the job such as rude customers and working under pressure. A review by Reilly, Brown, Blood, and Malatesta (1981) estimates the average effect of RJPs at 6 percent. In other words, one might expect a survival rate that is 6 percent higher for employees receiving an RJP. This percentage varies substantially from one setting or occupation to another, however. Wanous (1980) has suggested a model that attempts to explain how and why RJPs work. It appears in Figure 8–14. As you can see, both satisfaction and performance are involved. We will consider satisfaction in Chapter 11. In a recent study (Dean & Wanous, 1984), a second advantage of RJPs was identified. They studied the effects of different types of RJPs on bank teller applicants. Although there were no significant differences between those receiving RJPs and those who did not, there was a difference in terms of when new employees left. Those employees who received RJPs were more likely to leave during training. Those who did not receive RJPs tended to leave after 23 weeks. As indicated above, the latter group was more expensive to the organization than the former group.

Cascio and Phillips (1979) suggest that performance testing can play a major part in an RJP. Instead of traditional paper-and-pencil employment tests, they substituted various performance tests to be administered to applicants for employment in various operating departments of a city government. For example, individuals who applied for jobs as water and sewer workers were taken to actual work settings (e.g., underground sewage facilities) and asked to perform certain tasks. Other performance tests were also administered. During an evaluation period following the introduction of the RJP, Cascio and Phillips found that the turnover rate dropped from over 40 percent to less than 3 percent. Of course, many other things might have happened during the time period as well (e.g., a substantial increase in unemployment). Nevertheless, the possibility is an intriguing one. The actual methods that are used to test and inform applicants about positions may have an impact on their survival.

Recent meta-analyses of the RJP have been mixed. McEvoy and Cascio (1985) and Premack and Wanous (1985) report modest effects, but Guzzo, Jette, and Katzell (1985) report no effects. As Guion and Gibson (1988) suggest, the best conclusion is that "they work—a little bit and sometimes."

An RJP is not one thing. It is a label for a set of activities all directed toward the same end—providing a more realistic view of the job under consideration. As Wanous (1977) points out, expectations held by outsiders are almost always inflated. It makes sense to think of the selection decision adequacy as having a temporal characteristic to it. In addition to identifying correct and incorrect decisions based on measures of performance, turnover figures should also be kept in mind. Similarly, tests and selection procedures should be thought of not only as devices to gather information but also as strategies for providing information. I made this point in Chapter 7 in a different way. There, we considered the role that the interview might play in *informing* applicants with respect to the organization. The RJP is another example of the communication channel that could run from the organization to the applicant in the selection process.

Technical Appendix

1. CORRELATION AND PREDICTIVE EFFICIENCY

The relationship between correlation and predictive efficiency is described by the *coefficient of determination* r^2, which indicates that portion of the variance in Y accounted for by X. In the case $r = .50$, $r^2 = .25$, or 25 percent of the variance in Y is accounted for by X—better than nothing but less than

100. If $r = .50$, it means that if we know the X scores of a group of individuals, we can reduce the variance of their Y scores by 25 percent. This ability to reduce variability in one set of scores from knowledge of another set of scores is the essence of prediction. In the most basic terms, X predicts Y.

Another way of stating the same principle is that differential prediction of Y based on knowledge of X reduces the error variance in prediction by 25 percent. The reciprocal value, $1 - r^2$, is known as the coefficient of alienation, which with $r = .50$ would be .75. Therefore, from the point of view of classical measurement theory, a validity coefficient of .50 yields only a modest gain of 25 percent in predictive efficiency. Given the fact that validity coefficients seldom exceed .50, this is a rather disappointing interpretation. But even more disillusioning, perhaps, are the results obtained from applying another formula for evaluating predictive efficiency, the "index of forecasting efficiency," E. Whereas the coefficient of determination describes the reduction in the variance (σ^2) of the error distribution achieved by using predictor scores, E describes the reduction in the standard deviation of the errors in predicting the criterion scores. The index is obtained by the equation:

$$E = 1 - \sqrt{1 - r_{pc}^2}$$

With an $r_{pc} = .50$, as in our previous example, E is equal to only slightly more than .13, indicating a mere 13 percent improvement in predictive efficiency.

One final point should be made with respect to the coefficients of determination and alienation. These coefficients are misleading and result in too pessimistic a view of the value of low validity coefficients. The coefficients are based on the value r^2 rather than r. It is the latter statistic that is more appropriate for computational and inferential purposes (Brogden, 1946). The value r may be directly interpreted as the following ratio: the improvement in criterion scores that could be attained using the same selection ratio if *true* scores were known at the time of selection. With this in mind, the actual value of a predictor for selection is linearly related to r and not to r^2. This fact makes it clear that tests with low validities can have very high utilities associated with their use in selection.

2. THE TAYLOR-RUSSELL TABLES

Taylor and Russell (1939) provided a set of tables that show the percentages of new hires who will be successful as a function of (a) predictor validity, (b) selection ratio, and (c) preselection success rate. These tables summarize what happens to the proportion of true positives to total positives in Figure 8–2 as the predictor cutoff score (X_i) is moved left or right and as the criterion score (Y_c) separating successes from failures is moved up or down. Such an approach is practical: it does not speculate about the likelihood of false negatives (about which criterion data are not available, except in concurrent validation). However, the approach assumes that it is appropriate and feasible to dichotomize employees into successes and failures, as though all members of the success group had identical job proficiency scores and all failures were equally inept. This is not likely to be the case; performance can be expected to vary continuously as a function of individual differences (although, with either technological limits, such as the assembly line, or "social" limits, as found in restriction of production or in labor-management agreements on work quotas, the assumption may be more realistic: under these conditions, a successful employee makes quota, whereas an unsuccessful employee does not).

Thus, there were two limitations to the Taylor-Russell tables: (1) it was necessary to identify a single criterion score separating "success" from failure, and (2) they did not allow for degrees of success or failure.

THE NAYLOR-SHINE TABLES

Naylor and Shine (1965) presented tables that overcame these limitations of the Taylor-Russell approach to evaluating the payoff of a selection device. The tabled values describe the difference in average criterion scores for the selected as compared with the original group. Thus, job proficiency is treated as a continuous variable, and furthermore, this approach avoids the problem of identifying the criterion score separating the successful from the unsuccessful. Instead, as illustrated in Figure 8–15, the means of the two samples (selected and unselected) are subtracted to show the gain from selection.

PERCENTAGE INCREASE IN JOB PROFICIENCY

The Naylor-Shine tables are only one step removed from describing the payoff from selection in terms of a percentage increase in job proficiency. All that is required is to describe the "gain" in Figure 8–15 as a percentage of the mean of the original sample. Such an approach was summarized by Ghiselli and Brown (1955) in the nomograph shown in Figure 8–16. Here, the criterion of *percentage increase in job proficiency* is shown on the right-hand vertical scales. The graph is read by entering at the lower left with the appropriate selection ratio, moving vertically to the curve with the appropriate validity, then moving horizontally to the appropriate vertical scale. These latter scales introduce a new factor into the evaluation of a selection program: the *variability in job proficiency*. This is described at the top of Figure 8–16 as the ratio of the best to the poorest worker.

It may be noted that at a given selection ratio and validity the payoff decreases as the ratio of the best to the poorest worker (the "σ proficiency") decreases. This makes good intuitive sense. If the best worker produces 110 units and the poorest, 100 units (ratio 1.1:1.0, mean = 105 units), then we would never expect to exceed a 5 percent gain in proficiency, whereas with a ratio of 4:1 (e.g., 400:100 units, mean = 250 units), one might expect ideally to get everyone to the level of the best worker. While proficiency will vary

FIGURE 8–15 Comparison of Criterion Scores for Unselected and Selected Samples

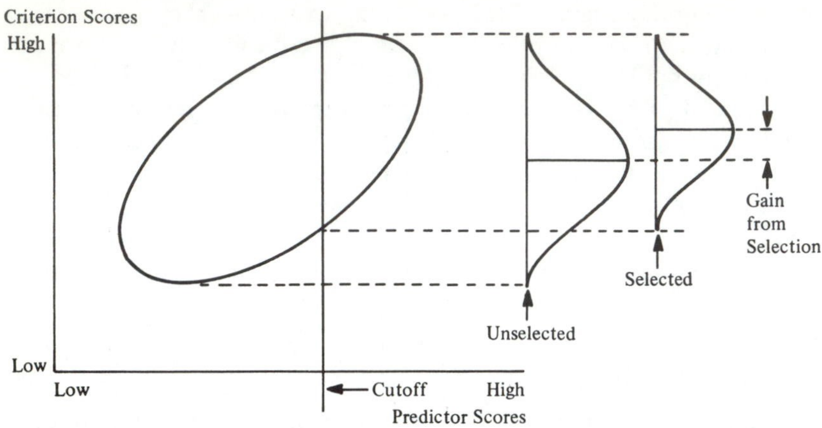

The difference in the means of these two samples represents the gain in job proficiency resulting from the selection program. This gain can be estimated when predictor validity and selection ratio are known (see Naylor and Shine, 1965).

from job to job, as a result both of true individual differences and of the technical and social restrictions discussed earlier, in only a few cases will the ratio reach or exceed 4:1. Hull (1928) summarized productive proficiency data for a number of semiskilled jobs. The ratio varied from 1.4:1–5.1:1, with an average of about 2:1. Thus, with a good predictive validity of .50, a reasonable selection ratio at 50 percent, and a 2:1 ratio of proficiency, one might expect about a 5 percent improvement in job proficiency. Although this may sound like a small gain, it could mean the difference between profit and loss or between successful and unsuccessful competition in many enterprises. For the relationships described in this procedure to hold, the scale of measurement for proficiency must be a ratio scale. Since a number of productivity indexes can be assumed to be ratio measurements (e.g., number of units produced or time required to complete a task), this technique is quite effective in describing the anticipated gain in productivity from the use of tests for various validity–selection ratio combinations.

3. MULTIPLE CORRELATION

The multiple correlation coefficient, *R*, indicates the degree of relationship between two or more sets of predictor scores and a set of predicted scores. When the predicted scores are a criterion measure, *R* is the validity coefficient

FIGURE 8–16 Percentage Increase in Job Proficiency

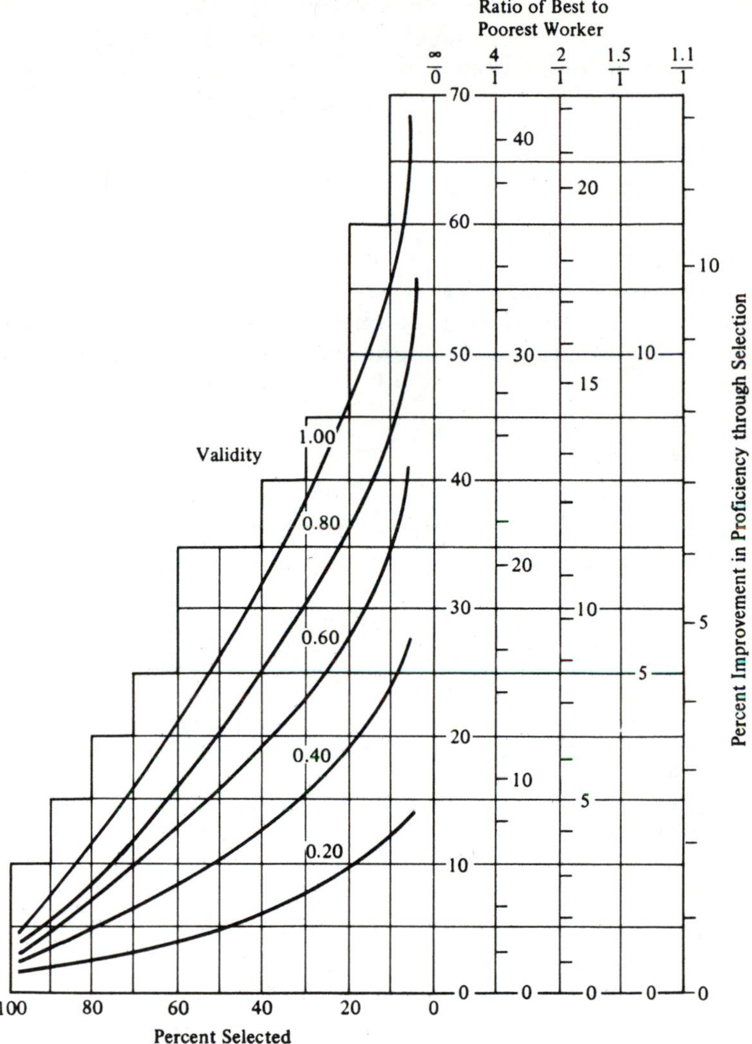

The relationship between validity, the selection ratio, variability in job proficiency (ratio of the best to the poorest worker), and percent improvement in proficiency.

SOURCE: From *Personnel and Industrial Psychology* (2nd ed.) (Fig. 5–4, p. 147) by E. E. Ghiselli and C. W. Brown, 1955, New York: McGraw-Hill.

for the combined predictors. It can be interpreted in the same way as a simple correlation coefficient. For example, if $R = .50$, the coefficient of determination, $R^2 = .25$, and the index of forecasting efficiency, E, is approximately .13. However, R cannot be obtained simply by adding the validity coefficients of the several predictors. Rather, it depends on their intercorrelations.

The equation for the squared multiple correlation coefficient, R^2, for two predictors, 1 and 2, is:

$$R^2_{c12} = \frac{r^2_{1c} + r^2_{2c} - 2r_{12}r_{1c}r_{2c}}{1 - r^2_{12}}$$

It takes into account the correlation between the two predictors, r_{12}. As r_{12} approaches 1, R^2_{c12} approaches the higher of the square of the two single validities as a lower limit. As r_{12} approaches zero, R^2_{c12} increases until, with $r_{12} = 0$,

$$R^2_{c12} = r^2_{1c} + r^2_{2c}$$

That is, with $r_{12} = 0$, the variance accounted for in the criterion is equal to the sum of variances accounted for by the individual predictors. However, this does not mean that we can simply *add* validity coefficients to obtain R even when $r_{12} = 0$, since

$$R^2_{c12} = r^2_{1c} = r^2_{2c} \text{ or } R = r^2_{1c} + r^2_{2c}$$

Thus, with $r_{1c} = r_{2c} = .40$, $R = (.40)^2 + (.40)^2 = \sqrt{.32}$ or .57, not the .80 that we would get from adding $r_{1c} + r_{2c}$.

As with the simple correlation, r, the multiple correlation coefficient does not tell us what criterion score to predict. For this we need to use the multiple regression equation discussed below.

MULTIPLE REGRESSION

Multiple correlation describes the relationship between two or more predictors and a criterion meaure. Multiple regression, like simple regression, defines the best estimate of the criterion score in terms of optimally weighted predictor scores, or

$$Y = b_1X_1 + b_2X_2 + \ldots b_nX_n$$

where Y is the predicted standard criterion score, X_1, $X_2 \ldots X_n$ are the standard scores on the n predictors, and b_1, $b_2 \ldots b_n$ are the weights assigned to each of the predictors (these weights essentially reflect the *unique* criterion variance accounted for by each predictor).

Multiple regression is a linear model. It assumes that the predictors are linearly related to the criterion. Furthermore, the fact that Y is a function of the *sum* of the weighted predictor scores indicates that scores on the predictors are additive and can compensate for one another. For example, in a two-predictor case with $b_1 = b_2$, persons with the following three combinations of scores would receive the same predicted criterion score: $X_1 = 50$, $X_2 = 50$; $X_1 = 100$, $X_2 = 0$; $X_1 = 0$, $X2 = 100$. Suppose, in a less extreme case, that X_1 and X_2 were "verbal" and "quantitative" scores, respectively. The multiple-regression model would assume that superior verbal ability compensates for inferior quantitative ability. While this system is the most precise and mathematically sophisticated, one may seriously doubt the extent to which the assumption of compensatory traits is tenable.

4. FORMULA FOR SHRINKAGE OF MULTIPLE CORRELATION

In computing a multiple correlation, there are two important numbers to keep in mind. The first is the sample size. If you compute a multiple R on a very small sample, the value will be in error to a greater extent than if the multiple R had been calculated on a larger sample. As an example, a sample of 10 is too small for multiple correlation, and a sample of 200 is suitable. The error most often results in an *overestimate* of the actual multiple correlation in the population.

The second number to keep in mind is the number of variables that enter into the correlation. As the number of variables increases, the amount of possible error also increases. In the situation where the sample size is small and the number of variables is large, error can be quite a serious problem. The formula below allows one to estimate how much error is represented in a multiple correlation as a function of the sample size and the number of variables.

$$\text{Corrected } R^2 = 1 - (1 - R^2)\frac{N - 1}{N - n}$$

where R^2 = the initial estimate, N = sample size, and n = the number of variables or predictors in the set (or, in the present case, tests in a battery).

This formula has been used commonly in the last several decades for obtaining shrinkage estimates. Recently, Schmitt, Coyle, and Rauschenberger (1977) have pointed out that it is based on some extreme assumptions. In particular, they suggest that while this formula may be appropriate for estimating a population R^2, that is seldom what we are after when testing for shrinkage. Instead, we are trying to estimate what the value of R^2 will be when the equation is applied to a new sample. As a result, they feel that it underestimates the shrinkage. As a substitute, they suggest the following shrinkage formula:

$$\text{Corrected } R^2 = 1 - \frac{N - 1}{N - n - 1}\,\frac{N + n + 1}{N}\,(1 - R^2)$$

CENTRAL POINTS FOR STUDY

1. A good personnel decision is one that results in a good match between the individual and the organization.
2. There are many factors other than validity that help to determine the effectiveness of a selection program.
3. Predictor information can be combined to yield more effective decisions.
4. Selection, placement, and classification are different processes.
5. There is a body of law and technical requirements that govern selection decisions.
6. Realistic job previews may be thought of as self-selection devices.

CHAPTER 9

Personnel Training and Development: Concepts, Models, and Techniques

Consider the following facts:

- Over 90 percent of the private corporations in the United States have some form of systematic training program (Goldstein & Buxton, 1982).
- During the period 1971 to 1981, training and instruction were the most commonly cited interventions to improve productivity in a sample of productivity improvement studies (Katzell & Guzzo, 1983).
- One large corporation reported spending over $75 million annually on the salaries of nonmanagement employees who were in training programs, and this did *not* include the actual cost of training programs or facilities (Holt, 1963).
- In 1971, the U.S. Civil Service Commission released a catalog of training programs for the disadvantaged. There were 50 different training programs listed *for reading alone* (Goldstein & Buxton, 1982).
- In the 1967 fiscal year, the U.S. Office of Education spent over $800 million on instructional materials and media (Grayson, 1972).
- In the 1977 fiscal year, the Department of Defense allocated over $6 billion for military training efforts.
- In the 1977 fiscal year, 555,544 civilians in the federal government received 37,469,999 hours of training at a reported cost of over $2.5 billion. This cost did not include trainees' salaries (Office of Personnel Management [OPM], 1979).
- In 1979, the cost of training an operator of an electronic switching system for the telephone company was $25,000 for each trainee (Reilly & Manese, 1979).

By any standard, training is big business. This should come as no surprise. There are few organizations that would not suffer from the poor performance of a new employee or the errors of a longtime employee who has just assumed new job duties. The object of training is to make sure that the employee has sufficient knowledge and proficiency to meet the demands of the job. As such, training is assumed to build on applicant motivations tapped in the recruiting phase and to refine and focus the basic competencies identified in the selection process. Further, it is assumed that training will provide the confidence necessary for skilled and motivated job performance. Training is a natural phase of the process by which applicants are transformed into successful employees.

From the point of view of the psychologist, training includes many different specific activities. The need for training must be documented, the training program developed, the training delivered, the program evaluated, and so forth. Table 9–1 provides a good description of the activities that might be carried out in a modern training department.

Although training can be directed toward improving motivation or changing attitudes, these topics will be taken up in later chapters where they are more central to chapter content. This chapter is concerned with fitting the individual to the job and to the organization by promoting the acquisition of information, skills, attitudes, and patterns of social behavior through training. We will consider the relationship of learning to training, various approaches that have characterized training programs, specific training devices and procedures, the evaluation of training efforts, and some miscellaneous issues such as training for the unemployed and the relationship of Equal Opportunity law to training.

TRAINING, LEARNING, AND PERFORMANCE

Training is a set of planned activities on the part of an organization to increase the job knowledge and skills or to modify the attitudes and social behavior of its members in ways consistent with the goals of the organization and the requirements of the job. *Learning* is a relatively permanent change in behavior that comes through experience and is not the direct result of body states such as fatigue or illness (Landy, 1987). By contrasting these two definitions, we see that they are really dealing with the same phenomenon from two different perspectives. Learning is something that takes place inside the person—a change of some sort. Training is something that is done to the person—it is a planned experience that is expected to lead to learning. All training does not result in learning, and all learning is not solely the result of training. To make matters even more complex, there is the issue of performance. Performance consists of a response of some sort. Good performance implies the correct response, and poor performance implies either an incorrect response or the absence of a response. Training may very well lead to learning, but learning does not guarantee satisfactory performance. Similarly, performance may be satisfactory even in the absence of training or learning. The point is that training increases the probability of learning, and learning increases the probability of performance. Nevertheless, it is reasonable to as-

TABLE 9–1 Training and Development Practitioner Roles

a. Needs analysis and diagnosis
Construct questionnaires and conduct interviews for needs analysis, evaluate feedback, etc.
b. Determine appropriate training approach
Evaluate the alternatives of "ready-made" courses or materials, use of programmed instruction, videotape, computer-managed, and other structured techniques versus a more process-oriented organization development/team-building approach.
c. Program design and development
Design program content and structure, apply learning theory, establish objectives, evaluate and select instructional methods.
d. Develop material resources (make)
Prepare scripts, slides, manuals, artwork, copy, programmed learning, and other instructional materials.
e. Manage internal resources (borrow)
Obtain and evaluate internal instructors/program resource persons, train others how to train, supervise their work.
f. Manager external resources (buy)
Hire, supervise, and evaluate external instructors/program resource persons; obtain and evaluate outside consultants and vendors.
g. Individual development planning and counseling
Counsel with individuals regarding career development needs and plans, arrange for and maintain records of participation in programs, administer tuition reimbursement, maintain training resource library, keep abreast of EEO.
h. Job/performance-related training
Assist managers and others in on-the-job training and development, analyze job skill and knowledge requirements, determine performance problems.
i. Conduct classroom training
Conduct programs, operate audio-visual equipment, lecture, lead discussion, revise materials based on feedback, arrange program logistics.
j. Group and organization development
Apply techniques such as team-building, intergroup meetings, behavior modeling, role-playing simulation, laboratory education, discussions, cases, issues.
k. Training research
Present and interpret statistics and data relating to training; communicate through reports, proposals, speeches, and articles; design data collection.
l. Manage working relationships with managers and clients
Establish and maintain good relations with managers as clients, counsel with them, and explain recommendations for training and development.
m. Manage the training and development function
Prepare budgets, organize, staff, make formal presentations of plans, maintain information on costs, supervise the work of others, project future needs, etc.
n. Professional self-development
Attend seminars/conferences and keep abreast of training and development concepts, theories, and techniques; keep abreast of activities in other organizations.

SOURCE: From "What Do Training and Development Professionals Really Do?" by P. R. Pinto and J. W. Walker, 1978, *Training and Development Journal, 28,* pp. 58–64. Copyright 1978 by the American Society for Training and Development, Inc. Reprinted by permission.

sume that training depends on having at least minimal amounts of certain basic abilities. Similarly, performance may well depend more heavily on motivational variables than on the adequacy of training programs.[1]

A Flowchart of the Training Process

Let's return for a moment to the logic of earlier chapters. When we considered the role of predictors in personnel decisions, we concluded that we must know something about the job demands before we can identify likely predictors of success on that job. A job analysis provided that information. The same is true of training programs. A particular form of analysis, called a *needs analysis,* tells us something about what will be expected of the training program. In the prediction context, once we know something about the job demands, we can consider the range of possible tests that might be used to identify potentially successful employees. In training, once a needs analysis has been completed, we can make a list of potentially valuable training approaches and devices that can be used to modify the knowledge structures, skilled performance, or attitudes of the trainee. Finally, we field test a predictor in order to determine its general utility by carrying out a validity study. In training, we use a particular method of collecting data that enables us to evaluate the effectiveness of the training intervention. In short, just as selection is aimed at developing some primitive theory of performance on the job in question, so too is training based on an elementary performance theory. Figure 9–1 describes the process by which this performance theory is proposed and evaluated.

The process begins with a needs assessment. This assessment provides a set of objectives for the training program. These objectives might include adding knowledge, developing specific skills, or helping to form attitudes. These objectives then play a dual role. First, they provide hints with respect to what learning principles and training devices should be included in the training program. In addition, the objectives become targets or methods for determining which aspect of the training was successful. In its simplest form, the goal of a training program is to meet the objectives identified in the needs assessment. In order to assess accurately the impact of the training, we usually need to know something about the status of the trainee *before* training took place. Thus, we need some pretraining information. In addition, after training has been completed, we need some posttraining information. Finally, since training is directed toward job performance, we need some information that addresses the extent to which the training transferred to on-the-job behavior.

---

[1]The important distinction between *performance* and *learning* should be kept in mind. Performance refers to observable, measurable behavior from which learning is *inferred.* However, changes (or lack of changes) in performance do not always accurately reflect the status of learning or the *ability* of the individual to perform.

FIGURE 9–1 An Instruction System

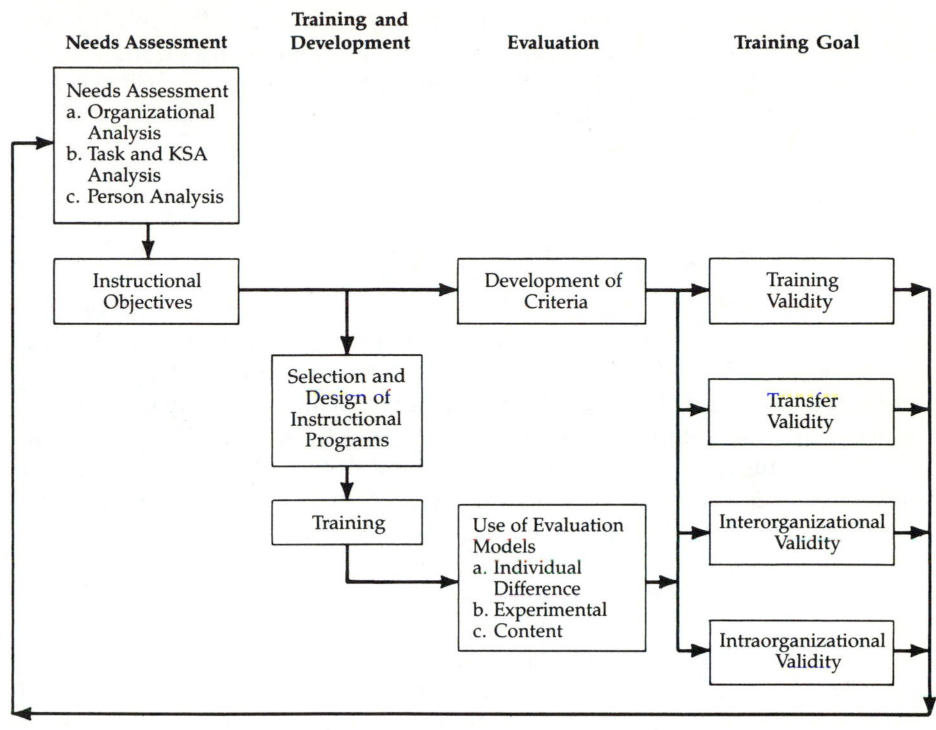

SOURCE: From *Training in Organizations* (2nd ed.) (Fig. 2–1, p. 16) by I. L. Goldstein, 1986, Monterey, CA: Brooks-Cole.

These, then, are the topics that compose the training area: learning, training program development, training devices and strategies, and training evaluation. Let's begin our consideration of training with needs assessment, since this process provides the initial impetus for considering a training program.

DETERMINING TRAINING NEEDS

Needs Analysis

As you could see in the newspaper article on pilot errors, the impetus for training is usually an identification of a need for improvement. In most work settings, the process of needs assessment is poorly understood. This is unfortunate since the care with which needs assessment is carried out will have strong implications for the eventual success of any training that is instituted. To most managers, needs assessment means telling the personnel department that there are production problems and maybe some people "need" training. Although such a statement may be the motivational foundation for needs assessment, it is hardly the substance of such a process. Needs assessment consists of three separate components: organizational analysis, task analysis, and person or worker analysis. We will consider each of these three components individually.

Organizational Analysis

Organizational analysis consists of an examination of the organizational goals, resources, and environment (Goldstein & Buxton, 1982). Goals include such things as quality, quantity, timeliness, and image. They are broad controlling influences. For example, one of the goals of a police department might be to reduce crime. Another goal might be to encourage safe behavior by motorists. Although these goals are not incompatible, they need to be recognized as separate in order to determine if they can be met through police officer training and, if resources (i.e., time and money) are scarce, which goal may be more important. In our newspaper article, it may not be apparent that delayed flights are creating public relations problems for airlines and that the airlines have put pressure on pilots and ground crews personnel to keep flights on time. This pressure might lead to shortcuts, and these shortcuts might lead to safety lapses. Similarly, in many nuclear power plants, there is pressure to keep the plants on-line and producing energy. This pressure often leads operators to ignore or reinterpret safety guidelines for plant operation. These examples point out the fact that in conducting a needs analysis stimulated by a "problem" of some kind, we should not ignore the influence of organizational goals (real *and* perceived) on the behavior of employees. Maybe they simply learned the wrong set of priorities.

There is a political flavor to some aspects of organizational analysis. If a training program does seem warranted, it is at this stage that agreements are (or should be) made with respect to what is expected from the training. Unless there is some discussion of the definition of what will be considered success and what will be considered failure of the training program, disputes about the value of the training (i.e., whether it "worked") are almost inevitable. As an example, in the late 1960s, the job corps program was introduced and targeted to the underemployed. Its broad purpose was to prevent the appearance of a new generation of hard-core unemployed citizens. After a few years of operation, there was a good deal of disagreement about whether the program was working. The program became a political football for the Democrats and Republicans, and they kicked it around vigorously. The reason it could be kicked around so easily was that there had been no agreement before the fact with respect to what would be considered "success."

Another interesting "political" aspect of organizational analysis can be the underlying motivations of the parties involved. In one organization with which I worked, a middle-level line manager suggested that production workers needed some training to improve the quality of the product and asked for some help in establishing a training program. A first-level supervisor of these employees heard of the training project and began developing a training program of his own. He also asked for help in developing this program. In working with these two individuals, I had the distinct impression that the first-level supervisor was operating from a "me, too" perspective. He felt that he was being indirectly criticized through the mere suggestion of training and felt strongly that he should be responsible for training, not the middle-level manager. This is an interesting situation because it highlights the fact that training is an intervention that must be viewed in the broader perspective of organizational structure and dynamics. The very process of training created a tension that had not been present before.

In addition to other organizational concerns, consideration should be given to the climate in which the trainee will be expected to perform. Safety training is a good example of the climate issue. In many settings, safe behavior (e.g., wearing ear protectors or safety glasses, using machine guards of various kinds) is looked down on as being "sissy" behavior. If that is the case, it is unlikely that any training will be effective until and unless attitudes are changed among members of the work group. Similarly, a manager may attend a training course that encourages her to adopt a new leadership style. When she returns to her home work setting, she may try out the new style and find that her subordinates are uneasy or uncomfortable with this new approach. They may make comments or give subtle hints that they want her to return to her old (more predictable) style. If she complies and reverts back to earlier styles, the effect of training will have been canceled out by an environment that would not accept change. It is important to consider what the environment or climate will allow from the trainee.

Task Analysis

The next level of needs assessment is a consideration of the actual duties and responsibilities that compose the job title(s) under consideration. The question being considered here has to do with performance standards. What skills, knowledges, or attitudes may be necessary for successful performance of the job duties being considered? This type of information is usually provided by a job analysis. As you remember from Chapter 4, a job analysis will identify the most important or frequently performed job duties. It answers the question, What is expected of someone with this job title? Consider a portion of a job analysis of a fire fighter that appears in Figure 9–2. As you can see, there are specific descriptions of behaviors that compose the fire fighter job. In this particular job analysis, there were over 200 such statements. As a group, these statements represent a task analysis of the job of fire fighter. They represent skills that may become part of the formal training program. In fact, virtually every fire academy training program would have specific components that would address each of these tasks.

FIGURE 9–2 Some Fire-Fighting Tasks

I. *Fire fighting*. Operates and advances charged hose lines, master stream appliances, and fire extinguishers from defensive positions or while advancing toward the fire area in order to extinguish the fire, while wearing full turnout gear.

I 1. Observes fire and smoke conditions, locates source of fire and applies knowledge of heat and fluid mechanics to anticipate fire behavior.

I 2. Operates hand lines (1 in. booster, 1¾ in. or 2 in. fabric or plastic) with straight stream or fog nozzles from a stationary position.

I 3. Advances and operates charged hand lines with straight stream or fog nozzles toward or into fire area.

I 4. Operates master stream appliances on the ground, from aerial ladders, or from elevating platforms.

I 5. Identifies and screens or saturates potential exposures using solid or fog streams.

I 6. Operates any class of fire extinguisher.

I 7. Operates deck gun from apparatus.

Person Analysis

The third aspect of needs assessment is a person or worker analysis. The question to be answered here is, Who should receive training? The answer to this question might seem obvious. There are two potential groups. The first group consists of those currently on the job who may be performing below expectation or standard on one or more tasks. The second group consists of individuals who are about to perform the job for the first time. Let's consider each of these groups separately.

Current Incumbents. The most obvious method for identifying performance weaknesses is performance evaluation. If the performance of individuals is evaluated with sufficient frequency and in sufficient detail, it should be possible to pinpoint areas of substandard performance that may be suitable for improvement through training. For example, the call for training of pilots working for Delta airlines in the newspaper article implies that all pilots need training. Perhaps it is only a subgroup of pilots who have a problem.

The simple identification of substandard performance does not necessarily answer the question of whether the performance deficiency is peculiar to one individual or a universal problem among employees. Further, it is not always clear if the problem is best solved through training or through a different type of intervention. In looking at performance problems, three aspects of the behavior should be considered. Kelley (1967) has labeled these aspects *consistency, consensus,* and *distinctiveness*. Consistency means that the performance problem is chronic rather than temporary—for example, have these

F.A.A. Opens Inquiry into Delta's Pilot Training

By Richard Witkin

Citing pilot error as a factor in a recent string of near accidents involving Delta Air Lines, the Federal Aviation Administration announced yesterday that it had begun a special investigation of the airline, with initial emphasis on pilot training and procedures.

Robert E. Whittington, acting head of the agency, said there was "no obvious pattern or link" among the incidents. But, he said, "Each incident apparently involved human error and this is a matter of great concern to us, as I'm sure it is to Delta."

Officials made it clear that the decisive event leading to the investigation was a near-collision over the North Atlantic on July 8 in which a Delta jumbo jet flew 60 miles off course and missed another westbound jumbo by less than 100 feet. One focus of the inquiry will be long-range navigation procedures that are used not only by Delta but by all airlines crossing both the Atlantic and Pacific.

The announcement of the special inquiry listed three other Delta incidents. In the first, late last month, a Delta jet descended to just 600 feet over the Pacific Ocean after the pilot inadvertently shut off both of the plane's engines. On July 7, a Delta jet landed at an airport 19 miles from its intended destination on a flight to Kentucky. And Sunday night, a Delta jet landed on the wrong runway at Boston's Logan International Airport.

Yesterday's announcement said that it would take three to six weeks to gather data on the incidents and that preliminary results should be available within 90 days.

Delta has said that all the incidents were isolated events and that there were no systemic safety problems at the airline.

The head of the F.A.A. division in charge of the inquiry, Anthony J. Broderick, an associate administrator, said in an interview that it would be a mistake to look at Delta in isolation.

"I'm confident," he said, "that what Delta has seen is an unusual cluster of incidents that doesn't reflect on the performance of the airline."

Mr. Broderick said a parallel effort was under way to determine what regulations might have been violated in the near-collision over the ocean and what enforcement actions his agency might take. He said the agency was "moving quite quickly" to gather information on the actions taken by the two crews directly involved and by the crews of other planes in the area.

Experts said the most likely explanation for the Delta plane straying off course was that the crew might have inserted the wrong latitude in the computerized navigation system automatically guiding their aircraft.

In the incident a Delta L-1011 passed just beneath a Continental Airlines Boeing 747. Government and industry officials have made critical comments on several aspect of the episode, including these:

- One or more pilots of the several airliners in the immediate area suggested in radio conversation that the incident not be reported.

(continued)

F.A.A. Opens Inquiry into Delta's Pilot Training—*(concluded)*

- All the pilots apparently failed to notify traffic controllers, who had no radar coverage of the over-ocean area, that the Delta jet was off course.
- Some of the pilots involved took unorthodox actions to help guide the Delta crew back to their proper course.

The Continental crew rejected the idea of hushing up the incident and eventually reported it to their own company and the aviation agency. The crew of an Air Force version of the Boeing 707, which was nearby and listening to the radio conversations, took steps to preserve the exchanges on a cockpit tape recorder. The Air Force has so far refused to make the tape available or provide a transcript.

The special inquiry into all the recent Delta incidents was welcomed by the airline.

"We want them here," said Jim Ewing, a Delta spokesman. "If they find something, we'll listen. We feel confident in our program."

The assistant vice president for flight operations, Harry C. Alger, sent a letter to all Delta pilots on Tuesday.

He said that Delta had amassed the best safety record in the industry. But he said that the recent incidents "reinforce the fact that we are only human and that by learning from our mistakes we can build on an even stronger foundation and work ethic."

In this regard, Mr. Alger concluded, management was immediately "initiating two programs to insure the necessary feedback." First, an oversight committee of selected pilots will conduct "an extensive internal audit of our line operations." Second, a safety review team will be formed to look at the recent chain of incidents to determine the causes and make recommendations.

SOURCE: *New York Times,* July 16, 1988, p. A16.

same Delta pilots been making these errors for years? In other words, does the individual in question *always* make the same mistake? Consensus relates to the extent to which many people have the same problem. Is it only this one employee, or is it anyone who holds this job—for example, do *all* pilots make these errors, and the Delta pilots were simply the most recent or obvious? Distinctiveness gets at the generality of the performance problem. Does it involve many different aspects of performance, or is it only one particular task? The answer to these questions has important implications for the introduction of a training program. For example, if the problem has never occurred before and is peculiar to this one person, you might simply monitor it for a while and see if it might correct itself. The correct approach might be to do nothing. If the problem is chronic and many people with similar jobs have the same problem, you might consider formal group training. In this situation, an alternative to training might be job redesign. It might be that a particular task is incompatible with another task or a particular work environment. It might be something as simple as moving a dispatcher's desk closer to a loading dock or providing an accounts clerk with a microcomputer or changing a shipping date from a Monday to a preceding Friday. The point is that it is not always appropriate to assume that a "problem" is the result of individual factors (either skill or motivational). The three issues of consistency, consensus, and distinctiveness should be considered part of a person analysis.

New Incumbents. Training current incumbents and training new incumbents are likely to be very different processes. A training program developed to solve the performance problems of an experienced worker may be useless in developing skill, knowledge, or attitudes in new incumbents. For one thing, training new incumbents usually involves providing opportunities for new learning. Training experienced incumbents who are having performance difficulties usually involves eliminating old habits that are competing with new ones. In other words, in addition to learning, the experienced incumbent often has to *unlearn*.

Similarly, many skills may be picked up in the course of performing the job. There are very few jobs that do not foster the development of techniques as the job is being performed. It is difficult to train a gas station attendant how to pump gas into three different cars at the same time while simultaneously checking oil, washing windshields, and engaging in small talk. Nevertheless, most good attendants learn how to do just this. They develop a sense of time so that they know when approximately 10 gallons of gas has gone into one car through the automatic nozzle. They learn to move back and forth among the three customers so that each feels some sense of personal attention. It would be fruitless to try and train this type of behavior. It comes with experience and exposure to job demands. On the other hand, the use of certain equipment (e.g., gas pump, tire pressure gauge) or a fixed knowledge base (e.g., position of hood latches, the correct method for checking antifreeze levels) can be a valuable part of a training program for the new employee. It is important to distinguish between those things that belong in a training program and those things that do not.

Demographic Analysis

In a recent review of the training literature, Latham (1988) suggests an additional level of analysis. He points out that many recent research articles have identified training needs peculiar to demographic subgroups of employees such as women, Hispanics, or older employees. He provides the following examples of demographic needs analysis:

1. A survey by Tucker (1985) in a federal agency discovered that workers between ages 40–49 desired training in management skills, workers between 50–59 wanted training in technological areas, and workers older than 60 wanted no training at all.
2. Bernick, Kindley, and Pettit (1984) found that first-level supervisors sought training in technical areas such as record keeping and written communications, middle-level managers wanted human resources training (e.g., leadership and motivation), and upper-level managers sought conceptual courses such as those dealing with goal-setting procedures and planning skills.
3. Berryman-Fink (1985) contrasted the training needs of male and female managers and found that survey respondents identified areas such as assertiveness, confidence building, public speaking, and dealing with males as most important for female managers, whereas their male counterparts seemed more in need of training in listening, verbal skills, nonverbal communication, empathy, and sensitivity.

One other study deserves mention in this section. Gordon, Cofer, and McCullough (1986) examined the relationship between seniority and trainability and discovered something interesting. In a sample of 106 textile workers, there was no relationship between seniority and trainability (after controlling for age). In fact, there was a slight tendency for those with more seniority to take longer in the training program. On the other hand, those with higher levels of on-the-job performance tended to be better trainees. Thus, one additional candidate for demographic consideration and analysis might be seniority.

The theme that comes out of these four examples is that there may be some broad skill areas that are appropriate for training programs presented to subgroups of employees identified by demographic characteristics.

Learning Objectives

On the basis of a task, person, or demographic analysis, it should be possible to specify some objectives or goals for the training program. What skills, behaviors, knowledges, or attitudes would you like the trainee to have after training that she did not have before training? Objectives are important for several reasons. In the first place, they represent information for both the trainer and the trainee about what is to be learned. In addition, they represent motivational forces. As you will learn in Chapter 10, goals exert a force on an individual. This helps to direct and sustain energy expenditure. Finally, learning objectives allow one to evaluate when training has been completed successfully. If a training goal is to develop the skill necessary to grind a piece of metal to a specified thickness, it should be easy enough to determine when that goal has been achieved.

Learning objectives come in many different forms. One major distinction is between the objectives that might be set for an individual who has been identified as substandard in his work performance and a new employee who is being trained for a job she never did before. Performance improvement objectives are usually tailored to the specific deficiencies of the incumbent. They are often negotiated with the trainee as a result of a performance appraisal. For example, a supervisor may agree to take a company course in machine maintenance, to audit a course offered at a local university in time management, and to complete a programmed instruction booklet related to first-aid treatment of chemical burns. In each instance, the objective is to acquire knowledge.

A SUMMARY STATEMENT

A training program should not be considered until a needs assessment has been completed. It is important to determine what the organizational training goals are and what the definition(s) of training success will be. It is important to know exactly what tasks are to be addressed in the training program. It is important to know who will take part in training and what should be done to tailor training to their particular needs. Once a needs assessment has been accomplished, the probability of introducing an *effective* training program is greatly enhanced.

Now that we have considered the needs assessment phase of training program development, we are faced with the problem of developing a training program that will bring about change in the trainee. In other words, we want the trainee to learn new skills or develop new attitudes or knowledge bases. In order to do this, we must have some appreciation for alternative learning approaches and principles that may help in training program development.

LEARNING THEORY AND LEARNING PRINCIPLES

Theory and principles are not the same thing. For one thing, they can exist independently. I may have a theory of electromagnetic action. In addition to or instead of that theory, I may have a principle that instructs me not to put my finger into light sockets. The same is true of learning theory and learning principles. In the course of examining possible learning theories, certain principles have been identified that seem conducive to efficient learning. For example, one principle is that in order to learn a person must *want* to learn. I do not necessarily need a theory to apply or appreciate the principle. Nevertheless, a theory might help me to apply the principle more efficiently. In the course of 100 years of learning research, several reasonable principles of efficient learning have been identified. First, we will consider the basic learning approaches or theories that might be usefully examined in a discussion of training. Then, we will briefly consider some specific principles that can make training more efficient.

Associationist Approaches to Learning

Classical Conditioning. There have been two basic variations of the associationist approach to learning. The first variation, called *classical conditioning,* assumes that the learner is passive and notices a connection between two stimuli. The first stimulus, called the *unconditioned* stimulus, has the capacity to elicit a particular response through its own power. For example, touching a hot radiator has an immediate result—discomfort. Once you touch a hot radiator, you are not likely to do it again voluntarily. The second stimulus is initially neutral and is called the *conditioned* stimulus. It assumes power from its association with the unconditioned stimulus. After many pairings of the two stimuli, the conditioned stimulus assumes the same response-eliciting properties as the unconditioned stimulus. Thus, it may be that every time you have had an interaction with the plant manager, you have been criticized. If criticism is the unconditioned stimulus (it makes you feel bad), this particular plant manager stands a good chance of becoming a conditioned stimulus (since she is the vehicle for the criticism). Furthermore, the association may spread beyond *this* plant manager to *any* plant manager. Keep in mind, however, that the learner is simply exposed to the association. No active response is required for learning to occur.

There is a good deal of both intentional and accidental classical conditioning in typical training programs. Trainers are often attempting to teach the trainee to relax or feel confident or even feel apprehensive in certain situations. In many police training programs, trainees are exposed to numerous situations that at first seem harmless but are actually life-threatening. The purpose of this exposure is to make the recruit feel uneasy and on guard in even apparently harmless situations. The fear is that if the officer is not constantly alert to danger, harm or death could result. Another example of this principle can be seen in maintenance training of nuclear power plant operators. This training often occurs at a simulation location constructed to be as much like a real control room as possible. A control room crew is given a problem to solve, and they are observed dealing with that problem. For example, the problem might be a leak in the cooling system. The crew might spend 25 minutes bringing the leak under control through the manipulation of valves and the reduction of power levels in the simulated plant. Just as they are calming down after stopping the leak, the person in charge of the simulation might throw in another emergency such as a rapidly increasing core temperature. The trainer wants the trainee to remember that the plant is a dynamic environment and that there is never a time when you can "relax."

Control room. (Philadelphia Electric Co.)

Simulated control room. (Philadelphia Electric Co.)

In addition to intentional conditioning, accidental learning can also occur without direct response by the learner. Virtually every aspect of the training program is a candidate for "conditioned stimulus" status. If a trainer is cruel or demanding, negative associations might easily be formed to the personnel department generally, or to all training programs, or even to sitting in classrooms. These associations may very well become obstacles in future situations. Many young adults experience anxiety in mathematics classes as a result of past failures and criticism in solving number problems. This anxiety, in turn, prevents effective use of skills and abilities. Failure in an earlier training program or exercise may very well inhibit performance in a current training program.

Operant Conditioning. A second associationist approach assumes that the learner plays an active role in the learning process. Instead of associating two stimulus variables, the operant approach proposes that learning results from the association between responses and rewards. The learner notices that a reward occurs shortly after a particular response. In order to get the reward again, the learner attempts to reproduce the response that originally led to the reward. Operant conditioning is really a complex technology. It involves such variables as the amount of the reward, the rate of reward (called the *reward* or *reinforcement schedule*), the time between the response and the reward, and the complexity of the behavior that composes the response.

The primary advocate of operant conditioning has been B. F. Skinner, although many have joined his ranks since he introduced the principles of behaviorism over 40 years ago (Skinner, 1938). The importance of rewards in training programs is a generally accepted learning principle that follows directly from the propositions of operant conditioning. In addition to the rather obvious value of rewarding trainees for new insights or skill levels, operant conditioning has played a major role in modifying the behavior of people on the job who are not enrolled in any formal training program.

As an example, in an industrial setting the time in obtaining customer request information was markedly reduced by having employees self-monitor the time elapsed between the request and the completion of the task (Emery Air Freight Corporation, 1971). In the same setting, a similar technique was used to gain a 100-percent increase in the efficiency in use of containers for air freight shipments. This latter application was estimated to have resulted in savings of $125,000 per month.

Similar results were obtained in a program that utilized operant conditioning techniques to increase the punctuality of six chronically tardy workers (Herman, De Montes, Dominquez, Montes, & Hopkins, 1973). Tardiness was reduced from a baseline of 15 percent to 2 percent under the treatment program.

By our earlier definition, these applications of operant conditioning methods qualify as training programs. The intervention was planned to modify permanently the behavior of organizational members and bring them into line with the requirements of the job. In general, whenever specific rewards and punishments are applied in the hope of modifying a particular employee behavior or introducing a new skill or knowledge base, we can assume that this was an attempt at training. As you will see in later chapters, the principles of operant conditioning play a major role in many areas of industrial behavior.

Cognitive and Social Learning Approaches

In both classical and operant conditioning, the recognition of and memory for associations is the most important part of the learning process. The associations may be between stimulus elements (classical) or between responses and rewards or punishments (operant). Many learning researchers feel that, at least with humans, there is a lot more to learning than simple associations. They feel that there are cognitive or mental operations well beyond simple memory for associations that must be part of the learning process. These mental activities would include such things as reasoning, concept formation, imagination, and judgment.

What are some of the implications of the cognitive approach for training? For one thing, it means that instructions to learn can be quite effective. If we ask trainees to pay attention to some specific aspect of the learning situation, they will learn faster than if they had not received those instructions. The important point here is that we can instruct the trainees using words and symbols. It is not necessary to provide practice trials. Similarly, training itself depends heavily on the symbolic representation and manipulation of critical concepts. When a trainee in an electronics repair program studies a schematic diagram, she is dealing with an abstract version of a real system—an idea, not a thing.

One very popular form of cognitive learning theory has been proposed by Albert Bandura (1969). It is called *social learning theory*, and it stresses the interactions among individuals as opportunities for learning. In addition to concepts such as memory and reasoning and judgment, Bandura includes processes such as motivation and emotion and changing levels of self-esteem in his learning approach. Simply put, Bandura suggests that there are many different ways in which we learn other than by doing. One of those ways is watching. He proposes that we often observe others perform an action and rehearse those actions mentally until we have an opportunity to try them. When we actually try to perform the action, we compare our action to the memory of that action as performed by others. On the basis of this comparison, we make any corrections necessary. It is common for new employees to be paired with a more experienced employee for some period of time to "learn the ropes." Learning the ropes typically means watching the experienced employee perform the tasks that constitute the job. There is an opportunity for questioning by the new employee, and often the experienced employee will point out certain things that are critical to success or not obvious to the casual observer. There is no unconditioned stimulus involved. There is no overt response on the part of the trainee. Instead, there is memory, reasoning, judgment, insight, and an increasing confidence provided by increased knowledge.

An interesting example of a social learning approach is one taken by Ross and Geller (in press) to train bartenders to detect patrons who were drinking too much and to intervene to reduce possible abuse and later problems with operating a vehicle. The training program included videotaped bar scenes, discussions, and role-playing sessions. All the trainees were real bartenders. After the training program, "pseudopatrons" (assistants to the experimenter) went to bars that were being tended by both those who were trained and those who had not taken part in training (the control group). The pseudopatrons did not announce their identity. The results demonstrated that the trained bartenders acted differently from the untrained bartenders when the pseudopatrons began drinking at a rapid rate. As a consequence, the pseudopatrons who were being served by the trained bartenders reached a blood alcohol level significantly lower than those served by a control bartender. Naturally, the pseudopatrons were blind to the status of the bartender—that is, they did not know if the bartender had been trained or not.

Which Approach Is Correct?

In the past, it has been popular for one learning theory to be pitted against another in an attempt to identify *the* correct approach. For our purpose, this is a waste of time. All three approaches have something to offer in the training context. There is no doubt that associations (both intended and unintended) play a role in the training process. Opinions, attitudes, biases, and expectations may all be thought of as classically conditioned responses or associations. Similarly, actions by the trainee can be rewarded or punished. These rewards or punishments can be concrete (e.g., cash bonus for early completion of training modules) or abstract (e.g., being recognized as the "top" trainee). Knowledge of results can play an important role in learning as well. For some people, it is not only information; it also represents a form of reward for appropriate behavior. Finally, every one has, at one time or another, tried to imitate the action of a model in performing a new task. This is particularly true in tasks that involve social interaction and interpersonal communication. Recently, a five-year-old boy saved his sister from choking to death on a piece of food by using the Heimlich maneuver. When asked how he knew what to do, he responded that he had seen the TV character Benson perform the action.

On the other hand, to say that *each* model or approach is "correct" is to obscure another more important point. Certain aspects of training may be more amenable to the principles of one approach rather than another. In other words, it may be easier to learn a given behavior using one particular theoretical orientation. As an example, operant conditioning principles suggest that learning steps should be small and become increasingly more complex. If part of the training program involves learning a set of rules or guidelines for equipment repair, it may be that a workbook and training module based on operant principles is the best approach. If, on the other hand, the task to be learned is how to provide counseling to a problem employee, then a social learning approach involving the observation of a model who performs the action correctly might be called for. As you will see in a later section dealing with training techniques, many of these techniques have their anchors in one or another of these basic approaches.

One of the most serious problems in training research has been the absence of any guiding principles or theoretical orientations in the development of training programs or devices (Campbell, 1971; Goldstein, 1980, 1986; Goldstein & Buxton, 1982). It is this atheoretical tendency that permits and encourages the appearance of fads and superficial training intervention that are expensive but useless. Something to keep in mind when a new training device or program appears is its relationship to any known learning theory. If it can be linked to an associationist or cognitive theory, it may have promise. If it has no theoretical roots or links, it is less likely to be valuable. For example, videotape devices can be shown to have links to social learning theory; teaching machines and programmed instruction have links to operant conditioning. Training based on listening to simple inspirational tape recordings is not closely linked to any particular theory of learning, and the expected outcome of this type of training is less clear. The point is that the greater the number of links between a training approach and an established theory of learning, the more valuable it is likely to be.

APPLICATIONS OF THE SOCIAL LEARNING APPROACH

As I implied above, many jobs include tasks involving interpersonal skills. These are the types of skills not easily learned by rote memorization of textual material. They require practice and self-confidence. In the last decade, there has been a good deal of experimentation with the social learning approach to teaching interpersonal skills, particularly to first-level managers. The application of the social learning principles to industrial training has been labeled the *behavioral modeling technique* (Goldstein & Sorcher, 1974). Instead of the haphazard pairing of the new and old employee implied by the "rub-off" model, behavioral modeling carefully sequences and controls the nature of the observation done by the trainee. A typical training sequence would involve observing the target behavior portrayed on film or videotape, rehearsing the behavior using a role-playing technique, receiving feedback on the rehearsal, and finally trying the behavior out on the job. Throughout the sequence, there is a strong emphasis on social reinforcement from trainees and eventually supervisors for appropriate behavior.

Kraut (1976) has identified another characteristic that distinguishes behavioral modeling from more traditional approaches. The traditional training model assumes the trainee is first presented with a theory of behavior to change attitudes and values. These changed attitudes and values presumably lead to changes in behavior, that, in turn, lead to superior results. In contrast, behavioral modeling teaches new behavior through observation, role playing, and practice. This new behavior, in turn, leads to superior results. The superior results change attitudes and values and encourage an understanding of the theory that explains the effectiveness of the new behaviors.

The research supporting this approach has been encouraging. Both the General Electric Corporation and IBM have devoted extensive time and resources to the examination of behavioral modeling training for first- and second-level supervisors. General Electric trained 2,700 first-line supervisors to deal with typical employee problems using the behavioral modeling approach and, as a result of the success of the training, developed a similar program for 1,200 middle-level managers (Burnaska, 1976). In an evaluation of this training, Burnaska examined differences between 62 managers who had been trained using behavioral modeling and 62 control managers who had received no training. Each group participated in role-playing exercises, and trainees were rated on various interpersonal skills by judges who did not know which participants had received training. The role playing was done both one month and four months after training. The analysis of the comparison showed that the trained group was rated higher in interpersonal skills by the judges than the control group. In addition, this difference *increased* from the one-month observation to the four-month observation, suggesting that the skills acquired in training improved with practice.

Moses and Ritchie (1976) examined the effect of behavior modeling training on first-level supervisors in various telephone companies that were part of American Telephone & Telegraph (AT&T). Two months after supervisors had been trained in interpersonal relations, both trainees and a control group of supervisors who had not experienced training were brought into an assessment center for evaluation. The assessment center was similar to the typical one described in Chapter 6. In this context, supervisors were asked to deal with three problems: absenteeism, discrimination against minority employees, and a theft case. Judges who were unfamiliar with both the training program and the subjects in the study rated supervisors on the way they handled the three situations. There were clear differences in favor of the group that received the behavioral modeling training.

In another study, Latham and Saari (1979) randomly assigned 40 first-line supervisors to either a behavior modeling training group or a control group. The training group received instruction in dealing with typical supervisor-subordinate problem areas such as the orientation of a new employee, the discussion of poor work habits, or the handling of a complaining employee. The training consisted of a film dealing with the particular problem, a group discussion of the behavior of the role model in the film, practice in imitating the behavior of the model, and feedback on the effectiveness of this imitation. There were nine consecutive weekly sessions, each lasting two hours.

Not all results have been uniformly positive. For example, Russell, Wexley, and Hunter (1984) found that behavioral modeling did seem to have an influence on attitudes and learning but did not actually change the behavior of trainees at the workplace. They suggest that this is because additional forces are necessary for behavior change—there must be the possibility of reward or punishment related to the trained behavior. In other words, if I learn a behavior in a training program and if my supervisor expects me to exhibit that behavior when I come back to the workplace, the chances are good that I will. On the other hand, if no one knows or cares that I was in a training program and I can do my job just as easily without exhibiting the behavior as I can with the behavior, then it is unlikely that I will exhibit the behavior. Performance evaluation and feedback is a good example. If I have never engaged in this behavior before with my subordinates, why should I start now? It will take time, it will annoy some subordinates, and it may result in some complaints to my supervisor. On the other hand, if my supervisor is looking for changes in my behavior as a result of the week seminar in performance techniques that I attended and will consider these changes when evaluating my performance, the chances are greater that I will try out this new behavior pattern.

A recent study by Hogan, Hakel, and Decker (1986) identified another interesting aspect of behavioral modeling procedures that might help explain some failures of behavioral modeling. As described above, most behavioral modeling programs present the trainee with opportunities to observe and apply certain rules that should govern a particular situation. If the material to be learned relates to performance feedback, the trainee might be told to apply rules such as "discuss behavior and not traits" or "permit the subordinate to explain various aspects of below average performance." Traditionally, these rules have been developed by the person who developed the rest of the training program. Hogan et al. decided to let a group of trainees (experimental group) derive the rules themselves from watching the behavior performed correctly and contrast the efficiency of learning with a group of trainees (control group). One week after training, both groups were given a practical test of application of the training material. The group that derived the rules for themselves performed significantly better on that test. Hogan et al. propose that this was the result of more efficient memory by the experimental group. It was suggested that since the experimental group derived the rules themselves, the rules and the material that the rules represented were encoded in memory in a more substantial way. This is based on work done by Craik and Lockhart (1972), a pair of cognitive psychologists who developed a memory model called the *depth-of-processing model.* The results of the Hogan et al. study are interesting because they suggest that the behavioral modeling training model can be enhanced with a modest change in technique.

You might wonder about what could be done if the trainees can't derive the rules. Hogan et al. suggest that if worse comes to worse, give the trainees the rules but have them reword or restate those rules. It is assumed that this will force the development of a cognitive structure and assist in remembering the rules at a later time.

It is often difficult to describe the effectiveness of a training program or approach because no formal evaluation was done. The Latham and Saari study described above is a refreshing exception. They considered four different measures of training effectiveness: (a) the reactions of the learners, (b) a posttraining test of supervisory principles, (c) behavioral measures consisting of tape-recorded role-playing sessions by the trainees, and (d) supervisory ratings of the trainees one month and one year after training. The initial reaction of the trainees to the modeling training was very positive. If anything, this positive attitude increased over the eight months following training. A comparison of the training and control group supervisors on a test of supervisory skill showed that those supervisors who had had the training received significantly higher scores than the control supervisors. Both trainee and control supervisors were asked to engage in a role-playing exercise related to the problems addressed in the training program several months after the completion of training. Judges rated the trained supervisors significantly higher than the control supervisors on the quality of the solutions. Finally, one year after training, supervisors of the training and control group members rated them on a series of behaviorally anchored scales. Once again, the training group was given significantly higher ratings than the control group. It is interesting to note that the organization in which this training was done was highly committed to the training program and had made it clear to the trainees that they were expected to apply this training back at the workplace. When they returned to the workplace, their behavior was monitored closely. This was exactly the facilitating environment that Russell et al. (1984) identified as resulting in behavioral change.

At this point, there are still too few careful studies of the outcomes associated with behavioral modeling. In addition, there are even fewer studies that *compare* the outcomes of behavioral modeling and other approaches. Such comparison should include cost-benefit analyses as well since behavioral modeling can be quite expensive, particularly for smaller organizations. For those reasons, it is inappropriate to label behavioral modeling an unqualified "success." Nevertheless, the available empirical data plus the strong ties to a well-established theoretical approach make the approach appealing. Future research should concentrate on comparisons with other techniques and an investigation of which training goals or objectives are best served by behavioral modeling. A recent review by Latham (1988) of the training literature emphasizes the role of feelings of competence (self-efficacy) in social learning and concludes that a combination of goal setting and behavioral modeling–social learning is an effective training approach. So far, the data seem to support such a conclusion.

LEARNING PRINCIPLES: TRANSFER OF TRAINING

On the basis of research that has been conducted on the various theories of learning outlined above, certain rules or guidelines have emerged with regard to efficient learning. These principles can be found in any basic learning textbook (e.g., Bower & Hilgard, 1981; Hall, 1982). They include such things as breaking learning sessions into small units rather than lumping all the training together (called the *principle of distributed practice*), reinforcing the learner for correct responses, training individuals to perform entire task units as a whole if the subtasks are organized and interrelated, providing learners with knowledge of results with respect to training performance, and providing opportunities for practicing the skills developed during training.

By far, the most important training issue from the learning perspective is that of transfer of training. When training experts speak of transfer of training, they are usually concerned with whether the knowledge, skills, or attitudes learned in the training situation will be available and utilized "back on the job." This is, of course, a critical issue in the evaluation of the utility of a training program. There is little value in training that does not carry over to the job situation. Transfer of training is evaluated as the extent to which the newly acquired knowledge or skill—that is, behavioral change—is evident in the posttraining performance. Sometimes transfer is easy, and sometimes it is difficult. Goldstein (1986) suggests that the ease or difficulty of transfer depends to some extent on how the new behavior (that behavior to be learned) differs from the old behavior. In addition, the similarity between new and old concepts and new and old environments will also affect transfer. Table 9–2 illustrates these principles. Transfer of training would be considerably easier to affect in situations described near the top of the table and would become increasingly difficult as one moved down toward the bottom of that table.

Wexley and Latham (1980) considered the issue of transfer of training in industrial situations. They provide the following suggestions for increasing the probability of transfer:

1. Maximize the similarity between the training situation and the job situation.
2. Provide as much experience as possible with the task being taught.
3. Provide for a variety of examples when teaching concepts or skills.
4. Label or identify important features of a task.
5. Make sure that general principles are understood.
6. Make sure that the trained behaviors and ideas are rewarded in the job situation.
7. Design the training content so that the trainees can see its applicability.

The Wexley-Latham suggestions represent only one of many schemes that might be applied to the development of a training strategy, but they are

TABLE 9–2 Examples of Changes in Job Methods, Content, and Context as a Function of Changes in Jobs

Methods Used (tasks, activity)	*Content Domain (concepts, objects acted upon)*	*Context (work situation)*	*Examples*
Same	Same	Same	a. Change in rank from Junior Programmer to Programmer to Senior Programmer. b. Change in rank from Associate Professor to Professor. c. Clerk-Steno III to Secretary I.
Same	Same	Different	a. Design Engineer for government research to Design Engineer for consumer product production, same employer. b. Navy Cook (retired) to Institutional Cook (civilian).
Same	Different	Different	a. Aerospace Systems Analyst for training requirements of new equipment to Systems Analyst for Public Vocational Education Systems. b. Medical Secretary to Legal Secretary. c. Business Data Programmer to Scientific Data Programmer.
Same	Different	Same	a. Secondary English Teacher to Secondary Social Studies Teacher. b. Flying Instructor (single-engine prop) to Flying Instructor (2-engine jet). c. Truck Driver (light panel) to Truck Driver (heavy tractor-trailer).
Different	Same	Same	a. Skilled Craftsman to Foreman. b. Secondary Teacher to Assistant Principal.
Different	Different	Same	a. Progress upward through key rungs of career ladder, from Orderly to LPN to RN to MD Intern. b. Flight Engineer to Commercial Pilot. c. Bricklayer (house construction) to Real Estate Agent.

SOURCE: From *Occupational Adaptability and Transferable Skills* (Information Series No. 129). Copyright 1978 by The National Center for Research in Vocational Education, Columbus, OH. Reprinted by permission.

TABLE 9–2 *(concluded)*

Methods Used (tasks, activity)	*Content Domain (concepts, objects acted upon)*	*Context (work situation)*	*Examples*
Different	Same	Different	a. Liberal Arts Major in Psychology to Salesman. b. Business Major to Auditor.
Different	Different	Different	a. Liberal Arts Major in Philosophy to Broker. b. Housewife to Riveter. c. Electronics Technician to Developmental Psychologist.

good suggestions that have firm anchors in instructional psychology. It would be a good idea to use them in evaluating a suggested training program or in planning your own program.

METHODS OF TRAINING

There are as many brand names for training programs as there are for cigarettes or laundry detergent. I will not catalog the brands. Instead, I will present some of the generic categories of training programs that can be used to sort through the various brands. I should, however, act as a "better business bureau" for a few seconds and mention "fads." Training is an area that seems more susceptible to gimmicks or fads than any other. Maybe it's because every manager intuitively believes that training of any kind is effective. You and I know that this type of overbroad generalization may be counterproductive (and often very expensive). A perfect case in point was the introduction of the "teaching machine." As you will see shortly, there is a legitimate place for a teaching machine in programmed instruction. The problem was that once a machine appeared, everyone wanted to use it to solve *his* training problem. As a result, virtually every problem was addressed using a teaching machine technology. This is a perfect example of a tail that wags a dog. In the late 1950s, the situation became so bad that Gilbert (1960) was provoked to offer the following advice:

> If you don't have a gadget called a teaching machine, don't get one. Don't buy one, don't borrow one, don't steal one; if you have such a gadget, get rid of it. Don't give it away, for someone else might use it. This is the most practical rule,

> based on empirical facts from considerable observation. If you begin with a device of any kind, you will try to develop a teaching program to fit that device.

Today a similar concern might be expressed concerning videotape. If a company training department has a videocassette device, it will inevitably be used in training programs dealing with everything from expanded employee benefits through tax accounting procedures. The devices used to support a program of training should be determined *after* training needs, target capabilities, and training models have been selected—not before. Now that I have finished with the consumer protection lecture, let's consider some general approaches that have been used in training.

In their extensive review of the literature and their survey of practices in managerial training, J. P. Campbell, Dunnette, Lawler, and Weick (1970) identified 22 different methods and techniques that were considered applicable to the training and development of managerial personnel. These techniques were categorized as (1) *information presentation techniques,* including the lecture, the conference or seminar, sensitivity training, laboratory education, systematic observation, closed-circuit television, programmed instruction, training by correspondence, motion pictures, and reading lists; (2) *simulation methods,* including the case method, the incident method, role playing, business games, the task model, and the in-basket technique; (3) *on-the-job training,* including job rotation, committee assignments (or junior executive boards), on-the-job coaching, and performance review.

I will not attempt to discuss each of these techniques. Some are well known or little used and need no further elaboration. Others, because they are novel or represent recent innovations in training technology, will be given more attention.

Information Presentation Techniques

Lectures, conference methods, correspondence courses, motion pictures, and reading lists are familiar methods in need of little further description. However, some attention will be given to them when we look at the research directed at evaluating methods.

Programmed Instruction. What characterizes programmed instruction is not the use of so-called teaching machines, since many instructional programs do not use machines at all, but instead are in a booklet form. The essence of programmed instruction is self-instruction through the use of tutorial devices without the direct participation of a human instructor. The learning materials are sequenced, together with questions and feedback of correct answers, in a way designed to provide optimum learning. Active involvement of the student in answering questions and systematic feedback at each point are characteristic. Also, the student typically is not allowed to progress beyond a point in the program until he shows evidence of having reached a criterion level of proficiency. Thus, each student may progress at his own rate; the slower learner is not allowed to fall behind, and the faster learner is not held up by a rate of instruction designed for the "average" learner. In Briggs's (1960) terms:

> In summary of the common features of all teaching machine [and other forms of programmed instruction], it may be said that they: (a) require of the student a series of responses to specially prepared materials and stimulus elements; (b) provide knowledge of the correctness or incorrectness of each overt response evoked; and (c) permit the individual student to proceed at his own rate (or at a specially computed rate) in order that each student may master the materials present. (p. 154)

Tutorial Models. Basically two different models of the tutorial instructional process are used in programmed instruction. The first of these has been labeled the *linear* or *compulsive tutor model* by Stolorow (1964). In this model, every trainee gets the same program in the same sequence. The basic assumption is the gradual modification of behavior through the systematic application of reinforcement (defined as the feedback of correct responses), that is, knowledge of results. This is essentially the model advocated by Skinner (1958), along with the notion of "vanishing" props or guidance cues as the trainee becomes more and more familiar with the concepts.

In contrast to the compulsive tutor model are the *branching* and *idiomorphic* models, which are more adaptive to the progress of the individual trainee, much like the computer adaptive testing programs are responsive to the performance of the testtaker. The notion of branching programs (Crowder, 1959) is that the sequencing of materials is made contingent upon the responses of the individual. Thus, depending on progress, the program may repeat a section, skip some material, or progress to the next section. The distinction between this branching method and so-called idiomorphic programming is that the latter uses information other than the trainee's immediately preceding responses to choose among alternative routes and rates of progress through the program. Thus, for example, information about previous training or experience or the diagnostic information might be used within the program itself to tailor the programmed instruction to the individual.

Teaching Cultural Values through Programmed Instruction. Programmed instruction has usually been linked to the teaching of easily sequenced verbal material. It is a popular technique for language and mathematics training. Recently, there have been some innovative uses of the approach that dramatically expand its scope. A good example of an innovative use is called the "culture assimilator" (Fiedler, Mitchell, & Triandis, 1971). In both the military and the private sector, it is often necessary to carry out job duties in a foreign country. This implies a change of culture for the individual. The question then becomes one of preparing or training the individual to function in this new culture. The objective of training would be to help the individual to assimilate to the new environment. This is where the term *culture* *assimilator* comes from. It is a programmed instruction component that provides the trainee with important information about the new environment. It accomplishes this by presenting the trainee with a situation similar to one she might encounter in the new environment. She is asked to choose one of several alternative responses. On the basis of that response, she is either reinforced for the correct choice or directed toward material that will explain why the choice was incorrect. If an incorrect choice is made, the trainee is given another similar situation to deal with. The trainee progresses to the next concept only after the current one is mastered. An example of one such situation and the various alternatives and program instructions appears in Figure 9–3. A 1977 study by O'Brien and Plooj further illustrated the potential for programmed instruction in cultural training. They demonstrated the effectiveness of a culture assimilator for training nurses in South Australia who would work with aboriginals.

Systematic Observation. This training method assumes that the trainee can learn managerial techniques and practices by observing an ideal manager in action. J. P. Campbell et al. (1970) thought that the method may be limited because the trainee must judge the relative importance of what he observes. This suggests that the method might well be combined with training in observation, including guidance of the trainee in classifying the situations, the types of problems the manager is solving, and the types of strategies and solutions involved. Observation without a system is seldom orderly, is subject to biases, and is not likely to be an effective or efficient training method.

Closed-Circuit Television. Closed-circuit television, particularly with videotape provisions allowing instant replays, has some unique properties as a training method. It permits trainees to see themselves in action shortly after the action has occurred. This sort of feedback may be valuable for a wide variety of training situations, from learning a golf swing to learning to be sensitive to one's own "stimulus value" in social situations. As an example of the latter, a program of research was conducted by the air force on the training of military personnel for interaction with people in cultures very different from their own. This contact interaction program (COIN) made extensive use of self-confrontation through videotape feedback. Trainees engaged in role playing specific social situations that were typical (and perhaps critical) in the foreign culture, and then they engaged in evaluative discussions that were centered around the videotape replay of the sessions (e.g., Haines, 1964; Haines & Eachus, 1965).

As I described earlier in the chapter, behavioral modeling has become a popular training approach. It has been common to present the model via videotape. Although there has been considerable research on the modeling aspect of the approach, there has not been much examination of the "delivery system"—videotape. Walter (1975) studied the effects of videotaped modeling and feedback on group problem solving. College students were asked to

FIGURE 9–3 An Example of a Culture Assimilator Incident

Page X-1

Sharon Hatfield, a school teacher in Athens, was amazed at the questions that were asked her by Greeks whom she considered to be only casual acquaintances. When she entered or left her apartment, people would ask her where she was going or where she had been. If she stopped to talk she was asked questions like, "How much do you make a month?" or "Where did you get that dress you are wearing?" She thought that Greeks were very rude.

Page X-2

Why did the Greeks ask Sharon such "personal" questions?

1. The casual acquaintances were acting like friends do in Greece, although Sharon did not realize it.

   Go to page X-3

2. The Greeks asked Sharon the questions in order to determine whether she belonged to the Greek Orthodox Church.

   Go to page X-4

3. The Greeks were unhappy about the way in which she lived, and they were trying to get Sharon to change her habits.

   Go to page X-5

4. In Greece, such questions are perfectly proper when asked of women but improper when asked of men.

   Go to page X-6

Page X-3

You selected 1: The casual acquaintances were acting like friends do in Greece, although Sharon did not realize it.

Correct. It is not improper for in-group members to ask these questions of one another. Furthermore, these questions reflect the fact that friendships (even "casual" ones) tend to be more intimate in Greece than in America. As a result, friends are generally free to ask questions which would seem too personal in America.

Go to page X-7

Page X-4

You selected 2: The Greeks asked Sharon the question in order to determine whether or not she belonged to the Greek Orthodox Church

No. This is not why the Greeks asked Sharon such questions. Remember, whether or not some information is "personal" depends upon the culture. In this case, the Greeks did not consider these questions too "personal." Why? Try again.

Go to page X-1

Page X-5

You selected 3: The Greeks were unhappy about the way in which she lived, and they were trying to get Sharon to change her habits.

No. There was no information given to lead you to believe that the Greeks were unhappy with Sharon's way of living. The episode states that the Greeks were acquaintances of Sharon.

Go to page X-1

(continued)

SOURCE: From "The Culture Assimilator: An Approach to Cross-Cultural Training," by F. E. Fiedler, T. Mitchell, and H. C. Triandis, 1971, *Journal of Applied Psychology, 55*, pp. 97–98. Copyright 1971 by the American Psychological Association. Reprinted by permission of the author.

FIGURE 9–3 *(concluded)*

Page X-5

You selected 4: In Greece, such questions are perfectly proper when asked of women, but improper when asked of men.

No. Such questions are indeed proper under certain situations. However, sex has nothing to do with it. When are the questions proper? Try to apply what you have learned about proper behavior between friends in Greece. Was Sharon regarded as a friend by these Greeks?

Go to page X-1

suggest solutions to some standard problems used for group problem-solving exercises. There were several control conditions involving verbal instructions. The experimental conditions included (1) a presentation of a videotape depicting a group dealing with a similar problem, (2) a presentation of the subjects' first efforts to solve the problem (i.e., feedback), and (3) a combination of feedback and modeling. The modeling condition produced the greatest number of novel and feasible solutions. The modeling-plus-feedback condition was also effective. The "feedback-only" condition was not significantly different from the control conditions. Walter concluded that the study clearly demonstrated the effectiveness of videotaped training inputs. I am inclined to agree but with one reservation: the study did not provide unequivocal support for the videotape machine. Instead, it suggested that there are certain kinds of information (behavior of models) that can be presented on videotape and have facilitating effects on trainee behavior. Walter suggests that this facilitating effect is due to the fact that the trainee is not bombarded with verbal and written information. By implication, he is hypothesizing that training often suffers because of information overload induced by instructions. This must remain speculation because although the effects of information overload have been examined carefully with respect to skilled performance, little research has been done on the issue with respect to training performance. It is a topic that deserves further examination.

Another more subtle point is contained in the Walter results. One of the more popular activities for trainers is to tape the performance of trainees and play it back to them, pointing out where mistakes were made and how to correct them. The results from the Walter study do not lend support to this technique. Instead, it seems as if it would be better to show the trainees tapes of models performing the action correctly. Unfortunately, this is an instance of the hardware wagging the program, a tendency described earlier in the chapter. It is fun to see yourself on TV, even when you are doing something stupid. Trainees are genuinely enthusiastic about having their performance taped. Unfortunately, it does not seem as if they learn much from looking at their mistakes. Although it would be precipitous to dismiss a technique such as videotaped feedback of performance to trainees on the basis of one study, in the absence of careful examinations of the use of videotape in industrial training, we would limit our generalizations of videotaped information presentation to modeling until more information becomes available regarding feedback.

Sensitivity Training: The "T-Group." Like the conference or seminar training method, the "T-group" is a discussion method involving participation by members in a small group. In contrast to the traditional conference, however, the subject matter for the T-group is the behavior of the members. Members are encouraged to reflect on, interpret, and evaluate the actions and reactions of others and of themselves. Members are expected to express freely their reactions to and interpretations of the others' behavior (verbal and other), pointing out evidence of hostility, insecurity, defensive reactions, and other behavior dynamics. J. P. Campbell et al. (1970) have pointed out some of many variations of the original National Training Laboratory (NTL) groups. These tend to vary with the degree of prominence and other aspects of the role of the group leader or trainer, who may be a passive resource person or an active interpreter of behavior and instigator of conflict. Nevertheless, these authors felt that certain objectives were common to the various sensitivity training techniques:

1. To give the trainee an understanding of how and why he acts toward other people as he does and of the way in which he affects them
2. To provide some insight into why other people act the way they do
3. To teach the participants how to "listen," that is, actually hear what the other people are saying rather than concentrating on a reply
4. To provide insights concerning how groups operate and what sorts of processes groups go through under certain conditions
5. To foster an increased tolerance and understanding of the behavior of others
6. To provide a setting in which an individual can try out new ways of interacting with people and receive feedback as to how these new ways affect them (p. 239).

An expansion of T-group training that may involve additional short lectures, role playing, and the like, is known as *laboratory education.* Such laboratories are usually held at a live-in training center away from the company. The most well-known laboratory education program is the NTL, but there are numerous innovators and imitators. (For a detailed description of NTL, see Bradford, Gibb, & Benne, 1964.)

Simulation Methods

Just as training can involve the simulation of a machine control task or of an entire multiple man-machine system, so also can it attempt to simulate certain aspects of the manager's situation. Various simulation methods are designed to provide realistic training in the decision-making or interpersonal relations aspects of the manager's job.

The Case Method. This method involves the written description of an organizational situation constituting a problem in need of a solution. The problem may be largely technical or logistical, or it may center on interpersonal or intergroup relations. Trainees are encouraged to offer solutions, usually in a conference or seminar setting, where proposals can be evaluated, providing feedback to the trainees. Sometimes the cases are descriptions of real situations where the outcomes of one or more attempted solutions are known. These results may be withheld by the trainer until solutions have been offered and evaluated by the training group and then presented as a basis for further evaluation and perspective on the proposals. J. P. Campbell et al. (1970) suggest that the case method may be most effective as a means of illustrating and providing practice in the application of general principles presented through lecture or other more direct methods. A variation of the case method is the *incident method* (Pigors & Pigors, 1955), in which a brief outline of the case is presented, and trainees are encouraged to seek additional information by questioning the trainer. After a solution has been reached, the trainer presents the case in full, whereupon the proposed solution is re-evaluated. On the face of it, this method offers practice not only in problem solving and decision making based on a static body of information but also in information-gathering skills necessary for problem solution.

Role Playing. Role playing is similar in many respects to the clinical technique known as *psychodrama*. The basic technique is that of acting out certain prescribed roles in problem situations, usually involving conflicting interests of individuals or of the groups they represent. The basic assumption is that true empathic appreciation of the position of another person is best achieved by "putting yourself in the other person's place." Role playing is thus designed to increase interpersonal sensitivity or human relations skills. At the same time, the actors are expected to work toward a solution of a problem. This problem constitutes the situation around which the acting takes place. There is no script; the participants are given only a brief description of their role and their position regarding the problem. Maier and his associates (Maier, 1952; Maier & Solem, 1952; Maier & Zerfoss, 1952) have advocated multiple role playing where the larger training group is divided into several role-playing teams and the various problem solutions are presented and discussed. This reduces the high cost and time consumption of a single session. Role playing shares the goals of sensitivity training with the T-groups and of decision making with the case method in a way that would appear to sensitize the decision maker to the participation method and to the impact of decisions on those whose jobs are affected.

Business Games. Decision making with a different emphasis appears to be the main goal of business games as they are used in management training and development. These games usually provide rather detailed information about a business or unit of an organization. This information describes rules and relationships between processes, prices, and departments. Trainees make decisions about prices, inventories, promotional campaigns, and the like. Such games vary from relatively modest cases to complex computer-based programs. Regardless of their complexity, most games operate on a few principles, which, once they are revealed, limit the challenge and the training value. At the same time, they may reinforce the notion that *this* principle is the one to guide all such decision making.

In-Basket Technique. The in-basket technique was described in Chapter 6 as a selection assessment device. However, a set of in-basket items such as correspondence, requests, or complaints, together with the trainees' report as to how each item would be dealt with, would appear to be a fruitful basis for discussion between trainer and trainees.

On-the-Job Methods

In addition to the unsystematic, often haphazard "sink-or-swim" policy that is frequently labeled "on-the-job training," there are some identifiable techniques for improving or broadening skill on the job. J. P. Campbell et al. (1970) identified four types of on-the-job training, some of which are unique to management development and some of which are more broadly applicable.

Job Rotation. Job rotation has very general applications as a training method. It may be used to develop and improve skills from the low-skill levels to top-level management. The goals of job rotation may be to increase the flexibility and adaptability of the work force or, at managerial and administrative levels, to increase the employee's effectiveness on her own job by providing firsthand knowledge of other operations within the organization.

If job rotation is treated as a trial-and-error learning method without some guidance or structuring, it may well be an ineffective and inefficient method, as its critics have suggested. However, as a part of a program that prepares the trainee for the experiences on the rotated job and uses the experiences as the basis for evaluating and coaching, the method may be quite valuable.

Other on-the-Job Methods. J. P. Campbell et al. (1970) list *committee assignments,* in which managers-in-training solve real problems in a committee structure, *coaching,* which reminds one of apprenticeship or tutorial training, and *performance evaluation,* which implies the notion of coaching, wherein the superior uses the evaluation interview to explore ways of improving the subordinate's performance, as additional on-the-job training techniques for managers.

The Local Expert. One of the most common training needs that has appeared on the industrial landscape in the last decade is the need for computer training. Most industries have come to rely on computer technology for accomplishing important goals. The computer might be used by office personnel for billing or word processing, it might be used by production floor personnel for keeping track of orders or inventory, it might be used by human resources personnel to keep track of work histories, and so on. Whenever a new piece of hardware or software is introduced, there is some need for training. In this situation, it is often assumed that training will occur through a manual of some sort or that the program itself will accomplish the training through the use of menus of "Help" screens. I have recently reviewed much of the literature dealing with such training (Landy, Rastegary, & Motowidlo, 1987), and there is some reason to question this assumption. In fact, in most such instances, workers will identify a "local expert," someone who has become proficient at the use of the software or hardware and depend on that person to help when things don't work as they should. In fact, many computer trainers suggest that a local expert be identified (or created) prior to the introduction of hardware or software to the entire working group. The interesting aspect of this is that a local expert will be used regardless of the quality or availability of manuals or on-line help. It seems as if people prefer to go to other people for training or help. This may be confirmation of what the social learning people knew all along, or it may be an identification of a problem. In my experience with computers, I have learned that the most effective way to learn a system is to experience a "crash" and get out of it yourself. Whenever I ask someone else to solve the problem, the solution remains in the mind of that other person and not in my own. Given the pervasiveness of computer technology, the phenomenon of the local expert deserves some careful attention from a training-learning perspective.

On-the-job training methods have the advantage that they avoid the problem of transfer of training from a separate training setting to the job setting. They represent the *whole-training method* in the broadest sense of this term. The trainee is expected to develop proficiency at the job tasks and, at the same time, adjust to the physical and social context in which these tasks are performed. On-the-job training also frequently offers opportunities for observing and imitating seasoned operators performing the same job. Obviously, there are many jobs in which at least the initial phases of training cannot be handled on the job. Thus, one cannot train an astronaut on board a space flight or turn loose a novice with a $100,000 airplane. On the other hand, most training programs begun off the job are continued on the job. Seldom is the trainee ready to meet standard production the first day on the job. A major question that apparently has received little attention has to do with providing for continued improvement and development of trainees once they have left training and are on the job.

The "whole-method" aspect of on-the-job training may produce an over-

Often when learning a new computer program, the learner will call on a "local expert" for help rather than look in a manual. (Penn State University)

load for the new employee. Preview of the job and orientation to the physical and social setting, as well as pretraining on the task itself, may facilitate job adjustment.

Miniature Job Training: A Multipurpose Intervention

A recent innovation with considerable promise is called *miniature job training* (or MJT). This technique has been used widely in the United Kingdom (Robertson & Downs, 1979) and has been applied to navy recruits in the United States (Siegel, 1983; Siegel & Bergman, 1975). In its simplest form, MJT is a structured and controlled period of learning that is used to identify those individuals most suitable for entry into the training program and eventually the job in question. Basically, a representative part of the training program is presented to the applicant, and after some standard exposure to this training sample, the applicant is tested in what she has been able to learn. The logic is that the best predictor of future learning and performance is past learning and performance.

Siegel (1983) has described the successful application of MJT in a project in which he administered MJT to 1,034 naval recruits who had been labeled "low aptitude." The correlations between MJT scores and later performance ratings were .56 after 9 months and .45 after 18 months. This is an impressive relationship. In addition, the trainees felt that the MJT was a "fair" measure of their ability. Thus, like assessment centers, MJT programs would seem to have built in face validity. One final advantage of the MJT approach is its realism. The MJT might easily function as a type of realistic job preview. Based on what you learned in the last chapter, this would imply that the MJT would provide information to the candidate that would allow for a more reasonable decision about whether the job was desirable.

TRAINING READINESS

Several recent studies have raised some interesting questions about the readiness of trainees for training. As an example, Noe and Schmitt (1986) examined the effect of trainee attitudes on the eventual effectiveness of training and discovered some interesting things. First, they found that if a trainee felt that her skills had been adequately assessed in the training program, then she was more satisfied with the training than if she had no confidence in the skill assessment. Second, and more important, they discovered that those who were most involved in their jobs and careers profited most from the training program. This is most likely the result of seeing the training as instrumental in career advancement or increased job proficiency. Based on these results, Noe and Schmitt make several suggestions. They suggest that you should not force low-involved employees into training since they will simply squander the training resources. Second, they suggest that it might be valuable to run some pretraining workshops devoted to increasing the involvement and job commitment of the eventual trainees. This would greatly enhance the utility of the training program from a cost-benefit perspective.

A second study addresses readiness from a very different perspective. Larsson (1987) investigated the impact of relaxation, meditation, and mental imagery training on recruits to the Swedish army. This training was presented several times each week for eight months by trained platoon leaders. He discovered that when such relaxation training occurred in conjunction with skill training (artillery, Morse code, etc.), the skill training was more effectively incorporated into the behavioral repertoire of the recruit. In some senses, he was suggesting that the relaxation training prepared the recruit mentally to receive the skill training.

The concept of readiness (e.g., reading readiness) has played a useful role in debates on educational training curricula, and it may very well play the same role in the consideration of industrial training. More research on this topic would be welcome and might substantially improve the delivery of training programs and their eventual effectiveness.

THE EVALUATION OF TRAINING PROGRAMS AND TECHNIQUES

Let's start with a definition. Goldstein (1980) defines training evaluation as "the systematic collection of descriptive and judgmental information necessary to make effective training decisions related to the selection, adoption, value and modification of various instructional activities" (p. 236). In plain

English, the question is whether it can be empirically demonstrated that one particular form of training is effective (or more effective than an alternative form). Evaluation is not necessarily an all-or-none activity. It is more an information-gathering process than an attempt to identify *the* best training program. There are multiple and occasionally contradictory criteria applied to training program "success." As an example, O'Leary (1972) reports a training program with mixed results. She presented training to a group of hard-core unemployed women who were enrolled in a federally sponsored work program. The training was intended to improve their self-esteem and pride. It worked so well that the women quit their low-paying boring jobs. By one standard, the program was a success; by another standard, it was a failure. It all depends on who is doing the counting.

As the title of this section suggests, it is one thing to evaluate a training program, but it may be quite another matter to evaluate a method or technique. Training programs often involve several methods, media, and specific techniques. When the overall effectiveness of the program is evaluated, little or nothing can be concluded about the component methods. Relative effectiveness of two methods or programs may be assessed by comparing two equivalent groups, each trained using one method or program, on a common criterion measure or measures. Evaluation of the absolute effectiveness of these methods would require the use of an appropriate control group receiving no formal training.

Criteria for Evaluation

As with any personnel program, the evaluation of training programs begins with a consideration of criteria and criterion measures. Although the general issues of criterion development and criterion selection were discussed in Chapter 6, there are some special considerations with respect to the choice of criteria for training research.

Kirkpatrick (1959) has suggested four criteria that are appropriate for training evaluation.

1. *Reaction criteria.* Measures of the impression of trainees. Was the training valuable? Did they learn much? Did they enjoy the program?
2. *Learning criteria.* Measures of how much was learned. These are typically gathered with traditional examinations. Your exam in this course is an example of a learning criterion.
3. *Behavioral criteria.* Measures of how much behavior changed back on the job. The real issue here is the extent to which transfer occurred from the training to the job.
4. *Results criteria.* Measures of payoff in organizational terms. The impetus for training may have been a scrap rate of 11 percent. The goal of training may have been to reduce the scrap rate to 3 percent. Did this reduction actually occur?

The choice of criteria should not be simply a matter of preference or convenience. Even though careful measurement of internal criteria—reactions and learning—in the context of an adequately designed study can provide valuable information to the trainer, these measurements cannot tell us what impact the training has on job behaviors or organizational goals. Evaluation of the payoff from a training program depends not on what is learned in training but on how and to what extent job behaviors and effectiveness are changed.

An excellent example of the collection of data on all four criteria is provided by the Latham and Saari (1979) study that was mentioned earlier in the context of social learning. Supervisors were given behavioral modeling training in order to improve their management skills. In order to evaluate the effectiveness of the program, the following data were collected:

1. *Reaction measures.* A questionnaire was administered immediately after training as well as eight months after training. The questions involved judgments concerning the perceived value of the training. Analysis showed that there was an initial positive reaction that did not diminish even after eight months.
2. *Learning measures.* Trainees were administered a test containing 85 situational questions that had been developed from a job analysis and critical incidents session. The group that received training scored significantly higher on that test than a control group that received no training.
3. *Behavioral measures.* Trainees were asked to role-play in situations that had been covered in training. These role-playing exercises were tape-recorded, and the tapes were reviewed and evaluated by a group of expert judges. Judges evaluated the behavior of both trainees and a control group but were unaware of which tapes represented the behavior of trainees and which were the tapes of the control subjects who received no training. The ratings of the trained group were significantly higher than those of the control group.
4. *Results measures.* As far as the organization was concerned, the real issue was whether there was any change back on the job in terms of job performance. Supervisors evaluated the trainees one month and one year after training. Trainees were rated significantly higher than control group subjects on various aspects of job performance. After one year, the control group subjects were also trained, and at that point the differences in rated performance between the graduates of the earlier training program and their control counterparts (who were now themselves graduates of the training program) disappeared.

This evaluation effort by Latham and Saari was impressive and, in many respects, a textbook illustration of how to do it. The only thing missing was a utility analysis or some sort of "bottom-line" evaluation that estimated the benefit in dollar terms of the training program in light of the cost of the program. Ultimately, the benefits of training should be cost accountable, as

FIGURE 9–4 Types of Validity in Training Evaluation

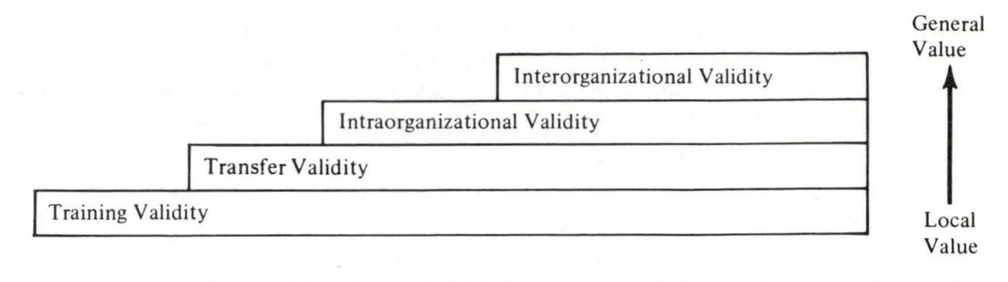

Odiorne (1964) insists, but this is a complex evaluation, and there are typically a host of uncontrolled factors (e.g., turnover, market changes) that are confounded with training effects so that accurate measures of gains and costs are not easily obtained.

The Validity of Training

Training evaluation really deals with the more basic issue of validity. Did the training accomplish what it purported to accomplish? Goldstein (1986) suggests that questions regarding the validity of a training program can be placed in one of four categories:

1. *Training validity.* Did the trainees match the criteria established for the training program?
2. *Transfer validity.* Did the trainees match the criteria established for success when they were back on the job?
3. *Intraorganizational validity.* Is the training program equally effective with different groups of trainees within the same company?
4. *Interorganizational validity.* Is the training program equally effective with different trainees in companies other than the one that developed the training program?

You would expect that a training program that can answer each of those four questions Yes would be evaluated very positively. The different kinds of validity might be arranged hierarchically, as is shown in Figure 9–4. This suggests that interorganizational validity is harder to achieve than intraorganizational validity, that transfer validity is harder to achieve than training validity, and so on. This is because there are more potential obstacles to training effectiveness as one proceeds up the hierarchy. Figure 9–5 describes some of the "threats" to validity at each of the levels in Figure 9–4. Keep in mind that the threats at one level include all the threats at the level below it. This should give you some appreciation for the difficulties in developing a

FIGURE 9–5 Threats to the Types of Training Validity

Type of Validity	*Threat*
Interorganizational	Dissimilarity between your organization and the one that developed the training program. This would include, among other variables: dissimilarity of tasks, jobs, needs, climates, products.
Intraorganizational	Unstable training effects, inadequate training evaluation, changes in organization over time, unintended changes in training program over time.
Transfer	Inadequate job or task analysis or both, no consideration of transfer mechanism, unspecified organizational goals, organization conflict.
Training	Availability of "cute" training hardware, lack of clear training objectives, biased assignments of individuals to training and control groups, failure to collect base-rate data.

generally applicable training program. More to the point, this suggests that it is important to determine the general purpose of the training prior to designing the evaluation of the training program.

Evaluation Designs

The basic issue in the design of training research, as J. P. Campbell (1971) points out, is whether we can set up our conditions so as to be able to say that changes in criterion behavior are, indeed, the result of training. Most designs and training studies leave us with an equivocal answer to this question. Since the fundamental purpose of training is to bring about a systematic *change* in behavior (knowledge, skills, attitudes), a simple after-training measure cannot document such training effects. A before-training measure is essential for comparison. However, the demonstration of a change from *before* to *after* measures for the training group does not unequivocally show that the change was due to the training. Since there was a time interval between before-and-after measures, only some portion of which was filled by training, the behavioral changes may have resulted from other experiences or events. As we saw in Chapter 2, uncontrolled third variables make interpretation very difficult. Thus, as MacKinney (1957) has argued, a control group is needed that receives the before-and-after measures but not the training. The training and control group should be comparable on the *before* measure, that is, essentially equivalent groups.

Even with before-after measures and a no-training control group, the interpretation of behavior changes is not simple. Suppose, for example, that both groups have *before* scores of 50, and even though the training group has an *after* score of 76, the control group has 63. Is the change in performance of the training group due to the *content* of the training course or to the mere fact that the trainees were selected for training, resulting in a positive effect on work motivation, that is, a "Hawthorne effect"?[2] What about the change in the control group scores? To what extent are these the result of simply having taken the pretest? From a practical point of view, it could be argued that if *any* "training" program will produce desired changes (via the Hawthorne effect), then by all means find the least expensive program that will satisfy the employee. On the other hand, if the administration of a simple *before* measure can result in half as much gain as an elaborate training program, then it may be reasonable simply to give *before* measures and forget the training. The first of these concerns can be evaluated by adding a "placebo" group. (This term refers to the "sugar-pill" type of control frequently used in drug research.) This group receives *before* and *after* measures, but in place of the training the group members are exposed to, this group receives a "sham" training program of some sort, which presumably can produce the Hawthorne effect. The second concern—that for the effects of the *before* measure per se—can be evaluated with a fourth group that receives no pretest and no training but does receive a posttest.

The Complete Design. This brings us to the training research design proposed by Solomon (1949). This design probably represents the ultimate in experimental elegance and control. Solomon suggested that pretests represent a validity threat of their own. They may have the effect of sensitizing the control group subjects to one or more of the components of the training program. As a result, the pretest may have an effect without any training taking place. As an example, consider a group of workers who receive a pretest on attitudes toward minority group coworkers. It is not hard to imagine the control group (i.e., no treatment group) becoming more sensitive to minority issues simply as a result of the pretest. Then suppose that the experimental and control groups are compared after training, and there is no difference in their attitudes. Should one conclude that the training did not work? A simple before-after design would not be able to answer the question. A more complex design would be necessary. Solomon suggested just such a design and it is illustrated in Figure 9–6. As you can see, two additional control groups have been added to the traditional trained and untrained groups. Neither of these additional groups receives a pretest and only one receives training. This allows one to evaluate the effects of the pretest independently of the effects of the training. This is a complicated and demanding

[2]The Hawthorne studies are discussed in Chapter 11. The *Hawthorne effect* refers to evidence noted in these studies that employees may respond to *any* change (or *perceived* change) in their work situation, or simply to the fact that they were chosen for the experiment, by increasing their productivity.

FIGURE 9–6

Group	*Time 1 (before)*	*Training*	*Time 2 (after)*
Experimental	Measure	Train	Measure
Control 1	Measure	Placebo	Measure
Control 2	No measure	Train	Measure
Control 3	No measure	No training	Measure

design that requires many subjects. Strange as it may seem, even this design is sometimes insensitive to subtle threats to validity. Bunker and Cohen (1977) found that pretest measures depressed certain skills and improved other skills in both trained and untrained (control) subjects, requiring some very sophisticated data analyses to untangle the web of training effects. It is important to keep in mind the possible sensitizing effects of pretest measures, particularly when attitude change is a training goal.

Quasi-Experimental Designs. Some less complete research designs have been proposed by D. T. Campbell and Stanley (1963). They allow for partial control and the elimination of at least some competing explanations of the changes accompanying training without requiring four comparable groups of subjects. The first of these is the *time series experiment,* a one-group design that requires a series of before-and-after measures at different points in time. Evidence for a training effect is a *discontinuity* in the series of measures, corresponding to the training program, and greater than point-to-point changes elsewhere in the measures—that is, an atypical change in the data. While this design is an improvement on the simple before-after design in that the criterion change corresponding to the training period can be compared with changes that occur at other times without intervening training, it does not rule out other nontraining explanations of the change, including Hawthorne effects. An excellent example of this type of design is provided by Komaki, Heinzmann, and Lawson (1980) in a study of industrial safety. They were interested in comparing the effects of training by itself to the effects of training and performance feedback. We will consider this study in more detail in the section on industrial safety (Chapter 15). For present purposes, I simply want to illustrate the evaluation design that was applied. Figure 9–7 presents the results of the intervention for four different job families. As you can see, the evaluation consisted of a series of treatments in which trainees moved from one condition to another over a period of 40+ weeks.

On the basis of an analysis of these data, the experimenters concluded that training plus feedback was more effective than training alone, although feedback was required three times per week in order to be effective. The longitudinal design of the evaluation permitted inferences that would have been obscured by other simpler designs.

FIGURE 9–7 Percentage of Incidents Performed Safely by Employees in Four Vehicle Maintenance Sections under Five Experimental Conditions

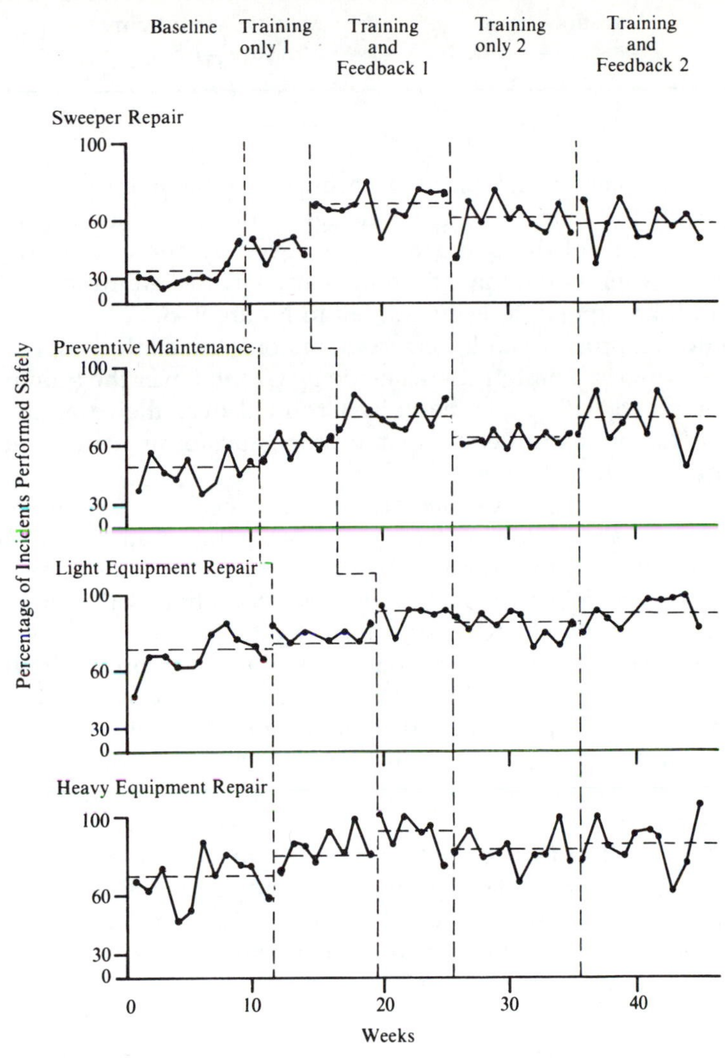

SOURCE: From "Effect of Training and Feedback: Component Analysis of a Behavioral Training Program" by J. Komaki, A. T. Heinzmann, and L. Lawson, 1980, *Journal of Applied Psychology, 65,* p. 265. Copyright 1980 by the American Psychological Association. Reprinted by permission of the authors.

Another design suggested by Campbell and Stanley seems to offer a reasonable compromise between experimental elegance and practical limitations. In this design, the target group is divided into two comparable groups. Both are given *before* tests followed by training of one group, no training of

FIGURE 9–8 A Quasi-Experimental Design Proposed by Campbell and Stanley

Group	*Time 1*	*Time 2*	*Time 3*
I	Measure—train	Measure—no train	Measure
II	Measure—no train	Measure—train	Measure

the other, and *after* measures for both groups. To this point the design does not differ from the simple two-group design. However, following the second measure, the roles of the two groups are reversed: the untrained group is now trained, whereas the trained group stands by for a third test given after the second training period, as illustrated in Figure 9–8.

This design provides additional comparisons and controls not offered by the simple two-group design. Gains made by Group I over the training period can be compared with gains made by Group II over their training period; gains made in training can be compared with gains (or no gains) made in the no-training period, and so on.

For the most part, the various designs described above could be applied to research comparing two or more training programs, methods, or variations by simply adding one experimental group for each method of training or by replacing the "sham" training of the placebo condition with a true training alternative. The methodological and logical pitfalls of comparative training research are many, however. The possibilities that certain methods are superior for instructing in specific content areas, that an outstanding lecture may be more effective than a mediocre programmed learning text, or that the novelty of a T-group experience may produce short-run superiority over an exercise in role playing suggest only a few of the problems in evaluating training methods.

In addition, it is important to remember the necessary conditions for interpreting any experiment (or quasi experiment). As you saw in the methods chapter, it is important that subjects be randomly assigned to conditions and that extraneous third variables be controlled. Without these assurances, any interpretation of training results is questionable.

The Problem of Control Groups

In the section on evaluation, we have concentrated heavily on the importance of control groups. They play a major role in the complete and quasi-experimental designs of Solomon (1949) and D. T. Campbell and Stanley (1963). There are also occasions where control groups actually create more problems than they solve. As an example, Pfister (1975) describes a study of police training techniques in which 24 of 78 police officers selected to be in the control group were angry and withdrawn and made "unpublishable comments about the research investigator" (Goldstein, 1980). In a training study that I conducted some years ago, the company was interested in training production workers to use automatic rather than manually operated machines for drilling and grinding. Employees were permitted to sign up to be in the training group. Those who did not sign up were designated as controls. As luck (i.e., bad luck) would have it, all the volunteers were young and had less tenure with the organization. All the control subjects were older and had been with the company for long periods of time. As the training progressed, the two groups grew more distant. The control group felt that the trainees were being given "special" treatment because they were young. They felt that the company was out to prove that the older employees were dead wood. The fact that the older employees had the opportunity to volunteer was of no importance in their attitudes. That fact had been forgotten almost immediately after the groups were formed. During the course of training, the control group varied between an attitude of hostility and obstructionism—making life as difficult for the trainees as possible—and competitiveness—trying to show the company that they could produce just as much as the "kids" using manual methods. From an evaluation standpoint, it was impossible to untangle the mess. The experimental group clearly produced more. There are many explanations that are equally appealing: (a) the training was effective, (b) the methods and equipment were superior, (c) the frustration of the control group depressed their performance, (d) the experimental group accepted a goal of increased output. There are many other possibilities that you could think of that could explain the results. The point I am making is that the mere presence of a control group can occasionally create a new and unintended experiment. In this instance, it might have been better to create two "training" programs and put the control group into an alternative training setting, for example, new methods for manual production, refreshers on equipment capabilities and standard methods. Control groups can be counterproductive.

TRAINING RESEARCH

The literature contains a large number of reports of training research. At least a few studies could be cited involving each of the methods, techniques, and media mentioned in this chapter. A thorough review of this body of research would require another book, however, and might well leave us with little more insight into which methods are best for which training purposes than we had when we began. Relatively few studies have been adequately controlled, and even those that were controlled frequently cannot be generalized to the field training situation. J. P. Campbell (1971) summarized his impression of the literature on training this way:

> By and large, the training and development literature is voluminous, nonempirical, nontheoretical, poorly written, and dull . . . it is faddish to an extreme.

> The fads center around the introduction of new techniques and follow a characteristic pattern. A new technique appears on the horizon and develops a large stable of advocates who first describe its "successful" use in a number of situations. A second wave of advocates busy themselves trying out numerous modifications of the basic technique. A few empirical studies may be carried out to demonstrate that the method "works." Then the inevitable backlash sets in and a few vocal opponents begin to criticize the usefulness of the technique, most often in the absence of data. Such criticism typically has very little effect. What does have an effect is the appearance of another new technique and a repetition of the same cycle.

Recent reviews of the training literature indicate that things have not improved appreciably (Goldstein, 1980, 1986; Goldstein & Buxton, 1982; Latham, 1988). The bad news is that the research in training has not been planned or executed in a manner that allows one to draw many solid conclusions. The good news is that there is plenty of room for progress!

Specific Training Targets

There are several content areas of training that can be considered. To this point, much of the discussion has implied that we were dealing with particular cognitive or motor skills in the training programs. Nevertheless, industrial training has been applied to many diverse content areas. These include such areas as leadership training, rater training, management training, and creativity training. It might be useful to consider briefly some training research that relates to these topics.

Leadership Training. As you saw earlier in the chapter, social learning theory is being used with greater frequency to instruct managers in methods of supervision. Latham and Saari (1979) have demonstrated the potential effectiveness of such programs of instruction. As you will see in Chapter 12, this is the equivalent of leadership training. There is no reason why these methods could not be applied to leaders in a wide variety of contexts including leaders of volunteer groups, political leaders, and academic leaders.

Another version of leadership training has been suggested by Fiedler and his colleagues (Fiedler & Mahar, 1979). Based on his theory of leader effectiveness, Fiedler has prepared a training program that instructs participants in the most important concepts of leadership. The program is called LEADER MATCH and uses a programmed instruction format.

A final and more traditional leadership training approach is based on teaching leaders how to be more people or task oriented, depending on where they may evidence a weakness.[3] Typically, a pretest is given to participants,

---

[3]It may be useful here to turn to Chapter 12 and read the section on the Ohio State Leadership Studies.

FIGURE 9–9 The New Managerial Grid

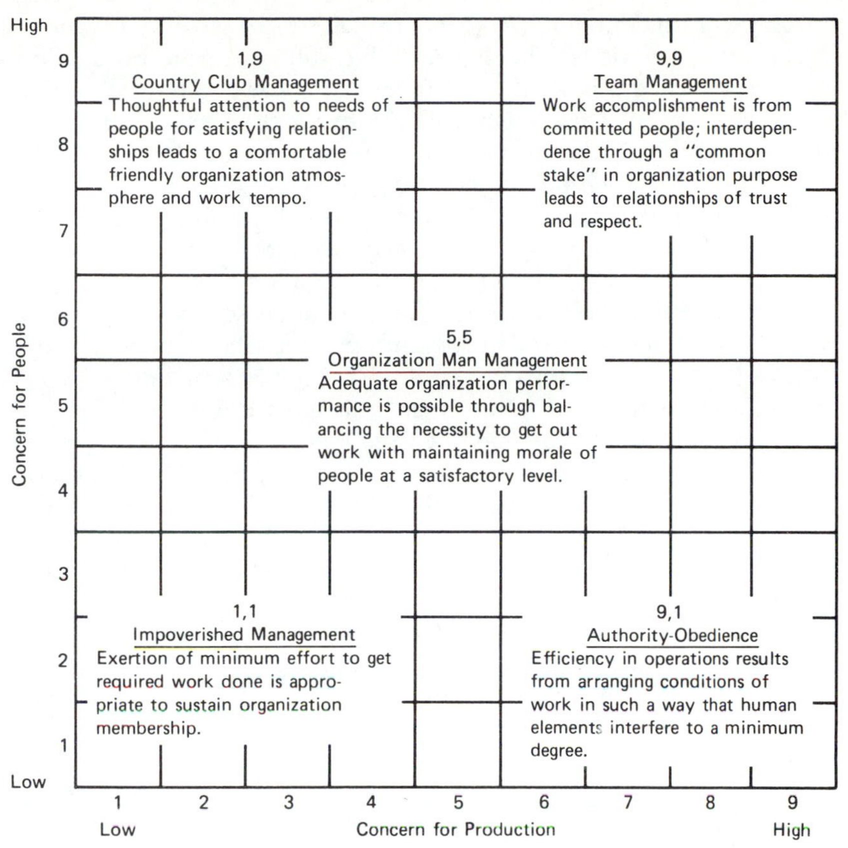

SOURCE: From *The Managerial Grid III: The Key to Leadership Excellence* (p. 12) by Robert R. Blake and Jane Srygley Mouton. Houston: Gulf Publishing Company, Copyright © 1985. Reprinted by permission.

and they are characterized as falling somewhere on the grid that appears in Figure 9–9. The goal of training is to improve on one or both of the two leadership dimensions. Training usually involves a combination of role-playing, lecture, and exercise-game activities. This type of training is by far the most common.

Latham (1988) reviews the leadership training literature and concludes that this area of training has advanced substantially in the past 10 years. This conclusion is supported by a meta-analysis conducted by Burke and Day (1986). They examined 70 studies related to management training and found that a wide range of these training programs could be considered effective, including many of the leadership training programs (such as LEADER MATCH) currently available.

Creativity Training. In many professions, a premium is placed on creativity. A good example is the research and development engineer. It is the responsibility of this individual to come up with technological advances and novel products or markets. This is somewhat different from production engineering in which the individual is required to solve some rather specific problems with known characteristics. The question then arises, Can creativity be taught? In one important respect, the answer seems to be yes. It appears that it is possible to teach people how to generate and evaluate ideas. They can be given a set of procedures to follow that will result in a large number of novel ideas. What is taught is the set of procedures. One example of such training is brainstorming (Basadur, Graen, & Green, 1982; Osborne, 1963; Parnes, 1976). One major obstacle to idea generation seems to be criticism—supplied either by other people or by the person who generates the idea. The quickest way to stifle idea generation is to have someone tell you that the idea you just suggested is the most ridiculous one she ever heard of. Brainstorming techniques teach people to separate idea generation from idea evaluation. Through group and individual exercises, individuals are encouraged to develop novel ideas—the wilder, the better. They also learn to defer criticism of their own ideas or those of others. They are encouraged to build on the ideas of others. Finally, the value of idea quantity rather than quality in the initial stages of creative thought is demonstrated.

Many studies have been conducted on these and similar training techniques (see Van Gundy, 1981). It does appear that people can be trained to develop an intra- and interpersonal environment that is conducive to creative thinking.

Observer Training. As you saw in Chapters 4 and 5, performance evaluation requires some fairly sophisticated operations on the part of the person doing the evaluation. Not only does it require skill in observation but also some skill in combining information and making judgments based on that combination. The various training techniques that have been used in preparing evaluators are described at length in Chapter 5 (e.g., frame-of-reference training). It seems safe to conclude that training has an impact on rating. The question is whether the impact is good or bad. As Bernardin and Pence (1980) have demonstrated, accuracy may actually suffer as a result of rater training (e.g., error avoidance training). But as McIntyre et al. (1984) and Pulakos (1984) contend, the right type of training can enhance rating accuracy.

Many rater training efforts have been directed toward information processing skills. There is something to be said, however, for improving the simple observation of behavior on the part of evaluators. In one of the earliest theoretical considerations of rating, Wherry (1983) suggested that observation skills were critical for accurate evaluation. Spool (1978) has reviewed training programs used for improving the accuracy of a wide range of observers of behavior including employment interviewers, performance raters, and those who record various behavior as dependent variables in psychological experiments. He concluded that modeling may be effectively used for such training. In particular, he suggested that the most effective steps include (a) observing models, (b) practicing what models do, (c) providing social reinforcement from trainers and other trainees, and (d) increasing the probability of transfer by increasing the realism of the training situation.

Management Training. It is virtually impossible to write a job description for the position of manager. It could include several dozen diverse behaviors. These behaviors vary from one job to another, from one day to another, and maybe even from one subordinate to another. For this reason, it is somewhat unclear as to what is actually covered by the term *management training*. To put it another way, there are few training programs that would *not* be legitimately included under this heading. J. P. Campbell et al. (1970) reviewed the literature and broke management training down into five distinct categories: (1) general management or general supervision training, (2) general human relations training, (3) training in problem solving and decision making, (4) laboratory education programs, and (5) specialized programs. On the basis of their review, they were able to draw some conclusions about management training:

1. General management and human relations training seems most likely to produce changes in attitudes rather than behaviors. Most of these training programs do not provide conditions that maximize transfer of training to work settings.
2. Even though results show that some permanent changes in behavior do occur as a result of management training, it is not clear if behavioral changes are accompanied by changes in performance efficiency. In other words, there is some question regarding the relevance of the training objectives and outcomes.
3. There is little evidence that training in problem solving is effective in work settings. Most of the positive results come from studies with student populations in university settings.
4. There is little comparative evidence about the relative effectiveness of one method of training compared with others. Most studies examine the effectiveness of only one method compared with a "do-nothing" control group. In this respect, the results of management training studies are no different from any other training studies.

While many of the Campbell complaints are still true to some extent, the recent meta-analysis by Burke and Day (1986) is encouraging. On the basis of that meta-analysis of 70 studies, they were able to conclude broadly that management training programs are effective and that this is true of a wide variety of such programs. To be sure, there were few direct comparative studies in the meta-analysis (i.e., comparing one type of training with another); nevertheless, it is still possible to come to some conclusions about the relative contributions of each method compared with a control. This is a step in the right direction. Examine what is happening at the workplace.

TRAINING THE UNEMPLOYED

There is one final type of training that deserves special attention, not so much because of what is taught but rather because of *who* is taught. During the 1960s a new vocabulary was born reflecting an intensified concern for the problems of large city ghettos, minority groups, and in general, the disadvantaged segments of our society. Programs were initiated to prepare the hard-core unemployed (HCU) for entry into the work force. The immediate answer to the question "Why are these people chronically unemployed or underemployed?" was in terms of inadequate marketable skills. However, it soon became apparent that the problems of hard-core unemployment were broader than this. They were bound up with the psychology of the ghetto, with expectancies, attitudes, motivational problems, even "language barrier" problems wherein the words of the trainers had different meaning for the trainees. Triandis, Feldman, Weldon, and Harvey (1975) labeled this syndrome "ecosystem distrust" and characterized it as a basic distrust of people and their motives and a rejection of authority. This type of distrust forms a formidable obstacle for any social system.

Recently, the problem of training the unemployed has reemerged, but in a slightly different form. Now the issue is how to train the *recently* unemployed—those who have worked for 5 or 10 or 15 years but have been put out of work by the recession. There is good reason to believe that employment will never be as "full" as it has been in past years. This means that we need to concern ourselves with the general issue of training the unemployed—both those who have not held jobs for long periods of time and those who are new to the ranks of the unemployed.

The "Hard-Core Unemployed"

Prerequisite to training the HCU is the need to understand something of their psychology. This has proved to be a complex and frustrating undertaking. As one example, Feldman (1973) found that some workers were less "afraid" of unemployment than others. As a matter of fact, they saw almost as many benefits from not working as from working. Searls, Braucht, and Miskimins (1974) examined the work values of the chronically unemployed in an attempt to gain some insight into their motivations. In comparing the HCU individual to blue-collar workers, they found that the HCU felt significantly more externally controlled and was less able to delay gratification than the blue-collar worker. The problem, of course, with data like these, is determining whether feelings of external control and an inability to delay gratification are *causes* of chronic unemployment or merely *symptoms*. A person who is unemployed and is used to eating will probably tap into the social welfare system available through local, state, and federal government. In the course of taking advantage of these systems, people often become "institutionalized"—they follow orders, fill out sheets, stand in lines, and would never consider deviating from a set routine. For many families, this has been a life-style for three generations. In cases such as these, it is extremely difficult to label "feelings of external control" as a cause rather than as a symptom of unemployment.

With respect to training programs directed toward HCUs, Goldstein (1974) suggests, "Programs that include motivational and attitudinal considerations are few; however, research indicates that programs that do not consider such factors are often doomed" (p. 203). Goldstein also pointed out that successful HCU training programs include, in addition to skill training, simulations to acquaint trainees with other aspects of the jobs, practice in job hunting, and interviewing assistance in contacting employers before the end of training, job placement, counseling, and follow-up programs.

An example of a program that appears to include some of these components has been developed by the Jewish Employment and Vocational Service (JEVS) of Philadelphia. This program was described briefly in the section on work sample tests in Chapter 6. Working in collaboration with a local Human Resources Development (HRD) Center of the Pennsylvania State Employment Service, JEVS has developed a program in a simulated industrial setting complete with workstations and time clocks. Trainees are observed and evaluated on work attitude, accuracy of performance, promptness in reporting to work, learning speed, acceptance of authority, expressed job interests, and other work-related behaviors. In this context, 28 work sample tasks related to available job and training opportunities are administered to each applicant over a two-week period. This testing–work experience phase is preceded and followed by vocational counseling and placement services in the HRD Center.

The work sample tasks simulate activities that trainees would face on regular jobs and require the use of standard tools and equipment. They range from simple operations like changing an automobile tire to more complex tasks involving reasoning and abstract thinking. Tasks are scheduled to progress from easy to more difficult. Since they are tasks rather than paper-and-pencil tests, they are seen as less threatening to the trainees. The combination of realistic work setting experiences and vocational counseling and placement services that utilize the data from the work sample testing and the observations of the trainees appears to provide an effective program for the hard-to-employ. Placement and job retention rates for the trainees have been relatively high, as indicated by follow-up studies.

The ultimate success of HCU programs—as reflected in placement and job retention records—may well depend on the social climate of the job in which the trainee is placed. This has been suggested by several studies (e.g., Friedlander & Greenberg, 1971). Coworkers and supervisors have attitudes about HCU employees. These attitudes set the tone for the social climate. In a study by DiMarco and Gustafson (1975), coworkers held much more positive attitudes than did the supervisors. In addition, the degree to which coworkers and supervisors had been previously exposed to HCU employees was examined. Individuals who had previous contact with HCU employees were more likely to express favorable opinions about them. When the two variables were combined (i.e., coworker/supervisor and know others/do not know others), the most negative attitudes were held by supervisors who had not had previous contact with HCU employees. It is reasonable to assume that supervisors with negative attitudes toward HCU employees will not go out of their way to help them. Thus, it may be somewhat unrealistic to introduce a HCU training program without at least examining the nature of the work group that will receive the trainee.

The plight of the HCU is a serious one. As a society, we must come to grips with the problems of all our members. We cannot simply "write off" a subgroup. In addition, the cost of the HCU problem does not go away by ignoring it. The problem is simply transferred from the specific arena of organizational profitability to the more general arena of social welfare. The HCU population represents a cost to our nation both in economic and in moral terms.

"Soft-Core" Unemployed

Occasionally, recessions occur, during which individuals who have spent the majority of their adult lives working find themselves among the unemployed. Further, they are individuals who had never even considered the possibility of unemployment. They have both the desire and the skill to work. The problem is that their jobs have disappeared. The blow to their psychological well-being is substantial. Consider the comments of Jim Hughes, a welder who was laid off:

> I had some anger because I had never been fired before. I felt my work performance was good. Excellent, really. I was doing three times the work they normally wanted on the day he fired me. So I went to the unemployment office. That kinda hurt my pride a little. More than a little. I didn't really want to go, but I felt I had to in this situation. I felt that I wanted to get them for all I could. I wanted a little bit of revenge. But even though I paid the money in, I still didn't like to go. I guess it was from the way I was brought up. Do things for yourself. Reward yourself. Nobody gives you anything for nothing. This is the attitude I had at that time. . . .
>
> And pretty soon, you start creating your own problems. I drank a little heavy. Started drinking when there was nothing to do. . . . And the wife and I had problems. We started to have little arguments. It wouldn't have happened if I

had been working. They were senseless. They were over little or nothing. We'd just bitch at each other for nothing. We had nothing else to do. Just bitch at each other.

These are the reactions of a man taken by surprise. We don't know anything about the reactions of his spouse or children or friends, but there were undoubtedly interpersonal waves and ripples. It is still too soon to see what lasting effects chronic unemployment will have on broad value systems like the work ethic. But one need not wait to see the effects of long periods of unemployment on job skills, self-esteem, and motivation. Warr and his colleagues (Warr, 1987; Warr & Jackson, 1984) have clearly demonstrated the effect of unemployment on mental health. The effect seems to be similar on physical health. As an example, Warr and Jackson (1984), in a study of unemployed British workers, found that there was a rapid deterioration of physical health for the first six months of unemployment and then a leveling off of health-related problems. From then on, the health of the unemployed worker was substantially below that of his employed counterpart.

The next decade will create some unique problems for training specialists—specifically, how to keep the soft-core from becoming the hard-core unemployed. We will come back to the issue of unemployment and its effects on individuals in the chapter on job satisfaction.

EQUAL EMPLOYMENT OPPORTUNITY GUIDELINES AND TRAINING

On Monday, December 11, 1978, the Supreme Court of the United States agreed to hear arguments regarding the potential adverse impact of training programs. Brian Weber, a Kaiser Aluminum and Chemical Corp. worker, claimed that he was a victim of reverse discrimination since, as a white employee, he was denied access to a company training program because half of all openings in the training program were reserved for blacks. If successful completion of a training program is a prerequisite for promotion within a company, then admission to that training program is, in effect, a type of selection decision. Although acceptance in the training program does not necessarily guarantee promotion, nonacceptance does guarantee that an individual will not be promoted. Thus, training programs must be responsive to the EEOC guidelines in a manner similar to testing programs.

Bartlett (1978) has considered the potential sources of discrimination in training programs:

1. *Training as a job prerequisite.* The most obvious example of this is the requirement that applicants for positions have certain academic credentials such as a high school or college diploma. As the Supreme Court stated in the 1971 *Griggs* v. *Duke Power* case, job relevance of the requirement must be established before it can be used for making selection decisions. To use

this prerequisite, it would be necessary to demonstrate that individuals without training perform more poorly than those with training.

2. *Selection for training.* As was implied in the earlier description of the reverse discrimination suit brought by Weber against Kaiser Aluminum, entry into training programs can be a critical issue in personnel decisions. In the past, the Court has ruled on several occasions that it is not sufficient to show that devices used for selecting trainees are correlated with training success. It must also be shown that training success is related to job success, in other words, the training program has some job relevance. Thus, the individual responsible for administration of the training program must give some thought to the manner by which individuals are selected for training. This may become a critical issue in training programs of the future.
3. *The training process.* The training activities themselves may have adverse impact on particular subgroups. Equipment may be designed for men rather than women, thus requiring strength or reach capabilities that are unrelated to job duties but largely determine training success. The same may be true of vocabulary levels or communication skills that are unrelated to ultimate job success but influence measured training success. For this particular problem, Bartlett suggests that the best way to address it reasonably is to go beyond a simple task analysis and do a "person" analysis, designed to uncover any individual difficulties related to the training process itself. This requires one actually to "look at" the trainee in the training situation—a good idea for lots of reasons.[4]
4. *Retention, progress, and graduation.* Occasionally, measures of training success are taken during the training program and are used to determine who will be "washed out" of training prior to completion. This might be thought of as the "football camp" approach where a certain percentage of the trainees are "cut" at various points in the training sequence. Unless these training measures are validated, there is the potential for unfair discrimination in these retention decisions.
5. *Job placement following training.* At the end of training, trainees are often

[4]A friend of mine, Irv Goldstein, delights in recalling an incident from his graduate school days as a research assistant. While assisting a professor doing operant conditioning of pigeons, Goldstein noticed that one pigeon was performing at much lower levels than the other subjects. In addition, the particular closed box that served as the experimental apparatus for this pigeon would occasionally shake, and there would be loud thumping noises accompanying the box movement. Goldstein asked the researcher for permission to observe this subject "in action"; the request was denied emphatically and immediately. The operant advocate felt that the pigeon would "shape up" shortly. Nevertheless, Goldstein looked into the box while the researcher was absent and discovered that the poor pigeon had somehow learned the wrong sequence of behaviors for producing the reward. It would go to the back of the box and run full speed to the front of the box, hitting the wall with an alarming impact. The impact was sufficient to trip the dispensing mechanism, thus releasing a reward. As far as the pigeon was concerned, this was the appropriate sequence in the "training" program. Trainers should be aware that it is often useful to "look in the box." In this case, the pigeon was saved, but Goldstein was chewed out.

assigned to jobs based on their success in the training program. Once again, there is the potential for unfair discrimination in these placement decisions unless the training measures have been shown to be job related.

6. *Promotion, advancement, and compensation.* If training is a prerequisite for promotion, advancement, or compensation increases, then the problem is similar to requiring training prior to employment. This was exactly the point of the *Weber* v. *Kaiser* case.

Validity of Training Programs

A recent review of court cases since Bartlett's review has been conducted by Russell (1984). In addition to identifying many of the same factors as Bartlett in court decisions, Russell also considered the issue of training as a criterion. In other words, he was interested in how courts considered the validity of training programs. He discovered that unless a training program could be shown to be job related, the courts tended to be skeptical of training success as a sole criterion for validating a selection device. Both Bownas, Bosshardt, and Donnelly (1985) and Goldstein (1986) confirm the importance of validating a training program. There are two different issues to be concerned with in considering the validity of a training program. The first is contamination, and the second is deficiency. *Contamination* means that there are elements in the training program that have nothing to do with job performance. For example, we might decide to train all our employees in the use of word processing equipment. But if many of our employees did not use word processing equipment in performing their job, then training success would be irrelevant (i.e., not job-related) for many of our employees. Keep in mind that validity in the training context means the same thing as validity in the selection context. We want to be able to infer that those who do better in training will do better on the job. To the extent to which that inference can be justified, we can claim validity for our training program. *Deficiency* in the training context would mean that important aspects of the job are not represented in the training program. The more of the job left out of the training program, the less confident we would be that those who do well in training will do well on the job. Thus, as was the case with contamination, deficiency is a threat to the validity of training programs.

It should be clear from the description above that in addition to evaluating training in terms of its effectiveness and cost, we must also consider whether the administration of the training program conforms to existing local, state, and federal regulations regarding employment decisions.

THE MAINTENANCE OF EFFECTIVENESS: RETRAINING AND UPDATING

Much of the emphasis of this chapter has been on the development of skills and knowledge in new employees so that they can reach a competency level of performance on the job for which they are hired. A major exception to this emphasis was found in the section on management development, in which the principal concern was with increasing proficiency on the job and promotability to higher levels of responsibility. In both cases, the emphasis has been on increasing the overall proficiency of employees and, consequently, their value to the organization.

In recent years, an increasing concern has developed for an area of training with a considerably more negative ring. Rather than expressing concern for broadening and increasing skills and adaptability of employees, researchers and theorists in this area have sounded an alarm for the problems of loss of proficiency as learned information and skills become "obsolete," as the applicability of knowledge "erodes," and as the effectiveness of once-valuable employees declines in the face of new knowledge and technology. The alarm may be relatively new but not the problem. Lukasiewicz (1971) estimated that in 1940 the "half-life" of the knowledge a newly trained engineer brought to a job was about 12 years. That is, in 12 years, one-half of this knowledge would be obsolete or no longer applicable. The basis for the increasing alarm is that the problem has been accentuated by an accelerated growth in knowledge and technology. Lukasiewicz estimated that the half-life of a 1970 graduating engineer was probably five years. Meanwhile, the half-life of the content in a university engineering course ("electronic circuits") was also estimated at about five years (Rosenstein, 1968).

One aspect of the problem of obsolescence is found in rapid changes in knowledge and technology, which, as previously suggested, makes the information and skills that are adequate to accomplish a job at one point in time insufficient, or at best inefficient, only a few years later. That is, obsolescence can come about because an employee's knowledge or skills remain static or change too slowly compared with changes in his field. A second problem—which is related to and yet different from that of technological obsolescence—is that of the loss of effectiveness as a result of the disuse or forgetting of information or skills. Thus, we can conceive of the problem as an increasing discrepancy between job demands and employee skills resulting from (1) changing demands with a relatively static skill level, (2) deteriorating skills such that job demands the employee could have handled earlier cannot now be met, or (3) some combination of these factors. The first situation requires training in new knowledge and techniques—what S. S. Dubin (1972a, 1972b) has called the *updating process*. The second situation is concerned with the *maintenance* of previously learned knowledge and skills through refresher training or through continued application on the job.

Electronics engineers may become obsolete because they were trained in a period before solid-state technology or because the job does not give them an opportunity to apply their knowledge of solid-state electronics, and they forget much of what they have learned. Physicians may become obsolete because they learned internal medicine 30 years too soon or, having subsequently specialized in pediatrics, have forgotten much knowledge about internal disorders.

Why Does Obsolescence Occur?

You may be thinking that the engineers or the physicians have become obsolete by choice, since in all likelihood they could have maintained skills and learned new ones had they been sufficiently motivated to do so. Others may say that the older workers simply cannot keep up with the new technology because they are older. Yet others may suggest that it is not so much that older employees cannot keep up but that they are not motivated to do so—they are either "fat, lazy, and secure" in the job, or they see nothing in it for them that is worth the effort to learn new techniques. No doubt there are kernels of truth in each of the pat answers, but such simplistic models are inadequate for understanding the problem.

Age and Performance. In a study of engineers, Dalton and Thompson (1971) explored the relationship between the age of engineers and three measures of effectiveness: performance ratings, job complexity ratings, and salary. The results of this analysis are shown in Figure 9–10. Clearly, ratings of performance and complexity rose and fell together with a steady decline after age 36–40. Meanwhile, salary continued to increase for about 10 years after the ratings peaked and had begun to decline.

At first blush, these data suggest a marked relationship between age and effectiveness as an engineer. However, since both the performance and job complexity criteria are based on subjective ratings, the close relationship between the two suggests some other possibilities. One possibility is that as the performance of engineers declines with age, their supervisors tend to assign them to less and less complex jobs. Another hypothesis is that supervision is biased toward the young "hotshots" who are fresh from university training and are given the more complex jobs, which leaves the less complex jobs for the older engineers. It may also be that despite efforts to distinguish between ratings of job performance and ratings of job complexity the supervisors may have had a built-in bias to rate *jobs* when they are supposed to rate *performance* (Levin & Butler, 1952). Thus, we have reason to question the meaning of the performance ratings, but even assuming their validity and freedom from contamination, we may well ask why performance goes down even on increasingly simple jobs at such a precipitous rate. It may well be a vicious cycle in which an engineer is given more and more routine assignments, which are less and less challenging and offer fewer opportunities to practice skills. Furthermore, unless the engineer believes that this cycle can be dramatically changed by extra efforts to keep up with new technology, he probably will not make the effort. It should be pointed out, however, that Dalton and Thompson (1971) found a good deal more variability in ratings *within* each age category than between them. The highest ratings for the "over-50" engineers were considerably higher than the average ratings at any age group. Therefore, it is necessary to be cautious when generalizing about *older workers*.

FIGURE 9–10 Age and Three Measures of Engineers' Effectiveness: Performance Ratings, Job Complexity Ratings, and Salary

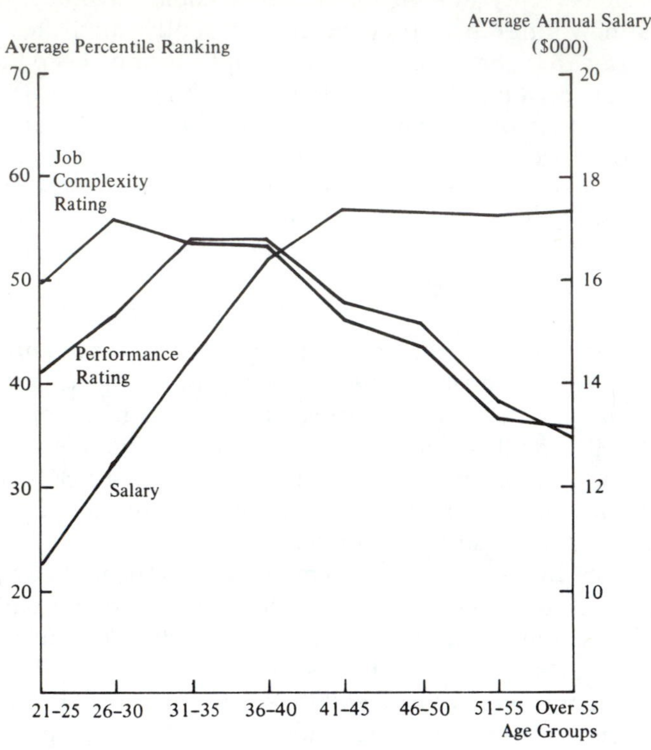

SOURCE: Adapted from "Accelerating Obsolescence of Older Engineers" by G. W. Dalton and P. H. Thompson, 1971, *Harvard Business Review, 49.*

Age, Performance, and Updating. The study by Dalton and Thompson provides some answers to the question, How do the "updating activities" of engineers compare at different ages and different performance levels? The three indicators of updating activity examined were (1) total (reported) hours per week reading professional journals; (2) total number of company courses taken; and (3) total number of college courses taken in the past three years. The first of these showed no systematic relationship with age or performance ratings, but both company and college course taking declined with age, relatively independently of performance ratings. Thus, in general, participation in activities that might be assumed to counteract obsolescence actually declines with age.

Age and Expectancies. Some insights as to why engineers do not show evidence of efforts to update themselves (the study also suggests less effort on the job as age increases) may be found in the Dalton and Thompson analyses of age and expectancies with respect to promotion and salaries. The engineers rated their chances for (1) promotion in engineering, (2) promotion into management, and (3) their maximum hoped-for salary. The results for four different age groups are shown in Figure 9–11.

The results are consistent and clear: age is associated with a marked decline in expectancies for advancement either through promotions or salary increases. Certainly these results suggest that two classes of incentives for job performance (and presumably for the maintenance of skills requisite to job performance)—advancement and salary—have lost some of their incentive value for the older engineers.

Combatting Obsolescence

D. T. Hall and Mansfield (1975) have suggested that professionals engaged in research and development activities (scientists, engineers) show three distinct stages to their careers. The first stage, called the *early career stage* (ages 20–34), is characterized by low job involvement, low intrinsic motivation, low needs for security, and high needs for self-actualization. The *mid-career stage* (ages 35–49) is characterized by greater job involvement, more intrinsic motivation, and a general personal stabilization. The *late career stage* (ages 50 and older) is characterized by high concerns for security and low needs for self-fulfillment and autonomy. In this stage, there is a great concern for holding on to the current job, with very little effort devoted to "breaking new ground."

If Hall and Mansfield are correct, it is not difficult to understand why obsolescence is a problem with older workers. In a sense, they have finally learned to do something well and are not excited about the prospects of attempting to develop new skills and to begin making errors all over again. As physicists have been trying to tell us for centuries, bodies at rest tend to stay at rest!

Nevertheless, simply labeling workers by stages does not help to alleviate the problem. Kaufman (1975) has examined the problem from a slightly different point of view. He has identified some variables that may help to get the potentially obsolete worker moving again. He found that those in less demanding jobs tended to engage in less demanding updating exercises. While this may be of some small comfort to organizations (i.e., obsolescence seems centered among those individuals who would do the least "damage" to the organization), Kaufman suggests that the organization may reverse this obsolescence trend by enriching the jobs of these workers. This would follow from the fact that those with more challenging jobs tend to treat updating requirements more seriously. Although it is inappropriate to draw causal inferences from this type of correlational data, Kaufman's suggestion does at least give the concerned manager a place to start. Recent research by Kozlowski and Farr (1988) seems to confirm this proposition. They found that engineers confronted with a need for new knowledge as a result of techno-

FIGURE 9–11 Engineers' Perceptions of Their Chances for Promotion to Management (lower curve), Chances for Promotion in Engineering (middle), and Maximum Hoped-for Salary (*upper) as Function of Age

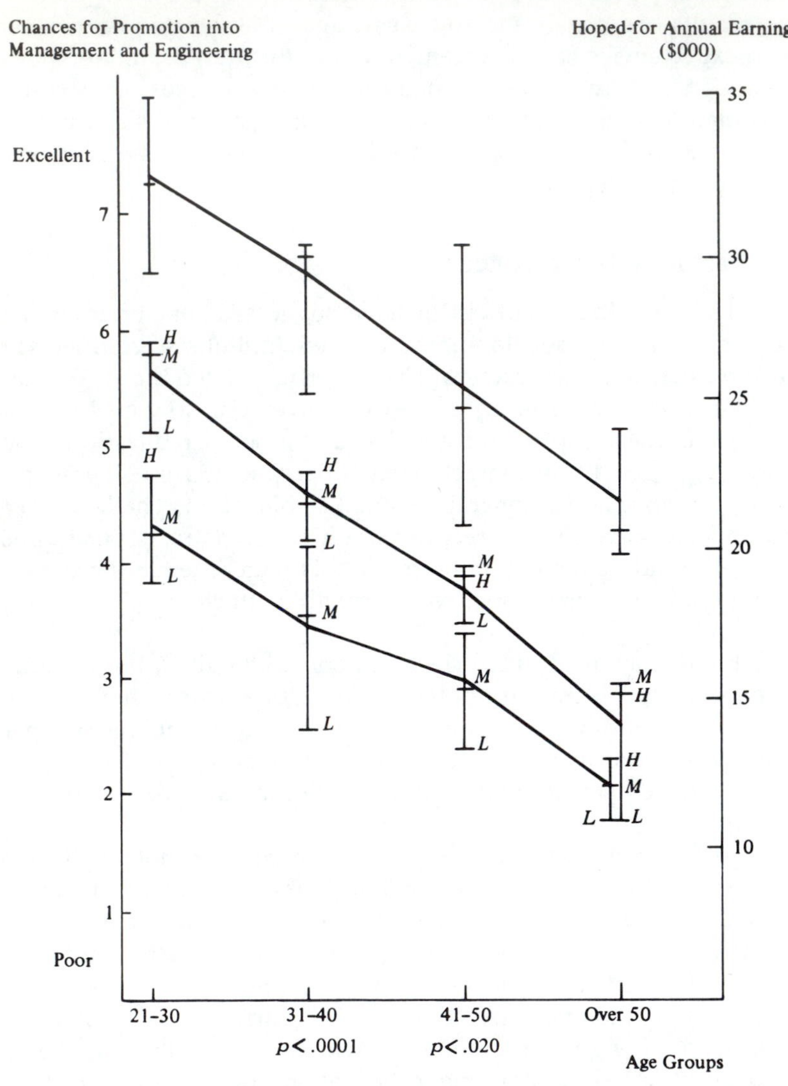

SOURCE: Adapted from exhibits 7, 8, and 9 of "Factors Contributing to the Effectiveness of the Older Engineer" by R. Kopelman, P. Thompson, and G. Dalton, in S. S. Dubin, H. Shelton, and J. McConnell (Eds.), *Maintaining Professional and Technical Competence of the Older Engineer*, 1974, Washington, D.C.: American Society of Engineering Education.

logical uncertainty in their jobs were more likely to seek updating than engineers simply told that training was good or provided external inducements for training. In fact, Kozlowski and Farr go so far as to suggest that it might not be a bad idea to *introduce* uncertainty to create a motivation to update in the professional employee.

In addition to the situation where the job requires new technical information on the part of the incumbent, there are also situations in which the work role systematically changes in some important way. There has been some research done that attempted to identify those individuals who would be most likely to adapt successfully to these role changes. Morrison (1977a) found that individuals who had engaged in many management development activities were more likely to adapt successfully to role changes. This is a rather important finding for an organization concerned about the value of nonspecific training, or what has come to be known as *generalized management development*. Morrison's results suggest that frequent management development activities keep people "loose" and flexible. It is almost as if they were continually learning to learn, a concept that has become popular in some more traditional learning circles (Harlow, 1959).

In summary, it seems as if there is a tendency for workers to become personally and professionally cautious in their work behavior as they get older. This effect is compounded by the diminishing importance of traditional incentives such as pay and promotion. The result is a strong emphasis on the status quo with respect to technical knowledge. In rapidly changing fields, to remain constant is to become obsolete. The meager research available suggests that this obsolescence might be reversed through job enrichment and continuing management development activity.

CENTRAL POINTS FOR STUDY

1. Training, learning, and performance are different concepts.
2. Training needs are established through a needs analysis.
3. Learning theory can be used to establish training programs.
4. Many conditions will affect the transfer of training to job situations.
5. The validity of a training program should be established.
6. A major challenge in training is dealing with the unemployed.
7. Training programs can be usefully directed toward combatting obsolescence.

CHAPTER 10

The Motivation to Work

The underlying assumption in an auto plant is that no worker wants to work. The plant is arranged so that employees can be controlled, checked and supervised at every point. The efficiency of an assembly line is not only in its speed but in the fact that the workers are easily replaced. This allows the employer to cope with high turnover. But it's a vicious cycle. The job is so unpleasantly subdivided that men are constantly quitting and absenteeism is common. Even an accident is a welcome diversion. Because of the high turnover, management further simplifies the job and more men quit. But the company has learned to cope with high turnover. So they don't have to worry if men quit or go crazy before they're forty. (Garson, 1972, p. 73)

Millwork ain't easy,
Millwork ain't hard,
Millwork it ain't nothin but an awful boring job.
I'm waitin' for my daydream,
To take me through the morning,
and put me in my coffee break,
where I can have a sandwich and remember.
Then it's me and my machine for the rest of the morning,
and the rest of the afternoon,
and the rest of my life.

SOURCE: From "Millworker," words and music by James Taylor, © 1979, Country Roads Music, Inc. Used by permission of Warner/Chappell Music, Inc. All rights reserved.

The first passage above is taken from an article by Barbara Garson about the nature of work at the General Motors plant in Lordstown, Ohio. The second passage is from a song written by James Taylor called "Millworker." These passages are not intended to represent all auto plants and mills accurately, but they do describe a point of view commonly held in many manufacturing settings, regardless of what is manufactured. It is a very pessimistic approach to work motivation. It implies

The assembly of circuit boards requires close attention to detail. (C-COR Electronics)

that motivational strategies are like heart-lung machines. As long as they are plugged in, the person continues to expend energy. Once they are unplugged, energy expenditure stops. The heart-lung machine in this case is control.

This chapter is intended to rebut this pessimistic view of motivated behavior. I will examine the theory and data that describe work motivation. As I hope you will see, there is virtually no evidence to support the heart-lung theory. Instead, there are data that suggest that motivation is a complex combination of perceptions, aspirations, and environmental interactions.

Even though many employers would reject the heart-lung approach to motivation, they are still at a loss to explain what forces affect the energy that workers invest in work-related activities. What is behind the decision to take one job rather than another? When they have decided on and accepted a job, why do they continue to come to that job every day, even when they may not "feel like going to work"? When they arrive at the job, why do they work hard to complete the task assigned on a particular day rather than discuss world affairs with coworkers?

These are questions that a theory of work motivation must answer. Given that the heart-lung theory is wrong, what theory is "right"? In the past, the answers were superficial. The most prevalent answer was money. This was a legacy of the scientific management approach of Frederick W. Taylor and other industrial engineers. But if we simply look at ourselves for data, we know that there are many things we would do even if we were not being paid to do them. For example, many workers are reluctant to retire even though their retirement benefits may be equal to or better than their take-home pay. In addition, there are an equal number of things we would not do, no matter how much money was offered. Not many of us would consider getting in a boxing ring with Mike Tyson regardless of the amount of money offered. It is common to hear someone say, "I wouldn't do that job no matter how much they paid me!" These simple data should be sufficient to convince us that we will need an explanation a little more complete than "money."

In the late 1950s and early 1960s, psychologists began to investigate seriously the relationships among job satisfaction, work motivation, and job performance. Soon after this research was begun, it became apparent that a framework for guiding the research—a theory of work behavior—was missing. For several decades, the only statement even coming close to a theory of work behavior was the commonplace belief that "a happy worker is a productive worker." But upon close examination, this theory was of little use. Did it mean that if you make a worker happy, she will *then* be productive, or did it mean that productive workers tend to be happier? Even more serious problems were presented by the fact that individuals could be found who were unhappy yet productive (not to mention the slightly larger group of happy and unproductive workers). Recent research has been directed at supplying the missing theoretical framework necessary for a reasonable discussion of the psychological aspects of work behavior.

Work motivation probably does not differ greatly from other kinds of motivation. For that reason, most of the models or theories of work motivation have their roots in the more general field of human motivation. There are a number of potential definitions of motivation, but the following one is most useful for the purposes of this chapter: *Motivation concerns the conditions responsible for variations in intensity, quality, and direction of ongoing behavior* (Vinacke, 1962). This definition makes it clear that work motivation is only one instance of a more general process. Although the conditions under which work is performed differ substantially from the conditions under which other behavior patterns occur, new theories are not needed to account for industrial behavior. The work context only requires some different ways of measuring the components of existing motivational models.

In this chapter, broad classes of work motivation theories will be presented. Within each class, variations and modifications will be described. Five general classes will be considered: (1) *need* theory, (2) *instrumentality* theory, (3) *comparison* theory, (4) *goal setting* theory, and (5) *reinforcement* theory. The various theories will be summarized and their similarities and dissimilarities described. In addition, some topics that are having a great impact on research in work motivation will be introduced. Finally, I will identify some principles that can be used to guide managers in improving the motivation of an individual or group.

THEORIES OF WORK MOTIVATION

There are several ways in which the theories of work motivation may be presented. A good framework was suggested by J. P. Campbell et al. (1970). They classified the theories as either "process" or "content." Process theories have as their objective explaining *how* behavior is initiated, directed, sustained, and stopped. Content theories search for the specific things within individuals that initiate, direct, sustain, and stop behavior. A silly example that might make the distinction clearer is a "theory of 10-speed bicycle riding." A process theory would concentrate on *how* energy is distributed from the rider to various devices, such as the pedals, hand brakes, and shifting levers. A content theory would focus on the nature of the energy source—why is it there to start with? This content-process distinction is a good one to keep in mind while reading the description of the motivational models, and it will be referred to often in the discussion of the five classes of motivation theories that follows.

An Introductory Comment

The development of various motivation theories has been sporadic. In the late 1950s and early 1960s, there was a great deal of activity in developing and testing need theories and comparison theories. After a dormant period, expectancy theory appeared and held sway for a decade or two. During the "expectancy era," goal setting theory began to build a head of steam, culminating in a coup that saw goal setting theory topple expectancy theory as the "preferred" theory of work motivation. In the past several years, there has been a flood of goal setting research in the journals. In the past two or three years, there has been a shift from straight goal setting to the role of personal efficacy (i.e., the belief that one can overcome task-related obstacles) in goal attainment.

The point of this brief history is that motivation theory is evolutionary and has experienced substantial change in the past few decades. But that does not mean that we can forget about theories that are not in vogue. In order to know where we are, we need to know where we have been. Nevertheless, I plan to give more coverage to those theories receiving the greatest attention currently. In particular, coverage of expectancy theory will be reduced in this edition compared with earlier editions to make room for goal setting and self-efficacy theory. More extensive reviews of expectancy theory can be found in earlier editions of this text (Landy, 1985; Landy & Trumbo, 1980).

Some Need Theories

Maslow's Need Hierarchy Theory. Maslow proposed that all individuals have basic sets of needs that they strive to fulfill over the course of their lives. As such, it is a broad theory of human development rather than a description of adult development or work motivation specifically. Nevertheless, I/O psychologists commonly consider only the adult years and, even then, seldom any other context than work. The industrial application assumes that individuals strive to meet their needs at the work setting and that understanding how these needs are met will lead to an understanding of work-related behavior. As a result, we will consider these work-related environments, but for a fuller appreciation of the theory, you should go to an early primary source and consider the broader perspective (Maslow, 1943).

Maslow's theory is, by far, the most popular and well known of the need hierarchy class. His theory is useful as a place to start because it emphasizes the idea of the hierarchical arrangement of needs. In 1943, he proposed that individuals have five basic set of needs:

1. *Physiological needs.* These are what learning theories generally refer to as basic needs or drives and are satisfied by such things as food, water, and sleep.
2. *Safety needs.* This category refers to the need an individual has to produce a secure environment—one free of threats to continued existence.
3. *Love needs.* These needs are concerned with interpersonal factors. They reflect an individual's desire to be accepted by peers.
4. *Esteem needs.* This describes the need an individual has to occupy a position in time and space as a function of who he is and what he is capable of. This need level transcends the previous level of love needs in that the affection of one's peers is not sufficient.
5. *Self-actualization needs.* This is generally described as the need for self-fulfillment; one strives toward the full realization of unique characteristics and potentials.

The most important characteristic of this need system is that it is arranged in predetermined levels. The arrangement of these needs is described in Figure 10–1.

The most basic unsatisfied need at any given time is considered to be the most important. Individuals will always strive to satisfy basic needs before higher-order needs. Furthermore, individuals will move up the hierarchy in a very systematic manner, satisfying first the physiological needs, then the safety needs, and so on.

If our concern is the motivation of employees, this theory tells us that it is essential to know what needs the individual is trying to satisfy. It implies that individuals will instigate, direct, and sustain activity to satisfy certain needs. It further implies that a personnel manager can set up a systematic program of motivation if she knows which needs are most important to an individual at a particular time and provides the environment necessary for the fulfillment of these needs.

What happens when an individual reaches the ultimate level of motivation—the self-actualization level? Is the self-actualized person no longer

FIGURE 10–1 Maslow's Hierarchy of Needs

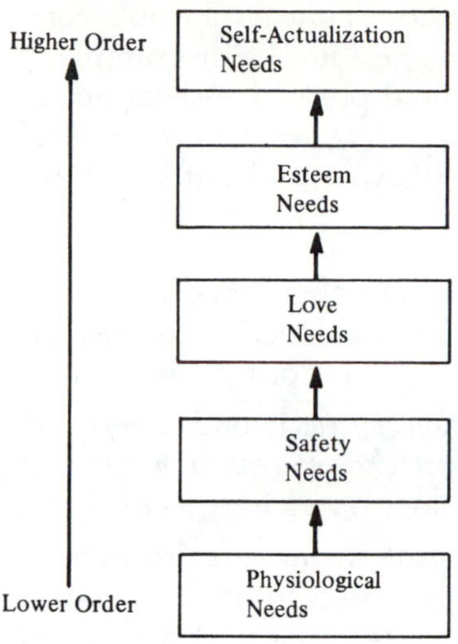

motivated? If that were the case, there would be good reason for managers to *prevent* workers from satisfying self-actualization needs. The theory takes this into account. It proposes that when an individual reaches the self-actualization level, the process changes—the self-actualization need feeds on itself. The more self-actualized the person becomes, the greater the need for self-actualization.

Even though a good deal of cross-sectional research has been done on Maslow's model, only a few longitudinal studies have been undertaken. There is an important difference between the two approaches. If Maslow's propositions are to have any value in the explanation of work motivation, they must be supported by data that describe the progress of individuals through the need hierarchy. For example, the theory must be supported with data that show that when an individual's love needs are satisfied, his esteem needs become more important. Most cross-sectional research designs in this area identify individuals at different organizational levels, gather information relating to the need level at which the individuals are operating, and make inferences about what conditions exist in the organizational environment that explain why the individual is operating at this need level. This is a *necessary* but not *sufficient* condition for support of the theory. For the model to receive strong support, these cross-sectional data must be backed up with longitudinal data.

Two studies yield data that contradict the Maslow model. D. T. Hall and Nougaim (1968) found that need intensity correlated *positively* with need satisfaction. This means that the more a need is satisfied, the more important it becomes. With the exception of the self-actualization level, this finding is in direct opposition to the need hierarchy theory of Maslow. The theory would predict that need satisfaction at one level would correlate positively with need importance scores for the *next* level. For example, an individual whose love needs were satisfied should perceive esteem needs as more important than love needs. The Hall and Nougaim data contradict that proposition.

A second study, by Lawler and Suttle (1972), tested three hypotheses related to Maslow's theory:

1. The *satisfaction* of needs in one category should correlate negatively with the *importance* of these same needs and positively with the *importance* of needs in the next higher level of the hierarchy.
2. *Changes in the satisfaction of needs* in one category should correlate negatively with *changes in the importance of needs in the same category* and positively with *changes in the importance of needs* in the next higher level of the hierarchy.
3. *High satisfaction of the needs* in one category at time one should be associated with *low importance of the needs* in the same category at time two and with *high importance of the needs* in the next higher category of the hierarchy at time two.

From hypotheses two and three it can be seen that a longitudinal design was used in this study. Since Lawler and Suttle had measurements on the subjects at more than one time, they were able to describe the behavior of individuals as these individuals supposedly moved through the hierarchy. Once again, no support was provided for the Maslow model. On the basis of the data analyses, all three hypotheses were rejected. A review of tests of the Maslow need hierarchy theory (Wahba & Bridwell, 1976) concluded that there is no longitudinal support for the theory and only weak support from cross-sectional studies. Wahba and Bridwell suggest that the need hierarchy theory suffers from both conceptual and operational shortcomings:

> The most problematic aspect of Maslow's theory, however, is that dealing with the concept of need itself. It is not clear what is meant by the concept of need. Does need have a psychological and/or physiological base? Does a need come to existence because of deficiency only or does need always exist even if it is gratified? How can we identify, isolate and measure different needs? There is ample evidence that people seek objects and engage in behavior that are in no way related to the satisfaction of needs. In a discussion of this point, Cofer and Apply (1964) concluded that this is probably also true for animals. Vroom (1964) does not use the concept of needs in his discussion of motivation. Lawler (1971) argued that concept of valence is related to that of need, e.g., objects acquire valence because of their instrumentality for meeting the basic needs of people. Lawler (1971), however, limits the use of the term to certain stimuli (or outcomes) that can be grouped together because they are sought by people. Even if we accept such a limited view of needs, the remaining question should be, why should needs be structured in a fixed hierarchy? Does this hierarchy vary for

different people? What happens to the hierarchy over time? How can we have a fixed hierarchy when behavior is multidetermined? (pp. 234–235)

Criticisms such as these are more than bothersome—they are terminal. The more recent research into Maslow's propositions has been sporadic and has involved the construction of new instruments to test the Maslow propositions (Mitchell & Moudgill, 1976). As a result, at the present time, Maslow's theory is of more historical than functional value. Nevertheless, it should be pointed out again that Maslow's theory is intended to be considerably broader than the typical research designs allow. It is unlikely that the changes in need levels occur as rapidly as implied by the research. Instead of weeks or months, it might be more appropriate to look at changes over years. Furthermore, instead of simply considering work-related behaviors and needs, it would seem critical to consider nonwork environments as well. As you will see in the next chapter, it is difficult and logically questionable to separate completely work from nonwork attitudes and behaviors.

Although it might be fair to say that Maslow's theory has still received no good empirical test in the industrial literature, the theoretical criticisms of Wahba and Bridwell are not as easily dismissed. They have been noted by psychologists in all areas where human motivation is of interest. The integrity of a "need" construct of any kind is dubious.

Need Achievement Theory. Independent of Maslow's theory, there have been some alternative motivational models suggested in which needs play an important role. The need for achievement (often referred to as *nAch* has been suggested by many as the primary basis for motivated behavior. Murray (1938) was one of the first to suggest this mechanism. He considered the need for achievement to be the desire "to overcome obstacles, to exercise power, to strive to do something difficult as well and as quickly as possible" (pp. 80–81). This was 1 of 20 needs that were thought to motivate action in human beings. It was in order to measure the strengths of needs such as this that Murray devised the Thematic Apperception Test (TAT) that has been used so widely by personality theorists and clinical psychologists.

McClelland (1955) developed a theory of motivation based predominantly on the need for achievement (and a related tendency called the *fear of failure).* He suggested that certain cues or stimuli in the environment acquire motivational properties by virtue of having been associated with success and failure in the past. If a person succeeded in the past in a particular situation, then the person would be more likely to engage in achieving behaviors in the future in a similar situation. Failure would have the opposite effect. Atkinson (1964) elaborated and tightened many of McClelland's notions and made the theory considerably more cognitive. We will not go into the general research literature on need achievement theory but will consider one rather specific and recent line of research in industrial settings. For those interested in learning more about need achievement theory, Beck (1983) does an excellent job of describing the theory and accompanying research. In addition, we will consider an offshoot of achievement theory in the leadership chapter. McClelland and his colleagues have suggested that certain types of individuals are motivated to lead or influence others. These leadership-prone individuals are characterized by strong needs in particular areas.

Steers (Steers, 1975; Steers & Spencer, 1977) has conducted some research suggesting that the need for achievement affects the relationship between performance and satisfaction. In particular, he finds that the correlations between performance and satisfaction are substantial for individuals with high needs for achievement but do not differ from zero for low-need achievers. In terms of the original statement of the theory, this means that work situations, generally, and work goals, specifically, have become associated in the past with achievement (and the accompanying pleasure derived from satisfying this need). Steers interprets this to mean that good performance is a reward *in and of itself* for high-need achievers. He further suggests that increasing the scope of the job by making it more autonomous and challenging can have positive effects on the performance of high-need achievers. This would suggest that job enrichment might be wasted on low-need achievers. In spite of these optimistic conclusions, Steers appropriately points out that these *nAch* effects on performance may be relatively minor when compared with the effects of reward levels and pressures for production.

ERG Theory. Alderfer (1969, 1972) has proposed a theory called the *ERG theory*. Instead of the five levels of need suggested by Maslow, Alderfer considers the individual to have three basic sets of needs:

1. *Existence needs.* These are material existence needs and are satisfied by environmental factors such as food, water, pay, fringe benefits, and working conditions.
2. *Relatedness needs.* These needs deal with maintaining interpersonal relatedness with significant other people such as coworkers, superiors, subordinates, family, friends, and enemies.
3. *Growth needs.* These needs are manifested in the individual's attempt to seek opportunities for unique personal development. They comprise all needs that involve a person attempting to have creative or productive effects on herself and the environment.

Although the rearrangement of the various needs from Maslow's hierarchy is interesting, the most noteworthy aspect of Alderfer's theory is the inclusion of a different "process" to explain how people move from one level to another. The process of Maslow's model may be expressed as one of "fulfillment-progression"; that is, an individual must satisfy one level of need before moving on to the next higher level. In addition to the fulfillment-progression component, Alderfer has added a "frustration-regression" component. Alderfer assumes that existence, relatedness, and growth vary on a

FIGURE 10–2 Dynamic Properties of Maslow's Model (fulfillment-progression)

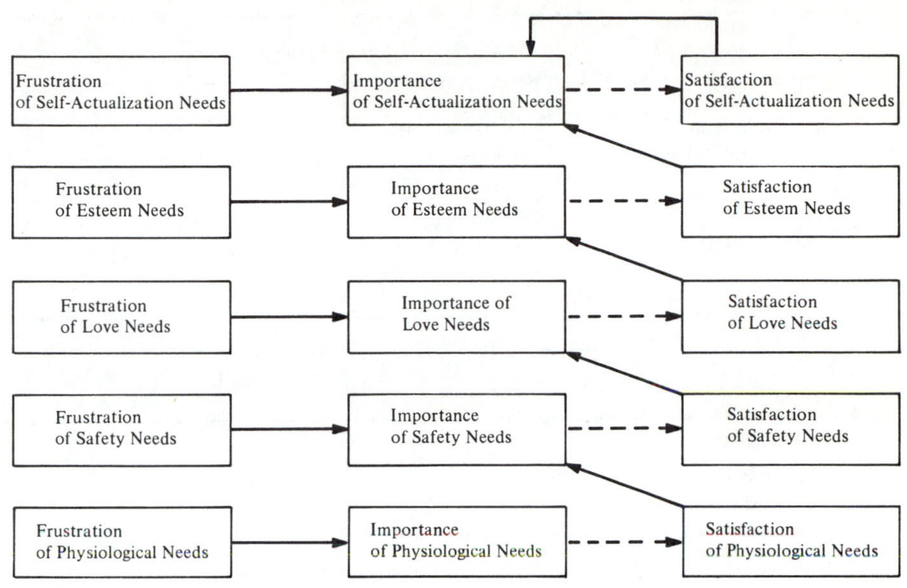

continuum of concreteness, with existence needs being the most concrete, relatedness needs being moderately concrete, and the growth needs being least concrete. He further assumes that when the less concrete needs are not met, more concrete need fulfillment is sought.

This means that the rigid ordering of Maslow's hierarchy is no longer appropriate. The difference between Alderfer and Maslow can be described in both *content* and *process* terms. They differ in content terms on the basis of the needs proposed: for Maslow there are five needs; for Alderfer there are three (although the substance of the needs themselves do not differ substantially in the two theories). They differ a good deal more in process terms: for Maslow, the process is one of fulfillment-progression; for Alderfer, both fulfillment-progression and frustration-regression are important dynamic elements. Figures 10–2 and 10–3 describe the differences between the two models in diagram form.

In a sense, Alderfer's view of motivation is a more hopeful one for managers. It provides them with the possibility of constructively channeling the energy of their subordinates even when the individual's higher-level needs are blocked. This energy can be directed toward lower-level needs. Even though the ERG variation was proposed almost two decades ago, there has been very little research conducted on it. What has been done provides mixed evidence for its value. For example, a study by Wanous and Zwany (1977) supported the existence of the three categories suggested by Alderfer. Nev-

FIGURE 10–3 Dynamic Properties of Alderfer's Model (fulfillment-progression; frustration-regression)

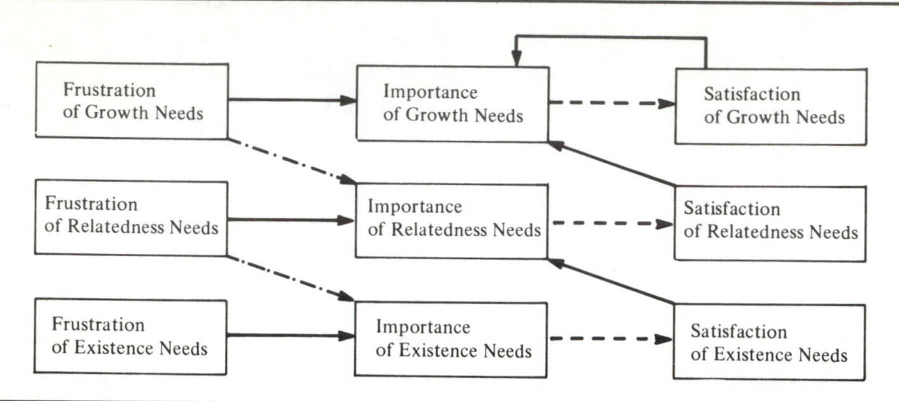

ertheless, they conclude that need hierarchy theories may be of little value in day-to-day management practices. Similarly, research by Rauschenberger, Schmitt, and Hunter (1980) does provide evidence that people tend to categorize their needs in the three-dimensional framework suggested by Alderfer, but there was no evidence for changes in these need levels over time. The same study provided additional evidence rejecting Maslow's hierarchical model.

In summary, it seems that when Maslow's model is put to the proper test, it leaves much to be desired. Models such as those in the need hierarchy group tend to be useful in the sense that they provide both process and content statements. As J. P. Campbell et al. (1970) point out, good theory must specify *both* content *and* process considerations. It may be that a redefinition of the need levels in Maslow's model as well as the process component of the model will yield more supportive data. In addition, the newer cognitive theories of motivation include a variable called *self-efficacy* or *personal efficacy* (Bandura, 1982, 1986, 1987). This variable is related to the extent to which the individual believes herself to be capable of overcoming environmental obstacles in pursuit of a goal. It may be that this variable is a more refined version of the earlier need constructs. We will consider this possibility in a later section of the chapter.

Two-Factor Theory. An extremely popular theory of work motivation over the past 25 years has been Herzberg's *motivator-hygiene* or *two-factor* theory. His theory has the same foundation as all need theories: the assumption that each individual is born with certain needs that must be satisfied. In contrast with the five-factor theory of Maslow, or the three-factor theory of Alderfer, Herzberg (1966) proposes that all individuals have two basic sets of needs, hygiene needs and motivator needs. The hygiene needs are basically maintenance needs. Herzberg likens them to those elements that provide us with a healthy environment. In a work setting, these needs would include such things as pay, security, coworkers, general working conditions, and company policies. Motivator needs are higher-order or growth needs. These needs are unique to humans and distinguish them from other animals. These needs seem to be related to some innate characteristic of individuals that requires them to seek challenge, stimulation, and autonomy. These needs are satisfied by things such as responsible work, independence of action, and recognition for the accomplishment of difficult tasks. In short, these needs are satisfied by things that are part of the work itself, rather than the context in which the work gets done.

According to Herzberg, there are two levels of functioning: motivation seeking and hygiene seeking. Motivation seeking is thought to be clearly preferable since it yields productive activity on the part of the worker and minimal "control" problems for management. In a sense, the theory suggests that if you can move individuals from hygiene-seeking levels to motivation-seeking levels, the individual will be self-motivated and the manager's problems will be over. The motivation seeker is probably best thought of as a person who "loves her work." It is interesting to note that Herzberg's two-factor theory was presented almost 30 years earlier by a Belgian psychologist named Henri DeMan (1929) in a book called *Joy in Work*. Figure 10–4 is taken from that book and illustrates the two-factor approach that DeMan discovered in interviews with workers. Thus, two individuals conducting research on work motivation separated by 30 years and conducted in two very different environments came to the same conclusion about the structure of motivation and satisfaction. More will be said about DeMan in the next chapter when we cover theories of job satisfaction.

Herzberg proposes a rather simple technique for accomplishing the movement from hygiene seeking to motivation seeking—*job enrichment*. He proposes that the only way you can give people an opportunity to satisfy motivator needs is to provide them with interesting work. If the tasks they are currently performing are dull and uninteresting, the tasks must be psychologically "enriched" or made more stimulating. We will cover the practice of job enrichment in greater detail later in this chapter and again in the chapter on organizational design.

Unlike Maslow's theory or the ERG theory, the motivator-hygiene theory is not arranged hierarchically in the formal sense. There is no hypothesis that motivator needs cannot be satisfied *until* hygiene needs are met. Nevertheless, in practice it would seem that individuals whose hygiene needs are not being met would be more likely to leave the organization, making it impossible to meet their motivator needs.

As with many needs theories, Herzberg leaves us in the dark concerning *where* these needs come from. The implication is that these needs are part of the defining characteristics of *Homo sapiens*—those things

FIGURE 10–4 Positive and Negative Factors Affecting the Worker's Attitude Toward His Work

Impulse to Joy in Work (+)	*Hindrances and Inhibitions (−)*
I. Primary motives 1. Instinct of activity 2. Instinct of play	I. Technical hindrances and inhibitions 1. Detail work 2. Repetitive work a. Monotony of motion b. Reduction of initiative c. Slackening of attention d. Hypnotic effects of rhythm
3. Constructive instinct 4. Instinct of curiosity	3. Fatigue 4. Unfavourable technical conditions
5. Instinct for self-assertion 6. Possessive instinct 7. Combative instinct	
II. Accessory motives	II. Intra-occupational social hindrances and inhibitions
1. Herd instinct	1. Dissatisfaction with working conditions
2. Longing for mastery and need for subordination	2. Unjust wage systems
3. Aesthetic gratification	3. Disciplinary subordination of the worker
4. Considerations of self-interest 5. Considerations of social advantage	
III. Sense of social obligation	III. Extra-occupational social hindrances and inhibitions 1. Permanent allocation to a lower class 2. Insecurity of livelihood 3. Conventional disparagement of manual labor

SOURCE: From *Joy in Work* (p. 223) by H. DeMan, 1929, New York: Henry Holt.

that distinguish us in the most basic sense from other species and that, as a result, do not have to be explained. One of the characteristics of the scientific community in general and psychologists specifically is an unwillingness to take anything as "given." As a result, there has been some reluctance to accept Herzberg's propositions on faith. Since many of the assumptions of the theory are more closely related to the topic of job satisfaction and the meaning of work, a discussion of the research on Herzberg's theory will be postponed until these topics are introduced in the next chapter.

The need theories are appealing and similar in many important respects. It is not difficult to see the same basic structure in each of them. Ronen, Kraut, Lingoes, and Aranya (1979) show how the same set of questions can be grouped in different ways, depending on the theory being considered. This structural translation can be seen in Figure 10–5. They all include certain elements that we recognize as being part of our own "psychological makeup." No one can deny that there is a good feeling that comes from accomplishing a difficult task; nor can one deny that as a result of that feeling the probability is increased that a difficult task will be attempted again. Nevertheless, there are too many elements that are left open to question. Under what conditions will a difficult task be attempted? What will occur if one *fails* at the task? How do individuals differ with respect to their willingness to approach difficult tasks? Why are needs arranged in one hierarchy rather than another? These are a few of the logical questions that arise when need hierarchy theory is used to explain the behavior of an individual in a work setting. Data supportive of need theories have been infrequent. Damaging data are commonplace. The only empirically positive thing that can be said about the need theories I have examined is that people seem to categorize the various needs in consistent ways semantically. This would explain why the theories of Maslow, McClelland, Herzberg, and others agree to such a great extent with respect to achieving (or self-actualizing or meeting motivator needs). They have all noted the same tendency in human behavior. Nevertheless, studies that confirm the tendency by asking subjects to complete questionnaires may be no more than an exercise in seeing whether subjects notice the same things or think in the same way as experimenters. In order to justify the title "theory," there should be a tight set of interrelated propositions that can be empirically tested. This is where most of the need approaches have fallen short. The proposed interrelationships have not been confirmed.

Instrumentality Theory

Whether we want to admit it or not, when we are deciding if we should expend some energy, we often ask ourselves the question, What's in it for me? We may not be so explicit, and we certainly don't say it out loud, but the principle is an important one. We usually decide to engage in the activity if it will provide us with something that we value. In that sense, the activity is *instrumental* in achieving some valued outcome. This logic is the backbone of a set of theories that will be referred to as *instrumentality theories*. They differ from the need theories in many respects. The most important of these

FIGURE 10–5 Questionnaire Wording of Fourteen Work Goals and Assignment to Various Motivational Taxonomies

		Category of Various Taxonomies		
Work Goal	*Questionnaire Wording*	*Maslow*	*Alderfer*	*Herzberg*
Physical	Have good physical working conditions (good ventilation and lighting, adequate work space, etc.)			
Area	Live in an area desirable to you and your family			
Time	Have a job which leaves you sufficient time for your personal or family life	Physiological and security	Existence	
Security	Have the security that you will be able to work for your company as long as you want to			
Benefits	Have good fringe benefits			Hygienes
Earnings	Have an opportunity for high earnings			
Co-workers	Work with people who cooperate well with one another	Social		
Manager	Have a good working relationship with your manager		Relatedness	
Recognition	Get the recognition you deserve when you do a good job			
Advancement	Have the opportunity for advancement to higher level jobs	Self-esteem		
Training	Have training opportunities (to improve your skills or to learn new skills)			Motivators
Autonomy	Have considerable freedom to adopt your own approach to the job		Growth	
Skills	Fully use your skills and abilities on the job	Self-actualization		
Challenge	Have challenging work to do—work from which you get a personal sense of accomplishment			

SOURCE: From "A Nonmetric Scaling Approach to Taxonomies of Employee Work Motivation" by S. Ronen, A. I. Kraut, J. C. Lingoes, and N. Aranya, 1979, *Multivariate Behavioral Research, 14,* p. 387–401.

respects is an emphasis on cognition. The instrumentality theories stress the process used by an individual to answer the implied question, Should I expend the energy?

The first work-related version of instrumentality theory was presented by Georgopolos, Mahoney, and Jones (1957) and was labeled "path-goal" theory. They proposed that if a worker sees high productivity as a path leading to the attainment of one or more personal goals, that worker will tend to be a high producer. Conversely, if low productivity is seen as a path to the achievement of goals, low production will result.

There are many examples of this principle: on the positive side, the young worker in a progressive company who sees that productivity is rewarded with rapid advancement and behaves accordingly; on the negative side, the new worker who actively restricts production to match the productivity level of a fellow worker rather than jeopardize a chance to be one of the gang.

In 1964, Vroom formalized many of the instrumentality hypotheses that were in the literature and constructed a theory that has since been labeled the valence, instrumentality, and expectancy (VIE) theory. Each of these components plays an important role in the theory. Valence is a component that describes the attracting or repelling capabilities of psychological objects in the environment and has much the same dynamic meaning as the valence of an element in chemistry. Money would have a positive valence for most of us; similarly, dirty and dangerous working conditions would have a negative valence. The instrumentality component of the theory is based on some earlier work by Peak (1955) and answers the question posed in the beginning of this section, What's in it for me? A person evaluates a potential outcome (e.g., a promotion) on the basis of her perception of the relationship between that outcome and other outcomes (e.g., increased money and responsibility) for which she has varying preferences or valences. The relationship between the first outcome, the promotion, and the second outcome, the money, is known as an *instrumentality relationship.* It answers the question, Is the promotion *instrumental* in providing me with money—an outcome I value? This logic can then be extended backward to include the activities necessary to get the promotion.

The expectancy component deals with the odds of receiving a particular outcome. The question a person asks is, If I expend the energy that is required for a promotion, what is the probability that I will get that promotion? An expectancy is a probability estimate of a relationship between an action and an outcome.

If these three components are put together (valence, instrumentality, and expectancy), the basic structure of VIE theory emerges. The theory assumes that individuals ask themselves (1) whether the action has a high probability of leading to an outcome (expectancy), (2) whether that outcome will yield other outcomes (instrumentality), and (3) whether those other outcomes are valued (valence). Since Vroom's formulation of VIE theory, there have been

FIGURE 10–6 Diagram of the Theoretical Model of Porter and Lawler

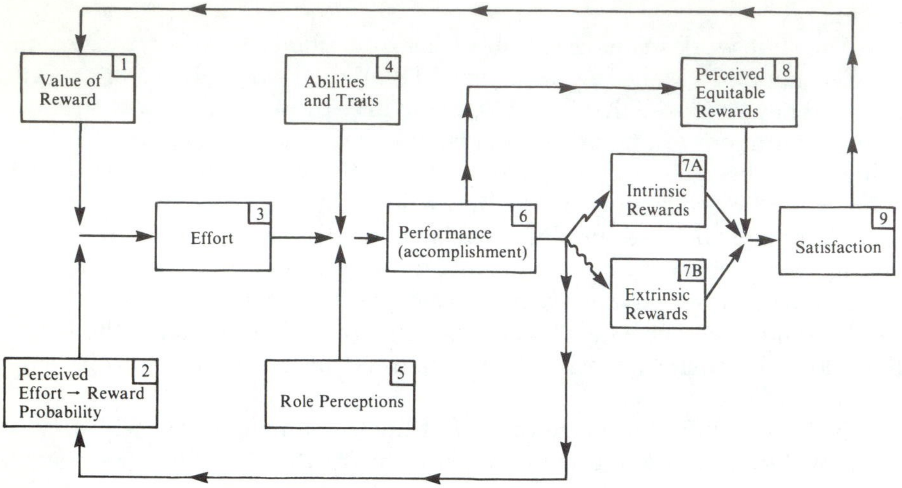

1 Value of Reward
4 Abilities and Traits
8 Perceived Equitable Rewards
7A Intrinsic Rewards
3 Effort
6 Performance (accomplishment)
9 Satisfaction
7B Extrinsic Rewards
2 Perceived Effort → Reward Probability
5 Role Perceptions

SOURCE: From *Managerial Attitudes and Performance* by L. W. Porter and E. E. Lawler, 1968, Homewood, IL: Irwin-Dorsey.

many variations proposed. Rather than present each of these variations, one representative treatment of the model will be described.

The Porter-Lawler Model. In a book dealing with managerial attitudes and performance, Porter and Lawler (1968) presented an instrumentality model of motivation and performance. They rejected the traditional drive approach of the need theories because of its emphasis on past response-reward connections. They felt that instrumentality theories more appropriately emphasized the anticipation of future events, an activity much more in keeping with the generally held view of individuals as organisms capable of delaying gratification and dealing with abstract concepts.

Having chosen the instrumentality approach, Porter and Lawler set out to test an initial model aimed at describing behavior in the industrial setting. This model appears in Figure 10–6. The definitions of the various components in Figure 10–6 are as follows:

1. *Value of Reward.* This component describes the valence or attractiveness of various outcomes to the individual. Past research in the area of job satisfaction makes it clear that people attach different preference values to outcomes; for example, while one person may value pay more than pleasant coworkers, a second person may value pleasant coworkers more than pay. Although the exact manner by which outcomes acquire preferential value, or valence, is unspecified in the model, at least one way is suggested

by the feedback loop from "satisfaction" to "value of reward"—rewards acquire valence as a function of their ability to "satisfy." This would be the position of the drive theorists.

2. *Perceived Effort-Reward Probability.* This component refers to the subjective estimate of the individual that increased effort will lead to the acquisition of some valued reward. As Porter and Lawler point out, this really comprises two specific subjective estimates or probabilities: (1) the probability that improved performance will lead to the valued reward (P→R) and (2) the probability that effort will lead to improved performance (E→P). These two probabilities are thought to have a multiplicative relationship such that if either one of the values is zero, the perceived effort-reward probability will be zero. An example of this would be the case of a student who values good grades but finds himself in a class being taught by a professor with a reputation for not giving many *A*s. Even though the student may see a high relationship between effort and performance, he would probably have a dimmer view of the relationship between performance and valued reward.

3. *Effort.* This component clarifies the distinction between effort (or expended energy) and performance, a distinction that was rarely clarified in earlier theory or research. This component is intended to supply an explanation of how hard an individual works, rather than how effectively an individual performs. To return to our example of the student striving for good grades, he may very well have expended a great amount of energy in the course but performed poorly on the tests.

4. *Abilities and Traits.* In the past, models have asked us to accept constant or fixed levels of abilities and traits, generally in the form of the statement "all other things being equal." Porter and Lawler appropriately include this component as an independent source of variation in their model. Abilities and traits refer to relatively stable characteristics of the individual such as intelligence, personality characteristics, and psychomotor skills. These abilities and traits are considered as "boundary conditions" for the individual's performance. They set upper limits for performance.

5. *Role Perceptions.* The role perception is an individual's definition of successful performance on a particular job. This is a critical factor in determining whether effort is transformed into good performance. If the person has an inappropriate definition of success, much of her effort might be wasted. For example, a police officer who defines her role as filling jail cells is likely to make a number of illegal arrests as well as enemies in the community. This would be an inappropriate role perception. Role perceptions might be thought of as the agreement or lack of agreement between a supervisor and a subordinate about the nature of good performance. If they agree, then effort can be transformed into effective performance. If they disagree, it is unlikely that effective performance (at least as defined by the immediate supervisor) will result.

6. *Performance.* Performance refers to the level of accomplishment the individual achieves. Performance has been the overriding concern of industry for decades. This is understandable, but it is important to consider the many components of successful performance as suggested by the model. Performance is the result of the combined effects of effort expenditure, role perceptions, and ability and trait patterns.
7. *Rewards.* Although the original model included rewards as a single component, Porter and Lawler decided to distinguish between intrinsic and extrinsic rewards. *Intrinsic rewards* (7A) are rewards that satisfy higher-order needs (in the Maslow sense) and are administered by the individual to himself rather than by some external agent. The wavy-line connection in Figure 10–6 implies that a direct relationship exists between performance and intrinsic rewards only when the job design is such that the worker feels challenged in the completion of job-related activities. *Extrinsic rewards* (7B) are rewards administered by an external agent such as the individual's immediate supervisor. This line is wavy owing to the sporadic nature of the relationship between successful performance and extrinsic rewards. External rewards are not always provided when a task is successfully completed; the supervisor may not be aware of the success or may not have the time or inclination to administer the appropriate reward.
8. *Perceived Equitable Rewards.* This component is a description of the level of reward that an individual *feels is appropriate.* It is determined by the individual's perception concerning how well she fits the role requirements of the job and her perceptions of how well she actually performs on the job.
9. *Satisfaction.* Porter and Lawler refer to satisfaction as a "derivative variable." It is derivative in the sense that its meaning or value is determined by the individual's comparison of what he considers an equitable reward with the amount of the actual reward. To the extent that the perceived equitable reward exceeds the actual reward, the individual is dissatisfied; if the actual reward exceeds the perceived equitable reward, the individual is satisfied. The larger the difference between these two values, the greater the degree of dissatisfaction or satisfaction.

The Porter-Lawler model is a good description of the components of a complete instrumentality description of work behavior. There have been no tests of the full model, and it is best to think of it as a heuristic device that help you to appreciate the various pieces and the complexity of the motivation and performance puzzle. As an explanatory mechanism, there are two problems with it. First, it places a heavy emphasis on rational decision making. This is unrealistic. Most humans could be characterized as displaying limited rationality. How else could we account for war, drug use, smoking, the American high school, and child abuse? Second, it assumes that effort is unaffected by abilities and traits and is exclusively a product of estimates of reward probabilities and values of rewards. Recent research and theory raises serious questions about this assumption (e.g., Bandura, 1986, 1987). Nevertheless, it is important to be aware of the research that has been done on various instrumentality predictions. In the following section, we will consider the results of that research in summary form. A more extensive review of this literature can be found in earlier editions of the text (Landy, 1985; Landy & Trumbo, 1980).

Recent Research on Instrumentality Models. In the past two decades, the amount of research being conducted on instrumentality models has grown considerably. This is due, in part, to the general acceptance by managers and researchers alike of the important role that cognitive activities play in motivation and performance. Excellent reviews of the early history of this research are provided by J. P. Campbell and Pritchard (1976) and T. R. Mitchell (1974).

The research on the general topic of "instrumentality" has taken several different forms. There are several studies that combine valence, instrumentality, and expectancy in particular ways in an attempt to predict either effort expenditure, performance, or both. Another class of studies deals with basic measurement problems in tests of the models, particularly the way in which each of these three variables is operationally defined or measured. A third class of studies deals with different approaches to testing the basic instrumentality model. Finally, several studies examine characteristics of workers or environments that affect the degree to which instrumentality models can predict worker behavior. I will try to synthesize the results of these studies.

Tests of VIE Models. Vroom's basic model (1964) has been expanded several times. The most comprehensive expansion was the Porter and Lawler version (1968) described above. Following that, revisions were also suggested by Graen (1969) and Lawler (1971, 1973). Perhaps the most elaborate expansion of the cognitive portion of the VIE model has recently been proposed by Naylor, Pritchard, and Ilgen (1980). Most of the tests of both the initial model and the later versions have yielded about the same results: effort is predicted more accurately than performance. This makes sense logically. Individuals have effort under their control but not always performance. The environment plays a major role in determining if and how effort will yield high levels of performance. Bandura (1987) criticizes this choice of dependent variable. He suggests that it was chosen because it is easy to operationalize in laboratory settings. Nevertheless, he feels that a good deal of variation in day-to-day activities is not the result of effort but is the result of ingenuity, perseverance, resiliency, and other variables that are equally "motivational" but not adequately described by the term *effort*.

One common finding is that even though the theory suggests that effort and the V, I, and E components are interrelated, this relationship is not particularly strong. Typical correlations between effort and the other components are in the .25 to .40 range. Correlations are occasionally higher, but this is usually when the measure of effort is a self-report.

In an early meta-analysis of VIE studies, Schwab, Olian-Gottlieb, and

Heneman, (1979) came to some very different and disturbing conclusions. They found that considering VIE studies on the whole a substantial percentage of variance in either effort or performance could be explained by things *other than* the cognitions (i.e., instrumentality and expectancy estimates) of the subjects. For example, more variance could be accounted for if self-report measures of effort or performance were used. More variance could be accounted for if a particular number of outcomes were evaluated. More variance could be accounted for if quantitative measures of performance or effort were used rather than ratings or rankings. Finally, more variance in effort or performance could be accounted for if only positive outcomes were considered rather than both positive *and* negative outcomes. In fact, Schwab et al. suggest that as much as 42 percent of the variance in effort or performance as measured in VIE studies could be accounted for by factors *other than* the subjects' responses to instrumentality, expectancy, and valence questions. This is a serious problem since it suggests that inferences drawn from past studies may have been influenced by methodology rather than theory. Wanous, Keon, and Latack (1983) also complain about the characteristics of the "typical" VIE study. For example, they suggest that in real life, subjects are dealing with a relatively small number of outcomes. In research studies, these same individuals may be asked to evaluate 15 or more outcomes. Bandura (1987) extends this argument by suggesting that people are satisficers rather than optimizers and are looking for "acceptable" levels of outcomes on a few number of variables rather than a maximal or optimal level on all variables. In addition, most VIE studies are carried out exclusively with questionnaires. Wanous et al. suggest that interviews might be equally appropriate. Finally, they criticize the choice of the "typical" subject, a highly educated professional or preprofessional. Bandura takes instrumentality theory to task because the joy of accomplishment is seldom included as an outcome. Instead, outcome sets tend to include mostly extrinsic (e.g., money, promotion) rather than intrinsic outcomes. In combination, the reviews of Schwab et al. and Wanous et al. and the criticisms of Bandura suggest that there is still a good deal of progress that can be made in refining VIE theory.

Another recent development in tests of VIE theories has been an examination of the basic multiplicative relationship between valence and expectancy that was proposed by Vroom and others. Stahl and Harrell (1981) have seriously questioned the generality of this assumption. In four studies, they examined the strategies used by 157 subjects in choosing among alternative courses of action. They found that over 65 percent of the subjects *did not* use a multiplicative model; instead, they simply added V to E to determine which course of action would be chosen. Slovic, Fischoff, and Lichtenstein (1977) suggest that this is not surprising. They feel that multiplicative relationships are very difficult for many people to deal with. Instead, the typical person reduces the situation to a simpler one. Cognitive theories must take into account the cognitive capacities of people. If it is reasonable to assume that individuals differ in cognitive abilities, then it is reasonable to assume that these same people will differ in how effective they are at the mental manipulations assumed by theories such as VIE theory.

Measurement of V, I, and E Components. Ilgen, Nebeker, and Pritchard (1981) have examined many different ways for measuring instrumentalities, expectancies, and valences. They have identified several methods that have greater integrity (i.e., reliability and validity) than others. In some senses, this reinforces the point of Schwab et al. (1979) that I discussed earlier. It seems as if the tests of VIE theory are very sensitive to peripheral variables. If questionnaire format can make such a difference in the integrity of the central variables of the theory, how should we interpret past research that failed to support the theory? Is it because the theory is wrong or because the variables have been measured poorly? At the present time, there is no answer to the question. There is the distinct possibility that past research has tested measurement procedures rather than theoretical relationships. This should remind you of our earlier discussions of reliability and validity. Without these characteristics, no inferences can be drawn. Reliability and validity are just as important to tests of motivation theory as they are for test validation.

Another measurement issue that has become important is the difference between positive and negative outcomes. The theory suggests that outcomes with positive valences and outcomes with negative valences can be averaged. This is important since seldom are situations all positive or all negative. Instead, situations are often characterized by multiple characteristics—some positive and some negative. A promotion may mean more status, but it may also mean an elimination of overtime pay and an increase in responsibility. A number of studies have demonstrated that VIE theory predictions are more accurate if only positive outcomes are considered. These studies are reviewed by Leon (1981). Leon looked more carefully at what was happening with negative outcomes and came to some interesting conclusions that fit in with more general models of information processing. He found that people evaluate positive outcomes in exactly the manner suggested by VIE theory. The more attractive the outcome, the stronger the relationship that outcome has to eventual choices of alternative courses of action. Negative outcomes showed no such relationship. If an outcome was negative, it had a fixed effect on eventual choice of actions. It did not matter *how* negative the outcome was. In other words, for positive outcomes, more was better; for negative outcomes, more was not necessarily worse. Leon pointed out that data from many different areas of applied psychology and information processing (e.g., the interview) confirm the fact that negative information is processed in a way different from positive information. It may simply be that we would prefer not to think about negative things. This has been called the *Pollyanna hypothesis* by Boucher and Osgood (1969). Once again, the data call for a rethinking of the original formulation of the model. For the time being, it makes sense to consider positive and negative outcomes qualitatively as well as quantitatively different even though VIE theory does not currently recognize that distinction.

Some Thoughts on Instrumentality Theory. As you can tell from the description of the Porter-Lawler model, instrumentality theory is a far cry from "a happy worker is a productive worker." It provides a comprehensive framework for dealing with complex industrial behavior. Recent research suggests that the model may be more useful as a descriptive device for organizing our thinking about work motivation. It seems less suitable as an actual theory of work motivation. Modifications are being made continually. Changing the model as new data are gathered in field and laboratory settings is an integral part of theory building. But in spite of its changing nature, the thrust of instrumentality theory is a good one. The cognitive nature of the approach does a good job of capturing the essence of energy expenditure. Very simply put, it says that the force on a person to perform a given action depends on the answers to a series of questions—Is a reward being offered that I value? If I expend the effort, will my performance improve? If I improve my performance, will I actually get the reward?—questions we ask ourselves day in and day out.

There are some differences between the instrumentality models and the need models. The process components are very different. The need models are based on inferred drives or needs that create tension in the person. To understand why an individual expends energy in a particular situation, we must know something of the history of responses and rewards of that individual. The instrumentality models are based on current estimates by the individual of the chances of obtaining some valued reward. Although it might be useful to have some information about the individual's reward history, it is sufficient to measure the individual estimates as cognitive variables rather than as historical facts. We must, however, keep in mind that the rationality of the person may be limited by a number of factors including cognitive skill, negative outcomes, and even the number of alternatives being considered. Rationality in most of us is bounded or limited rather than perfect and limitless.

Another difference between need models and instrumentality models is in the content portion of the models. Instrumentality models are very unclear about the nature of potential "rewards." The Porter-Lawler model goes so far as to distinguish between intrinsic and extrinsic rewards, but there is no very clear indication about where they come from, how they develop, or the effect of individual differences in personality characteristics on the potential of a reward to modify behavior. In this respect, most of the need theories are much more specific. Although they give little indication of where the needs come from, they are quite specific about the hierarchical or prepotent nature of needs and about the objects in the environment capable of satisfying those needs, and—at least in the case of Maslow's theory—they provide us with a framework for understanding individual differences in the strength of particular needs. In summary, instrumentality theories need some work on the *content* portion of the model, whereas need theories could be improved with a more reasonable consideration of the *process* of energy expenditure.

Equity Theory

Instrumentality theory was one type of cognitive theory. It implied that individuals assess the probability of outcomes and, as such, is future oriented. Another class of cognitive motivational theory holds that behavior is initiated, directed, and sustained by the attempts of the individual to maintain some internal balance of psychological tension. As a result, I will refer to this class of theories as *balance theory*. This balance is maintained by taking corrective actions based on past rewards and punishments. We will consider a specific instance of balance theory called *equity theory*.

Most industrial versions of balance theory are based on Festinger's (1957) *theory of cognitive dissonance*. The model is deceptively simple, proposing that (1) discrepant cognitions produce psychological tension within the individual; (2) tension is unpleasant for the individual; and (3) individuals will take action to reduce the tension. Even though this is a rather stripped-down version of the dissonance model, it is sufficient for our purposes. As you can see, a critical variable in the balance theories is tension. The fact that tension is thought to be unpleasant will be an important issue in the next chapter on job satisfaction. Is it reasonable? There have not been many direct studies of this question, but one recent study by Croyle and Cooper (1983) has documented a relationship between discrepant cognitions and physiological arousal. Subjects who engaged in behavior that was contrary to their attitudes displayed heightened arousal (in the form of galvanic skin response reactivity). Thus, the suggested mechanisms of dissonance theory seem plausible.

There are many different variations of balance theory. Some are based on personality considerations and suggest that individuals attempt to balance their own view of themselves with the view of them held by others or with their own self-concept. This is called *self-consistency theory* (e.g., Korman, 1970) and fits in with other broader theories of behavior such as the one proposed by Carl Rogers (1951) to explain normal and abnormal behavior.

The most common variation of the dissonance or balance theory in the examination of work motivation is known as *equity theory*. As suggested in a review of equity theory by Pritchard (1969), Adams's (1965) version of equity theory is perhaps the most extensive and explicit. The general proposition states that individuals form a ratio of their inputs in a given situation to their outcomes in that situation. *Inputs* are defined as anything the individual feels she personally contributes in a given work setting and may include things such as intellectual abilities, psychomotor skills, personality traits, seniority, or experience. *Outcomes* are all the factors that the individual perceives as having some personal value (e.g., money, promotions, or praise). The individual sets up the ratio of inputs to outcomes and compares the value of that ratio with the value of the ratio for "significant others." If the value of the ratio equals the values of the others' ratios, the situation is perceived as equitable and no tension exists; if the values are unequal—that is, the value of the person's ratio is larger or smaller than the value of some significant other's ratio—tension exists, and the individual will be motivated to reduce that tension. The force or intensity of the motivated behavior (amount of energy expended) is thought to be directly proportional to the amount of tension created by the inequality or inequity. This relationship of inputs to outcomes can be expressed in the form of simple equations:

Equity *Inequity*

$$\frac{O_p}{I_p} = \frac{O_o}{I_o} \qquad \frac{O_p}{I_p} > \frac{O_o}{I_o} \quad \frac{O_p}{I_p} < \frac{O_o}{I_o}$$

where $_p$ stands for *person* and $_o$ stands for *other*.

An example of an inequitable situation would be a case in which individual A contributes 5 units of input and receives 4 units of outcome, whereas individual B contributes 4 units of input and receives 5 units of outcome. The ratios would be 5:4 and 4:5, respectively. Since these values are not equal, inequity exists for both individual A and individual B (assuming of course that individuals A and B perceive each other as a "significant other"). But if individual A contributes 5 units of input and receives 4 units of outcome, whereas individual B contributes 10 units of input and receives 8 units of outcome, both perceive the situation as equitable. It is important to note that inputs and outcomes are defined as they are *perceived* by the individual.

The bulk of the equity studies have been done in laboratory settings, although there seems to be an increase in the number of studies using field simulations. In a typical equity experiment, subjects are randomly assigned to one of four conditions: (1) hourly rate–overpay condition, (2) hourly rate–underpay condition, (3) piece-rate–overpay condition, (4) piece-rate–underpay condition. Piece-rate pay means that the subjects are paid for each unit of production—the more they produce, the more money they make. Hourly pay means that the subjects will receive a fixed amount of money per unit time, regardless of the number of pieces produced. Each of these conditions is considered to be inequitable, two because of underpayment and two because of overpayment. The dissonance or tension is usually induced through instructions. For example, the overpayment subjects would be told, "More money has become available, and in spite of the fact that we told you your pay would be $1.75 per hour [or $0.07 per piece], we will pay you $2.25 per hour [or $0.10 per piece]." Those in the underpayment condition might be told, "We are sorry, but a terrible mistake has been made; we incorrectly advertised this position as paying $1.75 per hour [or $0.07 per piece]. Since we only have a limited amount of money, we cannot pay you what we advertised but will have to pay you $1.50 per hour [or $0.04 per piece]." Table 10–1 represents the expected results from such an experiment. From the table

TABLE 10–1 Equity Theory Predictions of Employee Reactions to Inequitable Payment

	Underpayment	*Overpayment*
Hourly payment	Subjects underpaid by the hour produce less or poorer-quality output than equitably paid subjects	Subjects overpaid by the hour produce more or higher-quality output than equitably paid subjects
Piece-rate payment	Subjects underpaid by piece rate will produce a large number of low-quality units in comparison with equitably paid subjects	Subjects overpaid by piece rate will produce fewer units of higher quality than equitably paid subjects

SOURCE: From "Equity Theory Predictions of Behavior in Organizations" by R. T. Mowday, in R. M. Steers and L. W. Porter (Eds.), *Motivation and Work Behavior* (2nd ed.), 1979, New York: McGraw-Hill.

you can see that the mode of tension reduction depends on the payment condition. In the piece-rate–overpayment condition, an increase in input only serves to *increase* the tension, since the individual will be paid more than before as a result of finishing more pieces. The prediction for this condition would be that the individual will improve the quality of the work while reducing the number of pieces produced. In the hourly rate–overpayment condition, the person will try to produce both greater quantity and higher quality to reduce the feelings of overpayment. In piece-rate underpayment, the person feels that she is being cheated. One good way of making more money and reducing the inequity is to turn out as many pieces as possible; quality will be irrelevant and probably low since the emphasis will be on numbers. In the hourly rate–underpayment condition, either quantity or quality or both will suffer. Since the person's income does not depend on quality or quantity of production (above some minimum level, at least), a good way of reducing inequity is to reduce inputs.

The general findings of the studies testing the equity model have been that equity predictions hold up fairly well in the underpayment conditions but not so well in the overpayment conditions.

Just as in the case of the other motivational theories, there is something quite appealing about equity theory. It describes the way we normally react to many work-related experiences. Everyone has had the experience at one time or another of feeling "cheated" because of an inappropriate reward. In addition, we all probably moderate our efforts to some degree according to what we consider "a fair day's work."

Nevertheless, we cannot let intuitive appeal or common sense substitute for scientific support. Pritchard (1969) and others have raised theoretical questions regarding: (1) the manner in which a comparison person is chosen by an individual; (2) the manner in which a strategy for tension reduction is chosen; (3) the emphasis on level of compensation as the independent variable in equity research; and (4) the role of individual differences in equity predictions. Let's consider these issues one at a time.

Choice of a Comparison Other. Equity theory places a rather heavy emphasis on the choice of a "referent" for the purpose of evaluating outcomes. In some studies, the referent is assumed to be another person with whom the individual works; in other studies, the referent is thought to be an idealized or internalized concept—possibly the average of all others with whom the individual ever worked. In any event, there is some confusion about the nature of the referent. Goodman (1974) has done some good research on this topic. In the course of this research, he was able to identify several different potential sources of referents that might be used when an individual evaluates his pay. Figure 10–7 presents these referents and their definitions. Goodman found that people may use more than one referent and that their felt satisfaction with pay was affected by a combination of comparisons with the appropriate referents. In addition, he found there were individual differences in referent choice. For example, college graduates were more likely to choose "other" referents from the outside than the inside. Perhaps this is because they see themselves as more mobile than noncollege graduates. This type of research, directed toward an understanding of the way in which referent sources are chosen and the effect of individual differences on these choices, is fascinating and deserves continued attention.

Another example of this type of research is a study by Middlemist and Peterson (1976). They were also interested in the role of the "other" in equity determination. They were able to demonstrate that individuals *do* pay attention to the efforts and qualifications of other group members; furthermore, they alter their own efforts in accordance with the efforts of coworkers. One finding is of particular interest. The researchers were able to manipulate the level of coworkers so that one group of subjects first worked with a "fast" coworker and then a slow one; a second group of subjects worked first with a "slow" coworker and then a fast one. When the coworker change was from a fast one to a slow one, the referent other chosen by the subject for equity purposes seemed to be an internalized other, similar to the fast coworker who had left; when the coworker change was from slow to fast, the referent other was the new coworker. This is important, since equity theory might be interpreted to suggest that the referent other is constant, regardless of whether that other is a real person called "my current coworker" or an internalized or idealized view of a coworker.

There is one important aspect of laboratory research as it relates to choice of significant other that must be mentioned. In lab studies, the significant other can be carefully controlled. Usually, it is a stranger, and the choice of that stranger is almost demanded by the experimental manipulations. The

FIGURE 10–7 Referent Measures: Conceptual and Operational Definitions

Referent	*Conceptual Definition*	*Operational Example*
Other-inside	Refers to others inside the organization with whom a person compares himself.	"Well, we only got a 5% raise . . . but the union got 8% and they have much less responsibility."
Other-outside	Indicates referents outside the organization.	"I get about the same as I would working in a similar job outside."
System-structure	Refers to whether the promised or stated structure of the pay system corresponds to the actual structure. For example, if an organization states that it operates on a merit raise system but the structure of the pay system does not distinguish between merit and cost of living raises, it is likely that a discrepancy between the expected structure and actual structure will exist and feelings of inequity will follow.	"The present raise system does not permit enough graduations to reflect changes in cost of living as well as superior performance."
System administration	Indicates referents that arise from the way the pay system is administered. For example, if the company policy were to provide an automatic raise at every promotion, then providing a raise at promotion would evoke an equitable referent, nonpayment an inequitable referent. In the case of system-administration referents, the issue is not the structure of the system but how the structure of that system is administered.	"When I was promoted I never got the 10% raise to bring me up to the lower pay range of that job."

(continued)

FIGURE 10–7 *(concluded)*

Referent	*Conceptual Definition*	*Operational Example*
Self-pay history	Refers to whether past or future job input-outcome ratios are used in evaluation of present pay.	"I have received good raises in the past and expect the same in the future."
Self-family	Refers to the individual's conception of the level of wages needed to maintain his family's standard of living. In this case the evaluation of present pay is a comparison of present input-outcome ratio with the ideal ratio relevant to meeting one's family role.	"I am able to provide for my family . . . we live well."
Self-internal	Refers to the individual's conception of his own worth. In the context of pay, this refers to the individual's internal standard of his worth to the company. While clearly shaped by external forces (e.g., parents, educational experiences, friends), the self-internal referent is entirely internal to the individual and represents a part of his general view of his self-worth.	"Given my length of service and education, I feel I am paid well for what I do."

SOURCE: From "An Examination of Referents Used in the Evaluation of Pay" by P. S. Goodman, 1974, *Organizational Behavior and Human Performance, 12,* pp. 180–181, table 1.

Middlemist and Peterson study is a perfect example of this control. This type of situation is seldom the case in the real world. We have a choice of a wide number of real and imaginary others. The very choice can be a strategy for inequity reduction. Lab research on equity theory may be a perfect example of an issue raised in Chapter 2: the control necessary for inference may be destroying the realism necessary for generalization.

Choice of Strategy. Industrial research on equity theory has suffered from an emphasis on performance modification strategies for the reduction of tension produced by inequity. From the behavioral perspective, a given

FIGURE 10–8

Proposition I: Individuals will try to maximize their outcomes (where outcomes equal rewards minus costs).

Proposition IIa: Groups can maximize collective reward by evolving accepted systems for equitably apportioning resources among members. Thus, groups will evolve such systems of equity and will attempt to induce members to accept and adhere to these systems.

Proposition IIb: Groups will generally reward members who treat others equitably and generally punish (increase the costs for) members who treat others inequitably.

Proposition III: When individuals find themselves participating in inequitable relationships, they will become distressed. The more inequitable the relationship, the more distress individuals will feel.

Proposition IV: Individuals who discover they are in an inequitable relationship will attempt to eliminate their distress by restoring equity. The greater the inequity that exists, the more distress they will feel, and the harder they will try to restore equity.

SOURCE: From *Equity: Theory and Research* (p. 6) by E. Walster, G. W. Walster, and E. Berscheid, 1978, Boston: Allyn & Bacon.

inequity may lead to quite different attempts to resolve it. These attempts might range from increased inputs to sabotage or quitting. Some research by Weick (Weick, Bougon, & Maruyama, 1976) suggests that there is a tendency to handle any inequity involving low outcomes by requesting higher outcomes for self. If this finding is supported, many of Pritchard's objections will be answered; at the same time, however, it will require a substantial revision of the theory to account for this phenomenon, since there are no elements currently in the theory that would explain the appeal of this strategy over others. Another finding in Weick's research was that increased effort due to overpayment was a lot less common than previously had been believed. One way of dealing with this prediction problem in the case of overpayment is to invoke expectancy theory. We might simply suggest that an overriding concern of all individuals is to maximize outcomes for self. This is a departure from Adams's version of equity theory that has been suggested by Walster, Walster, and Berscheid (1978). They reformulate equity theory around the propositions presented in Figure 10–8.

As you can see, it is possible to consider equity theory simply as a special case of expectancy theory. The two theories make identical predictions when the individual sees equitable behavior in his best interest. This possibility is still being widely discussed but has not yet been resolved (Mowday, 1979).

Goodman and Friedman (1971) have suggested that performance predictions from equity theory miss the point. The theory is a cognitive one and should have something to say about how people *perceive* their environment rather than simply how they act on it. In spite of the fact that little systematic research has been done on the cognitive strategies implied by equity theory, there is good reason to believe that the mental activities that a person engages in are complicated and important to understand. We will consider some of these mental activities shortly.

Compensation versus Other Outcomes. A majority of laboratory and field tests of equity theory have manipulated cognitions of compensation. Subjects have been told that they are being overpaid or underpaid or paid an average amount. This has been the strategy used to induce inequity and the accompanying tension. There is good reason to investigate the effects of payment schemes. Money is one of the most general rewards available. Its value is recognized from the preschool child to the senior citizen. Further, it is one of the major rewards used in industrial settings.

Unfortunately, the interest in compensation as an independent variable has slowed the investigation of other outcome variables that exist in the work setting. These other variables include such things as promotions, interesting work, pleasant coworkers, and increased status. As we saw earlier, Bandura (1987) suggests that one of the most substantial outcomes in the work setting is the satisfaction that derives from goal accomplishment. Recently, Greenberg and Ornstein (1983) have demonstrated the potential influence of variables other than compensation differences. They studied the effect of bestowing a high-status job title on an individual in terms of feelings of equity and behaviors intended to reduce inequity. In two studies, students were paid to proofread text and mark errors. Their proofreading activities were divided into three periods, and they were told they would be paid for one hour of work. During the initial 12-minute period, they simply checked the text for errors in four-to-six-member groups. At the end of the 12 minutes, they were called into another room and were treated in one of the following four ways:

Earned Title. The experimenter examined their work and indicated that he had never seen work that careful and accurate before. He indicated that there would be a need for a senior proofreader to check the work of the other students and asked if the subject were interested in assuming that responsibility. He added that there was no money to pay for this additional work (which would take another hour) but that it was an honor to be chosen for such a responsibility.

Unearned Title. In this condition, subjects were told that someone was needed for the position of senior proofreader and they had been selected. There was no mention made of the quality or quantity of their work, nor was it examined in their presence. They were told there would be no extra compensation and that it would take another hour of their time.

No Title. This group of subjects was told that someone was needed to check the work of the others and that there would be no pay for the additional hour. No mention was made of the job title of senior proofreader.

FIGURE 10–9 Mean Number of Lines Proofread per Work Session as a Title Bestowal

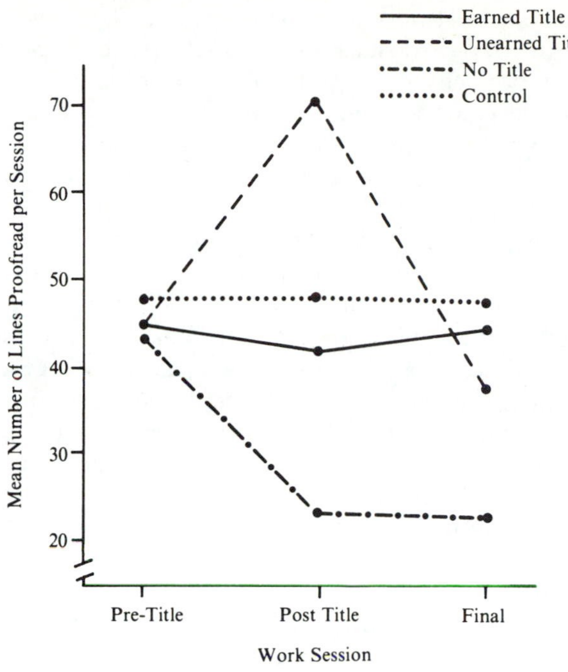

SOURCE: From "High Status Job Title as Compensation for Underpayment: A Test of Equity Theory" by J. Greenberg and S. Ornstein, 1983, *Journal of Applied Psychology, 68* (2), p. 288.

Control. The control subjects simply came into the room and discussed the nature of the work. No mention was made of extra work or the title of senior proofreader.

The hypotheses of the study involved various aspects of satisfaction and performance. It was proposed that both the No Title and the Unearned Title subjects would experience inequity—the No Title group because they were being asked for extra input with no additional outcomes and the Unearned Title subjects because they were receiving a desirable outcome (high-status job title) that was undeserved.

After being exposed to one of the four treatments, the subjects returned to their proofreading task for two additional 12-minute blocks. The results of the manipulation of title condition on performance are presented graphically in Figure 10–9. They are striking for two reasons. As you can see, there are dramatic differences between the No Title group and the other conditions. This was as predicted. What was not predicted was the strange behavior of the Unearned Title subjects in the second and third work sessions. In the second session (the posttitle session), their performance was the highest of any of the groups. In the final session, however, their performance dropped below that of the Control and Earned Title groups. The responses to questionnaires dealing with pay satisfaction administered at the end of the second and third sessions perfectly paralleled these performance findings. The No Title group felt underpaid at the end of both the second and third sessions. Both the Control and the Earned Title group felt equitably paid at the end of both sessions. The Unearned Title group felt overpaid at the end of the second session but underpaid at the end of the third session.

The unusual effect on the Unearned Title group was explained in terms of attributions made by the subjects. Greenberg and Ornstein speculate that the subjects in this condition felt flattered. They believed that the experimenter liked them particularly; this was the reason for being chosen as senior proofreaders. By the third session, perhaps the subjects had begun to doubt the motives of the experimenter. On reflection, the subjects in the Unearned condition might have concluded that they were being callously manipulated just to get some extra work out of them. This was thought to be responsible for the dramatic shift in both pay satisfaction and proofreading performance. The effect of the Unearned Title condition was replicated in a second similar study.

The Greenberg and Ornstein study has some important implications. In the first place, it demonstrates that a job title (and accompanying responsibilities) can act as a valued outcome under certain circumstances (i.e., when the title is seen as deserved). Under other circumstances (i.e., when no title accompanies the increased responsibility), the change may be seen as an input rather than an outcome, resulting in felt inequity. In still other circumstances (e.g., when the title is perceived as unearned), there is a shift over time. What is initially seen as a valued outcome is subsequently seen as additional input. This suggests a potential for using increased responsibilities and job titles as rewards in certain circumstances. From a theoretical perspective, it also suggests that many of the equity mechanisms examined in the compensation paradigm may hold for other outcomes as well. Finally, and perhaps most important from both a research and applied perspective, it suggests that perceptions are dynamic, not static. The perception of the Unearned Title group changed over a brief period of time from positive to negative. This fits neatly with some new approaches in cognitive psychology. In memory research (e.g., Loftus, 1979) as well as reading comprehension and concept formation research (Bransford & Franks, 1971), it has been proposed that cognition is constructive. In the simplest terms, this means that information is not simply stored and then retrieved in the form in which it was stored. Instead, things happen to that information to change it and mold it into something new. In other words, people continue to assess their views of the situation even after an initial impression has been formed. This line of reasoning is both fascinating and intimidating. It certainly makes for more complex models of motivation, but it also helps to draw theory and behavior closer together.

Individual Differences. One question that has arisen in research on equity theory has been the possible role of individual differences in equity calculation and tension reduction strategy. Are there variables on which people differ that change the predictions of equity theory? Prime candidates for such individual differences variables are cognitive factors. The input-outcome ratios that are estimated by individuals can be quite complex. These ratios might involve several "significant others," inputs and outcomes that are difficult to quantify (such as the experience brought to the task or the value of a new job title), and changing ratios over time. It is reasonable to assume that some people are less able to deal with the cognitive demands of equity operations than others. This does not mean that equity theory would not explain their behavioral choices or attitudes. Instead, it means that the combination rules that they use may be very different—possibly more primitive—than those rules used by people more cognitively capable. We considered a similar possibility in instrumentality theory. Remember that Stahl and Harrell (1981) found that 65 percent of their subjects used a combinatorial rule simpler than the one implied by the VIE model.

By *cognitive capability* I mean the capacity to form concepts, to reason inductively and deductively, to synthesize, to judge, and so on. Some studies have shown that the equity operations are difficult for young children and cannot be performed efficiently until adolescence. It is not unreasonable to assume that the same activities are difficult for some adults.

There is one cognitive variable that has been examined recently, and this variable does seem to have direct implications for the manner in which equity theory might operate. Vecchio (1981) proposed that since equity theory was based on the notion of "fairness" and social justice, perhaps moral maturity was involved in the operation of equity components. He contrasted instrumentality theory with equity theory. Instrumentality theory implies that individuals seek to maximize personal gain. Equity theory implies that individuals seek to balance personal gain against "fair" or deserved gain. Both traditional (Piaget, 1965) and contemporary (Kohlberg, 1976) theories of morality and moral behavior stress the importance of cognitive development and cognitive activity.

Vecchio suggested that the balancing operations of equity theory must involve the cognitive concept of morality. As a result, those who have developed moral maturity should be more "predictable" from an equity perspective than those who have not developed moral maturity. He was particularly interested in the overpayment condition since this is the circumstance in which morality is most likely involved. The subjects of the study were college students who had been hired to conduct interviews with fellow students about issues of importance on campus. The subjects were to be paid using a piece-rate scheme. They were to receive 40 cents per interview. The overpayment manipulation consisted of telling one-half the students that even though the normal rate was 40 cents per interview, they had been authorized to pay 75 cents and this would be the payment rate for these students. Vecchio's hunch was confirmed in his study. He found that moral maturity was negatively related to the number of interviews in overpayment conditions but positively related to the quality of those interviews. This means that the higher the moral maturity of the subject (measured using a standard questionnaire), the fewer the number of interviews conducted and the better those interviews. Conversely, those subjects low on moral maturity conducted more interviews of poorer quality. They maximized their pay levels. This means that high moral maturity subjects follow equity predictions for piece-rate payment, but low moral maturity subjects do not. Thus, moral maturity is conceivably an individual difference that modifies the predictions of equity theory. Of course, this is just one study. Replication would be necessary in other settings before we would incorporate moral maturity as a component in equity theory. Nevertheless, this gives you some idea of other variables that may interact with equity considerations.

The Concept of Equity. Virtually all tests of equity theory have been based, in one way or another, on a ratio of inputs to outcomes similar to the ones proposed earlier in this section. This is known as the *principle of proportionality*. Simply put, this principle states that fairness or equity exists when outcomes are proportional to inputs. If disproportionality exists, a state of inequity is present, and this state is accompanied by tension and strategies to reduce that tension. This assumed proportionality is critically important to theories such as Adams's. Mellers (1982) has shown that such a proportionality assumption is common to equity models dating back as far as Aristotle, so Adams is in good company.

Recently, research has begun to appear that raises serious questions about this proportionality assumption. The research is quite complicated, both statistically and procedurally, so I will not review it in detail but will simply highlight the implications. Michael Birnbaum (1983) has been examining the concept of fairness in salary increase allocation for many years. His research examines different potential definitions of perceived equity. He suggests three possible definitions:

Relative equity. Individuals of equal merit should receive salary increases that are equal in terms of percentage of current salary. This means that if you and I have performed with equal merit for the past year, we might both receive a 7-percent salary increase. If you received a 5-percent increase and I received a 9-percent increase, this would be considered inequitable by both of us. This is the equivalent of the Adams's formulation of equity.

Absolute equity. Individuals of equal merit should receive salary increases that are equal in dollar terms, regardless of current salary. In other words, if you and I have performed with equal merit for the past year, we might both receive a $1,000 salary increase. This would be viewed as equitable even though it represents 2 percent of your current salary and 4 percent of my current salary.

Adjustment equity. Individuals of equal merit should eventually receive salaries that are equal in dollar terms. This means that if you and I have performed with equal merit for the past year and my salary happens to be lower than yours (regardless of the reason), I will receive a salary increase that will bring our salaries closer together; that is, I will receive an increase that is larger than yours, both in terms of proportion of current salary and in absolute dollar terms. The object of a system such as this would be to make yearly adjustments to bring the salaries of individuals of equal merit into agreement.

Birnbaum's research has examined these alternative definitions from several different perspectives. One experimental task that he uses is an allocation task. He asks subjects to split up a fixed amount of money among hypothetical employees. The employees are described in terms of current merit and current salary. This allows for a determination of which variables play a role in salary increase decisions. Birnbaum finds that the strategy commonly used is that of adjustment equity. Subjects seem to concentrate on bringing overall salary into line for "employees" of equal merit. A second experimental task involves judgments by subjects about the fairness of decisions that have already been made. They are asked to consider a series of salary increases for hypothetical employees and make a judgment with respect to how "fair" these decisions were. Once again (Birnbaum, 1983), the adjustment model is best at explaining the fairness decisions of the subjects. In practical terms, this means that a person of high merit and low salary will be given a larger percentage increase than a person of high merit and high salary. Furthermore, this type of strategy will be perceived as "fairer" than either giving both individuals the same number of dollars or giving each individual the same percentage increase in salary.

Mellers (1982) has followed up Birnbaum's research and suggests that equity perceptions are based on some fairly complicated estimates on the part of the perceiver. She suggests that equity occurs when a person's relative position in a distribution of salaries is seen as similar to her relative position in a distribution of merit. Mellers suggests other variations in the traditional equity model that I won't detail. The point is that these data and propositions, if supported, suggest a completely new conceptualization of equity—one very different from that assumed in 30 years of industrial research. It may very well be that if the new (adjustment) model for calculating equity is applied to data, equity predictions may improve considerably. Furthermore, we may come to a better understanding of the implications of inequity for both emotional state and strategies for tension reduction. It is interesting to note that the recent discussions of comparable worth (see Chapter 4) are based on the adjustment model. It is argued that steps must be taken to bring individuals of equal worth (merit) closer together on the salary distribution scale. Neither relative nor absolute equity models can account for the dissatisfaction with pay expressed by the advocates of the comparable worth position.

A Concluding Statement. In summary, equity theory is due for some substantial (possibly even radical) modification. This modification will involve a reconsideration of individual differences, an extension to outcomes other than simply money, and possibly the adoption of a completely new definition of equity that abandons relative equity in favor of adjustment equity. For these reasons, the future of both research and application of equity theory is promising. I think that there will be a renewed interest in equity models in the next few years. This interest will be spurred by attempts to institute merit pay systems or performance-based reward systems such as those being discussed for teachers and federal employees.

Goal Setting

T. A. Ryan (1970), in his book on human motivation, presents a convincing logical, philosophical, and empirical argument for the role of intention in motivated behavior. He notes that "one of the commonly observed characteristics of intentional behavior is that it tends to keep going until it reaches completion. When we are interrupted before reaching the natural conclusion of the activity, we often experience irritation and resist the interruption" (pp. 95–96). More simply put, once we start something, we will not be happy until we reach a goal we have set for ourselves. Baldamus (1951) called this process one of "traction" (as opposed to distraction) and defined it as "the feeling of being pulled along by the inertia inherent in the particular activity" (p. 42). Ryan reviews a large body of literature suggesting that level of performance is closely related to the goals an individual has set for himself or accepted from someone else.

This emphasis on cognitive processes and the role of intentional behavior is most clearly brought out in the work of Locke (1968, 1970). In a series of carefully controlled and sequenced laboratory experiments, Locke has demonstrated the effect of goal setting on individual performance. His major proposition is that harder goals yield higher performance (but only if the individual *accepts* these goals). He has shown consistently that individuals who set or accept harder goals perform at levels higher than those who set or accept easier goals. Locke and his colleagues (Locke, Shaw, Saari, & Latham, 1981) have recently reviewed 15 years of goal setting research and come to some general conclusions:

1. An overwhelming number of field experiments, lab experiments, and correlational field studies (99 of 110, or 90 percent) have provided

support for the proposed relationship between goal setting and performance: the harder the (accepted) goal, the higher the performance.

2. ". . . Goals affect task performance by directing attention and action, mobilizing energy expenditure or effort, prolonging effort over time (persistence) and motivating the individual to develop relevant strategies for goal attainment" (Locke et al., 1981, p. 145).
3. Specific, hard goals will produce higher performance levels than either easy goals, "do-your-best" goals, or no goals at all.
4. Individuals must have the prerequisite ability for high performance in order for goal setting to have an effect on performance.
5. In addition to specific hard goals, an individual needs feedback or knowledge of results (KR) to perform at high levels. Either feedback or a hard goal alone will not have the optimum effect on performance.
6. Money and other concrete rewards may have the effect of increasing the commitment to an accepted goal.
7. There is no clear evidence that the performer must participate in goal setting for goals to exert their influence. Assigned goals seem to result in the same effect as goal setting in which the performer participated.
8. There have been no consistent findings with respect to individual differences variables other than ability (e.g., need for achievement, self-esteem) on goal setting behavior. Furthermore, when these nonability measures are included in analyses of performance, they seldom add any unique explanatory power to the variance in performance already explained by goal setting variables. That is not to say that individual differences can be discounted. Instead, the research in this area was said to be insufficient. (You will note that in a later section the evidence with respect to at least one individual difference variable—self-efficacy—has become quite clear and supportive—that is, self-efficacy does affect goal setting behavior.)

Let's stop for a moment and consider a graphic representation of what Locke proposes. What might be considered the "current" goal setting model appears in Figure 10–10. This figure illustrates many of the relationships suggested above. The review suggests that under certain circumstances goal acceptance may be affected by participation of the individual in setting the performance goals. Acceptance implies that the goal has been assigned or suggested by someone else. Similarly, goal commitment may be strengthened with the inducement of monetary or other rewards. In this case, the individual sets the goal and then determines the extent to which she is committed to that goal. In summary, money or participation in goal setting may increase the probability that a goal will actually be accepted (regardless of whether it is assigned by another or set by the person in question).

As you can see, goal acceptance and goal commitment (concepts that

FIGURE 10–10 A Diagram of Goal Theory

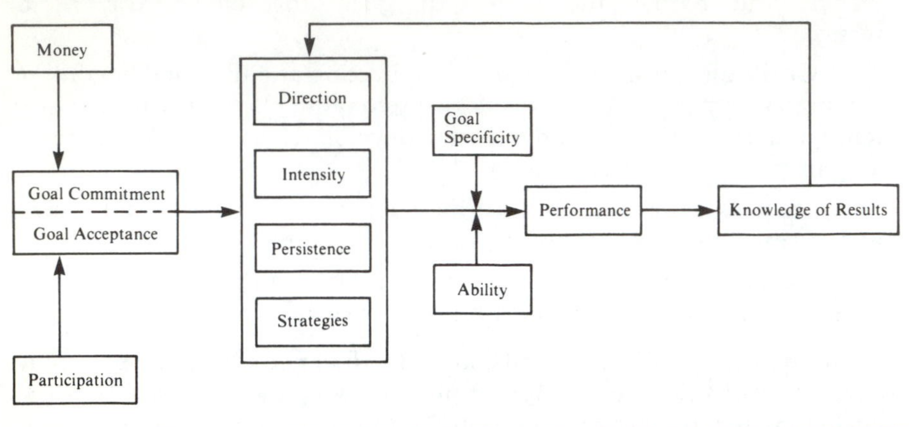

Locke et al. consider to be different) result in intermediate changes in direction, intensity, persistence, and strategic thinking. These changes, in turn, affect performance. If the individual is made aware of current performance levels (i.e., receives feedback in the form of knowledge of results), he or she may modify direction, intensity, persistence, or strategy to meet better the goal that has been accepted. This accounts for the loop connecting KR and intermediate states. In some senses, this loop represents a good example of control theory (see Figure 10-11), an approach taken by Ilgen and his colleagues to explain the effect of performance feedback in the performance appraisal context (Taylor, Fisher, & Ilgen, 1984). They liken control theory to the dynamics of the familiar room thermostat. When the temperature increases, the thermostat rises, and when it reaches a certain point, the heat is turned off in the room; when the temperature drops below a certain level, the thermostat once again energizes the heating system to bring the heat back to an acceptable level. Knowledge of results works in a similar fashion and, from the perspective of human behavior, might be thought of as part of a self-referent or self-regulatory mechanism.

A Cautionary Comment. In spite of the fact that goal setting literature seems to be unequivocal with respect to the facilitating effects of specific hard goals on performance, there is some concern that the results found in the laboratory may not generalize perfectly to field applications. Tubbs (1986), in a meta-analysis of goal setting research, found stronger effects in laboratory settings than in field settings. He suggested that this might be the case because subjects in short-duration laboratory studies would be willing to set or accept harder goals and to work harder to achieve them since they know that the activity will be of a short duration. For example, a common task assigned to

FIGURE 10–11 Simple Control Systems Model

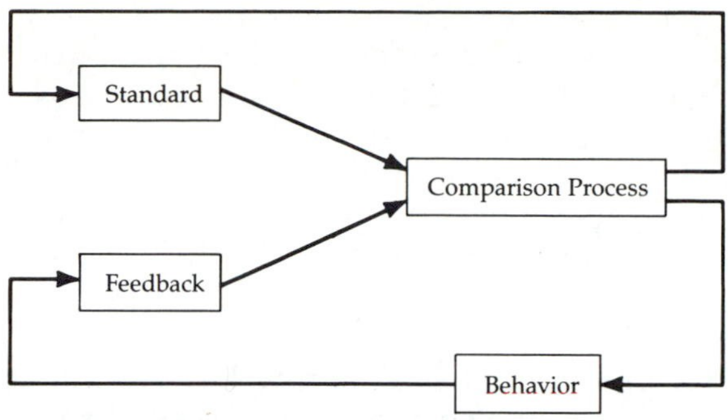

SOURCE: From "Individual's Reactions to Performance Feedback in Organizations" (Fig. 1, p. 84) by M. S. Taylor, C. D. Fisher, and D. R. Ilgen, in K. M. Rowland and G. R. Ferris (Eds.), *Research in Personnel and Human Resources Management* (Vol. 2), 1984, Greenwich, CT: JAI Press.

subjects in laboratory studies is the production of novel uses for a familiar object. Locke, Frederick, Lee, and Bobko (1984) asked 209 students to list as many uses as they could imagine for a coat hanger in one minute. Subjects were given several one-minute trials with different familiar objects. This is somewhat different from a worker at a rivet machine who has been at that rivet machine for 21 years and who is considering whether to produce 1,000 or 1,500 rivets each hour on a given day with a machine that occasionally breaks down and in the midst of the distraction of supervisors, lift trucks weaving in and out of machines, and comments from fellow workers. Bandura (1987) expresses similar concerns:

> The generality of evidence of unshaken pursuit of unreachable goals must be qualified, however, by the fact that laboratory situations may differ from actual conditions on several important dimensions—the (laboratory) endeavor usually involves only a brief effort, failure carries no costs, and no opportunities exist for alternative pursuits.

Locke (1986) argues vigorously that the goal setting results found in the laboratory do transfer to the real world. I do not disagree with the general conclusion that goals in the real world enhance effort and performance, as they do in laboratories. Nevertheless, I agree with Tubbs and Bandura that the *strength* of the relationship may well be mediated by various environmental constraints. There is reason to believe that an individual's willingness to set high goals may be affected by their beliefs regarding how long they will be required to sustain that activity. In discussing repetitive factory work with students in my classes, one student will inevitably claim that she worked in a bottling factory (or post office or fast-food restaurant) for a summer and didn't think it was so boring. I then ask her to consider what it would be like to do that job not for two months but for a lifetime. There is still work to be done in understanding the mechanisms of goal acceptance and effort expenditure.

Hollenbeck and Klein (1987) propose a model that directly addresses the possible complexity of the goal setting process and the various influences (including social and situational constraints) on that process. This model appears in Figure 10–12. We need more comparative data from the lab and field in order to understand completely what is going on in work settings. Lab data alone will not answer the questions implied in the Hollenbeck and Klein model.

An Integration of VIE and Goal Setting Theory. On the surface, goal setting theory would seem to be at odds with other theories of motivation. For example, expectancy theory would seem to predict the opposite: Easy goals (i.e., those that an individual feels certain can be achieved) will lead to greater effort (and therefore performance) than hard goals. As another example, achievement motivation theories (Atkinson & Feather, 1966) would seem to predict that moderately hard goals produce higher performance, whereas extremely easy or extremely hard goals yield lower performance. These relationships appear in Figure 10–13. In a test of these three different positions (Mento, Cartledge, & Locke, 1980), it was suggested that these different approaches are not necessarily mutually exclusive. As an example, it was suggested that expectancy and valence might influence whether a goal was accepted but that after acceptance, the difficulty of the goal is the primary influence on performance level. As we will see shortly, this type of revision of goal setting theory is both appropriate and informative.

To some extent, the early research in goal setting mechanisms implied that everyone sets goals and that they set goals in the same way. The recent research on goal setting has been more informative. As I indicated above, Mento et al. suggested the possibility that expectancies and valences play a role in goal setting. In effect, they proposed a two-phase process for explaining motivated behavior. The first phase, goal setting, was influenced by expectancies and valences. The second phase, energy expenditure, was affected by the actual goals that were set. In addition, since KR was thought to play a continuing role in energy expenditure, we could think of the theory as having 2+ phases.

Matsui and his colleagues (Matsui, Okada, & Inoshifa, 1983; Matsui, Okada, & Mizuguchi, 1981) have explored the role of valences and expectancies on goal setting in some detail. They hypothesized that from an expectancy perspective the effect of hard goals would be to *lower* the force to expend energy. On the other hand, they suggested that hard goals are attractive and have a positive valence since people value success on difficult tasks. This means that expectancy theory would predict that if an individual accepts a goal, it must be because the high valence overwhelms the low expectancy of success. This, in turn, should lead to a higher force on the person to expend

FIGURE 10–12 Expectancy Theory Model of the Antecedents and Consequences of Goal Commitment

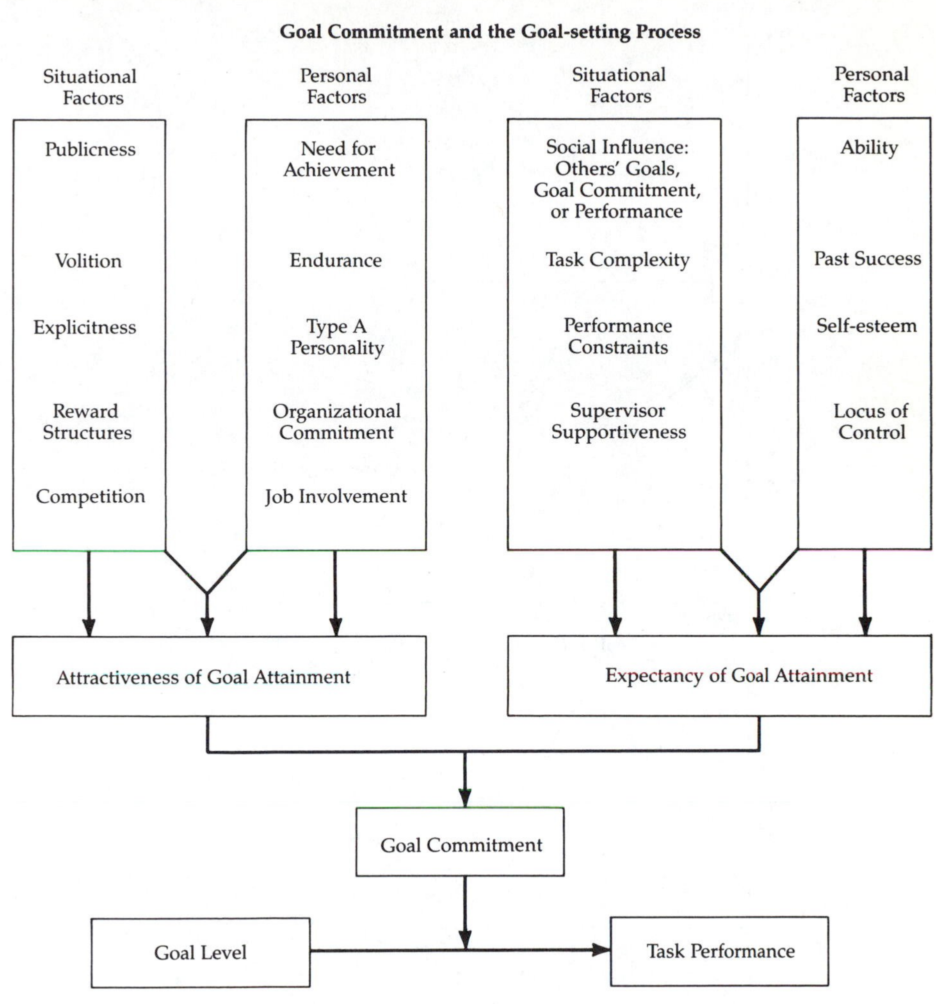

SOURCE: From "Goal Commitment and the Goal-Setting Process" by J. R. Hollenbeck and H. J. Klein, 1987, *Journal of Applied Psychology*, *72* (2), p. 15a. Copyright 1987 by the American Psychological Association, Reprinted by permission of the author.

energy (which, in turn, should lead to higher performance). Keep in mind that Matsui et al. are not proposing a different theory or trying to alter Locke's basic position with respect to the role of goals. They are simply suggesting a mechanism to explain *why* goals are accepted. Matsui conducted laboratory research with students performing a clerical accuracy task to test his propositions. As was the case with earlier studies, the hard-goal effect was found.

FIGURE 10–13 The Effect of Goal Difficulty in Three Different Theories

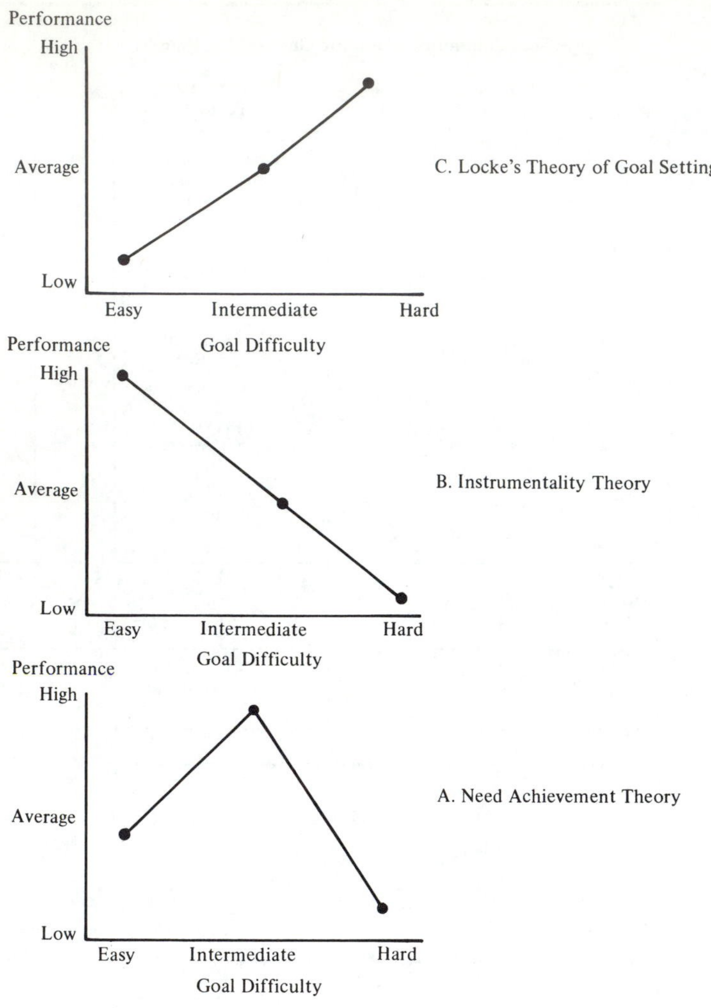

Those subjects who accepted a hard goal performed at a higher level than those accepting an easy goal. In addition, Matsui found that the valence of various outcomes that could occur from attaining the goals (e.g., increased self-confidence, increased clerical accuracy) was significantly higher for the hard-goal group than the easy-goal group. Finally, he found that hard-goal subjects had lower expectations that effort would lead toward goal attainment. These data do seem to indicate that valences and expectancies can influence goal adoption or choice. This should not be a great surprise since Vroom had originally proposed VIE theory as a theory of *choice* rather than as a theory of *action.* From these experiments, it follows that the critical issue in goal acceptance or commitment is valence. It is important to get the value of the outcome valence high enough to offset the low expectancy of success value. It would not make much sense to change the expectancy value since that would, in effect, change the goal from hard to easy, negating the well-established hard-goal effect. Borrowing again from Vroom's theory, the answer would seem to lie in instrumentalities. The person must be convinced that the outcomes of hard-goal attainment are associated with significantly greater payoff than the outcomes of easy-goal attainment or a condition where no goals are set.

In a later related study, Matsui and his colleagues (1983) demonstrated the effect of feedback on expectancies. They were able to show that feedback has very different effects on people performing at high or low levels of effectiveness. Student subjects were asked to solve 70 arithmetic problems in 10 minutes. This was considered a hard goal. After five minutes, the subjects received feedback about their progress toward that goal. Those who were making poorer progress significantly improved their performance in the second five minutes. Those who were making better progress did not change their behavior. Questionnaires administered at the five-minute mark asked the subjects to rate their expectation of meeting the goal. The expectancy value increased between the initial estimate and the intermediate estimate for the higher-performing group; it decreased for the lower-performing group. The experimenters concluded that feedback had its effect by influencing the intention to work fast on the part of the lower performers. A control group that was not given feedback showed no difference between first- and second-half performance or expectation of success. This further confirms the conclusion by Locke et al. (1981) that feedback is critical for goals to have their effect on performance.

Goal Setting: Assigned or Participative. A question that has received a good deal of attention in both research and application of goal setting methods is the extent to which the employee should be involved in actually deciding on goal levels. Would it be better or worse simply to assign goals to individuals rather than have them join in the goal selection? Locke et al. (1981) find little support in their literature review for the effectiveness of participation in goal setting. As an example of the type of study investigating the effect of participation, Dossett, Latham, and Mitchell (1979) created three goal conditions for clerical employees. One condition consisted of assigned goals. The second condition involved participative goal setting where employees were asked to set "difficult but obtainable" goals for themselves. In the third goal condition, employees were exhorted to "do your best." The results showed that there was no advantage to participative goal setting (although the researchers did suggest that the assigned group may have been assigned goals well below their ability levels).

Recently, some studies and reviews have come to different conclusions about the effect of participation in goal setting. For example, Earley and Kanfer (1985) found that when student subjects were given the opportunity to choose a goal level and to choose the strategy for meeting the goal, goal acceptance, satisfaction, and performance were higher. Similarly, Mento, Steel, and Karven (1987) conducted a meta-analysis of goal setting studies and concluded that there was some reason to believe that participation does have an effect. They were careful to note that only six studies were available and that not all those studies confirmed the effect of participation; nevertheless, they felt that the issue of participation was far from resolved.

Many researchers frame the participation question in a particular way. In effect, they ask, Is participation significantly more effective than assignment of goals in subsequent performance? The question might be framed somewhat differently. Instead, one might ask, Does participation cause harm? Does it suppress goal-directed behavior in any way? The answer seems to be no. Participation does not seem to do any harm. The issue may relate more closely to the organizational personality than to the nature of goal setting per se. In an autocratic organization, participation in goal setting might seem bizarre. In a democratic organization, assigning goals might seem equally bizarre. Ironically, participation in goal setting and work behavior is much more common in social democratic, socialist, and communist countries than in capitalist countries. As examples, there is heavy involvement of workers and first-level supervisors in determining output goals in countries such as Sweden, Hungary, Romania, and Yugoslavia. Such involvement is still the exception in the U.S. factory. I am not arguing that these forms of government are better than our capitalist-democratic model; I am pointing out that sociopolitical influences can be clearly seen in the behavior of industrial organizations and have those influences at the individual and work group level. Further, I am arguing that participation is not always an issue of effectiveness but, instead, may be a political and philosophical issue.

The Wave of the Future: Personal Efficacy

Much of the early research and a substantial amount of current research on goal setting theory relates to process issues: Is participation important? Do incentives make a difference? What happens when goals are unattainable? Recently, there has been a substantial shift in the tenor of goal setting research and discussion. This shift has been precipitated by the work of Bandura on a construct known as *self-efficacy* or *personal efficacy*. Bandura (1977, 1982) has carefully developed the construct from a set of theoretical propositions to a programmatic line of research that provides strong support for the notion that efficacy affects motivation and performance (Bandura, 1986, 1987). This development is one of the most exciting extensions of human motivation theory to occur since the expectancy-valence shift took place almost 30 years ago.

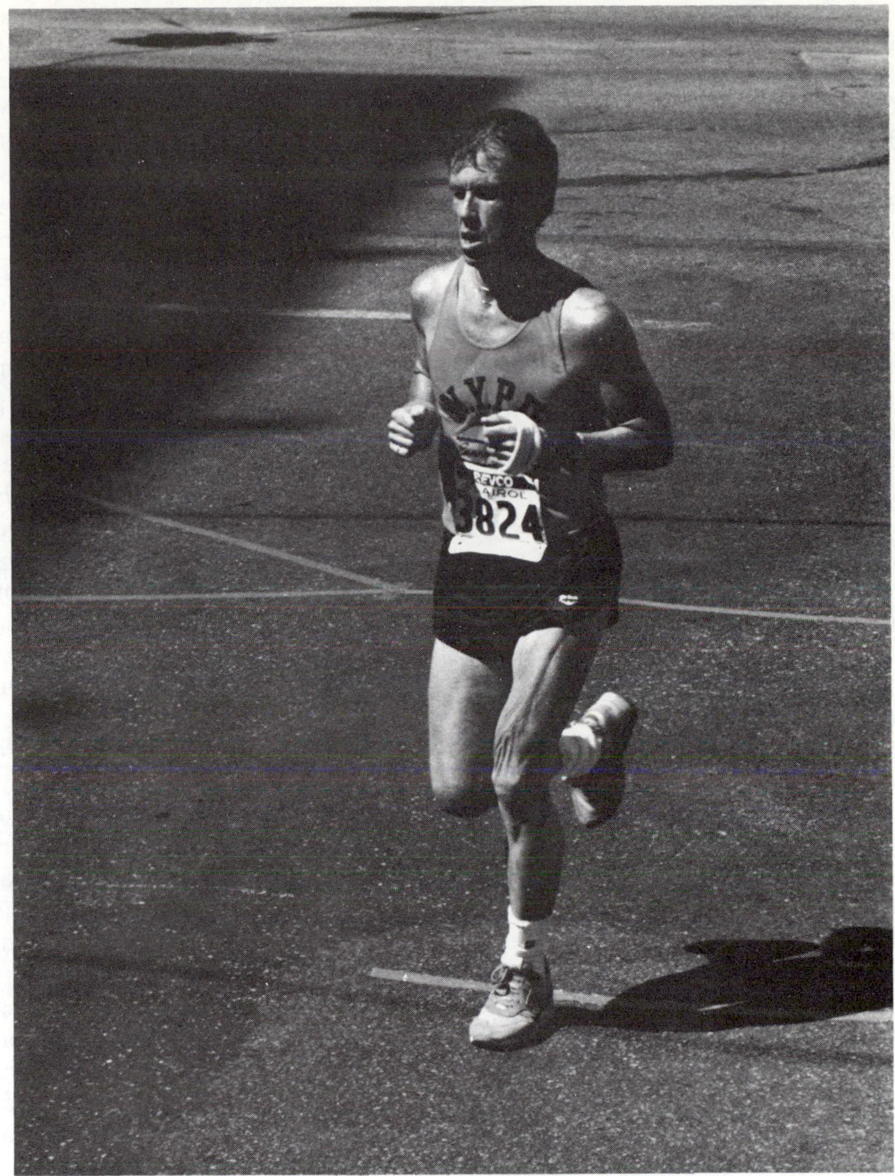

Marathon runners often push themselves to the limit of endurance because of confidence that they can complete the run of 26.2 miles.

Bandura's major proposition is simple but elegant: the extent to which a person believes that he or she possesses the necessary skills and abilities to accomplish a goal in the face of adversity is closely bound to the effort expenditure and level of accomplishment of that person. This belief has been labeled *self-efficacy* or *personal efficacy*. Bandura (1987) asserts that all motivational manipulations have their effects through a modification of self-efficacy. Thus, for example, he proposes that those individuals with high personal efficacy will set high goals, persist in the pursuit of those goals, and set even higher goals when the original goals have been met. In contrast, those with low efficacy will set lower initial goals, will abandon those goals in the face of any adversity, no matter how minor, and if they reach those initial goals, will set lower subsequent goals. Further, he suggests that success and failure histories will not directly affect future behavior but instead will affect feelings of efficacy, and that it is these feelings or beliefs that will impact directly on behavior. For example, a person with high efficacy who fails to meet a goal may double her effort and possibly even set higher goals. In contrast, a person with low efficacy may meet a goal and then *lower* subsequent goals, believing that he could never achieve that level again.

Bandura (1986) is quick to point out that efficacy is different from other variables such as locus of control or self-esteem or expectations. *Locus of control* is a broad belief about causal relations, not a specific belief about possessed skills and abilities. *Self-esteem* is a sense of worth or value, not an estimate of capability in the face of adversity. *Expectations* are beliefs about relationships between actions and outcomes. *Efficacy* is a belief on the part of an individual that he has "what it takes" to meet a difficult goal. Bandura is proposing that thought (in the form of beliefs of efficacy) mediates the relationship between knowledge and action.

There have been a number of studies that have provided supporting data for Bandura's propositions about efficacy, several conducted by Bandura and his colleagues (e.g., Bandura and Cervone, 1983, 1986). These studies have often involved performance on physical ability–type measures such as effort expended on an exercise bicycle. Support has also appeared in the industrial literature. Huber and Neale (1984) demonstrated the positive effect of feelings of interpersonal efficacy (i.e., the belief in one's ability to influence others) on the goal setting and performance of negotiators. Freedman and Phillips (1985) demonstrated that personal efficacy (which they referred to as a feeling of competence) overcame the effect of various environmental constraints on motivation and satisfaction. Those subjects who felt competent were not intimidated by various obstacles to high performance. That is not to say that these subjects *performed* at a level equal to subjects with no environmental constraints or obstacles. The point is that even in the presence of obstacles to effective performance, subjects who felt competent were not discouraged or unhappy. They continued to plug away. In a laboratory study mentioned earlier, Locke et al. (1984) found that efficacy was an effective predictor of effort and performance. Remember that this study dealt with novel uses of commonplace objects. Figure 10–14 presents the efficacy scale that was used in this study. The analysis of the data in this study showed that efficacy was affected by past performance (i.e., the extent to which goals were met) and affected future performance (i.e., the level of goals set and perseverance in

FIGURE 10–14 Self-Efficacy Scale

	Column A (Y = yes; N = no) *Can Do*	*Column B* (0 to 100%) *Certainty*
I can list 2 uses in 1 minute.	_____	_____
I can list 4 uses in 1 minute.	_____	_____
I can list 6 uses in 1 minute.	_____	_____
I can list 8 uses in 1 minute.	_____	_____
I can list 10 uses in 1 minute.	_____	_____
I can list 12 uses in 1 minute.	_____	_____
I can list 14 uses in 1 minute.	_____	_____
I can list 16 uses in 1 minute.	_____	_____

SOURCE: From "Effect of Self-Efficacy, Goals, and Task Strategies on Task Performance" by E. A. Locke, E. Frederick, C. Lee, and P. Bobko, 1984, *Journal of Applied Psychology, 69* (2), p. 243. Copyright 1984 by the American Psychological Association. Reprinted by permission of the publisher and author.

meeting those goals). Thus, efficacy was a fulcrum for cognition and behavior, as Bandura suggests. A graphic representation of this central role for efficacy appears in Figure 10–15.

Hill, Smith, and Mann (1987) present data that suggest that not only does efficacy affect a particular task; it also may affect related tasks. They studied the extent to which students felt efficacious in the use of personal computers and demonstrated that feelings of efficacy were related to the probability of taking computer-related courses. In addition, they showed a relationship between feelings of efficacy with respect to computers and the extent to which devices such as calculators and automated bank tellers were used by these students.

Finally, Taylor, Locke, and Lee (1985) demonstrated that feelings of efficacy were related to the extent to which faculty members at a university produced scientific publications. Anyone who attempts to publish scientific articles can easily understand the importance of efficacy in the process. Since the publication process involves review by peers, most manuscripts must be revised several times before they are actually published. When an article comes back with critical comments, there are two common types of reaction among authors. One reaction is to put the article and comments in the bottom of a deep drawer and forget that the article was ever written. The author may contemplate changing lines of work as well—possibly becoming a parking lot attendant or an optician. The second reaction is more positive. The individual sees the criticisms as minor, coming from reviewers who are slow to understand complex explanations. The second author might skip lunch and begin working immediately on a revision of the paper and possibly even expand the paper to include new material not covered in the earlier version.

FIGURE 10–15 Effect of Self-Efficacy and Goals on Performance

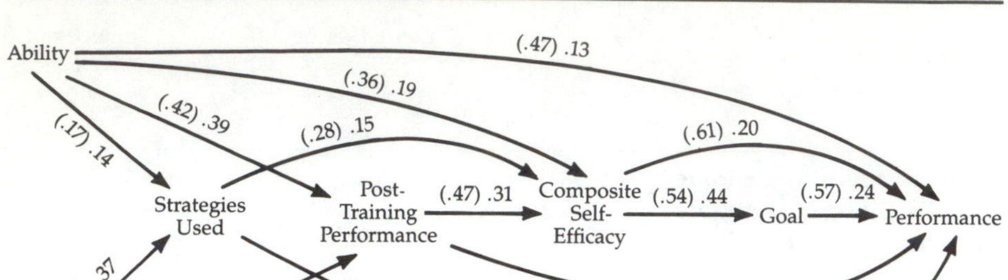

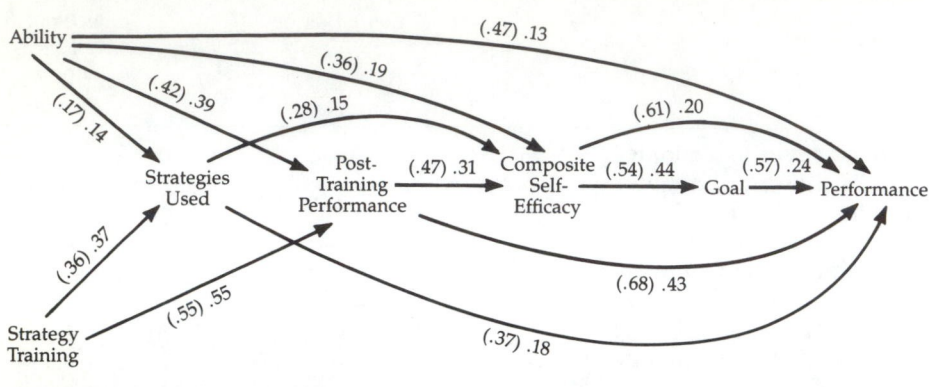

SOURCE: From "Effect of Self-Efficacy, Goals, and Task Strategies on Task Performance" by E. A. Locke, E. Frederick, C. Lee, and P. Bobko, 1984, *Journal of Applied Psychology, 69* (2), p. 247. Copyright 1984 by the American Psychological Association. Reprinted by permission of the publisher and author.

In this example, the first author would be thought to have low personal efficacy and the second author high self-efficacy. It is this difference that presumably controls the response to negative feedback.

In Bandura's approach, there are assumptions made that fit in nicely with what we have learned in other areas of motivational research. Some of these assumptions are as follows:

1. Motivation is a process of cognitive comparison.
2. People desire a positive self-image.
3. Comparison is aided by setting standards.
4. Goals are effective standards; the more specific the goal, the better as a standard for comparison.
5. In order to make the necessary comparison, people need feedback about goal attainment.

Bandura makes a compelling argument for the role of efficacy in theories of motivation. The assumptions listed above seem reasonable. Further, the data collected so far on the theory are supportive. Nevertheless, a good deal of additional data needs to be collected. We need to know more about the issue of the resiliency of efficacy. Even the efficacious author feels briefly nauseous when reading negative reviews for the first time. How is it that some people snap back from that experience and others do not? In addition, Bandura implies that it is more effective to err in the direction of optimism with respect to efficacy than to be veridical or realistic about skills and abilities. An efficacious person will not be as easily discouraged by failure and will persist and possibly even set a higher goal.

This last point raises a series of interesting questions in the work environment. For example, what is the role of the supervisor in determining the personal efficacy of subordinates? It would seem that the supervisor who is a cheerleader would be very helpful from a motivational perspective. Similarly, work group composition becomes a relevant issue. What is the effect of being placed in a work group with a majority of members high on personal efficacy? What is the effect of being in a group with low efficacy? There are literally dozens of interesting and relevant questions that relate to work motivation that are precipitated by the introduction of efficacy into the discussion.

To return to the evolutionary note struck in the beginning of the chapter, goal setting theory is in the process of radical transformation. The initial work of Locke and his colleagues in goal setting research (e.g., Locke 1968) was not particularly theoretical. It emphasized the effect of goals. In later research and writing, Locke emphasized the goal setting *process*, accepting some of the integrating suggestions of the expectancy theorists and researchers (e.g., Matsui et al., 1981). Recently, Locke has embraced the content contributions of Bandura and others who suggest that the "active ingredient" in goal setting behavior may be self-efficacy. In fact, I expect that within a relatively short period of time the emphasis in goal setting research will have shifted almost completely to the notion of efficacy and that goal setting behavior will be a specific manifestation of a broader theory of efficacy.

I am very enthusiastic about the future for this line of research. To be sure, there is a good deal of elaboration necessary for many of the theoretical propositions of efficacy theory, but I am convinced that this elaboration will occur quickly and effectively. In short, my feelings of personal efficacy related to efficacy theory development are quite strong!

Reinforcement Approaches (Behaviorism)

The reinforcement approach to work motivation is clearly an example of a "what-you-do-to-someone" tradition. The major thrust of this approach is to show that the behavior of an individual in an industrial setting can be accounted for by understanding various STIMULUS—RESPONSE—REWARD associations. Particular attention is paid to the RESPONSE—REWARD association. The term *reward schedule* has come to represent this association. There are two issues to consider. The first is the presence or absence of a *contingent* relationship between response and reward. The second issue relates to the *timing* (or schedule) of rewards.

Generally speaking, hourly pay or salary is noncontingent reinforcement. This means that the reward (in this case, money) does not depend on any particular behavior. It will come weekly or monthly independent of productivity. In fact, this is an exaggeration. Workers must appear at the workplace and must produce some minimum amount to warrant a paycheck, but beyond that minimum, level of productivity and reliability of attendance are unrelated to pay. Contingent rewards, on the other hand, imply that the rewards will occur only if certain behaviors occur. A piece-rate method of payment would be considered contingent reward. The person receives money in direct proportion to productive effort. A worker in a car wash may be paid according to the number of cars washed in a given day; a packer might be paid according to the number of boxes filled. The behaviorists argue that contingent rewards yield higher levels of effort and production than noncontingent rewards. By extension, they propose that energy expenditure (i.e., motivation) is the result of response-reward contingencies.

The issue of the schedule of rewards (assuming that they are contingent) represents an additional source of research and application for behaviorists. When Skinner first began his observation of the learning patterns of rats, he rewarded the rats each time they made a correct response. The reward was a food pellet. Although he had worked out an automatic reward dispenser, the fact was that the rats performed at such a high rate under the contingent reinforcement schedule that Skinner was forever making new food pellets and filling food dispensers. This was particularly annoying on weekends. As a result, he decided to see if he could reward the rats on something less than a 100-percent basis. As an example, he wondered if they would perform just as well if he only rewarded them for every third or fourth correct response. He discovered that not only did they continue to perform under these new reward conditions, but they actually performed at a more rapid rate. From that point on, Skinner devoted most of his attention to cataloging the effects of various reward schedules (Skinner, 1959). Skinner's initial method of rewarding the rats—that is, for every correct response—is called *continuous reinforcement*. The alternative method of reward—that is, only for a portion of correct responses—is called *intermittent reinforcement*. Both of these schedules of reinforcement are contingent. In both instances, correct responses must occur before a reward is presented. In industrial settings, there has been a good deal of interest in determining if intermittent schedules of reinforcement will lead to greater effort or productivity. Now might be a good time to review some of the more common schedules.

Reinforcement Schedules. There are many possible reinforcement schedules that could be employed in research or application, and entire books have been written on the intricacies of reinforcement schedules (e.g., Ferster & Skinner, 1957). Instead of listing all possible schedules, I will present descriptions of the more common schedules in industrial research as well as examples of studies examining the effects of these schedules. Studies often compare and contrast subsets of the following five schedules. The first schedule is noncontingent, and the other four are contingent.

1. *Hourly rate.* A noncontingent reinforcement schedule in which the individual is paid at a fixed rate regardless of performance. This is normally considered to be a "control" condition or a base rate for comparison purposes.

2. *Continuous reinforcement schedule.* A contingent reward presented after *each* correct response.
3. *Fixed-ratio schedule.* A contingent schedule in which rewards are presented after a fixed *number* (greater than one) of correct responses, for example, after five orders are processed.
4. *Variable-ratio schedule.* A contingent schedule in which the number of correct responses required before a reward occurs varies on some prearranged schedule (e.g., after 7 correct responses, then after 4 correct responses, then after 11 correct responses, etc.).
5. *Variable-amount schedule.* Contingent rewards vary in amount from one occasion to the next. For example, one correct response may result in a reward of $10, and another may result in a $50 reward (this commonly occurs in retail sales commissions. The salesperson does not know from one customer to another what the size of the commission might be). This is not actually a schedule of reinforcement in the strict sense, but it does represent an experimental condition that has been tested against other traditional schedules.

A good example of research on reinforcement schedules is illustrated in a series of experiments conducted by Pritchard and his associates (Pritchard, Hollenbeck, & DeLeo, 1980; Pritchard, Leonard, VonBergen & Kirk, 1976). In a study of the effect of reinforcement schedules on the training performance of students learning an electronics task, Pritchard et al. (1976) tested the hourly condition against fixed-ratio, variable-ratio, and variable-amount schedules and found that all contingent schedules yielded higher performance than hourly pay, but there were no differences among the various contingent schedules in terms of their performance effects. In a replication of this study, Pritchard et al. (1980) again found no evidence for the superiority of intermittent schedules of reinforcement.

Let's examine a typical study using reinforcement principles in the field as opposed to the laboratory or a simulated field setting. Luthans, Paul, and Baker (1981) considered the effect of contingent reinforcement on the behavior of sales personnel in a large department store. Three aspects of employee performance were of interest. They were:

Selling behavior. Assisting a customer within five seconds after the customer arrives in the sales area (or in a case where the clerk is already engaged with another customer, approaching the second customer within five seconds of the departure of the first customer)

Stocking behavior. Keeping the shelves stocked to within 70 percent of their capacity with appropriate merchandise

Attendance behavior. Being within three yards of the merchandise for which the salesperson was responsible

The study was carried out in a very large department store, and 16 departments were randomly chosen for the study. Eight departments were experimental departments and eight were control. The rewards in the experiment were cash and time off. For experimental group sales personnel, the rewards were as follows:

1. One hour per week of time off was accumulated for being absent from the workstation less than 10 percent of the workday.
2. Two hours per week of time off were awarded for meeting the sales standards (i.e., the five-second contact time).
3. If both attendance *and* sales performance standards were met in a given week, the person was awarded half a day off with pay or a cash bonus equal to pay for half a day of work. In addition, if all standards were met, the individual was eligible for a drawing that would award a week of paid vacation to the person whose name was chosen.

Control subjects were simply informed of performance standards but were promised no concrete rewards for meeting those standards. The authors noted that the most common method of motivation used by managers before the study (and presumably with the control subjects during the study) was scolding or threatening with punishment. The results of the experiment appear in Figures 10–16 and 10–17. As you can see, the contingent reinforcement seemed to have an immediate and dramatic effect. Figure 10–16 illustrates the effects of reinforcement on retailing behavior (a combination of selling and stocking behavior). For the first 20 days, the experimenters simply observed and recorded the behavior of the two groups. This was called the *baseline period,* since they were interested in identifying some preexperimental levels of retailing behavior. This would permit comparisons after the experimental variable (contingent reinforcement) was introduced. On the 21st day, the reinforcement schedule was introduced for the experimental subjects. The frequency of the various retailing behaviors jumped immediately and stayed high for the next 20 days. In contrast, the control subjects continued to behave as they had during the baseline period. On the 41st day, the contingent reinforcement was discontinued. This is called the *postintervention stage.* The experimental subjects continued to show high levels of retailing behavior, whereas the control subjects continued at the significantly lower performance level. Figure 10–17 presents similar data for the behavior related to absence from workstation. Keep in mind that with this variable high scores represent poor performance since they mean higher absence from the workstation. Once again, the effect of contingent reinforcement was immediate, dramatic, and long lasting.

These data represent a clear example of what behaviorists hope to achieve through the use of contingent reinforcement. They also represent something of a novelty. One of the problems with contingent reinforcement (particularly continuous reinforcement schedules) is that the effect usually disappears as soon as the reinforcement stops. In fact, sometimes the behavior in the post-

FIGURE 10–16 Aggregate Retailing Behavior

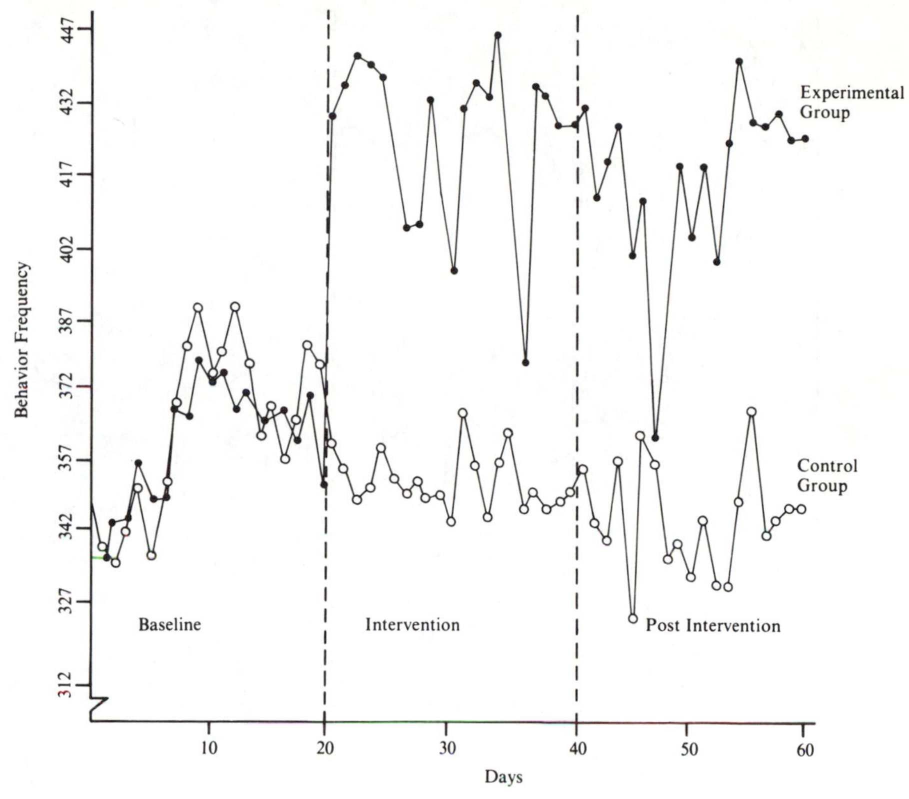

SOURCE: From "An Experimental Analysis of the Impact of Contingent Reinforcement on Sales and Persons' Performance Behavior" by F. Luthans, R. Paul, and D. Baker, 1981, *Journal of Applied Psychology, 66*(3), p. 319.

intervention phase even drops *below* the behavior in the baseline phase. In such a circumstance, one might argue that the intervention actually did more harm than good. In the present case, this did not occur. The authors suggest that the experimental sales personnel may have experienced the positive effect of good retail and attendance behavior. The scolding and threatening stopped, they were probably reinforced by customers for being attentive, and their skills in retail sales may have improved, resulting in higher sales and better self-image. For whatever reason, this experiment really represents the ideal in behaviorist interventions.

In industrial and organizational research, many of the studies that do find advantages for intermittent schedules are accompanied by other stranger results. As an example, in a study by London and Oldham (1979) contrasting piece-rate incentives with other payment schemes, they actually found that

FIGURE 10–17 Absence from the Workstation and Idle Time

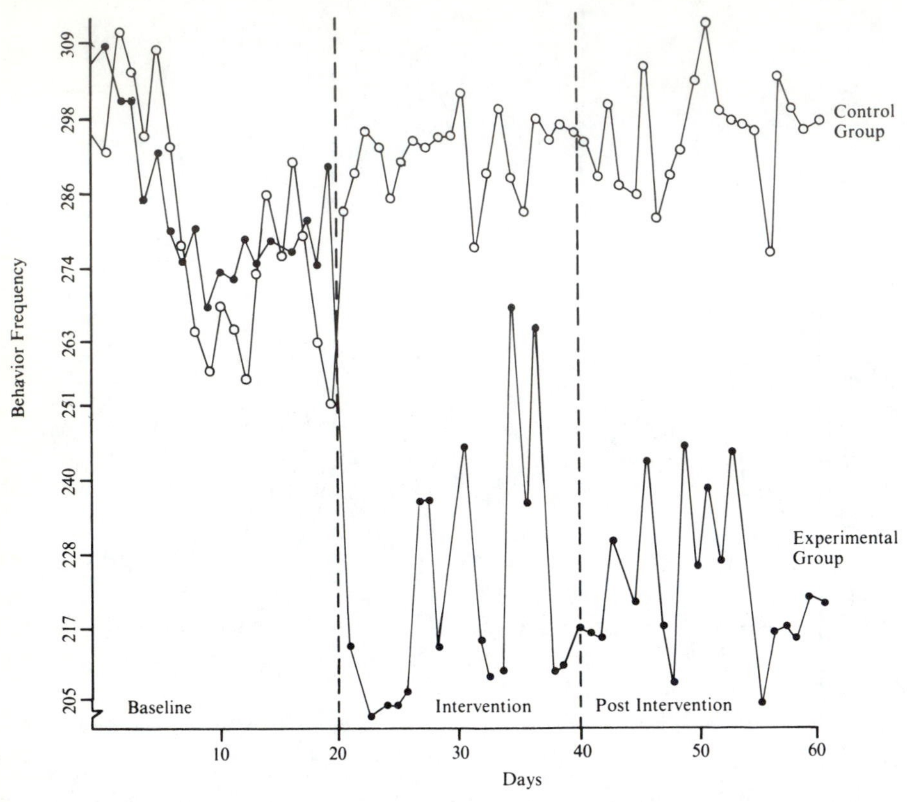

SOURCE: From "An Experimental Analysis of the Impact of Contingent Reinforcement on Sales and Persons' Performance Behavior" by F. Luthans, R. Paul, and D. Baker, 1981, *Journal of Applied Psychology, 66*(3), p. 320.

a no-pay condition produced superior performance. Similarly, other researchers have found intermittent schedules operating in a manner opposite to what might have been predicted from animal research (Yukl & Latham, 1975). Still other studies seem to indicate that the effect of a schedule will depend on the experience of the workers. For example, Latham and Dossett (1978) found that experienced workers were more productive on a variable-ratio schedule, whereas inexperienced workers were more productive on a continuous schedule. It is tempting to speculate that a good deal of this seeming confusion might be eliminated if we knew something about the efficacy beliefs of the subjects in these experiments. But since orthodox reinforcement researchers are loathe to consider internal cognitive variables in studying behavior, it is unlikely that such data would be gathered in the typical reinforcement study.

From an orthodox behaviorist perspective, the most reasonable conclusion to draw from this research with reinforcement schedules is that contingent reinforcement of any type is more effective than noncontingent reinforcement, but there are no reliable differences between or among various contingent schedules. Pritchard et al. (1980) state this position most directly: "The sum of evidence suggests that, for complex tasks in job settings, (intermittent) schedules such as variable ratio and variable ratio/variable amount have not shown any real superiority over more traditional fixed ratio or piece rate pay systems and, in fact, are probably inferior" (p. 352).

Why is this the case? Why don't the results from animal studies generalize to the workplace? There are several possible reasons. The first, and most obvious, is that the capacity to reason and conceptualize is infinitely greater in humans than in animals. The fact that an experimenter creates a given schedule does not mean that the schedule will be perceived in the intended manner by the subject. Most of us superimpose many different layers of meaning on environmental events. This is particularly true in the work setting. A reward (or lack thereof) carries lots of excess meaning. Furthermore, reinforcement represents information that is then transformed, stored, and retrieved in altered form. Another reason is related to the actual dispensing of rewards. In most field settings, it is virtually impossible to control reward presentation to the same extent that it can be controlled in laboratory settings. Finally, in field settings, there are many different reinforcers working simultaneously. The experimenter happens to control one of those reinforcers, but there are other concrete and social influences on behavior as well that cannot be controlled by the experimenter.

The Issue of Punishment

Punishment has always held a peculiar position in both the animal and human learning literature. The various reinforcement schedules that we have discussed so far have all involved the presentation of a *desired* object or environmental event (e.g., money, praise, a promotion) following an appropriate behavior. Punishment involves the presentation of an *undesirable* object or environmental event (e.g., suspension, verbal reprimand) following an inappropriate action. As an example, consider the policy of a state police agency that uses suspension without pay as a punishment for violations of a code of conduct established by the department. An officer who conducts private business while on duty may be suspended for two days without pay. Similarly, it is common in nuclear power companies to suspend operators or supervisors who make work-related errors that result in violations of the safety guidelines of the Nuclear Regulatory Commission. Thus, a control room supervisor who causes a plant "trip" (i.e., automatic shutdown) may be suspended for a week without pay. This may result in the loss of as much as $1,500 in regular and overtime pay.

The reason that punishment occupies a unique role is partly philosophical and partly empirical. Much of the laboratory data on learning experiments using punishment show that punishment makes subjects act very differently from those exposed to positive reinforcement. The punished subjects are more anxious, less clever, and less creative; tend to concentrate more on the presence of the punisher than on the task to be learned; and generally are more concerned with avoiding punishment than with learning. In the two examples of punishment systems described above, it is not unheard of for state police officers and nuclear power operators to continue with inappropriate behaviors but try to cover them up in order to avoid punishment.

Philosophically, many psychologists believe that punishment is unnecessary, cruel, unproductive, and possibly unethical. The belief is that for the most part workers are responsible, motivated, and interested in helping the organization meet its goals. As a result, punishment is seen as inappropriate. Consequently, there has been little formal research on the effect of punishment systems in spite of the fact that punishment of one form or another (even if it is only the "silent treatment" that is practiced by a supervisor on a subordinate after a subordinate error or omission) is virtually universal in organizations.

Recently, there has been a spark of interest in the comparative evaluation of punishment and reward systems. This has been initiated by the work of Arvey and his colleagues (Arvey, Davis, & Nelson, 1984; Arvey & Ivancevich, 1980). They suggest that punishment systems and reward systems are not mutually exclusive, as others seem to believe. In other words, it is possible (and effective) to have mixed systems of both rewards and punishments in the workplace. In a study of several thousand workers and supervisors, Arvey et al. (1984) discovered that there were two major dimensions to punishment behavior of supervisors. The first of these dimensions was called *disciplinary style* and was related to the tendency of a supervisor to abuse or overuse disciplinary measures. The second dimension was related to the consistency with which supervisors applied disciplinary measures within and across employees. Arvey discovered that discipline was correlated with the satisfaction that workers experienced with their supervisors but not with overall satisfaction. In particular, employees preferred to be disciplined immediately after the infraction rather than at a later time, they preferred supervisors who were less harsh in level of punishment, and they preferred supervisors who explained *why* the discipline was being administered. Further, Arvey et al. demonstrated that in terms of satisfaction with supervisors, both reward styles and punishment styles contributed *independently* to satisfaction. This means that a supervisor who is fair and consistent in administering punishment and rewards may be more favorably evaluated by subordinates than one who simply administers rewards.

This latter finding is not surprising for those who are familiar with work settings. From an equity perspective, workers often prefer a system that will punish fellow workers for violating rules of behavior (e.g., tardiness). They don't want to see the deviant worker "get away with" transgressions, particularly if the average worker is conscientious in following the rules. On the other hand, if the rules are only occasionally applied or applied too harshly or to the wrong person, then the workers resent the system, even if they are not directly affected by it.

Schnake (1986) conducted an interesting experiment in the application of punishment in a laboratory experiment. Students were working as proofreaders and observed a fellow "worker" (actually a confederate of the experimenter) being punished with a reduced wage for substandard performance. Those subjects who saw this punishment administered subsequently performed at a significantly higher level than a control group (i.e., those who were not exposed to the punishment manipulation). Further, simply *threatening* to cut the pay of the confederate did not have any appreciable effect on performance of the subjects. This is an interesting study because there is a common belief in industry that it is often necessary to show the workers that management is serious about a policy by making an example of a particular worker. It is assumed that by means of this vicarious punishment, other workers will have the rule in question "reinforced" in their minds. They will realize that the company is serious. Schnake's results would seem to confirm this belief. There is, however, one serious flaw in the study, a flaw that Schnake is quick to acknowledge. The subjects in the experiment did not know the "coworker" (confederate) who was punished. In many real-world situations, punishment meted out to a stranger is viewed neutrally or positively, but punishment delivered to a friend or colleague is resented, particularly if it is seen as unduly harsh or it appears that the friend was singled out in order to "make an example" for others to see.

Data on the comparative value of punishment and reward systems are virtually nonexistent. This is unfortunate, given the universality of punishment behavior in the workplace. The data of Arvey and Schnake are provocative. Additional data should be examined, particularly in the workplace with intact work groups, before punishment is dismissed as a reasonable mechanism for modifying behavior in the workplace. In addition, there is a clear need to examine the effect of labor unions on the administration and perception of punishment systems in industry. The grievance procedure fundamentally changes the application and interpretation of discipline.

Theoretical Status of Behaviorism in Industry

In all areas of psychology, there has been a continuing battle between the behaviorists and those of other theoretical persuasions, most notably the humanists and the cognitive psychologists. There are several areas of disagreement. The first and most fundamental disagreement is about the status of behaviorism. Opponents suggest that it is not a theory of behavior at all, that it is nothing more than a technology or a language. A second issue of controversy has been the role of mental activities in behavior. Radical behaviorism (adopted by the followers of Skinner) denies any importance to activities such as reasoning, judgment, creativity, concept formation, and feelings of efficacy. They claim that behavior can be understood by simply noting the associations between behavior and environmental events. In fact, from this perspective, there is no place for the concept of motivation. Humanists and cognitive psychologists point to the overwhelming evidence with respect to mental events, even in the data of the behaviorists. We can look at just such an example. Consider Figures 10–16 and 10–17 again. Consider the behavior of the experimental subjects on the very first day of the intervention. If this is not evidence of thinking, then the subjects are awfully quick learners! The behavior changes dramatically, suggesting cognitive activity. They had been told about the program, were prepared to try it out, and probably had even made plans for how to use the money or time off. In these same data, the postintervention phase also creates some problems for the behaviorist interpretation. Why didn't the behavior return to baseline levels for the experimental group? In some senses, the fact that the postintervention behavior remains at this high level means that the behavior must not be under the control of reinforcement (or at the very least, is *no longer* under the control of reinforcers).

Locke (1980) has done an excellent job of pointing to the problems of behaviorism as a sole or sufficient position for understanding industrial behavior. He suggests, as do others (e.g., Komaki, Collins, & Penn, 1982), that a more cognitive interpretation is appropriate for understanding the effects of contingent reinforcement. This is in keeping with changes in the broader approach to reinforcement theory. The radical anticognitive emphasis of Skinner has given way to a more complex information-processing and self-control orientation (Mahoney, 1974; Thoresen & Mahoney, 1974).

Most psychologists accept the fact that contingent reinforcement can affect behavior. But, as Locke suggests, "the behaviorist is happy to know *that* a reinforcer reinforces, whereas the cognitive psychologist wants to know *why* it does so" (p. 22). The needs of the practitioner and the theorist can be quite different. In the morning when I wake up, I have discovered that a cup of coffee will produce alertness more quickly than would have resulted without the coffee. I do not need to know how caffeine works on neurotransmission or the excretion of hormones in order to take advantage of this effect. I don't even need to know that coffee contains caffeine. Similarly, the manager who wants to improve attendance or sales behavior or work quality does not need to know anything about goals or reasoning. She only needs to be able to observe behavior and apply reinforcement contingently. It is my opinion that behaviorism is a technology rather than a theoretical position. It is a useful technology, to be sure. Nevertheless, an understanding of *why* contingent reinforcement is effective must come from another direction—possibly a cognitive direction such as the one suggested by goal setting theory or instrumentality theory.

Other Models

We have examined only five possible approaches to work motivation. Although they are the most popular of the current approaches, there are others that might be considered as well. For example, some (Gardner, 1984; Scott, 1966) have proposed that motivation is properly thought of from a physiological perspective. As a result, activation and arousal level are thought to be central in the motivational process. Some have suggested (Carver & Scheier, 1981; Taylor, Fisher, & Ilgen, 1984) that control theory be used to interpret motivated behavior. Frese (1986) has suggested an approach called *action theory* that assumes that individuals adopt certain styles (e.g., impulsive versus reflective) that govern motivated behavior through schematas or scripts. Each of these models has some merit. Unfortunately, there are simply too little data to warrant any extensive discussion from the industrial perspective.

SUMMARY OF THE MODELS

While each of the motivational categories has been summarized before, a capsule view of the way each of them treats the two major components of the motivational system—effort expenditure and performance—will prove useful. It should be noted that few of the theories actually claim to be able to predict performance directly. Nevertheless, many tests of the theories include an examination of work performance or more general work-related behavior (e.g., absence or turnover). There is little doubt that the theorists involved would be pleased if their propositions were able to account for performance differences. Thus, I think it is reasonable in this case to examine the issue of performance as well as energy expenditure and see how each of the theories might approach its prediction.

Effort Expenditure

The questions related to antecedents and consequences of work motivation in the various models really boil down to a consideration of the "whys" of effort expenditure or "content" questions. Need hierarchy and equity theory are in agreement that internal tension is the antecedent condition for directed behavior. They differ, however, on the causes of this tension. Equity theory is less rigid in the ordering of needs and more cognitive in dealing with the reduction of tension.

In a sense, neither the instrumentality theorists nor the behaviorists feel compelled to deal with motivation as a psychological construct. The behaviorists feel it is unnecessary to deal with it at all, avoiding, where possible, any reference to internal states of the individual and emphasizing the effects of the environment on behavior. If forced to explain the relationships between rewards and activity more extensively, they would probably consider "work motivation" to be a system of needs acquired through past reinforcements.

The instrumentality theorists prefer to consider motivation in a dual sense. Its first role is that of a simple measure of effort expended. Highly motivated people would be distinguished from poorly motivated people by the intensity of directed activity. The second sense in which they would use the concept of motivation is much broader. Their model, by definition, describes motivated behavior. It breaks down the phenomenon of motivated behavior into its functional components, such as perceived probabilities, valued rewards, and equitable reinforcement systems. The goal setting theorists would propose that hard goals lead to greater effort than easy goals if appropriate feedback is provided to the individual. More recent efficacy propositions add the notion that goal setting is a way of providing standards against which one can compare one's self. It is through such a comparison that one can derive feelings of personal satisfaction.

Job Performance

The explanation of why some people are good performers and others are poor performers has provided, and will continue to provide, a major impetus for research on models of work motivation. It should be obvious that performance is not exclusively the result of motivation. Equipment, ability, and opportunity play major roles as well. As a result, no theory of motivation should be able to account completely (or even substantially) for observable performance. Nevertheless, motivation theories should be able to account for some of the variation in industrial performance. As you have seen, some theories are more relevant to performance considerations than others.

Need hierarchy theories are particularly unsuited for making predictions about performance levels. They are too general and vague and must borrow heavily from other models to make such predictions. For instance, what are the performance implications of the fact that a particular individual is functioning at the security or safety level rather than the esteem level?

Equity theory is less vague in performance predictions. The unique shortcoming of equity theory so far has been an inability to specify *which* strategy an individual will use to reduce tension and *how* that strategy will relate to performance. This set of theories provides the temptation (to which some researchers have yielded) to add a new mode of tension reduction to the pool of strategies already available if none of those currently in the pool fit the data. As Goodman and Friedman (1971) suggest, the prediction of performance may be one of the *least* interesting applications of equity theory. Instead, one might concentrate on the possible intermediate states *between* equity perceptions and performance, for example, satisfaction/dissatisfaction. Furthermore, equity theory makes it clear that performance changes represent only *one* potential method for reducing inequity. There are other behaviors that might be chosen instead. For example, one might quit or stay home or change comparison others or devalue inputs. Each of these is an instance of a behavior—even the devaluation of inputs is a behavior. It is simply more difficult to observe than work performance.

The radical behaviorists see performance as a complex "operant." It is a function of behavior-reward contingencies. They tend to ignore relationships between successful performance and self-esteem or efficacy (since self-esteem or efficacy is an intraindividual construct and has no meaning in their theoretical system). They would also disregard the act of goal setting as well as any "sense of accomplishment" resulting from achieving a difficult goal (since goal setting implies cognitive activity, another internal construct). The role of performance in work motivation is probably more sterile and less interesting in this system than in any of the others reviewed. Less radical behaviorists accept the joint effects of things such as contingent rewards, goals, and feedback. They are less inclined to dismiss cognitive activity. Nevertheless, they would hold firm to the notion that contingent reinforcement is critical for high levels of performance.

The instrumentality theorists provide the richest and most explicit description of the role of performance in motivated behavior. Its antecedents are effort expenditure, abilities and traits, and role perceptions. The consequences of performance are both affective and cognitive. They are affective in their effects on satisfaction (through the medium of rewards). They are cognitive in their effects on perceived equitable outcomes and perceived effort-reward probabilities.

Goal setting and efficacy theorists would see high levels of performance as an *eventual* outcome but would be more confident in predicting that future goal setting behavior would be affected by past goal accomplishment. Further, they might suggest that if performance is *directly* affected, it is through changes in efficacy beliefs, not in actual goal levels.

A Conclusion

After examining the research that has attempted to test the various theories of work motivation, I see a recurrent emphasis that is causing some problems. Most research has been directed toward accepting or rejecting a theory in its entirety rather than modifying, refining, or reconceptualizing that theory. In this chapter, I have tried to present not only research aimed at supporting one position or another but also research that suggests modifications. As examples of "modification" research, the Birnbaum (1983) and Mellers (1982) studies suggest important changes in equity theory; Leon (1981) makes some important observations about the differences between positively and negatively valent outcomes in expectancy research; the new breed of cognitive behaviorist (e.g., Komaki et al., 1982) is enthusiastic about including cognitive variables in behaviorist frameworks. It is clear that efficacy propositions have radically transformed goal setting theory. These trends are healthy and necessary if the concept of motivation is to survive.

Another implication of the "modification" research is that any existing theory (e.g., need theory, expectancy theory, goal setting theory) has a mixture of useful and useless propositions. Every theory that I presented is still in the process of evolving. This means that the practitioner should be encouraged to take the reasonable and useful parts and discard the unreasonable or useless ones. There is no law that says that one must apply a theory in exactly the form in which it was originally proposed. By extension, then, I can suggest some principles of motivation in applied settings that are based on the current state of the science.

1. Rewards should be linked to good performance to whatever extent possible. The actual scheme or "schedule" is less important than the perceived contingent relationship.
2. Goals should be set whenever possible. To the extent feasible, the individual may be included in the goal setting process since it is not likely to do any harm and may, in some circumstances, provide certain advantages.
3. Steps should be taken to increase the feelings of personal efficacy that workers have about their work. It is better for them to have a slightly exaggerated view of their skills and abilities rather than a realistic view.
4. Individuals should receive accurate and timely feedback with respect to their level of performance as well as the level expected of them.
5. Negative outcomes test the limits of rationality. Performance may be less predictable when punishment or negative reinforcement is used by managers than when positive rewards are employed as incentives to outstanding performance.
6. Individuals may be more concerned with broad estimates of fairness (i.e., where they fit in a *distribution* of coworkers) than with specific comparisons (i.e., a particular coworker). As a result, if a manager is concerned with developing perceptions of equity, this broader context should be considered.

The common theme for these principles is that people *think* and that how and what they think will affect how they behave. It should come as no surprise to hear that perceptions are more important than reality for human behavior. Regardless of the motivational approach adopted, the manager must be as concerned with the management of perception as with the management of reality.

SOME OTHER ISSUES IN WORK MOTIVATION

Job Enrichment

As was mentioned in the section dealing with Herzberg's two-factor theory, job enrichment is considered to be a useful vehicle for increasing work motivation. An enriched job is one that provides a maximum amount of intrinsic satisfaction. This is not to say that extrinsic factors are ignored. Extrinsic factors are considered to be preconditions for motivated behavior, whereas intrinsic factors are more directly related to motivation. The procedure is one of redesigning the job to provide challenge and a sense of accomplishment to the individual. This is to be distinguished from *job enlargement,* which involves an increase in the variety of tasks the individual performs. Job enlargement does not imply job enrichment.

Job enrichment is generating a lot of interest among managers. There is little doubt that the procedure has proved valuable in many situations. When a particular job is enriched, the quality and quantity of work occasionally improve, satisfaction generally increases, and absences and turnover generally decrease. In short, it seems that motivation increases. The real question is, Why do these changes occur? The two-factor group would contend that enriched jobs satisfy the motivator needs of the individual. They would further contend that enlarged jobs will not necessarily have the same effect. The simple addition of tasks to an individual's organizational role does not necessarily provide challenge.

Porter and Lawler would explain the effect of job enrichment on the basis of the different nature of intrinsic and extrinsic rewards. Their model suggests that intrinsic rewards are more likely to be effective than extrinsic rewards. Since enriched jobs, by definition, provide intrinsic rewards, enriched jobs should have a more direct effect on satisfaction, motivation, and performance than extrinsic reward systems.

Activation theory (Scott, 1966) would propose that stimulus variety or intensity has predictable effects on energy expenditure and performance. Enriched jobs provide exactly that—stimulus variety. Therefore, activation theory would predict that job enrichment will increase activation or arousal level. Activation level would, in turn, affect both job satisfaction and job performance. An interesting implication of this approach is that job enrichment can adversely affect some individuals. A worker who is optimally aroused on this present job would be overstimulated if his job were enriched. In this case, enrichment might actually act as a stressor. Activation theorists would not dismiss job enlargement as easily as the two-factor group. In activation terms, an enlarged job also provides stimulus variety and has the potential for increasing activation level.

The behaviorists would contend that enriched jobs simply bombard the individual with an expanded set of positive rewards. In other words, the opportunity for achieving valued rewards is greatly increased. Since enriched jobs are accompanied by a larger set of potential rewards, the probability of "turning on" or motivating any single individual is increased. In addition, since intrinsic rewards are self-administered, the schedule of reinforcement is continuous.

In the same sense, it is possible to derive an explanation from equity theory. An enriched job greatly increases the outcomes in the input-outcome ratio. This would provide the individual with a greater number of benefits to offset costs (i.e., units of input), thus making inequities (and the resulting tension) less probable. It is interesting to note that some reviews of the job enrichment literature have concluded that enrichment is more likely to affect satisfaction than productivity (see Katzell & Yankelovich, 1975, for example). This would support such an equity interpretation of job enrichment effects.

The goal setting theorists would embrace job enrichment as an opportunity for additional standards (in the form of goals) to be established. This expanded set of standards would enhance the opportunity for self-evaluation and would provide facilitating information in the presence of beliefs of self-efficacy.

A Model for Enrichment. As you can see, enrichment could be considered a motivational technique. The principle is straightforward: Enriched jobs lead to greater energy expenditure than unenriched jobs. Stated this way, enrichment is simply a matter of environmental engineering and is not substantially different from the propositions of the behaviorists that we have examined earlier in the chapter. There is, however, another version of the job enrichment approach that combines both environmental (task) characteristics and individual characteristics. Hackman and Oldham (1975, 1976) have proposed that the actual duties and responsibilities that make up a job have the capacity to motivate certain individuals. They suggest that every job (collection of tasks) occupies a position on a "potential to motivate" scale. Some jobs are very high on the scale (i.e., are very motivating), and some jobs are very low on the scale (i.e., are unlikely to motivate those who hold them). They have developed a method for estimating the potential of a job to motivate its holder. By having incumbents answer a series of questions about the nature of their work, it is possible to calculate a *motivating potential score* (MPS). These questions tap five distinct areas: skill variety, task identity, task significance, autonomy, and feedback. A job that is high on all these characteristics has the potential to be very motivating; a job that is low on these characteristics has little motivating potential. Hackman and Oldham further propose that the difference between *potential* motivation and *actual* motivation lies in a characteristic of the person being considered. They believe that a high MPS job will only motivate those individuals who are also high on *growth need strength* (GNS). GNS scores are similar to a person's position on a need hierarchy similar to the one suggested by Maslow or Alderfer. An individual functioning at the self-actualization level (Maslow) or at the growth level (Alderfer) would be considered high on GNS. In contrast, a person at the security level (Maslow) or at the existence level (Alderfer) would be considered low on GNS.

As you can see, the Hackman-Oldham theory is a "some people" theory, since it only tells us how to motivate high GNS employees. For those people, motivation can be increased by adding to one or more of the five components of the MPS. By extension, the theory says that steps must be taken to get the person up the need hierarchy before job enrichment schemes will have any effect. This seems to be what Herzberg was saying as well: Until hygiene needs are satisfied, motivator needs cannot be met. The Hackman-Oldham theory has received more criticism than support. There are questions about the computation of the MPS score (Arnold & House, 1980; Brief & Aldag, 1975; Dunham, 1976), the conceptual importance of both MPS and GNS (Aldag, Barr, & Brief, 1981), and the effect of task characteristics on psychological states (Wall, Clegg, & Jackson, 1978). Regardless of the support for this *particular* theory, it does represent an example of an attempt to account for the effects of job enrichment on individuals. It also represents an interesting example of the combination of two quite different motivational approaches (behaviorism/environmentalism and need theory). As you have already seen, combinations of motivational theories (e.g., instrumentality and equity theory, goal setting theory and reinforcement theory) seem more promising than single theoretical approaches.

One recent study reintroduces an issue that we considered in the goal setting research—the effect of participation. As we saw earlier, there is some debate about the value of participation in setting goals. Locke et al. (1981) assert that participation has little impact on behavior. Tubbs (1986), on the other hand, found that there did seem to be some positive advantage to participation. Griffeth (1985) looked at the effect of participation in a job enrichment field experiment. The subjects were 76 receptionists in various departments of a university. They were randomly assigned to one of four cells in a 2 by 2 design. Their jobs were either enriched or not enriched, and they either participated or did not participate in designing the enrichment program. In the nonenriched participative cell, subjects were told that their jobs would be redesigned, and they made suggestions about job changes, but they were subsequently informed that the job would not be changed after all. Interestingly enough, participation did not exert any substantial influence on the perceptions of the workers with respect to their jobs; that is, there were no differences between those who participated and those who did not. There were substantial effects related to redesign. Those workers whose jobs were redesigned were considerably more positive than those whose jobs remained unchanged. Thus, we are still left with a puzzle with respect to participation. This result would seem to favor the interpretation of Locke et al. (1981). There is a clear need for continued research in this area.

In practice, most attempts to enrich jobs have also involved changing pay schedules, methods of supervision, planning and decision-making strategies, and work group interaction patterns. For that reason, it might be better to think of job enrichment as a reorganization of the job or task. In Chapter 13, which deals with the concept of organization in the work setting, we will look more specifically at job enrichment programs and the Hackman-Oldham model of enrichment.

Intrinsic versus Extrinsic Factors

A great deal of research effort has been spent on the question of the importance of intrinsic and extrinsic factors in work motivation. Herzberg's two-factor theory proposes that these two classes of factors are distinct. Intrinsic factors (motivators) primarily affect job satisfaction, whereas extrinsic factors (hygiene) affect job dissatisfaction. Maslow's five levels have been collapsed into lower-level and higher-level needs that parallel the intrinsic-extrinsic distinction. Porter and Lawler distinguish between the power of intrinsic and extrinsic rewards. Behaviorists contend that the difference between the effects of intrinsic and extrinsic rewards is primarily a difference in the schedule of rewards, rather than in their unique nature.

It is common for both researchers and managers to think of intrinsic and extrinsic factors as additive. It is assumed that if high levels of pay are combined with interesting work, the result is a greater potential for motivation than if either of these rewards were offered alone. This assumption has been challenged recently (DeCharms & Muir, 1978; Deci 1972, 1976; Lepper & Greene, 1975; Lepper, Greene, & Nisbet, 1973). It has been suggested that when extrinsic rewards are tied to performance, intrinsic motivation suffers. Lepper et al. (1973) conducted an experiment that illustrates the point. Children were given the choice of a number of activities. One of the most popular was drawing with a felt-tip pen. Some children were then reinforced for this activity by receiving a "good player" certificate. Compared with a control group, the children who received the certificate subsequently chose to draw with the felt-tip pen less frequently. It appeared that the extrinsic reward had actually diminished the desire to draw with the pens. Similar studies have been carried out with college students in work and nonwork environments.

There are two different lines of explanation that have been provided (DeCharms & Muir, 1978). One explanation has been suggested by Deci and has been labeled *cognitive evaluation theory*. Dynamically, he proposes that external reinforcement makes people feel there are "external" forces controlling their behavior. On the other hand, intrinsic rewards—rewards individuals provide to themselves—strengthen the feeling of control. Thus, Deci suggests that the combination of extrinsic and intrinsic rewards is *subtractive*, not additive; that using both types of reinforcement together yields a lesser potential for motivation than if either were used alone. The second type of explanation has been called the *overjustification* (Lepper & Greene, 1975) theory and is similar in some respects to the balance or dissonance theory that you encountered earlier in the chapter. The overjustification hypothesis proposes that people evaluate their own actions and attempt to justify them. Individuals who engage in activities with no extrinsic reward present perceive themselves as intrinsically motivated. When a concrete reward is attached to an activity that has already been "justified" (i.e., I do it because it is interesting), then the activity becomes overjustified. When overjustification occurs, there is a need to bring the cognitive system back into balance, and this is accomplished by reducing the intrinsic motivation to do the task. When the reward is removed, the activity is then underjustified and is stopped or at least engaged in less frequently.

Just as Herzberg's work on satisfaction (Herzberg, Mausner, Peterson, & Capwell, 1957; Herzberg, Mausner, & Snyderman, 1959) was a radical departure from the orthodox thinking of the time, so were the cognitive evaluation theory and the overjustification hypotheses. Predictably, many people were upset with this formulation, since it challenged some long-standing assumptions. This was particularly true of the reinforcement theorists. This struck at the heart of behaviorism for two reasons. First, it purported to identify circumstances in which reinforcement diminished rather than increased activity. In addition, it suggested that people's thoughts controlled their behavior. Since radical behaviorists deny the importance of mental activities in accounting for behavior, the proposed explanations for the phenomenon were as offensive as the phenomenon itself.

A good deal of research has been generated on the topic since it was introduced. A good review has been provided by DeCharms and Muir (1978). Criticism takes two forms. One form is conceptual. As examples, W. E. Scott (1976) points out the confusion surrounding the term *intrinsic.* Is this something that belongs to the task in question, or is it primarily a perception of an individual independent of the task? Dyer and Parker (1975) provide additional evidence suggesting some fuzzy concepts in the intrinsic-extrinsic discussion. They found that industrial psychologists could not agree on the definitions of "intrinsic" and "extrinsic" rewards. Furthermore, they could not agree as to which of a series of possible rewards were intrinsic and which extrinsic. As a result, they questioned the meaning of Deci's propositions, since it seemed impossible to distinguish the two types of rewards conceptually.

The second form of attack has been empirical. Several studies have failed to replicate the basic findings of people like Deci (1972) and Lepper and Greene (1975) (Arnold, 1976; Farr, 1976; Hamner & Foster, 1975; Salancik, 1975; Scott & Erskine, 1980). One study even went so far as to reanalyze Deci's original data and show that there never *was* any such relationship between extrinsic and intrinsic motivation (Farr, Vance, & McIntyre, 1977). The results of this follow-up research have been useful. There is now a greater willingness to accept the idea that the relationship among various rewards is not a simple additive one (Pritchard, Campbell, & Campbell, 1977). There do seem to be instances where adding an extrinsic reward to an already interesting task may diminish interest (Mossholder, 1980). It is also becoming clear that the situation is more complicated than originally suggested. As an example, Mossholder (1980) has demonstrated that setting specific hard goals can reduce intrinsic motivation for an interesting task. In contrast, the same specific hard goals will *increase* intrinsic motivation for a dull and tedious task. This extended the results of an earlier study by Calder and Staw (1975) that examined the effects of extrinsic rewards on intrinsic motivation. In the Calder and Staw study, extrinsic rewards were found to increase intrinsic motivation on boring tasks.

It seems that there is a good deal more here than meets the eye. The effects of extrinsic rewards can be shown to interact in complicated ways on interesting tasks. Whether something called "intrinsic motivation" actually exists, and if it does, whether it is a property of a person or a task, has not been decided. *Why* the effects are found is also an open question. Possible answers include multiple schedules of reinforcement (Scott, 1976), cognitive evaluation (Deci, 1975), and overjustification (Lepper & Greene, 1975). It has even been suggested that the extrinsic reward elicits responses that get in the way of the original activity. This has been labeled the *competing response hypothesis* (Reiss & Sushinsky, 1976). At this point, there are no clear answers, but after reading the research reports, one is reminded of the central role that cognition plays in behavior. The only safe conclusion that can be drawn at this point is that rewards interact in a complex manner with task characteristics. More is not always better.

CONCLUDING COMMENTS

We have covered a lot of ground in this chapter. An attempt has been made to present, as clearly as possible, alternative explanations for motivated behavior in the work setting. A basic understanding of the various approaches is a prerequisite for interpreting research results. Motivational programs such as job enrichment will continue to emerge. If such programs are to be of maximum utility, they must be tied to some theoretical framework.

The sophistication and potential value of research in the area of work motivation have grown tremendously in the past decade. There is every reason to believe that the value will continue to increase.

Technical Appendix

In experimental design terminology, two different types of VIE studies have been conducted. The first is called a *between-subjects design,* and the second is termed a *within-subjects design.* In a between-subjects VIE study, subjects would be asked to rate the attractiveness of an outcome on a scale from 1 to 5. In using valences to predict effort or performance, this rating would be taken at face value and would not be considered relative to any other rating that the subject provided for any other outcome. Consider the following valence ratings of outcomes as gathered from hypothetical subjects

A, B, and C. High ratings will represent desired outcomes, and low ratings will represent unattractive outcomes.

	Outcomes		
Subjects	*I*	*II*	*III*
A	5	4	3
B	4	3	2
C	3	2	1

If we consider columns one at a time, we can contrast the ratings that the subjects have given to any particular alternative. Thus, for outcome I, it would appear that subject C finds that outcome a good deal less desirable than does subject A. This would be a between-subjects comparison. In contrast, let's consider the relative desirability of the outcomes *within* a single subject. We would do this by looking at the *rows* of the matrix rather than the columns. When we look at the data from this perspective, each subject has chosen the same outcome as most attractive compared with the other outcomes in the set. This would be a within-subjects analysis.

As originally stated by Vroom, VIE theory only makes sense in terms of a within-subjects analysis. Effort and performance should be determined by how much an individual values one outcome compared with another, not by how much greater one individual values that outcome than another individual. The VIE approach predicts that individuals will be guided by the outcome that is most preferred in a set of outcomes. Comparisons of within- and between-subjects analysis confirm that a within-subjects analysis provides greater support for VIE theory than a between-subjects analysis (Matsui, Kagawa, Nagamatsu, & Ohtsuka, 1977; Parker & Dyer, 1976). Effort is predicted more accurately when an individual's actions are considered in light of his ordering rather than when those actions are viewed in light of his preference for an outcome compared with another individual's preference for that outcome.

CENTRAL POINTS FOR STUDY

1. There are five broad classes of motivation theory: need, instrumentality, balance, reinforcement, and goal setting.
2. Theories of motivation have both process and content components.
3. Need theories have not received much empirical or logical support.
4. Instrumentality theory is a cognitive approach to motivation based on the principle that individuals are rational and attempt to maximize gain.
5. Instrumentality theory can be fruitfully combined with goal setting theory to yield an explanation of motivated behavior.

6. Hard goals seem to have a motivating effect on individuals.
7. Equity theory is a cognitive approach to motivation based on the principle of reducing psychological tension produced by imbalance.
8. Reinforcement approaches to motivation represent a technology rather than a theory.
9. Personal efficacy affects motivation.
10. Motivation theories should be combined rather than contrasted.
11. Intrinsic and extrinsic motivation seem to represent substantially different systems.

CHAPTER 11

Job Satisfaction: The Meaning of Work

"My job was stacking the Ping-Pong paddles into piles of fifty. Actually, I didn't have to count all the way up to fifty. To make it a little easier, they told me to stack 'em in circles of four with the first handle facing me. When there got to be thirteen handles on the second one from the front, then I'd know I had fifty. After a while of stacking, I didn't have to count anyway. I could tell fifty by just looking at the pile.

"Maybe it wouldn't have been so bad if I could have seen all the piles I stacked at the end of the day. But they were taking them down as fast as I was piling them up. That was the worst part of the job.

"No," she corrected herself, "that wasn't the worst part. The worst part was that you had to stand up all day doing it.

"You couldn't talk either. You wouldn't want to anyway because it was too noisy and the way we were all spaced apart, you'd have to lean over and shout. But if you ever tried to talk, Alma would come running over with a whole lot more paddles. Or she'd yell, 'Why aren't you finished yet?' So you were alone with your head all day." (Garson, 1975, pp. 1–2)

* * *

"The job wasn't really that great. I washed big pans that were used to cook the short ribs. They were about five feet long and two feet wide. They were covered with grease and I would push this cart along the line and collect all the dirty pans and then bring them over to the washer. I would stack them on these racks and then wheel the racks into this big washer. Then I would start the pulley and open the wash valve and wait for them to come out the other end. This might take a minute, maybe two. I don't really remember. When they came out, I would wheel them back to the other end of the line, unload them, and pick up some more dirty pans.

"I used to joke at lunch. I'd say, 'If anybody hears that layoffs are comin', do me a favor. Send in my name.' Then a funny thing happened. I got laid off. I couldn't believe it. First, I thought it was one of the guys pulling a joke. But then I heard other people got notices, too, and I knew it wasn't a joke. I felt like a kid who wet his pants. I was afraid to go home and tell my wife. The rest of the day, nobody talked to me. They looked at me like I had cancer. I tried to smile, but I wanted to puke. The end of the day, I didn't want to leave. I even thought about just working through the next shift. It was crazy, like I thought if I didn't leave the pan washer, they couldn't lay me off. But the afternoon shift guy came and I had to leave."

Above, you see excerpts from two interviews. The first interview gives a glimpse of a tedious job—a woman who stacks Ping-Pong paddles. There is no redeeming feature to the job. You have the feeling that the job is punishment—that she would like to take a walk out the door and not come back. The second interview describes the reaction of a man who was asked to do just that—leave his job as a pan washer and not come back. He was devastated by the experience. Both had difficult, tedious, and dehumanizing work, yet one couldn't wait to leave and the other couldn't stand the thought of leaving. George Bernard Shaw noted some time ago that the two tragedies of life were not getting your heart's desire and getting your heart's desire. If we examine the reaction of people to work, we see many of these contradictions. It is a love-hate relationship. What makes me happy today makes me angry tomorrow. What excites you, bores me.

We have just finished an examination of the circumstances of motivated behavior. This examination implied that there were aspects of the work environment that could be changed to yield higher motivation or greater energy expenditure. This, in turn, suggests that stimuli have general and predictable effects on individuals. In many of the theories that we considered, emotional responses played a major role. In need theory, we saw the impact of need *satisfaction* on behavior. In equity theory, it was proposed that *dissatisfaction* resulted from the discrepancy between expectations and reality. In instrumentality theory, it was suggested that *satisfaction* increased the value of a future reward and that *dissatisfaction* reduced that value. In self-efficacy theory, it was noted that individuals derive *satisfaction* from a favorable comparison of their behavior with some standard (goal) that they have set for themselves and that they are *dissatisfied* when they compare themselves unfavorably to that standard. In each instance, satisfaction represented a hedonic variable—a point on a pleasant-unpleasant continuum that had implications for action. This catches the flavor of much of the research and theory that addresses job satisfaction. Researchers have attempted to discover one of two things: (1) What are the antecedents or causes of various levels of satisfaction or dissatisfaction? and (2) What are the consequences of these emotional states? Managers have been more interested in the latter, particularly with respect to phenomena such as productivity, absence, and turnover.

SATISFACTION AND MENTAL HEALTH

Recently, Warr (1987) has provided quite a strong case for the importance of studying job satisfaction for its own sake rather than because of a concern for productivity, turnover, or absence. This is an uncommon motive for the "modern" applied psychologist. The modern I/O psychologist expresses an interest to the manager to affect the "bottom line" somehow. It is interesting to note that one of the pioneers of our field, Arthur Kornhauser, expressed a similar concern in 1932, a challenge to study satisfaction in its own right. The challenge was widely ignored then and is widely ignored now. This is a mistake. We still need to know a great deal about the phenomenon of job satisfaction, and until we know more about it, there is not much hope of using it to predict, understand, or control other behaviors.

In keeping with the two examples that opened this chapter, Warr notes that work is anomalous—the very same job can be responsible for curing depression in one person and causing depression in another. I remember a discussion I had with a middle-level manager one day. He expressed anguish and frustration about his job. I asked him what the problem seemed to be. He said that he had to control the behavior of a dozen people, predict an unpredictable market demand, cope with mechanical systems that failed without warning, and motivate people who seemed immune to any motivational interventions. I asked what he liked about his job. He grinned sheepishly and said that he liked the thought of being responsible for a dozen people, enjoyed the uncertainty of the consumer demand, enjoyed fixing broken systems, and felt that there was no one who he couldn't motivate somehow. In a comic strip called "POGO" that was common years ago, the main character said, "We have met the enemy and we are them!" My manager friend realized the inherent contradictions implied in his comments, but he was reporting his feelings realistically. He felt that it was my job to disentangle those feelings and help him work out an effective system to cope with them.

Warr feels that there is more than enough evidence to conclude that work and the satisfaction with that work are centrally involved in determining the adjustment of adults in virtually every culture. He is convinced that there is a fundamental association between work and mental health. I agree. He lists nine different sources of evidence for this conclusion. These sources of evidence are as follows:

1. Studies of the effect of unemployment clearly demonstrate the devastating effect of the loss of a job.
2. Studies of the effects of job satisfaction on job holders show the emotional consequences of different jobs and work environments on those individuals.
3. Qualitative studies of particular occupations illustrate differential occupational effects, for example, studies of suicide rates among physicians, rates of alcoholism among police officers, burnout in social workers.
4. Quantitative studies of job satisfaction illustrate differing levels of satisfaction associated with various occupations.
5. Certain job features can be shown to affect mental and physical well-being; for example, short-cycle jobs and jobs with little opportunity for control seem to lead to stress reactions in work.

TABLE 11–1 Recent Instances of Assault at Workplace

Date	*Headline*
January 1987	Fired worker returns to office with rifle and takes six coworkers hostage
February 1987	Worker critically injures fellow worker by assaulting him with a shovel
August 1987	Postal worker kills 14 coworkers and commits suicide
October 1987	Naval recruit shoots three instructors after flunking a training course
December 1987	Former airline employee kills boss in flight, causing crash which kills 43
February 1988	Silicon Valley worker shoots eight coworkers at company offices
March 1988	Two guards shot by fellow worker at naval supply yard
April 1988	Broker trainee kills manager after being fired

6. Workers who change jobs often experience a reduction in various somatic symptoms characteristic of emotional turmoil.
7. Clinicians who treat individuals for various adjustment disorders note the frequency with which work-related issues seem to play a role in the etiology of the disorder.
8. It has been demonstrated that the simple *fact* of employment can be an effective intervention in treating the mentally ill.
9. Research on the relationship between work satisfaction and life satisfaction shows clear associations between work-related tension and low-quality family life.

This list provides eloquent testimony to the relationship between work and emotional well-being. There is additional evidence of a more dramatic variety that seems to demonstrate the most extreme instances of this relationship. Instances of violence at the workplace seem to be increasing. Consider the list of recent incidents that appears in Table 11–1. One need not conclude from this list that work *causes* psychopathology. It is sufficient to note that individuals often choose the workplace as the stage for acting out destructive impulses. They do not choose the neighborhood park, the bowling alley, the public library. They choose the workplace. There are hundreds of less dramatic events such as punches, pushes, and threats that are not reported in *The New York Times* but, nevertheless, suggest that the workplace is a central and defining environment for emotional well-being. In a recent study, Barling and Rosenbaum (1986) show that there is the possibility of work affecting nonwork violence as well. They discovered that stressful work events experienced by husbands were associated with wife abuse in the home. Certainly, this should not be interpreted as if the job were *causing* wife abuse (thus freeing the husband from any personal responsibility for his actions). If that were the case, one would expect wives experiencing work-related stress to abuse husbands physically as well, and there is little evidence of this pattern. Further, as the authors themselves suggest, this may be a matter of husbands simply rationalizing their abusive behavior patterns. Nevertheless, the statistical association exists and supports the notion that emotions at work are tied to emotions in other settings.

In this chapter, much of what we consider will be a good deal less dramatic than the studies that Warr reviews or the incidents in Table 11–1. Traditional research on job satisfaction has a tendency to produce narrow thinking. The research deals with measurement issues, or the relationship of satisfaction to performance or the extent to which satisfaction is similar to organizational climate. Keep in mind that there is a broader question that is equally deserving of our attention: What is the *meaning* of work to individuals? This broader question may be more important in the long run since it leads us more easily into discussions of unemployment, education and training, retirement, life satisfaction, mental health, and social systems. In this chapter, we will deal with both types of questions. First, we will take a traditional trip through job satisfaction research. This will include theory, measurement, and application. Then we will consider some of the broader issues implied by the preceding discussion, issues such as the contribution of job satisfaction to the quality of life and the consequences of unemployment on individual well-being. I will begin with a brief review of the history of the area.

A SHORT HISTORY OF SATISFACTION RESEARCH

As a formal area for research, job satisfaction did not really exist until the mid-1930s. Recently, I had a discussion with Morris Viteles, the father of modern industrial psychology. He wrote one of the first modern textbooks in the area in 1932, one recognized as the building block for today's theory and research in I/O psychology. I noted that *job satisfaction* did not appear in the index of that book, and I asked him why. His response was simple—there was not enough research in the area to warrant a separate treatment. In fact, empirical research in this area did not develop a decent head of steam until the late 1930s and early 1940s. After a late start, however, researchers more than made up for this dearth of early research. Well over 3,000 studies on job satisfaction were *published* by 1972 (Locke, 1976). This is a small percentage of the studies actually *conducted,* since many were never published. Further, there seems to have been no slackening in the rate of satisfaction research between 1976 and today.

Although there was little empirical research prior to the 1930s, there was a good deal of qualitative research and theorizing about the concept of job satisfaction. For example, Freud (1922) and Janet (1907) both felt that unconscious impulses were implicated in emotions displayed at the workplace. Freud felt that esprit de corps or morale acted to suppress negative tendencies toward narcissistic behavior, encouraging instead personal sacrifice and commitment to group goals. Janet was convinced that factory work required too little thought on the part of workers and, as a result, permitted them to dwell on negative thoughts, thus producing various forms of psychopathology such as paranoia, neurotic behavior patterns, and other forms of obsessive thinking. He termed this condition "obsession reverie," and it was later to play a major role in the theories and interventions of Elton Mayo, a leading architect of programmatic research in work attitudes. Theories of job satisfaction were also suggested by William James (1890), Hugo Munsterberg (1913), E. L. Thorndike (1922), Whiting Williams (1925), and Henri De Man (1929). Thus, it appears that satisfaction had been of interest to basic and applied psychologists for some time before extensive empirical research began.

Measurement Issues

The quantitative research period was triggered by a methodological breakthrough—the appearance of the job satisfaction questionnaire or attitude survey. The attitude is so commonplace today that it is hard to believe that there was a period when it was not used in industry. In fact, the survey as we know it was not used prior to 1927. Instead, work attitudes were measured through interviews with managers about the happiness of workers, observations of psychologists masquerading as workers (e.g., W. Williams, 1925), or extensive open-ended questionnaires. J. D. Houser (1927) was one of the first to suggest that a standard set of questions could be used and that the responses to those questions could be categorized in terms of positive and negative emotions. Further, he suggested that it might be better to have these structured interviews with workers rather than managers. But this was not the insight that it might appear to be. His suggestion about talking with workers was motivated by a concern for determining whether managers were doing their jobs or telling the truth, rather than a concern for the well-being of the workers. A worker would be interviewed and responses to standard questions would be given a rating by the interviewer on a scale from 1 to 5, with a 1 being given to responses that seemed to be most positive and a 5 representing a "hostile" response.

Even though the method suggested by Houser was a clear improvement from a standardization perspective, it was administratively inefficient since it still required one-on-one interviews. Houser began to develop a technology for mass paper-and-pencil administration, but by then another development had occurred that overshadowed the efforts of Houser. The attitude scale was developed by L. L. Thurstone (1938) and was widely applied as a method for determining attitudes toward all sorts of psychological objects, including religion, political events and political figures, and work. The Thurstone scale consisted of hundreds of statements of positive, neutral, and negative aspects of a particular psychological object. These statements had been previously scaled by judges in terms of their favorability toward the object in question.

Thus, a person's attitude was inferred from the types of statements that he endorsed as representing his feelings about the object in question. One of the most extensive developmental efforts in applying Thurstone's technique to work attitudes was carried out by Uhrbrock (1948).

There were some problems with Thurstone scaling, however, when applied to the measurement of work attitudes. First, the method required the development, scaling, and response to hundreds of individual statements. Managers then were like managers now—they were reluctant to spend the time necessary to ensure a scale of high psychometric integrity, required to use this technique. In addition, negative statements (i.e., statements that described unfavorable reactions to the work) made the managers uncomfortable. Fortunately, in 1932, Rensis Likert introduced an attitude measurement technique that solved both those problems. His technique (a technique that has come to be known as *Likert scaling*) required respondents to use a five-choice standardized response format (strongly agree to strongly disagree) to register their attitudes toward a series of positive statements about the job. This solved both problems simultaneously. First, the number of statements could be radically reduced. Additionally, negative attitudes could be inferred from the use of the "strongly disagree" response to positive statements; thus, no negative statements were necessary. Likert demonstrated that there was good agreement between the results of his method and the results of Thurstone's method, and the Likert technique became widely used. After the introduction of standardized questionnaires and the Likert format, attitude surveys in industry became almost universal, and comparisons among occupations, divisions of a company, male and female workers, blue-collar and white-collar workers, and so on, began to appear in the scientific literature with some regularity. In the popular press, the *Fortune* magazine attitude survey of a national sample of workers became a regular feature in the 1940s and was widely referred to in the newspapers at the time.

THEORETICAL ISSUES

The Hawthorne Studies

As we will see in more detail in the chapter on organizational theory, the approach to understanding work behavior that pervaded the early part of this century was classic organization theory, generally, and scientific management theory, specifically. Frederick W. Taylor proposed scientific management theory in the late nineteenth century as a way of making the conduct of work-related activities more efficient. Scientific management was also known as "Taylorism." The major motivational assumption of the approach was that individual workers valued economic incentives and would be willing to work hard for monetary rewards. It is important to note the rigidity of this assumption. It was assumed that *all* workers valued money more than any other reward. If this were true, it certainly would make the lives of managers easier and the behavior of workers more predictable.

The published psychological literature provides ample evidence that this assumption was accepted in the application of behavior principles to work settings. As a matter of fact, one of the pioneers in industrial psychology, Hugo Munsterberg (1914), in a book on general psychology, describes industrial psychology as "economic psychology." Munsterberg was an ardent and vocal supporter of scientific management principles. Most of the published research on work behavior was conducted by considering the influences of physical working conditions—things such as heating and lighting—on productivity and absence. Psychologists, economists, and industrial engineers were collaborating in an attempt to identify *the one most efficient system for the production of goods and services,* the one production method suitable for *all* workers in a particular job. The worker was considered a potential error in that system and was treated accordingly. As a matter of fact, most training programs of the time were directed at reducing or eliminating completely individual differences in behavior. Scientific management had another important goal, however. It was used widely as a method for undermining the trade union movement. Unions vigorously resisted the principles of scientific management. There were congressional hearings to deal with this conflict. In particular, scientific management was intended to eliminate the restriction of output by workers (what was known as "soldiering"). Managers were convinced that this restriction was orchestrated by the labor unions to ensure continued work for union members and to drive up wages. Scientific management systems involved individual contracts between supervisors and workers that eliminated any role for the union in determining wages. Instead, productive workers were paid at a high rate and unproductive workers at a low rate.

There were many psychological researchers and theorists both in the United States and in other countries who were appalled by the implications of scientific management for work motivation and satisfaction. In fact, Viteles (1932) asserts that he decided to study industrial psychology to protect workers from the excesses of the industrial engineers such as Taylor, Gilbreth, and Emerson. Viteles and many of his colleagues felt that the industrial engineer was prone to treating people as machines. The psychologists were convinced that work would lose all its meaning as it became routinized and standardized. Advocates of scientific management claimed that work would become more interesting since it required closer attention of the worker (e.g., Gilbreth & Gilbreth, 1917). One of the first substantial research efforts that made a break with this restricted view of the worker was conducted at the Hawthorne plant of the Western Electric company in Cicero, Illinois. These studies, which spanned a period of over 12 years, have come to be known as the "Hawthorne studies" and deserve some attention for several reasons.

1. The authors concluded with the radical suggestion that workers have feelings that affect their work behavior.

2. Their approach of field experimentation demonstrated both the strengths and the weaknesses of that particular research design.
3. They suggested that the way in which workers *perceive* objective reality may be more important in understanding behavior than the *facts* of objective reality.

In a sense, these studies represent the beginning of the study of the social aspects of industrial and organizational psychology. These studies will be briefly described, but there are some excellent sources for examining them in their entirety (Roethlisberger & Dickson, 1939).

The studies began with a harmless research question: What is the effect of illumination on productivity? Three departments were involved. Initial performance data were gathered as base-rate information for the evaluation of any changes in performance due to illumination changes. Subsequently, illumination was systematically varied, but the performance data showed no clear effect. The experimenters, suspecting that they had not exercised appropriate experimental control, redesigned the experiment with subjects chosen for experience and base-rate production. Experimental and control groups were matched on these two dimensions and physically separated from each other. Lighting was systematically varied for the experimental subjects, whereas the matched control group worked under constant illumination conditions. This time *both* the experimental *and* control groups increased production to the same degree. This result made it impossible to conclude that performance increases were due to illumination, since the illumination did not change in the control group.

In another series of studies in which experimental control was tightened even more, the experimental group maintained their initial level of performance in spite of the fact that illumination had been reduced by 70 percent. The crowning blow to the simple illumination-productivity hypothesis came when the experimenters only *pretended* to change the illumination level by replacing light bulbs with other light bulbs *of the same intensity*. The workers expressed pleasure with the "increased illumination" and continued to increase their production.

This last result—the fact that a constant level of illumination was perceived as changing—was the first hint that the perception of events may have been as important as the events themselves. Nevertheless, the experimenters chose to refine their experimental procedures and controls even more. In addition, they began to focus on possible confounding variables such as fatigue. The experimental manipulations now included the introduction of work breaks, the shortening of the workday, and the shortening of the workweek. A series of experimental periods were run to determine the effect of these variables on productivity. Table 11–2 gives a description of each of the manipulations. As expected, the introduction of work breaks and shortened work periods had a positive effect on performance. However, something unexpected was found. As the work breaks were removed and the workday and -week were lengthened to their original status, production continued to in-

TABLE 11–2 Hawthorne Studies—Changes in Work Schedules and the Effect of These Changes on Productivity

Period	*Length in Weeks*	*Experimental Conditions of Work*	*Percent of Standard Output*
1	2	Standard	100
2	5	Standard	101
3	8	Standard	105
4	5	Two 5 min. rests	109
5	4	Two 10 min. rests	112
6	4	Six 5 min. rests	113
7	11	15 min. A.M. rest and lunch; 10 min. P.M. rest	116
8	7	Same as 7, but 4:30 stop	123
9	4	Same as 7, but 4:00 stop	125
10	12	Same as 7	124
11	9	Same as 7, but Sat. A.M. off	123
12	12	Standard	122
13	31	Same as 7	131

SOURCE: Adapted from *Management and the Worker* (p. 57) by F. J. Roethlisberger and W. J. Dickson, 1939, Cambridge, MA: Harvard University Press.

crease, as can be seen in the right-hand column of Table 11–2. On the basis of diaries kept by the workers during these studies, it became increasingly obvious that attitudes toward supervision and coworkers were having an effect on the results.

The possibility of the feelings and attitudes of the workers affecting production rate put an entirely new slant on the efforts of the Hawthorne researchers. An interviewing program was introduced to assess the nature of the relationship between methods of supervision and worker attitudes. As a result of these interviews, it became apparent that the effect of wages, working conditions, and other job-related stimuli could not be *legislated* by management. The meaning of these factors was determined by the individual's personal history and work environment.

Later studies showed that group production rates were affected by the guidelines of the informal work group as well as the goals of the organization and the behavior of the immediate supervisor. On the basis of interviews, a counseling program was begun to improve communication in the organization. After the studies and counseling program were completed, the general feeling was that interpersonal relations within the company had improved. This was an incredible leap from the simple illumination-productivity hypothesis that had launched the studies.

The Hawthorne studies do not, by any means, represent the ultimate in field experimentation. They had many problems. Landsberger, in a book titled

Hawthorne Revisited (1958), points out that two of the most important economic influences of the period were ignored—the depression and the rise of trade unionism. These two factors must have affected the responses of the workers. Nevertheless, the Hawthorne studies do represent a breakthrough in understanding both the nature of work behavior and the process of field experimentation.

A major figure in these studies was Elton Mayo. Mayo was an Australian who had come to the United States in the mid-1920s on a research sabbatical and stayed here for the rest of his career. He was a frustrated physician (Landy, 1988a; Trahair, 1984) who continually looked for physical explanations for anomalies in work behavior. He began his career in the United States by studying the work patterns of textile workers in Philadelphia (Trahair, 1984). He suggested that the drop in productivity that could be noted during the working day was the result of an imbalance of the pulse rate in the upper and lower body extremities (later developing an index or ratio of this difference called the "pulse index"). He prescribed a treatment of rest pauses to cure this problem and actually brought cots onto the work floor for workers to recline on during the workday. Mayo was also an ardent opponent of both trade unionism and scientific management. He opposed trade unionism on philosophical grounds and scientific management on theoretical grounds. He had been heavily influenced by the early writings of the French psychiatrist Janet and believed firmly that scientific management (like the factory system of assembly-line work) produced "reverie obsession" and was responsible for most of the adjustment problems and unhappiness displayed by industrial workers. Further, he came to believe that union activity was a *symptom* of reverie obsession and that if scientific management could be eliminated, then unions would probably disappear as well. Mayo introduced the notion of human relations as a substitute for scientific management. It was a clever intervention because it eliminated the regimentation of work behavior but at the same time retained the notion of individual relations between workers and supervisors. It was the supervisor's responsibility to develop an individual and personal relationship with each worker, to discover what the worker desired and what were the sources of happiness and unhappiness. It is important to note that Mayo was not advocating workplace democracy. On the contrary, the supervisor was still a key figure in the work group. Once again, the value of any collective negotiation between workers and management (e.g., through the medium of labor unions) was diminished. There is no way of really determining what Mayo was trying to accomplish with the Hawthorne studies and their popularization, but it is clear that the research was not value-free, as many would prefer to believe (Walter-Busch, 1986). Mayo most certainly had a political and social agenda in mind.

Regardless of Mayo's motivation, as a function of the Hawthorne studies, interests were shifted from lighting to interpersonal communications, from work rate curves and boredom to work motivation, from company policy to the perception of this policy by the workers, from variables in the physical

The Early Years of I/O: "Dr." Mayo

Frank J. Landy
Penn State University

George Elton Mayo (1880–1949) came from a family of physicians. His grandfather and father were classically trained physicians in South Australia. Mayo had every intention of following their footsteps and enrolled in medical school to seek his degree. He failed his second year examinations and returned home in disgrace. In the following years, he made several other attempts to pursue a medical degree, but each failed.

Having made little progress in medicine, Mayo decided to pursue a degree in philosophy and was awarded a bachelor's degree in 1911. In the years following his graduation he became a lecturer in psychology and was particularly interested in clinical applications. Prior to coming to the United States, he began examining the issue of fatigue and its role in psychopathology at work.

When he arrived at the Wharton School of the University of Pennsylvania in 1924 for a temporary position, he immediately began applying his notions of fatigue to industrial work in Philadelphia and conducted several projects in which rest pauses were shown to affect productivity, health, and feelings of depression. In these studies, he had cots brought onto the factory floor for workers to use when taking their rest pauses. In addition, he often took various physiological measures such as heart rate and blood pressure and occasionally collected blood samples for analysis.

Throughout his life, he was sensitive to his failure in medical school and was not reluctant to permit, and on occasion encourage, misconceptions about his "credentials." While still in Australia, he claimed that he was denied his M.A. by the University of Adelaide because of "red tape." This did not stop him from fostering the notion later in his career in America that he was a "doctor"—though whether this was meant to suggest an M.D. or Ph.D. was left attractively ambiguous.

This attraction to medicine pervaded a good deal of Mayo's professional work. He identified more closely with clinical psychology than other subareas. He was a firm believer in Janet's notions of the unconscious, and in particular, he felt that obsessive reveries were caused by factory work. Janet proposed a close link between reverie obsession and psychopathology. Mayo believed that the rest pauses that he introduced reduced such obsessive thought and thus reduced psychopathology. In one case that he described, he suggested that the rest pauses cured a worker of alcoholism and several other self-destructive behavior patterns.

At one point, several of the participants in the Hawthorne experiments showed a disaffection with their work and productivity dropped sharply. The managers were concerned that perhaps the human relations propositions of Mayo and his collaborators had been wrong. Mayo went to talk with one of the workers and concluded that she was suffering from anemia and "prescribed" a change in diet and some rest. This seemed to solve the problem, and her work returned to the previous level.

The Early Years of I/O: "Dr." Mayo *(concluded)*

At Harvard, Mayo expected people to address him as "doctor" and his secretary wore the uniform of a nurse. He was acutely aware of any criticism directed toward his work by the medical community. He never was able to shake the feeling of failure developed from his unsuccessful medical school studies nor to avoid the seemingly compensating behavior patterns that smacked of the medical profession.

SOURCE: From "The Early Years of I/O" by F. Landy, *The Industrial-Organizational Psychologist*, 1988, *25*, (3), pp. 53-54.

environment to variables in the social environment of the employee, and from rigid assumptions about the nature of workers to a consideration of individual differences. From a methodological and analytic perspective, the results were attacked almost immediately by leaders in the field of industrial psychology (e.g., Kornhauser, 1931; Viteles, 1930). There were so many uncontrolled variables that it was impossible to draw any firm conclusions from the results. The view of many of the contemporaries of Mayo was that he was an eloquent spokesperson for a point of view, a man with a genuine concern for the well-being of workers but also a man with little or no appreciation for the importance of rigorous experimental designs. Mayo remained an enigmatic and solitary figure until his death in 1949. In spite of the fact that he had never received a doctorate, he preferred to be called Dr. Mayo and was prone to be assisted by a nurse in uniform rather than a secretary when he did his research (Landy, 1988a).

The Hoppock Study

In the early 1930s, Robert Hoppock was a graduate student and was encouraged by his adviser to apply the new scaling techniques of Thurstone to job satisfaction. As a result, for his doctoral dissertation he studied the job satisfaction of workers in the community of New Hope, Pennsylvania. The study was interesting for several reasons. One of these reasons was that he analyzed interviews of almost all the working adults in New Hope. This was quite a substantial undertaking. Interestingly enough, this came about as a result of the availability of a research assistant. His father-in-law had recently retired and had time on his hands. He agreed to go to all the houses in town and ask questions that his son-in-law had formulated (Hoppock, 1935). Hoppock's analysis addressed two basic questions: On an absolute level, are workers in New Hope happy? On a relative level, are workers in some occupations happier than others? The answer to the first question seemed to be yes. Only 12 percent of the workers surveyed could be classified as dis-

TABLE 11–3 Job Satisfaction of Various Occupational Levels—Hoppock Study

Occupational Classification	*Number of Cases*	*Range of Indexes*	*Mean Index*
1 Unskilled manual	55	100–650	401
2 Semiskilled	74	125–650	483
3 Skilled manual and white-collar	84	125–675	510
4 Subprofessional, business, and minor supervisory	32	250–700	548
5 Professional, managerial, and executive	23	300–700	560

SOURCE: From *Job Satisfaction* (p. 255) by R. Hoppock, 1935 New York: Harper.

satisfied. The basic finding has been replicated time and time again. Workers *reporting* dissatisfaction are usually in the minority.

The answer to the second question can be found in Table 11–3. Again the answer was yes: different levels of satisfaction are related to different occupational levels, with the highest occupational level being accompanied by the highest satisfaction. This is another finding that has been replicated numerous times. We will deal specifically with the relationship between occupational level and satisfaction in a later section.

The data bearing on the effect of occupational level make the data relating to the absolute levels of satisfaction somewhat arbitrary. It is clear that not all occupational levels are equally satisfied. There were more unskilled manual workers who reported dissatisfaction than professionals. The 12-percent figure is an average number across all occupational categories.

A final interesting point from these data can be seen in Table 11–3 under the column heading "Range of Indexes." A person responding to Hoppock's questionnaire could have received a score ranging from 100 (extreme dissatisfaction) to 700 (extreme satisfaction). The range of values reported for each of the occupational groups shows the wide variation of satisfaction even *within* occupations. Attempts at understanding this variation have not been overwhelmingly successful. One possible conclusion that might be drawn from this within-job variation is similar to one of the conclusions of the Hawthorne researchers: perceptions may be more important than objective reality. As we will see later in the chapter, there is some reason to believe that people bring a frame of reference to the work setting. This frame of reference influences how and what they see. One of my colleagues once described this circumstance succinctly by saying, "I'll see it when I believe it!" This emphasis on perception can be seen clearly in the work of Robert Schaffer.

Schaffer's Theory

Hoppock's initial approach to the phenomenon of job satisfaction suggested that certain variables outside of the individual worker affected levels of satisfaction—variables such as occupational group. R. H. Schaffer (1953) emphasized variables *within* the individual as contributing to satisfaction and dissatisfaction. He felt there was some psychological "set" or mechanism that operated to make people satisfied or dissatisfied in general. This set was thought to affect satisfaction with work as well. When certain needs the individual had were not fulfilled, tension was created, the amount of tension being directly related to the strength of the unfulfilled need. In other words, the objective characteristics of the job were only part of the "equation" of job satisfaction; another part was related to the needs of the individual. In effect, Schaffer proposed that workers looked at jobs through "need-colored" glasses.

This conception was much closer to many of our current theories of satisfaction and motivation than any of the work that preceded it. Schaffer proposed that individuals had 12 basic needs. These needs had the same characteristics as the five need categories in Maslow's hierarchy or the three of Alderfer's model. The set was composed of needs such as recognition, affection, mastery, and economic security. Since it was unrealistic to think that the 12 needs were equally important to all individuals, an analysis was done to identify those needs that contributed substantially to overall job satisfaction. This was done by first asking for three pieces of information from each respondent: (1) the importance of each of the 12 needs; (2) the degree to which each of the needs was being satisfied, and (3) an indication of overall job satisfaction. Schaffer was able to determine that the overall job satisfaction of an individual could be predicted from information concerning only the first two most important needs of that individual. In short, if the individual's two most important needs were being satisfied by the job, the individual would report overall job satisfaction; if the two most important needs were not being satisfied, overall dissatisfaction would be reported. The importance of Schaffer's work was not in the identification of the two most important needs of an individual; it was in the demonstration that there are reliable individual differences in the importance of needs. This approach can be seen in the dynamics of modern motivation theories (e.g., in Maslow's theory the most important needs would be found at the level in the hierarchy that has not yet been satisfied). In instrumentality theory, these most important needs would be represented by "valences," or in the Porter-Lawler version, the "value of the reward." Even though Schaffer's work was crude by current standards, the results anticipated (or possibly provided the foundation for) some important theories of work motivation.

CURRENT RESEARCH AND THEORY

Schaffer's work was followed closely by the publication of two important reviews of the literature in job satisfaction. The first was conducted by Brayfield and Crockett (1955) and the second by Herzberg et al. (1957). The Herzberg et al. review provided the basis for the two-factor theory discussed in Chapter 10. These two reviews are often contrasted with each other because they came to different conclusions. Both reviews set out to examine the relationship between job satisfaction and job performance. Brayfield and Crockett concluded that there was no demonstrable relationship between job satisfaction and performance. Herzberg et al. concluded that there was a systematic relationship between job satisfaction and certain work behaviors, as well as between job dissatisfaction and other work behaviors. Katzell (1957) provides reasons for the discrepancies in conclusions from the two reviews:

> [Herzberg] finds that, among studies in which performance was compared with favorability of job attitudes, 54 percent reported a positive relationship, 35 percent no relationship, and 11 percent a negative relationship. Most of the relationships were low. They also conclude that there is more unequivocal evidence of a relationship (negative) between job attitudes and both turnover and absenteeism, with some data also supporting the same trend as regards accidents and psychosomatic illnesses. In general, they conclude with "the belief that positive job attitudes are a tremendous asset to industry is supported by much of the experimental evidence now available."
>
> Brayfield and Crockett, on the contrary, infer in their review that "there is little evidence in the available literature that employee attitudes . . . bear any simple . . . or appreciable relationship to performance on the job." It should be noted that their definition of "performance on the job" excludes absenteeism, accidents, etc. (they do infer that attitudes are related to absenteeism and turnover). This is one source of difference in the tone of the two conclusions. Another reason for the difference is that the two studies do not cover exactly the same literature. Moreover, Herzberg et al. are more receptive to suggestive findings, whereas Brayfield and Crockett slight anything not statistically significant. (Whereas the latter position is more "correct," it also entails the danger of Type II errors regarding the null hypothesis, since most of the studies were based on small N's because the unit measured was more often the group than the individual.) But perhaps the main reason for the disparity is that Brayfield and Crockett state their generalization prior to their consideration of the parameters involved in the relationships between attitudes and performance, whereas Herzberg et al. more appropriately take such influences into account in arriving at their overall judgment. Both sets of authors make good suggestions on how improved methodology and research design may result in better clarification of these relationships.

The Two-Factor Theory

In their own ways, both reviews have had a great impact on the field of industrial and organizational psychology. Brayfield and Crockett were much more concerned with methodological considerations in their review. In the long run, however, the conclusions of Herzberg et al. have had a more serious impact on the field. This is probably due to the fact that while the things said by Brayfield and Crockett were more traditional and more frequently heard, the Herzberg review led indirectly to some revolutionary proposals. On the basis of the review, Herzberg concluded that satisfaction and dissatisfaction were two completely different phenomena. As I indicated in the motivation chapter, DeMan had come to a similar conclusion in 1929. It was proposed that satisfaction and dissatisfaction developed from quite different sources and had different initial effects on behavior and different long-term effects on behavior. Subsequently, Herzberg et al. (1959) conducted a study with 203 accountants and engineers from the Pittsburgh area. These individuals were interviewed and asked to describe a time when they felt particularly good or bad about their jobs. The responses were examined for indications of:

1. The situations that led to the feelings
2. The needs or drives that were activated by these situations
3. The amount of time the feelings lasted

(Again, it is interesting to note that DeMan [1929] used a similar technique, asking workers to write essays about the things that made them happy and the things that made them unhappy about their work.) The results of the Herzberg study indicated that the following factors were related to good feelings about a job: achievement and recognition, the nature of the work itself, responsibility, advancement, and salary. Bad feelings about a job seemed to be related to the following factors: company policy and administration, technical supervision, salary, interpersonal relations with supervisors, and working conditions. In addition, good feelings seemed to persist long after the events or situations that caused them had disappeared. This seemed to suggest that negative attitudes had a weaker effect on performance than positive attitudes, if for no other reason than the fact that they did not last as long.

These findings led Herzberg to propose what has come to be known as the *two-factor theory* or the *motivator-hygiene theory*. The basic propositions of the theory are straightforward:

1. Every individual has two sets of needs. One set, labeled *hygiene* (DeMan called them *health factors* 30 years earlier), relates to the physical and psychological environment in which the work is done. These needs would be met by such persons or things as coworkers, supervisors, working conditions, and company policy. The second set of needs, labeled *motivator needs*, relates to the nature and challenge of the work itself. These needs would be met by such things as the stimulation provided by job duties and responsibility attached to the job.
2. When hygiene needs are not met, the individual is dissatisfied. When the hygiene needs are met, the individual is no longer dissatisfied (but is not satisfied either).
3. When motivator needs are not met, the individual is not satisfied (but not dissatisfied either). When motivator needs are met, the individual is satisfied.

Figure 11–1 graphically depicts this relationship. Increasing amounts of hygiene factors will bring a person from a state of dissatisfaction to a neutral

FIGURE 11–1 The Effects of Motivator and Hygiene Factors on Job Satisfaction

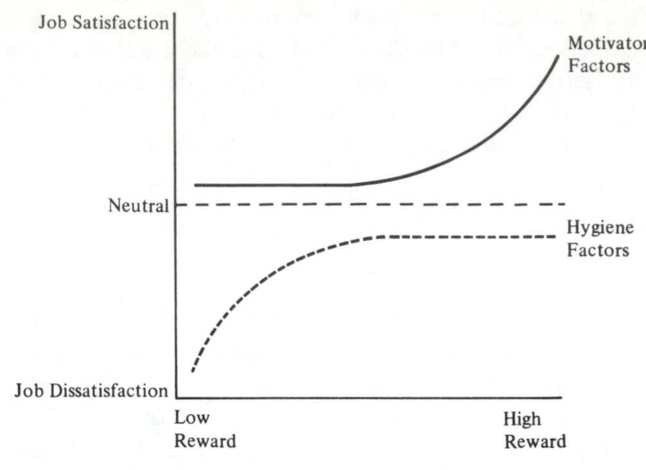

point. Increasing the motivator factors will bring a person from a neutral point to a state of satisfaction.

Tests of Two-Factor Theory. The research on two-factor theory has been voluminous and generally discouraging. Two-factor theory came under attack almost immediately on methodological grounds. The major argument was that since the data were gathered in face-to-face interviews, possibly the respondents were acting defensively when they responded. People might be unwilling to admit to an interviewer that a bad experience was their own fault. Consequently, when relating a dissatisfying time, they would attribute the cause of the dissatisfaction to someone or something other than themselves (e.g., a supervisor, coworker, or company policy). On the other hand, they would be more likely to take personal responsibility for good events (e.g., accomplishing a difficult task, receiving recognition for meeting a goal). Because of this potential confounding factor, numerous researchers have tried to replicate Herzberg's findings using methods other than face-to-face interviews. In most of these cases, they did not find the same results as Herzberg (Ewen, 1964; Ewen, Smith, Hulin, & Locke, 1966; Hinrichs & Mischkind, 1967; Hulin & Smith, 1965). But it is interesting to note that DeMan *had* used a different data gathering technique (written essays) and suggested a framework similar to the one that Herzberg eventually proposed.

In addition to the lack of empirical support, Herzberg has been severely criticized on conceptual grounds. King (1970) identified no less than five distinctly different "theories" suggested by Herzberg at various times. These "versions" are presented in Figure 11–2.

FIGURE 11–2 Five Versions of the Two-Factor Theory

I. All motivators combined contribute more to job satisfaction than to job dissatisfaction; all hygienes combined contribute more to job dissatisfaction than to job satisfaction.
II. All motivators combined contribute more to job satisfaction than do all the hygienes combined; all hygienes combined contribute more to job dissatisfaction than do all motivators combined.
III. Each motivator contributes more to job satisfaction than to job dissatisfaction; each hygiene contributes more to job dissatisfaction than to job satisfaction.
IV. Theory III holds and, in addition, each principal motivator contributes more to job satisfaction than does any hygiene factor; each principal hygiene contributes more to job dissatisfaction than does any motivator.
V. Only motivators determine job satisfaction, and only hygiene factors determine job dissatisfaction.

SOURCE: From "Clarification and Evaluation of the Two-Factor Theory of Job Satisfaction" by N. King, 1970, *Psychological Bulletin 74*.

In comparing the versions, it can be seen that version I is the weakest (i.e., would be easiest to support) and version V is the strongest (would be the most demanding to support). In examining the studies that applied to the various versions, King concluded that there was little evidence to suggest that any of the theories were supported.

Owing to the conceptual and empirical problems in supporting Herzberg's propositions, there has been a substantial decrease in research on the two-factor theory. This might be one way of saying that it has "fallen into disrepute." Every few years, however, Herzberg publishes a restatement of the theory and research conducted 30 years ago, so many of today's managers are still familiar with the propositions of two-factor theory. In spite of the absence of empirical support, Herzberg's theory is probably a reasonable one at the descriptive level. It does a good job of describing what a manager might expect to find—*on the average*. The factors listed as motivators are probably important to a majority of the work force in a particular organization (e.g., the stimulation provided by the job duties). But description is not explanation. Being able to describe the characteristics of a majority of the work force is a long way from understanding the relationships among satisfaction, motivation, and performance. One valuable research line that continues to maintain the interest of investigators is the difference between "intrinsic," or job content (motivator), and "extrinsic," or job context (hygiene), factors. Some of the differences will be examined in a later section of this chapter. On the whole, Herzberg has had a positive effect on the research in job satisfaction. As a result of his theory, variables are more clearly understood, the operations involved in measuring important variables are more reasonable, and people are thinking more flexibly about the meaning of job satisfaction than they did before his theory appeared.

FIGURE 11–3 Model of the Determinants of Satisfaction

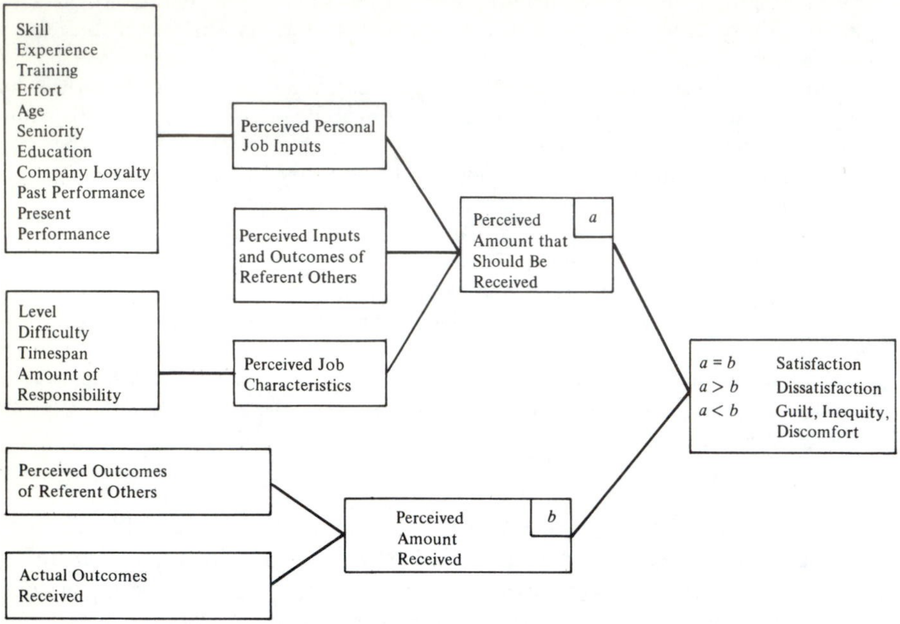

Skill
Experience
Training
Effort
Age
Seniority
Education
Company Loyalty
Past Performance
Present Performance

Perceived Personal Job Inputs

Perceived Inputs and Outcomes of Referent Others

Level
Difficulty
Timespan
Amount of Responsibility

Perceived Job Characteristics

Perceived Amount that Should Be Received *a*

$a = b$ Satisfaction
$a > b$ Dissatisfaction
$a < b$ Guilt, Inequity, Discomfort

Perceived Outcomes of Referent Others

Actual Outcomes Received

Perceived Amount Received *b*

SOURCE: From *Motivation in Work Organizations* (p. 75) by E. E. Lawler III, 1973, Monterey, CA: Brooks/Cole. Copyright © 1973 by Wadsworth Publishing Company, Inc. Reprinted by permission of the publisher, Brooks/Cole Publishing Company, Monterey, CA.

The Lawler Model of Facet Satisfaction

A book on motivation in work organizations by Lawler (1973) proposes a model of job satisfaction that differs from most others. It is really an expansion of the section in the Porter-Lawler model of work motivation dealing with the relationship between actual rewards for performance and perceived equitable rewards. You will remember that the model predicted that when perceived equitable rewards exceeded actual rewards, dissatisfaction would result. On the other hand, if actual rewards exceeded or equaled perceived equitable rewards, satisfaction resulted. The Lawler model, which appears in Figure 11–3, is a more specific statement of the factors leading to satisfaction and dissatisfaction.

The single most important process implied in the model is *perception*. This process takes the form of *perceived* personal job inputs, *perceived* inputs and outcomes of significant others, *perceived* job characteristics, and *perceived* outcomes (rewards). The importance of the *perception* of reality as opposed to reality itself was first recognized by the Hawthorne researchers and has remained a critical factor since. This model of satisfaction differs in one important respect from the treatment of satisfaction in the motivation model of Porter and Lawler. In the current model, if actual rewards *exceed* perceived equitable rewards, guilt, discomfort, and presumably tension are the result. If perceived equitable rewards exceed actual rewards, dissatisfaction results. In the earlier motivation model of Porter and Lawler, satisfaction was thought to result if actual rewards met or *exceeded* perceived equitable rewards. This change in operation moves the phenomenon of job satisfaction much closer to cognitive dissonance ("equity") theory. It says that some psychological discomfort results from the knowledge that we are receiving more than we deserve. This psychological discomfort is synonymous with physical discomfort (tension) and provides the impetus for actions necessary to relieve this tension.

Although this model describes the satisfaction an individual will experience with any particular aspect or facet of the job (e.g., pay, coworkers, challenge), Lawler feels that the combination of the feelings a worker has about all aspects of the job defines *overall job satisfaction.* He qualifies this somewhat by saying that facets or aspects contribute to overall satisfaction according to their importance to the individual. Although Lawler's model was one of the earliest explicit facet models, it remains a generally accepted structure for thinking about job satisfaction. Most researchers assume that there is some algebraic operator in us that calculates the sum of various facet satisfactions in coming to a conclusion about overall satisfaction.

SOME RECENT THEORIES

A number of unique theories of job satisfaction have appeared in the last decade and are worthy of brief mention simply because of their novelty. Unfortunately, there is little research available at this time either supporting or rejecting the theories, but from a conceptual perspective, they illustrate the range of thinking about job satisfaction that is possible beyond the simple facet model.

Locke's Value Theory

Locke (1976) distinguishes between value and need. He thinks of needs as elements that ensure an individual's survival, much in the sense that we use the term *biological need.* He considers needs to be objective, existing regardless of the desires of the individual. Values, on the other hand, are subjective and represent what a person *desires* at either a conscious or subconscious level. Given this distinction, Locke's theory of job satisfaction might be stated as follows:

> Job satisfaction [is] the pleasurable emotional state resulting from the perception of one's job as fulfilling or allowing the fulfillment of one's important job values, providing these values are compatible with one's needs. (p. 1342)

At present, Locke's theory is philosophically rather than empirically based. His argument with the need theorists would seem to be more semantic

FIGURE 11–4 Relationship of Importance to Satisfaction

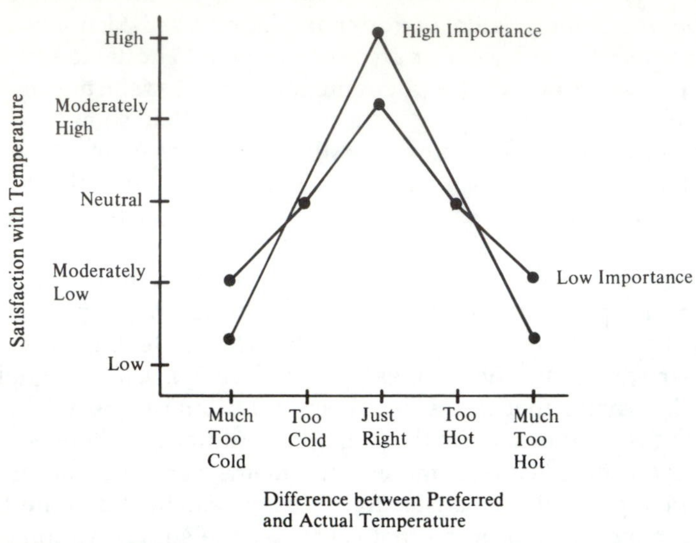

SOURCE: Adapted from "The Nature and Causes of Job Satisfaction" (p. 1305) by E. A. Locke, in M. D. Dunnette (Ed.), *Handbook of Industrial and Organizational Psychology*, 1976, Chicago: Rand McNally. Copyright 1976 by John Wiley & Sons, Inc. Reprinted by permission.

than ideological. Nevertheless, in the course of presenting his theory, he does suggest an interesting role for the concept of "importance." As we have already seen, it is reasonable to expect that job satisfaction is not the simple sum of satisfactions with individual elements of the job. One component that might play a role is the relative *importance* of each of the factors being considered. Thus, if pay is extremely important to you and pleasant coworkers are relatively unimportant, pay should play a greater role in determining your overall satisfaction than pleasant coworkers. This would mean that we should get a more accurate prediction of an individual's overall satisfaction if we weight satisfaction with each specific job element by its importance. In spite of the appeal of this operation, a number of studies have shown that weighting by importance does not improve the prediction of overall job satisfaction (Ewen, 1967; Mikes & Hulin, 1968). Locke suggests that the importance of a particular job aspect affects the *range* of emotional response a given job element can produce, rather than the actual satisfaction with that element. In other words, if something is relatively unimportant to me, I will not be either very satisfied or very dissatisfied with it; I will be indifferent regardless of the amount of that element I receive. On the other hand, if I value a particular job element very highly, then slight variations from optimal amounts of that element will produce wide variations in satisfaction. Figure 11–4 presents this principle in graphic form. As you can see, when room temperature is unimportant to an individual, wide variation in temperature will produce little variation in satisfaction with temperature; on the other hand, when temperature is of critical importance to an individual, small variations in actual temperature will produce wide variations in expressed satisfaction with temperature.

From a broader perspective, the prevailing theory of emotions, that of Schachter and Singer (1962), supports Locke's propositions. The Schachter-Singer theory suggests that the major predisposing element for emotional experience is arousal. Without arousal, there is little or no emotional reaction. It is reasonable to assume that important factors are arousing factors, predisposing individuals to emotional reactions. The Schachter-Singer theory will be covered in greater detail later in the chapter. For the time being, it is fair to say that there is theoretical support for Locke's propositions regarding importance.

Opponent-Process Theory

I have suggested an approach to job satisfaction that departs radically from the more traditional approaches outlined earlier (Landy, 1978b). It is called the *opponent-process theory* and differs from other approaches in proposing that an individual's satisfaction with a particular reward will systematically change over time, even though the reward itself remains constant. As an example, a job tends to be more interesting in the first week than it is after six years on the same job. In the past, this has been dismissed as simply an instance of "boredom," as if labeling the phenomenon somehow explained it. Opponent-process theory proposes that there are some mechanisms within individuals that help maintain some equilibrium in emotional states. Since job satisfaction and dissatisfaction are thought to be, at least in part, emotional phenomena, these mechanisms of emotional balance are thought to play a role in job satisfaction.

As the name implies, opponent-process theory holds that there are opposing processes for dealing with emotional states. For example, whenever we are extremely happy, there is a mechanism that automatically attempts to keep that happiness from getting out of control. Conversely, when we are unhappy, there is a mechanism that opposes that emotional state and attempts to bring the individual back to some neutral level. This "mechanism" sounds somewhat mystical, but in actuality it is thought to be a central nervous system function. The theory assumes that extremely emotional states (either positive or negative) are damaging to the individual and that physiological mechanisms attempt to protect the individual from these extreme states. This certainly fits in well with current conceptions of stress and mechanisms for coping with stress (Frankenhauser, 1974; Selye, 1974). Opponent-process theory suggests that this "protection" function is responsible for the fact that individuals differ in job satisfaction. Figure 11–5 represents the way the opponent process works. There are three components in the figure: *primary emotion, opponent process, and stimulus*. The figure suggests that when a stimulus is introduced,

FIGURE 11–5 Underlying Opponent Processes after Few Stimulus Presentations

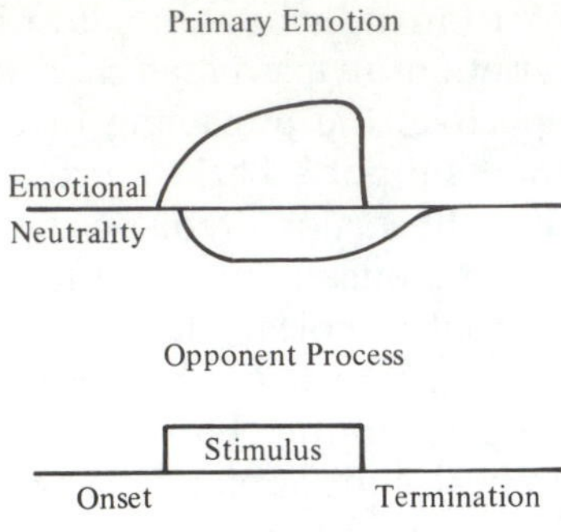

SOURCE: From "An Opponent Process Theory of Job Satisfaction," by F. J. Landy, 1978b, *Journal of Applied Psychology, 63* (5), p. 536. Copyright 1978 by the American Psychological Association. Reprinted by permission of the author.

it produces an emotion, either positive or negative. Once this primary emotion passes some threshold, an opponent process is automatically activated to bring this primary emotion under control. When the stimulus disappears, the primary emotion disappears immediately, and the opponent process disappears more gradually. Figure 11–5 is a view of each of the two processes independent of each other. Now look at Figure 11–6. This figure represents the actual changes in the emotional state of an individual during and after stimulus (reward or punishment) presentation. This suggests that shortly after the presentation of a reward, an individual is elated. This elation levels out after a period of time, and when the stimulus that originally elicited the elation disappears, the individual is somewhat depressed or unhappy. This can be

FIGURE 11–6 Emotional Response after Few Stimulus Presentations

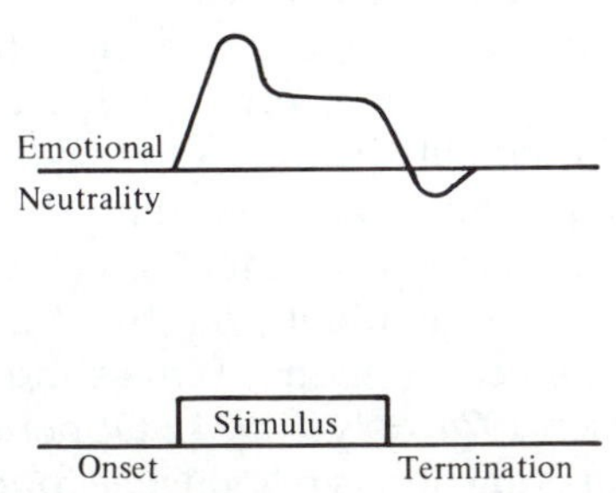

SOURCE: From "An Opponent Process Theory of Job Satisfaction" by F. J. Landy, 1978b, *Journal of Applied Psychology, 63* (5), p. 536. Copyright 1978 by the American Psychological Association. Reprinted by permission of the author.

FIGURE 11–7 Underlying Opponent Processes after Many Stimulus Presentations

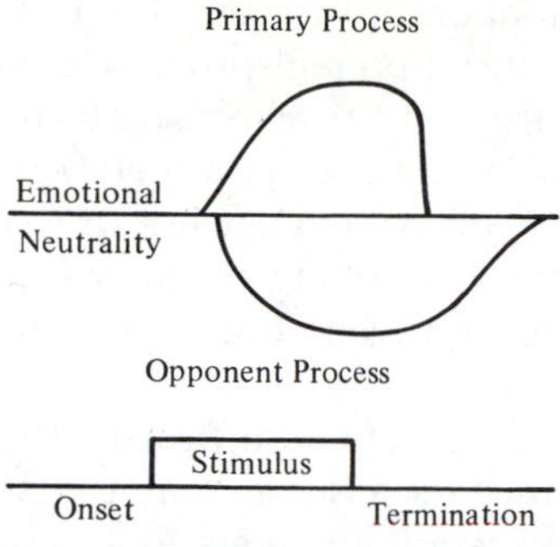

SOURCE: From "An Opponent Process Theory of Job Satisfaction" by F. J. Landy, 1978b, *Journal of Applied Psychology, 63* (5), p. 538. Copyright 1978 by the American Psychological Association. Reprinted by permission of the author.

seen by the fact that the curve representing the emotional state of the individual dips below the line representing emotional neutrality.

Another proposition of the theory makes it even more intriguing. It is assumed that the opponent process becomes stronger each time it is activated. This means the same stimulus can have different effects on the satisfaction of an individual, depending on how often the individual has encountered the stimulus in the past. Figure 11–7 presents a picture of what the primary emotional state and opponent process might look like after many presentations of the same reward or punishment. As you can see, the primary emotion remains exactly the same as it was in Figure 11–5, but the opponent process has grown dramatically in strength. It is both more intense and longer lasting than it was in Figure 11–5. Figure 11–8 represents the changes in emotional state that the individual would be likely to experience during the presence

FIGURE 11–8 Emotional Response after Many Stimulus Presentations

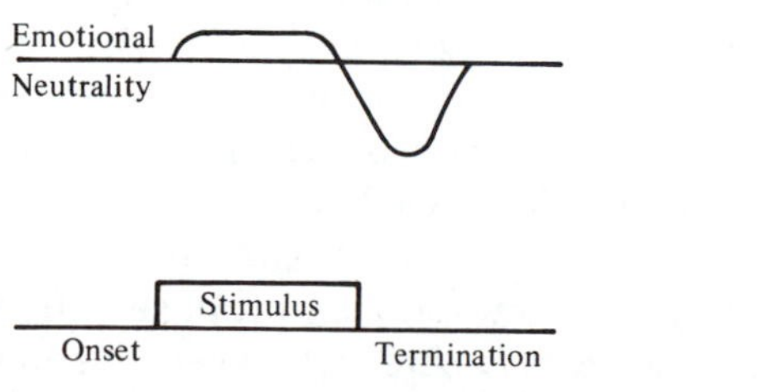

SOURCE: From "An Opponent Process Theory of Job Satisfaction" by F. J. Landy, 1978b, *Journal of Applied Psychology, 63* (5), p. 538. Copyright 1978 by the American Psychological Association. Reprinted by permission of the author.

and disappearance of the stimulus (reward or punishment). As you can see, the initial presentation of the stimulus has little observable effect on the individual, but the termination of the stimulus has a rather dramatic effect.

The implications of the opponent-process theory are rather extensive. For one thing, it suggests that studies of job satisfaction should be longitudinal rather than cross-sectional in nature. The theory implies that *when* you ask satisfaction questions may affect the answers. If you ask the question when the primary process is the controlling influence, you will get one kind of answer. If you ask the question when the opponent process is operating, the answer will be different.

Another implication of the opponent-process theory is related to the issue of "boredom." Most managers assume that the work itself diminishes in "stimulation value," thus resulting in a state of boredom. Opponent-process theory suggests that the stimulus value of the work itself remains unchanged, but the opponent process has become stronger. Further, the theory implies that a worker can become bored with any work-related stimulus (including coworkers, pay, and working conditions).

The Vitamin Model

Warr (1987) and his colleagues have suggested a model of job satisfaction that is patterned after the notion of how various vitamins work on physical health. He suggests that there are nine particular attributes of work that produce variations in satisfaction. This is similar to the notion that various vitamins, as a group, affect physical health. Warr further suggests that like vitamins, we need some minimum daily "dosage" of these nine attributes to remain satisfied with our jobs. It is here, however, that Warr departs from conventional thinking. Still using the vitamin notion, he suggests that although meeting the minimum daily requirements will bring an individual to a state of positive mental health, too much of some of the attributes will lead to "toxic" reactions. In other words, too little of any attribute can be harmful, but too much of some of these attributes will also cause problems. He likens this circumstance to that of taking too much of certain vitamins (i.e., vitamin A and vitamin D). Figure 11–9 presents the theory graphically. Certain environmental attributes will not cause any harm in an overabundance (identified in the figure as CE factors and similar in action to vitamins C and E that are excreted when they are consumed in abundance), but other attributes (identified as AD factors and similar in action to vitamins A and D) will actually cause a decrease in emotional well-being (just as individuals may experience toxic reactions to overdoses of vitamins A and D). Table 11–4 illustrates these two different types of factors and their proposed effects. Warr's vitamin model is interesting from a process perspective because few other theories propose that too *much* of an attribute can cause problems in and of itself. For example, Herzberg implied that too much of either motivator or hygiene factors had no effect beyond some critical value. Instrumentality theory implies that

FIGURE 11–9 Schematic Representation of Two Assumed Relationships between Environmental Features and Mental Health

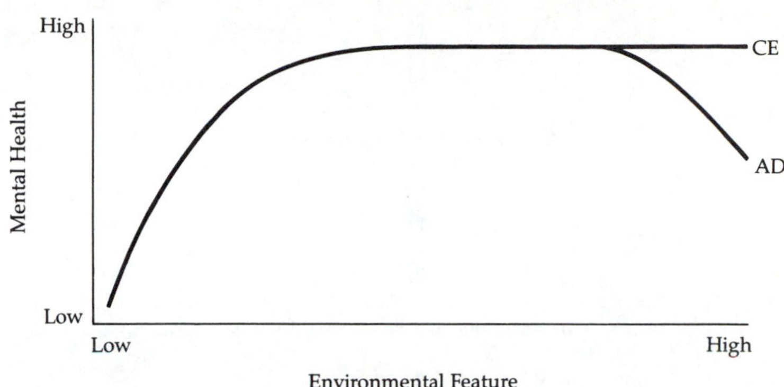

CE = constant effect, AD = additional decrement.

SOURCE: From *Work, Unemployment and Mental Health* (Fig. 1.1, p. 10) by P. B. Warr, 1987, Oxford: Clarendon Press.

greater rewards yield more effort. Equity theory suggests that too much of a reward causes imbalance (or dissonance), but Warr's theory takes a substantially different approach to the issue of emotional distress. In addition, Warr suggests that *particular* attributes cause "toxic" reactions, but equity theory implies that *any* imbalance causes tension. Thus, there are substantive differences between the vitamin model and equity theory as well. Warr's theory

TABLE 11–4 Effects of High Levels of CE and AD Variables

	Variable	*Effect*
High levels of CE variables	Money	Constant effect at high levels
	Physical security	Constant effect at high levels
	Valued social position	Constant effect at high levels
High levels of AD variables	Externally generated goals	Overload; stress
	Variety	Low concentration and achievement
	Clarity	Little control or opportunity for development
	Control	Overload; stress
	Skill use	Overload; stress
	Interpersonal contact	Lack of personal control; overcrowding

SOURCE: Adapted from *Work, Unemployment and Mental Health* (pp. 13–14) by P. B. Warr, 1987, Oxford: Clarendon Press.

FIGURE 11–10 Schachter-Singer Theory of Emotion

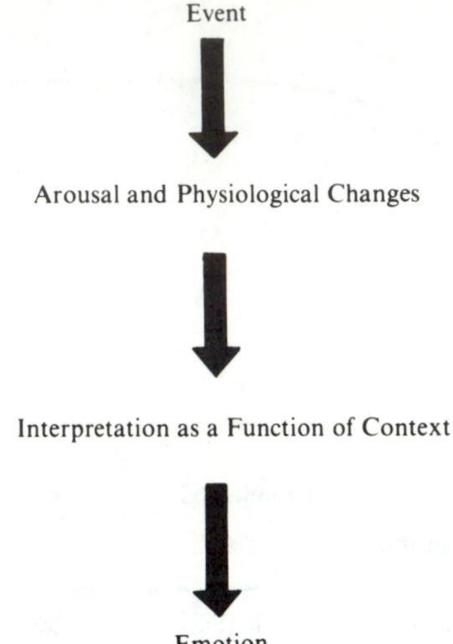

In the Schachter-Singer theory of emotion, an event causes arousal and psychological changes, which are noticed by the person, who looks to the environment for clues as to what caused the arousal and then picks an emotional label that fits the clues.

SOURCE: From *Psychology: The Science of People* (2nd ed.) (p. 381) by F. J. Landy, 1987, Englewood Cliffs, NJ: Prentice-Hall. © 1987. Reprinted by permission of Prentice-Hall, Inc.

is an interesting one and should receive the careful attention of researchers. On the surface, it would appear considerably easier to test than either Locke's value theory or the opponent-process theory.

AN EMERGING POSITION: SATISFACTION AS ATTRIBUTION

Mechanisms of Emotion

There is a gap between theory and research in job satisfaction. Most researchers would accept the proposition that job satisfaction has emotional or affective components. In everyday language, satisfaction/dissatisfaction is a *feeling*. In spite of this consensus, there has been little reference to general theories of emotion in satisfaction research. The most widely accepted theory of emotions has been suggested by Schachter and Singer (1962). They proposed that there are two critical processes that compose any emotion—arousal and attribution. Figure 11–10 graphically illustrates their theory. It suggests that some environmental event causes arousal in an individual and that the individual looks around for cues that might explain this arousal. In this framework, there are no unique emotions—only arousal. This means that there is no physiological distinction between satisfaction and dissatisfaction as far as the individual is concerned. Further, it means that any particular stimulus or situation is capable of producing either satisfaction or dissatisfaction. The particular emotional state will depend on the interpretation of cues by the individual trying to account for the arousal. Let's take a few concrete examples.

Arousal and Satisfaction

Job enrichment involves a substantial increase in scope of job duties, breadth of job duties, or both. If done correctly, it is reasonable to assume that arousal will be increased for the incumbent. This is the first component of an emotion. The second component, however, would be attribution. The aroused individual might find herself in a work group that is opposed to job enrichment. The group might feel that the company is trying to increase job duties without increasing pay. In such a circumstance, you might find that the worker is dissatisfied with the enriched job. In contrast, the work group might be very positive about the changed jobs. They might believe that the company is trying to make the work more interesting and fulfilling. In this case, the worker would be expected to report satisfaction with her enriched job. In fact, there are instances in which job enrichment seems "not to work." The incumbents are less satisfied after the change than they were before. This could be explained using the attributional model of Schachter and Singer.

Satisfaction and Cognition

If the Schachter-Singer position is correct, it puts satisfaction in a very different light. Reports of satisfaction and dissatisfaction become social and cognitive constructions—attempts by the individual to make sense of a change in arousal level. That does not make satisfaction a useless or artificial construct since emotional states have consequences for other aspects of behavior. It does suggest, however, that reported satisfaction or dissatisfaction depends on many things other than level of the particular environmental variable being studied. If the variable in question is not arousing, there is no emotional reaction at all. If it does increase arousal, other cues will determine whether the felt emotion is positive or negative.

There have been a number of recent studies that support the view of satisfaction as a cognitive or social-cognitive construction. A good example is a study conducted by Caldwell and O'Reilly (1982). In this study, 77 MBA students were asked to imagine themselves in a particular job. Half of them were told to imagine that they were very satisfied with that job. The other half were told to imagine that they were dissatisfied in that job. Based on the job descriptions that they were given, the subjects were then asked to evaluate the extent to which their job was "enriched." The subjects who had been asked to imagine satisfaction rated their job as more enriched than those who imagined dissatisfaction. Remember, all subjects were given the *same* job description. In a field replication of the study, 88 sales representatives for a single organization were asked questions about their satisfaction and the extent to which they saw their jobs as enriched. All the sales representatives had the same basic job duties and work environments. The satisfied representatives reported more enriched jobs than the dissatisfied representatives. Caldwell and O'Reilly conclude that the conventional wisdom about satisfaction is wrong. Job redesign and job enrichment experiments assume that the enriched job leads to greater satisfaction. Caldwell and O'Reilly suggest that satisfaction leads to changed perception. L. R. James and Jones (1980) had reached a similar conclusion in a study of the relationship between job satisfaction and organizational climate. In a study of 642 nonsupervisory workers, they concluded that job satisfaction had a strong influence on job perceptions. Once again, these results run counter to conventional wisdom and many of the previous cognitive models of job satisfaction.

A Cognitive Puzzle: Job Enrichment. The relationship between job enrichment and job satisfaction is particularly puzzling. As we saw above, Caldwell and O'Reilly found differences in satisfaction with imaginary enriched jobs in spite of the fact that all subjects were to imagine the same enriched job. To be sure, the experimental design was artificial in the student sample, but the result was replicated in the employed sample. In another study in a work setting, Rafaeli (1985) found that quality circles (i.e., a form of job enrichment in which employee groups meet and consider improvements to the work or work setting) did not affect job satisfaction. Marks, Mirvis, Hackett, and Grady (1986) suggest that quality circles and similar enrichment programs involving social interaction do not function to increase job satisfaction but instead act as a buffer and represent a form of emotional support against assaults by the environment (e.g., economic pressures, poor supervision). Finally, Loher, Noe, Moeller, and Fitzgerald (1985) conducted a meta-analysis of 27 studies dealing with the effects of enrichment on satisfaction and concluded that there is a substantial positive relationship between enrichment efforts and experienced satisfaction of workers. Clearly, the relationship is a complicated one. Perhaps a model such as Warr's might solve the riddle. It may be that some of the enrichment studies are dealing with job attributes that have exceeded the "minimum daily requirements" but have not become toxic yet; other studies may be dealing with toxic levels of certain attributes for some of the subjects in the study.

Satisfaction as a Disposition

It has often been suggested that some people are simply more satisfied with all aspects of life than others. Certainly, the recent work of Bandura (1986, 1987) on self-efficacy leans in that direction. As an example, in a study of job choice and satisfaction, O'Reilly and Caldwell (1981) found that individuals who felt that they had made a job choice freely without pressure and who perceived the decision to be irrevocable were more satisfied and committed to their jobs six months later. O'Reilly and Caldwell interpreted this relationship to mean that job satisfaction could have been a function of past influences having nothing to do with the objective characteristics of the job or work environment. From this perspective, job satisfaction is more an example of retrospective rationality or postdecisional justification than of current situational influences. Another possible interpretation might be that those individuals predisposed to be satisfied with their jobs do express satisfaction at a later point in time. Pulakos and Schmitt (1983) offer additional evidence of the possibility of a more basic traitlike mechanism for understanding job satisfaction. In their study, they asked students to anticipate the reactions to various aspects of future work. The data showed that beliefs about future job characteristics correlated significantly with the reported feelings of these students about their jobs 20 months later. Pulakos and Schmitt prefer a cognitive interpretation of this result. They propose that students created a cognitive structure and turned it into a self-fulfilling prophecy. In other words, the students "saw it when they believed it." Motowidlo and Lawton (1984) suggest that the cognitive mechanism involved is one of information processing. Individuals develop expectations about future outcomes, and these expectations work as filters allowing only confirming data to be registered and excluding disconfirming data from the information-processing loop.

Staw and Ross (1985) present even more impressive data that job satisfaction may be an enduring disposition of people rather than a response to an environment. They examined the satisfaction responses of 5,000 men in a national sample over a five-year period and discovered that attitudes toward their work (i.e., job satisfaction) remained very stable over this period regardless of changes in employers and occupations. Staw and Ross go so far as to speculate that employers may do well to *select* satisfied people rather than try to make dissatisfied people satisfied. The implications (and ethics) of such a possibility are startling and require serious evaluation but do point to an interesting extension of the dispositional view of job satisfaction.

A final study by Arvey, Bouchard, Segal, and Abraham (1987) in this area is equally startling. In a study of the job satisfaction of identical twins reared apart, these authors concluded that as much as 30 percent of the variance in job satisfaction might be the result of *genetic* factors. This would certainly explain the stability of the attitudes identified by O'Reilly and Caldwell, and Pulakos and Schmitt, as well as the consistency found by Staw and Ross. These four studies represent single investigations of complex phenomena and must be considered as "preliminary" evidence. Nevertheless, the results are different enough from conventional thinking to warrant replication and serious discussion.

In contrasting the facet models of satisfaction, the cognitive models, and the dispositional models, there is a basic issue that is in dispute here. Many theories of job satisfaction imply that thinking precedes feeling. This is certainly the case in equity theory and Lawler's facet satisfaction model. It is assumed that the individual evaluates some environmental condition and chooses an appropriate emotional reaction. An alternative position is that the individual experiences a feeling of some sort and then tries to figure out why that feeling occurred. Zajonc (1980) has presented a clear and provocative statement of this latter position. He proposes that feeling comes first and thinking second.

Two new research lines seem to be emerging in the study of job satisfaction. The first line is a cognitive one. The second is a dispositional-constitutional-genetic one. It is time to entertain some novel and possibly unpopular approaches to understanding job satisfaction. The cognitive emphasis is long overdue. As I indicated in the first chapter, the cognitive revolution has swept through many other areas of psychology. Although the revolution has been slow in coming to industrial and organizational theories, I think it is here to stay. It is important for industrial and organizational psychologists to integrate their work with mainstream theory in psychology. The fact that we have learned so little about job satisfaction after 50+ years and 4,000+ studies is testimony in favor of such integration. Since there is general agreement that satisfaction and dissatisfaction are emotions, we should try to apply theories of emotion to our study of job satisfaction. The work of Caldwell and O'Reilly, Pulakos and Schmitt, and James and Jones suggests that general theories of emotion such as those proposed by Schachter and Singer or by Zajonc may provide a good framework for a reconceptualization of job satisfaction.

Interestingly enough, however, much of the same research (i.e., Caldwell & O'Reilly, Pulakos & Schmitt) can be interpreted in a radically different manner in light of the findings of Staw and Ross and Arvey and his colleagues. These latter researchers seem to argue for a trait-based approach to satisfaction, an approach that had been abandoned in many areas of psychology several decades ago. I suspect that within a very few years the "pretheoretical" status of the type of studies described above will change to theoretical with the appearance of a cohesive set of propositions relating dynamic cognitive variables, on the one hand, and stable dispositional characteristics, on the other hand, to job satisfaction.

SOURCES OF JOB SATISFACTION

Up to this point, formal models of job satisfaction have been presented. Another way of studying satisfaction is to examine data that have been gathered on the topic, independent of a particular theoretical orientation. Several reviews have attempted such an examination (Herzberg et al., 1957; Vroom, 1964). But the amount of research is accumulating so rapidly that one must depend on the most recent review available for drawing any general conclusions. In 1976, Locke estimated that there were more than 3,300 articles or dissertations that had been published on job satisfaction. You will be happy

"I find this work truly fulfilling in many ways—there's the exercise, the sense of accomplishment, and, most important, the opportunity to make lots of noise."
From *The Wall Street Journal,* with permission of Cartoon Features Syndicate.

to know that I have decided against presenting the results of each of these studies to you. Instead, I will take advantage of the extensive review that Locke (1976) accomplished and present a synthesis of his conclusions.

Locke has suggested that studies be placed in one of two categories: (1) *events and conditions* or (2) *agents.* While events and conditions are thought to be directly responsible for feelings of happiness or unhappiness, agents are responsible for events and conditions. Thus, the amount of work, the task activity, and compensation are examples of events and conditions; supervi-

FIGURE 11–11 Effects of Various Events, Conditions, and Agents on Job Satisfaction[a]

Source	*Effect*
Events or conditions	
Work itself: challenge	Mentally challenging work that the individual can successfully accomplish is satisfying.
Work itself: physical demand	Tiring work is dissatisfying.
Work itself: personal interest	Personally interesting work is satisfying.
Reward structure	Just and informative rewards for performance are satisfying.
Working conditions: physical	Satisfaction depends on the match between working conditions and physical needs.
Working conditions: goal attainment	Working conditions that facilitate goal attainment are satisfying.
Agents	
Self	High self-esteem is conducive to job satisfaction.
Supervisors, coworkers, subordinates	Individuals will be satisfied with colleagues who help them attain rewards. Individuals will be satisfied with colleagues who see things the same way they do.
Company and management	Individuals will be satisfied with companies that have policies and procedures designed to help the individual attain rewards. Individuals will be dissatisfied with conflicting roles or ambiguous roles imposed by company, management, or both.
Fringe benefits	Benefits do not have a strong influence on job satisfaction for most workers.

[a]The interested reader is directed to Locke's (1976) review for a more detailed presentation of these conclusions.

sors, coworkers, and customers are examples of agents. Figure 11–11 presents Locke's conclusions. There is not really much to say about these results other than the fact that they represent some conclusions that might be drawn from a series of studies that varied dramatically in emphasis, sample, hypotheses, and measures. In other words, they probably tell us little about the nature of satisfaction. On the other hand, as was the case with Herzberg's propositions, the effects in Figure 11–11 have been observed, so they represent more than simply idle speculation. They might represent a point of departure for a manager who would like to set about improving the satisfaction of his work force.

Individual Differences and Job Satisfaction

A popular hypothesis in job satisfaction research has been that certain individual differences are associated with levels of satisfaction or dissatisfaction. These individual differences have varied from the demographic (e.g., age, race, or gender) to the functional (e.g., self-esteem or ability level). This approach implies that satisfaction is something that is inherent in the person rather than in the situation or the environmental stimuli. Newspapers and magazines periodically report that blacks or women or older employees are more (or less) satisfied than they were two years ago or more (or less) satisfied than white middle-aged male employees.

Data presented by Weaver (1977, 1978) would seem to disconfirm this general belief. There do not seem to be any dramatic differences in job satisfaction among demographic subgroups, particularly when variables such as education, occupational status, and pay level are held constant. This would seem to contradict the earlier discussion about dispositional-genetic variables, but the contradiction is more apparent than real. We have known for some time that demographic variables are surrogates of what we are interested in and not the variables of interest themselves. The dispositional data suggest that we should go beyond the issue of gender, race, age, or education and discover what are the important *psychological* variables associated with those demographic characteristics. The dispositional, constitutional, or genetic characteristics that may be responsible for the variations in job satisfaction could well be demographically unbiased mechanisms, affecting individuals regardless of race, sex, age, or national origin.

THE MEASUREMENT OF JOB SATISFACTION

So far, the history, logic, theory, and research base of job satisfaction have been presented, but nothing has been said about how satisfaction information is gathered today—that is, how the variable is measured in current research studies. Figure 11–12 shows several different ways in which *satisfaction with the work itself* might be measured.

At *A* in the figure is a format known as the *semantic differential*. The worker is asked to place a mark on the line separating the two bipolar adjectives; this mark indicates how well one or the other of the adjectives describes the concept "my work." At *B* is a checklist format in which the worker is asked to place a check or mark next to those items that best describe the work itself. This might be thought of as a version of a Thurstone scale described earlier. At *C* is the format known as a Likert scale. This format and its development

FIGURE 11–12 Ways of Measuring Job Satisfaction

A. *The Work Itself*

Fascinating _ _ _ _ _ _ _ _ _ Boring
Monotonous _ _ _ _ _ _ _ _ _ Challenging
Simple _ _ _ _ _ _ _ _ _ Difficult
Creative _ _ _ _ _ _ _ _ _ Routine
Useless _ _ _ _ _ _ _ _ _ Useful

B.

My work is routine ________
My work is difficult ________
I seem to do many useless things on my job ________
I have the opportunity to be creative in my work ________

C.

1. My work is routine SA A N D SD
2. My work is difficult SA A N D SD
3. I seem to do many useless things on my job SA A N D SD
4. I have the opportunity to be creative in my work SA A N D SD

SA = strongly agree
A = agree
N = neither agree nor disagree (neutral)
D = disagree
SD = strongly disagree

D. *Work*

Yes ? No Fascinating
Yes ? No Routine
Yes ? No Satisfying
Yes ? No Boring
Yes ? No Good
Yes ? No Creative
Yes ? No Respected
Yes ? No Hot
Yes ? No Pleasant
Yes ? No Useful
Yes ? No Tiresome
Yes ? No Healthful
Yes ? No Challenging
Yes ? No On your feet
Yes ? No Frustrating
Yes ? No Simple
Yes ? No Endless
Yes ? No Gives sense of accomplishment

SOURCE: The scale (Part D, Work) is copyrighted by Bowling Green State University. Information may be obtained from Patricia Cain Smith, Department of Psychology, Bowling Green State University, Bowling Green, OH 43403.

were also described earlier in the chapter. The worker is asked to read each of the statements and circle one of the alternatives (SA = strongly agree; A = agree; N = neither agree nor disagree—neutral; D = disagree; SD = strongly disagree). At *D* is a portion of a measuring instrument known as the *Job Descriptive Index* (JDI) (Smith, Kendall, & Hulin, 1969). Workers are asked to circle one of the three alternatives—Yes, ?, or No—to indicate whether the word describes their jobs. In a sense, this is actually a combination of checklist format and the Likert format. These methods are known collectively as *rating scales*. In Chapter 5, rating scales were described as aids used to help the supervisor make performance statements about subordinates. In this case, rating scales are aids for workers in making statements about their jobs.

Overall job satisfaction or satisfaction with a specific aspect of the job has generally been measured as an attitude. An attitude might be defined as a feeling, belief, and action tendency toward a psychological object. You might have a feeling about your job—disgust, fear, excitement, apprehension, or enthusiasm. Independent of this feeling, you might have a belief about your job—it is an interesting job, or it is a high-status job. Finally, you might have an action tendency related to your job—you rush to your job, or you tend to talk more to your coworkers than you do to your family. Each of these three components describes an aspect of your attitude toward your job.

Job satisfaction scales usually measure one of the first two components of an attitude—feeling or belief. It is not always clear which of the two components is being considered. This presents a problem for interpretation, since the *feelings* about a job or job aspect are quite different from the *beliefs* about that aspect. For example, we might feel apprehensive every time we get into the car to go to work, yet believe that our job is the best in the world. If beliefs were measured in this instance, it might be concluded that you had a "good attitude" toward your work; if your feelings were measured, you might be described as having a "poor attitude" toward your work.

Over the years, an interesting characteristic of satisfaction measurement has been the unwillingness of one researcher to make use of the satisfaction questionnaire developed by another researcher. There has been the tendency to develop a new satisfaction questionnaire for each study. This is the equivalent of every carpenter in the world developing an individual way of measuring lengths. One carpenter might use the standard ruler marked off in inches, whereas a second uses a ruler marked off in metric units, and a third prefers to measure lengths with a screwdriver (e.g., this page is one screwdriver length long). This preference for varying measuring methods presents no problem until the carpenters try to talk to one another. The same is true of job satisfaction research. Since different ways were used to measure job satisfaction, and even different components of attitudes toward the job were being measured, the literature is very confusing. Fortunately, this is changing. The JDI shown in Figure 11–12 at *D* is being widely used in satisfaction research. It was very carefully developed and documented, is relatively easy for workers to use and understand, and relates logically and empirically to other measures of job satisfaction. Two recent studies (Johnson, Smith, & Tucker, 1982; Schneider & Dachler, 1978) have reconfirmed the reliability and validity of the JDI. In addition to the five separate scores for the various aspects of job satisfaction, it has also been suggested that the JDI can be used as a measure of general job satisfaction (Hulin, Drasgow, & Komocar, 1982; Parsons & Hulin, 1982).

The major drawback of the JDI is practical rather than technical. There are many potential aspects of a job that might be related to satisfaction or dissatisfaction. The JDI certainly covers the major categories. Nevertheless, there are other areas that are not covered. Some of these areas might be quite important in a given situation. As an example, some people are unhappy with the reputation of the company they work for; others may be unhappy with the nature of the product they are associated with. In the nuclear power industry, workers are often concerned with exposure to radiation. It would be difficult to express such concern with the JDI. In addition, the JDI devotes little attention to processes in the organization. As we have seen earlier, people express pleasure and displeasure with the manner in which performance appraisal is carried out (independent of their satisfaction with the person doing the evaluation). The JDI is a good instrument for measuring attitudes toward several aspects of the job. Occasionally, supplementary questionnaires might be called for as well.

Attitude scales are the most common measuring instruments in job satisfaction research. The tendency for investigators to develop their own scales has led to the existence of more scales than there is space to describe them. Fortunately, Cook, Hepworth, Wall, and Warr (1981) have done the work for us. They have reviewed 4,000 research reports in an attempt to provide information concerning over 249 measures of work-related attitudes. There are two separate chapters dealing directly with job satisfaction. One chapter reviews 17 measures of overall or general job satisfaction; the second chapter covers 29 measures of satisfaction with specific aspects of work. This book is an enormous aid for both research and practice. For each satisfaction measure, the authors cover the following areas:

Description and background. Title and source; constructs, subscales; number of items, response format, scoring, etc.

Descriptive statistics. Means and standard deviations from the original source material as well as published research studies; description of sample characteristics for published studies

Scale reliability and validity. Reported reliability and validity estimates from original source as well as other studies

Scale usage. Listing of every published application of the scale

Scale items and response format. A listing of the actual items on the instrument as well as the scoring instructions

With this type of information, it is relatively easy to choose the best measure to satisfy the particular project need. Be warned, however! A major conclusion of Cook et al. after reviewing all these measures is that many of these scales are poorly documented.

Measures of Satisfaction Other than Attitude Scales

In addition to attitude scales, Locke (1976) lists the following techniques that might be considered in gathering job satisfaction information:

1. *Overt behavior* (e.g., everyone in attendance on a particular day must be satisfied with his work or he would not be there).
2. *Action tendency scales* (e.g., ask an individual how she *feels like acting*).
3. *Interviews*.
4. *Critical incidents* (e.g., ask individuals to remember a time when they were particularly happy or unhappy with their work and describe the circumstances).

Each of these approaches has its own advocates. The behaviorists would favor overt action; Herzberg based his theory on the results of critical incidents; Lawler depends heavily on attitude rating scales. There is no *best* way. But no matter how satisfaction is measured, the technique must be capable of producing reliable and valid data, or those data are worthless.

THE CONSEQUENCES OF JOB SATISFACTION AND DISSATISFACTION

Most managers implicitly assume some relationship between job satisfaction and certain organizational outcomes, such as absenteeism, turnover, and productivity. In fact, a large number of studies have explored these possible relationships. We will consider the conclusions of these studies.

Satisfaction and Withdrawal from the Workplace

Managers commonly believe that unhappy workers are less likely to come to work than happy workers. Since absenteeism is costly to an organization, it would seem logical that one way of reducing absence would be to increase job satisfaction. There is also the general belief among managers that turnover is the result of job dissatisfaction. Support of these beliefs comes from Brayfield and Crockett (1955), Herzberg et al. (1957), and Vroom (1964). They all conducted reviews of studies dealing with the satisfaction-withdrawal (absence and turnover) relationship and concluded that the two variables were substantially related; that is, unhappy workers were more likely to leave or stay away from the job.

Recently, these time-honored beliefs have been called into question. Several recent reviews have come to quite different conclusions. In the first place, they have questioned the assumption that quitting and absenteeism are similar. In addition, they have been critical of the types of absenteeism studies that are conducted. Finally, they are skeptical of the role of satisfaction in either absenteeism or turnover. We will review these conclusions in some detail.

In 1973, Porter and Steers suggested that absenteeism and turnover should not be thought of as similar responses. It is commonly believed that if a worker is dissatisfied with his job but cannot find another one easily, he is more likely to be absent than quit. Porter and Steers disagree with this assumption. They felt that absenteeism was much more "spontaneous," whereas the decision to quit, owing to its economic implications, was a much more carefully considered decision. Their review did point to a relationship between satisfaction and turnover, but they were much more cautious about suggesting a satisfaction-absence relationship. They did, however, accept the possibility that under certain extreme conditions absenteeism might function as a short-term substitute for quitting.

Absenteeism. Nicholson, Brown, and Chadwick-Jones (1976) reviewed 29 studies of the satisfaction-absenteeism relationship and concluded that most of the results that supported the relationship were artifactual and were due to either a flawed experimental design or an inappropriate analysis. They conducted their own study of absenteeism in a sample of 1,200 workers from 16 different organizations and concluded that there was no relationship between job satisfaction and absence rate. They then analyzed the absence data from a different perspective, attempting to explain the absence rate on the basis of demographic characteristics such as age and sex. They found that older workers had fewer absences; also, the finding was stronger for men than for women in their sample. Nicholson et al. suggested that this might be due to a greater "need for regularity" in older workers. In addition, older workers are more likely to have increased levels of economic responsibility for family members, which would seem to require steady attendance. Since the Nicholson et al. study was cross-sectional rather than longitudinal, we cannot be sure that individual workers actually *become* more responsible with respect to attendance as they get older; the differences may be due to the fact that the older workers and the younger workers in the sample came from different generations with different values and expectations. Nevertheless, the research of Nicholson and his colleagues is important because it seriously damages the assumed satisfaction-absence relationship.

Steers and Rhodes (1978), after reviewing 104 empirical studies of the satisfaction-absence relationship, proposed a process model for helping to understand the relationship. This model appears in Figure 11–13.

In a recent treatment of the social psychology of absenteeism, Chadwick-Jones, Nicholson, and Brown (1982) completely dismiss the traditional view of absenteeism as an individual phenomenon influenced by the particular

FIGURE 11–13 Major Influences on Employee Attendance

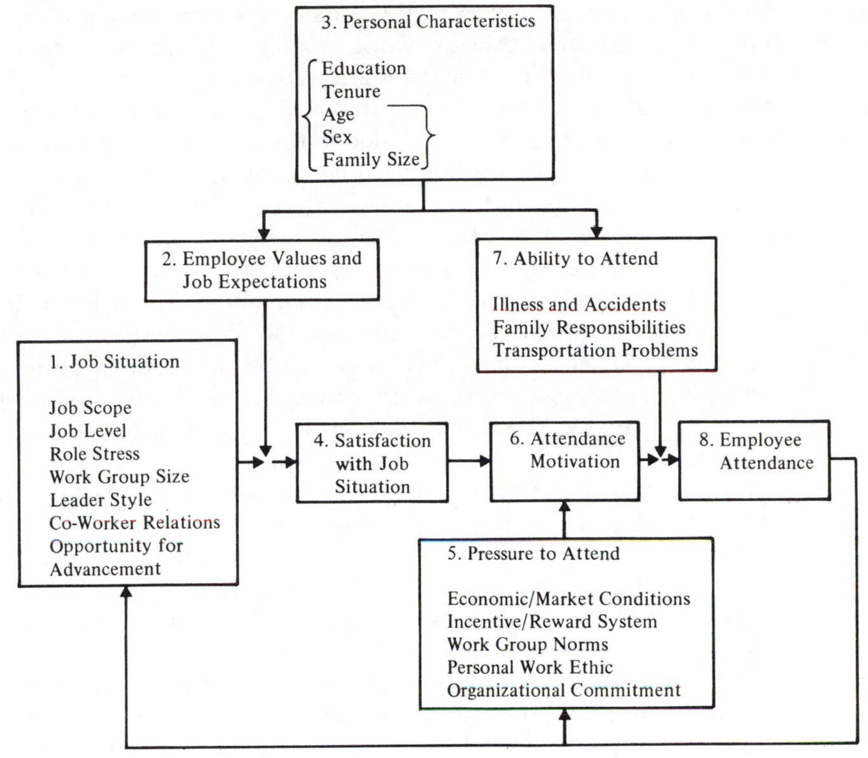

SOURCE: From "Major Influences on Employee Attendance: A Process Model" by R. M. Steers and S. R. Rhodes, 1978, *Journal of Applied Psychology, 63,* p. 393. Copyright 1978 by the American Psychological Association. Reprinted by permission of the author.

worker's opportunity or satisfaction or motivation to attend (as illustrated by the Steers and Rhodes model). Instead, they suggest that absenteeism is a social phenomenon that depends on things other than individual motivations and abilities. Chadwick-Jones et al. propose a social exchange theory of absenteeism in which absence rates and patterns depend on group norms and expectations. This is a form of social exchange between the individual and the group. Further, they assume that there is an exchange relationship between employer and employee and that absence behavior is influenced by that relationship as well. From this perspective, absence rates have less to do with satisfaction than with learning something about the "acceptable" levels of absence from the perspective of the work group and the organization and then applying what was learned. The social exchange approach considers stable individual differences or motivations as trivial contributors to absenteeism.

Another problem with the work motivation–job satisfaction approach to absence is that it ignores the positive valence of nonwork activities and goals. I have a friend who likes to dance to the music of a particular group. He drives a bus and is required to begin work at 6:00 A.M. When his favorite group is in town, he dances most of the night and skips work the next day. The fact that he missed work has nothing to do with his relative satisfaction with work. It has a lot to do with his satisfaction with music. But even with his love for this dance music, he knows how many days he can take off without getting into trouble, and he does not exceed that number. His supervisor knows he isn't sick. Nevertheless, the supervisor doesn't call to check on my friend, nor does the supervisor demand a doctor's certificate attesting to the illness. The supervisor simply expects that my friend will not brag about what he does or make the company look foolish. Further, the supervisor expects that when my friend comes to work (which is almost always) he will do a "good" job. This type relationship characterizes many supervisor-subordinate pairs. It is, as Chadwick-Jones et al. suggest, a form of social exchange.

Youngblood (1984) suggests an interesting mechanism for dealing with the joint effect on absence of negative influences on the job and positive influences off the job. He proposes that the *initiation* of an absence is more likely to be the result of a weak attachment to the work role (i.e., low satisfaction and limited job responsibilities or scope) but that the *duration* of the absence may be more closely associated with positive aspects of the nonwork activities that the individual engages in while absent. Experience and empirical data seem to agree that the relationship between satisfaction and absence is indirect, complex, and tenuous, at best. There is no reason to think that improving satisfaction will substantially reduce absenteeism frequency or, equally important, absence duration.

Turnover. Mobley, Horner, and Hollingsworth (1978) have pursued the issue of turnover along parallel lines. They suggested that dissatisfaction was not the only, or even the most important, variable contributing to turnover. They proposed a model of the turnover process, which I have presented in Figure 11–14. As you can see, once again, job satisfaction is several steps removed from the actual process of quitting. They tested the model in a hospital setting. They collected questionnaire data from 203 hospital employees on all the variables in the model. They then examined the turnover data 47 weeks later to see who had quit and who had stayed. The results were encouraging for their model. They found that job satisfaction was most closely related to thoughts of quitting and intentions to search for another job; further, they found that the intention to quit was significantly related to actually quitting. Mobley et al. seem to be describing a series of stages that an individual goes through. Job satisfaction seems to play a rather important role early in the process, but this role becomes less important as the individual progresses through the stages. Once again, this is pure conjecture, since we

FIGURE 11–14 A Simplified Representation of Intermediate Linkages in the Employee Withdrawal Decision Process

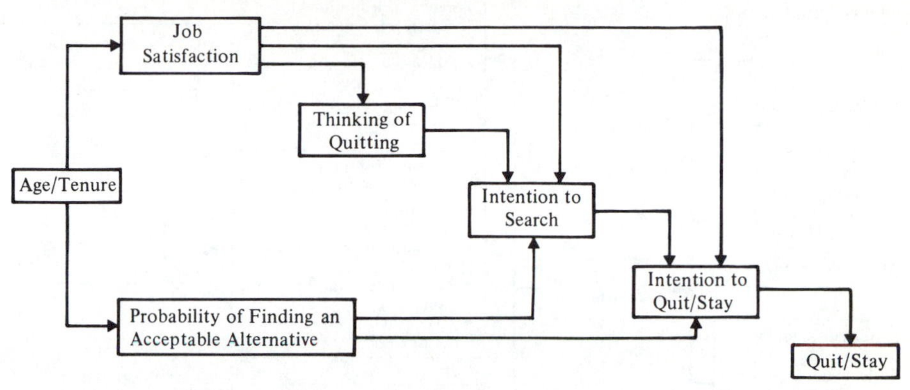

SOURCE: From "An Evaluation of Precursors of Hospital Employee Turnover," by W. H. Mobley, S. O. Horner, and A. T. Hollingsworth, 1978, *Journal of Applied Psychology*, 63, p. 410. Copyright 1978 by the American Psychological Association. Reprinted by permission of the author.

have not examined the individual at each of the stages but have tried to "reconstruct" what might have occurred through correlational analyses. Nevertheless, this model fits nicely with the earlier conclusion of Porter and Steers that turnover is a less spontaneous process than absenteeism.

The decision to quit is a substantial one. It represents an upheaval in one's life, a rupturing of many supportive social bonds, and the apprehension of learning the "rules" of a completely new organization. As a result, the decision is seldom made casually. The picture of a worker swaggering up to a supervisor and saying, "Take this job and shove it" is appealing but uncommon. Most of us have put up with distasteful and unpleasant aspects of various jobs for long periods of time with only an infrequent and casual thought of quitting. Students must often experience the same anguish by sitting in a boring and trivial course for a semester. A part of the student wants to drop the course, but another part of that same student knows that it will be necessary to find a substitute course, make up work missed already in that substitute course, trot around to a dozen offices getting a drop-add slip signed, and eventually schedule the course they don't like again.

Finally, with respect to turnover, a major controlling factor is the extensiveness of unemployment generally as well as in the field of the particular individual. The more difficult it is to get a job, the less likely it is to quit the one you have, regardless of your level of satisfaction. Carsten and Spector (1987) confirm that link. In a meta-analysis of 47 studies of turnover conducted between 1947 and 1984, they discovered that the relationship between satisfaction and turnover when unemployment was high was minimal (e.g., −.18) but that the relationship became stronger as the unemployment rate

FIGURE 11–15 Heuristic Model of Affect-Intention-Withdrawal Behavior

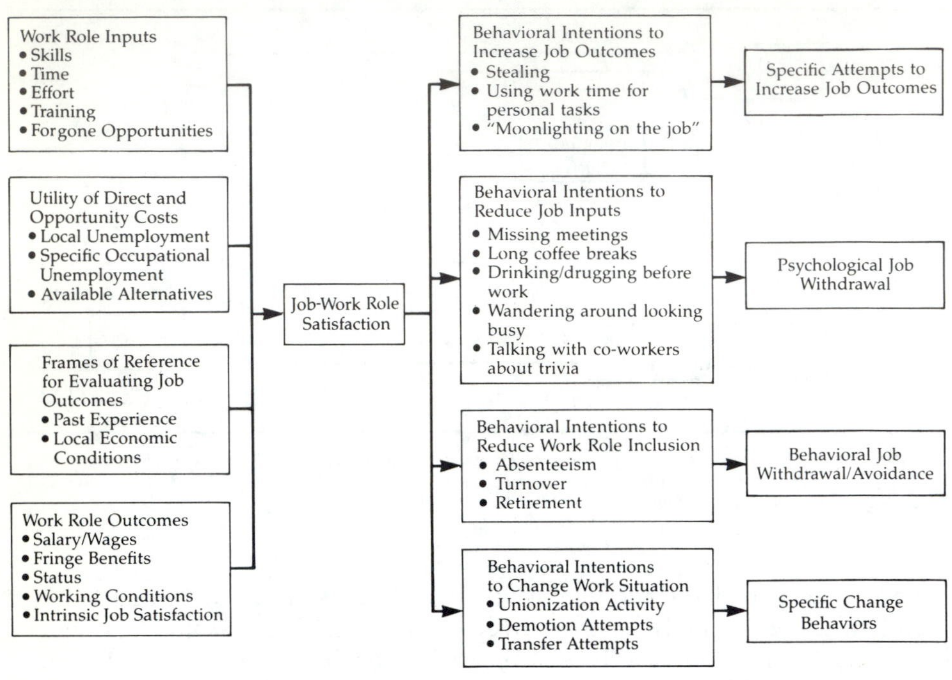

SOURCE: From "Alternative Opportunities and Withdrawal Decisions" by C. L. Hulin, M. Roznowski, and D. Hachiya, 1985, *Psychological Bulletin, 97*, p. 246.

decreased (e.g., −.52). Keep in mind, however, that the relationship between satisfaction and turnover is only modest under the most conducive of circumstances to quit (i.e., low unemployment). Only 27 percent of the variance (i.e., $.52^2$) can be accounted for. This means that quitting is only one of many responses that might be made even when the opportunity to quit is available. Hulin, Roznowski, and Hachiya (1985) provide an excellent model describing the multiple influences on decisions to remain or leave a job as well as the multiple mechanisms other than quitting that are available for coping with dissatisfaction. The model is presented in Figure 11–15.

Turnover as a Communicable Disease. One recent study is interesting from an "epidemiological" perspective. It suggests that turnover is something that is infectious. Krackhardt and Porter (1986) studied the quitting behavior of adolescent workers in the fast-food industry. They discovered that these teenage workers were more likely to quit if they saw a peer quit. The implication was that if others are quitting, something must be wrong with this job. My daughters report to me that "anyone who is anyone" in the high school has quit McDonald's. The implication in their description is that quitting

McDonald's is the "thing to do." At a more basic psychological level, the phenomenon might be explained with a social modeling mechanism. Krackhardt and Porter come to the conclusion that it might be better for an employer to concentrate on limiting the spread of the infection by "treating" subgroups of workers than to introduce broad organizational programs intended to increase the satisfaction of all workers. There is good reason to believe that adults are not quite so prone to the "me, too" responses of younger workers, but there is some reason to examine whether there are some of the same epidemiological influences (although less intense) in other employment settings.

Advantages of Turnover. Some recent research confirms what should be obvious about turnover. It is not always bad. Hollenbeck and Williams (1986) distinguish between functional and nonfunctional turnover. They classify functional turnover as the departure of employees who were not making a contribution to the organization. They suggest that this type of turnover can be good. In fact, they discovered that 53 percent of the turnover among a group of 112 department store sales clerks was functional. Further, they estimated that replacing these below-average individuals with average performers would lead to an increase in sales of $112,000 per person per year at a cost of $2,500 per person.

Job Satisfaction and Performance

From the earliest days of industrial psychology, the relationship between satisfaction and performance represented a kind of "holy grail." The Hawthorne studies and the subsequent human-relations movement sanctified the search for the relationship. Unfortunately, the search has been a discouraging one. Brayfield and Crockett (1955) concluded that "no appreciable relationship" existed. Vroom (1964) came to a similar conclusion. A decade later, Locke (1976) conducted an extensive review of the satisfaction literature and concluded that "job satisfaction has no direct effect on productivity" (p. 1334). Finally, a recent meta-analysis by Iaffoldino and Muchinsky (1985) of 74 studies and 213 correlations examining the satisfaction-performance relationship came to the same conclusion. The average correlation was +.14—a value bordering on the trivial.

There is an important difference between the early conceptions of the satisfaction-performance relationship and some more recent considerations of the issue. Historically, researchers attempted to show that satisfaction *caused* productivity. It has been clearly demonstrated that this relationship does not hold. More recently, the opposite relationship has been suggested; that is, successful performance causes satisfaction (Locke, 1970; Porter & Lawler, 1968). A good deal of Locke's research in goal setting and goal accomplishment, as well as the recent research and theory of Bandura, seems to support this hypothesis.

The major problem with most studies of the satisfaction-performance relationship is that it is impossible to control other variables that might be influencing one or both of the variables in question. For example, Mirvis and Lawler (1977) have used cost-accounting procedures to show that a modest increase in job satisfaction in a midwestern bank would result in a savings of $17,664 to the organization. They came to this conclusion after examining correlations between various satisfaction measures and employee behaviors (absenteeism, turnover, and productivity). Unfortunately, a significant correlation between satisfaction and behavior does not allow one to conclude that the satisfaction caused the performance. As suggested by Locke, the reverse might have been true—performance might have caused satisfaction. If this were the case, instead of spending time and money on improving the attitudes of employees, it might be better to work directly on performance aids and expanded training programs to increase profits and decrease costs and think of improved job attitudes as a "fringe benefit" of increased productivity.

In 1971, Cherrington, Reitz, and Scott conducted a laboratory experiment that illustrated the possibly fickle nature of the satisfaction-performance relationship. The subjects were 90 college students and the job was scoring tests. A subgroup of these subjects was appropriately rewarded (i.e., good performers received rewards and poor performers received no rewards). Another subgroup was inappropriately rewarded (i.e., good performers were not rewarded and poor performers were). All subjects were asked to complete a satisfaction questionnaire as well. The results are interesting and are presented in Table 11–5. As you can see, the two conditions produced quite different performance-satisfaction relationships. When performance was appropriately rewarded, the satisfaction-performance relationship was positive; when performance was inappropriately rewarded, the relationship was negative. Across the entire group of subjects (some rewarded appropriately and others inappropriately), the relationship was zero. These data point out again the indirect role of satisfaction in many relationships. In this case, the reward structure mediated the relationship between satisfaction and performance. Considering the experimental design, it would be difficult to conclude that satisfaction *caused* performance or that performance *caused* satisfaction. Both variables were influenced by a third process—reward administration. Theoretically and empirically, there is no reason to accept the notion that only satisfied workers are productive or that productivity breeds happiness. The relationship is much more complex and indirect than that.

WORK AND LIFE

It is natural to question the contribution of work to life in general. This is a broad but important issue that has been overshadowed by research on particular scales or demographic differences in satisfaction levels. In this section, we will consider this broader question.

Some things are obvious; jobs provide economic stability, which allows

TABLE 11–5 Correlations between Performance during Second Hour and Satisfaction at End of Second Hour

Satisfaction Indexes	*All Ss*[a]	*Appropriately Reinforced Ss*[b]	*Inappropriately Reinforced Ss*[b]
General affective tone	−.03	.55‡	−.51‡
General arousal	.02	.42†	−.26
Personal competence	.13	.48†	−.16
General satisfaction with pay	.03	.67‡	−.56‡
Equity of pay	−.09	.45†	−.51‡
Adequacy of pay	−.03	.59‡	−.57‡
Attractiveness of fellow workers	.20	.44†	.04
Attractiveness of task	−.06	.32*	−.16

[a] $n = 90$.
[b] $n = 42$.
* $p < .05$.
† $p < .01$.
‡ $p < .001$.

SOURCE: From "Effect of Contingent and Noncontingent Reward on the Relationship between Satisfaction and Task Performance by D. J. Cherrington, H. J. Reitz, and W. E. Scott, 1971, *Journal of Applied Psychology*, 53, p. 535.

for nonwork enjoyment and long-range planning unrelated to occupational goals. A less obvious question has to do with whether the very act of working adds to or detracts from the life experience of an individual or members of that individual's family. As an example, Staines, Pottick, and Fudge (1986) discovered that husbands of working wives (i.e., wives who worked more than 20 hours per week outside the home) were less satisfied with their own work (*in spite of* increased family income) than husbands whose wives did not work outside the home. As another example, recall the study by Barling and Rosenbaum (1986) suggesting a relationship between dissatisfaction and wife abuse, or consider the sufferings of the "workaholic" (Oates, 1971). With respect to workaholism, the point is made that work can easily get out of hand, occupying inordinate amounts of time, often to the detriment of those around such individuals and eventually even to the individuals themselves. And yet organizations are constantly trying to "involve" their members, to get them to accept organizational goals as individual ones—in short, to derive life satisfaction from job satisfaction. Once again, we have met the enemy and we are them.

On the other hand, there are many studies that demonstrate a relationship between positive mental health and job satisfaction, the implication being that job satisfaction *induces* mental well-being (Gechman & Wiener, 1975; Warr, 1987). Thus, the question remains, Does job satisfaction contribute to or detract from the quality of life? Recently, London, Crandall, and Seals (1977) analyzed the responses of a sample of 1,297 individuals from various backgrounds and with various demographic characteristics. Their results were surprising. The degree to which an individual was satisfied with a job seemed to have very little impact on general life satisfaction. In addition, for disadvantaged respondents, job satisfaction was *completely unrelated* to life satisfaction. Although these results must be viewed with caution, they do suggest that work is less important than we might have suspected once the individual is outside the work setting. Because we spend so much time at work, it is natural to assume that it has a major impact on our emotional well-being. This does not seem to be true. It may be that work is viewed more as a necessity by many workers, much like eating and sleeping. Often, if you ask someone, "How's work?" the response will be, "Work is work!" For some people, it is unlikely that work would have a major impact on our lives, under normal circumstances. I once conducted a study of absenteeism of underground coal miners. In the course of a conversation with a group of young miners, the question was asked, "Why do you come to work four days a week when your contract calls for five?" One of the miners immediately answered, "Because I can't afford to come to work only three days a week." During the same conversation, another miner was asked, "Do you like your work?" and he answered, "Compared to what?" Such conversations give me the uneasy feeling that job satisfaction may be viewed differently by industrial psychologists and managers than by workers.

In the last few years, the work-life relationship has been studied extensively, and the picture that is emerging is a complicated one. It has often been assumed that job satisfaction contributes to or at least precedes life satisfaction. Schmitt and Mellon (1980) found evidence that suggested the opposite relationship: life satisfaction leads to job satisfaction. On the other hand, Orpen (1978) found the reverse to be true: satisfaction with work factors had a greater impact on nonwork satisfaction. In an excellent review of the work-nonwork relationship, Kabanoff (1980) suggests that it is necessary to take a much broader view of satisfaction. He proposes that understanding of the complex work-nonwork relationship will come from identifying patterns of activity and satisfaction based on work, leisure, and family pursuits. The workaholic is a perfect example of this interrelationship. In a study of the marital satisfaction of the workaholic, J. R. Burke, Weir, and DuWors (1979) found that in addition to dissatisfying home and family lives, the wives of male workaholics had fewer friends, fewer social contacts with those friends, and a deficient social network from which to draw emotional support. Since these data are correlational, there is no way of telling whether the behavior of the workaholic was *responsible* for or *the result of* the dissatisfactions and behavior of the wives. For the sake of discussion, it really doesn't matter. One would still conclude that work and nonwork are substantially related. Keep in mind, however, the results of the studies cited earlier on dispositional characteristics of job satisfaction. It is possible that both job satisfaction and life satisfaction are the result of traitlike attributes (or as Arvey et al. have suggested, genetic predispositions).

Korman (1980) has considered the issue of work and nonwork from a different perspective. He discovered that many middle-aged executives were experiencing professional success and personal failure. By most objective standards, the individuals in question had "made it" in their professions. They had moved rapidly up the ladder of success and were well paid and widely respected and had apparently unlimited autonomy with respect to their lives. Many of these people reported feelings of intense depression. When asked how they would sum up their overall feelings regarding their career and life in general, they would occasionally respond, "I would like to walk in front of a train"—a statement in stark contrast to the apparent reality of their success. Korman attributes this depression to the fact that many individuals are ill-prepared for success. In particular, they are not aware of the negative consequences of success. In the left-hand column of Figure 11–16, you will find many of the expectations of those who have not yet achieved success. These individuals believe that success will help them achieve many of the goals implied in this list. Contrast these expectations with reality as portrayed in the right-hand column. As you can see, contradictions abound. For present purposes, concentrate on some of the work-nonwork relationships. The individual believes that professional success will provide more time for family and friends. Actually, success leaves less time, not more. The person believes that success will act as an immunization against age and disease. In fact, success offers no protection and may even lead to the deterioration of health and well-being, as is the case with many highly stressed individuals. Finally, the individual believes that success will result in the maximum amount of self-control and self-direction. In fact, the more successful the individual, the more she sees herself as controlled by others. The entrepreneur who builds a technical business in her garage to a multimillion dollar operation with 100 employees falls asleep each night worrying about making the payroll next month. She begins to feel that she is working for her employees rather than the other way around. The theme of Korman's analysis is the effect of unrealistic expectations on happiness and behavior. It seems likely that work is a major component in a broader "life-plan" as Kabanoff suggests.

UNEMPLOYMENT AND JOB SATISFACTION

Most studies of the role of work in life satisfaction deal with a select group of subjects: those who are employed. But as you saw in the opening vignette describing the reaction of a pan scrubber to the prospect of unemployment, we may be missing something important if we concentrate only on the employed. In the past decade, levels of unemployment have reached near-record proportions. The decline of basic industries, the dramatic gains

FIGURE 11–16 Outcomes of Success

Expected (positive) Outcomes of Career Success and Effective Work Performance	*Unexpected Outcomes of Career Success and Effective Work Performance*
1. Societal approbation for having achieved societal value	1. Realization that all positions involve routine and repetitive tasks
2. Freedom from the drudgery of jobs calling for common everyday routine, repetitive tasks	2. Decreasing social value of work success
3. Higher income and the resulting ability to purchase an ever-increasing variety of consumer goods	3. Increasing tax rates, inflation, and aspiration levels
4. Greater ability to control one's life in both a career and noncareer sense	4. Transitory sensory quality of consumer satisfaction and goods and their likelihood of being overpromised by TV and other media
5. Greater ability to control the task activity of others and to assert power over others in general	5. Realization that career success has not protected self from upsets of midlife years
6. A more viable, cohesive family life because of greater income and presence of a more desirable role model as the successful individual	6. Continued presence of legal restrictions, government control, and union constraints
7. Relative freedom from the cares and woes of middle- and old-age (due to greater income, greater status, and the more viable family that this has generated)	7. Continued societal and personal demand for success
8. In addition, to the benefit of the organization, it has also been assumed that the values derived by individuals have also generated an increased work commitment and intent	8. Decline of nuclear familial relationships because of work commitment and geographic mobility
	9. Decline of parental and extended family relationships because of changes in social status and geographic mobility
	10. Lack of affiliative relationships with other individuals in the work setting
	11. Decline of ability to establish affiliative relationships with others
	12. Inability to reconcile needs of organizational superiors with those of subordinates
	13. Inability to meet sufficiently needs relevant to other dimensions of human experience (e.g., humanistic interests, religious activities, affiliative desires)

SOURCE: From *Career Success and Work Performance,* by A. Korman, 1980, paper presented at meetings of the American Psychological Association, Montreal, Canada.

of high-technology manufacturing, and the energy crisis were all partially responsible for this circumstance. Many people who found themselves out of work had never anticipated such an event. These were not the "hard-core unemployed" of the 1960s or the disenfranchised counterculture youth of the early 1970s. These people were the core of the traditional working class. As a result of the personal devastation and the political disenchantment that resulted from rising unemployment, many psychologists have begun to consider the effect of unemployment on physical and psychological well-being. This is instructive for the purposes of this chapter since it provides evidence about the meaning that work holds for individuals.

Warr and his colleagues have studied the problem of unemployment in the United Kingdom extensively. In a review of this work (Warr, 1983, 1987), certain conclusions have been reached about the effect of unemployment. Briefly, some of these conclusions are:

1. The psychological health of the unemployed is poorer than that of employed individuals.
2. This poorer health is the result of (not the *cause* of) unemployment since a return to paid employment is commonly followed by an improvement in psychological health.
3. Losing one's job often results in depression, insomnia, irritability, lack of confidence, listlessness, inability to concentrate, and general anxiety.
4. In a small percentage of cases (about 8 percent), people report that unemployment *improved* mental health.

In considering *why* unemployment results in poor psychological well-being, Warr suggests the following mechanisms. Unemployment reduces both income level and daily variety in experience. There are also fewer goals to guide day-to-day activities. There is also a considerably reduced opportunity to make decisions. There is little to decide about. When decisions are made, they are usually small and often repetitive—for instance, when to get up, when to shop, when to look for a job. There are fewer opportunities to develop and practice valued skills. Another obvious effect is the substantial increase in threat that results from diminished income. From Maslow's perspective, security needs become critically important. From Bandura's perspective, the assault on beliefs of self-efficacy are massive. Finally, the individual's social relations are changed considerably. The absolute number of contacts is reduced, and the person's status among friends, relatives, and neighbors is also dramatically altered. Jahoda (1981) has taken a similar view of the role of employment in psychological well-being. She describes the latent effects of employment as follows:

> First, employment imposes a time structure on the waking day; second, employment implies regularly shared experiences and contacts with people outside the nuclear family; third, employment links individuals to goals and purposes

FIGURE 11–17 Characteristics of Psychologically 'Good' and Psychologically 'Bad' Unemployment

	'Good' Unemployment Has	*'Bad' Unemployment Has*
1. Money	More	Less
2. Variety	More	Less
3. Goals, traction	More	Less
4. Decision latitude	More	Less
5. Skill use/development	More	Less
6. Psychological threat	Less	More
7. Security	More	Less
8. Interpersonal contact	More	Less
9. Valued social position	More	Less

SOURCE: From "Work, Jobs and Unemployment" by P. B. Warr, 1983, *Bulletin of the British Psychological Society, 36*, p. 306.

> that transcend their own; fourth, employment defines aspects of personal status and identity; and finally, employment enforces activity. (p. 188)

As you can see, Jahoda sees work as a central aspect of behavior and adjustment. She notes that even Freud (1930) saw work as "a person's strongest tie to reality." This tie to reality prevents us from being controlled by fantasy and emotion. This is heavy stuff. It is far removed from questionnaires and rating scales and satisfaction with the color of the locker room walls. It deals with the basic components of the human condition.

Warr (1983) comes to a fascinating conclusion after reviewing the research on unemployment. He suggests that there is "good" and "bad" unemployment just as there are "good" and "bad" jobs. The differences between good and bad unemployment are illustrated in Figure 11–17. He suggests that psychologists should be actively involved in eliminating the bad aspects of unemployment. A broader conclusion might be drawn: for most people, the *fact* of employment is critical but widely unrecognized. The importance and meaning of work to individuals can be seen clearly when work is denied.

There is an interesting sidelight to this line of discussion. Warr and Parry (1982) studied the effect of paid employment on depression in various groups of women. They discovered that paid employment of *any* kind can be particularly beneficial to mothers in working-class homes. They propose that this is because the daily lives of working-class women are more likely to be "psychologically impoverished" than their middle-class or nonmother counterparts. This places the nature of work in a very different light. It casts it in a therapeutic light (a phenomenon that occupational psychologists have recognized for a long time!). It further suggests that instead of simply concentrating on how we might eliminate dissatisfaction with aspects of work, societal benefits might accrue from considering how work can be used to improve the general psychological and physical well-being of members of that society. This is a nontraditional question that may well lead to a substantial improvement in our understanding of job satisfaction. It is also ironic to consider the results of the Warr and Parry study in contrast to the findings of Staines et al. (1986). Remember that the latter researchers discovered that if a wife worked outside the home for more than 20 hours per week, the husband was less satisfied with his work. This would seem to represent a dilemma. The answer, of course, is that the family is a system, and one must be concerned with balancing the entire system, not just a piece of it. Most couples have realized that adjustments are necessary by both partners for a successful relationship. The role of work and nonwork happiness is part of this adjustment process.

Warr and Jahoda agree that now is the time for industrial and organizational psychologists to make a substantial contribution to the quality of life. They feel that continued and perhaps increasing world unemployment is inevitable, both citing technological advances as a major contributing factor. As a result, they suggest that psychologists should now be heavily involved in planning for that future. This will involve novel work schedules (e.g., alternating weeks of work), satisfying circumstances of unemployment (e.g., opportunities for decision making and varied personal contacts), and national programs of employment as opposed to unemployment insurance or welfare payments. In a recent study by Brenner and Bartell (1983), it was suggested that there is a critical period that occurs shortly after unemployment begins. What happens during this period has a major influence on the extent to which unemployment will be debilitating. As a result, they suggest that early intervention and preparation for unemployment is something that can and should be done by psychologists.

The time is right to move from the narrower issue of job satisfaction to the broader issue of the meaning of work, and I/O psychologists are well suited to effect that shift.

JOB SATISFACTION FROM AN INTERNATIONAL PERSPECTIVE

Although it may not be obvious to you, job satisfaction research, theory, and practice has a national character to it. European psychologists dominated the early discussions (1900–1920) of job satisfaction. Levenstein in Germany had conducted satisfaction interviews with thousands of German workers prior to 1911. Otto Lippmann had written extensively on job satisfaction and scientific management by 1920. As mentioned earlier, Henri DeMan (1929) had anticipated Herzberg's two-factor theory by almost 30 years. Non–U.S. I/O psychologists are often amused (and more often annoyed) by the lack of appreciation by their U.S. colleagues for alternate sociopolitical systems (i.e., systems other than capitalism) in considering issues of satisfaction and motivation.

Several years ago, Nord (1977) illustrated the capitalist flavor of U.S. job satisfaction research. For example, there is little concern or discussion of the possibilities of giving real power to lower-level workers. As I mentioned earlier, the human-relations movement had no intention of giving workers control of the workplace; it was not democratization. Similarly,the discussion of satisfaction usually occurs in the context of a broader consideration of worker productivity. In discussions with eastern European psychologists and workers, I have seen similar differences between the "U.S." approach and the approach adopted by others. In Yugoslavia and Romania, for example, a major issue is the extent to which workers feel committed to the workplace rather than the family farm. Another issue relates to the political attitudes of workers and their effects on work behavior. In contrast to the United States, there is little or no discussion concerning work or task redesign. The major characteristic of equipment and design decisions is cost rather than its potential for "humanizing" work. In many of these countries, rewards are controlled by the work group and collective decisions are made about economic rewards and punishments for individual workers. Managers are often paid the same as (or less than) blue-collar workers. Gorbachev's new liberalization policies are having substantial effects on the attitudes and behavior of industrial workers in Warsaw Pact nations. It seems clear that studies of job satisfaction in these cultures would provide data and suggest inferences that are very different from the ones to which U.S. I/O psychologists are accustomed. There is much to be learned from contacts with workers and psychologists in other cultures.

CENTRAL POINTS FOR STUDY

1. The Hawthorne studies represented a revolution in I/O psychology and the beginning of serious interest in worker satisfaction.
2. The two-factor theory of satisfaction proposed different mechanisms for satisfaction and dissatisfaction.
3. Recent approaches to satisfaction emphasize discrepancies of desired versus obtained rewards.
4. There seem to be few stable demographic differences of any magnitude in terms of reported levels of satisfaction.
5. There are several different ways of measuring job satisfaction.
6. An important question for I/O psychology is what role work plays in the broader perspective of life satisfaction and well-being.

CHAPTER 12

The Supervisor as Leader

The previous chapters on work motivation and job satisfaction considered the relationship between the individual worker and the physical and psychological environment. There are, however, at least two major intervening influences to take into account before we can understand work behavior: the supervisor and the organization. This chapter will deal with the supervisor in the role of "leader" and consequently will consider many of the problems related to the study of leadership. First, a very general perspective of previous leadership research will be presented. Then, some organizational influences that interact with leader behavior will be introduced. Finally, the current status of selected models of leadership will be considered.

SOME WARNINGS

It is easy to become confused in reading the leadership literature. Over the years, the term *leadership* has been used to represent several different behaviors. It has not always been clear which behavior is being considered in a particular theory or study. In addition, it is tempting to take the "here and now" perspective in considering the behavior of a given leader and ignore the history that the leader brings to the position or the extent to which the situation influences leader characteristics. In other words, it is easy to forget both the past and the future of the leader. These two issues—the definition of leadership and the larger context of leader behavior—need to be considered before moving on to specific issues and theories of leadership.

Leader Effectiveness versus Leader Emergence

The effectiveness-emergence distinction has been a source of confusion for a number of years. As a dependent variable, leader emergence is quite different from leader effectiveness. In the former case, we are considering the relationship between the behavior or characteristics of an individual (or both) and the probability that she will emerge as a leader (either formal or informal) in a demand situation of some kind. In the latter case, that of leader effectiveness, we are considering the relationship between the behavior or characteristics of an individual (or both) in a leadership position (either formal or informal) and some form of outcome that is valued by a group or organization.

In addition, both of these variables, emergence and effectiveness, may be affected differently by situational factors such as the nature of the group, stress, or the management philosophy of the organization. Crooked or incompetent political leaders are examples of ineffective leaders who emerge. Studies that have examined leader emergence often attempt to find characteristics or traits of individuals that are correlated with the probability that a person will emerge as a leader. In fact, many of these studies have successfully isolated leadership emergence variables (Lord, DeVader, & Alliger, 1986). On the other hand, studies of leader effectiveness seem to take a quite different approach. Instead of looking at traits of emerging leaders, they examine the *behavior* of leaders for clues to behavioral correlates of effectiveness. Traits have been much less successful in the prediction of leader effectiveness.

We have used a lot of terms in the preceding paragraph that should be defined before we continue. The first term, of course, would be *leader*. For the purposes of this chapter, Fiedler's (1967) definition is most suitable:

> a leader is *"the individual in the group given the task of directing and coordinating task-relevant group activities, or who, in the absence of a designated leader, carries the primary responsibility for performing these functions in the group"* (p. 8).

Some other definitions are necessary to distinguish among *attempted* leadership, *successful* leadership, and *effective* leadership. Bass (1960) has done a good job of separating these terms:

1. *Attempted leadership.* Person A accepts the goal of changing person B and, in fact, can be observed attempting to change person B.
2. *Successful leadership.* Person B changes his behavior as a function of person A's effort.
3. *Effective leadership.* As a function of person B's behavior change, person B will be more satisfied, will be better rewarded, or will have attained an important goal.

These will be important distinctions to keep in mind when looking at studies of leadership. The way in which leadership is defined (i.e., attempted, successful, or effective) should have systematic effects on the relationship between leadership behaviors and individual or organizational outcomes. For example, the relationship between group productivity and attempted leadership should be quite different from the relationship between group productivity and effective leadership.

The Historical Character of Leader Behavior

Much of the research on leadership has been concerned with the effects of leadership rather than the leadership process itself. As you will see, the result has been that we have learned a good deal about how to direct the

FIGURE 12–1

Billy Martin Fired Again*

John Poindexter Resigns

Gary Hart's Influence Diminished in Wake of Donna Rice Scandal

*On June 23, 1988, Billy Martin set a new personal and league record by being fired as manager for the fifth time by the New York Yankees. As a result of this accomplishment, he maintains his position in this figure, a position he has now held through four editions. In his honor, we may retire this figure number after he retires from baseball.

behavior of subordinates but not quite as much about the nature of leadership. Similarly, there has been a tendency to consider the various *parts* of leadership behavior patterns rather than the entire *process* of leadership (Hollander & Julian, 1969). The full leadership cycle might also include both emergence and acceptance of a leader. Still another aspect that may be included is the *decline* of a leader. We know something about how leaders are chosen or appointed; we know something about how leaders behave in varying situations; we know little or nothing about the conditions or behaviors leading to a decline or fall from power. Figure 12–1 reminds us of some recent examples of leadership decline. Parenthetically, there is one thing that I must point out about this figure. In the first, second, and third editions of this book (published in 1976, 1980, and 1985, respectively), the entry "BILLY MARTIN AXED . . . " appeared. In the first edition, he was fired by the Houston Astros; in the second edition, it was the New York Yankees; in the third edition, he had repeated his departure from the Yankees. Unfortunately, I am writing this chapter at the beginning of the season in 1988, and Billy Martin has not been fired yet this year. But if the copyediting takes longer than expected, I might be able to identify one of the most stable patterns of leader decline in the twentieth century by simply presenting the chronicle of Martin's fifth slide from grace. On the other hand, my friends from New York suggest that I may be looking at the wrong leader. I should be watching George Steinbrenner rather than Billy Martin. Regardless of which of the pair we watch, this type of consistency makes a good case for the trait approach to the study of behavior.

The fact that leaders rise and fall suggests that it might be useful to consider something like a "leadership life span" or leadership cycle that would include emergence, performance, and decline. Since so few studies and theories deal with leadership behavior from the historical perspective, it will be important for you to keep this perspective in mind. The description of leader behavior at any one point in time is a single, time-bounded sample of a much more complex pattern of behavior.

SUPERVISION VERSUS LEADERSHIP

The most obvious symbol of leadership in the industrial setting is the supervisor. Although the terms *leader* and *supervisor* are often used interchangeably, there is a clear difference. *Supervisor* is a job title. It implies that there are certain responsibilities for directing that are part of the job of the person who holds the title. The title specifies *what* must be done. Leadership, on the other hand, implies *how* these responsibilities will be met. As any supervisor will tell you, being called a supervisor does not immediately provide the holder of that title with the skills necessary for effective leadership.

Historically, many definitions of supervisory roles have actually represented suggestions for methods of leadership. In essence, these definitions have functioned as informal theories of leadership. It might be useful to take a look at the kinds of activities often included in the supervisory role before considering formal theories of leadership.

Descriptions of supervisory responsibilities vary from a one-dimensional description (e.g., the primary responsibility of a supervisor is the motivation of subordinates) to elaborate job descriptions including dozens of major and minor job duties. As an example of the former type, F. C. Mann (1965) suggests the following role for the supervisor.

> One of the basic problems of organizations, then, is how to reconcile, coordinate, or integrate member needs or goals with organizational requirements and objectives. This social-psychological aspect of the role of the supervisor in the complex organization is of key importance; it is here that the supervisor must deal with the motivational problem of relating man and system. (p. 71)

Some time ago, French and Raven (1959) proposed a different way of examining the leadership process. They suggested that one should examine the different types of power available to a leader and how that power is typically used. The kinds of power commonly available to a supervisor are as follows:

1. *Reward power.* The potential of a supervisor to mediate or dispense rewards to a subordinate is reward power. It should be clear from our discussion of work motivation that this is a demonstrable source of power for the supervisor. If rewards valuable to the subordinate can be controlled, the behavior of that subordinate can be influenced.
2. *Coercive power.* The potential of a supervisor to mediate or dispense punishments to a subordinate is coercive power. Historically, it was the

prerogative of the first-line supervisor or foreman to "hire and fire"; the power to "fire" is, of course, an implied threat and a form of coercive power.

3. *Legitimate power.* The *right* of a supervisor to influence a subordinate and the obligation of a subordinate to accept that influence constitute legitimate power. McGregor (1967) referred to this as the "right" to govern, or the "consent of the governed."
4. *Referent power.* The identification of the subordinate with the supervisor is referent power. In this case, the subordinate accepts the supervisor's goals as her own. McGregor refers to this form of power as the "power of example." He further points to this particular form of power as the best example of the nature of the leadership process. The worker perceives the supervisor achieving desired goals; the identification of the worker with the supervisor provides an attractive means for achieving those same desired goals; the worker will continue to identify with the supervisor as long as movement toward those desired goals is perceived. As soon as movement toward those goals stops, identification stops. McGregor uses this paradigm to highlight his belief that leadership is no more a property of the individual "than gravitation is a property of objects" (p. 145). A recent study serves to verify this type of power base. Weiss (1977) studied 130 supervisors and their immediate superiors. He found that the lower-level supervisors tended to imitate the leadership style of their superiors when they viewed their superior as being both competent and successful. Interestingly enough, the probability of supervisors imitating their superiors was *not* related to the number of rewards they received from their superiors. Perhaps the songs are right—love can't be bought!
5. *Expert power.* The knowledge or expertise that a supervisor has in a special area is expert power.

Yukl (1981) has considered these various sources of power and suggested the range of outcomes that might be expected as a result of using one or another of these power bases. This range of response can be seen in Table 12–1.

It has been popular and useful to view leadership in terms of sources of power. Recently, two of the categories have been combined to form a sixth base of power. Referent power and expert power have been combined to form *incremental power* or *incremental influence.* Incremental influence is considered to be that degree of control a leader has over subordinates that cannot be explained simply on the basis of prescribed power or reward-punishment power. In the past, it has been called *charisma* or *magnetism.* It is the power that the leader is able to accrue. An important characteristic of incremental influence is that it is the interaction of referent and expert power and considered as a *sixth power base, not just another name for one of the existing power bases.*

TABLE 12–1 Major Sources of Leader Influence over Subordinates and Likely Outcomes

Source of Leader Influence	*Type of Outcome*		
	Commitment	*Compliance*	*Resistance*
Referent power	Likely If request is believed to be important to leader	Possible If request is perceived to be unimportant to leader	Possible If request is for something that will bring harm to leader
Expert power	Likely If request is persuasive and subordinates share leader's task goals	Possible If request is persuasive but subordinates are apathetic about task goals	Possible If leader is arrogant and insulting, or if subordinates oppose task goals
Legitimate power	Possible If request is polite and very appropriate	Likely If request or order is seen as legitimate	Possible If arrogant demands are made or request does not appear proper
Reward power	Possible If used in a subtle, very personal way	Likely If used in a mechanical, impersonal way	Possible If used in a manipulative, arrogant way
Coercive power	Very unlikely	Possible If used in a helpful, nonpunitive way	Likely If used in a hostile or manipulative way

SOURCE: From "The Bases of Social Power" by J. R. P. French and B. H. Raven, in D. Cartwright (Ed.), *Studies in Social Power,* 1959, Ann Arbor: University of Michigan, Institute for Social Research.

A study by Student (1968) might serve to clarify the nature of incremental influence. The study was done in a large manufacturing organization in which 486 hourly employees described the forms of power exercised by their first-line supervisors. Student found that incremental influence was positively related to four of eight production measures, whereas referent power by itself was related to withdrawal measures (absenteeism, etc.), and expert power was related to accidents. Interestingly enough, legitimate power was *unrelated* to performance measures. The relationship between accidents and expert power makes sense, he suggests, because a good deal of variance in accidents is due to a breakdown in technical knowledge. Therefore, a supervisor who does not have the knowledge base (expertise) necessary to rely on as a source of power will also be less likely to provide the technical knowledge base necessary for the reduction of accidents.

The study by Student poses some interesting questions about the choice of a power base in applied settings. If we are to understand the nature of leadership completely, there are a few things that we will have to know about the use and abuse of power. For example, if a particular leader has more than one power base to work from in a given situation, which one is most appropriate? Do situational or personal characteristics (or both) modify the decision as to which power base to use? Kipnis and Cosentino (1969) conducted a study aimed at answering some of these questions. They studied the range of social power at the disposal of supervisors for the correction of subordinate behavior. They also investigated the personal and situational factors that could possibly influence the use of those powers. They gathered data from five different manufacturing companies. The participants in the study were 131 blue-collar, hourly paid supervisors. The supervisors were asked to describe a supervision problem they had recently encountered. They were also asked to describe the corrective action they took. The problems fell into one of four categories:

1. *Attitude.* The subordinate displayed lack of interest.
2. *Discipline.* The subordinate disobeyed a company rule.
3. *Work.* The subordinate failed to maintain minimum standards.
4. *Appearance.* The subordinate was inappropriately dressed.

The corrective actions used by the supervisors to deal with these problems fell into one of eight categories:

1. *Verbal.* Diagnostic or corrective talk.
2. *Increased supervision.* Extra instruction, inspection, and so on.
3. *Situational change.* Reassignment, transfer, and so on.
4. *Penalty.* Reprimand, extra work, reduced privileges.
5. *Refer.* Referred to superior or personnel office.
6. *Written warning.*
7. *Termination.*
8. *Example.* Supervisor acting as a model.

Kipnis and Cosentino found that diagnostic talks were used for problems of attitude or discipline, whereas increased supervision was used for problems of work. Complex problems were likely to be handled by a transfer. Less experienced supervisors were more likely to refer a problem to their superior or the personnel office. Finally, as the size of the work group increased, the use of the official written warnings also increased. The major importance of these findings is that the decision as to which form of power to exercise in the solution of a particular problem seemed to be as much a function of the situation and of the individual as a function of the particular problem. While the categories of power may be slightly better defined than those currently used by first-line supervisors, there are very few supervisors who do not have to make a decision relating to the way in which a subordinate will be "handled" (i.e., coddled or clobbered, persuaded or punished).

In a later study, Goodstadt and Kipnis (1970) suggest that supervisory self-confidence has an effect on the power choice for a problem solution. They found that less confident leaders depended more heavily on formally prescribed powers, whereas the more confident supervisors used both informal and formal power but more often attempted to persuade subordinates informally. Podsakoff (1982) has recently reviewed studies of how and when supervisors use rewards and punishments. His conclusions are both reassuring and disturbing, at the same time. The reassuring part is the fact that he found subordinate performance to have the greatest influence on the use of rewards and punishments. Good performers were rewarded; poor performers were punished. The disturbing conclusions have to do with individual differences of supervisors. Punishment was used more frequently by less experienced and less confident supervisors. Organizational factors also seem to play a role in dispensing rewards and punishments. Supervisors with larger work groups were more likely to use punishment as a means of directing subordinate behavior.

Interestingly enough, Rosen and Jerdee (1974) found that managers tend to respond more to the severity of the *consequences* of a rule violation than the violation itself. This, unfortunately, suggests to the employee that rules may be broken as long as the consequences are not disastrous. The unfortunate part of this principle is that workers have complete control over the act of violation but seldom have any control over the consequences of the violation. In a study in which the same hypothesis was tested, Mitchell and Wood (1980) found similar results. Punitive responses were more likely when the consequences of poor performance were serious. In addition, when the consequences were serious, leaders tended to blame the performer for these consequences rather than the situation.

It seems clear from the results presented above that supervisors will choose different methods for directing the efforts of subordinates. These choices seem to be influenced by things such as age, experience, and the consequences of poor performance. If supervisors choose among methods of supervision, it would stand to reason that some methods might be better than others. If that were the case, there would be some value in identifying the "best" method of supervision and training all supervisors in the use of that method. Historically, this has been the goal of many leadership theories—to identify those behaviors, styles, or characteristics of leaders that are associated with increased subordinate satisfaction, motivation, and performance, on the one hand, and decreased absenteeism, turnover, and accidents, on the other. The studies cited above are really pretheoretical. There are theories implied by the findings, but these theories are seldom stated directly. In the next section, we will consider some formal theories of leadership.

AN OVERVIEW OF LEADERSHIP RESEARCH

We often identify someone who is successful at something and ask that person to set forth a package of guidelines that will enable us to be as successful as they. We ask the 100-year-old man how he managed to stay alive so long. He will answer in one of two ways. He will either say, "You get to be ninety-nine and then you are very careful for one more year" or "I have been smoking five cigars and eating two pounds of turnips every day since my fourteenth birthday." We have a tendency to ask the same questions of "successful" leaders: What makes successful leaders? Unfortunately, we usually get answers. The following description of a successful leader is taken from a book written by Field Marshal Montgomery (1961) on the topic of leadership.

> The leader must have infectious optimism, and the determination to persevere in the face of difficulties. He must also radiate confidence, relying on moral and spiritual principles and resources to work out rightly even when he himself is not too certain of the material outcome. He must have a sound judgment in which others will have confidence, and a good knowledge of human nature. He must be able to see his problems truly and whole. Self-control is a vital component of his make-up. (p. 11)

It might have been just as useful had the field marshal described the successful leader as one who smokes five cigars and eats two pounds of turnips every day.

It should be obvious that Montgomery was implicitly accepting a trait theory of leadership. He was assuming that people possess certain enduring characteristics that guarantee effective leadership. Research following that trait tradition abounds. Both psychological and physical characteristics have been examined. A partial list of characteristics studied appears in Figure 12–2. Most of the research takes the same general form. The major hypothesis reads something like this: "Effective leaders will be *XXXXX*er than ineffective leaders." In the space filled with *X*s, you can fill in any of the characteristics appearing in Figure 12–2. In addition, the hypothesis is generally a linear one, although not always stated as such. This means that one can never have too much of *XXXX;* as *X* increases, leadership effectiveness increases. The more, the better.

Brown (1954) quotes Tredgold on the topic of leader characteristics: "The longer and more comprehensive the list of qualities, the more obvious it must be that their possession would be of no use as a junior leader in industry, for he would inevitably be in demand elsewhere as a Prime Minister, or maybe as an Archangel" (p. 219). Citing as examples Hitler, Napoleon, and Cromwell, Brown includes that insanity or injustice, per se, do not prevent an individual from being an effective leader "so long as he is insane in the appropriate direction."

Both logical and empirical investigations of leadership and leader effectiveness from the trait approach have been disappointing. Reviews of the literature by Stogdill (1948) and Mann (1959) have demonstrated little or no

FIGURE 12–2 Some Characteristics of Leaders That Have Been Studied

Adjustment	Height	Popularity
Age	Intelligence	Psychoticism
Altruism	Introversion	Responsibility
Ambition	Judgment	Scholarship
Authoritarianism	Kindness	Self-confidence
Compatibility	Lability	Sensitivity
Conservatism	Masculinity	Sex
Deference	Maturity	Sociability
Dominance	Motivation	Stature
Empathy	Neuroticism	Supportiveness
Esteem	Originality	Surgency
Extroversion	Perceptiveness	Verbal facility
Fear of failure	Persistence	Vocabulary usage
		Weight

relationship between personality factors and leadership effectiveness. More recent reviews have come to the same conclusion (Hollander & Julian, 1969).

Disenchantment with the trait approach gave rise to the *behavioral approach*. The essence of this approach is to determine what effective leaders *do*, rather than concentrating on their personal characteristics or traits. Extensive survey and observational studies are conducted to determine the activities of people in leadership positions. These activities are then systematically categorized. The resulting categories are subsequently used to form profiles or descriptions of leaders. The profiles or descriptions are then related to the judged effectiveness of the leaders as well as to other organizational outcomes such as turnover, grievances, or worker morale. As a line of inquiry, the behavioral approach has been considerably more fruitful than the trait approach. It is still generating new lines of research, but it has not yet resulted in any comprehensive theory of leadership.

Hollander and Julian (1969) suggest that the failure of the trait approach and the relative success of the behavioral approach has been due to the unwillingness or the inability of the trait theorists to distinguish between leadership as a process and the leader as a person. Current theories of leadership emphasize both the dynamics of leadership effectiveness (leadership as a process) and situational factors affecting leader effectiveness. Another distinction between the earlier studies of leadership and current research is the nature of the dependent variable. As Dubin suggested in 1965, there are many possible outcomes related to leadership, and only one of them is productivity. Outcomes such as subordinate satisfaction, subordinate interest in longtime membership in the organization, and the effectiveness of peer cooperation are also affected.

As you saw in several earlier chapters, the cognitive revolution is being felt in many areas of psychology. Leadership research is one of those areas. There is a growing body of literature that questions the meaning and the measurement of leadership. Briefly, it is proposed that leadership is in the eye of the beholder—that followers *attribute* leadership behaviors to supervisors in particular situations independent of what the supervisors actually do at the workplace. An extension of this line of theorizing is that individuals carry around theories of leadership in their heads and invoke those theories to describe their own behavior (if they are supervisors) or the behavior of their supervisors when they fill out a questionnaire intended to tap leadership style or behavior. If these cognitive propositions are correct, the effect on the study of leadership would be enormous. In the first place, most of the research carried out to this point must be reinterpreted. Instead of the study of leader behavior, this research would represent the study of people *perceiving* the behavior of leaders. Thus, we would be dealing with perceiver behavior rather than leader behavior. A second effect would be to make most leadership training programs irrelevant. It is still too early to tell whether this implicit theory position is tenable, but we will review the available research. For present purposes, the point is that an increasingly popular theoretical framework for studying leadership is the cognitive one.

THEORIES OF LEADERSHIP

Leadership models are much more tentative and speculative than models of selection or training. This is because of the inherent complexity of the phenomenon of leadership. If we want to consider leadership, we have to consider the abilities of the leader, the motivation of the leader, the organizational context in which the leading is done, the nature of the work group, and so on. Leadership represents a capsule view of the whole of industrial and organizational psychology. No wonder it is difficult to come up with a single model that efficiently explains leader behavior. In this section, I will present some of the current approaches to leadership. The presentation is intended to be representative rather than exhaustive. The choice of leadership models is not meant to imply that those chosen are "good" and those not chosen "bad." I have made these choices on the basis of approaches that are (1) most divergent, (2) representative of a class of studies, and (3) accompanied by a substantial body of data.

Leader Behaviors: The Ohio State Studies

In the early 1950s researchers at Ohio State University abandoned the trait approach to leadership and adopted the behavioral approach. This approach is well described as follows:

> Focusing on the kinds of behavior engaged in by people in leadership roles, these investigators developed over 1,800 items (for example, "He calls the

Often, leaders are called on as a resource in problem solving, and most provide both structure and consideration. (Penn State University)

group together to talk things over"; "He knows about it when something goes wrong") descriptive of what supervisors do in their leadership roles. These items were then classified into ten broad categories of leader behavior (for example, initiation, domination, evaluation, communication). Questionnaires were developed by means of which leader behavior could be described and scored on these ten dimensions. Each supervisor was described in terms of how frequently (for example, always, often, . . . never) he did what each item stated. Repeated use of these questionnaires in a variety of leader-group situations (foreman-worker, executive-subordinate, school principle–teacher, university department head–professor, aircraft commander–crew, submarine officer–crew) showed that these ten categories overlapped with one another and that the items could be grouped into two more basic dimensions of leader behavior. These were labeled *consideration* and *initiating structure.* (Fleishman, 1967b, p. 362)

Since the introduction of the Ohio State studies, literally hundreds of studies have been done in an attempt to determine how these two dimensions relate to leadership effectiveness, group productivity, group morale, and other relevant dependent variables. Before reviewing this research, we should define the two dimensions in question.

Consideration. Includes behavior indicating mutual trust, respect, and a certain warmth and rapport between the supervisor and his group. This does not mean

FIGURE 12–3 Sample Items from the LOQ

Structure	*Consideration*
1. Put the welfare of your unit above the welfare of any person	1. Give in to your subordinates in your discussions with them
2. Encourage after-duty work by persons of your unit	2. Back up what persons under you do
3. Try out your own new ideas in the unit	3. Get approval of persons under you on important matters before going ahead

SOURCE: *Leadership Opinion Questionnaire* by E. A. Fleishman, 1960, Chicago: Science Research Associates.

> that this dimension reflects a superficial "pat-on-the-back, first-name calling" kind of human-relations behavior. This dimension seems to emphasize a deeper concern for group members' needs and includes such behavior as allowing subordinates more participation in decision making and encouraging more two-way communication.
>
> *Structure.* Includes behavior in which the supervisor organizes and defines group activities and his relation to the group. Thus, he defines the role he expects each member to assume, assigns tasks, plans ahead, establishes ways of getting things done, and pushes for production. This dimension seems to emphasize overt attempts to achieve organizational goals. (Fleishman & Harris, 1962, pp. 43–44)

The similarity between these two terms and other terms can be readily seen. *Consideration* is very much like *employee-centered supervision, supportive, participative,* and *human-relations–oriented* supervision. *Initiating structure,* on the other hand, is most similar in meaning to terms like *job-centered, directive,* and *task-oriented* supervision.

Two basic instruments or questionnaires have been used to measure the degree of consideration or initiating structure present in a particular supervisor. The first of these is known as the LOQ (Leadership Opinion Questionnaire) and asks the *supervisor* questions dealing with ideal methods of supervision. The second instrument is known as the LBDQ (Leader Behavior Description Questionnaire) and is usually completed by a *subordinate* whose task is to describe how the supervisor behaves in varying situations. Some sample items from the LOQ appear in Figure 12–3.

The general findings of the Ohio State studies have been replicated a number of different times, with different instruments, different theoretical approaches, and different subject populations. Although most of the follow-up studies have proposed additional factors, consideration and initiating structure usually account for approximately 80 percent of the variance in descriptions of leader behavior. One study (Tscheulin, 1971) attempted to replicate the findings of the Ohio State group after 20 years and in a different culture. When leader behavior was measured in German industry, the factors that emerged were very clearly consideration and initiating structure. There is little doubt that consideration and initiating structure represent reliable phenomena in the measurement of leader behavior. As we will see shortly, however, this reliability may be more in the conceptual behavior of the person filling out the questionnaire rather than in the behavior of the person being described.

The independence of the two dimensions is an important practical and theoretical issue. Various studies have shown consideration and initiating structure to be positively correlated, uncorrelated, and negatively correlated. Theoretically, the direction and sign of the relationship could tell us a good deal about the dynamics of leadership. If the two dimensions are positively correlated, this could be taken as evidence for the existence of a "style" as described earlier, a habitual way of responding that pervades most situations. If the two dimensions are negatively correlated, we may be observing sets of behaviors that are mutually exclusive; if this were the case, it would be virtually impossible for a leader high on initiating structure to exhibit considerate behavior. If the two dimensions are uncorrelated, the variations in leader behavior are more numerous, and the effects of various combinations of consideration and initiating structure on work group behavior would be much more complex.

For the sake of argument, let's assume that the two dimensions are sufficiently correlated to suggest a unitary leader "style." This is only part of the picture. A more sophisticated view of the situation is provided by looking at various *combinations* of the two factors. Fleishman and Harris (1962) gathered data in a truck-manufacturing company and looked at the relationship between supervisory behavior and dependent measures such as turnover and grievances. Leader behavior was measured by a variation of the LBDQ. The most interesting relationships they discovered appear in Figures 12–4, 12–5, 12–6, and 12–7. Figure 12–4 depicts the relation between grievance rate and consideration, and Figure 12–5 shows the relation between turnover and consideration. There seems to be a clear relationship between consideration and the two dependent variables. High consideration is related to low grievance rate and low turnover. Low consideration is related to high grievance rate and high turnover. Both of the relationships seem to have the same general curvilinear shape such that beyond a certain point increases in consideration do not further decrease turnover or grievance rate. Figures 12–6 and 12–7 describe the relationship between levels of initiating structure and the two dependent variables. The results seem to be the mirror image of those obtained with consideration. Increased initiation of structure leads to increased grievance rate and increased turnover. Once again, both relationships seem to have the same general curvilinear shape.

FIGURE 12–4 Relation between Consideration and Grievance Rate

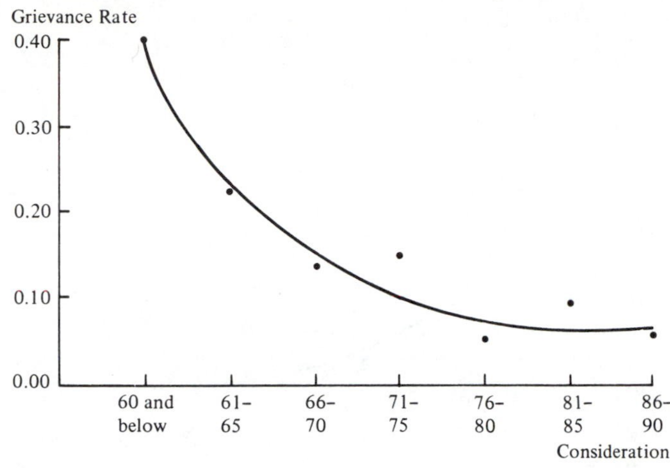

SOURCE: From "Patterns of Leadership Behavior Related to Employee Grievances and Turnover," by E. A. Fleishman and E. F. Harris, 1962, *Personnel Psychology, 15.*

These data seem to be clear. They tell us to avoid too much structuring and be considerate of subordinates—or do they? Figure 12–8 really tells the tale. It presents data related to the *interaction* of the two dimensions. Supervisors were separated into three groups, which fell along the consideration continuum: high, medium, and low. The relationship between each of the dependent variables and degree of structure was then examined separately for each of the three groups. As Figure 12–8 clearly shows, the relationship between structuring behavior on the part of the supervisor and grievance rate was very different for each of the groups. For *high*-consideration leaders, structuring behavior could be sharply increased without any dramatic effect on grievances, so the grievance rate remained minimal. Supervisors designated as *low* on consideration could also increase structuring behavior without affecting grievance rates, so the rate stayed high. The major effect of initiating structure on grievance rate was found in the *medium*-consideration group. For that group, there was a very strong positive relationship between structuring behavior and grievance rate. One of the conclusions Fleishman and Harris drew concerning this interaction was that while supervisors can compensate for high structure by increasing consideration, low-consideration supervisors cannot erase the negative effects of lack of concern for subordinates by reducing structure. This finding may mean consideration acts as a threshold or releaser mechanism, a precondition for effective supervision. It may be that the perception of "structuring" behavior changes when a leader is described as considerate; it may be that the structuring behavior is thought to be just

FIGURE 12–5 Relation between Consideration and Turnover Rate

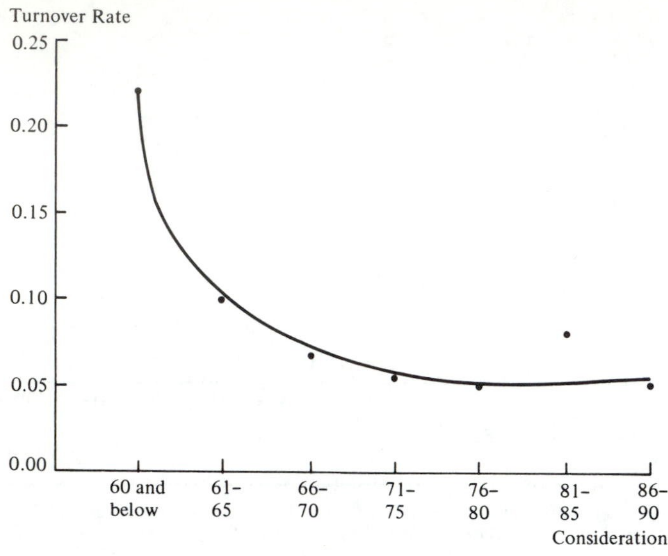

SOURCE: From "Patterns of Leadership Behavior Related to Employee Grievances and Turnover," by E. A. Fleishman and E. F. Harris, 1962, *Personnel Psychology, 15.*

FIGURE 12–6 Relation between Structure and Grievance Rate

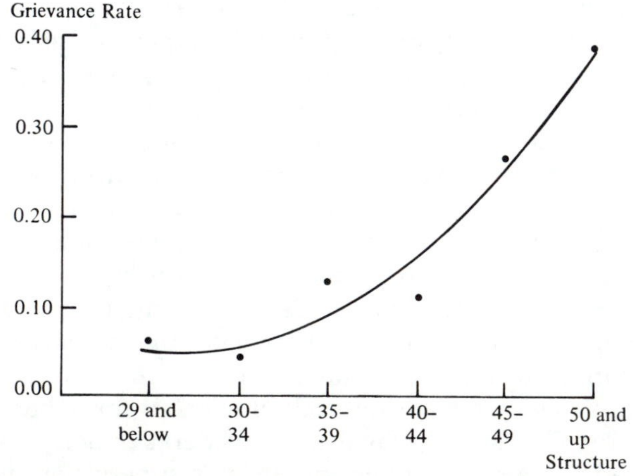

SOURCE: From "Patterns of Leadership Behavior Related to Employee Grievances and Turnover," by E. A. Fleishman and E. F. Harris, 1962, *Personnel Psychology, 15.*

FIGURE 12–7 Relation between Structure and Turnover Rate

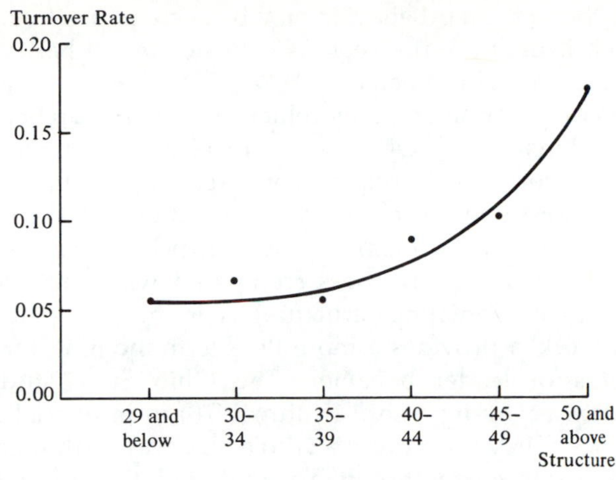

SOURCE: From "Patterns of Leadership Behavior Related to Employee Grievances and Turnover," by E. A. Fleishman and E. F. Harris, 1962, *Personnel Psychology, 15.*

FIGURE 12–8 Combinations of Consideration and Structure Related to Grievance Rate

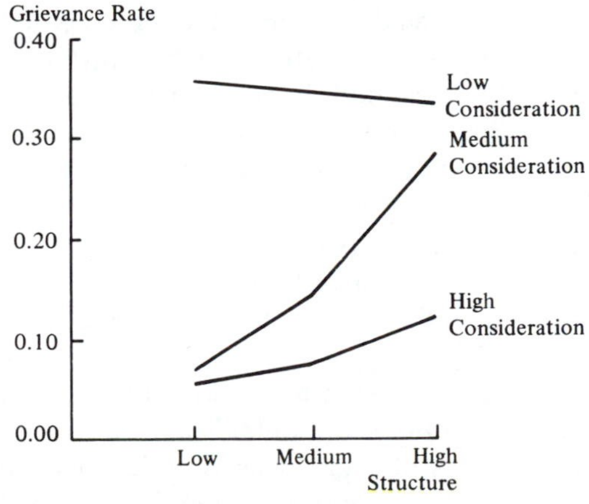

SOURCE: From "Patterns of Leadership Behavior Related to Employee Grievances and Turnover," by E. A. Fleishman and E. F. Harris, 1962, *Personnel Psychology, 15.*

another example of consideration by subordinates of highly considerate supervisors. This may mean that if leaders are viewed as considerate (i.e., liked or approved), then all their behavior may be seen as positive, an asset. On the other hand, if they are not seen as considerate, all behaviors might be viewed in a negative light, a liability.

There has been an increasing reluctance by researchers to consider the two dimensions of the Ohio State model as *the* dimensions of leadership. Instead, work has continued on breaking down these broad dimensions into more specific ones. As an example, Yukl (1981) has suggested a more refined taxonomy of leader behaviors, which is reproduced in Figure 12–9. The richness (compared with the two dimensions of consideration and initiating structure) is immediately obvious. A taxonomy such as Yukl's provides a more flexible foundation for the examination of patterns of leader behavior. The Ohio State studies represent the equivalent of a paradigm shift (Kuhn, 1970) in industrial and organizational psychology. They introduced a whole new way of thinking about leadership. Yukl's taxonomy represents a useful evolutionary shift in the new paradigm.

Situational Influences: Fiedler's Contingency Model

One of the most active lines of leadership research is related to Fiedler's contingency model. He has been gathering data related to the propositions of the model since 1951, and the model "emerged" from this mass of data. Although the model has changed form significantly over the years, the general thrust has remained the same: *Effective leadership is a joint function of leader characteristics and situational characteristics.*

In some early research, Fiedler (1951) noticed that clinical therapists who were considered to be "good" therapists tended to view their patients as similar to themselves, whereas therapists considered "bad" saw their patients as quite dissimilar to themselves. Fiedler took this finding and extended it to the leadership setting. He reasoned that effective leaders might be those who saw their followers as similar to themselves. He labeled this measure of similarity the *least preferred co-worker* (LPC) index. It measures the extent to which the leader describes ineffective subordinates in positive terms. A high LPC score indicates that the leader has some good things to say even about ineffective workers. Conversely, a low LPC score means that the leader describes ineffective workers in negative terms. Fiedler considered LPC to represent the style of the leader.

In addition to this basic element of leadership style, Fiedler also introduced situational variables into his model. He felt that the situational variables moderated the effectiveness of a given leadership style; that is, a high LPC leader might be more effective in one situation than in another. He proposed three major determinants of the leadership situation: leader-member relations, task structure, and position power.

FIGURE 12–9 Definition of Managerial Behaviors in Yukl's Taxonomy

Performance emphasis. The extent to which a leader emphasizes the importance of subordinate performance and encourages subordinates to make a maximum effort

Role clarification. The extent to which a leader informs subordinates about their duties and responsibilities, clarifies rules and policies, and lets subordinates know what is expected of them

Training-coaching. The extent to which a leader provides any necessary training and coaching to subordinates or arranges for others to provide it

Goal setting. The extent to which a leader, either alone or jointly with a subordinate, sets specific, challenging, but realistic performance goals for each important aspect of the subordinate's job

Planning. The extent to which a leader plans in advance how to organize and schedule the work efficiently, coordinate work unit activities, accomplish task objectives, and avoid or cope with potential problems

Innovating. The extent to which a leader looks for new opportunities for the work unit to exploit, proposes new activities to undertake, and offers innovative ideas for strengthening the work unit

Problem solving. The extent to which a leader takes prompt and decisive action to deal with serious work-related problems and disturbances

Work facilitation. The extent to which a leader provides subordinates with any supplies, equipment, support services, and other resources necessary to do their work effectively

Monitoring operations. The extent to which a leader keeps informed about the activities within his/her work unit and checks on the performance of subordinates

External monitoring. The extent to which a leader keeps informed about outside events that have important implications for his/her work unit

Information dissemination. The extent to which a leader keeps subordinates informed about decisions, events, and developments that affect their work

Discipline. The extent to which a leader takes appropriate disciplinary action to deal with a subordinate who violates a rule, disobeys an order, or has consistently poor performance

Representation. The extent to which a leader promotes and defends the interests of his/her work unit and takes appropriate action to obtain necessary resources and support for the work unit from superiors, peers, and outsiders

Consideration. The extent to which a leader is friendly, supportive, and considerate in his/her behavior toward subordinates

Career counseling and facilitation. The extent to which a leader offers helpful advice to subordinates on how to advance their careers, encourages them to develop their skills, and otherwise aids their professional development

Inspiration. The extent to which a leader stimulates enthusiasm among subordinates for the work of the group and says things to build their confidence in the group's ability to attain its objectives successfully

(continued)

SOURCE: From *Innovations in Research on Leader Behavior* by G. Yukl, paper presented at a meeting of the Eastern Academy of Management, Baltimore, May 14, 1982.

FIGURE 12–9 *(concluded)*

Praise recognition. The extent to which a leader provides appropriate praise and recognition to subordinates with effective performances and shows appreciation for special efforts and contributions made by subordinates

Structuring reward contingencies. The extent to which a leader rewards effective subordinate performance with tangible benefits, such as a pay increase, promotion, better assignments, better work schedule, or extra time off

Decision participation. The extent to which a leader consults with subordinates before making work-related decisions and otherwise allows subordinates to influence his/her decisions

Autonomy delegation. The extent to which a leader delegates responsibility and authority to subordinates and allows them discretion in determining how to do their work

Interaction facilitation. The extent to which a leader emphasizes teamwork and tries to promote cooperation, cohesiveness, and identification with the group

Conflict management. The extent to which a leader discourages unnecessary fighting and bickering among subordinates and helps them settle conflicts and disagreements in a constructive manner

Constructive criticism. The extent to which a leader criticizes subordinate mistakes and poor performance in a constructive, calm, and helpful manner

Leader-Member Relations. This particular dimension of the situation is straightforward. It concerns whether the members of the group like the leader. If they do, the situation should be favorable for leading; if they do not, the situation should not be favorable for leading. Fiedler suggests that leader-member relations would also include such things as trust of the leader and loyalty to the leader. This seems similar to the concept of incremental influence that was considered earlier in the chapter. Of the three dimensions of the situation, leader-member relations is considered to be, by far, the most important dimension.

Task Structure. The structure or specificity of the task is determined by a taxonomy of task structure developed by Shaw (1963). Four of Shaw's scales have been used in Fiedler's research. These scales are:

1. *Decision verifiability.* The degree to which the correctness of a solution or decision can be verified
2. *Goal clarity.* The degree to which task requirements are clearly stated and known by group members
3. *Goal path multiplicity.* The number of different ways that the problem can be solved
4. *Solution specificity.* The degree to which there is more than one correct solution

TABLE 12–2 The Favorability of the Leadership Situation

Situational Factors[a]								
Leader-member relations	High	High	High	High	Low	Low	Low	Low
Task structure	High	High	Low	Low	High	High	Low	Low
Position power	High	Low	High	Low	High	Low	High	Low
Situation favorability	High—							—Low

[a]Leader-member relations is the most important; task structure, the next most important; and position power, the least important in determining favorability. This accounts for the variable arrangement of the high and low cells in the table.

The general idea is that a structured situation is more favorable for a leader than an unstructured situation.

Position Power. The third dimension of the situation that helps determine its favorability is what Fiedler refers to as "fate control," the capacity of the leader for dispensing rewards and punishments. *Position power* is very close in meaning to the earlier notion of *legitimate power*. It is the power inherent in a particular organizational role, such as "supervisor." Situations in which the leader has strong position power are thought to be more favorable than those in which the position power is weak.

Simply as a way of progressing with the research, Fiedler dichotomized each of the situational characteristics. Leader-member relations, task structure, and position power were each categorized as either high or low. This dichotomization yielded eight distinct kinds of situations. These situations are described in Table 12–2. Fiedler suggested that these situations differed in terms of "favorability," with some being positive leadership climates (e.g., high on each of the three situational characteristics) and some being negative climates (e.g., low on each of the situational characteristics).

Leadership Style. High LPC leaders use the positive terms in describing ineffective individuals. According to Fiedler, the high LPC leader describes the least preferred coworker as reasonably nice, intelligent, and so on. On the other hand, the low LPC leader describes the least preferred coworker in negative terms such as uncooperative and unintelligent. The high LPC leader seems to be able to distinguish between the individual and the work, whereas the low LPC leader appears unable to do that. The low LPC leader seems to link the performance of the least preferred coworker to personality characteristics. These two styles, high and low LPC, suggest variations on the theme of consideration and initiating structure. This is further supported by Fiedler's description of the high and low LPC leaders. Both seek esteem, but the high LPC individual seeks esteem through interpersonal relations, whereas the low LPC leader seeks it through successful task completion. Nevertheless, Fiedler is quick to point out that the interpretation of LPC scores is considerably more complex than just initiating structure and consideration. While the LPC score has also been considered a possible measure of cognitive complexity, the currently favored interpretation is that LPC scores represent a measure of goal hierarchy, with low LPC leaders having significantly different goal structures from those of high LPC leaders. In short, Fiedler is saying that the LPC is a motivational measure of some sort.

The Contingency Theory. On the basis of the data he has gathered over the years, Fiedler has constructed a model that attempts to predict the effectiveness of certain combinations of leadership style (as identified by LPC scores) and situation favorability. Simply put, he contends that low LPC leaders will be effective in either very favorable or very unfavorable situations, whereas high LPC leaders will be most effective in situations of moderate favorability. This leads to the major hypothesis of the contingency model: *"The effectiveness of a group is contingent upon the relationship between leadership style and the degree to which the group situation enables the leader to exert influence"* (Fiedler, 1967, p. 15).

Figure 12–10 describes the proposed relationship between leadership style, situation favorability, and group effectiveness. This is a rather complex relationship, but it is an important one to understand. The graph demonstrates that as the situation moves from high favorability to moderate favorability for the leader (from the extreme left to the center of the horizontal axis), the correlation between LPC scores and group effectiveness changes from negative to positive. In other words, in the extremely favorable situation, the lower the LPC score, the higher the group effectiveness. In the moderately favorable situation, the higher the LPC score, the higher the group effectiveness. The opposite effect occurs when we move from a situation of moderate favorability to a very unfavorable situation (from the center to the extreme right on the horizontal axis). The sign of the correlation coefficients between LPC score and group effectiveness changes from positive to negative. In the very unfavorable situation, the lower the LPC score, the higher the group performance.

The conclusion Fiedler draws from these data is that low LPC is most appropriate in either very favorable or very unfavorable situations. As a function of this conclusion, he recommends a program of "organizational engineering." The function of organizational engineering would be to change the nature of the situation to match the style of a particular leader. This suggestion flows from Fiedler's belief that leadership style is a relatively enduring characteristic of the individual and tied to a motivational system. Although we could, of course, opt to change the individual, Fiedler thinks it would be more efficient in the long run to change the situation.

The most complete presentation of the studies supporting the theory and its propositions appears in Fiedler's book *A Theory of Leadership Effectiveness*

FIGURE 12–10 Fiedler's View of the LPC-Group Effectiveness Relationship

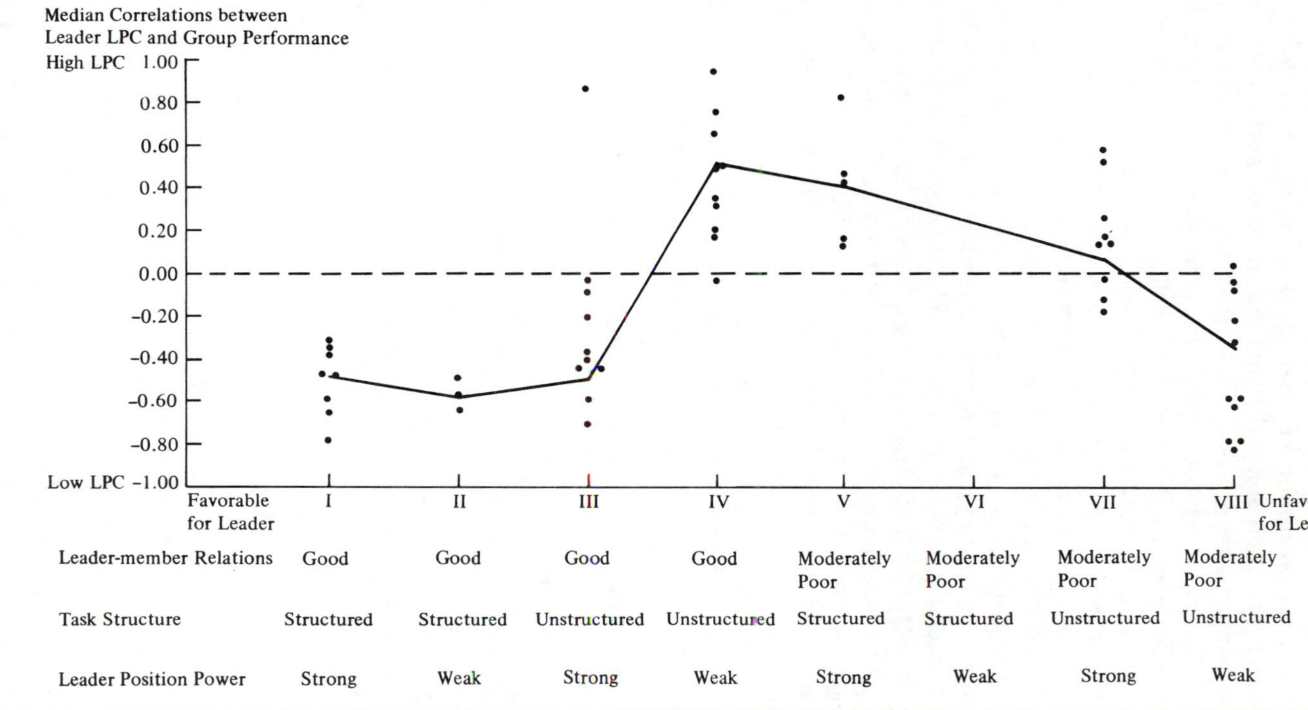

SOURCE: From *Leadership*, F. E. Fiedler, 1971, Morristown, NJ: General Learning Press. © 1971, General Learning Corporation.

(1967). A recent meta-analysis of 145 tests of contingency theory (Strube & Garcia, 1981) claims widespread support for the theory. Nevertheless, there is a good deal of nonsupportive research as well (e.g., Vecchio, 1977, 1983). Most research has been somewhat limited in scope and has not permitted inferences about the theory as a whole. Instead, researchers have examined parts of the theory. The most popular focus for this research is the meaning of LPC. Fiedler and his followers have settled on a cognitive-motivational interpretation of LPC scores. Low LPC leaders are thought to be cognitively simple and somewhat rigid in response patterns. Unfortunately, there is less than unanimous agreement that LPC represents cognitive complexity. Evans and Derner (1974) agree that the low LPC leaders are cognitively simple, but they found that the high LPC leaders were not necessarily complex. Green and Nebeker (1977) found that high LPC leaders seem to be able to differentiate situational characteristics very well, whereas low LPC leaders are relatively constant in their response regardless of the situational characteristics. Finally, Stinson and Tracy (1974) found that LPC scores were not particularly stable. An individual who is characterized as high LPC today may be characterized differently if the LPC scales are administered at another time. This is another way of saying that these authors question the reliability of the scale. In addition to the independence of LPC and situational characteristics, Fiedler's contingency theory proposes that each of the situational variables (task structure, leader-member relations, and position power) is independent of the other two variables. But Ilgen and O'Brien (1974) found that leader-member relations were related to task characteristics, particularly the degree of coordination among members required. In addition, member compatibility seemed to affect leader-member relations.

Finally, Justis, Kedia, and Stephens (1978) found that position power had a main effect on the effectiveness of trainers. Trainers who were perceived as high in position power were able to have a greater influence on trainees than trainers with low position power. If Fiedler is correct, one would expect the effect of position power to depend on the trainer's LPC score.

Kennedy (1982) has presented results that broadly support some propositions of contingency theory. He studied middle-LPC leaders—those whose scores fall between the high and low extremes. He found that the middle-LPC leader was more effective across all the variations of situation favorability. He suggested that this was because they were more flexible and found it easier to adopt varying styles, depending on the situation. These findings are in line with contingency theory predictions. There have been other studies that have supported Fiedler's model, but they have been either limited in scope (Schnier, 1978) or lacking in sufficient control to justify serious consideration.

There have been persistent criticisms of contingency theory. Three particular categories of criticism deserve discussion. I will present these criticisms and then provide a brief rebuttal and personal evaluation of each of them.

1. The first criticism relates to the nature of the dependent variable in most of the studies. Look again at Figure 12–10. Notice that if we consider situation favorability as the independent variable (or antecedent variable), the *correlation between LPC and group effectiveness becomes the dependent variable, not group effectiveness itself.* If we consider the correlation coefficient to be the dependent variable, we know nothing about the absolute level of performance. It may be of little comfort to know that LPC and group effectiveness are negatively related in one situation and positively related in another. Without knowing something about absolute levels of group performance, it is impossible to conceive of "organizational engineering" as proposed by Fiedler. It is distinctly possible that the best match of situation and leader style could yield the lowest levels of performance in an absolute sense.

In addition to the issue of absolute levels of performance, there is a problem at the individual level since the model predicts *group* performance, not individual performance. As we will see shortly, there is some evidence to suggest that there are idiosyncratic relationships between specific supervisor-subordinate pairs in addition to the possible general style effects of a supervisor. Fiedler's propositions make no allowance for individual performance or individual supervisor-subordinate relationships. This is a serious shortcoming of the model.

The criticism is a serious one. The practical applications and implications of any leadership theory add or detract from its status. The practical value of the theory will remain questionable until data relating to absolute levels and individual levels of performance begin to appear with more regularity. This criticism does not in any sense "destroy" the theory. It simply questions the relevance of the dependent variable. It is silly to contend that the LPC-group effectiveness correlation is *totally* irrelevant; it is not. It provides some useful dynamic information about the *process* of leadership. Unfortunately, the correlation can say little about one class of outcomes of that process—absolute levels of group or individual performance. In addition, some have suggested that leader effectiveness is not the *only* dependent variable of interest. Rice (1981) suggests that member satisfaction is an equally important result of leadership style and deserves equal attention from contingency theory.

2. Another criticism of contingency theory relates to the meaning of LPC. There is a general feeling of uneasiness that surrounds the use of the LPC score. It is felt that LPC should have systematic relationships with other logically related variables to qualify as a construct; in other words, construct validity should be demonstrated.

In response, it might be argued that the fact that LPC does not seem to relate systematically to other variables is not the fault of the contingency researchers. They document numerous attempts to find out what LPC means. Again, this criticism is not sufficient to destroy the theory. It would be nice if we knew a little more about the meaning of LPC, but this will not be the first or last time in psychological research that an ambiguous construct has led to advances in one way or another (e.g., "intelligence," "instincts"). Furthermore, data are accumulating that point to LPC as indicative of some type of cognitive construct.

3. One final criticism has to do with the nature of the "situational" determinants of favorability. Critics claim that the characteristics of the *situation* are not independent of the *leader*. In other words, it is possible that some of the LPC score is also represented in the measures of situation favorability, thereby confounding some of the relationships predicted by the model.

This third criticism concerning the relative independence of leader characteristics and situational characteristics speaks directly to the purpose of leadership research for the past several decades, that is, a description of the interaction between the leader and the situation, a description of the leadership *process*. Available data seem to indicate that leader characteristics and situational characteristics are *not* independent. If Fiedler's contingency theory is to be of any value, this relationship must be better understood.

Recently, there have been additional meta-analyses (Peters, Hartke, & Pohlmann, 1985) and sophisticated computer simulations (Jago & Regan, 1986b) of the contingency theory and the LEADER MATCH training program, which teaches leaders how to adopt the contingency model of leading. You will remember that we considered the LEADER MATCH program in the training chapter. The meta-analysis suggests that Fiedler's theory receives more support in the laboratory than in the field. The computer simulation of LEADER MATCH suggests that there are some internal inconsistencies in the theory. As you would expect, Fiedler and his colleagues (Chemers & Fiedler, 1986) were not amused by these attacks and suggested that the unflattering data were gathered by researchers who did not understand the theory and who violated various assumptions in testing that theory. The original antagonists responded that the situation was even *worse* than they first thought and that contingency theory was on extremely shakey ground (Jago & Regan, 1986a). Fistfights aside, Fiedler's theory and data have been controversial from their first introduction. In 1967, one might have been justified in suggesting that Fiedler be given more time to explore and develop his theory systematically. In the intervening 22 years, not much new has been offered, and the attacks continue. It is becoming increasingly clear that the contingency theory of Fiedler has not sufficiently illuminated the phenomenon of leadership. Contingency theory represents a good example of a situational approach to leadership, but its stature as an explanatory mechanism remains questionable.

Leadership as Decision Making: The Vroom-Yetton Contingency Theory

Vroom and Yetton (1975) have proposed a model of leadership that deals with one particular aspect of the leadership process: decision making. They reviewed past research on leader decision making and found that it was possible to describe a limited number of strategies or styles a manager might use to make decisions or solve problems. Figures 12–11 and 12–12 graphically illustrate the propositions of the theory. In Figure 12–11, you will find the various alternatives available to the leader faced with a group or individual problem to be solved. Figure 12–12 is a diagram that allows one to arrive at the "correct" decision-making style by answering a series of yes-no questions.

Vroom and Yetton proposed that the effectiveness of decisions could be judged on the following three dimensions: the *quality* of rationality of the decision, the *acceptance* of the decision by subordinates, and the *time* required to make the decision. These dimensions represent the *attributes* of the problem. Thus, as was the case with Fiedler's model, the leader behavior is *contingent* on other variables, in this case, problem attributes. As an example, consider the case of a manager who is trying to make a decision about a new pay plan. It may be that her superior wants a recommendation in a matter of days; this would make the problem a *time* problem. On the other hand, the issue might be one of acceptance; for example, it may be that she will lose some key people to other organizations if she does not get acceptance for the new pay plan. As you can see by examining the decision styles in Figure 12–12 again, some of these strategies seem better suited to quick decisions, whereas others are more suited to high levels of decision acceptance. These various characteristics of the decision are represented in the questions that appear in Figure 12–12. This is exactly the nature of the theory: it identifies the styles or strategies of decision making that a manager should use in solving problems with specific attributes.

Vroom and Yetton label their theory a *normative* or *prescriptive* theory. This means that they intend to tell managers how they *should* behave in certain situations. The Ohio State approach and Fiedler's model are less obviously normative (but are normative, nonetheless); they *imply* that leaders will be more effective if they adopt some particular consideration–initiating structure balance or modify the situation to match their particular LPC level. Vroom and Yetton specify exactly which strategies to use with problems having particular attributes.

Since the theory was introduced, there has been little substantive research on it. The research that has been done has been of a confirmatory rather than exploratory nature. Jago and Vroom (1977) found that managers who used "acceptable" decision strategies (as determined by the problem attributes) were more likely to report that the decision was an "effective" one than managers who used "unacceptable" strategies. Hill and Schmitt (1977) studied the decision strategies of 33 students asked to play the role of manager.

FIGURE 12–11 Decision Procedures for Group and Individual Problems

Group Problem	*Individual Problem*
AI. You solve the problem or make the decision yourself, using information available to you at the time.	AI. You solve the problem or make the decision by yourself, using information available to you at the time.
AII. You obtain the necessary information from your subordinates, then decide the solution to the problem yourself. You may or may not tell your subordinates what the problem is in getting the information from them. The role played by your subordinates in making the decision is clearly one of providing the necessary information to you rather than generating or evaluating alternative solutions.	AII. You obtain the necessary information from your subordinate, then decide on the solution to the problem yourself. You may or may not tell the subordinate what the problem is in getting the information from him. His role in making the decision is clearly one of providing the necessary information to you, rather than generating or evaluating alternative solutions.
CI. You share the problem with the relevant subordinates individually, getting their ideas and suggestions without bringing them together as a group. Then, *you* make the decision, which may or may not reflect your subordinates' influences.	CI. You share the problem with your subordinate, getting his ideas and suggestions. Then you make a decision, which may or may not reflect his influence.
CII. You share the problem with your subordinates as a group, obtaining their collective ideas and suggestions. Then you make the decision, which may or may not reflect your subordinates' influence.	GI. You share the problem with your subordinate, and together you analyze the problem and arrive at a mutually agreeable solution.
GII. You share the problem with your subordinates as a group. Together you generate and evaluate alternatives and attempt to reach agreement (consenses) on a solution. Your role is much like that of chairman. You do not try to influence the group to adopt "your" solution, and you are willing to accept and implement any solution which has the support of the group.	DI. You delegate the problem to your subordinate, providing him with any relevant information that you possess but giving him responsibility for solving the problem by himself. You may or may not request him to tell you what solution he has reached.

SOURCE: From *Leadership and Decision-Making*, by V. H. Vroom and P. W. Yetton, 1973, by permission of the University of Pittsburgh Press.

FIGURE 12–12 The Vroom-Yetton Contingency Model of Leadership Behavior

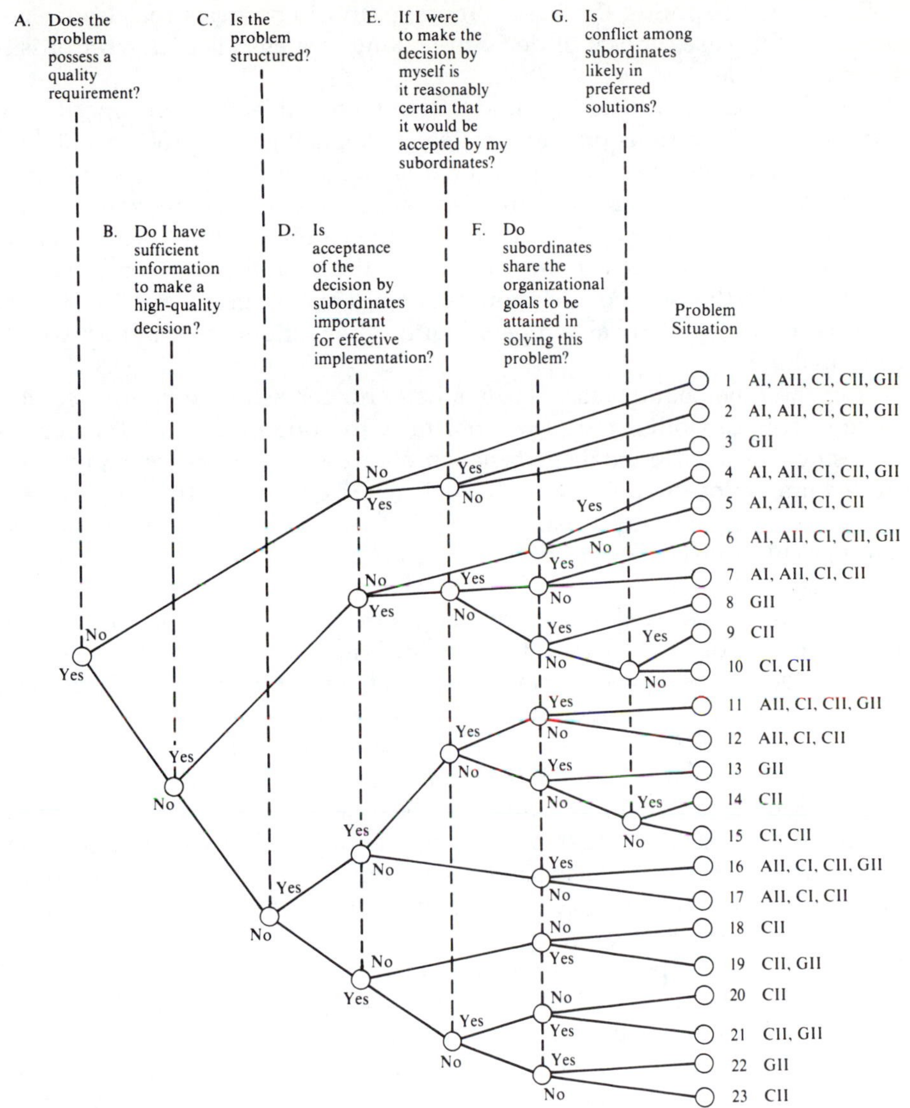

SOURCE: From *Leadership and Decision-Making*, by V. H. Vroom and P. W. Yetton, 1973, by permission of the University of Pittsburgh Press. Copyright 1973 by the University of Pittsburgh Press.

They found that the nature of the problem (i.e., the problem attributes) had a major influence on the strategy the "manager" selected to solve a particular problem. This supports the basic Vroom-Yetton hypothesis that leader behavior (in this case, choice of decision-making strategy) is *contingent* on situational variables.

Field (1982) conducted a study in which subjects were specifically instructed to use various decision strategies in small-group problem solving. He found that the "correct" styles (i.e., as suggested by the Vroom-Yetton model) resulted in more effective decisions. This was the good news. The bad news was that the nature of the problem (e.g., easy versus hard) accounted for much more variance in the ultimate decision effectiveness than did the style of decision making. This suggests that the model might be correct but trivial compared with other influences on effective decision making.

On the other hand, many leaders have no consistent style for decision making. This can often create a problem with subordinates and superiors alike, since the decision maker's behavior often seems capricious or arbitrary. The Vroom-Yetton model is an attractive scheme for both training and administration. At the very least, it imposes a certain consistency in decision making. This consistency is bound to be an advantage in decision-making situations.

Some recent research casts some doubt on the generality of the Vroom-Yetton model from two perspectives. First, it appears that supervisors may choose to delegate when they have considerable trust in the subordinate and when the issue is less important. On the other hand, if the decision is an important one, or if the supervisor is not completely confident in the capabilities of the subordinate(s), the decision is made autocratically or with some limited form of participation. Thus, it appears that leaders pick and choose their willingness to delegate or participate carefully. This does not necessarily argue that the prescriptive aspect of the Vroom-Yetton model is *wrong*, but it does suggest that considerable training might be necessary to get supervisors to abandon typical strategies.

A different perspective is provided by Heilman, Hornstein, Cage, and Herschlag (1984). They asked subjects to consider the various decision strategies from the point of view of both a subordinate and a supervisor. The subordinate perspective was unwavering with respect to the preference for participation in all situations. On the other hand, when subjects were asked to take the role of supervisor, the Vroom-Yetton model predicted the preference for decision-making choice almost perfectly. The moral was that effectiveness of a decision-making strategy may reside in the eye of the beholder.

On the basis of this limited research, it is impossible to come to any firm conclusion about the Vroom-Yetton model. In its current form, the model is somewhat limited. It would seem to deal with only one aspect of a manager's job: decision making. This may be a reasonable approach to management, since almost everything a manager does (or any worker, for that matter) can be translated into a "problem" of one kind or another, requiring a decision. But if it is to occupy a role as a "full-fledged" theory of leadership, the Vroom-Yetton model will have to be modified to deal more specifically with a wider range of problems, including interpersonal relations, rewarding-punishing decisions, and planning and scheduling. In addition, more work will have to be done on understanding how leaders naturally choose decision styles. There is a developing interest in the decision-making styles of leaders (Beach & Mitchell, 1978; McAllister, Mitchell, & Beach, 1979). This area of investigation will evolve considerably in the next few years.

Participative Decision Making. An underlying issue that characterizes the Vroom-Yetton model is that of participation in decision making. The question is, When should subordinates be allowed or encouraged to participate in making unit decisions, and what will the effect of that participation be? This has been a popular topic for research for some time, and some opinions have been formed about the potential benefits and disadvantages. The Vroom-Yetton model suggests *when* it might be advantageous to encourage group or individual participation. Let's consider some of the reasons *why* it would be advantageous. Some are obvious from the theory, but some are not so obvious. Yukl (1981) has summarized these assumed advantages.

1. Participation helps subordinates understand the circumstances requiring a decision.
2. Participation results in the individual identifying with the decision and, consequently, working hard to make the solution work.
3. Participation makes objectives and plans necessary to meet those objectives clear to the participant.
4. Participation makes the potential rewards and punishments clearer. This increases employee motivation.
5. Participation is a normal, mature behavior and satisfies needs for autonomy and achievement.
6. Participatory group decisions result in social pressures on members to accept the decision.
7. Group decision making provides opportunities for cooperative social interaction.
8. Participative procedures can improve communications and provide opportunities for conflict resolution between manager and subordinate.
9. Participation results in better decisions to the extent that the talent and skills of the group are tapped.

This is an impressive list of advantages. Nevertheless, the Vroom-Yetton model implies that there are some occasions when participation is inappropriate. This implies that there must be some perceived disadvantages. Yukl has listed the drawbacks of participation. Again, some of these are implied by the Vroom-Yetton model, but some are not so obvious.

1. Participatory decisions take more time.
2. Participation in some decisions makes employees think that they should be involved in all decisions.
3. Managers who use participatory techniques frequently may be perceived as lacking the necessary skill or confidence to make the decision.
4. If the participants lack the skills or knowledge to make the correct decision, participatory decision making will result in lower-quality decisions.
5. Participatory group decision making lessens the feeling of responsibility of any one person.
6. Participatory decision making is not conducive to individual reward systems.
7. Participatory decision strategies require a skilled leader. Without the necessary skill, the process will be frustrating and the decision suboptimal.

The debate about the value of participation is not only an empirical one—it is also a philosophical one. We saw a bit of this in the motivation chapter when we considered goal setting. From one perspective, it was suggested that since participation did not positively affect goal setting or performance, it could be ignored. From another perspective, however, it might be suggested that since it does no harm and does produce feelings of worth in the individual, participation should be encouraged whenever possible. Participation in decision making is the one issue that most clearly separates the U.S. manager and worker from European counterparts. In many countries, particularly the Scandinavian countries, laws have been passed that *require* managers to share decision making with subordinates. Surprisingly to some people, the same is true in many of the eastern bloc countries such as Hungary, Romania, and Yugoslavia. The feeling is that this is the right of the worker and that this right cannot be abridged for economic or administrative reasons, no matter how compelling these reasons might be. In some countries, worker councils have delegates on the board of directors of their company, making decisions about issues of such magnitude as product diversification, capital investment, and long-term human-resource planning. If you want a glimpse of this clear philosophical division between proponents and opponents of participation, read the positive evaluation by Dachler and Wilpert (1978) and the critical evaluation of Locke and Schweiger (1979). It is clear that participation is not natural in many U.S. work settings. But, as the Vroom-Yetton model suggests, there are many situations that suggest the value of this approach. A reasonable conclusion might be that participation should be situationally determined. The Vroom-Yetton model is an excellent start toward defining the appropriate situations.

LEADERSHIP FROM THE BEHAVIOR MODIFICATION PERSPECTIVE

Supervisory Behavior Description Research

Recently, several researchers have specifically studied the minute-to-minute activities of supervisors in an attempt to identify dimensions on which effective and ineffective leaders might be separated. While earlier researchers used questionnaires and asked for opinions of supervisors regarding various behaviors, the "new" behavioral research depends on observation checklists and contemporaneous diaries kept by supervisors. Gioia and Sims (1986) carefully decomposed the verbal behavior of supervisors in their interactions with subordinates. They identified 15 different types of verbal behavior that a supervisor might engage in with a subordinate. In addition, they identified 11 different verbal behaviors that a subordinate might engage in while interacting with a supervisor. The Gioia and Sims study was able to demonstrate, among other things, that supervisors engage in different verbal interactions when discussing failure than when discussing success with their subordinates. Unfortunately, the research did not necessarily identify *effective* types of verbal interaction, only common ones. Thus, there were few practical implications of the research.

Komaki and her colleagues (Komaki, 1986; Komaki, Zlotnick, & Jensen, 1986) also developed a taxonomy of supervisory behavior. The Komaki taxonomy of supervisory behavior had seven major categories. As a result of this research, an observation checklist was developed for categorizing the behavior of supervisors. This checklist was sensitive enough to distinguish between various occupations. For example, the researchers were able to demonstrate that theater managers and bank managers engaged in different types of managerial behaviors to varying extents. For example, theater managers monitored the performance of subordinates to a greater extent than bank managers. The research also demonstrated that the observation checklist could be used quite reliably by independent observers. This led Komaki (1986) to hypothesize that the checklist could be used to distinguish between effective and ineffective managers. If this were possible, Komaki might have backed into a theory of leadership from the behaviorist perspective. Unfortunately, the checklist was of no help in differentiating between effective and ineffective managers, although Komaki claims otherwise. She notes that effective managers monitor performance 2.9 percent of the time but that marginal managers only monitor performance 2.0 percent of the time. Although this difference is statistically significant, it is trivial from a practical perspective. Her claim that effective managers spend "close to 50 percent more time collecting performance information" seems almost silly when you realize that one is spending 2.0 percent and the other 2.9 percent of their time. This new behaviorist trend of collecting supervisory behaviors like butterfly collectors identify rare species has not provided a good deal of illumination to the study of leadership behavior.

Reward and Punishment as Leadership

A number of researchers have examined the effect of positive versus punitive behavior on the part of the supervisor. These studies have sought to document the differential effects of positive reinforcements and punishments on subordinate behavior (Keller & Szilagyi, 1978; Sims & Szilagyi, 1975a, 1975b). To some extent, they have been successful, demonstrating that the appropriate use of reinforcement principles can have a facilitating effect on performance levels. It is difficult, however, to see what this has to do with leadership. It may constitute a prescription for supervisory action, but it represents, at best, a technology rather than a theory, and a limited one at that. For example, one of the more interesting aspects of rewards and punishments in the leadership context has been generally ignored. What is the effect of a reward or punishment administered to one person on other persons in the immediate environment or work group? O'Reilly and Weitz (1980) suggest that punishment, when appropriately applied to a member of the work group, can give rise to feelings of equity by other work group members. If someone is goofing off at work, coworkers often feel some satisfaction in seeing that person punished. This aspect of the reward-punishment environment is seldom examined by the reinforcement researchers. They typically look at the relationships between rewarding or punishing person A and the subsequent satisfaction or performance of person A. Perhaps they should examine the effect of punishing person A on the behavior or satisfaction of person B. In the motivation chapter, we saw a study that seemed to indicate that punishment did not engender hostility in coworkers, but if you remember, the subjects were students who had not known each other before the experiment began. The effect of punishment of one member of a closely knit work group (such as a company of fire fighters or a work team of coal miners) may have quite different results than the laboratory study.

Influences on Leader Behavior

The line of research represented by the application of behavior modification to the leadership issue has had some unintended effects that are valuable. In the context of reinforcement research, investigators began to look at *when* and *how* supervisors used rewards and punishments. Hinton and Barrow (1975) found that supervisors often used positive rewards as *incentives* with poorer performers in the hope of inducing better performance. They also found that supervisors who *received* positive economic rewards were much more likely to *give* positive economic rewards to subordinates. In short, they concluded that there was a good deal more discretionary use of rewarding strategies than any existing theories of leadership would suggest. In a later study (Hinton & Barrow, 1976), these same researchers found that the personality characteristics of supervisors who were prone to positive reward strategies differed from those of punitive supervisors. Finally, Butler and Jaffee (1974) looked at leadership behavior in small discussion groups. They found that when leaders received positive feedback, they were more likely to engage in task-oriented behavior; however, when they received negative feedback, they became tense, antagonistic, and disagreeable (not a surprising finding to children who have the temerity to correct parents, or students who dare to criticize teachers).

As I indicated earlier in the chapter, the attributions and subsequent actions of a supervisor confronted with poor performance represent examples of leadership as a *dependent* variable. To review briefly, Mitchell and Wood (1980) found that when the poor performance had serious consequences (as opposed to trivial ones), supervisors were more likely to place blame on the employee rather than on the situation. They were also more likely to choose punitive responses. In a related study, Mitchell and Kalb (1982) found that leaders who had actually *performed* the task in question (i.e., the one related to the poor performance) were more likely to place blame on the situation rather than on the employee. Presumably, this would also lead to a lower probability for punitive responses. Podsakoff (1982) was able to identify both personal characteristics (e.g., experience, self-confidence) and situational characteristics (e.g., group size) that influenced the choice of rewarding or punishing response modes by supervisors.

Recently, Manz and Sims (1986) have presented some intriguing data relating to how supervisors develop and modify various leadership strategies. It is reasonable to assume that, at least to some extent, supervisors develop supervision schemes by watching other supervisors. Social learning theory (Bandura, 1977) suggests the plausibility of such a mechanism. Thus, it is reasonable to expect that if you watch a model demonstrate reinforcing behavior, you might be more likely to engage in reinforcing behavior yourself; similarly, if you see a model engage in goal setting as a supervisory strategy, you may be more likely to use goal setting techniques yourself. Regardless of how reasonable this mechanism might seem, Manz and Sims found much more complex relationships between the model's behavior and the subject's behavior. For example, when a subject watched a punitive model, that subject not only increased punitive behavior but also *decreased* rewarding and goal setting behavior. Similarly, when a model was seen engaging in goal setting behavior, the subject actually increased punitive behavior. Manz and Sims conclude that interpretations of what you *think* a model is doing are more critical than the actual behavior of the model. Thus, it would appear that the goal setting model is actually seen as controlling and disapproving. In any event, it seems clear that we need to be concerned not only about the *apparent* type of behavior that the leader is engaged in but also about the behavior as perceived by an observer. They are not always seen as the same behaviors.

This recent research on variables that influence leader behavior is very exciting. It suggests that there is considerable value in examining leader behavior as a dependent variable. While this line of research has been suggested in the past (Nebeker & Mitchell, 1974), it is only recently that it has received substantial theoretical attention. Two theories have been proposed dealing with leader behavior as a dependent variable—Hollander's social exchange theory and the vertical dyad model. I will refer to both of these as "reciprocal" theories, because they both emphasize the reciprocal or exchange relationship between leader and follower.

RECIPROCAL THEORIES OF LEADERSHIP

Some time ago, Lowin and Craig (1968) were able to show that subordinate behavior affected leader behavior. Subjects were recruited for a position advertised in a newspaper as "office manager." Confederates of the experimenters played the role of "subordinate" and were either "high performers" or "low performers." The effect on the subjects (supervisors) was revealing. The high-performing subordinates were treated with high consideration and low initiating structure; the low performers, on the other hand, received little consideration and a lot of structure. These data suggest, at the very least, a reciprocal relationship between leader and follower, each influencing the other. Green's results, described earlier in the chapter, fit nicely into this reciprocal framework. You will remember that the level of performance of the subordinate changed the balance between consideration and initiating structure. Surprisingly, there are only a few theories that give explicit attention to the issue of factors influencing the *leader's* behavior. Indirectly, Vroom and Yetton (1975) suggest that the nature of the problem dictates, to some degree, the decision style of the leader. Similarly, Fiedler (1967) suggests that leaders might change the situation to fit their style; this implies that current situation favorability would have an influence on future leader behavior. But these theories do not directly address the dynamic aspects of leader behavior, the spontaneous choices that a leader makes among alternative courses of action. In short, they do not describe how a leader *does* lead but rather how she *should* lead.

There are two current theories that stress the dynamic and reciprocal aspects of leader behavior. We will describe them briefly.

Hollander's Social Exchange Theory of Leadership

Hollander (1978) suggests that the leadership "problem" is one of coordinating situational variables, leader characteristics and expectations, and follower characteristics and expectations. Figure 12–13 graphically depicts the interrelationships of these variables. It implies that a leader's behavior can be understood only in light of the variables included in the *situation, follower, and leader* components. Further, it implies that the critical interaction is between follower expectations and leader behaviors and that this interaction is embedded in a particular situation or context. Hollander proposes that leaders change or maintain their behavior to conform to the expectations of the subordinates. This is done because the leader *needs* certain things from the group:

FIGURE 12–13 Hollander's Social Exchange Theory

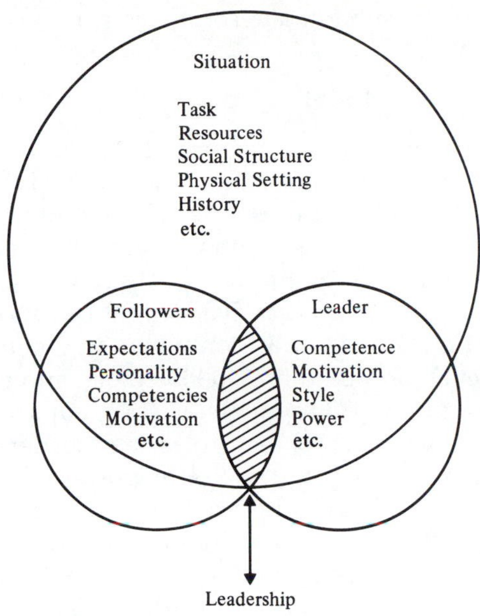

SOURCE: From *Principles and Methods of Social Psychology*, Third Edition, by Edwin P. Hollander. Copyright © 1976 by Oxford University Press, Inc. Reprinted by permission.

loyalty, energy expenditure, praise, and so on. Similarly, the group accepts or rejects the behavior of the leader according to expectations, anticipated rewards, and probability estimates of goal attainment. This process clearly implies an *exchange* between leader and follower. The theory further suggests that this exchange must be seen as an *equitable* one by both leader and follower. Thus, the propositions of equity theory, as described in Chapter 10, would be important propositions for the social exchange theory of leadership as well. This takes the results of Lowin and Craig (1968) and Greene (1975) one step further by suggesting *why* the leader behavior changed in response to poor subordinate performance: the leader may have felt that the exchange had become an inequitable one, with too much being contributed by the leader and too little by the follower.

At this point, Hollander's propositions are primarily conceptual. The specific hypotheses suggested by the theory have not been tested. As a matter of fact, the theory itself has probably not stopped growing or changing yet. Nevertheless, it is extremely promising because it considers leadership as both a dependent and independent variable. As a simple example, consider the discussion of absence in the last chapter. Chadwick-Jones et al. (1982)

suggest that absence is a concrete example of the exchange that occurs between supervisor and leader. It would not be difficult to identify other examples in the supervisor-subordinate social system.

The Vertical Dyad Model

A second theory that stresses the variables influencing the leader's behavior has been proposed by Dansereau, Graen, and Haga (1974). They suggest that leadership behaviors represent a role that develops over time and is based on the quality of supervisor-subordinate relationships. Any follower and leader form a two-person group called a *dyad;* since the two persons are at different organizational levels, the dyad might be called a *vertical dyad.*

On the basis of a research study conducted in a manufacturing organization, Dansereau et al. proposed that followers fall into two distinct groups: in-group members and out-group members. In-groups are characterized by high latitude for negotiating their own roles, and leaders tend to deal with these groups without resorting to the use of power stemming from formal authority; these types of relationships are thought of as "high-quality" interactions. Out-groups are characterized by low latitude for negotiating their roles and have leaders who commonly attempt to influence them by using formal authority. These two groups of followers are not naturally occurring; that is, people are not "born" to be in- or out-group members (regardless of what your cousin says). Group membership is a role that develops on the basis of leader-follower interaction.

Their results also suggested that managers typically play two roles simultaneously. They play a supervisory role with out-group members and a leadership role with in-group members. This strongly suggests that follower characteristics have an influence on a manager's behavior. Once again, we are confronted with the reciprocal nature of the leader-follower relationship. In addition, we are reminded of the substantial difference between supervision (the simple direction of effort) and effective leadership (the motivation of subordinates).

In a test of the theory, Graen and Scheimann (1978) demonstrated that in-group members agreed more highly with their supervisors about the nature of work-related situations than did out-group members. This is an unusual finding. It is much more common to find that employees and supervisors agree to only a limited extent about work-related variables. Graen and Scheimann propose that leaders are closer to in-group members, thus are more likely to share common points of view. Studies that do not separate subordinates into in- and out-groups would be unlikely to find high levels of agreement. These results suggest two things: (1) as a classification scheme, the in-group–out-group distinction is a valuable one, and (2) leader behaviors are dynamic and are substantially affected by follower characteristics.

The exchange relationship between supervisor and subordinate is receiving increasing attention. Graen, Liden, and Hoel (1982) looked at high-

and low-quality exchange relationships in an attempt to understand turnover. They found that members tended to remain in an organization if they saw themselves as actively exchanging support and emotional resources as well as *extra* effort with their supervisors. On the other hand, if the exchange involved only the contractually agreed upon elements—for example, eight hours work for eight hours pay—there was a greater tendency to leave the organization. Graen extended the characterization to include high- and low-quality exchange relationships. In low-quality relationships, leaders seldom talked to subordinates about effectiveness or helped them with different assignments. In high-quality exchanges, leaders discussed performance with subordinates, initiated discussions about personal matters and problems, and appeared genuinely interested in work-related difficulties. At least on the surface, the issue seems to be one of a social or personal bonding between supervisor and subordinate. It may be that this is the critical bond that immunizes against alienation and encourages worker commitment. There is one discordant note supplied by a recent study by Duchon, Graen, and Taber (1986). Out-group members, in spite of being aware that they are not among the "favored," do not see themselves as having less influence, as having less enriched jobs, or as experiencing less satisfaction with their leader. One might expect that part of the out-group identification process is the feeling of second-class citizenship, but this does not seem to be the case. This is puzzling.

It is interesting to note that the nature of the leader-member exchange influences the extent to which followers will be given a decision-making role. In two studies, Graen and his colleagues (Scandura, Graen, & Novak, 1986; Wakabayashi & Graen, 1984) found that if a subordinate had good relations with her superior and high ability, she would be given opportunities for influence. But if either a high-quality relationship with the supervisor or high ability was missing, little decision influence would be offered to the subordinate.

Vecchio (1982) has also examined the vertical dyad linkage (VDL) model and come to some interesting conclusions. He contrasted two positions. The first position is the traditional one as emphasized in the Ohio State model or Fiedler's contingency theory. It suggests that leaders bring one constant style or behavior pattern to all their interactions with subordinates. Vecchio calls this the *average leadership style* (ALS) approach. In contrast, the VDL approach suggests that there are specific relationships between the supervisor and *each* subordinate and that it is this special relationship that influences leader effectiveness. This was the point of the Graen et al. (1982) discussion of high-quality and low-quality exchanges described above. Vecchio found that VDL did seem to influence subordinate attitudes but not their performance. Miner (1980) suggests a possible explanation for Vecchio's results. It may be that VDL relationships are peculiar to upper organizational levels. Supervisors of blue-collar workers may feel pressure to treat everyone the same. In fact, a pattern of idiosyncratic leader behavior similar to that described by the VDL model might even lead to a grievance in a work group represented by a union.

In addition, the performance of blue-collar and lower-level workers is often homogeneous and constrained by job descriptions, equipment, and interdependent tasks.

An interesting position seems to be emerging from the ALS-VDL contrast. It is tempting to choose *between* the two approaches. That would be a mistake. Instead, it would seem valuable to examine the balance between a leader's ALS and VDL behaviors. From this perspective, leadership is seen as the superimposition of unique or idiosyncratic supervisor-subordinate relationships on a backdrop of habitual response patterns (such as those represented by LPC scores or consideration scores). The issue of leader-member exchange deserves continuing attention.

SUBSTITUTES FOR LEADERSHIP

Most of us have noted situations that seem to contradict the leadership theories that we have just examined. The first situation is characterized by effective work groups or individuals with poor or missing leaders. The second situation is characterized by leaders who would seem on the surface to have all the prerequisites for effective leadership yet seem not to be able to make use of those talents. In simple terms, there seem to be situations when leadership is redundant or unimportant, and there seem to be other situations when attempts at leadership are blocked. Kerr and Jermier (1978) have considered those situations and proposed two different sets of variables to account for these events. One group of variables has been labeled *leadership substitutes*, and the other, *leadership neutralizers.* Substitutes make leadership unnecessary or redundant; neutralizers prevent a leader from acting in a particular way. Table 12–3 presents a sample of the variables that might function as either substitutes for or neutralizers to supportive (considerate) or instrumental (structuring) leadership behaviors. From the perspective of this table, the theories that we have considered to this point assume some set of ideal circumstances that make the leader behavior in question important or at least guarantee that the leader may behave in a particular way. This table suggests some of the realistic limits to the practice of leadership. As Kerr and Jermier point out, there is an important difference between substitutes and neutralizers. Substitutes represent a "person or thing acting or used in place of" the missing influence of the leader. Neutralizers, on the other hand, create a leadership vacuum. This vacuum will probably result in some serious organizational dysfunction.

There are several important implications of the concepts of substitutes and neutralizers. The first implication relates to research. If such variables do exist, they can be invoked to account for the wide variation in tests of various leadership theories. For example, if a cohesive work group is a substitute for supportive leadership, then leader's consideration scores may be unrelated to the satisfaction or performance of cohesive work groups. Similarly, if the rewards offered by the organization are unimportant or undervalued, the

TABLE 12–3 Specific Substitutes and Neutralizers: Supportive and Instrumental Leadership

Substitute or Neutralizer	*Supportive Leadership*	*Instrumental Leadership*
A. Subordinate characteristics		
1. Experience, ability, training		Substitute
2. "Professional" orientation	Substitute	Substitute
3. Indifference toward rewards offered by organization	Neutralizer	Neutralizer
B. Task characteristics		
1. Structured, routine, unambiguous task		Substitute
2. Feedback provided by task		Substitute
3. Intrinsically satisfying task	Substitute	
C. Organization characteristics		
1. Cohesive work group	Substitute	Substitute
2. Low position power (leader lacks control over organizational rewards)	Neutralizer	Neutralizer
3. Formalization (explicit plans, goals, areas of responsibility)		Substitute
4. Inflexibility (rigid, unyielding rules and procedures)		Neutralizer
5. Leader located apart from subordinates with only limited communication possible	Neutralizer	Neutralizer

SOURCE: From *Leadership in Organizations* (p. 163) by G. A. Yukl, 1981, Englewood Cliffs, NJ: Prentice-Hall. Based on Kerr and Jermier, 1978.

extent to which a leader can remove obstacles from the path of the subordinate may be irrelevant. From examples like these, it can be seen that the presence or absence of certain situational variables can have a major influence on the potency of a proposed independent variable, such as LPC score or consideration score.

There is another, more practical implication of the substitute-neutralizer hypotheses. Consider the cells in Table 12–3 where the word *substitute* appears. It should be possible to develop the substitute variable in work groups or individuals when the leader is weak or inexperienced or ineffective. In fact, when you consider the issue of leaderless or autonomous work groups—groups without hierarchical leaders—you will probably find that the principles guiding their formation include the presence of many of the substitutes that appear in Table 12–3. To take the final step, you might even replace the word *substitute* with the phrase *self-motivating* and the word *neutralizer* with the phrase *demotivating*. This would permit the entire concept of leadership to be replaced with the concept of motivation—a possibility implied by several of the theories that we have examined.

There is a recent research trend that ties into the substitute-neutralizer framework quite well. It is the concept of self-monitoring. Sarason and Potter

(1983) find that individuals who are taught to monitor their own performance (act as their own leaders) perform better and are more satisfied than counterparts who do not have these skills. Manz and Sims (1979) suggest that self-management makes leadership efforts redundant. This thought is easily extended. It may be that self-monitoring or self-management is a neutralizer to instrumental leadership. Individuals or groups capable of monitoring their own activities may actively resist attempts by leaders to direct their activities. The relationship between self-management and leadership substitutes-neutralizers deserves close attention.

The concepts of substitutes and neutralizers are useful. They help to remind us that leaders occasionally lead at the pleasure of followers. Similarly, it serves to remind us that even in situations where the leader seems to be making a difference, she may be redundant. The effective performance may be the result of a substitute variable rather than a leader behavior.

AN OVERVIEW OF THE THEORIES

Dismissing for the moment the problems of substitutes and neutralizers, the theories of leadership that we have examined to this point actually fall into two separate categories. One of these categories might be more appropriately called *theories of followership.* This is because these theories consider leadership as an independent variable and are mainly concerned with the effect of leader behaviors on followers. They tend to be prescriptive and suggest the "best" ways of leading. There is, of course, something to be learned from an examination of the effects of leaders' behavior, particularly if the leader strives to improve his effectiveness. Nevertheless, these theories represent the *application* of knowledge regarding leader behavior. They are based solely on a distinction between successful and unsuccessful leaders. The Ohio State studies, Fiedler's contingency theory, and to a certain extent, the Vroom-Yetton model all fall into this group. In Figure 12–14, these models are represented by arrows running from left to right. These arrows imply that the important perspective is what leaders *do* to other people.

Other theories deal with the *dynamics* of leadership. They attempt to understand why leaders behave the way they do. They view leadership as a role or system, capable of being influenced at any time by a number of other variables within the same system. Hollander's social exchange theory and the vertical dyad model fall into this category. Most of the atheoretical studies of management style also fall into this category (e.g., types of power used by leaders). Although this second group of theories may also be used prescriptively to improve leader effectiveness, this is not the primary purpose. In Figure 12–14, these theories have arrows running from right to left or in both directions. This implies that the important perspective for leadership research is understanding why leaders act the way they do or how reciprocal relationships develop between leaders and followers.

FIGURE 12–14 General Approaches in Research on Leader Effectiveness

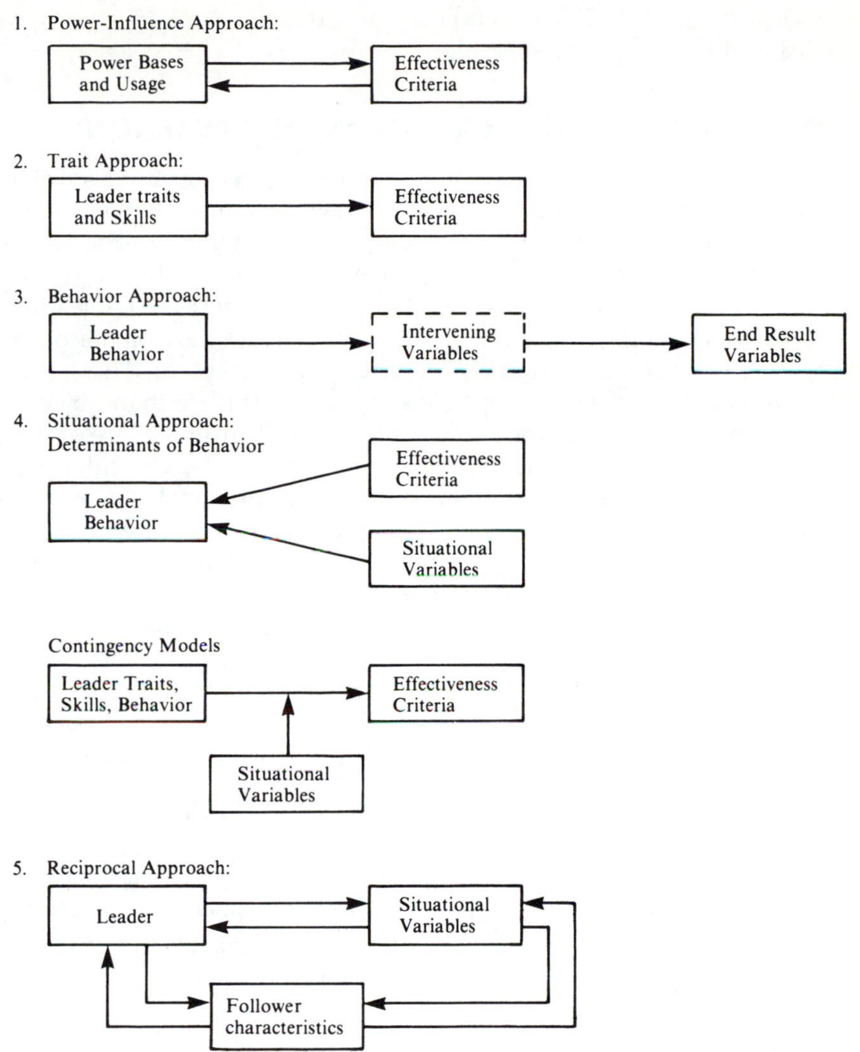

SOURCE: From *Leadership in Organizations,* (p. 7) by G. A. Yukl, 1981, Englewood Cliffs, NJ: Prentice-Hall. Reprinted by permission of Prentice-Hall, Inc.

More than 20 years of research devoted to the first kind of theory has not brought us much closer to an understanding of leader behavior (although they have provided us with a useful vocabulary; e.g., "consideration," "initiating structure"). It may be time to concentrate research efforts on theories like those in the second group. The first set of theories can be adequately covered by theories of worker motivation and satisfaction. It is the second class of theories that represents a unique contribution to understanding work behavior in the context of leadership.

LEADERSHIP AS AN ATTRIBUTIONAL PHENOMENON

You may not have noticed it, but we have begged a rather substantial question up to this point in the chapter. We have assumed that leadership is something that exists and can be identified in the behavior of the leader or supervisor. There is a counterposition. It may be that leadership is something that exists in the eye of the beholder—the follower. It may be that leadership is nothing more than a cognitive construction on the part of the observer (follower) that is used to account for events in the workplace. This has some serious implications. If leadership is a subjectively (rather than objectively) perceived construct, most of the theories presented to this point are off-target. The same might be said for leadership training programs. Consider the following example that puts this dilemma in the simplest light. A researcher goes into an organization and administers a leadership questionnaire. In addition, measures of individual and group performance are collected. A correlation between leadership style scores (e.g., consideration) and performance measures is calculated and turns out to be positive and significant. The researcher concludes that leader consideration results in high performance. But consider an alternative explanation: high-performing groups and individuals describe their leaders as more considerate than low-performing groups and individuals. In other words, consider the possibility that performance levels are affecting leader descriptions rather than the other way around. This is a radical point of view. We will examine it and some related points in this section. There are two different aspects that deserve attention. The first is concerned with general theories of leadership that individuals might hold, independent of the actual behavior of the leader. These are called *implicit theories*. The second aspect that bears on the question relates to variables that seem to influence an individual's perception of leadership behaviors.

Implicit Theories of Leadership

In a study of the leadership perceptions of undergraduate students, Rush, Thomas, and Lord (1977) found that there were few differences between the perceptions by these subjects of fictitious and superficially described leaders and the perceptions of employed samples rating the leader behaviors of real supervisors. In addition, it was discovered that the ratings of the students were significantly influenced by cues regarding the effectiveness of the performance of the individual being rated. This led Rush et al. to conclude that rather than leader behavior, leadership questionnaires were actually tapping the cognitive sets of the respondents. In a later study, Phillips and Lord (1981) found some evidence that subjects may develop global impressions of leadership effectiveness and then use those global impressions to describe leader behavior on specific dimensions of leadership. In a recent study, Phillips (1984) extended the phenomenon even further. He found that if subjects were told beforehand that leaders were effective or ineffective, these subjects reported leader behaviors consistent with these labels after watching the leaders perform in a group problem-solving setting for 15 minutes. The important point to note here is that an impression held prior to observing the leader accounted for substantial variance in subsequent descriptions of that leader.

The studies listed above were noninteractive. The observers and raters of leader behavior were not really subordinates. They were subjects told to adopt the role of observers. This raises the question of how implicit theories or preconceptions work when there are real supervisor-subordinate pairs. Eden and Shani (1982) conducted a fascinating study in the Israeli army. Trainees in the armed forces were labeled as "high expectations" (likely to move quickly to a command position), "regular expectations" (average movement), or "unknown." The supervisors of these trainees were exposed to these bogus labels four days prior to the arrival of the trainees at boot camp. The results showed that trainees who were labeled as "high expectations" perceived their leaders as more positive and also achieved higher scores in an objective achievement test at the end of the training period. This suggests that these implicit theories or preconceptions that individuals have may actually affect their behavior. In this case, it is plausible to assume that the leaders developed expectations about the trainees, acted in a way that was necessary to confirm those expectations, and produced higher-quality trainees who noted the special attention that they received. From this perspective, leader behaviors were instrumental in fulfilling prophecies that the leaders had accepted in the form of labels. This study suggests one additional intriguing possibility. Since the "regular expectations" and "unknown" candidates did not score particularly high on the objective achievement test and did not perceive the leaders as unusually positive, the leaders must have acted differently toward these "less talented" trainees. This suggests that leadership behavior may be dispensed by the leader as would a scarce resource. It is used sparingly or suboptimally on particular individuals. In some senses, this is exactly what Graen was suggesting with the vertical dyad linkage model. This should not be particularly surprising. It has been found to occur frequently in classroom settings where teachers interact with students based on expectations created by test scores and past academic history.

Recently Lord and his colleagues (Lord, Foti, & Phillips, 1986) have been pursuing the issue of leadership from a more traditional cognitive framework. They have been examining the possibility that individuals carry around conceptions of prototypic leaders in their heads and use these conceptions to analyze and store information about actual leaders. The implications of this are serious for the measurement of leadership behavior using the standard leadership questionnaires. It means that people use simplifying mechanisms to store and recover information about leader behavior. In the process of simplifying the actual behavior, distortions and biases are introduced. Thus, we return to the question, What is being measured by leadership scales—the behavior of the leader or the cognitive categories of the observer? There is no answer to this question yet, but there is the possibility that typical leadership questionnaires may have to be abandoned as methods for measuring leader behavior.

Additional Distorting Factors in Leadership Perception

Implicit theories and methods of categorization are descriptions of abstract processes that individuals may use to store and retrieve data. Let's consider some concrete examples of distorting influences on leadership perceptions. One way to demonstrate the distorting effect is to consider the traditional demographic characteristic of sex. Consider the evaluations of autocratic styles of supervision as practiced by men and women. Jago and Vroom (1982) found that women who adopted autocratic styles of supervision were evaluated more negatively than male counterparts who adopted the same style. This finding parallels the results of an earlier study by Haccoun, Haccoun, and Sallay (1978). Male and female leaders acting in a similar manner are perceived differently. This certainly suggests that some variance in the perception of leaders is in the eye of the beholder rather than in the behavior of the leader. Recently, Trempe, Rigny, and Haccoun (1985) suggest that there is some confounding going on. They suggest that the reason why women are perceived of as less effective is not necessarily because they are women but because they find themselves stuck with jobs that have little possibility of upward influence. Since it is upward influence that often affects the subordinate's view of the leader, it may be the influence variable rather than the sex variable that is causing the harm.

There are many studies that document disagreements among observers regarding leader behavior. Graen and Scheimann (1978) have demonstrated such discrepancies as a function of high- and low-quality exchange relationships; Mitchell, Larson, and Green (1977) demonstrated that groups who perceived themselves as high performers were more positive in their descriptions of their leaders than those who perceived themselves as poor performers. Many similar studies could be cited. They all suggest the same thing: At least some of the variance in the description of leader behavior is the result of perceptual processes of the observers. This is not to say that there is *no* relationship between leader behavior and observer description, but the relationship may be far from perfect. Once again, we are left with the uneasy feeling that the typical questionnaire measures of leadership are not telling us what we want to know. If the problem is simply one of the method of measurement, then there is reason for optimism. The thing that I/O psychologists do *best* is develop new methods of measurement. For the time being, the most reasonable conclusion that might be drawn is that standard questionnaires for measuring leadership behavior are under suspicion and should be used cautiously.

CENTRAL POINTS FOR STUDY

1. Leader effectiveness and leader emergence are different variables.
2. The Ohio State studies of leadership were based on a behavioral approach.
3. Fiedler's contingency theory of leadership emphasizes situational characteristics and leader behaviors.
4. The Vroom-Yetton model is a theory of decision making.
5. Behavior modification principles have been applied to leader behavior.
6. Reciprocal theories of leadership emphasize both the behavior of leaders and the behavior of followers.
7. It may be the case that substitutes for leadership and neutralizers of leader behavior exist.
8. Leader behavior may be an attribution of followers.

CHAPTER 13

The Organization of Behavior

One of your tasks as a student in this course is understanding the behavior of individuals in work settings. So far, the identification, selection, and training of appropriate applicants, theories for understanding why energy is expended at work and the relationship between the behavior of leaders and the behavior of subordinates have been described. There is another element that must be introduced to understand fully the relationship between a worker and a job; that element is *organization.*

In every work setting, there are dozens of organizing forces acting simultaneously on the behavior of people in that setting. The most obvious organizing influence is the leader of the group. In fact, it has been suggested that all organizing is really an example of leadership of one variety or another (Hosking, 1988). Hosking proposes that organizing is simply a matter of negotiating, since it involves individuals who are seldom in the same power structure. As a result, it is not possible to "command" that an action be carried out. Instead, it is necessary to persuade others to carry out actions. It is this pattern of coordinated action that best represents the process of organization. To some extent, then, the efficiency in an organization is thought to be the result of the efficiency of the *organizer*—the leader. It is best to keep in mind that many organizations will have more than one leader (or organizer). For example, there might be three leaders in the night shift of a manufacturing organization. The first leader might be the person designated as the supervisor. The second leader could be the most experienced machine operator. The third leader might be the union steward assigned to that shift. Each of these individuals might have a unique point of view and goal for that night shift. The efficiency of the shift (and by extension, the organization) will be determined by how well these individuals are able to negotiate their different roles.

Hosking's view of the organizing process is a radical one from a historical viewpoint. It implies that we should be studying the organizing *process* rather than organizational characteristics. This is an appealing perspective for the psychologist since it involves variables such as values, motivations, cognitions, and attitudes. More traditional views of organizations (and organizational behavior) emphasize less dynamic and more static variables. As an example of this more traditional perspective, one might examine the formal characteristics of the organization itself. These characteristics would include such things as chain of command, permissible communication channels, and policies regarding compensation. Each of these factors is an attempt to organize a person's efforts, to have the person behave within certain boundaries. In addition to these formal organizational characteristics, there are informal characteristics. In a sense, these informal characteristics might be thought of as the "personality" of the organization. Consider the personality of the organization that might issue the memo that appears in Figure 13–1. This would be a very "special" type of organization—one that most of us would rather not join. Organizations might have innovative or traditional reputations; they might be thought of as cold and impersonal or warm and familylike to their employees; they might be participative or authoritarian. Each of the personality characteristics also influences the behavior of organizational members. As an example, employees in authoritarian organizations learn not to bother putting ideas into the suggestion box, and employees of "cold" organizations don't bother the personnel manager with personal problems. In these ways behavior has been organized. Other mechanisms of organization would include the nature of the job (e.g., assembly lines have an enormous organizing impact) and work groups (e.g., individual workers are often discouraged from doing too much work).

Although informal characteristics may define the personality of an organization, there is no doubt that the formal characteristics of an organization play a role in the formation of this personality as well. Just as individuals with unusual physical characteristics often develop styles of behavior that reflect these characteristics, so do organizations develop styles that fit a particular configuration of characteristics. Big organizations act one way; small organizations act another. To return to the individual level again for a second, those who are interested in looking at the influence of stable characteristics on behavior might be called *trait psychologists.* You saw examples of this approach in the leadership chapter. This has been a popular approach over the years, although its popularity is quickly giving way to situational and interactional theories. There is a counterpart to the trait theme in theories of organizational behavior. Researchers have sought to find relationships between particular stable characteristics of organizations (e.g., size, number of levels of supervision) and the behavior of organizational members. Schneider (1985) has labeled this pursuit of a relationship between factors that might describe an organization and factors that might describe an individual as *schizophrenic,* a matter of mixing apples and oranges. Nevertheless, as you will see shortly, this was a popular approach for many years. It was called the classic approach. That approach is now giving way to more dynamic systems of understanding that consider stable characteristics as one influence, although not the only or even most important influence. The real issue is not what the characteristic is but how that characteristic is interpreted by members of an organization and used by them in their organizational negotiations. Size, per se, is uninteresting to the psychologist. What is interesting is how size gets "coded" by organizational members. Does it imply impersonality to

FIGURE 13–1 Organization Personality

Restroom Policy Keeps Workers on Edge of Seats

By Gary T. Marx

Marx, a sociology professor at MIT, is engaged in research on the monitoring of work and workers. This article originally appeared in the Los Angeles Times.

CAMBRIDGE, Mass.—As part of a research project on productivity, I recently came across the following innovative policy just adopted by a major corporation. It might serve as a model for other companies wrestling with this problem.

TO: ALL EMPLOYEES
FROM: PERSONNEL DEPT.
SUBJECT: RESTROOM POLICY

An internal audit of employee restroom time (ERT) has found that this company significantly exceeds the national ERT standard recommended by the President's commission on Productivity and Waste. At the same time, some employees complained about being unfairly singled out for ERT monitoring. Technical Division (TD) has developed an accounting and control system that will solve both problems.

Effective 1 April 1987, a Restroom Trip Policy (RTP) is established.

A Restroom Trip Bank (RTB) will be created for each employee. On the first day of each month employees will receive a Restroom Trip Credit (RTC) of 40. The previous policy of unlimited trips is abolished.

Restroom access will be controlled by a computer-linked voice-print recognition system. Within the next two weeks, each employee must provide two voice prints (one normal, one under stress) to Personnel. To facilitate familiarity with the system, voice-print recognition stations will be operational but not restrictive during the month of April.

Should an employee's RTB balance reach zero, restroom doors will not unlock for his/her voice until the first working day of the following month.

Restroom stalls have been equipped with timed tissue-roll retraction and automatic flushing and door-opening capability. To help employees maximize their time, a simulated voice will announce elapsed ERT up to 3 minutes. A 30-second warning buzzer will then sound. At the end of the 30 seconds the roll of tissue will retract, the toilet will flush and the stall door will open. Employees may choose whether they wish to hear a male or female "voice." A bilingual capability is being developed, but is not yet on-line.

To prevent unauthorized access (e.g., sneaking in behind someone with an RTB surplus, or use of a tape-recorded voice), video cameras in the corridor will record those seeking access to the restroom. However, consistent with the company's policy of respecting the privacy of its employees, cameras will not be operative within the restroom itself.

An additional advantage of the system is its capability for automatic urine analysis (AUA). This permits drug-

SOURCE: From "Restroom Policy Keeps Workers on Edge of Seats" by G. T. Marx, April 3, 1987, *Atlanta Constitution*, p. 21.

FIGURE 13–1 *(concluded)*

testing without the demeaning presence of an observer and without risk of human error in switching samples. The restrooms and associated plumbing are the property of the company. Legal Services has advised that there are no privacy rights over voluntarily discarded garbage and other like materials.

In keeping with our concern for employee privacy, participation in AUA is strictly voluntary. But employees who choose to participate will be eligible for attractive prizes in recognition of their support for the company's policy of a drug-free workplace.

Management recognizes that from time to time employees may have a legitimate need to use the restroom. But employees must also recognize that their jobs depend on this company's staying competitive in a global economy. These conflicting interests should be weighed, but certainly not balanced. The company remains strongly committed to finding technical solutions to management problems. We continue to believe that machines are fairer and more reliable than managers. We also believe that our trusted employees will do the right thing when given no other choice.

them? Coldness? Lack of accountability? Unwillingness to reward appropriately? Why does one individual see the organization as impersonal and another individual see the same organization as close-knit and supportive? Those are the real questions for the psychologist.

THEORIES AS ALTERNATIVE PERSPECTIVES

In this chapter, we will consider some of the organizing influences described above. These influences will be examined from several different perspectives. Historically, theories of organization have played a major role in research and practice. These theories are formal attempts to describe "correct" organizing principles that might be used to design and administer an organization. They are prescriptive—they tell you "how to" and are a view of the world of work through the glasses of the designer—the engineer whose task it is to build the organization. Many of these theories are the "trait" variety described above. A very different perspective of organizational influences is provided when we look through the glasses of the worker—the target of the designer. We will consider that point of view by looking at some of the *effects* of organizational characteristics and design on the organizational members. This point of view can be seen in the newer theories of organization. We will consider two of these newer approaches—human-relations theory and sociotechnical theory.

A third area that we will cover in the chapter is more practical than theoretical, although it has theoretical implications. It has become clear that we are not always aware of the variables that help shape (or organize) our behavior. The gestalt principles of perception are good examples. We are more likely to see some patterns than others. Similarly, we are often ready to make negative judgments about people who are not members of our own group. In organizational psychology, a major line of activity is helping to make people aware of the influences working on their behavior within certain organizational settings. This activity is not prescriptive. The intention is not so much to tell people *how* to behave as it is to make them aware of how they are behaving. This gives them the choice of maintaining or changing that behavior. The goal is to support or facilitate change within the organization. This general area has become known as *organizational development* (OD), and we will sample some of its content.

THE IMPORTANCE OF ORGANIZATION

Organization is key to understanding human behavior. It does not matter whether that behavior occurs in the middle of the desert, hundreds of miles from another person, or in a major airport, in the midst of thousands of fellow travelers. Each of us has almost 100 billion neurons at birth. We are capable of producing hundreds of chemicals (neurotransmitters and hormones) that will influence our behavior. We have perceptual mechanisms that are dedicated to making sense out of apparent nonsense. Without the hierarchical organization of the central nervous system, the temporal organization of the autonomic nervous system and the built-in interpretation mechanisms of the perceptual system, life would be unbearable. In fact, life does become difficult when one or another mechanism of organization does not work properly. Brain damage, chemical imbalance, and sensory-perceptual deficiencies all lead to disordered behavior. The same is true in work settings. Consider our three "leaders" of the night shift. What happens when one of them is characterized as a "loose cannon," unpredictable and unable or unwilling to negotiate with the other two leaders? The result is inefficiency at best and chaos at worst. Job actions and wildcat strikes often result from such organizational deficiencies. In all work settings, there are certain principles of organization in operation. If any two of these principles are incompatible (e.g., organizing efforts of the work group and organizing efforts of the upper-level administration), problems arise. These problems can be emotional, behavioral, or both. This is why the analogy between the personality of an individual and the personality of an organization is an apt one. Personality implies integration. It suggests that the various forces acting on an individual are in balance. Disordered personalities involve imbalances and unusual behavior. The same is true of organizations. When forces are out of balance, disorder and disintegration occur. Thus, in this chapter, we will consider the forces present in work settings that help or hinder integration of the efforts and emotions of organizational members.

FORMAL THEORIES OF ORGANIZATION

An Overview

Organizations without people have no meaning. IBM has an image. This image is one of an operationally conservative, individually creative company with bottom-line orientation. We can point to rules, reporting relationships, decision-making strategies, and work group design that maintain this image. On the other hand, without people to react to these rules, to report in a particular direction, to produce innovative designs, or to respond to pressure from the competition, the image is without substance or meaning, much like a snapshot of a stranger. IBM's competition with Apple computers is not a competition between companies—it is a competition among individuals inside and outside of those companies. In order to understand completely the influence of organizational principles on behavior, we must consider both the characteristics of the environment and the characteristics of the people who function in that environment.

Early theories of organization tended to emphasize the importance of the immediate organizational environment on work behavior. Further, there was an emphasis on certain "key" variables in that environment. These theories have been commonly referred to as *classic* organization theories. Classic organization theorists proposed that variables such as size and number of levels of supervision determined the success or efficiency of organizations. These variables were generally considered independently of the individuals in an organization. This approach was prescriptive, in that it suggested the "one best way" to organize the efforts of organizational members. This approach is reflected in the early works of the sociologist Durkheim, who implied that people could be characterized *as a function of* the structural properties of the society in which they lived. From this perspective, it was important to build the skeleton of the organization carefully, since the behavior of the people in the organization would be a *product* of this skeleton. This view was made more concrete in the propositions of Weber (1947) regarding bureaucracies. We will consider these propositions in some detail shortly.

A second group of theorists took issue with the broad "one best way" emphasis of the classical theories. Instead, they suggested that there were a number of "best ways." It was proposed that there were certain situations that were more conducive to one skeleton than to another. For example, if a company wanted accuracy and timeliness in production efforts, one type of organization was called for. On the other hand, if the organization wanted innovation, another type of organization was called for. In other words, they were suggesting that the best way depended on certain other conditions—that the best way was contingent on particular situational characteristics. This emphasis should be familiar to you. In the last chapter, you saw examples of leadership theories that suggested the existence of multiple best ways to lead. The Vroom and Yetton decision-making model and Fiedler's contingency theory were examples of this approach. In keeping with that terminology, I will refer to this second group of organizational theories as *contingency* theories of organization.

There is something that these two approaches—classic and contingency—have in common: neither places much emphasis on the properties of the actors in these idealized organizational environments, the individual workers. Neither of the approaches has much to say about things like satisfaction, motivation, interpersonal conflict, or leadership. This personal perspective has been taken by a third group of organization theorists. I will label this group the *human relations* group. This approach was popularized by Elton Mayo as a result of his conclusions based on the Hawthorne studies. He concluded that the attitudes of workers toward management and their fellow workers influenced their behavior at the workplace. The human relations theorists begin with the characteristics of the individual organism—the worker—in forming their theory. They propose that it is practically impossible to understand or predict the "behavior" of an organization (if, in fact, an organization can "behave") without understanding or being able to predict the behavior of the people making up that organization. Implied in the human relations approaches is the idea that the formal organization, as it exists today, is a reflection (although not by any means a perfect one) of the problem-solving, decision-making, and general thought processes of the human being. This view of the organization is very different from that of either the classical or the contingency theorists. The role of the individual is of maximum importance in human relations theories but of questionable value in classical or contingency theories. As Argyris (1972) has so aptly put it in attacking the peripheral role given the individual in a recent form of classic theory, "The variable human seems to be minimally variable and minimally human" (p. 33). To some extent, this criticism is equally applicable to contingency theories.

Although all the variations of the classical versus contingency versus human relations argument cannot be discussed here, it is important for you to understand the basic differences among the three approaches. In the following sections, I will present examples and descriptions of each of these approaches. Because I will present each of the approaches individually, it will be tempting for you to view this as a "competition," as if your task were to choose one of these approaches as "correct," thus eliminating the others from consideration. This would be a serious mistake. As we have seen in theories of satisfaction, motivation, and leadership, different approaches offer different advantages. There are certain appealing characteristics of classical theory. The same can be said of contingency and human relations theory. Consider Figure 13–2. This is a staggering yet realistic view of any organization, regardless of whether that organization is a cub scout troop or General Motors. The specific aspect of the organization that interests you will dictate which of the theoretical approaches might be most helpful. The left side of the figure would benefit more from the classical approaches. The right side suggests that human relations propositions will be more helpful. The bridges between major subsections (e.g., external environment and organization, organization and subsystem) seem prime candidates for the application of contingency theories. Thus, it is not particularly helpful to think of various theories as competitors. Instead, it is best to consider each approach as a different perspective on how behavior is organized.

Now that you have been introduced to the nature of the problem to be explored, the approaches will be presented in some detail. The first approach to be considered will be the classical one.

CLASSIC ORGANIZATION THEORY

One of the best known classical organization theories was proposed by Max Weber (1947) in his propositions in favor of *bureaucracy* as the ideal model for organizational efficiency. For Weber, the bureaucratic form of organization was a form of social protest against the excesses of the entrepreneurial system as it existed in the early days of the Industrial Revolution. It was an attempt to describe a system that could function free of the injustices of nepotism and favoritism; it was a system that was predictable, allowing the individual worker to make long-range plans; it was also a system that allowed an individual to advance on the basis of merit rather than on the basis of predetermined classes or castes.

Weber proposed that such a system could be characterized or described along a number of dimensions. Those most often mentioned are division of labor, delegation of authority, structure, and span of control. Before dealing with each of these components in turn, let's look in a global sense at the role of these components in solving the basic organizational problem of successfully completing a complex operation. The operation is first broken down into a number of smaller, specifiable components; this is known as the *division of labor* or *specialization* and is thought to be necessary for the assignment and discharge of complex responsibilities. This division of labor, in turn, creates a problem of the coordination of these complex responsibilities. Coordination is thought to be best handled through the systematic *delegation of authority*. Figure 13–3 depicts a traditional organizational chart. The vertical dimension of the figure represents the delegation of authority. The horizontal dimension represents division of labor or specialization. It was felt that only through this hierarchical arrangement of authority could supervisors hope to guide the activities of subordinates. The chart implies the formal authority vested in each position. The higher the level in the chart, the more authority in the position. Leadership activities are the way in which this authority is manifested in the work setting.

The third and fourth components, *structure* and *span of control*, are interrelated. Structure is basically the height of an organization relative to its width. The structure continuum varies from tall to flat. Span of control, in its simplest form, is the number of subordinates controlled by a single supervisor. Tallness or flatness, then, is dependent on the number of hierarchical levels of au-

FIGURE 13–2 A Framework for the Study of Behavior in Organizations

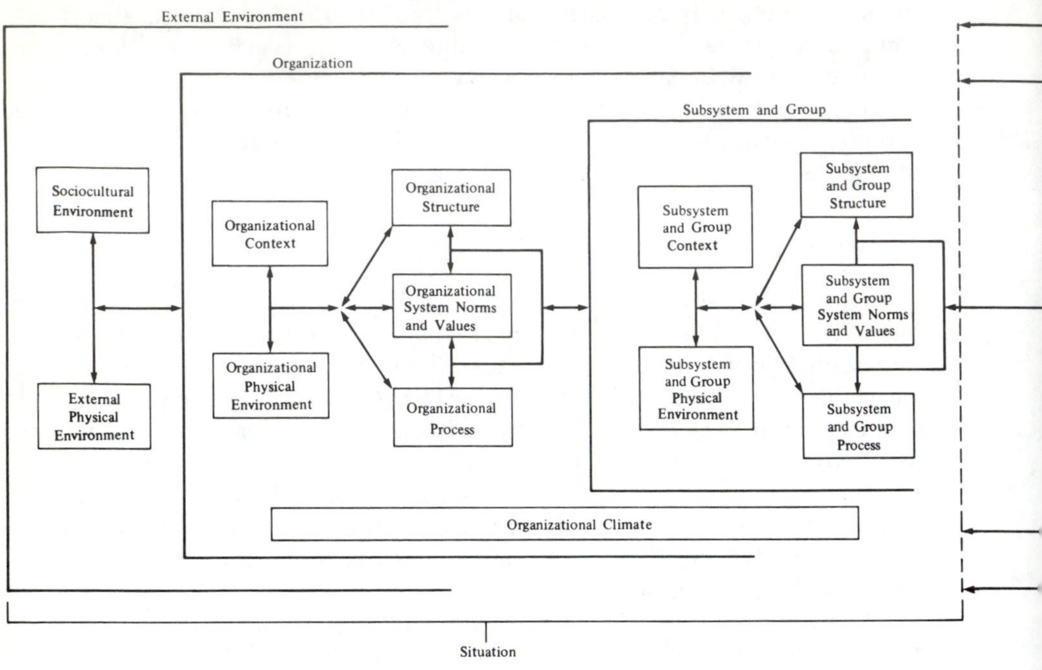

SOURCE: From "Organizational Structure: A Review of Structural Dimensions and Their Conceptual Relationships with Individual Attitudes and Behaviors" by L. R. James and A. P. Jones, 1976, *Organizational Behavior and Human Performance, 16,* pp. 96–97.

thority and the span of control of each of these levels. Figure 13–4 **(A)** depicts the relationship between levels of authority, span of control, and organizational structure. Assuming that organizational size remains constant (i.e., a fixed number of employees), the organization becomes flatter as span of control increases and levels of authority decrease. This is shown by contrasting **(A)** and **(B)**. The bureaucratic model implied that there was one best span of control as well as one best structure. These two variables, structure and span of control, have received most of the attention of researchers, followed by delegation of authority (in the form of models of decision making). Research on the division of labor usually combines this component with the structure component and deals with *line-staff* distinctions, where *line* roles are defined as those having direct responsibility for goods and services, whereas *staff* roles assume indirect responsibility for such activities. Most of the recent work in the classic tradition has taken the form of a compacting or expansion

FIGURE 13–2 *(concluded)*

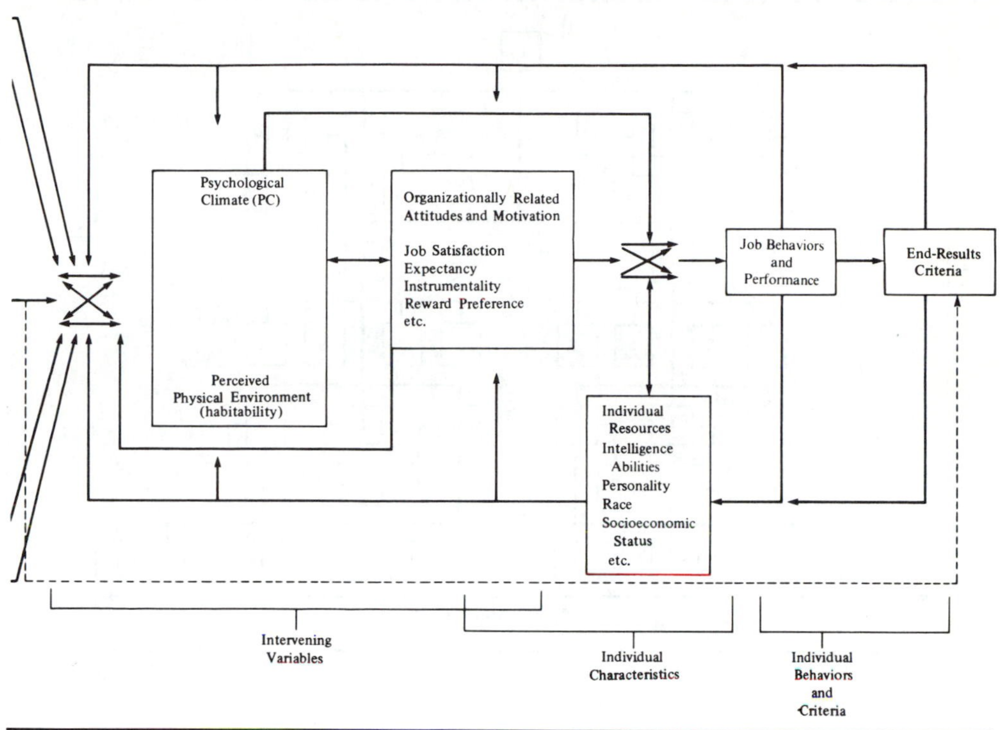

of these four basic components. One thing that should be apparent from this description of classical organization theory is the perspective of the organization as a closed and depersonalized system. If you push in on one variable (e.g., size), there is a bulge in another variable (e.g., span of control). There is little recognition that an external environment exists or that the internal environment is affected by the characteristics of the inhabitants of that environment. As an example, Miller and Droge (1986) presented data suggesting that the personality of the chief executive officer (CEO) had a profound effect on the structure of the organization. They found that in small and young firms, CEOs with a strong drive to achieve and succeed centralized power with tall and tight organizational structures. These structures were characterized as having many formal policies, very controlled communications channels, and a strong general emphasis on control by the CEO. It is this type of insight that seemed to escape the early organizational theorists. Before introducing recent variations in classic theory, the research relevant to the role of some of the traditional components will be reviewed briefly.

FIGURE 13–3 A Representation of Specialization and Delegation Dimensions of a Hypothetical Organization (*L = line; S = staff*)

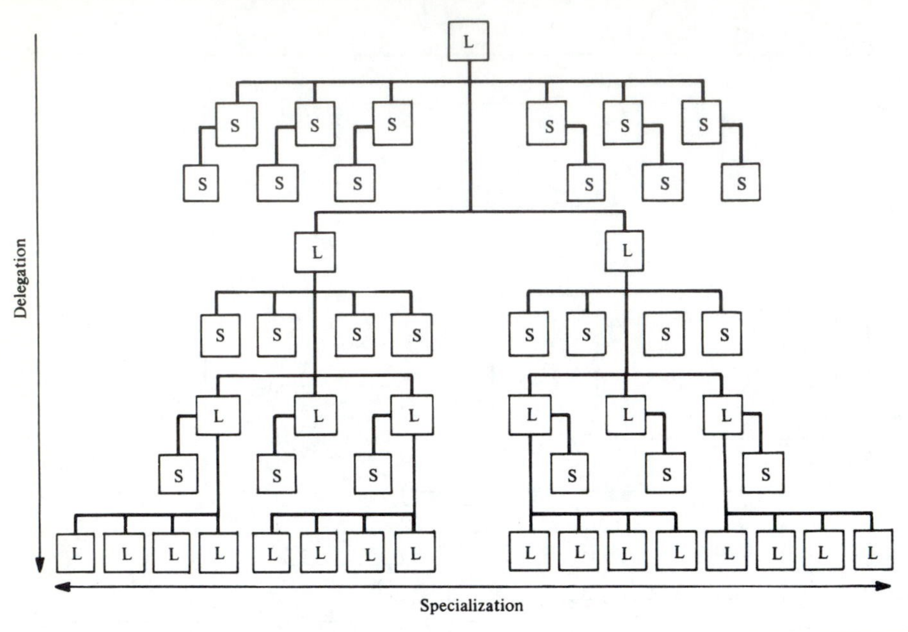

Span of Control

Try to visualize a football coach directing the efforts of all the individual members of a football team. You would predict that it would be an impossible task for one individual. The coach needs a staff of specialist coaches (e.g., a backfield coach and a line coach). Without such a system, the performance of the team (or organization) would be unrelated to the wishes and goals of the head coach. But the use of specialist coaches could be carried to an extreme. Suppose there were a coach for every two players, a supervisor for every two coaches, and an administrator for every two supervisors. The control would be so extreme that it would be miraculous if a play ever got from the coach to the team in enough time to run the play. In fact, many quarterbacks have complained that games were lost because the coaching staff on the sidelines was disorganized and sending conflicting or garbled communications into the game. These examples describe the extremes of the span of control. A span of control of 80 is too large; a span of control of 2 is too small.

The search for the most efficient span of control assumed major importance in classic organization theory. Investigations of span of control have

FIGURE 13–4 Span of Control Company (*size* = *1,000*)

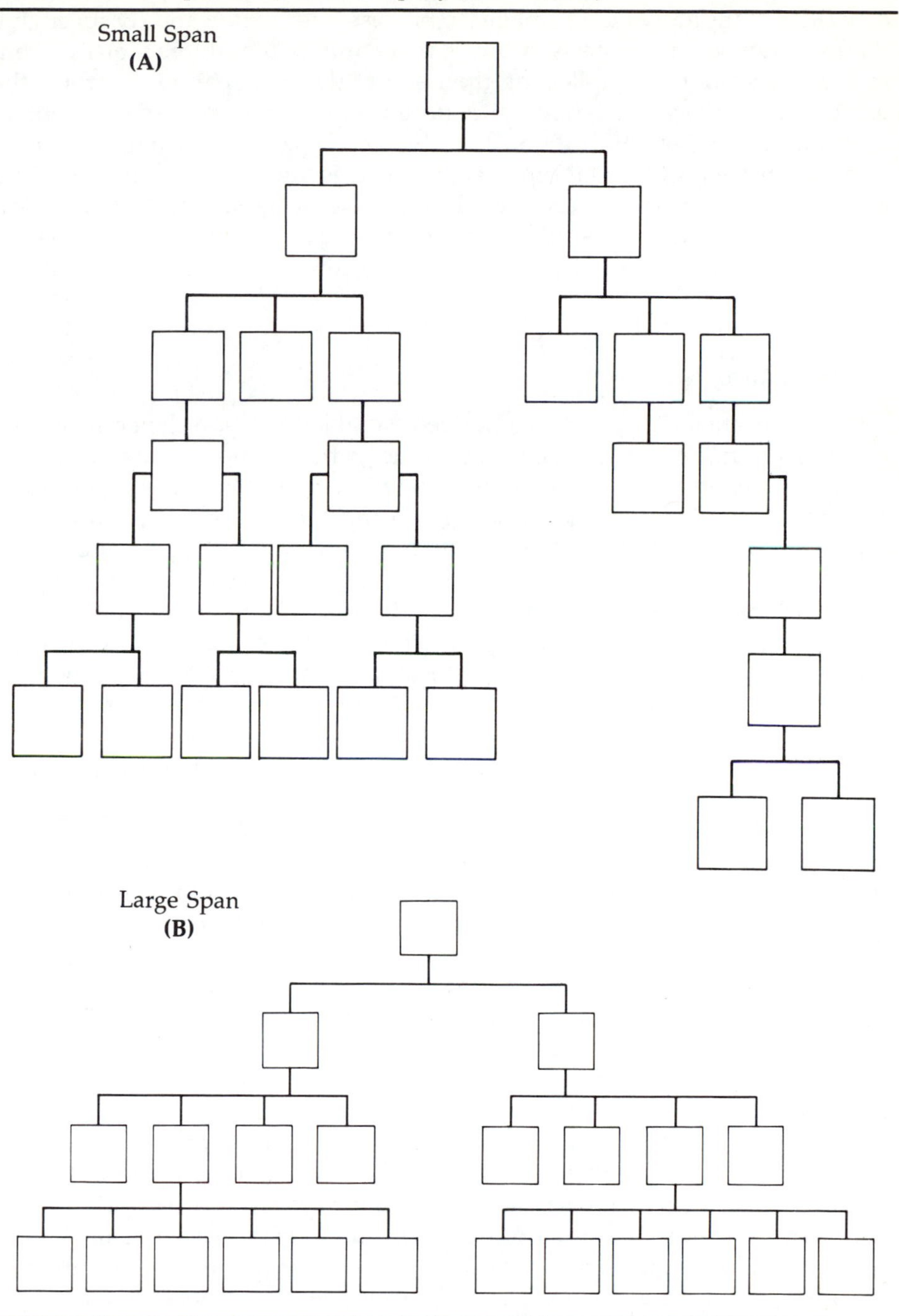

taken one of two forms: (1) specifying the best number on the basis of the capacities of the individual manager to process information and (2) specifying the best number on the basis of the number and kind of interactions present in the work group. Complicating the issue of the best span of control is the fact that there are several different definitions of *control span.* As an example, Ouchi and Dowling (1974) found that the *actual* span of control often differs from the organizationally approved span. This is due to the fact that workers may report to several supervisors. In addition, workers may report to supervisors other than those they are formally assigned to. These types of informal reporting relationships affect the accuracy of span of control estimates.

Structure

Organizational structure is a derived variable; that is, it depends on several other variables for its definition. Some of these variables are size, span of control, centralization of decision making, number of levels of supervision, and division of labor. All these things go together to form a picture of an organization's structure. The most commonly used label for organizational structure is "tall" or "flat." Tall organizations are characterized by small spans of control, many levels of supervision, and centralization of decision making; on the other hand, flat organizations are thought to be characterized by large spans of control, fewer levels of supervision, and decentralized decision making. The terms *tall* and *flat* are not particularly useful to the organizational psychologist in understanding the interactions of individuals and organizations. They are the equivalent of traits of the organization. On the other hand, the extent and type of supervision or the decision-making process used by work groups might provide a better understanding of motivation, satisfaction, or efficiency. Structure, more than any other concept in organizational psychology, typifies the static view of the organization as a closed and disembodied system. Nevertheless, it undoubtedly has a role in shaping perceptions of organizational members.

It is important to remember that structure may be different in various departments of an organization or even within the same department. Consider the two different levels of detail provided in Figures 13–5 and 13–6. In Figure 13–5, you can see a rather traditional view of a company involved in the production of sophisticated medical equipment. Consider now the organization depicted in Figure 13–6. This is the magnification of the engineering department pictured in Figure 13–5. It is like looking at a drop of water or a human hair with and without the aid of a high-powered microscope. You will note that in Figure 13–6, in addition to having much greater detail, there is also a hybrid structure. The left portion of the chart (the triangular group of job titles) depicts a high-expertise group of engineers who serve as a resource to both upper management (in terms of market strategy and product development) and fellow engineers (as technological resources for the production

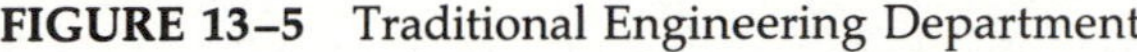

FIGURE 13–5 Traditional Engineering Department

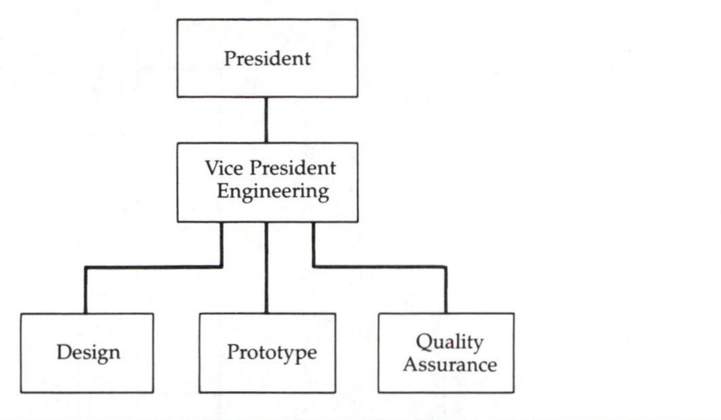

of particular pieces of high-tech equipment). In the jargon of the field, the design of the engineering department of this particular company would be called a *matrix* design because it extracts from the traditional structure certain resources (high-expertise engineers) and makes those resources available to many different projects on an "as-needed" basis. This is often a more effective use of scarce resources (both money and time) than a traditional structure in which the resources (such as technical expertise) would be made available in *each* project line. This latter strategy leads to substantial duplication and difficult communication across projects.

Relationships among Size, Structure, and Behavior

Some studies have investigated the effect of various aspects of organizational structure on individual and organizational behavior. Evers, Bohlen, and Warren (1976) examined 153 farmer cooperatives and found that less formal structures evolved in smaller firms (less than 10 employees), whereas the structure became much more formal (with rules, regulations, standardization pressures, and so on) as size increased above 10. This would suggest that size has certain constraining effects on behavior. Perhaps as organizations grow in size, the limits of the information-processing capacities of humans become more apparent. On the other hand, Moch (1976) examined over 400 hospitals and concluded that increased size led to functional differentiation and decentralization of decision making; these conditions, in turn, led to greater ease in the adoption of innovation. These two studies, in combination, suggest that size per se is not the critical variable in organizational functioning. Rather, one must consider the effect size has on other interrelated variables such as specialization and decision making. So it would seem that largeness

FIGURE 13–6 Matrix Organization

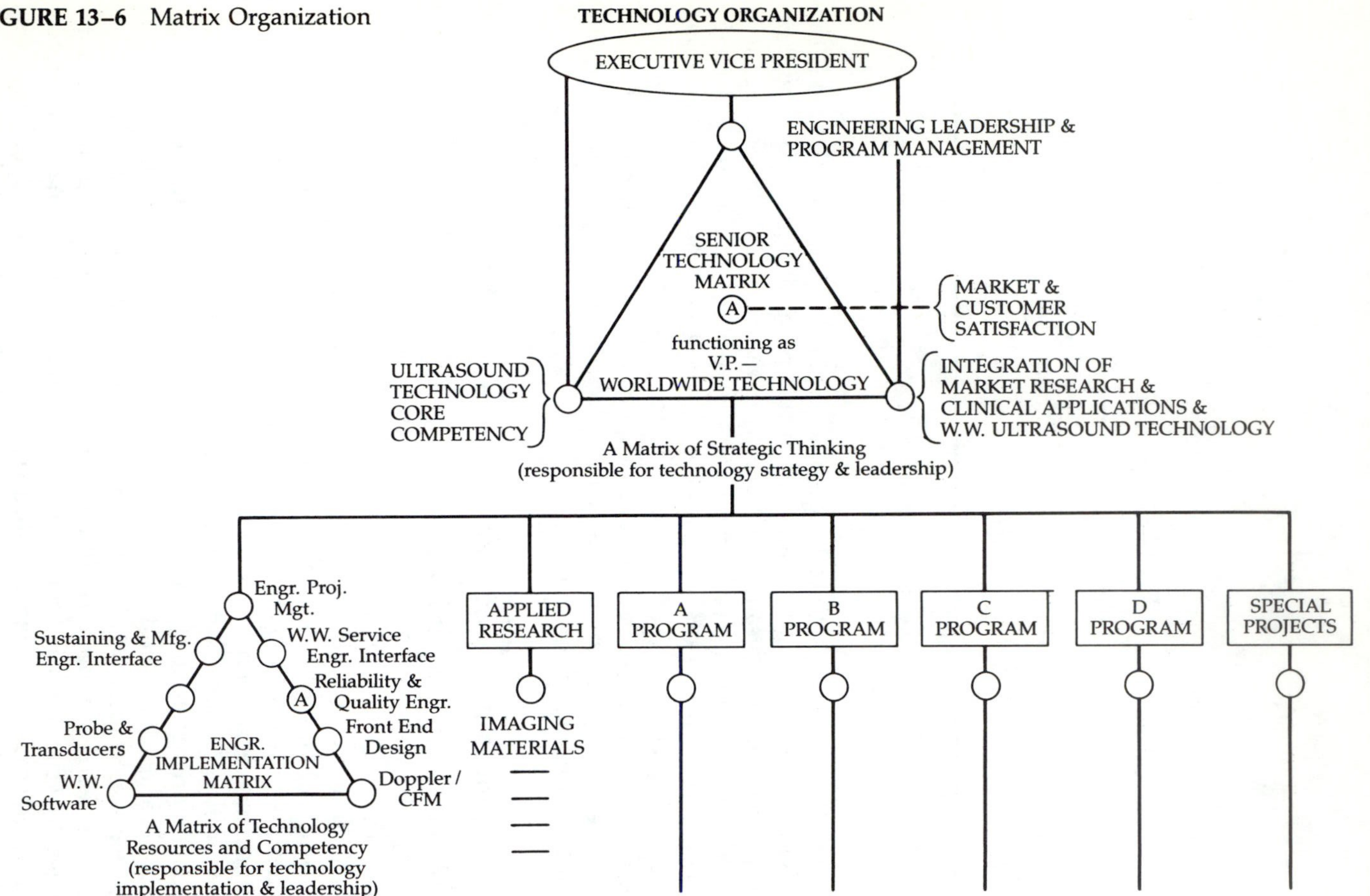

SOURCE: Figure supplied by Gene Larson, Advanced Technology Laboratories.

or smallness in an organization is not, by itself, good or bad. There must be other things involved.

In 1950, Worthy suggested that flat organizations were "better" than tall ones. Flat organizations were thought to have characteristics appropriate for both organizational and individual efficiency. They are administratively decentralized and less complex. In addition, satisfaction is thought to be higher in flat organizations, since there would seem to be less punitive control over the individual worker and ample opportunity for increased responsibility and initiative. The technology matrix described in Figure 13–6 has led to a substantial increase in the satisfaction of the engineers in that matrix. They report more opportunity to communicate with fellow engineers, a quicker resolution of work-related problems of a technical variety, and a much shorter project completion time. A "before-after" view of that engineering department would reveal that the department had been flattened by the matrix intervention.

Ivancevich and Donnelly (1975) questioned 195 sales personnel in 3 organizations and found that the individuals in flat organizations reported more satisfaction with self-actualization and autonomy motives, felt they were under less stress, and performed more efficiently than sales personnel in either medium or tall organizations. Although these data are generally supportive of Worthy, we must remember that the terms *tall* and *flat* cover a multitude of variables whose impact could not have been adequately assessed in only three organizations. Nevertheless, based on this and similar research, it seems probable that organizational structure is implicated in organizational behavior.

A more direct example of the fruitfulness of considering organizational characteristics from the perspective of their effect on behavior is provided by Ghiselli (1969). He looked at the relationships between the type of advancement system used in a particular organization and the organizational structure (tall versus flat). He defined two different types of advancement systems. The first, the *open personnel-procurement system,* is characterized by organizations that fill vacancies at all levels of the organization from both inside *and* outside the organization. The second, the *closed personnel-procurement system,* is characterized by organizations that fill only the lowest-level vacancy from outside the organization and all other vacancies from inside (e.g., military organizations). Ghiselli proposed that the efficiency of these two systems of filling vacancies would vary as a function of the type of advancement policy used and the flatness or tallness of the organization. He proposed that in flat organizations with a closed procurement system, advancement on the basis of *merit* might be a good policy. He reasoned that since the number of individuals in the work group is relatively large, the competition should be stiff. On the other hand, in a tall organization with a closed procurement system, merit may not be the best advancement procedure to use. Instead, something like an aptitude test might provide a more valid basis for the advancement decision. In an open procurement system, these relationships are modified.

This concept is similar to the "selection ratio" logic introduced in Chapter 8. If you are making a promotional decision for a work group member in a closed personnel-procurement system, the size of that group is analogous to the concept of a selection ratio. This work by Ghiselli suggests important relationships between organizational characteristics and personnel policies. More important, this work illustrates the advantages of breaking out of the closed system view of organizations. The open procurement system suggests an important interactional process between the organization and its external environment. As another example, consider once again the organization of the engineering department depicted in Figure 13–6. Prior to the introduction of that new matrix structure, there had been considerable concern expressed by the individual engineers that it was difficult to advance up the organizational ladder or to develop new skills and capabilities. The creation of the technology matrix on the left side of that structure opened a whole new avenue for advancement as well as an opportunity to develop new skill sets. In addition, it permitted the development of a "mentoring" atmosphere in which members of the matrix could assume tutorial relationships for less senior members of the project teams in the center of the chart.

The Value of Classic Theory

Classic organization theory is more appropriately viewed as a starting point for the development of organization theory from the psychological perspective. It provides a convenient taxonomy for describing certain characteristics of organizational environments. It is a point of departure in that it provides a historical and empirical foundation for current models of organizational behavior. What must be avoided, however, is taking the prescriptive or directional view. Classical theorists would have us believe that the only thing worth examining is the effect that structure has on behavior. But an equally interesting question is what effect behavior has on structure. Earlier, I reported the results of the study of Miller and Droge (1986) showing the effect of CEO personality (i.e., need for achievement) on organizational structure. You will remember a similar discussion from the last chapter in considering the effect of follower behavior on leadership style. As another example of this alternative perspective of organizational characteristics, Lowin (1968) showed that participative decision making changes the nature of the traditional hierarchical model of the organization. Specifically, he contended that in the classic model of organization the individual who makes the decision and more the individual who *implements* that decision occupy different positions in the organization chart—decisions are handed down to be implemented. In the traditional model, the decision function and the implementation function are separated. Participative decision making has the effect of giving a single individual both decision and action functions. The segregation of function existing in the traditional model is eliminated. From this per-

FIGURE 13–7 Organizational Chart of a Small Insurance Company Showing Bypassing of a Hierarchical Level

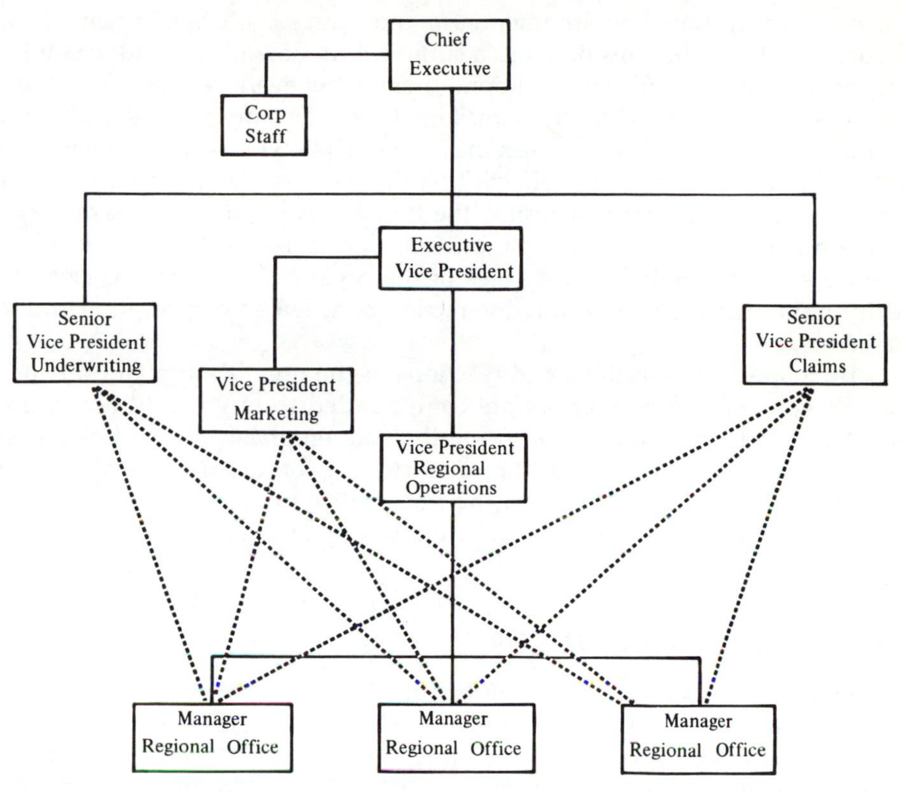

SOURCE: From "Multiple Hierarchies and Organizational Control" by P. B. Evans, 1975, *Administrative Science Quarterly, 20,* p. 256.

spective, we can describe the organization from a classical point of view, introduce some intervention (e.g., participative decision making), and then note how the organization has changed from the preintervention state. This is a considerably less prescriptive use of classical organization theory. It does not suggest the one best way; instead, it accepts the key variables of classical theory as targets for change and assesses the effects of certain interventions on these parameters. In this way, classical theory can be useful without being "correct." As we will see in the section on organizational development, many interventions have change in structure as a *goal.*

Figure 13–7 is just one example of the differences between the idealized view of an organization implied by classical theory and the observable events that compose real organizational behavior. An organizational chart implies (or more formally, *demands*) certain interrelationships among and between levels of the organization. As you can see from this figure, reality is often at odds with this ideal. Regardless of what the organization chart *says*, people will develop patterns of behavior to accommodate their own needs and the current organizational environment. For those reasons, classic organization theory should not be considered as a sufficient framework for understanding organizational behavior. In addition, there may even be negative consequences from adopting the principles of the classic approach as a guide to administrative action. This is seen in Korman's (1971) pessimistic view, presented in Figure 13–8, of the effect of traditional organizational structure on creative expression. Parenthetically, the figure also points out that the organization is just as much under the control of organizational members as the members are controlled by the rules of the organization. There is clearly a reciprocal rather than a one-way interaction between an organization and its members.

By following the actions and reactions of the organization and the individual, you can see how errors are compounded through reciprocal action and feedback loops. You can also see that the emphasis on controlling, so characteristic of classic organization theory, is a counterproductive strategy in many cases. This emphasis on the personalized organization has been a primary characteristic of the second class of organization theories—the human relations theories.

HUMAN RELATIONS THEORY

Figure 13–8 is a case study of dysfunction. It illustrates how organizations disintegrate. In contrast, consider Figure 13–9. Here, we have a much more normal view of organizational activity. It is a representation of the "organization" of an orchestra from a behavioral perspective. More important, it is the view of the organization through the eyes of its members rather than from the point of view of an outside observer. Specifically, it reflects the causal variables that influence the organization of work for individual orchestra members. This is a very different view of organization than one that might be provided by classical theory. There is no identification of variables such as span of control, delegation, or subunit size. In fact, the organization members tend to emphasize the organizing *process* rather than any fixed components of the organization itself.

W. G. Scott (1967) proposed a scheme for understanding the behavior of individuals in organizations. He contends that there are three essential elements that must be examined: (1) the requirements of the organization, (2) the characteristics of the individuals who populate the organization, and (3) the relationship between the organizational requirements and the characteristics of the people in it. The human relations approach to organization theory is best described by the third element. Below, we will consider some human relations theories in detail.

FIGURE 13–8 A Critical View of Behavior in an Organization Built upon Classic Organization Theory

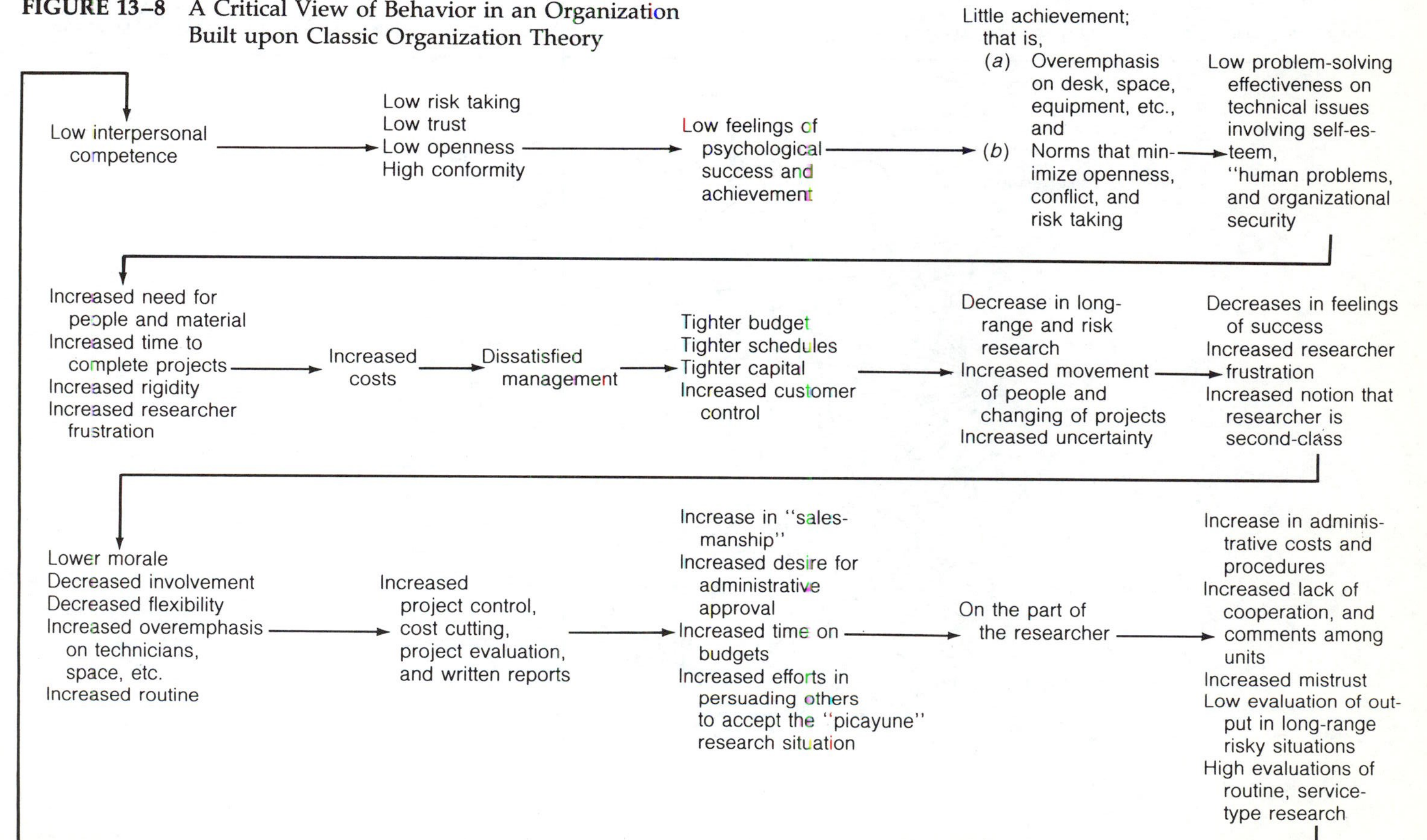

SOURCE: From *Industrial Organizational Psychology* (p. 95) by A. K. Korman, 1971, Englewood Cliffs, NJ: Prentice-Hall. Adaptation from *Organization and Innovation* (pp. 230–237) by C. Argyris, 1965.

FIGURE 13–9 Cause Relationships Mentioned by a Significant Number of Orchestra Members

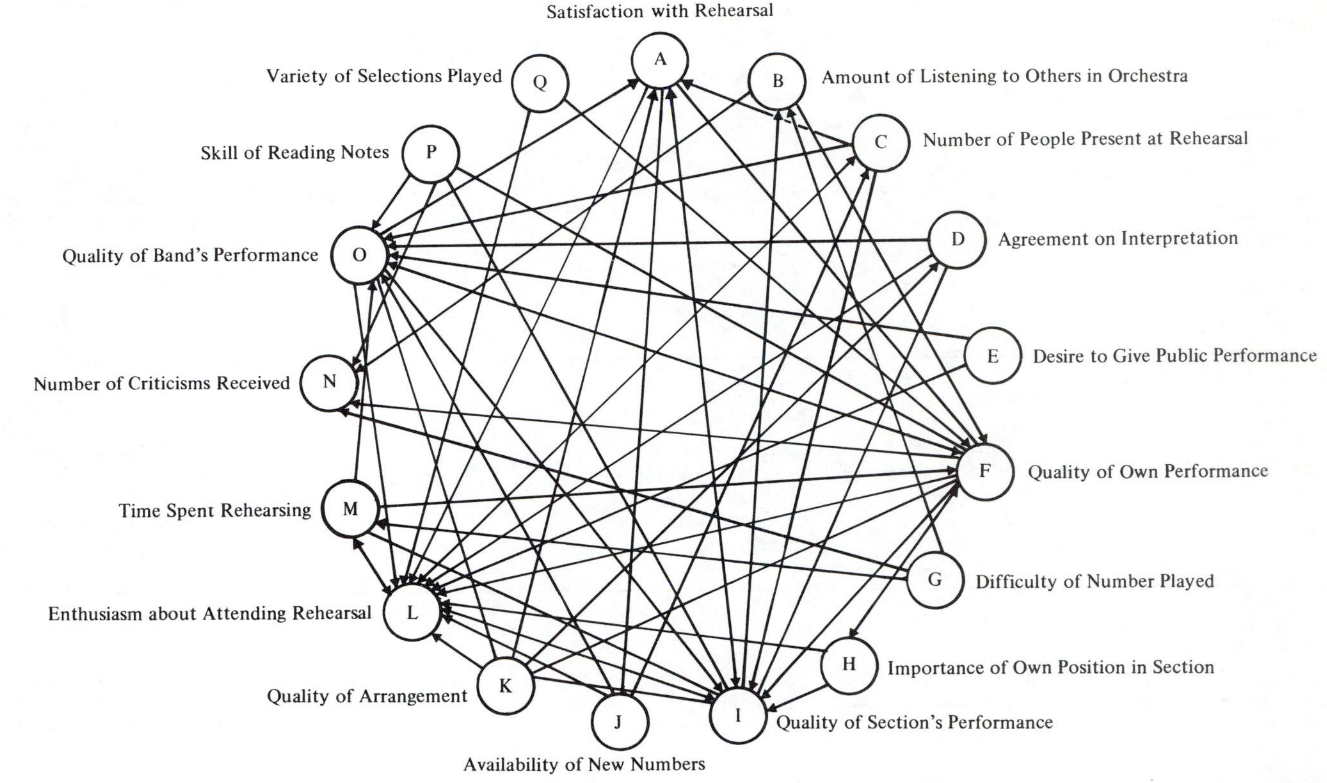

SOURCE: From "Cognition in Organizations: An Analysis of the Utrecht Jazz Orchestra" by M. Bougon, K. Y. Weick, and D. Binkhorst, 1977, *Administrative Science Quarterly*, 22, p. 610.

McGregor's Theory X/Theory Y

The thoughts of Douglas McGregor have had a profound effect on managers. In his book *The Human Side of Enterprise* (1960), he developed the logical relationships between the beliefs managers hold about subordinates and the behavior of those subordinates. In an effort to describe the effect of various belief systems, he developed the two fictional belief systems that he labeled *Theory X and Theory Y.* These terms have been widely used and often misunderstood since they were introduced. McGregor intended the belief systems to be considered as simply *examples* of belief systems that might exist. He states in a work (1967) published after his death:

> It should be apparent that one could find managerial beliefs about the nature of man sufficiently different from X or Y that they might be labeled Theory A or O or S. How many differnt theories there are would thus become a matter for empirical investigation and classification. (p. 80)

In spite of McGregor's warning, it is commonplace to hear managers discuss organizations, departments, or other individuals in terms of Theory X versus Theory Y as if the two belief systems exhausted the possibilities for beliefs held by managers. Unfortunately, McGregor was not able to describe alternative belief systems clearly before his death in 1964. Therefore, while the generally accepted descriptions of Theory X and Theory Y will be presented, you should not take them as rigid cornerstones of a theory but as examples of managerial philosophies that, in turn, lead to certain managerial strategies. We will also consider the recent propositions of Ouchi (1981) in which he describes theories that are commonly found in American firms (Theory A), those that are more frequently found in Japanese firms (Theory J), and a hybrid theory that Ouchi sees as an effective combination of American emphasis on accountability and Japanese emphasis on affiliation. But first, let's examine McGregor's propositions.

Theory X managers believe that in the interest of meeting organizational goals, the behavior of subordinates must be modified, controlled, and directed to meet the needs of the organization. If managers did not engage in these controlling and directing activities, the subordinates would be either apathetic or actively resistant to meeting organizational goals. It is further assumed by Theory X managers that such controlling and directing should be accomplished through persuasions, punishments, and rewards—more generally, by controlling mechanisms outside the individual.

Managers holding beliefs labeled Theory Y assume that individual workers are motivated to seek out responsibility and can easily accept responsibility for meeting organizational goals. In addition, this belief system implies that any resistance or apathy encountered in the individual is a function *not* of the basic nature of the individual but of the individual's experience with the organization. In short, resistance and apathy are learned.

The major component in McGregor's theory of organizational functioning is the integration of the goals of the organization with the goals of the individual. He felt that only through collaborative effort could both sets of goals be met. The task of management—by extension, the task of the organization and its structure—is to create conditions that facilitate the goal achievement of organization members at all levels. In addition, this goal achievement should result from the direction of individual efforts toward organizational goals. In other words, it is important that the individual see that the goals of the organization and her goals are not mutually exclusive. Instead, the two goal systems should be viewed as closely related.

It is the component of integration through collaboration that highlights the importance of the two belief systems. The environment or organizational conditions that exist at any given moment can either help or hinder the process of integration. Theory X belief systems were seen as creating a hindering environment, whereas Theory Y systems were seen as creating a helping environment.

McGregor's statements imply that if employees see the satisfaction of organizational goals as a path to achieving personal goals, they will expend energy in the direction of satisfying organizational goals. In addition, collaboration as a vehicle for integration suggests management by objectives, a technique by which supervisors and subordinates jointly set performance goals and explore strategies for achieving those goals.

McGregor's theory is of interest for two reasons. The first is historical. It played a major role in the development of many systems of motivation and attempts to increase satisfaction among employees. But in retrospect, it appears as a symbol—an "early warning" of the cognitive revolution in psychological theory. McGregor was suggesting that beliefs influence behavior and that this resultant behavior, in turn, strengthens the original beliefs. We have seen this type of reciprocity in earlier theories of satisfaction, performance evaluation, motivation, and leadership. The difference here is that the beliefs are not specific to one individual. Instead, they function as stereotypes: beliefs about large groups of people—beliefs that exist in spite of behavior that might suggest alternative beliefs to be more reasonable or accurate.

Chris Argyris's Theory

The work of Argyris (1972) is quite specific about the possible effect of organizational structure on employee behavior. He makes quite a leap from the demands of the formal system to the probable behavior of people in the system. He makes this leap on the basis of certain assumptions about human nature and, more specifically, about the way the individual progresses from child to adult. In that sense, his theory has been called a *developmental* theory. He contrasts the way individuals develop with the restrictions put on that development by the formal organization.

Argyris contends that individuals develop:

1. From passive organisms to active organisms
2. From dependent organisms to independent organisms
3. From organisms requiring immediate need gratification to organisms able to tolerate delays in gratification
4. From organisms able to deal only with concrete operations to those able to deal in abstractions
5. From organisms with few abilities to organisms with many abilities

If we accept those assumptions (and they seem quite reasonable), then we must also accept the fact that some forms of work and some strategies for technological control (e.g., assembly-line work) are not suited to the level of development of the individual entering the organization. This lack of congruence inevitably leads to tension on the part of the individual, who subsequently engages in certain kinds of activities to relieve this tension. Some of these activities are absenteeism, turnover, unionization, and apathy. The traditional organization, viewing these actions on the part of the worker, comes to the conclusion that more control is needed, institutes such control, and consequently exaggerates rather than eliminates the maladaptive behavior of the individual.

There are some striking similarities between the thinking of McGregor and that of Argyris. It would not be too difficult to translate Argyris's developmental assumptions into the Theory Y belief system. In addition, the process of matching the goal system of the individual and the demands of the organization plays a crucial role in both approaches.

Ouchi's Theory Z: Human Relations Theory Gone Astray

McGregor described an approach in which certain assumptions about individual motivational systems resulted in organizational responses and structures that either fostered or hindered satisfaction, creativity, and efficiency. Argyris's observations of the consequences of inappropriate assumptions on organizational adaptation provided a stark warning to managers and companies that might impose constraints that were opposed to normal trends in human development. Both of these theories suggested that individuals should be free from control and unnecessary direction—that individual workers were the best judges of how their efforts should be directed. All workers needed was some guidance in the process of planning and implementation. But as E. H. Schein (1981) points out, managers who adopted this perspective became disillusioned. They discovered that

1. High morale did not necessarily correlate with high productivity.
2. Autocratic systems could outproduce democratic systems.
3. High productivity could lead to high morale even when productivity was achieved through autocratic methods.

FIGURE 13–10 Characteristics of Two Familiar Organizational Ideal Types: A and J

Type A (American)	*Type J (Japanese)*	*Type Z (Modified American)*
Short-term employment	Lifetime employment	Long-term employment
Individual decision making	Consensual decision making	Consensual decision making
Individual responsibility	Collective responsibility	Individual responsibility
Rapid evaluation and promotion	Slow evaluation and promotion	Slow evaluation and promotion
Explicit, formalized control	Implicit, informal control	Implicit, informal control with explicit, formalized measures
Specialized career path	Nonspecialized career path	Moderately specialized career path
Segmented concern	Holistic concern	Holistic concern, including family

4. Worker participation in decision making was expensive.

It has been noted that the Japanese system of management is paternalistic. Japanese organizations accept responsibility for all aspects of worker well-being, not just those aspects that involve work activity. As a result, the typical Japanese worker encounters a substantially different organizational environment than his American counterpart. The left and center columns of Figure 13–10 present a simplified view of the differences between the two systems. Type A is the prototypic American organization and Type J the Japanese counterpart. Ouchi (1981) suggests that there are appealing characteristics to both systems and that the "best" organization is one that combines these characteristics. He calls this hybrid type of organization *Type Z*. By extension, he argues that the closer an organization can come to Type Z characteristics, the more likely it is to be characterized by high productivity, high morale, and general feelings of well-being. Type Z characteristics appear in the right-hand column of Figure 13–10. As you can see, the Type Z organization allows for independence but provides support and security (though less than that suggested in the Type J organization).

From a theoretical perspective, there is little new in Ouchi's propositions. As E. H. Schein (1981) has suggested, it is based on some earlier propositions of Maslow (1971). We have already seen that there are serious problems with need theories of any kind. Theory Z is open to the same forms of criticism as Maslow's theory of hierarchical needs. Unfortunately, many organizations have simply accepted Theory Z on faith at this point. As a result, there is little enthusiasm for gathering data that might confirm or refute its value. Nevertheless, we can consider the data that are currently available and used to support the theory and raise some questions. The major empirical foundation for the theory is that Theory Z characteristics have been noted in successful organizations. There are several alternative explanations in addition to the standard Theory Z proposition that these characteristics *caused* the organizational success. Consider two of these alternative explanations. First, it may very well be that successful organizations adopt Type Z characteristics as a *result of* their success. Another interpretation might be that Type Z is one of many ways in which organizations can become successful but that Ouchi's sampling techniques tended to uncover only this type of organization. In fact, there is usually very little serious sampling that goes on in the verification of broad theories such as Theory Z. Instead, proponents set out to discover instances that support the a priori position set forth in the theory.

As it now stands, conceptually, Theory Z is simply a recent fad, remarkable for its popularity rather than its substance. If this fad follows the pattern of others, counterexamples (i.e., failing organizations with Type Z characteristics or successful firms having Type A characteristics) will appear with greater frequency. This will set the stage for the appearance of a "new" theory to take its place, and the fad cycle will begin again.

Contingency Theories

At the beginning of this chapter, I identified three major theoretical movements in organizational theories. The first of these, the classical approach, sought the one best configuration of organizational characteristics. Presumably, this one best configuration would yield maximum employee satisfaction or productivity with correlated advantages of low absence and turnover. The human relations approach, on the other hand, saw the salvation of organizations in recognizing certain immutable psychological characteristics of individuals who populate the organization—needs for independence or affiliation or stimulation. An alternative to both classical theory and human relations theory is the contingency approach. From the contingency perspective, the choice of organizational configuration depends on certain environmental variables. As you will see, some contingency theories consider the technological aspects of the environment, others emphasize the social aspects, and a few emphasize both.

Why are they called "contingency" theories? You will remember the principles of contingency from the last chapter. In Fiedler's theory of leadership, the "correct" leader style depended on the extent to which the situation (or work environment) was favorable. Contingency theories of organizational behavior function in a similar manner. The correct or most suitable organizational configuration depends on some set of circumstances that are part of the broader environment with which the organizational members interact. We will consider three contingency theories. The work of Joan Woodward suggests that span of control depends on the type of technology. The propositions of Lawrence and Lorsch suggest that organizational characteristics depend on the amount of change being experienced by the organization. Finally, the sociotechnical movement argues that organizations should be arranged with an eye toward the interaction of social patterns and technological demand.

Woodward's Contingency Approach

Joan Woodward, a British industrial sociologist, was one of the first to point out the importance of technology on the administrative characteristics of the organization. In a series of studies published in 1958, she looked at span of control in three different types of technology:

1. *Small-batch organizations.* Those engaged in producing specialty products one at a time
2. *Large-batch and mass-production organizations.* Those producing large numbers of discrete units—essentially, assembly-line operations
3. *Continuous process organizations.* Those depending on a continuous process for output or product, including operations such as chemical operations and distilleries

Figure 13–11 depicts the relationship between type of technology and span of control. The median span of control for small-batch firms was between 21 and 30, the median span of control for mass-production firms was between 41 and 50, and the median for continuous process firms was between 11 and 20. R. Dubin (1965) points out that part of the reason for the decreased span of control in continuous process operations is the relative costliness of a mistake. Since the cost of a mistake tends to be higher in continuous process, high-speed operations, more of the responsibilities for inspection and quality control are passed on to first-level management and taken away from the worker. Consequently, the number of supervisory personnel tends to increase, so that all managerial functions can be attended to as well as the additional responsibilities for inspection and quality control. Woodward's work (1958) illustrates the relationship between the structural characteristics of an organization and the social patterns of its members. While Woodward did not look directly at technological change, it should be apparent that if a technology is changed from unit to mass production, there will probably be some accompanying changes in span of control and supervisory processes. If that is the case, careful human resource planning must accompany technological change if the organization is to realize advantages from the technical innovation. Furthermore, these findings suggest that there is no one best span of control. The best supervisor-subordinate ratio will depend on the nature of the technology. This point will be examined again in much greater detail in the section dealing with the sociotechnical approach to organizations.

FIGURE 13–11 Span of Control in First-Line Supervision

Number of Persons Controlled \ System of Production	Unit Production	Mass Production	Process Production
Unclassified	□	□	
81–90		□ □ □	
71–80		□	
61–70		□ □ □ □ □	
51–60	□	□ □ □ □	
41–50	□ □ □	□ □ □ □ □ □ □ □ □ ★	
31–40	□ □ □ □	□ □ □ □ □	□ □
21–30	□ □ □ □ □ □ □ □ ★	□ □	□ □ □ □ □
11–20	□ □ □ □ □ □	□	□ □ □ □ □ □ □ □ □ □ □ □ ★
10 or Less	□		□ □ □ □ □ □

□ Firm
★ Median

SOURCE: From *Management and Technology* by J. Woodward, 1958, London: Her Majesty's Stationery Office.

Recent Considerations of Technology Impact

Woodward concentrated on span of control in her consideration of technology. Her findings were revolutionary at the time. Nevertheless, her characterization of technology was somewhat primitive. T. A. Mahoney and Frost (1974) have suggested an approach to technology that is more realistic. It is based on earlier work by Thompson (1967) and consists of three types of technology:

1. *Long-linked technology*. Implies knowledge and predictability of cause-effect relationships, and high structuring of jobs and work processes; the type of technology described is analogous to mass-production assembly line.
2. *Mediating technology*. Involves the choice among a number of alternative

FIGURE 13–12 Proposed Relationships among Types of Technology, Criteria of Effectiveness for Those Technologies, and Variables Contributing to Effectiveness in Those Technologies

Technology	*Effectiveness Criteria*	*Variables Contributing to Effectiveness*
Long-linked	Planning Performance Reliability	Supervisory control of work Supervisory emphasis on results Group cohesion
Mediating	Flexibility Planning Performance Supervisory control	Low interchange with other units Limited coordination with other units
Intensive	Performance Cooperation Development Staffing	Minimal delegation Low coordination with other units Emphasis on meeting work commitments to other units

processes or programs; jobs are first classified in some way, and then processes appropriate to the classification category are applied. An example of a mediating technology would be an insurance claims unit processing the claims of individuals. In this case, claims must first be grouped and then processed by applying the right set of decision rules.

3. *Intensive technology*. Considered as highly specialized with a good deal of discretionary performance. The individual receives feedback from the object under consideration, and this feedback determines the nature of the procedure, process, or treatment applied next to the object of interest. Research and development units are representative of intensive technologies. They are constantly involved in evaluating the effects of one treatment and using those results to decide on the next treatment. They propose that each technology is suited to a particular kind of performance criterion or effectiveness. In addition, they suggest that certain types of variables contribute to these different types of effectiveness. In other words, to a certain extent, the technology determines which effectiveness criteria can be maximized as well as *how* they can be maximized. Figure 13–12 describes the effectiveness criteria and the variables that affect them.

As an example of how this information might be used, we would expect that a mass-production unit should be evaluated in terms of the reliability of the final product, the long- and short-range planning for future production, and production level. Furthermore, we would expect planning, reliability, and performance to be facilitated by high work group cohesion, an emphasis on turning out high quality and high quantity, and strong initiating-structure behavior on the part of the leader.

The work of Mahoney and Frost is just an example of a different type of contingency relationship. They suggest that the variables used to *evaluate* an organization or organizational subunit depend on the technology employed. Different variables should be examined for varying technologies. Hammer and Turk (1987) provide a different perspective of the interaction between technology and behavior. In a study of 160 supervisors of 12 sections of a manufacturing plant, they were able to demonstrate that supervisors in long-linked technologies devoted more time to maintaining internal work group processes. This was in contrast to supervisors of intensive technologies who spent more of their time developing links with other work groups and functions. Similarly, it appeared that supervisors in intensive technologies had more authority than those in long-linked technologies.

Research on the relationship between technology and organizational effectiveness has become quite complex—too complex for the purposes of this chapter. It is becoming increasingly obvious that technology (like some of its earlier predecessors in organizational research, i.e., size, span of control, etc.) does not exist independent of many other variables. As a final example, Sutton and Rousseau (1979) show that parent organizations have a suppressing effect on their dependent subunits. The dependence relationship must be considered simultaneously with variables such as technology and structure when examining organizational behavior. It seems that there are many complex components of the organizational environment. Each of these components adds another "it depends" caution. This is what makes the contingency approach both the most exciting and the most demanding.

Woodward's research and the Mahoney and Frost extension represent substantial departures from the earlier propositions of classical organization theory. These two approaches do much more than simply add a few more best ways to the tool kit of the organizational designer. They point to the fact that departments and organizational units function in a broader environment. They are not closed systems but receive input from external sources. This environmental theme can be seen clearly in the propositions of other recent contingency theorists such as Lawrence and Lorsch.

Lawrence and Lorsch's Theory

Lawrence and Lorsch (1967) characterized the classical approach as one directed toward finding the best possible organizational structure for coping with all situations. They suggested that this quest was fruitless, since an "average" organizational structure would be useless in any one situation (although it would be invaluable in the "average" situation). For Lawrence and Lorsch, change was the most important component of an organization. Their goal was to describe the best form of organization for coping with environmental change. In fact, environmental change versus environmental stability is one of the most important components of their approach.

They base their position both on their own data and also on that of Burns and Stalker (1961). Burns and Stalker found that organizations in stable industries tend to be more "mechanistic." *Mechanistic* is defined as dependent on formal rules and regulations, decisions reached at higher levels of the organization, and smaller spans of control. In contrast, organizations in dynamic, changing industries tended to be more "organic." *Organic* is defined as having larger spans of control, less formalization of procedures, and decisions made at middle levels of the organization. Consequently, they believe that certain environments lead to certain forms of organization.

While these propositions seem straightforward, Lawrence and Lorsch go on to deal with organizational behavior as a function of intraorganizational variables as well as the environment described above. The intraorganizational variables are described in the form of three basic questions, which must be answered to understand organizational behavior:

1. What are the differences among managers with different functional jobs in their orientation toward particular goals?
2. What are the differences in time orientations of different managers in different parts of the organization?
3. What are the differences in interpersonal orientations of managers in different parts of the organization?

The answers to these three questions characterize a single dimension along which organizations differ. This dimension has been labeled *differentiation* and is defined as the difference in cognitive and emotional orientation of managers in different parts of the organization. This is a unique form of differentiation, not at all like that proposed by the classical theorists. For the early traditionalists, differentiation appeared in the form of specialization and division of labor and was thought to be essential for meeting organizational goals. The inconvenience of coordination of the various special functions was eliminated by the "chain of command" or hierarchical authority levels. Lawrence and Lorsch contend the very act of specialization produces side effects that were not considered by the early theorists. These side effects appear in the new definition of differentiation: inconveniences and inefficiencies caused by different orientations toward time, goals, and interpersonal relations.

Like McGregor, Lawrence and Lorsch consider collaborative effort to be the best form of activity when unity of organizational movement is demanded by the environment. Their term for collaboration is *integration*, and it is defined as the quality or state of collaboration that exists among departments. Integration cannot be realized until the conflicts between departments—conflicts caused by differentiation—are resolved. As an example, the structure of the engineering department of the high-tech medical company depicted in Figure 13–6 was intended to develop a cooperative rather than competitive environment for the individual project groups. Rather than competing with each other, the expert engineers with the most project experience were formed into a new group (called the *technology matrix*) and rewarded for collaborating with individual project engineers. What at first might appear as fractionation (creating a new engineering group in addition to the old groups) is actually intended to accomplish the opposite—integration.

The Lawrence and Lorsch brand of contingency theory is much broader and more dynamic than that of Woodward. They imply that managers and organizations should prepare for dealing with change. In that sense, every organizational response is a contingent response—it depends on the extent of differentiation and the speed with which this differentiation occurs. Woodward was concerned with technology in a limited sense. Lawrence and Lorsch consider the broader environmental context of technology. They also move down a level of aggregation from Woodward and suggest that the point at which the organization *meets* the environment is at the department level, not the corporate level. Thus, in our example, the major issue was how the engineering department was able to cope with the competition from engineers in other companies in similar departments and how the engineering department was able to interact with the needs of their own marketing department. Departments must be prepared to adapt to changing environments. If departments can cope with externally imposed change, their parent organization will certainly prosper.

The Lawrence and Lorsch approach is important since it is the empirical and intellectual predecessor of many current approaches to organizational change. It also pushed well beyond Woodward's contingency notions in recognizing a more dynamic external environment in which the organization was embedded.

The Sociotechnical Approach

The sociotechnical approach to understanding and designing organizations is a contingency theory based on both classical and human relations considerations. From the sociotechnical perspective, an organization consists of structural and process characteristics (as emphasized by the classic theorists, e.g., size and chain of command) as well as social and personal characteristics (as emphasized by the human relations theorists, e.g., needs for mastery or recognition). The social and technical characteristics are inextricably bound to form a *system*. It is assumed that the best type of organization will depend on the unique interactions of the structural-procedural variables and personal-social variables.

In the chapters dealing with satisfaction, motivation, and leadership, we tended to treat individuals in the workplace as social entities, influenced by attitudes, beliefs, feelings, and aspirations. In the chapters dealing with human engineering and machine design, we will consider individuals as important components in larger man-machine systems. Sociotechnical organizational theory emphasizes the relationship between individuals and *technologies* rather than individuals independent of those technologies or individuals with respect to tasks or machines. From the contingency perspective, the sociotechnical approach implies an attempt to find the best match between social systems and technical systems rather than exaggerate the importance of one at the expense of the other.

The sociotechnical approach has become almost synonymous with the Tavistock Institute. The Tavistock Institute of Human Relations in London became involved in examining the social consequences of technological change in the British coal-mining industry in the late 1940s. Until then, coal mining had been done by small work groups and primarily by hand. Mass technology was introduced by means of what has become known as the *long-wall method*. Long-wall mining was accomplished by the use of mechanical equipment that carved out substantial amounts of coal from the face or wall and transported it back to a central location for processing. The old days of small autonomous cohesive work groups were gone. Specialization had arrived. New jobs were created. Old social interdependencies were swept away and new ones put in their place.

Trist and Bamforth (1951) examined the results of the change and discovered that all sorts of dysfunctional behavior (rivalry, absenteeism, and so on) could be directly traced to the changes in social patterns demanded by the new technology. On the basis of these observations, Trist and Bamforth suggested that technological change must be accompanied by planned integration for new social relations patterns. Further work in the mining industry demonstrated that particular combinations of social and technical systems yielded high productivity, high satisfaction, low absenteeism, and so on. In these studies, it seemed that the way work groups were formed and the manner in which labor was divided were critical issues. In some later studies by other Tavistock researchers (A. K. Rice, 1958), the sociotechnical principles were again demonstrated in weaving mills in India. The conclusion from these studies was that meaningful tasks, satisfying primary work group relations, and social organization arranged with task accomplishment in mind were critical for productive and satisfied workers. The sociotechnical approach is both important and interesting. For that reason, I will present a rather detailed description of a recent sociotechnical experiment.

An Application of the Sociotechnical Systems Approach. As a result of his interest in the quality of working life, Trist and his colleagues (Trist, Susman, & Brown, 1977) applied the sociotechnical model of the Tavistock Institute to a U.S. coal-mining operation. They were conducting an action research project to see if optimizing the match between social and technical systems could improve the perceived quality of working life.

They were able to interest the United Mine Workers, the United States Commission on Productivity and Work Quality, and a small independent deep coal mine in jointly sponsoring a project designed to assess the effect of autonomous or self-supervised work groups on various individual and organizational outcomes. The experiment was to last for slightly over one year, and the decision to continue with the new sociotechnical system would be made on the basis of the results of the first year.

Prior to the beginning of the experiment, several conditions were agreed to by the management of the mine. These agreements were as follows:

1. In experimental groups, all workers would be paid the same amount rather than the amount typically suggested by the job classification plan; in other words, miners, mechanics, roof bolters, and so on, would all be paid the same amount as opposed to the typical differential rate based on job duties.
2. Normal grievance procedures were eliminated for experimental groups, and a joint worker-management council was established for handling grievances.
3. Members of the experimental groups would be allowed to try out all the different mining jobs (e.g., mechanic, helper, or bolter) without these jobs being posted or made available to other employees of the company.
4. The company relinquished the right to direct experimental crew members at the work site.

These were rather remarkable concessions made on the part of both union and management. From them, you can begin to get a feel for the notion of a sociotechnical system. The typical experiment would change one of those factors but not all. But the essence of the sociotechnical approach is that one deals with a *system,* not a single component.

After management and union representatives agreed to the conditions of the experiment, job openings were posted for three eight-man crews. Volunteers for the experimental groups were chosen on the basis of seniority and qualifications. Those workers chosen for the experiment went through an orientation period that included both on-the-job training and classroom exposure to the principles of autonomous work groups. In addition, the workers were given classroom exercises in group relations and problem solving. A work group consisted of mining machine operators, mechanics, helpers, roof bolters, shuttle car operators, and support men. Although each worker bid on only one job, during the orientation period the workers were encouraged to try out as many of the jobs as possible. There was no pressure for production from the management during this orientation period.

The researchers then began a sociotechnical analysis of the work itself. The major source of production is a machine called the *continuous miner.* This machine consists of a large rotating drum studded with sharp bits. The drum is brought into contact with the wall to be mined. It gouges out coal and scoops the coal underneath the drum toward the rear, and then the coal is transported to a central location for further processing. The continuous miner bites out sections of the wall and creates a "room" 20 feet wide and 18 feet deep. This is done in several different areas until there is a series of adjacent rooms divided by pillars of coal. These pillars are then cut away, allowing

Coal mining represents a complex sociotechnical system, not simply a physically demanding job. (International Labor Organization)

for a "controlled collapse" of the mine roof. Theoretically, this is a very efficient way of mining coal. The capacity of the continuous miner is 4,000 tons per shift. In reality, the typical shift produces between 350 and 400 tons of coal. The discrepancy is due to time consumed in moving equipment, waiting time between cars carrying the coal, mechanical breakdowns, poor communications, and unnecessary movements on the part of the work groups. After examining the technical aspects of the work, the researchers identified the following potential problems in the psychosocial environment:

1. The work group members were isolated from one another during the performance of their work.

2. Instead of cooperating with one another, shifts competed.
3. Conditions were very uncertain from one day to the next: there were new geological conditions to be faced every time the next room was started, it was difficult to anticipate equipment breakdowns, and the distance between actual mining operations and support services was constantly changing.
4. Foremen were in a double bind with concerns for both safety and production.

As a result of this analysis, the researchers introduced the following changes in the operation of the work groups:

1. They attempted to change the view of the mining process from one of production of coal to one of transportation of coal.
2. They fed back performance information in terms of large blocks of time instead of by shift; additionally, they fed back information to entire mine sections rather than to each work group on each shift.
3. They attempted to ensure that group members had several different skills so that uncertainty could be more effectively dealt with.
4. They redistributed responsibilities so group members made day-to-day decisions rather than counting on the foreman for structure.
5. They changed the foreman's role to that of a resource person who provided information rather than directed work.

A number of different strategies were used for accomplishing these changes. In a later section on organizational development, we will describe the specific purpose of several of these techniques. Every six weeks, work group members and experimenters met to discuss the progress of the last six weeks and the plans for the next six weeks. Researchers visited the actual mine faces twice each week to collect information and provide reinforcement for changed procedures. In addition, there were irregular meetings of the joint worker-management council to handle grievances. Finally, foremen of the experimental work groups met every two weeks to discuss issues with the researchers and general management. As you can see, this was an ambitious undertaking for researchers, workers, and management. Table 13–1 presents some of the results of the experiment. Preexperiment data were available for both experimental and nonexperimental work groups for 1973. These data were compared with figures for the experimental year 1974. In addition to these figures, there was a rather substantial decrease in the cost of mining for the experimental groups. The actual production figures were difficult to interpret, but the researchers were able to conclude that production did not *decrease* during the experimental period for the autonomous work group. Finally, the attitudes of the experimental group about the work improved considerably during the experimental period.

A dramatic success such as this should have a happy ending. Unfortu-

TABLE 13–1 Results of the Autonomous Work Group Experiment

Variable	*Year*	*Experimental Group*	*Comparison Group A*	*Comparison Group B*
Safety violations	1973	18	19	10
	1974	7	37	17
Accidents	1973	6	5	4
	1974	7	14	11
Man-hours absent (percent)	1974	2.5	4.4	2.4

nately, that is not the case. The workers were given the opportunity to extend the experiment to the entire mine through their union. The union members voted *not* to expand the experiment by a vote of 79 to 75. The researchers examined the causes for the vote and identified the following possible contributing factors:

1. There were certain wage inequities built into expanding the experiment.
2. Many of the older miners were upset by the fact that the experimental groups contained many young workers and apprentices. They felt that these young workers were receiving concrete and abstract "benefits" that they had not yet earned through years of hardship in the mines.
3. There was the fear that the autonomous work groups were subtle attempts to bust the union.
4. The experimental work groups were resented as "elitist."

A recent evaluation of the long-term effects of the experiment was encouraging. Most of the changes seen in 1974 remained, although somewhat diluted. In addition, most of the structural changes in work groups and work process were also intact. The Rushton study is one example of a broad-based sociotechnical approach to organizational effectiveness. Similar but less ambitious efforts are common. Pasmore and Sherwood (1978) have described the "typical" sociotechnical experiment:

> It includes male, blue-collar, unionized workers who perform industrial tasks. These employees number about forty, and they participate directly in the change program. The experimental changes involve forming an autonomous work group; specific modifications include increases in autonomy, interpersonal/group processes, feedback of results, and task variety, with parallel changes in the technical/physical setting to form whole task groups and in the pay/reward system to reinforce group performance. If the necessary conditions for autonomous group functioning are implemented, the likely results are increases in productivity and worker satisfaction (p. 268).

In many senses, this is an idealized version of the sociotechnical experiment.

It is a version that might be at odds with the reality of a physical and technical environment that may be influenced by the quasi-rational characteristics of the actors in that environment. DeGreene (1988) is pessimistic in his consideration of the likelihood of the ultimate success of sociotechnical experiments. He proposes that:

> the top management of institutions is likely to tolerate, even encourage, small scale alternative sociotechnical (re)designs for reasons that range from necessary public relations to hope that such efforts might somehow improve productivity. However, management is likely to resist strongly those alternative designs that might threaten the existing structure of power, privilege, and control. (p. 20)

I think that this is an unduly pessimistic view of the possibilities of sociotechnical redesign. From a psychological perspective, we need to know more about the types of environments and the types of leaders who will genuinely embrace sociotechnical design and redesign as an opportunity rather than as an obstacle.

IMPROVING THE QUALITY OF WORKING LIFE THROUGH JOB DESIGN

Up to this point, the discussion has been somewhat abstract. We have considered different approaches that *might* be taken to designing organizations. What concrete activities are organizations *actually* engaging in that are responsive to some of the propositions of the theories of organizational behavior that we have just examined? The Rushton Mine experiment was a good example of a broad system-based approach to organizational intervention, but it is unusual. It is seldom that management, labor, and organizational representatives agree to a joint intervention of any consequence. Even in the instance of the Rushton experiment, it was eventually discontinued in spite of its success.

True sociotechnical interventions are the exception rather than the rule. What is more common is a limited intervention that addresses one or another principle of an organization theory. For example, an organization might add planning and budgeting responsibilities to the duties of a machine operator. This would be called *job enrichment*. The organization might simply add a greater variety of tasks to the operator's duties. This would be *job enlargement*. Alternatively or additionally, the organization might change the role of the supervisor of the machine operator from a directing to an advising function and allow a group of machine operators and support personnel to direct their own efforts. This would be called an *autonomous work group*. In fact, there are many different programs that might be introduced, all of which are compatible with one or more of the formal approaches to organizational behavior that we have considered. A broad term that has been used to refer to these interventions collectively has been *quality of working life* programs. It is also referred to often as the *process of humanizing work*. Walton (1980) identifies

TABLE 13–2 Variations on Worker Participation Strategies

Location	*Strategy*	*Purported Result*
Lowes Co.	6,000 employees own most of stock	Sales 3 × competitor's
Donnelly Mirrors	Employees elected to corporate decision-making body	Return on equity tripled
Carborundum Co.	Employees redesigned plant	Saved $3.5 million in design costs
New England Telephone	Group problem solving	Complaints reduced, performance improved
National Steel Corp.	Group problem solving	$600,000 saving
General Motors	Replaced supervisors with elected team leaders	Absenteeism down 90%; scrap down 50%

SOURCE: Adapted from "Reforming Work" by J. Simmons and W. J. Mares, October 25, 1982, *New York Times*, p. 22.

some typical characteristics of a high-quality work environment. These include:

1. Adequate and fair pay
2. A safe environment
3. A bill of rights including equity and due process
4. An environment that actively develops human capacities
5. Advancement opportunities
6. An environment that promotes positive human relations
7. An environment that recognizes the total life space of the individual (including the family)
8. An organization that has social relevance
9. An environment that allows for some control by the worker over decisions that affect her

If these are the characteristics of a high-quality environment, it follows that organizational interventions should be directed toward creating or maintaining one or more aspects of this type of psychosocial environment. Sociotechnical experiments are very ambitious; they address all the elements listed above. On the other hand, there are less ambitious efforts that address only one or a few of these elements. These less global interventions are much more characteristic of the typical U.S. company. One popular intervention has been the attempt to involve employees in important aspects of decision making. Table 13–2 presents some examples of such attempts. These programs attempt to strengthen the bond between a worker and the employing organization, to reduce the gap between the concepts of *management* and *worker*.

These participation programs are heterogeneous. Some are directed at work groups, some at units as large as departments, and some at boards of directors. There is no overriding theory guiding the application of the programs. In the last chapter, we saw that there may be both advantages and disadvantages to developing schemes of worker participation. Different theories suggest different outcomes for participation.

Another popular intervention that is often coupled with participation programs is task design (or redesign) experiments. These programs are directed to the things that a worker actually does in a working day—the specific duties and responsibilities that compose the "job" of the individual. The goal is to design tasks and jobs that will be most compatible with the motivational characteristics of those who hold the jobs and perform the task. In that sense, it seems to be a practical extension of the human relations approach described earlier. Let's consider the logic, theoretical foundations, and results of job and task design projects.

The Effect of Task and Job Design on Behavior

Within certain limits, technology will influence task design, although these influences are not always positive. Thus, mass-production jobs do not typically give the person performing the job much discretion in work behavior. Things are to be done in a particular way, and there is little room for variation. On the other hand, other technologies (e.g., writing software for microcomputers) commonly involve a good deal of discretion on the part of the employee in the choice of work methods and processes. We have seen in the motivation and satisfaction chapters that individuals can be influenced by a multitude of variables in the environment. The design of the particular job the individual is doing might be one of those variables. Certainly Herzberg (1966) suggested that "enriched" jobs had dramatically different effects on individuals than "deprived" jobs. The object of task design programs is to match the task characteristics with the psychological characteristics of the person who will perform that task.

The effect of task design on employee behavior has been closely examined in the last several years. The most popular model or theory guiding these examinations has been that of Hackman and Oldham (1976). They have proposed a model that has been labeled the *job characteristics model* to explain relationships between technology and worker motivation. This model is reproduced in graphic form in Figure 13–13. The model suggests that certain job characteristics (core job dimensions) produce certain perceptions in individuals (critical psychological states), which in turn lead to certain organizational and individual outcomes (personal and work outcomes). They further suggest that workers who are high in growth need strength will react more positively to jobs with high amounts of the core job dimensions than indi-

FIGURE 13–13 The Job Characteristics Model of Work Motivation

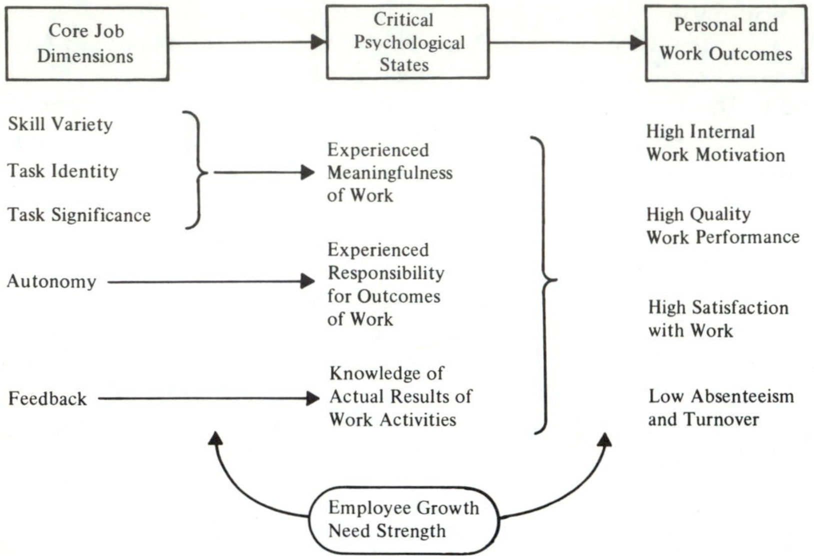

SOURCE: From "Motivation through the Design of Work: Test of a Theory" by J. R. Hackman and G. R. Oldham, 1976, *Organizational Behavior and Human Performance, 16,* p. 256.

viduals with low growth need strength. Level of growth need strength is related to the level in the Maslow-type hierarchy that best describes the individual in question. Thus, an individual currently functioning at the self-actualization level is thought to be high on growth need strength, whereas an individual who considers security needs as most important would be thought to have low growth need strength. The core job dimensions are defined as follows:

Skill variety. The degree to which the tasks require different skills

Task identity. The degree to which the individual completes a "whole" piece of work rather than simply a part

Task significance. The degree to which the job has an impact on the lives or work of other people

Autonomy. Freedom and independence of action

Feedback. The degree to which the job provides clear and direct information about individual effectiveness

The theory suggests that these five core dimensions can be combined in a particular way to provide an index of the motivating potential of any job. In other words, each job can give a score on each of the five dimensions, and these scores can be used to distinguish jobs that have motivating potential from those that do not. The motivation potential of a job is its capacity to spur an individual to personal and professional growth and development. This score (the motivating potential score, or MPS) is a measure of the adequacy of job design. The score is computed by means of the following formula:

$$\text{MPS} = \frac{\text{Skill variety} + \text{Task identity} + \text{Task significance}}{3} \times \text{Autonomy} \times \text{Feedback}$$

The formula suggests that skill variety, task identity, and task significance have additive relationships, and more of one of them can make up for a deficiency in another. This is not the case with autonomy and feedback. If either of these values is zero, the MPS is also zero.

Hackman and Oldham (1975) have produced an instrument that measures the core job dimensions. It is called the *Job Diagnostic Survey* (JDS) and provides measures of objective dimensions, individual psychological states resulting from these characteristics, affective reaction to the job characteristics, and measures of growth need strength.

In spite of the fact that the Hackman and Oldham model has been widely used in attempts to improve task and job design, the results have been mixed. In addition, critics have questioned the instruments used to measure the various components of the model, the form of the equation for calculating MPS, and the very theoretical foundation of the model (i.e., need theory). Brief and Aldag (1975) and Dunham (1976) both expressed reservations about the independence of the five core dimensions. Dunham conducted a factor analysis of responses to the JDS and found a single factor he labeled "job variety." In addition, Brief and Aldag expressed concern about the proposed mediating influence of growth need strength. This variable did not seem to function in the way suggested by Hackman and Oldham. Wall et al. (1978) attempted to test the job characteristics model and concluded that critical psychological states were not produced or affected by the core job dimensions. In addition, they questioned the independence of the core job dimensions as measured by the JDS.

Recent research has uncovered some of the possible reasons for the disappointing results in testing the model. This research seems to indicate that the five core dimensions suggested by the theory do not always appear for two reasons. First, there seems to be a difference between the responses of younger or well-educated workers, on the one hand, and older or less well educated workers, on the other hand. The young–well-educated respondents do seem to see their jobs along the five dimensions suggested by Hackman and Oldham. The older–less-well-educated workers see their jobs in much less complex terms, differentiating on only three or four dimensions (Fried & Ferris, 1986). P. Birnbaum, Farh, and Wong (1986) found that supervisors see incumbent jobs in more complex terms than incumbents themselves see their own jobs. Another possible source of confusion with the JDS questionnaire has been suggested by Idaszak and Drasgow (1987). They discovered that the five dimensions represented in the questionnaire are obscured by the fact that some of the statements are negatively worded. The negative wording may be confusing for workers with less education and lower reading comprehension ability (Fried & Ferris, 1986). In short, the value of the theory may not be fully realized until some of the measurement problems are resolved. Idaszak and Drasgow showed that the proposed five-factor structure could be identified when the negative items were reworded to be positive items.

A recent meta-analysis of the studies testing the job characteristics model has been generally supportive of the propositions of the theory (Loher et al., 1985). In a review of 28 studies testing the model, the average correlation between the job characteristics index and job satisfaction was +.39. This suggests that enriched jobs are more satisfying than unenriched jobs. Actual correlations ranged from +.32 (task identity) to +.46 (autonomy). Even more supportive was the differential relationship between these two variables for high and low GNS subjects. The correlation between the job characteristics index and job satisfaction for high GNS subjects was +.68 in contrast with a value of +.38 for those low in GNS. Loher et al. suggest that an enriched job itself may be sufficient to satisfy high GNS workers but that low GNS workers might need to experience external inducements (e.g., work group or management support for growth activities) actually to respond to the characteristics of an enriched job. It may also be that low GNS subjects are less well educated. If this were the case, it would be a simple matter to combine the results of Fried and Ferris (1986) with the results of Idaszak and Drasgow (1987) to propose that, in order to see truly the relationship between individual differences (such as GNS) and job enrichment results, it will be necessary to develop a more sophisticated measurement instrument to gather information about job characteristics as seen by the worker. In any event, the model seems more promising now than it has at any time since it was introduced.

The quality of working life is undoubtedly affected by task and job design. The characteristics suggested by the Hackman and Oldham model are good places to start in this examination of design issues, but it would seem that the instruments currently used to test and extend the theory need attention. It seems as if the work that should have followed the original statement of the model never got done. As was the case with Maslow's model, people were more interested in using the model than testing or developing it. If the issue of task design is to make any contribution to the understanding of organizational behavior, it will be necessary to move beyond the initial statements of the Hackman and Oldham model.

DESIGN FOR WHAT?

Before leaving the topic of job design and redesign, it might be useful to explore alternative models of design/redesign. Campion and Thayer (1985) propose that there are four distinctly different models that might be used to design jobs and that each model could be expected to impact on different variables. The four models they suggest are as follows:

1. *Motivational model.* Design guided by changes in feedback, social interaction, goal clarity, and so on; characteristic of the job enrichment literature such as the Hackman-Oldham model we just examined.
2. *Mechanistic model.* Based on the principles of time-and-motion study and scientific management; design of jobs is guided by changes in task specialization, economy of motion, and skill simplification.
3. *Biological model.* Based on principles of biomechanics; design of jobs is guided by attempts to make jobs easier to carry out physically (e.g., noise reduction, vibration reduction, tool design).
4. *Perceptual motor model.* Based on the principles of human engineering; design of jobs is guided by display-control compatibility, information-processing requirements, and so on.

Campion and Thayer suggest that the underlying model will dictate what type of outcome variables are affected by the design changes. Thus, jobs characterized by the motivational model of design will yield changes in satisfaction and motivation. Mechanistically designed jobs will have higher productivity and lower training requirements. Biologically designed jobs will be less fatiguing and effortful, leading to fewer aches, pains, and medical complaints. Finally, jobs designed using the human engineering model will produce fewer accidents, errors, and stress-related symptoms and require fewer mental demands. Campion and Thayer have developed a questionnaire that can be used to illuminate the underlying logic for the design of any job. They propose that this questionnaire can be used as a template either to determine if design goals are being or have been achieved, or to determine what the primary underlying influence is in terms of the design characteristics of a job under consideration. This research is still too new to determine the ultimate value of their suggestions, but their arguments are persuasive. It is likely that different design considerations will yield different results. One might not expect an enriched job to lead to fewer accidents or errors, although it might increase motivation and satisfaction; similarly, one should not expect a mechanistically designed job to lead to high satisfaction, although it might lead to higher productivity with limited talent. These issues are worth considering in job design interventions.

ORGANIZATIONAL DEVELOPMENT

As I indicated in the earlier discussion, organizational theory has evolved from a narrow, impersonal, and closed-system view of the behavior of individuals in organizations to a broader, socially oriented open-systems approach. As part of this evolution, a new specialty area has arisen. The area is called organizational development (OD). It is both a profession and a discipline. It is a profession in the sense that there are practitioners who have developed unique skills and experience bases that allow them to work more effectively with organizations than one who does not have the same skills or experience base. It is a discipline in the sense that it deals with a bounded substance area. Friedlander (1980) suggested that the essence of OD is its aim of helping organizations to explore and implement their need for change by increasing their awareness of how and why organizational members behave the way they do.

The issue of producing *awareness* is central to OD. Friedlander suggests that OD consultants do not provide answers to organizational questions. Instead, they promote awareness by *asking* questions. As examples, the OD consultant might question:

The methods used by a group to discover issues such as production problems

The methods used by a group to utilize resources such as a sales staff or a product image

Relationships within groups that help or hinder problem solving such as the often uneasy relationship between quality control and production departments

The effect of autocracy versus participation in attempts to change

The extent to which job design causes social dysfunction

As you can see, each of these questions relates to some aspect of an organizational theory that we have considered. But instead of emphasizing organizational structure or task significance or theory X beliefs, OD concentrates on the strategies of making these issues obvious to those that are affected by them. This means that OD draws from a wide range of specialties (Friedlander, 1980). For example, OD draws from social psychology (group dynamics and small group theory), from clinical and counseling psychology (diagnosis and counseling methods), and industrial psychology (attitude and motivation theory).

In many ways, organizational development is similar to clinical psychology. It is an attempt to help an organization develop, to adjust, to meet its own expectations. Clinical psychology and counseling have much the same goal in mind except that adjustment is the goal of an individual, a couple, or a family. Similarly, just as the clinical psychologist gathers information and prepares a plan of treatment or counseling based on that information, so does the OD consultant. Although the area of OD is much too broad to cover in a few pages, you can get a feel for it by considering a sampling of topics central to OD activities. First, we will consider the issue of organizational diagnosis, and in particular the determination of an organization's *climate*. Next, we will consider some dysfunctions created by the attempts to organize individual effort through the specification of work roles. Finally, we will consider some common interventions initiated by OD consultants.

Organizational Diagnosis: The Case of Climate

The climate of an organization is thought to represent the *perception* of objective characteristics by organization members. As an example, the size of an organization is objective, but a person's feeling about that size is subjective; it is the perception of these objective characteristics that is thought to be represented by the climate of an organization. Figure 13–14 presents a graphic representation of this view of climate and how it differs from organizational structure and the subjective characteristics of individuals. Climate is at the heart of many OD interventions. It is the individual's view of the "personality" of the organization that is thought to prevent or precipitate many organizational changes or dysfunctions.

Litwin and Stringer (1966) conducted some of the earliest research into the nature of organizational climate. They proposed that climate is made up of six distinct factors: (1) structure, (2) individual responsibility, (3) rewards, (4) risks and risk taking, (5) warmth and support, and (6) tolerance and conflict. Campbell et al. (1970) have suggested that these factors of climate actually describe the way an organization treats its members. This is why I refer to climate as the "personality" of the organization. Just as some individuals are aggressive in their dealings with other individuals, some organizations are aggressive in their dealings with members. Of course, organizations do not exist in the same way that single individuals do; nevertheless, traditions and styles of organizations do endure over time and seem to have a rather strong influence on managers and upper-level executives. Whyte's (1956) classic description of the "organization man" is a vivid example of the type of force we are considering.

There has been a good deal of empirical research on organizational climate. In a study of the success of a training program for the hard-core unemployed, Friedlander and Greenberg (1971) found that the sole correlate of performance was the degree of perceived organizational supportiveness. They suggested that training could be facilitated by paying more attention to climate variables. Using the suggestion of Campbell et al. (1970), they might have concluded that the *way* in which the training program was administered was just as important as *what* was taught.

From the measurement perspective, a good deal of research has been directed toward identifying the general components of organizational climate. Campbell et al. reviewed most of the work done to that point and concluded there were four major factors: (1) individual autonomy, (2) degree of structure imposed by the position, (3) reward orientation, and (4) consideration, warmth, and support. Similar factors have been found by Sims and LaFollette (1975) and Muchinsky (1976). There have been many similar studies attempting to identify *the* parameters of organizational climate. Unless researchers are careful, climate research may get sidetracked in the same way as satisfaction research a decade earlier. You will remember from the chapter on job satisfaction that until the JDI was published (Smith et al., 1969), there was

FIGURE 13–14 Major Influences on Organizational Structure and Climate

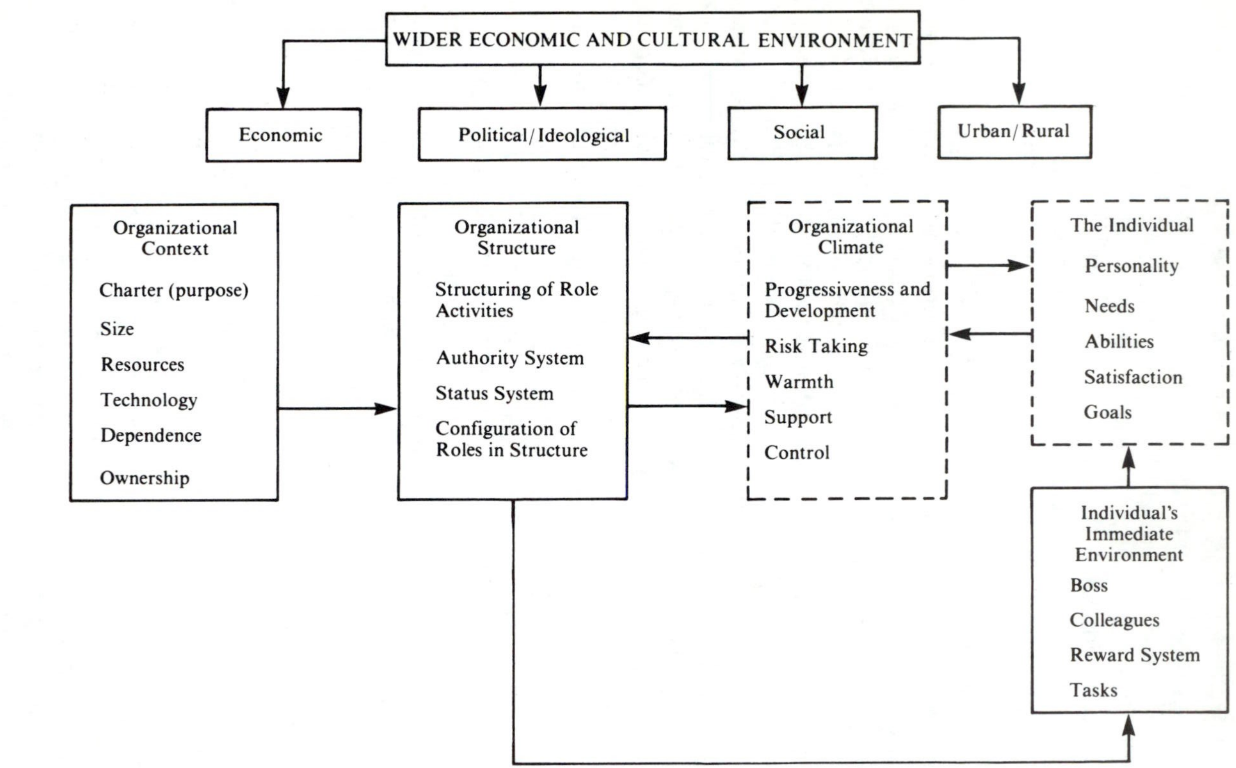

SOURCE: From "Organizational Structure and Climate" (Fig. 1, p. 1127) by R. Payne and D. S. Pugh, in M. D. Dunnette (Ed.), *Handbookof Industrial and Organizational Behavior*, 1976, Chicago: Rand McNally.

no way to compare results from study to study, since different measures of satisfaction were used in each study. The same will be true of climate research until a single measure is agreed on. The review of Campbell et al. was well done and the subsequent research reasonably supportive. Thus, it seems that climate is well described by the characteristics of autonomy, structure, reward, and consideration orientation.

In general, research supports the existence of the construct of organizational climate. It also seems as if this construct is distinct from job satisfaction, although occasionally individuals may have a difficult time divorcing their feelings about a job from their description of that job (Schnake, 1983). One line of research (Franklin, 1975; Lawler, Hall, & Oldham, 1974), and theory building (Schneider & Snyder, 1975), has begun to focus on the organizational process rather than on structural components. Thus, current investigations of climate are more likely to focus on variables such as *how* performance is appraised or *how* promotions are made than on organizational size or span of control. Climate will clearly play a role in most organizational theories of the future. It will represent the organizational members' perceptions of the organization—its personality. As you can see from Figure 13–14, climate represents an excellent point of entry into the open system that includes the individual, the organization, and the environment. It provides information relevant to the match between organizational structure and individual characteristics.

Recently, the term *organizational culture* has been used interchangeably with the concept of *climate* (Schneider, 1985). It is not clear if this is really a difference in concepts or simply a difference in jargon and methodology. As Schneider points out, *culture* seems to be a more popular term in business circles and is often "measured" through case studies and qualitative forms of analysis. Although the concept of culture may prove to be a unique and useful way of characterizing organizations, the empirical justification for introducing a "new" concept has not yet been provided. As a result, we might consider the concept to be old wine in new bottles.

Organizational Dysfunctions: Role Conflict and Ambiguity

I began the section on organizational development by defining it as the process by which organizations are assisted in growth and development. As we saw in the earlier discussions of organizational theory, the very fact of specialization (i.e., different people assigned to different jobs) implies the possibility of confusion or suboptimal effort expenditure. In fact, this confusion and counterproductive effort is almost an inevitable by-product of organizational growth. Several terms are used to describe this negative by-product. Two popular terms are *role conflict* and *role ambiguity*. The study of role conflict and role ambiguity plays an important part in the organizational development process.

Miles and Perreault (1976) described four different types of role conflict:

1. *Person-role conflict.* The individual would like to do things in a manner different from that suggested by the job description.
2. *Intrasender conflict.* The individual receives an assignment without sufficient personnel to complete the assignment successfully.
3. *Intersender conflict.* The individual is asked to behave in such a manner that one person will be pleased with the result, whereas others will not be.
4. *Role overload.* The individual is assigned more work than can be effectively handled.

Most of us have been in one or more of the situations described. For example, it is common to perform an action that pleases our parents but annoys our friends (intersender conflict) or to receive assignments from three different instructors that, in combination, might take more than a term or semester to complete (role overload). Those studying the effect of role conflict believe that competing demands such as these produce stress in individuals. This stress, in turn, is thought to produce dissatisfaction and performance problems.

Role conflict is often studied in the context of a second, similar concept: role ambiguity. Role ambiguity is concerned with the degree to which an individual actually understands what is required on the job. This is different from role conflict in which the individual perfectly understands the competing demands being made. It is common for students completing term papers to feel that they do not understand what the instructor expects. Role ambiguity is also thought to produce tension that may negatively affect satisfaction, performance, or both.

Rizzo, House, and Lirtzman (1970) suggested that role conflict and ambiguity were related to dissatisfaction and inappropriate organizational behavior. They proposed that conflict and ambiguity resulted in stress, and stress, in turn, resulted in dissatisfaction and poor performance. They developed a questionnaire to measure the degree of conflict and ambiguity individuals experienced in their work, and this questionnaire has been widely used. Schuler, Aldag, and Brief (1977) analyzed responses of individuals from six samples to the Rizzo et al. scales and concluded that the questions did measure the two variables of conflict and ambiguity. Furthermore, these variables did seem to be related to negative states such as dissatisfaction and stress. In a similar study, Keller (1975) found that employees were more satisfied when expectations were clear and nonconflicting. From the practical point of view, several studies have pointed out the possible value of a supervisor in reducing the potentially damaging effects of conflict and ambiguity. Randolph and Posner (1981) found negative correlations between role conflict and ambiguity, on the one hand, and supervisory support, on the other hand. They suggested that group cohesiveness might act in a manner similar to supervisory support. Fisher and Gitelson (1983) completed a meta-analysis of studies of conflict and ambiguity and concluded that both ambiguity and conflict were associated with dissatisfaction. This suggests the possibility that conflict and ambiguity might be part of a more pervasive dysfunctional syndrome rather than caused directly and specifically by competing or unclear job demands. As with many other variables in psychology, we can not be sure if conflict and ambiguity are causes, effects, or reciprocally related to other variables such as satisfaction and motivation.

Interpersonal Conflict: A Special Case. Recently, Kabanoff (1985) has suggested a structure for helping to understand why interpersonal conflict occurs and how to relieve it. He has proposed that there are six sources of influence that might be applied in an interpersonal situation. He further suggests that any one of these six sources of influence might be in conflict with any other of the sources of influence in a given situation. All the possible conflicts are then arranged in a matrix form, as depicted in Figure 13–15. Further, Kabanoff suggests ways of relieving or resolving these various conflicts. An example of several conflicts and methods for resolving them appear in Table 13–3. This framework for considering conflict and its resolution is quite new but does warrant close attention and empirical study. Like the Vroom-Yetton model of decision making, its prescriptive characteristics make it potentially useful, and it is intuitively appealing.

We are at a very early stage in the understanding of the concepts of role ambiguity and role conflict. If you remember the development of concepts such as leadership and job satisfaction, you can infer that it often takes ten or more years before a new concept's conceptual and operational problems are ironed out. We have not yet reached that stage with the conflict and ambiguity concepts. Nevertheless, they are appealing from both an empirical and a theoretical point of view. The implications for theories of work motivation are pretty clear. If we examine the Porter-Lawler cognitive model in light of role conflict propositions, we can easily see that there are instrumentalities, valences, and expectancies canceling one another in situations of conflict. Thus, when high production is expected by a supervisor and moderate production is expected by co-workers, the individual must somehow balance these forces. Similarly, when the job description calls for one behavior, whereas common sense calls for another, there will be some problems in defining good performance (this would be an example of inappropriate role perception in the Porter-Lawler model). Similarly, with respect to role ambiguity, an individual who does not know what is expected probably cannot perform his duties with maximum efficiency. Conflict and ambiguity also have implications for theories of goal setting and a wide range of theories dealing with leadership effectiveness. The notion of work roles and their accompanying demands and pressures is an important one. Research on conflict and ambiguity is likely to increase considerably our understanding of work-related stress, job satisfaction, and leader effectiveness. This type of research is important for another reason as well: it clearly describes some dysfunctional characteristics of organizations—the flaws of organizational personalities.

FIGURE 13–15 Examples of the 15 General Types of Conflict Situations

	Informal	*Ability/ Knowledge*	*Assignment (communication)*	*Authority*	*Allocation*	*Precedence*
Ability/ knowledge	A person's actual ability does not match (e.g., exceeds) their expertise as perceived by other members					
Assignment	A person with low commitment to the group is placed in a central communication position	A person's ability is incongruent with the ability requirements of the position, i.e., selection problem				
Authority	A disliked person exercises authority over others	A person of low ability exercises authority over others	A position has limited opportunities for communication with positions over which it has authority			

Allocation	Persons with incompatible needs are required to collaborate in the performance of a task	A person is allocated tasks that are incongruent with the ability specifications of the position, i.e., job design problem	A position has limited communication channels but is allocated many tasks	The number of tasks allocated to a position are not matched by its authority	
Precedence	A person's informal status is mismatched with the importance of their task in the work flow	Ability of the person is incongruent with the criticality of the task in the work flow	A position where task performance depends on others has limited opportunities to communicate with these other positions	A low authority position is allocated a high precedence or critical task	The amount of time allocated for task performance does not match the criticality of the task

SOURCE: From "Potential Influence Structures as Sources of Interpersonal Conflict in Groups and Organizations" by B. Kabanoff, 1985, *Organizational Behavior and Human Decision Processes, 36*, p. 131.

TABLE 13–3 Suggested Solutions for Various Conflict Combinations

Conflict Type	*Example*	*Resolution*
Informal versus ability	Person has more ability than others believe	Change person's informal status through public praise
Ability versus authority	Person of low ability in charge of others	Retrain person; decrease authority
Assignment versus allocation	A position has limited communication channels but many tasks	Increase channels; decrease tasks
Informal versus authority	Disliked person in position of authority	Increase people skills; decrease authority

SOURCE: Adapted from "Potential Influence Structures as Sources of Interpersonal Conflict in Groups and Organizations" by B. Kabanoff, 1985, *Organizational Behavior and Human Decision Processes, 36.*

Organizational Development Techniques

As you saw in the introduction to this section, OD is often action oriented rather than theory or substance oriented. The practicing clinical psychologist is often only vaguely interested in theory or research. He is interested in what works. He wants to help his client feel better. The same is true of the OD consultant. She wants to help her client organization change and develop. She wants to help the members of that organization feel better and act in a way that is both personally satisfying and organizationally productive. OD examines, and often precipitates, change.

Beer (1976) provides a good description of the background and technology of OD. I will simply review some of the more frequently used techniques. There are four major categories of organizational intervention practiced by the typical OD consultant. These are survey feedback, laboratory training, team building, and process consultation.

Survey feedback consists of gathering data (e.g., climate perceptions) from different sources in the work unit or organization (e.g., supervisors and subordinates, maintenance and production) and using discrepancies in these perceptions as the background for precipitating a discussion between the contrasted groups. One of the most popular versions of this type of intervention is one developed by Rensis Likert (1961, 1967). He asks participants in the survey to describe where they see their department now and where they would like to see their department in several years. By contrasting the response profiles of subgroups of individuals, he can identify discrepancies between these groups. For example, one group might indicate that they anticipate little organizational change in five years, but another group might expect rapid and massive change. This suggests that there will be problems

FIGURE 13–16 Survey Feedback to One School in a School District

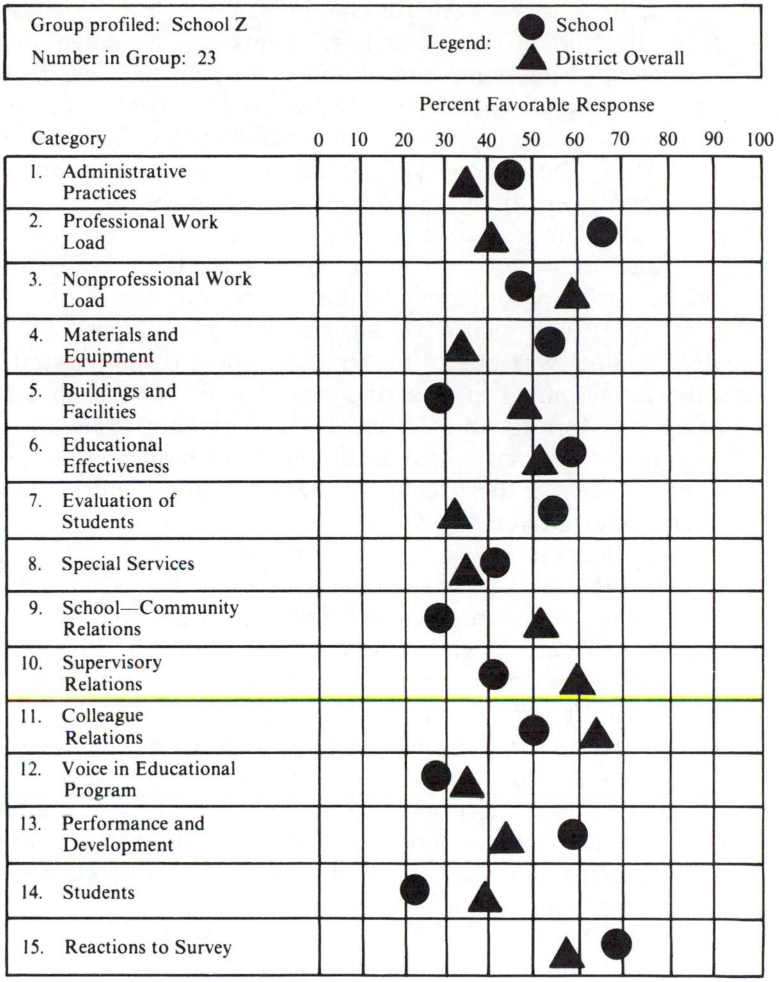

Group profiled: School Z
Number in Group: 23

Legend: ● School ▲ District Overall

Percent Favorable Response

Category 0 10 20 30 40 50 60 70 80 90 100

1. Administrative Practices
2. Professional Work Load
3. Nonprofessional Work Load
4. Materials and Equipment
5. Buildings and Facilities
6. Educational Effectiveness
7. Evaluation of Students
8. Special Services
9. School—Community Relations
10. Supervisory Relations
11. Colleague Relations
12. Voice in Educational Program
13. Performance and Development
14. Students
15. Reactions to Survey

SOURCE: From *Failures in Organization Development and Change"* (p. 152) by P. H. Mirvis and D. N. Berg, 1977, New York: John Wiley & Sons.

in coordinating the efforts of these two groups. At the very least, one would expect resistance on the part of the group anticipating no change. In survey feedback techniques, the validity of the data is emphasized. The participants are faced with the fact that real people (i.e., co-workers) have provided these responses and that the responses imply action (or inaction) on the part of those who provided them. Figure 13–16 is an example of some feedback used in discussion in a school district. The discussions were intended to precipitate change in School Z so that they would meet or exceed district standards on some of the behavior categories listed. These data are self-explanatory to the people receiving them. If you were a teacher in School Z, it would be apparent to you that the teachers in your school see themselves as above the district average in terms of professional output and quality of materials and equipment. On the other hand, your fellow teachers see themselves as below the average in terms of community relations and buildings and facilities. It would not be that difficult, given these data, to begin a discussion of areas where your school is perceived to be below average. These discussions would be the first step in a program of change.

Questionnaires represent only one of several methods available for collecting the data necessary for survey feedback interventions. Table 13–4 presents other methods with their advantages and disadvantages.

Laboratory training was one of the first and most common strategies of organizational development in its early years. The first institutionalized approach to OD was through the National Training Laboratories in Bethel, Maine. It was here that many of currently used techniques were first introduced. The best known of these techniques was the unstructured laboratory, more commonly referred to as *sensitivity training,* or the formation of T-groups. The unstructured laboratory was based on the notion that individuals will learn much about themselves by examining the way in which they attempt to impose structure on an unstructured environment. Typically, groups of individuals who were unknown to one another would be brought together and provided with no structure or agenda. If there was any task, it was simply the structuring of a situation completely lacking in structure. It was felt that the absence of structure or an agenda of some type would create tension in the group members, and this tension would create action of some sort. Group members were asked to observe and comment on the actions taken by others in the group but to comment in nonevaluative terms rather than critical ones. It was thought that this type of feedback might help individuals become aware of their attitudes, values, and behaviors.

The logic of the unstructured laboratory is based on the notion that attitude change is a three-stage process. The first stage is one of *unfreezing,* in which individuals become aware of values and beliefs they hold. The second phase is one of *changing,* in which new beliefs, values, and attitudes are adopted. Finally, comes a third stage called *refreezing,* which consists of the stabilization of new attitudes and values. Sensitivity training was thought to facilitate these three stages. Feedback from the group begins the unfreezing process. A supportive environment enables the individual to try out new attitudes and behavior patterns (i.e., the changing process), and the group reinforces the individual for new attitudes (refreezing). It should be kept in mind that sensitivity training or the formation of T-groups is just a conceptual label; there are almost as many variations in the actual process as there are groups.

A different approach to the same process is that of *instrumented laboratory*

TABLE 13–4 A Comparison of Different Methods of Data Collection

Method	*Major Advantages*	*Major Potential Problems*
Interviews	1. Adaptive—allows data collection on a range of possible subjects 2. Source of "rich" data 3. Empathic 4. Process of interviewing can build rapport	1. Can be expensive 2. Interviewer can bias responses 3. Coding/interpretation problems 4. Self-report bias
Questionnaires	1. Responses can be quantified and easily summarized 2. Easy to use with large samples 3. Relatively inexpensive 4. Can obtain large volume of data	1. Nonempathic 2. Predetermined questions may miss issues 3. Data may be overinterpreted 4. Response bias
Observations	1. Collects data on behavior rather than reports of behavior 2. Real-time, not retrospective 3. Adaptive	1. Interpretation and coding problems 2. Sampling is a problem 3. Observer bias/reliability 4. Costly
Secondary data/ unobtrusive measures	1. Nonreactive—no-response bias 2. High face validity 3. Easily quantified	1. Access/retrieval possibly a problem 2. Potential validity problems 3. Coding/interpretation

SOURCE: From *Feedback and Organizational Development* (table 7.1, p. 119) by D. A. Nadler, 1977, Reading, MA: Addison-Wesley.

training. As opposed to the unstructured approach of the sensitivity training group, the instrumented training approach typically involves a group of individuals who are given a particular problem to solve. In the process of solving the problem, the group members are asked to observe the behaviors of others in the group and provide feedback to those individuals with respect to their social behavior. As an example, the group might be given a supervisor-subordinate problem to resolve. In the course of dealing with the problem, their attitudes toward leadership are revealed, these attitudes are made apparent to them by fellow group members, and they are asked to consider alternative attitudes toward supervisor-subordinate relations.

Both the unstructured and the instrumented approaches have a common theme: they both attempt to create a social environment in which the individual can try out or practice new behaviors or attitudes with relative impunity. Nevertheless, these laboratory settings were thought to be somewhat artificial, and the more modern approaches to OD emphasize using local work-related issues to accomplish the unfreezing, changing, and refreezing goals.

Laboratory training (and in particular, sensitivity or T-group training) is not without critics. It can be a traumatic experience for some people, particularly when carried out by poorly prepared trainers. In many respects, it is the equivalent of group psychotherapy. Values, beliefs, and habitual response mechanisms are assaulted. These assaults can affect psychological well-being. One cannot simply shrug off a three-day training session devoted to changing values or interpersonal perceptions. It is likely that this type of intervention creates both positive and negative change. One must be aware of both possibilities. It is interesting to note that since 1975 sensitivity training has been formally prohibited by the Swedish government in any training efforts conducted in local, state, or national governmental agencies. This is the result of some negative sensitivity training experiences.

Process consultation or *intervention* is a distinctly different type of OD. Whereas survey feedback might deal with a group's reaction to a perceived state of affairs (e.g., favorable or unfavorable as depicted in Figure 13–16), process consultation deals more directly with the behavior in question than with the attitudes toward the behavior. Typically, a group is asked to engage in a social process that is part of their job. Critiques of these activities are then presented to group members, and they are encouraged to try alternative ways of accomplishing their goals. Consider the example in Figure 13–17. This might be used with a group after the completion of a meeting. They would be asked to answer the questions and then discuss these answers as a way of analyzing what happened in the meeting that was productive and counterproductive. There is a basic difference between process interventions and other OD techniques. Process interventions assume that the behavior must change before the attitudes; other approaches assume that attitudes change first, and subsequently, behavior changes. Thus, behavioral modeling, described in Chapter 9, is an example of a process intervention.

Another commonly used technique is known as *team building*. This technique is frequently used to prepare groups of people to accomplish particular tasks. It may be that a team will be formed for the design of a new product or for the development of a marketing plan or for deciding how to deal with mandated budget cuts. Often, these teams consist of individuals who each have specific areas of expertise but no allegiance (or even familiarity) with each other. Team building techniques are geared toward developing an appreciation among team members for what the task is, what roles must be filled, and who will fill them. In addition, individual strengths are highlighted as they pertain to the tasks. Finally, it is hoped that cohesion will develop among team members.

Recently, it was my responsibility to help two engineering groups from different divisions of the same organization develop a common plan for a

FIGURE 13–17 Sample Form for Analyzing Group Effectiveness

A: Goals

(poor)	1 2 3 4 5 6 7 8 9 10	(good)
Confused; diverse; conflicting; indifferent; little interest.		Clear to all; shared by all; all care about the goals, feel involved.

B: Participation

(poor)	1 2 3 4 5 6 7 8 9 10	(good)
Few dominate; some passive; some not listened to; several talk at once or interrupt.		All get in; all are really listened to.

C: Feelings

(poor)	1 2 3 4 5 6 7 8 9 10	(good)
Unexpected; ignored or criticized.		Freely expressed; empathic responses.

D: Diagnosis of group problems

(poor)	1 2 3 4 5 6 7 8 9 10	(good)
Jump directly to remedial proposals; treat symptoms rather than basic causes.		When problems arise the situation is carefully diagnosed before action is proposed; remedies attack basic causes.

E: Leadership

(poor)	1 2 3 4 5 6 7 8 9 10	(good)
Group needs for leadership not met; group depends too much on single person or on a few persons.		As needs for leadership arise various members meet them ("distributed leadership"); anyone feels free to volunteer as he sees a group need.

SOURCE: Edgar Schein, *Process Consultation* © 1969, Addison Wesley Publishing Co., Inc., Reading, Massachusetts. Fig. 4.3 on page 42. Reprinted with permission.

FIGURE 13–17 *(concluded)*

F: Decisions

(poor)	1 2 3 4 5 6 7 8 9 10	(good)
Needed decisions don't get made; decision made by part of group; others uncommitted.		Consensus sought and tested; deviates appreciated and used to improve decision; decisions when made are fully supported.

G: Trust

(poor)	1 2 3 4 5 6 7 8 9 10	(good)
Members distrust one another; are polite, careful, closed, guarded; they listen superficially but inwardly reject what others say; are afraid to criticize or to be criticized.		Members trust one another; they reveal to group what they would be reluctant to expose to others; they respect and use the responses they get; they can freely express negative reactions without fearing reprisal.

H: Creativity and Growth

(poor)	1 2 3 4 5 6 7 8 9 10	(good)
Members and group in a rut; operate routinely; persons stereotyped and rigid in their roles; no progress.		Group flexible, seeks new and better ways; individuals changing and growing; creative; individually supported.

new product. The two groups would be required to work closely with each other over a period in excess of one year to design an electronic device that would be profitable and would satisfy the needs of *both* divisions of the corporation. These groups could not have been more different if the differences had been planned. One group contained predominantly older members;

the other, younger members. One group was located in a rural western area; the other, in the industrialized northeast. One group had gone through many similar design projects; the other group had never brought a project to completion. One group considered themselves creative and uninterested in detail; the other group thought of themselves as contributing via reliability and cost consciousness rather than through creative breakthroughs. The two groups were brought together in a wooded retreat area for three days. The first day began with some group exercises in brainstorming (e.g., how many uses can you find for a coat hanger) in which participants were encouraged to build on the ideas that others had already suggested. Next, small groups were formed (with equal numbers of engineers from both locations), and the groups solved an unusual problem. In this case, the problem was what resources to carry with them from a plane that had crashed on the desert. After several hours of these types of activities, mixed-location groups were formed to suggest a project-related agenda for the next two days. During these next two days, the engineers developed a plan of action for developing the new product. In the course of the three days, the participants were encouraged to eat with their counterparts from the other location, to find out something about their backgrounds, and to develop an appreciation of the strengths and weaknesses of the people they would work with during the next year. At the end of the three-day period, there was a much greater feeling of cohesion than had been present at the start of the sessions. This feeling could never have been produced by telephone conversations or the exchange of documents or memos.

The Choice of OD Techniques. The discussion of particular techniques makes it appear as if one must choose among these techniques. This is not the case. In many instances, several different techniques are used simultaneously to achieve different purposes. Consider the intervention program introduced by the U.S. Army for dealing with organizational change at an army communications processing center. Table 13–5 lists the problems to be addressed and the techniques chosen to address those problems. As you can see, four different interventions were used to address different problem areas.

The Evaluation of OD Efforts. A particularly thorny question in the organizational development literature has been how to evaluate the relative success of various interventions. Most interventions are complex and involve both process and substance changes. In addition, the possibilities of identifying reasonable control groups are few and far between. Terpstra (1981) has looked at the relationship between methodological rigor and positive results and come to the conclusion that there is a positive bias in the reporting of OD results. Specifically, he proposes that when sample sizes are small, control groups are missing or nonexistent, random assignment to conditions is not possible, and sampling strategies are inappropriate, the chances for finding a "success" are good. This implies that the evaluation is not objective by

TABLE 13–5 Some Problem/Strategy Combinations

Problem Areas Identified
1. Lack of peer group norms which encourage good performance
2. Insufficient performance feedback
3. Need for training in supervisory techniques
4. Role ambiguity and conflict
5. Inadequate intergroup communication patterns
6. Lack of motivating job content
7. Ambiguous performance evaluation standards

OD Strategies Selected to Address Problem Areas

Strategies	*Problem Address*
Survey feedback	#4,5,7
Participative problem-solving/team building	#4,5,7
Management training	#2,3
Job enrichment	#1,6

SOURCE: From "Intervening at the Bottom: Organizational Development with Enlisted Personnel in an Army Work Setting" by S. L. Cohen and J. R. Turney, 1978, *Personnel Psychology, 31,* table 2, p. 721.

commonly accepted standards of the scientific community. Bass (1983) suggests some alternative interpretations of Terpstra's findings. He suggests that it may be that those who are unconvinced of the worth of OD efforts have a negative bias in reviewing results. Alternatively, he suggests that those in favor and those opposed to OD interventions look at different criteria as indicators of success. The critics look for "real" changes in productivity or absence or some other observable variable. The proponents of OD techniques look for changes in attitudes, emotional levels, or perceptions.

CONCLUDING COMMENTS

It should be quite clear to you now that organizations are more complicated than even the most complex organization charts imply. K. E. Weick (1976) has suggested that organizations are analogous to a soccer game played on a round, sloped field with several different goals appearing at random locations on the field; players are permitted to enter and leave the field freely and use any number of soccer balls, depending on their preference. The players can arbitrarily "define" a goal whenever they feel like it. This is a very appealing analogy for both organizational members and organizational researchers. It highlights the desperation and frustration implicit in dealing with a complex social system.

In a more serious vein, it is reasonable to wonder if organizational psychology is the study of organizations or of the organizing process of members of those organizations. There is no doubt that current research and theory are directed toward the organizing process. This is as it must be for psychology. We must not lose sight of the fact that the subject matter for the behavioral sciences is *behavior* of individuals and groups of individuals. Thus, the formal characteristics of organization are of importance only to the degree that they (1) are manifestations of values, beliefs, attitudes, predispositions, or behaviors of the organizational members or (2) have the capacity to function as "treatments" in the classic experimental sense, helping to explain variance in the behavior of organizational members. Viewed in this light, the evolution of organization theory from the classic approach to the contingency approach mirrors the growth of psychology from infant stages in the late nineteenth century to adulthood 100 years later. The next challenge will be in developing meaningful ways of evaluating the impact of these organizational environments on specific behaviors as well as the impact of changes in these environments.

CENTRAL POINTS FOR STUDY

1. Classic organization theory implies that there is one best form for an organization.
2. Human relations theory presents organizations through the eyes of the members.
3. Contingency theories propose an interaction between the external environment and the form and process of the organization.
4. The sociotechnical approach to organization emphasizes the interactions between individuals and technologies.
5. Organizational development is both a profession and a discipline.
6. Role conflict and role ambiguity are symptoms of organizational dysfunction.
7. Organizational development addresses the issue of organizational change.

CHAPTER 14

Work and Well-Being

In one sense, work is something that *happens* to an individual. It is a treatment of sorts. People go to a work setting and are exposed to various elements. These elements include things such as heat and light and noise. In addition, there are such elements as pay and supervisory style and coworkers. Even the duties and responsibilities that make up the "job" are treatments. Workers are exposed to a work pace, a certain demand for productivity, and accountability. As we saw in the last chapter, they may be asked to tolerate conflicting or ambiguous demands. In earlier chapters, we have considered ways in which work may be made more motivating and satisfying. We have examined methods of selecting and training workers so that they might be prepared to carry out their duties in a more satisfying and efficient manner. But as we all know, few jobs are perfect. Instead, most jobs have one or more aspects that can be harmful. A particular job might be too hot or pay too little or demand too much or have poorly defined responsibilities or even be too exciting. In these cases, we expect that to some extent the worker will be adversely affected by the job—the treatment will be aversive. There have been many examinations of this relationship, and all have come to the same conclusion: certain work situations can adversely affect physical and psychological health (e.g., Hamburg, Elliott, & Parron, 1982). Work can be a threat to well-being.

In this chapter, we will consider the "cost" of work to the worker from several perspectives. One traditional approach is to examine the concept of safety. It is self-evident that work represents an opportunity for injury and death. A second common perspective of the consideration of well-being is the identification of aversive elements in the work environment, both physical and psychological. These are commonly called *stressors*—circumstances that put a "strain" on the worker.

More recently, a broader approach to work and well-being has emerged in the literature of industrial and organizational psychology. It is the concern for psychological demands and the extent to which work contributes to those demands. It is this broader concern that will be the major theme of this chapter. The generally accepted term for examining such issues is *stress*. We will examine some aspects of the relationship between work and stress. First, we will consider the objective work situation in the form of a discussion of stressors and reactions to stress. Second, we will deal with characteristics of individuals that might make them more or less vulnerable to environmental stressors. Third, we will consider some theories of stress that might be applicable to the work context as well as suggestions regarding how stress might be controlled or reduced. Fourth, we will note the practical elements of safety and the prevention of industrial accidents. As you can see, all these topics relate to well-being but in slightly different ways.

ENVIRONMENTAL STRESSORS

One way to look at factors in the physical environment is to view them as a class of potential "stressors" of the worker. In this way, they may be included with a larger set of conditions that "push" the performance or endurance limits or both under which one can work. This larger set of stressors includes *task-induced* stresses—those conditions of speed or load demands of the task or job itself that test the limits of one's ability to perform. Situational and psychological factors resulting from job insecurity, excessive competition, hazardous working conditions, long or unusual working hours, and the like, represent another class of stressors on the worker. Finally, the worker may be stressed by loss of sleep, disease, alcohol, drugs, or other personal factors that affect the physiological equilibrium of the body.

All stressors pose some degree of threat—physical or psychological—to the worker. In this sense, stressors are somewhat analogous to the stress tests that engineers apply to metals, alloys, structures, or systems to determine the limits of strength, flexibility, or other properties of inanimate objects. Although tasks are not created deliberately to test a person to the "breaking point," it is of considerable importance to know the limits within which one can adapt and perform efficiently. Equally important, since many workers do adapt to stress, we need to know the price paid for adaptation to suboptimal conditions, even though the stressors may not appreciably interfere with efficient performance.

In the case of physical environmental stresses, the worker has a certain range of adaptability and tolerance within which he can operate without mobilizing emergency systems and with no appreciable effect on his performance. For example, our bodies are continuously making minor adjustments to temperature change through the thermal regulating systems, our eyes accommodate to the distance of the field of view, and our ears adjust to the prevailing noise level. Thus, the question is not whether one can adapt, for one does so continually, but rather the limits and the costs one pays for adaptation to conditions that represent stresses on these adaptive mechanisms. Of course, it is also of interest to know something about the ideal or optimal levels of environmental stimulation for physical and psychological well-being (as well as for performance).

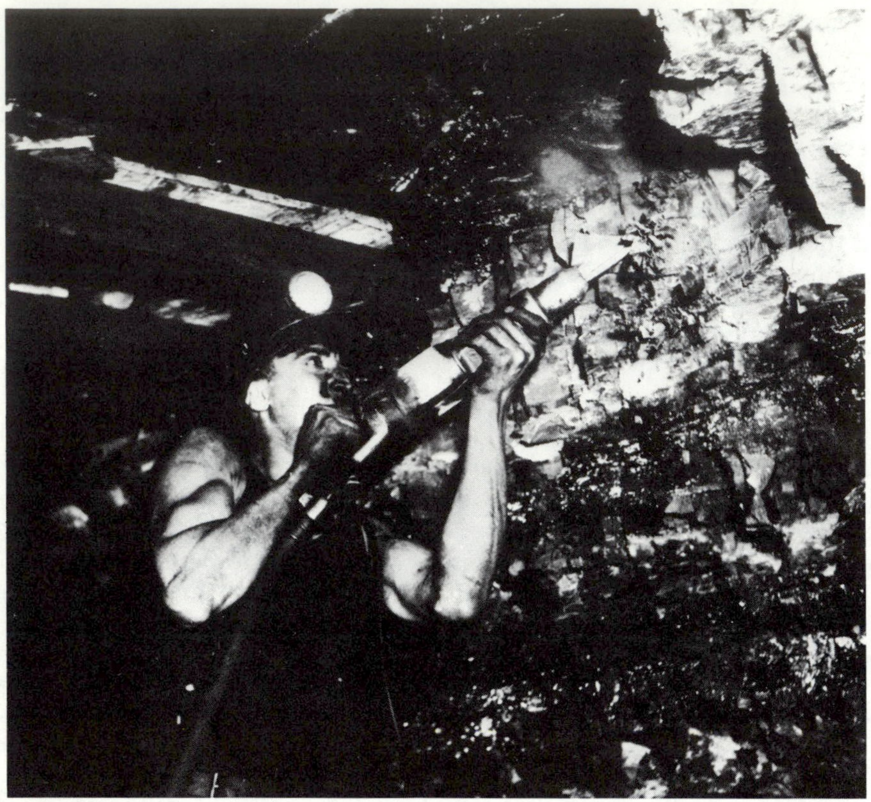

Many jobs, such as that of a coal miner, require substantial physical adaptation. (International Labor Organization)

EFFECTS OF SINGLE ENVIRONMENTAL STRESSORS

Sound and Noise

Let's begin our consideration of stress with a simple example of an environmental stimulus that has often been labeled a stressor—noise. It is not so much that noise is a critical issue in the workplace. But noise is an easy variable to deal with in the laboratory, so it has been a favorite independent variable for considerations of environmental stress. As a result, there are lots of studies describing its effects. In addition, at one time or another, most of us have been bothered by noise. Perhaps it was the sound of children playing while we were trying to concentrate on material for a test, or it might have been the sound of traffic outside our window while we were trying to sleep, or maybe even the enraging sound of a dripping spigot in an otherwise quiet environment. The effects that these sounds have on our behavior will depend, at least to some degree, on the nature of the behavior in question. In spite of the traffic noises, we often manage to get back to sleep. On the other hand, disruptive environmental conditions, such as children playing, can have substantial effects on learning and memory; consequently, we might justifiably blame poor test performance on a noisy roommate or dormitory floor.

These examples are pale reflections of the forces that confront many industrial workers. When an individual first encounters the "environment" of a typical production site of a manufacturing company, the first thing she notices is the noise! Students on field trips to companies often comment that they "couldn't hear themselves think" when they were on the production floor. If those same students had remained on the production floor for several days, they would have been surprised to discover that the noise no longer seemed so aversive. In the material that follows, we will consider the role of noise in industrial performance, adaptation to noise, individual differences in reaction to noise, and the interpretation of noise as a source of physical and psychological stress, but keep in mind the fact that many environmental stressors have effects similar to those of noise.

The scientist has no problem defining sound. We can measure its intensity in decibels, we can measure its frequency in cycles per second, and thanks to psychophysical research, we can specify the psychological properties of loudness and pitch. Unfortunately, even though *noise* must be related to *sound*, it is much more difficult to define. Noise is often thought to be an unwanted or an annoying sound, but this means that *noise* must be more *subjective* than *sound*. Parents and children seldom agree about the "annoyance index" of popular music (this difficulty is exaggerated because adolescents seem to pass through a period in which intensities of sound less than 100 decibels cannot be perceived).

I will attempt to clarify these problems by using the term *sound* to refer to physical (or psychophysical) properties of any auditory stimulus and to define *noise* as irrelevant sounds, that is, any sounds that are unimportant to the task at hand. Using such an approach, any sound may be defined unequivocally as noise in a given situation, independent of its effect on physiological or subjective measures of annoyance. Most of our interest in this section will be with the effects of noise on people working at some task, either in the real world or in the laboratory.

Noise and Performance. Unfortunately, there is no simple relationship between noise and task performance. Common sense might suggest that noise always has detrimental effects on performance, but this is not the case. Sometimes it has no effect, and sometimes it even *improves* performance. As an example, think of what you do when you are driving alone on a large empty highway and beginning to get sleepy: you turn on the radio—LOUD! This has the effect of improving your performance in spite of the fact that the sounds from the radio would be viewed as unrelated to the task of getting your car from one point to another. The only way to make sense out of the seemingly contradictory evidence on the noise-performance relationship is to consider specific characteristics of both the noise and the task in question.

Dimensions of Noise. Noises may differ in intensity, frequency, and complexity. Noise sources may produce either continuous or intermittent noise. Each of these dimensions is an important determinant of the effects of noise on performance. For example, when the sound is irrelevant to the task (i.e., noise), high frequencies tend to be associated with more errors in performance than low frequencies. On the other hand, when the sound is relevant, as in a task requiring quick reactions to tones, high-frequency tones produce faster reactions than low-frequency tones (Broadbent, 1957). Thus, we can see that in the case of irrelevant sounds high-frequency tones are distracting; but when the tone is relevant to the task at hand, high-frequency tones actually do a better job of capturing our attention. Similarly, loud noises seem to have adverse effects on performance, whereas less intense noises often have no effect or even benefit performance. Finally, intermittent or on-off noises generally interfere with performance more than continuous noises. Thus, we can see that testing the hypothesis that "noise affects performance" is simpleminded; one must specify which dimension of noise is being considered. This has been one of the primary reasons for contradictory findings in the past—poor descriptions of the dimensions of noise being considered.

Noise and Communication. There is little question that noise may interfere with job performance when the job requires conversation between workers. Noise not only makes communication difficult, resulting in errors; it may also increase the total energy costs of the job. If one has to shout all day long above the roar of an engine, her fatigue level at the end of the day may be as much due to the noise as to the work itself. A good deal of work has been done on determining the conditions under which noise will inhibit communication (this research is reviewed in McCormick [1957] and Poulton [1970]). As a general principle, noise at a particular frequency tends to interfere with speech sounds at the same frequency. This phenomenon is known as *masking*. Higher-frequency speech sounds are particularly vulnerable to masking.

Noise and Low-Input Tasks. Often, workers are required to look for infrequent, temporally uncertain signals of near-threshold intensity; in addition, they may be required to look for these signals over long periods of time. The task might be auditory, as described above, or visual. A perfect example of a visual type of task of this sort would be that of the radar operator responsible for alerting national defense units to the possibility of an enemy attack. This type of task is known as a *vigilance task* and is common in quality control operations, guarding duties, and even general maintenance operations. You might guess that noise might have particularly damaging effects on this type of task. Research by Broadbent (1954) and by Jerison (1957) indicates that noise may interfere with, improve, or have no effect on vigilance performance, depending on its intensity, continuity, and the length of time

Airline ramp workers are subjected to frequent periods of intense noise.

the worker is continuously on the job. High-intensity noise (about 95 decibels or higher) does not appear to interfere with the detection of signals in a vigilance task until after an hour or an hour and a half of continuous watch-keeping. Meanwhile, low-intensity noise seems to improve performance, again after considerable time at the task, especially if the noise is intermittent.

Noise and High-Input Tasks. High-input tasks are characterized by frequent signals. While noise does not seem to have a dramatic effect on rate of performance, it does seem to increase errors; furthermore, these errors seem to occur much more quickly than was the case in vigilance or low-input tasks, sometimes occurring as soon as 20 minutes after beginning the task (Wilkinson, 1963). The problem seems to be one of overload. The individual may have to process more information than is reasonable. As I indicated earlier, noise (particularly high-frequency noise) *demands* our attention. Thus, when it is necessary to share our attention between the task at hand and environmental noise, problems arise. A study of driver performance (Finkelman, Zeitlin, Filippi, & Friend, 1977) showed that when the driver was required to concentrate on two tasks simultaneously (driving and arithmetic calculations), noise had a negative effect on performance. This suggests that the environment is placing an inappropriate load on the individual. In heavy traffic, it is common for drivers to reduce the volume of a car radio or even turn it off completely. This would seem to be a way of reducing the information-processing load on the driver.

Even though the accumulation of evidence on noise effects is confusing, there are some things we can conclude. For example, intense noise (95 decibels or higher) does seem to have negative effects on performance, particularly when the noise is intermittent. In contrast, low-intensity noise (less than 95 decibels) has little or no degrading effect on performance.

Changes in Noise Level. Teichner, Arees, and Reilly (1963) suggested that the complex effects of noise on performance might be better understood in the context of *changing* levels of noise rather than *constant* levels. They felt that the evidence on the effects of intermittent versus continuous noise strongly suggested that noise *change* was a source of distraction rather than any absolute characteristic of the noise. In a series of experiments, Teichner and his associates were able to show that more errors were made by groups that experienced a change in noise level (e.g., 81 to 69 decibels or 81 to 93 decibels) than in groups that had a constant noise level. Furthermore, they were able to demonstrate that the loss of proficiency on the task was proportional to the *amount* of change in the noise level, regardless of whether the level was increased or decreased. These results could not be explained by any simple reference to frequency or intensity of noise, such as implied in the earlier sections on noise research. Consequently, Teichner proposed that the results of noise can be understood by considering psychological factors and physiological factors simultaneously. He suggested that physiologically the individual experiences auditory adaptation, and arousal; psychologically the individual experiences distraction and eventually habituation when a new noise level is introduced. Teichner was able to predict the conditions under which performance would be adversely affected by changes in noise levels. These studies introduce the concepts of *arousal* and *adaptation*. These processes will be important in understanding the effects of environmental variables on human performance, and we will return to them in a later section.

Noise and Satisfaction. There is one final issue that should be considered with respect to noise. Independent of the effects of noise on performance, people *complain* about noise at the workplace. To some degree, this might be thought of as an indication of dissatisfaction with working conditions. While there has been little research directly addressing the issue of emotional reactions to noise in the work setting, studies in nonwork environments may provide some useful data. Several studies suggest that some people may be more vulnerable to noise than others, at least with respect to its annoyance value. Fiedler and Fiedler (1975) considered the noise complaints of residents in an area immediately adjacent to a large airport.[1] It is interesting to note that they found the complaints of individuals in this high-noise area to be roughly the same as complaints from individuals in control low-noise areas. In interviews with residents of the high-noise zone, the residents often said that they adopted a strategy of "not letting the noise bother them." Fiedler and Fiedler concluded that the source, the type, or the intensity of noise might have less to do with its annoyance potential than the individual's "vulnerability" to noise. This suggests that noise vulnerability may be a trait or at the very least that there are interactions between individual characteristics and situational characteristics and that it is the *interaction* that is responsible for annoyance.

Weinstein (1978) considered the issue of individual differences in sensitivity to noise more directly. As many of you know, college dormitories are noisy places. On the basis of a questionnaire administered to college students prior to their arrival on campus as first-year students, Weinstein was able to distinguish between those students who were bothered by noise and those who were not. He called these groups "sensitive" and "insensitive" subjects, respectively. After the students arrived on campus, Weinstein monitored both their academic progress and their satisfaction/dissatisfaction with dormitory living. The sensitive group was significantly more unhappy with the noise level in the dormitories than the insensitive students. This dissatisfaction increased over the course of the year. In addition, the academic work of the sensitive students seemed to suffer as a result of the noise.

These findings add another dimension to noise research: individual differences. They suggest several things:

1. All individuals are not equally annoyed by the same amount of noise, the same type of noise, or both.
2. It may be possible to use cognitive strategies to reduce the annoyance caused by noise—that is, tell yourself that it is not as annoying as other sounds that might be present.
3. Rather than adapting, some individuals may in fact become *more* aware of noise.

Historically, the human-engineering approach has tended to deal with the human as constant and the environment as variable. Data such as those presented above suggest that it may be critical to examine individual differences when considering the effect of environmental variables on efficiency or satisfaction. Humans are seldom as uniform or "constant" as psychologists might wish.

---

[1] If puns were criminal offenses, Fiedler and Fiedler would have been given a stiff sentence. The title of their article was "Port Noise Complaints."

Heat and Cold

As was the case with noise, the effects of heat and cold on performance are not simple. It is clear that extremes of temperature can have dramatic effects on performance. One would not expect a brain surgeon to work well with fingers numbed by cold. The indirect effects of heat and cold represent just as great a threat to the efficiency of the typical industrial worker. Consequently, we will consider the role of these indirect effects as environmental stressors.

Like noise, temperature would seem to have simple and obvious characteristics. One need only specify the scale units (i.e., Fahrenheit or centigrade) to talk about high and low temperatures. Unfortunately, the human does not react quite so simply. As you are well aware, a temperature of 100°F on a dry desert may not be as uncomfortable as 85°F in a jungle; our impressions are further modified by the rate of air movement. This has led to the use of the concept of *effective temperature* in place of *objective temperature*. The effective temperature scale combines temperature, humidity, and air movement in computing the comfort index of a particular environment. Some research suggests that humidity may be more important than either of the other two variables in determining relative comfort and efficiency (Pepler, 1958). Unfortunately, most of the research in the use of effective temperature has involved subjects not engaged in actual work but merely moving back and forth from one room to another, reporting relative comfort. To use the effective temperature concept in industrial settings, it will be necessary to calculate these values in the actual industrial environment. In addition, as we will see shortly, the critical issue may be the combination of temperature extremes and other stressors, rather than temperature by itself.

Cold. Much of the research on the effects of low temperatures on performance has been of the more obvious type where numbness of fingers or skin temperature of the hands has been related to proficiency on tasks involving manual operations. The purpose of such research is not so much to demonstrate such effects as it is to assess their magnitude, that is, to describe in a quantitative way the losses in performance that can be expected by the direct effects of cold. Research results suggest that manual performance is adversely affected by lowered body temperature, even when hands are kept warm (Lockhart, 1966). This suggests that, in addition to the direct effect of cold on finger and hand dexterity, there is also an indirect effect of lowered body temperature acting as a stressor or detractor. Similar effects have been found for vigilance tasks (Poulton, Hitchings, & Brooke, 1965). Both accuracy and speed of detection of signals dropped as a result of lowered body temperature. Finally, there is some evidence that people may adapt to cold conditions over time (Teichner & Kobrick, 1955), although this is more likely due to increased motivation in stressful conditions or changes in strategies for completing the task than to physiological adaptation.

Stressors and Information Processing

In 1958, Bursill reported the results of three experiments in which he used heat as an environmental stressor. Subjects engaged in two tasks simultaneously: a tracking task (in which the subject was required to follow a moving object) and a visual detection task (in which the subject was required to detect light signals occurring at 20 degrees, 50 degrees, and 80 degrees of visual angle from either side of the tracking display). The most interesting result of these studies was that subjects missed higher proportions of signals at the wider visual angles under heat than under normal temperature conditions. These results suggested that a specific effect of heat stress was to reduce the field of visual attention, either as a direct effect on the visual mechanism or as a more central effect of narrowing or "funneling" of attention. When Bursill made the task easier, subjects no longer made a larger number of errors on wide-angle signals. He took this as evidence that attention, rather than a visual mechanism, was affected by heat stress.

Bursill's experiment was repeated by Hockey (1970) but with noise rather than heat as a stressor. Similar results were found: noise was related to greater errors at wide visual angles. In a second experiment, Hockey was able to demonstrate *how* attention was affected by stress. Bursill's results implied that subjects tended to pay attention to those things closest to them (or immediately in front of them). Hockey systematically changed the probability that the lights at various angles would come on and was able to demonstrate that subjects paid more attention to those lights that were more likely to come on, regardless of the central or peripheral position of those lights. It was almost as if the individual "oriented" herself or positioned herself in preparation for responding.

The results of these studies indicate that stressors tend to limit the capacity of subjects to attend to task-relevant information—perhaps because the stressor "uses up" some attention capacity. As a result of these data, we might draw the following conclusion about the way in which stress affects information processing.

Under stress, an operator's attention will be directed toward the more probable sources of information, and she will be more likely to miss information from less probable sources.

THE INTERACTION OF TWO OR MORE STRESSORS

A low level of noise has been found to increase the percentage of signals detected in vigilance tasks, but more intense noise has a detrimental effect, decreasing signal detections. Therefore, in a task with a low and unpredictable signal rate, noise can be either beneficial or detrimental, depending on its intensity. On the other hand, noise appears to have no effect on the rate of responding in a serial reaction task, where the signal rate is higher than in vigilance tasks, but noise does increase errors in this task. As another example, loss of a night's sleep results in an increase in the number of slow reactions on the serial reaction task, whereas heat increases errors on the same task.

These effects are presented to show that the simple, or "main," effects of environmental stressors are not simple at all. Rather, they depend on the performance task and even on the measure of task performance that one observes. In other words, there are important *interaction effects* between stressors and tasks and between stressors and measures of performance, as well as between stressors and states of the organism. To complicate the picture further, we will find that the stressors themselves interact, producing accumulative effects in some cases and compensatory, or canceling, effects in other cases.

Thus far we have looked at the effects of single stressors as they influence the performance of human operators. In doing so, I have often found it difficult to avoid complicating the story with references to the ways in which environmental stressors interact with other stressors of various kinds. No doubt it has become apparent already that to speak of the effects of stress on performance one must specify the conditions under which the stress is experienced. As Wilkinson (1969) has pointed out, stress effects are dependent on (1) the duration of work on the task, (2) the familiarity of the operator with the stress and with the work he has to do under stress, (3) the level of incentive of the operator, (4) the kind of work he has to do, (5) the aspect of performance (i.e., speed or accuracy) that is most important, and (6) the presence of other stresses in the working situation, as well as the nature and level of the stressor itself.

We have seen evidence that the stress, the task, time on the task, adaptation to the stress, familiarity with the task, and the measures of task performance all interact with one another to determine the nature and the magnitude of stress effects. The present section is devoted largely to examining how stressors may interact with one another or with the incentive conditions of the task.

A Model of Multiple-Stressor Effects

Before looking at stressor interactions, it may be useful to have a conceptual model of what we might expect to find. Such a model has been suggested by Broadbent (1971) in an attempt to determine whether two or more stressors were acting independently on performance. To illustrate how the model works, let's assume that when two different stressors are applied singly in a given task situation, each results in a 10-percent decrement in performance. Now the question is, What would be the expected result if the effects of the two stressors acting together are *strictly additive?* At first glance, one may conclude that the answer is 20 percent, arrived at simply by adding the two percentages obtained for each stressor acting alone. That is, if the two stressors were combined and the net effect was a 20-percent decrement

FIGURE 14–1 A Model to Illustrate the "Superadditive" Effects of Stressors

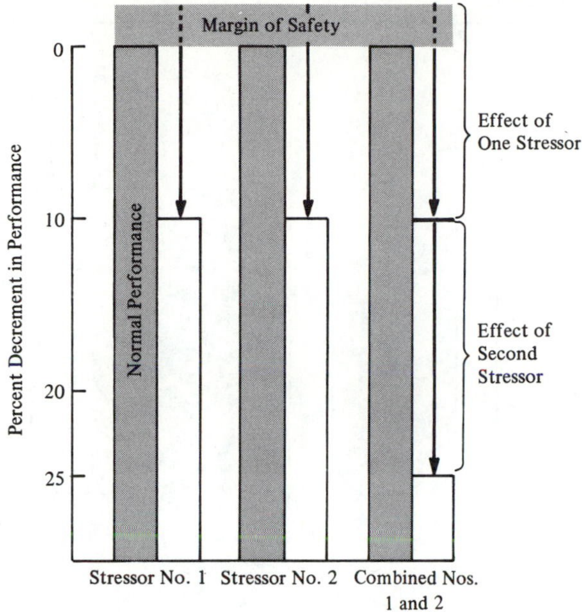

When presented alone, stressors 1 and 2 first overcome the "margin of safety," then decrease performance by 10 percent. When presented together, however, one stressor uses up the margin of safety, allowing the second stressor to have full effect on performance.

in performance, it would be tempting to conclude that the effects of one stressor were simply added to the other.

Suppose, on the other hand, that one reasons, as Broadbent did, that human performance in the normal unstressed condition leaves a small reserve, or a *margin of safety*, whereby one can compensate for or "absorb" a moderate degree of stress before the performance is affected. From this view, the initial effect of a stressor is to overcome or "use up" this margin of safety, and this effect is not apparent in the performance measures. Now, assume for the moment that this safety margin is equal to 5 percent of the operator's normal performance level; that is, the operator works at 95 percent of his "true" capacity. This notion is illustrated in Figure 14–1 by the region labeled the "Margin of Safety." It will then be seen that the effect of each stressor alone should be described as the sum of the 10-percent decrement in performance *plus* the 5 percent used up in overcoming the margin of safety. As indicated in the figure, when either stressor is presented alone, part of its effect is absorbed, but when the two stressors are combined, it is reasonable to assume that one of the two overcomes the safety margin, so that the total effect of the second would be seen in reduced performance. Therefore, in our example,

FIGURE 14–2 Performance under Single and Combined Stressors (alcohol, meclozine, and hyoscine), Showing the Superadditive Effects of Pairs of Stressors

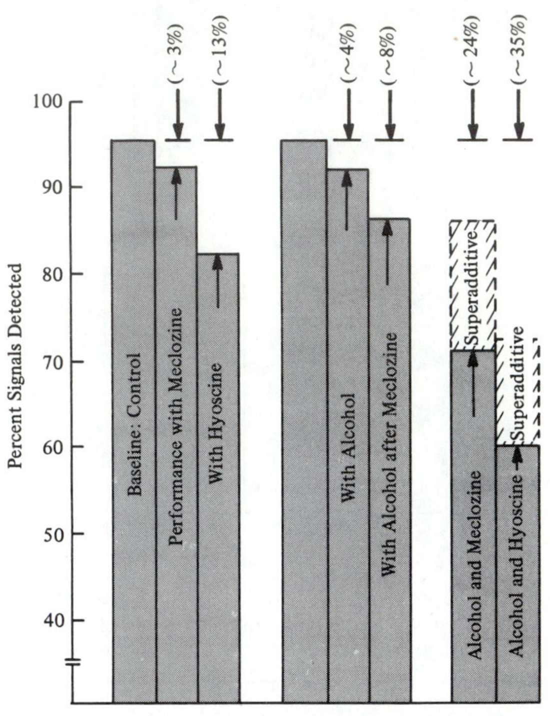

SOURCE: From "Effects of Hyoscine and Meclozine on Vigilance and Short-term Memory" by W. P. Colquhoun, 1962, *British Journal of Industrial Medicine, 19.*

simple additive effects of the two stressors would be to reduce performance by 25 percent, rather than the 20 percent suggested by adding the independent values, even though this appears to be a case of "superadditivity." You often hear people refer to the "straw that broke the camel's back." This may be the explanation for that phenomenon. A single stressor may not appear to have a major impact on behavior, but the addition of another stressor—regardless of its nature—represents the "last straw."

The first question to be raised about the model in Figure 14–1 is whether there is any evidence that such apparently superadditive effects occur when two or more stressors are combined. The answer to this question is a rather convincing yes, as shown in Figure 14–2. This figure summarizes the results of a study by Colquhoun (1962) in which alcohol and two drugs, meclozine and hyoscine, were administered separately and in combination. These substances are all considered stressors if the doses are sufficiently high. Performance was evaluated on a vigilance task. As shown in the figure, neither alcohol nor meclozine had much effect on the percentage of signals detected as compared with the control ("placebo") condition. However, when alcohol was given the day after the subjects had taken meclozine ("alcohol plus meclozine residue"), the effect was at least as great as the original effect of the meclozine plus the effect of alcohol alone. When alcohol and either of the drugs were administered on the same day, the results were much more convincing, as shown on the right in Figure 14–2. The combined effects of alcohol and meclozine are more than twice as great as one would expect by adding their separate effects, and this outcome is repeated, somewhat less dramatically, for alcohol and hyoscine.

But, you may ask, why all this concern for the question of the additivity of the combined effects of different stressors? First, Colquhoun's results with drugs suggest that stressors may have much greater effects in combination than would be expected from their simple effects. In other words, a hot, noisy work environment may degrade performance to a greater extent than one would predict from the results of studies of noise or heat tested separately. This in itself argues for the need to study stressors in combination. It also argues for the model that includes the concept of a safety margin in performance. Furthermore, there is a theoretical significance to Colquhoun's findings that ultimately has some important implications for our understanding of the process by which stressors affect behavior.

To illustrate the last point, let us consider a case in which the combined effects of two stressors are strictly additive and another case in which the combined effects of two other stressors are superadditive, as in Colquhoun's study. Now, if we assume further that the margin of safety is specific to some behavioral mechanism or to some stage in the processing of information (e.g., short-term memory, stimulus classification, or response selection), then it appears that the stressors with superadditive effects act upon the *same* mechanism or process, whereas stressors with additive effects act upon *different* mechanisms or processes (i.e., each stressor "uses up" a different margin of safety involving a different mechanism). It would also follow that two stressors that individually interfere with performance but in combination produce *less* than the sum of their separate effects are, in some way, compensatory. This suggests that such stressors may act in opposite or antagonistic ways on the same mechanism or process.

Noise and Sleep Loss. With respect to the last point, it is again appropriate to ask whether there is any evidence that one stressor may act to cancel or reduce the effects of another. An affirmative answer to this question was provided by Wilkinson (1963) in a study of the effects of sleep deprivation and noise on performance in a serial reaction task. As shown in Figure 14–3, both noise and loss of sleep resulted in increases in errors on the task. However, when the subjects had lost a night's sleep, performance under noise was better than performance in the quiet condition. Thus, the two stress-

FIGURE 14–3 The Effect of Combinations of Sleep *(S)* and Sleep Deprivation *(SD)* with Noise *(N)* and Quiet *(Q)* upon Proportional Errors (errors as a percentage of all responses)

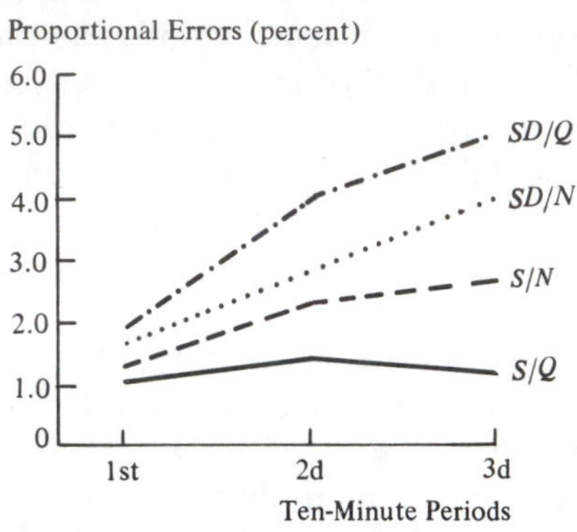

SOURCE: From "Interaction of Noise with Knowledge of Results and Sleep Deprivation" by R. T. Wilkinson, 1963, *Journal of Experimental Psychology, 66.*

ors, noise and loss of sleep, each of which interfered with performance when presented separately, tended to cancel each other when presented together.

Performance Feedback and Sleep Loss. Another example of the compensatory effects of two stressors presented in combination comes from a second study by Wilkinson (1963). In this study, subjects who had slept and were given feedback about their performance on the task performed much better than subjects who had slept but were given no feedback. Such positive effects of feedback are, of course, not surprising. However, when subjects were deprived of a night's sleep before the test, their performance suffered only when no feedback was given. In other words, feedback compensates for the effects of sleep loss, and this effect is much greater than the positive effect of feedback when there has been no loss of sleep.

From these two examples, it appears that feedback operates very much as noise does when it is combined with loss of sleep; that is, both factors tend to compensate for the negative effects of sleep loss. Does this mean that feedback should be considered as a stressor in the same sense as noise or other environmental conditions? Given our earlier definition of stressors as conditions that "press" the individual to greater effort or a higher level of performance, it may not be unreasonable to consider feedback and other incentives or inducements to performance as a class of stressors. In this connection, Poulton (1970) has defined feedback as a "mild threat" to the operator, presumably because it increases his awareness of and anxiety about poor performance.

Performance Feedback and Other Stressors. When feedback is combined with noise, the results are not at all what one would predict from the separate effects of the two stressors. By itself, loud noise interferes generally with performance, whereas feedback, almost without exception, enhances performance. Taken together, one might expect that feedback would tend to reduce the negative effects of noise or, vice versa, that noise might reduce the positive effects of the feedback. However, when Wilkinson (1963) combined these two stressors for subjects working on the serial reaction task, he found that accuracy was poorer under noise with feedback than without, whereas in the quiet condition, feedback markedly reduced the error rate.

A Summary of Combined Effects

While an exhaustive review of the research on stressors would yield additional examples of interaction effects, perhaps enough evidence has been presented to illustrate how complex these interactions are. It appears that there is good evidence that different stressors presented together may act upon the same underlying mechanism, either in the same way, resulting in superadditive effects, or in a compensatory manner wherein either (1) two stressors, which by themselves impair performance, cancel each other (e.g., noise and sleep loss) or (2) the negative effect of one stressor is actually reduced when combined with the negative condition of the other (e.g., performance without feedback is better in noise than in quiet). The studies combining sleep loss and heat suggest, at least tentatively, additive and independent effects with the two stressors conceivably acting on two different mechanisms or processes.

With the possible exception of the results with heat and sleep loss, none of the evidence reviewed thus far rules out the possibility that all stressor effects can be accounted for in terms of a single underlying mechanism. Thus, it is conceivable, as I have tried to show, that the superadditive effects are not superadditive at all but are additive effects of two stressors acting on the same mechanism. Similarly, when two stressors appear to cancel each other, it could be because they act on one mechanism in opposite ways. Even the interactions of single stressors with time on task, adaptation to the stress, familiarity with the task, the task itself, and the measures of performance could conceivably be accounted for by a single mechanism.

STRESS AND THE CONCEPT OF AROUSAL

In this chapter, I have emphasized the importance of relating stressor effects to underlying processes or mechanisms that govern performance or activity in general. In seeking to describe a general mechanism or process to account for the stressor effects, it seems reasonable to assume that all stressors acting on the worker, from the physical environment, social environment, work, and physical condition as affected by illness, drugs, or loss of sleep, summate in some way to determine a general level of stress. However, as we have seen, the summing of stressors is not a matter of simple addition. Some effects seem to add, but others seem to cancel one another, as with loss of sleep and noise. Furthermore, some stressors appear to have one effect at one level of intensity and a different effect at another level. Thus, for example, a low level of noise may aid performance in a vigilance task. However, when the noise is loud enough or the task itself is sufficiently stimulating, the combination of task and environmental stressors interferes with performance. In the first case, noise seems to provide needed stimulation. In the second, it appears to overstimulate the operator.

The concept of *arousal* has been suggested to account for these stressor effects. Arousal is variously defined by different theorists, but broadly speaking, it refers to the dimension of general alertness, or activation, ranging from sound sleep at one extreme to a state of rage or shock at the other. Arousal has been defined in terms of various physiological measures, such as heart rate, electroencephalogram, galvanic skin response, or other measures of autonomic nervous system activity. Stress is assumed to govern the arousal level of the individual. Furthermore, it is assumed that there is a level, or range, of arousal that is optimal for performing certain activities. Above or below this optimal level, performance suffers because the individual is "under- or overaroused." This is the notion of the "inverted-**U**" relation between arousal level and performance. This relationship is illustrated by the curve in Figure 14–4.

If the job has a low rate of input, or the worker has lost a night's sleep, or there is little incentive to produce, the worker's arousal level will be low and his performance will be impaired. If, on the other hand, the task is demanding, the noise level is high, and incentives are strong, he may be too highly aroused to produce well on the same task.

Figure 14–4**(A)** also shows how the effects of noise on performance in a vigilance task can be described in terms of arousal. First, it is assumed that the arousal level in quiet *(Q)* is not very high, because the low-input vigilance task itself is not very stimulating. The addition of noise *(N)* increases the arousal level of the operator, and performance improves. However, if the noise is too loud *(LN)*, it increases arousal beyond the optimal level and performance falls off.

A hypothetical example of a task with a higher input rate (e.g., the choice-reaction task or a tracking task) is shown in Figure 14–4**(B)**. Here, performance in quiet *(Q)* is high because the task is sufficiently demanding, or stimulating, to keep the operator aroused. The addition of noise *(N)* to this task increases arousal beyond the optimal level, and performance suffers. This example also shows a decrease in performance from sleep loss *(SL)*. Notice, however, that while sleep loss and noise are both shown as degrading performance to about the same extent, they are seen to operate in opposite directions on arousal. Loss of sleep reduces the arousal level below the optimal, but noise increases arousal above the optimal level in this example. The effect of combining these

FIGURE 14–4 Arousal and Performance

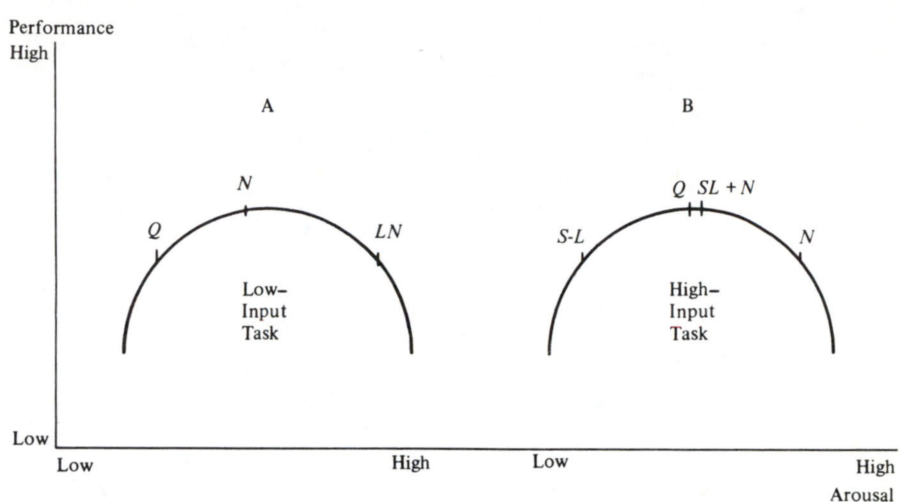

Model of the relation of arousal to performance on a low-input task **(A)** and on a high-input task **(B)**. *Q* = quiet, *N* = noise, *LN* = loud noise, *S-L* = sleep loss.

two stressors *(SL + N)* is to leave the arousal level somewhere near the optimum for performance. Thus, the tendency toward sleep ("underarousal") resulting from sleep loss is counteracted by the noise, and in turn, the tendency toward overarousal by the noise is counteracted by the sleep loss.

A final example of the way in which the inverted-**U** hypothesis may be used to account for stress effects is shown in Figure 14–5. In this illustration, the two factors are noise and performance feedback. It will be recalled that while feedback nearly always improves performance, the effects of noise are less predictable. They depend, in part, on the task and the intensity of the noise. The example in Figure 14–5 is taken from Wilkinson (1963), who found little effect of noise by itself but a large positive effect of feedback. Noise without feedback tended to improve performance over the quiet condition. However, noise added to feedback tended to produce more errors than feedback alone. Apparently, noise plus feedback resulted in overarousal of the operators, interfering with performance.

It is tempting to conclude that the concept of arousal provides a complete explanation of the effects of stressors on performance. It is true that many of the complex relationships and interactions seem to be "explained" in a satisfying way when we apply the notion of the inverted-**U** relationship. In fact, one of the difficulties with the arousal explanation may be that it can too readily "account for" nearly any combination of results. However, Broadbent (1971), for one, has pointed out some evidence from the research on stress

FIGURE 14–5 Noise, Feedback, and Performance

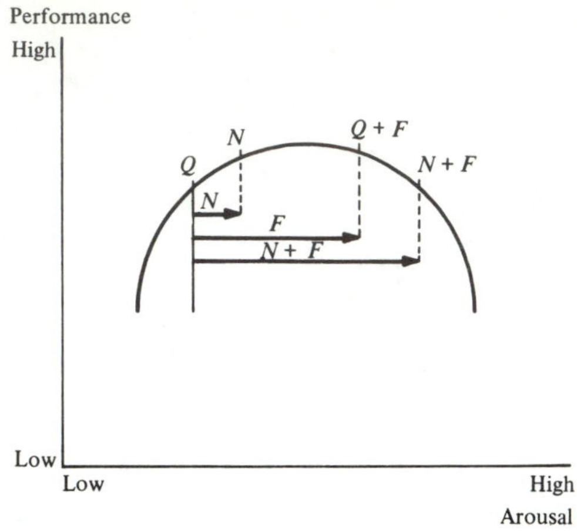

Low performance under quiet *(Q)* corresponds to low arousal. Noise *(N)* increases arousal and performance, as does feedback *(F)*. However, both noise and feedback produce overarousal and performance declines.

that is difficult to handle with the inverted-**U** curve. I will not develop Broadbent's arguments here. However, an example of the difficulties he finds is the fact that the effects of noise and sleep loss both show up late in the work session, even though their effects on arousal are presumably in opposite directions. Another difficulty for arousal theory is found in the results on heat. The fact that small and large increases of body temperature have different effects on performance, and these effects appear to be *opposite* for different tasks, is not easily explained in terms of a single mechanism of arousal. In addition, as we have seen, the effects of heat and feedback seem to be independent and strictly additive, suggesting that they effect two different mechanisms rather than one. Finally, the very notion of the inverted-**U** relationship between arousal and performance has been challenged by Näätänen (1973), a Finnish pychologist. In part, Näätänen urges that the decrease in task performance attributed to overarousal may reflect instead that the operator is sharing his attention and his responding between the task and the stressor introduced to raise his arousal level. In other words, the stressor is seen as a secondary task, demanding some coping responses by the operator that may compete with task-relevant responses. This is similar to the explanation of noise effects offered by Teichner et al. (1963), presented earlier in this chapter. At any rate, Näätänen argued that one's true performance efficiency at any level of arousal should be assessed in terms of some measure of how well one handles both the task *and* the stressor, not just the task alone.

The arousal concepts that we have just discussed suggest that stress is not a figment of someone's imagination. Extreme intensities of various stimuli may have the effect of pushing the man-machine system past reasonable limits. The arousal model proposes that interactions of various environmental stressors should also be considered, not just the effects of single stressors.

There is one common work condition that is often mentioned by workers in discussions of stress and fatigue: the scheduling of work hours. Most of us feel less than efficient when we are required to put in overtime on an arduous task. A good example of this that might be found in student life is the "all-nighter"—the attempt to read 10 weeks of class assignments in 15 hours. In addition to efficiency losses, we often feel emotionally drained after such an experience. In the next chapter, we will consider the issue of the work schedule as a potential stressor in the work environment.

Some Aftereffects of Stressors

We have seen that some stressors such as heat and noise appear to have significant effects on the performance of certain tasks, the nature of these effects depending on the tasks, the stressors, and possibly individual differences in workers. In other cases, experiments have failed to find any influence of the stressor on the behavioral measures they have recorded. One possible reason for lack of noticeable effect may be that individuals devote more effort to tasks that are performed under stress—that is, to maintain a given level of efficiency under difficult conditions, they try harder. This possibility has led researchers to look for possible aftereffects of environmental stress. If the worker does maintain performance levels through extra effort, the effects of this increased effort may accumulate over time and appear at some time after the actual presentation of the stressor (minutes later, hours later, or even weeks later). As we will see in the next chapter, there is good reason to believe that shift work (particularly the night shift) has such cumulative aftereffects.

C. G. Glass and Singer (1972) have provided some evidence regarding the aftereffects of noise. They began with the assumption that "while man is adaptable, he pays a price for adaptation," a price more obvious after the stress is over than during the stressful conditions.[2] Subjects were exposed to either loud or soft noise. Furthermore, noise was presented either predictably (on/off at regular intervals) or unpredictably (on/off at random intervals). Response measures taken during the experimental conditions indicated that there was a generalized stress response to noise that decreased with re-

[2] A similar situation was suggested with respect to job satisfaction by Landy's Opponent Process Theory. The same basic mechanism would apply here: While the stimulus is present, the person experiences one state, but when the stimulus disappears, another state takes its place.

peated stimulation. This was equally true for predictable and unpredictable noise.

However, Glass and Singer were more interested in the aftereffects of noise than the immediate effects. Consequently, they administered two types of tests to subjects after the experimental sessions. These consisted of a set of insoluble puzzles and a proofreading task. The number of attempts to solve the puzzles was taken as a measure of the subject's tolerance for frustration, whereas the number of proofreading errors found by the subject was interpreted as a measure of ability to cope with a task requiring care and attention.

Their results showed:

1. Subjects who had been exposed to noise made fewer attempts to solve puzzles and missed more proofreading errors than subjects who had previously worked in quiet.
2. Unpredictable noise had a much more negative effect than predictable noise.

As an explanation of why the unpredictable noise condition had a more serious effect than predictable noise, the authors proposed that unpredictability created a feeling of lack of control over the environment, which raised the anxiety of the subjects. As a test of this hypothesis, Glass and Singer simply repeated the experiment but added a "noise control switch" for the subjects. Half the subjects were told that if the noise became intolerable, they could turn it off by throwing the switch. The other half were told nothing about the switch. All subjects were exposed to the unpredictable noise condition and given the same task and postnoise tests. The results showed that access to the noise switch did not help performance during the noise conditions, but the effect of the switch on postnoise tests was dramatic. Subjects who had access to the switch made many more attempts at the puzzles and missed fewer proofreading errors than the subjects who were told nothing about the switch. The results supported the experiments' predictions, and they concluded "that unpredictable noise produced adverse after-effects because it is more aversive than predictable noise, its greater aversiveness being a function of the same helplessness induced in an individual who is unable to control and/or predict its onset or offset" (p. 462).

The results of the work by Glass and Singer suggest that it may not be appropriate to examine the effects of stressors only during the stress situation. In spite of the fact that adaptation seems to occur, it may be that the negative effects are simply being postponed rather than being eliminated. The degree to which these stresses accumulate over time and the effects of these accumulations on worker behavior both in and outside of the work setting are unknown. But there is good reason to believe that the effects of stressors must be examined over long periods of time if we are to understand their impact fully. It is this longer-term perspective that has come to characterize the investigation of stress in recent years.

THEORIES OF STRESS

Up to this point, we have considered stress in a very limited way. We have examined specific objective characteristics of the work environment. We have seen how stressors combine to yield their effects on performance, and in the work of Glass and Singer, we have seen some hints that stress has long-term as well as short-term consequences. In the last decade, there has been tremendous interest in the issue of psychological and physiological responses to stress. Selye (1976) was one of the first to recognize the frequently damaging long-term effects of stress. He suggested that when we encounter a stressor, there is a general bodily reaction that acts to protect us against the stressor. He called this reaction the *general adaptation syndrome* and considered it an automatic chain reaction involving internal glands, the hormones that they produced, and organs affected by those hormones. The organ most frequently considered in this general stress reaction is the heart (and more generally, the entire cardiovascular system). It was assumed that since the body is very much like a machine, it could only work so hard before breaking down. As a result, there has been a good deal of research on the relationship between chronic or continuing levels of stress and heart attacks and other cardiovascular diseases. Thus, in addition to the behavioral aftereffects documented by Glass and Singer, there has also been a great deal of interest in physiological aftereffects. This concern for the long-term consequences of stress has been the driving force behind the development of stress theories for obvious reasons: it was assumed that once we knew the causes of stress, we could develop effective programs for controlling or reducing that stress and thereby eliminate its dangerous side effects. I should warn you that there is no *one* generally accepted theory. This whole area is quite new, and there are several attractive alternative approaches to understanding industrial stress.

The Life Events Theory

One of the simplest models for explaining stress has been suggested by the work of Holmes and Rahe (1967). They were able to develop a list of life events and attach scale values to these events that represented the extent to which an individual was required to adapt to a new situation. As we saw in our earlier discussion of stress, a common theme is one of adaptation and, more important, the cost of that adaptation. Selye believed that adaptation could only go on for so long. He thought of adaptation energy as a bank account that would only allow withdrawals, not deposits.

The life events with their scale values appear in Figure 14–6. The higher the value, the more adaptation required of the individual (and presumably, the greater the "cost" to that individual). The scale values were referred to as *life change units* (LCUs). Holmes and Rahe proposed that an individual would develop physical stress symptoms in direct proportion to the number

FIGURE 14–6 Social Readjustment Rating Scale

Rank	*Life Event*	*Mean Value*
1	Death of spouse	100
2	Divorce	73
3	Marital separation	65
4	Jail term	63
5	Death of close family member	63
6	Personal injury or illness	53
7	Marriage	50
8	Fired at work	47
9	Marital reconciliation	45
10	Retirement	45
11	Change in health of family member	44
12	Pregnancy	40
13	Sex difficulties	39
14	Gain of new family member	39
15	Business readjustment	39
16	Change in financial state	38
17	Death of close friend	37
18	Change to different line of work	36
19	Change in number of arguments with spouse	35
20	Mortgage over $10,000	31
21	Foreclosure of mortgage or loan	30
22	Change in responsibilities at work	29
23	Son or daughter leaving home	29
24	Trouble with in-laws	29
25	Outstanding personal achievement	28
26	Wife begins or stops work	26
27	Begin or end school	26
28	Change in living conditions	25
29	Revision of personal habits	24
30	Trouble with boss	23
31	Change in work hours or conditions	20
32	Change in residence	20
33	Change in schools	20
34	Change in recreation	19
35	Change in church activities	19
36	Change in social activities	18
37	Mortgage or loan less than $10,000	17
38	Change in sleeping habits	18
39	Change in number of family get-togethers	15
40	Change in eating habits	15
41	Vacation	13
42	Christmas	12
43	Minor violations of the law	11

SOURCE: From "Social Readjustment Rating Scale" by T. H. Holmes and R. H. Rahe, 1967, *Journal of Psychosomatic Research, 11*. Pergamon Press, Ltd., © 1967. Reprinted with permission.

of LCUs accumulated in a one-year period. As a rough guide, scores from 150 to 199 are thought to represent a mild life crisis; scores from 200 to 299, a moderate life crisis; and scores of 300 and above, a major life crisis. Thus, if in one year, your spouse died, you lost your job, several family members became ill, and you had several run-ins with your boss, you would be undergoing a major life crisis. Of course, it would not require a questionnaire for you to figure that out! It was further proposed that the more severe the crisis, the more likely that the individual would become ill.

There are several explanations for this proposed relationship between crisis and illness, but they all revolve around the notion of the natural immunity system of the body. The body has its own internal protection system to fight off infection and disease. This system depends on the production of white blood cells to aid in the protection process. Some studies have suggested that when a person is under stress, the production of white blood cells is substantially reduced. When this occurs, the individual is more easily infected or more susceptible to diseases.

The Holmes and Rahe model is a simple one. It suggests that environmental events have certain stress values (as was implied in our earlier discussion of heat and noise) and that these events had a cumulative effect on well-being. Naismith (1975) has developed a stress scale based on the Holmes and Rahe scale but dealing specifically with the work environment. He includes items such as the cancellation of a work project, getting a new boss, being transferred involuntarily, and moving to a new office location. H. Weiss, Ilgen, and Sharbaugh (1982) have examined the value of this general model in considering the effect of environmental changes in the activity of workers. They proposed that stress precipitated an increase in examination of search of the environment by the individual. Presumably, the goal of the searching was the reduction of stress. They contrasted stress that was the result of work-related events with stress that was unrelated to work and found some interesting differences. First, both types of stress precipitated search behavior, and the extent of this search behavior was proportional to the level of stress. But more interestingly, they found that the particular form of that search varied as a function of the source of the stress. If the stress was caused by work events, the resulting behavior was a search for alternative styles of work behavior. For example, if a worker was having problems with a supervisor, she might ask the supervisor to review her work more frequently or ask a coworker for a suggestion about different work methods. On the other hand, if the stress was coming from nonwork events, the search behavior was more likely to involve much more global or radical changes. For example, the individual might begin looking in the classified ads for a new job or consider taking a continuing education course of some type. This latter type of adjustment seemed to involve a complete reconsideration of the person's approach to work generally. An extreme example of this would be an individual who learns that he has a serious illness. Work loses its meaning very quickly. Shortly after announcing that he would run for another term in the U.S.

Senate, Senator Paul Tsongas abruptly announced he would *not* seek reelection. He had been diagnosed as having a life-threatening illness and had decided to spend more time with his family. Weiss et al. see an interesting positive aspect to stress. They suggest that it may have a facilitating effect on individuals in the long run since it blasts them out of complacency. The search behavior requires them to encounter novel stimuli.

There are also some recent data that contradict the propositions of the LCU approach. Brett (1982) studied the relationship between job transfer and many different aspects of well-being. In particular, she looked at the relationship between particular work-related events and job satisfaction. As you will see shortly, it is commonly proposed that one symptom of work-related stress is job dissatisfaction. It is generally assumed that being transferred from one work location to another represents quite a trauma for an individual worker. If you consider the scale in Figure 14–6, a job relocation might include the following life events: 16, 20, 22, 24, 25, 26, 28, 29, 31, 32, 33, 34, 35, 36, and 39. This represents a substantial accumulation of LCUs. One might expect a good deal of stress to result from that move. In fact, in Brett's comparison of mobile (moved once every 2 years) and stable families (stayed in one place for 10 or more years), there were almost no differences in work and nonwork satisfactions. Although the mobile workers seemed somewhat less satisfied with social relations outside of the immediate family, they were *more* satisfied with their marriage and their family, and they believed that they had a more interesting life than their more stable counterparts and displayed a more positive self-concept. This is a fascinating finding since it seems to run counter to both the logic of the Holmes and Rahe model as well as "conventional wisdom." The results might be explained in several ways. In the first place, most of the moves of the mobile groups were considered promotions and were accompanied by increased compensation. This made the economic pressure less critical. In addition, there were few, if any, involuntary moves included in the mobile groups. It would be interesting to see if the findings would hold up with a group of laid off autoworkers who pulled up stakes and moved to the Sunbelt in the hope of finding employment. In any event, the research line is so new that it is of little value to try to identify any trend in the results.

Total Life Stress. The LCU approach to stress is an interesting one and will receive considerably more attention in the next few years. One of its advantages is that it assumes that stress is the by-product of all the influences in a person's environment, not just heat and noise and work place. A leading Swedish stress researcher, Marianne Frankenhauser, and her colleagues have been recently emphasizing the concept of *total life stress*. They have argued that we often play multiple roles in our lives and that each of these roles may require unique adaptation on our part. Thus, the traditional working mother must adapt to stresses of a job, of a parent, and of a housekeeper. In contrast, her traditional husband may accept only the role of "bread winner" and thus have considerably less adaptation (and stress). Bhagat, McQuaid, Lindholm, and Segovis (1985) have presented evidence confirming the value of the construct of total life stress in understanding worker behavior and adjustment.

The LCU model also recognizes that social interactions may play a major role in stress. This fits in nicely with the conceptions of stress being suggested by I/O psychologists. As an example, consider Figure 14–7. This illustrates the open systems concept of stress in which the manager can be affected by many different stress sources both within and outside of the work environment. This is the type of complexity with which we must deal in considering stress at the workplace.

The Person-Environment Fit Model

Another model of stress that has been quite popular for several years is one suggested by J. R. P. French. It is called the *person-environment fit* (P-E) model and emphasizes the match between the characteristics of the individual and the characteristics of the environment. The model is presented in graphic form in Figure 14–8. In this model, stress is represented in box *G*, labeled the "Subjective Person-Environment Fit." This model is substantially different from the LCU model in several ways. In the first place, it suggests that environmental events are not universal stressors. Instead, their stress value depends on perceptions of the individual. These perceptions involve not only estimates of the demands being made by the environment but also estimates by the individual of his capability and motivation to meet those demands. This emphasis represents the cognitive view of stress and is mirrored in a popular definition of stress as provided by McGrath (1970), an active stress researcher: *Stress is a perceived substantial imbalance between demands and response capabilities under conditions where failure to meet demands has important perceived consequences.*

In addition to the emphasis on perception, the P-E fit model suggests that individuals can be protected from stress by two mechanisms. The first is social support, and the second is an ego defense network. These defenses include the classic mechanisms such as repression (ignoring the demands) and projection (seeing weaknesses in others rather than yourself). Nevertheless, if neither of these mechanisms is operating, the P-E fit model assumes that stresses will be converted into strains. These strains include poor performance, psychosomatic disorders, and dissatisfaction. The French model is well described in a recent book that documents the research that supports its propositions (French, Caplan, & Van Harrison, 1982).

The Role of Social Support. Early research on the fit model was mixed. Parkes (1982) found that social support decreased depression in student nurses exposed to work-related stressors. On the other hand, La Rocco and Jones (1978) found that social support and stress were independent of one another. Each affected various organizational outcomes independently. Social

FIGURE 14–7 Sources of Managerial Stress

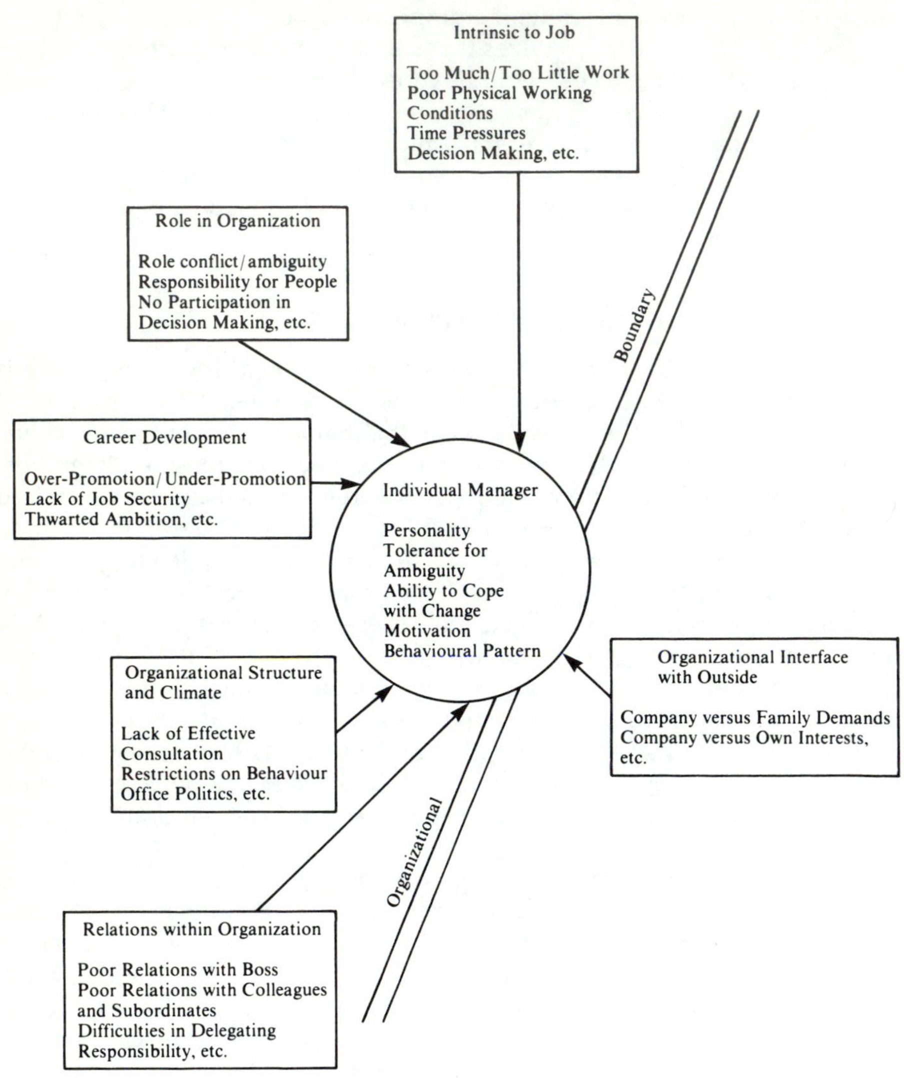

SOURCE: From "An Empirical Investigation of Job Stress, Social Support, Service Length, and Job Strain" by G. Blau, 1981, *Organizational Behavior and Human Performance, 27,* p. 281.

support did not seem to moderate the experience of stress. Blau (1981) came to a similar conclusion in a study of bus operators. Blau did, however, find limited support for other aspects of the model, noting that there was a significant relationship between stress, as conceptualized in the fit model, and job satisfaction. He found no relationship between stress and performance,

FIGURE 14–8 A General Model of the Effects of the Social Environment on Psychological Strain and Health

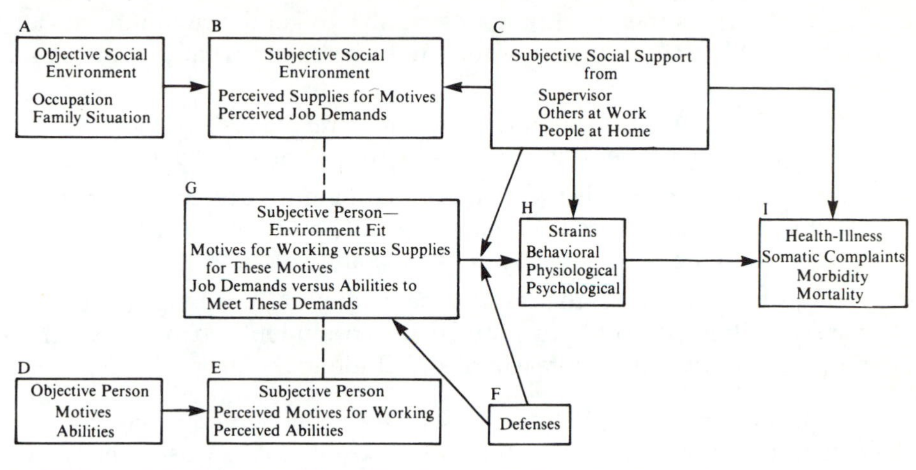

SOURCE: From *Stress at Work* (p. 83) by C. Cooper and R. L. Payne, 1978, New York: John Wiley & Sons.

however. More recently, the data related to social support have been less equivocal. It seems clear that social support is a main effect, not a moderator (S. L. Cohen & Wills, 1985; Dooley, Rook, & Catalano, 1987; Ganster, Fusilier, & Mayes, 1986). In other words, social support is not a buffer between stressful events and experienced strain. Instead, social support is seen to be a major contributor to perceived well-being regardless of whether there are stressors present. Cohen and Wills (1985) suggest an exception to this main-effect rule. In their review of studies examining the role of social support, they discovered that support could be a buffer if part of the social network were necessary to deal directly with the stressful events. As an example, if you received a rush order that you could not process by yourself but were able to prevail on a colleague to help you out of the jam, the fact of social support would be less important than the additional resource to cope with the new demand. In this instance, it would appear that social support was acting as a buffer by reducing stress.

If the P-E fit model is reasonable, there should be some change in stress levels when the objective person or the objective environment changes. There are several studies that document change in stress as a function of changes in these two components. Let's look at changes in the person first.

The Objective Person. Koch, Tung, Gmelch, and Swent (1982) examined stress in school administrators. They asked 1,156 administrators to complete a 35-item questionnaire describing stressful events. Through factor analysis, they were able to identify four sources of stress that were relatively independent of one another.

1. *Role-based stress* is the result of not being able to get the right information, not being able to satisfy supervisors, not being sure what the job is, and so on.
2. *Task-based stress* comes from having too much responsibility, meetings that take up too much time, interruptions by telephone calls, and the like.
3. *Boundary-spanning stress* is the result of planning for budgets, engaging in collective bargaining sessions, following state and federal regulations regarding personnel and educational issues, and so on.
4. *Conflict-mediating stress* is the result of being required to discipline students as well as trying to settle disputes between students, between teachers and parents, and between teachers and students.

Of all these sources of stress, task-based stress would seem the most likely candidate for change as a function of experience. Most effective administrators develop schemes for dealing with interruptions, meetings, and work load. They might set aside particular times for meetings (e.g., Monday and Wednesday afternoons). They might give a receptionist or secretary particular instructions with respect to *who* is allowed to interrupt them with a visit or telephone call. They might develop effective delegation skills so that the work load is moved to other locations in the organization. In fact, this is what Koch et al. (1982) found. Task-based stress decreased as the individual became more experienced and moved up the administrative hierarchy. Interestingly enough, conflict-mediating stress and role-based stress did not change with experience, and boundary-spanning stress actually increased with experience. Perhaps this is because in boundary-spanning situations the individual is controlled by other institutional forces and may have diminished influence. For example, negotiations might depend on the school board and the teacher's union. In this case, the administrator is the spokesperson but may have little authority or decision discretion. The same may be true with the administrator's interactions with the state and federal departments of education. The administrator is controlled by circumstances. This fits in nicely with the Glass and Singer notion of perceived control and its relation to stress.

The Objective Social Environment. There have been many studies that have demonstrated that stress is reality based—that it rises and falls depending upon certain characteristics of the objective environment. Frankenhauser and Gardell (1976) contrasted two groups of sawmill workers. One group performed self-paced functions, and the other group engaged in machine-paced work. The results showed substantial stress for the machine-paced work. This stress was evident not only in the complaints of the machine-paced workers about fatigue, depression, and illness but also in elevated levels of catecholamines (hormones that are implicated in adaptation to stress as well as cardiovascular disease). Recently, Hurrell (1985) studied several thousand postal workers and discovered that those working in machine-paced jobs (e.g., working with sorting machines) experienced greater stress than those working on non–machine-paced jobs of a similar nature. It is clear from data such as these that the external environment does play a role in stress. It is not just "in your head."

The Frankenhauser and Gardell and the Hurrell studies were cross-sectional rather than longitudinal. They sampled workers from various jobs (some machine-paced and some self-paced) at a fixed point in time and made inferences about the effect of machine pacing on stress. There have been several experimental studies and longitudinal studies that have come to similar conclusions about the effect of environmental change on stress. Eden (1982) studied student nurses and found that anxiety, blood pressure, and pulse rate all increased in response to what Eden called *critical job events* (CJEs). Examples of CJEs were the student nurse's first patient and the final exam for the nursing program. One interesting sidelight of this study was the finding that these changes occurred even when increases in stress were not reported. This means that we may not always be aware of the stress that we are under.

In an experimental study of student nurses, Parkes (1982) studied the effects of different ward assignments on stress. In a counterbalanced design, nurses were assigned to either medical or surgical wards. It was found that there was considerably more stress in the medical than in the surgical ward. As the nurses moved from one ward to the other, stress levels went up or down, depending on which ward they had come from. Stress was measured as reported dissatisfaction and depression.

Finally, a study by J. B. Shaw and Riskind (1983) using the PAQ to assess task-based stress provides some relevant data. As you remember, the PAQ is an instrument developed by McCormick and his colleagues (McCormick et al., 1972) for job analysis. Since the instrument actually decomposes jobs in terms of various task demands (e.g., decision making and reasoning, manipulation coordination activities, use of stored information), it would seem perfectly suited to identifying the aspects of jobs that are related to stress. In the long run, this type of analysis will be more effective than a gross identification of entire jobs that are stressful. It is not likely that every aspect of a job is equally stressful. Shaw and Riskind were able to identify several subdivisions of work activities that were most closely related to stress. I will single out one in particular. They found that the subdivision of tasks labeled CONTROLLED MANUAL AND/OR RELATED ACTIVITIES was the category most closely associated with heart disease, hypertension, anxiety, depression, dissatisfaction, and various cardiovascular problems. I single this category out because we have already seen similar data in earlier studies. The study of Frankenhauser and Gardell with the sawmill workers concluded that workers performing machine-paced tasks were at greatest risk. The Hurrell study would

Machine-paced jobs in the postal service. (U.S. Postal Service)

seem to lead to a similar conclusion. In addition, the early work of Glass and Singer on unpredictable noise also emphasized the issue of control. In a later section, we will have occasion to make this point again. Karasek (1979) suggests that the most stressful jobs are those that offer little opportunity for control in the form of decision making. It seems clear that some aspects of jobs are more likely to blame for perceived stress than others. The PAQ and other similar devices can be very useful in identifying those aspects.

These data, experimental and correlational, do suggest that the objective environment (and changes in it) play a substantial role in perceived stress. The data are not sufficient by themselves to confirm French's notions of the P-E fit. Nevertheless, if the objective environment could not be linked to perceived stress, the model would be in serious trouble.

The Stress-Vulnerability Model: Type A Behavior

Let's review where we have been. The LCU model suggested that stressful events accumulated and resulted in negative effects for the individual. Although the LCU model did not deal specifically with work stress, it seems safe to extend those assumed negative effects to include not only illness but also dissatisfaction, poor performance, and withdrawal in the form of absence and turnover. The P-E fit model suggested that stressors alone were not sufficient to account for the *experience* of stress. One should consider both the perception of the objective world as well as the presence of mechanisms to defend against stress-produced strain (e.g., defense mechanisms). The next logical model, then, might be one that emphasizes the characteristics of people rather than the characteristics of environments or the person-environment fit. This model is represented in the research on the Type A personality.

Two medical researchers, Friedman and Rosenman (1974) suggested that there might be a relationship between a particular pattern of behavior and heart disease. They described two different patterns of behavior. The first, labeled *Type A behavior,* is found in individuals who show an intense striving for achievement, competitiveness, impatience, a sense of time urgency, abrupt gestures and speech, overcommitment to a profession, and excess drive and hostility. This pattern was contrasted with *Type B behavior,* which is characterized by people who were easygoing, less frantic, less likely to do two things at once, and considerably less hostile. Friedman and Rosenman demonstrated that Type A individuals were much more likely to suffer from heart disease than Type B individuals. It is generally assumed that the reason for this is related to increased levels of hormones in the blood stream of the Type A individual. In terms of Selye's notions of stress, these individuals are continually making withdrawals from their adaptation account. In effect, the implication is that Type A individuals experience potential stressors with greater intensity. It is this "enhanced" experience that leads to the feeling of subjective stress. Motowidlo, Packard, and Manning (1986) have developed a model that illustrates this mechanism. It appears in Figure 14–9.

FIGURE 14–9 Preliminary Model of the Causes of Occupational Stress and Its Consequences for Job Performance

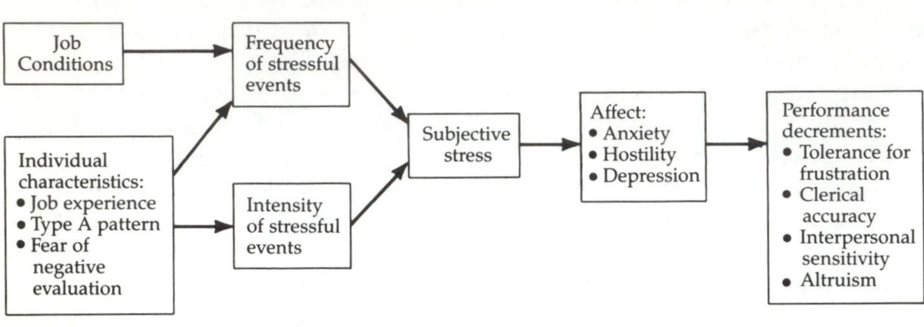

SOURCE: From "Occupational Stress: Its Causes and Consequences for Job Stress" by S. J. Motowidlo, J. S. Packard, and M. R. Manning, 1979, *Journal of Applied Psychology*, *71*, 618–629.

Friedman and Rosenman made their observations on the basis of interviews with subjects. C. D. Jenkins, Zyzanski, and Rosenman (1979) developed a structured questionnaire that taps Type A behavior tendencies. Some typical questions appear in Figure 14–10. D. C. Glass (1977) has suggested that at the base of Type A behavior is the desire (or obsession) to control the environment. This fits in nicely with his earlier research on the aftereffects of noise, since he was able to demonstrate that perceived control reduced the effects of stressors. Recently, there has been a good deal of disenchantment with the Jenkins Activity Survey as a measure of Type A behavior (Landy, Thayer, & Colvin, 1988; Spence, Helmreich, & Pred, 1987). Nevertheless, the disenchantment is related to measurement methodology rather than to the concept of individual vulnerability.

In the Type A propositions, we have the basis of a different model of stress. It suggests that some people are more vulnerable than others to certain environmental demands. You might see this model as an extension of the French P-E fit model. To some extent, it is, but there is a much greater emphasis on habitual characteristics of the individual, particularly the need for control, than is obvious in the P-E model. Another difference is that Type A tendencies are seen as predispositions that can be activated by particular environmental stressors and that these predispositions are individual vulnerabilities much like allergies. Some people have them and some don't.

Research on Type A behavior in industry has been scattered and, again, too recent to draw any firm conclusions. For example, Sanders and Malkis (1982) seemed to confirm that Type A individuals had a need to control the situation. Problem-solving groups were formed by mixing Type A and Type B individuals. The Type A members were most often seen as leaders and were generally considered as helpful in attempts to solve the problem. Interestingly, their solutions were rated as lower than the solutions of Type B

FIGURE 14–10 Sample Items from a Questionnaire Used to Assess Type A Behavior

1. Do you ever have trouble finding time to get your hair cut or styled?
   a. Never
   b. Occasionally
   c. Almost always
2. When you are under pressure or stress, what do you usually do?
   a. Do something about it immediately.
   b. Plan carefully before taking any action.
3. Ordinarily, how rapidly do you eat?
   a. I'm usually the first one finished.
   b. I eat a little faster than average.
   c. I eat at about the same speed as most people.
   d. I eat more slowly than most people.
4. How often do you find yourself doing more than one thing at a time, such as working while eating, reading while dressing, or figuring out problems while driving?
   a. I do two things at once whenever practical.
   b. I do this only when I'm short of time.
   c. I rarely or never do more than one thing at a time.
5. When you listen to someone talking, and this person takes too long to come to the point, how often do you feel like hurrying the person along?
   a. Frequently
   b. Occasionally
   c. Almost never
6. Would people who know you well agree that you enjoy a "contest" (competition) and try hard to win?
   a. Definitely yes
   b. Probably yes
   c. Probably no
   d. Definitely no

SOURCE: From *Manual for the Jenkins Activity Survey* (table 20–3, p. 520) by C. O. Jenkins, S. J. Zysanski, and R. H. Rosenman, 1979, New York: Psychological Corporation, a subsidiary of Harcourt Brace Jovanovich.

counterparts. Frankenhauser, Lundberg, and Forsman (1980) report a fascinating aspect of Type A individuals: they found that the problems of the Type A individual might center more around coping with inactivity than with a need to control. Frankenhauser et al. suggested that the actual coping cost for Type As is seen in their attempts to deal with inactivity. By implication, this means that attempting to get Type As to "slow down" and relax will actually exaggerate the stress that they feel. This may be due to the fact that the Type A has a strong need to control, and there is nothing to control in the case of inactivity. As was the case with the French P-E fit model, the Type A syndrome deserves serious consideration by I/O psychologists since the workplace abounds with opportunities for the Type A vulnerabilities to show themselves.

One recent study casts some doubt on the viability of the Type A construct. Hurrell (1985) found that machine-paced work did produce significant effects on mood states, but there was no indication that Type As suffered greater stress than non–Type As.

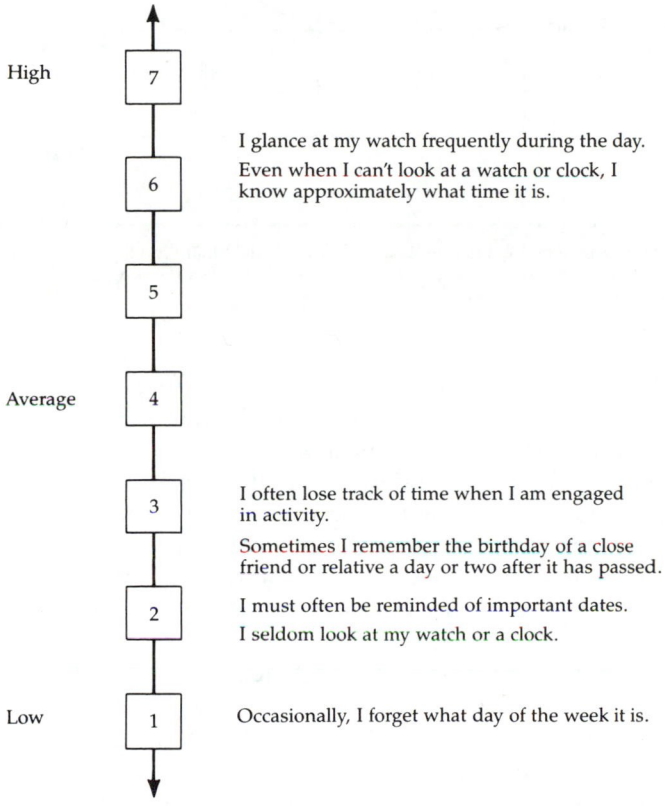

Time Urgency. One of the major factors in Type A behavior has been thought to be time urgency—the feeling that there is not enough time to get everything done. It was this factor that was initially proposed as the primary culprit in coronary heart disease. Recently, Spence et al. (1987) found that an irritability and impatience factor was correlated with psychosomatic complaints in college students. In other words, the more impatient students had significantly more psychosomatic complaints than the less impatient students. In the Jenkins Activity Survey, time urgency or impatience is seen as a unidimensional construct. This may not be the case. We (Landy et al., 1988) have just completed a research project on the construct of time urgency and discovered that there are as many as seven different facets to time awareness. We were able to develop behaviorally anchored scales for measuring the following facets: awareness of time, eating behavior, speech patterns, deadline control, scheduling, nervous energy, and list making. An example of one of these scales appears in Figure 14–11. Schriber and Gutek (1987) have uncovered as many as 13 different aspects of time awareness in organizations. It appears as if there is still a good deal of work to be done in understanding the role of Type A behavior patterns in the subjective experience of stress. It also seems clear that time urgency will continue to play a central role in the construct.

Demands and Constraints

There is one final model that deserves description. Karasek (1979) notes that the stress literature often seems contradictory. For example, he cites some studies by Quinn et al. (1971) that found high demand characteristics in the jobs of both assembly-line workers and executives, yet assembly-line workers were dissatisfied and executives were satisfied. Presumably, job dissatisfaction is one of the outcomes (strains) associated with stress. Karasek suggested that the problem was the emphasis on environmental stressors (task demands) without a recognition that decision latitude was a mediating influence. He proposed that two factors were necessary for an individual to perceive stress. Environmental stressors in the form of job demands represented one of these factors. In this respect, Karasek agreed with all the earlier theories. But he suggested that the extent to which the individual had control over important decisions also played a role. His formal hypothesis is that "psychological strain results not from a single aspect of the work environment but from the joint effects of the demands of a work situation and the range of decision making freedom (discretion) available to the worker facing those demands" (p. 287). The absence of decision latitude was seen as a constraint on effective action,

FIGURE 14–11 One Facet of Time Urgency

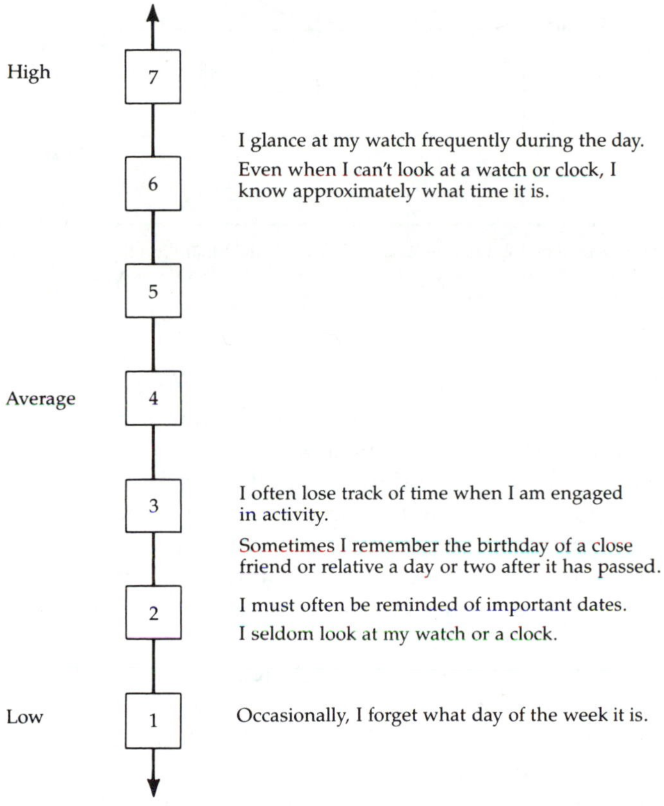
Awareness of Time
The extent to which an individual is aware of the exact time of day, regardless of the environment or circumstances. The extent to which a person is aware of important dates such as birthdays and tests.
High
7
6
I glance at my watch frequently during the day.
Even when I can't look at a watch or clock, I know approximately what time it is.
5
Average
4
3
I often lose track of time when I am engaged in activity.
Sometimes I remember the birthday of a close friend or relative a day or two after it has passed.
2
I must often be reminded of important dates.
I seldom look at my watch or a clock.
Low
1
Occasionally, I forget what day of the week it is.

an obstacle to meeting job demands. Figure 14–12 presents the theory graphically. As you can see from this figure, there are various possible combinations of demands and decision latitude (the opposite of constraints on decision making). In the high demand–low latitude cell, strain is highest (and presumably, negative effects of this strain are greatest). In the high demand–high latitude cell, the situation fosters personal growth and development since the individual has the capacity to deal with the strain through personal action. In the low demand–low latitude cell, Karasek assumes that the job holder will experience a reduction in activity level and general problem-solving skills will decline. The implications of the low demand–high latitude

FIGURE 14–12 Job Strain Model

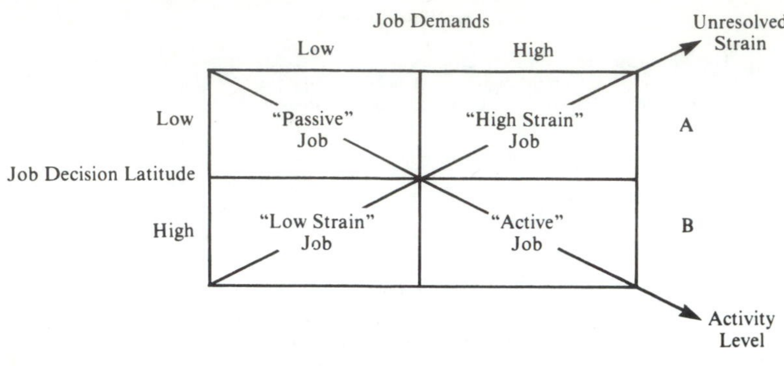

SOURCE: From "Job Demands, Job Decision Latitude, and Mental Strain: Implications for Job Redesign" by R. A. Karasek, Jr., 1979, *Administrative Science Quarterly*, 24, p. 288, fig. 1. Copyright 1979 by *Administrative Science Quarterly*. Reprinted by permission.

cell are unclear, but we might speculate that the effects would be similar to the low demand–low latitude since there is really nothing in the environment to respond to. Karasek's model is based on two data sets—one U.S. and one Swedish. Consider the data that describe the U.S. sample ($n = 911$) in terms of job dissatisfaction as presented in Figure 14–13. In some senses, Karasek's model signals a return to the environmental approach. He emphasizes two aspects of the environment—job demands and decision latitude—but does not formally emphasize perception or cognition in his consideration of job strain. His major interest is in job design. He suggests that jobs should be arranged so that those with the greatest demands also have the greatest decision latitude. He presents an example of how his model applies to an examination of various occupational titles. In Figure 14–14, you can see this distribution of jobs. The jobs in the lower right corner are those with the greatest strain potential. These are the jobs most likely to contribute to cardiovascular illness, according to the model. Karasek clearly has job design and redesign in mind. He concludes that many job demands are realistic and contribute to organizational productivity. As a result, it might be self-defeating simply to reduce demands. Instead, the suggested treatment is to increase decision latitude.

Payne (1979) has suggested an alternative model that extends Karasek's theory in two ways. First, he returns to the P-E fit notion of perception and proposes that it is the individual's *perceptions* of demands and decision latitude that are critical. Second, he introduces the notion of *supports* into the model. Thus, Payne has a three-dimensional model in which he suggests that strain is the result of high demand, high constraint (i.e., low perceived decision latitude), and low support. *Support* is defined as the degree to which the environment makes available resources (natural, physical, intellectual, tech-

FIGURE 14–13 Test of the Job Strain Model with Reports of Dissatisfaction

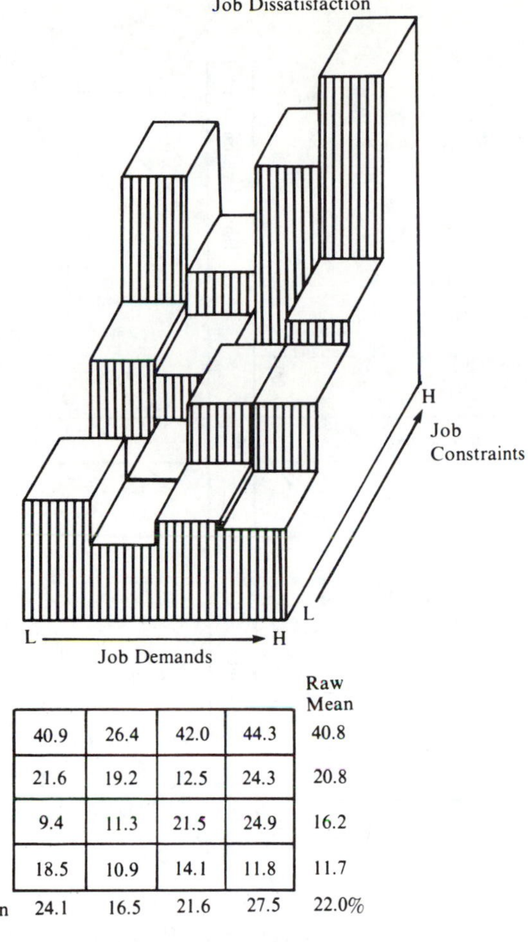

					Raw Mean
	40.9	26.4	42.0	44.3	40.8
	21.6	19.2	12.5	24.3	20.8
	9.4	11.3	21.5	24.9	16.2
	18.5	10.9	14.1	11.8	11.7
Column Mean	24.1	16.5	21.6	27.5	22.0%

SOURCE: From "Job Demands, Job Decision Latitude, and Mental Strain: Implications for Job Redesign" by R. A. Karasek, Jr., 1979, *Administrative Science Quarterly*, *24*, p. 298, table 3, "Job Dissatisfaction" only.

nical, and social) relevant to the demands made upon the person. In general, Payne suggests that greater support means that less adaptive energy has to be used to cope with the demands of the job under conditions of low decision latitude. As a result, Payne would suggest that stress might be reduced by adding various supports to the system. These supports might come in the form of extra personnel, training, or supervisory consideration.

Neither Karasek's model nor Payne's variation on it have received any

FIGURE 14–14

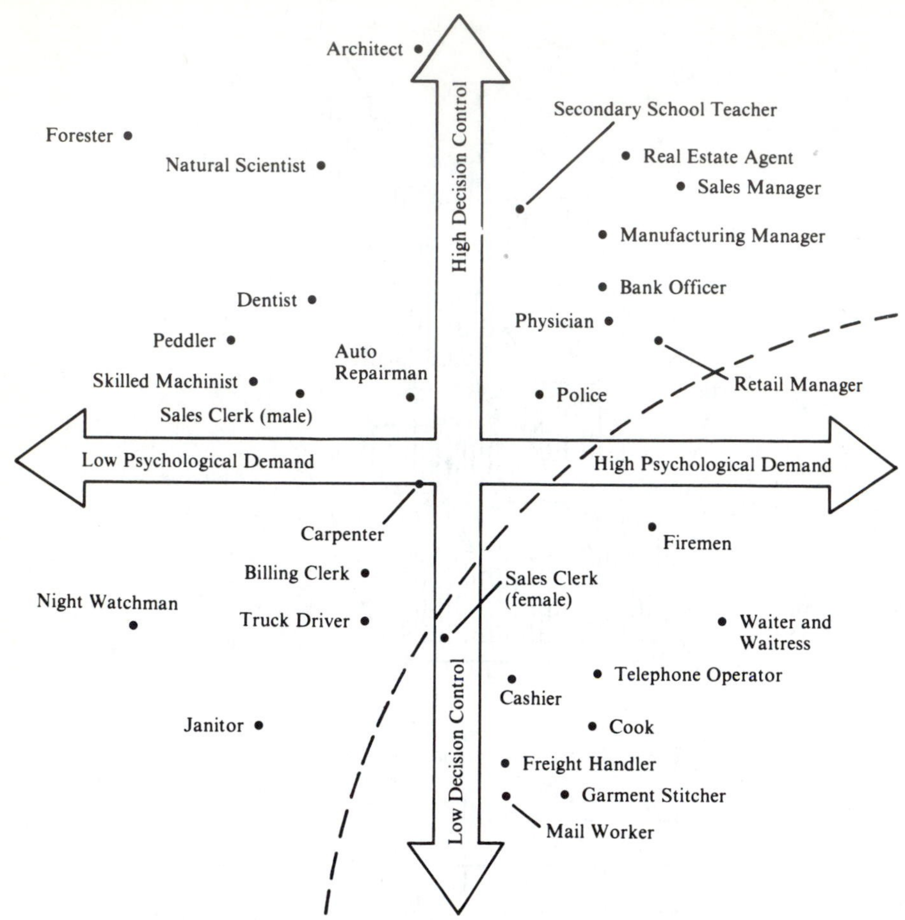

Some jobs are considered more stressful than others. The chart shows a number of familiar jobs and how they would be rated in terms of control or ability to make decisions and in terms of the demand on the person. The most stressful jobs are those shown in the lower right area of the chart. These jobs are characterized by low control and high demand.

substantial test as of yet. A recent study by Bromet, Dew, Parkinson, and Schulberg (1988) does suggest that the low control–high demand environment is not a healthy one. This combination led to a higher incidence of alcohol problems in blue-collar power plant employees. It is reasonable to assume that the bridge between the work environment and the use of alcohol was stress. No doubt, additional research will accumulate in the next few years. Both models are exciting and immediately suggest hypotheses to test. It is refreshing in industrial and organizational psychology to have many theories to choose from. Too often, the problem has been having too many empirical relationships and *no* theory to rely on. As you can see from these various theoretical positions, I/O psychology finds itself in a position to make both theoretical and practical contributions in the area of stress in the near future. But what is to be done in the meantime? In the next section, we will consider some of the approaches that are currently available to manage or reduce stress. Most of these strategies are implied by one or more of the models above.

DEALING WITH STRESS

There are several headings that might have been chosen for this section, but each one implies a theory of stress. For example, some people refer to stress *management*. This implies that environmental stress is inevitable and that individuals must learn to "handle" stress. The same is true of the concept of *coping* with stress. As we have already seen, H. Weiss et al. (1982) even suggest that stress can have facilitating effects on search activities. Stress management often involves a cognitive reorientation toward the stressful event or object. The individual is asked to think about the situation in a different way.

A second heading that appears frequently is *stress reduction*. This heading implies that actions can be taken that will reduce the perceived stress on the individual. These actions usually include physiological or behavioral intervention, on the one hand, or work-task redesign, on the other. I chose the heading "Dealing with Stress" so that we might consider a range of possible interventions. This seems to make the most sense until the various models of stress outlined above have had more extensive testing.

There are four basic approaches that might be taken to dealing with stress. These approaches include the following:

1. *Behavioral intervention*. This technique implies that individuals will be taught to act in a different way. For example, the behavior of Type As might be changed using behavior modification techniques. It is assumed that if they can be made to act more like Type Bs, the risk of stress effects is reduced.
2. *Physiological intervention*. This technique addresses the secondary effects of perceived stress. Through the use of biofeedback or relaxation techniques, or both, the individual is taught to control certain autonomic nervous system response levels (e.g., heart rate, blood pressure). It is assumed that this will minimize the use of adaptive energy. In Selye's terms, the withdrawals from the "adaptation account" will be smaller. L. R. Murphy and Sorenson (1988) compared muscle relaxation with biofeedback and found a slight advantage for muscle relaxation in reducing absenteeism, but in general, the results only weakly supported this type of intervention.
3. *Job design and redesign*. This approach suggests that there are certain characteristics that are part of the work environment or task arrangement that are contributing to perceived stress. By changing these objective charac-

teristics, the level of stress can be reduced. We have seen several examples of such strategies in the work of Frankenhauser and Gardell, Shaw and Riskind, and Karasek. They all emphasize the control aspects of the task. The "treatment" would be to increase decision latitude.

4. *Cognitive intervention.* In several of the approaches that we have examined, the role of perception has been central. The P-E fit model, Type A behavior, and Payne's reformulation of Karasek's demand-constraint model are all examples of this emphasis. It follows from this line of reasoning that stress can be reduced by changing an individual's perception of the environment, on the one hand, and her capacities to meet the demands of the environment, on the other. The work of Meichenbaum (1977) is particularly relevant in this approach. The individual is taught to replace self-defeating cognitions (e.g., the work is too hard for me; I do not have the necessary skill to do this task) with more adaptive cognitions (e.g., I can handle this if I take it one step at a time; I should have some more people to help me with this task). A recent study by Firth and Shapiro (1986) indicates that treating those suffering from stress reactions as patients and using traditional forms of psychotherapy might, in the long run, be more beneficial than trying to prevent stress in much larger numbers of people.

There is very little comparative research on the efficacy of various strategies for dealing with stress in the industrial and organizational literature. It does appear as if most of these techniques have some positive effect on reducing subjective stress. As examples of this research, Jackson (1983) demonstrated that participation in staff meetings reduced role conflict and role ambiguity, although the effect of this intervention did not really begin to appear for several months after the staff meetings were initiated. This type of intervention might be classified as either a behavioral intervention or a job redesign strategy or both.

Ganster, Mayes, Sime, and Tharp (1982) took a different approach. They instituted a combined program of cognitive reorientation (based on the Meichenbaum model) and relaxation training combined with biofeedback. This would fall under the physiological and cognitive intervention headings. The treatment was effective. Forty treatment subjects were contrasted with 39 control subjects, and those receiving the combined cognitive-physiological program showed reduced depression and lower epinephrine levels (a hormone thought to be a by-product of stress). The interesting aspect of this study was that the authors came to the conclusion that this method of treatment should *not* be used. This conclusion was based on the following considerations:

1. The effects were modest even after 16 hours of exposure stretched over eight weeks.
2. These modest effects were produced by the joint efforts of an experienced clinical psychologist and a stress physiologist.
3. The program was not intended to eliminate the actual stressor.

These authors were very pessimistic about the quality of treatment programs generally available to industrial organizations. They estimated that the typical stress reduction program lasted a few hours and was conducted by consultants poorly equipped to teach the critical techniques. Instead, they suggest a more careful examination of the environment in the hope of identifying elements that might be modified. As an example, they cite the work of Timio and Gentili (1976) that purports to show a substantial effect of methods of payment on perceived stress. Piece-rate payment is thought to produce considerable stress in the worker. Ganster et al. suggest that in the long run changing environmental characteristics such as method of payment will have a considerably greater effect on perceived stress than helping a person adapt to the environmentally induced stress. Ganster et al. are following in the footsteps of clinical psychologists who argue that individual psychotherapy aimed at helping an individual to "adjust" to unreasonable environmental demands is inappropriate. I/O psychologists should be particularly careful in the area of treatment of stress. If the object is to promote worker well-being, coping or adapting strategies might not always be in the best interest of that worker. The approach should be a balanced one, considering both adaptation and environmental redesign possibilities.

Latack (1986) suggests that there are three ways in which individuals might cope with stress in industrial settings: control, escape, and symptom management. Controlling means discussing issues with supervisors, customers, or fellow workers. It also involves devoting more time to work and spending more time on planning and scheduling. In contrast, escape includes activities such as avoiding the situation that produces the stress, delegating work to others, anticipating negative consequences of actions, or just reconciling oneself to a situation. Symptom management includes doing physical exercise, drinking alcoholic beverages, eating, watching TV, using biofeedback and relaxation, and so on. This three-parameter model might provide a useful point of departure for comparing those who successfully cope with stress with those who do not cope so well.

We have now considered some traditional as well as more recent issues in work and well-being. The data and theories strongly suggest that there are elements of the objective environment that may combine with elements of the worker to produce threats to that worker's well-being. There is another threat to well-being that is more immediate and of equal consequence—the industrial accident. Safety has always been a topic of concern for the I/O psychologist. Below, I will consider recent theory and research in the area of industrial safety.

SAFETY AT THE WORKPLACE

If I were to ask you to identify the product of a man-machine system, you would probably suggest an auto body, a bolt, or a computer printout. But another product of a man-machine system is an accident. Errors depend on the particular combination of both man and machine error. This combination often results in death and permanent disability for the worker. It has been estimated that more than 12,500 workers die and over 2.2 million workers are disabled by industrial accidents in a typical year (Komaki, Barwick, & Scott, 1978). If you assume that this is only a portion of the workers who engage in unsafe behavior (the others were "lucky" enough to escape injury), you can see the enormity of the problem.

The issue of safety, more than any other area in I/O psychology, points out the diversity of approaches that might be taken to the same problem. The problem would seem to be relatively simple: reduce accidents. The question is, How shall we begin? There have been three common approaches to the problem. The first has been the *engineering approach.* This approach has assumed that by modifying the nature of the equipment or process that a worker uses errors (and subsequently accidents) can be reduced. The second has been the *personnel-psychology approach.* In this approach, the psychologist attempts to identify particular traits, response patterns, or individual characteristics of workers that seem to be correlated with accident frequency. Subsequently, this correlation is used to select workers with lower probabilities of accident occurrence. Alternatively, training programs are developed to modify those traits, response patterns, or individual characteristics that are correlated with accidents. The third method of addressing the issue of safety is the *industrial-social approach.* The assumption is made that accidents are basically motivational problems. While workers may *know* what the safe behavior is, there is no motivation for performing an action in a safe manner. Each of these three different approaches has met with some success.

The Engineering Approach

In Chapter 2, we considered the delicate art of driving a cab. In that chapter, I described a field experiment conducted in order to evaluate the effect of deceleration lights on rear-end collisions (Voevodsky, 1974). A brief review of that experiment might be in order. A San Francisco cab company was concerned about the number of accidents in which their cabs were hit from behind by other cars. They reasoned that the other drivers did not have sufficient warning when the cabs were about to stop or slow down. The experiment involved putting lights on the trunks of the cabs. These lights began to blink when the cab slowed down; the lights blinked faster when the cab decelerated faster. A total of 343 cabs were fitted with these lights. A control group of 160 cabs had no deceleration lights.

If you keep in mind that the company was trying to reduce rear-end collisions, one might interpret the cab and cab driver as the machine and the following motorist as the man in this man-machine system. The company was attempting to reduce errors in the system by changing the nature of the machine—by making it more efficient in terms of the information it provided the man (the unsuspecting motorist).

As you saw earlier, after 10 months, the results were dramatic. In almost every category, the experimental cabs outperformed the control cabs. The number of rear-end collisions, the costs of repairs necessitated by rear-end collisions, and injuries to cab drivers were all reduced by over 60 percent. The statistics for the control cabs remained unchanged over the 10-month period. It was concluded that the engineering modification had resulted in accident reduction. Remember, front-end accidents did not decline at all, so it was not simply a matter of the cab driver being more cautious. Instead, it would seem that a new and useful display was added to the man-machine system—the blinking light. This study is an interesting example of reducing system error (and accidents) through system design. It is interesting to note that experiments such as these can often have an impact on the wider social system. U.S. automobiles manufactured after 1985 are required to have eye-level brake lights. These lights are mounted inside or outside the rear window. The U.S. Department of Transportation estimated that this would have the effect of eliminating 40,000 injuries and $434 million in property damages annually. It might be useful if the Transportation Department also added deceleration lights to the new law. Nevertheless, it is likely that the cab experiment was testing not only the effect of deceleration lights but also the effect of eye-level feedback. For that reason, the Transportation Department's expectations are reasonable.

As we will see in the next chapter, there is more to engineering a job than simply reducing noise or heat or providing adequate lighting. In addition, work schedule can play a critical role in safe behavior. Consider the risks to an individual who has been at the workplace for 24 or 36 hours. Consider the risks to someone who has just switched from a day shift to a night shift. We will consider these issues in some detail in the next chapter, but Rhodes and Schuster completed a study in 1983 that has direct implications for the relationship between working hours and safety. They considered the issue of overtime and the extent to which overtime hours were related to industrial accidents. Although there were some sampling limitations to their study, they tentatively concluded that overtime hours were positively related to both accident probability and accident severity. This is an important line of research to pursue since a popular strategy for many organizations in times of recession is to reduce the absolute work force level and increase overtime for remaining workers.

The Personnel Approach

"Accident proneness" has been a popular concept in safety research. It is seductively simple. The psychological principle is one of selection: identify the characteristics of individuals likely to have accidents and do not hire individuals who possess those characteristics. An alternative strategy would be to identify those worker characteristics that are most highly correlated with accidents and attempt to change those characteristics in workers. The latter strategy is a training approach based on the measurement of individual differences.

Since the measurement of individual differences is usually accomplished through testing of one form or another, it is not surprising to find that over the past several decades clues to the mystery of the accident-prone employee have been sought in the full range of test types: personality, attitude and interest, psychomotor, intellectual, and perceptual. Unfortunately, the concept of accident proneness has not received much empirical support. While it is clear that some individuals have more accidents than others, it is difficult to equate the rate of exposure to accidents. Miners have a higher rate of accidents than people in other occupations, but one suspects that miners are no more accident-prone as a group. They simply are exposed to potential accident situations at a higher rate than, say, retail clerks. Furthermore, the fact that some people have more accidents than others is to be expected on the basis of chance. For example, if in a given year there are 1,000 workers in a plant and 500 accidents, it is obvious that *at least* 500 workers will be accident free. Of those who have accidents, the vast majority will have only one; relatively few will have two; even fewer will have three; and so on. The point is that essentially the same distribution would have occurred had we placed the names of the workers in a hat and drawn from the hat 500 times, replacing each name after it was drawn. That is, we could identify as "lucky" (in this case, "accident-prone") those workers whose names were drawn more than once, but actually the results could be accounted for by chance alone.

In spite of the fact that it is fruitless to search for individuals who can be stamped "AP" for accident-prone, there may be some value in seeking attributes of individuals that are predictive of accident behavior in a specific task or occupational setting. This approach has been taken in several studies. In one study (Barrett & Thornton, 1968), it was discovered that measures of basic perceptual skill were predictive of accidents and near-accidents with pedestrians in a simulated driving situation. Subjects were given a test that required them to find a hidden figure in a complicated background. Those who were better at finding the hidden figure also had fewer accidents in the driving simulation.

Mihal and Barrett (1976) examined individual differences in selective attention and perceptual-motor reaction time in addition to capacity to find hidden figures. They administered various perceptual and reaction-time tests to drivers for a utility company and then examined the accident rates of those drivers for the five previous years. *Selective attention* was the capacity of the individual to select information differentially in making a decision; *perceptual-motor reaction time* was a complex reaction time requiring both perceptual and motor responses rather than the traditional simple motor reaction–time measures. As in the earlier study, individuals who were able to find the hidden figure had fewer accidents; in addition, those who were able to select certain pieces of information differentially rather than try to process all information available had fewer accidents. There has been some recent research showing that 3-D or stereoscopic perceptual tests are also predictive of accident occurrence (J. R. Williams, 1977).

This approach is an interesting one and, as can be seen from the studies described above, a potentially fruitful one. An examination of all the literature that has been published on this approach seems to indicate that traditional trait approaches are not as valuable as "work sample" or simulation approaches. In addition, recent research and theory in cognitive psychology suggests that the way in which people process information may be a critical individual difference that contributes to safe behavior at the workplace.

The Industrial-Social Approach

A distinctly different hypothesis about the causes of safe behavior and accidents is reflected in the industrial-social approach. This approach proposes that the worker must be *motivated* to behave safely; there must be a *reason*. Common sense would suggest that the protection of life and limb would be sufficient reason for workers to behave safely, but this is clearly not the case, since there are an enormous number of accidents occurring every day. The survival motive is probably not as strong as it could be, since workers engage in unsafe behaviors every day but seldom have accidents. In addition, safe behavior often requires a greater expenditure of energy than careless behavior. Finally, in many work settings, it is considered macho to perform work activities in dangerous ways—at the very least, it is unmacho to use safety goggles, ear protectors, special safety equipment, and so on. Thus, the motivational approach to safety tries to change workers' preferences for and satisfactions with safe behavior.

A good example of this approach is a study by Komaki et al. (1978). They instituted a program of goal setting, positive reinforcement, and feedback in an attempt to stimulate safe job performance by employees in a food manufacturing plant. The subjects were workers from two departments in the plant—the production (makeup) and the wrapping departments. There were 38 employees involved in the study. An analysis of the job led the researchers to conclude that the high accident rate in the plant was a result of a combination of the following forces:

1. Safety was ignored in training and educational programs at the plant.
2. Safe behavior took more time than unsafe behavior.
3. Safe behavior was seldom rewarded by management or coworkers.
4. Unsafe behavior seldom caused actual injuries.

As a result of observation and interviews with workers, the research team was able to identify safe and unsafe behaviors in each of the two departments. Some examples of these behaviors are presented in Figure 14–15.

The behaviors described in Figure 14–15 were made into slides depicting the safe and unsafe ways of going about the same activity. The workers were assembled for discussions of these slides. First, they were shown the unsafe version of the activity and asked to describe what was unsafe about it. After discussion, the workers were shown the slide depicting the safe way of car-

FIGURE 14–15 Sample Items on Observational Codes

Makeup Department

When picking up pans from the conveyor belt, no more than two pans are picked up prior to placing the pans on the pan rack.

Roll pans are stacked no higher than the rear rail of the pan rack.

When lifting or lowering dough trough, hand holds and at no time loses contact with dump chain.

When pulling dough trough away from dough mixer, hands are placed on the front rail of the dough trough and not on the side rails.

Wrapping Department

There are no cardboard spacers (defined as cardboard 30 mm square or larger) on the floor.

When cutting wire bands from stacks of boxes or spacers, employee cuts with one hand and holds the metal strap above the cut with the other hand.

When moving conveyor, at least one person is on each end.

When handling a skid, employee attempts to break its fall in some manner, for example, sliding it off rather than letting it fall flat on the floor.

Both Departments

When mechanical problems arise (e.g., pans jam on conveyor belt, belt breaks), the machine is turned off (the machine is off when the on-off switch is in the off position and machine moving parts have stopped), or maintenance is notified.

SOURCE: From "A Behavioral Approach to Occupational Safety: Pinpointing and Reinforcing Safe Performance in a Food Manufacturing Plant" by J. Komaki, K. D. Barwick, and L. R. Scott, 1978, *Journal of Applied Psychology, 63*, p. 438.

rying out the task, and the general principle for safe behavior in the particular situation was identified. Workers were then shown graphs that described their own proportion of safe and unsafe behaviors; this was done in confidentiality so that none of the workers was aware of the data for any other worker. The workers were then asked to set a department goal for percentage of safe behaviors. This goal was placed on a conspicuous graph, which was prominently displayed at the work site. The research team continuously observed work behavior and provided frequent feedback and encouragement with respect to safe behavior. In addition, levels of safe behavior were recorded on the public graph.

The results of the safety program are shown in Figure 14–16. As you can see, the results were both immediate and impressive. Shortly after the program was begun, the percentage of safe behaviors in the wrapping department increased from 70 percent to 95 percent; in the makeup department, the percentage of safe behaviors increased from 77 percent to 99 percent! After the safe behavior had been clearly established and maintained, the feedback and reinforcement were terminated. As you can see from the figure, safe behavior diminished to levels similar to the preintervention period.

During the course of the experiment, workers became very involved in

FIGURE 14–16 Percentage of Items Performed Safely by Employees in Two Departments of a Food Manufacturing Plant during a 25-Week Period of Time

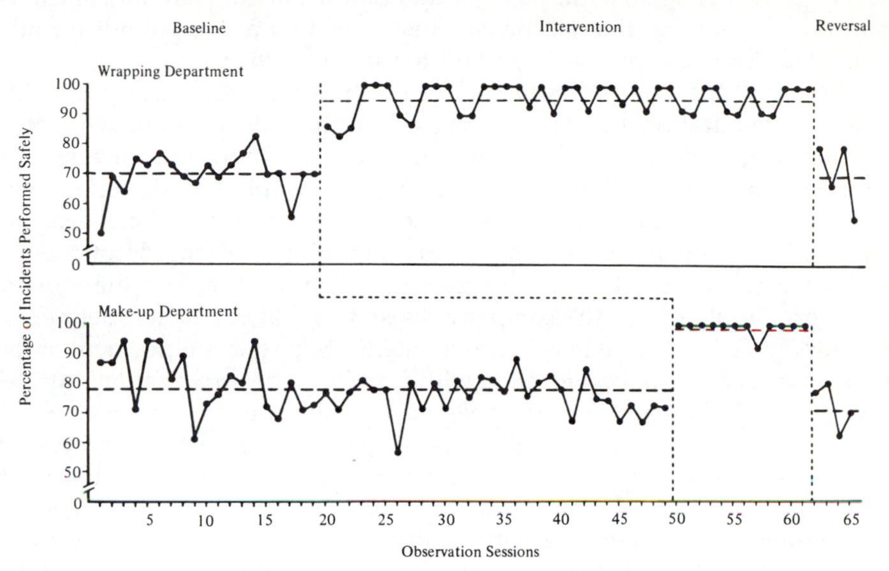

SOURCE: From "A Behavioral Approach to Occupational Safety: Pinpointing and Reinforcing Safe Performance in a Food Manufacturing Plant" by J. Komaki, K. D. Barwick, and L. R. Scott, 1978, *Journal of Applied Psychology, 63*, p. 439. Copyright 1978 by the American Psychological Association. Reprinted by permission of the author.

the safety program. They were aware of increases and decreases in safety percentage and occasionally cheered when the graph showed an increase in safe behavior. In addition, they often put pressure on fellow workers to eliminate unsafe behaviors that were "ruining the graph." In short, the workers reacted favorably to the program. One might conclude that their motivation to behave safely had been increased through the experimental intervention. While the results are positive and make the point that I originally intended—that accidents may be reduced by addressing motivational issues—there is some disconcerting information in Figure 14–16 as well. The fact that the workers reverted to earlier levels of unsafe behavior *as soon as the motivational program was suspended* (the section labeled "Reversal" in the figure) is a little scarey. It implies that safe behavior is very fragile and requires almost constant attention from supervisors.

This last approach was represented by only one of the motivational strategies that might have been used: the reinforcement strategy. It might be possible to adapt other motivational approaches such as the need, the social comparison, or the cognitive approach to motivating safe behavior. For example, in a more recent study by Komaki and her colleagues (Komaki, Heinzmann, & Lawson, 1980), it was demonstrated that feedback is critically important in maintaining safe behavior. Without feedback, safety training has limited impact. We reviewed this study in detail in the training chapter, so I won't go over it again. The point is that safe behavior may be considered *motivated* activity and that all the circumstances that are important for other motivated activities are also important for safe behavior.

Recently, the issue of industrial safety has been approached from the broader, organizational perspective as well. Zohar (1980) conducted a study in which he measured the safety climate in an organization. You will remember from our earlier discussion that climate is the perception that workers have of some collection of objective organizational characteristics. Zohar reasoned that workers probably have some guess regarding the attitude of their organization toward safety, and this guess is likely to influence the worker's behavior. Simply put, if the company doesn't care about safety, neither will the worker. Zohar was able to demonstrate that there was agreement among workers in a particular organization with respect to the organization's attitude toward safety. Furthermore, it appeared that this climate (as perceived by workers) was related to safety program effectiveness as estimated by safety inspectors. The two most important aspects of this climate seemed to be the worker's perceptions of management attitudes about safety (as evidenced in job training programs emphasizing safety, relegation of executive authority to safety officials, and adjusting work pace to meet safety demands) and their perceptions of the extent to which safety played a role in the general production process. Zohar suggests that until and unless management commitment to safety is obvious to the workers, poster campaigns, safety slogan contests, and additional safety regulations may not be particularly effective in decreasing accident and injury. The industrial-social approach is distinctly different from either the engineering or the personnel approach described earlier. It shows a good deal of promise.

Safety Legislation

The federal government has formed an agency to deal with the issue of industrial safety. This agency is called the Occupational Safety and Health Administration (OSHA), and its mission is administering and enforcing the Occupational Safety and Health Act of 1970 (Public Law 91–596, December 29, 1970). This act has as its stated purpose "to insure so far as possible every working man and woman in the nation safe and healthful working conditions and to preserve our human resources." Everyone agrees with the goals of OSHA, at least in principle. In practice, however, such goals run into economic realities and the conflicting interests of special-interest groups. In addition, the goals often conflict with behavioral patterns of workers. It is common to see workers totally disregarding safeguards placed in their environment to protect their health. Asbestos workers often refuse to wear masks; farm workers often refuse to install roll bars on tractors; riveters often refuse to wear ear protectors. This suggests that while environmental legislation may be the precondition for worker safety, it is a far cry from a guarantee of an accident-free workplace.

Safety from a Systems Perspective

Safe behavior, like many other behaviors examined by the psychologist, is best considered in a systems context. In that respect, the industrial psychologist would be well advised to consider all three approaches—engineering, personnel, and motivational—when dealing with accident reduction. Consider the recent "findings" of the National Transportation Safety Board concerning the causes for the crash of an Air Florida flight at Washington's National Airport on an icy day in January 1982. They concluded that the ultimate cause was "pilot error." The facts suggest a much more complex situation. The contributing factors included the following (R. D. Shaw, 1982):

- A 49-minute delay between the last de-icing of the plane and takeoff. This delay was due to the fact that the airport was closed for a period of time, resulting in a backup of planes for departure.
- The failure to turn on the plane's automatic de-icers.
- The use of the plane's reverse thrusters and exhaust from other planes to melt the ice on the wings. This actually added to the amount of snow and water on the wings.
- The prodding of an air traffic controller to hurry the takeoff because another plane was approaching and would need the runway. This prevented the pilot from revving the engines—a procedure that would have provided critical information regarding the danger of a takeoff under the existing circumstances.
- Incorrect information from cockpit gauges that led to an overestimate of engine power. This was a direct result of the failure to turn on the engine de-icers.
- The unwillingness of the pilot to listen to the warnings of the copilot or the copilot to take direct action to prevent the takeoff. In fact, the pilot had only flown in snow on four earlier occasions and was "inexperienced" in those conditions by most standards.

As you can see, there are implications here for training, job design, equipment design, organizational control, stress management, and a myriad of other factors. Labeling a disaster such as the crash of the Air Florida flight "pilot error" is ludicrous. What is required is a decomposition of the event and an examination of the many different simultaneous interventions that might prevent such accidents in the future.

ERRORS BY A TENSE U.S. CREW LED TO DOWNING OF IRAN JET, INQUIRY IS REPORTED TO FIND

STRESS OF COMBAT

High-Tech Gear Used by Radar Operators Is Found Not at Fault

In some respects, the shooting down of an Iranian civil airliner might be considered a stress-related accident.

Stress and Safety

We have considered the issues of stress and safety individually, as if they were different topics. This is not the case. It should be obvious from the theories and studies that describe the physiological, psychological, and behavioral effects of stress that any of these effects could result in an accident if the situation is right. Jumpiness, depression, fatigue, searching activities directed to eliminating a stressor can all contribute to an accident. This is one more reason for organizations to introduce programs related to the identification and elimination of sources of stress in the work environment.

Biorhythms and Safety

In the discussion of safety in the workplace, I would be remiss if I did not treat the topic of biorhythm. In the past decade, there has been a growing tendency to blame accidents on the parents of the accident victim for having poorly planned the instant of conception of the person in question. Biorhythm advocates suggest that there are three major cycles that might be used to characterize the human being. These cycles are begun at the moment of birth (although to be exact, they surely must begin at some earlier point—possibly some point between conception and birth) and have different temporal lengths. The *physical* cycle has 23 days, the *emotional* cycle has 28 days, and the *intellectual* cycle has 33 days (except for individuals born in remote sections of northwestern Ohio). Each of these cycles has a high and a low phase. The theory suggests that individuals are particularly susceptible to accidents on days corresponding to the low phases of their cycles. Presumably, the very worst days for accident probability are those days in which all three cycles are at their lowest points.

There have been many accounts in newspapers and magazines about companies that have adopted the strategy of helping employees keep track of their biorhythms in the hope of reducing accidents. If an employee is entering a low phase of one or more cycles, he may be assigned to a relatively harmless operation until the low phase is passed; alternatively, he may be warned to be particularly careful on certain days. Many organizations have claimed that accidents were reduced by the use of the biorhythm system. Unfortunately, there have been few controlled studies of the value of this approach.

From the psychological point of view, the "theory" borders on the ridiculous. Nevertheless, even industrial psychologists are not above the ridiculous if accidents can be reduced. A group of researchers (Wolcott, McKeeken, Burgin, & Yanowitch, 1977) examined the biorhythms of pilots involved in general aviation accidents to see if the accidents might have been predicted on the basis of low phases in one or more of the pilots' cycles. Biorhythms were calculated for over 4,000 pilots involved in accidents in 1972. Exact dates and times of the accidents were recorded, and they were separated into two groups: those in which the pilot was considered to be at fault and those in which the pilot had no responsibility for the accident.

The results of the analysis clearly showed that there was no relationship between the biorhythm of pilots and aviation accidents. As a matter of fact, if there was any trend in the data, it was that accidents were slightly more probable on "good" days. Similar results were obtained by Carvey and Nibler (1977) in an analysis of vehicular and industrial accidents of city employees in Tacoma, Washington.

The lack of a relationship between biorhythms and accidents for pilots is comforting for those of us who worry about the well-being of those who fly the planes we ride in; when a commercial airline has an accident, others often share that accident. The results are also reassuring for scientists who are generally annoyed with mystical techniques. But if we accept the reports of positive results at face value, how can we explain them? Wolcott et al. suggest a plausible explanation. If all three cycles are considered independently, critical periods in one or more of those cycles occur approximately six times per month. If the employee is cautioned to be careful for one day before and one day after the critical day (as well as the day itself), the employee is being sensitized to safety for more than 50 percent of the month! In addition, the introduction of biorhythm systems is like the introduction of many other employee relations programs—it implies a concern on the part of management for the worker and may have a positive value similar to that of the "Hawthorne effect" described in Chapter 11. The fact that biorhythm can be shown to have effects on accidents only after workers have been made aware of the theory and their own cycles says something about the nature of the approach. A verification of the theory would require that it be able to predict accidents even when the victims were ignorant of the theory and their cycles. In spite of the fact that the theory has no scientific credibility, I have no argument with attempts to increase safety consciousness, no matter how silly they may be. On the other hand, if organizations are going to great lengths to introduce biorhythm principles into work scheduling, with an accompanying increase in overhead and direct production costs, they might be better off spending their money on designing safer machines or procedures.

One final point that deserves some attention is the possibility of bias in the studies that purport to demonstrate a biorhythm effect. Two recent studies suggest that bias does play a role in the "success" stories. Prytula et al. (1980) were able to demonstrate that subjects who listened to favorable descriptions of biorhythm theory were more likely to perceive the predictions as accurate. Chaffin and Skadburg (1979) found that when subjects were instructed to score accident charts by looking for correct biorhythm predictions, they overreported correct predictions by almost 50 percent. These two studies taken together show once again that without the safeguards that are built into the scientific method, many people will "see it when they believe it."

In summary, I find nothing to suggest that biorhythm is anything other than an amusing gimmick. If an organization is truly interested in reducing accidents, I would suggest one or more of the strategies described in the earlier sections.

CENTRAL POINTS FOR STUDY

1. Certain physical characteristics of the workplace can be considered stressors.
2. Single stressors have different effects on behavior.
3. Multiple stressors have complex effects on behavior.
4. The major theories of stress include the life events theory, the person-environment fit model, and the stress-vulnerability model.
5. Stress can be dealt with in two ways: it can be reduced, or it can be managed.
6. Safety can be approached from the personnel, social, or engineering perspective.

CHAPTER 15

Designing Work for People

Typically, people work in a social environment, and they work with machines. There are many questions regarding the effects of the social environment and the machine, or "systems environment," on a person's efficiency and well-being that have intrigued psychologists and other scientists. It seems fair to say that the evidence reviewed earlier leaves little doubt as to the importance of both the social context and the machines as factors determining the satisfactoriness of performance and the satisfaction that the worker experiences in connection with the job. Many questions remain unanswered, and science is far from ready to specify the details either of ideal social systems or of ideal machine systems. Nevertheless, some progress has been made in formulating more appropriate questions and in designing research and theory that is more likely to provide the answers. It remains for us to consider what is perhaps the most obvious aspect of the work environment, the conditions under which one works.

People are highly adaptable creatures and can work under a fairly wide range of physical conditions if other conditions in their "psychological environment" motivate them to do so. For example, two girls in a minor experiment in the Hawthorne studies worked under a moonlight level of illumination without loss of production and without reporting excessive eyestrain.

This is not to deny the importance of physical environment factors, however. The fact that people *can* adapt to a wide range of conditions does not mean that they always *will* adapt or that they do not pay a price, either physiologically or psychologically, for their adaptation. In the last chapter, we considered the impact of heat and noise and sleep loss on behavior and saw several instances of adverse effects. These subjects did not behave in the same manner as the Hawthorne subjects who worked in poorly lighted environments.

From both the pragmatic and the humanistic points of view, science has an obligation to identify those conditions that minimize the need for excessive adaptation and the attendant costs of such adaptation in manpower resources and human well-being. In connection with the latter point, it may be recalled that in Herzberg's theory of work motivation (see Chapters 10 and 11) the *context* of the job, including the physical work conditions, is seen as the primary determinant of negative job attitudes or job dissatisfaction. Furthermore, there is sufficient evidence for adverse physiological effects of extreme environmental conditions to warrant their systematic study from the standpoint of either productive efficiency or human values. We saw that evidence in our consideration of work-related stress. But we should consider the other side of the coin as well. Comfort and efficiency are not always well matched. As Wilkinson (1974) points out, if the job being considered is that of a diesel train driver, efficiency at seeing the occasional but unexpected signal will not be maximized by giving that driver a warm cab and insulating the cab so that all noise is eliminated. This means that when we are considering the conditions of work, we must concern ourselves with the full range of conditions that affect efficiency and comfort rather than those conditions that affect only one or the other of these variables.

In the last chapter, we looked at the ways by which work and work environments can create stress in the worker. This was a sobering and negative view of the workplace. So what is to be done about these circumstances of stress? The implication of Chapter 14 was that once we recognize the symptoms of stress, we can set about redesigning the job or environment, on the one hand, or helping the individual worker to manage or cope with the stress, on the other hand, or where appropriate, instituting both. Although there are many occasions that require this reactive type of response from I/O psychologists, there are an equal number of opportunities to design the job and environment correctly in the first place. Similarly, there are many reasons (both humanistic and economic) to design or redesign jobs even though they may *not* lead to stress. To take a stark but simple example, it is unlikely that the worker who loses her hand in a punch press accident feels much stress in the minutes or seconds before the accident. Similarly, the driver who misreads a traffic sign and goes the wrong way on a highway ramp may not experience any stress in the brief instant before he is hit head on by the 18-wheel semi. In this chapter, we will consider the broader issue of man-machine systems and the implications of this concept for theory, research, and practice of I/O psychology. We will consider both traditional and novel topics. The traditional topics include issues such as the essence of the human engineering approach, the relationship of displays and controls, the capacities and limitations of human operators, and some important characteristics of physical environments (in addition to those particularly stressful characteristics considered in the last chapter). The novel topics include issues of automation, computerization and robotics, and work schedules. Although the research on these novel topics is somewhat skimpy, they are of sufficient interest and importance to warrant some discussion.

It is tempting to present a broad survey of human engineering and environmental design in this chapter. Instead, however, I will try to emphasize those issues that are central to a broad sociotechnical approach to work as well as those issues that relate directly to the cognitive components of work, a theme I have tried to emphasize in every chapter. The more traditional treatments of display and control design—sometimes facetiously referred to as "advanced knobology"—are well covered in other specialized and widely available texts and technical sources. As an example, the *Applied Ergonomics Handbook* (Applied Ergonomics, 1974) and the *Human Factors Handbook* (Salvendy, 1987) both provide a wealth of information on design issues.

THE HUMAN ENGINEERING APPROACH

We have seen that from its early beginnings industrial psychology has been concerned with the identification and measurement of individual differences predictive of differential performance on different jobs. This approach to the efficiency of technological systems may be summarized in the phrase, "Find the person to fit the machine [or job]." The machine was accepted largely as a "given"—an unalterable creation of engineers and designers, beyond the domain of psychologists. The industrial psychologist's role was to contribute to productive efficiency through improved selection procedures. To the extent that selection devices and strategies were inadequate to the task, the psychologist sometimes was expected to "fit" the individual to the job through training programs. In a sense, then, the total personnel approach may be described as, "Find the right people (through selection techniques) and fit them (through training programs) to the jobs."

Personnel selection and training continue to be major activities of industrial psychologists. As we have seen in other sections of this book, new and promising devices and models for selection and for the evaluation of selection strategies are being developed. Furthermore, in the areas of management development and personnel training, new theories and techniques as well as empirical findings are being applied, and vigorous attempts are being made to realize the implications for industry of basic research on learning and performance. Taken together with recent developments in industrial-social psychology, which emphasize the role of the social context of work, personnel selection and training continue to be major areas within which psychologists contribute to technological efficiency and to human effectiveness. But in spite of the contributions that personnel psychology can make toward efficiency or happiness, there are certain harsh realities imposed by environments. Unless these realities are considered in the design of workplaces and equipment, certain mismatches will occur, and there may be no modifications of selection or training procedures that will eliminate those mismatches. As an example, consider Figure 15–1. Many lathes that are currently in use seem to assume that the operators of those lathes are very unusually constructed or proportioned human beings. The top portion of the figure shows the current match between operator and machine. The bottom portion illustrates what the "perfect" operator should look like, given the characteristics of lathes most commonly used. One solution would be to search

FIGURE 15–1 Man-Machine Mismatch

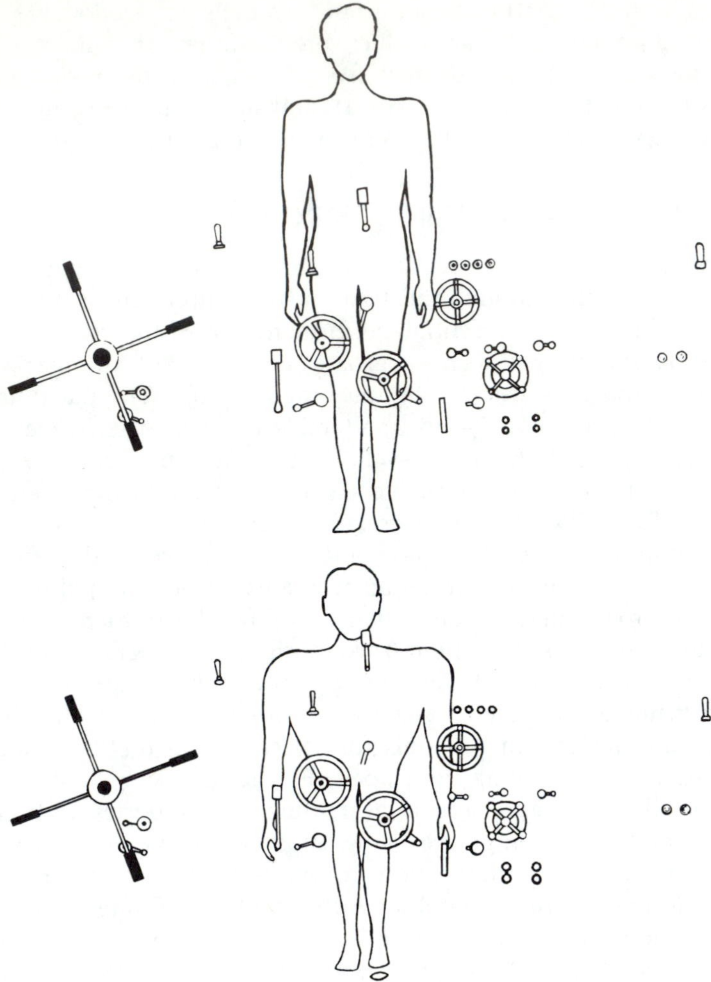

The controls of a lathe in current use are not within easy reach of the average man but are so placed that the ideal operator should be 4½ feet tall, 12 feet across the shoulders, and have an 8-foot arm span.

SOURCE: From *Applied Ergonomics Handbook* (p. 3) by Applied Ergonomics, 1974, Surrey, England: IPC Science and Technology Press.

for (or breed, if time is not a problem) operators who have those "perfect" characteristics. A more realistic solution would be to redesign the equipment so that it more closely matches the characteristics of the "average" operator. This latter approach has been labeled the *human factors* or *human engineering*

FIGURE 15–2 The Simple but Important Frame of Reference for the Worker

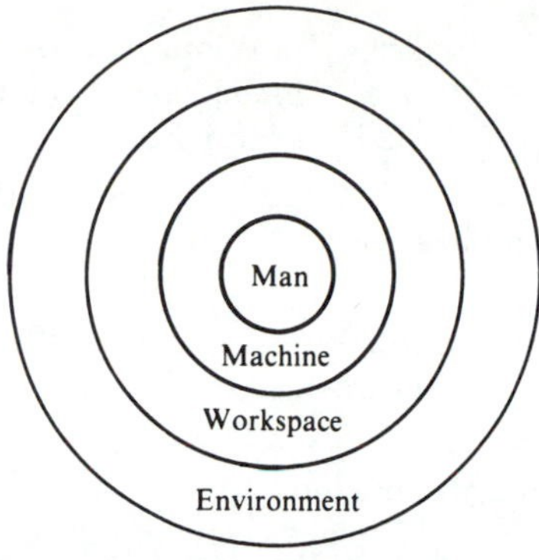

SOURCE: From *Applied Ergonomics Handbook* (p. 10) by Applied Ergonomics, 1974, Surrey, England: IPC Science and Technology Press.

approach. In Chapter 13, in the section on organizational design, you may remember the article by Campion and Thayer (1985) that proposed four underlying models of job design. In their taxonomy, redesigning machinery to fit the average operator and thus (on the average) reduce fatigue would have been guided by the biological model.

Human engineering (as well as *biomechanics, ergonomics, psychotechnology,* or *applied experimental psychology*) is the study of man-machine systems that vary in complexity and reliability. For our purposes, it is appropriate to consider a system as including several components sharing a common purpose and a common information flow network. The goal of this particular approach is to design machines and systems that can be more easily and more efficiently used by human beings. Perhaps the most complex and unreliable system the psychologist studies is the *human being.* But the human system is embedded in a larger system, which includes the equipment the human uses to accomplish work, the physical environment in which the work is done, and the social-psychological environment of which the worker is a part. It might seem as if there are two elements, then, to the study of man-machine systems—the person and the equipment. This is too simple a view. Both operator and machine are embedded in two large systems—the workspace and the broader social-psychological environment. This larger view is illustrated in Figure 15–2. This means that when an analysis is prepared for designing a job or a workstation, a series of questions must be considered. Figure 15–3 presents examples of some issues that might be covered in such an analysis. It can be very detailed, much like the job analysis procedures we considered in Chapter 4. Unlike a job analysis, however, it concentrates on the *interactions* between operator and machine, operator and workspace, and operator and environ-

FIGURE 15–3 Workstation Analysis Outline

Man

Consideration of — sex, age, size; physique, intelligence, experience; training, motivation

Definition of operational modes — searching, tracking; monitoring, decision making

Required in final situation and thus consideration of abilities and limitations of human operator for all aspects of the task.

Man-Machine Interaction

Influence, on operator and his decisions, of
- displays—sensory input to operator
- controls—motor output from operator
- panel layouts—display-control compatibility

Based upon study of human, equipment and task operational sequences.

Man-Workspace Interaction

Influence, on operator's position, posture, and reach of
- machine size
- chairs, desks, etc.
- adjacent machines, structures, and material

Man-Environment Interaction

Influence upon behaviour and performance of
- physical aspects
- chemical aspects
- biological aspects
- psychological aspects

Physical:	light and color, noise, heat, ventilation, gravity, movement, electromagnetic, and nuclear radiation
Chemical:	gas or liquid, composition, pressure, smell
Biological:	microbes, insects, animals
Psychological:	workteam, command structure, pay and welfare, shift conditions, discomfort or risk, socio-psychological aspects of the particular factory, neighborhood, town, and type of industry concerned

Special Questions

Consideration of nonstandard conditions, such as errors, exceptional circumstances, or similar factors not included in the previous analysis of normal operation. Consideration of problems peculiar to the specific case under investigation.

SOURCE: From *Applied Ergonomics Handbook* (p. 11) by Applied Ergonomics, 1974, Surrey, England: IPC Science and Technology Press.

ment. Figure 15–4 takes the design process through to its final conclusion. In this case, the issue is the design of a drill press. What are the particular issues or questions that arise in the course of examining the work process? These issues appear in the right-hand column and, in some senses, are the raw material for the human engineer. Design, whether equipment, workspace, or environmental, can be quite exciting. As Figures 15–1 and 15–2 imply, however, our concern in the present chapter will not be with equipment design per se but will be with matching individuals to environments.

PREDECESSORS TO HUMAN ENGINEERING

Efforts to fit the job to the operator began largely within engineering and scientific management rather than within psychology. Especially important were those efforts to arrange the work and the workplace optimally. These efforts are embodied in such principles as *work simplification* and *standardization* and utilized the methods of the time-and-motion analysts. The early work of F. W. Taylor (1911) in time analysis and of Gilbreth and Gilbreth (1917) in motion analysis paved the way for human engineering because this research made it apparent that neither the job nor the machine were unalterable but could be analyzed and redesigned for greater efficiency and greater compatibility with the characteristics of the human operator.

Other predecessors of human engineering are to be found in early experimental work on the physical work environment. Thus, as we have seen, the initial phases of the Hawthorne studies were designed to determine the optimum level of illumination at the workplace. While such studies did not investigate the design of the machines or of the job per se, they were concerned with the physical conditions in which workers and machines were expected to function. Today, research on the effects of extreme, unusual, even "hostile" environmental conditions on human performance is an important part of human engineering. It should be noted that human performance and, consequently, the performance of any technological system of which people are a part is always evaluated in the context of a particular physical environment. Factors and principles in the design of such systems that hold true for the usual or "normal" working environment may not be appropriate when environmental conditions are changed. Studies seeking principles of human performance and systems design go hand in hand with the investigation of the physical conditions of work. Extreme, unusual, and hostile environmental conditions can often produce unexpected results. In spite of all the simulation in conjunction with the space program, little was learned about the problem of motion sickness that affects a large number of the astronauts.

AWARENESS OF HUMAN ENGINEERING PROBLEMS

It was not until World War II that the need for the discipline we now call human engineering began to be recognized. Prior to that time, some efforts were made to increase efficiency through job design and improved working

FIGURE 15–4 General Analysis of Bench Drill Operation and Detailed Operational Sequence of the "Drill" Section

Sections of Job

Preliminaries

- Receive drawings and instructions. Get materials and tools
- Mark off and punch workpiece

Man-machine task

- Mount workpiece
- Mount drill
- Set drill depth
- Set drill speed
- Center workpiece
- Drill
- Check hole depth
- Dismount drill
- Deburr hole edge (Mount, run, dismount burr)
- Dismount workpiece

Detailed Operational Sequence of the 'Drill' Section

State at start: Drill Mounted and Depth Set: Drill Speed Set: Workpiece Mounted, Centered, and Clamped

Operational sequence	Notes of questions to be checked as design progresses
Final check of drawing ↓	Where will the drawing be?
Final check drill suitability, size, depth setting and machine speed setting ↓	Can operator easily see and measure drill size, depth setting and machine speed?
Check safety guards in place ↓	Are guards *really easy* to put on? Check with safety officer?
Switch on machine ↓	Which hand? Easy to reach? Emergency off even easier?
Supply lubricant	Which hand? Where is lubricant stored?
Grasp operating lever Lower drill ↓	Which hand? Easy to do? Position comfortable? Control good? Gear ratio, etc—refer to ergonomic data?
Drill tip touches and dimples material ↓	Lighting good enough? Need light on the machine?
Raise drill ↓	
Check position of dimple with punch mark ↓	Lighting good enough?
Lubricate ↓	
Lower drill ↓	
Drill starts to bite ↓ (branches)	
Normal resistance to hand, sound, smell, etc., normal ↓ / Hand feels excessive resistance or sound of binding or smell of over-heating ↓	Is position of operator, workpiece, etc, such that this information will be received by operator easily and quickly?

Check hole position

Clear and clean drill machine

Finishing off

Deliver product to foreman
Return tools, etc,

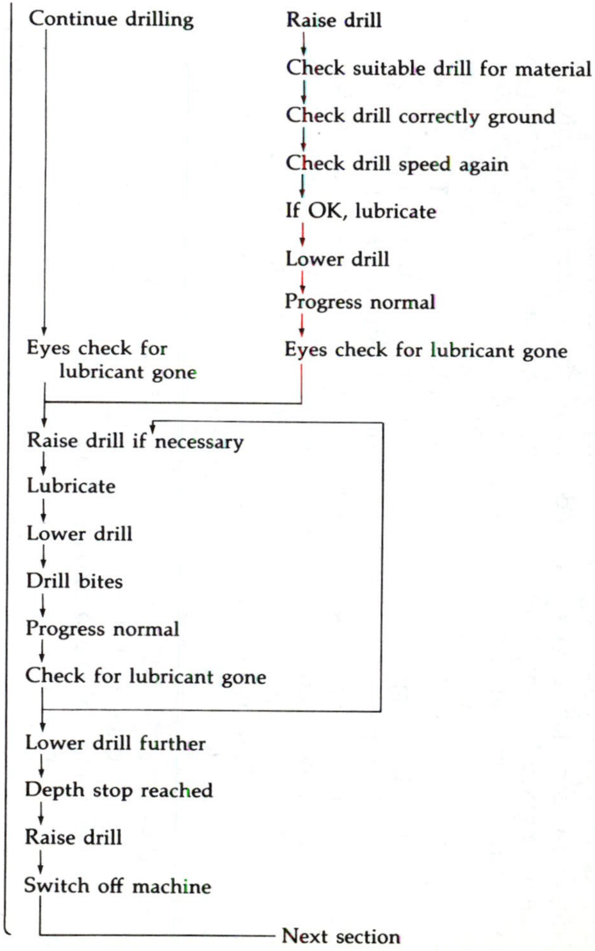

Continue drilling → Eyes check for lubricant gone

Raise drill → Check suitable drill for material → Check drill correctly ground → Check drill speed again → If OK, lubricate → Lower drill → Progress normal → Eyes check for lubricant gone

→ Raise drill if necessary → Lubricate → Lower drill → Drill bites → Progress normal → Check for lubricant gone (→ back to Raise drill if necessary)

→ Lower drill further → Depth stop reached → Raise drill → Switch off machine → Next section

Depth stop securely lockable? No risk of crashing through it?

Is this very easy to do (for safety reasons)?

SOURCE: From *Applied Ergonomics Handbook* (p. 13) by Applied Ergonomics, 1974, Surrey, England: IPC Science and Technology Press.

conditions, but it took the rapid technological developments spurred on by the wartime emergency to foster the realization that machines could be designed that would effectively outrun the operator's ability to control these machines. In this period, rapid developments in technology drastically changed the work tasks of thousands of people. Pilots, trained on an old generation of aircraft, were familiarized with a second generation but often required to fly a third by the time they reached the war zone. They were faced with new dials, gadgets, previously unheard of speeds, and dramatically different maneuvering capabilities. Submarine crews found themselves with sonar equipment, air traffic controllers with radar and with greatly increased air traffic moving at high speeds. In nearly every such situation, tasks were in some respects more complex. It is true that there generally was less physical demand placed on the operator, since muscle power was replaced by motor power, but the number of decisions required and the amount of information to be processed from a variety of sources increased tremendously.

Frequent complaints were received that machines carrying highly respectable engineering specifications for reliable and accurate performance simply were not performing up to standards in field operations. Radar, known to be accurate to within a few yards at, say, ten miles, showed no such accuracy, it was reported. Similarly, airplanes with the potential for maneuverability and safety of operation fell short on both counts. Thus, the evidence piled up that the rapid technological developments fostered by the war had left the human operator far behind. The failures of airplanes, radar, sonar, and other machines were chalked up to "human error," but this was little more than an admission that the performance of technological systems is restricted by the limitations of the humans who must operate them. (We saw some vivid examples of system failure in the last chapter when we looked at all the factors that contributed to the crash of the Air Florida flight into the Potomac River.) Failures dismissed as due to human error could have been avoided in many cases by better equipment design. Increased efforts to improve selection and training programs, though meeting with some success, were not the complete answer to the problem.

It is interesting to note that human engineers are often at odds with design engineers when it comes to the issue of human error. Perrow (1983) has clearly described this tension:

> Human factors engineers are much more tolerant of operators than design engineers, or top management. They see the deceptive designs that produce errors; the overload and inaccessible controls that produce forced errors; the systematic barriers to system comprehension that forces operators to just follow the book when the events are novel and never conceived of by the book's authors. They are often aware of production pressures that are built into the equipment by designers and which override procedural safeguards. Their concern with operators, however, may result in top management and designers associating them with error-prone operators. (p. 533)

The disdain that design engineers have for human engineers seems to be reciprocal. One human engineer resigned from the Institute for Nuclear Power Operations because he felt that the behavioral aspects of safety were being ignored. The design engineers were unwilling to listen to the human engineers: "The idea is if you're an engineer and you're a human, you are a human engineer. If you are a psychologist, you are soft in the head" (Cordes, 1983). Perrow provides an excellent analysis of the interplay between human engineering and organizational psychology that deserves careful consideration. Human factors engineering is not done in a vacuum. Part of the environment in which the research goes on is political. Another part is interpersonal. The manner by which organizations decompose "error" will continue to represent a battlefield for the human engineer until there is a greater appreciation in industrial settings for the man part of the man-machine system. Let's consider the issue of a system in greater detail.

SYSTEMS

An extremely important development in human engineering was the adoption of the notion of *systems*. A system means many different things to different people, and *general systems theory* has developed into a very complex and sophisticated area of study, with applications in many areas of science and engineering. Today, the term *system* is applied to such diverse phenomena as nervous systems, communication systems, and solar systems. In the chapter on organizational behavior, we saw the value of viewing the work organization as an open system, influenced by its specific and general environment.

While there are a number of issues in the definition of a system, the term generally implies some "communication" or interaction among the component parts of some identifiable entity or aggregate. These issues go beyond the scope and purpose of this chapter, however. Our concern is with man-machine systems. Such systems have component parts, some of which are machines, other of which are people. These components interact to determine the behavior, or performance, of the system. Any system under consideration may, in fact, be a subsystem when viewed in a larger context. Thus, a worker and a drill press define a man-machine system, which is at the same time a subsystem of the machine room that in turn is a subsystem of the factory, and so on. This was implied in Figure 15–2.

Man-machine systems are typically designed for some purpose, and the adequacy of the design can be evaluated in terms of how completely and efficiently it achieves this purpose. Among human engineers, the purpose of a system is often referred to as its *mission*. Given a certain mission—"Place a person on the moon and return her safely to earth"—systems designers are able to specify the *systems functions* that must be fulfilled if the mission is to be accomplished. These functions may be grouped into categories such as

FIGURE 15–5 The Communication of Man and Machine

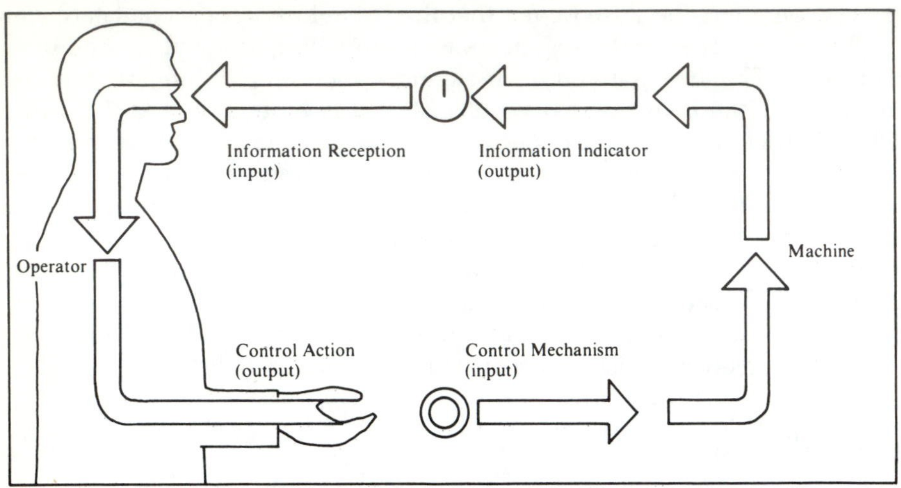

The communication between man and machine can be viewed as an information flow loop connecting their respective inputs and outputs.

SOURCE: From *Applied Ergonomics Handbook* (p. 12) by Applied Ergonomics, 1974, Surrey, England: IPC Science and Technology Press.

"systems guidance functions," "personnel (or 'life') support functions," "systems maintenance functions," and the like. Having identified such functions, systems designers must decide on the *allocation of functions* to human and machine components of the system. In the design of a spaceship, for example, questions arise as to whether certain systems guidance functions should be carried out by humans or by machines, and whether some of the systems maintenance functions should be handled through the use of standby equipment that can be switched on in case of the failure of a subsystem or allocated to human components, who then repair the faulty subsystem or replace it by manually guiding the ship.

A MODEL FOR MAN-MACHINE SYSTEMS

What are the characteristics of a man-machine system? They can be described in a simple way. Consider Figure 15–5. As you can see, the essence of the system is a communication process. The operator sends information through the controls (knobs, levers, switches) and receives information through the displays (dials, gauges). The machine simply reverses these elements. The machine receives information by means of the controls and sends information through the displays. These information sources constitute *potential* sources of input to the human components. The word *potential* is used to indicate that the machine may send information not received by the operator because his sensing equipment is too limited, because his limited attention capacity is occupied with other sources of information, or because he fails to attend at all.

While man and machine do form a system, there are some issues that may be considered from either a human or a machine perspective. You will remember from Chapter 4 that one technique for job analysis (McCormick's PAQ) breaks the job into several components including *input, mediation, and output*. I will use these categories to discuss man-machine systems.

Input from the Man-Machine Perspective

The issue of input seems simple enough. The operator receives an instruction from somewhere and carries it out. The heart of the "problem" lies in the concept of an *instruction*. I will substitute the term *information* for *instruction*. This will enable us to take advantage of a large body of research that tells us something about how individuals deal with stimulation received from the external environment.

It is possible to consider input from two different points of view. First, we have the mechanism *receiving* that input—the human being. To a certain extent, the human operator is limited by sensory capacities. On the other hand, we might consider the nature of the machinery used to *present* that information or input. In engineering terms, we might study the characteristics of *displays*. We will begin our consideration of input issues with an examination of the capacities of the person receiving the information.

Humans as Sensing Devices. The operator receives information about the machine and its performance through the senses. Here we run into the first point in the model where human capabilities and limitations must be considered. As every student of introductory psychology should know, human sensory capabilities, sensitivity, and sensory acuity are limited, often much more severely than we realize. The traditional study of sensory psychology and psychophysics has sought to determine what these limitations are, and a good deal of information has been accumulated. However, human engineers have frequently found that this information is limited to the world of the research laboratory, and many questions have to be asked again under more realistic performance situations. For example, the absolute thresholds for vision and audition as determined by psychophysicists were obtained in highly controlled laboratory environments designed to yield optimum estimates of sensitivity under ideal conditions of sensory adaptation. Only rarely have these scientists been concerned with the operator's ability to detect a signal presented against a noisy background or to see a light flash in the peripheral visual field while busily reading instruments directly in the line of sight.

There are several issues that must be considered in trying to understand

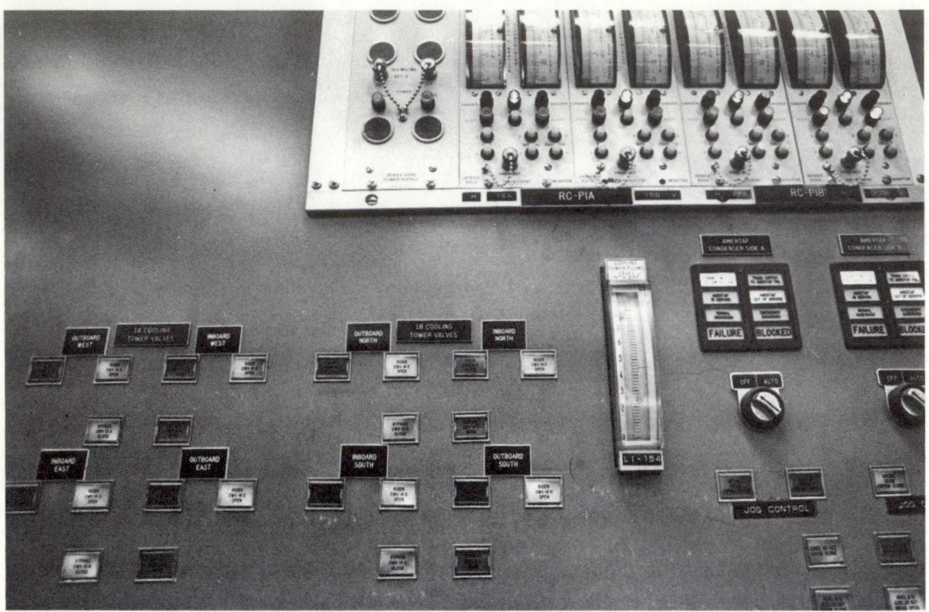

Picture A

Displays can often be enhanced to help the worker find information quickly. Picture A is a section of a nuclear power control room display panel before being modified. Picture B shows the modified panel. It is much easier to isolate information in picture B. (General Public Utility Nuclear Corporation)

how the human senses deal with input. First, we must consider *ranges* of sensation or the capacity of the individual to detect a stimulus. Next, we must consider the efficiency with which an individual *discriminates* among various stimuli, separating the irrelevant from the important. Finally, we must consider the sheer *amount* of input or information that confronts the individual. This last point implies that the more information confronting the individual, the greater the information load (and the greater the demand on the person). There is an exception to this rule, however. If several different inputs are redundant (i.e., the same information being presented in several different forms), then accuracy may be enhanced without being appreciably slowed (Lewandowski & Kobus, 1988).

Displays. The previous section implies that the "answer" to man-machine problems is to build equipment providing information or input to the operator in a form and at a rate that best matches her sensory capacities. This is the way in which the pure experimental psychologist might approach the situation. A different, perhaps more problem-oriented, approach would be to study the relative efficiency of different ways of providing the same information—the advantages and disadvantages of various *displays*. Look at your watch. It most likely has specific marks that break the face into hours

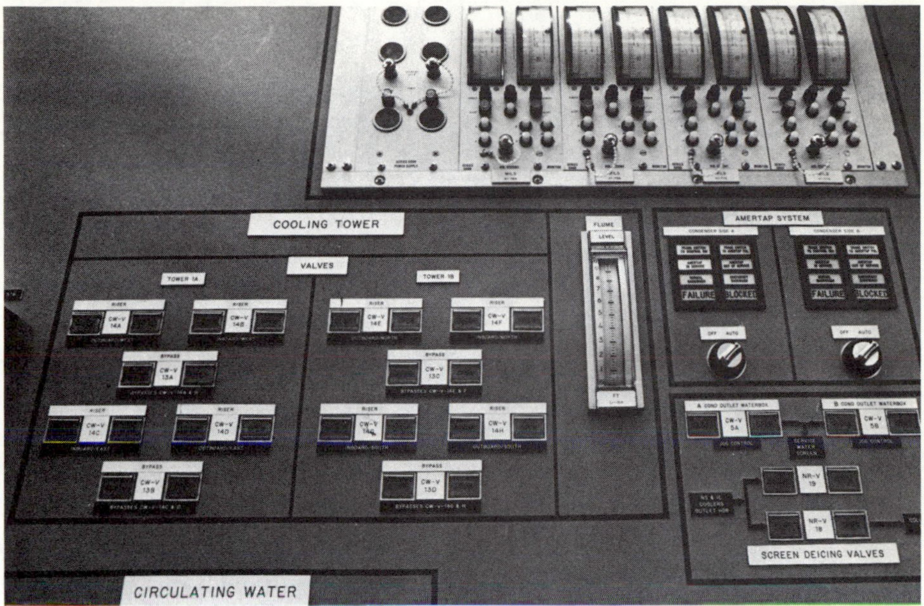

Picture B

and possibly minutes. This is a display. What if there were no such marks but only two hands on a round, unmarked face? Which of these two displays do you think would be more efficient in helping you arrive at class on time? A good deal of the human engineering research that was done in the early days of the field was of this type—the identification of efficient displays. This was probably because the engineering psychologist was more often called upon to *redesign* a system that was causing problems than to design a new system. In looking at system failures, engineering psychologists often found evidence that the load of sensory information on the human operator exceeded his capacity to take it in.

A typical problem faced by the engineering psychologist during World War II was the rapid change in the design of fighter aircraft. The pilot was faced with a bewildering array of dials, gauges, and lights. Even control knobs in many instances required visual monitoring, first to be certain that the appropriate control was being manipulated, then to assume that it was moved to the correct setting. Figure 15–6 shows the interior of the cockpit of an aircraft, with its numerous displays, many of them at wide angles to the normal line of sight of the pilot.

One approach to these problems of overloading of the visual system included attempts to present some types of information through other sensory channels, such as the auditory or tactile senses. It is interesting to note that the visual overload often experienced by busy air traffic controllers is the

FIGURE 15–6 The Cockpit of a Boeing 747-400

SOURCE: Courtesy of Boeing Corporation.

result of redesigning the equipment to eliminate auditory overload. In earlier decades, a great deal more conversation between pilot and controller went on. In order to cut down on this auditory load, information was moved to the visual mode.

This approach assumed, implicitly at least, that people could process more information, "in parallel," as it were, when the information was addressed to different senses, than when it was presented to a single sensory system. Certainly in the case of vision, involving as it does the fixation or focusing of the eye to different display locations, this assumption may be valid. However, we will explore some models of human information processing, including a "single-channel" model, that suggest that information is only processed serially, not in parallel. This might explain why presenting *redundant* information in two different forms does not negatively affect performance. There is really no new *information* being presented in the additional channel. At any rate, this approach was valuable because it revealed some human capabilities for processing auditory and tactile information.

Early attempts at auditory signaling systems included variations on Radio

Range, a system of interlocking tonal signals whereby pilots can chart their course in "blind" approaches to the runway, and Flybar (flying by auditory reference), a system of signals to indicate the "attitude" of the plane (roll, bank, and turn). In the latter system, various combinations of signal intensities and frequencies were explored to determine a pilot's ability to discriminate and use auditory information to control the attitude of the plane. Although such systems have important limitations (see Chapanis, Garner, & Morgan, 1949, for an evaluation), these studies provide valuable information about human performance. For example, it was noted that when three different signals were used to indicate the three aspects of the plane's attitude, pilots frequently attended to one signal and lost track of the others. Also, it was discovered that signal systems requiring absolute identification of signal properties (frequency or intensity) were less reliable than those that included a constant reference tone, thus requiring comparative rather than absolute judgments (Chapanis et al., 1949; Forbes, 1946).

Later on, other sensory systems, particularly the sense of touch, were to be investigated as potential channels of information whereby signals from machines could be communicated to the operators.

The second approach to the problem of overloading of the visual channel included attempts to develop more efficient visual displays. Research on the design of visual displays increased rapidly as the result of evidence gathered from interviews with pilots by Fitts and Jones (1947b). These researchers collected reports of 270 errors, which they then classified into 9 categories. These errors, summarized in Table 15–1, served to identify many research problems in display design. Much of the subsequent research has been reviewed by Fitts (1951) and by Grether (1968). Fitts (1951) reviewed the problems and the research findings in this area under headings such as "problems involving visibility" (size, brightness contrast, color, discrimination of velocity and acceleration, and so on), "problems related to pattern discrimination" (size of numerals and letters, size of dials, spacing of scale markers, pointer design, and so on), and problems related to the "design of quantitative displays" (interpretation of scales, graphs, and tables, for example). Special attention was given to multiple-pointer instruments, such as the standard three-pointer altitude indicator.

The Arrangement of Displays. In addition to research on the design of specific information displays, investigations were directed toward the arrangement of displays on an instrument panel. Little attention had been paid to the location of displays relative to one another or to the operator. Equally significant were instances where the same information display was to be found in one location in one model and in quite a different place in another model of the same equipment.

The problems of visual displays in complex systems were compounded by the fact that information displays designed by one manufacturer were different from those of another manufacturer, even for the same type of information. The "null" position, or safety region, might be at the twelve

TABLE 15–1 Classification of 270 Errors Made by Aircraft Pilots in Responding to Instruments and Signals

	Relative Frequency
1. *Misinterpreting multirevolution instruments.* Mistakes in comprehending information presented by two or more pointers or by a pointer plus a rotating dial viewed through a "window."	18
2. *Misinterpreting direction of indicator movement (reversal errors).* Improper interpretation of an instrument indication with the result that subsequent actions increase rather than reduce an undesirable condition.	17
3. *Misinterpreting visual and auditory signals.* Failing to respond appropriately to hand signals, warning lights or sounds, or radio range signals.	14
4. *Errors involving poor legibility.* Difficulty in seeing numerals, scale markings, or pointers clearly enough to permit quick and accurate reading.	14
5. *Failing to identify a display.* Mistaking one instrument for another or confusing pointers on a multiple-pointer display.	13
6. *Using an inoperative instrument.* Accepting as valid the indication of an instrument that is inoperative or operating improperly.	9
7. *Misinterpreting scale values.* Difficulty in interpolating between numbered scale graduations or failure to assign the correct value to a numbered graduation.	6
8. *Errors associated with illusions.* Difficulties arising out of a conflict between body sensations and information given by visual displays.	5
9. *Omitting the reading of an instrument.* Failing to refer to an instrument at the proper time.	4
Total	100

SOURCE: From *Psychological Aspects of Instrument Display. I. Analysis of 270 "Pilot-Error" Experiences in Reading and Interpreting Aircraft Instruments* (Report No. TSEAA-694–12A, table 1, slightly modified) by P. M. Fitts and R. E. Jones, 1947a, Dayton, OH: Aero Medical Laboratory, Air Material Command.

o'clock position on one dial but at the three, six, or nine o'clock position on another model. Little wonder that a pilot, swamped with a myriad of decisions to be made within a few seconds, might make an error, especially when she has been transferred suddenly from one type of aircraft to another.

The answer to these problems may seem quite simple: standardize the dial design and arrangement of displays for all models. Certainly, this is a sensible suggestion and, no doubt, a valid one as far as it goes. Standardization in this sense is quite consistent with the principles of efficient learning and transfer of training. Standardization even of suboptimally designed instruments would almost surely improve human performance and reduce human error, but how much better it would be to standardize with optimally designed displays, arranged in an optimal configuration. Thus, "standardization" as an answer to these problems immediately leads to questions about the optimal way to design certain kinds of information: What kinds of information are to be displayed? What use must be made of the information? Is the interpretation of the information dependent upon information from other sources? If so, how should these sources be arranged relative to one another? Finally, questions are raised as to the optimum design of the individual information display, its size, markings, pointers, and other properties.

All these questions are legitimate starting points for psychological research. They focus attention on the nature of the physical equipment rather than sensory processes of the operator. Nevertheless, both approaches—the sensory approach and the display approach—deal with the information-input part of the man-machine system. In the next section, we will consider what happens to this information when it is received by the human operator.

Mediation in Man-Machine Systems

As you could see from the earlier diagram of the man-machine system, the human component mediates or intervenes between two machine components. Information is presented through some mechanical means, and the operator responds through the use of mechanical devices of some type. The mechanical means for input may be as simple as a memo or as complicated as a radar display; similarly, the mechanical devices by which the human responds may be as simple as a telephone or as complicated as the controls in the cab of a multistory crane. Regardless of the sophistication of the physical system, the human being is required to *process* the information before making the appropriate response. It is the information-processing activities of the worker that represent both the strength and the weakness of the *man* part of the man-machine system.

Humans as Processors of Information. The operator is not simply a channel through which the information in a man-machine system flows. Once the information is sensed, it must be coded, or classified and interpreted in some way. In a way, it is as though the operator says, "I see a signal; now what does it mean?" Classifying and interpreting the signal is, in effect, answering the question, What does it mean? To classify signals, the operator must compare them with information stored in long-term memory. Thus, the sound of a buzzer in a particular context means something only when the sound can be matched with the memorial representation of a similar experi-

Many jobs require complex and rapid sensory information processing. (Federal Aviation Administration)

ence with which a certain sound has been associated. The sound may be identified as "the signal that it is lunchtime" or "the signal that the cake is baked" only if, through prior learning, the signal has been coded in such a way.

Even though the signal is coded and its meaning is precisely understood, there is no guarantee that the correct response will be made. Consider the worker watching the needle of a pressure gauge climb steadily into the "danger" zone. He "gets the message," the meaning is unequivocally clear, but instead of closing the shutoff valve, he calls for help or scurries to a safe place. The problem is that while he can *encode* the message, he cannot *decode* it into an appropriate response. Efficient processing of information involves the learning of both stimulus and response codes and the appropriate relationships between them. It may also involve complex transformations of the

FIGURE 15–7 A Diagram Showing What Occurs in Sensation

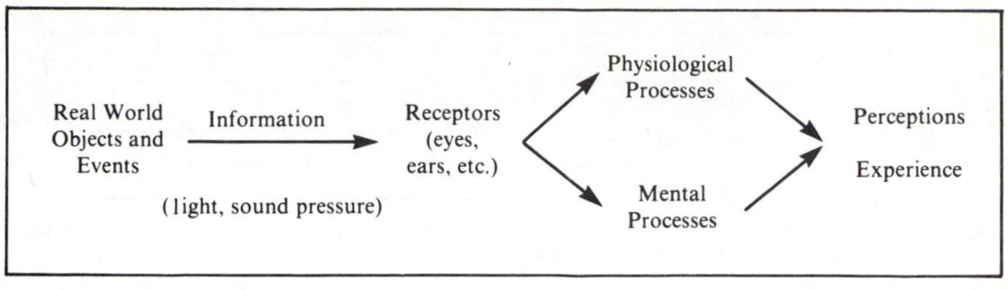

SOURCE: From *Psychology: The Science of People* (2nd ed.) (p. 94) by F. J. Landy, 1987, Englewood Cliffs, NJ: Prentice-Hall.

incoming information, including arithmetic operations, estimates of probabilities, and decisions with respect to the choices among alternative responses. It should be apparent that to predict human performance in a complex man-machine-environment system a good deal must be known about the ways in which people operate on the information they receive.

An Information-Processing Model. A number of models of varying complexity have been offered by psychologists to describe human information processing. All these models include both sensation and perception. Figures 15–7 and 15–8 detail those two processes. But for our purposes, we need a more detailed view of what happens in the organization-interpretation-action chain. This view is provided by Figure 15–9. It describes the major cognitive steps or stages of processing and some of the principal mechanisms involved. It is characterized by four stages. The first stage is the "Stimulus Preprocessing" stage, in which physical stimuli are received, registered through the sensory mechanisms, and converted to neural impulses. The

FIGURE 15–8 A Diagram of the Three Basic Elements of Perception: Search/Attention, Organization, and Interpretation

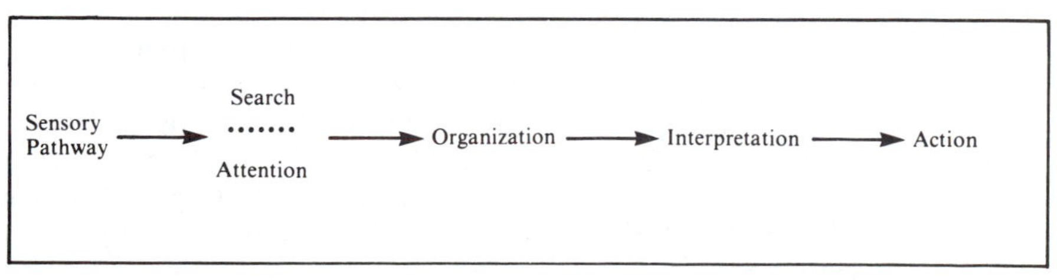

SOURCE: From *Psychology: The Science of People* (2nd ed.) (p. 127) by F. J. Landy, 1987, Englewood Cliffs, NJ: Prentice-Hall.

FIGURE 15–9 A Simple Model of Stages in the Processing of Information

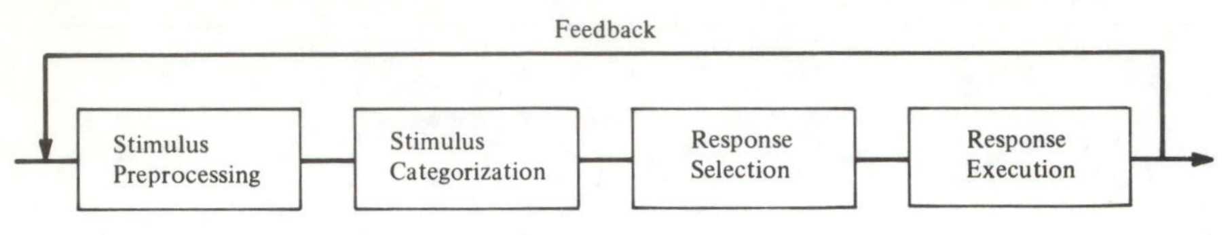

SOURCE: Based on the model suggested in "Choice Reaction Time: An Analysis of the Major Theoretical Positions" by E. E. Smith, 1968, *Psychological Bulletin, 69*.

second stage is the "Stimulus Categorization" stage at which the signals are classified or categorized. At this second stage, the signal is identified or "recognized"; that is, it is compared with information stored in memory and can then be labeled as, for example, "a police siren," "a skyrocket," "frying onions," or whatever, including "an unfamiliar signal." This last case implies that the signal does not match anything stored in the person's memory—it is unrecognized.

The third stage of this model, labeled "Response Selection," refers to the process following stimulus registration and classification in which an "appropriate" response is selected. In the case of a red traffic light, the response might be to press the brake pedal of the car. The choice of responses and the predictability of response selection, of course, depends on memory. However, it may be meaningful to consider this a different type of memory from that referred to in the classification stage. An example may help to make this point clear.

Consider the example just used of the person who saw the pointer on a pressure gauge climbing into the danger zone. The signal was registered and categorized. The person clearly recognized the meaning of the signal from past experiences stored in memory but did not make the most appropriate response, because that response had not been learned or associated with the signal. In other words, stimulus categorization or recognition depends on what is sometimes called *perceptual memory*, whereas response selection depends on having associated certain responses with certain signals, or what is often called *associative memory*. Whether we choose to consider these two types of learning as involving different memory processes depends in part on how we choose to treat the recognition process. If we take the position that recognition ("a red traffic light" or "a danger signal") is a response learned to a particular signal—a cognitive response—but not different in kind from the overt response of pressing the brake pedal, then we may find it unnecessary to include two different memory processes in our model of information processing.

The final stage ("Response Execution") in this simple model is the *execution* of the responses that have been selected. Ability to execute the appropriate response with speed and precision obviously depends, among many other things, on the nature of the response and on how well it has been learned. In a sense, the difference between response selection and response execution is analogous to the difference between theory and practice. People may learn what the appropriate response is; they "know" which response to make and what the desired effects of the response are, but their ability to execute it may be limited by their ability to differentiate a response of one amplitude, force, direction, or duration from another. One can argue at this point that the limitation we are describing is really a limitation of response selection—not of response execution. From this view, response execution is simply the highly automatic "running off" of whatever response was selected, and if it is in error, that is because an inappropriate response—one having the wrong amplitude, force, direction, or duration—was selected. We need not pursue this question at this point, although it obviously is related to the way in which we model the processing of information.

Feedback. Humans are not "open-loop" systems; rather, they receive information about their responses themselves. Without such feedback, or knowledge of results, about the outcomes of one's responses, it would be impossible for a person systematically to modify, adapt, and improve performance. When, for example, we push the brake pedal in response to the traffic light, we may feel ourselves thrown forward by the sudden deceleration and may hear our tires squeal and our passengers complain. We have received feedback about our response that enables us to evaluate its appropriateness. At the same time, we receive information about the response itself—its rate, force, amplitude, direction, pressure, and so on—from the kinesthetic receptors in the muscles, tendons, and joints of our legs and from the touch receptors on the bottom of our feet. The latter information defines "that response" and we know that "that response" was inappropriate, since it did not lead to the desired effect on the environment. This information is stored in memory and serves as a basis for evaluating subsequent responses selected in reaction to similar signals.

If one can assume either that a person can compare the response that has been selected for execution with some *memorial representation* of the "right" response or that such a memorial representation actually governs the response selection process, then it makes sense to conceive of the learning of skilled performance as the *perfecting of the memorial representation of the appropriate response.* This "sharpening" of the criterion for behavior obviously depends on the feedback of information of two sorts: (1) information about the discrepancy of the outcome of the response as compared with some "intended" or "desired" outcome and (2) information about the characteristics of the response itself. Whenever possible, it makes sense to minimize the necessity for tapping memory. This can be accomplished by providing the individual with an example of what she should be looking for. In quality control functions, this might be a sample of a barely acceptable item or product. This would define the border between an item accepted and one rejected. In electronics testing, this might represent a picture of the correct wave form that is displayed next to an oscilloscope on which actual components are being tested.

As you can see from even this brief presentation of an information-processing model, the concepts are very complicated. In the past two decades, these issues have become the focus of an increasingly important area of psychology known as *cognitive psychology.* I cannot hope to present you with all the relevant issues with respect to information processing. Nevertheless, by looking at the model I have presented, you can see that there are distinct *operations* that the worker performs on the information prior to executing a response. It should be clear that these operations can be helped or hindered by work design. In particular, it seems as if *feedback* is a critical aspect of the environment that is under the direct control of the organization. One might also consider the possibility of improving the general information-processing capabilities of the work force through selection and training procedures. But even with a select and highly trained work force, the nature of information presentation and environmental feedback can have substantial effects on the efficiency with which the system functions. We will consider the issue of feedback and its value in efficient action again when we examine the use of computers and robots at the workplace.

Output from the Man-Machine Perspective

In considering the input portion of the man-machine model that I presented, I distinguished between input issues that were primarily human in orientation (e.g., sensory mechanisms) and those that were more related to the machine component (displays). We can make similar distinctions when we consider the *output* of a man-machine system. In our model of information processing, we dealt with a component called *response execution.* The issue of execution is a crucial one in performance. We may be perfectly aware of which response is called for and yet be incapable of making it correctly. This is the point at which the skills and abilities of the worker typically enter the system. While you may *know* what the task of a tennis player is, the fact that you continually miss the ball when you swing at it says something about your capacity to execute the desired response.

Human Performance Abilities. Psychologists have devoted a good deal of effort to the development of selection and training programs designed to ensure that the requisite skills will be attained. However, as Fleishman (1967a) pointed out, much of the information regarding predictor tests (and training procedures) that has been gathered in the past proves to be inapplicable as new systems are considered. This is true in part because each new system is somewhat different, placing new demands or a new combination of demands on the operator. It is also true in part because we do not have an adequate system for classifying the tasks that people perform, that is, a *taxonomy of tasks.* Neither do we have a clear conception of the *structure of human abilities* that underlies performance on different tasks.

Many psychologists have bemoaned this state of affairs and have called for a taxonomy of tasks that will allow more accurate prediction from one set of operations or functions to another. One approach to this problem used the methodology of correlation and factor analysis, as well as experimentation. An outstanding example of this approach is the work of Fleishman and his associates (e.g., Fleishman, 1966, 1967a; Fleishman & Parker, 1962; Fleishman & Rich, 1963). Fleishman made the distinction between *abilities,* which he defines as the more general traits of individuals inferred from intertask correlations, and *skills,* which are defined in terms of performance of specific tasks. Thus, *abilities* are seen as the attributes the individual has inherited or acquired in previous situations and brings to the new task situation. *Skill* is the level of proficiency attained on the task as a function of the level of ability, or abilities, the individual possesses and the particular strategies developed in the task situation. Acquiring a skill, then, refers to developing the sequence of responses or the degree of precision of behavior required on a specific task. By definition, abilities are related to performance on a number of tasks.

Fleishman's approach has been to describe tasks and to identify a taxonomy of basic tasks in terms of the abilities that are required to perform them. Typically, he has given a large battery of performance tests to a large sample of individuals. The scores from the various tasks are then intercorrelated, providing some notion of which tasks "go together," that is, call upon some of the same abilities. Further information about the abilities common to different tasks is obtained when the intercorrelations are factor analyzed (see the "Technical Appendix" of Chapter 2 for a description of factor analysis). The outcome of the factor analysis is a set of factors defined in terms of the "loadings" of the different tests on a common factor. These loadings are then examined in an attempt to describe or label the ability common to all the tests that have significant loadings on the factor. This description, or labeling, of the factors can be thought of as a process of hypothesizing the existence of an underlying ability with certain characteristics.

The hypothesized abilities are tested further by attempts to develop more "pure" performance tests to measure the ability as it has been conceptualized. These *reference tests,* as Fleishman calls them, are then used to predict performance on the tasks that defined the factor. In this way, a set of reference tests are developed and refined, which in turn define a set of abilities.

As a result of several years of research involving over 200 different tasks and several thousand subjects, Fleishman and his associates have identified and refined 11 factors that account for a large part of the variance in human motor performance. These factors were listed and described earlier, in Figure 6–8. To review briefly, the factors were labeled as follows: control precision, multilimb coordination, response orientation, reaction time, speed of arm movement, rate control, manual dexterity, finger dexterity, arm-hand steadiness, wrist and finger speed, and aiming.

These 11 factors are relatively independent of one another; that is, the possession of a high level of ability on one factor does not necessarily mean a high level of ability on the other factors. This means that the reference test developed to measure one of the abilities should be predictive of performance on tasks or jobs if and only if that particular ability is important in the performance of that task. Fleishman, like Seashore (1951) and others before him, found little evidence to support the notion of a general factor of perceptual-motor performance. Therefore, it is probably fallacious to predict that an operator who is highly skilled at assembling very small parts will necessarily be highly skilled at, say, driving a car or steering a ship, assuming that the first task involves *finger dexterity* and the second involves *control precision*.

Another significant finding from this approach is the consistent evidence that, with practice, performance on a given task is increasingly a function of habits and skills specific to that task. In other words, abilities that were highly related to performance in the early stages of skill development tend to be less important after much practice. It is as though the abilities give the trainee a "head start" but do not necessarily guarantee that a high level of performance will be attained. In addition to the "group" factors that define the abilities, the factor-analytic studies frequently yield evidence for such "task-specific" factors with a high factor loading for a single task. These loadings increase with practice. This means that as skill increases, performance is less dependent on the more general ability factors and more dependent on the strategies developed to cope with the task. This evidence led Seashore (1951) to state what he called the *work-methods hypothesis:*

> Individual differences in any human ability (not just motor skills) are attributed to three groups of factors: (1) the physical constant of the various organs (especially sense organs, nervous system, and musculature) employed, (2) the general qualitative pattern of component actions involved, and (3) the refinement of the component actions with respect to both strength and timing so as to produce an optimal pattern of action, [but that superior performance is usually the result of] . . . hitting upon qualitative patterns of action, or *work methods,* that make the work easier. (p. 1353)

Skilled performance was seen by Seashore as more often limited by inadequate patterning or sequencing of actions than by sensory, nervous system, or muscular limitations of the operator. On the other hand, a high level of performance was seen by Seashore to be a function of work methods "hit upon rather than carefully thought out or even recognized afterward" (p. 1354). He felt that such work methods or strategies were largely a matter of trial and error and rather impervious to attempts to train the operator. The work-methods hypothesis is consistent with the evidence that task-specific factors increase in importance as practice continues, whereas the more general abilities tend to decrease or drop out: performance in a given task is increasingly a function of the particular work methods hit upon by the operator and less and less a function of the pattern of abilities that he brings to the task situation.

This point is well illustrated in Figure 15–10 from Fleishman (1966). Here it can be seen that the factor specific to the task (in this case, a reaction-time task) accounts for an increasing amount of the total variance in the task performance, whereas the reference measures of the more general abilities become less and less important.

In one sense, Figure 15–10 presents a discouraging picture. It suggests that although we may be able to develop measures of abilities that rather successfully predict performance and the rate of improvement early in the development of a skill, it may be much more difficult to predict really high levels of performance. Such results also provide an explanation of the fact that early performance on a task is seldom very predictive of later performance: the abilities that give the trainee a "running start" are not necessarily those that ensure the development of a high level of skill. Furthermore, the operator who starts out badly may fortuitously hit upon a strategy at a later time that leads to skillful performance. However, while some abilities (e.g., spatial relations) become less predictive of performance with practice, other abilities (e.g., reaction time and rate of movement) become more predictive as skill develops.

This last point is illustrated in a study by Fleishman and Rich (1963) involving performance on a two-hand coordination task. In this study, 40 subjects were given practice on the task, then divided into two groups on the basis of their scores on a test of spatial ability. Performance on the two-hand coordination task was then compared for these two groups. The results are shown in Figure 15–11. This figure shows that those subjects with high spatial ability had a head start on the task. They performed better during the early stages of practice. However, their advantage was short-lived: after about a half hour of practice, they were no better than the group with low spatial ability scores. When these same subjects were divided into two groups on the basis of their scores on a test of kinesthetic sensitivity, the results were quite different. As Figure 15–12 shows, kinesthetic sensitivity was not related to performance on the coordination task early in training; subjects with high scores on the measure showed an advantage only after the first half of the training session. Thus, the ability (visual spatial orientation) that was important for performance early in practice was not the same as the ability (kinesthetic sensitivity) related to achievement of a high level of skill on the task. Incidentally, this finding also supports the notion that people rely relatively more on feedback from their environment (via the exteroceptors: vision, audition, etc.) in the early stages of the development of perceptual-motor skills but come to rely more and more on kinesthetic information as the skill is being perfected.

This emphasis on human performance abilities can be quite useful in

FIGURE 15–10 Factors Related to Skilled Performance

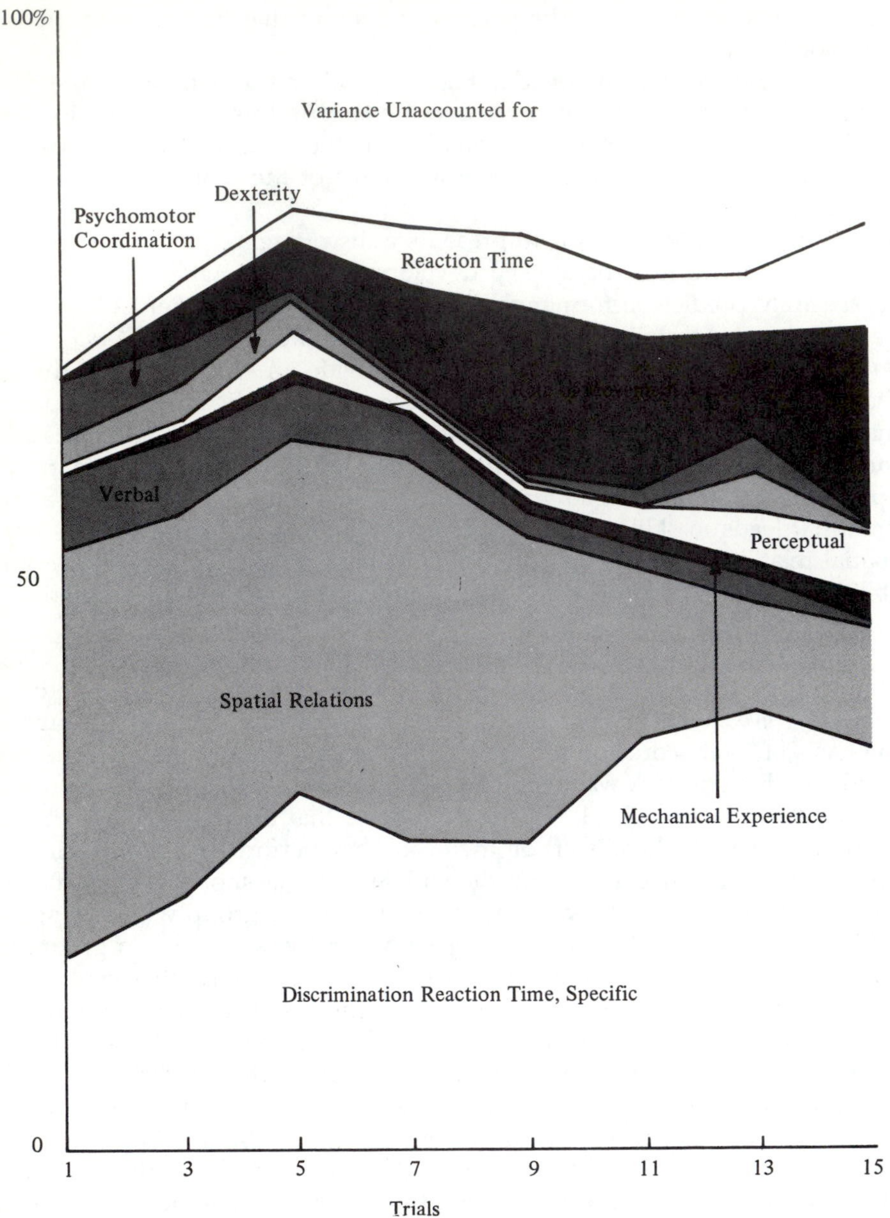

Percentage of variance represented by each factor at different stages of practice on the Discrimination Reaction Time Task. Percentage of variance is represented by the area shaded in for each factor.

SOURCE: From "Human Abilities and the Acquisition of Skill" (p. 160) by E. A. Fleishman, in E. A. Bilodeau (Ed.), *Acquisition of Skill*, 1966, New York: Academic Press.

FIGURE 15–11 Comparison of Two-Hand Coordination Acquisition Curves for Groups High and Low on the Aerial Orientation Test

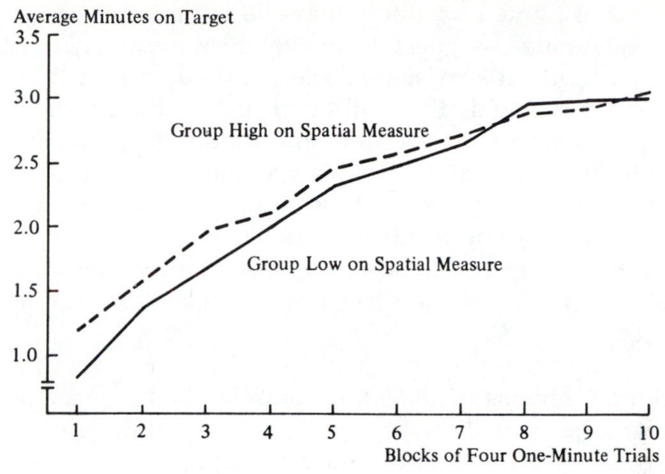

SOURCE: From "Role of Kinesthetic and Spatial-Visual Abilities in Perceptual Motor Learning" by E. A. Fleishman and S. Rich, 1963, *Journal of Experimental Psychology, 66.*

FIGURE 15–12 Comparison of Two-Hand Coordination Acquisition Curves for Groups High and Low on the Kinesthetic Sensitivity Measure

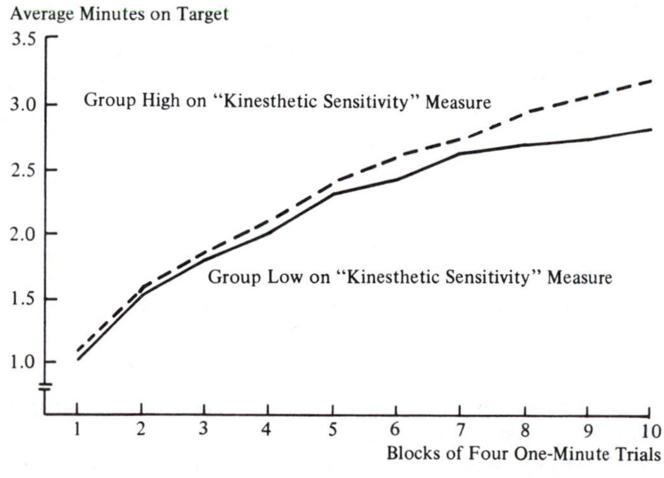

SOURCE: From "Role of Kinesthetic and Spatial-Visual Abilities in Perceptual Motor Learning," by E. A. Fleishman and S. Rich, 1963, *Journal of Experimental Psychology, 66.*

developing man-machine systems. Knowing the capabilities and limitations of human operators tells us a good deal about what properties the machine components of the man-machine system should have. In addition, knowledge of requirements of human operators that will be imposed by machine and equipment configurations suggests a way in which the engineering approach can be integrated with the personnel selection and training approach. One can determine the demands that will be placed on the operator before the fact and develop appropriate selection and training mechanisms to prepare the operator for those demands. But, as was the case with the input to the man-machine system, the psychologist is often consulted after a problem has occurred. This requires one to identify problems with existing control and execution systems rather than to design completely new ones. Thus, a second approach that one might take to system output would be an examination of control devices.

Identifying Problems of Machine Control. Many of the issues raised in the earlier discussion of displays also apply to the control devices by which a worker communicates with and guides the equipment. In many machine systems, the number of controls—knobs, levers, buttons, toggle switches, handwheels, and the like—might increase as rapidly as the number of displays. This is likely to be the case, since most displays imply some control action, at least when some critical level is indicated by the display. Thus, in many systems, such as the aircraft in Figure 15–6, the cockpit space not filled with displays is filled with controls.

One of the early investigations of control problems by psychologists is significant for a number of reasons. In the first place, it demonstrates the first step in any systematic investigation—identify and describe the problem. Second, the study, despite its relative simplicity, gave a good deal of direction to human engineering research in the 1940s and 1950s. The study, conducted by Fitts and Jones (1947a), involved interviews with about 500 pilots and former pilots. Essentially, the researchers applied the critical-incident technique. Pilots were asked to "describe in detail an error in the operation of a cockpit control (flight control, engine control, toggle switch, selector switch, trim-tab control, etc.) which was made by yourself or another person whom you were watching at the time."

The researchers analyzed the replies given by the pilots and found that they could be classified into six categories, shown in Figure 15–13. The following examples of some of these types of errors were provided by an experienced pilot.

1. *Substitution errors.* In the early days of the retractable landing gear, pilots often mistakenly raised the wheels immediately after landing, causing considerable danger, embarrassment, and damage to the airplane. This was because it had been habit to raise the flaps shortly after landing, and the pilot simply pulled the wrong lever—the landing gear retraction lever.

FIGURE 15–13 Classification of 460 Errors Made by Pilots in Operating Aircraft Controls

1. *Substitution errors.* Confusing one control with another or failing to identify a control when it was needed. In general, most of these errors were due to (a) lack of uniformity in the placement of controls, (b) inadequate separation of controls, and (c) lack of a coding system to help the pilot identify controls positively by the sense of touch alone.
2. *Adjustment errors.* Operating a control too slowly or too rapidly, moving a switch to the wrong position, or following the wrong sequence in operating several controls. The most common single kind of error in this category was made by turning the fuel-selector switch so that it was halfway between two tanks and leaving it in a position where fuel could flow from neither tank, or actually turning the switch to the wrong tank.
3. *Forgetting errors.* Failing to check, unlock, or use a control at the proper time.
4. *Reversal errors.* Moving a control in a direction opposite to that necessary to produce the desired result. Many such errors could be traced to the fact that controls sometimes would not move in "expected" directions.
5. *Unintentional activation.* Accidentally operating a control without being aware of it.
6. *Inability to reach.* Difficulty in reaching a control.

SOURCE: Adapted from *Analysis of 460 "Pilot-Error" Experiences in Operating Aircraft Controls* (Report No. TSEAA-649–12) by P. M. Fitts and R. E. Jones, 1947a, Dayton, OH: Engineering Division, Air Material Command.

When the general substitution error became obvious, the locations of the actuation levers were standardized. The gear lever was placed on the left of the throttles, and the flap lever on the right of the throttles. They have also been coded for touch by making the gear lever handle in the shape of a small tire. The flap lever is shaped like a wing cross section. There are still occasional substitution errors, but they have been greatly reduced.

2. *Adjustment errors.* In Cessna aircraft in the mid-1960s, the fuel selector switch was on the floor between the two pilot seats. It had four positions—off at the six o'clock position, left tank at nine, both tanks at twelve, and right tank at three. The selector handle was rotated to point at the desired position. It was required to be in the "both" or twelve o'clock position for landing. In one incident, a student pilot was making his before-landing check as he approached the landing field. When he called, "Fuel selector, both," he put his hand on the selector lever and felt that the instructor pilot had moved it to the three o'clock position. That was a common practice to determine the student's proficiency in performing the checklist items. Without looking at the selector lever, the student pilot turned it so that it was in line with the twelve o'clock position (or so he thought). This was a serious error because the instructor pilot had placed the indicator in the nine o'clock position, not the three o'clock position. Approximately 30

seconds later, the engine stopped running—the student had accidentally adjusted the selector to the six o'clock "off" position. Returning the selector to "both" quickly restored engine power, and the student had learned a valuable lesson: Look at the fuel selector switch before adjusting it.

3. *Forgetting errors.* The pilot was giving six people a ride to a work site on a cold winter day in Alaska. He did not use his checklist because he was in a hurry and it was very cold. He forgot to remove an external control lock in his haste. The control lock keeps the ailerons and elevator control surfaces from moving to protect them from damage by the wind when the airplane is on the ground. The rudder controls worked normally and were used to position the aircraft for takeoff. The pilot initiated his takeoff, and as the airplane reached flying speed, it lifted off the ground approximately 10 feet. At that point, the pilot found that he could not control roll and pitch, and the aircraft crashed, killing all aboard, because of the forgotten control lock.[1]

The fruitfulness of Fitts and Jones's critical-incident study should be obvious. Each of the six categories of errors suggests a number of problems in the design of machine controls, some of which may be unique to the task of piloting an airplane but many of which may be common to the design of a wide range of machines. This analysis led to a host of studies on the design of control devices, on location size, on shape coding of controls, and on human abilities to perform control operations.

Figure 15–14 shows the device used in one study of control design (W. C. Jenkins, 1947). The purpose of this study was to determine the tactile discriminability of various control knob shapes, so that a set of knobs could be prescribed that would not be confused by the operator. In the experiment, 25 different knob designs were used. The experimental subject, who was blindfolded, was allowed to grasp one of the knobs for one second. Then the "lazy Susan" on which the knobs were mounted was rotated to a randomly chosen starting position. The subject then felt each knob in turn until he thought he recognized the original knob. In this way, it was possible to determine which shapes were confused with which other shapes. Subjects were tested with and without gloves. As a result of the study, two sets of eight knobs were identified such that the shapes within each set were rarely confused with one another. Thus, the use of either set, together with location coding in a machine system, would allow essentially errorless performance, without the need for visual monitoring.

The Interactions of Controls and Displays. Thus far, we have treated problems of display and control design separately, as though you could determine the optimum design and arrangement of one without considering the other. Up to a point, this is probably a safe assumption. We can assess

---

[1]I am indebted to Ronald T. Talcott for these examples (personal communication, 1974).

FIGURE 15–14 Shape-Coded Controls

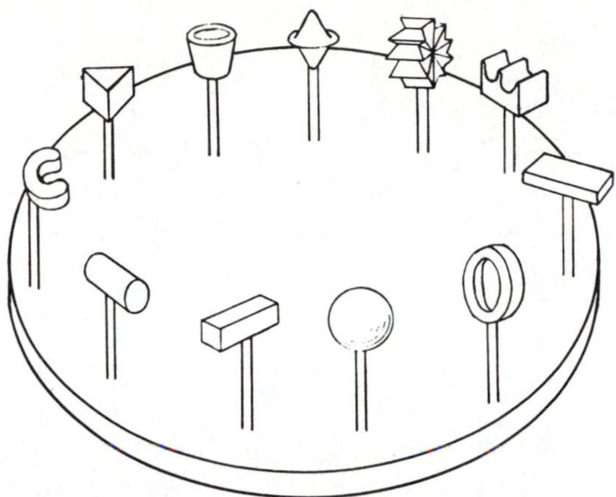

The apparatus used by Jenkins (1947) to select knobs for shape coding of controls. The 11 knob shapes shown were found to be readily identifiable by touch.

SOURCE: From "The Tactual Discrimination of Shapes for Coding Aircraft-Type Controls" by W. O. Jenkins, in P. M. Fitts (Ed.), *Psychological Research on Equipment Design*, 1947, Washington, D.C.: U.S. Government Printing Office.

the visibility, legibility, and error rates of dials of different designs; the discriminability of different control shapes; locations; and the precision of control movements in this manner. However, when questions arise as to the optimum design of a display *for a specific control operation*, then both the design of the control and of the display must be considered. In such a situation, we are concerned with the extent to which particular display configurations "command" certain control actions rather than others.

Our everyday experiences provide many examples in which information displays command or fail to command appropriate control responses. For example, the selector display on a radio may have a pointer that moves across a fixed horizontal scale of radio wave frequencies. The pointer is controlled by a knob, which may be turned either clockwise or counterclockwise to move the pointer. What should be the linkage between the knob and the pointer? Should a clockwise turn of the knob move the pointer to the left or to the right? Should the linkage be reversed if the pointer is fixed and the scale is moved past the pointer? Suppose the display is placed on the front of the radio, but the knob is on the side (as with many small portable models); what should then be the relation between control and pointer movement?

Many questions such as these arise in the design of equipment controls and displays. Figure 15–15 illustrates one problem with which most of us are familiar. Four models of ordinary kitchen stoves are presented, each with a different configuration of controls and burners ("displays"). Now, suppose

FIGURE 15–15 Models of Four Stoves Tested by Chapanis and Lindenbaum

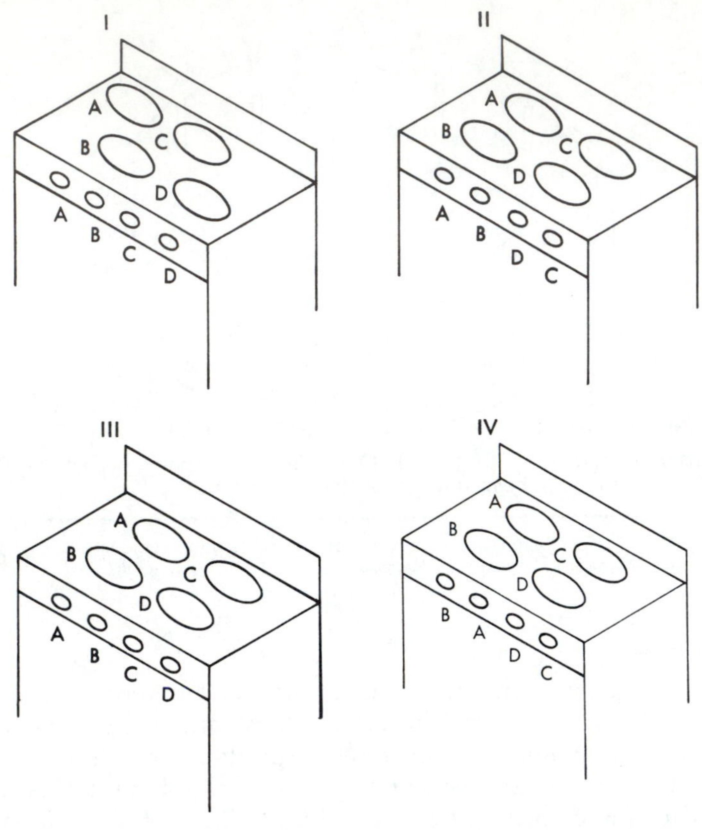

SOURCE: From "A Reaction Time Study of Four Control-Display Linkages" by A. Chapanis and L. E. Lindenbaum, 1959, *Human Factors*, 2. © 1959, by the Human Factors Society, Inc. and reproduced by permission.

that your favorite dinner is burning or boiling over on one of the burners. Which configuration will ensure the quickest and most accurate control action? Chapanis and Lindenbaum (1959) conducted an experiment to answer this question.

In their experiment, a small light came on near the center of one of the burners on one of the stoves shown in Figure 15–15. The subjects' task was to turn off the light as quickly as possible by turning one of the knobs. In all, 1,200 trials were recorded for each stove, 20 trials for each of 60 experimental subjects. The results showed that with stove I there were no errors, whereas stoves II, III, and IV had 26 percent, 38 percent, and 43 percent errors, respectively. The speed with which responses were made agreed perfectly with the error data: stove I was operated with the shortest average response times; stove IV, the longest response times.

A basic method in the study of control-display relationships is to determine the *population stereotype* for responses to information displays. This term refers to the "norm" or typical response of a large sample of people when they are faced with a control-display configuration. A simple example is a situation in which subjects are asked to turn a doorknob to open a door. The experimenter simply records the percentages of people who initially turn the knob clockwise or counterclockwise. The *index of stereotypy* is directly proportional to the percentage of people choosing the preferred response. Thus, in the "doorknob" example, the index of stereotypy would be zero if half the subjects turned the knob closkwise, whereas the other half turned it counterclockwise. Stereotypes can be weak or strong. A strong stereotype is one that is found in a large percentage of people. A weak stereotype is the modal response in a sample, but it may not be a majority or even a large percentage.

Data on population stereotypes have been recorded for many display-control configurations. Such information is of obvious value for designing the linkage between controls and displays. The more often a particular control action is chosen in response to a particular display of information, the more *compatible* the display-control arrangement is said to be. In Figure 15–16, I have presented a number of questions dealing with response stereotypes. Match your choices to those of an expert group of human factors specialists, engineers, and a group of female friends and relatives of the engineers. As you can see from the results that are presented in Figure 15–17, some choices are clear and some are not so clear. How did you do?

The concept display-control, or stimulus-response (S-R) compatibility, refers to the "ease" or naturalness with which a set of responses is linked to a set of signals by the operator. Population stereotypes constitute one of the determinants of S-R compatibility: the higher the index of stereotypy, the more compatible the display-control arrangement.

In a study dealing with response stereotypy to auditory information, Simon and his associates (J. R. Simon, Mewaldt, Acosta, & Hu, 1976) suggested that population stereotypes might be thought of as examples of performance limitations of the worker. They found that it was more natural for subjects to move a switch up in response to a high tone and down to a low tone than vice versa. In this case, if we designed a system that required the worker to move a switch *up* in response to a *low* tone, we could expect frequent errors. One way of viewing this situation is that the performance of the operator is limited to the degree to which the machine requires a response that is incompatible with a natural tendency. This is not to say that natural tendencies cannot be overcome—most can. But the point is that if we are aware of these tendencies before the fact, we may design the system in such

FIGURE 15–16 Population Stereotype Quiz

1. Knob turn

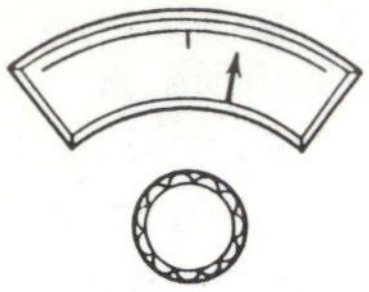

1. To move the arrow-indicator to the center of the display, how would you turn the knob?

_____ Clockwise
_____ Counterclockwise

2. Quadrant labels

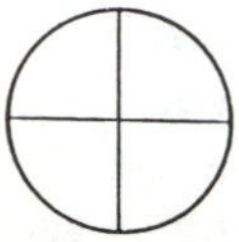

2. In what order would you label the four quadrants of a circle?

Write in the letters A, B, C, and D, assigning one letter to each quadrant.

3. Numbered keys

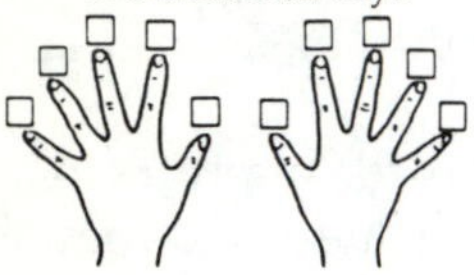

3. A worker is required to duplicate numbers as they appear on a screen, by pressing 10 keys, one for each finger.

Label the diagram to show how you would assign the 10 numerals to the 10 fingers.

4. Cross faucets

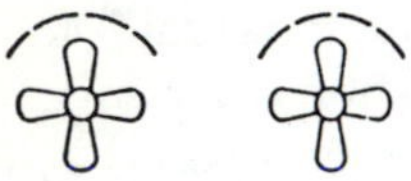

4. Here are two knobs on a bathroom sink, looking down at them.

Put an arrow on each dotted line to show how you would operate these knobs to turn the water on.

5. *"Pressure High"*

Working with a fire crew, the hoseman yells "Pressure high."

What should be done to the water pressure?

_____ Lower the pressure
_____ Raise the pressure

6. River bank

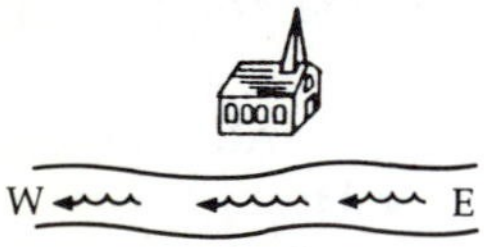

W E

6. Here is a river, flowing from east to west.

Is the church on the

_____ Left bank?
_____ Right bank?

7. Highway lanes

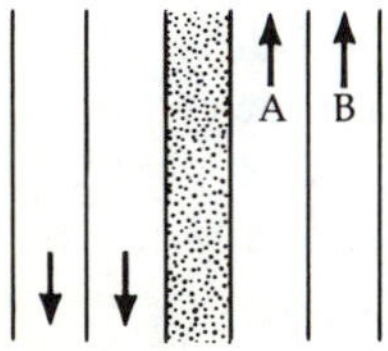

A B

7. On the four-lane divided highway pictured here, which is the outside lane?

_____ A
_____ B

SOURCE: From *Human Factors* by B. H. Kantowitz and R. D. Sorkin, 1983, Wiley, pp. 325 & 326.

FIGURE 15–17 Answers to Population Stereotype Quiz

Answers

1. Counterclockwise: Engineers (%) 97%
   Women (%) 94%
   HF (%) 91%

2.

	Engineers (%)	Women (%)	HFS (%)
Clockwise from upper right	33	26	45
Clockwise from upper left	19	11	5
Counterclockwise from upper right	34	3	5
"Reading" order	14	54	43
Other		6	2

3.

	Engineers (%)	Women (%)	HFS (%)
Ascending left to right	70	70	84
Ascending outwards from thumbs	18	16	5
Other	12	14	11

4.

Left faucet	Right faucet	Engineers (%)	Women (%)	HFS (%)
C	C	17	34	22
C	CC	23	20	13
CC	C	13	26	16
CC	CC	47	20	49

5.

	Engineers (%)	Women (%)	HFS (%)
"Lower the pressure" (Error)	66	48	78
"Raise the pressure" (Command)	34	53	22

6.

	Engineers (%)	Women (%)	HFS (%)
Left bank	18	16	13
Right bank	82	84	80
Other (not answered)			7

(continued)

SOURCE: From *Human Factors* (p. 327, 329) by B. H. Kantowitz and R. D. Sorkin, 1983, New York: Wiley.

FIGURE 15–17 *(concluded)*

Answers	7.	Engineers (%)	Women (%)	HFS (%)
	A outside	50	51	20
	B outside	50	49	80

a way that instead of having a performance limitation built into the system, we have a performance strength—a required response that is compatible with a natural tendency.

A Brief Review

In this chapter, I have chosen to redefine *work* as an example of a man-machine system. The worker has certain *input* capacities and limitations; these can be seen primarily in the functions of sensory mechanisms. The machine also has capacities and limitations, which interact with those of the worker. The machine may display input information in a variety of ways. Once the worker has received the input, she must do something with it. The process of using input is called *information processing*. This is something that *people* do and as such is of great interest to the industrial psychologist, since the individual worker mediates between input and output of the system.

The *output* part of the man-machine system has two components as well. The human component defines what responses can be executed by the worker in terms of skills and abilities. The machine contribution to the system at this point is a series of *control* mechanisms by which the worker physically makes a response. The human engineer dissects work in a way that is completely different from that of the personnel or industrial social psychologist. Consequently, these three different types of I/O psychologists should be thought of as complementing one another in attempting to understand the relationship between people and work.

AUTOMATION AND MAN-MACHINE SYSTEMS

The phrase *human error* or *pilot error* often crops up in the discussion of systems failures. The clear implication is that if the individual could be eliminated from the system, things would go more smoothly. Since people are very likely to be implicated if not directly responsible for faulty system performance, this would, at first glance, appear to be a reasonable approach. How is it accomplished? The immediate response is, "Automation. Develop automated systems that operate without people." Many examples of automated and partially automated systems such as oil refineries, spaceships, and engine-block plants can be cited. Yet, while it is obvious that automation has greatly reduced the ratio of men to machine components and drastically changed the remaining jobs, it seldom "gets the person out of the system" completely. Instead, people are kept in the system, fulfilling the functions of monitors and troubleshooters. Rather than performing operations directly on the material with direct sensory feedback about the effects of their actions, they are removed to remote stations where they monitor the system indirectly through symbolic and abstract information displays. The magnitude of the errors that the operator is capable of committing is frequently much greater than in the days of "one worker–one operation" mechanization. The decisions that must be made are often critical to the well-being and successful operation of equipment worth hundreds of thousands of dollars. Nevertheless, to keep things in perspective, when automated systems go out of control, they often go wildly out of control. Humans, on the other hand, seem capable of much greater flexibility and adaptation to environmental change. This is because humans can "reprogram" themselves. Automated equipment, on the other hand, cannot spontaneously reprogram itself.

A dramatic and sobering example of the critical nature of the interaction between operators and "automatic" equipment is the nuclear accident that occurred at Three Mile Island in Pennsylvania. This accident was the result of compounded man-machine failures. As part of a routine maintenance program, the secondary or backup system for cooling the superheated water from the nuclear reactor was shut down. Through oversight on the part of plant personnel, this secondary system was not turned back on after the maintenance. Two weeks after this backup machine was shut down, a pump failed in the *primary* cooling system. Since the secondary system was inoperable, the temperature began to climb in the reactor chamber. Then a valve stuck; an "automatic" emergency system went into operation, exaggerating the negative effect of the stuck valve, and control room personnel misinterpreted information from faulty instruments. The situation came close to a genuine disaster in which the lives of thousands of people might have been in jeopardy. While it is impossible to "blame" the accident on one thing or one person, it is clear that human decisions played a major role in the accident, in spite of (or possibly *because* of) automated systems or subsystems.

As you would expect, an immediate reaction to this accident was a demand for improved mechanical, electrical, and chemical systems that would prevent a reoccurrence. But in addition, the role of the operator in the man-machine system also received close attention. For example, as a result of the accident, the Swedish Nuclear Industry has proposed rigid standards for the selection, training, and licensing of control room personnel in nuclear power plants. Similar suggestions are being considered in all countries with substantial nuclear facilities. It is ironic to note that in the United States there is a good deal more training and certification testing required of those who will receive a pilot's license than of those who will work in a nuclear facility, in spite of the fact that the general public welfare can be more directly affected by workers in the nuclear facility than by the private or commercial pilot.

It is true that automation and its forerunner, mechanization, have taken much of the drudgery, inhumanity, and danger out of work and, for those reasons, ought to be pursued vigorously. What the human engineer needs to attend to, however, are the ways in which automation has changed the nature of work, the system's functions that are increasingly allocated to human operators, and those that are likely to be part of the operator's role in future systems. Two recent studies highlight what those concerns should be. The first deals with the use of computers, first in a clerical office, then in a bakery. The second is an evaluation of a program to introduce robots into a plant that forged and machined various pieces of metal alloy.

Computers

Anecdotal stories of the way in which computers change the nature of work abound. One example is the Blue Shield of Massachusetts office in Plymouth, Massachusetts. The claims processors were introduced to microcomputers and video-display terminals (VDTs) recently. Many of the workers there feel that the workplace has been turned into an assembly line through computerization. With the Blue Shield system, the use of the electronic device to record and retrieve claims information is only one of the many operations the computer performs. In addition, the machine monitors the operator's performance and produces a report detailing the worker's productivity each week on a *minute-by-minute basis!* These figures are compared to production standards, and the pay of the workers is adjusted depending on whether they exceeded or fell short of the "standard." In effect, the work has become piece-rate work. The workers are complaining of sore eyes, backaches, and headaches. The culprit has been identified as "the computer." Perhaps it is, but one could not come to that conclusion from these kinds of reports. A number of other possible culprits are available, including method of payment, organizational controls, organizational climate, and supervisory methods. In other words, when you introduce a computer, you are not simply replacing one piece of equipment with another. You are intervening in a *system.* Recently, two colleagues and I (Landy, Rastegary, et al., 1987) have outlined the psychosocial aspects of the VDT revolution. It seems clear that there are an enormous number of potential "culprits" in the VDT mystery. Ironically, bills are now being passed at the state and local level mandating working conditions for VDT users. For example, Suffolk County, New York, just passed a bill requiring rest breaks for VDT users. From our perspective, it would have been better if the bill had dealt with payment systems, training programs, and extent of standardization. VDTs may represent the Taylorism of the 1980s.

As such, legislation such as that passed by Suffolk County would be akin to having passed legislation in 1911 governing the size of the shovel that the pig iron handlers were permitted to use. The crux of the scientific management problem was not equipment—it was a respect for the dignity of the worker. We are facing similar issues with VDT use.

Let's consider another application of computers to another industrial system and context. Buchanan and Boddy (1983) describe the introduction of a computer into the process of cookie making. The computer was used to control dough mixing and to monitor the weight and size of the cookies shortly after baking. These two operations are crucial in cookie making—the former, since it clearly affects taste and composition, and the latter, because it provides information both about mixing and about the oven temperature and baking time. One of the interesting aspects about the introduction of a computerized system was that it had very different effects on the two processes. Consider the descriptions of "before" and "after" for each of the jobs. Before the introduction of the computer, the mixing was done by master bakers. They directed the efforts of subordinates who brought the raw material to large mixing machines and combined the ingredients that would become the cookie dough. Like any good cook, they were able to see and feel and taste (and even hear) the process of dough mixing. They could add a pinch of this or a dash of that. The dough could be moistened if it were too dry or dried if it were too wet. They were recognized in the plant for their experience and special skills. After the computerized mixing process was introduced, the job was greatly simplified. It took only twenty minutes to complete, and there was need for only one worker who was not required to have any special skills (other than those necessary to start the machine, add material when the computer requested it, take a sample of the completed dough, and move the dough on to the person running the oven, called the *ovensman*).

The effect of computerization on the ovensman was very different. Before computerization, the ovensman was required to check periodically the weight and size of the cookies as they came out of the oven. This was important both for purposes of quality control and in order to alert the wrapping department if there were any adjustments necessary in the wrapping machinery or process as a result of bulk or weight variations. All this was done manually and, as a result, was inefficient. A computerized weighing system was introduced to the process. This made it much easier to weigh every cookie (rather than a sample) and to get the information at a much earlier time in the baking process. As a result of the earlier information, the ovensman could either instruct the machine operator to adjust the rollers to make thinner or thicker cookies, or speed up/slow down the oven to change size, or instruct the wrappers to put more/fewer cookies in a package to maintain weight standards. In this case, pressure on the ovensman was reduced dramatically. In the past, there had been frequent disputes about whose "fault" it was when there were wrapping difficulties. The new system was able to pinpoint process problems more quickly and accurately, thus reducing conflict. As a result of the computerization, the ovensman felt that his job was more responsible. In addition, he received bonus pay since production improved.

As a result of the introduction of the computer, Buchanan and Boddy concluded that the following changes occurred in the two jobs:

Mixer

- Poorer understanding of production process and equipment
- Could not see the consequences of personal action or inaction
- Could not trace process failures
- Became bored and apathetic
- Rejected responsibility for breakdowns
- Developed no new skills, thus became less promotable

Ovensman

- Retained monitor and control functions
- Got more rapid feedback on performance
- Developed a better understanding of production process
- Developed more control over process
- Had a visible goal that could be personally influenced
- Perceived the job to be more interesting and challenging

As you can see from these results, there is no generalization that can be made about the introduction of computers into this cookie factory. This is so for several reasons. First, the equipment was only *one* of the things that changed. Other things included social relations, pay, feedback, and status, to mention just a few. For reasons such as these, any general statements about what "computers do to jobs" should be ignored. It is critical to understand what secondary effects occur in other parts of the entire man-machine system as well as how the sociotechnical environment of each job that the computer touches has changed.

There is very little informative research regarding human-computer interaction at the sociotechnical level. To be sure, there is a good deal of traditional information available about the design characteristics of screens and keyboards. Unfortunately, there is little information available about the sociotechnical changes implied by the introduction of computers. That is unfortunate because the computer revolution is upon us. Technology is galloping ahead of behavioral theory. The next few years should see a rapid increase of information that will allow for the design of effective computer-controlled systems from the psychological perspective.

Robotics

Contrary to the magical image of robots presented in movies such as *Star Wars* or in science fiction books such as those written by Isaac Asimov, industrial robots are unexciting to look at and even less exciting to talk to. Their functions are quite limited, and they are often dedicated to a particular task such as welding, holding and turning engines or car bodies, or simply moving material from one place to another. As such, they are really nothing more than the extension of programming capabilities that have been part of machine operations for several decades. For example, machinists have been constructing paper tape programs for multiple turret lathe machines and drill presses without ever thinking of them as "robots," yet that is exactly what these machines are. The dictionary definition of a *robot* is "any automatic device that performs functions ordinarily ascribed to human beings." A more useful definition of a robot for our purposes might be "electro[mechanical] devices with multiple task capability and programmability" (Argote, Goodman, & Schkade, 1983). The question for psychologists to consider is what effect these electromechanical devices might have on their human coworkers. As we have just seen, computerized work flow can have an impact on the efficiency, motivation, and happiness of workers. It follows that robots will have similar impact.

If there were few studies of the effects of computers on work behavior, there are even fewer of the effects of robots. As a result, I will base the following discussion on some recent work done by Argote et al. (1983). They observed the effects of introducing a robot into a department that did milling and grinding on metal bars. The function of the robot was to load and unload the milling machines. The researchers interviewed several dozen employees of the department 2½ months prior to (Time 1) and 2½ months after (Time 2) the time at which the robots were introduced.

They first considered the beliefs that workers held about robots before and after their introduction to the workplace. These beliefs were derived from the various descriptions of the robots that workers used in the course of the interviews. Specifically, they were asked, "How would you describe the robot to a friend?" These data are presented in Table 15–2. There were three broad response categories used: general beliefs (the first five responses), beliefs about functions (the next two responses), and beliefs about consequences (the last three responses). As you can see, some beliefs changed over time. Fewer workers thought of the robots as a "mechanical man"; more described them as hydraulic arms. There was less of a tendency to see the robots as increasing productivity but an increased tendency to see them as lessening the manual work load. Table 15–3 presents additional data concerning the general beliefs of the workers about robots after having been exposed to them for 2½ months. Although there was the perception that the robots would be an advantage in the economic competition between the United States and other nations, there was also the belief that in order to use the robots to their full advantage

Sparks fly as a robot applies one of more than 2,000 welds to a Sentra automobile in the Body, Frame, and Stamping Plant at Nissan Motor Manufacturing Corporation. U.S.A. (Nissan)

considerable job retraining would be necessary. This is often a source of stress for older workers who fear that the learning will be too difficult or will involve concepts that they have not previously been exposed to in school or work settings.

Table 15–4 provides fascinating data regarding the workers' changing perceptions about the results of robots on productivity, accidents, costs, quality, and job displacement. As we have already seen in Table 15–2, beliefs about increased productivity become less optimistic. In addition, there is the perception that the risk of an accident has increased, that costs have increased, and that the quality of work will probably not change. Also, the fear of being displaced by robots seemed to diminish.

As you would expect, there were substantial changes in the activities of the workers. Before, they loaded the machine, started and tended it, and unloaded it. After the introduction of the robots, they did a good deal more watching and aiding in machine setup, and they now had the added task of

TABLE 15–2 Workers' Descriptions of Robots

	Percent of Total Mentions	
	Time 1	*Time 2*
Type of robot		
Mechanical man	15%	9%
Hydraulic arm	2	9
Computer	6	0
Preprogrammed machine	15	16
TV image	10	7
Function		
Moves material	4	9
Loads machine	12	14
Consequences		
Better productivity	15	5
Reduces manual work	15	23
Works continuously	6	8
	100%	100%

SOURCE: Reprinted from "The Human Side of Robotics: How Workers React to a Robot" by L. Argote, P. Goodman, and D. Schkade, *Sloan Management Review*, 24, 1983, p. 33, by permission of the publisher.

TABLE 15–3 Workers' Beliefs about Robots in General at Time 2

	*Percent of Workers Agreeing/ Strongly Agreeing**
Robots Will:	
Make United States more competitive	87%
Be capable of doing my job	29
Be capable of doing clerical jobs	8
Be capable of doing management jobs	17
Displace workers	50
Create less desirable jobs	21
Require more job retraining	87

*Questions were asked in this order.

SOURCE: Reprinted from "The Human Side of Robotics: How Workers React to a Robot" by L. Argote, P. Goodman, and D. Schkade, *Sloan Management Review*, 24, 1983, p. 33, by permission of the publisher.

TABLE 15–4 Perceptions of the Effect of a Robot in a Production Department

	*Percentage of Respondents Who Said Robot Had Effect on:**									
	Productivity		*Accidents*		*Costs*		*Quality*		*Number of People Employed*	
Effect	*Time 1*	*Time 2*	*Time 1*	*Time 2*	*Time 1*	*Time 2*	*Time 1*	*Time 2*	*Time 1*	*Time 2*
Increase	81%	67%	11%	29%	10%	33%	51%	17%	6	0
No effect	8	12	32	46	7	4	30	54	44	83
Decrease	3	12	41	21	55	42	3	21	44	17

*The percent of respondents who said "Don't know" is not included in this table; hence, percentages for some outcomes will total less than 100 percent.

SOURCE: Reprinted from "The Human Side of Robotics: How Workers React to a Robot" by L. Argote, P. Goodman, and D. Schkade, *Sloan Management Review*, 24, 1983, p. 33, by permission of the publisher.

programming the robot to carry out its material handling functions. As a result of these changes, the workers reported more stress and more responsibility. There were also some fears about having the responsibility for an expensive piece of equipment. Another subtle change occurred. A form of "competition" seemed to develop between worker and robot. In the initial interviews, there was speculation about whether the workers could "beat" the robot. As Argote et al. report, "By our second visit, workers seemed resigned to the fact that the robot would always be able to outproduce a worker: The reason was simple. Robots do not take breaks or go to lunch." This seems like a modern version of John Henry, the "steel drivin' man." Like John Henry, these workers could not beat the new equipment. As is commonly the case in other machine work, particularly when it is piece-rate or machine paced, the workers felt controlled by the robot—in spite of the fact that they programmed its operations. The workers also reported that the robots left little time for communication and interaction with other workers. Social patterns of long standing were altered by the introduction of the robots.

Argote et al. complete their description with a list of recommendations for managers who are contemplating the introduction of robots (or other similar technological innovations) at the workplace. Some of these recommendations were:

1. Resolve workers' fears about pay and security before making the change.
2. Anticipate the effect that the change will have on the entire sociotechnical system. This would include work activities, social interactions, and beliefs.
3. Get workers involved in the introduction of the new technology. This will increase understanding and may increase commitment to the change.
4. Use demonstrations of the new equipment/process as a means of communication rather than written descriptions or lectures or formal presentations.
5. Consider what the "new" job will be like and make sure that the characteristics that the worker will bring to that new job meet its demands.
6. If the change will result in less "doing" and more "observing," be prepared to counter boredom with job rotation or some similar technique.
7. If the change destroys certain social patterns, allow the workers to help plan the change so that new patterns may be developed to take the place of the old ones.

This evaluation by Argote and her colleagues is not rigorous by common scientific standards, but it is informative. It identifies a number of critical areas of concern. These areas make sense because they are suggested by other research and theory that we have examined in earlier chapters. Although there are probably fewer than 6,000 robots in operation in U.S. industry today, that number is bound to increase as more powerful microchips are introduced and more user-friendly software becomes available. Now is the time for I/O psychologists to explore this new aspect of man-machine interaction. The more sophisticated the robots become, the more complex will be the interface of man, machine, workplace, and environment. This, in turn, will result in a greater need for understanding the behavioral implications of these technological changes.

In a more recent study, Chao and Kozlowski (1986) identified four general areas of employee concern with respect to the introduction of robots. These areas were: general robotics orientation (i.e., beliefs about the value of robots in terms of organizational survival), job security, management concern (distrust of managements' motivation for introducing robots), and expected changes (a feared depersonalization of the work environment). In general, the study demonstrated that low-skill workers were most threatened by the introduction of robots and high-skill workers were enthusiastic about the change. It seems clear that robots (and more generally, any new technology) represent different things to different workers. The challenge is the introduction of the new technology so that all workers see opportunities for positive outcomes, not just some workers. This would suggest differential training and orientation programs for those most likely to believe that they will "lose" if robots are introduced.

WORK SCHEDULES

As you have seen, the man-machine system is a complex one when you include the workplace and the environment. This system is influenced by equipment, temperature, patterns of social interaction, pay rates, and supervisory relations, to name just a few of the factors we have considered. There is one factor, however, that we have not considered yet that has a substantial influence on the efficiency of the man-machine system. Two simple examples make the point. The first is the way you study. At least once in your life, you have probably stayed up all night to prepare for an examination, that is, "pulled an all-nighter." Did you feel alert and efficient when you took that test the next day? Did you feel that the last two hours of study were as worthwhile as the first two? Did you follow your normal sleep-wake pattern on the day after you took the exam? The answer to all these questions is probably no. You did two things that unbalanced your system—you disturbed your normal 24-hour (circadian) cycle and you deprived yourself of sleep. Work schedules can have a similar effect. We will consider these effects in an examination of shift work—both fixed and rotating.

The second example is a little more upbeat, although it involves exams again. It is the last week of the semester and you will be taking exams in four different courses. Naturally, the exams are scheduled at the most inconvenient times and conflict with your work schedule at the restaurant where you work. Something has to give so you talk with your boss at the restaurant, and she tells you not to worry about showing up exactly as scheduled. She reasons that since the real rush won't begin until 6:00 P.M. and since there will be three other people on duty from 3:00 on, that there shouldn't be any problem. The only thing she asks is that you be there from 6:00 to 10:00 and that you even your hours out by the end of the week so that you have put in the expected twenty-seven hours. This modification allows you to work and take your exams. Your work schedule has been made more flexible. This is an example of a phenomenon called *flexitime* that has been formally introduced into many workplaces. It is an example of a positive contribution that work schedules can make to well-being and system efficiency. We will examine some of the recent research on this scheduling system.

Shift Work

In most of our discussion so far, we have assumed that the individuals in question arrive at work at 9:00 A.M. and leave at 4:30 or 5:00 P.M., having enjoyed a leisurely lunch with coworkers. But in many work settings, this is little more than a fantasy. In continuous process operations, such as the steel industry, it has been common to keep the work activities going around the clock. In part, this is a function of the fact that it would be quite expensive (and in some cases, impossible) to restart furnaces each day at 8:00 A.M. Shift work is common in many other settings that require constant monitoring (e.g., police and fire departments). These types of work settings require special systems of manpower allocation. The need has been met by devising various work schedules that allow for the "shifting" of job duties from one group of workers to another group. This type of scheduling has come to be known as *shift work* and seems to be a symptom of industrialized societies. In Europe, "odd" working hours represent about 20 percent of total working hours; the figure is probably similar in the United States.

Shift work is a complicated concept to deal with, owing to the almost infinite number of variations available. For example, consider three shifts: *day* (7:00 A.M. to 3:00 P.M.), *swing or afternoon* (3:00 P.M. to 11:00 P.M.), and *night* (11:00 P.M. to 7:00 A.M.). When you add the variable of *days off,* you might have any one of the following possible shift patterns:

5 day—2 off—5 day—2 off
2 day—2 swing—2 off—3 night—2 off—2 day
6 night—4 off—6 night—4 off
5 night—2 off—5 day—2 off—5 swing—2 off

Since there are so many possibilities for scheduling shifts, psychologists have become interested in whether some shift schedules might be more satisfying, healthy, safe, or productive than others. We will review some research that deals with this issue.

The Michigan Study. In spite of the long history of shift work in U.S. industry, there has been little serious consideration of its effects on workers until relatively recently. In 1965, a group of researchers at the University of Michigan (Mott, Mann, McLoughlin, & Warwick) published the results of their investigations of the effect of shift schedules on workers. The investigators gathered information from workers and their wives with respect to the social, psychological, and physiological effect of shift work.

The subjects were blue-collar workers from several continuous process plants in the eastern United States. Several hundred questionnaires were distributed and interviews conducted with workers and their wives. The response rate was 87 percent, an extremely high figure, possibly indicating the importance of the topic to shift workers and their families.

In considering the results of this study, remember that they represent the verbal report of the workers rather than "hard" measures of the variables in question; as such, they are open to question. Nevertheless, they are interesting.

Sleep-related problems seemed to be at the heart of shift work difficulties. Loss of sleep seemed to have negative effects on both physical and social patterns. This suggested that there might be some natural rhythms that are disturbed by unusual shifts. It is generally accepted that human beings are characterized by rhythms of approximately 24 hours in duration—*circadian* rhythms. The results of the study seemed to point to a mismatch between work requirements and these circadian rhythms. Night shift and rotating shift workers complained of constant fatigue, poor appetites, constipation, and a variety of other disorders. In addition, these workers reported that they were less interested in the typical social activities that characterized the leisure-time pursuits of their day shift colleagues.

A more detailed examination of the various shifts showed that steady day shift seemed to have the greatest advantage for the individual worker. Steady afternoon (swing) shift had the greatest negative impact on social patterns both inside and outside the family (the father was often asleep while the children were preparing for school, and by the time the father returned from work, the children were in bed). Steady night shift work was not as disruptive to social relations as the swing shift, but it did seem to have negative effects on self-reported health. By far, the worst schedule seemed to be a weekly rotating shift system in which the worker was on day shift for five days with two days off, followed by the swing shift with two days off, and then the night shift with two days off. This not only prevented physical adaptation; it also isolated the worker from normal social patterns for two of every three weeks.

The Michigan study was not carefully controlled; in addition, it was not widely representative of either shifts or work settings. Nevertheless, it did point to shift work as a potential stressor in the work environment. In some respects, it was a unique stressor, however, since it had rather immediate effects on family and friends. As the Michigan researchers noted, when you ask a worker to adapt to a shift other than a typical day shift, you are asking the worker's family to adapt as well.

The British Steel Corporation Study. From 1970 to 1972, Alexander Wedderburn, a Scottish I/O psychologist, conducted a series of studies of the effect of shift work on British steelworkers. The 315 workers came from three different locations and were on one of the following shifts:

1. 6 on–2 off. A rotating system in which the workers changed shifts about every week.
2. 2 × 2 × 3 rotating. A rapidly rotating shift system in which the individual spent 2 days on one shift (e.g., day), 2 days on another shift (e.g., swing), and 3 days on the last shift (e.g., night); days off were wedged between various shift changes.
3. 5 × 4 rotating. 5 days on one shift (e.g., day), followed by several days off and 4 days on another shift (e.g., night).

As was the case with the Michigan research, Wedderburn found that sleeping problems and distorted social relations were frequent sources of dissatisfaction for shift workers. In addition, he found that there were definite shift types; that is, some workers preferred the night shift, whereas others preferred afternoon or day. These preferences were unrelated to age, marital status, number of children in the family, or experience on shift work. Also, he found that 18 percent of the workers said that they liked shift work, whereas only 8 percent disliked it. When the various types of shift were compared, the 6 on–2 off workers were most negative, and the 2 × 2 × 3 workers were the most positive.

Workers on various shifts (day, swing, night) were asked to describe the relative advantages and disadvantages of each shift. The day shift was valued for the social flexibility it provided; in contrast, the afternoon shift seemed to restrict social life and yet was thought to be the least tiring of the three shifts and the shift most likely to provide sufficient sleep opportunity. The night shift was described as tiring, socially restrictive, poor for family life, and physiologically disruptive. In spite of these disadvantages, even the night shift was thought to have some things in its favor: it was judged to provide more spare time and provided greater freedom from supervision while at work.

Wedderburn also discussed problems of performance. The issue of safety and performance seems to be critical when considering the night shift. A phenomenon generally known to night shift workers is the "3:00 A.M. dip." This is a rather substantial drop in vigilance that occurs about three to four hours after the beginning of night shift work (at about 3:00 A.M. if the shift begins at 11:00 P.M.). The solution to this problem depends on whether physiological cycles can be changed to meet the required work rhythms. If physiological cycles can change over time (or "phase shift"), then the dip should gradually disappear on its own; in this case, performance of workers just beginning the night shift is monitored closely until they have adapted to night work (this might take anywhere from several weeks to several months). If, on the other hand, the worker must be rotated around the three shifts, making adaptation more difficult, it might be better to rearrange the starting and stopping times for the night shift so that workers begin their shift immediately after "dip" period (at about 4:00 A.M.). There are also individual differences in the nature of this dip[2]—it does not occur for the same length of time and at the same time of night for all workers. But in spite of the individual-differences component in this phenomenon, there is sufficient anecdotal evidence to suggest that the dip occurs and that it is potentially dangerous. In an article in a Stockholm, Sweden, newspaper, it was reported that 9 out of 10 freight locomotive operators "blacked out" occasionally at night. One engineer described the experience of passing through a railway station and waking up almost 60 miles further down the track! Most of us have had a similar experience in driving an automobile, arriving at our destination and finding that we could remember *nothing* of the last hour of the drive.

Additional Research on Shift Work. Agervold (1976) reviewed much of the research that has been done on shift work in Scandinavia. On the basis of this literature review, he voiced strong opposition to night shift work. He suggested that if night shift work was absolutely essential, it would be better to use constant assignment to night shift rather than rotating shifts over time. Once again, the question of adaptation arises. While Agervold may be right with respect to work efficiency or satisfaction, if a phase shift actually *does* occur, this must mean that the worker will be out of phase with respect to some other activity—sleeping, playing golf, doing the laundry, talking with the children. The clear lesson to be learned from much of this research is that whenever one departs from a regular 8:30 to 4:30 schedule, some compromises will have to be made. These compromises will define the relative balance of health, family, work, and leisure in the individual worker's life. We need to know much more about the effects of shift work on workers before we can help them make the best available compromise between working and non-working hours.

Characteristics of Shifts

There is a tendency to speak of shift work as if it were a homogeneous phenomenon with the same characteristics in every location. Nothing could be further from the truth. There are so many variations in shift work patterns that the concept loses all meaning at the general level. The biggest difference

---

[2]An excellent review of research in the area of sleep, shift work, and performance can be found in a book entitled *Aspects of Human Efficiency* edited by W. P. Colquhoun (London: English Universities Press, 1972). In addition, the September 1978 issue of the journal *Ergonomics* gives careful consideration to many of these issues.

is between fixed and rotating shifts. The problems that confront the worker who is assigned to steady night work are very different than the problems of workers who change shifts every four days. The fixed shift worker eventually develops particular patterns (both behavioral and physiological). She adapts. This almost guarantees that the worker is poorly adapted to some other activities that are nonwork related. The rotating shift worker, however, may never adapt since she is exposed to any one shift for too short a period before changing to another schedule. It is reasonable to assume that the body will *try* to adapt as soon as the schedule changes but fails. This means that there is constant stress on the individual. To borrow Selye's analogy one more time, constant withdrawals are being made from the adaptation account.

Once you have distinguished between fixed and rotating shifts, there are still many variations to be considered *within* the class of rotating shifts. Consider some of the following.

Forward versus Backward Rotation. Does the worker move from day shift to afternoon shift to night shift (forward) or from day shift to night shift to afternoon shift (backward)? There is some evidence that jet lag has differing effects depending on whether we go from east to west or west to east (west to east has longer-lasting effects). This suggests that backward shift changes might be more problematic than forward rotations. Although the industrial data are scarce, one highly publicized study of shift rotation in the United States seems to bear this out (Wolinsky, 1982). The Great Salt Lake Minerals and Chemicals Corporation experimented with changes in both the direction of shift change and length of shift cycle. Previously, workers had shifted backward on a weekly basis. Two experimental and one control group were compared after the following changes were made: one experimental group (n = 52) changed their schedule so that they were on the same shift for 21 days rather than 7. In addition, when this group changed to a new shift, the movement was forward rather than backward. The second experimental group also changed to a 21-day cycle but continued to change shifts in a backward direction. The control group was composed of 68 fixed day and night shift workers. As is commonly the case, anecdotal reports of the results are glowing. Workers who experienced the direction change and lengthening of cycle time report less stress and greater happiness. Management estimates 15 percent to 20 percent improvements in productivity. By now, you should recognize that many different factors might have been responsible for changes in behavior or attitudes. The simple fact of intervention might have been responsible for some of the positive effects. In addition, supervisory methods, work procedures, coworker patterns, leisure patterns, or any of several dozen other factors might have changed simultaneously. No one can say exactly *what* factor or factors were most influential, but this study does point out two important variables to consider in rotating shift work research—rotation direction and cycle length.

Days Off. Another issue of concern in rotating shift work should be the nature of days off. For one thing, days off can be fixed or variable. If you are on a 2 × 2 × 3 rotating shift, your days off could be the same days every week (e.g., Monday and Tuesday), or they might shift as your work shifts. In the latter case, your days off might be Monday and Tuesday this week, Saturday and Sunday next week, and Wednesday and Thursday during the third week. The fixed versus rotating nature of days off can have a substantial impact on your nonwork patterns. If the days are fixed, it is possible to plan leisure, education, and family activities on a long-term basis. If the days off rotate, this type of planning is much more difficult.

A related issue has to do with where the days off come within your shift cycle. Do they come in the middle of a shift or at the point when you shift from one schedule to another. For example, on a 2 × 2 × 3 rotating pattern, your days off might always come in the middle of the night shift. Contrast this with days off that appear *between* shifts. If the days off come between day and night shifts (in a forward rotation scheme), you might work Monday from 8:00 A.M. to 4:00 P.M. and not report to work again until Thursday night at 11:00 P.M. That is three full days off. If, on the other hand, your days off come between night shift and day shift, you might leave work on Tuesday morning at 7:00 A.M. and be expected back to work on Thursday morning at 7:00 A.M., a total of 48 hours off. Most organizations have recognized the problems of where days off come so that this latter circumstance would be unusual. The point I am making is that there are many variations to keep in mind.

Other Factors. In addition to rotation direction, cycle length, and days off variations, shifts also vary in terms of absolute shift length (some shifts are 8 hours, others 10 hours, and still others 12 hours), the extent to which overtime is allowed/encouraged/discouraged, and the extent to which the different shift workers receive different levels of compensation (i.e., in most companies, workers on swing and night shifts receive extra pay).

Shifts are incredibly complicated and represent a substantial influence on the intersection of worker, equipment, workplace, and environment. As a result, I/O psychologists should be less interested in the fact of shift work than in the components of shift schedules. A simple statement to the effect that "shift work is damaging to workers" is of little value. We need to know what aspect of this many-headed monster is responsible for threats to physical or psychological well-being. Is it the number of hours worked, the workers' feelings that they have no control, the disrupted or nonexistent social patterns outside of work, or disruption of the natural forward-moving circadian rhythm of the worker? For example, Jamal (1981) considers the effect of rotating shifts on job attitudes, social participation, and anticipated turnover and comes to the conclusion that rotating shifts are disruptive (and presumably, should be eliminated). The reader is told *nothing* about length of shift cycle, direction of change, days off, and so forth. Can it be that all rotating shifts are bad? It is possible but not likely. More to the point, there are some aspects of rotating shift work that need attention.

Further, it is critical to distinguish between fixed and rotating shifts when considering the effects of shift work. For example, Frost and Jamal (1979) report that rotating shifts are disruptive and have negative effects on such things as mental health, satisfaction, social involvement, and absenteeism. They combine nonday fixed shifts and rotating shifts into one group that is compared with day shift workers. These types of studies are of little value in developing theories or effective interventions that address the issue of shift work. A good deal more basic research is needed on shift effects before broad, condemning statements are justified.

Studies of Ex-Shift Workers

There is one final issue that should be mentioned. Many studies of the effect of shift work (either fixed or rotating) focus on the aftereffects. These studies collect data from workers who had previously been on the implicated shift arrangement. This implies that some adaptation model underlies the research. It is assumed that the costs incurred in the adaptation to the offending shift can still be identified or measured. Frese and Okonek (1984) argue that this type of design needs to be refined. He suggests that there are two different types of ex-shift worker. One type left the shift in question on a voluntary basis, but the other type was forced to leave as a result of health problems (or in anticipation of serious threats to health). They find that the former category of shift worker has spent considerably less time on the shift (6 years versus 10 years), is less concerned about job security, and has higher skill levels. To Frese and Okonek, this suggests that there may be a critical level of exposure or a "breaking point" and that if you stay long enough on the shift in question (e.g., night), you will probably develop one or more serious symptoms. According to these authors, the net effect of these differences is to lead to a substantial underestimate of the effects of shift work on well-being. This is a good point and one that must be considered in dealing with retrospective data on shift work effects.

Shift Work and Absence

If there is such a great interplay between working hours and nonworking activities, one might expect to see symptoms of stress in absence data. Nicholson, Jackson, and Howes (1978) studied the absence trends of workers on various shifts. The subjects were 150 male maintenance engineers with a steel corporation in the United Kingdom. The workers were assigned to a 6 on–2 off schedule, as described earlier. The investigators were able to examine the independent effects of shift (day, swing, night), time during the six-day cycle (first two, middle two, last two days), and days of the week (Monday,

Tuesday, and so on). All three of these effects were significant. Weekend absences were higher and Thursdays (payday) lower; absences were higher in the day and lower in the swing shifts; absences were much higher in the last two days of the six-day cycle than in either the first two or middle two days. In addition, there were complicated interactions among these variables. For example, swing shift workers were much more likely to be absent toward the end of the six-day cycle when the end of the cycle fell on a weekend. Nicholson et al. concluded that rest days seemed to "infect" the workdays closest to them and, further, that certain shifts increased this effect.

It seems clear from the research described that shift work is a very potent (though complex) variable in the work environment. It affects satisfaction, performance, safety, family life, physical and psychological well-being, and absences. The results to date suggest that shift work should be considered as a potential stressor on the worker. As was the case with temperature and noise, we need to know much more about the mechanisms by which shifts affect behavior. There are some particular pitfalls in doing cross-sectional research in this area. For example, it might be reasonable to assume that night shift workers represent a "survivor" population—those who are left after those who cannot or will not adapt to the pressures of night work move to other shifts or other companies. Consequently, it is misleading to compare the responses of cross sections of night shift workers and other shift workers. We have also seen how retrospective studies of shift work effects can also be misleading. In addition, there is evidence that suggests that circadian rhythms may be only part of the problem; mealtime changes and changes in drinking habits may account for variations in physical complaints as well, and the general level of noise around the house may account for sleeping problems. In short, the problem is a very complicated one and will require careful study. Currently, a great deal of research is being conducted on the topic of sleep, shift work, stress, cycles, and so on (see, for example, Akerstedt, Patkai, & Dahlgren, 1977; Gillberg, 1983; Patkai, Akerstedt, & Pettersson, 1977). You can expect rapid advances in the understanding of the relationship between "hostile" working hours and behavior in the next few years.

The Peach Bottom Syndrome. Recently, a new term has been added to the human factors glossary. It has been called the *Peach Bottom syndrome.* The term was developed to describe a situation at the Peach Bottom plant of the Philadelphia Electric Company. This is one of several nuclear plants run by the company. It was discovered that many of the workers on the night shift were falling asleep at their posts—including control room operators. This was and is a serious problem. With a technology as potentially devastating as nuclear power, the highest levels of vigilance are necessary. Many different causes for the sleeping were explored, ranging from circadian rhythms to poor supervisory practices. There is no clear understanding yet of what the root causes of the sleeping were, but it is clear that it is, at least in part, a human factors problem. Several nuclear power companies have designed their work schedules so that the night shifts are very busy, with lots of routine and nonroutine maintenance tasks to be accomplished. This goes a long way toward eliminating the long, quiet hours that induce sleep. One person suggested in a letter to the *New York Times* that the solution to the problem had been found several decades earlier by the TNT manufacturing industry. They had workmen sit on one-legged stools. Whenever they began to doze off, the stool would begin to tip, and they would awaken, thus averting a disaster. Perhaps until an answer is found, the workers at the Peach Bottom plant might be issued some of these one-legged stools.

Alternative Schedules for Day Work

Work scheduling has also received some attention in traditional 8-to-4 jobs. Two different concepts have been introduced. The first is known as *"flexible working hours"* (FWH) and implies variable start and stop times for job duties. Thus, one individual may begin work at 7:00 A.M. and finish at 3:30 P.M., whereas a second individual may begin at 9:30 A.M. and finish at 6:00 P.M. There are many variations to this general theme. Three of these are:

Flexitime. Variable starting and stopping times with a fixed or constant "core" of working hours every day. The individual is required to put in 40 hours each week.

Flexitour. Individuals develop their own work schedule but follow that schedule every day.

Gliding time. Starting and stopping time can vary, but eight hours must be put in each day.

We will consider the flexitime schedule.

The second concept is related to the length of the workweek. It has various names, but one common label is the *4–10 plan,* which stands for four 10-hour workdays instead of five 8-hour workdays. In both cases, the worker devotes 40 hours to the job, but in the former case, the individual is free from work for three days instead of the typical two-day break. We will consider these two scheduling systems independently.

Flexitime. The appeal of flexitime is that the worker is given a degree of discretion in arranging her work hours. To a certain extent, she can choose when to arrive at work and when to leave. This should enable the worker to arrange work and nonwork schedules more effectively. A recent study provides a good example of a flexitime arrangement (Narayanan and Nath, 1982). The workday was considered 12 hours long, running from 7:00 A.M. until 7:00 P.M. Within that 12-hour block, workers were expected to arrive anytime between 7:00 A.M. and 9:00 A.M., work from 9:00 to 11:30 A.M., work from 1:30 to 3:30 P.M., and leave anytime between 3:30 P.M. and 7:00 P.M. Thus, the core working period was 4½ hours long, and the workers could arrange noncore time to suit themselves. The only requirement was that the worker should have put in 40 hours during the week. A more common schedule is for a fixed block of core time with no break. For example, workers might be expected to be at their jobs between 10:00 A.M. and 2:00 P.M. but would be free to arrive anytime before 10:00 A.M. and leave anytime after 2:00 P.M.

There are both advantages and disadvantages to such a system. Clearly, a flexible time system is totally unsuitable for certain types of work. Bus drivers, police officers, nurses, and schoolteachers would all be poor candidates for such a system, at least as far as the clients of their services are concerned. In addition, any work that requires close coordination and cooperative effort on the part of the workers or groups of workers would be ill suited to such an arrangement. Nevertheless, in situations where it is possible to schedule collective and client-centered activities in a specific block of time during the day, flexitime is an interesting possibility. At least on the surface, it would seem to have the potential for allowing individuals to eliminate various stresses placed on them by competing schedules (e.g., the coordination of the working schedules of husbands and wives); additionally, it would seem to provide workers with a greater degree of autonomy in their work environment.

Data are beginning to accumulate that make the flexitime schedule look attractive. One early study was conducted by Golembiewski, Hilles and Kagno (1974). They examined the effect of flexitime on a group of R&D employees and concluded that the effect was positive on the attitudes of both workers and their supervisors, but the authors were cautious to point out that the effect could have been more the result of the simple fact of intervention rather than the result of a specific change in working hours. V. E. Schein, Maurer, and Novak (1977) examined the effects of FWH on the productivity of various groups of clerical workers in a large financial institution. In this organization, workers were required to work for 7¾ hours every day but could arrive anytime between 7:30 A.M. and 10:00 A.M. and were permitted to leave between 3:15 P.M. and 5:45 P.M. The effects of this schedule were examined after four months. The researchers looked at work volume, work quality, time to completion on various tasks, and other aspects. They were able to compare the work of groups on flexible schedules with other groups on fixed schedules. Their conclusions were cautious. They felt that it could be said with some certainty that FWH did not have any *adverse* effects on productivity, but they were unwilling to claim that it increased worker performance. Unfortunately, they did not gather measures of satisfaction, felt stress, motivation, and so on, which might allow us to make inferences about any psychological changes that occurred in the workers. In addition, they did not report how many workers actually took advantage of the opportunity for flexible scheduling. It was entirely possible that all workers continued to come in at 9:00 A.M. and leave at 4:45 P.M.

This issue of what really happens when workers are given the opportunity to schedule their arrival and departure time is an important one for several reasons. From a theoretical perspective, if they do not change their times yet feel better about their job, then the effect must surely be related to perceptions of control. From a practical perspective, many managers are afraid that when flexitime is introduced, the variability of workers' schedules will increase dramatically, making planning and scheduling of work impossible. Ronen (1981) has provided data that answer this question. In a study of the effect of flexitime on the actual starting and stopping times of Israeli workers, he found that the average starting time was 8 minutes later than before the flexitime change, and the average stopping time was 22 minutes later than before. Furthermore, and more importantly in some respects, each worker followed a predictable and stable pattern. They developed a new, slightly modified start-stop sequence and stayed in that pattern. This makes sense since there are many other factors that help to determine when a worker will choose to start and stop work. These include spouses' work schedules, school schedules for children, traffic patterns, car pool characteristics, and so on. Since the introduction of flexitime is unlikely to affect many of those other factors, stability is ensured, at least to some extent. Ronen reports another benefit of the flexitime schedule. In this particular setting, tardiness disappeared. It had been a serious problem prior to the flexitime change. On the average, 35 percent of the employees were tardy in a given week. After flexitime was introduced, fewer than 5 percent of the employees failed to arrive by the beginning of the core period. Thus, supervisors' fears of chaos may be exaggerated. In fact, they may actually find that their job becomes easier since the issue of tardiness diminishes.

The studies that have been done to evaluate the effect of flexitime have, on the whole, been carefully planned. There have been before and after measures of behavior and attitude. To the extent possible, workers (or work units) have been randomly assigned to experimental and control conditions. A wide range of possible effects—both attitudinal and behavioral—have been sampled. The results have been generally positive. The typical study (e.g. Narayanan & Nath, 1982; Orpen, 1981) finds that:

1. Production levels do not change much.
2. Work quality does not change much.
3. Overall and facet satisfaction does not change much.
4. Workers are happier with their life in general, particularly their new-found flexibility.
5. Supervisors are pleased with the new arrangement.
6. Absenteeism drops.
7. Tardiness drops dramatically.
8. Workers express satisfaction with the new schedule format.

The federal government introduced flexitime to the jobs of 325,000 workers under the Carter administration. These jobs were spread through 1500 different units. An evaluation of the effect of this intervention was carried out at the end of the three-year trial period (Kirk, 1981). The results were virtually identical to those reported above. This led to an interesting battle between the Reagan administration and Congress. The Reagan administration contended that since there were no clear productivity gains, the program should be discontinued. Congress, on the other hand, contended that since there were no productivity *losses,* the program should be continued since the people directly affected by flexitime were positive. Of the supervisors and workers affected by the change, 85 percent of the supervisors and 90 percent of the workers were positive about the program. It is interesting to note that when the program was first introduced, only 60 percent of the supervisors were positive. With experience in the new schedule, their attitudes became more positive. The attitudes of the workers had been extremely positive to begin with and stayed positive. In March 1982, there was some serious lobbying against continuing the flexitime program. The vote was delayed until July 1982, when the flexitime program received an almost unanimous vote of support from both the Senate and the House. It was continued for another three years and was scheduled for reconsideration in July 1985. A decision was made at that time to continue the program. It has been an overwhelming success.

Recently, a study has been published that points to one possible moderator of the value of flexitime. Ralston, Anthony, and Gustafson (1985) distinguish between the use of flexitime when scarce resources (e.g., equipment) are shared and when resources are plentiful. When resources are scarce, flexitime can have a substantial positive effect on productivity. But when there is no competition for resources, there seem to be few obvious production gains from the introduction of flexitime. This suggests that organizations who experience a high demand for certain resources or support services might consider flexitime as a productivity booster (as well as a morale booster).

As I said earlier, it is not possible to tell the extent to which the effect is an OD effect and the extent to which this effect is tied to the scheduling of time specifically. Many of the federal workers reported satisfaction in being finally "treated like adults" after years of being treated like children. In addition, unlike other OD programs (e.g., process consultation, team building), this intervention had an immediate and obvious effect on the way in which the organization functioned. More work needs to be done on decomposing these sources of influence, but I see no serious reasons for misgivings about flexitime programs. Of course, there will be local disasters. In some situations, the flexitime schedules will not work, but this is true of virtually any intervention. On the average, one might expect positive results.

The Four-Day Workweek. The opportunity to work for four days rather than five provides a unique opportunity to workers. It allows for more uninterrupted blocks of free time, the possibility of second part-time jobs, expanded familial activities, and so on. But it also implies the possibility that fatigue will affect work quality, safety, and worker satisfaction. The four-day workweek has received considerably more attention in the popular press and in locker rooms than it has in scientific circles. Nevertheless, the few studies that have been done of the effects of the four-day system have been enlightening.

Nord and Costigan (1973) examined the reactions of workers in a pharmaceutical company that had switched to a 4–10 plan. There was a very favorable reaction among the workers: 81 percent favored the four-day week, and this favorable margin remained even one year after the introduction of the plan; but workers reported that they slept less after the change, and there were some negative effects on home life (presumably as a result of longer working hours for the four days).

Goodale and Aagaard (1975) found similar mixed results. They examined the reactions of over 400 clerical and supervisory personnel to a four-day workweek. In this organization, the extra day off was a rotating day, so that four-day weekends were not uncommon. In spite of the fact that 86 percent of the workers were satisfied with the four-day schedule, 62 percent found the new schedule "more tiring"; in addition, many workers reported that work was more difficult toward the end of the day. There was another interesting difference: younger workers were much more positive about the four-day week than older workers. As a result, they concluded that the four-day schedule may be a problem for the older workers. Several investigators have suggested that an individual on the night shift experiences fatigue similar to that of a worker with diminished physical resources. The work of Goodale and Aagaard leads one to a similar conclusion with respect to the four-day workweek. It may be important to consider the nature of the work force prior to making a switch.

Ivancevich investigated the effects of the four-day week on worker satisfaction and performance in a manufacturing organization in two different studies (Ivancevich, 1974; Ivancevich & Lyon, 1977). In the first study, 13 months after the introduction of the new system, he found that workers were generally positive toward the four-day week and that some specific measures of productivity showed some improvements. There were no changes in absenteeism rates or in the workers' perceptions of autonomy or self-actualization. In a follow-up study (1977), he again found positive performance effects after 13 months and no effects on absenteeism, satisfaction, autonomy, or self-actualization. In addition, he found that the differences in performance disappeared after 25 months!

In spite of the fact that there is a need for much more research in this area, some things are clear. First, the glowing reports of the effects of the four-day workweek in the popular press seem to be exaggerated. Second, the studies of Goodale and Aagaard (1975) and Nord and Costigan (1973) both suggest that workers may express preferences for schedules that have negative effects on their physical and social well-being. Finally, the work described in

Chapter 13 on sociotechnical systems suggests that there may be some rather far-reaching and unanticipated effects of changes in work scheduling. In contrast to my feelings about flexitime, I have some doubts about the proposed advantages that the 4–10 plan holds over the more traditional 5–8 plan. Latack and Foster (1985) suggest that many of the potential shortcomings of compressed work schedules can be overcome by having employees involved in making the decision to switch to the compressed schedule. Further, they suggest that the greatest benefits will be seen in reducing turnover in middle-aged, skilled personnel in high-technology jobs that cannot be enriched. The compressed work schedule represents an opportunity to "escape" from the environment. While that may be the case, I would hope that I/O psychologists might accept the challenge of enriching those jobs rather than encourage the "escape" mentality.

The Interaction of Working Hours and Pay

With the advent of flexitime and the four-day workweek, an immediate problem arises: How will we define "overtime"? If overtime is defined as "more than eight hours," there are added costs to the four-day workweek. If overtime is defined as "time spent after 5:00 P.M. or before 9:00 A.M., regardless of the number of hours worked," then FWH plans are in trouble. These alternative scheduling schemes may finally force us to consider carefully the nature of human effort. Payment should be at least roughly correlated with the amount of effort required to produce a fixed level of performance (at least within job titles). Thus, if a person is working on the ninth hour of a 10-hour shift, it may very well be that he will have to exert extra energy to yield the same level of performance as a person doing the same task in the sixth hour of an 8-hour shift. It may be that payment schemes will have to be matched carefully to the new demands of alternate working hour schedules.

Comment

While the data reported are somewhat scarce and do not answer all the important questions about work scheduling, I feel that they do support the contention that alternative methods of scheduling working hours may have a significant effect on the worker, the worker's family, and the company. Furthermore, it is likely that some of these effects are short term and others long term. It seems to me that this is another excellent opportunity for the behavioral scientist to work closely with other scientists in making a genuine contribution to workers as individuals and to society as a whole.

In the last chapter, the discussion of the effects of specific stressors (such as noise) required us to consider the dangers involved in many working environments. It is my feeling that work schedules represent both a stressor and a possible adaptive mechanism in the work environment. Shift work, either rotating or fixed, can represent a threat to well-being. Flexitime can represent an aspect of control that is sorely missing from many work environments. In addition, work scheduling is one of the most obvious ways to work out an effective compromise between the worlds of work and nonwork. It deserves the attention of managers and psychologists alike.

CENTRAL POINTS FOR STUDY

1. The human engineering approach includes a consideration of the system formed from the interaction of man and machine.
2. Man-machine systems involve information input, information processing, and response output.
3. Both input and output depend on the capabilities and limitations of both man and machine.
4. Controls and displays interact to affect efficiency.
5. The schedule of working hours has an effect on efficiency and well-being.
6. Shift work, flexitime, and four-day workweeks are examples of alternative schedules of work.
7. Flexitime seems to have positive effects on employees with few costs.

References

Adams, J. S. (1965). Inequity in social exchange. In K. Berkowitz (Ed.), *Advances in experimental social psychology* (Vol. 2, pp. 267–299). New York: Academic Press.

Agervold, M. (1976). Shiftwork: A critical review. *Scandinavian Journal of Psychology, 17,* 181–188.

Ahern, E. (1949). *Handbook of personnel forms and records.* New York: American Management Association.

Akerstedt, T., Patkai, P., & Dahlgren, K. (1977). Field studies of shiftwork: II. Temporal patterns in psychophysiological activation in workers alternating between night and day work. *Ergonomics, 20,* 621–631.

Aldag, R. J., Barr, S. H., & Brief, A. P. (1981). Measurement of perceived task characteristics. *Psychological Bulletin, 90*(3), 415–431.

Alderfer, C. P. (1969). An empirical test of a new theory of human needs. *Organizational Behavior and Human Performance, 4,* 142–175.

Alderfer, C. P. (1972). *Existence, relatedness, and growth: Human needs in organizational settings.* New York: Free Press.

American Psychological Association. (1954). *Technical recommendation for psychological tests and diagnostic techniques.* Washington, DC: APA.

American Psychological Association. (1976). *A career in psychology.* Washington, DC: APA.

American Psychological Association. (1981). Ethical principles of psychologists. *American Psychologist, 36*(6), 633–638.

American Society for Personnel Administration and American Compensation Association. (1981). *Elements of sound base pay administration.* Washington, DC.

Anastasi, A. (1981). Coaching, test sophistication and developed abilities. *American Psychologist, 36*(10), 1086–1093.

Anastasi, A. (1982). *Psychological testing* (5th ed.). New York: Macmillan.

Anastasi, A. (1988). *Psychological testing* (6th ed.). New York: Macmillan.

Applied Ergonomics. (1974). *Applied ergonomics handbook.* Surrey, England: IPC Science and Technology Press.

Argote, L., Goodman, P., & Schkade, D. (1983). The human side of robotics: How workers react to a robot. *Sloan Management Review, 24,* 31–41.

Argyris, C. (1972). *The applicability of organizational sociology.* Cambridge, England: Cambridge University Press.

Arnold, H. J. (1976). Effects of performance feedback and extrinsic reward upon high intrinsic motivation. *Organizational Behavior and Human Performance, 17,* 275–288.

Arnold, H. J., & House, R. J. (1980). Methodological and substantive extensions to the job characteristics model of motivation. *Organizational Behavior and Human Performance, 25,* 161–183.

Arnold, J. D., Rauschenberger, J. M., Soubel, W. G., & Guion, R. M. (1982). Validation and utility of a strength test for selecting steelworkers. *Journal of Applied Psychology, 67*, 588–604.

Arvey, R. D. (1979). Unfair discrimination in the employment interview: Legal and psychological aspects. *Psychological Bulletin, 86*(4), 736–765.

Arvey, R. D. (1986). Sex bias in job evaluation procedures. *Personnel Psychology, 39*(2), 315–335.

Arvey, R. D., Bouchard, T. J., Segal, N. L., & Abraham, L. M. (1987). *Job satisfaction: Environmental and genetic components*. Unpublished manuscript.

Arvey, R. D., & Campion, J. E. (1982). The employment interview: A summary and review of recent literature. *Personnel Psychology, 35*, 281–322.

Arvey, R. D., Davis, G. A., & Nelson, S. M. (1984). Use of discipline in an organization: A field study. *Journal of Applied Psychology, 69*(3), 448–460.

Arvey, R. D., & Ivancevich, J. M. (1980). Punishment in organizations: A review, propositions, and research suggestions. *Academy of Management Review, 5*(1), 123–132.

Asher, J. J., & Sciarrino, J. A. (1974). Realistic work samples: A review. *Personnel Psychology, 27*, 519–534.

Astrand, P. O., & Rohdahl, K. (1977). *Textbook of work physiology* (2nd ed.). New York: McGraw-Hill.

Athey, T. R., & McIntyre, R. M. (1987). Effect of rater training on rater accuracy: Levels-of-processing theory and social facilitation theory perspectives. *Journal of Applied Psychology, 72*(4), 567–572.

Atkinson, J. W. (1964). *An introduction to motivation*. New York: Van Nostrand Reinhold.

Atkinson, J. W., & Feather, N. T. (Eds.). (1966). *A theory of achievement motivation*. New York: John Wiley & Sons.

Ax, A. F. (1953). The physiological differentiation between fear and anger in humans *Psychosomatic Medicine, 15*, 433–442.

Baldamus, W. (1951). Type of work and motivation. *British Journal of Sociology, 2*, 44–58.

Bandura, A. (1969). *Principles of behavior modification*. New York: Holt, Rinehart, & Winston.

Bandura, A. (1977). Self-efficacy: Toward a unifying theory of behavioral change. *Psychological Review, 84*(2), 191–215.

Bandura, A. (1982). Self-efficacy mechanism in human agency. *American Psychologist, 37*(2), 122–147.

Bandura, A. (1986). *Social foundation of thought and action: A social cognitive theory*. Englewood Cliffs, NJ: Prentice-Hall.

Bandura, A. (1987). Self-regulation of motivation and action through goal systems. In V. Hamilton & N. H. Fryda (Eds.), *Cognition, motivation, and affect: A cognitive science view*. Dordrecht: Martinus Nijholl.

Barling, J., & Rosenbaum, A. (1986). Work stressors and wife abuse. *Journal of Applied Psychology, 71*(2), 346–348.

Barnes-Farrell, J. L., & Weiss, H. M. (1984). Effects of standard extremity on mixed standard scale performance ratings. *Personnel Psychology, 37*(2), 301–316.

Baron, R. A. (1983). Sweet smell of success: The impact of pleasant artificial scents on the attractiveness of job applicants. *Journal of Applied Psychology, 68,* 709–711.

Baron, R. A. (1984). Reducing organizational conflict: An incompatible response approach. *Journal of Applied Psychology, 69*(2), 272–279.

Barr, S. H., & Hitt, M. A. (1986). A comparison of selection decision models in manager versus student samples. *Personnel Psychology, 39*(3), 599–618.

Barrett, G. V., Phillips, J. S., & Alexander, R. A. (1981). Concurrent and predictive validity designs: A critical reanalysis. *Journal of Applied Psychology, 66*(1), 1–6.

Barrett, G. V., & Thornton, C. L. (1968). The relationship between perceptual style and driver reaction to an emergency situation. *Journal of Applied Psychology, 52,* 169–176.

Bartlett, C. J. (1978). Equal employment opportunity issues in training. *Human Factors, 20,* 179–188.

Basadur, M., Graen, G. B., & Green, S. G. (1982). Training in creative problem solving: Effects on ideation and problem finding and solving in an industrial research organization. *Organizational Behavior and Human Performance, 30,* 41–71.

Bass, B. M. (1954). The leaderless group discussion. *Psychological Bulletin, 51,* 465–492.

Bass, B. M. (1960). *Leadership, psychology, and organizational behavior.* New York: Harper.

Bass, B. M. (1983). Issues involved in relations between methodological rigor and reported outcomes in evaluations of organizational development. *Journal of Applied Psychology, 68*(1), 197–199.

Bass, B. M., & Norton, F. T. M. (1951). Group size and leaderless discussion. *Journal of Applied Psychology, 6,* 397–400.

Baxter, J. C., Brock, B., Hill, P. C., & Rozelle, R. M. (1981). Letters of recommendation: A question of value. *Journal of Applied Psychology, 66*(3), 296–301.

Beach, L. R., & Mitchell, T. R. (1978). A contingency model for the selection of decision strategies. *Academy of Management Review, 3,* 439–449.

Beck, R. C. (1983). *Motivation: Theory and principles.* Englewood Cliffs, NJ: Prentice-Hall.

Beer, M. (1976). The technology of organizational development. In M. D. Dunnette (Ed.), *Handbook of industrial and organizational psychology.* Chicago: Rand McNally.

Ben-Shukhar, G., Bar-Hillel, M., Bilu, Y., Ben-Abba, E., & Flug, A. (1986). Can graphology predict occupational success? Two empirical studies and some methodological ruminations. *Journal of Applied Psychology, 71*(4), 645–653.

Bernardin, H. J. (1977). Behavioral expectation scales versus summated ratings: A fairer comparison. *Journal of Applied Psychology, 62*(4), 422–427.

Bernardin, H. J., Alvares, K. M., & Cranny, C. J. (1976). A recomparison of behavioral expectation scales to summated scales. *Journal of Applied Psychology, 61,* 564–570.

Bernardin, H. J., & Bownas, D. A. (Eds.). (1985). *Personality assessment in organizations.* New York: Praeger.

Bernardin, H. J., & Kane, J. S. (1980). A second look at behavioral observation scales. *Personnel Psychology, 33,* 809–814.

Bernardin, H. J., & Pence, E. C. (1980). Effects of rater training: Creating new response sets and decreasing accuracy. *Journal of Applied Psychology, 65*(1), 60–66.

Bernick, E. L., Kindley, R., & Pettit, K. K. (1984). The structure of training courses and the effects of hierarchy. *Public Personnel Management, 13,* 109–119.

Berryman-Fink, C. (1985). Male and female managers' views of the communication skills and training needs of women in management. *Public Personnel Management, 14,* 307–313.

Bhagat, R. S., McQuaid, S. J., Lindholm, H., & Segovis, J. (1985). Total life stress: A multimethod validation of the construct and its effects on organizationally valued outcomes and withdrawal behaviors. *Journal of Applied Psychology, 70*(1), 202–214.

Birnbaum, M. H. (1983). Perceived equity of salary policies. *Journal of Applied Psychology, 68*(1), 49–59.

Birnbaum, P. H., Farh, J. L., & Wong, G. Y. Y. (1986). The job characteristics model in Hong Kong. *Journal of Applied Psychology, 71*(4), 598–605.

Blanz, F., & Ghiselli, E. E. (1972). The mixed standard scale: A new rating system. *Personnel Psychology, 25,* 185–200.

Blau, G. (1981). An empirical investigation of job stress, social support, service length, and job strain. *Organizational Behavior and Human Performance, 27,* 279–302.

Boehm, V. R. (1977). Differential prediction: A methodological artifact? *Journal of Applied Psychology, 62*(2), 146–154.

Borman, W. C. (1982). Validity of behavioral assessment for predicting military recruiter performance. *Journal of Applied Psychology, 67*(1), 3–9.

Boucher, J., & Osgood, C. E. (1969). The Pollyanna hypothesis. *Journal of Verbal Learning and Verbal Behavior, 8,* 1–8.

Bower, G. H., & Hilgard, E. R. (1981). *Theories of learning.* Englewood Cliffs, NJ: Prentice-Hall.

Bownas, D. A., Bosshardt, M. J., & Donnelly, L. F. (1985). A quantitative approach to evaluating training curriculum content sampling adequacy. *Personnel Psychology, 38,* 117–131.

Bradford, L. P., Gibb, J. R., & Benne, K. D. (1964). *T-group theory and laboratory method.* New York: John Wiley & Sons.

Bransford, J. D., & Franks, J. J. (1971). The abstraction of linguistic ideas. *Cognitive Psychology, 2,* 331–350.

Bray, D. W., Campbell, R. J., & Grant, D. L. (1974). *Formative years in business: A long-term AT&T study of managerial lives.* New York: John Wiley & Sons.

Bray, D. W., & Grant, D. L. (1966). The assessment center in the measurement of potential for business management. *Psychological Monographs: General and Applied, 80*(17), 53.

Brayfield, A. H., & Crockett, W. H. (1955). Employee attitudes and employee performance. *Psychological Bulletin, 52,* 396–424.

Brenner, S. O., & Bartell, R. (1983). The psychological impact of unemployment: A structural analysis of cross-sectional data. *Journal of Occupational Psychology, 56,* 129–136.

Brett, J. M. (1982). Job transfer and well-being. *Journal of Applied Psychology, 67*(4), 450–463.

Brief, A. P., & Aldag, R. J. (1975). Employee reactions to job characteristics: A constructive replication. *Journal of Applied Psychology, 60,* 182–186.

Brief, A. P., Fulk, M., & Barr, S. H. (1981). Correlates of perceived fairness and accuracy of performance evaluations: Trimming of a model. Mimeo. Los Angeles: University of Southern California, Annenberg School of Communications.

Briggs, L. J. (1960). Teaching machines. In G. Finch (Ed.), *Educational and training media: A symposium.* Washington, DC: National Academy of Sciences–National Research Council.

Broadbent, D. E. (1954). Some effects of noise on visual performance. *Quarterly Journal of Experimental Psychology, 6,* 1–5.

Broadbent, D. E. (1957). Effects of noise on behavior. In C. M. Harris (Ed.), *Handbook of noise control.* New York: McGraw-Hill.

Broadbent, D. E. (1971). *Decision and stress.* New York: Academic Press.

Brown, J. A. C. (1954). *The social psychology of industry.* Baltimore: Penguin Books.

Buchanan, D. A., & Boddy, D. (1983). Advanced technology and the quality of working life: The effects of computerized controls on biscuit making operators. *Journal of Occupational Psychology, 56,* 109–119.

Bunker, K. A., & Cohen, S. L. (1977). The rigors of training evaluation. A discussion of field demonstration. *Personnel Psychology, 30,* 525–541.

Burke, M. J., & Day, R. R. (1986). A cumulative study of the effectiveness of managerial training. *Journal of Applied Psychology, 71*(2), 232–245.

Burke, R. J., Weir, T., & DuWors, R. E. (1979). Type A behavior of administrators and wives reports of marital satisfaction and well-being. *Journal of Applied Psychology, 64,* 57–65.

Burke, R. J., Weitzel, W., & Weir, T. (1978). Characteristics of effective employee performance review and development interviews: Replication and extension. *Personnel Psychology, 31,* 903–919.

Burnaska, R. F. (1976). The effects of behavior modeling training upon managers' behaviors and employees' perceptions. *Personnel Psychology, 29,* 329–335.

Burns, T., & Stalker, G. M. (1961). *The management of innovation.* London: Tavistock Publications, Ltd.

Buros, O. K. (1938). *The first mental measurements yearbook.* Highland Park, NJ: Gryphon.

Buros, O. K. (1972). *The seventh mental measurements yearbook.* Highland Park, NJ: Gryphon.

Buros, O. K. (1978). *The eighth mental measurements yearbook.* Highland Park, NJ: Gryphon.

Bursill, A. E. (1958). The restriction of peripheral vision during exposure to hot and humid conditions. *Quarterly Journal of Experimental Psychology, 10,* 113–129.

Butler, R. P., & Jaffee, C. L. (1974). Effects of incentive feedback and manner of presenting the feedback on leader behavior. *Journal of Applied Psychology, 59,* 332–336.

Calder, B. J., & Staw, B. M. (1975). Self-perception of intrinsic and extrinsic motivation. *Journal of Personality and Social Psychology, 31,* 599–605.

Caldwell, D. F., & O'Reilly, C. A., III. (1982). Task perceptions and job satisfaction: A question of causality. *Journal of Applied Psychology, 67,* 361–369.

Campbell, D. T., & Stanley, J. C. (1963). *Experimental and quasi-experimental designs for research.* Chicago: Rand McNally.

Campbell, J. P., (1971). Personnel training and development. *Annual Review of Psychology.* Palo Alto, CA: Annual Review.

Campbell, J. P., Dunnette, M. D., Lawler, E. E., & Weick, K. E. (1970). *Managerial behavior, performance, and effectiveness.* New York: McGraw-Hill.

Campbell, J. P., & Pritchard, R. D. (1976). Motivation theory in industrial and organizational psychology. In M. Dunnette (Ed.), *Handbook of industrial and organizational psychology.* Chicago: Rand McNally.

Campion, M. A. (1983). Personnel selection for physically demanding jobs: Review and recommendations. *Personnel Psychology, 36,* 527–550.

Campion, M. A., & Thayer, P. W. (1985). Development and field evaluation of an interdisciplinary measure of job design. *Journal of Applied Psychology, 70*(1), 29–43.

Cardy, R. L., & Kehoe, J. F. (1984). Rater selective attention ability and appraisal effectiveness: The effect of a cognitive style on the accuracy of differentiation among ratees. *Journal of Applied Psychology, 69*(4), 589–594.

Carlson, R. E. (1967a). Selection interview decisions: The effect of interviewer experience, relative quota situation, and applicant sample on interviewer decisions. *Personnel Psychology, 20,* 259–290.

Carlson, R. E. (1967b). Selection interview decisions: The relative influence of appearance and factual written information on an interviewer's final rating. *Journal of Applied Psychology, 51,* 461–468.

Carlson, R. E. (1968). Employment decisions: Effect of mode of applicant presentation on some outcome measures. *Personnel Psychology, 21,* 193–207.

Carlson, R. E. (1972, May). *The current status of judgemental techniques in industry.* Paper presented at the symposium "Alternatives to paper and pencil personnel testing." University of Pittsburgh.

Carsten, J. M., & Spector, P. E. (1987). Unemployment, job satisfaction, and employee turnover: A meta-analytic test of the Muchinsky model. *Journal of Applied Psychology, 72*(3), 374–381.

Carter, L., Haythorn, W., Shriver, B., & Lanzetta, J. (1951). The relation of categorizations and ratings in the observation of group behavior. *Human Relations, 4,* 239–253.

Carter, R. (1979). *Visual and color coding.* Unpublished manuscript, University Park, PA: Penn State University, Department of Psychology.

Carver, C. S., & Scheier, M. F. (1981). *Attention and self-regulation: A control theory approach to human behavior.* New York: Springer-Verlag.

Carvey, D., & Nibler, R. G. (1977). Biorhythmic cycles and the incidence of industrial accidents. *Personnel Psychology, 30,* 447–454.

Cascio, W. F. (1975). Accuracy of verifiable biographical information blank responses. *Journal of Applied Psychology, 60,* 767–769.

Cascio, W. F. (1976). Turnover, biographical data, and fair employment practice. *Journal of Applied Psychology, 61,* 576–580.

Cascio, W. F. (1982). *Applied psychology in personnel management* (2nd ed.). Reston, VA: Reston Publishing.

Cascio, W. F., & Bernardin, H. J. (1981). Implications of performance appraisal litigation for personnel decisions. *Personnel Psychology, 34,* 211–226.

Cascio, W. F., & Phillips, N. F. (1979). Performance testing: A rose among thorns. *Personnel Psychology, 32,* 751–765.

Chadwick-Jones, J. K., Brown, C., Nicholson, N., & Sheppard, C. (1971). Absence measures: Their reliability and stability in an industrial setting. *Personnel Psychology, 23,* 463–470.

Chadwick-Jones, J. K., Nicholson, N., & Brown, C. (1982). *The social psychology of absenteeism.* New York: Praeger.

Chaffin, R., & Skadburg, J. (1979). Effect of scoring set on biorhythm data. *Journal of Applied Psychology, 63,* 213–217.

Chao, G. T., & Kozlowski, S. W. (1986). Employee perception on the implementation of robotic manufacturing technology. *Journal of Applied Psychology, 71*(1), 70–76.

Chapanis, A., Garner, W. R., & Morgan, C. T. (1949). *Applied experimental psychology: Human factors in engineering design.* New York: John Wiley & Sons.

Chapanis, A., & Lindenbaum, L. E. (1959). A reaction time study of four control-display linkages. *Human Factors, 1,* 1–7.

Chemers, M. M., & Fiedler, F. E. (1986). The trouble with assumptions: A reply to Jago and Ragan. *Journal of Applied Psychology, 71*(4), 560–563.

Cherrington, D. J., Reitz, H. J., & Scott, W. E. (1971). Effect of contingent and noncontingent reward on the relationship between satisfaction and task performance. *Journal of Applied Psychology, 55,* 531–536.

Cleary, T. A., Humphreys, L. G., Kendrick, S. A., & Wesman, A. (1975). Educational uses of tests with disadvantaged students. *American Psychologist, 30,* 15–41.

Cofer, C. N., & Appley, M. H. (1964). *Motivation: Theory and research.* New York: Wiley.

Cohen, J., & Lefkowitz, J. (1974). Development of a biographical inventory blank to predict faking on personality tests. *Journal of Applied Psychology, 59*(3), 404–405.

Cohen, S. L., & Turney, J. R. (1978). Intervening at the bottom: Organizational development with enlisted personnel in an army work setting. *Personnel Psychology, 31,* 715–730.

Cohen, S. L., & Wills, T. A. (1985). Stress, social support, and the buffering hypothesis. *Psychological Bulletin, 98*(2), 310–357.

Colquhoun, W. P. (1962). Effects of hyoscine and meclozine on vigilance and short-term memory. *British Journal of Industrial Medicine, 19,* 287–296.

Cook, J. D., Hepworth, S. J., Wall, T. D., & Warr, P. B. (1981). *The experience of work.* New York: Academic Press.

Cooper, C., & Payne, R. L. (1978). *Stress at work.* New York: John Wiley & Sons.

Cordes, C. (1983, June). Human factors and nuclear power: Nose to the grindstone or lip service? *Monitor, 14,* 3.

Craik, F. I. M., & Lockhart, R. S. (1972). Levels of processing: A framework for memory research. *Journal of Verbal Learning and Verbal Behavior, 11,* 671–684.

Cronback, L. J. (1970). *Essentials of psychological testing.* New York: Harper & Row.

Cronback, L. J., & Gleser, G. C. (1965). *Psychological tests and personnel decisions.* Urbana, IL: University of Illinois Press.

Crowder, N. A. (1959). Automatic tutoring by means of intrinsic programming. In E. H. Galanter (Ed.), *Automatic teaching: The state of the art* (pp. 109–116). New York: John Wiley & Sons.

Croyle, R. T., & Cooper, J. (1983). Dissonance arousal: Physiological evidence. *Journal of Personality and Social Psychology, 45,* 782–791.

Cummings, L. L. (1973). A field experimental study of the effects of two performance appraisal systems. *Personnel Psychology, 26,* 489–502.

Dachler, H. P., & Wilpert, B. (1978). Conceptual dimensions and boundaries of participation: A critical evaluation. *Administrative Science Quarterly, 23,* 1–39.

Dalton, G. W., & Thompson, P. H. (1971). Accelerating obsolescence of older engineers. *Harvard Business Review, 49,* 57–67.

Dansereau, F., Graen, G., & Haga, W. J. (1974). *A vertical dyad linkage approach to leadership within the formal organization.* Unpublished report, State University of New York, Buffalo.

DAT Space Relations Test Manual. (1973, 1974). Reproduced by permission. Copyright 1973, 1974 by The Psychological Corporation, New York, NY. All rights reserved.

Davis, B. L., & Mount, M. K. (1984). Effectiveness of performance appraisal training using computer assisted instruction and behavior modeling. *Personnel Psychology, 37*(3), 439–452.

Dean, R. A., & Wanous, J. P. (1984). Effects of realistic job previews on hiring bank tellers. *Journal of Applied Psychology, 69,* 61–68.

DeCharms, R., & Muir, M. S. (1978). Motivation: Social approaches. *Annual Review of Psychology, 29,* 91–113.

Deci, E. L. (1972). The effects of contingent and noncontingent rewards and controls on intrinsic motivation. *Organizational Behavior and Human Performance, 8,* 217–229.

Deci, E. L. (1976). Notes on the theory and metatheory of intrinsic motivation. *Organizational Behavior and Human Performance, 15*(1), 130–145.

Decker, P. J., & Cornelius, E. T., III. (1979). A note on recruiting sources and job survival rates. *Journal of Applied Psychology, 64,* 463–464.

DeMan, H. (1929). *Joy in work.* New York: Henry Holt.

DenGreene, K. B. (1988). Long wave cycles of sociotechnical change and innovation: A macropsychological perspective. *Journal of Occupational Psychology, 61*(1), 7–23.

DeNisi, A. S., Cornelius, E. T., III, & Blencoe, A. G. (1987). Further investigation of common knowledge effects on job analysis ratings. *Journal of Applied Psychology, 72*(2), 262–268.

DiMarco, N., & Gustafson, D. P. (1975). Attitudes of co-workers and management toward hard-core employees. *Personnel Psychology, 28*, 65–76.

Dooley, D., Rook, K., & Catalano, R. (1987). Job and non-job stressors and their moderators. *Journal of Occupational Psychology, 60*(2), 115–132.

Dossett, D. L., Latham, G. P., & Mitchell, T. R. (1979). Effects of assigned versus participatively set goals, knowledge of results, and individual differences on employee behavior when goal difficulty is held constant. *Journal of Applied Psychology, 64*, 291–298.

Doverspike, D., Carlisi, A. M., Barrett, G. V., & Alexander, R. A. (1983). Generalizability analysis of a point method job evaluation instrument. *Journal of Applied Psychology, 68*(3), 476–483.

Dreher, G. F., & Sackett, P. R. (1983). *Perspectives on staffing and selection*. Homewood, IL: Irwin.

Dubin, R. (1965). Supervision and productivity: Empirical findings and theoretical considerations. In R. Dubin (Ed.), *Leadership and productivity*. San Francisco, CA: Chandler.

Dubin, S. S. (1972a). Obsolescence of life-long education: A choice for the professional. *American Psychologist, 27*, 486–498.

Dubin, S. S. (Ed.). (1972b). *Professional obsolescence*. Lexington, MA: Health.

DuBois, P. (1970). *A history of psychological testing*. Boston: Allyn & Bacon.

Duchon, D., Green, S. G., & Taber, T. D. (1986). Vertical dyad linkage: A longitudinal assessment of antecedents, measures, and consequences. *Journal of Applied Psychology, 72*(1), 56–60.

Dunham, R. B. (1976). The measurement and dimensionality of job characteristics. *Journal of Applied Psychology, 61*, 404–409.

Dunnette, M. D. (Ed.). (1976). *Handbook of industrial and organizational psychology*. Chicago: Rand McNally.

Dunnette, M., & Borman, W. (1979). Personnel section and classification systems. In M. Rosenzweig & L. Porter (Eds.), *Annual Review of Psychology, 30*, 477–526.

Dyer, L., & Parker, D. F. (1975). Classifying outcomes in work motivation research: An examination of the intrinsic-extrinsic dichotomy. *Journal of Applied Psychology, 60*, 455–458.

Earley, C., & Kanfer, R. (1985). The influence of component participation and role models on goal acceptance, goal satisfaction, and performance. *Organizational Behavior and Human Decision Processes, 36*(3), 378–390.

Eberhardt, B. J., & Muchinsky, P. M. (1982a). Biodata determinants of vocational typology: An integration of two paradigms. *Journal of Applied Psychology, 67*(2), 714–727.

Eberhardt, B. J., & Muchinsky, P. M. (1982b). An empirical investigation of the factor stability of Owens' biographical questionnaire. *Journal of Applied Psychology, 67*(2), 138–145.

Eden, D. (1982). Critical job events, acute stress, and strain: A multiple interrupted time series. *Organizational Behavior and Human Performance, 30,* 312–329.

Eden, D., & Shani, A. B. (1982). Pygmalion goes to boot camp. Expectancy, leadership, and trainee performance. *Journal of Applied Psychology, 67*(2), 194–199.

Emery Air Freight Corporation. (1971). *Feedback systems.* Wilton, CT: System Performance Division.

England, G. W., & Patterson, D. G. (1960). Selection and placement: The past ten years. In H. G. Heneman, R. L. C. Brown, M. K. Chandler, R. Kahn, H. S. Parnes, & G. P. Shultz (Eds.), *Employment relations research: A summary and appraisal* (pp. 43–72). New York: Harper & Brothers Publisher.

Equal Employment Opportunity Commission. (1974). *Guidelines on employee selection procedures.* Washington, DC: U.S. Government Printing Office.

Equal Employment Opportunity Commission. (1978a). Adoption by four agencies of uniform guidelines on employee selection procedures. *Federal Register, 43,* 38290–38309.

Equal Employment Opportunity Commission. (1978b). *Guidelines on employment testing procedures.* Washington, DC: Equal Employment Opportunity Commission.

Evans, M. G., & Derner, J. (1974). What does least preferred co-worker scale really measure? A cognitive interpretation. *Journal of Applied Psychology, 59,* 202–206.

Evers, F. T., Bohlen, J. M., & Warren, R. D. (1976). The relationships of selected size and structure indicators in economic organizations. *Administrative Science Quarterly, 21,* 326–342.

Ewen, R. B. (1964). Some determinants of job satisfaction: A study of the generality of Herzberg's theory. *Journal of Applied Psychology, 48,* 161–163.

Ewen, R. B. (1967). Weighting components of job satisfaction. *Journal of Applied Psychology, 51,* 68–73.

Ewen, R. B., Smith, P. C., Hulin, C. L., & Locke, E. A. (1966). An empirical test of the Herzberg two-factor theory. *Journal of Applied Psychology, 50,* 544–550.

Farh, J. L., & Werbel, J. D. (1986). Effects of purpose of the appraisal and expectation of validation on self-appraisal leniency. *Journal of Applied Psychology, 71*(3), 527–529.

Farr, J. L. (1976). Task characteristics, reward contingency, and intrinsic motivation. *Organizational Behavior and Human Performance, 16,* 294–307.

Farr, J. L., Vance, R. J., & McIntyre, R. M. (1977). Further examinations of the relationship between reward contingency and intrinsic motivation. *Organizational Behavior and Human Performance, 20,* 31–53.

Feild, H. S., & Holley, W. H. (1980). *The relationship of performance appraisal system characteristics in verdicts in selected employment discrimination cases.* Mimeo. Auburn University.

Feldman, J. M. (1973). Race, economic class, perceived outcomes of work, and unemployment. *Journal of Applied Psychology, 58,* 16–22.

Feldman, J. M. (1981). Beyond attribution theory: Cognitive processes in performance appraisal. *Journal of Applied Psychology, 66*(2), 127–148.

Ferguson, L. W. (1962). *The heritage of industrial psychology.* Hartford, CT: Finlay Press.

Ferster, C. B., & Skinner, B. F. (1957). *Schedules of reinforcement.* New York: Appleton-Century-Crofts.

Festinger, L. (1957). *A theory of cognitive dissonance.* Evanston, IL: Row, Peterson.

Fiedler, F. E. (1951). A method of objective quantification of certain countertransference attitudes. *Journal of Clinical Psychology, 7,* 101–107.

Fiedler, F. E. (1967). *A theory of leadership effectiveness.* New York: McGraw-Hill.

Fiedler, F. E., & Fiedler, J. (1975). Port noise complaints: Verbal and behavioral reactions to airport-related noise. *Journal of Applied Psychology, 60,* 498–506.

Fiedler, F. E., & Mahar, L. (1979). The effectiveness of contingency model training: A review of the validation of Leader Match. *Personnel Psychology, 32,* 45–62.

Fiedler, F. E., Mitchell, T., & Triandis, H. C. (1971). The culture assimilator: An approach to cross-cultural training. *Journal of Applied Psychology, 55,* 95–102.

Field, R. H. G. (1982). A test of the Vroom-Yetton normative model of leadership. *Journal of Applied Psychology, 67*(5), 523–532.

Finkelman, J. M., Zeitlin, L. R., Filippi, J. A., & Friend, M. A. (1977). Noise and driver performance. *Journal of Applied Psychology, 62,* 713–718.

Finkle, R. B. (1976). Managerial assessment centers. In M. D. Dunnette (Ed.), *Handbook of industrial and organizational psychology* (pp. 861–888). Chicago: Rand McNally.

Firth, J., & Shapiro, D. A. (1986). An evaluation of psychotherapy for job-related distress. *Journal of Occupational Psychology, 59*(2), 111–119.

Fisher, C. D., & Gitelson, R. (1983). A meta-analysis of the correlates of role conflict and ambiguity. *Journal of Applied Psychology, 68*(2), 320–333.

Fitts, P. M. (1951). Engineering psychology and equipment design. In S. S. Stevens (Ed.), *Handbook of experimental psychology* (pp. 1287–1340). New York: John Wiley & Sons.

Fitts, P. M., & Jones, R. E. (1947a). *Analysis of factors contributing to 460 "pilot-error" experiences in operating aircraft controls* (Report No. TSEAA-694-12). Dayton, OH: Engineering Division, Air Materiel Command.

Fitts, P. M., & Jones, R. E. (1947b). *Psychological aspects of instrument display. I: Analysis of 270 "pilot-error" experiences in reading and interpreting aircraft instruments* (Report. No. TSEAA-694-12A). Aero Medical Laboratory, Air Materiel Command.

Flanagan, J. C. (1954). The critical incident technique. *Psychological Bulletin, 51*(4), 327–358.

Fleishman, E. A. (1966). Human abilities and the acquisition of skill. In E. A. Bilodeau (Ed.), *Acquisition of skill.* New York: Academic Press.

Fleishman, E. A. (1967a). The development of a behavior taxonomy for describing human tasks: A correlational-experimental approach. *Journal of Applied Psychology, 51,* 1–10.

Fleishman, E. A. (1967b). Performance assessment based on an empirically derived task taxonomy. *Human Factors, 9,* 349–366.

Fleishman, E. A. (1975). Toward a taxonomy of human performance. *American Psychologist, 30,* 1127–1149.

Fleishman, E. A. & Harris, E. F. (1962). Patterns of leadership behavior related to employee grievances and turnover. *Personnel Psychology, 15,* 43–56.

Fleishman, E. A., & Parker, J. F. (1962). Factors in the retention and relearning of perceptual motor skill. *Journal of Experimental Psychology, 64,* 215–226.

Fleishman, E. A., & Quaintance, M. K. (1984). *Taxonomies of human performance, the description of human tasks.* Broedling, FL: Academic Press.

Fleishman, E. A., & Rich, S. (1963). Role of kinesthetic and spatial-visual abilities in perceptual motor learning. *Journal of Experimental Psychology, 66,* 6–11.

Forbes, T. W. (1946). Auditory signals for instrument flying. *Journal of Aeronautical Science, 13,* 255–258.

Ford, K., Kraiger, K., & Schechtman, S. L. (1986). Study of race effects in objective indices and subjective evaluations of performance: A meta-analysis of performance criteria. *Psychological Bulletin, 99,* 330–337.

Frankenhauser, M. (1974). Overstimulation—A threat to the quality of life. In *Man in the communications system of the future.* Stockholm: Swedish Cabinet Office, Secretariat for Future Studies.

Frankenhauser, M., & Gardell, B. (1976). Underload and overload in working life: Outcline of a multidisciplinary approach. *Journal of Human Stress, 2,* 34–46.

Frankenhauser, M., Lundberg, U., & Forsman, L. (1980). Note on arousing Type A persons by depriving them of work. *Journal of Psychosomatic Research, 24*(1), 45–47.

Franklin, J. L. (1975). Relations among four social-psychological aspects of organizations. *Administrative Science Quarterly, 20,* 422–433.

Freeberg, N. E. (1969). Relevance of rater-ratee acquaintance in the validity and reliability of ratings. *Journal of Applied Psychology, 53*(6), 518–524.

Freedman, S. M., & Phillips, J. S. (1985). The effects of situational performance constraints on intrinsic motivation and satisfaction: The role of perceived competence and self determination. *Organizational Behavior and Human Decision Processes, 35,* 397–416.

French, J. R. P., Jr., Caplan, R. D., & Van Harrison, R. (1982). *The mechanisms of job stress and strain.* New York: John Wiley & Sons.

French, J. R. P., Jr., & Raven, B. H. (1959). The bases of social power. In D. Cartwright, (Ed.), *Studies in social power.* Ann Arbor: University of Michigan, Institute for Social Research.

Frese, M. (1986). Coping as a moderator and mediator between stress at work and psychosomatic complaints. In M. H. Appley & R. Trumbull (Eds.), *Dynamics of stress* (pp. 183–206). N.Y. London: Plenum.

Frese, M., & Okonek, K. (1984). Reasons to leave shiftwork and psychological and psychosomatic complaints of former shiftworkers. *Journal of Applied Psychology, 69*(3), 509–514.

Freud, S. (1922). *Beyond the pleasure principle* (C. J. M. Hubback, Trans.). London, Vienna: The International Psychoanalytical Press.

Freud, S. (1930). *Civilization and its discontents.* London: Hogarth Press.

Fried, Y., & Ferris, G. R. (1986). The dimensionality of job characteristics: Some neglected issues. *Journal of Applied Psychology, 71*(3), 419–426.

Friedlander, F. (1980). The facilitation of change in organizations. *Professional Psychology, 11,* 520–530.

Friedlander, F., & Greenberg, S. (1971). Effect of job attitudes, training, and organization climate on performance of the hard-core unemployed. *Journal of Applied Psychology, 55*(4), 187–195.

Friedman, L., & Harvey, R. J. (1986). Can raters with reduced job descriptive information provide accurate Position Analysis Questionnaire (PAQ) ratings? *Personnel Psychology, 39*(4), 779–790.

Friedman, M., & Rosenman, R. H. (1974). *Type A behavior and your heart.* New York: Alfred A. Knopf.

Frost, P. J., & Jamal, M. (1979). Shift work, attitudes, and reported behavior: Some associations between individual characteristics and hours of work and leisure. *Journal of Applied Psychology, 64,* 77–81.

Fryer, D. H., & Henry, E. R. (1950). *Handbook of applied psychology* (Vols. I & II). New York: Holt, Rinehart, & Winston.

Ganster, D. C., Fusilier, M. R., & Mayes, B. T. (1986). Role of social support in the experience of stress at work. *Journal of Applied Psychology, 71*(1), 102–110.

Ganster, D. C., Mayes, B. T., Sime, W. E., & Tharp, G. S. (1982). Managing organizational stress: A field experiment. *Journal of Applied Psychology, 67*(5), 533–542.

Gardner, D. G. (1986). Activation theory and task design: An empirical test of several new predictions. *Journal of Applied Psychology, 71*(3), 411–418.

Garner, W., & Wigdor, A. (1982). *Ability testing: Use, consequences and controversies.* Washington, DC: National Academy Press.

Garson, B. (1972, June). Luddities in Lordstown. *Harpers Magazine,* pp. 67–73.

Garson, B. (1975). *All the livelong day.* New York: Penguin Books.

Gechman, A. S., & Wiener, Y. (1975). Job involvement and satisfaction as related to mental health and personal time devoted to work. *Journal of Applied Psychology, 60,* 521–523.

Georgopoulos, B. S., Mahoney, G. M., & Jones, N. W. (1957). A path-goal approach to productivity. *Journal of Applied Psychology, 41,* 345–353.

Ghiselli, E. E. (1955). The measurement of occupational aptitude. *University of California Publications in Psychology, 8,* 101–216.

Ghiselli, E. E. (1966). *The validity of occupational aptitude tests.* New York: John Wiley & Sons.

Ghiselli, E. (1969). The efficacy of advancement on the basis of merit in relation to structural properties of the organization. *Organizational Behavior and Human Performance, 4,* 402–413.

Ghiselli, E. E. (1973). The validity of aptitude tests in personnel selection. *Personnel Psychology, 26,* 461–477.

Ghiselli, E. E., & Brown, C. W. (1948). *Personnel and industrial psychology.* New York: McGraw-Hill.

Ghiselli, E. E., & Brown, C. W. (1955). *Personnel and industrial psychology* (2nd ed.). New York: McGraw-Hill.

Gifford, R., Ng, C. F., & Wilkinson, M. (1985). Nonverbal cues in the employment interview: Links between applicant qualities and interviewer judgments. *Journal of Applied Psychology, 70*(4), 729–736.

Gilbert, T. F. (1960). On the relevance of laboratory investigation of learning to self-instructional programming. In A. A. Lumsdaine & R. Glaser (Eds.), *Teaching machines and programmed instruction* (pp. 475–485). Washington, DC: Department of Audio-Visual Instruction, National Education Association.

Gilbreth, F. B., & Gilbreth, L. M. (1917). *Applied motion study.* New York: Sturgis & Walton Company.

Gillberg, M. (1983). *The human sleep-wake cycle: Circadian and homeostatic influences.* Stockholm, Sweden: Karolinska Institute.

Gioia, D. A., & Sims, H. P., Jr. (1986). Cognition-behavior connections: Attribution and verbal behavior in leader-subordinate interactions. *Organizational Behavior and Human Decision Processes, 37,* 197–229.

Glass, C. G., & Singer, J. E. (1972). Behavioral after effects of unpredictable and uncontrollable aversive events. *American Scientist, 60,* 457–465.

Glass, D. C. (1977). *Behavior patterns, stress, and coronary disease.* Hillsdale, NJ: Erlbaum Associates.

Glass, G. V. (1976). Primary, secondary and meta-analysis of research. *Educational Researcher, 5,* 308.

Goldstein, I. L. (1974). *Training: Program development and evaluation.* Monterey, CA: Brooks/Cole Publishing.

Goldstein, I. L. (1980). Training in work organizations. *Annual Review of Psychology, 31,* 229–272.

Goldstein, I. L. (1986). *Training in organizations* (2nd ed.). Monterey, CA: Brooks-Cole.

Goldstein, I. L., & Buxton, V. M. (1982). Training and human performance. In M. D. Dunnette & E. A. Fleishman (Eds.), *Human performance and productivity* (Vol. 1, pp. 135–177). Hillsdale, NJ: Erlbaum.

Goldstein, I. L., & Sorcher, M. (1974). *Changing supervisory behavior.* Elmsford, NY: Pergamon Press.

Golembiewski, R. T., Hilles, R., & Kagno, M. S. (1974). A longitudinal study of flexitime effects: Some consequences of an OD structural intervention. *Journal of Applied Behavioral Sciences, 10,* 403–531.

Goodale, J. G., & Aagaard, A. K. (1975). Factors relating to varying reactions to four-day workweeks. *Journal of Applied Psychology, 60,* 33–38.

Goodman, P. S. (1974). An examination of referents used in the evaluation of pay. *Organizational Behavior and Human Performance, 12,* 170–195.

Goodman, P. S., & Friedman, A. (1971). An examination of Adams' theory of inequity. *Administrative Science Quarterly, 16,* 271–288.

Goodstadt, B. T., & Kipnis, D. (1970). Situational influence on the use of power. *Journal of Applied Psychology, 54*(3), 201–207.

Gordon, M. E., Cofer, J. L., & McCullough, P. M. (1986). Relationships among seniority, past performance, interjob similarity, and trainability. *Journal of Applied Psychology, 71*(3), 518–521.

Gordon, M. E. & Cohen, S. L. (1973). Training behavior as a predictor of trainability. *Personnel Psychology, 26,* 261–272.

Gordon, M. E., & Fitzgibbons, W. J. (1982). Empirical test of the validity of seniority as a factor in staffing decisions. *Journal of Applied Psychology, 67,* 311–319.

Gordon, M. E. & Johnson, W. A. (1982). Seniority: A review of its legal and scientific standing. *Personnel Psychology, 35,* 225–280.

Gordon, M. E., & Kleiman, L. S. (1976). The prediction of trainability using a work sample test and an aptitude test: A direct comparison. *Personnel Psychology, 29*(2), 243–253.

Gorman, C. D., Clover, W. H., & Doherty, M. E. (1978). Can we learn anything about interviewing real people from "interviews" of paper people? Two studies of the external validity of a paradigm. *Organizational Behavior and Human Performance, 22,* 165–192.

Gottfredson, L. (1986). Societal consequences of the g factor in employment. *Journal of Vocational Behavior, 29,* 379–411.

Gould, S. J. (1981). *The mismeasure of man.* New York: Norton.

Graen, G. (1969). Instrumentality theory of work motivation. *Journal of Applied Psychology, 53*(2, Pt. 2).

Graen, G. B., Liden, R. C., & Hoel, W. (1982). Role of leadership in the employee withdrawal process. *Journal of Applied Psychology, 67*(6), 868–872.

Graen, G., & Scheimann, W. (1978). Leader member agreement: A vertical dyad linkage approach. *Journal of Applied Psychology, 63,* 206–212.

Grayson, L. P. (1972). Costs, benefits, effectiveness: Challenge to educational technology. *Science, 175,* 1216–1222.

Green, S. G., & Nebeker, D. M. (1977). The effects of situational factors and leadership style on leader behavior. *Organizational Behavior and Human Performance, 19,* 368–377.

Green, S. B., & Stutzman, T. (1986). An evaluation of methods to select respondents to structured job-analysis questionnaires. *Personnel Psychology, 39*(3), 543–564.

Greenberg, J. (1986). Determinants of perceived fairness of performance evaluations. *Journal of Applied Psychology, 71*(2), 340–342.

Greenberg, J., & Ornstein, S. (1983). High status job title as compensation for underpayment: A test of equity theory. *Journal of Applied Psychology, 68*(2), 285–297.

Greene, C. N. (1975). The reciprocal nature of influence between leader and subordinate. *Journal of Applied Psychology, 60,* 187–193.

Greenwood, J. M., & McNamara, W. J. (1967). Interrater reliability in situational tests. *Journal of Applied Psychology, 51,* 101–106.

Grether, W. F. (1968). Engineering psychology in the United States. *American Psychologist, 23,* 743–751.

Griffeth, R. N. (1985). Moderation of the effects of job enrichment by participation: A longitudinal field experiment. *Organizational Behavior and Human Decision Process, 35*(1), 73–93.

Gross, M. L. (1962). *The brain watchers.* New York: Random House.

Guion, R. M. (1965). *Personnel testing.* New York: McGraw Hill.

Guion, R. M. (1966). Employment tests and discriminatory hiring. *Industrial Relations, 5,* 20–37.

Guion, R. M. (1967). Personnel selection. *Annual Review of Psychology, 18,* 191–216.

Guion, R. M. (1976). Recruiting, selection, and job replacement. In M. D. Dunnette (Ed.), *Handbook of industrial and organizational psychology* (pp. 777–828). Chicago: Rand McNally.

Guion, R. M. (1987). Changing views for personnel selection research. *Personnel Psychology, 40*(2), 199–213.

Guion, R. M., & Cranny, C. J. (1982). A note on concurrent and predictive validity designs: A critical re-analysis. *Journal of Applied Psychology, 67*(2), 239–244.

Guion, R. M., & Gibson, W. M. (1988). Personnel selection and placement. *Annual Review of Psychology, 39,* 349–374.

Guion, R. M., & Gottier, R. F. (1965). Validity of personality measures in personnel selection. *Personnel Psychology, 18,* 135–164.

Guzzo, R. A., Jette, R. D., & Katzell, R. A. (1985). The effects of psychologically based intervention programs on worker productivity: A meta-analysis. *Personnel Psychology, 38*(2), 275–292.

Haccoun, D. M., Haccoun, R. R., & Sallay, G. (1978). Sex differences in the appropriateness of supervisory styles: A nonmanagement view. *Journal of Applied Psychology, 63,* 124–127.

Hackman, J. R., & Oldham, G. R. (1975). Development of the job diagnostic survey. *Journal of Applied Psychology, 60,* 159–170.

Hackman, J. R., & Oldham, G. R. (1976). Motivation through the design of work: Test of a theory. *Organizational Behavior and Human Performance, 16,* 250–279.

Haines, D. B. (1964). *Training for culture-contact and interaction skills.* USAF AMRL-TR No. 64–109.

Haines, D. B., & Eachus, H. T. (1965). *A preliminary study of acquiring cross-cultural interaction skills through self-confrontation.* USAF AMRL-TR No. 65–137.

Hakel, M. D. (1982). Employment interviewing. In K. M. Rowland & G. R. Ferris (Eds.), *Personnel management.* Boston: Allyn & Bacon.

Hakel, M. D. (1986). Personnel selection and placement. *Annual Review of Psychology, 37,* 351–380.

Hall, D. T., & Mansfield, R. (1975). Relationships of age and seniority with career variables of engineers and scientists. *Journal of Applied Psychology, 60,* 201–210.

Hall, D. T., & Nougaim, K. E. (1968). An examination of Maslow's need hierarchy in an organizational setting. *Organizational Behavior and Human Performance, 3,* 12–35.

Hall, J. F. (1982). *An invitation to learning and memory,* Boston, MA: Allyn & Bacon.

Hamburg, D. A., Elliott, G. R., & Parron, D. L. (1982). *Health and behavior: Frontiers of research in the biobehavioral sciences.* Washington, DC: National Academy Press.

Hamner, W. C., & Foster, L. W. (1975). Are intrinsic and extrinsic rewards additive: A list of Deci's cognitive evaluation theory of task motivation. *Organizational Behavior and Human Performance, 14,* 398–415.

Harlow, H. (1959). Learning to learn. In S. Koch (Ed.), *Psychology: A study of a science* (Vol. II). New York: McGraw-Hill.

Harris, D. A. (1987). Joint-service job performance measurement enlistment standards project. *The Industrial/Organizational Psychologist, 24,* 36–42.

Hedrick, K. (1983). *The influence of gender and job type on absenteeism.* Unpublished master's Thesis, Penn State University, Department of Psychology, University Park, PA.

Heilman, M. E., Hornstein, H. A., Cage, J. H., & Herschlag, J. K. (1984). Reactions to prescribed leader behavior as a function of role perspective: The case of the Vroom-Yetton Model. *Journal of Applied Psychology, 69*(1), 50–60.

Heneman, R. L. (1986). The relationship between supervisory ratings and results-oriented measures of performance: A meta-analysis. *Personnel Psychology, 39*(4), 811–826.

Herman, J. A., de Montes, A. E., Dominquez, B., Montes, F., & Hopkins, B. L. (1973). Effects of bonuses for punctuality on the tardiness of industrial workers. *Journal of Applied Behavioral Analysis. 6,* 563–572.

Herzberg, F. (1966). *Work and the nature of man.* Cleveland: World Publishing.

Herzberg, F., Mausner, B., Peterson, R. O., & Capwell, D. F. (1957). *Job attitudes: Review of research and opinion.* Pittsburgh: Psychological Service of Pittsburgh.

Herzberg, F., Mausner, B., & Snyderman, B. (1959). *The motivation to work.* New York: John Wiley & Sons.

Hill, T., & Schmitt, N. (1977). Individual differences in leadership decision making. *Organizational Behavior and Human Performance, 19,* 353–367.

Hill, T., Smith, N. D., & Mann, M. F. (1987). Role of efficacy expectations in predicting the decision to use advanced technologies: The case of computers. *Journal of Applied Psychology, 72*(2), 307–313.

Hinrichs, J. R., & Haanpera, S. (1976). Reliability of measurement in situational exercises: An assessment of assessment center testing. *Personnel Psychology, 29,* 31–40.

Hinrichs, J. R., & Mischkind, L. A. (1967). Empirical and theoretical limitations of the two-factor hypothesis of job satisfaction. *Journal of Applied Psychology, 51,* 191–200.

Hinton, B. L., & Barrow, J. C. (1975). The supervisor's reinforcing behavior as a function of reinforcements received. *Organizational Behavior and Human Performance, 14,* 123–143.

Hinton, B. L., & Barrow, J. C. (1976). Personality correlates of the reinforcement propensities of leaders. *Personnel Psychology, 29,* 61–66.

Hockey, G. R. J. (1970). Signal probability and spatial locations as possible bases for increased selectivity in noise. *Quarterly Journal of Experimental Psychology, 22,* 37–42.

Hogan, P. M., Hakel, M. D., & Decker, P. J. (1986). Effects of trainee-generated versus trainer-provided rule codes on generalization in behavior-modeling training. *Journal of Applied Psychology, 71*(3), 469–473.

Hollander, E. P. (1978). *Leadership dynamics: A practical guide to effective relationships.* New York: Free Press.

Hollander, E. P., & Julian, J. W. (1969). Contemporary trends in the anlaysis of the leadership process. *Psychological Bulletin, 71*, 387–397.

Hollenbeck, J. R., & Klein, H. J. (1987). Goal commitment and the goal-setting process: Problems, prospects, and proposals for future research. *Journal of Applied Psychology, 72*(2), 212–220.

Hollenbeck, J. R., & Williams, C. R. (1986). Turnover functionality versus turnover frequency: A note on work attitudes and organizational effectiveness. *Journal of Applied Psychology, 71*(4), 606–611.

Holmes, T. H., & Rahe, R. H. (1967). Social readjustment rating scale. *Journal of Psychosomatic Research, 11*, 213–218.

Hoppock, R. (1935). *Job satisfaction*. New York: Harper & Row.

Hosking, D. M. (1988). Chairperson's address: Organizing through skillful leadership. *The British Psychological Society. The Occupational Psychologists*, no. 4, pp. 4–11.

Hough, L. M. (1984). Development and evaluation of the "accomplishment-record" method of selecting and promoting professionals. *Journal of Applied Psychology, 69*(1), 135–146.

Hough, L. M., Keyes, M. A., & Dunnette, M. D. (1983). An evaluation of three "alternative" selection procedures. *Personnel Psychology, 36*(2), 261–276.

Houser, J. D. (1927). *What the employer thinks*. Cambridge, MA: Harvard University Press.

Huber, V. L., & Neale, M. A. (1984). Effects of self and competitor goals on performance in an interdependent bargaining task. *Journal of Applied Psychology, 72*(2), 197–203.

Hulin, C. L. (1982). Some reflections on general performance dimensions and halo rating error. *Journal of Applied Psychology, 67*, 165–170.

Hulin, C. L., Drasgow, F., & Komocar, J. (1982). Applications of item response theory to analysis of attitude scale translations. *Journal of Applied Psychology, 67*(6), 818–825.

Hulin, C. L., Roznowski, M., & Hachiya, D. (1985). Alternative opportunities and withdrawal decisions: Empirical and theoretical discrepancies and an integration. *Psychological Bulletin, 97*, 233–250.

Hulin, C. L., & Smith, P. C. (1965). A linear model of job satisfaction. *Journal of Applied Psychology, 49*, 209–216.

Hull, C. L. (1928). *Aptitude testing*. New York: Harcourt Brace Jovanovich.

Hunter, J. E., & Hunter, R. F. (1984). Validity and utility of alternative predictors of job performance. *Psychological Bulletin, 96*(1), 72–98.

Hunter, J. E., Schmidt, F. L., & Hunter, R. (1979). Differential validity of employment tests by race: A comprehensive review and analysis. *Psychological Bulletin, 86*, 721–735.

Hunter, J. E., Schmidt, F. L., & Jackson, G. B. (1982). *Meta-analysis: Cumulating research findings across studies*. Beverly Hills: Sage Publications.

Hurrell, J. J., Jr. (1985). Machine-paced work and the type A behaviour pattern. *Journal of Occupational Psychology, 58*, 15–25.

Iaffaldano, M. T., & Muchinsky, P. M. (1985). Job satisfaction and job performance: A meta-analysis. *Psychological Bulletin, 97*(2), 251–273.

Idaszak, J. R., & Drasgow, F. (1987). A revision of the job diagnostic survey: Elimination of a measurement artifact, *Journal of Applied Psychology, 72*(1), 69–74.

Ilgen, D. R., Fisher, C. D., & Taylor, M. S. (1979). Consequences of individual feedback on behavior in organizations. *Journal of Applied Psychology, 64*(4), 349–371.

Ilgen, D. R., Nebeker, D. M., & Pritchard, R. D. (1981). Expectancy theory measures: An empirical comparison in an experimental simulation. *Organizational Behavior and Human Performance. 28,* 189–223.

Ilgen, D. R., & O'Brien, G. (1974). Leader-member relations in small groups. *Organizational Behavior and Human Performance, 12,* 335–350.

Ivancevich, J. M. (1974). Effects of the shorter workweek on selected satisfaction and performance measures. *Journal of Applied Psychology, 59,* 717–721.

Ivancevich, J. M. (1979). Longitudinal study of the effects of rater training on psychometric error in ratings. *Journal of Applied Psychology, 64,* 502–508.

Ivancevich, J. M., & Donnelly, J. H., Jr. (1975). Relation of organizational structure to job satisfaction, anxiety-stress, and performance. *Administrative Science Quarterly, 20,* 272–280.

Ivancevich, J. M., & Lyon, H. L. (1977). The shortened workweek: A field experiment. *Journal of Applied Psychology, 62,* 34–37.

Jackson, S. E. (1983). Participation in decision making as a strategy for reducing job related strain. *Journal of Applied Psychology, 68*(1), 3–19.

Jago, A. G., & Regan, J. W. (1986b). The trouble with Leader Match is that it doesn't match Fiedler's contingency model. *Journal of Applied Psychology, 71*(4), 555–559.

Jago, A. G., & Regan, J. W. (1986b). The trouble with Leader Match is that it doesn't match Fiedler's contingency model. *Journal of Applied Psychology, 71*(4), 555–559.

Jago, A. G., & Vroom, V. H. A. (1977). Hierarchical level and leadership style. *Organizational Behavior and Human Performance, 18*(1), 131–145.

Jago, A. G., & Vroom, V. H. (1982). Sex differences in the incidence and evaluation of participate leader behavior. *Journal of Applied Psychology, 67*(6), 776–783.

Jahoda, M. (1981). Work, employment, and unemployment: Values, theories, and approaches in social research. *American Psychologist, 36,* 184–191.

Jamal, M. (1981). Shift work related to job attitudes, social participation, and withdrawal behavior: A study of nurses and industrial workers. *Personnel Psychology, 34,* 535–548.

James, L. R., Demaree, R. G., & Mulaik, S. A. (1986). A note on validity generalization procedures. *Journal of Applied Psychology, 71*(3), 440–450.

James, L. R., & Jones, A. P. (1980). Perceived job characteristics and job satisfaction: An examination of reciprocal causation. *Personnel Psychology, 33,* 87–135.

James, W. (1890). *The principles of psychology.* New York: H. Holt and Company.

Janet, P. (1907). *The major symptoms of hysteria.* New York: Macmillan.

Jansen, A. (1973). *Validation of graphological judgment.* Paris: Mouton.

Jenkins, C. D., Zyzanski, S. J., & Rosenman, R. H. (1979). *Manual for the Jenkins Activity Survey*. New York: Psychological Corporation.

Jenkins, W. C. (1947). The tactual discrimination of shapes for coding aircraft-type controls. In P. M. Fitts (Ed.), *Psychological research on equipment design*. Washington, DC: U.S. Government Printing Office.

Jerison, H. J. (1957). Performance on a simple vigilance task in noise and quiet. *Journal of the Acoustical Society of America, 29*, 1163–1165.

Johnson, S. M., Smith, P. C., & Tucker, S. M. (1982). Response format of the job descriptive index: Assessment of reliability and validity by the multitrait-multimethod matrix. *Journal of Applied Psychology, 67*, 500–505.

Justis, R. T., Kedia, B. L., & Stephens, D. B. (1978). The effect of position power and perceived task competence on trainer effectiveness: A partial utilization of Fiedler's contingency model of leadership. *Personnel Psychology, 31*, 83–93.

Kabanoff, B. (1980). Work and nonwork: A review of models. *Psychological Bulletin, 88*, 60–77.

Kabanoff, B. (1985). Potential influence structures as sources of interpersonal conflict in groups and organizations. *Organizational Behavior and Human Decision Processes, 36*, 113–141.

Kantowitz, B. H., & Sorkin, R. D. (1983). *Human factors*. New York: Wiley.

Karasek, R. A., Jr. (1979). Job demands, job decision latitude, and mental strain: Implications for job redesign. *Administrative Science Quarterly, 24*, 285–308.

Katzell, R. A. (1957). Industrial psychology. *Annual Review of Psychology*. Palo Alto, CA: Annual Review.

Katzell, R. A., & Dyer, F. J. (1977). Differential validity revived. *Journal of Applied Psychology, 62*, 137–145.

Katzell, R., & Guzzo, R. (1983). Psychological approaches to productivity improvement. *American Psychologist, 38*, 468–472.

Katzell, R., & Yankelovich, D. (1975). *Work productivity and job satisfaction*. New York: Psychological Corporation.

Kaufman, H. G. (1975). Individual differences, early work challenge, and participation in continuing education. *Journal of Applied Psychology, 60*, 405–408.

Kay, E., Meyer, H., & French, J. R. P. (1965). Effects of threat in a performance appraisal interview. *Journal of Applied Psychology, 49*, 311–317.

Keating, E., Patterson, D. G., & Stone, C. H. (1950). Validity of work histories obtained by interview. *Journal of Applied Psychology, 34*, 6–11.

Keller, R. T. (1975). Role conflict and ambiguity correlates with job satisfaction and values. *Personnel Psychology, 28*, 57–64.

Keller, R. T., & Szilagyi, A. D. (1978). Employee reactions to leader reward behavior. *Academy of Management Journal, 19*, 619–627.

Kelley, H. (1967). Attribution theory in social psychology. In D. Levine (Ed.), *Nebraska symposium on motivation*. Lincoln: University of Nebraska Press.

Kennedy, J. K. (1982). Middle LPC leaders and the contingency model of leadership effectiveness. *Organizational Behavior and Human Performance, 30*, 1–14.

Kerr, S., & Jermier, J. M. (1978). Substitutes for leadership: Their meaning and measurement. *Organizational Behavior and Human Performance, 22,* 375–403.

King, N. (1970). Clarification and evaluation of the two-factor theory of job satisfaction. *Psychological Bulletin, 74,* 18–31.

Kipnis, D., & Cosentino, J. (1969). Use of leadership powers in industry. *Journal of Applied Psychology, 53*(6), 460–466.

Kirk, R. J. (1981, September). Interim report to the president and Congress: Alternative work schedules experimental program. Washington, DC: Office of Personnel Management.

Kirkpatrick, D. L. (1959, 1960). Techniques for evaluating training programs. *Journal of the American Society of Training Directors, 13,* 3–9, 21–26, *14,* 13–18, 28–32.

Kleiman, L. S., & Faley, R. H. (1985). The implications of professional and legal guidelines for court decisions involving criterion-related validity: A review and analysis. *Personnel Psychology, 38*(4), 803–834.

Klimoski, R., & Brickner, M. (1987). Why do assessment centers work? The puzzle of assessment center validity. *Personnel Psychology, 40*(2), 243–260.

Klimoski, R. J., & Strickland, W. J. (1977). Assessment centers—valid or merely prescient. *Personnel Psychology, 30,* 353–361.

Knouse, S. B. (1983). The letter of recommendation: Specificity and favorability of information. *Personnel Psychology, 36*(2), 331–342.

Koch, J. L., Tung, R., Gmelch, W., & Swent, B. (1982). Job stress among school administrators: Factorial dimensions and differential effects. *Journal of Applied Psychology, 67,* 493–499.

Kohlberg, L. (1976). Moral stages and moralization: The cognitive developmental approach. In T. Lickona (Ed.), *Moral development and behavior: Theory, research, and social issues.* New York: Holt, Rinehart & Winston.

Komaki, J. L. (1986). Toward effective supervision: An operant analysis and comparison of managers at work. *Journal of Applied Psychology, 71*(2), 270–279.

Komaki, J., Barwick, K. D., & Scott, L. R. (1978). A behavioral approach to occupational safety: Pinpointing and reinforcing safe performance in a food manufacturing plant. *Journal of Applied Psychology, 63,* 434–445.

Komaki, J. L., Collins, R. L., & Penn, P. (1982). The role of performance antecedents and consequences in work motivation. *Journal of Applied Psychology, 67*(3), 334–340.

Komaki, J., Heinzmann, A. T., & Lawson, L. (1980). Effect of training and feedback: Component analysis of a behavioral safety program. *Journal of Applied Psychology, 65*(3), 260–270.

Komaki, J. L., Zlotnick, S., & Jensen, M. (1986). Development of an operant-based taxonomy and observational index of supervisory behavior. *Journal of Applied Psychology, 71*(2), 260–269.

Korman A. (1970). Toward an hypothesis of work behavior. *Journal of Applied Psychology, 54,* 32–41.

Korman, A. K. (1971). *Industrial and organizational psychology.* Englewood Cliffs, NJ: Prentice-Hall.

Korman, A. (1980). *Career success and work performance.* Paper presented at meetings of the American Psychological Association, Montreal, Canada.

Kornhauser, A. W. (1933). The technique of measuring employee attitudes. *Personnel, 9,* 99–107.

Kozlowski, S. W. J., & Farr, J. L. (1988). An integrative model of updating and performance. *Human Performance, 1,* 5–29.

Krackhardt, D., & Porter, L. W. (1986). The snowball effect: Turnover embedded in communication networks. *Journal of Applied Psychology, 71*(1), 50–55.

Kraut, A. I. (1976). Developing managerial skills via modeling techniques—Some positive research findings: A symposium. *Personnel Psychology, 29,* 325–328.

Kuhn, T. S. (1970). *The structure of scientific revolutions* (2nd ed.). Chicago: University of Chicago Press.

Landsberger, H. A. (1958). *Hawthorne revisited: Management and the worker, its critics and developments in human relations in industry.* Ithaca: New York State School of Industrial and Labor Relations.

Landy, F. J. (1978a). Adventures in implied psychology: The value of true negatives. *American Psychologist, 33*(8), 756–760.

Landy, F. J. (1978b). An opponent process theory of job satisfaction. *Journal of Applied Psychology, 63*(5), 533–547.

Landy, F. J. (1985). *Psychology of work behavior* (3rd ed.). Homewood, IL: Dorsey Press.

Landy, F. J. (1986). Stamp collecting versus science: Validation as hypothesis testing. *American Psychologist, 11,* 1183–1192.

Landy, F. J. (1987). *Psychology: The science of people* (2nd ed.). Englewood Cliffs, NJ: Prentice-Hall.

Landy, F. J. (1988a). The early years of I/O: "Dr." Mayo. *Industrial Organizational Psychologist (TIP), 25*(3), 53.

Landy, F. J. (in press). *Test validity yearbook: Organizational.* Hillsdale, NJ: Lawrence Erlbaum Associates.

Landy, F. J., Barnes, J. L., & Murphy, K. R. (1978). Correlates of perceived fairness and accuracy of performance evaluation. *Journal of Applied Psychology, 63*(6), 751–754.

Landy, F. J., & Farr, J. L. (1980). Performance rating. *Psychological Bulletin, 87,* 72–107.

Landy, F. J., & Farr, J. L. (1983). *The measurement of work performance: Methods, theory, and applications.* New York: Academic Press.

Landy, F. J., & Rastegary, H. (1988). Current issues in performance evaluation. In I. Robertson & M. Smith (Eds.), *Personnel evaluation of the future.* New York: Wiley.

Landy, F. J., Rastegary, H., & Motowidlo, S. (1987). Human computer interactions in the workplace: Psychosocial aspects of VDT use. In M. Frese, E. Ulich, & W. Dzida (Eds.), *Psychological issues of human-computer interaction in the workplace* (pp. 3–22). North-Holland: Amsterdam.

Landy, F. J., Thayer, J., & Colvin, C. (1988). *The measurement of time urgency.* Unpublished manuscript.

Landy, F. J., & Trumbo, D. A. (1976). *Psychology of work behavior.* Homewood, IL: Dorsey Press.

Landy, F. J., & Trumbo, D. A. (1980). *Psychology of work behavior* (rev. ed.). Homewood, IL: Dorsey Press.

Landy, F. J., & Vasey, J. (1988). *Effect of demographic variables on job analysis results.* Unpublished manuscript.

Landy, F. J., Zedeck, S., & Cleveland, J. (1983). *Performance measurement and theory.* Hillsdale, NJ: Erlbaum Associates.

La Rocco, J. M., & Jones, A. P. (1978). Co-worker and leader support as moderators of stress-strain relationships in work situations. *Journal of Applied Psychology, 63,* 629–634.

Larsson, G. (1987). Routinization of mental training in organizations: Effects on performance and well-being. *Journal of Applied Psychology, 72*(1), 88–96.

Latack, J. C. (1986). Coping with job stress: Measures and future directions for scale development. *Journal of Applied Psychology, 71*(3), 377–385.

Latack, J. C., & Foster, L. W. (1985). Implementation of compressed work schedules: Participation and job redesign as critical factors for employee acceptance. *Personnel Psychology, 38*(1), 75–92.

Latham, G. P. (1988). Human resource training and development. *Annual Review of Psychology, 39,* 545–582.

Latham, G. P., & Dossett, D. L. (1978). Designing incentive plans for unionized employees: A comparison of continuous and variable reinforcement schedules. *Personnel Psychology, 31,* 47–61.

Latham, G. P., Fay, C., & Saari, L. (1979). The development of behavioral observation scales for appraising the performance of foremen. *Personnel Psychology, 32,* 299–311.

Latham, G. P., & Saari, L. M. (1979). Application of social learning theory to training supervisors through behavioral modeling. *Journal of Applied Psychology, 64*(3), 239–246.

Latham, G. P., & Saari, L. M. (1984). Do people do what they say? Further studies on the situational interview. *Journal of Applied Psychology, 69*(4), 569–573.

Latham, G. P., Saari, L. M., Pursell, E. D., & Campion, M. A. (1980). The situational interview. *Journal of Applied Psychology, 65,* 422–427.

Latham, G. P., & Wexley, K. N. (1977). Behavioral observation scales for performance appraisal purposes. *Personnel Psychology, 30,* 225–268.

Latham, G. P., & Wexley, K. N. (1981). *Increasing productivity through performance appraisal.* Reading, MA: Addison-Wesley.

Lawler, E. E. (1971). *Pay and organizational effectiveness: A psychological review.* New York: McGraw-Hill.

Lawler, E. E. (1973). *Motivation in work organizations.* Monterey, CA: Brooks/Cole Publishing.

Lawler, E. E., Hall, D. T., & Oldham, G. R. (1974). Organizational climate: Relationship to organizational structure, process, and performance. *Organizational Behavior and Human Performance, 11,* 139–155.

Lawler, E. E., & Suttle, J. L. (1972). A causal correlational test of the need hierarchy concept. *Organizational Behavior and Human Performance, 7,* 265–287.

Lawrence, P. R., & Lorsch, J. (1967). *Organization and environment.* Cambridge, MA: Harvard University Press.

Lee, R., & Booth, J. M. (1974). A utility analysis of a weighted application blank designed to predict turnover from clerical employees. *Journal of Applied Psychology, 59,* 516–518.

Lefkowitz, J. (1980). Pros and cons of "truth in testing" legislation. *Personnel Psychology, 33,* 17–24.

Leon, F. R. (1981). The role of positive and negative outcomes in the causation of motivational forces. *Journal of Applied Psychology, 66*(1), 45–53.

Lepper, M. R., & Greene, D. (1975). Turning play into work: Effects of adult surveillance and extrinsic rewards on children's intrinsic motivation. *Journal of Personality and Social Psychology, 31,* 479–486.

Lepper, M. R., Green, D., & Nisbett, R. E. (1973). Undermining children's intrinsic interest with extrinsic rewards: A test of the overjustification hypothesis. *Journal of Personality and Social Psychology, 28,* 129–137.

Lerner, B. A. (1980a). The war on testing: David, Goliath, and Gallup. *Public Interest, 60,* 119–147.

Lerner, B. A. (1980b). The war on testing: Detroit Edison in perspective. *Personnel Psychology, 33,* 11–16.

Levin, J., & Butler, J. (1952). Lecture versus group decision in changing behavior. *Journal of Applied Psychology, 36,* 29–33.

Levine, E. L., Flory, A., & Ash, R. A. (1977). Self-assessment in personnel selection. *Journal of Applied Psychology, 62,* 428–435.

Lewandowski, L. J., & Kobus, D. A. (in press). Bimodal information processing in sonar performance. *Human Performance.*

Likert, R. (1961). *New patterns of management.* New York: McGraw-Hill.

Likert, R. (1967). *The human organization.* New York: McGraw-Hill.

Lindzey, G. (1965). Seer versus sign. *Journal of Experimental Research in Personality, 1,* 17–26.

Litwin, G. H., & Stringer, R. (1966, March). *The influence of organizational climate on human motivation.* Paper presented at a conference on organizational climate, Foundation for Research on Human Behavior, Ann Arbor, MI.

Locke, E. A. (1968). Toward a theory of task motivation and incentives. *Organizational Behavior and Human Performance, 3,* 157–189.

Locke, E. A. (1970). Job satisfaction and job performance: A theoretical analysis. *Organizational Behavior and Human Performance, 5,* 484–500.

Locke, E. A. (1976). The nature and causes of job satisfaction. In M. D. Dunnette (Ed.), *The handbook of industrial and organizational psychology.* Chicago: Rand McNally.

Locke, E. A. (1980). Latham versus Komaki: A tale of two paradigms. *Journal of Applied Psychology, 65*(1), 16–23.

Locke, E. A. (1986). *Generalizing from laboratory to field settings.* Lexington, MA: Lexington Books.

Locke, E. A., Cartledge, N., & Knerr, C. S. (1970). Studies of the relationship between satisfaction, goal-setting and performance. *Organizational Behavior and Human Performance, 5,* 484–500.

Locke, E. A., Frederick, E., Lee, C., & Bobko, P. (1984). Effect of self-efficacy, goals, and task strategies on task performance. *Journal of Applied Psychology, 69*(2), 241–251.

Locke, E. A., & Schweiger, D. M. (1979). Participation in decision making: One more look. *Research on Organizational Behavior, 1,* 265–339.

Locke, E. A., Shaw, K. N., Saari, L. M., & Latham, G. P. (1981). Goal setting and task performance: 1969–1980. *Psychological Bulletin, 90,* 125–152.

Lockhart, J. M. (1966). Effects of body and hand cooling on complex manual performance. *Journal of Applied Psychology, 50,* 57–59.

Loftus, E. F. (1979). *Eyewitness testimony.* Cambridge, MA: Harvard University Press.

Loher, B. T., Noe, R. A., Moeller, N. L., & Fitzgerald, M. P. (1985). A meta-analysis of the relation of job characteristics to job satisfaction. *Journal of Applied Psychology, 70*(2), 280–289.

London, M. (1976). Employee perceptions of the job reclassification process. *Personnel Psychology, 29,* 67–77.

London, M., & Bray, D. W. (1980). Ethical issues in testing and evaluation for personnel decisions. *American Psychologist, 35,* 890–901.

London, M., Crandall, R., & Seals, G. W. (1977). The contribution of job and leisure satisfaction to the quality of life. *Journal of Applied Psychology, 62,* 328–334.

London, M., & Oldham, G. R. (1979). Effects of varying goal types and incentive systems on performance and satisfaction. *Academy of Management Journal, 19,* 537–546.

Lord, R. G., DeVader, C. L., & Alliger, G. M. (1986). A meta-analysis of the relation between personality traits and leadership perceptions: An application of validity generalization procedures. *Journal of Applied Psychology, 71*(3), 402–410.

Lord, R. G., Foti, R., & Phillips, J. S. (1982). A theory of leadership categorization. In J. G. Hunt, U. Sekaran, & C. Schriesheim (Eds.), *Crosscurrents in leadership.* Carbondale: Southern Illinois Press.

Lowin, A. (1968). Participative decision making: A model, literature critique, and prescriptions for research. *Organizational Behavior and Human Performance, 3*(1), 68–106.

Lowin, A., & Craig, J. R. (1968). The influence of level of performance on managerial style: An experimental object lesson in the ambiguity of correlational data. *Organizational Behavior and Human Performance, 3,* 440–458.

Lukasiewicz, J. (1971). The dynamics of science and engineering education. *Engineering Education, 61,* 880–882.

Luthans, F., Paul, R., & Baker, D. (1981). An experimental analysis of the impact of contingent reinforcement on sales persons' performance behavior. *Journal of Applied Psychology, 66*(3), 314–323.

Lykken, D. (1981). *A tremor in the blood: Uses and abuses of the lie detector.* New York: McGraw-Hill.

Lykken, D. (1983). Polygraph prejudice. *Monitor, 14,* 4.

Mabe, P. A., III, & West, S. G. (1982). Validity of self-evaluation of ability: A review and meta-analysis. *Journal of Applied Psychology, 67*(3), 280–296.

MacKinney, A. C. (1957). Progressive levels in the evaluation of training programs. *Personnel, 34,* 72–77.

Madigan, R. M. (1985). Comparable worth judgments: A measurement properties analysis. *Journal of Applied Psychology, 70*(1), 137–147.

Mahoney, M. J. (1974). *Cognition and behavior modification.* Cambridge, MA: Ballinger.

Mahoney, T. A., & Frost, P. J. (1974). The role of technology in models of organizational effectiveness. *Organizational Behavior and Human Performance, 11,* 122–138.

Maier, N. R. F. (1952). *Principles of human relations: Applications to management.* New York: John Wiley & Sons.

Maier, N. R. F., & Solem, A. R. (1952). The contribution of a discussion leader to the quality of group thinking: The effective use of minority opinions. *Human Relations, 52,* 277–288.

Maier, N. R. F., & Zerfoss, L. F. (1952). A technique for training large groups of supervisors and its potential use in social research. *Human Relations, 5,* 177–186.

Mann, F. C. (1965). Toward an understanding of the leadership role in formal organization. In R. Dubin, G. C. Homans, & D. C. Miller (Eds.), *Leadership and productivity.* San Francisco, CA: Chandler.

Mann, R. D. (1959). A review of the relationships between personality and performance in small groups. *Psychological Bulletin, 56,* 241–270.

Manz, C. C., & Sims, H. P. (1979). Self-management as a substitute for leadership: A social learning theory perspective. *Academy of Management Review, 20,* 221–232.

Manz, C. C., & Sims, H. P., Jr. (1986). Beyond imitation: Complex behavioral and affective linkages resulting from exposure to leadership training models. *Journal of Applied Psychology, 71*(4), 571–578.

Marks, M. L., Mirvis, P. H., Hackett, E. J., & Grady, J. F., Jr. (1986). Employee participation in a quality circle program: Impact on quality of work life, productivity, and absenteeism. *Journal of Applied Psychology, 71*(1), 61–69.

Marino, K. E. (1980). A preliminary investigation into the behavioral dimensions of affirmative action compliance. *Journal of Applied Psychology, 65*(3), 346–350.

Maslow, A. H. (1943). A theory of motivation. *Psychological Review, 50,* 370–396.

Maslow, A. H. (1971). *The farthest reaches of human nature.* New York: Viking Press.

Matsui, T., Kagawa, M., Nagamatsu, J., & Ohtsuka, Y. (1977). Validity of expectancy theory as a within-person behavioral choice model for sales activities. *Journal of Applied Psychology, 62,* 764–767.

Matsui, T., Okada, A., & Inoshita, A. (1983). Mechanism of feedback affecting task performance. *Organizational Behavior and Human Performance, 31,* 114–122.

Matsui, T., Okada, A., & Mizuguchi, R. (1981). Expectancy theory prediction of the goal theory postulate "the harder the goals, the higher the performance." *Journal of Applied Psychology, 66,* 54–58.

Maurer, H. (1979). *Not working.* New York: Holt.

Mayfield, E. C. (1964). The selection interview: A reevaluation of published research. *Personnel Psychology, 17,* 239–260.

McAllister, D. W., Mitchell, T. R., & Beach, L. R. (1979). The contingency model for the selection of decision strategies: An empirical test of the effects of significance, accountability and reversibility. *Organizational Behavior and Human Performance, 24,* 228–244.

McClelland, D. C. (1955). Some social consequences of achievement motivation. In M. R. Jones (Ed.), *Nebraska symposium on motivation.* Lincoln: University of Nebraska Press.

McCormick, E. J. (1957). *Human engineering.* New York: McGraw-Hill.

McCormick, E. J. (1981). Minority report. In D. J. Treimand & H. I. Hartmann (Eds.), *Women, work and wages: Equal pay for jobs of equal value.* Washington, National Academy Press.

McCormick, E. J., Jeanneret, P., & Mecham, R. C. (1972). A study of job characteristics of job dimensions as based on the position analysis questionnaires [Monograph]. *Journal of Applied Psychology, 36,* 347–368.

McDaniel, M. A., Schmidt, F. L., & Hunter, J. E. (1986). The evaluation of a causal model of job performance: The relation of job experience and general mental ability to job performance.

McEvoy, G. M., & Cascio, W. F. (1985). Strategies for reducing employee turnover: A meta-analysis. *Journal of Applied Psychology, 70*(2), 342–353.

McGrath, J. E. (1970). A conceptual formulation for research on stress. In J. E. McGrath (Ed.), *Social psychological factors in stress.* New York: Holt, Rinehart & Winston.

McGregor, D. (1960). *The human side of enterprise.* New York: McGraw-Hill.

McGregor, D. (1967). *The professional manager.* New York: McGraw-Hill.

McIntyre, R. M., Smith, D. E., & Hassett, C. E. (1984). Accuracy of performance ratings as affected by rater training and perceived purpose of rating. *Journal of Applied Psychology, 69*(1), 147–156.

McMurray, R. N. (1945). Validating the patterned interview. *Personnel, 23,* 263–272.

McNamara, W. J., & Hughes, J. L. (1961). A review of research on the selection of computer programmers. *Personnel Psychology, 14,* 39–51.

Meehl, P. E. (1954). *Clinical versus statistical prediction.* Minneapolis: University of Minnesota Press.

Meehl, P. E. (1957). When shall we use our heads instead of a formula? *Journal of Counseling Psychology, 4,* 268–273.

Meehl, P. E. (1965). Seer over sign: The first good example. *Journal of Experimental Research in Personality, 1,* 27–32.

Meichenbaum, D. (1977). *Cognitive behavior modification: An integrative approach.* New York: Plenum.

Mellers, B. A. (1982). Equity judgment: A revision of Aristotelian views. *Journal of Experimental Psychology, 111,* 242–270.

Mento, A. J., Cartledge, N. D., & Locke, E. A. (1980). Maryland vs. Michigan vs. Minnesota: Another look at the relationship of expectancy and goal difficulty to task performance. *Organizational Behavior and Human Performance, 25,* 419–440.

Mento, A. J., Steel, R. P., & Karven, R. J. (1987). A meta-analytic study of the effects of goal setting on task performance. *Organizational Behavior and Human Decision Processes, 39,* 52–83.

Meyer, H. H. (1961). The in-basket as a measure of managerial aptitude. *Behavioral Research Service.* General Electric, 52.

Middlemist, R. D., & Peterson, R. B. (1976). Test of equity theory by controlling for comparison worker's efforts. *Organizational Behavior and Human Performance, 15,* 335–406.

Mihal, W. L., & Barrett, G. (1976). Individual differences in perceptual information processing and their relation to automobile accident involvement. *Journal of Applied Psychology, 61,* 229–233.

Mikes, P. S., & Hulin, C. L. (1968). Use of importance as a weighting component of job satisfaction. *Journal of Applied Psychology, 52,* 394–398.

Miles, R. H., & Perreault, W. D. (1976). Organizational role conflict: Its antecedents and consequences. *Organizational Behavior and Human Performance, 17,* 19–44.

Miller, D., & Droge, C. (1986). Psychological and traditional determinants of structure. *Administrative Science Quarterly, 31,* 539–560.

Miner, J. B. (1980). *Theories of organizational behavior.* Hinsdale, IL: Dryden Press.

Mirvis, P. H., & Lawler, E. E., III. (1977). Measuring the financial impact of employee attitudes. *Journal of Applied Psychology, 62*(1), 1–8.

Mitchell, J. V. (1983). *Tests in print* III. Lincoln: University of Nebraska Press.

Mitchell, J. V. (1985). *Ninth mental measurements yearbook.* Lincoln: University of Nebraska Press.

Mitchell, T. R. (1974). Expectancy models of job satisfaction, occupational preference, and effort: A theoretical, methodological, and empirical approach. *Psychological Bulletin, 81,* 1053–1077.

Mitchell, T. R., & Kalb, L. S. (1982). Effects of job experience on supervisor attributions for a subordinate's poor performance. *Journal of Applied Psychology, 67*(2), 181–188.

Mitchell, T. R., Larson, J. R., & Green, S. G. (1977). Leader behavior, situational moderators, and group performance: An attributional analysis. *Organizational Behavior and Human Performance, 18,* 254–268.

Mitchell, T. R., & Wood, R. E. (1980). Supervisor's responses to subordinate poor performance: A test of an attribution model. *Organizational Behavior and Human Performance, 25,* 123–138.

Mitchell, T. W., & Klimoski, R. J. (1982). Is it rational to be empirical? A test of methods for scoring biographical data. *Journal of Applied Psychology, 67*(4), 411–418.

Mitchell, V. F., & Moudgill, P. (1976). Measurement of Maslow's need hierarchy. *Organizational Behavior and Human Performance, 16,* 334–349.

Mobley, W. H., Horner, S. O., & Hollingsworth, A. T. (1978). An evaluation of precursors of hospital employee turnover. *Journal of Applied Psychology, 63,* 408–414.

Moch, M. K. (1976). Structure and organizational resource allocation. *Administrative Science Quarterly, 21,* 661–674.

Montgomery of Alamein, Bernard Law Montgomery, 1st viscount. (1961). The path to leadership. New York: G. P. Putnam's Sons.

Morrison, R. F. (1977a). Career adaptivity: The effective adaptation of managers to changing role demands. *Journal of Applied Psychology, 62*(5), 549–558.

Morrison, R. F. (1977b). A multivariate model for the occupational placement decision. *Journal of Applied Psychology, 62*(3), 271–277.

Moses, J. L., & Ritchie, R. J. (1976). Supervisory relationships training: A behavioral evaluation of the behavioral modeling program. *Personnel Psychology, 29,* 337–343.

Mossholder, K. W. (1980). Effects of externally mediated goal setting on intrinsic motivation: A laboratory experiment. *Journal of Applied Psychology, 65*(2), 202–210.

Motowidlo, S. J., & Lawton, G. W. (1984). Affective and cognitive factors in soldiers' reenlistment decisions. *Journal of Applied Psychology, 69*(1), 157–166.

Motowidlo, S. J., Packard, J. S., & Manning, M. R. (1986). Occupational stress: Its causes and consequences for job performance. *Journal of Applied Psychology, 71*(4), 618–629.

Mott, P. E., Mann, F. C., McLoughlin, Q., & Warwick, D. P. (1965). *Shift work.* Ann Arbor: University of Michigan Press.

Mowday, R. T. (1979). Equity theory predictions of behavior in organizations. In R. M. Steers & L. W. Porter. *Motivation and work behavior* (2nd ed.). New York: McGraw-Hill.

Muchinsky, P. M. (1976). An assessment of the Litwin and Stringer organization climate questionnaire: An empirical and theoretical extension of the Sims and LaFollette study. *Personnel Psychology, 29,* 371–392.

Muchinsky, P. M. (1977). Employee absenteeism: A review of the literature. *Journal of Vocational Behavior, 10,* 316–340.

Munsterberg, H. (1913). *Psychology and industrial efficiency.* New York: Houghton-Mifflin.

Murphy, K. R. (1983). Fooling yourself with cross-validation: Single sample designs. *Personnel Psychology, 36,* 111–118.

Murphy, K. R., & Balzer, W. K. (1986). Systematic distortions in memory-based behavior ratings and performance evaluations: Consequences for rating accuracy. *Journal of Applied Psychology, 71*(1), 39–44.

Murphy, K. R., & Constans, J. I. (1987). Behavioral anchors as a source of bias in rating. *Journal of Applied Psychology, 72*(4), 573–577.

Murphy, K. R., Garcia, M., Kerkar, S., Martin, C., & Balzer, W. K. (1982). Relationship between observational accuracy and accuracy in evaluating performance. *Journal of Applied Psychology, 67,* 320–325.

Murphy, K. R., Martin, C., & Garcia, M. (1982). Do behavioral observation scales measure observation? *Journal of Applied Psychology, 67,* 562–567.

Murphy, L. R., & Sorenson, S. (1988). Employee behaviors before and after stress management. *Journal of Organizational Behavior, 9*(2), 173–182.

Murray, H. J. (1938). *Explorations in personality*. New York: Oxford University Press.

Näätänen, R. (1973). The inverted-U relationship between activation and performance: A critical review. In S. Kornblum (Ed.), *Attention and performance IV*. New York: Academic Press.

Naismith, D. C. (1975). Stress among managers as a function of organizational change. *Dissertation Abstracts International, 36*, 401-A.

Narayanan, V. K., & Nath, R. (1982). A field test of some attitudinal and behavioral consequences of flexitime. *Journal of Applied Psychology, 67*(2), 214–218.

Naylor, J. C., Pritchard, R. D., & Ilgen, D. R. (1980). *A theory of behavior in organizations*. New York: Academic Press.

Nebeker, D. M., & Mitchell, T. R. (1974). Leader behavior: an expectancy theory approach. *Organizational Behavior and Human Performance, 11*, 355–367.

Neiner, A. G., & Owens, W. A. (1982). Relationships between two sets of biodata with seven years separation. *Journal of Applied Psychology, 67*, 146–150.

Nevo, B. (1976). Using biographical information to predict success of men and women in the army. *Journal of Applied Psychology, 61*, 106–108.

Nicholson, N., Brown, C. A., & Chadwick-Jones, J. K. (1976). Absence from work and job satisfaction. *Journal of Applied Psychology, 61*, 728–737.

Nicholson, N., Jackson, P., & Howes, G. (1978). Shiftwork and absence: A study of temporal trends. *Journal of Occupational Psychology, 51*, 127–137.

Nisbett, R., & Ross, L. (1980). *Human inference: Strategies and shortcomings of social judgment*. Englewood Cliffs, NJ: Prentice-Hall.

Noe, R. A., & Schmitt, N. (1986). The influence of trainee attitudes on training effectiveness: Test of a model. *Personnel Psychology, 39*(3), 497–523.

Nord, W. R. (1977). Job satisfaction reconsidered. *American Psychologist, 22*, 1026–1035.

Nord, W. R., & Costigan, R. (1973). Worker adjustment to the four-day week: A longitudinal study. *Journal of Applied Psychology, 58*, 60–66.

Oates, W. E. (1971). *Confessions of a workaholic*. Cleveland: World.

O'Brien, G. E., & Plooj, D. (1977). Comparison of programmed and prose culture training upon attitudes and knowledge. *Journal of Applied Psychology, 62*, 499–505.

O'Connor, E. J., Wexley, K. N., & Alexander, R. A. (1975). Single group validity: Fact or fallacy? *Journal of Applied Psychology, 60*, 352–355.

Odiorne, G. S. (1964). The need for an economic approach to training. *Journal of the American Society of Training Directors, 18*(3), 3–12.

Office of Personnel Management (1979). *Report of the training evaluation demonstration project: Issues and recommendations*. Washington, DC: Office of Personnel Management.

Oldham, G. R. (1976). The motivational strategies used by supervisors: Relationships in effectiveness indicators. *Organizational Behavior and Human Performance, 15*, 66–86.

O'Leary, V. E. (1972). The Hawthorne effect in reverse: Effects of training and practice on individual and group performance. *Journal of Applied Psychology, 56,* 491–494.

O'Reilly, C. A., & Caldwell, D. F. (1981). The commitment and job tenure of new employees: Some evidence of postdecisional justification. *Administrative Science Quarterly, 26,* 597–616.

O'Reilly, C. A., & Weitz, B. A. (1980). Managing marginal employees: The use of warnings and dismissals. *Administrative Science Quarterly, 25,* 467–484.

Orpen, C. (1978). Work and nonwork satisfaction: A causal-correlational analysis. *Journal of Applied Psychology, 63,* 530–532.

Orpen, C. (1981). Effect of flexible working hours on employee satisfaction and performance. *Journal of Applied Psychology, 66,* 113–115.

Orpen, C. (1985). Patterned behavior description interviews versus unstructured interviews: A comparative validity study. *Journal of Applied Psychology, 70*(4), 774–776.

Osborn, A. F. (1963). *Applied imagination* (3rd ed.). New York: Schribner.

Ouchi, W. (1981). *Theory Z: How American business can meet the Japanese challenge.* Reading, MA: Addison-Wesley.

Ouchi, W. G., & Dowling, J. B. (1974). Defining the span of control. *Administrative Science Quarterly, 19,* 357–365.

Overall, J. E., & Hollister, L. E. (1964). Computer procedures for psychiatric classification. *Journal of the American Medical Association, 187,* 538–588.

Owens, W. A., & Schoenfeldt, L. F. (1979). Toward a classification of persons. *Journal of Applied Psychology, 64,* 569–607.

Panone, R. D. (1984). Predicting test performance: A content valid approach to screening applicants. *Personnel Psychology, 37*(3), 507–514.

Parker, D. F., & Dyer, L. (1976). Expectancy theory as a within-person behavioral choice model: An empirical test of some conceptual and methodological refinements. *Organizational Behavior and Human Performance, 17,* 97–117.

Parkes, K. R. (1982). Occupational stress among student nurses: A natural experiment. *Journal of Applied Psychology, 67,* 784–796.

Parnes, S. J. (1976). Idea stimulation techniques. *Journal of Creative Behavior, 10,* 126–129.

Parsons, C. K., & Hulin, C. L. (1982). An empirical comparison of item response theory and hierarchical factor analysis in applications to the measurement of job satisfaction. *Journal of Applied Psychology, 67,* 826–834.

Pasmore, W. A., & Sherwood, J. J. (Eds.). (1978). *Sociotechnical systems: A source book.* LaJolla, CA: University Associates.

Patkai, P., Akerstedt, T., & Pettersson, K. (1977). Field studies of shiftwork I: Temporal patterns in physiological activation in permanent night workers. *Ergonomics, 20,* 611–619.

Payne, R. L. (1979). *Demands, supports, constraints, and psychological health* [Memo No. 302]. Sheffield, England: University of Sheffield, Department of Psychology.

Payne, R., & Pugh, D. S. (1976). Organizational structure and climate. In M. D. Dunnette (Ed.), *Handbook of industrial and organizational psychology.* Chicago: Rand McNally.

Peak, H. (1955). Attitude and motivation. In M. R. Jones (Ed.), *Nebraska symposium on motivation* (pp. 149–188). Lincoln: University of Nebraska Press.

Pearce, J. L., & Porter, L. W. (1986). Employee responses to formal performance appraisal feedback. *Journal of Applied Psychology, 71*(2), 211–218.

Pearlman, K., Schmidt, F. L., & Hunter, J. E. (1980). Validity generalization results for tests used to predict training success and job proficiency for clerical occupations. *Journal of Applied Psychology, 65,* 373–406.

Pepler, R. D. (1958). Warmth and performance: An investigation in the tropics. *Ergonomics, 2,* 63–88.

Perrow, C. (1983). The organizational context of human factors engineering. *Administrative Science Quarterly, 28,* 521–541.

Peters, L. H., Hartke, D. D., & Pohlmann, J. T. (1985). Fiedler's contingency theory of leadership: An application of the meta-analysis procedures of Schmidt and Hunter. *Psychological Bulletin, 97*(2), 274–285.

Peters, L. H., & Terborg, J. (1975). The effects of temporal placement of unfavorable information and of attitude similarity on personnel selection decisions. *Journal of Applied Psychology, 13,* 279–293.

Pfister, G. (1975). Outcomes of laboratory training for police officers. *Journal of Social Issues, 31,* 115–121.

Phillips, J. (1984). The accuracy of leadership ratings: A cognitive categorization perspective. *Journal of Applied Psychology, 33,* 125–138.

Phillips, J. S., & Lord, R. G. (1981). Causal atributions and perceptions of leadership. *Organizational Behavior and Human Performance, 28,* 143–163.

Piaget, J. (1965). *The moral judgment of the child* (Marjorie Gabain, Trans.). New York: Free Press.

Pigors, P., & Pigors, F. (1955). *The incident process: Case studies in management development.* Washington, DC: Bureau of National Affairs.

Plutchik, R. (1980). *Emotion: A psychoevolutionary synthesis.* New York: Harper & Row.

Podsakoff, P. M. (1982). Determinants of a supervisor's use of rewards and punishments: A literature review and suggestions for future research. *Organizational Behavior and Human Performance, 29,* 58–83.

Porter, L. W., & Lawler, E. E. (1968). *Managerial attitudes and performance.* Homewood, IL: Dorsey.

Porter, L. W., & Steers, R. M. (1973). Organization, work, and personal factors in employee turnover and absenteeism. *Psychological Bulletin, 80,* 151–176.

Poulton, E. C. (1970). *Environment and human efficiency.* Springfield, IL: Charles C Thomas.

Poulton, E. C., Hitchings, N. B., & Brooke, R. B. (1965). Effect of cold and rain upon the vigilance of lookouts. *Ergonomics, 8,* 163–168.

Premack, S. L., & Wanous, J. P. (1985). A meta-analysis of realistic job preview experiments. *Journal of Applied Psychology, 70,* 706–719.

Prien, E. P., & Hughes, G. L. (1987). The effect of quality control revisions on mixed standard scale rating errors. *Personnel Psychology, 40*(4), 815–823.

Pritchard, R. D. (1969). Equity theory: A review and critique. *Organizational Behavior and Human Performance, 4,* 176–211.

Pritchard, R. D., Campbell, C. M., & Campbell, D. J. (1977). Effects of extrinsic financial rewards on intrinsic motivation. *Journal of Applied Psychology, 62,* 9–15.

Pritchard, R. D., Hollenback, J., & DeLeo, P. J. (1980). The effects of continuous and partial schedules of reinforcement on effort, performance, and satisfaction. *Organizational Behavior and Human Performance, 25,* 336–353.

Pritchard, R. D., Leonard, D. W., VonBergen, C. W., & Kirk, R. J. (1976). The effects of varying schedules of reinforcement on human task performance. *Organizational Behavior and Human Performance, 16,* 205–230.

Prytula, R. E., Sadowski, C. J., Ellisor, J., Corritore, D., Kuhn, R., & Davis, S. F. (1980). Studies on the perceived predictive accuracy of biorhythms. *Journal of Applied Psychology, 65*(6), 723–727.

Pulakos, E. D. (1984). A comparison of rater training programs: Error training and accuracy training. *Journal of Applied Psychology, 69*(4), 581–588.

Pulakos, E. D., & Schmitt, N. (1983). A longitudinal study of a valence model approach for the prediction of job satisfaction of new employees. *Journal of Applied Psychology, 68*(2), 307–312.

Quinn, R., Seashore, S., Kahn, R., Mangione, T., Campbell, D., Staines, G., & McCullough, M. (1971). *Survey of working conditions: Final report on univariate and bivariate tables* (Document No. 2916–001). Washington, DC: U.S. Government Printing Office.

Rafaeli, A. (1985). Quality circles and employee attitudes. *Personnel Psychology, 38*(3), 603–615.

Rafaeli, A., & Klimoski, R. J. (1983). Predicting sales success through handwriting analysis: An evaluation of the effects of training and handwriting sample content. *Journal of Applied Psychology, 68*(2), 212–217.

Ralston, D., Anthony, W., & Gustafson, D. (1985). Employees may love flexitime, but what does it do to the organization's productivity? *Journal of Applied Psychology, 70,* 272–279.

Randolph, W. A., & Posner, B. Z. (1981). Explaining role conflict and role ambiguity via individual and interpersonal variables in different job categories. *Personnel Psychology, 34,* 89–102.

Rauschenberger, J., Schmitt, N., & Hunter, J. E. (1980). A test of the need hierarchy concept by a Markov model of change in need strength. *Administrative Science Quarterly, 25,* 654–670.

Reilly, R. R., Brown, B., Blood, M. R., & Malatesta, C. Z. (1981). The effects of realistic previews: A study and discussion of the literature. *Personnel Psychology, 34,* 823–834.

Reilly, R. R., & Manese, W. R. (1979). The validation of a mini-course for telephone company switching technicians. *Personnel Psychology, 32,* 83–90.

Reilly, R. R., Zedeck, S., & Tenopyr, M. (1979). Validity and fairness of physical ability tests for predicting performance in craft jobs. *Journal of Applied Psychology, 64,* 262–274.

Reiss, S., & Sushinsky, L. W. (1976). The competing response hypothesis of decreased play effects: A reply to Lepper and Greene. *Journal of Personality and Social Psychology, 33,* 233–244.

Rhodes, S. R., & Schuster, M. (1983). *The effect of overtime work on industrial accidents.* Final Report. Syracuse, NY: Syracuse University School of Management.

Rice, A. K. (1958). *Productivity and social organization: The Ahmedabad experiment.* London: Tavistock Publications.

Rice, R. W. (1981). Leader LPC and follower satisfaction: A review. *Organizational Behavior and Human Performance, 28,* 1–25.

Richardson, M. W., & Kuder, G. F. (1939). The calculation of test reliability coefficients based on the method of rational equivalence. *Journal of Educational Psychology, 30,* 681–687.

Rizzo, J., House, R. E., & Lirtzman, J. (1970). Role conflict and ambiguity in complex organizations. *Administrative Science Quarterly, 15,* 150–163.

Robertson, I., & Downs, S. (1979). Learning and prediction of performance: Development of trainability testing in the United Kingdom. *Journal of Applied Psychology, 64,* 42–50.

Roethlisberger, F. J., & Dickson, W. J. (1939). *Management and the worker.* Cambridge, MA: Harvard University Press.

Rogers, C. R. (1951). *Client-centered therapy, its current practice, implications, and theory.* Boston: Houghton-Mifflin.

Ronen, S. (1981). Arrival and departure patterns of public sector employees before and after implementation of flexitime. *Personnel Psychology, 34,* 817–822.

Ronen, S., Kraut, A. I., Lingoes, J. C., & Aranya, N. (1979). A nonmetric scaling approach to taxonomies of employee work motivation. *Multivariate Behavioral Research, 14,* 387–401.

Roose, J. E., & Doherty, M. E. (1976). Judgment theory applied to the selection of life insurance salesmen. *Organizational Behavior and Human Performance, 16,* 231–249.

Rosen, B., & Jerdee, T. H. (1974). Factors Influencing disciplinary judgments. *Journal of Applied Psychology, 59,* 327–331.

Rosen, B., & Mericle, M. F. (1979). Influence of strong versus weak fair employment policies and applicant's sex on selection decisions and salary recommendations in a management simulation. *Journal of Applied Psychology, 64,* 435–439.

Rosenstein, A. (1968). *Study of profession and professional education* (Report No. EDP7-68). Los Angeles: University of California Press.

Rothe, H. F., & Nye, C. T. (1959). Output rates among machine operators: II—Consistency related to methods of pay. *Journal of Applied Psychology, 43,* 417–420.

Rush, M. C., Thomas, J. C., & Lord, R. G. (1977). Implicit leadership theory: A potential threat to the internal validity of leader behavior questionnaires. *Organizational Behavior and Human Performance, 20,* 93–110.

Russ, N. W., & Geller, E. S. (in press). Training bar personnel to prevent drunken driving: A field evaluation. *American Journal of Public Health.*

Russell, J. S. (1984). A review of fair employment cases in the field of training. *Personnel Psychology, 37*(2), 261–276.

Russell, J. S., Wexley, K. N., & Hunter, J. E. (1984). Questioning the effectiveness of behavior modeling in an industrial setting. *Personnel Psychology, 37*(3), 465–482.

Ryan, A. M., & Sackett, P. R. (1987). A survey of individual assessment practices by I/O psychologists. *Personnel Psychology, 40*(3), 455–488.

Ryan, T. A. (1970). *International behavior*. New York: Ronald Press.

Rynes, S. L., & Miller, H. E. (1983). Recruiter and job influences on candidates for employment. *Journal of Applied Psychology, 68*(1), 147–154.

Saal, F. E. (1979). Mixed standard rating scale: A consistent system for numerically coding inconsistent response combinations. *Journal of Applied Psychology, 64*, 422–428.

Sackett, P. R., & Decker, P. J. (1979). Detection of deception in the employment context: A review and critical analysis. *Personnel Psychology, 32*, 487–506.

Sackett, P. R., & Dreher, G. (1984). Situation specificity of behavior and assessment center validation strategies: A rejoinder to Neidig and Neidig. *Journal of Applied Psychology, 69*(1), 187–190.

Sackett, P. R., & Harris, M. M. (1984). Honesty testing for personnel selection: A review and critique. *Personnel Psychology, 37*(2), 221–246.

Sackett, P. R., Tenopyr, M. L., Schmitt, N., & Kehoe, J. (1985). Commentary on forty questions about validity generalization and meta-analysis. *Personnel Psychology, 38*(4), 697–798.

Sackett, P. R., & Wilson, M. A. (1982). Factors affecting the consensus judgment process in managerial assessment centers. *Journal of Applied Psychology, 67*, 10–17.

Sackett, P. R., Zedeck, S., & Fogli, L. (1988). Relationship between measures of typical and maximum job performance. *Journal of Applied Psychology, 73*(3), 482–486.

Salancik, G. R. (1975). Interaction effects of performance and money on self-perception of intrinsic motivation. *Organizational Behavior and Human Performance, 13*, 339–351.

Salvendy, G. (1987). *Handbook of human factors*. New York: Wiley.

Sanders, G. S., & Malkis, F. S. (1982). Type A behavior, need for control, and reactions to group participation. *Organizational Behavior and Human Performance, 30*, 71–86.

Sarason, I. G., & Potter, E. H., III. (1983, December). *Self-monitoring: Cognitive processes and performance* (Technical Report No. CO-ONR-009). Seattle: University of Washington.

Scandura, T. A., Graen, G. B., & Novak, M. A. (1986). When managers decide not to decide autocratically: An investigation of leader-member exchange and decision influence. *Journal of Applied Psychology, 71*(4), 579–584.

Schachter, S., & Singer, J. E. (1962). Cognitive, social, and physiological determinants of emotional state. *Psychological Review, 69*, 379–399.

Schaffer, D. R., Mays, P. V., & Ethridge, K. (1976). Who shall be hired: A biasing effect of the Buckley amendment on employment practices. *Journal of Applied Psychology, 61*, 571–575.

Schaffer, R. H. (1953). Job satisfaction as related to need satisfaction in work. *Psychological Monographs, 67* (No. 304).

Schein, E. H. (1981). Does Japanese management style have a message for American managers? *Sloan Management Review, 23,* 55–68.

Schein, V. E., Maurer, E. H., & Novak, J. F. (1977). Impact of flexible working hours on productivity. *Journal of Applied Psychology, 62,* 463–465.

Schmidt, F. L., Caplan, J. R., Bemis, S. E., Decuir, R., Dunn, L., & Antone, L. (1979). *The behavioral consistency method of unassembled examining.* Washington, DC: U.S. Office of Personnel Management.

Schmidt, F. L., Gast-Rosenberg, I., & Hunter, J. E. (1980). Validity generalization results for computer programmers. *Journal of Applied Psychology, 65,* 643–661.

Schmidt, F. L., & Hunter, J. E. (1981). Employment testing: Old theories and new research findings. *American Psychologist, 36,* 1128–1137.

Schmidt, F. L., & Hunter, J. E. (1984). A within setting empirical test of the situational specificity hypothesis in personnel selection. *Personnel Selection, 37*(2), 317–326.

Schmidt, F. L., Hunter, J. E., & Outerbridge, A. N. (1986). Impact of job experience and ability on job knowledge, work sample, performance, and supervisory ratings of job performance. *Journal of Applied Psychology, 71*(3), 432–439.

Schmidt, F. L., Hunter, J. E., & Pearlman, K. (1981). Task differences as moderators of aptitude test validity in selection: A red herring. *Journal of Applied Psychology, 66*(2), 166–185.

Schmidt, F. L., Hunter, J. E., Pearlman, K., & Hirsh, H. R. (1985). Forty questions about validity generalization and meta-analysis. *Personnel Psychology, 38,* 697–798.

Schmidt, F. L., Hunter, J. E., Pearlman, K., & Shane, G. S. (1979). Further tests of the Schmidt-Hunter Bayesian validity generalization procedure. *Personnel Psychology, 32,* 257–281.

Schmitt, N. (1976). Social and situational determinants of interview decisions: Implications for the employment interview. *Personnel Psychology, 29,* 79–101.

Schmitt, N., & Cohen, S. (in press). Internal analyses of task ratings by incumbents. *Journal of Applied Psychology.*

Schmitt, N., Gooding, R. Z., Noe, R. D., & Kirsch, M. (1984). Metaanalyses of validity studies published between 1964 and 1982 and the investigation of study characteristics. *Personnel Psychology, 37*(3), 407–422.

Schmitt, N., & Mellon, P. M. (1980). Life and job satisfaction. Is the job central? *Journal of Vocational Behavior, 16,* 51–58.

Schnake, M. E. (1983). An empirical assessment of the effects of affective response in the measurement of organizational climate. *Personnel Psychology, 36*(4), 791–807.

Schnake, M. E. (1986). Vicarious punishment in a work setting. *Journal of Applied Psychology, 71*(2), 343–345.

Schneider, B. (1985). Organizational behavior. *Annual Review of Psychology, 36,* 573–611.

Schneider, B., & Dachler, H. P. (1978). A note on the stability of the Job Descriptive Index. *Journal of Applied Psychology, 63,* 650–653.

Schneider, B., & Schmitt, N. (1986). *Staffing organizations.* Glenview, IL: Scott-Foresman.

Schneider, B., & Snyder, R. A. (1975). Some relationships between job satisfaction and organizational climate. *Journal of Applied Psychology, 60,* 318–328.

Schnier, C. F. (1978). The contingency model of leadership: An extension of emergent leadership and leader's sex. *Organizational Behavior and Human Performance, 21,* 220–239.

Schoenfeldt, L. F. (1974). Utilization of manpower: Development and evaluation of an assessment-classification model for matching individuals with jobs. *Journal of Applied Psychology, 59,* 583–595.

Schoorman, F. D. (1988). Escalation bias in performance appraisals: An unintended consequence of supervisor participation in hiring decisions. *Journal of Applied Psychology, 73*(1), 58–62.

Schriber, J. B., & Gutek, B. A. (1987). Some time dimensions of work: Measurement of an underlying aspect of organization culture. *Journal of Applied Psychology, 72*(4), 642–650.

Schuler, R. S., Aldag, R. J., & Brief, A. P. (1977). Role conflict and ambiguity: A scale analysis. *Organizational Behavior and Human Performance, 20,* 111–128.

Schwab, D., Heneman, H. G., III, & DeCotiis, T. (1975). Behaviorally anchored rating scales: A review of the literature. *Personnel Psychology, 28,* 549–562.

Schwab, D., Olian-Gottlieb, J., & Heneman, H., III. (1979). Between subjects expectancy theory research: A statistical review of studies predicting effort and performance. *Psychological Bulletin, 86,* 139–147.

Scott, W. D., Clothier, R. C., & Spriegel, W. R. (1949). *Personnel management: Principles, practices, and point of view* (4th ed.). New York: McGraw-Hill.

Scott, W. E. (1966). Activation theory and task design. *Organizational Behavior and Human Performance, 1,* 3–30.

Scott, W. E. (1976). The effects of extrinsic rewards on "intrinsic motivation." *Organizational Behavior and Human Performance, 15,* 117–129.

Scott, W. E., Jr., & Erskine, J. A. (1980). The effects of variations in task design and monetary reinforcers on task behavior. *Organizational Behavior and Human Performance, 25,* 311–335.

Scott, W. G. (1967). *Organization theory: A behavioral analysis for management.* Homewood, IL: Richard D. Irwin.

Searls, D. J., Braucht, G. N., & Miskimins, R. W. (1974). Work values of the chronically unemployed. *Journal of Applied Psychology, 59*(1), 93–95.

Seashore, R. H. (1951). Work and motor performance. In S. S. Stevens (Ed.), *Handbook of experimental psychology.* New York: John Wiley & Sons.

Selye, H. (1974). *Stress without distress.* Philadelphia: J. B. Lippincott.

Selye, H. (1976). *The stress of life* (2nd ed.). New York: McGraw-Hill.

Shaffer, D. R., & Tomarelli, M. (1981). Bias in the ivory tower: An unintended consequence of the Buckley amendment for graduate admissions. *Journal of Applied Psychology, 66,* 7–11.

Shaffer, G. S., Saunders, V., & Owens, W. A. (1986). Additional evidence for the accuracy of biographical data: Long-term retest and observer ratings. *Personnel Psychology, 39*(4), 791–810.

Sharf, J. C. (1988). APA and Civil Rights Bar opposed by justice, EEOC, ASPA, IPMA and EEAC before Supreme Court in *Clara Watson* vs. *Fort Worth Bank and Trust. Industrial-Organizational Psychologist (TIP), 25*(2), 27–34.

Shaw, J. B., & Riskind, J. H. (1983). Predicting job stress using data from the Position Analysis Questionnaire. *Journal of Applied Psychology, 68*(2), 253–261.

Shaw, M. E. (1963). *Scaling group tasks: A method for dimensional analysis.* Gainesville: University of Florida.

Shaw, R. D. (1982, August 11). Safety board says Air Florida crash caused by pilot error, chain of events. *Philadelphia Inquirer*, p. 3.

Shrauger, J. S., & Osberg, J. W. (1981). The relative accuracy of self-predictors and judgments by others in psychological assessment. *Psychological Bulletin, 90,* 322–351.

Siegel, A. I. (1983). The miniature job training and evaluation approach: Additional findings. *Personnel Psychology, 36,* 41–56.

Siegel, A. I., & Bergman, B. A. (1975). A job learning approach to performance prediction. *Personnel Psychology, 28,* 325–339.

Silverman, S. B., & Wexley, K. N. (1984). Reactions of employees to performance appraisal interviews as a function of their participation in rating scale development. *Personnel Psychology, 37*(4), 703–710.

Simon, H. A. (1960). *The new science of management decision.* New York: Harper & Row.

Simon, J. R., Mewaldt, S. P., Acosta, E., & Hu, J. (1976). Processing auditory information. *Journal of Applied Psychology, 61,* 354–358.

Sims, H. P., & LaFollette, W. (1975). An assessment of the Litwin and Stringer organization climate questionnaire. *Personnel Psychology, 28,* 19–38.

Sims, H. P., & Szilagyi, A. D. (1975a). Leader reward behavior and subordinate satisfaction and performance. *Organizational Behavior and Human Performance, 14,* 426–438.

Sims, H. P., Jr., & Szilagyi, A. D. (1975b). Leader structure and subordinate satisfaction for two hospital administrative levels: A path analysis approach. *Journal of Applied Psychology, 60,* 194–197.

Skinner, B. F. (1938). *The behavior of organisms.* Englewood Cliffs, NJ: Prentice-Hall.

Skinner, B. F. (1958). Teaching machines. *Science, 128,* 969–977.

Skinner, B. F. (1959). *Cumulative record.* New York: Appleton-Century-Crofts.

Slovic, P., Fischoff, B., & Lichtenstein, S. (1977). Behavioral decision theory. *Annual Review of Psychology, 28,* 1–39.

Smith, P. C., & Kendall, L. M. (1963). Retranslation of expectations: An approach to the construction of unambiguous anchors for rating scales. *Journal of Applied Psychology, 47,* 149–155.

Smith, P. C., Kendall, L. M., & Hulin, C. L. (1969). *The measurement of satisfaction in work and retirement: A strategy for the study of attitudes.* Chicago: Rand McNally.

Snyderman, M., & Herrnstein, R. J. (1983). Intelligence tests and the Immigration Act of 1924. *American Psychologist, 38,* 986–995.

Sokal, M. (1987). *Psychological testing and American society, 1890–1930.* New Brunswick, NJ: Rutgers University Press.

Solomon, R. L. (1949). An extension of control group design. *Psychological Bulletin, 46,* 137–150.

Specter, P., & Levine, E. (1987). Meta-analysis for integrating study outcomes: A Monte Carlo study of its susceptibility to type I and type II errors. *Journal of Applied Psychology, 72*(1), 3–9.

Spool, M. D. (1978). Training programs for observers of behavior: A review. *Personnel Psychology, 31,* 853–888.

Srinivas, S., & Motowidlo, S. J. (1987). Effects of raters' stress on the dispersion and favorability of performance ratings. *Journal of Applied Psychology, 72*(2), 247–251.

Stahl, M. J., & Harrell, A. M. (1981). Effort decisions with behavioral decision theory: Toward an individual differences model. *Organizational Behavior and Human Performance, 27,* 303–325.

Staines, G. L., Pottick, K. J., & Fudge, D. A. (1986). Wives' employment and husbands' attitudes toward work and life. *Journal of Applied Psychology, 71*(1), 118–128.

Stapp, J., Fulcher, R., Nelson, S. D., Pallak, M. S., & Wicherski, M. (1981). The employment of recent doctorate recipients in psychology: 1975 through 1978. *American Psychologist, 36,* 1211–1254.

Staw, B. M., & Ross, J. (1985). Stability in the midst of change: A dispositional approach to job attitudes. *Journal of Applied Psychology, 70*(3), 469–480.

Stead, W. H., & Shartle, C. L. (1940). *Occupational counseling techniques.* New York: American Book Company.

Steers, R. M. (1975). Effects of need for achievement on the job performance–job attitude relationship. *Journal of Applied Psychology, 60,* 678–682.

Steers, R. M., & Rhodes, S. R. (1978). Major influences on employee attendance: A process model. *Journal of Applied Psychology, 63,* 391–407.

Steers, R. M., & Spencer, D. G. (1977). The role of achievement motivation in job design. *Journal of Applied Psychology, 62,* 472–479.

Stern, R. M., Botto, R. W., & Herrick, C. D. (1972). Behavioral and physiological effects of false heart rate feedback: a replication and extension. *Psychophysiology, 9,* 21–29.

Stern, R. M., & Lewis, N. L. (1968). Ability of actors to control their GSRs and express emotions. *Psychophysiology, 4,* 294–299.

Stinson, J. E., & Tracy, L. (1974). Some disturbing characteristics of the LPC score. *Personnel Psychology, 27,* 477–486.

Stogdill, R. M. (1948). Personal factors associated with leadership. *Journal of Psychology, 25,* 35–71.

Stolorow, L. M. (1964). *Some educational problems and prospects of a systems approach to instruction.* Alexandria, VA: Defense Documentation Center. (Report No. A.D. 435032) [Office of Naval Research Contract Nonr. 3985 (04), 1964, Report #2]

Stone, D. L., Gueutal, H. G., & McIntosh, B. (1984). The effects of feedback sequence and expertise of the rater on performance feedback accuracy. *Personnel Psychology, 37*(3), 487–506.

Strube, M. J., & Garcia, J. E. (1981). A meta-analytic investigation of Fiedler's contingency model of leadership effectiveness. *Psychological Bulletin, 90,* 307–321.

Student, K. (1968). Supervisory influence and work group performance. *Journal of Applied Psychology, 52* (3), 188–194.

Sutton, R. I., & Rousseau, D. M. (1979). Structure, technology, and dependence on a parent organization: Organizational and environmental correlates of individual responses. *Journal of Applied Psychology, 64,* 675–687.

Task force on the practice of psychology in industry. (1971). *American Psychologist, 26,* 974–991.

Taylor, F. W. (1911). *The principles of scientific management.* New York: Harper & Row.

Taylor, H. S., Fisher, C. D., & Ilgen, D. R. (1984). Individuals' reactions to performance feedback in organizations: A control theory perspective. In K. M. Rowland & G. R. Ferris (Eds.), *Research in personnel and human resources management* (Vol. 2). Greenwich, CT: JAI Press.

Taylor, M. S., Locke, E. A., Lee, C., & Gist, L. E. (1984). Type A behavior and faculty research productivity: What are the mechanisms? *Organizational Behavior and Human Performance, 34*(3), 402–418.

Teichner, W. H., Arees, E., & Reilly, R. (1963). Noise and human performance: A psychophysiological approach. *Ergonomics, 6,* 83–97.

Teichner, W. H., & Kobrick, J. L. (1955). Effects of prolonged exposure to low temperature on visual-motor performance. *Journal of Experimental Psychology, 49,* 122–126.

Terman, L. M. (1917). A trial of mental and pedagogical tests in a civil service examination for policemen and firemen. *Journal of Applied Psychology, 1,* 17–29.

Terpstra, D. E. (1981). Relationship between methodological rigor and reported outcomes in organizational development evaluation research. *Journal of Applied Psychology, 66,* 541–543.

Thompson, J. D. (1967). *Organizations in action.* New York: McGraw-Hill.

Thoresen, C. E., & Mahoney, M. J. (1974). *Behavioral self-control.* New York: Holt, Rinehart & Winston.

Thorndike, E. L. (1922). The psychology of labor. *Harper's Magazine, 144,* 799–806.

Thurstone, L. L. (1938). Primary mental abilities. *Psychometric Monographs,* 1.

Timio, M., & Gentili, S. (1976). Adrenosympathetic overactivity under conditions of work stress. *British Journal of Preventive Social Medicine, 30,* 262–265.

Trahair, R. C. S. (1984). *The humanist temper.* New Brunswick, NJ: Transaction, Inc.

Treiman, D. J., & Hartmann, H. I. (1981). *Women, work, and wages: Equal pay for jobs of equal value.* Washington, DC: National Academy Press.

Trempe, J., Rigny, A-J., & Haccoun, R. R. (1985). Subordinate satisfaction with male and female managers: Role of perceived supervisory influence. *Journal of Applied Psychology, 70*(1), 44–47.

Triandis, H. C., Feldman, J. M., Weldon, D. E., & Harvey, W. M. (1975). Ecosystem distrust and the hard-to-employ. *Journal of Applied Psychology, 60*(1), 44–56.

Trist, E. L., & Bamforth, K. W. (1951). Some social and psychological consequences of the long-wall method of coal getting. *Human Relations, 4,* 3–38.

Trist, E. L., Susman, G. I., & Brown, G. R. (1977). An experiment in autonomous working in an American underground coal mine. *Human Relations, 30,* 201–236.

Tscheulin, D. (1971). Leader behavior measurement in German industry. *Journal of Applied Psychology, 56*(1), 28–31.

Tubbs, M. E. (1986). Goal setting: A meta-analytic examination of the empirical evidence. *Journal of Applied Psychology, 71*(3), 474–483.

Tucker, F. D. (1985). A study of the training needs of older workers: Implications for human resources development planning. *Public Personnel Management, 14,* 85–95.

Uhrbrock, R. S. (1948). The personnel interview. *Personnel Psychology, 1*(3), 273–302.

Ulrich, L., & Trumbo, D. (1965). The selection interview since 1949. *Psychological Bulletin, 63,* 100–116.

Uniform Guidelines on Employee Selection Procedures. (1978). *Federal Register, 43,* No. 166, 38290–38309.

Van Gundy, A. B. (1981). *Techniques of structured problem solving.* New York: Van Nostrand Reinhold.

Van Zelst, R. H. (1952). Sociometrically selected work teams increase production. *Personnel Psychology, 5,* 175–185.

Vaughn, C. L., & Reynolds, W. A. (1951). Reliability of personal interview data. *Journal of Applied Psychology, 35,* 61–63.

Vecchio, R. P. (1977). An empirical examination of the validity of Fiedler's model of leadership effectiveness. *Organizational Behavior and Human Performance, 19,* 180–206.

Vecchio, R. P. (1981). An individual differences interpretation of the conflicting predictions generated by equity theory and expectancy theory. *Journal of Applied Psychology, 66,* 470–481.

Vecchio, R. P. (1982). A further test of leadership effects due to between-group and within-group variation. *Journal of Applied Psychology, 67,* 200–208.

Vinacke, E. (1962). Motivation as a complex problem. *Nebraska Symposium on Motivation, 10,* 1–45.

Viteles, M. (1932). *Industrial psychology.* New York: Norton.

Voevodsky, J. (1974). Evaluations of a deceleration warning light for reducing rear-end automobile collisions. *Journal of Applied Psychology, 59,* 270–273.

Vroom, V. H. (1964). *Work and motivation.* New York: John Wiley & Sons.

Vroom, V., & Yetton, P. W. (1973). *Leadership and decision-making.* Pittsburgh: University of Pittsburgh Press.

Wagner, R. (1949). The employment interview: A critical review. *Personnel Psychology, 2,* 17–46.

Wahba, M. A., & Bridwell, L. B. (1976). Maslow reconsidered: A review of research on the need hierarchy theory. *Organizational Behavior and Human Performance, 15,* 212–240.

Wakabayashi, M., & Graen, G. (1984). The Japanese career progress study: A seven year follow-up. *Journal of Applied Psychology, 69,* 603–614.

Wall, T. D., Clegg, C. W., & Jackson, P. R. (1978). An evaluation of the job characteristics model. *Journal of Occupational Psychology, 51*(2), 183–196.

Walster, E., Walster, G. W., & Berscheid, E. (1978). *Equity: Theory and research.* Boston: Allyn & Bacon.

Walter, G. A. (1975). Effects of videotape training inputs on group performance. *Journal of Applied Psychology, 60,* 308–313.

Walter-Busch, E. (1986, August 14). *The sudden restlessness of relay assembly operator 2A.* Paper presented at Academy of Management Meetings, Chicago.

Walton, R. (1980). Quality of work life activities: A research agenda. *Professional Psychology, 11,* 484–493.

Wanous, J. P. (1977). Organizational entry: Newcomers moving from outside to inside. *Psychological Bulletin, 84,* 601–618.

Wanous, J. (1980). *Organizational entry: Recruitment, selection, and socialization of newcomers.* Reading, MA: Addison-Wesley.

Wanous, J. P., Keon, T. L., & Latack, J. C. (1983). Expectancy theory and occupational/organizational choices: A review and test. *Organizational Behavior and Human Performance, 32,* 66–86.

Wanous, J. P., & Zwany, A. (1977). A cross-sectional test of need hierarchy theory. *Organizational Behavior and Human Performance, 18,* 78–79.

Warr, P. B. (1983). Work, jobs, and unemployment. *Bulletin of the British Psychological Society, 36,* 305–311.

Warr, P. B. (1987). *Work, unemployment and mental health.* Oxford: Clarendon Press.

Warr, P. B., & Jackson, P. (1984). Men without jobs: Some correlates of age and length of unemployment. *Journal of Occupational Psychology, 57*(1), 77–85.

Warr, P. B., & Parry, G. (1982). Paid employment and women's psychological wellbeing. *Psychological Bulletin, 91,* 498–516.

Weaver, C. N. (1977). Relationships among pay, race, sex, occupational prestige, supervision, work autonomy, and job satisfaction in a national sample. *Personnel Psychology, 30,* 437–445.

Weaver, C. N. (1978). Black-white correlates of job satisfaction. *Journal of Applied Psychology, 63,* 255–258.

Weber, M. (1947). *The theory of social and economic organization* (A. M. Henderson & T. Parsons, Trans. and Eds.). New York: Oxford University Press.

Webster, E. C. (1982). *The employment interview: A social judgment process.* Schomberg, Ontario, Canada: S.I.P. Publications.

Weick, E. E., Bougon, M. G., & Maruyama, G. (1976). The equity context. *Organizational Behavior and Human Performance, 15,* 32–65.

Weick, K. E. (1976). Educational organizations as loosely coupled systems. *Administrative Science Quarterly, 21,* 1–19.

Weinstein, N. D. (1978). Individual differences in reactions to noise: A longitudinal study in a college dormitory. *Journal of Applied Psychology, 63,* 458–466.

Weiss, D. J., & Dawis, R. V. (1960). An objective validation of factual interview data. *Journal of Applied Psychology, 44,* 381–385.

Weiss, H. M. (1977). Subordinate imitation of supervisor behavior: The role of modeling in organizational socialization. *Organizational Behavior and Human Performance, 19,* 89–105.

Weiss, H., Ilgen, D., & Sharbaugh, M. E. (1982). Effects of life and job stress on information search behaviors of organizational members. *Journal of Applied Psychology, 67,* 60–66.

Wexley, K., & Latham, G. P. (1980). *Developing and training human resources in an organization.* Santa Monica, CA: Goodyear Publishing.

Wexley, K. N., & Yukl, G. A. (1984). *Organizational behavior and personnel psychology.* Homewood, IL: Richard D. Irwin.

Wherry, R. J. (1983). The control of bias in rating: A theory of rating (Personnel Research Board Report 922). In F. J. Landy & F. L. Farr, *The measurement of work performance: Methods, theory, and applications.* New York: Academic Press.

Whyte, W. H. (1956). *The organization man.* New York: Simon & Schuster.

Wiersma, U., & Latham, G. P. (1986). The practicality of behavioral observation scales, behavioral expectation scales, and trait scales. *Personnel Psychology, 39*(3), 619–628.

Wigdor, A., & Green, B. F. (1986). *Assessing the performance of enlisted personnel: Evaluation of joint service project.* Washington, DC: National Academy Press.

Wiggins, J. S. (1973). *Personality and prediction: Principles of personality assessment.* Reading, MA: Addison-Wesley.

Wilkinson, R. T. (1963). Interaction of noise with knowledge of results and sleep deprivation. *Journal of Experimental Psychology, 66,* 332–337.

Wilkinson, R. T. (1969). Some factors influencing the effect of environmental stressors upon performance. *Psychological Bulletin, 72,* 260–272.

Wilkinson, R. T. (1974). Individual differences in response to the environment. *Ergonomics, 17,* 745–756.

Williams, J. R. (1977). Follow-up study of relationships between perceptual style measures and telephone company vehicle accidents. *Journal of Applied Psychology, 62,* 751–754.

Williams, W. (1925). *Mainsprings of men.* New York: Scribner's.

Wolcott, J., McKeeken, R., Burgin, R., & Yanowitch, R. (1977). Correlation of general aviation accidents with biorhythm theory. *Human Factors, 19,* 283–294.

Wolinsky, J. (1982, December). Beat the clock. *Monitor,* pp. 28–29.

Woodward, J. (1958). *Management and technology.* London: Her Majesty's Stationery Office.

Worthy, J. C. (1950). Organizational structure and employee morale. *American Sociological Review, 15,* 169–179.

Wright, O. R., Jr. (1969). Summary of research on the selection interview since 1964. *Personnel Psychology, 22,* 391–413.

Youngblood, S. A. (1984). Work, nonwork, and withdrawal. *Journal of Applied Psychology, 69*(1), 106–117.

Yukl, G. A. (1981). *Leadership in organizations.* Englewood Cliffs, NJ: Prentice-Hall.

Yukl, G. A., & Latham, G. P. (1975). Consequences of reinforcement schedules and incentive magnitudes for employee performance: Problems encountered in an industrial setting. *Journal of Applied Psychology, 60,* 294–298.

Zajonc, R. (1980). Feeling and thinking: Preferences need no inferences. *American Psychologist, 35,* 151–175.

Zohar, D. (1980). Safety climate in industrial organizations: Theoretical and applied implications. *Journal of Applied Psychology, 65,* 96–102.

Name Index

Subject Index